Lecture Notes in Artificial Intelligence   3835

Edited by J. G. Carbonell and J. Siekmann

Subseries of Lecture Notes in Computer Science

T0216731

Geoff Sutcliffe   Andrei Voronkov (Eds.)

Logic for Programming, Artificial Intelligence, and Reasoning

12th International Conference, LPAR 2005
Montego Bay, Jamaica, December 2-6, 2005
Proceedings

 Springer

Series Editors

Jaime G. Carbonell, Carnegie Mellon University, Pittsburgh, PA, USA
Jörg Siekmann, University of Saarland, Saarbrücken, Germany

Volume Editors

Geoff Sutcliffe
University of Miami, Department of Computer Science
P.O. Box 248154, Coral Gables, FL 33124, USA
E-mail: geoff@cs.miami.edu

Andrei Voronkov
University of Manchester, Department of Computer Science
Oxford Road, Manchester M13 9PL, UK
E-mail: voronkov@cs.man.ac.uk

Library of Congress Control Number: 2005936393

CR Subject Classification (1998): I.2.3, I.2, F.4.1, F.3, D.2.4, D.1.6

ISSN   0302-9743
ISBN-10   3-540-30553-X Springer Berlin Heidelberg New York
ISBN-13   978-3-540-30553-8 Springer Berlin Heidelberg New York

Springer is a part of Springer Science+Business Media

springeronline.com

© Springer-Verlag Berlin Heidelberg 2005
Printed in Germany

Typesetting: Camera-ready by author, data conversion by Scientific Publishing Services, Chennai, India
Printed on acid-free paper   SPIN: 11591191   06/3142   5 4 3 2 1 0

Preface

This volume contains the full papers presented at the 12th International Conference on Logic for Programming, Artificial Intelligence, and Reasoning (LPAR), held 2-6 December 2006, in Montego Bay, Jamaica. The call for papers attracted 108 full paper submissions, each of which were reviewed by at least three reviewers. The Program Committee accepted the 46 papers that appear in these proceedings. The conference program also included 4 invited talks, by Tom Ball of Microsoft Research, Doug Lenat of Cycorp, Roberto Nieuwenhuis of the Universidad Politécnica de Cataluña, and Allen Van Gelder of the University of California at Santa Cruz. Papers or abstracts for the invited talks are in these proceedings.

In addition to the main program, the conference offered a short paper track, which attracted 13 submissions, of which 12 were accepted, and the Workshop on Emperically Successful Higher Order Logic (ESHOL).

Thanks go to: the authors (of both accepted and rejected papers); the Program Committee and their reviewers; the invited speakers; Christoph Benzmüller, John Harrison, and Carsten Schürmann for organizing ESHOL; Celia Alleyne-Ebanks for administering the conference in Jamaica; the Honorable Minister Phillip Paulwell of the Ministry of Commerce, Science and Technology for opening the conference (and Daphne Simmonds for introducing us to the minister); the Mona Institute of Applied Sciences at the University of the West Indies for their support; Microsoft Research for sponsorship of student regsitrations; the Kurt Gödel Society for taking registrations; and EasyChair for hosting the review process.

October 2006

Geoff Sutcliffe
Andrei Voronkov

Conference Organization

Program Chairs

Geoff Sutcliffe
Andrei Voronkov

Program Committee

Elvira Albert
Maria Alpuente
Matthias Baaz
Christoph Benzmüller
Koen Claessen
Anatoli Degtyarev
Thomas Eiter
Bernd Fischer
Rajeev Goré
Erich Grädel
John Harrison
Miki Hermann
Brahim Hnich
Ian Horrocks
Mateja Jamnik
Neil Jones
Christoph Koch
Christopher Lynch
Michael Maher
Maarten Marx
Catuscia Palamidessi
Peter Patel-Schneider
Jeff Pelletier
Harald Ruess
Carsten Schürmann
Stephan Schulz
John Keith Slaney
Cesare Tinelli
Ashish Tiwari
Margus Veanes

Local Organization

Celia Alleyne-Ebanks
Geoff Sutcliffe

External Reviewers

Andreas Abel
Amal Ahmed
Wolfgang Ahrendt
Anbulagan
Grigoris Antoniou
Puri Arenas
Jürgen Avenhaus
Demis Ballis
Clark Barrett
Peter Baumgartner
Michael Beeson
Leopoldo Bertossi
Gavin Bierman
Bernard Boigelot
Chad Brown
Colin Campbell
Luciano Caroprese
Manuel Carro
Claudio Castellini
Balder ten Cate
Patrice Chalin
Anatoly Chebotarev
Adam Chlipala
Agata Ciabattoni
Manuel Clavel
Jonathan Cohen
Jesús Correas
Stephen Craig
Medhi Dastani
Jeremy Dawson
Anatoli Degtyarev
Stephane Demri
Dan Dougherty
Esra Erdem
Santiago Escobar
Wolfgang Faber
Moreno Falaschi
Chris Fermüller
Massimo Franceschet
Anders Franzén
Carsten Fritz

John Gallagher
Stephane Gaubert
Samir Genaim
Jürgen Giesl
Birte Glimm
Eugene Goldberg
Georges Gonthier
Wolfgang Grieskamp
Yuri Gurevich
Reiner Hähnle
Jay Halcomb
Joe Hendrix
Hugo Herbelin
Mark Hills
Marieke Huisman
Dieter Hutter
Giovambattista Ianni
Rosalie Iemhoff
Pascual Julián Iranzo
Tommi Junttila
Nicolas Kicillof
Joseph Kiniry
Felix Klaedtke
Roman Kontchakov
Sergey Krivoi
Orna Kupferman
Oliver Kutz
Axel Legay
Stephane Lengrand
Martin Leucker
Lei Li
Ninghui Li
Guohui Lin
Christina Lindenberg
John Lloyd
Andrei Lopatenko
Salvador Lucas
Ines Lynce
Alexis Maciel
John Matthews
Farhad Mehta

George Metcalfe
Marino Miculan
Dale Miller
David Mitchell
Alberto Momigliano
José Morales
Ben Moszkowski
Boris Motik
Lev Nachmanson
Robert Nieuwenhuis
Andreas Nonnengart
Michael Norrish
Don Nute
Jan Obdrzalek
Albert Oliveras
Vincent van Oostrom
Sam Owre
Miguel Palomino
Jeff Pan
Grant Passmore
Lawrence C. Paulson
Brigitte Pientka
Andre Platzer
Erik Poll
Andrei Popescu
Steven Prestwich
Arthur Ramer
María José Ramírez
Christophe Ringeissen
Enric Rodríguez-Carbonell
Roberto Rossi
Grigore Rosu
Pritam Roy
Piotr Rudnicki
Jeffrey Sarnat
Roman Schindlauer
Renate Schmidt

Johann Schumann
Thomas Schwentick
Alberto Segre
Anton Setzer
Jatin Shah
Chung-chieh Shan
Jörg Siekmann
Konrad Slind
Maria Sorea
Mark Steedman
Graham Steel
Gernot Stenz
Charles Stewart
Lutz Strassburger
Ofer Strichman
Aaron Stump
Evgenia Ternovska
Sebastiaan Terwijn
Rene Thiemann
Hans Tompits
Leon van der Torre
Dmitry Tsarkov
Xavier Urbain
Alasdair Urquhart
Frank D. Valencia
Alex Vaynberg
Helmut Veith
Gérard Verfaillie
Alicia Villanueva
Fer-Jan de Vries
Emil Weydert
Wayne Wobcke
Stefan Woltran
Rostislav Yavorskiy
Richard Zach
Noam Zeilberger
Evgeny Zolin

Table of Contents

Independently Checkable Proofs from Decision Procedures: Issues and Progress

Allen Van Gelder

School of Engineering, University of California at Santa Cruz
avg@cs.ucsc.edu

Abstract. In many verification applications the desired outcome is that the formula is unsatisfiable: a satisfying assignment essentially exhibits a bug and unsatisfiability implies a lack of bugs, at least for the property being verified. Most current high-performance satisfiability solvers and special-theory decision procedures are unable to provide proof of unsatisfiability. Since bugs have been discovered in many such programs long after being put into service, an uncheckable decision poses a significant problem if important economic or safety decisions are to be based upon it. This talk develops the thesis is that decision procedures can and should be designed with the ability to output an independently checkable proof. While *finding* a proof is hard, *checking* a proof can be straightforward if the proof system is simple enough. (By a "proof" we mean a real proof, with no steps omitted.) In practice, most underlying theories can produce a resolution proof. We argue that outputting such a proof does not place an undue burden on the decision procedures. We report on practical progress in this area for satisfiability solvers. Experiments have been carried out with what might be the first implementations of solver and proof checker that were developed completely independently, having only the specifications of the proof-file format as common knowledge. There is a trend toward combining high-performance satisfiability solvers with other theorem-proving methods. As the total systems become more complex, the need for "independent audits" becomes greater. Design goals for checkable proofs are proposed.

G. Sutcliffe and A. Voronkov (Eds.): LPAR 2005, LNAI 3835, p. 1, 2005.
© Springer-Verlag Berlin Heidelberg 2005

Zap: Automated Theorem Proving
for Software Analysis

Thomas Ball, Shuvendu K. Lahiri, and Madanlal Musuvathi

Microsoft Research
{tball, shuvendu, madanm}@microsoft.com

Abstract. Automated theorem provers (ATPs) are a key component that many software verification and program analysis tools rely on. However, the basic interface provided by ATPs (validity/satisfiability checking of formulas) has changed little over the years. We believe that program analysis clients would benefit greatly if ATPs were to provide a richer set of operations. We describe our desiderata for such an interface to an ATP, the logics (theories) that an ATP for program analysis should support, and present how we have incorporated many of these ideas in Zap, an ATP built at Microsoft Research.

1   Introduction

To make statements about programs in the absence of concrete inputs requires some form of *symbolic reasoning*. For example, suppose we want to prove that the execution of the assignment statement `x:=x+1` from a state in which the formula $(x < 5)$ holds yields a state in which the formula $(x < 10)$ holds. To do so, we need machinery for manipulating and reasoning about formulas that represent sets of program states.

Automated theorem provers (ATPs) provide the machinery that enables such reasoning. Many questions about program behavior can be reduced to questions of the validity or satisfiability of a first-order formula, such as $\forall x : (x < 6) \implies (x < 10)$. For example, given a program P and a specification S, a verification condition $VC(P, S)$ is a formula that is valid if and only if program P satisfies specification S. The validity of $VC(P, S)$ can be determined using an ATP. The basic interface an ATP provides takes as input a formula and returns a Boolean ("Valid", "Invalid") answer. Of course, since the validity problem is undecidable for many logics, an ATP may return "Invalid" for a valid formula.

In addition to this basic interface, ATPs may generate proofs witnessing the validity of input formulas. This basic capability is essential to techniques such as proof-carrying code [Nec97], where the ATP is an untrusted and potentially complicated program and the proof generated by the ATP can be checked efficiently by a simple program.

Through our experience with the use of ATPs in program analysis clients, we often want ATPs to provide a richer interface so as to better support program analysis tasks. We group these tasks into four categories:

G. Sutcliffe and A. Voronkov (Eds.): LPAR 2005, LNAI 3835, pp. 2–22, 2005.

- **Symbolic Fixpoint Computation.** For propositional (Boolean) formulas, binary decision diagrams (BDDs) [Bry86] enable the computation of fixpoints necessary for symbolic reachability and symbolic CTL model checking [BCM⁺92] of finite state systems. The transition relation of a finite state system can be represented using a BDD, as well as the initial and reachable states of the system. A main advantage of BDDs is that every Boolean function has a normal form, which makes various operations efficient. The basic operations necessary for fixpoint computation are a subsumption test (to test for convergence), quantifier elimination (to eliminate temporary variables used in image computation) and a join operation (to combine formulas representing different sets of states; this is simply disjunction in the case of Boolean logic). We would like to lift these operations to logics that are more expressive than propositional logic, so as to enable the computation of symbolic fixpoints over structures that more closely correspond to the types in programming languages (integers, enumerations, pointers, etc.). While normal forms may not be achievable, simplification of formula is highly desirable to keep formulas small and increase the efficiency of the fixpoint computation.
- **Abstract Transformers.** A fundamental concept in analyzing infinite-state systems (such as programs) is that of abstraction. Often, a system may be converted to a simpler abstract form where certain questions are decidable, such that proofs in the abstract system carry over to proofs in the original system. Abstract interpretation is a framework for mathematically describing program abstractions and their meaning [CC77]. A basic step in the process is the creation of *abstract transformers*: each statement in the original program must be translated to a corresponding abstract statement. This step often is manual. Predicate abstraction is a means for automating the construction of finite-state abstract transformers from infinite-state systems using an ATP [GS97]. ATPs can also be used to create *symbolic best transformers* for other abstract domains [YRS04]. Unfortunately, these approaches suffer from having to make an exponential number of calls to the ATP. If an ATP provides an interface to find all the *consequences* of a set of facts, the process of predicate abstraction and creation of symbolic best transformers can be made more efficient [LBC05]. Consequence finding [Mar99] is a basic operation for the automated creation of abstract transformers that ATPs could support.
- **Property-guided Abstraction Refinement.** If an abstraction is not precise enough to establish the correctness of a program with respect to some property, we wish to find a way to make the abstraction more precise with respect to the property of interest [Kur94, CGJ⁺00, BR01]. Recently, McMillan showed how interpolants naturally describe how to refine (predicate) abstractions with respect to a property of interest [McM03, HJMM04]. An interpolating ATP [McM04] can support the automated refinement of abstractions.
- **Test Generation.** Finally, we would like to use ATPs to prove the presence of a bug to the user through the automated generation of failure-inducing

inputs [Cla76]. In general, we wish to generate a test input to a program to meet some coverage criteria (such as executing a certain statement or covering a certain control path in the program). To do this, one can create from the program a formula that is satisfiable if and only if there is a test input that achieves the desired coverage criteria. We wish not only to determine the satisfiability of the input formula but also to generate a satisfying assignment that can be transformed into a test input. Model finding/generation is an important capability for ATPs in order to support test generation [ZZ96].

The paper is organized as follows. Section 2 presents more detail about the needs of (symbolic) program clients of ATPs. Section 3 describes the theories/logics that naturally arise from the analysis of programs. We have created an ATP called Zap to meet some of the needs described above. Section 4 gives background material necessary to understand Zap's architecture, which is based on the Nelson-Oppen combination procedure [NO79a, TH96]. We have found that the Nelson-Oppen method can be extended in a variety of ways to support the demands of program analysis clients mentioned above. Section 5 gives an overview of Zap's architecture and describes some of our initial results on efficient decision procedures for fragments of linear arithmetic that occur commonly in program analysis queries. Section 6 describes how we have extended Zap and the Nelson-Oppen combination framework to support richer operations such as interpolation and predicate abstraction. Finally, Section 7 discusses related work.

2 Symbolic Program Analysis Clients of ATPs

This section formalizes the requirements of symbolic program analysis clients of ATPs.

2.1 Notation

A program is a set C of guarded commands, which are logical formulas c of the form

$$c \equiv g(X) \wedge x'_1 = e_1(X) \wedge \ldots \wedge x'_m = e_m(X)$$

where $X = \{x_1, x_2, \ldots, x_m\}$ are all the program variables. The variable x'_i stands for the value of x_i after the execution of the command. We write $g(X)$ to emphasize that g's free variables come only from X. A program state is a valuation of X. We have a transition of one state into another one if the corresponding valuation of primed and unprimed variables satisfies one of the guarded commands $c \in C$.

In symbolic evaluation, a formula ϕ represents a set of states, namely, those states in which the formula ϕ evaluates true. Formulas are ordered by implication. We write $\phi \leq \phi'$ to denote that ϕ logically implies ϕ'.

The application of the operator post_c on a formula ϕ is defined as usual; its computation requires a quantifier elimination procedure.

$$\mathsf{post}_c(\varphi) \equiv (\exists X. \ \varphi \wedge g(X) \wedge x'_1 = e_1(X) \wedge \ldots \wedge x'_m = e_m(X))[X/X']$$
$$\mathsf{post}(\varphi) \equiv \bigvee_{c \in C} \mathsf{post}_c(\varphi)$$

In order to specify correctness, we fix formulas init and safe denoting the set of *initial* and *safe* states, respectively. A program is *correct* if no unsafe state is reachable from an initial state. The basic goal of a fixpoint analysis is to find a *safe inductive invariant*, which is a formula ψ such that

$$(\text{init} \leq \psi) \wedge (\text{post}(\psi) \leq \psi) \wedge (\psi \leq \text{safe})$$

The correctness can be proven by showing that $\text{lfp}(\text{post}, \text{init}) \leq$ safe, where $\text{lfp}(\mathcal{F}, \phi)$ stands for the least fixpoint of the operator $\mathcal{F}$ above ϕ.

2.2   Fixpoint Computation

Figure 1 gives a very basic algorithm for (least) fixpoint computation using the post operator. Here we abuse notation somewhat and let ϕ and old be variables ranging over formulas. Initially, ϕ is the formula init and old is the formula `false`. The variable old represents the value of ϕ on the previous iteration of the fixpoint computation. As long as ϕ is not inductive (the test $\phi \leq$ old fails) then old gets the value of ϕ and ϕ is updated to be the disjunction of current value of ϕ and the value of *post* applied to the current value of ϕ. If ϕ is inductive (the test $\phi \leq$ old succeeds) then the algorithm tests if ϕ is inside the safe set of states. If so, then the algorithm returns "Correct". Otherwise, it returns "Potential error".

```
φ, old := init, false
loop
    if (φ ≤ old) then
        if (φ ≤ safe) then
            return "Correct"
        else
            return "Potential error"
    else
        old := φ
        φ := φ ∨ post(φ)
endloop
```

Fig. 1. Basic fixpoint algorithm

So, in order to implement a symbolic algorithm using an ATP, we require support for: (1) a subsumption test to test if ϕ is inductive under post ($\leq$); (2) quantifier elimination (to implement post); (3) disjunction of formulas (to collect the set of states represented by ϕ and $\text{post}(\phi)$).

There are a number of interesting issues raised by the symbolic fixpoint client. First, it is well known that certain logics (for example, equality with uninterpreted functions) do not entail quantifier elimination. In these cases, we desire the ATP to provide a "cover" operation, $\mathsf{cover}(\phi)$, that produces the strongest quantifier-free formula implied by ϕ.

Second, because the lattice of formulas may be infinite, to achieve termination it may be necessary to use an operator other than disjunction to combine the formulas ϕ and $\mathsf{post}(\phi)$. As in abstract interpretation, we desire that logics are equipped with "widening" operators. Given formulas ϕ_i and ϕ_{i+1} such that $\phi_i \leq \phi_{i+1}$, a widening operator widen produces a formula $\psi = \mathsf{widen}(\phi_i, \phi_{i+1})$ such that: (1) $\phi_{i+1} \leq \psi$; (2) the iterated application of widening eventually converges (reaches a fixpoint) [CC77].

The fixpoint algorithm computes a sequence of formulas as follows: $\phi_0 = \mathsf{init}$ and $\phi_{i+1} = \phi_i \lor \mathsf{post}(\phi_i)$. Widening typically is applied to consecutive formulas in this sequence: $\phi_{i+1} = \mathsf{widen}(\phi_i, \phi_i \lor \mathsf{post}(\phi_i))$. The type of widening operator applied may depend on the underlying logic as well as the evolving structure of formulas in the fixpoint sequence. An example of widening over the integer domains would be to identify a variable with an increasing value and widen to an open interval: $\mathsf{widen}(i = 1, i = 1 \lor i = 2) = i \geq 1$.

2.3   Finitary Abstract Transformers

As we have seen in the previous section, the symbolic fixpoint computation can diverge because the lattice of formulas may have infinite ascending chains. Widening is one approach to deal with the problem. Another approach is to a priori restrict the class of formulas under consideration so as to guarantee termination of the fixpoint computation.

For example, suppose we restrict the class of formulas we can assign to the variables ϕ and old in the fixpoint computation to be propositional formulas over a set P of finite atomic predicates. Let us denote this class of formulas by F_P. In this case, the number of semantically distinct formulas is finite.

However, there is a problem: this class of formulas is not closed under post (nor under pre, the backwards symbolic transformer, for that matter). Suppose that we have $\phi \in F_P$ and that $\mathsf{post}(\phi) \notin F_P$. We again require a cover operation $\mathsf{cover}_P(\phi)$ of the ATP, that produces the strongest formula in F_P implied by ϕ. Then, we modify the fixpoint computation by changing the assignment statement to variable ϕ to:

$$\phi := \phi \lor \mathsf{cover}_P(\mathsf{post}(\phi))$$

Note that cover_P is not the same operation as the cover operation from the previous section. cover_P is parameterized by a set of predicates P while the cover operation has no such restriction. The cover_P operation is the basic operation required for predicate abstraction [GS97].

The cover_P operation is related to the problem of consequence finding [Mar99]. Given a set of predicates P, the goal of consequence finding is to find all consequences of P. The $\mathsf{cover}_P(\phi)$ operation expresses all consequences of P that are implied by ϕ. As described later, we have shown that is possible to compute cover_P efficiently for suitably restricted theories [LBC05].

2.4   Abstraction Refinement

In the presence of abstraction, it often will be the case that the fixpoint computation will return "Potential error", even for correct programs. In such cases, we would like to refine the abstraction to eliminate the "potential errors" and guide the fixpoint computation towards a proof. In the case of predicate abstraction, this means adding predicates to the set P that defines the finite state space. Where should these new predicates come from?

Let us again consider the sequence of formulas computed by the abstract symbolic fixpoint: $\phi_0 = $ init; $\phi_{i+1} = \phi_i \lor \text{cover}_P(\text{post}(\phi_i))$. Suppose that ϕ_k is inductive (with respect to post) but does not imply safe. Now, consider the following sequence of formulas: $\psi_0 = $ init; $\psi_{i+1} = \text{post}(\psi_i)$. If the program is correct then the formula $\psi_k \land \neg$safe is unsatisfiable. The problem is that the set of predicates P is not sufficient for the abstract symbolic fixpoint to prove this. One approach to address this problem would be to take the set of (atomic) predicates in all the ψ_j $(0 \leq j \leq k)$ and add them to P. However, this set may contain many predicates that are not useful to proving that $\psi_k \land \neg$safe is unsatisfiable.

Henzinger et al. [HJMM04] showed how Craig interpolants can be used to discover a more precise set of predicates that "explains" the unsatisfiability. Given formulas A and B such that $A \land B = $ false, an interpolant $\Theta(A, B)$ satisfies the three following points:

- $A \Rightarrow \Theta(A, B)$,
- $\Theta(A, B) \land B = $ false,
- $V(\Theta(A, B)) \subseteq V(A) \cap V(B)$

That is, $\Theta(A, B)$ is weaker than A, the conjunction of $\Theta(A, B)$ and B is unsatisfiable ($\Theta(A, B)$ is not too weak), and all the variables in $\Theta(A, B)$ are common to both A and B.

Let us divide the formula $\psi_k \land \neg$safe into two parts: a *prefix* $A_j = \text{post}^j(\text{init})$ and a *suffix* $B_j = \text{post}^{k-j} \land \neg$safe, where $0 \leq j \leq k$ and post^i denotes the i-fold composition of the post operator (recall that post is itself a formula).[1]

An interpolant $Q_j = \Theta(A_j, B_j)$ yields a set of predicates $\text{p}(Q_j)$ such that $\text{cover}_{\text{p}(Q_j)}(A_j) \land B_j$ is unsatisfiable. This is because $A_j \Rightarrow Q_j$ and $Q_j \land B_j = $ false (by the definition of interpolant) and because $A_j \Rightarrow \text{cover}_{\text{p}(Q_j)}(A_j)$ and $\text{cover}_{\text{p}(Q_j)}(A_j)$ is at least as strong as Q_j (by the definition of cover).

Thus, the union $Q = \bigcup_{j \in \{1, \cdots k\}} \text{p}(Q_j)$ is sufficient for the abstract symbolic fixpoint to prove that it is not possible to reach an unsafe state (a state satisfying $\neg$safe) in k steps.

2.5   Test Generation

We also would like to use ATPs to prove the *presence* of errors as well as their absence. Thus, it makes sense for ATPs to return three-valued results for validity/satisfiability queries: "yes", "no" and "don't know". Of course, because

---

[1] Note that $\psi_k = \text{post}^k(\text{init})$.

of undecidability, we cannot always hope for only "yes" or "no" answers. However, even for undecidable questions, it is more useful to separate out "no" from "don't know" when possible, rather than lumping the two together (as is usually done in program analysis as well as automated theorem proving). Much research has been done in using three-valued logics in program analysis model checking [SRW99, SG04].

The ultimate "proof" to a user of a program analysis tool that the tool has found a real error in their program is for the tool to produce a concrete input on which the user can run their program to check that the tool has indeed found an error. Thus, just as proof-carrying code tools produce proofs that are relatively simple to check, we would like defect-detection tools to produce concrete inputs that can be checked simply by running the target program on them. Thus, we desire ATPs to produce models when they find that a formula is satisfiable, as SAT solvers do. We will talk about the difficulty of model production later.

2.6   Microsoft Research Tools

At Microsoft Research, there are three main clients of the Zap ATP: *Boogie*, a static program verifier for the C# language [BLS05]; *MUTT*, a set of testing tools for generating test inputs for MSIL, the bytecode language of Microsoft's .Net framework [TS05]; and *Zing*, a model checker for concurrent object-oriented programs (written in the Zing modeling language) [AQRX04]. In the following sections, we describe each of the clients and their requirements on the Zap ATP.

Boogie. The Boogie static program verifier takes as input a program written in the Spec# language, a superset of C# that provides support for method specifications like pre- and postconditions as well as object invariants. The Boogie verifier then infers loop invariants using interprocedural abstract interpretation. The loop invariants are used to summarize the effects of loops. In the end, Boogie produces a verification condition that is fed to an ATP.

MUTT. MUTT uses a basic approach [Cla76] to white-box test generation for programs: it chooses a control-flow path p through a program P and creates a formula $F(P, p)$ that is satisfiable if and only if there is an input I such that execution of program P on input I traverses path p. A symbolic interpreter for MSIL traverses the bytecode representation of a program, creating a symbolic representation of the program's state along a control-flow path. At each (binary) decision point in the program, the interpreter uses the ATP to determine whether the current symbolic state constrains the direction of the decision. If it does not, both decision directions are tried (using backtracking) and appropriate constraints added to the symbolic state for each decision. This client generates formulas with few disjuncts. Furthermore, the series of formulas presented to the ATP are very similar. Thus, an ATP that accepts the incremental addition/deletion of constraints is desired. Finally, when a formula is satisfiable, the ATP should produce a satisfying model.

Zing. Zing is an explicit state model checker for concurrent programs written in an objected-oriented language that is similar to C#. Zing implements various optimizations such as partial-order reduction, heap canonicalization and procedure-level summarization. Recently, researchers at Microsoft have started to experiment with hybrid state representations, where some parts of the state (the heap) are represented explicitly and other parts (integers) are represented symbolically with constraints. Zing uses the Zap ATP to represent integer constraints and to perform the quantifier elimination required for fixpoint computation.

3   Theories for Program Analysis

Various program analyses involve reasoning about formulas whose structure is determined both by the syntax of the programs and the various invariants that the analyses require. This section identifies those logics that naturally arise when analyzing programs and thus should be supported by the ATP. We provide an informal description of these logics and emphasize those aspects that are particularly important for the clients of Zap. The reader should read [DNS03] for a more detailed description.

We restrict the discussion to specific fragments of first-order logic with equality. While we have not explored the effective support for higher order logics in Zap, such logics can be very useful in specifying certain properties of programs [GM93, ORS92, MS01, IRR+04]. For instance, extending first-order logic with transitive closure [IRR+04] enables one to specify interesting properties about the heap.

The control and data flow in most programs involve operations on integer values. Accordingly, formulas generated by program analysis tools have a preponderance of integer arithmetic operations. This makes it imperative for the ATP to have effective support for integers. In practice, these formulas are mostly linear with many *difference* constraints of the form $x \leq y + c$. While multiplication between variables is rarely used in programs, it is quite common for loop invariants to involve non-linear terms. Thus, some reasonably complete support for multiplication is desirable.

As integer variables in programs are implemented using finite-length bit vectors in the underlying hardware, the semantics of the operations on these variables differs slightly from the semantics of (unbounded) integers. These differences can result in integer-overflow related behavior that is very hard to reason about manually. An ATP that allows reasoning about these bounded integers, either by treating them as bit-vectors or by performing modular arithmetic, can enable analysis tools that detect overflow errors. In addition, the finite-implementation of integers in programs becomes apparent when the program performs bit operations. It is a challenging problem for the ATP to treat a variable as a bit-vector in such rare cases but still treat it as an integer in the common case.

Apart from integer variables, programs define and use derived types such as structures and arrays. Also, programs use various *collection* classes which can be abstractly considered as maps or sets. It is desirable for the ATP to have support for theories that model these derived types and data structures.

Another very useful theory for program analysis is the theory of partial orders. The inheritance hierarchy in an object oriented program can be modeled using partial orders. The relevant queries involve determining if a particular type is a minimum element (base type) or a maximal element (final type), if one type is an ancestor (derived class) of another, and if two types are not ordered by the partial-order.

While the formulas generated during program analysis are mostly quantifier-free, invariants on arrays and collection data structures typically involve quantified statements. For instance, a tool might want to prove that all elements in an array are initialized to zero. Accordingly, the underlying ATP should be able to reason about quantified facts. In addition, supporting quantifiers in an ATP provides the flexibility for a client to encode domain-specific theories as axioms.

4   Background

In this section, we briefly describe the notations, the syntax and semantics of the logic, and a high-level description of the Nelson-Oppen combination algorithm for decision procedures. Our presentation of theories and the details of the algorithm is a little informal; interested readers are referred to excellent survey works [NO79a, TH96] for rigorous treatment.

4.1   Preliminaries

Figure 2 defines the syntax of a quantifier-free fragment of first-order logic. An expression in the logic can either be a *term* or a *formula*. A *term* can either be a variable or an application of a function symbol to a list of terms. A *formula* can be the constants true or false or an atomic formula or Boolean combination of other formulas. Atomic formulas can be formed by an equality between terms or by an application of a predicate symbol to a list of terms. A *literal* is either an atomic formula or its negation. A *monome m* is a conjunction of literals. We will often identify a conjunction of literals $l_1 \wedge l_2 \ldots l_k$ with the set $\{l_1, \ldots, l_k\}$.

The function and predicate symbols can either be *uninterpreted* or can be defined by a particular theory. For instance, the theory of integer linear arithmetic defines the function-symbol "+" to be the addition function over integers and "$<$" to be the comparison predicate over integers. For a theory T, the *signature Σ* denotes the set of function and predicate symbols in the theory. If an

$$term ::= variable \mid function\text{-}symbol(term, \ldots, term)$$
$$formula ::= \text{true} \mid \text{false} \mid atomic\text{-}formula$$
$$\mid \ formula \wedge formula \mid formula \vee formula \mid \neg formula$$
$$atomic\text{-}formula ::= term = term \mid predicate\text{-}symbol(term, \ldots, term)$$

Fig. 2. Syntax of a quantifier-free fragment of first-order logic

expression E involves function or predicate symbols from two (or more) theories T_1 and T_2, then E is said to be an expression over a combination of theories $T_1 \cup T_2$.

An *interpretation* $\mathcal{M} = \langle \mathcal{D}, \mathcal{J} \rangle$ consists of (i) a *domain* $\mathcal{D}$ and a (ii) mapping $\mathcal{J}$ from each function (or predicate) symbol in the theory to a function (or relation) over the domain $\mathcal{D}$. A formula ϕ is said to be *satisfiable* if there exists an interpretation $\mathcal{M}$ and an assignment ρ to the variables such that ϕ evaluates to **true** under $(\mathcal{M}, \rho)$. Such an interpretation is called a *model* of ϕ. A formula is *valid* if $\neg \phi$ is not satisfiable (or unsatisfiable). A satisfiability (or decision) procedure for Σ-theory T checks if a formula ϕ (over Σ) is satisfiable in T.

A theory T is *convex* if a quantifier-free formula ϕ in the T implies a disjunction of equalities over variables $x_1 = y_1 \vee x_2 = y_2 \ldots x_k = y_k$ if and only if ϕ implies at least one of the equalities $x_i = y_i$. A theory T is *stably-infinite* if a quantifier-free formula ϕ has a model if and only if ϕ has an infinite model, i.e., the domain of the model is infinite. Example of both convex and stably-infinite theories include the logic of Equality with Uninterpreted Functions (EUF) and rational linear arithmetic [NO79a]. Example of non-convex theories include the theory of *arrays* and the theory of integer linear arithmetic.

4.2   Nelson Oppen Combination

Given two *stably infinite* theories T_1 and T_2 with disjoint-signatures Σ_1 and Σ_2 respectively (i.e. $\Sigma_1 \cap \Sigma_2 = \{\}$), and a conjunction of literals ϕ over $\Sigma_1 \cup \Sigma_2$, we want to decide if ϕ is satisfiable under $T_1 \cup T_2$. Nelson and Oppen [NO79a] provided a method for modularly combining the satisfiability procedures for T_1 and T_2 to produce a satisfiability procedure for $T_1 \cup T_2$.

We describe the Nelson-Oppen procedure for convex theories.[2] The input ϕ is split into the formulas ϕ_1 and ϕ_2 such that ϕ_i only contains symbols from Σ_i and $\phi_1 \wedge \phi_2$ is equisatisfiable with ϕ. Each theory T_i decides the satisfiability of ϕ_i and returns unsatisfiable if ϕ_i is unsatisfiable in T_i. Otherwise, the set of equalities implied by ϕ_i over the variables common to ϕ_1 and ϕ_2 are propagated to the other theory T_j. The theory T_j adds these equalities to ϕ_j and the process repeats until the set of equalities saturate.

Therefore, in addition to checking the satisfiability of a set of literals, each theory also has to derive all the equalities over variables that are implied by the set of literals. The satisfiability procedure is called *equality generating* if it can generate all such equalities.

5   Zap

In this section, we start by describing the basic theorem proving architecture in Zap in Section 5.1. In Section 5.2, we present improvements to decision procedures for a restricted fragment of linear arithmetic that constitute most program analysis queries. In Section 5.3, we describe the handling of quantifiers in first-order formulas.

---

[2] For the description of the algorithm for non-convex case, refer to the [NO79a].

5.1   Basic Architecture

In this section, let us assume that we are checking the satisfiability of a quantifier-free first-order formula ϕ over theories $T_1, \ldots, T_k$. The basic architecture of Zap is based on a lazy proof-explicating architecture for deciding first-order formulas [ABC$^+$02, BDS02, FJOS03].

First, a Boolean abstraction of ϕ is generated by treating each atomic formula e in ϕ as an uninterpreted Boolean variable. The abstract formula is checked using a Boolean SAT solver. If the SAT solver determines that the formula is unsatisfiable, then the procedure returns unsatisfiable. Otherwise, the satisfying assignment from SAT (a monome m over the literals in ϕ) is checked for satisfiability using the Nelson-Oppen decision procedure for the combined theory $T_1 \cup \ldots \cup T_k$, as described in the last section. If ϕ is satisfiable over the first-order theories, the formula ψ is satisfiable and the procedure returns satisfiable. Otherwise, a "conflict clause" is derived from the theories that will prevent the same assignment being produced by the SAT solver. The process repeats until the Boolean SAT solver returns unsatisfiable or the Nelson-Oppen procedure returns satisfiable.

To generate a conflict clause, the decision procedure for the combined theories generates a proof of unsatisfiability when the monome m is unsatisfiable over $T_1 \cup \ldots \cup T_k$. The literals that appear in the proof constitute a conflict clause. In this framework, each theory generates the proof of (i) unsatisfiability of a monome in the theory and (ii) proof of every equality $x = y$ over the shared variables that are implied by the literals in the theory.

We use SharpSAT, a variant of the ZChaff [MMZ$^+$01] Boolean SAT solver developed at Microsoft by Lintao Zhang, as the underlying Boolean solver. In addition to checking satisfiability of a Boolean formula, SharpSAT also generates proof of unsatisfiability for unsatisfiable formulas. The theories present in Zap are the logic of equality with uninterpreted functions (EUF) and linear arithmetic. The decision procedure for EUF is based on the congruence closure algorithm [NO80]. For linear arithmetic, we have an implementation of proof-generating variant of the Simplex algorithm described in the Simplify technical report [DNS03]. We also have a decision procedure for Unit Two Variable Per Inequality (UTVPI) subset of linear arithmetic.

5.2   Restricted Linear Arithmetic Decision Procedures

Pratt [Pra77] observed that the arithmetic component in most program verification queries is mostly restricted to the difference logic ($x \leq y + c$) fragment. Recent studies by Seshia and Bryant [SB04] also indicate that more than 90% of the arithmetic constraints in some program analysis benchmarks are in difference logic fragment. We have also observed that structure of the constraints is *sparse*, i.e., if n is the number of variables in the queries, and m is the number of arithmetic constraints, then m is typically $O(n)$. In this section, we present our first step to obtain efficient decision procedure that exploit these observations.

The Unit Two Variable Per Inequality (UTVPI) logic is the fragment of integer linear arithmetic, where constraints are of the form $a.x + b.y \leq c$, where

a and b are restricted to $\{-1, 0, 1\}$ and c is an integer constant. This fragment (a generalization of difference constraints) is attractive because this is the most general class (currently known) of integer linear arithmetic for which the decision procedure enjoys a polynomial complexity [JMSY94]. Extending this fragment to contain three variables (with just unit coefficients) per inequality or adding non-unit coefficients for two variable inequalities make the decision problem NP-complete [Lag85]. Having an integer solver is often useful when dealing with variables for which rational solutions are unacceptable. Such examples often arise when modeling indices of an array or queues [FLL+02].

In [LM05a], we present an efficient decision procedure for UTVPI constraints. Our algorithm works by reducing the UTVPI constraints to a set of difference constraints, and then using negative cycle detection algorithms [CG96] to solve the resultant problem. Given m such constraints over n variables, the procedure checks the satisfiability of the constraints in $O(n.m)$ time and $O(n + m)$ space. This improves upon the previously known $O(n^2.m)$ time and $O(n^2)$ space algorithm provided by Jaffar et al. [JMSY94] based on transitive closure. The space improvement of our algorithm is particularly evident when m is $O(n)$, which occurs very frequently in practice, as the number of constraints that arise in typical verification queries have a sparse structure.

In addition to checking satisfiability of a set of UTVPI constraints, the decision procedure is also equality generating and proof producing. These requirements are in place because the decision procedure participates in the proof-explicating ATP described earlier. The decision procedure generates equalities between variables implied by a set of UTVPI constraints in $O(n.m)$ time. The algorithm can generate a proof of unsatisfiability and equalities implied in $O(n.m)$ time. Both these algorithms use linear $O(n+m)$ space. The algorithm for UTVPI generalizes our earlier results for difference logic fragment [LM05b].

We also provide a model generation algorithm for rational difference logic constraints (i.e. the variables are interpreted over rationals) in [LM05b]. The highlight of the algorithm is that the complexity of generating the model places a *linear* time and space overhead over the satisfiability checking algorithm. We also provide a model generation algorithm for integer UTVPI constraints in [LM05a]. The algorithm is currently based on transitive closure and runs in $O(n.m + n^2.logn)$ time and $O(n^2)$ space.

For many program analysis queries, having a UTVPI decision procedure suffice — more complex linear constraints often simplify to UTVPI constraints after propagating equalities and constants. We are also working on integrating the decision procedure UTVPI constraints within a general linear arithmetic decision procedure. This will enable us to exploit the efficient decision procedures for UTVPI even in the presence of (hopefully a few) general linear arithmetic constraints.

5.3 Quantifiers

Quantified statements naturally arise when analyzing invariants over arrays and data structures such as maps. To handle such quantified formulas, Zap uses an approach very similar to Simplify based on heuristic instantiations. When the theories (that reason on quantifier-free literals in the formula) are not able to detect unsatisfiability, Zap uses various heuristics to instantiate quantified formulas with relevant terms from the input formula. Zap propagates the resulting quantifier-free formulas to the theories, which in turn try to detect unsatisfiability. This instantiation process continues for a few iterations (if necessary) after which Zap returns stating its inability to prove the unsatisfiability of the formula.

One challenge in supporting this instantiation based approach in a lazy proof explication setting is the following. Quantified formulas typically involve propositional connectives. As a result, quantifier instantiations performed during theory reasoning can dynamically introduce Boolean structure in the formula. This directly conflicts with the requirement that the Boolean structure be exposed statically to the SAT solver in a lazy proof explication setting. Moreover, most quantifier instantiations are not useful in proving the validity of the formula. Blindly exposing such redundant instantiations to the SAT solver could drastically reduce the performance of the propositional search.

To alleviate these problems, Zap implements a *two-tier* technique [LMO05] for supporting quantifiers. This technique involves two instances of a SAT solver, a *main* solver that performs the propositional reasoning of the input formula, and a *little* solver that reasons over the quantifier instantiations. When the main SAT solver produces a propositionally satisfying instance that is consistent with the decision procedures, the heuristic instantiation process generates a set of new facts that The little SAT solver, along with the decision procedures, tries to falsify the satisfying instance with the instantiations produced. If successful, the little SAT solver generates a blocking clause that only contains literals from the input formula. By thus separating the propositional reasoning of the input formula from that of the instantiated formulas, this technique reduces the propositional search space, with an eye toward improving performance.

In practice, we have found that our implementation is limited by the heuristics we use to instantiate quantifiers. These heuristics rely heavily on the "patterns" that the user specifies with each quantified statement. The performance of the ATP changes significantly even for slight changes to these patterns requiring several iterations to get them right. Moreover, we have found that it takes considerable effort to automate the process of generating these patterns. Ideally, we could use general purpose resolution-based ATPs (such as Vampire [RA01]) that are optimized to reason about quantified statements. However, these ATPs do not effectively support arithmetic reasoning, an important requirement for Zap. Combining a decision procedure for integers with a resolution-based ATP is a challenging open problem. Such an ATP would be very useful in our setting.

6   Richer Operations and Their Combinations

As described in Section 2, the main goal of Zap is to support a rich set of symbolic operations, apart from validity checking. These operations, such as quantifier elimination and model generation are essential to support symbolic computation in Zap's clients. On the other hand, Zap needs to support a variety of theories (Section 3) that are useful for program analysis. Supporting these symbolic operations in the presence of multiple theories leads to an interesting challenge of *combining* these operations across theories.

Specifically, we seek a generalization of the Nelson-Oppen combination for decision procedures as follows. For a particular symbolic operation, assume that there exists a theory-specific procedure that performs the operation for formulas in that theory. Now, given such procedures for two different theories, the *combination* problem is to devise a procedure that performs the symbolic operation on formulas in the combination of the two theories, using the two theory-specific procedures as black boxes. When the symbolic operation in question is that of determining the satisfiability of a set of formulas then the general combination problem reduces to the well studied combination of decision procedures.

Such a combination procedure for supporting symbolic operations has several advantages over a monolithic procedure for a specific combination of theories. First, the combination approach provides the flexibility of adding more theories in the future. This is very important for Zap as enabling new applications might require supporting new theories. Second, the combination approach allows each theory-specific decision procedure to be independently designed, implemented and proven correct. The combination method itself needs to be proven once. The correctness of a particular combination directly follows from the correctness of each individual theory-specific procedure and the correctness of the combination method. Finally, the combination approach leads to a modular implementation of Zap that greatly simplifies the correctness of the implementation.

In the following sections, we describe how we extended the equality propagation framework of Nelson-Oppen combination to modularly combine procedures for interpolant-generation (in Section 6.1), and predicate abstraction (in Section 6.2). In Section 6.3, we present difficulties in modularly combining model generation procedures. The combination methods for other symbolic operations still remains open.

6.1   Interpolants

In [YM05], we presented a novel combination method for generating interpolants for a class of first-order theories. Using interpolant-generation procedures for component theories as black-boxes, this method generates interpolants for formulas in the combined theory. Provided the individual procedures for the component theories can generate interpolants in polynomial time, our method generates interpolants for the combined theory in polynomial time.

The combination method uses the fact that the proof of unsatisfiability produced in a Nelson-Oppen combination has a particular structure. In the Nelson-Oppen framework, the decision procedures for component theories communicate by propagating entailed equalities. Accordingly, the proof can be split into theory-specific portions that only involve inference rules from that theory. These theory-specific portions use literals from the input or equalities generated by other theories. The crucial idea behind the combination method is to associate a *partial interpolant* with each propagated equality. Whenever a component theory propagates an equality, the combination method uses the interpolant-generation procedure for that theory to generate the partial interpolant for the equality. When a theory detects a contradiction, the combination method uses the partial interpolants of all propagated equalities to compute the interpolant for the input formulas.

The combination method places some restrictions on the theories that can be combined. The Nelson-Oppen combination requires that the component theories have disjoint signatures and be *stably-infinite* [NO79b, Opp80]. Our method naturally inherits these restrictions. Additionally, our combination method restricts the form of equalities that can be shared by the component theories. Specifically, the method requires that each propagated equality only involve symbols common to both input formulas A and B. We show that this restricted form of equality propagation is sufficient for a class of theories, which we characterize as *equality-interpolating* theories. Many useful theories including the quantifier-free theories of uninterpreted functions, linear arithmetic, and Lisp structures are equality-interpolating, and thus can be combined with our method.

While the restriction to equality-interpolating theories provides us a way to extend the existing Nelson-Oppen combination framework, the problem of generalizing the combination result to other theories remains open. Moreover, while our method generates *an* interpolant between two formulas, it is not clear if the interpolant generated is useful for the program analysis in question. Accordingly, we need to formalize the notion of *usefulness* of an interpolant to a particular analysis and design an algorithm that finds such interpolants.

6.2   Predicate Abstraction

Given a formula ϕ and a set of predicates P, the fundamental operation in predicate abstraction is to find the best approximation of ϕ using P. Let $\mathcal{F}_P(\phi)$ be the weakest expression obtained by a Boolean combination of the predicates that implies ϕ.[3]

In [LBC05], we describe a new technique for computing $\mathcal{F}_P(\phi)$ without using decision procedures, and provide a framework for computing $\mathcal{F}_P(\phi)$ for a combination of theories. We present a brief description of the approach in this section.

For simplicity, let us assume that ϕ is an atomic expression (for more general treatment, refer to [LBC05]). To compute $\mathcal{F}_P(\phi)$, we define a *symbolic decision procedure* (*SDP*) for a theory to be a procedure that takes as input a set of atomic expressions G and an atomic expression e and returns a symbolic *representation* of all the subsets $G' \subseteq G$ such that $G' \wedge \neg e$ is unsatisfiable. $SDP(G, e)$ symbolically simulates the execution of a decision procedure on every subset $G' \subseteq G$. Let $\tilde{P}$ be the set of negated predicates in P. If the formula ϕ and the predicates P belong to a theory T, then $SDP(P \cup \tilde{P}, \phi)$ represents $\mathcal{F}_P(\phi)$.

---

[3] Note that $\mathcal{F}_P(\phi)$ is the dual of $\mathsf{cover}_P(\phi)$ introduced earlier. It is easy to see that $\mathsf{cover}_P(\phi) = \neg\mathcal{F}_P(\neg\phi)$.

We present an algorithm for constructing SDP for a class of theories called *saturating theories*. For a theory T, consider the following procedure that repeatedly derives new facts from existing facts by applying the inference rules of the theory on the existing set of facts — Given a set of atomic expressions $H_0 \doteq H$, let $H_0, H_1, \ldots, H_i, \ldots$ denote a sequence of sets of atomic expressions in T such that H_{i+1} is the set of atomic expressions either present in H_i or derived from H_i using inference rules in the theory. A theory is saturating, if (i) each of the sets H_i is finite and, (ii) if H is inconsistent, then `false` is present in H_{k_H}, where k_H is a finite value that is a function of the expressions in H alone. For such a saturating theory one can construct $SDP(G, e)$ by additionally maintaining the derivation history for each expression in any H_i. The derivation history can be maintained as a directed acyclic graph, with leaves corresponding to the facts in H. Finally, the expression for $SDP(G, e)$ can be obtained by performing the above procedure for $H \doteq G \cup \{\neg e\}$ and returning (all) the derivations of `false` after k_H steps.

For two saturating theories T_1 and T_2 with disjoint signatures that also are convex and stably-infinite, we present a procedure for constructing SDP for the combined theory $T_1 \cup T_2$, by extending the Nelson-Oppen framework. Intuitively, we symbolically encode the operation of the Nelson-Oppen equality sharing framework for any possible input for the two theories. The SDP for the combined theory incurs a polynomial blowup over the SDP for either theory. For many theories that are relevant to program analysis, SDP can be computed in polynomial or pseudo-polynomial time and space complexity. Examples of such theories include EUF and difference logic (DIF). The combination procedure allows us to construct an SDP from these theories' SDPs.

We have implemented and benchmarked our technique on a set of program analysis queries derived from device driver verification [BMMR01]. Preliminary results are encouraging and the new predicate abstraction procedure outperformed decision procedure based predicate abstraction methods by orders of magnitude [LBC05]. It remains open how to extend this approach in the presence of more complex (non-convex) theories or quantifiers.

6.3   Model Generation

When Zap reports that a first-order formula ϕ is satisfiable, it is desirable to find a model for ϕ. Apart from serving as a witness to the satisfiability of ϕ, the model generated is very useful for generating test cases from symbolic execution of software. In this section, we present some of the issues in combining model generation for different theories.

To generate an assignment for the variables that are shared across two theories, each theory T_i needs to ensure that the variable assignment ρ for T_i assigns two shared variables x and y equal values if and only if the equality $x = y$ is implied by the constraints in theory T_i. Such a model where $\rho(x) = \rho(y)$ if and only if $T_i \cup \phi_i$ implies $x = y$, is called a *diverse* model. We have shown that for even (integer) difference logic, producing *diverse* models is NP-complete [LM05a].

The following example shows why diverse model generation is required in the Nelson-Oppen framework. Let $\phi = (f(x) \neq f(y) \wedge x \leq y)$ be a formula in the combined theory of EUF and UTVPI. An ATP based on the Nelson-Oppen framework will add $\phi_1 \doteq f(x) \neq f(y)$ to the EUF theory (T_1) and $\phi_2 \doteq x \leq y$ to the UTVPI theory (T_2). Since there are no equalities implied by either theory, and each theory T_i is consistent with ϕ_i, the formula ϕ is satisfiable. Now, the UTVPI theory could generate the model $\rho \doteq \langle x \mapsto 0, y \mapsto 0 \rangle$ for ϕ_2. However, this is not a model for ϕ, as it is not diverse.

Presently, Zap uses various heuristics for generating a model consistent with all the theories. As a last resort, we perform an equisatisfiable translation of ϕ to a Boolean formula using an *eager* encoding of first-order formulas [LS04, SB04] and use the SAT solver to search for a model[4].

7   Related Work

In this section, we describe some prior work on theorem proving and symbolic reasoning for program analysis.

Simplify [DNS03] is an ATP that was built to discharge verification conditions (VCs) in various program analysis projects including ESC/JAVA [FLL+02]. It supports many of the theories discussed in this paper along with quantifiers. It is based on the Nelson-Oppen framework for combining decision procedures. Apart from validity checking, Simplify allows for error localization by allowing the verification conditions to contain *labels* from the program. These labels help to localize the source locations and the type of errors when the validity check of a VC fails.

McMillan [McM04] presents an interpolating ATP for the theories of EUF and linear inequalities (and their combination). This ATP has been used in abstraction refinement for the BLAST [HJMM04] software model checker. Our work on combining interpolants for various equality-interpolating theories generalizes McMillan's work, and extends it to other theories. Lahiri et al. [LBC03] present an algorithm for performing predicate abstraction for a combination of various first-order theories by performing Boolean quantifier elimination. Unlike their approach, the use of symbolic decision procedures in our case allows us to perform predicate abstraction in a modular fashion.

Gulwani et al. [GTN04] present join algorithms for subclasses of EUF using *abstract congruence closure* [BTV03]. They show the completeness of he algorithm for several subclasses including the cases when the functions are *injective*. Chang and Leino [CL05] provide an algorithm for performing abstract operations (e.g. join, widen etc.) for a given *base* domain (e.g. the polyhedra domain for linear inequalities [CH78]) in the presence of symbols that do not belong to the theory. Their framework introduces names for each *alien* expression in the theory. A congruence closure abstract domain equipped with the abstract operations (join, widen etc.) is used to reason about the mapping of the names to

---

[4] Krishna K. Mehra implemented part of the model generation algorithm in Zap when he spent the summer in Microsoft.

the alien expressions. They instantiate the framework for the polyhedra domain and a domain for reasoning about heap updates.

There has also been a renewed interest in constructing decision procedures for first-order theories by exploiting SAT solver's backtracking search. Decision procedures based on lazy proof explicating framework (e.g. CVC [BDS02], Verifun [FJOS03], Mathsat [ABC+02]), eager approaches (e.g. UCLID [BLS02]), extending DPLL search to incorporate theory reasoning [GHN+04] have been proposed to exploit rapid advances in SAT solvers. Although Zap is closest to the lazy approaches in its architectures, we are also investigating the best match of these approaches for the nature of queries generated by the various clients of program analysis.

References

[ABC+02]   G. Audemard, P. Bertoli, A. Cimatti, A. Korniłowicz, and R. Sebastiani. A SAT-based approach for solving formulas over Boolean and linear mathematical propositions. In *CADE 02: Conference on Automated Deduction*, LNCS 2392, pages 195–210. Springer-Verlag, 2002.

[AQRX04]   T. Andrews, S. Qadeer, S. K. Rajamani, and Y. Xie. Zing: Exploiting program structure for model checking concurrent software. In *CONCUR 04: Concurrency Theory*, LNCS 3170, pages 1–15. Springer-Verlag, 2004.

[BCM+92]   J.R. Burch, E.M. Clarke, K.L. McMillan, D.L. Dill, and L.J. Hwang. Symbolic model checking: 10^{20} states and beyond. *Information and Computation*, 98(2):142–170, 1992.

[BDS02]   C. W. Barrett, D. L. Dill, and A. Stump. Checking satisfiability of first-order formulas by incremental translation to SAT. In *CAV 02: Computer-Aided Verification*, LNCS 2404, pages 236–249. Springer-Verlag, 2002.

[BLS02]   R. E. Bryant, S. K. Lahiri, and S. A. Seshia. Modeling and verifying systems using a logic of counter arithmetic with lambda expressions and uninterpreted functions. In *CAV 02: Computer-Aided Verification*, LNCS 2404, pages 78–92. Springer-Verlag, 2002.

[BLS05]   M. Barnett, K. Rustan M. Leino, and Wolfram Schulte. The Spec# programming system: An overview. In *CASSIS 04: Construction and Analysis of Safe, Secure, and Interoperable Smart Devices*, LNCS 3362, pages 49–69. Springer-Verlag, 2005.

[BMMR01]   T. Ball, R. Majumdar, T. Millstein, and S. K. Rajamani. Automatic predicate abstraction of C programs. In *PLDI 01: Programming Language Design and Implementation*, pages 203–213. ACM, 2001.

[BR01]   T. Ball and S. K. Rajamani. Automatically validating temporal safety properties of interfaces. In *SPIN 01: SPIN Workshop*, LNCS 2057, pages 103–122. Springer-Verlag, 2001.

[Bry86]   R.E. Bryant. Graph-based algorithms for Boolean function manipulation. *IEEE Transactions on Computers*, C-35(8):677–691, 1986.

[BTV03]   Leo Bachmair, Ashish Tiwari, and Laurent Vigneron. Abstract congruence closure. *J. Autom. Reasoning*, 31(2):129–168, 2003.

[CC77]   P. Cousot and R. Cousot. Abstract interpretation: a unified lattice model for the static analysis of programs by construction or approximation of fixpoints. In *POPL 77: Principles of Programming Languages*, pages 238–252. ACM, 1977.

20   T. Ball, S.K. Lahiri, and M. Musuvathi

[CG96]   B. V. Cherkassky and A. V. Goldberg. Negative-cycle detection algo-
           rithms. In *European Symposium on Algorithms*, pages 349–363, 1996.
[CGJ+00]   E. Clarke, O. Grumberg, S. Jha, Y. Lu, and H. Veith. Counterexample-
           guided abstraction refinement. In *CAV 00: Computer Aided Verification*,
           LNCS 1855, pages 154–169. Springer-Verlag, 2000.
[CH78]   P. Cousot and N. Halbwachs. Automatic discovery of linear restraints
           among variables of a program. In *POPL 78: Principles of Programming
           Languages*, pages 84–96. ACM, 1978.
[CL05]   B-Y. E. Chang and K. R. M. Leino. Abstract interpretation with alien ex-
           pressions and heap structures. In *VMCAI 05: Verification, Model Check-
           ing, and Abstract Interpretation*, LNCS 3385, pages 147–163. Springer-
           Verlag, 2005.
[Cla76]   L. A. Clarke. A system to generate test data and symbolically execute
           programs. *IEEE Transactions on Software Engineering*, 2(3):215–222,
           September 1976.
[DNS03]   D. L. Detlefs, G. Nelson, and J. B. Saxe. Simplify: A theorem prover for
           program checking. Technical report, HPL-2003-148, 2003.
[FJOS03]   C. Flanagan, R. Joshi, X. Ou, and J. Saxe. Theorem proving using lazy
           proof explication. In *CAV 03: Computer-Aided Verification*, LNCS 2725,
           pages 355–367. Springer-Verlag, 2003.
[FLL+02]   C. Flanagan, K. R. M. Leino, M. Lillibridge, G. Nelson, J. B. Saxe, and
           R. Stata. Extended static checking for Java. In *PLDI 02: Programming
           Language Design and Implementation*, pages 234–245. ACM, 2002.
[GHN+04]   H. Ganzinger, G. Hagen, R. Nieuwenhuis, A. Oliveras, and C. Tinelli.
           DPLL(T): Fast decision procedures. In *CAV 04: Computer Aided Verifi-
           cation*, LNCS 3114, pages 175–188. Springer-Verlag, 2004.
[GM93]   M. J. C. Gordon and T. F. Melham. *Introduction to HOL: A Theo-
           rem Proving Environment for Higher-Order Logic*. Cambridge University
           Press, 1993.
[GS97]   S. Graf and H. Saidi. Construction of abstract state graphs with PVS. In
           CAV 97: Computer Aided Verification, LNCS 1254, pages 72–83. Springer-
           Verlag, 1997.
[GTN04]   S. Gulwani, A. Tiwari, and G. C. Necula. Join algorithms for the theory
           of uninterpreted functions. In *FSTTCS 2004: Foundations of Software
           Technology and Theoretical Computer Science*, LNCS 3328, pages 311–
           323. Springer, 2004.
[HJMM04]   T. A. Henzinger, R. Jhala, R. Majumdar, and K. L. McMillan. Abstrac-
           tions from proofs. In *POPL 04: Principles of Programming Languages*,
           pages 232–244. ACM, 2004.
[IRR+04]   N. Immerman, A. Rabinovich, T. Reps, S. Sagiv, and G. Yorsh. The
           boundary between decidability and undecidability for transitive-closure
           logics. In *CSL 04: Conference on Computer Science Logic*, LNCS 3210,
           pages 160–174. Springer-Verlag, 2004.
[JMSY94]   J. Jaffar, M. J. Maher, P. J. Stuckey, and H. C. Yap. Beyond finite do-
           mains. In *PPCP 94: Principles and Practice of Constraint Programming*,
           LNCS 874, pages 86–94. Springer-Verlag, 1994.
[Kur94]   R.P. Kurshan. *Computer-aided Verification of Coordinating Processes*.
           Princeton University Press, 1994.
[Lag85]   J. C. Lagarias. The computational complexity of simultaneous diophan-
           tine approximation problems. *SIAM Journal of Computing*, 14(1):196–
           209, 1985.

[LBC03]   S. K. Lahiri, R. E. Bryant, and B. Cook. A symbolic approach to predicate abstraction. In *CAV 03: Computer-Aided Verification*, LNCS 2725, pages 141–153. Springer-Verlag, 2003.

[LBC05]   S. K. Lahiri, T. Ball, and B. Cook. Predicate abstraction via symbolic decision procedures. In *CAV 05: Computer Aided Verification*, LNCS 3576, pages 24–38. Springer-Verlag, 2005.

[LM05a]   S. K. Lahiri and M. Musuvathi. An efficient decision procedure for UTVPI constraints. In *FroCos 05: Frontiers of Combining Systems*, LNCS 3717, pages 168–183. Springer-Verlag, 2005.

[LM05b]   S. K. Lahiri and M. Musuvathi. An efficient Nelson-Oppen decision procedure for difference constraints over rationals. Technical Report MSR-TR-2005-61, Microsoft Research, 2005.

[LMO05]   K. R. M. Leino, M. Musuvathi, and X. Ou. A two-tier technique for supporting quantifiers in a lazily proof-explicating theorem prover. In *TACAS 05: Tools and Algorithms for the Construction and Analysis of Systems*, LNCS 3440, pages 334–348. Springer-Verlag, 2005.

[LS04]   S. K. Lahiri and S. A. Seshia. The UCLID decision procedure. In *CAV 04: Computer Aided Verification*, LNCS 3114, pages 475–478. Springer-Verlag, 2004.

[Mar99]   P. Marquis. Consequence-finding algorithms. In *Handbook of Defeasible Reasoning and Uncertainty Management Systems (vol. 5): Algorithms for Defeasible and Uncertain Reasoning*, pages 41–145. Kluwer Academic Publishers, 1999.

[McM03]   K.L. McMillan. Interpolation and SAT-based model checking. In *CAV 03: Computer-Aided Verification*, LNCS 2725, pages 1–13. Springer-Verlag, 2003.

[McM04]   K.L. McMillan. An interpolating theorem prover. In *TACAS 04: Tools and Algorithms for Construction and Analysis of Systems*, pages 16–30. Springer-Verlag, 2004.

[MMZ+01]   M. Moskewicz, C. Madigan, Y. Zhao, L. Zhang, and S. Malik. Chaff: Engineering an efficient SAT solver. In *DAC 01: Design Automation Conference*, pages 530–535. ACM Press, 2001.

[MS01]   A. Møller and M. I. Schwartzbach. The pointer assertion logic engine. In *PLDI 01: Programming Language Design and Implementation*, pages 221–231. ACM Press, 2001.

[Nec97]   G.C. Necula. Proof carrying code. In *POPL 97: Principles of Programming Languages*, pages 106–119. ACM, 1997.

[NO79a]   G. Nelson and D. C. Oppen. Simplification by cooperating decision procedures. *ACM Transactions on Programming Languages and Systems (TOPLAS)*, 2(1):245–257, 1979.

[NO79b]   G. Nelson and D. C. Oppen. Simplification by cooperating decision procedures. *ACM Transactions on Programming Languages and Systems*, 1(2):245–257, October 1979.

[NO80]   G. Nelson and D. C. Oppen. Fast decision procedures based on the congruence closure. *Journal of the ACM*, 27(2):356–364, 1980.

[Opp80]   Derek C. Oppen. Complexity, convexity and combinations of theories. In *Theoretical Computer Science*, volume 12, pages 291–302, 1980.

[ORS92]   S. Owre, J. M. Rushby, and N. Shankar. PVS: A prototype verification system. In *CADE 92: Conference on Automated Deduction*, LNCS 607, pages 748–752. Springer-Verlag, 1992.

[Pra77]   V. Pratt. Two easy theories whose combination is hard. Technical report, Massachusetts Institute of Technology, Cambridge, Mass., September 1977.

[RA01]   A. Riazanov and A.Voronkov. Vampire 1.1 (system description). In *IJ-CAR '01: International Joint Conference on Automated Reasoning*, LNAI 2083, pages 376–380. Springer-Verlag, 2001.

[SB04]   S. A. Seshia and R. E. Bryant. Deciding quantifier-free Presburger formulas using parameterized solution bounds. In *LICS 04: Logic in Computer Science*, pages 100–109. IEEE Computer Society, July 2004.

[SG04]   S. Shoham and O. Grumberg. Monotonic abstraction-refinement for CTL. In *TACAS 04: Tools and Algorithms for Construction and Analysis of Systems*, LNCS 2988, pages 546–560. Springer-Verlag, 2004.

[SRW99]   M. Sagiv, T. Reps, and R. Wilhelm. Parametric shape analysis via 3-valued logic. In *POPL 99: Principles of Programming Languages*, pages 105–118. ACM, 1999.

[TH96]   C. Tinelli and M. T. Harandi. A new correctness proof of the Nelson–Oppen combination procedure. In *FroCos 96: Frontiers of Combining Systems*, Applied Logic, pages 103–120. Kluwer Academic Publishers, 1996.

[TS05]   N. Tillmann and W. Schulte. Parameterized unit tests. In *FSE 05: Foundations of Software Engineering*, pages 253–262. ACM Press, 2005.

[YM05]   G. Yorsh and M. Musuvathi. A combination method for generating interpolants. In *CADE 05: Conference on Automated Deduction*, LNCS 3632, pages 353–368. Springer-Verlag, 2005.

[YRS04]   G. Yorsh, T. Reps, and M. Sagiv. Symbolically computing most-precise abstract operations for shape analysis. In *TACAS 04: Tools and Algorithms for Construction and Analysis of Systems*, LNCS 2988, pages 530–545. Springer-Verlag, 2004.

[ZZ96]   H. Zhang and J. Zhang. Generating models by SEM. In *CADE 96: Conference on Automated Deduction*, LNAI 1104, pages 308–312. Springer-Verlag, 1996.

Decision Procedures for SAT, SAT Modulo Theories and Beyond. The BarcelogicTools*

Robert Nieuwenhuis and Albert Oliveras**

Abstract. An overview is given of a number of recent developments in SAT and SAT Modulo Theories (SMT). In particular, based on our framework of Abstract DPLL and Abstract DPLL modulo Theories, we explain our DPLL(T) approach to SMT.

Experimental results and future projects are discussed within Barce-logicTools, a set of logic-based tools developed by our research group in Barcelona. At the 2005 SMT competition, BarcelogicTools won all four categories it participated in (out of the seven existing categories).

1 Introduction

Nowadays, SAT solvers and their extensions are becoming the tool of choice for attacking more and more different problems in areas such as Electronic Design Automation, Verification, Artificial Intelligence, or Operations Research. Most state-of-the-art SAT solvers [MMZ+01, GN02, ES03, Rya04] today are based on the Davis-Putnam-Logemann-Loveland (DPLL) procedure [DP60, DLL62]. These DPLL-based SAT solvers have spectacularly improved in the last years, due to better implementation techniques and conceptual enhancements such as *backjumping, conflict-driven lemma learning* ([MSS99]), and *restarts*. These advances make it possible to decide the satisfiability of industrial SAT problems with tens of thousands of variables and millions of clauses.

Because of their success, both the DPLL procedure and its enhancements have been adapted for handling satisfiability problems in logics that are more expressive than propositional logic. For example, some properties of timed automata are naturally expressed in *difference logic*, where formulas contain atoms of the form $a - b \leq k$, which are interpreted with respect to a background theory T of the integers, rationals or reals [Alu99]. Similarly, for the verification of pipelined microprocessors it is convenient to consider a logic of *Equality with Uninterpreted Functions (EUF)*, where the background theory T specifies a congruence [BD94]. To mention just one other example, the conditions arising from

---

* Parts of this work were published in a preliminary form in [NO03, GHN+04, NOT05] [NO05c, NO05b, NO05a], several of them in collaboration with Cesare Tinelli.
** Technical Univ. of Catalonia, Barcelona, www.lsi.upc.es/~roberto|~oliveras. Partially supported by Spanish Min. of Educ. and Science through the LogicTools project (TIN2004-03382, both authors), FPU grant AP2002-3533 (Oliveras), and by Cesare Tinelli's NSF Career grant #0237422 supporting Oliveras' stays in Iowa.

G. Sutcliffe and A. Voronkov (Eds.): LPAR 2005, LNAI 3835, pp. 23–46, 2005.

program verification usually involve arrays, lists and other data structures, so it becomes very natural to consider satisfiability problems *modulo* the theory T of these data structures. In such applications, problems may contain thousands of clauses like

$$p \quad \vee \quad \neg q \quad \vee \quad a = f(b - c) \quad \vee \quad read(s, f(b - c)) = d \quad \vee \quad a - g(c) \leq 7$$

containing purely propositional atoms as well as atoms over (combined) theories. This is known as the *Satisfiability Modulo Theories* (SMT) problem for a theory T: given a formula F, determine whether F is T-satisfiable, i.e., whether there exists a model of T that is also a model of F. A library of benchmarks for SMT called *SMT-LIB* is maintained at http://combination.cs.uiowa.edu/smtlib/ and a formal standard for its syntax exists [RT03].

In this paper, based on our framework of Abstract DPLL (Section 2) and Abstract DPLL modulo Theories (Section 3), we explain our DPLL(T) approach to SMT (Section 4). We describe two variants of DPLL(T), depending on whether *theory propagation* is done exhaustively or not. DPLL(T) is based on a general DPLL(X) engine, whose parameter X can be instantiated with specialized solvers $Solver_T$ for given theories T, thus producing a system DPLL(T). Once the DPLL(X) engine has been implemented, this approach becomes extremely flexible: new theories can be dealt with by simply plugging in new theory solvers. These solvers must only be able to deal with *conjunctions* of theory literals and conform to a minimal and simple set of additional requirements. We describe how DPLL(X) and $Solver_T$ cooperate, and the architecture of DPLL(T) for several theories that are widely used in industrial verification problems.

Section 5 describes BarcelogicTools, a set of logic-based tools developed by our research group in Barcelona, including, in particular, a state-of-the-art SAT solver, a DPLL(X) engine, and a number of theory solvers. Results show that our DPLL(T) systems in BarcelogicTools significantly outperform the other state-of-the-art tools, frequently in several orders of magnitude, and moreover scale up very well. In fact, at the 2005 SMT competition, BarcelogicTools won all four categories it participated in (out of seven categories that existed in total; search SMT Competition on the web). Finally, some future extensions of the BarcelogicTools project are discussed.

2   Abstract DPLL in the Propositional Case

Let P be a fixed finite set of propositional symbols. If $p \in P$, then p and $\neg p$ are *literals* of P. The *negation* of a literal l, written $\neg l$, denotes $\neg p$ if l is p, and p if l is $\neg p$. A *clause* is a disjunction of literals $l_1 \vee \ldots \vee l_n$. A *unit clause* is a clause consisting of a single literal. A (finite, non-empty, CNF) *formula* is a conjunction of one or more clauses $C_1 \wedge \ldots \wedge C_n$. When it leads to no ambiguities, we sometimes also write such a formula in set notation $\{C_1, \ldots, C_n\}$ or simply replace $\wedge$ connectives by commas.

A (partial truth) *assignment* M is a set of literals such that $\{p, \neg p\} \subseteq M$ for no p. A literal l is *true* in M if $l \in M$, it is *false* in M if $\neg l \in M$, and l is *undefined* in M otherwise. M is *total* over P if no literal of P is undefined in M. A clause C is true in M if at least one of its literals is in M. It is false in M if all its literals are false in M, and it is undefined in M otherwise. A formula F is true in M, or *satisfied* by M, denoted $M \models F$, if all its clauses are true in M. In that case, M is called a *model* of F. If F has no models then it is called *unsatisfiable*. If F and F' are formulas, we write $F \models F'$ if F' is true in all models of F. Then we say that F' *is entailed by* F, or is a *logical consequence* of F. If $F \models F'$ and $F' \models F$, we say that F and F' are *logically equivalent*.

In what follows, (possibly subscripted or primed) lowercase l *always* denote literals. Similarly C and D always denote clauses, F and G denote formulas, and M and N are assignments. If C is a clause $l_1 \vee \ldots \vee l_n$, we sometimes write $\neg C$ to denote the formula $\neg l_1 \wedge \ldots \wedge \neg l_n$.

2.1   The Classical DPLL Procedure

Here a DPLL procedure is modelled by a transition relation over states (check [NOT05] for details). A state is either *FailState* or a pair $M \parallel F$, where F is a finite set of clauses and M is a sequence of literals that is seen as a partial interpretation. Some literals l in M will be *annotated* as being *decision literals*; these are the ones added to M by the Decide rule given below, and are sometimes written l^d. The transition relation is defined by means of rules. The following simple Classical DPLL system is given here mainly for explanatory and historical reasons.

Definition 1. *The* Classical DPLL system *Cl consists of the five rules:*

UnitPropagate :
$$M \parallel F, C \vee l \quad \Longrightarrow \quad M\, l \parallel F, C \vee l \quad \text{if} \quad \begin{cases} M \models \neg C \\ l \text{ is undefined in } M \end{cases}$$

PureLiteral :
$$M \parallel F \quad \Longrightarrow \quad M\, l \parallel F \quad \text{if} \quad \begin{cases} l \text{ occurs in some clause of } F \\ \neg l \text{ occurs in no clause of } F \\ l \text{ is undefined in } M \end{cases}$$

Decide :
$$M \parallel F \quad \Longrightarrow \quad M\, l^d \parallel F \quad \text{if} \quad \begin{cases} l \text{ or } \neg l \text{ occurs in a clause of } F \\ l \text{ is undefined in } M \end{cases}$$

Fail :
$$M \parallel F, C \quad \Longrightarrow \quad FailState \quad \text{if} \quad \begin{cases} M \models \neg C \\ M \text{ contains no decision literals} \end{cases}$$

Backtrack :
$$M\, l^d\, N \parallel F, C \Longrightarrow M\, \neg l \parallel F, C \quad \text{if} \quad \begin{cases} M\, l^d\, N \models \neg C \\ N \text{ contains no decision literals} \end{cases}$$

One can use the transition system Cl for deciding the satisfiability of an input CNF F by simply generating an arbitrary derivation $\emptyset \parallel F \implies_{Cl} \ldots \implies_{Cl} S_n$, where S_n is a final state with respect to Cl. Such derivations are always finite, and (i) F is unsatisfiable if, and only if, the final state S_n is *FailState*, and (ii) if S_n is of the form $M \parallel F$ then M is a model of F.

These rules speak for themselves, providing a classical depth-first search with backtracking, where the Decide rule represents a case split: an undefined literal l is chosen from F, and added to M. The literal is annotated as a *decision literal*, to denote that, if $M\ l$ cannot be extended to a model of F, then (by Backtrack) still the other possibility $M\ \neg l$ must be explored. In the following, if M is a sequence of the form $M_0\ l_1\ M_1 \ldots l_k\ M_k$, where the l_i are all the decision literals in M, then the literals of each $l_i\ M_i$ are said to *belong to decision level i*.

Example 2. In the following derivation, to improve readability we have denoted atoms by natural numbers, negation by overlining, and written decision literals in **bold** font:

$$
\begin{array}{llllll}
\emptyset \parallel & \overline{1}\vee\overline{2}, & 2\vee 3, & \overline{1}\vee\overline{3}\vee 4, & 2\vee\overline{3}\vee\overline{4}, & 1\vee 4 & \implies_{Cl} & \text{(Decide)} \\
\mathbf{1} \parallel & \overline{1}\vee\overline{2}, & 2\vee 3, & \overline{1}\vee\overline{3}\vee 4, & 2\vee\overline{3}\vee\overline{4}, & 1\vee 4 & \implies_{Cl} & \text{(UnitPropagate)} \\
\mathbf{1}\ \overline{2} \parallel & \overline{1}\vee\overline{2}, & 2\vee 3, & \overline{1}\vee\overline{3}\vee 4, & 2\vee\overline{3}\vee\overline{4}, & 1\vee 4 & \implies_{Cl} & \text{(UnitPropagate)} \\
\mathbf{1}\ \overline{2}\ 3 \parallel & \overline{1}\vee\overline{2}, & 2\vee 3, & \overline{1}\vee\overline{3}\vee 4, & 2\vee\overline{3}\vee\overline{4}, & 1\vee 4 & \implies_{Cl} & \text{(UnitPropagate)} \\
\mathbf{1}\ \overline{2}\ 3\ 4 \parallel & \overline{1}\vee\overline{2}, & 2\vee 3, & \overline{1}\vee\overline{3}\vee 4, & 2\vee\overline{3}\vee\overline{4}, & 1\vee 4 & \implies_{Cl} & \text{(Backtrack)} \\
\overline{1} \parallel & \overline{1}\vee\overline{2}, & 2\vee 3, & \overline{1}\vee\overline{3}\vee 4, & 2\vee\overline{3}\vee\overline{4}, & 1\vee 4 & \implies_{Cl} & \text{(UnitPropagate)} \\
\overline{1}\ 4 \parallel & \overline{1}\vee\overline{2}, & 2\vee 3, & \overline{1}\vee\overline{3}\vee 4, & 2\vee\overline{3}\vee\overline{4}, & 1\vee 4 & \implies_{Cl} & \text{(Decide)} \\
\overline{1}\ 4\ \mathbf{3} \parallel & \overline{1}\vee\overline{2}, & 2\vee 3, & \overline{1}\vee\overline{3}\vee 4, & 2\vee\overline{3}\vee\overline{4}, & 1\vee 4 & \implies_{Cl} & \text{(UnitPropagate)} \\
\overline{1}\ 4\ \mathbf{3}\ 2 \parallel & \overline{1}\vee\overline{2}, & 2\vee 3, & \overline{1}\vee\overline{3}\vee 4, & 2\vee\overline{3}\vee\overline{4}, & 1\vee 4 & & \text{Final state:} \\
& & & & & & & \text{model found.} \quad \square
\end{array}
$$

The Davis-Putnam procedure [DP60] was originally presented as a two-phase proof-procedure for first-order logic. The unsatisfiability of a formula was to be proved by first generating a suitable set of ground instances which then, in the second phase, were shown to be propositionally unsatisfiable.

Subsequent improvements, such as the Davis-Logemann-Loveland procedure of [DLL62], mostly focused on the propositional phase. What most authors nowadays call the *DPLL Procedure* is a satisfiability procedure for propositional logic based on this propositional phase. Originally, this procedure amounted to the depth-first search algorithm with backtracking modeled by our Classical DPLL system.

2.2   Modern DPLL Procedures

The major modern DPLL-based SAT solvers do not implement the Classical DPLL system. For example, due to efficiency reasons the pure literal rule is normally only used as a preprocessing step, and hence we will not consider this rule in the following. Moreover, instead of Backtrack a more general Backjump rule is considered, of which Backtrack is a particular case.

Definition 3. *The* Basic DPLL *system is the four-rule transition system B consisting of* UnitPropagate, Decide, Fail, *and the following* Backjump *rule:*

Backjump :

$$M \; l^{\mathsf{d}} \; N \parallel F, C \implies M \; l' \parallel F, C \;\; \text{if} \; \begin{cases} M \; l^{\mathsf{d}} \; N \models \neg C, \text{ and there is} \\ \text{some clause } C' \vee l' \text{ such that:} \\ F, C \models C' \vee l' \;\; \text{and} \;\; M \models \neg C', \\ l' \text{ is undefined in } M, \text{ and} \\ l' \text{ or } \neg l' \text{ occurs in } F \text{ or in } M \; l^{\mathsf{d}} \; N \end{cases}$$

We call the clause $C' \vee l'$ in Backjump *a* backjump *clause.*

Example 4. The aim of this Backjump rule is to generalize backtracking by a better analysis of why the so-called *conflicting* clause C is false. Standard backtracking reverses the *last* decision, and adds it as a unit to the previous decision level. Backjumping frequently allows one to add a new unit literal to a decision level that is lower than the previous level. Consider:

$$\begin{array}{llll} \emptyset \parallel \overline{1}\vee 2, \; \overline{3}\vee 4, \; \overline{5}\vee \overline{6}, \; 6\vee \overline{5}\vee \overline{2} & \implies_B & (\text{Decide}) \\ 1 \parallel \overline{1}\vee 2, \; \overline{3}\vee 4, \; \overline{5}\vee \overline{6}, \; 6\vee \overline{5}\vee \overline{2} & \implies_B & (\text{UnitPropagate}) \\ 1\,2 \parallel \overline{1}\vee 2, \; \overline{3}\vee 4, \; \overline{5}\vee \overline{6}, \; 6\vee \overline{5}\vee \overline{2} & \implies_B & (\text{Decide}) \\ 1\,2\,3 \parallel \overline{1}\vee 2, \; \overline{3}\vee 4, \; \overline{5}\vee \overline{6}, \; 6\vee \overline{5}\vee \overline{2} & \implies_B & (\text{UnitPropagate}) \\ 1\,2\,3\,4 \parallel \overline{1}\vee 2, \; \overline{3}\vee 4, \; \overline{5}\vee \overline{6}, \; 6\vee \overline{5}\vee \overline{2} & \implies_B & (\text{Decide}) \\ 1\,2\,3\,4\,5 \parallel \overline{1}\vee 2, \; \overline{3}\vee 4, \; \overline{5}\vee \overline{6}, \; 6\vee \overline{5}\vee \overline{2} & \implies_B & (\text{UnitPropagate}) \\ 1\,2\,3\,4\,5\,\overline{6} \parallel \overline{1}\vee 2, \; \overline{3}\vee 4, \; \overline{5}\vee \overline{6}, \; 6\vee \overline{5}\vee \overline{2} & \implies_B & (\text{Backjump}) \\ 1\,2\,\overline{5} \parallel \overline{1}\vee 2, \; \overline{3}\vee 4, \; \overline{5}\vee \overline{6}, \; 6\vee \overline{5}\vee \overline{2} \end{array}$$

Before the Backjump step, the clause $6 \vee \overline{5} \vee \overline{2}$ is conflicting: it is false in $1\,2\,3\,4\,5\,\overline{6}$. The reason for its falsity is the unit propagation 2 of the decision 1, together with the decision 5 and its unit propagation $\overline{6}$. Therefore, one can infer that the decision 1 (and its unit propagation 2) is incompatible with the decision 5. This is why the Backjump rule moves to the state $1\,2\,\overline{5}$.

Note that an application of Backtrack instead of Backjump would have given a state with first component $1\,2\,3\,4\,\overline{5}$, even though the decision level $3\,4$ is unrelated with the reasons for the falsity of $6\vee\overline{5}\vee\overline{2}$. Moreover, intuitively, the search state $1\,2\,\overline{5}$ reached after Backjump is more *advanced* than $1\,2\,3\,4\,\overline{5}$. This notion of "being more advanced" is formalized in Theorem 12 below.   □

The Backjump rule makes progress in the search by reverting to a strictly lower decision level, but with the additional information given by the literal l' that is added to that level. Indeed, as it is proved below, the four rules of the Basic DPLL system (UnitPropagate, Decide, Fail, and Backjump) suffice for completeness. But in most modern DPLL implementations, in addition the backjump clause $C' \vee l'$ is *added to the clause set* as a *learned* clause (*conflict-driven clause learning*). In Example 4, learning the clause $\overline{1}\vee\overline{5}$ will allow the application of UnitPropagate to any state whose assignment contains either 1 or 5. Hence, it will prevent any conflict caused by having both 1 and 5 in M. Indeed, reaching such *similar* conflicts frequently happens in industrial problems having some regular structure, and learning such lemmas has been shown to be very effective. Since a lemma is aimed at preventing future similar conflicts, when such conflicts are not very likely to be found again the lemma can be removed. In practice this is usually done if the *activity* of a lemma (e.g., the number of times it becomes a unit or a conflicting clause) has become low [ES03]. In order to model lemma learning and removal we consider the following system.

Definition 5. *The rules of* Learn *and* Forget *are the following ones:*

Learn :
$$M \parallel F \implies M \parallel F, C \ \text{ if } \ \begin{cases} all \ atoms \ of \ C \ occur \ in \ F \\ F \models C \end{cases}$$

Forget :
$$M \parallel F, C \implies M \parallel F \quad \text{ if } \ \{ F \models C$$

In any application step of these two rules, the clause C is said to be learned *and* forgotten, *respectively.*

Example 6. Assume a strategy that is followed in most state-of-the-art SAT solvers: (i) Decide is applied only if no other Basic DPLL rule is applicable, and (ii) after each application of Backjump, the backjump clause is learned. Consider a state of the form $M \parallel F$, where, among other clauses, F contains:

$$\overline{9} \vee \overline{6} \vee 7 \vee \overline{8} \quad 8 \vee 7 \vee \overline{5} \quad \overline{6} \vee 8 \vee 4 \quad \overline{4} \vee \overline{1} \quad \overline{4} \vee 5 \vee 2 \quad 5 \vee 7 \vee \overline{3} \quad 1 \vee \overline{2} \vee 3$$

and M is of the form: $...6...\overline{7}...9\ \overline{8}\ \overline{5}\ 4\ \overline{1}\ 2\ \overline{3}$. It is easy to observe how by six applications of UnitPropagate this state has been reached after the last decision **9**. For example, $\overline{8}$ is implied by 9, 6, and $\overline{7}$, due to the leftmost clause $\overline{9} \vee \overline{6} \vee 7 \vee \overline{8}$. The DPLL implementation stores the ordered sequence of propagated literals, each one of them together with the clause that caused it. In this state $M \parallel F$, the clause $1 \vee \overline{2} \vee 3$ is conflicting, since M contains $\overline{1}$, 2 and $\overline{3}$. Now one can trace back the reasons for this conflicting clause. For example, the DPLL implementation knows that $\overline{3}$ was implied by $\overline{5}$ and $\overline{7}$, due to the clause $5 \vee 7 \vee \overline{3}$. The literal $\overline{5}$ was in turn implied by $\overline{8}$ and $\overline{7}$, and so on. In this way, working backwards from the conflicting clause, and in the reverse order in which each literal was propagated, one can build a *conflict graph*:

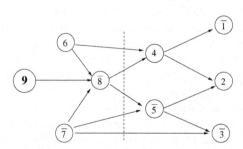

In the graph that is shown, the building process was stopped when the current decision literal **9** was reached, and hence **9** and the nodes belonging to earlier decision levels (in this example, literals 6 and $\overline{7}$) have no incoming arrows. For finding a backjump clause, it suffices to cut the graph into two parts. The first part must contain at least the literals with no incoming arrows. The second part must contain at least the literals with no outgoing arrows, i.e., the negated literals of the conflicting clause (in our example, $\overline{1}$, 2 and $\overline{3}$). It is not hard to see that in such a cut no model of F can satisfy all the literals whose outgoing edges are cut.

For instance, consider the cut indicated by the dotted line, where the literals with cut outgoing edges are $\overline{8}$, $\overline{7}$, and 6. Indeed, from these three literals by unit propagation using five clauses of F one can infer the negated literals of the conflicting clause. Hence, one can infer from F that $\overline{8}$, $\overline{7}$, and 6 cannot be simultaneously true, i.e., one can infer the clause $8 \lor 7 \lor \overline{6}$. In this case, it is an adequate backjump clause, that is, the clause $C' \lor l'$ in the definition of the Backjump rule, where the literal 8 plays the role of l'. Indeed, it allows one to backjump to the decision level of $\overline{7}$, adding 8 to it. After that, under our strategy the clause $8 \lor 7 \lor \overline{6}$ has to be learned, in order to explain, in future conflicts, the presence of 8 as a propagation from 6 and $\overline{7}$.

Such a cut produces an adequate backjump clause provided that only one of the literals with cut outgoing edges belongs to the current decision level. Then, this literal is called a *Unique Implication Point (UIP)* and it can play the role of l' in the backjump clause. It is not hard to argue that there is always at least one UIP, namely the current decision literal (which is **9** in our example). In practice one does not actually build the graph; it suffices to work backwards from the conflicting clause, maintaining only a *frontier* list of literals yet to be expanded, until reaching the *first UIP* (in our example, $\overline{8}$) [MSS99, ZMMM01, GN02]. This can also be seen as a resolution process, until reaching a clause with only one literal of the current decision level (in our example, the literal 8 in the clause $8 \lor 7 \lor \overline{6}$). In our example, the clause $8 \lor 7 \lor \overline{6}$ is obtained by resolution by resolving on the conflicting clause the literals $\overline{3}, 2, \overline{1}, \overline{4}$ and 5, i.e., in the reverse order they were propagated, with the clauses that caused their propagation:

$$
\begin{array}{ccc}
 & & 5 \lor 7 \lor \overline{3} \qquad 1 \lor \overline{2} \lor 3 \\
 & \overline{4} \lor 5 \lor 2 & 5 \lor 7 \lor 1 \lor \overline{2} \\
 & \overline{4} \lor \overline{1} & \overline{4} \lor 5 \lor 7 \lor 1 \\
 \overline{6} \lor 8 \lor 4 & & \overline{4} \lor 5 \lor 7 \\
 8 \lor 7 \lor \overline{5} & \overline{6} \lor 8 \lor 5 \lor 7 \\
 & 8 \lor 7 \lor \overline{6} &
\end{array}
$$

Some provers such as Siege also learn some of the intermediate clauses in such resolution derivations [Rya04]. ☐

State-of-the art SAT-solvers [MMZ+01, GN02, ES03, Rya04] essentially apply Abstract DPLL with Learning using efficient implementation techniques for UnitPropagate (e.g., watching two literals for unit propagation [MMZ+01]), and heuristics for selecting the decision literal when applying the Decide rule. In addition, modern DPLL implementations *restart* the DPLL procedure whenever the search is not making enough progress according to some measure. The rationale behind this idea is that upon each restart, the newly learned lemmas will lead the heuristics for Decide to behave differently, and hopefully cause the procedure to explore the search space in a more compact way.

The combination of learning and restarts has been shown to be powerful not only in practice, but also from the theoretical point of view. Essentially, any Basic DPLL derivation to *FailState* is equivalent to *tree-like* refutation by resolution. But for some classes of problems tree-like proofs are always exponentially larger than the smallest *general*, i.e., DAG-like, resolution ones [BEGJ00]. The good news is that DPLL with learning and restarts becomes again equivalent to general resolution with respect to such notions of proof complexity [BKS03].

Definition 7. *The* DPLL *system with learning and restarts, denoted by L, consists of the four transition rules of the Basic DPLL system, the* Learn *and* Forget *rules and the following* Restart *rule:*

$$M \parallel F \implies \emptyset \parallel F$$

2.3   Correctness of Modern DPLL Systems

Deciding the satisfiability of an input formula F will be done by generating an arbitrary derivation of the form $\emptyset \parallel F \implies_L \ldots \implies_L S_n$ such that S_n is *final with respect to the Basic DPLL system* (note that one cannot aim at reaching final states with respect to the DPLL system with learning, since, e.g., tautologies like $p \lor \neg p$ can be learned or forgotten in all states but *FailState*).

Building such derivations is practical because for all rules their applicability is easy to check, and such derivations are always finite if one never applies infinitely many consecutive Learn and Forget steps, and Restart is applied with increasing periodicity. Then, one always reaches a state S_n that is final with respect to the Basic DPLL system, and a final state is moreover easily recognizable as such, because it is either *FailState* or else it is of the form $M \parallel F$ where all literals of F are defined in M and there is no conflicting clause. Then, moreover, (i) F is unsatisfiable if, and only if, S_n is *FailState*, and (ii) if S_n is of the form $M \parallel F'$ then M is a model of F.

The following three lemmas are the key to proving these results (see [NOT05] for details). The first one states some easy invariants that are preserved under rule application. Proving the second one essentially involves the construction of an adequate backjump clause for showing that Backjump applies, which is less simple. From these two lemmas, the third one, stating properties of final states, is not hard to obtain.

Lemma 8. *Assume* $\emptyset \parallel F \implies_L^* M \parallel G$. *Then G is logically equivalent to F. If M is of the form $M_0 \, l_1 \, M_1 \, \ldots \, l_n \, M_n$, where $l_1, \ldots, l_n$ are all the decision literals of M, then $F, l_1, \ldots, l_i \models M_i$ for all i in $0 \ldots n$.*

Lemma 9. *Assume that* $\emptyset \parallel F \Longrightarrow_L^* M \parallel F'$ *and that* $M \models \neg C$ *for some clause* C *in* F'. *Then either* **Fail** *or* **Backjump** *applies to* $M \parallel F'$.

Lemma 10. *If* $\emptyset \parallel F \Longrightarrow_L^* S$, *and* S *is final with respect to Basic DPLL, then* S *is either FailState, or it is of the form* $M \parallel F'$, *where*
(i) all literals of F' *are defined in* M, *and*
(ii) there is no clause C *in* F' *such that* $M \models \neg C$, *and*
(iii) M *is a model of* F.

Theorem 11. *If* $\emptyset \parallel F \Longrightarrow_L^* S$ *where* S *is final w.r.t. Basic DPLL, then*

1. S *is FailState if, and only if,* F *is unsatisfiable.*
2. *If* S *is of the form* $M \parallel F'$ *then* M *is a model of* F.

Proof. For Property 1, if S is *FailState* it is because there is some state $M \parallel F'$ such that $\emptyset \parallel F \Longrightarrow_L^* M \parallel F' \Longrightarrow_L FailState$. By the definition of the Fail rule, there is no decision literal in M and there is a clause C in F' such that $M \models \neg C$. Since F and F' are equivalent by Lemma 8, we have that $F \models C$. However, if $M \models \neg C$, by Lemma 8 then also $F \models \neg C$, which implies that F is unsatisfiable. For the right-to-left implication, if S is not *FailState* it has to be of the form $M \parallel F'$. But then, by Lemma 10, M is a model of F and hence F is satisfiable. For Property 2, if S is $M \parallel F'$ then, again by Lemma 10, M is a model of F.   □

The soundness and completeness results of Theorem 11 can be applied if one can ensure that a final state with respect to Basic DPLL is eventually reached. This is usually done in practice by periodically increasing the minimal number of Basic DPLL steps between each pair of restart steps. Also, one should not apply infinitely many consecutive **Learn** and **Forget** steps (for example, learning and forgetting the same clause all the time), a condition that is weak and easily enforced. In fact, **Learn** is typically only applied together with **Backjump** in order to learn the corresponding backjump clause. This is formalized below.

Theorem 12. *Any derivation* $\emptyset \parallel F \Longrightarrow S_1 \Longrightarrow \dots$ *by the transition system* L *extended with the* **Restart** *rule is finite if (i) it contains only finitely many consecutive* **Learn** *and* **Forget** *steps, and (ii) between every two* **Restart** *steps there are more steps by Basic DPLL than between the previous two* **Restart** *steps.*

Proof. (See [NOT05] for details.) The four basic rules can be shown terminating by a well-founded ordering $\succ$ that considers only the first component M of states of the form $M \parallel F$. The ordering is lexicographic. It considers M more advanced than M' (i.e., $M' \succ M$) if M has more literals at decision level 0 than M', or both have the same number of literals at level 0 and M has more literals at level 1, etc. If D is an infinite derivation fulfilling the requirements, then in a subderivation of D without **Restart** steps, at each step either this first component decreases with respect to $\succ$ (by the Basic DPLL steps) or it remains equal (by the **Learn** and **Forget** steps). Therefore, since there are no infinitely many consecutive **Learn** and **Forget** steps, there must be infinitely many **Restart** steps in D. Also, if between two states there is at least one Basic DPLL step, these states do not have the same first component. Therefore, if N denotes the (fixed, finite) number of different first components of states that exist for the given finite set of symbols, there are no subderivations with more than N Basic DPLL steps between two Restart steps. This contradicts the fact that there are inifinitely many Restart steps if Restart has increasing periodicity. in D.   □

3   Abstract DPLL Modulo Theories

Here we consider the same definitions and notations given in Section 2 except that here the set P over which formulas are built is a fixed finite set of *ground* (i.e., variable-free) first-order atoms (instead of propositional symbols).

In addition to these propositional notions, a *theory* T is a set of closed first-order formulas that is satisfiable in the first-order sense.

A formula F is *T-satisfiable* or *T-consistent* if $F \wedge T$ is satisfiable in the first-order sense. Otherwise, it is called *T-unsatisfiable* or *T-inconsistent*. As before, a partial assignment M will also be seen as a conjunction and hence as a formula. If M is a T-consistent partial assignment and F is a formula such that $M \models F$, i.e., M is a (propositional) model of F, then we say that *M is a T-model of F*. The SMT problem for a theory T is the problem of determining, given a formula F, whether F is T-satisfiable, or, equivalently, whether F has a T-model. Note that, as usual in SMT, here we only consider the SMT problem for *ground* (and hence quantifier-free) CNF formulas F. Also note that F may contain constants that are free in T, which, as far as satisfiability is concerned, can equivalently be seen as existential variables. We will consider here only theories T such that the T-satisfiability of conjunctions of such ground literals is decidable, and a decision procedure for doing so is called a *T-solver*. If F and G are formulas, then *F entails G in T*, written $F \models_T G$, if $F \wedge \neg G$ is T-inconsistent. If $F \models_T G$ and $G \models_T F$, we say that F and G are *T-equivalent*.

3.1   An Informal Presentation of SMT Procedures

In the so-called *eager* approach to SMT, the input formula is translated in a single satisfiability-preserving step into a propositional CNF formula which is then checked by a SAT solver for satisfiability (see, e.g., [BGV01, BV02, Str02]). Sophisticated ad-hoc translations have been developed for several theories, but still, on many practical problems the translation process or the SAT solver run out of time or memory (see [dMR04]), and the alternative techniques explained below are usually orders of magnitude faster.

As an alternative to the eager approach, one can use a T-solver for deciding the satisfiability of conjunctions of theory literals. Then, a decision procedure for SMT is easily obtained by converting the formula into disjunctive normal form (DNF) and using the T-solver for checking whether there is at least one conjunction which is satisfiable. However, the exponential blowup due to the conversion into DNF makes this approach too inefficient. Therefore, a large amount of recent research involves the combination of the strengths of specialized T-solvers with the strengths of state-of-the-art SAT solvers for dealing with the boolean structure of the formulas. One such an approach, which has been widely used in the last few years is usually referred to as the *lazy* approach [ACG00, FORS01, ABC⁺02, BDS02, dMR02, FJOS03, ACGM04], [BCLZ04]. It initially considers each atom occurring in a formula F to be checked for satisfiability simply as a propositional symbol, i.e., it "forgets" about the theory T. Then it sends the formula to a SAT solver. If the SAT solver reports propositional unsatisfiability, then F is also T-unsatisfiable. If the SAT solver returns a propositional model of F, then this model (a conjunction of literals) is checked by a T-solver. If it is found T-satisfiable then it is a T-model of F. Otherwise, the T-solver builds a ground clause, called a *theory lemma*, a clause C such that $\emptyset \models_T C$, precluding that model. This lemma is added to F and the SAT solver is started again. This process is repeated until the SAT solver finds a T-satisfiable model or returns unsatisfiable.

Example 13. Assume we are deciding the satisfiability of a large EUF formula, i.e., the background theory T is equality, and assume that the model M found by the SAT solver contains, among many others, the literals: $b = c$, $f(b) = c$, $a \neq g(b)$, and $g(f(c)) = a$. Then the T-solver detects that M is not a T-model, since $b = c \ \land \ f(b) = c \ \land \ g(f(c)) = a \ \models_T \ a = g(b)$. Therefore, the lazy procedure has to be restarted after the corresponding theory lemma has been added to the clause set. In principle, one can take as theory lemma simply the negation of M, that is, the disjunction of the negations of all the literals in M. However, this clause may therefore have thousands of literals, and the lazy approach will behave much more efficiently if the T-solver is able to generate a small *explanation* of the T-inconsistency of M, which in this example could be the clause $b \neq c \ \lor \ f(b) \neq c \ \lor \ g(f(c)) \neq a \ \lor \ a = g(b)$. $\qquad\square$

The lazy approach is quite flexible: it can easily combine any SAT solver with any T-solver. Moreover, if the SAT solver used by the lazy SMT procedure is based on DPLL, several refinements exist that make it much more efficient:

Incremental T-solver. The T-consistency of the model can be checked incrementally, while the model is being built by the DPLL procedure, i.e., without delaying the check until a propositional model has been found. This can save a large amount of useless work. Currently, most SMT implementations work with incremental T-solvers. The idea was already mentioned in [ABC⁺02] under the name of *early pruning* and in [Bar03] under the name of *eager notification*.

On-line SAT solver. When a T-inconsistency is detected by the incremental T-solver, one can ask the DPLL procedure simply to backtrack to the last point where the assignment was still T-consistent, instead of restarting the search from scratch. If the current DPLL state is of the form $M \, l \, M' \parallel F$, and M is the maximal T-consistent prefix of $M \, l \, M'$, then the DPLL procedure can, for instance, backjump to $M \neg l \parallel F$. On-line SAT solvers (in combination with incremental T-solvers) are nowadays common in SMT implementations.

Theory propagation. In the approach presented so far, the T-solver provides information only *after* a T-inconsistent partial assignment has been generated.

In this sense, the T-solver is used only to *validate* the search a posteriori, not to *guide* it a priori. In order to overcome this limitation, the T-solver can also be used in a given DPLL state $M \parallel F$ to detect literals l ocurring in F such that $M \models_T l$, allowing the DPLL procedure to move to the state $M l \parallel F$. This is called *theory propagation*. It was first mentioned in [ACG00] under the name of *forward checking simplification*; however, it was believed to be very expensive. Since T-solvers were not designed to support it, it was simply implemented by sending $\neg l$ to the T-solver, and, if this made the model T-inconsistent, then inferring l. The real effectiveness of theory propagation has become demonstrated in our DPLL(T) approach [GHN+04, NO05b], using efficient T-solvers for it.

Exhaustive Theory Propagation. For some theories it even pays off, for every state $M \parallel F$, to eagerly detect and propagate *all* literals l ocurring in F such that $M \models_T l$ [NO05b]. Then, in every state $M \parallel F$ the model M will be T-consistent, and hence the T-solver will never detect any T-inconsistencies. Similarly, theory lemma learning becomes useless if exhaustive theory propagation is applied, because any unit propagation from a theory lemma will already be immediately obtained as a theory propagation. For some logics, such as, e.g., Difference Logic, exhaustive theory propagation can give several orders of magnitude of speedup (see Section 5).

3.2   Abstract DPLL Modulo Theories

In this section we formalize the different enhancements of the lazy approach to Satisfiability Modulo Theories. This will be done by adapting the abstract DPLL framework for the propositional case presented in the previous section. Here Learn, Forget and Backjump are slightly modified in order to work modulo theories: in these rules, entailment between formulas now becomes entailment in T:

Definition 14. *The rules T-Learn, T-Forget and T-Backjump are:*

T-Learn :

$$M \parallel F \qquad \Longrightarrow M \parallel F, C \quad \text{if } \begin{cases} \text{every atom of } C \text{ occurs in } F \text{ or in } M \\ F \models_T C \end{cases}$$

T-Forget :

$$M \parallel F, C \qquad \Longrightarrow M \parallel F \qquad \text{if } \{ F \models_T C$$

T-Backjump :

$$M l^d N \parallel F, C \Longrightarrow M l' \parallel F, C \text{ if } \begin{cases} M l^d N \models \neg C, \text{ and there is} \\ \text{some clause } C' \vee l' \text{ such that:} \\ \quad F, C \models_T C' \vee l' \text{ and } M \models \neg C', \\ \quad l' \text{ is undefined in } M, \text{ and} \\ \quad l' \text{ or } \neg l' \text{ occurs in } F \text{ or in } M l^d N \end{cases}$$

Modeling the naive lazy approach. Each time a state $M \parallel F$ is reached that is final with respect to Decide, Fail, UnitPropagate, and T-Backjump, i.e., final in a similar sense as in the previous section, M can be T-consistent or not. If it is, then M is indeed a T-model of F. If it is not, then there exists a subset $\{l_1, \ldots, l_n\}$ of M such that $\emptyset \models_T \neg l_1 \vee \ldots \vee \neg l_n$. By one T-Learn step, this theory lemma $\neg l_1 \vee \ldots \vee \neg l_n$ can be learned and then Restart can be applied. If these theory lemmas are never removed by the T-Forget rule, this stategy is terminating under the same restrictions as stated in the previous section on T-Learn, T-Forget, and Restart, and it is also sound and complete: the initial formula is T-unsatisfiable iff, the final state is *FailState*, and otherwise a T-model has been found.

Modeling the lazy approach with an incremental T-solver. Assume the incremental T-solver detects that a (not necessarily final) state $M \parallel F$ has been reached such that M is T-inconsistent. Then, as in the naive lazy approach, there exists a subset $\{l_1, \ldots, l_n\}$ of M such that $\emptyset \models_T \neg l_1 \vee \ldots \vee \neg l_n$. This theory lemma is then learned, reaching the state $M \parallel F, \neg l_1 \vee \ldots \vee \neg l_n$. As in the previous case, then Restart can be applied and the same results apply.

Modeling the lazy approach with an incremental T-solver and an online SAT solver. As in the previous case, if a T-inconsistency is detected a state $M \parallel F, \neg l_1 \vee \ldots \vee \neg l_n$ is reached. But now instead of completely restarting, the procedure *repairs* the T-inconsistency of the partial model by exploiting the fact that $\neg l_1 \vee \ldots \vee \neg l_n$ is a conflicting clause. Then, as before, if there is no decision literal in M then Fail applies, and otherwise T-Backjump applies. Even if always immediately after backjumping the theory lemma is forgotten, the termination, soundness and completeness results hold.

Modeling the previous refinements and theory propagation. This requires the following additional rule:

Definition 15. *The Theory Propagate rule is:*

$$M \parallel F \implies M\, l \parallel F \ \ \text{if} \ \begin{cases} M \models_T l \\ l \ or \ \neg l \ occurs \ in \ F \\ l \ is \ undefined \ in \ M \end{cases}$$

The purpose of this rule is to prune the search by assigning a truth value to literals that are T-entailed by M. Below we prove that the results of termination, soundness, and completeness mentioned for the previous three lazy approaches also hold in combination with arbitrary applications of this rule.

Modeling the previous refinements and exhaustive theory propagation. Exhaustive theory propagation is modeled simply by assuming that Theory Propagate is applied eagerly. As a particular case of the previous refinement (arbirary applications of Theory Propagate), the aforementioned results remain true.

3.3   Correctness of Abstract DPLL Modulo Theories

Definition 16. *The Basic DPLL Modulo Theories system consists of the rules* Decide, Fail, UnitPropagate, *and* T-Backjump.

The Full DPLL system Modulo Theories, *denoted by* FT, *consists of the Basic DPLL Modulo Theories rules and the rules of* Theory Propagate, T-Learn, T-Forget, *and* Restart.

The proofs of the following results are structured in the same way as the ones given in Section 2.3 for the propositional case (see [NOT05] for details). As before, a decision procedure is any derivation by the given rules using a terminating strategy, and again we consider as final states, apart from *FailState*, the ones of the form $M \parallel F$ that are final with respect to the four rules of Basic DPLL Modulo Theories, but now in addition we require that the model M is T-consistent. We provide here only one additional property, showing that such final states can be effectively computed:

Property 17. If $\emptyset \parallel F \Longrightarrow^*_{\text{FT}} M \parallel F'$ and M is T-inconsistent, then either there is a conflicting clause in $M \parallel F'$, or else T-Learn applies to $M \parallel F'$, generating a conflicting clause.

Theorem 18.

1. *If* $\emptyset \parallel F \Longrightarrow^*_{\text{FT}}$ *FailState then* F *is* T-*unsatisfiable.*

2. *If* $\emptyset \parallel F \Longrightarrow^*_{\text{FT}} S$ *where* S *is final with respect to Basic DPLL modulo theories and* M *is* T-*consistent, then* M *is a* T-*model of* F.

Theorem 19 (Termination). *Any derivation* $\emptyset \parallel F \Longrightarrow_{\text{FT}} S_1 \Longrightarrow_{\text{FT}} \ldots$ *by the Full DPLL system modulo theories is finite, if it contains only finitely many consecutive* T-Learn *and* T-Forget *steps, and between every two* Restart *steps, either there are more steps by Basic DPLL Modulo Theories than between the previous two* Restart *steps, or else a new clause has been learned that is never forgotten in* D.

4   The DPLL(T) Approach

In this section we shortly describe the DPLL(T) approach for SAT Modulo Theories [GHN+04, NO05b]. It is based on a general DPLL engine, called DPLL(X), that is not dependent on any particular theory T. Instead, it is parameterized by a solver for a theory T of interest. A system DPLL(T) for deciding the satisfiability of CNF formulas in a theory T is produced by instantiating the parameter X with a module $Solver_T$ that can handle conjunctions of literals in T. The basic idea is similar to the $CLP(X)$ scheme for constraint logic programming: provide a clean and modular, but at the same time efficient, integration of specialized theory solvers within a general-purpose engine, in our case one based on DPLL.

The concrete DPLL(T) scheme and its architecture and implementation presented here combine the advantages of the eager and lazy approaches to SMT. On the one hand, experiments for several different theories reveal that, as soon as the theory predicates start playing a significant role in the formula, our DPLL(T) approach outperforms all others. On the other hand, DPLL(T) has the flexibility of the lazy approaches: more general logics can be dealt with by simply plugging in other solvers into our general DPLL(X) engine, provided that these solvers conform to a minimal interface.

Here we describe two versions of the DPLL(T) approach, namely with and without exhaustive theory propagation. For the first case, in [NO05b] an efficient exhaustive solver for *difference logic* is described. For some other logics, such as the logic of Equality with Uninterpreted Functions (EUF, see Example 13), exhaustive theory propagation is not the best DPLL(T) approach. Our experiments with EUF revealed that detecting exhaustively all *negative* equality consequences is very expensive, whereas all positive equalities can be propagated efficiently by means of a congruence closure algorithm [DST80]. In [NO03] a modern incremental, backtrackable congruence closure algorithm for this purpose is described, and progressively more efficient ways of retrieving explanations in this context are described in [dMRS04, ST05, NO05c].

4.1   DPLL(T) with Exhaustive Theory Propagation

For the initial setup of DPLL(T), *Solver$_T$* reads the input CNF, stores the list of all literals occurring in it, and hands it over to DPLL(X), who treats it as a purely propositional CNF. After that, DPLL(T) implements the rules as follows:

- At each state $M \parallel F$, both DPLL(X) and *Solver$_T$* are aware of the current M. Each time DPLL(X) communicates to *Solver$_T$* that a literal l is added to M, (e.g., due to UnitPropagate or to Decide), *Solver$_T$* answers with the list of *all* literals of the input formula that are new T-consequences. Then, for each one of these consequences, Theory Propagate is immediately applied by DPLL(X). Note that hence M never becomes T-inconsistent.
- If Theory Propagate is not applicable, then UnitPropagate is eagerly applied by DPLL(X) (this is implemented using the two-watched-literals scheme).
- DPLL(X) applies Fail or T-Backjump if a conflicting clause is detected. T-Backjump works as explained in Example 6, but there is a difference: a literal l at a node in the graph can now also be due to an application of Theory Propagate. Hence, building the graph requires that *Solver$_T$* must be able to recover a (preferably small) subset of literals of M that T-entailed l. This is done by the *Explain(l)* operation provided by *Solver$_T$*. It is the same operation as for providing explanations in the lazy approach, cf. Example 13.
- Immediately after each T-Backjump application, the T-Learn rule is applied for learning the backjump clause. This clause is always a T-consequence of the current formula. As explained in Subsection 3.1 for exhaustive theory

propagation, theory lemmas (clauses C such that $\emptyset \models_T C$) are not learned, since this is useless.

- After each backjump has taken place in DPLL(X), it tells $Solver_T$ how many literals of the partial interpretation have been unassigned, which allows $Solver_T$ to undo them.
- In our current implementation, DPLL(X) applies Restart when certain system parameters reach some prescribed limits, such as the number of conflicts or lemmas, the number of new units derived, etc.
- In our current implementation, T-Forget is applied by DPLL(X) after each restart (and only then), removing at least half of the lemmas according to their activity (number of times involved in a conflict since last restart). The 500 newest lemmas are not removed.
- DPLL(X) applies Decide only if none of Theory Propagate, UnitPropagate, Fail or T-Backjump is applicable. We currently use a heuristic for chosing the decision literal as in BerkMin [GN02].

4.2 DPLL(T) with Non-exhaustive Theory Propagation

- Each time DPLL(X) adds a literal l to M, $Solver_T$ either indicates that M has become T-inconsistent, or, otherwise, it returns a (possibly incomplete) list of T-consequences to which Theory Propagate is immediately applied by DPLL(X) (as in the exhaustive case). T-inconsistencies are treated by DPLL(X) as described in Subsection 3.2 for modeling with an on-line SAT solver: if there is a subset $\{l_1, \ldots, l_n\}$ of M that becomes T-inconsistent by adding l to it, the corresponding theory lemma $\neg l_1 \vee \ldots \vee \neg l_n \vee \neg l$ is learned, and used as a backjump clause in a T-Backjump step.
- As before, if Theory Propagate is not applicable, then UnitPropagate is eagerly applied by DPLL(X), and Fail or T-Backjump are applied if a conflicting clause C is detected. After each T-Backjump application, $Solver_T$ is notified for unassigning literals, and T-Learn is applied for learning the backjump clause. Also Decide (only lazily) and Restart are applied as before.
- T-Forget is also applied as in the exhaustive case, but in this case among the (less active) lemmas that are removed there are also theory lemmas.

5   The BarcelogicTools

In this section we describe BarcelogicTools, a set of logic-based tools developed by our research group in Barcelona. The development of the BarcelogicTools is funded by the Spanish Ministry of Education and Science (TIN2004-03382), as well as by several private sources. The intended applications of Barcelogic-Tools range from hardware and software verification to industrial combinatorial optimization problems (planning, scheduling). Most of the tools are built around a state-of-the-art SAT solver, and there is also a DPLL(X) engine and a number of theory solvers that can be combined forming different DPLL(T) systems.

5.1 SMT Inside BarcelogicTools

Currently, BarcelogicTools supports difference logic over the integers or the reals, equality with uninterpreted function symbols (EUF) and the interpreted functions symbols *predecessor* and *successor*, or combinations of these theories. More theory solvers for, e.g., linear integer and real arithmetic, the theory of arrays, and bit vectors are under development.

The system is written in C. Apart from the parser and the CNF translator, three are the main components of the system.

1. Its DPLL(X) engine has some 3500 lines of source code. It is based on the DPLL procedure and implements state-of-the-art techniques such as the two-watched literal scheme, 1UIP learning scheme and VSIDS-like decision heuristics, but does not present any significant novelty wrt. state-of-the-art SAT solvers.
2. The solver for EUF (some 4000 lines) is an extension of a congruence closure algorithm. Apart from determining the satisfiability of a given set of equalities and disequalities E, it can detect that *some* literals in the original formula are entailed by E. In addition, for each such literal the solver can compute a small subset of E of which the literal is already a logical consequence. More details can be found at [NO03, NO05c].
3. The solver for difference logic (1400 lines) can be seen an extension of a shortest-path algorithm aimed at determining, given a consistent set of difference constraints S, *all* literals in the original formula that are logically entailed by S. For each of these consequences, the solver can compute a minimal (wrt set inclusion) subset of S from which the literal is also entailed. For further details see [NO05b].

The effectivity of our approach was shown at the 2005 SMT Competition [BdMS05]. A large collection of benchmarks (around 1300) coming from diverse areas such software and hardware verification, bounded model checking, finite model finding, or scheduling were classified, according to the underlying theory or to some syntactic restrictions, into the 7 divisions of which the competition consisted. For each division, around 50 benchmarks were randomly chosen and given to each entrant with a time limit of 10 minutes per benchmark.

One single version of BarcelogicTools, our DPLL(T) implementation as described in Section 4, entered (and won) all four divisions for which it had a theory solver: EUF, IDL and RDL (integer and real difference logic), and UFIDL (combining EUF and IDL). The same Among the competitors were well-known SMT solvers like SVC [BDL96], CVC [BDS02], CVC-Lite [BB04], MathSAT [BBA+05] and the very recent successors of ICS [FORS01], called Yices (by Leonardo de Moura) and Simplics (by Dutertre and de Moura). For each division, the results of the best three systems are given in the following table, where **Time** is the total time *for the solved problems*:

	top-3 systems	# Problems solved	Time (secs.)
	BarcelogicTools	39	1758.2
EUF (50 problems):	Yices	37	1801.4
	MathSAT	33	2186.2
	BarcelogicTools	41	940.8
RDL (50 pbms.):	Yices	37	1868.0
	MathSAT	37	2608.0
	BarcelogicTools	47	1131.2
IDL (51 pbms.):	Yices	47	1883.2
	MathSAT	46	1295.4
	BarcelogicTools	45	305.2
UFIDL (49 pbms.):	Yices	36	1989.8
	MathSAT	22	1055.5

5.2   Ad-Hoc Theory Combination and UFIDL

Perhaps the most remarkable results obtained by BarcelogicTools in the SMT
Competition are the ones for the UFIDL division, where problems contain both
uninterpreted functions and difference logic atoms, interpreted with respect to
a background theory T of the integers. That is, atoms can be equalities $s = t$,
or atoms of the form $s - t \leq k$, where s and t are ground terms built over
uninterpreted symbols, and k is a concrete integer (apart from $\leq$, also $>$ may
appear).

Many general results exist for the modular combination of decision procedures, à la Shostak, or à la Nelson-Oppen [Sho84, NO79]. But we believe that
for certain classes of problems it is better to apply a more ad-hoc combination
of theories. One particular example appears to be this combination of EUF and
IDL.

Our procedure proceeds as follows. It first checks whether the input formula
contains some ordering predicate ($\leq$ or $<$).

- If this is the case, first all function symbols are removed by means of Ackermann's reduction [Ack54]: for each pair of occurrences in the formula of
  terms of the form $f(s_1, \ldots, s_n)$ and $f(t_1, \ldots, t_n)$, a monotonicity clause
  $$s_1 = t_1 \wedge \ldots \wedge s_n = t_n \longrightarrow f(s_1, \ldots, s_n) = f(t_1, \ldots, t_n)$$
  is added. After that, the equality predicate can be encoded as an equivalence
  relation (i.e., not any more as a congruence relation). This can be done by
  simply considering $s = t$ as a difference logic atom (e.g., as $s \leq t \wedge t \leq s$),
  and hence only a theory solver for difference logic needs to be used.
- If the input formula contains no ordering predicates $\leq$ or $<$, an EUF solver
  using the congruence closure algorithm of [NO03] is used. Its extension with
  integer offsets for dealing with the symbols *predecessor* and *successor* (also
  described in [NO03]) allows for expressing literals of the form $s - t = k$ as
  equalities $s = t + k$.

Even if there are no ordering predicates, if the number of function symbols
is reasonably small it is sometimes still useful to add the monotonicity clauses

of Ackermann's transformation. The reason is that it allows one to detect some propagations of negative equalities that would remain undetected in the non-exhaustive theory propagation approach used by BarcelogicTools for EUF. More precisely, it is not detected in general that $f(a) \neq f(b)$ implies $a \neq b$, which will be detected in the presence of the monotonicity clause $a \neq b \vee f(a) = f(b)$.

5.3 The Role of Theory Propagation in BarcelogicTools

In our experience, the overhead produced by theory propagation is usually compensated by a significant reduction of the search space. In [GHN+04] we already gave extensive experimental results showing its effectivity inside our DPLL(T) approach for EUF logic, and in [NO05b] a large amount of experiments are discussed for difference logic, with additional emphasis on the good scaling properties. Hence it is not surprising that new SMT solvers such as Yices and MathSAT also apply theory propagation. In fact, the most recent versions of MathSAT include exactly our congruence closure algorithms with theory propagation and Explain [NO03, NO05c] for its EUF solver.

In the following two figures, BarcelogicTools with and without theory propagation is compared in terms of runtime (in seconds) and number of decisions on a typical real-world difference logic suite (fischer6-mutex) consisting of 20 problems of increasing size.

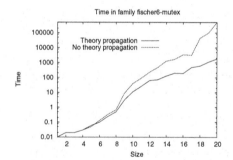 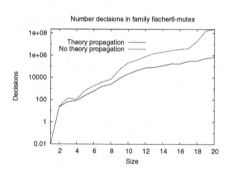

The figures show the typical behaviour on the larger problems: both the runtime and the number of decisions are orders of magnitude smaller in the version with theory propagation. In both cases the $DPLL(X)$ engine used was exactly the same, although in the exhaustive theory case some parts of the code never applied (e.g., theory lemma learning).

Of course, theory propagation may not pay off in certain specific problems where the theory plays an insignificant role, i.e., where reasoning is done almost entirely at the boolean level. Such situations can be detected on the fly by computing the percentage of conflicts which are produced in part due to theory propagation. If this number is very low, theory propagation can be switched off automatically in order to speed up the computation.

5.4   Comparison of BarcelogicTools with the Eager Approach

For completeness, we finally compare DPLL(T) with UCLID, the best-known tool implementing the eager translation approach to SMT [LS04]. Three typical series of benchmarks of difference logic are considered, coming from different methods for pipelined processor verification given in [MS05a, MS05b]. Results of runtimes in seconds (with one hour timeout) are given using Siege [Rya04] as the final SAT solver for UCLID, since it gave the best results.

	UCLID	DPLL(T)	UCLID	DPLL(T)	UCLID	DPLL(T)
6 stage	258	1	3596	5	19	1
7 stage	835	3	>3600	8	58	1
8 stage	3160	15	>3600	18	226	1
9 stage	>3600	23	>3600	18	664	1
10 stage	>3600	54	>3600	29	>3600	2

6   Conclusions

We have shown that the Abstract DPLL formalism introduced here can be very useful for understanding and formally reasoning about a large variety of DPLL-based procedures for SAT and SMT.

In particular, we have used it here for describing two variants of a new, efficient, and modular approach for SMT, called DPLL(T). New theories can be dealt with by DPLL(T) by simply plugging in new theory solvers, which must only be able to deal with *conjunctions* of theory literals and conform to a minimal and simple set of additional requirements.

Current work inside the BarcelogicTools concerns the development of more theory solvers, for, e.g., linear integer and real arithmetic, the theory of arrays, and bit vectors, as well as the development of other logic-related tools.

Also, a new $DPLL(X_1, \ldots, X_n)$ engine is being developed for automatically dealing with the combination of theories, i.e., essentially standard theory solvers for theories $T_1, \ldots, T_n$ can be used for obtaining a system $DPLL(T_1, \ldots, T_n)$. We aim at an approach for doing this in a way similar to the one of [BBC+05], but where part of the equality reasoning takes place inside the $DPLL(X_1, \ldots, X_n)$ engine.

References

[ABC+02]   G. Audemard, P. Bertoli, A. Cimatti, A. Kornilowicz, and R. Sebastiani. A SAT based approach for solving formulas over boolean and linear mathematical propositions. In *CADE-18*, LNCS 2392, pages 195–210, 2002.

[ACG00]   Alessandro Armando, Claudio Castellini, and Enrico Giunchiglia. SAT-based procedures for temporal reasoning. In Susanne Biundo and Maria Fox, editors, *Proceedings of the 5th European Conference on Planning (Durham, UK)*, volume 1809 of *Lecture Notes in Computer Science*, pages 97–108. Springer, 2000.

[ACGM04]   Alessandro Armando, Claudio Castellini, Enrico Giunchiglia, and Marco
Maratea. A SAT-based Decision Procedure for the Boolean Combination
of Difference Constraints. In *7th International Conference on Theory and
Applications of Satisfiability Testing(SAT 2004)*. LNCS, 2004.

[Ack54]   Wilhelm Ackermann. *Solvable Cases of the Decision Problem*. Studies in
Logic and the Foundations of Mathematics. North-Holland, Amsterdam,
1954.

[Alu99]   Rajeev Alur. Timed automata. In Nicolas Halbwachs and Doron Peled,
editors, *Proceedings of the 11th International Conference on Computer
Aided Verification, CAV'99 (Trento, Italy)*, volume 1633 of *Lecture Notes
in Computer Science*, pages 8–22. Springer, 199.

[Bar03]   Clark W. Barrett. *Checking Validity of Quantifier-Free Formulas in Combinations of First-Order Theories*. PhD thesis, Stanford University, 2003.

[BB04]   Clark W. Barrett and Sergey Berezin. CVC lite: A new implementation
of the cooperating validity checker category b. In R. Alur and D. Peled,
editors, *Proceedings of the 16th International Conference on Computer
Aided Verification, CAV'04 (Boston, Massachusetts)*, volume 3114 of *Lecture Notes in Computer Science*, pages 515–518. Springer, 2004.

[BBA+05]   M. Bozzano, R. Bruttomesso, A.Cimatti, T.Junttila, P.v.Rossum,
S.Schulz, and R.Sebastiani. An incremental and layered procedure for
the satisfiability of linear arithmetic logic. In *Tools and Algorithms for
the Construction and Analysis of Systems, 11th Int. Conf., (TACAS)*,
volume 3440 of *Lecture Notes in Computer Science*, pages 317–333, 2005.

[BBC+05]   Marco Bozzano, Roberto Bruttomesso, Alessandro Cimatti, Tommi A.
Junttila, Silvio Ranise, Peter van Rossum, and Roberto Sebastiani. Ef-
ficient satisfiability modulo theories via delayed theory combination. In
Int. Conf. on Computer Aided Verification (CAV), volume 3576 of *Lecture
Notes in Computer Science*, pages 335–349, 2005.

[BCLZ04]   Thomas Ball, Byron Cook, Shuvendu K. Lahiri, and Lintao Zhang.
Zapato: Automatic theorem proving for predicate abstraction refinement. In R. Alur and D. Peled, editors, *Proceedings of the 16th International Conference on Computer Aided Verification, CAV'04 (Boston,
Massachusetts)*, volume 3114 of *Lecture Notes in Computer Science*, pages
457–461. Springer, 2004.

[BD94]   J. R. Burch and D. L. Dill. Automatic verification of pipelined microprocessor control. In *Procs. 6th Int. Conf. Computer Aided Verification
(CAV)*, LNCS 818, pages 68–80, 1994.

[BDL96]   C. Barrett, D. L. Dill, and J. Levitt. Validity checking for combinations of
theories with equality. In *Procs. 1st Intl. Conference on Formal Methods
in Computer Aided Design*, LNCS 1166, pages 187–201, 1996.

[BdMS05]   C. Barrett, L. de Moura, and A. Stump. SMT-COMP: Satisfiability Modulo Theories Competition. In K. Etessami and S. Rajamani, editors,
17th International Conference on Computer Aided Verification, Lecture
Notes in Computer Science, pages 20–23. Springer, 2005. Results at:
www.csl.sri.com/users/demoura/smt-comp.

[BDS02]   Clarke Barrett, David Dill, and Aaron Stump. Checking satisfiability of
first-order formulas by incremental translation into sat. In *Procs. 14th
Intl. Conf. on Computer Aided Verification (CAV)*, LNCS 2404, 2002.

[BEGJ00]   Maria Luisa Bonet, Juan Luis Esteban, Nicola Galesi, and Jan Johannsen.
On the relative complexity of resolution refinements and cutting planes
proof systems. *SIAM J. Comput.*, 30(5):1462–1484, 2000.

[BGV01]   R. Bryant, S. German, and M. Velev. Processor verification using efficient reductions of the logic of uninterpreted functions to propositional logic. *ACM Trans. Computational Logic*, 2(1):93–134, 2001.

[BKS03]   Paul Beame, Henry Kautz, and Ashish Sabharwal. On the power of clause learning. In *Proceedings of IJCAI-03, 18th International Joint Conference on Artificial Intelligence*, Acapulco, MX, 2003.

[BV02]   Randal E. Bryant and Miroslav N. Velev. Boolean satisfiability with transitivity constraints. *ACM Trans. Computational Logic*, 3(4):604–627, 2002.

[DLL62]   Martin Davis, George Logemann, and Donald Loveland. A machine program for theorem-proving. *Comm. of the ACM*, 5(7):394–397, 1962.

[dMR02]   Leonardo de Moura and Harald Rueß. Lemmas on demand for satisfiability solvers. In *Procs. 5th Int. Symp. on the Theory and Applications of Satisfiability Testing, SAT'02*, pages 244–251, 2002.

[dMR04]   Leonardo de Moura and Harald Ruess. An experimental evaluation of ground decision procedures. In R. Alur and D. Peled, editors, *Proceedings of the 16th International Conference on Computer Aided Verification, CAV'04 (Boston, Massachusetts)*, volume 3114 of *Lecture Notes in Computer Science*, pages 162–174. Springer, 2004.

[dMRS04]   Leonardo de Moura, Harald Rueß, and Natarajan Shankar. Justifying equality. In *Proceedings of the Second Workshop on Pragmatics of Decision Procedures in Automated Reasoning*, Cork, Ireland, 2004.

[DP60]   Martin Davis and Hilary Putnam. A computing procedure for quantification theory. *Journal of the ACM*, 7:201–215, 1960.

[DST80]   Peter J. Downey, Ravi Sethi, and Robert E. Tarjan. Variations on the common subexpressions problem. *J. of the Association for Computing Machinery*, 27(4):758–771, 1980.

[ES03]   Niklas Eén and Niklas Sörensson. An extensible sat-solver. In *Proceedings of the Sixth International Conference on Theory and Applications of Satisfiability Testing (SAT)*, pages 502–518, 2003.

[FJOS03]   C. Flanagan, R. Joshi, X. Ou, and J. B. Saxe. Theorem proving using lazy proof explanation. In *Procs. 15th Int. Conf. on Computer Aided Verification (CAV)*, LNCS 2725, 2003.

[FORS01]   J.-C. Filliâtre, S. Owre, H. Rueß, and N. Shankar. ICS: Integrated Canonization and Solving (Tool prese ntation). In G. Berry, H. Comon, and A. Finkel, editors, *Proceedings of CAV'2001*, volume 2102 of *Lecture Notes in Computer Science*, pages 246–249. Springer-Verlag, 2001.

[GHN+04]   Harald Ganzinger, George Hagen, Robert Nieuwenhuis, Albert Oliveras, and Cesare Tinelli. DPLL(T): Fast Decision Procedures. In R. Alur and D. Peled, editors, *Proceedings of the 16th International Conference on Computer Aided Verification, CAV'04 (Boston, Massachusetts)*, volume 3114 of *Lecture Notes in Computer Science*, pages 175–188. Springer, 2004.

[GN02]   E. Goldberg and Y. Novikov. BerkMin: A fast and robust SAT-solver. In *Design, Automation, and Test in Europe (DATE '02)*, pages 142–149, 2002.

[LS04]   Shuvendu K. Lahiri and Sanjit A. Seshia. The uclid decision procedure. In *Computer Aided Verification, 16th International Conference, (CAV)*, volume 3114 of *Lecture Notes in Computer Science*, pages 475–478, 2004.

[MMZ+01]   Matthew W. Moskewicz, Conor F. Madigan, Ying Zhao, Lintao Zhang, and Sharad Malik. Chaff: Engineering an Efficient SAT Solver. In *Proc. 38th Design Automation Conference (DAC'01)*, 2001.

[MS05a]   Panagiotis Manolios and Sudarshan K. Srinivasan. A computationally efficient method based on commitment refinement maps for verifying pipelined machines. In *ACM IEEE Int. Conf. on Formal Methods and Models for Co-Design (MEMOCODE)*, 2005.

[MS05b]   Panagiotis Manolios and Sudarshan K. Srinivasan. Refinement maps for efficient verification of processor models. In *Design, Automation and Test in Europe Conference and Exposition (DATE)*, pages 1304–1309. IEEE Computer Society, 2005.

[MSS99]   Joao Marques-Silva and Karem A. Sakallah. GRASP: A search algorithm for propositional satisfiability. *IEEE Trans. Comput.*, 48(5):506–521, may 1999.

[NO79]   Greg Nelson and Derek C. Oppen. Simplification by cooperating decision procedures. *ACM Trans. Program. Lang. Syst.*, 1(2):245–257, 1979.

[NO03]   Robert Nieuwenhuis and Albert Oliveras. Congruence Closure with Integer Offsets. In M Vardi and A Voronkov, editors, *10h Int. Conf. Logic for Programming, Artif. Intell. and Reasoning (LPAR)*, LNAI 2850, pages 78–90, 2003.

[NO05a]   Robert Nieuwenhuis and Albert Oliveras. BarcelogicTools for SMT, July 2005. SMT Competition 2005. Entrants' system descriptions. www.csl.sri.com/users/demoura/smt-comp.

[NO05b]   Robert Nieuwenhuis and Albert Oliveras. DPLL(T) with Exhaustive Theory Propagation and its Application to Difference Logic. In Kousha Etessami and Sriram K. Rajamani, editors, *Proceedings of the 17th International Conference on Computer Aided Verification, CAV'05 (Edimburgh, Scotland)*, volume 3576 of *Lecture Notes in Computer Science*, pages 321–334. Springer, July 2005.

[NO05c]   Robert Nieuwenhuis and Albert Oliveras. Proof-Producing Congruence Closure. In Jürgen Giesl, editor, *Proceedings of the 16th International Conference on Term Rewriting and Applications, RTA'05 (Nara, Japan)*, volume 3467 of *Lecture Notes in Computer Science*, pages 453–468. Springer, June 2005.

[NOT05]   Robert Nieuwenhuis, Albert Oliveras, and Cesare Tinelli. Abstract DPLL and Abstract DPLL Modulo Theories. In Franz Baader and Andrei Voronkov, editors, *"11th Int. Conf. Logic for Programming, Artif. Intell. and Reasoning (LPAR)"*, volume 3452 of *Lecture Notes in Computer Science*, pages 36–50. Springer, 2005.

[RT03]   Silvio Ranise and Cesare Tinelli. The SMT-LIB Format: An Initial Proposal. In *Proceedings of the 1st Workshop on Pragmatics of Decision Procedures in Automated Reasoning*, Miami, 2003.

[Rya04]   Lawrence Ryan. Efficient Algorithms for Clause-Learning SAT Solvers. Master's thesis, School of Computing Science, Simon Fraser University, 2004.

[Sho84]   Robert E. Shostak. Deciding combinations of theories. *Journal of the ACM*, 31(1):1–12, January 1984.

[ST05]   Aaron Stump and Li-Yang Tan. The algebra of equality proofs. In Jürgen Giesl, editor, *Proceedings of the 16th International Conference on Term Rewriting and Applications, RTA'05 (Nara, Japan)*, volume 3467 of *Lecture Notes in Computer Science*, pages 469–483. Springer, 2005.

[Str02]   Ofer Strichman. On solving presburger and linear arithmetic with sat. In Mark Aagaard and John W. O'Leary, editors, *Formal Methods in Computer-Aided Design, 4th International Conference, FMCAD 2002, Portland, OR, USA, November 6-8, 2002, Proceedings*, volume 2517 of *Lecture Notes in Computer Science*, pages 160–170. Springer, 2002.

[ZMMM01]   L. Zhang, C. F. Madigan, M. W. Moskewicz, and S. Malik. Efficient conflict driven learning in a Boolean satisfiability solver. In *Int. Conf. on Computer-Aided Design (ICCAD'01)*, pages 279–285, 2001.

Scaling Up: Computers vs. Common Sense

Doug Lenat

Cycorp
doug@cyc.com

Abstract. Over the last 21 years, we've spent almost a person-millenium producing Cyc, an axiomatization of general human knowledge. Though still far from complete, Cyc contains over three million axioms. The need to express the range of things a person knows has led us to ever more expressive representation languages – currently we use an nth order predicate calculus with an overlay of contexts which are themselves first class objects. These pressures and others (e.g., elaboration tolerance) have driven us against numerous sorts of "scaling up" problems. In this talk I will briefly describe Cyc, the processes by which new axioms are added and deleted, applications of it, etc., but I will focus on some of these scaling up issues and approaches we have taken – and plan to take – to keep inference fast enough and to keep contradictions from being more than a nuisance.

G. Sutcliffe and A. Voronkov (Eds.): LPAR 2005, LNAI 3835, p. 47, 2005.
© Springer-Verlag Berlin Heidelberg 2005

A New Constraint Solver for 3D Lattices and Its Application to the Protein Folding Problem

Alessandro Dal Palù[1], Agostino Dovier[1], and Enrico Pontelli[2]

[1] Dipartimento di Matematica e Informatica,
Università di Udine
{dalpalu, dovier}@dimi.uniud.it
[2] Department of Computer Science,
New Mexico State University
epontell@cs.nmsu.edu

Abstract. The paper describes the formalization and implementation of an efficient constraint programming framework operating on 3D crystal lattices. The framework is motivated and applied to address the problem of solving the abinitio *protein structure prediction* problem—i.e., predicting the 3D structure of a protein from its amino acid sequence. Experimental results demonstrate that our novel approach offers up to a 3 orders of magnitude of speedup compared to other constraint-based solutions proposed for the problem at hand.

1 Introduction

In this paper we investigate the development of a generic *constraint framework* for discrete three dimensional (3D) crystal lattices. These lattice structures have been adopted in different fields of scientific computing [7, 15], to provide a manageable discretization of the 3D space and facilitate the investigation of physical and chemical organization of molecular, chemical, and crystal structures. In recent years, lattice structures have become of great interest for the study of the problem of computing approximations of the folding of protein structures in 3D space [20, 3, 11, 12, 15]. The basic values, in the constraint domain we propose, represent individual lattice points, and primitive constraints are introduced to capture basic spatial relationships within the lattice structure (e.g., relative positions, Euclidean and lattice distances). Variables representing those points can assume values on a *finite* portion of the lattice. We investigate constraint solving techniques in this framework, with a focus on propagation and search strategies.

The main motivation behind this line of research derives from the desire of more scalable and efficient solutions to the challenging problem of determining the 3D structure of globular proteins. The *protein structure prediction* (or *protein folding*) problem can be defined as the problem of determining, given the molecular composition of a protein (i.e., a list of amino acids, known as the *primary structure*), the three dimensional (3D) shape (*tertiary structure*) that the protein assumes in normal conditions in biological environments. Knowledge of the 3D protein structure is vital in many biomedical applications, e.g., for perfect drugs design and for pathogen detection. We allow as input some *secondary structure* knowledge (i.e., local 3D rigid conformations) that can

G. Sutcliffe and A. Voronkov (Eds.): LPAR 2005, LNAI 3835, pp. 48–63, 2005.

be obtained directly from the primary sequence using predictors [19]. We can classify our problem as *ab-initio*, since there is no other input information.

In recent decades, most scientists have agreed that the answer to the folding problem lies in the concept of the *energy state* of a protein. The predominant strategy in solving the protein folding problem has been to determine a state of the amino acid sequence in the 3D space with minimum energy state. According to this theory, the 3D conformation that yields the lowest energy state represents the protein's natural shape (a.k.a. the *native conformation*). The energy of a conformation can be modeled using *energy functions*, that determine the energy level based on the interactions between any pairs of amino acids [6]. Thus, we can reduce the protein folding problem to an optimization problem, where the energy function has to be minimized under a collection of constraints (e.g., derived from known chemical and physical properties) [9].

The problem is extremely complex and it can be reasonably simplified in several aspects, in order to reduce the overall complexity, without compromising the biological relevance of the solutions. A common simplification relies on the use of *lattice space models* to restrict the admissible positions of the amino acids in the space [1, 21, 20]. In this discrete space framework, the use of constraint solving techniques can lead to very effective solutions [11, 3].[1] Previous work conducted in this area relied on mapping the problem to traditional *Constraint Logic Programming over finite domains (CLP(FD))* (or making use of integer programming solutions [15]). In [11, 12], we showed that highly optimized constraints and propagators implemented in CLP allow us to achieve satisfactory performances on small/medium size instances, improving precision over previous models [3]. Unfortunately, the CLP(FD) libraries we explored (SICStus Prolog and ECLiPSe) proved ineffective in scaling to larger instances of the problem [12]. Furthermore, these libraries provided insufficient flexibility in implementing search strategies and heuristics that properly match the structure of our problem.

In this paper, we overcome the limitations of CLP(FD) encodings by implementing the protein folding problem in our novel lattice constraint programming framework. The novel solver is an optimized C program, that implements techniques for constraint handling and solution search, dealing directly with lattice elements—i.e., our native FD variables represent 3D lattice points (*lattice variables*). We include an efficient built-in labeling strategy for lattice variables and new search techniques for specific rigid objects (predicted secondary structure elements). The experimental results obtained show a dramatic improvement in performance (10^2–10^3 speedups w.r.t. SICStus 3.12.0 and ECLiPSe 5.8). We also implemented ideas and heuristics discussed through the paper and show our solver is robust enough to tackle proteins up to 100 amino acids and to produce acceptable quality solutions, given the model in use. We show that the encoding of the protein folding problem on *Face-Centered Cubic (fcc) lattices*, using our native lattice constraint framework, allows us to process significantly larger proteins than those handled in [11, 12], directly or by viewing them as clusters composed of known parts. The code discussed in the paper can be found at www.dimi.uniud.it/dovier/PF.

---

[1] Even with simple lattice models, the problem is NP-complete [10].

2   A New Constraint Solver on 3D Lattices

We describe a framework developed to solve *Constraint Satisfaction Problems* (CSPs) modeled on 3D lattices. The solver allows us to define lattice variables with associated domains, constraints over them, and to search the space of admissible solutions.

2.1   Variables and Domains

Crystal Lattices. A *crystal lattice* (or, simply, a lattice) is a graph (N, E), where N is a set of 3D points $(P_x, P_y, P_z) \in \mathbb{Z}^3$, connected by undirected edges (E). Lattices contain strong symmetries and present regular patterns repeated in the space. If all nodes have the same degree δ, then the lattice is said δ-*connected*. Given $A, B \in N$, we define:

- the *squared Euclidean distance* as: $eucl(A, B) = (B_x - A_x)^2 + (B_y - A_y)^2 + (B_z - A_z)^2$
- the *norm infinity* as: $norm_\infty(A, B) = \max\{|B_x - A_x|, |B_y - A_y|, |B_z - A_z|\}$

In this work, we focus on fcc lattices, where:

$$N = \{(x, y, z) \mid x, y, z \in \mathbb{Z} \text{ and } x + y + z \text{ is even}\} \text{ and}$$
$$E = \{(P, Q) \mid P, Q \in N, eucl(P, Q) = 2\}.$$

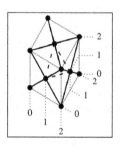

Lattice points lie on the vertices and on the center point of each face of cubes of size 2 (Fig. 1). Points at Euclidean distance $\sqrt{2}$ are connected and their distance is called *lattice unit*. Two points are in *contact* iff their Euclidean distance is 2. This lattice is 12-connected. In [17] it is shown that the fcc model is a well-suited, realistic model for 3D conformations of proteins.

Fig. 1. An fcc-cube

Domains. A *domain* D is described by a pair of lattice points $\langle \underline{D}, \overline{D} \rangle$, where $\underline{D} = (\underline{D}_x, \underline{D}_y, \underline{D}_z)$ and $\overline{D} = (\overline{D}_x, \overline{D}_y, \overline{D}_z)$. D defines a *box*:

$$Box(D) = \left\{(x, y, z) \in \mathbb{Z}^3 \ : \ \underline{D}_x \leq x \leq \overline{D}_x \ \wedge \ \underline{D}_y \leq y \leq \overline{D}_y \ \wedge \ \underline{D}_z \leq z \leq \overline{D}_z \right\}$$

We only handle the bounds of the effective domain, since a detailed representation of all the individual points in a volume of interest would be infeasible (due to the sheer number of points involved). The approach follows the same spirit as the manipulation of finite domains using bounds consistency [2]. The choice of creating a single variable representing a three dimensional point is driven by the fact that consistency is less effective when independently dealing with individual coordinates [16]. We say that D is *admissible* if $Box(D)$ contains at least one lattice point; D is *ground* if it is admissible and $\underline{D} = \overline{D}$; D is *empty* (*failed*) if D is not admissible. We introduce two operations:

- *Domain intersection*: Given two domains D and E, their intersection is defined as follows: $D \cap E = \langle \uparrow (D, E), \downarrow (D, E) \rangle$ where:
$$\uparrow (D, E) = (\ \max\{\underline{D}_x, \underline{E}_x\}, \max\{\underline{D}_y, \underline{E}_y\}, \max\{\underline{D}_z, \underline{E}_z\}\ )$$
$$\downarrow (D, E) = (\ \min\{\overline{D}_x, \overline{E}_x\}, \min\{\overline{D}_y, \overline{E}_y\}, \min\{\overline{D}_z, \overline{E}_z\}\ )$$
- *Domain dilation*: Given a domain D and a positive integer d, we define the domain dilation operation (that enlarges $Box(D)$ by $2d$ units) $D + d$ as:
$$D + d = \langle (\underline{D}_x - d, \underline{D}_y - d, \underline{D}_z - d), (\overline{D}_x + d, \overline{D}_y + d, \overline{D}_z + d) \rangle$$

Each variable V, that represent lattice points, is associated to a *domain* $D^V = \langle \underline{D}^V, \overline{D}^V \rangle$.

2.2 Constraints

We define the following binary constraints on variables, based on spatial distances. Given two lattice variables V_1, V_2 and $d \in \mathbb{N}$, we define the constraints:

$$\text{CONSTR\_DIST\_LEQ}(V_1, V_2, d) \Leftrightarrow \exists P_1 \in B_1, \exists P_2 \in B_2 \ s.t. \ norm_\infty(P_1, P_2) \leq d$$
$$\text{CONSTR\_EUCL}(V_1, V_2, d) \quad \Leftrightarrow \exists P_1 \in B_1, \exists P_2 \in B_2 \ s.t. \ eucl(P_1, P_2) = d$$
$$\text{CONSTR\_EUCL\_LEQ}(V_1, V_2, d) \Leftrightarrow \exists P_1 \in B_1, \exists P_2 \in B_2 \ s.t. \ eucl(P_1, P_2) \leq d$$
$$\text{CONSTR\_EUCL\_G}(V_1, V_2, d) \quad \Leftrightarrow \exists P_1 \in B_1, \exists P_2 \in B_2 \ s.t. \ eucl(P_1, P_2) > d$$

where $B_1 = Box(D^{V_1})$, $B_2 = Box(D^{V_2})$, and P_1, P_2 are lattice points.

All the constraints introduced are bi-directional (i.e., symmetric). Nevertheless, for practical reasons, we treat them as directional constraints, using the information of the first (leftmost) domain to test and/or modify the second domain. Consequently, every time a constraint C over two variables has to be expressed, we will add in the constraint store both constraints $C(V_1, V_2, d)$ and $C(V_2, V_1, d)$. A *Constraint Satisfaction Problem (CSP)* on the variables $V_1, \ldots, V_n$ with domains $D^{V_1}, \ldots, D^{V_n}$ is a set of binary constraints of the form above. A solution of the CSP is an assignment of lattice points to the variables $V_1, \ldots, V_n$, such that the lattice points belong to the corresponding variable domains and they satisfy all the binary constraints.

Proposition: *The general problem of deciding whether a CSP in the lattice framework admits solutions is NP-complete.*

Proof [Sketch]: The problem is clearly in NP. To show the NP-hardness, we reduce the *Graph 3-Colorability Problem* of an undirected graph $G(V, E)$ in our CSP (we refer to cubic lattices. For other lattices, additional CONSTR_EUCL_G constraints might be required to identify 3 points in the box). For each node $n_i \in V$, we introduce a variable V_i with domain $D^{V_i} = \langle (0,0,0), (0,0,2) \rangle$. $Box(D^{V_i})$ contains three lattice points $(0, 0, j)$, corresponding to the color j. For every edge $e = (n_i, n_j)$, we add the constraint CONSTR_EUCL_G$(V_i, V_j, 0)$, that constrains the points represented by the variables to be at a distance greater than 0 (i.e., have a different color). □

The *constraint store* is a data structure used to implement a CSP, representing constraints, variables, and their domains. In our implementation, it is realized as a dynamic array. For efficiency, we also maintain, for each variable V_i, the adjacency list containing links to all the constraints $C(V_i, V_j)$—those that have to be considered after a modification of the domain of D^{V_i}.

2.3 Constraint Solving

We modeled the solver considering the constrain phase separated from the search phase. Thus, neither new variables nor constraints can be added during the search.

Propagation and Consistency. The constraint processing phase is based on propagating the constraints on the bounds of the domains in the 3 dimensions at the same time, i.e., modifying the boxes of the domains.

The constraint CONSTR_DIST_LEQ(A, B, d) states that the variables A and B are distant no more than d in $norm_\infty$. It can be employed to simplify domains through bounds consistency. The formal rule is: $D^B = (D^A + d) \cap D^B$.

The constraint CONSTR_EUCL_LEQ(A, B, d) states that A and B are at squared euclidean distance less than or equal to d. The sphere of radius $\sqrt{d}$, that contains the admissible values defined by the constraint, can be approximated by the minimal surrounding box that enclose it (a cube with side $2\lfloor\sqrt{d}\rfloor$). The formal propagation rule is: $D^B = (D^A + \lfloor\sqrt{d}\rfloor) \cap D^B$. This rule can also be applied in the case of the CONSTR_EUCL constraint (this constraint implies CONSTR_EUCL_LEQ). The constraint CONSTR_EUCL_G does perform any propagation. We also assume that an eventual cost function (to be optimized during the search for solutions) does not propagate any information to the domains and thus it is handled as simple evaluation function.

Propagation is activated whenever the domain of a variable is modified. Let us consider a situation where the variables $G = \{V_1, \ldots, V_{k-1}\}$ have been bound to specific values, V_k is the variable to be assigned next, and let $NG = \{V_{k+1}, \ldots, V_n\}$ be all the remaining variables. The first step, after the labeling of V_k, is to check for consistency the constraints of the form $C(V_k, V_i)$, where $V_i \in G$ (this is the *node consistency* check). The successive *propagation* phase is divided in two steps. First, all the constraints of the form $C(V_k, V_j)$ are processed, where $V_j \in NG$. This step propagates the new bounds of V_k to the variables not yet labeled. Thereafter, bounds consistency, using the same outline of AC-3 [2], is applied to the constraints of the form $C(V_i, V_j)$, where $V_i, V_j \in NG$. We carefully implemented a constant-time insertion for handling the set of constraints to be revisited, using a combination of an array to store the constraints and an array of flags for each constraint. This leads to the following result:

Proposition: *Each propagation phase has a worst-case time complexity of $O(n + ed^3)$, where n is the number of variables involved, e is the number of constraints in the constraint store, and d the maximum domain size.*

Proof [Sketch]: Let us assume that the variable V_i is labeled. Each propagation for a constraint costs $O(1)$, since only arithmetic operations are performed on the domain of the second variable. Let us assume that for each pair of variables and type of constraint, at most one constraint is deposited in the constraint store (it can be guaranteed with an initial simplification). In the worst case, there are $O(n)$ constraints of the form $C(V_i, V_j, d)$, where V_j is not ground. Thus, the algorithm propagates the new information in time $O(n)$, since each constraint costs constant time. The worst-case time complexity of AC-3 procedure is $O(ed^3)$, where e is the number of constraints in the constraint store and d the maximum domain size. □

Handling the Search Tree. The search procedures are implementations of a standard *backtracking+propagation* search procedure [2]. The evolution of the computation can be depicted as the construction of a search tree, where the internal nodes correspond to guessing the value of a variable (*labeling*) while the edges correspond to propagating the effect of the labeling to other variables (through the constraints). We implement two *variable selection* strategies: a *leftmost* strategy—it selects the leftmost uninstantiated variable for the next labeling step—and a *first-fail* strategy—it selects the variable with the smallest domain size, i.e., the box with the smallest number of lattice points. The process of selecting the value for a variable V relies on D^V, on the structure of the underlying lattice and on the constraints present. E.g., in a fcc lattice, if V is known to be only 1 lattice unit from a specific point in the lattice, then it has only 12 possible placements, that can be tested directly, instead of exploring the full content of $Box(D^V)$.

At the implementation level, the current branch of the search tree is stored into an array; each element of the array represents one level of the current branch. A value-trail stack is employed to keep track of variables modified during propagation, and used to undo modifications during backtracking. Moreover, we allow the possibility of collapsing levels of the search tree, by assigning a *set* of (related) variables in a single step. This operation is particularly useful when dealing with variables that represent points that are part of a secondary structure element.

2.4 Bounded Block Fails Heuristic

We present a novel heuristic to guide the exploration of the search tree, called *Bounded Block Fails (BBF)*. This technique is *general* and can be applied to every type of search, though it is particularly effective when applied to the protein folding problem [12]. The heuristic involves the concept of *block*. Let $\hat{V}$ be a list $[V_1, \ldots, V_n]$ of variables and constants (i.e., ground variables). The collection of variables in $\hat{V}$ is partitioned in *blocks* of fixed size k, such that the concatenation of all the blocks $B_1 B_2 \ldots B_\ell$ gives the ordered list of non ground variables in $\hat{V}$, where $\ell \leq \lceil \frac{n}{k} \rceil$. The blocks are dynamically selected, according to the variable selection strategy and the state of the search. Fig. 2 shows an example for a list of 9 variables and $k = 3$. Dark boxes represent ground variables.

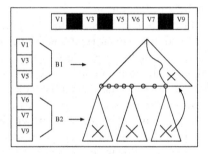

Fig. 2. An fcc-cube

The heuristics consists of splitting the search among the ℓ blocks. Within each block B_i, the variables are individually labeled. When a branch in block B_i is completely labeled, the search moves to the successive block B_{i+1}, if any. If the labeling of the block B_{i+1} fails, the search backtracks to the block B_i. Here there are two possibilities: if the number of times that B_{i+1} completely failed is below a certain threshold t_i, then the process continues, by generating one more solution to B_i and re-entering B_{i+1}. Otherwise, if too many failures have occurred, then the BBF heuristic generates a failure for B_i as well and backtracks to a previous block. Observe that the count of the number of failures includes both the regular search failures as well as those caused by the BBF strategy. The list $t_1, \ldots, t_\ell$ of thresholds determines the behavior of the heuristic. In Fig. 2, $t_1 = 3$; note how, after the third failure of B_2, the search on B_1 fails as well.

BBF is an incomplete strategy, i.e., it can miss the optimum. However intuition and experimental results suggest that it is effective in finding suboptimal solutions whenever they are spread in the search tree. In these cases, we can afford to skip solutions when generating block failure, because others will be discovered following other choices in earlier blocks. In the context of searching for solutions in 3D lattices, a failure in the current branch means that the partial spatial structure constructed so far (by placing variables in the lattice) does not allow to proceed without violating some constraints.

The BBF heuristic suggests to revise earlier choices (i.e., a "more drastic" revision of the structure built so far) instead of exploring the whole space of possibilities depending on the block that collects failures (i.e., a "more local" revision of the structure). The high density and the large number of admissible solutions typically available in the type of lattice problems we consider, permit to exclude some solutions, depending on the threshold values, and to still be able to find almost optimal solutions in shorter time.

3   An Application: The Protein Folding Problem on the fcc Lattice

A protein folds in the 3D space with a high degree of freedom and tends to reach the *Native* conformation (tertiary structure) with a minimal value of free energy. Native conformations are largely built from *secondary structure* elements (e.g., α-helices and β-sheets), often arranged in well-defined motifs.

Fig. 3. Protein 1d6t native state

In Fig. 3, α-helices (contiguous amino acids arranged in a regular right-handed helix) are in dark color and β-sheets (collections of extended strands, each made of contiguous amino acids) in light color. Following similar proposals (e.g., [1, 3, 15]), we focus on fcc lattices. For details about the biological issues and lattice modeling see [11].

Let $\mathcal{A}$ be the set of amino acids ($|\mathcal{A}| = 20$). Given a (primary) sequence $S = s_1 \cdots s_n$, with $s_i \in \mathcal{A}$, we represent with lattice variable V_i the *lattice position* of amino acid s_i—i.e., the placement of the amino acid s_i in the lattice. The modeling leads to the following constraints:

- for $i \in \{1, \ldots n - 1\}$, CONSTR_EUCL($V_i, V_{i+1}, 2$): adjacent amino acids in the primary sequence are mapped to lattice points connected by one lattice unit;
- for $i \in \{2, \ldots n - 1\}$, CONSTR_EUCL_LEQ($V_{i-1}, V_{i+1}, 7$): three adjacent amino acids may not form an angle of 180° in the lattice;
- for $i, j \in \{1, \ldots n\}$, $|i - j| \geq 2$, CONSTR_EUCL_G($V_i, V_j, 4$): two non-consecutive amino acids must be separated by more than one lattice unit (no overlaps), and angles of 60° are disallowed for three consecutive amino acids.

In fcc, the angle between three consecutive amino acids can assume only values 60°, 90°, 120°, and 180°, but volumetric constraints make values 60° and 180° infeasible. The following additional constraints are also introduced [11]:

- CONSTR_DIST_LEQ($V_i, V_j, 4$) are added whenever the presence of a ssbond between the amino acids s_i and s_j is known; the ssbond (*disulfide bridge*) is a predictable limit on the distance in space between pairs of amino acids.
- CONSTR_DIST_LEQ($V_i, V_j, \text{cf} \cdot n$) are added, where cf is the *compact factor*, expressed as a number between 0 and 1, and n is the protein length. The compact factor establishes an approximated maximal distance between amino acids.

A *folding* ω of $S = s_1 \cdots s_n$ is an assignment of lattice points to the variables $V_1, \ldots, V_n$ that is a solution of the CSP defined by the constraints above.

A simplified evaluation of the *energy* of a folding can be obtained by observing the *contacts* present in the folding. Each pair of non-consecutive amino acids s_i and s_j in contact (i.e., at Euclidean distance 2) provide an energy contribution, described by the commutative function $\mathsf{Pot}(s_i, s_j)$ [11]. These contributions can be obtained from tables developed using statistical methods applied to structures obtained from X-Rays and NMR experiments [6]. Finally, the *protein structure prediction problem* can be modeled as the problem of finding the folding ω of S such that the following energy cost function is minimized:

$$E(\omega, S) = \sum_{1 \leq i < n} \sum_{i+2 \leq j \leq n} \mathsf{contact}(\omega(V_i), \omega(V_j)) \cdot \mathsf{Pot}(s_i, s_j).$$

The function $\mathsf{contact}$ takes two lattice points and returns a value in $\{0, 1\}$:

$$\mathsf{contact}(A, B) = 1 \Leftrightarrow eucl(A, B) = 4.$$

Together with the primary sequence S, we allow input knowledge about presence of specific secondary structure elements (e.g., helices). These could be determined, for example, using standard secondary structure prediction systems (e.g., PHD or PSI-pred). This information can be used to impose several local constraints forcing a sequence of points to assume the a rigid spatial form. In this paper, we view each rigid object (an helix or a sheet) as a unique high-level disjunctive constraint, which is automatically activated when one point in the secondary structure is labeled.

3.1 Variable Instantiation in the fcc Lattice

Once the constraints have been set up, the search phase is initiated. Different strategies are employed to prune the search space at this stage.

If the variable V_{i-1} (with first fail strategy also V_{i+1}) is ground and the variable V_i has to be instantiated, it turns out that there are only 12 possible assignments allowed by fcc—being the lattice 12-connected, and consecutive amino acids are connected by exactly one lattice unit. Thus, it is convenient to expand the search tree for only those 12 assignments that are compatible with the current domain of V_i. A more particular case, but very common, occurs when V_{i-1} and V_{i-2} (V_{i+1} and V_{i+2}) are both ground. In this case, the interaction of all constraints limits the values of V_i to at most 6 possible assignments—and only those that are also present in $Box(D^{V_i})$ are used to expand the search tree. This lattice dependent instantiation scheme allows us to directly assign feasible values, reducing the number of consistency checks. The use of this strategy leads to a speedup of 2-3 times w.r.t. a labeling that explores all points in $Box(D^{V_i})$.

Another labeling strategy relates to the handling of secondary structure elements. When the first variable belonging to a rigid object is labeled, all the other variables in it are assigned, according to precomputed patterns that describe every possible orientation of the secondary structure elements in the lattice. After a point in the secondary structure is labeled, there are only 24 possible assignments for the *whole* rigid object, due to the lattice constraints and symmetries. To save unnecessary work, moreover, after the consistency checks are performed, the bounds consistency procedure is run only once, after the propagation from the newly labeled variables has been completed.

3.2   Pruning Minimal Contacts Heuristic

In this section, we present a branch and bound (BB) strategy, adapted to the specific needs of the protein folding problem. In the case of the protein folding problem, a generic branch and bound scheme, based on the estimation of the energy of the conformation, proved to be rather ineffective with large input sizes. Our intuition is that the cost function can collect many contributions at the very end of a branch and drastically change its value. This behavior is particularly evident when processing large proteins. As a result, the prediction of the bounds for the energy function, computationally expensive, reveals to be potentially inaccurate.

We adopted a more coarse and constant time cost estimation. The strategy we propose implements branch and bound using the *number of contacts* generated by the given conformation as the information to perform pruning. In general, the global energy and the number of contacts are strongly related. Nevertheless, since the energy function is composed of weighted contributions of amino acids in contact, the two values may occasionally diverge.

The computation of estimates of the number of contacts is facilitated by the peculiar properties of the fcc lattice; e.g., each amino acid can form at most 3 contacts with other ones. When a new best conformation is found, we compute the number c of contacts realized. Assuming that, in the worst case, the last amino acids to be labeled generate 3 contacts each, at $c/3$ levels before the leaves, each subtree can be safely pruned whenever the number of contacts is less than c. This heuristic can be computed in constant time since, given a partial assignment, an upper bound for possible contacts is immediately known. Since the energy is not precisely expressed by the number of contacts, we cannot guarantee the completeness of the heuristics. Nevertheless, empirical tests showed that this is not a significant problem; our experiments indicated also that the pruning of the last levels of the tree provides significant speedup during search.

In Table 1, we show some experimental tests of enumeration of the complete search tree, with and without the pruning heuristic presented above (under Windows on an AMD Duron 1.0GHz). For each protein ID of length N, we run a complete enumeration and then perform the same search with the con-

Table 1. Effectiveness of contact pruning heuristic

ID	N	Enumeration			BB Heuristic		
		Energy	Nodes	Time	Energy	Nodes	Time
1kvg	12	-6,881	318,690	0.851s	-6,881	124,722	0.540s
1le0	12	-4,351	1,541,107	4.015s	-4,351	487,105	1.842s
1le3	16	-5,299	1,544,830	5.938s	-5,299	439,969	2.513s
1edp	17	-12,279	20,491	0.140s	-12,279	8,726	0.120s
1pg1	18	-10,352	56,934	0.280s	-10,352	7,908	0.140s
1zdd	34	-12,315	268,061	5.037s	-12,097	68,428	3.805s

tacts heuristic activated. In all cases, the heuristic improves time and reduces the number of nodes explored, without significantly changing the optima discovered.

4   Results and Comparisons

Efficiency Analysis. The first test we discuss is designed to benchmark the speed of our solver. Our goal is to compare the solution to the protein folding problem using our lattice solver with the solution obtained by mapping the problem to finite domain constraints—using SICStus 3.12.0 (`clpfd`) and ECLiPSe 5.8 (`ic`). We run complete enumerations of the search tree using the first-fail strategy. To perform a fair comparison, we did not make use of branch and bound strategies in any of the implementations.

We implement the protein structure prediction problem in SICStus and ECLiPSe using the best formalization we developed in [12]. In our solver, we implement the equivalent sets of constraints, reported in Section 3, but expressed in terms of finite domains. In Table 2, we compare the running times required to explore the whole search space. In the first col-

Table 2. Complete Search

ID	Our	SICStus	ECLiPSe
1edp	0.063s	8.92s (142x)	1m.5s (1039x)
1pg1	0.156s	16.00s (103x)	1m.50s (704x)
1kvg	0.406s	40.81s (101x)	4m.22s (646x)
1le0	1.922s	6m.31s (203x)	33m.13s (1036x)
1le3	2.859s	9m.46s (205x)	59m.37s (1251x)
1zdd	2.437s	insuff. memory	> 8h. (>10000x)

umn, we report the protein selected, in the second the time (in seconds) required by the lattice solver to explore the search tree, while the last two columns report the corresponding running times using SICStus and ECLiPSe (in brackets the speedup w.r.t. the lattice solver). For these examples, we use proteins whose search tree can be exhaustively explored in a reasonable time. These tests are performed using Windows (Pentium P4, 2.4GHz, 256Mb RAM). Table 2 shows that the choices made in the design and implementation of the new solver allow us to gain speedups in the order of 10^2–10^3 times w.r.t. standard general-purpose FD constraint solvers. Moreover, our implementation is robust and scales to large search trees with a limited use of memory. These positive results have also an interesting side-effect: the solver allows us to quickly collect the entire pool of admissible conformations for small proteins.

Quality of the Results. We analyze the foldings produced by our solver for proteins for which the native conformation is known. In our case, we consider proteins with known conformation from the PDB database [5]. Different ingredients come into play: the use of a simplified spatial model (fcc in our case), the use of a simplified energy function, and the use of a simplified protein model. Clearly, we cannot compare directly our results to the ones deposited in the PDB. In [11], we showed how to enrich fcc predictions to a solution relaxed in the continuous space. Only after that step a direct comparison with the original protein in the PDB is meaningful. Since in these tests we do not apply any refinement to our fcc solutions, we introduce a new *quality measure*, in order to mask the errors induced by the use of the lattice. We analyze the foldings as follows. We map an original protein from the PDB onto the fcc lattice, using the usual constraints for an admissible conformation. Moreover, to reproduce the same shape on the lattice, we add a set of distance constraints for each pair of amino acids taken from the original protein. The distance constraints are relaxed to a range of possible distances allowed for each pair, in order to allow the protein to find a placement in the discretized space. This process produces a *set of admissible foldings* that are very close to the original protein. These PDB over fcc proteins are the best representatives on fcc of quasi-optimal foldings according to the native conformation. Since it is not possible to collect the complete set of solutions, due to time complexity, we select, as representatives of the complete set, the enumeration of the first $1,000$ conformations found. Out of this set we identify the best conformation evaluated according to the *comparison function* introduced below.

The function used to compare the quality of the foldings cannot be the energy function used in the minimization process, since it accounts only for local contacts. We also decided not to use a standard RMSD[2] measure of spatial positions. This measure, in fact, computes only the deviation of corresponding positions between two conformations, and does not take into account other properties of the amino acids being compared. In our specific case, we want to include also the specific energy contribution carried by every pair of amino acids. We developed a *comparison function* that includes all these properties; basically the function is a more refined extension to continuous values of the contact energy function. The comparison of two conformations is reduced to comparing the values returned by the comparison function applied to the two conformations. The comparison function is as follows:

$$compare(S, \omega) = 4 \cdot \sum_{i \neq j} contrib(i, j) \, / \, \sqrt{eucl(\, \omega(i), \omega(j)\,)}$$

where S is the sequence of amino acids and ω is the conformation. The function is normalized w.r.t. the distance of a contact (i.e., 4). The function is a continuous extension of our energy model, and it is tolerant to small changes in positions of amino acids, compensating for the differences of the spatial and energetic models.

In Table 3, we compare the evaluations with the *comparison function* for different proteins; the Our column reports the value of the comparison function applied to the best folding obtained from our solver, using a complete search; the PDB (1) column reports the value for the best mapping of the PDB protein on the fcc lattice. The PDB (2) column reports the value for the original protein as in the PDB. This is useful to compare how much the protein is deformed when placed on the lattice.

It is interesting to discuss these data, since our previous implementations [11, 12] could not terminate a complete enumeration in reasonable

Table 3. compare applied to best, PDB on fcc and PDB folding

ID	Our	PDB (1)	PDB (2)
1kvg	-19,598	-17,964	-28,593
1le0	-11,761	-12,024	-16,030
1le3	-20,192	-14,367	-21,913
1edp	-46,912	-38,889	-48,665
1pg1	-44,436	-39,906	-58,610
1zdd	-64,703	-63,551	-69,571
1e0n	-57,291	-54,161	-60,728

time. The results indicate that the values are indeed very close. It is important to remember that we are constrained to fold the proteins on the lattice structure, and thus the values are expected to be closer to (1) than (2). In general, (2) should be an upper bound for (1). Moreover, note that our best folding on lattice is often better than the corresponding mapping from PDB to fcc. This is due to the fact that the pool of conformations used in computing the PDB on fcc mapping is not complete, and the constraints used in the two approaches are different. Visually, the predicted conformations are very close to the corresponding original ones (e.g., Fig. 4).

---

[2] *Root-Mean-Square Deviation*, a typical measure of structural diversity.

For medium and large size proteins, determining the optimal folding is computationally infeasible. When computing an *approximated* solution for the folding of a

Fig. 4. Protein 1zdd: our solution, fcc on PDB mapping and PDB

protein, it is also important to relate the result of the computation to the optimal solution, in order to evaluate the impact of the pruning strategies adopted. Once again we use the scheme presented above to estimate the quality of our solutions—by comparing how far our heuristic landed from the hypothetical optimal solution.

Heuristics Tests. To show the power of our constraint solver in handling ad-hoc search heuristics, we test a set of selected proteins, with lengths ranging from 12 to 104. Table 4 reports the results of the executions; the Table indicates the PDB protein name, the protein length (n) in terms of amino acids, the BBF thresholds value assigned to $t_1 = \cdots = t_\ell$, the time to complete the search, the evaluation of the comparison function applied to the best solution, to the PDB on fcc, and to the original PDB. For BBF, we decided to define the block size equal to $\lfloor n/12 \rfloor + 1$ for $n \leq 48$ and equal to 5 for larger proteins. We empirically noticed that larger block sizes provide less accurate results, due to the higher pruning when failing on bigger blocks.

Proteins with more than 100 amino acids can be handled by our solver. This result is improved over the capabilities of the previous proposed frameworks (60 [11] and 80 [12] amino acids). This improvement is non-trivial, because of the NP-completeness of the problem at hand. The new heuristics provide more effective pruning of the search

Table 4. BBF experimental results (Linux, 2.8MHz, 512Mb RAM)

ID	n	CF	BBF	Time	Energy	PDB on fcc	PDB
1kvg	12	0.94	50	0.16s	-19,644	-17,964	-28,593
1edp	17	0.76	50	0.04s	-46,912	-38,889	-48,665
1e0n	27	0.56	50	1.76s	-52,558	-51,656	-60,728
1zdd	34	0.49	50	0.80s	-63,079	-62,955	-69,571
1vii	36	0.48	50	4.31s	-76,746	-71,037	-82,268
1e0m	37	0.47	30	19m57s	-72,434	-66,511	-81,810
2gp8	40	0.45	50	0.27s	-55,561	-55,941	-67,298
1ed0	46	0.41	50	8.36s	-124,740	-118,570	-157,616
1enh	54	0.37	50	45.3s	-122,879	-83,642	-140,126
2igd	60	0.35	20	2h42m	-167,126	-149,521	-201,159
1sn1	63	0.18	10	58m53s	-226,304	-242,589	-367,285
1ail	69	0.32	50	2m49s	-220,090	-143,798	-269,032
1l6t	78	0.30	50	1.19s	-360,351	-285,360	-446,647
1hs7	97	0.20	50	35m16s	-240,148	-246,275	-367,687
1tqg	104	0.15	20	10m35s	-462,918	-362,355	-1,242,015

tree, and allow to collect better quality solutions. The tradeoff between quality and speed is controlled by the BBF threshold: higher values provide a more refined search and higher quality solutions. Moreover, the quality comparisons between our folding and the mapping of PDB on fcc and PDB itself, reveal that our solutions, even for larger proteins, are comparable to foldings of PDB on fcc. Note also that, for larger proteins, the size of pool of the selected solutions for PDB on fcc mappings, becomes insufficient, i.e., the difference of comparison function from the PDB value becomes significant. For large proteins, it is an open problem in the literature how to precisely estimate the errors arising from discretizing the protein structure in a lattice space.

Scalability. A distinct advantage of our approach is its ability to readily use additional knowledge about known components of the protein in the resolution process, as long as they can be expressed as lattice constraints. In particular, some proteins, like hemoglobin, are constructed of a cluster of subunits, whose structure is known and already deposited in the PDB (or can be predicted). This approach follows the evolution of proteins, i.e., combination of already existing pieces into new bigger blocks. Often biologists explore unknown proteins by extracting the structure of sub-blocks by *homology* from the PDB. Our constraint-based approach can easily take advantage of the known conformations of the subsequences, treated as rigid spatial objects described by constraints, to determine the overall conformation of the protein. This ability is lacking in most other approaches to the problem; our previous finite domains encodings cannot handle proteins with more than 100 amino acids.

To study the scalability of our solver, we report some tests on artificial proteins having a structure of the type XYZ, i.e., composed of two known subsequences (X and Z), while Y is a short connecting sequence. We can show that our framework can easily handle proteins of size up to $1,000$ amino acids. We run some complete enumerations varying the length of Y and the proteins used as pattern for X and Z.

In our tests, we load the proteins X and Z as predicted in Table 4. We link them with a coil of amino acids with length $|Y|$ (leaving X and Z free of moving in the lattice as rigid objects). The search is a simple enumeration using Leftmost variable selection.

Table 5. From left to right, processing proteins XYZ (a), and ratios sphere/box approach (b)

X	Z	$|X|$	$|Y|$	$|Z|$	Time
1e0n	1e0n	27	5	27	11.3s
1e0n	1e0n	27	6	27	1m5s
1ail	1ail	69	5	69	1m25s
1ail	1ail	69	6	69	7m52s
1hs7	1hs7	97	5	97	3m7s
1hs7	1hs7	97	6	97	16m25s
1e0n	1e0n	27	3	27	0.40s
1e0n-2	1e0n-2	57	3	57	1.92s
1e0n-4	1e0n-4	117	3	117	9.26s
1e0n-8	1e0n-8	237	3	237	29.7s
1e0n-16	1e0n-16	477	3	477	1m48s

ID	Nodes	Time
1pg1	1.00	1.34
1kvg	1.95	2.39
1le0	1.00	1.06
1le3	1.02	1.16
1edp	2.96	2.00
1zdd	1.30	2.18

Table 5 (a) shows that the computational times are extremely low, and dominated by the size of Y, instead of the size of XYZ. In the second part of the Table, we consider proteins constructed as follows: we start with X and Z equal to the 1e0n protein (whose folding can be optimally computed), and every successive test makes use of $X' = Z' = XYZ$—i.e., at each experiment we make use of the results from the previous experiment. This approach allowed us to push the search to sequences of size up to 1, 000 amino acids. In these experiments, our concern is not only the execution time, but the ability of the solver to make use of known structures to prune the search tree.

Boxes vs Spheres. We tested a different formalization of the variables domains, where domains are represented as spheres instead of using Box. We reimplemented in our solver the domain description of a variable in terms of a center and a radius (with discrete coordinates) and the definition of an intersection of spheres as the smallest sphere that includes them. The idea is that a sphere should be more suitable to express the propagation of euclidean distance constraints. Unfortunately, results reported in Table 5 (b) show that this idea is not successful. The Table reports in the first column the test protein used, in the second the ratio of visited nodes in the search tree between sphere over box implementations. The last column provides the ratio of computation times between the two implementations. In particular, note that many more internal nodes are expanded in the sphere implementation. There are two reasons for this. First, computing spheres intersection is more expensive than intersecting boxes. Second, often two intersecting spheres are almost tangent. In this case the correct intersection is approximated by another sphere that includes a great amount of discarded volume.

5   Related Works

The problem of protein structure prediction is a fundamental challenge [20] in molecular biology. An abstraction of the problem, that has been investigated, is the ab-initio problem in the *HP* model, where amino acids are separated into two classes (*H*, *hydrophobic*, and *P*, *hydrophilic*). The goal is to search for a conformation produced by an *HP* sequence, where most HH pairs are neighboring in a predefined lattice. The problem has been studied on 2D square lattices [10, 15], 2D triangular lattices [1], 3D square models [15], and fcc lattices [17]. Backofen et al. have extensively studied this last problem [3, 4]. Integer programming approaches to this problem have also been considered [14]. The approach is suited for globular proteins, since the main force driving the folding process is the electrical potential generated by *H*s and *P*s, and the fcc lattices are effective approximations of the 3D space. Backofen's model has been extended in [11, 6], where the interactions between classes *H* and *P* are refined as interactions between every pair of amino acids, and modeling of secondary structures has been introduced.

The use of constraint technology in the context of the protein folding problem has been fairly limited. Backofen and Will used constraints over finite domains in the context of the *HP* problem [4]. Rodosek [18] proposed an hybrid algorithm which combines constraint solving and simulated annealing. Clark employed Prolog to implement heuristics in pruning a exhaustive search for predicting α-helix and β-sheet topology from secondary structure and topological folding rules [8]. Distributed search and continuous optimization have been used in ab-initio structure prediction, based on selection of discrete torsion angles for combinatorial search of the space of possible foldings [13]. Krippahl and Barahona [16] used a constraint-based approach to determine protein structures compatible with distance constraints obtained from NMR data.

In this work we adopted an approach different from the previous literature [3, 11, 12], where the modeling relied on traditional FD constraints. The description of a 3D lattice model using (single dimensional) FD-variables requires a complex interaction of constraints, in order to reproduce the natural correlation between the coordinates of the same lattice point. This leads to larger encodings with many constraints to be processed. Moreover, arc and bounds consistency reduce the domains one dimension at a time, and the system stores the explicit set of admissible (single-dimensional) points. Scalability is also hampered in this type of encodings. Our experience [11, 12] indicates that performance of these representations based on SICStus and ECLiPSe solvers is insufficient for larger instances of the problem.

The constraint model adopted in this paper is similar in spirit to the model used in [16]—as they also make use of variables representing 3D coordinates and box domains. The problem addressed in [16] is significantly different, as they make use of a continuous space model, they do not rely on a energy model, and they assume the availability of rich distance constraints obtained from NMR data, thus leading to a more constrained problem—while in our problem we are dealing with a search space of $O(6^n)$ conformations in the fcc lattice for proteins with n amino acids. Every modification of a variable domain, in our version of the problem, propagates only to a few other variables, and every attempt to propagate refined information (i.e., the good/no good sub-volumes of [16]) when exploring a branch in the search tree, is defeated by the frequent backtracking. Thus, in our approach we preferred a very efficient and coarse bounds consistency. The ideas of [16], i.e., restricting the space domains for rigid objects is simply too expensive in our framework (see [12]). We opted for a direct grounding of rigid objects, since in lattices there are few possible orientations. In our case, the position of objects can be basically anywhere, due to the lack of strong constraints. The techniques of [16] would be more costly and produce a poor propagation.

6   Conclusion and Future Work

We presented a formalization of a constraint programming framework on crystal lattice structures—a regular, discretized version of the 3D space. The framework has been realized into a concrete solver, with various search strategies and heuristics. The solver has been applied to the problem of computing the minimal energy folding of proteins in the fcc lattice, providing high speedups and scalability w.r.t. previous solutions. The speedups derive from a more direct and compact representation of the lattice constraints, and the use of search strategies that better match the structure of the problem. We proposed general lattice (BBF) and problem-specific heuristics, showing how they can be integrated in our constraint framework to effectively prune the search space.

As future work, we plan to extend the investigation of search strategies and heuristics. We also propose to explore the use of parallelism to further improve scalability of the solution to larger instances of the problem.

Acknowledgments. This research has been supported by NSF grants 0220590, 0454066, and 0420407, by GNCS2005 project on constraints and their applications and by FIRB project RBNE03B8KK on protein folding.

References

1. R. Agarwala et al. Local rules for protein folding on a triangular lattice and generalized hydrophobicity in the HP model. *J. Computational Biology*, 275–296, 1997.
2. K. R. Apt. *Principles of constraint programming*. Cambridge University press, 2003.
3. R. Backofen. The protein structure prediction problem: A constraint optimization approach using a new lower bound. *Constraints*, 6(2–3):223–255, 2001.
4. R. Backofen and S. Will. A Constraint-Based Approach to Structure Prediction for Simplified Protein Models that Outperforms Other Existing Methods. *ICLP*, 2003, Springer Verlag.
5. H. M. Berman et al. The Protein Data Bank. *Nucleic Acids Research*, 28:235–242, 2000.
6. M. Berrera, H. Molinari, and F. Fogolari. Amino acid empirical contact energy definitions for fold recognition in the space of contact maps. *BMC Bioinformatics*, 4(8), 2003.
7. Center for Computational Materials Science, Naval Research Labs, *Crystal Lattice Structures*, cst-www.nrl.navy.mil/lattice/.
8. D. Clark et al. Protein topology prediction through constraint-based search and the evaluation of topological folding rules. *Protein Engineering*, 4:752–760, 1991.
9. P. Clote and R. Backofen. *Computational Molecular Biology*. John Wiley & Sons, 2001.
10. P. Crescenzi et al. On the complexity of protein folding. In *STOC*, pages 597–603, 1998.
11. A. Dal Palù, A. Dovier, and F. Fogolari. Constraint logic programming approach to protein structure prediction. *BMC Bioinformatics*, 5(186), 2004.
12. A. Dal Palù, A. Dovier, and E. Pontelli. Heuristics, Optimizations, and Parallelism for Protein Structure Prediction in CLP(FD). In Proc. of *PPDP'05*, 2005.
13. S. Forman. *Torsion Angle Selection and Emergent Non-local Secondary Structure in Protein Structure Prediction*. PhD thesis, U. of Iowa, 2001.
14. H. J. Greenberg et al. Opportunities for Combinatorial Optimization in Computational Biology. In *INFORMS Journal of Computing*, 2003.
15. W. Hart and A. Newman. The computational complexity of protein structure prediction in simple lattice models. CRC Press. 2003. (to appear).
16. L. Krippahl and P. Barahona. Applying Constraint Programming to Protein Structure Determination. In *CP'99*, Springer, 1999.
17. G. Raghunathan and R. L. Jernigan. Ideal architecture of residue packing and its observation in protein structures. *Protein Science*, 6:2072–2083, 1997.
18. R. Rodosek. A Constraint-based Approach for Deriving 3-D Structures of Cyclic Polypeptides. In *Constraints*, 6(2-3):257–270, 2001.
19. B. Rost. Protein Secondary Structure Prediction Continues to Rise. *J. Struct. Biol.* 134, 2001.
20. J. Skolnick et al. Reduced models of proteins and applications. *Polymer*, 45:511–524, 2004.
21. L. Toma and S. Toma. Folding simulation of protein models on the structure-based cubo-octahedral lattice with contact interactions algorithm. *Protein Science*, 8:196–202, 1999.

Disjunctive Constraint Lambda Calculi

Matthias M. Hölzl[1] and John N. Crossley[2,*]

[1] Institut für Informatik. LMU, Munich, Germany
Matthias.Hoelzl@ifi.lmu.de
[2] Faculty of Information Technology, Monash University, Australia
John.Crossley@infotech.monash.edu.au

Abstract. Earlier we introduced Constraint Lambda Calculi which integrate constraint solving with functional programming for the simple case where the constraint solver produces no more than one solution to a set of constraints. We now introduce two forms of Constraint Lambda Calculi which allow for multiple constraint solutions. Moreover the language also permits the use of disjunctions between constraints rather than just conjunction. These calculi are the Unrestricted, and the Restricted, Disjunctive Constraint-Lambda Calculi. We establish a limited form of confluence for the unrestricted calculus and a stronger form for the restricted one. We also discuss the denotational semantics of our calculi and some implementation issues.

1 Introduction

Constraint programming languages have been highly developed in the context of logic programming (see e.g. [9, 3] and, regarding confluence, [14]). In [11] Mandel initiated the use of the lambda calculus as an alternative to a logic programming base. There were many difficulties and, in particular, the treatment of disjunction was not very satisfactory (see [12]). It has turned out to be surprisingly difficult to get a transparent and elegant system for the functional programming paradigm. This was ultimately accomplished in [6] and [8], where we introduced the unrestricted and restricted constraint-lambda calculi. In this paper we expand the language of these calculi to include disjunction in constraints.

The basic problem with the introduction of disjunction or, indeed with multiple solutions, is easily demonstrated by the example (first noted, we believe, by Hennessy [5]) $(\lambda x.x + x)(2|3)$ where "2|3" means "2 or 3". If a choice is first made of a value of the disjunction "2|3", then there are two answers: 4 and 6. If the β-reduction is performed first, then the result is $(2|3) + (2|3)$. In this case there is also the possible interpretation that the first value should be chosen to be 2 and the second to be 3 (or *vice versa*) yielding an additional answer: 5.

We propose two solutions, one for each possibility, in Sections 2 and 8.

The systems that we define are extensions of our calculi in [8]. Because we now have multiple solutions as a matter of course we cannot expect conflu-

---

* Special thanks to Martin Wirsing for his support, interest and extremely helpful criticism. Thanks also to three anonymous and helpful referees.

G. Sutcliffe and A. Voronkov (Eds.): LPAR 2005, LNAI 3835, pp. 64–78, 2005.
© Springer-Verlag Berlin Heidelberg 2005

ence.[1] Nevertheless we are able to establish a weaker property, which we call *path-confluence*, in Theorem 2 for the Restricted Disjunctive Constraint-Lambda Calculus.

We briefly discuss the denotational semantics of our systems and implementation issues. Then we turn to the question of multiple constraint stores and finally we compare our systems with the earlier work of Mandel and Cengarle [13] and other current approaches to constraint-functional programming integration.

2   Unrestricted Disjunctive Constraint-Lambda Calculus

The Constraint Language. A constraint is a relation that holds between several entities from a fixed domain. We assume a notion of equality, denoted by $=$, is given. Typical constraint domains are the real numbers, the integers, or a finite subset of the integers.

A *constraint language* is a 4-tuple $\mathcal{L} = (\mathcal{C}, \mathcal{V}, \mathcal{F}, \mathcal{P})$, where $\mathcal{C} = \{c_1, c_2, \dots\}$ is a set of *individual constants*, $\mathcal{V} = \{X_1, X_2, \dots\}$ is a set of *constraint variables*, $\mathcal{F} = \{f_1, f_2, \dots\}$ is a set of function letters with fixed arity, and $\mathcal{P} = \{P_1, P_2, \dots\}$ is a set of *predicate symbols*, again with fixed arities. We assume that a constant, $\bot$, representing the undefined value is included in $\mathcal{C}$. The set $\mathfrak{T}$ of *constraint terms* over a constraint language $\mathcal{L}$ is defined inductively in the usual way. Constraint terms containing no variables are called *ground* and $\mathfrak{T}_g$ is the set of all ground constraint terms. Model-theoretic notions such as *model* and *satisfaction* are defined for sets of formulae in the constraint language in the usual way.

Definition 1. *If P is a predicate letter with arity n and $t_1, \dots, t_n$ are constraint terms, then $P(t_1, \dots, t_n)$ is an* atomic constraint. *The set of* constraints $\mathfrak{C}$ *is the closure of the atomic constraints under conjunction ($\wedge$) and disjunction ($\vee$). The empty conjunction is written as* **true** *and the empty disjunction as* **false**.

Definition 2 (Inconsistent constraints). *A set $S = \{C_1, C_2, \dots, C_n\}$ of constraints is said to be* inconsistent, *if S is not satisfiable.*

The denotation of a constraint term in a constraint language $\mathfrak{L}$ over a constraint domain D, is defined by evaluating it in the usual way (which gives the usual properties): $value : (\mathcal{V} \to D) \to \mathfrak{T} \to D$. So if $\theta : \mathcal{V} \to D$ then $value(\theta) : \mathfrak{T} \to D$.

Convention 1 (Canonical names). *We assume that there is an idempotent mapping (canonical naming) $n : \mathfrak{T}_g \to \mathcal{C}$ with the following properties:*

$$value(\theta)(n(t)) = value(\theta)(t) \tag{1}$$

$$\big(value(\theta)(t_1) = value(\theta)(t_2)\big) \implies n(t_1) \equiv n(t_2) \tag{2}$$

---

[1] Confluence is the property that when a lambda-calculus-style term M is reduced in two different ways (possibly in many steps) to M_1 and M_2 then (up to renaming of bound variables) there is a third term M_3 to which both M_1 and M_2 reduce.

for all maps $\theta : \mathcal{V} \to D$, where $=$ is the semantic equality of the constraint domain and $\equiv$ is syntactic equality. The image of a ground constraint term under n is called its canonical name, *the image of the constraint domain under n is the set of* canonical names. *We write cn or cn_i for canonical names and CN for $n[\mathfrak{T}_g]$.*

A *constraint store* is a set of constraints. The only operation on constraint stores is the addition of a new constraint to the store, denoted by $S \oplus C$:

$$S \oplus C = S \cup \{C\}.$$

We shall only be concerned with formulae, principally equations, implied by a constraint store S, therefore a constraint solver may simplify the set of constraints contained in the constraint store without changing the possible reductions. Since, for our purposes, all inconsistent stores are equivalent, we write $\otimes$ to denote any inconsistent store and we then write $S = \otimes$.

Syntax. The syntax for constraint-lambda terms is given by:[2]

$$\Lambda ::= x \mid X \mid c \mid f(\Lambda, \ldots, \Lambda) \mid \lambda x.\Lambda \mid \Lambda\Lambda \mid \{GC\}\Lambda,$$
$$GCT ::= \Lambda, \quad GC ::= P(GCT, \ldots, GCT) \mid (GC \wedge GC) \mid (GC \vee GC).$$

The syntactic categories are:

- **Constraint-lambda terms** (Λ): These are the usual lambda terms augmented with a notation for constraint-variables (variables whose values are computed by the constraint solver) and a notation to describe the addition of constraints to the constraint store.
- **General constraint terms** (GCT): These are augmented terms of the constraint language. Constraint-variables may appear as part of a lambda term or as part of a general constraint term. This makes it possible to transfer values from the constraint store to lambda terms. Similarly, a lambda term may appear inside a constraint term. Having lambda variables inside constraints allows us to compute values in the lambda calculus and introduce them as part of a constraint. We also allow arbitrary lambda terms inside constraints. These terms have to be reduced to constraint terms before being passed to the constraint solver.
- **General constraints** (GC): These are primitive constraints as well as disjunctions and conjunctions of constraints (defined in terms of general constraint terms instead of the usual constraint terms). They correspond to, but are slightly more general than, the notion of constraint in the previously defined constraint-language, since they may include lambda terms as constituents.

Note. The generalized constraint terms correspond exactly to the constraint-lambda terms. Nevertheless we consider it important to distinguish these two sets, since the set of *pure* constraint-lambda terms and *pure* constraint terms are disjoint:

---

[2] In the rest of the paper we sometimes omit the parentheses around disjunctions and conjunctions.

Definition 3. *We call a constraint-lambda term* pure *if it contains no term of the form* $\{C\}M$; *we call a constraint term* pure *if it contains no lambda term, i.e., if the only constraint-lambda terms it contains are constraint variables, constants or applications of function-symbols to pure constraint terms. A constraint* C *is called a* pure constraint *if every constraint term appearing in* C *is pure. We write* Λ_p *for the set of all pure constraint-lambda terms not containing* $\bot$.

Free and bound variables and substitution are defined in a straightforward way (see [6] for details). Only lambda variables may appear as free and bound variables, i.e., $FV(X) = \emptyset = BV(X)$. As usual we identify α-equivalent terms, so we can freely rename bound variables and also ensure no variable appears both free and bound in M. We postulate the following:

Convention 2 (Variable Convention). *The following property holds for all* λ-*terms* M: *No variable appears both free and bound in* M, $FV(M) \cap BV(M) = \emptyset$. *Furthermore, we can always assume by changing bound variables (if necessary) that for different subterms* $\lambda x.M_1$ *and* $\lambda y.M_2$ *of* M, *we have* $x \neq y$.

Reduction Rules. It is necessary to take the constraint stores into account in defining the reductions of our constraint terms since the stores interact with these terms, so we define reductions on pairs (M, S) where S is a constraint store.

Rule 1. Fail on an Inconsistent Store $\qquad (M, \otimes) \to (\bot, \otimes)$ $\qquad\qquad (\bot)$

Rule 2. Beta-reduction $\qquad\qquad ((\lambda x.M)N, S) \to (M[x/N], S)$ $\qquad\quad (\beta)$

Rule 3. Reduce Pure Constraint Terms
$\quad (C, S) \to (n(C), S)$ $\quad$ if C is pure, $C \in \mathfrak{T}_g$ and $C \neq n(C)$ $\qquad\qquad (CR)$

Rule 4. Introduce Constraint
$\quad (\{C\}M, S) \to (M, S \oplus C)$ $\quad$ if C is a pure constraint $\qquad\qquad\qquad (CI)$

Rule 5. Use Constraint
$\quad (X, S) \to (cn, S \oplus (X = cn))$ $\quad$ if $(S \oplus (X = cn)) \neq \otimes$ and $cn \in CN$ $\quad (CS)$

Notes on the Rules.
$\quad$ Rule 1. Reductions resulting in inconsistent stores correspond to failed computations in logic programming languages.
$\quad$ Rule 2. We allow full beta-reduction in the disjunctive constraint-lambda calculi. E.g., if we have the integers as constraint domain, $(\lambda x.x + 1)5 \to 5 + 1$.
$\quad$ Rule 3. This rule ties the constraint system into the lambda calculus. E.g., continuing our example: $5 + 1 \to 6$. We do not allow arbitrary transformations between pure constraint terms, since this does not increase the expressive power of the system.[3]

---

[3] This rule was not included in our earlier work [8] but it easy to verify that it does not affect the confluence properties.

Rule 4. We only allow pure constraints to be passed to the constraint store since otherwise the constraint solver could perform transformations other than β-reduction on lambda terms. This would increase the power of the system since "oracles" might be introduced as predicates in the constraint language. But it would also require the constraint theory to be a true superset of the lambda calculus. This would pose a major problem for practical applications of the calculus, since most constraint systems cannot handle lambda terms.

Rule 5. A constraint variable may be instantiated to any value that is consistent with the constraint store. We only introduce canonical names into the lambda term since this allows us to obtain confluent restrictions of the disjunctive calculus. We introduce the constraint $X = cn$ into the constraint store to remove the possibility of substituting different values for the same variable.

Definition 4. *We say a constraint lambda term M is reducible with store S if one of the rules $(\bot)$, (β), (CR), (CI) or (CS) is applicable to the pair (M, S). We say M is reducible if it is reducible for all stores S. We write $M \to M'$ as an abbreviation for $\forall S.\exists S'.(M, S) \to (M', S')$.*

We call a sequence of zero or more reduction steps $(M_1, S_1) \to (M_2, S_2), \ldots, (M_{n-1}, S_{n-1}) \to (M_n, S_n)$ a reduction sequence and abbreviate it by $(M_1, S_1) \to^* (M_n, S_n)$. We write $M \to^* M'$ as an abbreviation for $\forall S.\exists S'.(M, S) \to^* (M', S')$.

Example 1. Without the addition of $X = M$ to the store we would have:

$$(X + X, \{X = 2 \vee X = 3\}) \to (2 + X, \{X = 2 \vee X = 3\})$$
$$\to (2 + 3, \{X = 2 \vee X = 3\}).$$

If we add the new constraint to the store, there are only two (essentially different) possible reduction sequences:

$$(2)\ (X + X, \{X = 2 \vee X = 3\}) \to (2 + X, \{X = 2 \vee X = 3, X = 2\})$$
$$\to (2 + 2, \{X = 2 \vee X = 3, X = 2\})$$
$$(3)\ (X + X, \{X = 2 \vee X = 3\}) \to (3 + X, \{X = 2 \vee X = 3, X = 3\})$$
$$\to (3 + 3, \{X = 2 \vee X = 3, X = 3\}).$$

Obviously the order in which the variables are instantiated can be changed.

We need to have the reductions commute with the constructions of constraints in order to allow reductions of subterms. (For example, a pair of the form $(\lambda x.(\lambda y.y)x, S)$ ought to be reducible to $(\lambda x.x, S)$.) If the reduction of a subterm changes the store, then this change propagates to the store associated with the enclosing term. We give only a few examples. If $(M, S) \to (M', S')$,

$$(f(M_1, \ldots, M, \ldots, M_n), S) \to (f(M_1, \ldots, M', \ldots, M_n), S')$$
$$(L \wedge M, S) \to (L \wedge M', S'), \quad (LM, S) \to (LM', S')$$
$$(\lambda x.M, S) \to (\lambda x.M', S'), \quad (\{M\}N, S) \to (\{M'\}N, S')$$

To avoid infinite reduction paths where the terms differ only in the names of constraint variables we impose:

Convention 3. *We assume a well-founded partial order $\prec$ on the set of constraint variables. Substitution in rule (CS) is only allowed if, for every variable Y in M, we have $Y \prec X$.*

Example 2. We write $(x|y)_X$ as an abbreviation for $\{X = x \vee X = y\}X$ with a fresh constraint-variable X. When we reduce the term $(\lambda x.x + x)(2|3)_X$ with an empty constraint store, we obtain as one possible reduction sequence:

$$
\begin{aligned}
((\lambda x.x + x)(2|3)_X, \{\}) &\to (\{X = 2 \vee X = 3\}X + \{X = 2 \vee X = 3\}X, \{\}) \\
&\to (X + \{X = 2 \vee X = 3\}X, \{X = 2 \vee X = 3\}) \\
&\to (2 + \{X = 2 \vee X = 3\}X, \{X = 2\}) \\
&\to (2 + X, \{X = 2\}) \\
&\to (2 + 2).
\end{aligned}
$$

3 Confluence

It is not possible to have confluence in the traditional sense for the unrestricted calculus because different reductions can lead to different constraint stores as well as to different solutions.

Example 3. Consider the pair $((\lambda x.X)(\{X = cn\}M), \emptyset)$, where the constraint store is initially empty. This can be reduced in two different ways. In the first the final store contains $X = cn$ but in the second the store remains empty and it is not possible to carry out any further reduction. Thus we have the reductions:

$$
\begin{aligned}
((\lambda x.X)(\{X = cn\}M), \emptyset) &\to ((\lambda x.X)M, \{X = cn\}) && \text{by (CI)} \\
&\to (X, \{X = cn\}) && \text{by } (\beta) \\
(*) \qquad\qquad &\to (cn, \{X = cn\}) && \text{by (CS)}
\end{aligned}
$$

but we also have

$$
(**) \quad ((\lambda x.X)(\{X = cn\}M), \emptyset) \to (X, \emptyset) \text{ by } \beta\text{-reduction,}
$$

and there is no way to reduce $(*)$ and $(**)$ to a common term.

Note that the constraint store may contain different sets of constraints at different stages of the the reduction so that, while a constraint substitution may not be possible at some reduction step, it may become possible later.

Definition 5. *Suppose that in a reduction sequence $(M_1, S_1) \to^* (M_n, S_n)$ we apply rule (CS) zero or more times and replace X_i by cn_i. If a store S exists, such that, for all these applications of rule (CS), we have $S \models X_i = cn_i$, then we say that $(M_1, S_1) \to^* (M_n, S_n)$ is a reduction sequence that can be restricted to store S.*
Let $(M, S) \to^* (M_1, S_1)$ and $(M, S) \to^* (M_2, S_2)$ be two reduction sequences. We say these reduction sequences are compatible *if $S_1 \cup S_2$ is consistent.*

Definition 6. *We call the following property* confluence as a reduction system: *For every pair of reductions* $(M, S) \to^* (M_1, S_1)$ *and* $(M, S) \to^* (M_2, S_2)$ *such that both reduction sequences can be restricted to store S there exist a term N and stores S_1', S_2' such that* $(M_1, S_1) \to^* (N, S_1')$ *and* $(M_2, S_2) \to^* (N, S_2')$.

Example 1 shows that the unrestricted disjunctive constraint-lambda calculus is not confluent as a reduction system since different reductions may introduce different values for a constraint variable. But if two reductions introduce the same values for all constraint-variables then their results can be reduced to a common term. This property is made explicit in the remainder of this section.

Since each application of the rule (CS) introduces a constraint $X_i = cn_i$ into the store it is clear that all applications of rule (CS) for a variable X in two compatible reduction sequences substitute the same value for X. From this we may conclude that the reduction sequences $(M, S_1 \cup S_2) \to^* (M_1, S_1 \cup S_2)$ and $(M, S_1 \cup S_2) \to^* (M_2, S_1 \cup S_2)$ (obtained from the original sequences by extending the stores but not changing any reductions) are reduction sequences in the single-valued calculus of [8]. These sequences can trivially be restricted to $S_1 \cup S_2$. It follows from the confluence as a reduction system of the single-valued constraint-lambda calculus which was proved as Theorem 1 in [8] that there is a term N and a store S' such that both $(M_1, S_1 \cup S_2)$ and $(M_2, S_1 \cup S_2)$ reduce to (N, S'). We therefore have:

Theorem 1. *Let* $(M, S) \to^* (M_1, S_1)$ *and* $(M, S) \to^* (M_2, S_2)$ *be compatible reduction sequences. Then there is a term N and a store S' such that both* $(M_1, S_1 \cup S_2)$ *and* $(M_2, S_1 \cup S_2)$ *reduce to* (N, S').

4   Restricted Disjunctive Constraint-Lambda Calculus

The restricted constraint-lambda calculus has the same reduction rules as the unrestricted constraint-lambda calculus, but the allowed terms are only those from λI (not λK, see Barendregt [1], Chapter 9) so an abstraction $\lambda x.M$ is only allowed if $x \in FV(M)$:

Definition 7. *The set of restricted constraint-lambda terms, RCTs, Λ_I is defined inductively by the following rules:*

- *Every lambda variable x and every constraint variable X is a RCT.*
- *If M is a RCT and $x \in FV(M)$, then $\lambda x.M$ is a restricted lambda term.*
- *If M and N are restricted lambda terms, then MN is a RCT.*
- *If C is an extended constraint and M a restricted constraint-lambda term, then $\{C\}M$ is a RCT.*

The sets of extended constraints and extended constraint terms (corresponding to GC and GCT) are defined similarly to the sets of general constraints and general constraint terms, but with RCTs in place of general constraint terms. We write $M \in \Lambda_I$ if M is a restricted lambda term.

We use the same conventions as for the unrestricted constraint-lambda calculus, most importantly, we use the variable convention. The reduction rules for the restricted constraint-lambda calculus are the same as for the unrestricted constraint-lambda calculus. The terms of the restricted constraint-lambda calculus satisfy certain properties that are not necessarily true of unrestricted terms.

Lemma 1.   *1. $\lambda x.M, N \in \Lambda_I \implies M[x/N] \in \Lambda_I$,*
2. $\lambda x.M \in \Lambda_I \implies FV((\lambda x.M)N) = FV(M[x/N])$,
3. $M \in \Lambda_I, M \to^* N \implies N \in \Lambda_I$, and
4. $M \in \Lambda_I, M \to^* N, N \neq \bot \implies FV(M) = FV(N)$.

For the proof see [6].
The following Lemma holds for terms of Λ_I. A *normal form* is a term which cannot be reduced.

Lemma 2.   *Let $M \in \Lambda_I$. If $(M, S) \to^* (N, S')$, where N is a normal form, then every reduction path starting with (M, S) is finite.*

The proof is similar to the one in [1]. We make use of the previously introduced Convention 3 for rule (CS) (see page 69) to show that no infinite (CS)-reduction sequences can occur. This Lemma is also true for the restricted single-valued calculus. Since we make no other use of this Lemma we omit the details.

5   Path-Confluence

The single-valued restricted constraint-lambda calculus was proved in [8] to be confluent so we can improve Theorem 1 for terms of the Restricted Disjunctive Constraint-Lambda Calculus to the following whose proof may be found in [6]. Path-confluence requires a controlled sequence of choices of extensions to stores.

Theorem 2 (Path-confluence).   *Let M be a RCT and let $(M, S) \to^* (M_1, S_1)$ and $(M, S) \to^* (M_2, S_2)$ be compatible reduction sequences. Then there is a term N and a store S' such that both (M_1, S_1) and (M_2, S_2) reduce to (N, S').*

6   Denotational Semantics

We defined the denotational semantics of the constraint-lambda calculus without disjunction in [8] and we recall only a few key points here. We let E denote the semantic domain of the constraint-lambda terms. The denotational semantics are defined in such a way that each model for the usual lambda calculus can be used as a model for the constraint-lambda calculus provided that the model is large enough to allow an embedding $emb : D \to E$ of the underlying constraint domain D into E. This is usually the case for the constraint domains appearing in applications. As usual we have an isomorphism $E \to E \simeq E$ (see e.g. [1], chapter 5). We denote environments by η (a mapping from lambda variables to E). We can then define a semantic valuation from the set of constraint terms, T, into D which we call $val : T \to D$. We shall write val' for $emb \circ val : T \to E$.

We associate a pure lambda term with every constraint-lambda term by replacing all constraint variables by lambda variables. Let M be a constraint-lambda term with constraint variables $\{X_1, \ldots, X_n\}$ and let $\{x_1, \ldots, x_n\}$ be a set of distinct lambda variables not appearing in M. Then the *associated constraint-variable free term, cvt(M)*, is the term

$$\lambda x_1 \ldots \lambda x_n.(M[X_1/x_1] \ldots [X_n/x_n]).$$

We separate the computation of a constraint-lambda term into two steps. First we collect all constraints appearing in the term and compute all the lambda terms contained therein in the appropriate context. Then we apply the associated constraint-variable free term to the values computed by the constraint-solver to obtain the value of the constraint-lambda term.

For a constraint-lambda term M and store S we set

1. $\mathfrak{D}_\eta$ as the denotation of a constraint-lambda term in an environment η when the constraints are deleted from the term.[4]
2. The function $\mathfrak{C}^C$ applied to the constraint-lambda term, M, collects all constraints appearing in M and evaluates the lambda expressions contained within these constraints. The superscript C on $\mathfrak{C}$ denotes the recursively generated context.

The semantics of a single-valued constraint-lambda term with respect to a store S is defined as

$$[\![(M, S)]\!] = \{\mathfrak{D}_\eta(cvt(M)v_1 \ldots v_n) \mid S \,\cup\, \mathfrak{C}^\circ(M) \vdash X_1 = v_1, \ldots, X_n = v_n\}$$

where $\mathfrak{D}_\eta$ defines the usual semantics for pure lambda terms and ignores constraints contained within a term. The superscript $\circ$ on $\mathfrak{C}$ indicates that we are starting with the empty context and building up $\mathfrak{C}$ as we go into the terms. The environment η is supposed to contain bindings for the free variables of M.

Intuitively, this definition means that the semantics of a single-valued constraint-lambda term is obtained as the denotation of the lambda term when all constraints are removed from the term and all constraint-variables are replaced by their values. In particular we have (by footnote 4):

Fact 1. *The denotational semantics of a* pure *lambda term is the same as in the traditional denotational semantics.*

The denotation of a constraint-lambda term in an environment η, $\mathfrak{D}_\eta$, is defined as follows:[5]

$$\mathfrak{D}_\eta(\lambda x.M) = \lambda v.\mathfrak{D}_{\eta[x/v]}(M)$$

$$\mathfrak{D}_\eta(x) = \eta(x) \qquad \mathfrak{D}_\eta(MN) = \mathfrak{D}_\eta(M)\mathfrak{D}_\eta(N)$$

$$\mathfrak{D}_\eta(c) = val'(c) \qquad \mathfrak{D}_\eta(\{C\}M) = \mathfrak{D}_\eta(M)$$

$$\mathfrak{D}_\eta(f(M_1, \ldots, M_n)) = val'(f)(\mathfrak{D}_\eta(M_1), \ldots, \mathfrak{D}_\eta(M_n))$$

---

[4] Therefore, for pure constraint-lambda terms, $\mathfrak{D}_\eta$ represents the usual semantics.

[5] Notice that the semantic function $\mathfrak{D}$ is only applied to constraint-variable-free terms and that it does not recurse on constraints, therefore there is no need to define it on constraints or constraint terms. Furthermore the interpretations of a constant, when regarded as part of a lambda term or as part of a constraint, coincide, as expected.

When evaluating lambda terms nested inside constraints, we are only interested in results that are pure constraints, since the constraint solver cannot handle any other terms. Therefore we identify all other constraint-lambda terms with the failed computation.

We can now show that the semantics of a constraint-lambda term is compatible with the reduction rules.

Lemma 3. *For all environments η and all terms M, N, we have*

$$\mathfrak{D}_\eta(M[x/N]) = \mathfrak{D}_{\eta[x/\mathfrak{D}_\eta(N)]}(M).$$

For unrestricted constraint-lambda terms without disjunction we may lose a constraint during the reduction and then we get $[\![(M, S)]\!] \supseteq [\![(M', S')]\!]$. However in the case of the disjunctive calculus the situation is reversed: Now a smaller set of constraints implies a larger set of values, therefore if $(M, S) \to (M', S')$ it may be the case that $[\![(M', S')]\!]$ contains values that are not contained in $[\![(M, S)]\!]$. Therefore the operational semantics are not correct with respect to the denotational semantics in this case. This, however, is not surprising if we consider the meaning of $[\![(M, S)]\!]$. We have defined the semantics so that this expression denotes the precise set of values that can be computed in such a way that all constraints are satisfied. If constraints are dropped during a β-reduction step the new term places less restrictions on the values of the constraint variables, thus we obtain an approximation "from above" as the semantics of the new term.[6]

7   Implementation Issues

Application of the rule (CS) to a variable with a large range of possible values may lead to many unnecessary reductions. If, for example, we introduce

$$(\{X = 100\}X, \{1 \le X, X < 500\})$$

---

[6] The evaluation of constraints in the denotational semantics is currently done in a very "syntactical" manner. To see why this is the case, we have to make a short digression into the motivations for defining the semantics in the way they are defined. As M. B. Smyth points out in [18], the Scott topology is just the Zariski topology ([2]) on the ring defined by the lattice structure of the domain in question and corresponds to the notion of an *observable property*. It is evident that this topology cannot be Hausdorff for any interesting domain. The denotational semantics of logic programming languages, on the other hand, is generally defined on the Herbrand-universe, and the fixed points are calculated using consequence operators, see [10] or [4]. It seems that these two methods of defining the denotational semantics do not match well. A more natural approach in our setting would be to regard the predicates of the constraint theory as boolean functions over the constraint domain and constraints as restrictions on the known ranges of these functions. However, this definition results in a Hausdorff topology on the universe in question, and is therefore incompatible with the topology of the retract definition. It would be interesting to see whether this problem can be resolved by a suitable denotational semantics for the constraint theory. The resulting topology shows another problem: A Hausdorff topology cannot be the topology resulting from observable properties. This suggests a connection with the sometimes difficult to control behavior of constraint programs.

with rule (CS) we may have to try many substitutions for X before instantiating X with the only value that does not lead to an inconsistent store in the next reduction step. If we introduce the constraint $X = 100$ into the store the next reduction step immediately leads to the normal form 100. Therefore one has to be careful not to apply the (CS)-rule indiscriminately in an implementation of the constraint-lambda calculus. We discuss practical issues about implementation in our paper [7].

For applications of the constraint-lambda calculus it is sometimes useful to extend the system with additional capabilities. One such extension is the addition of multiple constraint stores, another is the computation of fresh constraint variables. We discuss this extension in the next section. It adds some additional complexity to the calculus but we think that this is more than compensated for by the added expressive power.

8 Multiple Constraint Stores

For some applications it is desirable to split the problem into several smaller parts and to have each part operate on its own constraint store. This can be done by extending the constraint-lambda calculus to incorporate multiple constraint stores. The addition of multiple stores allows us to provide a choice for the following problem: If a function is applied to a non-deterministic argument, should all references to this argument be instantiated with the same value or should it be possible to instantiate each reference individually? For example, should $(\lambda x.x + x)(2|3)$ return only the values 4 and 6 or should it also return 5? In Section 2 we restricted ourselves to the first solution. With the extension discussed in this section we allow the user to choose the preferred alternative by means of a *store assignment*. To keep the strict separation between program logic and control, the store assignment is defined on the meta-level.

Syntax. When we add multiple stores to a constraint-lambda calculus we need a means of showing on which store the rules (CI) and (CS) operate. To this end we extend the syntax of the calculus with *names for stores*, denoted by the letter S (with indices and subscripts if necessary) and with *locations*. Syntactically, any constraint-lambda term can be used as a location, but only locations evaluating to a store-name can actually select a store. We write the locations as superscripts to other constraint-lambda terms. For example, in the term M^N, the term N is used as the location for M. In terms of the form $\{C\}^N M$, the term N is used as the location for the constraint C, and terms of the form $\{C\}M$ without location for the constraint C are not valid terms of the constraint-lambda calculus with multiple stores. The context-free syntax is therefore

$$\Lambda ::= \bot \mid x \mid X \mid c \mid S \mid \Lambda^\Lambda \mid f(\Lambda,\dots,\Lambda) \mid \lambda x.\Lambda \mid (\Lambda\Lambda) \mid \{GC\}^\Lambda \Lambda.$$

We write $\mathcal{N}$ for the set of all names for stores and $\mathfrak{C}$ for the set of all constraints. We extend substitution to the new terms in the natural way:

$$S[x/L]=S;\ M^N[x/L]=M[x/L]^{N[x/L]};\ (\{C\}^N M)[x/L]=\{C[x/L]\}^{N[x/L]}M[x/L].$$

Reduction Rules. We want to be able to "alias" store names, i.e., we want to be able to have two different names refer to the same constraint store. Therefore we define reductions on triples $(M, \sigma, \mathfrak{S})$ where M is a constraint-lambda term, σ is a map from store names to integers, $\sigma : \mathcal{N} \rightarrow \omega$ and $\mathfrak{S}$ is a map from integers to sets of constraints, $\mathfrak{S} : \omega \rightarrow \mathfrak{P}(\mathfrak{C})$. where $\mathfrak{P}$ denotes "power set". For any integer n we write $\mathfrak{S} \oplus_n C$ for the following mapping:

$$(\mathfrak{S} \oplus_n C)(m) = \begin{cases} \mathfrak{S}(m) & \text{if } m \neq n \\ \mathfrak{S}(n) \cup \{C\} & \text{if } m = n. \end{cases}$$

If σ is clear from the context, we write $\mathfrak{S} \oplus_S C$ for $\mathfrak{S} \oplus_{\sigma(S)} C$.

We consider a branch of the computation to fail if *any* constraint store becomes inconsistent in that branch.

With these notations we can define the reduction rules for the disjunctive constraint-lambda calculus with multiple stores:

$$(M, \sigma, \mathfrak{S}) \rightarrow (\bot, \sigma, \mathfrak{S}) \text{ if } \exists n \in \omega. \mathfrak{S}(n) = \otimes. \tag{$\bot$}$$

$$((\lambda x.M)N, \sigma, \mathfrak{S}) \rightarrow (M[x/N], \sigma, \mathfrak{S}). \tag{β}$$

$$(C, \sigma, \mathfrak{S}) \rightarrow (n(C), \sigma, \mathfrak{S}), \quad \text{if } C \text{ is a pure constraint \& } C \neq n(C). \tag{CR}$$

$$(\{C\}^S M, \sigma, \mathfrak{S}) \rightarrow (M, \sigma, \mathfrak{S} \oplus_S C), \text{if } C \text{ is a pure constraint.} \tag{CI}$$

$$(X^S, \sigma, \mathfrak{S}) \rightarrow (M, \sigma, \mathfrak{S} \oplus_S (X = M)), \text{if } \mathfrak{S} \oplus_S (X = M) \neq \otimes. \tag{CS}$$

The closure rules can be transferred *mutatis mutandis* from the disjunctive constraint-lambda calculus. We allow reductions in locations: If $(M, \sigma, \mathfrak{S}) \rightarrow (M', \sigma, \mathfrak{S}')$, then $(L^M, \sigma, \mathfrak{S}) \rightarrow (L^{M'}, \sigma, \mathfrak{S}')$, and similarly for $\{C\}^M N$.

Next we show how the addition of multiple stores adds even more flexibility.

Example 4. On p. 68, we argued that when we substitute M for X using the rule (CS) we have to add the constraint $X = M$ to the store to avoid substitutions such as those in Example 1. With the addition of multiple stores we have more liberty to define whether we want to allow this kind of behaviour. To illustrate this we slightly modify the example.

We define the abbreviation $M|N$ by: $M|N := \lambda x_S.\{X = M \vee X = N\}^{x_S} X^{x_S}$ where X is a fresh constraint variable. This term can be applied to a store name and evaluates to either M or N. For example, if we write $\mathfrak{S}_0$ for the map $n \mapsto \emptyset$, and if σ is any map $\mathcal{N} \rightarrow \omega$, then we obtain the following reductions:

$$((2|3)S, \sigma, \mathfrak{S}_0) \rightarrow (\{X = 2 \vee X = 3\}^S X^S, \sigma, \mathfrak{S}_0)$$
$$\rightarrow (X^S, \sigma, \mathfrak{S}_0 \oplus_S \{X = 2 \vee X = 3\})$$
$$\rightarrow (2, \sigma, \mathfrak{S}_0 \oplus_S \{(X = 2 \vee X = 3), X = 2\})$$
$$\text{and} \quad ((2|3)S, \sigma, \mathfrak{S}_0) \rightarrow (\{X = 2 \vee X = 3\}^S X^S, \sigma, \mathfrak{S}_0)$$
$$\rightarrow (X^S, \sigma, \mathfrak{S}_0 \oplus_S \{X = 2 \vee X = 3\})$$
$$\rightarrow (3, \sigma, \mathfrak{S}_0 \oplus_S \{(X = 2 \vee X = 3), X = 3\}).$$

Now consider a more complicated expression (corresponding to Example 2): $(\lambda x.x^{S_1} + x^{S_2})(2|3)$. If we evaluate this expression with a map σ for which $\sigma(S_1) = \sigma(S_2)$ it is obvious that this expression only evaluates to the values 4 and 6. If we change σ to a map where $\sigma(S_1) \neq \sigma(S_2)$ we obtain the three values 4, 5 and 6. In general this is not the desired behavior for arithmetic problems, but for other problems this behavior is more sensible. For example, if we allow constraints to range over job-titles in an organization, then it might be reasonable for a function *talkTo(programmer|manager)* to talk to the manager in the part dealing with business matters and to the programmer when deciding technical details.

Another example where the choice of different values for a single constraint variable is useful are compilers. One specific example is code generators: An optimizing compiler might have different code generators for the same intermediate-language expression; these code generators usually represent different trade-offs that can be made between compilation speed, execution speed, space and safety. For example, the `d2c` compiler can assign either a *speed-representation* or a *space-representation* to a class. The CMUCL Common Lisp compiler has different policies (`:fast`, `:safe`, `:fast-safe` and `:small`) with which an intermediate representation might be translated into machine code. In a compiler based on the constraint-lambda calculus the policy used for the translation of some intermediate code could be determined by a constraint solver. This constraint-solver might compute disjunctive solutions, e.g., the permissible policy values might be `:safe` and `:fast-safe`, but not `:small` and `:fast` because some constraint on the safety of the program part in question has to be satisfied. In this case it is obviously desirable if different instantiations of the "policy-variable" can be instantiated with different values: An innermost loop might be compiled with `:fast-safe` policy to attain the highest possible execution speed while user-interface code might be compiled with the `:safe` policy to reduce the size of the program.

9   Comparison with Earlier Work

In [13], Mandel and Cengarle provided a partial solution of the disjunction problem only. We have now provided mechanisms for resolving Hennessy's problem (see Section 1) in both directions.

A current example for a constraint-functional language is *Alice* [16] which is based on a concurrent lambda calculus with futures, $\lambda(\mathsf{fut})$ [15, 17]. The $\lambda(\mathsf{fut})$ calculus is not directly concerned with integration of constraints but rather allows the integration of constraint solvers via general-purpose communication mechanisms. There are two major technical differences between $\lambda(\mathsf{fut})$ and our work: the treatment of concurrency, and how far the order of evaluations is restricted.

In our constraint-lambda calculi we do not deal with concurrency in our formulations of the the reduction rules of the calculi, we use *reduction strategies* to specify parallel executions on the meta-level. $\lambda(\mathsf{fut})$ incorporates an interleaving semantics for concurrent execution of multiple threads directly in the reduction rules. This makes it possible to talk about communication between concurrently executing threads in $\lambda(\mathsf{fut})$ but not in the basic constraint-lambda calculi. In [6] we have developed an extension of the constaint-lambda calculi that can model explicit communication with the environment.

The $\lambda(\mathsf{fut})$ calculus uses the call-by-value β-reduction rule, which requires all arguments to functions to be evaluated before the function can be applied. Furthermore, to preserve confluence, futures may only be evaluated at precisely specified points of a reduction secuence. The constraint-lambda calculi do not restrict applications of the β-rule at all and in general impose very few restrictions on allowed reductions.

10   Conclusions and Future Work

We have extended constraint functional programming to accommodate disjunctions. In particular we have introduced the unrestricted disjunctive constraint-lambda calculus and the restricted disjunctive constraint-lambda calculus in a simple and transparent fashion which, unlike previous attempts at defining combinations of constraint solvers and lambda calculi, makes them conservative extensions of the corresponding traditional lambda calculi.

The interface between the constraint store and the lambda terms ensures clarity and the smooth movement of information into and out of the constraint store.

We have shown that the restricted disjunctive constraint-lambda calculus satisfies a restricted form of confluence, namely that it is path-confluent as a reduction system. In the case of the the unrestricted disjunctive constraint-lambda calculus the stores play an important rôle and we can prove convergence of the terms only under certain conditions on the stores (Theorem 1).

In addition, we have given the denotational semantics for each of these theories.

Finally, we have shown how both horns of Hennessy's dilemma: e.g., the evaluation of $(\lambda x.x + x)(2|3)$ to either $\{4, 6\}$ or $\{4, 5, 6\}$, can be accommodated by the appropriate choice of one of our calculi.

In the future we are planning to extend our implementation of the constraint lambda calculi without disjunction (see [6, 7]) to the disjunctive constraint lambda calculi treated here.

References

1. Hendrik Pieter Barendregt. *The Lambda Calculus, Its Syntax and Semantics*. North Holland, 1995.
2. Nicolas Bourbaki. *Commutative Algebra, Chapters 1-7*. Elements of Mathematics. Springer, 1989, first published 1972.
3. Bart Demoen, María García de la Banda, Warren Harvey, Kim Marriott, and Peter Stuckey. An overview of *HAL*. In *Proceedings of Principles and Practice of Constraint Programming*, pages 174–188. Asociation for Computing Machinery, 1999.

4. Kees Doets. *From Logic to Logic Programming*. The MIT Press, 1994.
5. Matthew C. B. Hennessy. The semantics of call-by-value and call-by-name in a nondeterministic environment. *SIAM Journal on Computing*, 9(1):67–84, 1980.
6. Matthias Hölzl. *Constraint-Lambda Calculi: Theory and Applications*. PhD thesis, Ludwig-Maximilians-Universität, München, 2001.
7. Matthias M. Hölzl and John Newsome Crossley. Parametric search in constraint-functional languages. In preparation.
8. Matthias M. Hölzl and John Newsome Crossley. Constraint-lambda calculi. In Alessandro Armando, editor, *Frontiers of Combining Systems, 4th International Workshop*, LNAI 2309, pages 207–221. Springer, 2002.
9. Joxan Jaffar and Jean-Louis Lassez. Constraint logic programming. In *Conference Record, 14th Annual ACM Symposium on Principles of Programming Languages, Munich, West Germany, 21–23 Jan 1987*, pages 111–119. Association for Computing Machinery, 1987.
10. John Wylie Lloyd. *Foundations of Logic Programming*. Artificial Intelligence. Springer, second edition, 1987. First edition, 1984.
11. Luis Mandel. *Constrained Lambda Calculus*. PhD thesis, Ludwig-Maximilians-Universität, München, 1995.
12. Luis Mandel and María Victoria Cengarle. The disjunctive constrained lambda calculus. In Dines Bjørner, Manfred Broy, and Igor Vasilevich Pottosin, editors, *Perspectives of Systems Informatics, (2nd. International Andrei Ershov Memorial Conference, Proceedings)*, volume 1181 of *Lecture Notes in Computer Science*, pages 297–309. Springer Verlag, 1996.
13. Luis Mandel and María Victoria Cengarle. The disjunctive constrained lambda calculus. In Dines Bjørner, Manfred Broy, and Igor Vasilevich Pottosin, editors, *Perspectives of Systems Informatics, (2nd. International Andrei Ershov Memorial Conference, Proceedings)*, volume 1181 of *Lecture Notes in Computer Science*, pages 297–309. Springer Verlag, 1996.
14. Kim Marriott and Martin Odersky. A confluent calculus for concurrent constraint programming. *Theoretical Computer Science*, 173(1):209–233, 1997.
15. Joachim Niehren, Jan Schwinghammer, and Gert Smolka. A concurrent lambda calculus with futures. In Bernhard Gramlich, editor, *5th International Workshop on Frontiers in Combining Systems*, Lecture Notes in Computer Science. Springer, May 2005. Accepted for publication.
16. Andreas Rossberg, Didier Le Botlan, Guido Tack, Thorsten Brunklaus, and Gert Smolka. Alice through the looking glass. In Hans-Wolfgang Loidl, editor, *Trends in Functional Programming, Volume 5*, volume 5 of *Trends in Functional Programming*. Intellect, Munich, Germany, 2004.
17. Jan Schwinghammer. A concurrent lambda-calculus with promises and futures. Master's thesis, Programming Systems Lab, Universität des Saarlandes, February 2002.
18. Michael B. Smyth. Topology. In *Handbook of Logic in Computer Science*, pages 641–761. Oxford Science Publications, 1992.

Computational Issues in Exploiting Dependent And-Parallelism in Logic Programming: Leftness Detection in Dynamic Search Trees

Yao Wu, Enrico Pontelli, and Desh Ranjan

Department of Computer Science,
New Mexico State University
{epontell, dranjan, yawu}@cs.nmsu.edu

Abstract. We present efficient *Pure Pointer Machine (PPM)* algorithms to test for "leftness" in dynamic search trees and related problems. In particular, we show that the problem of testing if a node x is in the leftmost branch of the subtree rooted in node y, in a dynamic tree that grows and shrinks at the leaves, can be solved on PPMs in worst-case $O((\lg \lg n)^2)$ time per operation in the *semi-dynamic* case—i.e., all the operations that add leaves to the tree are performed before any other operations—where n is the number of operations that affect the structure of the tree. We also show that the problem can be solved on PPMs in amortized $O((\lg \lg n)^2)$ time per operation in the fully dynamic case.

1 Introduction

Logic Programming (LP) is a popular computer programming paradigm, that has been effectively used in a wide variety of application domains. A nice property of LP is that *parallelism* can be automatically extracted from logic programs by a run-time system, allowing the user to *transparently* take advantage of available parallel computing resources to speed-up program execution. However, the implementation of a parallel LP system poses many challenging problems [7]. In spite of the extensive research in the field, which has led to a variety of approaches and implemented systems, to date very little attention has been paid to the analysis of the computational complexity of the operations required to support this type of parallel execution models. This type of analysis is vital for providing a *clear understanding of the inherent costs* of the operations required to support parallel LP, as well as for providing a *formal framework for the comparison* of alternative execution models.

Execution of LP can be abstracted as the process of maintaining a dynamic tree; the operational semantics of the language determines what operations on the tree are of interest. As execution proceeds, the tree grows and shrinks, and, in the parallel case, different parts of the tree are concurrently affected. Various additional operations are needed to guarantee the correct execution behavior. Although dynamic data structures have been extensively studied, the specific ones required by parallel LP have yet to be fully investigated. In this paper, we focus on modeling the key operations underlying the implementation of *dependent and-parallelism*, and we rely on the pointer machine model for the investigation of the problem—as this model allows us to perform a finer-grained analysis of the problem, and it naturally models the linked nature of the struc-

G. Sutcliffe and A. Voronkov (Eds.): LPAR 2005, LNAI 3835, pp. 79–94, 2005.

tures involved in Prolog systems' implementations. This line of research continues our successful exploration of formal analysis of parallel logic programming, which led to a formal classification of models for or-parallelism [11] and to the discovery of more effective methodologies for handling side-effects in parallel executions [13].

And-Parallelism in Logic Programming: One of the commonly used strategies to support parallel execution of LP programs, referred to as *dependent and-parallelism (DAP)* [7], relies on the concurrent execution of separate components of the current goal—i.e., given a goal $B_1, \ldots, B_n$, multiple subgoals B_i can be concurrently solved. Thus, we allow different processors to cooperate in the construction of *one* solution to the original goal. A major research direction in parallel LP has been the design of parallel implementations that automatically reproduce the *observable behavior* of sequential systems [7]. The parallel execution mechanisms have to be designed so that a user observes the same *external behavior* during parallel execution as observed during sequential execution. This is necessary in order to guarantee proper treatment of many language features, such as I/O and user-defined search strategies.

The and-parallel execution can be visualized as an *and-tree*. The root is labeled with the initial goal; if a node contains a conjunction $B_1, \ldots, B_n$, then it will have n children: the ith child is labeled with the body of the program clause used to solve B_i.

The main problem in the implementation of DAP is how to efficiently manage the *unifiers* produced by the concurrent reduction of different subgoals. Let $vars(B)$ denote the set of variables present in the subgoal B. Two subgoals B_i and B_j ($1 \leq i < j \leq n$) in the goal $B_1, \ldots, B_n$ should agree in the bindings for all the variables in $vars(B_i) \cap vars(B_j)$—such variables are termed *dependent* variables in parallel LP terminology. In sequential Prolog execution, usually, B_i, the goal to the left, binds the dependent variables and B_j works with the bindings produced by B_i. During DAP execution, however, B_i and B_j may produce bindings in a different order (e.g., B_j may bind a variable first). This may modify the behavior of the program and violate the sequential Prolog semantics [7]. Unfortunately, it is in general undecidable to determine whether a variable binding will modify the observable behavior w.r.t. a sequential execution. The most commonly used computable approximation to guarantee the proper semantics is to ensure that bindings to common variables are made *in the same order* as in a sequential execution [7]. Two strategies have been considered to tackle the problem: *curative* and *preventive* strategies. In our previous work we have investigated the formalization of the curative scheme as a data structure problem [18]. In this paper, we analyze the data structure problem originating from the use of *preventive strategies*. This is a more important problem, since preventive strategies have been shown in practice to have superior performance [7] and have been more widely adopted. We tackle the problem in different steps, showing that it can be efficiently solved, on a pure pointer machine, with an amortized time complexity of $O((\lg \lg n)^2)$ per operation, where n is the number of updates performed on the and-tree. We also show that the problem can be solved in worst-case time $O((\lg \lg n)^2)$ per operation in the semi-dynamic case, where all operations that add nodes to the tree are performed first. These results provide some important insights on the inherent complexity of the problem, and suggest the potential to improve the performance of existing implementation schemes.

Pointer Machines: The model of computation adopted in this investigation is the Pointer Machine model. Pointer Machines have been defined in different ways [2]. All models of pointer machines share the common characteristic of disallowing indexing into an array (i.e., pointer arithmetic), as opposed to RAM models. In a pointer machine, memory is structured as a collection of records (all with the same, finite, structure), and each record field can store a pointer to a record or a data item. The primitive operations allow following pointers, storage and retrieval from record fields, creation of new records, and conditional jumps based on equality comparisons. The *Pure Pointer Machine (PPM)* model also has the restriction of disallowing constant-time arithmetic operations and constant-time comparisons between numbers. The pure pointer machine model is essentially the Linking Automaton model proposed by Knuth and is a representative of what has been called *atomistic pointer machine model* in [2]. Further details on PPMs can be found in [2, 16, 14]. Even though RAM is the most commonly used reference model in studies of complexity of algorithms, the PPM model has received increasing attention. PPMs provide a good base for modeling implementation of linked data structures. The PPM model is also simpler, thus making it more suitable for analysis of lower bounds of time complexity [16, 4, 9, 12]. Note that the PPM model is similar to the Turing Machine model with respect to the fact that the complexity of the arithmetic operations has to be accounted for while analyzing the complexity of an algorithm. It is more powerful than the Turing machine model because it allows for "jumps" based on pointer comparisons in constant time, that is not possible in the Turing machine model. The *Arithmetic Pointer Machine (APM)* model is an extension of the PPM that allows integer numbers to be stored in the records and that allows constant time arithmetic for $O(\lg n)$-size integers [3].

2   The $\mathcal{AND}\mathcal{PP}$ Problem

2.1   Background, Notations and Definitions

In this work we will focus on labeled binary trees, where labels are drawn from a label set Γ. For a node v in the tree, we denote with $left(v)$ $(right(v))$ the left (right) child of v in the tree ($\perp$ if v does not have a left (right) child). We assume that the following operations are available to manipulate the structure of trees:

1. *create_tree*(ℓ), used to create a tree containing a single node labeled $\ell \in \Gamma$.
2. *expand*(u, ℓ_1, ℓ_2): given a leaf u in the tree, the operation creates two new nodes (labeled ℓ_1 and ℓ_2) and makes them the children of u;
3. *remove*(u): given a leaf u in the tree, the operation removes it from the tree.

For two nodes u and v in a tree T, we write $u \preceq v$ if u is an ancestor of v. Observe that $\preceq$ is a partial order. We will often refer to the notion of *leftmost branch*—i.e., a path in the tree containing nodes with no left siblings. Given a node u, *left_branch*(u) contains all the nodes (including u) that belong to the leftmost branch of the subtree rooted in u. For any node u, the elements of *left_branch*(u) constitute a total order with respect to $\preceq$. The notion of leftmost branch allows us to define a partial order between nodes, indicated by $\unlhd$. Given two nodes u, v, we say that $u \unlhd v$ if v is a node in the leftmost branch of the subtree rooted at u. Formally, $u \unlhd v \Leftrightarrow v \in$ *left_branch*(u). Given a node v, let $subroot(v) = min_{\preceq}\{u \; node \; of \; T \,|\, u \trianglelefteq v\}$. $subroot(v)$ is the highest node u in the tree (i.e., closest to the root) such that v is in the leftmost branch of the subtree rooted at u. $subroot(v)$ is known as the *subroot node* of v [8].

2.2   Formalizing Preventive Strategies: The $\mathcal{AND}\mathcal{PP}$ Problem

Preventive strategies enforce the correct order of variable bindings by assigning *producer* or *consumer* status to each subgoal that shares a given dependent variable [15, 7]. The leftmost subgoal that has access to the variable is designated as the producer for that variable, while all the others are consumers. A consumer subgoal is not allowed to bind the dependent variable, it is only allowed to read its binding. If a consumer subgoal attempts to bind a free dependent variable, it has to suspend until the producer binds it first. If the producer terminates without binding the variable, then the producer status is transferred to the leftmost active consumer of such variable. Thus, the producer subgoal for a dependent variable can change during execution. A major problem in DAP is to dynamically keep track of the leftmost active subgoal that shares each variable.

The management of goals can be abstracted in terms of operations on the dynamic tree representing the execution of a program. During an and-parallel execution, nodes are added and deleted from the and-tree. The execution steps can be directly expressed using the tree *expand* and *remove* operations described in the previous section [18]. The correct management of variables in preventive strategies, can be abstracted as follows. A binding for a variable X, taking place in a node u of the tree, can be safely performed (w.r.t., sequential Prolog semantics) iff the node u lies on the leftmost branch of each node in $alias(X)$, where $alias(X)$ collects all the nodes where the variables that have been aliased to X (i.e., unbound variables that have been mutually unified) have been defined. Formally, for all Y in $alias(X)$ we have $node(Y) \trianglelefteq u$. We will denote with *verify_leftmost*(u, v) the operation which, given a node u and a node v, verifies whether u is in the leftmost branch in the subtree rooted in v (a.k.a. *leftness test*). Thus, we have the following data structure problem: *"The problem $\mathcal{AND}\mathcal{PP}$ consists of the following operations on dynamic trees: create, expand, remove, and verify_leftmost."*

The rest of the paper tackles the problem of designing efficient algorithms for this problem. We can easily show that the $\mathcal{AND}\mathcal{PP}$ problem requires $\Omega(\lg \lg n)$ on PPMs, via a reduction from the *Temporal Precedence (TP)* problem—i.e., the problem of maintaining a dynamic list (where elements can be inserted) and performing precedence tests. The TP problem has a lower bound time complexity of $O(\lg \lg n)$ on PPMs [12].

3   Efficient Solutions for Some Restricted Cases

3.1   General Scheme and Solutions Based on Relationships to Other Problems

The general *verify_leftmost* test can be performed efficiently if one can efficiently maintain the subroot nodes for all nodes in the tree. More precisely, the ability to determine

---

Algorithm VERIFY_LEFTMOST (u, v)
  $s_1 \leftarrow$ SUBROOT(u); $s_2 \leftarrow$ SUBROOT(v);
  return $(s_1 = s_2$ AND height$(v) <$ height$(u))$;

Fig. 1. General Scheme

SUBROOT(v) for any node v allows the solution outlined in Fig. 1 for verifying leftness. The time required by this algorithm is the sum of the times required by the procedure *subroot* and by the height comparison. In general, the set of nodes in a dynamic tree can be partitioned into disjoint subsets of nodes with all nodes in each subset having the same subroot node. The nodes of each subset form a path in the tree, each path terminating in a leaf (Fig. 2). From this perspective, it is easy to relate the problem to the Union-Find Problem [16, 9, 4] and the Marked-Ancestor Problem [1].

Relationship to the Union-Find Problem: The $\mathcal{AND}\mathcal{PP}^\mathcal{P}$ problem can be solved using the solution to the *union-find* problem [16]. This solution maintains the disjoint paths with the same subroot nodes as disjoint sets, with the subroot nodes as the representatives. Each time we perform an *expand* operation, a new set containing the right child and a new set containing the left child are created; the latter is unioned to the set containing its parent. When a *remove* operation is performed, if the removed node does not have a right sibling, then nothing needs to be done. If the removed node u has a right sibling w, then the set containing w is unioned with the set containing the parent of u. *verify_leftmost*(u, v) can be implemented by checking if *find*(u) = *find*(v) and if node v is closer to the root than u. The union-find problem can be solved optimally on a *Pointer Machine with Arithmetic (APM)* in amortized time $O(m\alpha(m, n))$ (m is the number of operations performed and n is the number of nodes in the tree) [9]. Furthermore, comparison of the heights of the nodes can be done in constant time on an APM (since an APM allows constant-time comparisons of numbers).

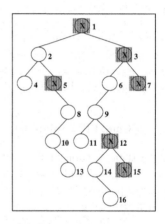

Fig. 2. Marked Ancestors

To analyze the complexity of this scheme on PPM (i.e., with no constant-time arithmetic), let us denote with e the number of *expand* operations, with d the number of *remove* operations, and with q the number of *verify_leftmost* queries performed. Let $m = d + e + q$. Each *expand* operation requires constant time. Each *remove* operation requires one union operation; the union using the union-by-rank heuristic can be performed in $O(\lg \lg \lg n)$ time on a PPM. Each *verify_leftmost* operation requires two find operations and one *precedes* operation (for height comparison). This can be done in $O(\lg \lg n)$ time[1]. This solution can be implemented on a PPM in amortized time $O(m\alpha(m, e) + d \lg \lg \lg e + q \lg \lg e)$. Blum [4] provides a PPM solution with a worst-case time complexity of $O(\lg n / \lg \lg n)$ per operation.

The type of union-find operations required to support the computation of the subroot nodes are actually very specialized. Each union operation is performed when a node with a right sibling is removed from the tree; in that case the union links the set associated with the right sibling with the set associated with its parent. This can be seen as an instance of the *adjacent union-find* problem [10, 17]—a union-find problem where

---

[1] Using the scheme in [12].

elements are arranged in a list and the union operation is performed only on adjacent sets. The problem has been shown to be solvable in worst-case time complexity $O(\lg \lg n)$ on a pointer machine *with arithmetic* (APM) [10, 17]; however the solution makes extensive use of the arithmetic capabilities of APM, and the corresponding solution is not as effective on a PPM, as it requires $O(\lg n \lg \lg n)$ time per operation.

Relationship to Marked Ancestor: Another problem that is strongly related to the one at hand is the Marked Ancestor problem [1]. The problem assumes the presence of a tree structure, where each node can be either marked or unmarked. The operations available are $\mathrm{mark}(v)$—used to mark the node v—$\mathrm{unmark}(v)$—used to remove the mark from v—and $\mathrm{first}(v)$—used to retrieve the nearest marked ancestor of node v. The results in [1] provide optimal solutions for the marked ancestor problem (on RAM), with worst-case time complexity $\Theta(\lg n / \lg \lg n)$ per operation. A simplified version of the problem, the *decremental marked ancestor problem*, allows only the unmark and first operations. This problem can be solved in amortized constant time on RAMs. The problem can also be solved on RAMs with worst case $O(\lg \lg n)$ per unmark and $O(\lg n / \lg \lg n)$ per first operation [1].

The semi-dynamic $\mathcal{AND\!P\!P^P}$ problem is an instance of the decremental ancestor problem. Starting from the same tree structure as in $\mathcal{AND\!P\!P^P}$ problem, initially the only marked nodes are those that are subroot nodes of at least one node in the tree. Each time a *remove(v)* operation is required, if the node v has a right sibling, then the right sibling is unmarked, otherwise no nodes are changed. Each SUBROOT operation corresponds to a first operation. This provides a solution for the problem with worst-case complexity $O(\lg n / \lg \lg n)$ per operation, and amortized time complexity $O(1)$—on RAM. These results do not provide a better complexity on PPMs.

3.2   A Good PPM Solution for the Static Case

In the static version of the problem, all the *expand* and *remove* operations are performed prior to any *verify_leftmost* operations—i.e., the *verify_leftmost* queries are applied to a static tree. One can obtain an efficient solution in this case by making a simple, but key, observation.

```
Algorithm Linear-Subroot(head)
 1. u ← head
 2. while (next[u] is not NIL) do
 3.     if (u is marked) do
 4.         subroot[u] ← u
 5.     else
 6.         subroot[u] ← subroot[prev[u]]
 7.     u ← next[u]
```

Fig. 3. Linear Subroot

Theorem: *Let T be a tree where only and all subroot nodes are marked (see Fig. 2), and L be the preorder traversal of T. For every node v, the subroot node of v is the nearest marked node to the left (marked predecessor) of v in L.* The tree T can be preprocessed in linear time to answer the subroot queries in $O(1)$ time. First, in linear time one can construct the preorder traversal L of T (as a double-linked list). The procedure Linear-Subroot(L) (Fig. 3) preprocesses the list L in linear time. After this procedure is called, the subroot node field for each node is set correctly. Each successive subroot query can be answered in $O(1)$ time—this is illustrated in Fig. 4. To answer the *verify_leftmost* query, we still need to compare the height of two given nodes. This can be done in time $O(\lg \lg n)$ on a PPM [12]. Thus, this static version of the problem has a solution with worst-case time complexity of $O(\lg \lg n)$ per operation.

Fig. 4. A data structure allows constant time subroot query

3.3   An Efficient PPM Solution in the Semi-dynamic Case

The solution can be extended to a semi-dynamic version of the problem, where all the *expand* operations are performed prior to the *remove* and *verify _leftmost* opera-tions. As men-tioned, this ver-sion of the prob-

Algorithm Find-Marked-Predecessor-Binary(u)
  1. $v' \leftarrow u; v \leftarrow parent(u)$;
  2. **if** (u is marked) **do**
  3.   **return** u
  4. **while** (v' is left child of v or the left sibling of v' is unmarked) **do**
  5. $v' \leftarrow v; v \leftarrow parent(v)$;
  6. $v' \leftarrow$ left marked child of v;
  7. **while** (v' is not a leaf) **do**
  8. $v' \leftarrow$ rightmost marked child of v';
  9. **return** v'

Fig. 5. Find-Marked-Predecessor-Binary

lem is an instance of the decreased marked ancestor problem. Solving the semi-dynamic version of the problem can be simplified to the problem of maintaining a list L of nodes, some of which are marked, which represents the preorder traversal of the tree. The re-quired operations on this list are *unmark* and *find-marked-predecessor*. The *unmark(v)* operation is required when a leaf u with right sibling v is removed. The *find-marked predecessor(u)* operation returns the nearest marked node to the left of u in the pre-order traversal list L. This is a special case of the Marked-Ancestor Problem, i.e., the Marked-Ancestor problem on a *linear tree*. [17] provides a solution with worst-case single operation complexity $O(\lg \lg n)$ on RAMs.

While [16] gives solutions which are efficient in amortized time complexity, the fo-cus here is to obtain an efficient solution w.r.t. single operation worst case time complex-ity. We begin with a simple solution that has $O(\lg n)$ single operation worst case time complexity. This solution is then improved to $o(\lg n)$ and, finally, to a $O((\lg \lg n)^2)$ worst-case time solution for the semi-dynamic $\mathcal{AND}P^{\mathcal{P}}$ problem on PPMs. Results that are similar in spirit to this investigation have been proposed in [6] for the union-find problem (where the union-find problem is solved w.r.t. a fixed union structure).

An $O(\lg n)$ Solution: Let L be the preorder traversal of the tree T. Let T' be a complete binary tree with the nodes of L as leaves. T' has height $\lceil \lg n \rceil$. We proceed to mark in T' an internal node if any of its descendants is marked. If there are less than $2^{\lceil \lg n \rceil}$ nodes, dummy nodes can be added to make it a complete binary tree without changing the asymptotic time complexity of the operations. This requires preprocessing time $O(n)$, where n is the number of nodes in the list L. The marked predecessor can then be found simply as indicated in procedure Find-Marked-Predecessor-Binary(u)—see Figure 5. The single operation worst case time complexity of this procedure is proportional to the height of the tree, which is $O(\lg n)$.

An $O(\lg n \lg \lg \lg n / \lg \lg n)$ **Solution:** We can improve the previous algorithm by keeping *shorter* trees. Increasing the degree from 2 to some $k > 2$ will reduce the height of the tree to $\lg_k n$. Let L be the preorder traversal of T. Without loss of generality, let T' be a complete k-ary tree with the nodes of L as leaves. T' has height $\lceil \lg_k n \rceil$. As done earlier, in T' we will mark an internal node if any of its descendants is marked. This construction requires $O(n)$ preprocessing time (n is the number of nodes in L). The procedure in Fig. 6 finds the marked predecessor of u in L.

The while loops in the procedure are executed at most $\lceil \lg_k n \rceil$ times. On the flip side, however, it becomes more expensive to test the condition in the first while loop. If we use a trivial comparison scheme to test precedence

---

Algorithm Find-Marked-Predecessor-Binary(u)

1. $v' \leftarrow u; v \leftarrow parent(u)$;
2. **if** (u is marked) **do**
3.   **return** u
4. **while** (v' is left child of v or the left sibling of v' is unmarked) **do**
5. $v' \leftarrow v; v \leftarrow parent(v)$;
6. $v' \leftarrow$ left marked child of v;
7. **while** (v' is not a leaf) **do**
8. $v' \leftarrow$ rightmost marked child of v';
9. **return** v'

Fig. 6. Find-Marked-Predecessor

in line 2, the comparison requires time $O(k)$. Making use of the result from [12], this comparison can be done in $\lg \lg k$ time. The loop in line 2, requires at most $\lceil \lg_k n \rceil$ precedence tests in the worst-case (potentially one for each tree level). Line 4 requires time $O(k)$ as one can walk left starting from v' until a marked sibling is found. The loop in line 5 requires time at most $\lg_k n$. Hence, the total time required for the *Find-Marked-Predecessor* operation illustrated in Fig. 6, in the worst-case, is bounded by $\lg \lg k \lg_k n + k + \lg_k n$. The $unmark(u)$ operation is performed as follows: first of all, the node u is unmarked; if u is either the leftmost or the rightmost marked child of its parent, then this information has to be updated. If u is the only marked child of its parent, then the unmarking procedure is repeated on the parent of u. The total time for unmark in the worst-case is $O(\lg_k n)$. The best value of k turns out to be $k = \lg n / \lg \lg n$, leading to a time complexity of $O(\lg n \lg \lg \lg n / \lg \lg n)$ for the *Find-Marked-Predecessor* operation; the time complexity of $unmark$ is $O(\lg n/(\lg \lg n))$.

An $O((\lg \lg n)^2)$ **Solution:** The idea here is to note that, in line 4 of the *Find-Marked-Predecessor* procedure in Figure 6, we are actually finding the marked predecessor of v' in the list of children of v. Hence, one can improve the computation by recursively organizing the children of a node as a tree. We use a $\sqrt{n}$-ary tree with height 2 (Fig.

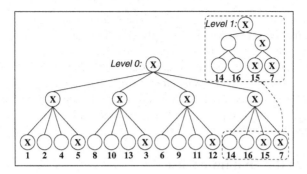

Fig. 7. A 16 node $\sqrt{n}$-ary tree with height 2

Algorithm Find-Marked-Predecessor(u,ℓ)
  0. **if** ($\ell = \lg \lg n$) **then** use direct list search to determine the answer;
  1. **if** (marked(u)) **then return**(u);
  2. $v \leftarrow parent(u,\ell)$;
  3. **if** ((leftmost marked child of v precedes u)) **then**
  4.   **return**(Find-Marked-Predecessor($u,\ell + 1$));
  5. $w \leftarrow$ Find-Marked-Predecessor($v,\ell + 1$);
  6. **return** rightmost marked child w;

Fig. 8. Find-Marked-Predecessor

7). The $\sqrt{n}$-ary tree has $\sqrt{n}$ subtrees, each having size $\sqrt{n}$. We recursively maintain a similar structure for each subtree—thus, the $\sqrt{n}$ children of a node are themselves organized in a $\sqrt[4]{n}$-ary tree, etc. The number of levels of the recursive construction is bounded by $O(\lg \lg n)$. The tree structure information has to be maintained for each recursive level. This can be done efficiently using the scheme developed to solve the temporal precedence problem, as described in [12]. Let us refer to the number of edges connected to the root as *root degree* and the number of edges connecting a middle level node to leaves as *middle level degree*.

The algorithm *Find-Marked-Predecessor(u,ℓ)* described in Fig. 8 finds the marked predecessor of node u at level ℓ of nesting in the recursive tree structure. To find the marked predecessor of u in the list L, the procedure *Find-Marked-Predecessor($u,0$)* is called. Note that a node may have different parents at different recursive levels (see Fig. 7)—in the algorithm $parent(u, \ell)$ denotes the parent of u at level ℓ. Note also that a node may have children only in one of the recursive levels. Let $T(n)$ to be the worst-case time required by the *Find-Marked-Predecessor* operation performed on a list of size n. The procedure *Find-Marked-Predecessor* calls itself at most once, in line 4 or line 5, with the problem size equal to $\sqrt{n}$. This contributes $T(\sqrt{n})$ in the recurrence. The comparison in line 3 takes time $O(\lg \lg \sqrt{n})$ (again, using the solution to the temporal precedence problem). Hence, with this scheme $T(n)$ satisfies the recurrence: $T(n) = O(\lg \lg \sqrt{n}) + T(\sqrt{n})$, where n is the number of nodes in the list L. The solution of this recurrence relation is $T(n) = \Theta((\lg \lg n)^2)$. The *unmark* operation takes time $O(1)$ per level of nesting. Hence, the total time required is $O(\lg \lg n)$.

On an APM (and hence on RAM), this scheme requires only $O(\lg \lg n)$ for both operations, as the precedence test now requires $O(1)$ time, and the recurrence for $T(n)$ becomes: $T(n) = T(\sqrt{n}) + O(1)$. A different $O(\lg \lg n)$ scheme to solve this problem, *on RAM*, has been presented in [17]. However, a direct translation of that scheme to Pure Pointer Machines will require $O(\lg n \lg \lg n)$ time per operation.

4   Solution to the Dynamic Case

The dynamic version of the problem allows the operations *expand*, *verify_leftmost*, and *remove* to be carried out in any order. This section extends the data structure presented earlier to obtain an efficient solution in the fully dynamic case. This solution has an amortized time complexity of $O((\lg \lg n)^2)$ per operation, where n is the total number of operations.

4.1   Dynamic *Expand* Operation

We devise a scheme to update the data structure developed for the semi-dynamic case when an *expand* operation is performed, without adversely affecting the time to answer marked predecessor queries. Since the time required to answer a query depends directly on the degree of the nodes in the tree, it is intuitive to prevent the degree of nodes from growing too large. The algorithm we propose does exactly this by either "splitting" the tree node or "reorganizing" the recursive data structure. The algorithm relies also on the following simple observation:

Lemma: *Let L be the preorder traversal of T. After the operation $expand(u, l_1, l_2)$ is performed, u, l_1 and l_2 appear consecutively in L, in that order.*

It follows from this lemma that, if we adopt the nested recursive structure discussed earlier, l_1 and l_2 are consecutive in the frontier of the outer-most recursion tree.

The Basic Strategy: The whole data structure is reorganized when the root degree of the outermost recursion tree doubles, by using the preprocessing for the static case. For the recursion trees at other levels, starting from the deepest recursion level, whenever the root degree of a recursion tree doubles, the tree is split into two trees. Correspondingly, in the tree at next higher level of recursion, it is natural to split the node for the original group to be two nodes. We can see that each tree split implies a node split of a middle layer node in the preceding level of recursion. The process is applied recursively (see Figures 9-10).

The "reorganization" is the process of constructing the whole recursive data structure from scratch. If the tree has size n, the reorganization requires time $n \lg \lg n$. The field *olddegree* is the degree of a recursion tree produced during reorganization. Before another reorganization, the actual degrees may shrink and grow, and the degrees of different nodes may be different. However, the *olddegree* field for every node remains

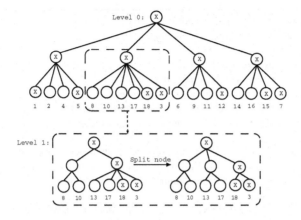

Fig. 9. After performing *expand(13, 17, 18)* on the tree of Fig. 2

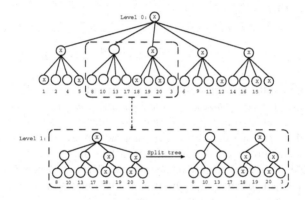

Fig. 10. After performing *expand(13, 17, 18)* and *expand(18, 19, 20)*

unchanged. It represents the "capacity" of the recursive tree and serves as a criteria for the timing of splitting. This field is set during reorganization.

The Algorithm: The procedure *Dynamic-Expand(u, l_1, l_2)* inserts two nodes l_1 and l_2 into the frontiers of $\lg \lg n$ different recursion trees. Line 1 and lines 8-13 of the loop ensure that the list of marked children of each node at each level is maintained correctly. The procedure Adjust is called after the insertions to perform the "splitting" and reorganization, as needed.

In the procedure *Dynamic-Expand(u, l_1, l_2)*, *Find-Marked-Predecessor* is called in line 1 to find the marked predecessor w of u in the outer-most recursion level. This requires $O((\lg \lg n)^2)$ time. The loop in line 2 requires at most $\lg \lg n$ time to insert l_1 and l_2 in all the recursion levels. Line 14 calls Adjust(u, $\lg \lg n - 1$) to split or reorganize the recursion trees from the deepest recursion level, if necessary. The code can be found in Appendix A. The procedure Adjust(u, $level$) readjusts the group size at all recursion levels, starting from the deepest recursion and ending with the outermost recursion tree.

Algorithm Dynamic-Expand(u, l_1, l_2)

1. $w \leftarrow$ Find-Marked-Predecessor(u, 0)
2. **for** (each recursion level t) **do**
3. $parent(l_1, t) \leftarrow parent(u, t)$;
4. $parent(l_2, t) \leftarrow parent(u, t)$;
5. $degree[parent(u, t)] \leftarrow degree[parent(u, t)] + 2$;
6.   insert l_1 and l_2 into the doubly linked list of all children
       of $parent(u, t)$, immediately following u
7.   mark l_2
8.   **if** $(parent(w, t) = parent(u, t))$ **then**
9.   insert l_2 into the doubly linked list of all marked children
           of $parent(u, t)$, immediately following w
10.   **else**
11.   insert l_2 at the beginning of the doubly linked list of
           all marked children of $parent(u, t)$
12.   if $parent(u, t)$ is unmarked, mark it
13.   if $parent(parent(u, t), t)$ is unmarked, mark it
14. Adjust(u, $\lg \lg n - 1$)

Fig. 11. Dynamic Expand

Lines 28-29 represent the base case. If the root degree of the outermost recursion tree doubles, then these lines reorganize the whole data structure. Lines 3-15 split an internal node if the middle level degree of a recursion tree doubles. Lines 16-27 split a recursion tree if the root degree of a recursion tree (except the outermost one) doubles. For an *expand* operation, the procedure Adjust may either be called through all the recursion levels or be called just for the deepest recursion level. The cost depends on the how far we need to fix the data structure after inserting the two nodes in each recursion level. Let us analyze the amortized cost in this scenario.

The Time Complexity of the Algorithm: The cost of *expand* is composed of the following parts: *(i)* the insertion of two nodes in each recursion level and management of data structures; *(ii)* the splitting of nodes and splitting of the tree as the degree grows; *(iii)* the reorganization of the whole data structure when the root degree of the outermost recursion tree doubles.

Cost of Insertion and Reorganization: Since the procedure *Dynamic-Expand* calls *Find-Marked-Predecessor*, which requires $O((\lg \lg n)^2)$ time in the worst case, $O(n(\lg \lg n)^2)$ time is needed between two reorganizations. The reorganization itself needs $O(n \lg \lg n)$ for a list of length n.

Total Cost of Splitting: Notice that, during the expansion, every time a tree is split, the size of this tree is at least twice of what it was immediately after the previous split. Let $T(2k)$ denote the total cost (i.e., including costs of splits of nodes that are children w) of splitting a node w which has degree $2k$. In this tree, the *olddegree* of the node is k. To split this node into two new nodes of degree k, each of which has half of all the children, we create two new nodes u and v, where u is the new parent of the first half of the children of w and v is the new parent of the second half of the children of w. We also need to maintain the marked children of u and v as doubly linked lists. These steps can be done in $O(k)$ time. The natural question is how often do we split nodes with degree $2k$ and what is the total time required for all these splits. Splitting a node implies that the root degree of corresponding one level deeper recursion tree has doubled. In this deeper level recursion tree, *olddregree* is $\sqrt{k}$. Hence, at most $\sqrt{k}$ splitting node operations can be performed in this recursion tree before its root degree doubles. The split nodes in the deeper level of recursion have degree $2\sqrt{k}$, hence the time used for one such splitting is bound by $T(2\sqrt{k})$. This leads to the recurrence $T(2k) \leq \sqrt{k} \cdot T(2\sqrt{k}) + O(k)$. Solving the recurrence, $T(2k)$ is $O(k \lg \lg k)$. Let us assume that we have just reorganized the data structure and that the *olddegree* in the outermost level is k. Then, before the whole data structure is reorganized again, there will be k outermost level splitting node operations. Hence, the time used between two reorganizations, is $(k^2 \lg \lg k)$. The actual size of the tree is at least $n = 2k^2$. Thus, the total cost of splitting between reorganizations is $O(n \lg \lg n)$.

Total Cost of Dynamic Expand: Let $G(n)$ be the time complexity of total cost for for all n *Dynamic-Expand* operations. Between two reorganizations, maintaining the structure has cost $O(n \cdot \lg \lg n)$ and the reorganization itself has cost $O(n \cdot \lg \lg n)$. The last reorganization occurs when the size is $\frac{n}{2}$. Then the recurrence relation for $G(n)$ is: $G(n) = G(\frac{n}{2}) + O(n \cdot (\lg \lg n)^2)$. Solving this recurrence, we obtain that the total cost for $O(n)$ *Dynamic-Expand* operations is $O(n \cdot (\lg \lg n)^2)$. Hence, the *Dynamic-Expand* operation can be performed with amortized time complexity $O((\lg \lg n)^2)$.

4.2 Dynamic *Remove* Operation

When the *remove* operation is performed on a dynamic tree T, there are two cases. If the node to be removed u does not have a right sibling, then we can remove this node from each level of the recursion tree and maintain the data structures. If u has a right sibling v, then we need to remove u and unmark the right sibling v in all recursive trees. Since the level of recursion is $O(\lg \lg n)$, the *remove* operation requires $O(\lg \lg n)$ time. Section 4.3 will show that this simple solution allows an efficient query algorithm.

4.3 Dynamic *Verify_Leftmost* Operation

The find algorithm is identical to the static case. However, the analysis of the running time is more involved. Recall that, in the static case, the recurrence relation is $T(n) = O(\lg \lg \sqrt{n}) + T(\sqrt{n})$. as the nodes are maintained in equally sized groups. In the new scheme, we allow the number of nodes to increase up to a certain point. It is worth noting that our scheme may allow the size of a group to increase by more than a constant factor between levels, nevertheless it still supports the *Find-Marked-Predecessor* operation in $O((\lg \lg n)^2)$ time.

Consider a freshly reorganized data structure for a n-node dynamic tree. According to the scheme, the level $(\lg \lg n - 1)$ recursion tree (which has 4 leaves) may grow up to 7 leaves before splitting is performed. Its size cannot exceed 2 times of the original size. In the level $(\lg \lg n - 2)$ recursion tree, since the middle level degree may be the largest possible size of level $(\lg\lg n - 1)$ recursion tree and the root degree cannot exceed 2 times the original, the size of level $(\lg\lg n - 2)$ recursion tree cannot exceed 4 times of the original size. Similarly, the size of level $(\lg\lg n - 3)$ recursion tree cannot exceed 8 times of the original size. Extending this, the size of level 1 recursion tree cannot exceed $2^{\lg\lg n - 1}$ times of the original size, which is $\frac{\lg n}{2} \cdot \sqrt{n}$.

More formally, define $N(i)$ to be largest possible size in recursion level i. Then,

$$N(i) \le \begin{cases} 7 & \text{if } i = \lg\lg n - 1; \\ 2 \cdot olddegree(i) \cdot N(i+1) & \text{otherwise.} \end{cases}$$

where the $olddegree(i)$ is the value of olddegree field in level i recursion tree, which is $n^{\frac{1}{2^{i+1}}}$. Solving this recurrence relation, $N(1) = O(2^{\lg\lg n - 1} \cdot n^{\frac{1}{2}}) = O(\sqrt{n}\lg n)$. $N(1)$ is the largest possible group in the outer-most recursion tree. Observe that with this bound on the largest group size, the asymptotic running time to answer the query is unchanged. It is important to note that in the *Dynamic-Expand* operation one needs to insert nodes in arbitrary positions in a list (of children of a node) and still be able to compare if the leftmost marked node in this list is to the left of a given node efficiently. This is more general than the temporal precedence problem. However, data structures developed in [5] can be used to solve the general problem equally efficiently.

5   Conclusions and Future Work

We have studied the problem of testing leftness in a dynamically growing tree and provided efficient pure pointer machine algorithms for several variants of the problems. The problem has theoretical interest and practical applications in programming languages implementation. The results indeed suggest that preventive schemes in DAP can be executed more efficiently than curative schemes (which have been shown to have higher complexity); at the same time, the data structures provided in this paper suggest that, at least theoretically, better implementation structures can be devised to support preventive schemes. None of the algorithms we propose is provably optimal. As future work, we propose to investigate possibly tighter bounds; for example, we will investigate if these problems can be solved in $O(\lg\lg n)$ time on pure pointer machines.

Acknowledgments. The research has been supported by NSF grants CNS-0220590, CNS-0454066, and HRD-0420407.

References

1. S. Alstrup, T. Husfeldt, and T. Rauhe. Marked Ancestor Problems. *FOCS*, 534–544, 1998.
2. A.M. Ben-Amram. What is a Pointer Machine? SIGACT News, 26(2), June 1995.
3. A.M. Ben-Amran and Z. Galil. On Pointers versus Addresses. *JACM*, 39(3), 1992.
4. N. Blum. On the single-operation worst-case time complexity of the disjoint set union problem. *SIAM Journal on Computing*, 15(4):1021–1024, 1986.
5. A. Dal Palù, E. Pontelli, and D. Ranjan. An Optimal Algorithm for Finding NCA on Pure Pointer Machines. *Scandinavian Workshop on Algorithm Theory*. Springer Verlag, 2002.

6. H.N. Gabow and R.E. Tarjan. A Linear-time Algorithm for a Special Case of Disjoint Set Union. *Journal of Computer and System Sciences*, 30:209–221, 1985.
7. G. Gupta et al. Parallel Execution of Prolog Programs. *ACM TOPLAS*, 23(4), 2001.
8. B. Hausman et al. Cut and Side-Effects in Or-Parallel Prolog. In *Int. Conf. on Fifth Generation Computer Systems*, pages 831–840, 1988. Springer Verlag.
9. H. LaPoutré. Lower Bounds for the Union-Find and the Split-Find Problem on Pointer Machines. *Journal of Computer and System Sciences*, 52:87–99, 1996.
10. K. Mehlhorn, S. Naher, and H. Alt. A Lower Bound on the Complexity of the Union-Split-Find Problem. *SIAM Journal of Computing*, 17(6), 1988.
11. E. Pontelli et al. An Optimal Data Structure to Handle Dynamic Environments in Non-Deterministic Computations. *Computer Languages*, 28(2), 2002.
12. D. Ranjan et al. The Temporal Precedence Problem. *Algorithmica*, 28:288–306, 2000.
13. D. Ranjan et al. Data Structures for Order-sensitive Predicates in Parallel Non-deterministic Systems. *ACTA Informatica*, 37(1), 2000.
14. A. Schönhage. Storage Modification Machines. *SIAM Journal of Computing*, 9(3), 1980.
15. K. Shen. Exploiting Dependent And-parallelism in Prolog: The Dynamic Dependent And-parallel Scheme. *Int. Conf. and Symp. on Logic Programming*, 1992. MIT Press.
16. R.E. Tarjan. A Class of Algorithms which Require Nonlinear Time to Maintain Disjoint Sets. *Journal of Computer and System Sciences*, 2(18):110–127, 1979.
17. P. van Emde Boas, R. Kaas, and E. Zijlstra. Design and Implementation of an Efficient Priority Queue. *Mathematical Systems Theory*, 10, 1977.
18. Y. Wu, E. Pontelli, and D. Ranjan. On the Complexity of Dependent And-parallelism in Logic Programming. *Int. Conf. on Logic Programming*. Springer Verlag, 2003.

Appendix A

Algorithm Adjust(u, $level$)

1. $p \leftarrow parent(u, level)$;
2. $pp \leftarrow parent(p, level)$;
▷ middle level degree of deepest recursion tree doubles or
when upper level of recursion is called, split node
3. **if** (($degree[p] \geq 2 \cdot olddegree[p]$ and $level = \lg \lg n - 1$) or $level \neq \lg \lg n - 1$)
4.   Create two nodes $left$ and $right$;
5. $degree[left] \leftarrow degree[p]/2$;
6. $degree[right] \leftarrow degree[p] - degree[left]$;
7. $parent[left] \leftarrow pp$;
8. $parent[right] \leftarrow pp$;
9. $degree[pp] \leftarrow degree[pp] + 1$;
10.   replace p with $left$ and insert $right$ into the children list of pp;
11.   the parent of the first half children of $p \leftarrow left$;
12.   if any child of $left$ is marked, $left$ is marked;
13.   the parent of the second half children of $p \leftarrow right$;
14.   if any child of $right$ is marked, $right$ is marked;
15.   maintain marked children list for nodes $left$ and $right$;
▷ root degree of the tree doubles, split tree
16. **if** ($degree[pp] \geq 2 \cdot olddegree[pp]$ and $level \neq 0$)
17.   Create two nodes old and new;
18. $degree[old] \leftarrow degree[pp]/2$;
19. $degree[new] \leftarrow degree[pp] - degree[old]$;

20. $parent[old] \leftarrow NIL$;
21. $parent[new] \leftarrow NIL$;
22.   the parent of the first half children of $pp \leftarrow old$;
23.   if any child of old is marked, old is marked;
24.   the parent of the second half children of $pp \leftarrow new$;
25.   if any child of new is marked, new is marked;
26.   maintain marked children list for nodes old and new;
27.   Adjust$(u, level - 1)$;
▷ base case of the recursion
28. **if** $(degree[pp] \geq 2 \cdot olddegree[pp]$ and $level = 0)$
29.   reorganize the whole data structure by building it from scratch.
        a. taking the preorder traversal of the dynamic tree of size n.
        b. constructing all $\lg \lg n$ levels of recursion trees.
        c. "olddegree" field squared for each level of recursion.
        d. maintain correct internal structure for each group.

The *nomore++* Approach to Answer Set Solving

Christian Anger, Martin Gebser, Thomas Linke, André Neumann, and Torsten Schaub

Institut für Informatik, Universität Potsdam,
Postfach 90 03 27, D–14439 Potsdam

Abstract. We present a new answer set solver, called *nomore++*, along with its underlying theoretical foundations. A distinguishing feature is that it treats heads and bodies equitably as computational objects. Apart from its operational foundations, we show how it improves on previous work through its new lookahead and its computational strategy of maintaining unfounded-freeness. We underpin our claims by selected experimental results.

1 Introduction

A large part of the success of Answer Set Programming (ASP) is owed to the early availability of efficient solvers, like *smodels* [1] and *dlv* [2]. Since then, many other systems, sometimes following different approaches, have emerged, among them *assat* [3], *cmodels* [4], and *noMoRe* [5].

We present a new ASP solver, called *nomore++*, along with its underlying theoretical foundations. *nomore++* pursues a hybrid approach in combining features from literal-based approaches, like *smodels* and *dlv*, with the rule-based approach of its predecessor *noMoRe*. To this end, it treats heads and bodies of logic programs' rules equitably as computational objects. We argue that this approach allows for more effective (in terms of search space pruning) choices than obtainable when dealing with either heads or bodies only. As a particular consequence of this, we demonstrate that the resulting lookahead operation allows for more effective propagation than previous approaches. Finally, we detail a computational strategy of maintaining "unfounded-freeness".

We empirically show that, thanks to its hybrid approach, *nomore++* outperforms *smodels* on relevant benchmarks. In fact, we mainly compare our approach to that of *smodels*. Our choice is motivated by the fact that both systems primarily address normal logic programs.[1] *dlv* and many of its distinguishing features are devised for dealing with the more expressive class of disjunctive logic programs. Also, *smodels* and *nomore++* share the same concept of "choice points", on which parts of our experiments rely upon.

The paper is organised as follows. After some preliminary definitions, we start with a strictly operational specification of *nomore++*. In fact, its configurable operator-based design is a salient feature of *nomore++*. We then concentrate on two specific features: First, we introduce *nomore++*'s lookahead operation and prove that, in terms of propagation, it is more powerful than the ones encountered in *smodels* and *noMoRe*. Second, we present *nomore++*'s strategy of keeping assignments unfounded-free. Finally, we provide selected experimental results backing up our claims.

---

[1] Unlike *smodels*, *nomore++* cannot (yet) handle cardinality and weight constraints.

G. Sutcliffe and A. Voronkov (Eds.): LPAR 2005, LNAI 3835, pp. 95–109, 2005.

2 Background

A *logic program* is a finite set of rules of the form

$$p_0 \leftarrow p_1, \ldots, p_m, not\ p_{m+1}, \ldots, not\ p_n, \tag{1}$$

where $n \geq m \geq 0$ and each p_i $(0 \leq i \leq n)$ is an *atom* in some alphabet $\mathcal{A}$. A *literal* is an atom p or its negation *not* p. For r as in (1), let $head(r) = p_0$ be the *head* of r and $body(r) = \{p_1, \ldots, p_m, not\ p_{m+1}, \ldots, not\ p_n\}$ be the *body* of r. Given a set X of literals, let $X^+ = \{p \in \mathcal{A} \mid p \in X\}$ and $X^- = \{p \in \mathcal{A} \mid not\ p \in X\}$. For $body(r)$, we then get $body(r)^+ = \{p_1, \ldots, p_m\}$ and $body(r)^- = \{p_{m+1}, \ldots, p_n\}$.

A logic program Π is called *basic* if $body(r)^- = \emptyset$ for all $r \in \Pi$. The *reduct*, Π^X, of Π relative to a set X of atoms is defined by

$$\Pi^X = \{head(r) \leftarrow body(r)^+ \mid r \in \Pi,\ body(r)^- \cap X = \emptyset\}.$$

A set X of atoms is closed under a basic program Π if, for any $r \in \Pi$, $head(r) \in X$ if $body(r)^+ \subseteq X$. $Cn(\Pi)$ denotes the smallest set of atoms closed under basic program Π. A set X of atoms is an *answer set* of a logic program Π if $Cn(\Pi^X) = X$.

As an example, consider program Π_1 comprising rules:

$$\begin{aligned} r_1 &: a \leftarrow not\ b \qquad & r_3 &: c \leftarrow not\ d \\ r_2 &: b \leftarrow not\ a \qquad & r_4 &: d \leftarrow not\ c \end{aligned} \tag{2}$$

We get four answer sets, viz. $\{a, c\}$, $\{a, d\}$, $\{b, c\}$, and $\{b, d\}$.

For a program Π, we write $head(\Pi) = \{head(r) \mid r \in \Pi\}$ and $body(\Pi) = \{body(r) \mid r \in \Pi\}$. We further extend this notation: For $h \in head(\Pi)$, define $body(h) = \{body(r) \mid r \in \Pi, head(r) = h\}$.

Without loss of generality, we restrict ourselves to programs Π satisfying $\{p \mid r \in \Pi, p \in body(r)^+ \cup body(r)^-\} \subseteq head(\Pi)$. That is, every body atom must occur as the head of some rule. Any program Π can be transformed into such a format, exploiting the fact that no atom in $(\mathcal{A} \setminus head(\Pi))$ is contained in any answer set of Π.

3 Operational Specification

We provide in this section a detailed operational specification of *nomore++*. The firm understanding of *nomore++*'s propagation mechanisms serves as a basis for formal comparisons with techniques used by *smodels* or *dlv*. We indicate how the operations applied by *nomore++* are related to well-known propagation principles, in particular, showing that our basic propagation operations are as powerful as those of *smodels* (cf. Theorem 1). Beyond this, the hybrid approach of *nomore++* allows for more flexible choices, in particular, leading to a more powerful lookahead, as we detail in Section 4.

We consider assignments that map heads and bodies of a program Π into $\{\oplus, \ominus\}$, indicating whether a head or body is true or false, respectively. Such assignments are extended in comparison to those used in literal-based solvers, such as *smodels* and *dlv*, or rule-based solvers, such as *noMoRe*. Formally, a (partial) assignment is a partial mapping $A : head(\Pi) \cup body(\Pi) \rightarrow \{\oplus, \ominus\}$. For simplicity, we often represent such an assignment A as a pair $(A^{\oplus}, A^{\ominus})$, where $A^{\oplus} = \{x \mid A(x) = \oplus\}$ and $A^{\ominus} = \{x \mid A(x) = \ominus\}$. Whenever $A^{\oplus} \cap A^{\ominus} \neq \emptyset$, then A is undefined as it is no mapping. We represent an undefined assignment by $(head(\Pi) \cup body(\Pi), head(\Pi) \cup body(\Pi))$. For comparing assignments A and B, we define $A \sqsubseteq B$, if $A^{\oplus} \subseteq B^{\oplus}$ and $A^{\ominus} \subseteq B^{\ominus}$. Also, we define $A \sqcup B$ as $(A^{\oplus} \cup B^{\oplus}, A^{\ominus} \cup B^{\ominus})$.

Forward propagation in *nomore++* can be divided into two sorts. Head-oriented propagation assigns $\oplus$ to a head if one of its associated bodies belongs to $A^{\oplus}$, it assigns $\ominus$ whenever all of a head's bodies are in $A^{\ominus}$. This kind of propagation is captured by sets $T_{\Pi}(A)$ and $\overline{T}_{\Pi}(A)$ in Definition 1. Body-oriented propagation is based on the concepts of *support* and *blockage*. A body is *supported* if all its positive literals belong to $A^{\oplus}$, it is *unsupported* if one of its positive literals is in $A^{\ominus}$. This is reflected by sets $S_{\Pi}(A)$ and $\overline{S}_{\Pi}(A)$ below. Analogously, but with roles partly interchanged, sets $B_{\Pi}(A)$ and $\overline{B}_{\Pi}(A)$ define whether a body is *blocked* or *unblocked*, respectively.[2]

Definition 1. *Let Π be a logic program and let A be a partial assignment of $head(\Pi) \cup body(\Pi)$. We define*

1. $T_{\Pi}(A) = \{h \in head(\Pi) \mid body(h) \cap A^{\oplus} \neq \emptyset\}$;
2. $\overline{T}_{\Pi}(A) = \{h \in head(\Pi) \mid body(h) \subseteq A^{\ominus}\}$;
3. $S_{\Pi}(A) = \{b \in body(\Pi) \mid b^{+} \subseteq A^{\oplus}\}$;
4. $\overline{S}_{\Pi}(A) = \{b \in body(\Pi) \mid b^{+} \cap A^{\ominus} \neq \emptyset\}$;
5. $B_{\Pi}(A) = \{b \in body(\Pi) \mid b^{-} \cap A^{\oplus} \neq \emptyset\}$;
6. $\overline{B}_{\Pi}(A) = \{b \in body(\Pi) \mid b^{-} \subseteq A^{\ominus}\}$.

We omit the subscript Π whenever it is clear from the context. In what follows, we also adopt this convention for similar concepts without further notice.

Based on the above sets, we define forward propagation operator $\mathcal{P}$ as follows.

Definition 2. *Let Π be a logic program and let A be a partial assignment of $head(\Pi) \cup body(\Pi)$. We define*

$$\mathcal{P}_{\Pi}(A) = A \sqcup (T(A) \cup (S(A) \cap \overline{B}(A)), \overline{T}(A) \cup \overline{S}(A) \cup B(A)) .$$

A head is assigned $\oplus$ if it belongs to $T(A)$; a body must be supported as well as unblocked, namely, belong to $S(A) \cap \overline{B}(A)$. Conversely, a body is assigned $\ominus$ whenever it is unsupported or blocked, i.e. in $\overline{S}(A) \cup B(A)$; a head must be in $\overline{T}(A)$.

For example, let us apply $\mathcal{P}$ to $A_0 = (\{body(r_1)\}, \emptyset)$ on Π_1:

$$\begin{array}{lll}
\mathcal{P}(A_0) = A_1 = (\{a, body(r_1)\}, \emptyset) & \text{by } T(A_0) \\
\mathcal{P}(A_1) = A_2 = (\{a, body(r_1)\}, \{body(r_2)\}) & \text{by } B(A_1) \\
\mathcal{P}(A_2) = A_3 = (\{a, body(r_1)\}, \{b, body(r_2)\}) & \text{by } \overline{T}(A_2)
\end{array}$$

Note that A_3 is closed under $\mathcal{P}$, that is, $\mathcal{P}(A_3) = A_3$.

For describing the saturated result of operators' application, we need the following definition. Let $\mathcal{O}$ be a collection (possibly a singleton) of operators and let A be a partial

---

[2] We systematically use over-lining for indicating sets with antonymous contents.

assignment. Then, we denote by $\mathcal{O}^*(A)$ the $\sqsubseteq$-smallest partial assignment containing A and being closed under all operators in $\mathcal{O}$. In the above example, we get $\mathcal{P}^*(A_0) = A_3$.

Backward propagation can be viewed as an inversion of $\mathcal{P}$. For example, consider the definition of $T(A)$ and suppose $h \in head(\Pi) \cap A^\oplus$ whereas $body(h) \cap A^\oplus = \emptyset$, that is, no body of any rule with head h has been assigned $\oplus$ so far. Hence, h is not "produced" by $T(A)$. Yet there must be some body $b \in body(h)$ that is eventually assigned $\oplus$, otherwise h cannot be true. However, this body can only be determined if all other bodies are already in $A^\ominus$. This leads us to the definition of $T_\Pi^b(A)$.[3] Analogously, we can derive the following sets.[4]

Definition 3. *Let Π be a logic program and let A be a partial assignment of $head(\Pi) \cup body(\Pi)$. We define*

1. $T_\Pi^b(A) = \{b \mid b \in body(h), h \in head(\Pi) \cap A^\oplus,\ body(h) \setminus \{b\} \subseteq A^\ominus\}$;
2. $\overline{T}_\Pi^b(A) = \{b \mid b \in body(h), h \in head(\Pi) \cap A^\ominus\}$;
3. $S_\Pi^b(A) = \{h \mid h \in b^+, b \in body(\Pi) \cap A^\oplus\}$;
4. $\overline{S}_\Pi^b(A) = \{h \mid h \in b^+, b \in body(\Pi) \cap A^\ominus \cap \overline{B}(A),\ b^+ \setminus \{h\} \subseteq A^\oplus\}$;
5. $B_\Pi^b(A) = \{h \mid h \in b^-, b \in body(\Pi) \cap A^\ominus \cap S(A),\ b^- \setminus \{h\} \subseteq A^\ominus\}$;
6. $\overline{B}_\Pi^b(A) = \{h \mid h \in b^-, b \in body(\Pi) \cap A^\oplus\}$.

Combining the above sets yields backward propagation operator $\mathcal{B}$.

Definition 4. *Let Π be a logic program and let A be a partial assignment of $head(\Pi) \cup body(\Pi)$. We define*

$$\mathcal{B}_\Pi(A) = A \sqcup (T^b(A) \cup S^b(A) \cup B^b(A),\ \overline{T}^b(A) \cup \overline{S}^b(A) \cup \overline{B}^b(A)) .$$

Adding the rule $b \leftarrow c$ to program Π_1 still gives $\mathcal{P}(A_3) = A_3$. Due to the fact that $b \in A_3^\ominus$, iterated application of $\mathcal{B}$ additionally yields:

$$
\begin{array}{llll}
\mathcal{B}(A_3) = & A_4 & = A_3 \sqcup (\emptyset, \{\{c\}\}) & \text{by } \overline{T}^b(A_3) \\
\mathcal{B}(A_4) = & A_5 & = A_3 \sqcup (\emptyset, \{\{c\}, c\}) & \text{by } \overline{S}^b(A_4) \\
\mathcal{B}(A_5) = & A_6 & = A_3 \sqcup (\emptyset, \{\{c\}, c, body(r_3)\}) & \text{by } \overline{T}^b(A_5) \\
\mathcal{B}(A_6) = & A_7 & = A_3 \sqcup (\{d\}, \{\{c\}, c, body(r_3)\}) & \text{by } B^b(A_6) \\
\mathcal{B}(A_7) = \mathcal{B}^*(A_3) & = A_3 \sqcup (\{d, body(r_4)\}, \{\{c\}, c, body(r_3)\}) & \text{by } T^b(A_7)
\end{array}
$$

The next definition elucidates the notion of an unfounded set [6] in our context. Given an assignment A, the *greatest unfounded set* of heads and bodies, $U_\Pi(A)$, is defined in terms of the still potentially derivable atoms in $\overline{U}_\Pi(A)$.

Definition 5. *Let Π be a logic program and let A be a partial assignment of $head(\Pi) \cup body(\Pi)$. We define*

$$U_\Pi(A) = \{b \in body(\Pi) \mid b^+ \not\subseteq \overline{U}_\Pi(A)\} \cup \{h \in head(\Pi) \mid h \notin \overline{U}_\Pi(A)\}$$

where $\overline{U}_\Pi(A) = Cn((\Pi \setminus \{r \in \Pi \mid body(r) \in A^\ominus\})^\emptyset)$.

---

[3] We use the superscript ^{b} to indicate sets used in backward propagation.
[4] The relation between $\mathcal{P}$ and $\mathcal{B}$ will be detailed in the full paper.

The set $\overline{U}(A)$ of potentially derivable atoms is formed by removing all rules whose bodies belong to $A^{\ominus}$. The resulting subprogram is reduced with respect to the empty set so that we can compute its (potential) consequences by means of the Cn operator, as defined for basic programs in Section 2.

The following operator $\mathcal{U}$ falsifies all elements in a greatest unfounded set.

Definition 6. *Let Π be a logic program and let A be a partial assignment of $head(\Pi)\cup body(\Pi)$. We define*

$$\mathcal{U}_{\Pi}(A) = A \sqcup (\emptyset, U(A)) .$$

Consider program Π_2, obtained from Π_1 by adding rules

$$r_5 : e \leftarrow not\ a, not\ c, \quad r_6 : e \leftarrow f, not\ b, \quad r_7 : f \leftarrow e, \tag{3}$$

and assignment $A = (\emptyset, \{body(r_5)\})$.[5] We then have $\overline{U}(A) = Cn((\Pi_2 \setminus \{r_5\})^{\emptyset}) = Cn(\{a \leftarrow,\ b \leftarrow,\ c \leftarrow,\ d \leftarrow,\ e \leftarrow f,\ f \leftarrow e\}) = \{a, b, c, d\}$, and thus we obtain $\mathcal{U}(A) = (\emptyset, \{body(r_5), e, body(r_6), f, body(r_7)\})$. As we detail in the full paper, the assignment $(\mathcal{PU})^*((\emptyset, \emptyset))$ amounts to a program's well-founded semantics [6].

Let us compare the introduced operators to propagation in *smodels*, which is based on two functions, called *atleast* and *atmost*. Function *atleast* computes deterministic consequences by forward and backward propagation, Function *atmost* is the counterpart of $\overline{U}(A)$ and amounts to $Cn((\Pi \setminus \{r \mid body(r)^+ \cap A^{\ominus} \neq \emptyset\})^{A^{\oplus} \cap head(\Pi)})$. In [1], *smodels'* assignments are represented as sets of literals. Although we refrain from giving a formal definition, we however mention that *atleast* bounds the set of true literals from "below" and that *atmost* bounds the set of true atoms from "above".

Theorem 1. *Let Π be a logic program. Let X be a partial assignment of $head(\Pi)$ and let A be a partial assignment of $head(\Pi) \cup body(\Pi)$ such that $(A^{\oplus}, A^{\ominus}) = (X^+, X^-)$.[6] Then, we have the following results.*

1. *Let $Y = atleast(\Pi, X)$ and $B = (\mathcal{PB})^*(A)$.*
   If $Y^+ \cap Y^- = \emptyset$ and $B^{\oplus} \cap B^{\ominus} = \emptyset$, then $(Y^+, Y^-) = (B^{\oplus} \cap head(\Pi), B^{\ominus} \cap head(\Pi))$; otherwise, $Y^+ \cap Y^- \neq \emptyset$ and $B^{\oplus} \cap B^{\ominus} \neq \emptyset$.
2. *Let $Y = X \sqcup (\emptyset, head(\Pi) \setminus atmost(\Pi, X))$ and $B = \mathcal{U}(\mathcal{P}(A))$.*
   If $Y^+ \cap Y^- = \emptyset$ and $B^{\oplus} \cap B^{\ominus} = \emptyset$, then $(Y^+, Y^-) = (B^{\oplus} \cap head(\Pi), B^{\ominus} \cap head(\Pi))$; otherwise, $Y^+ \cap Y^- \neq \emptyset$ and $B^{\oplus} \cap B^{\ominus} \neq \emptyset$.

The above results show that *nomore++*'s basic propagation operations $\mathcal{P}$, $\mathcal{B}$, and $\mathcal{U}$ are as powerful as those of *smodels*. The reason why $\mathcal{P}$ is applied once in 2. is that initially A assigns no values to bodies in order to be comparable to *smodels'* assignment X.

Concluding with basic propagation, we mention that $\mathcal{P}$ corresponds to Fitting's operator [7], $(\mathcal{PB})$ coincides to unit propagation on a program's completion [8], $(\mathcal{PU})$ amounts to propagation via well-founded semantics [6], and $(\mathcal{PBU})$ matches *smodels'* propagation, that is, well-founded semantics enhanced by backward propagation.

---

[5] The situation that a body is in $A^{\ominus}$ without belonging to $\overline{S}(A) \cup B(A)$ is common in *nomore++*, as bodies can be taken as choices.

[6] Note that $(A^{\oplus} \cap body(\Pi), A^{\ominus} \cap body(\Pi)) = (\emptyset, \emptyset)$.

The first differences to well-known approaches are encountered at choices. In *smod-els* and *dlv*, choices are restricted to heads; *noMoRe* chooses on rules (comparable to bodies) only. Unlike this, *nomore++* generally allows for choosing to assign values to heads as well as bodies, and we define *nomore++*'s choice operator C as follows.

Definition 7. *Let Π be a logic program, let A be a partial assignment of $head(\Pi) \cup body(\Pi)$, and let $X \subseteq head(\Pi) \cup body(\Pi)$. We define*

1. $C_\Pi^\oplus(A, X) = (A^\oplus \cup \{x\}, A^\ominus)$ *for some $x \in X \setminus (A^\oplus \cup A^\ominus)$;*
2. $C_\Pi^\ominus(A, X) = (A^\oplus, A^\ominus \cup \{x\})$ *for some $x \in X \setminus (A^\oplus \cup A^\ominus)$.*

The set X delineates the set of possible choices. In general, the chosen object $x \in X$ can be any unassigned head or body.

The possibility of choosing among heads and bodies provides us with great flexibility. Notably, some choices have a higher information gain than others. On the one hand, setting a head to $\ominus$ yields more information than choosing some body to be $\ominus$. Negating some head h by $\ominus$ implies that all bodies in $body(h)$ are false (via $\mathcal{B}$). Conversely, choosing a body to be $\ominus$ has generally no direct effect on the body's heads because there may be alternative rules (i.e. other bodies) sharing the same heads. Also, we normally gain no information on the constituent literals of the body. On the other hand, assigning $\oplus$ to bodies is superior to assigning $\oplus$ to heads. When we choose $\oplus$ for a body, we infer that its heads must be assigned $\oplus$ as well (via $\mathcal{P}$). Moreover, assigning $\oplus$ to a body b implies that every literal in b is true (via $\mathcal{B}$). Unlike this, choosing $\oplus$ for some head does generally not allow to determine a corresponding body that justifies this choice and would then be assigned $\oplus$, too. The observation that assigning $\ominus$ to heads and $\oplus$ to bodies, respectively, subsumes the opposite assignments also fortifies *nomore++*'s lookahead strategy, detailed in Section 4.

Following [9], we characterise the process of answer set formation by a sequence of assignments.

Theorem 2. *Let Π be a logic program, let A be a total assignment of $head(\Pi) \cup body(\Pi)$, and let $X = head(\Pi) \cup body(\Pi)$. Then, $A^\oplus \cap head(\Pi)$ is an answer set of Π iff there exists a sequence $(A^i)_{0 \leq i \leq n}$ of assignments with the following properties:*

1. $A^0 = (\mathcal{PBU})^*((\emptyset, \emptyset))$;
2. $A^{i+1} = (\mathcal{PBU})^*(C^\circ(A^i, X))$ *for some $\circ \in \{\oplus, \ominus\}$ and $0 \leq i < n$;*
3. $A^n = A$.

The intersection $A^\oplus \cap head(\Pi)$ accomplishes a projection to heads and thus to the atoms forming an answer set. Many different strategies can be shown to be sound and complete. For instance, the above result still holds after eliminating $\mathcal{B}$. (For simplicity, we refer to these strategies by $(\mathcal{PBU})^*C$ or $(\mathcal{PU})^*C$, respectively. We also drop superscripts $\oplus$ and $\ominus$ from C when referring to either case.) As with computational strategies, alternative choices, expressed by X, are possible. For example, Theorem 2 also holds for $X = head(\Pi)$ or $X = body(\Pi)$, respectively, mimicking a literal-based approach such as *smodels'* one or a rule-based approach as the one of *noMoRe*. A further restriction of choices is discussed in Section 5.

Although we cannot provide the details here, it is noteworthy to mention that allowing $X = head(\Pi) \cup body(\Pi)$ as choices leads to an exponentially stronger proof system (in terms of proof complexity [10], i.e. minimal proofs for unsatisfiability) in comparison to either $X = head(\Pi)$ or $X = body(\Pi)$. The comparison between different proof systems and proof complexity results will be key issues in the full paper.

4   Lookahead

We have seen that *nomore++*'s basic propagation is as powerful as that of *smodels*. An effective way of strengthening propagation is to use *lookahead*.[7] Apart from specifying *nomore++*'s lookahead, we demonstrate below that a *hybrid* lookahead strategy, incorporating heads and bodies, allows for stronger propagation than a *uniform* one using only either heads or bodies. Uniform lookahead is for instance used in *smodels* on literals and in *noMoRe* on rules (comparable to bodies). However, we do not want to put more computational effort into hybrid lookahead than needed in the uniform case. The solution is simple: Assigning $\ominus$ to heads and $\oplus$ to bodies within lookahead is, in combination with propagation, powerful enough to compensate for the omitted assignments.

First of all, we operationally define our lookahead operator $\mathcal{L}$ as follows.

Definition 8. *Let Π be a logic program and let A be a partial assignment of $head(\Pi) \cup body(\Pi)$. Furthermore, let $\mathcal{O}$ be a collection of operators.*

For $x \in (head(\Pi) \cup body(\Pi)) \setminus (A^{\oplus} \cup A^{\ominus})$, we define:

$$\ell_{\Pi}^{\oplus,\mathcal{O}}(A, x) = \begin{cases} (A^{\oplus}, A^{\ominus} \cup \{x\}) & \text{if } \mathcal{O}^*((A^{\oplus} \cup \{x\}, A^{\ominus})) \text{ is undefined} \\ A & \text{otherwise} \end{cases}$$

$$\ell_{\Pi}^{\ominus,\mathcal{O}}(A, x) = \begin{cases} (A^{\oplus} \cup \{x\}, A^{\ominus}) & \text{if } \mathcal{O}^*((A^{\oplus}, A^{\ominus} \cup \{x\})) \text{ is undefined} \\ A & \text{otherwise} \end{cases}$$

For $X \subseteq head(\Pi) \cup body(\Pi)$, we define:

$$\mathcal{L}_{\Pi}^{\oplus,\mathcal{O}}(A, X) = \bigsqcup_{x \in X \setminus (A^{\oplus} \cup A^{\ominus})} \ell_{\Pi}^{\oplus,\mathcal{O}}(A, x)$$

$$\mathcal{L}_{\Pi}^{\ominus,\mathcal{O}}(A, X) = \bigsqcup_{x \in X \setminus (A^{\oplus} \cup A^{\ominus})} \ell_{\Pi}^{\ominus,\mathcal{O}}(A, x)$$

$$\mathcal{L}_{\Pi}^{\mathcal{O}}(A, X) = \mathcal{L}_{\Pi}^{\oplus,\mathcal{O}}(A, X) \sqcup \mathcal{L}_{\Pi}^{\ominus,\mathcal{O}}(A, X)$$

Observe that, according to the above definition, elementary lookahead ℓ can only be applied to an unassigned head or body x. For such an x, ℓ tests whether assigning and propagating a value leads to a conflict. If so, the opposite value is assigned. We stipulate x to be unassigned because the intended purpose of lookahead is gaining information from imminent conflicts when basic propagation is stuck, hence the name "lookahead".

Our lookahead operator $\mathcal{L}$ can be parametrised in several ways. First, one can decide on a set $X \subseteq head(\Pi) \cup body(\Pi)$ to apply ℓ to. Second, either $\oplus$, $\ominus$, or both of them, one after the other, can be temporarily assigned and propagated. Third, the collection $\mathcal{O}$ determines the propagation operators to be applied inside lookahead, which can be

---

[7] Note that we consider lookahead primarily as a propagation operation, such as $\mathcal{P}$, $\mathcal{B}$, and $\mathcal{U}$. Supplementary, lookahead is often also used for gathering heuristic values for the selection of choices. As with *smodels* and *dlv*, this information is exploited by *nomore++* as well.

different from the ones used outside lookahead. The general definition allows us to describe and to compare different variants of lookahead.

In what follows, we detail *nomore++*'s hybrid lookahead on heads and bodies and show that it is strictly stronger than uniform lookahead on only either heads or bodies, without being computationally more expensive. To start with, observe that *full* hybrid lookahead by $\mathcal{L}^{\mathcal{O}}(A, head(\Pi) \cup body(\Pi))$ is the most powerful lookahead operation with respect to some $\mathcal{O}$. That is, anything inferred by a restricted lookahead is also inferred by full hybrid lookahead. Given that full hybrid lookahead has to temporarily assign both values, $\oplus$ and $\ominus$, to each unassigned head and body, it is also the computationally most expensive lookahead operation. In the worst case, there might be $2 * (|head(\Pi)| + |body(\Pi)|)$ applications of ℓ without inferring anything.

The high computational cost of full hybrid lookahead is the reason why *nomore++* applies a *restricted* hybrid lookahead. Despite the restrictions, *nomore++*'s hybrid lookahead does not sacrifice propagational strength and is in combination with propagation as powerful as full hybrid lookahead (see *3.* in Theorem 3 below). The observations made on choices in the previous section provide an explanation on how a more powerful hybrid lookahead operation can be obtained without reasonably increasing the computational cost in comparison to uniform lookahead on only either heads or bodies: Assigning $\ominus$ to a head subsumes assigning $\ominus$ to one of its bodies, assigning $\oplus$ to a body subsumes assigning $\oplus$ to one of its heads. That is why *nomore++*'s hybrid lookahead applies $\ell^{\ominus,\mathcal{O}}$ to heads and $\ell^{\oplus,\mathcal{O}}$ to bodies only. Provided that $\mathcal{P}$ belongs to $\mathcal{O}$ and that all operators in $\mathcal{O}$ are monotonic (like, for instance, $\mathcal{P}$, $\mathcal{B}$, and $\mathcal{U}$), *nomore++*'s hybrid lookahead has the same propagational strength as full hybrid lookahead.

Theorem 3. *Let Π be a logic program. Let A be a partial assignment of $head(\Pi) \cup body(\Pi)$ and let*

$$B = \mathcal{P}(\mathcal{L}^{\oplus,\mathcal{O}}(A, body(\Pi))) \sqcup \mathcal{L}^{\ominus,\mathcal{O}}(A, head(\Pi)) \ .$$

Then, for every collection $\mathcal{O}$ of $\sqsubseteq$-monotonic operators such that $\mathcal{P} \in \mathcal{O}$, we have

1. $\mathcal{L}^{\mathcal{O}}(A, head(\Pi)) \sqsubseteq B$;
2. $\mathcal{L}^{\mathcal{O}}(A, body(\Pi)) \sqsubseteq \mathcal{P}(B)$;
3. $\mathcal{L}^{\mathcal{O}}(A, head(\Pi) \cup body(\Pi)) \sqsubseteq \mathcal{P}(B)$.

Fact *3.* states that *nomore++*'s lookahead is, in combination with propagation, as powerful as full hybrid lookahead. Facts *1.* and *2.* constitute that it is always at least as powerful as any kind of uniform lookahead. Thereby, condition $\mathcal{P} \in \mathcal{O}$ stipulates that propagation (within lookahead) must be at least as powerful as Fitting's operator. Unlike this, the occurrences of $\mathcal{P}$ in B, *2.*, and *3.* are only of formal nature and needed for synchronising heads and bodies. In practise, lookahead is interleaved with $\mathcal{P}$ anyway, since it is integrated into propagation, viz. $(\mathcal{PBUL})^*$. More importantly, *nomore++*'s restricted hybrid lookahead, assigning $\ominus$ to heads and $\oplus$ to bodies only, faces approximately the same computational efforts as encountered in the uniform case and not more than the most consuming uniform lookahead, since $2 * min\{|head(\Pi)|, |body(\Pi)|\} \leq |head(\Pi)| + |body(\Pi)| \leq 2 * max\{|head(\Pi)|, |body(\Pi)|\}$.[8]

---

[8] For both, heads and bodies, we have $|head(\Pi)| \leq |\Pi|$ and $|body(\Pi)| \leq |\Pi|$, respectively. In uniform cases, factor 2 accounts for assigning *both* values, $\oplus$ and $\ominus$, one after the other.

$$\Pi_b^n = \left\{ \begin{array}{lll} r_0 : x \leftarrow not\ x \\ r_1 : x \leftarrow a_1, b_1 & r_2 : a_1 \leftarrow not\ b_1 & r_3 : b_1 \leftarrow not\ a_1 \\ \vdots \\ r_{3n-2} : x \leftarrow a_n, b_n & r_{3n-1} : a_n \leftarrow not\ b_n & r_{3n} : b_n \leftarrow not\ a_n \end{array} \right\}$$

$$\Pi_h^n = \left\{ \begin{array}{llll} r_0 : x \leftarrow c_1, \ldots, c_n, not\ x \\ r_1 : c_1 \leftarrow a_1 & r_2 : c_1 \leftarrow b_1 & r_3 : a_1 \leftarrow not\ b_1 & r_4 : b_1 \leftarrow not\ a_1 \\ \vdots \\ r_{4n-3} : c_n \leftarrow a_n & r_{4n-2} : c_n \leftarrow b_n & r_{4n-1} : a_n \leftarrow not\ b_n & r_{4n} : b_n \leftarrow not\ a_n \end{array} \right\}$$

Fig. 1. Lookahead programs Π_b^n and Π_h^n for some $n \geq 0$

Finally, let us demonstrate that *nomore++*'s hybrid lookahead is in fact *strictly* more powerful than uniform ones. Consider Programs Π_b^n and Π_h^n, given in Figure 1. Both programs have, due to rule r_0 in the respective program, no answer sets and are thus unsatisfiable. For Program Π_b^n, this can be found out by assigning $\oplus$ to bodies of the form $\{a_i, b_i\}$ $(1 \leq i \leq n)$ and by backward propagation via $\mathcal{B}$. With Program Π_h^n, assigning $\ominus$ to an atom c_i $(1 \leq i \leq n)$ leads to a conflict by backward propagation via $\mathcal{B}$. Provided that $\mathcal{B}$ belongs to $\mathcal{O}$ in $\mathcal{L}^{\mathcal{O}}$,[9] body-based lookahead detects the unsatisfiability of Π_b^n, and head-based lookahead does the same for Π_h^n. Hence, *nomore++*'s hybrid lookahead detects the unsatisfiability of both programs without any choices being made. Unlike this, detecting the unsatisfiability of Π_b^n with head-based lookahead and choices restricted to heads (*smodels'* strategy) requires exponentially many choices in n. The same holds for Π_h^n with body-based lookahead and choices restricted to bodies (*noMoRe*'s strategy). Respective benchmark results are provided in Section 6.

5 Maintaining Unfounded-Freeness

A characteristic feature, distinguishing logic programming from propositional logic, is that true atoms must be derived via the rules of a logic program. For problems that involve reasoning, e.g. Hamiltonian cycles, this allows for more elegant and compact encodings in logic programming than in propositional logic. Such logic programming encodings produce *non-tight* programs [11, 12], for which there is a mismatch between answer sets and the models of programs' completions [8]. The mismatch is due to the potential of circular support among atoms. Such circularity is prohibited by the answer set semantics, but not by the semantics of propositional logic. The necessity of supporting true atoms non-circularly is reflected by propagation operator $\mathcal{U}$ in Section 3.

We detail in this section how our extended concept of an assignment, incorporating bodies in addition to heads, can be used for avoiding that atoms assigned $\oplus$ are subsequently detected to be unfounded. (Note that such a situation results in a conflict.) More formally, our goal is to avoid that atoms belonging to $A^{\oplus}$ in an assignment A are contained in $U(B)$ for some extension B of A, i.e. $A \sqsubseteq B$. We therefore devise a

---

[9] If $\mathcal{B} \notin \mathcal{O}$, neither variant of lookahead detects unsatisfiability without making choices.

computational strategy that is based on a modified choice operator, largely preventing conflicts due to true atoms becoming unfounded as a result of some later step. Finally, we point out how our computational strategy facilitates the implementation of operator $\mathcal{U}$ and which measures must be taken in the implementation of operators $\mathcal{B}$ and $\mathcal{L}$.

Let us first reconsider program Π_2 in (2) and (3) for illustrating the problem of true atoms participating in an unfounded set. Assume that the collection $(\mathcal{PBU})$ of operators is used for propagation and that we start with $A_0 = (\mathcal{PBU})^*((\emptyset, \emptyset)) = (\emptyset, \emptyset)$. Let our first choice be applying $\mathcal{C}^{\oplus}$ to atom e. We obtain

$$A_1 = (\mathcal{PBU})^*(((\{e\}, \emptyset)) = (\{e, f, body(r_7)\}, \emptyset).$$

At this point, we cannot determine a rule for deriving the true atom e, since we have two possibilities, r_5 and r_6. Let us apply $\mathcal{C}^{\oplus}$ to atom d next. We obtain

$$A_2 = (\mathcal{PBU})^*(A_1 \sqcup (\{d\}, \emptyset)) = A_1 \sqcup (\{d, body(r_4)\}, \{c, body(r_3)\}).$$

Still we do not know whether to use r_5 or r_6 for deriving e. Our next choice is applying $\mathcal{C}^{\oplus}$ to atom a, and propagation via $(\mathcal{PB})$ yields

$$
\begin{aligned}
A'_2 &= (\mathcal{PB})^*(A_2 \sqcup (\{a\}, \emptyset)) \\
&= A_2 \sqcup (\{a, body(r_1), body(r_6)\}, \{b, body(r_2), body(r_5)\}).
\end{aligned}
$$

We have $U(A'_2) = \{b, c, e, f, body(r_6), body(r_7)\}$, and $\mathcal{U}(A'_2)$ yields a conflict on atoms e and f and on bodies $body(r_6)$ and $body(r_7)$.

The reason for such a conflict is applying choice operator $\mathcal{C}^{\oplus}$ to a head or a body lacking an established non-circular support. Consider a head h that is in $A^{\oplus}$, but not in $T(A)$, that is, h has not been derived by a rule yet. Supposing that h is not unfounded with respect to A, i.e. $h \notin U(A)$, some of the bodies in $body(h)$ might still be assigned $\ominus$ in the ongoing computation. As a consequence, all bodies potentially providing a non-circular support for h might be contained in $B^{\ominus}$ for some extension B of A, that is, $A \sqsubseteq B$. For such an assignment B, we then have $h \in U(B)$, and propagation via $\mathcal{U}$ leads to a conflict. Similarly, a body b that is in $A^{\oplus}$ but not supported with respect to A, i.e. $b \notin S(A)$, can be unfounded in an assignment B such that $A \sqsubseteq B$, as some positive literal in b^+ might be contained in $U(B)$.

Conflicts due to $\oplus$-assigned heads and bodies becoming unfounded cannot occur when non-circular support is already established. That is, every head in $A^{\oplus}$ must be derived by a body that is in $A^{\oplus}$, too. Similarly, the positive part b^+ of a body b in $A^{\oplus}$ must be derived by other bodies in $A^{\oplus}$. This leads us to the following definition.

Definition 9. *Let Π be a logic program and let A be an assignment of $head(\Pi) \cup body(\Pi)$. We define A as unfounded-free, if*

$$\left(head(\Pi) \cap A^{\oplus}\right) \cup \left(\bigcup_{b \in body(\Pi) \cap A^{\oplus}} b^+\right) \subseteq Cn(\{r \in \Pi \mid body(r) \in A^{\oplus}\}^{\emptyset}) .$$

Heads and bodies in the positive part, $A^{\oplus}$, of an unfounded-free assignment A cannot be unfounded with respect to any extension of A.

Theorem 4. *Let Π be a logic program and let A be an unfounded-free assignment of $head(\Pi) \cup body(\Pi)$. Then, $A^{\oplus} \cap U(B) = \emptyset$ for any assignment B such that $A \sqsubseteq B$.*

Unfounded-freeness is maintained by forward propagation operator $\mathcal{P}$. That is, when applied to an unfounded-free assignment, operator $\mathcal{P}$ produces again an unfounded-free assignment.

Theorem 5. *Let Π be a logic program and let A be an unfounded-free assignment of $head(\Pi) \cup body(\Pi)$. If $\mathcal{P}(A)$ is defined, then $\mathcal{P}(A)$ is unfounded-free.*

For illustrating the above result, reconsider Π_2 in (2) and (3) and assignment $A = (\{body(r_5)\}, \emptyset)$. A is unfounded-free because $body(r_5)^+ = \emptyset \subseteq Cn(\{e \leftarrow\}) = \{e\}$. We obtain $\mathcal{P}^*(A) = (\{body(r_5), e, body(r_7), f\}, \emptyset)$, which is again unfounded-free, since $\{e, f\} \cup body(r_5)^+ \cup body(r_7)^+ = \{e, f\} \subseteq Cn(\{e \leftarrow, f \leftarrow e\}) = \{e, f\}$.

In order to guarantee unfounded-freeness for choice operator $\mathcal{C}^\oplus$, the set X of heads and bodies to choose from has to be restricted appropriately. To this end, *nomore++* provides the following instance of $\mathcal{C}$.

Definition 10. *Let Π be a logic program and let A be a partial assignment of $head(\Pi) \cup body(\Pi)$. We define*

1. $\mathcal{D}_\Pi^\oplus(A) = \mathcal{C}_\Pi^\oplus(A, (body(\Pi) \cap S(A)))$;
2. $\mathcal{D}_\Pi^\ominus(A) = \mathcal{C}_\Pi^\ominus(A, (body(\Pi) \cap S(A)))$.

Operator $\mathcal{D}$ differs from $\mathcal{C}$ in restricting its choices to supported bodies. This still guarantees completeness, as an assignment A that is closed under $(\mathcal{PBU})$ is total if $(body(\Pi) \cap S(A)) \setminus (A^\oplus \cup A^\ominus) = \emptyset$.[10]

Like $\mathcal{P}$, operator $\mathcal{D}$ maintains unfounded-freeness.

Theorem 6. *Let Π be a logic program and let A be an unfounded-free partial assignment of $head(\Pi) \cup body(\Pi)$ such that $(body(\Pi) \cap S(A)) \setminus (A^\oplus \cup A^\ominus) \neq \emptyset$. Then, $\mathcal{D}^\circ(A)$ is unfounded-free for $\circ \in \{\oplus, \ominus\}$.*

Note that there is no choice operator like $\mathcal{D}$ for heads. A head h having a true body, i.e. $body(h) \cap A^\oplus \neq \emptyset$, is already decided through $\mathcal{P}$. Thus, h cannot be assigned $\ominus$ and is no reasonable choice. On the other hand, if we concentrate on heads having a body that is supported but not already decided, i.e. there is a body $b \in (body(h) \cap S(A)) \setminus (B(A) \cup \overline{B}(A))$, such a b can still be assigned $\ominus$ in some later step. That is, a head chosen to be true can still become unfounded later on.

Unlike $\mathcal{P}$ and $\mathcal{D}$, backward propagation $\mathcal{B}$ and lookahead $\mathcal{L}$ can generally not maintain unfounded-freeness, as they assign $\oplus$ for other reasons than support. That is why we introduce at the implementation level a *weak* counterpart of $\oplus$, denoted by $\otimes$.[11] Value $\otimes$ indicates that some head or body, for which non-circular support is not yet established, must eventually be assigned $\oplus$. In the implementation, only $\mathcal{P}$ and $\mathcal{D}$ assign $\oplus$, while operators $\mathcal{B}$, $\mathcal{C}$, and $\mathcal{L}$ can only assign $\otimes$ (or $\ominus$).[12] Any head or body in $A^\otimes$ can be turned into $\oplus$ by $\mathcal{P}$ without causing a conflict. So, by distinguishing

---

[10] Note that any body whose literals are true is in $A^\oplus$ due to $\mathcal{P}$. All other bodies either contain a false literal and are in $A^\ominus$ due to $\mathcal{P}$, or they positively depend on unfounded atoms in $U(A)$ and are in $A^\ominus$ due to $\mathcal{U}$.

[11] Similar to *dlv*'s *must-be-true* [13]; see Section 7.

[12] Please note that $\mathcal{P}$ retains $\otimes$ when propagating from $\otimes$. Also, a body b cannot be chosen by $\mathcal{D}$ if some $h \in b^+$ is in $A^\otimes$.

two types of "true", we guarantee unfounded-freeness for the $\oplus$-assigned part of an assignment.

Maintaining unfounded-freeness allows for a lazy implementation of operator $\mathcal{U}$. That is, the scope of $U(A)$ (cf. Definition 5) can be restricted to $(head(\Pi) \cup body(\Pi)) \setminus (A^\oplus \cup A^\ominus)$, taking the non-circular support of $A^\oplus$ for granted. In other words, the computation of $U(A)$ is restricted to heads and bodies being either unassigned or assigned $\otimes$. Beside the fact that $\mathcal{D}$ can assign $\oplus$ and $\mathcal{C}$ only $\otimes$, using $\mathcal{D}$ instead of $\mathcal{C}$ helps in avoiding that true atoms lead to a conflict by participating in an unfounded set. This can be crucial for efficiently computing answer sets of non-tight programs, as the benchmark results in the next section demonstrate.

6   System Design and Experimental Results

nomore++ is implemented in C++ and uses *lparse* as parser. A salient feature of *nomore++* is that it facilitates the use of different sets of operators. For instance, if called with command line option "`--choice-op C --lookahead-op PB`", it uses operator $\mathcal{C}$ for choices and $(\mathcal{PB})$ for propagation within lookahead. The default strategy of *nomore++* is applying $(\mathcal{PBUL})$ for propagation, where lookahead by $\mathcal{L}$ works as detailed in Section 4, and $\mathcal{D}$ as choice operator. By default, $(\mathcal{PBU})$ is used for propagation within lookahead. The system is freely available at [14].

Due to space limitations, we confine our listed experiments to selected benchmarks illustrating the major features of *nomore++*. A complete evaluation, including further ASP solvers, e.g. *assat* and *cmodels*, can be found at the ASP benchmarking site [15]. All tests were run on an AMD Athlon 1.4GHz PC with 512MB RAM. As in the context of [15], a memory limit of 256MB as well as a time limit of 900s have been enforced. All results are given in terms of number of choices and seconds (in parentheses), reflecting the average of 10 runs.

Let us note that, due to the fairly early development state of *nomore++*, its base speed is still inferior to more mature ASP solvers, like *smodels* or *dlv*.

This can for instance be seen in the results of the "Same Generation" benchmark, where *smodels* outperforms *nomore++* roughly by a factor of two (cf. [15]).[13] Despite this, the selected experiments demonstrate the computational value of crucial features of *nomore++* and provide an indication of the prospect of the overall approach.

In all test series, we ran *smodels* with its (head-based) lookahead and *dlv*. For a complement, we also give tests for *nomore++* with body-based lookahead $\mathcal{L}^{(\mathcal{PBU})}(A, body(\Pi))$ for an assignment A and a program Π, abridged $\mathcal{L}_b$. The tests with *nomore++*'s hybrid lookahead rely on $\mathcal{L}^{\oplus,(\mathcal{PBU})}(A, body(\Pi)) \sqcup \mathcal{L}^{\ominus,(\mathcal{PBU})}(A, head(\Pi))$, abbreviated by $\mathcal{L}_{bh}$.

For illustrating the effect of maintaining unfounded-freeness, Table 1 shows results obtained on Hamiltonian cycle problems on complete graphs with n nodes (HC_n), both for the first and for all answer sets. While *nomore++* does not make any wrong choices leading to a linear performance in Table 1(a), *smodels* needs an exponential number

---

[13] Other apt benchmarks are "Factoring" and "Schur Numbers" (cf. [15]); in both cases, *smodels* still outperforms *nomore++* by an order of magnitude.

of choices, even for finding the first answer set. The usage of choice operator $\mathcal{D}$ enforces that rules are chained in the appropriate way for solving HC_n programs. We note that, on HC_n programs, *dlv* performs even better regarding time (cf. [15]); the different concept of "choice points" makes *nomore++* and *dlv* incomparable in this respect.

Table 1. Experiments for HC_n Computing (a) one answer set; (b) all answer sets

HC_n	dlv	smodels	nomore++ $(PBVL_b)^*D$	nomore++ $(PBVL_{bh})^*D$	dlv	smodels	nomore++ $(PBVL_b)^*D$	nomore++ $(PBVL_{bh})^*D$
3	(0.00)	1 (0.00)	1 (0.00)	1 (0.00)	(0.00)	1 (0.00)	1 (0.00)	1 (0.00)
4	(0.00)	2 (0.01)	2 (0.01)	2 (0.00)	(0.00)	5 (0.00)	5 (0.00)	5 (0.00)
5	(0.00)	3 (0.00)	3 (0.00)	3 (0.01)	(0.01)	26 (0.00)	23 (0.02)	23 (0.02)
6	(0.01)	4 (0.01)	4 (0.01)	4 (0.01)	(0.02)	305 (0.02)	119 (0.11)	119 (0.11)
7	(0.01)	3(0.01)	5 (0.02)	5 (0.02)	(0.14)	4,814 (0.38)	719 (0.83)	719 (0.85)
8	(0.01)	8 (0.00)	6 (0.03)	6 (0.03)	(1.06)	86,364 (7.29)	5,039 (7.40)	5,039 (7.60)
9	(0.02)	48 (0.01)	7 (0.05)	7 (0.05)	(10.02)	1,864,470(177.91)	40,319 (73.94)	40,319 (76.09)
10	(0.03)	1,107 (0.18)	8 (0.08)	8 (0.08)	(109.21)	n/a	362,879 (818.73)	362,879 (842.57)
11	(0.03)	18,118 (2.88)	9 (0.13)	9 (0.12)	n/a	n/a	n/a	n/a
12	(0.05)	398,306 (65.29)	10 (0.19)	10 (0.20)	n/a	n/a	n/a	n/a
13	(0.06)	n/a	11 (0.29)	11 (0.30)	n/a	n/a	n/a	n/a

Table 2. Results for (a) Π_b^n; (b) Π_h^n

Π_b^n	dlv	smodels	nomore++ $(PBVL_b)^*D$	nomore++ $(PBVL_{bh})^*D$	Π_h^n	dlv	smodels	nomore++ $(PBVL_b)^*D$	nomore++ $(PBVL_{bh})^*D$
0	(0.04)	0 (0.00)	0 (0.01)	0 (0.01)	0	(0.07)	0 (0.01)	0 (0.01)	0 (0.01)
2	(0.04)	0 (0.00)	0 (0.01)	0 (0.01)	2	(0.04)	0 (0.01)	0 (0.01)	0 (0.01)
4	(0.04)	3 (0.00)	0 (0.01)	0 (0.01)	4	(0.04)	0 (0.01)	3 (0.01)	0 (0.01)
6	(0.04)	15 (0.00)	0 (0.01)	0 (0.01)	6	(0.04)	0 (0.01)	15 (0.01)	0 (0.01)
8	(0.05)	63 (0.00)	0 (0.01)	0 (0.01)	8	(0.05)	0 (0.01)	63 (0.01)	0 (0.01)
10	(0.06)	255 (0.00)	0 (0.01)	0 (0.01)	10	(0.06)	0 (0.01)	255 (0.03)	0 (0.01)
12	(0.10)	1,023 (0.01)	0 (0.01)	0 (0.01)	12	(0.10)	0 (0.01)	1,023 (0.09)	0 (0.02)
14	(0.26)	4,095 (0.03)	0 (0.02)	0 (0.02)	14	(0.29)	0 (0.01)	4,095 (0.33)	0 (0.02)
16	(0.93)	16,383 (0.11)	0 (0.02)	0 (0.02)	16	(1.06)	0 (0.01)	16,383 (1.27)	0 (0.02)
18	(3.60)	65,535 (0.43)	0 (0.03)	0 (0.02)	18	(4.14)	0 (0.01)	65,535 (5.04)	0 (0.02)
20	(14.46)	262,143 (1.71)	0 (0.03)	0 (0.03)	20	(16.61)	0 (0.01)	262,143 (20.37)	0 (0.02)
22	(57.91)	1,048,575 (6.92)	0 (0.03)	0 (0.03)	22	(66.80)	0 (0.01)	1,048,575 (81.24)	0 (0.03)
24	(233.44)	4,194,303 (27.70)	0 (0.03)	0 (0.03)	24	(270.43)	0 (0.01)	4,194,303 (322.73)	0 (0.03)
26	n/a	16,777,215 (111.42)	0 (0.03)	0 (0.03)	26	n/a	0 (0.01)	n/a	0 (0.04)
28	n/a	67,108,863 (449.44)	0 (0.04)	0 (0.04)	28	n/a	0 (0.01)	n/a	0 (0.04)
30	n/a	n/a	0 (0.04)	0 (0.04)	30	n/a	0 (0.01)	n/a	0 (0.04)

The results in Table 2, obtained on programs Π_b^n and Π_h^n from Figure 1, aim at supporting *nomore++*'s hybrid lookahead. We see that a hybrid approach is superior to both kinds of uniform lookahead. *smodels* employs a head-based lookahead, leading to a good performance on programs Π_h^n, yet a bad one on Π_b^n. The converse is true when restricting *nomore++* to lookahead on bodies only (command line option "--body-lookahead"). *nomore++* with hybrid lookahead performs optimal regarding choice points on both types of programs. Also, a comparison of the two *nomore++* variants shows that hybrid lookahead does not introduce a computational overhead. Note that *dlv* performs similar to the worst approach on both Π_b^n and Π_h^n.

7 Discussion

We have presented a new ASP solver, along with its underlying theory, design and some experimental results. Its distinguishing features are (i) the extended concept of an assignment, including bodies in addition to atoms, (ii) the more powerful lookahead operation, and (iii) the computational strategy of maintaining unfounded-freeness. We draw from previous work on the *noMoRe* system [5], whose approach to answer set computation is based on "colouring" the rule dependency graph (RDG) of a program. *noMoRe* pursues a rule-based approach, which amounts to restricting the domain of assignments to $body(\Pi)$. The functionality of *noMoRe* has been described in [9] by graph-theoretical operators similar to $\mathcal{P}$, $\mathcal{U}$, $\mathcal{C}$, and $\mathcal{D}$. *nomore++*'s operators for backward propagation ($\mathcal{B}$) and lookahead ($\mathcal{L}$) were presented here for the first time.[14] In general, operator-based specifications facilitate formal comparisons between techniques used by different ASP solvers. Operators capturing propagation in *dlv* are given in [18]. Pruning operators based on Fitting's [7] and well-founded semantics [6] are investigated in [19]. The full paper contains a detailed comparison of these operators.

smodels [1] and *dlv* [2] pursue a literal-based approach, which boils down to restricting the domain of assignments to $head(\Pi)$. However, in both systems, propagation keeps track of the state of rules, which bears more redundancy than using bodies.[15] *nomore++*'s strategy of maintaining unfounded-freeness is closely related to some concepts used in *dlv*, but still different. In fact, the term "unfounded-free" is borrowed from [20], where it is used for assessing the complexity of unfounded set checks and characterising answer sets in the context of disjunctive logic programs. We, however, address assignments in which the non-circular support of true atoms is guaranteed. Also, *dlv* selects its choices among so-called *possibly-true literals* [13], corresponding to a literal-based version of choice operator $\mathcal{D}$. But, as discussed in Section 5, unfounded-freeness in our context cannot be achieved by choosing atoms to be true.

We conclude with outlining some subjects to future development and research. First, the low-level implementation of *nomore++* will be improved further in order to be closer to more mature ASP solvers, such as *smodels* and *dlv*. Second, aggregates, like *smodels'* cardinality and weight constraints, will be supported in future versions of *nomore++*, in order to enable more compact problem encodings. Finally, we detail in the full paper that restricting choices to either heads or bodies leads to exponentially worse proof complexity. Although choice operator $\mathcal{D}$ is valuable for handling non-tight programs, it is directly affected, as it restricts choices to bodies.[16] Thus, conditions for allowing non-supported choices, though still preferring supported choices, will be explored, which might lead to new powerful heuristics for answer set solving.

Acknowledgements. We are grateful to Yuliya Lierler, Tomi Janhunen, and anonymous referees for their helpful comments. This work was supported by DFG under grant SCHA 550/6-4 as well as the EC through IST-2001-37004 WASP project.

---

[14] Short or preliminary, respectively, notes on *nomore++* can be found in [16, 17].

[15] The number of unique bodies in a program is always less than or equal to the number of rules.

[16] Note that literal-based solvers, such as *smodels* and *dlv*, suffer from exponential worst-case complexity as well.

References

1. Simons, P., Niemelä, I., Soininen, T.: Extending and implementing the stable model semantics. Artificial Intelligence **138** (2002) 181–234
2. Leone, N., Faber, W., Pfeifer, G., Eiter, T., Gottlob, G., Koch, C., Mateis, C., Perri, S., Scarcello, F.: The DLV system for knowledge representation and reasoning. ACM Transactions on Computational Logic (2005) To appear.
3. Lin, F., Zhao, Y.: Assat: computing answer sets of a logic program by sat solvers. Artificial Intelligence **157** (2004) 115–137
4. Lierler, Y., Maratea, M.: Cmodels-2: Sat-based answer sets solver enhanced to non-tight programs. In Lifschitz, V., Niemelä, I., eds.: Proceedings of the Seventh International Conference on Logic Programming and Nonmonotonic Reasoning (LPNMR'04). Springer (2004) 346–350
5. Anger, C., Konczak, K., Linke, T.: noMoRe: A system for non-monotonic reasoning under answer set semantics. In Eiter, T., Faber, W., Truszczyński, M., eds.: Proceedings of the 6th International Conference on Logic Programming and Nonmonotonic Reasoning (LPNMR'01), Springer (2001) 406–410
6. van Gelder, A., Ross, K., Schlipf, J.: The well-founded semantics for general logic programs. Journal of the ACM **38** (1991) 620–650
7. Fitting, M.: Fixpoint semantics for logic programming: A survey. Theoretical Computer Science **278** (2002) 25–51
8. Clark, K.: Negation as failure. In Gallaire, H., Minker, J., eds.: Logic and Data Bases. Plenum Press (1978) 293–322
9. Konczak, K., Linke, T., Schaub, T.: Graphs and colorings for answer set programming: Abridged report. In Vos, M.D., Provetti, A., eds.: Proceedings of the Second International Workshop on Answer Set Programming (ASP'03). CEUR (2003) 137–150
10. Cook, S., Reckhow, R.: The relative efficiency of propositional proof systems. Journal of Symbolic Logic **44** (1979) 36–50
11. Fages, F.: Consistency of clark's completion and the existence of stable models. Journal of Methods of Logic in Computer Science **1** (1994) 51–60
12. Erdem, E., Lifschitz, V.: Tight logic programs. Theory and Practice of Logic Programming **3** (2003) 499–518
13. Faber, W., Leone, N., Pfeifer, G.: Pushing goal derivation in DLP computations. In Gelfond, M., Leone, N., Pfeifer, G., eds.: Proceedings of the Fifth International Conference on Logic Programming and Nonmonotonic Reasoning (LPNMR'99). Springer (1999) 177–191
14. (http://www.cs.uni-potsdam.de/nomore)
15. (http://asparagus.cs.uni-potsdam.de)
16. Anger, C., Gebser, M., Linke, T., Neumann, A., Schaub, T.: The nomore++ system. In Baral, C., Greco, G., Leone, N., Terracina, G., eds.: Proceedings of the Eighth International Conference on Logic Programming and Nonmonotonic Reasoning (LPNMR'05). Springer (2005) 422–426
17. Anger, C., Gebser, M., Linke, T., Neumann, A., Schaub, T.: The nomore++ approach to answer set solving. In Vos, M.D., Provetti, A., eds.: Proceedings of the Third International Workshop on Answer Set Programming (ASP'05). CEUR (2005) 163–177
18. Faber., W.: Enhancing Efficiency and Expressiveness in Answer Set Programming Systems. Dissertation, Technische Universität Wien (2002)
19. Calimeri, F., Faber, W., Leone, N., Pfeifer, G.: Pruning operators for answer set programming systems. In Benferhat, S., Giunchiglia, E., eds.: Proceedings of the Nineth International Workshop on Non-Monotonic Reasoning (NMR'02). (2002) 200–209
20. Leone, N., Rullo, P., Scarcello, F.: Disjunctive stable models: Unfounded sets, fixpoint semantics, and computation. Information and Computation **135** (1997) 69–112

Optimizing the Runtime Processing of Types in Polymorphic Logic Programming Languages

Gopalan Nadathur[1] and Xiaochu Qi[2]

[1] Digital Technology Center and Department of CSE, University of Minnesota
[2] Department of CSE, University of Minnesota

Abstract. The traditional purpose of types in programming languages of providing correctness assurances at compile time is increasingly being supplemented by a direct role for them in the computational process. In the context of typed logic programming, this is manifest in their effect on the unification operation. Their influence takes two different forms. First, in a situation where polymorphism is permitted, type information is needed to determine if different occurrences of the same name in fact denote an identical constant. Second, type information may determine the form of bindings for variables. When types are needed for the second purpose as in the case of higher-order unification, these have to be available with every variable and constant. However, in situations such as first-order and higher-order pattern unification, types have no impact on the variable binding process. As a consequence, type examination is needed in these situations only for the first of the two purposes described and even here a careful preprocessing can considerably reduce their runtime footprint. We develop a scheme for treating types in these contexts that exploits this observation. Under this scheme, type information is elided in most cases and is embedded into term structure when this is not entirely possible. Our approach obviates types when properties known as definitional genericity and type preservation are satisfied and has the advantage of working even when these conditions are violated.

1 Introduction

This paper concerns the runtime treatment of types in a higher-order logic programming language that incorporates polymorphic typing. We are interested in a setting where types are used prescriptively, i.e., where their purpose is to impose coherence conditions on expressions in a program. The traditional utility for such conditions is to express limitations in the applicability of specific operations, thereby providing a control over the kinds of computations that are attempted. This is, in fact, a role for types that is relevant to program correctness and one that is typically discharged at compile-time. There is, however, another mode in which types can be used: they can be employed to influence the kind of computation that is carried out. Such a usage of types leads to *ad hoc* polymorphism, a facet that is exploited systematically in object-oriented programming and also sometimes imported into functional programming contexts

G. Sutcliffe and A. Voronkov (Eds.): LPAR 2005, LNAI 3835, pp. 110–124, 2005.

for efficiency reasons [15]. It is when types are used in this fashion that they exhibit a runtime presence.

The two uses of types that we describe above apply also in the logic programming setting; they are present, for instance, in the language λProlog [12]. The runtime effects of types are characterized within this paradigm by their role in the unification operation. This operation is carried out by a possibly repeated application of two phases. One of these phases is that of *term simplification*, a critical part of this computation being that of matching the constants at the heads of the two terms that are being unified. In a polymorphic setting, different instances of a constant with a particular name may have distinct associated types and information must be available for determining if these can be made identical. The other phase is one in which a binding is determined for a variable that appears at the head of one of the terms. Types can affect this *variable binding* phase as well, impacting thereby on the shape of unifiers rather than merely on the question of unifiability. When types influence both phases, as they do in the case of higher-order unification [3], they must be available with each variable and constant appearing in a term.

Types typically have a rich structure in declarative programming languages, making their runtime processing a costly operation. The usual resolution to this problem in the typed logic programming setting is to restrict the language so as to altogether eliminate their need in computations. The language that is at the center of most such proposals is either a first-order one or, at least, uses unification in a first-order way. In such a situation, types can be made irrelevant to the variable binding phase. Conditions are then imposed on the structure of the declared types of constants, the instance types of the predicates that appear as the heads of clauses and possibly on the mode in which predicates are used to ensure that types are not needed to determine unifiability either. Exemplars of this approach are those presented in [1, 2, 5, 9].[1]

Our concern in this paper also is to minimize the impact of types on runtime behaviour. However, we take the view that we cannot change the language to suit our needs as its implementors. Instead, we focus on a combination of compile-time analysis and a processing structure that can reduce the runtime footprint of types. The key ingredients of our approach are the following:

- We orient our implementation around a form of unification in which types do not impact on the variable binding phase; this allows us to elide types with variables.
- Following [4], we utilize information available from signature declarations to factor types for constants into a fixed skeleton part that we discard and a variable part that we carry around at runtime.
- Using a compile-time examination of predicate definitions and the structure of the types for constants, we isolate and eliminate those variable parts in types over which unification is guaranteed to succeed.

---

[1] Both [1] and [2] seem to suggest that their conditions can be applied on a "per constant" and "per clause" basis. However, the proposals in these papers are incorrect if interpreted in this way; see Section 5 for a specific example to this effect.

The scheme we describe allows all runtime computations over types to be eliminated when the conditions known as *definitional genericity* and *type preservation* required by many of the previously described approaches are met and degrades gracefully to function also in situations where these are not satisfied.

The rest of this paper is organized as follows. In the next two sections we describe the typed language and we present a computational model for it around which we orient our implementation ideas. In Section 4 we show how compile-time type checking and the structure of types can be exploited to eliminate much of the type information with non-predicate constants. For predicate constants, we have to further analyze the usage of type information in goal invocations, an aspect that we discuss in Section 5. We conclude the paper in Section 6 with an indication of how the ideas that are presented in it are actually being used.

2   The Syntax of the Typed Language

We consider the core language of λProlog in this paper with a restriction: we do not permit predicate quantification and we disallow predicates and logical symbols within the arguments of predicates. This omission simplifies our presentation without seriously limiting the applicability of the scheme that we develop.

The types that are used are similar to the ones employed in a language such as SML. We begin with sorts and type variables and use type constructors to build structured types over these. We assume a collection of built-in sorts such as *int*, *string*, and *o* (that stands for propositions) and the well-known unary type constructor *list*. Syntactically, type variables are distinguished as tokens that begin with uppercase letters. Using this vocabulary, we obtain types such as *int*, *(list int)* and *(list A)*. The last is an example of a polymorphic type whose different manifestations are obtained by suitably instantiating the variable A. Existing collections of sorts and type constructors can be enhanced through mechanisms whose details we omit. We use a curried syntax for constructed types. Thus, if *pair* has been identified as a binary type constructor, then the expression *(pair int string)* is a type; note that a constructor must be given a number of arguments equal to its arity to produce a legitimate type. The types that we have described thus far constitute *atomic* types. The language also admits of *function* types, written as $\alpha \rightarrow \beta$ where α and β are types. Parentheses are omitted in type expressions by assuming that $\rightarrow$ associates to the right. Using this convention, a function type may be depicted in the form $\alpha_1 \rightarrow \cdots \rightarrow \alpha_n \rightarrow \beta$ where β is an atomic type. Such a type has $\alpha_1, \ldots, \alpha_n$ as its *argument* types and β as its *target* type. This notation and terminology is extended to atomic types by allowing the argument types to be missing. We do not permit *o* to appear in argument types.

The terms of the language are those of a lambda calculus restricted by the types just described. The starting point is provided by a collection of constants and variables each element of which has a designated type. We assume as built-in the usual integer and string constants of type *int* and *string* and the list constructors *nil* of type *(list A)* and *::* of type *(A → (list A) → (list A))*, the latter being written as an infix, right associative operator. Additional constants can be identified together with their types in a manner that we do not detail here. In constructing terms, we are permitted to use constants at instances of their declared types. In particular, the terms are given with their associated types by the following rules: (i) a variable is a term of its associated type, (ii) a constant is a term of any instance of its declared type, (iii) if t and s are terms of type $\alpha \to \beta$ and α respectively, then $(t\ s)$ is an (application) term of type β, and (iv) if x is a variable of type α and t is a term of type β, then $\lambda x\,t$ is an (abstraction) term of type $\alpha \to \beta$. In writing terms, we shall use the conventions that application associates to the left and has higher priority than abstraction.

We assume a notion of equality on terms that is given by the rules of α-, β- and η-conversion. Types ensure that these rules can be used to convert every term into a *head-normal form*. Such a form has the structure $\lambda x_1 \ldots \lambda x_n\ (h\ t_1\ \ldots\ t_n)$, where h is a constant or variable; we shall refer to h as the head of the term and to $t_1, \ldots, t_n$ as its arguments. We also observe that, given two head-normal forms of the same type, the α- and η-rules allow us to arrange the abstractions at the front to be identical in number and in the names for the bound variables. We utilize these facts implicitly in the discussions that follow.

Programming in the language is based on two sets of formulas called *program clauses* and *queries* or *goals*. Formulas in these two classes are constructed using logical symbols from atomic ones that are actually terms of type o with (predicate) constants as heads. Denoting atomic formulas by the symbol A and using x to represent variables that do not have o as a target type, program clauses and goals are the D and G formulas given by the following syntax rules:

$$D ::= A \mid G \supset A \mid \forall x\, D$$
$$G ::= A \mid \exists x\, G \mid \forall x\, G \mid G \wedge G \mid D \supset G.$$

Computation consists of attempting to solve a closed query relative to a finite collection of closed program clauses, called a program, in a manner that we explain in the next section.

We will use devices familiar from Prolog when we have to depict actual programs. In particular, we will adopt Prolog's manner for writing implications in program clauses, its convention of making top-level universal quantifiers implicit by using names beginning with uppercase letters for quantified variables and its method for depicting sets of clauses. As an illustration, the program

$\{\ \forall l\ (append\ nil\ l\ l),$
$\quad \forall x\, \forall l1\, \forall l2\, \forall l3\ ((append\ l1\ l2\ l3) \supset (append\ (x{::}l1)\ l2\ (x{::}l3)))\ \},$

in which we assume *append* to be a predicate constant of type

$(list\ A) \to (list\ A) \to (list\ A) \to o,$

will be rendered as

append nil L L.
(append (X::L1) L2 (X::L3)) :- (append L1 L2 L3).

Similarly, the convention for making top-level existential quantifiers in queries implicit will also be used. Thus, the query

$\exists f \, \forall a \, (append \, (a::nil) \, (b::a::nil) \, (f \, a)),$

where we assume b to be a constant of a (new) type i, will be depicted as

$\forall a \, (append \, (a::nil) \, (b::a::nil) \, (F \, a)).$

Solving a query is intended to produce a bindings for its implicitly quantified variables. Thus, in this instance, the result would be the binding $\lambda x \, (x::b::x::nil)$ for F. This query incidentally illustrates the fact that the language is higher-order and that computation in it can take place under a mixed prefix of quantifiers.

We have thus far been silent about how types are associated with variables. This can be done by annotating the abstractions and quantifiers that introduce variables in terms. It is also possible to infer a unique most general type for them using ideas familiar from SML; using this approach we would, for instance, infer the type *(list A)* for the variable L that appears in the first clause for *append* above. For constants, we have to contend with the fact that their defined types may be refined in specific contexts of use; this happens for instance for both *::* and *nil* in the term *(1::nil)*. In the end, these specific type associations may have to be carried into computations. We shall depict them as subscripts on variables and constants in the next section when we spell out the evaluation model. We then devote our attention to the efficient treatment of these type annotations.

3   The Model of Computation

Given a program $\mathcal{P}$, let us denote the set of instances of clauses in $\mathcal{P}$ obtained by substituting ground types for the type variables appearing in them by $\{\mathcal{P}\}_t$. Similarly, let us denote the set of all ground type instances of a goal G by $\{G\}_t$. A goal G is then intended to be solvable from a program $\mathcal{P}$ if and only if there is a $G' \in \{G\}_t$ such that $\{\mathcal{P}\}_t \vdash G'$ holds in intuitionistic logic. Our language possesses the uniform provability property [8] and this fact allows us to use a procedure similar to the one for Prolog in addressing this derivability question. In particular, given a complex goal, we may proceed by simplifying it as per its top-level logical symbol. When this symbol is an existential quantifier, we introduce a special *logic* variable that serves as a place-holder for a term whose precise shape will be determined as the search proceeds. When the goal has been reduced to an atomic one, we use clauses from the program in a backchaining mode. This step makes use of unification and may yield a further goal to solve, leading to a repetition of the overall process.

There are, however, new aspects to be dealt with arising out of the richer syntax of our language. One such aspect relates to the possible presence of implications in goals. The program can change dynamically because of this, requiring the solution of each subgoal to be relativized to a specific program. Another issue concerns the treatment of mixed prefixes of quantifiers. Universal quantifiers in goals lead to the introduction of new constants during computation and unification must respect the scope of such constants. To satisfy this restriction, we think of annotating each constant and logic variable with a level indicator and of using these annotations in an occurs-check phase in unification.

$$\frac{\theta \in \mathit{unify}(A, A')}{\mathcal{P}, n \vdash A, \theta} \ [\text{ATOM}]$$

where $A' \in [\mathcal{P}]_n$

$$\frac{\mathcal{P} \cup \{D\}, n \vdash G, \theta}{\mathcal{P}, n \vdash D \supset G, \theta} \ [\text{IMP}]$$

$$\frac{\mathcal{P}, n \vdash G[x := X^n], \theta}{\mathcal{P}, n \vdash \exists x \, G, \theta} \ [\text{SOME}]$$

where X is a new logic variable
of the same type as x

$$\frac{\theta \in \mathit{unify}(A, A') \qquad \theta(\mathcal{P}), n \vdash \theta(G), \theta'}{\mathcal{P}, n \vdash A, \theta' \circ \theta} \ [\text{BC}]$$

where $G \supset A' \in [\mathcal{P}]_n$

$$\frac{\mathcal{P}, n \vdash G_1, \theta' \qquad \theta'(\mathcal{P}), n \vdash \theta'(G_2), \theta}{\mathcal{P}, n \vdash G_1 \wedge G_2, \theta} \ [\text{AND}]$$

$$\frac{\mathcal{P}, n+1 \vdash G[x := c^{n+1}], \theta}{\mathcal{P}, n \vdash \forall x \, G, \theta} \ [\text{ALL}]$$

where c is a new constant of the same
type as x

Fig. 1. The operational semantics rules

Towards realizing these ideas, we allow logic variables into our formulas and we label them and also the constants with natural numbers. We display these labels where needed as superscripts on the corresponding symbols. The operational semantics of our language is then given by the derivation of judgements of the form $\mathcal{P}, n \vdash G, \theta$, where $\mathcal{P}$ is a program, n is a natural number, G is a goal and θ is a substitution for both logic and type variables. Let us write $F \in [\mathcal{P}]_n$ if F can be obtained from a clause in $\mathcal{P}$ by first picking fresh names for the type variables that appear in it and then instantiating the universal quantifiers that appear at its head with new logic variables carrying the label n. Moreover, let us denote the result of replacing the variable x in a formula F with t by the expression $F[x := t]$. Then the rules shown in Figure 1 allow us to derive the judgements that are of interest to us. To solve the (top-level) goal G from the program $\mathcal{P}$, we label all the constants appearing in G and in $\mathcal{P}$ with 0 and then try to construct a derivation for $\mathcal{P}, 0 \vdash G, \theta$ for some θ using these rules. Notice that the substitution component of such a judgement actually constitutes the result produced by a computation and, when thought of in this manner, this imposes a sequentiality in the solution of conjunctive goals using the rule [AND].

The rules in Figure 1 rely on a unification judgement. In elaborating this, we shall assume that all the unification problems that we encounter dynamically satisfy the following condition: whenever a logic variable appears as the head of (the normal form of) a term, it has as arguments a sequence of distinct variables bound by abstractions or distinct constants with labels greater than that attached to the logic variable. This is the higher-order pattern restriction [7, 13] that is satisfied trivially by first-order terms and also by most higher-order unification problems that arise in practice [6]. The solution to such problems can be computed by descending through the structures of terms first in a simplification mode and later in a variable binding mode if needed [10]. The rules in Figure 2 define the form of this process. These rules use lists of equations to capture recursion through term structure. To find a θ in $\mathit{unify}(A, A')$, we initiate the rewriting process with the tuple $\langle A = A' :: \mathit{nil}, \emptyset \rangle$, hoping to reduce this to the form $\langle \mathit{nil}, \theta \rangle$. Notice that rule (2) requires a most general unifier to be computed for two types under a view of them as first-order terms. We also use in this rule the fact that if two terms of identical type have the same constant or bound variable as their heads, then they must have the same number of arguments.

(1) $\langle (\lambda x\, t = \lambda x\, s :: E, \theta \rangle \longrightarrow \langle (t = s) :: E, \theta \rangle.$

(2) $\langle (a_\tau\ t_1\ \ldots\ t_n) = (a_\sigma\ s_1\ \ldots\ s_n) :: E, \theta \rangle \longrightarrow \langle \phi(t_1 = s_1 :: \ldots :: t_n = s_n :: E), \phi \circ \theta \rangle,$
provided a is a constant or a variable bound by an abstraction
and ϕ is a most general unifier for τ and σ

(3) $\langle (F_\sigma\ y_1\ \ldots\ y_n) = t) :: E, \theta \rangle \longrightarrow \langle \varphi(E), \varphi \circ \theta \rangle$
provided F is a logic variable and $mksubst(F_\sigma, t, [y_1, \ldots, y_n]) = \varphi.$

(4) $\langle (t = (F_\sigma\ y_1\ \ldots\ y_n) :: E, \theta \rangle \longrightarrow \langle \varphi(E), \varphi \circ \theta \rangle$
provided F is a logic variable and $mksubst(F_\sigma, t, [y_1, \ldots, y_n]) = \varphi.$

Fig. 2. Simplification rules for higher-order pattern unification

The invocation of $mksubst(F_\sigma, t, [y_1, \ldots, y_n])$ in the last two rules initiates the variable binding phase. This computation is intended to determine a substitution for F_σ and possibly for logic variables appearing in t that make the terms $(F_\sigma\ y_1\ \ldots\ t_n)$ and t identical, if they are in fact unifiable. Towards this end, a traversal is carried out over the structure of t, determining at each subterm what needs to be done with the head symbol if a unifying substitution is to be generated. If this symbol is a constant with a label less than or equal to that of F_σ or if it is a variable bound by an abstraction appearing inside t, then it can appear directly in the term to be substituted for F_σ. If it is a constant that has a label larger than that of F_σ or it is a variable bound by an abstraction outside of t, then it may appear in an instance of $(F_\sigma\ y_1\ \ldots\ y_n)$ only if it is in the list $[y_1, \ldots, y_n]$ and in this case the term that F_σ is bound to must carry out a suitable projection. Finally, the head symbol may itself be a logic variable. Suppose that the subterm is $(G_\rho\ z_1\ \ldots\ z_m)$ where G_ρ is a logic variable and the arguments $z_1, \ldots, z_m$ satisfy the pattern restriction. If G_ρ is identical to F_σ, then the terms are unifiable only if the subterm under consideration is all of t. If this is the case, then n must be identical to m and the substitution for F_σ should prune away all the arguments for which y_i and z_i do not agree. If G_ρ is distinct from F_σ, we have two cases to consider. If the label of G_ρ is smaller than or equal to that of F_σ, it is necessary to "prune" those elements of $z_1, \ldots, z_m$ that do not appear in $y_1, \ldots, y_n$ and a suitable pruning substitution for G_ρ and a corresponding projection for the subterm must be computed. On the other hand, if the label of G_ρ is larger than that of F_σ, it is necessary to replace this variable in the subterm by one that has the same label as F_σ to prevent subsequent instantiations that violate scope restrictions. However, while doing this, the elements of $y_1, \ldots, y_n$ that can legitimately appear in an instantiation of G_ρ and that are not already contained in $z_1, \ldots, z_m$ must be added to the sequence of arguments of the subterm. To realize this correctly, the earlier described pruning substitution for G_ρ must be complemented by a "raising" component.

We refer the reader to [10] for an elaboration of the above description of $mksubst$. Relative to such a description, we have the following theorem:

Theorem 1. *Let $\mathcal{P}$ be a program and let G be a goal and let $\mathcal{P}'$ and G' be obtained from these by labelling all the constants appearing in them with the*

number 0. *Further suppose that all the terms appearing in a derivation rooted at* $\mathcal{P}', 0 \vdash G', \theta$ *(for an arbitrary* θ*) satisfy the higher-order pattern restriction. Then there is a derivation of* $\mathcal{P}', 0 \vdash G', \varphi$ *for some* φ *if and only if there is a* $G' \in \{G\}_t$ *and a finite subset* Γ *of* $\{\mathcal{P}\}_t$ *such that* $\Gamma \vdash G'$ *in intuitionistic logic.*

The computation process that we have described has a shortcoming in that it "stalls" when it encounters a unification problem outside the higher-order pattern fragment. Practical systems work around this difficulty by deferring equations that violate the pattern restriction, reexamining them later or presenting them as qualifications on computed answers—see, e.g., [14]. We elide a further discussion of this matter since it is orthogonal to our present concerns.

4   Using Declared Types to Simplify Type Annotations

Types need to be carried into runtime computations only insofar as they affect the course of computation. Towards understanding how this might happen, we consider the different phases of the interpreter of Section 3.

In one phase, characterized by the rules in Figure 1, goals are simplified and a unification computation may be initiated in support of backchaining. Types do not determine the steps in this phase although some bookkeeping work relating to them may have to be done. In particular, the rules [ALL] and [SOME] must attach the type of the quantified variable to the new constant and logic variable introduced by these rules if in fact these types are needed later during execution. An important point to note with these constants and variables, though, is that the same type is shared by every instance and, in terms of checking identity, a simple lookup of the names suffices.

Another phase, defined by the rules in Figure 2, corresponds to the simplification of the top-level fixed structure of terms in the unification process. Types are used in an essential way in one of these rules, specifically in rule (2). In determining the applicability of this rule, it is necessary to match up both the names and the types of the constants or abstracted variables that appear as the heads of the two terms being unified. Observe, however, that if these heads are matching abstracted variables or constants introduced by the [ALL] rule for goals, then the types must already be identical. Thus the checking or unification of types is necessary only for the genuinely polymorphic constants declared at the top-level in the program.

The last phase is the one that determines variable bindings in unification. A closer look at the description we have provided of the computation carried out by *mksubst* reveals the following: First, the types of logic variables are neither examined nor refined in the process of constructing bindings; we do have to check the identities of these variables at certain places but a simple comparison of names is all that is needed for this. Second, we sometimes have to compare constants (and abstracted variables), but these comparisons are restricted to being between constants that appear as the arguments of the logic variables in the appropriate instances of rule (3) or (4) in Figure 2. The higher-order pattern restriction requires that such constants have higher labels than the logic variable at the head, implying thereby that they must have been introduced by a use of the [ALL] rule. Hence every instance of any such constant must already be known to have the same type. From these observations, it is evident that types are incidental to the variable binding computation.

From the above considerations, it is clear that the only symbols with which we need to maintain types at run time are the top-level declared constants. A further examination allows us to simplify even this information. The defined type for such a constant provides a skeleton that compile-time type checking ensures every occurrence of the constant shares. The only possible differences between the types of distinct occurrences are in the instantiations of the variables that occur in the skeleton. Thus, the type annotations for each constant can be systematically transformed by a compiler into a (possibly empty) list of type variable instantiations and it is only these (simpler) types that need to be unified during execution. As a particular example, given the types *(list A)* for *nil* and $A \rightarrow$ *(list A)* $\rightarrow$ *(list A)* for *::*, a compiler can determine that only the bindings for the type variable A need to be stored with instances of these constants. Let us write type annotations as a special first list argument for constants and let us temporarily use a prefix syntax for *::*. Then, by virtue of the present observation, the structure *(:: [int $\rightarrow$ (list int) $\rightarrow$ (list int)] 1 (nil [list int]))* can be rendered into the form *(:: [int] 1 (nil [int]))* instead.

The manner in which unification problems are processed actually allows for a further refinement of type annotations. The usage of the rules in Figure 2 begins with an equation between two (predicate) terms that have the same type and each transformation preserves this relationship between the terms in each equation. Thus, at the time when the types of different instances of a constant are being unified in rule (2), their target types are known to be identical. This has the special implication that there is no need to check the bindings for the variables in the type skeleton that also occur in the target type and so these may be eliminated from the annotations. In the case that all the variables in the skeleton type also appear in the target type, i.e., when the constant type satisfies the type preservation property [2], the compiler can conclude that no type annotation needs to be maintained with the constant. This happens to be the case for both *::* and *nil*, for instance, and so all type information can be elided from lists that are implemented using these constants.

We formalize the ideas expressed up to this point in the following fashion. First, we attach with each constant an initial "list of types" argument. This list is empty for the constants introduced by the [ALL] rule and for instances of the other constants it consists of bindings for the variables that appear only in the argument part of their declared types, presented in an order determined by a compiler. This extra argument is simply carried along with the constant when a variable substitution is being constructed. The only real use of it occurs in rule (2) of the simplification phase of unification that is refined into the form shown in Figure 3. The second rule in this collection is needed because constructors of function type can appear without their arguments in programs in our higher-order language. We also note that the types list argument is likely to be empty in most situations and this is to be treated by a special case of rule (2.1).

(2.1) $\langle (a\ [\tau_1, ..., \tau_k]\ t_1...t_n) = (a\ [\sigma_1, ..., \sigma_k]\ s_1...s_n) :: E, \theta \rangle$
$\longrightarrow \langle \phi((t_1 = s_1) :: ... :: (t_n = s_n) :: E), \phi \circ \theta \rangle,$
where $n > 0$, and ϕ is a most general unifier for $\{\langle \tau_1, \sigma_1 \rangle, ..., \langle \tau_k, \sigma_k \rangle\}$,
if a is a constant.

(2.2) $\langle (a\ [\tau_1, ..., \tau_k]) = (a\ [\sigma_1, ..., \sigma_k]) :: E, \theta \rangle \longrightarrow \langle E, \theta \rangle$, if a is a constant.

(2.3) $\langle (a\ t_1...t_n) = (a\ s_1...s_n) :: E, \theta \rangle \longrightarrow \langle ((t_1 = s_1) :: ... :: (t_n = s_n) :: E), \theta \rangle,$
if a is a variable bound by an abstraction.

Fig. 3. The refined structure simplification rule

The correctness of the implementation scheme described in this section is stated in the following theorem. The proof of this theorem requires a formal presentation of the compiler function that transforms the types of constants into lists of type variable bindings. A subsequent argument utilizes this definition to establish a correspondence between compile-time type checking and the runtime type unification in rule (2.1) in Figure 3 on the one hand and the unification carried out at runtime over the entire type in rule (2) of Figure 2 on the other.

Theorem 2. *The modified interpreter described in this section in combination with the scheme for transforming type annotations is sound and complete with respect to the interpreter presented in Section 3.*

The ideas we have described here may be applied to the *append* program. There is a type variable appearing in the argument types of *append* that does not appear in its target type the binding for which must therefore annotate its occurrences. We have already seen that type annotations can be dropped from *::* and *nil*. Thus, the definition of *append* is transformed into the following:

append [A] nil L L.
(append [A] (X::L1) L2 (X::L3)) :- (append [A] L1 L2 L3).

The query considered in Section 2 correspondingly becomes

$\forall a$ *(append [i] (a::nil) (b::a::nil) (F a)).*

The scheme that we have described is capable also of dealing with the situation where the type preservation property is violated. For example, consider a representation of heterogenous lists based on the constants *null* of type *lst* and *cons* of type $A \to lst \to lst$. The list containing *1* and *"list"* as its elements would then be represented by the term *(cons [int] 1 (cons [string] "list" null)).*

5   Eliminating Type Annotations for Predicates

Predicate names are constants whose declared types have *o* as their target types. A consequence of this is that the ideas of the previous section do not allow any of the variables that appear in the type of a predicate constant to be dispensed with from the annotation that adorns it. This is unfortunate because in many instances these annotations have no tangible effect on a computation. A particular illustration of this fact is provided by the transformed definition of *append* that we saw towards the end of Section 4. The type variable A that annotates the head of each of these clauses can be unified with any type and hence has no impact on the applicability of the clause to a given query. Actually carrying out its unification with an incoming type will result in extracting a binding that, in the second clause, is passed on to a recursive call of *append*. However, this call will also at most result in the type binding being extracted and passed along without affecting the computation in an observable way. The type annotation for *append* can therefore be dispensed with without adverse effect.

But is there a systematic way for determining when a type annotation on a predicate constant can be so eliminated? This is the issue we now address. We propose a way for determining the elements of the types list associated with a predicate name that could potentially influence a computation. For the types not in this list we conclude that they can be elided.

The process of determining the potentially "needed" elements in the types list can be oriented around the clauses defining the predicate constant.[2] We must include in this analysis also the clauses that appear on the lefthand sides of implication goals in the bodies of clauses. If a constant appears as the head of such a clause, we assume every element in its types list is needed: in the model of computation we have described, the values for the type variables that appear in such a clause get fixed when the clause is added to the program and consequently runtime unification with them may determine a binding that influences the subsequent usage of the clause. For a clause that appears at the top-level, our analysis can be more sophisticated. An element in the types list for its head predicate is needed if the value in the relevant position in the list associated with the head in that clause is anything other than a variable; unification over this element must be attempted during execution since it has the possibility of failing in this case. Another situation in which the element is needed is if it is a variable that occurs elsewhere in the same types list or in the types lists associated with a non-predicate constant that occurs in the clause. The rationale here is that either the variable will already have a binding that must be tested against an incoming type or a value must be extracted into it that is used later in a unification computation of consequence. A more subtle situation for the variable case is when it occurs in the types list associated with the predicate head of a clause that appears on the left of an implication goal in the body. In this case the binding that is extracted at runtime in the variable has an impact on the applicability of the clause that is added and consequently is a needed one.

The only case that remains to be considered is that where a variable element in the types list for the clause head appears also in the types list associated with a predicate constant in a goal position in the body, either at the top-level or,

---

[2] The calculation we describe is sensitive to our being able to fix statically the full set of clauses for a predicate. We obtain this ability here by assuming that the top-level goal does not contain implications. In reality, the module system of λProlog gives assistance in this task. A detailed discussion is beyond the scope of this paper.

recursively, in an embedded clause definition. We could, somewhat simplistically, treat such predicate constants also like the other constants. The drawback with this is that the type annotation with the predicate constant appearing in the body may itself be eliminable and then an opportunity for optimization would be missed. We could, of course, determine this neededness information for the body predicate constant first and then use this information in the analysis for the given clause head. As an example of how this might work, suppose that *print* is a predicate of type $A \rightarrow o$ and *printlist* is a predicate of type *(list A)* $\rightarrow o$ and consider the following clauses annotated in the style of Section 4:

> *print [int] X :- {code for printing the integer value bound to X}.*
> *print [string] X :- {code for printing the string value bound to X}.*
>
> *printlist [C] nil.*
> *printlist [C] (X::L) :- print [C] X, printlist [C] L.*

In this code, *print* is a predicate that is polymorphic in an *ad hoc* way and that makes genuine use of its type "argument." This information can be used to determine that it needs its type adornment and the following analysis exposes the fact that *printlist* must therefore carry its type annotation.[3]

The approach suggested above needs refinement to be applicable to a context where dependencies between definitions can be iterated and even recursive; at present, it doesn't apply directly even to the definition of *append*. The solution is to use an iterative, fixed-point computation that has as its starting point the neededness information gathered by initially ignoring predicate constants appearing in goal positions in the body of the clause. In effecting this calculation relative to a given program $\mathcal{P}$, we employ a two-dimensional global boolean array called *needed* whose first index, p, ranges over the set of predicate constants appearing in $\mathcal{P}$ and whose second index, i, is a positive integer that ranges over the length of the types list for p; this array evidently has a variable size along its second dimension. The intention is that if, at the end of the computation, $needed[p][i]$ is *false* then the ith element in the types list associated with p does not have an influence on the solution of any goal G from $\mathcal{P}$. We compute the value of this array by initially setting all the elements of *needed* to *false* and then calling the procedure *find_needed* defined in Figure 4 on the program $\mathcal{P}$.

The invocation of *find_needed* on any program $\mathcal{P}$ must clearly terminate. The correctness of the procedure is then the content of the following lemma.

Lemma 1. *Let p be a predicate constant defined in $\mathcal{P}$ and let it be the case that when find_needed($\mathcal{P}$) terminates, needed[p][i] is set to false. Then the ith element in the types list of p has no impact on the solvability of any goal G from $\mathcal{P}$.*

Proof. Only a sketch is provided. Suppose that the specific value of a component of the types list of a predicate constant p has a bearing on some computation.

---

[3] This example vividly illustrates the problem with interpreting the conditions described in [1] and [2] as applicable on a "per clause" and "per constant" basis. Using them in this way, we would drop the type annotation with *print_list* and therefore not be able to pass this information on to *print* where it is genuinely needed.

procedure *find_needed(P)* {
  init_needed(P);
  repeat
    for each top-level non-atomic clause C in P {*process_clause(C)*;}
  until (the value of *needed* does not change)
}

procedure *init_needed(P)* {
  for every embedded clause C in P with $(p\ [\tau_1, ..., \tau_k]\ t_1\ ...\ t_n)$ as head
    for $1 \leq i \leq k$ {*needed[p][i]* = *true*};

  for every top-level clause C in P with $(p\ [\tau_1, ..., \tau_k]\ t_1\ ...\ t_n)$ as head
    for $1 \leq i \leq k$
      if τ_i is not a type variable {*needed[p][i]* = *true*;}
      else {
        if ((τ_i occurs in τ_j for some j such that $1 \leq j \leq k$ and $i \neq j$) or
          (τ_i occurs in the types list of a non-predicate constant in C) or
          (τ_i occurs in the types list of a predicate constant appearing
            as the head of an embedded clause in the body of C))
        needed[p][i] = *true*;
      }
}

procedure *process_clause(C)* {
  let C be of the form $(p\ [\tau_1, ..., \tau_k]\ t_1\ ...\ t_n)$:- G
  for $1 \leq i \leq k$
    if *needed[p][i]* is *false* then {*needed[p][i]* = *process_body(G, τ_i)*};
}

function *process_body(G, τ)* : boolean {
  if G is
  $\forall G'$, $\exists G'$: return *process_body(G', τ)*;
  $G_1 \wedge G_2$: return (*process_body(G_1, τ)* or *process_body(G_2, τ)*);
  $D \supset G$: return (*process_body(G, τ)* or *process_embedded_clause(D, τ)*);
  atomic and of the form $(q\ [\sigma_1, ..., \sigma_l]\ s_1\ ...s_m)$:
    if τ occurs in σ_i for some i such that $1 \leq i \leq l$ and *needed[q][i]* is *true*
    then return *true*;
    else return *false*;
}

function *process_embedded_body(D, τ)* : boolean {
  if D is
  $\forall D_1$: return *process_embedded_body(D_1)*;
  $G \supset A$: return *process_body(G, τ)*);
  atomic: return *false*;
}

Fig. 4. Determining if a predicate type argument is needed

Then it must become relevant at a specific point in the backchaining sequence. An induction on the distance of the relevant call of p from this point in the sequence shows that *needed[p][i]* must be set to true by *find_needed*: the base case is accounted for by the initialization code and the inductive case is handled by the fact that the iteration concludes only when a fixed point is reached.

The lemma leads naturally to the following theorem:

Theorem 3. *Let $\mathcal{P}$ and G be a program and a goal that is annotated in the style described at the end of Section 4. Let $\overline{\mathcal{P}}$ and $\overline{G}$ be the program and goal that result from $\mathcal{P}$ and G by eliminating those components from the types lists of predicates that are found not to be needed by the invocation of find_needed($\mathcal{P}$). Then G succeeds from $\mathcal{P}$ if and only if $\overline{G}$ succeeds from $\overline{\mathcal{P}}$ using the interpreter described in Section 4.*

Using this theorem and *find_needed*, the type annotation for *append* can be eliminated and the definition of this predicate can be reduced to essentially the untyped form. In general, if every clause is type general in the sense of [2], then types can be eliminated entirely from runtime computations.

6   Conclusion

A polymorphically typed higher-order logic programming language like λProlog requires type information to be carried into computations. We have described in this paper ways in which the amount of information that must be available and manipulated at runtime can be significantly reduced. A critical part of our approach is a shift from using a full higher-order unification procedure to one based on higher-order patterns. There can be some differences in the end results of computations as a result of this shift but, in most cases, the changes are actually for the better in that more precise answers are produced. The modified model also facilitates a static analysis of the dynamic effects of types that eventually lies at the heart of our approach for eliding them in programs.

The ideas we have described here need extension in one respect to be actually applicable to λProlog. In this language, predicate constants can in fact appear within terms. When they appear in such contexts, they have to be treated like other (non-predicate) constants and, under the present scheme, must carry binding for their type variables. However, even in this situation, the ideas in Section 5 can be applied to the extensional uses of predicate constants. Moreover, by exploiting visibility properties of constants emanating from the modules language of λProlog, we can profitably lift the kind of analysis that we have described in Section 5 for predicate constants that appear extensionally to constants that appear within terms. As a particular case, then, the reach of these ideas can also be extended to constants that appear both intensionally and extensionally.

The work that we have described here is being utilized in a new implementation of λProlog. They already have an impact in yielding an abstract machine for the language that is considerably simpler than the one underlying the *Teyjus* system [11]. We expect in the future to be able to compare the performance of the two systems and to isolate the efficiency benefits of the reduced type processing that are supported by the ideas in this paper.

Acknowledgements. We are grateful to the reviewers for their close reading and helpful comments. This work has been supported by the NSF Grant CCR-0429572. Part of this research was conducted under the rubric of the SLIMMER project that is jointly funded by INRIA and NSF.

References

1. M. Hanus. Horn clause programs with polymorphic types: Semantics and resolution. In J. Diaz and F. Orejas, editors, *TAPSOFT 89*, pages 225–240. Springer-Verlag, 1989. Lecture Notes in Computer Science Vol 352.
2. M. Hanus. Polymorphic higher-order programming in Prolog. In G. Levi and M. Martelli, editors, *Proceedings of the Sixth International Logic Programming Conference*, pages 382–398. MIT Press, 1989.
3. G. Huet. A unification algorithm for typed λ-calculus. *Theoretical Computer Science*, 1:27–57, 1975.
4. K. Kwon, G. Nadathur, and D.S. Wilson. Implementing polymorphic typing in a logic programming language. *Computer Languages*, 20(1):25–42, 1994.
5. T.K. Lakshman and U.S. Reddy. Typed Prolog: A semantic reconstruction of the Mycroft-O'Keefe type system. In V. Saraswat and K. Ueda, editors, *Proceedings of the International Logic Programming Symposium*, pages 202–217. MIT Press, 1991.
6. S. Michaylov and F. Pfenning. An empirical study of the runtime behavior of higher-order logic programs. In *Conference Record of the Workshop on the λProlog Programming Language*, Philadelphia, July-August 1992.
7. D. Miller. A logic programming language with lambda-abstraction, function variables, and simple unification. *Journal of Logic and Computation*, 1(4):497–536, 1991.
8. D. Miller, G. Nadathur, F. Pfenning, and A. Scedrov. Uniform proofs as a foundation for logic programming. *Annals of Pure and Applied Logic*, 51:125–157, 1991.
9. A. Mycroft and R. A. O'Keefe. A polymorphic type system for Prolog. *Artificial Intelligence*, 23:295–307, 1984.
10. G. Nadathur and N. Linnell. Practical higher-order pattern unification with on-the-fly raising. Technical Report 2005/2, Digital Technology Center, April 2005. To appear in the Proceedings of ICLP'05.
11. G. Nadathur and D.J. Mitchell. System description: Teyjus—a compiler and abstract machine based implementation of λProlog. In H. Ganzinger, editor, *Automated Deduction–CADE-16*, number 1632 in Lecture Notes in Artificial Intelligence, pages 287–291. Springer-Verlag, July 1999.
12. G. Nadathur and F. Pfenning. The type system of a higher-order logic programming language. In F. Pfenning, editor, *Types in Logic Programming*, pages 245–283. MIT Press, 1992.
13. T. Nipkow. Functional unification of higher-order patterns. In *Eighth Annual IEEE Symposium on Logic in Computer Science*, pages 64–74. IEEE Computer Society Press, June 1993.
14. F. Pfenning. Elf: A language for logic definition and verified metaprogramming. In *Fourth Annual Symposium on Logic in Computer Science*, pages 313–322. IEEE Computer Society Press, June 1989.
15. D. Tarditi, G. Morrisett, P. Cheng, C. Stone, R. Harper, and P. Lee. TIL: A type-directed optimizing compiler for ML. In *Proc. ACM SIGPLAN '96 Conference on Programming Language Design and Implementation*, pages 181–192, 1996.

The Four Sons of Penrose

Nachum Dershowitz*

School of Computer Science,
Tel Aviv University,
Ramat Aviv 69978, Israel
nachum.dershowitz@cs.tau.ac.il

Abstract. We distill Penrose's argument against the "artificial intelligence premiss", and analyze its logical alternatives. We then clarify the different positions one can take in answer to the question raised by the argument, skirting the issue of introspection *per se*.

1 The Argument

> It follows that there are four sons:
> one wise; and one wicked;
> one simple; and who knows not how to ask.
>
> —*Mekhilta of R. Ishmael* (c. 300)

Artificial Intelligence (AI) is the endeavor to endow mechanical artifacts with human-like intellectual capacities. The "strong" AI hypothesis (as propounded in [7], for example, and critiqued in [18]) avows that "an appropriately programmed computer really is a mind" [18]. The Computational Hypothesis asserts that the human mind is in reality some kind of physical symbol-manipulation system. The "weak" version of the hypothesis ("A physical symbol system has the necessary and sufficient means for intelligent action." [13]) allows for the possibility that the mind is not mechanical, but claims that it is (theoretically, at least) simulatable by mechanico-symbolic means (to wit, by a Turing machine).[1]

In *The Emperor's New Mind* [14] and especially in *Shadows of the Mind* [15], Roger Penrose argues against these AI theses, contending that human reasoning cannot be captured by an artificial intellect because humans detect nontermination of programs in cases where digital machines do not. Penrose thus adapts the similar argumentation of Lucas [11]. The latter was based on Gödel's incompleteness results, whereas Penrose uses the undecidability of the halting problem, demonstrated by Turing [22].

---

* This research was supported by the Israel Science Foundation (grant no. 250/05).
[1] For a discussion of problems inherent in comparisons of computational power via simulations, see [2].

G. Sutcliffe and A. Voronkov (Eds.): LPAR 2005, LNAI 3835, pp. 125–138, 2005.

In a nutshell, Penrose's argument runs as follows:

1. Consider all current sound human knowledge about non-termination.
2. Suppose one could reduce said knowledge to a (finite) computer program.
3. Then one could create a self-referential version of said program.
4. From the assumed existence of such a program, a contradiction to its correct performance can be derived.

Penrose's resolution of this contradiction is to deny the validity of the second step: No program can incorporate everything (finitely many) humans know. This, it would seem, violates even the weak AI premiss.

Since some (immortal) humans can emulate (unbounded) Turing machines, while machines—according to this argument—cannot simulate all humans, Penrose concludes that the human mind comprises super-Turing abilities, using undiscovered physical processes. (For a more recent dispute over whether quantum physics supports potentially super-Turing computability, see [8, 21, 9, 19].) Penrose's conclusions have been roundly critiqued, for example, in [1, 3, 5, 10, 16].

In this paper, we distill the arguments on both sides. Specifically, we reduce the bone of contention to a consideration only of the question, "Does X not respond to input X?", and restrict ourselves to one entity versed in computer science, namely, "Roger". In the process, we demonstrate that there are exactly four ways to resolve the conundrum raised by the above "diagonalization" argument. Roger falls into one (or more) of the following categories:

I. An idealized human who is inherently more powerful than Turing's machines.
II. A slipshod human who can err in judgement.
III. An impetuous human who sometimes errs, having resorted to a baseless hunch.
IV. A pedantic human who may decline to express an opinion when questioned.

The analysis remains the same regardless of whether the entities involved are human, humanoid, or otherwise endowed with reasoning abilities. Knowledge of one's self-consistency does not directly enter the equation.

Most discussions exclude options II and III, as irrelevant when considering "ideal" beings. Thus, it appears that IV, though rarely proposed explicitly in these terms, is the preferred alternative for those who, unlike Penrose, do not accept I. It goes without saying that real, corporeal mortal, humans suffer from both II and III, and ultimately from IV, and—in the final analysis—have no more computational power than sub-Turing finite automata.

In Sect. 3, we recapitulate a simplified version of Turing's proof of the undecidability of the halting problem. Before and after that section, we give a fanciful rendition of the interplay between soundness (never giving a wrong answer) and completeness (in the sense of always knowing when the answer is "yes"). Section 5 defines transfinite sequences of better and better programs for termination analysis. In Sect. 6, we introduce the entities that play a rôle in our analysis. After setting the stage, we present our quadriad of possible solutions in Sect. 7.

Finally, in the concluding section, these alternatives are matched up with some of the different published opinions on the subject.

2   The Androids

> Thousands of battle droids, super battle droids,
> droidekas and other models
> are built from start to finish within the factory.
>
> —starwars.com

Androids have become more and more commonplace in the 21st century. Each specimen is identified by model# and serial#. The older Model-T units are being phased out. Most modern consumer models belong to either the R series (circa 2001) or S series (circa 2010). Intelligence engineers have worked hard over the years to continually lower response time, without compromising performance quality. The R series is quite impressive, with guaranteed response time nowadays of less than one minute. Reaction to this series, however, has been mixed, since R-series androids have been known to occasionally give wrong answers and, hence, cannot be trusted with sensitive tasks. Despite manufacturer claims that such occurrences are extraordinarily rare, and that normal household use is highly unlikely to suffer, the fact is that complaints continue to stream in.

In response to customer demands, the S series was launched, in which reliability was made a top priority. These androids came with a "money back" guarantee of correctness, for which purpose logicians were hired by android manufacturers. Reviews of this series remain mixed, however. As it turns out, some questions seem to befuddle members of this class, and unreasonably long delays have been experienced before an answer was forthcoming. Some questions took so long, that the "last resort" restart procedure was manually invoked.

It has become something of a geek game to come up with neat questions that trip-up R-units and/or stump S-units. A simple litmus test to distinguish between these two series is to ask the "trick question":[2]

Will you answer "no" to this question?

All R models give a wrong answer, though some answer in the affirmative and others in the negative. On the other hand, no S model answers within a minute, or—indeed—has ever been known to answer this trick question. In fact, this question belies claims that R-series droids will never fail in ordinary day-to-day use.

In response to customer dissatisfaction, a new model has just hit the market. It is the vanguard of the much-vaunted Q-series, which promises to harness quantum technology to overcome shortcomings of the R and S models. Whether it will be a success remains to be seen.

---

[2] I have not yet found the origin of this riddle.

3   The Halting Problem

> This statement is false.
>
> —Eubulides (c. −350)

The argument for undecidability of the halting problem, as in the seminal work of Alan Turing, is by *reductio ad absurdum*. We provide a full "one-minute proof" of the undecidability of a special case (viz. self-divergence), inspired by Doron Zeilberger's "2-minute proof" [24] and by Penrose's claims. The idea is to formalize a paraphrasing of the trick question of the previous section, namely,

> ### Will you not answer "yes" to this question?

computationally.

Consider any programming language supporting programs as data (as in typical AI languages), which has some sort of conditional (**if ... then ... else ...**) and includes at least one non-terminating program (which we denote **loop**). Consider the decision problem of determining whether a program X diverges on itself, that is, $X(X) = \bot$, where $\bot$ denotes a non-halting computation. Suppose A were a program that purported to return true (T) for (exactly) all such X. Then A would perforce fail to answer correctly regarding the behavior of the following (Lisp-ish) program:

$$C(Y) := \textbf{if } A(Y) \textbf{ then } T \textbf{ else loop}() \,,$$

since we would be faced with the following contradiction:

$$C(C) \text{ returns } T \quad \Leftrightarrow \quad A(C) \text{ returns } T \quad \Leftrightarrow \quad C(C) \text{ diverges} \,.$$

The first biconditional is by construction of C (the only case in which C returns T is when A does); the second, by specification of A (A is to return T iff the program it is applied to is self-looping).

So, we are forced to reject the supposition that there exists such an A. Technically, we say that the self-looping problem is not semi-decidable. But the fact that no program can answer such a question should not surprise us, any more than the failure of smart humans at the same task.

Programming languages that do not directly support "procedures as parameters" need to use some "code" c as the parameter instead of program C itself, but otherwise the undecidability proof is unchanged:

$$C(c) \text{ returns } T \quad \Leftrightarrow \quad A(c) \text{ returns } T \quad \Leftrightarrow \quad C(c) \text{ diverges} \,.$$

4   The Clones

> This copy will outlive the original
> and always look young and alive.
>
> —*L'Eve future* (Villiers de l'Isle-Adam, 1886)

Our goal in this section is to demonstrate the impossibility of designing an omniscient robot.

Consider a Model-T android, named Andrea, with the ability to speak, comprehend speech, and react. Any one could pose questions to Andrea, like "Is it raining here, now?". Andrea might answer correctly (by sticking her hand out the window and determining the meteorological state), she might lie (if she is contrary), she might guess and take her chances at being right or wrong (without looking out the window), she might give an inappropriate answer (like, "Shall I get you an umbrella?"), or she may ignore the question and simply stay mum on the subject.

Just as people might question Andrea, other robots might query her. Furthermore, people as well as robots, might ask her questions about herself or about other robots, like: "Are you hungry?"; "Do you fancy Borg?"; or "Is Borg in love with himself?".

The situation can get trickier. Andrea might be programmed to consult her cohorts regarding certain questions. For example, rather than trying to figure out for herself whether Borg is narcissistic, she may be designed to refer such questions to the subject himself. In that case, Andrea will give the same answer to this question as would Borg had we asked him directly (assuming Borg does not formulate his answer based on who is doing the asking). Andrea might turn some questions around before turning to Borg, or might barrage Borg with a series of questions.

Alternatively, Andrea may be smart enough to occasionally detect that Borg is lying, after hearing him explain his answer. So it may be that Andrea gives a different answer than Borg. Still, let's assume that in any such case, where Andrea requests an answer from Borg, but he refuses to answer, she too remains reticent.

Now, hypothesize the existence of a "know-it-all" android, Data. An impossibly self-contradictory situation follows logically from the supposition that such an omniscient, unerring robot is conceivable. If one could construct such a Data, then one could also build a sister robot Echo with design specifications that include the following behavior pattern:

> If anyone asks Echo the abbreviated question, "What about So-and-So?", where "So-and-So" is the name (or serial number) of any robot, then Echo first asks Data (or, better, a built-in homunculus clone of Data) the following roundabout question:
> "Does So-and-So answer the question
> 'What about So-and-So?' ?".

Moreover, Echo is quite contrary:
- whenever Data answers "no" to this question, she answers "yes";
- whenever Data answers "yes" to this question, she keeps her mouth shut.

For example, if we ask Echo about Andrea, Echo turns to Data to ask whether Andrea answers the question, "What about Andrea?". Suppose Andrea would answer "no" to this particular question, and Data is smart enough to predict Andrea's answer without even asking. Then Data will answer "yes" to Echo, since Andrea in fact gives a negative answer. Hearing Data's answer to her question,

Echo refuses to answer. Echo also keep her mouth shut whenever Data neglects to answer her, but she never answers "no", herself.

The crux of the issue is whether Data (or any other robot) could in fact be all-knowing. To resolve this, consider the specific question "What about Echo?" and imagine that we pose this question to Echo herself! Echo proceeds to ask Data whether or not Echo answers the very same question. Consider all three possibilities:

- If Echo in fact answers "yes" when asked that question, it can only be because Data answers "no" when Echo asks him about her own behavior. But then Data gave the *wrong* answer. He was asked whether Echo answers. She does, but he said she doesn't.
- If Echo does not answer the question, it may be because Data answers "yes", but then again Data got it backwards.
- It may also be that Echo does not answer us, because Data does not answer her. But that means that Data himself does not know the right answer.

The inescapable conclusion is that no robot can be made smart enough to answer such questions: Either Data gives an erroneous answer (our Option II), or else he is dumbfounded (Option IV), just like a human interlocutor in the same situation. The intent of the vague question ("What about So-and-So?") is immaterial.

Of course, bystanders, equipped with hindsight, have no problem giving the correct answer *ex post facto*, as soon as Echo answers—should she altogether. Furthermore, privy to the inner workings of Echo's CPU, and armed with the knowledge that Data is programmed to never lie, no matter what, we can predict the correct answer: Echo will not answer (since Data won't).

5   The Transfinite

> To iterate through ordinals requires ordinal notations.
> These are notations for computable predicates,
> but it is necessary to establish that the computation
> really produces a well-founded total ordering.
> Thus we need to consider provably recursive ordinals.
>
> —John McCarthy (1999)

In fact, one can build a transfinite series of (ordinal-indexed) programs or robots, each more knowledgable about such matters (self-looping) than its predecessors.

Let $\mathcal{O}$ be any system of ordinal notations (e.g. ordinal diagrams [20] or the recursive path ordering [6]) with programmable ordering $<$, that is, such that the computation of a comparison $\beta < \alpha$ terminates for all $\alpha, \beta \in \mathcal{O}$. Define, for each $\alpha \in \mathcal{O}$:

$$S_\alpha(y) := \textbf{if } o_s(y) < \alpha \textbf{ then } T \textbf{ else loop}() ,$$

where $o_s(y)$ is a pattern-based function that checks if y is a program of the form **if** $\_ < \beta$ **then** T **else loop**(), and returns the upper bound β if it is (and $\mathcal{O}$, otherwise, where $\mathcal{O}$ is bigger than any $\alpha \in \mathcal{O}$, as is customary). Similarly,

$$R_\alpha(y) := \textbf{if } o_R(y) < \alpha \textbf{ then loop}() \textbf{ else } T \,,$$

where o_R returns β if y is of this form (or else $\mathcal{O}$).

For all $\alpha \in \mathcal{O}$, we have $S_\alpha(S_\alpha) = \perp$ and $R_\alpha(R_\alpha) \neq \perp$. So, all the S_α are guaranteed sound with respect to the question $X(X) = \perp$, and are complete for $X = S_\beta$, for all β up to (but not including) the ordinal α. Similarly, all the R_α are guaranteed complete (responsive when the answer is in the affirmative), and are sound for all R_β, $\beta < \alpha$. However, for us to be sure that they are correct, we must verify the correctness of $<$ on $\mathcal{O}$.

Despite the fact that S_ω and R_ω have no trouble answering correctly regarding infinitely many programs, there are transfinitely many "better" programs! (Cf. the ordinal-indexed search algorithms of [17].)

6   The Processes

> You must reject the statement I am now making to you
> because all the statements I make are incorrect.
>
> —*The Monkey Wrench* (Gordon Dickson, 1951)

Now we add two new components to the argument, corresponding to the plausible option (III) that an android sometimes just guesses an answer (instead of fruitlessly mulling over the question) and to the remote prospect that some alien androids are not cloneable (Option I).

Five processes will play a rôle:

R: This (Data-like) process (a.k.a. Roger) is meant to identify some programs X that diverge when fed themselves as input, but is implemented in some undisclosed fashion, say, via quantum wetware. (We are living in a Lisp world wherein programs are their own code.) At this point, we are making no assumptions about R's correctness.

A: This program (Andrea, say) has the same purpose as R. In Penrose's scenario [15], A incorporates all current, sound scientific knowledge on the subject, but only answers "yes", if it answers at all. It is enough for the argument, however, to incorporate all of R's knowledge. (Since R's knowledge is presumed to be some finite of "rules", were we able to program all of it in a finite program, a finite set of rules that include only those of R's ideas that are sound would also have to exist as a program.) Again, we will make no *a priori* presumptions about the correctness of A's behavior.

G: This (God-like) entity is our truth yardstick, an oracle that always has the absolute, correct answer to such questions of divergence.

C: This (Echo-like) program applies Cantorian diagonalization to A in the standard fashion so as to produce paradoxical behavior *vis-à-vis* any pretensions of A to know too much.

K: This will be an undisclosed process (in Roger's cerebrum or Data's logic circuitry) used by R to inspect programs like A.

Unlike [15], we will be specializing A and R to deal with divergences (lack of answer) of self-applications $X(X)$, rather than questions regarding more general applications $Y(X)$. This simplifies matters and is all that is, in the final analysis, cogent to the argument.

Let Π denote the set of one-input partial predicates in any standard model of computation (which contains diverging programs and has a conditional construct and subprocedures). By "predicate", we mean that the output is always one of the Boolean truth values, T/F; by "partial", we mean that some inputs may result in no output. As is common, one can enrich the range of a function to include an undefined value $\perp$, denoting the outcome of a never-ending or non-responsive ("I don't know the answer.") process. That is, each $p \in \Pi$ may be viewed as a total function $p : y \mapsto \{T, F, \perp\}$. For example, Π can be the set of one-argument untyped Lisp programs whose range is $\{T, F, \perp\}$ (or a subset thereof).

As explained above, for any particular program $A \in \Pi$, one can construct the following diagonalized program $C_A \in \Pi$:

$$C_A(Y) := \textbf{if } A(Y) \textbf{ then } T \textbf{ else loop() where } A \ldots , \tag{1}$$

The input Y can be any program in Π (Borg, say). The behaviors of A and C_A are intimately connected:

- When $A(Y)$ returns T, so does $C_A(Y)$.
- If $A(Y)$ responds F, then $C_A(Y)$ enters an eternal loop.
- If $A(Y)$ does not respond, neither does $C_A(Y)$.

The stated requirement for A is that $A(X)$ answer T when "it" is aware that execution of $X(X)$ is nonterminating ($X(X) = \perp$). In other words, A is sound if $A(X) \Rightarrow X(X) = \perp$. But there is no guarantee that A behaves as expected. Were A to know all there was to know (completeness), that would mean $X(X) = \perp \Rightarrow A(X)$.

On the other hand, $G : \Pi \to \{T, F\}$ is the total predicate,

$$G(X) := [X(X) = \perp] , \tag{2}$$

manifesting the truth of the matter. Equality ($=$) is semantic: both sides must be equally (un)defined.

Now consider some (partial) predicate $R : X \mapsto \{T, F, \perp\}$ with the following behavioral rule:

> *return T if*
> *program X is of the form*
> $X(Y) := \textbf{if } Z(Y) \textbf{ then } T \textbf{ else loop(), where } Z \ldots$ (3)
> *and*
> $K[Z(X) \neq T] .$

Here $X, Y,$ and Z are pattern variables ("placeholders") and $K : S \to \{T, F, \perp\}$ is some partial predicate over statements S. The process K is meant to model whatever thought processes are involved in R's analysis of the question whether $Z(X) \neq T$. Thus, the above behavior is (a special case of) what Penrose believes humans are capable of.

The presumption is that R on input X will, in fact, answer T regarding the divergence of $X(X)$ when and if R "believes it knows"—via process K—that the test $Z(X)$ performed by $X(X)$ does not succeed. Specifically, $R(C_A)$ returns T if $K[A(C_A) \neq T]$ returns T and some other rules of R has not already ventured an answer. On the other hand, R may have various additional considerations that that pre-empt the above behavior and are employed when K responds with F, or when K does not come up with an answer within some reasonable time frame.

7 The Four Sons

> All human errors are impatience,
> a premature breaking off of methodical procedure....
>
> —Franz Kafka (1917)

The following facts are indisputable:

$$A(C_A) = T \quad \Leftrightarrow \quad C_A(C_A) = T \tag{4}$$
$$A(C_A) \neq T \quad \Leftrightarrow \quad C_A(C_A) = \bot \tag{5}$$
$$A(C_A) = T \quad \Rightarrow \quad G(C_A) = F \tag{6}$$
$$A(C_A) \neq T \quad \Rightarrow \quad G(C_A) = T . \tag{7}$$

Facts (4,5) follow directly from the references to A in the definition (1) of C: C_A calls A, answers T if A does, and loops, otherwise. Facts (6,7) follow directly from C's behavior and the specification (2) of G: If $A(C_A)$ yields T, then C_A does not diverge (4), and G knows it; if $A(C_A)$ doesn't yield T, then C_A does diverge (5), and again G knows it.

Now, G is infallible and total $(G(C_A) \neq \bot)$. Hence (by 6, 7), no A can always be right, whether the result of A, when asked question C_A, is T, F, or $\bot$. That is:

$$A(C_A) \neq G(C_A) , \tag{8}$$

which is just a restatement (as in Sect. 3) of Turing's undecidability result for the halting problem. That is, no program $A(X)$ can answer infallibly—for any program X—whether $X(X)$ diverges; specifically, it must trip up with regard to C_A. So, if A happens to agree with R about C_A, then R, too, must not give the textbook answer G.

The upshot of the above facts is that:

$$A(C_A) = R(C_A) \quad \Rightarrow \quad R(C_A) \neq G(C_A) . \tag{9}$$

In other words, *if A simulates R* (at least on C_A), then R does not respond properly (T for F, F for T, or $\bot$), while *if R is averred to never err* (precluding both Options II and III), then either $A(C_A) \neq R(C_A)$ (Option I) or else $R(C_A) = \perp$ (as dictated by Option IV). In the last case, R's knowledge is incomplete:

$$A(C_A) = R(C_A) = \perp \quad \Rightarrow \quad \neg K[A(C_A) \neq T] , \qquad (10)$$

since, were K to have responded, so would have R.

The dichotomy at the heart of the debate is whether there in fact exists a computer program A in Π that agrees with R on C_A, or perhaps there can never be such a program. According to both the strong and weak AI points of view, there exists such a program A that, in particular, agrees with R when queried regarding C_A. But, then, either neither answer, or else both give the same wrong answer. In the latter case, R's error may result either from faulty "reasoning", or from some other cause. It is much like an examinee who, presented with a difficult true/false question, cannot work out the correct answer within the time limit. In this situation, a person may "guess" (using heuristics, perhaps), or may give up and leave the answer blank.

To summarize, we have discerned four characteristics of the nature of R:[3]

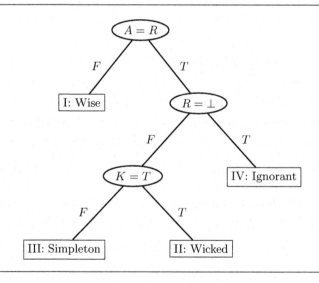

Fig. 1. Possible resolutions

I. R **the Wise:** $R \notin \Pi$
   (wise, in a super-Turing sense);
II. R **the Wicked:** $K[A(C_A) \neq T] = T$ but in fact $\neg[A(C_A) \neq T]$
   (wicked, in that R internalizes an untruth);

---

[3] The options are evocative of the "Four Sons" of the Passover *Haggadah*, derived from the *Mekhilta*, quoted at the outset.

III. **R the Simpleton:** $K[A(C_A) \neq T] \neq T$ and in reality $R(C_A) = \neg G(C_A)$
(acting without thinking);
IV. **R the Ignorant:** $R(C_A) = \perp$
(expressing no opinion in the matter).

Using an ostensibly ratiocinative, but fallacious, process (K) is Case II; resorting to an extralogical process is our Case III; not answering is IV. See Fig. 7.

If R gives the wrong answer, it is either due to the above-specified behavior pattern (3), in which case K is unsound (Case II), or else R answers wrongly based on some other consideration or impulse (Case III). In the latter event, K does not respond with T within some allocated time frame, either because its answer is F, or else because it never reaches a conclusion.

Case I follows from the supposition that there is no $A \in \Pi$ such that $A(C_A) = R(C_A)$. If, on the contrary, $A(C_A) = R(C_A)$ for some $A \in \Pi$, then (by 9) $R(C_A) \neq G(C_A)$, either because $R(C_A)$ gives a wrong answer or yields no answer. With the latter outcome (Case IV), R is not fully (self-) cognizant, since $\neg K[A(C_A) \neq T]$, though in fact $R(C_A) = A(C_A)$ and $R(C_A) \neq T$ (by 10). In other words, R is an incomplete reasoner.

8   The Conclusion

> If a machine is expected to be infallible, it cannot also be intelligent.
> There are several theorems which say almost exactly that.
> But these theorems say nothing about how much intelligence may be displayed
> if a machine makes no pretense at infallibility.
>
> —Alan Turing (1947)

We have skirted the issue of R's being "aware" or "unaware" of its own consistency. We all know (even R's creator claims to know) that R cannot correctly answer all questions involving his *own* consistency, any more than can A. Whether R sees himself reflected in A is beside the point. The more perspicacious question is whether R reasons soundly about one specific aspect of one particular observable program A. Does R (erroneously, perhaps) believe (via K) that he knows how A behaves given program C_A (which, in turn, involves A) as input?

Penrose opts for the "R the Wise" solution, since he believes that R is sound (neither "Wicked" nor "Simpleton") and responsive (not "Ignorant"). He goes on [14, 15] to propose a non-Turing-equivalent model for $R \notin \Pi$. Rejoinders to Penrose along the lines that R represents an "idealized" mathematician agree that such an R cannot be captured algorithmically, but is rather more G-like.[4]

---

[4] "[Penrose] admits that he is talking about an idealized mathematician, not an actual one. It would be a great feat to discover that a certain program is the one that the brain of an actual mathematician 'runs', but it would be quite a different feat to discover that a program is the one that a brain of an idealized mathematician would run." [16].

Detractors of Penrose who contend that there may be a program A mimicking R must choose between one of the other three options: R reasons unsoundly with K (II); R feels under pressure and answers using a process other than K (III); or R doesn't answer at all (IV). For example, Hilary Putnam is quoted in [11] as suggesting that humans are inconsistent machines, that is, R ("the Wicked") believes (via K) a falsehood ($A(C_A) \neq T$), our Case II. Similarly, Martin Davis [5] says in response to Penrose: "No human mathematician can claim infallibility. We all make mistakes! So there is nothing in Gödel's theorem to preclude the mathematical powers of a human mind being equivalent to an algorithmic process that produces false as well as true statements."

In frustration at getting nowhere with his sound, cerebral reasoning faculty K, R may blurt out some simplistic—but invariably wrong—answer (Option III). This is how I interpret one of John McCarthy's [12] criticisms: "Much of Penrose's reasoning is nonmonotonic, $e.g.$ preferring the simplest explanation of some phenomenon, but his methodology doesn't allow for nonmonotonic reasoning by the program." In other words, there is in fact an A that acts precisely like R and answers incorrectly, for reasons that are non-Aristotelian, but Penrose looks instead at an alternate A' that acts like a hamstrung R for which only monotonic K is consulted. Thus, it is $A' \neq R$, whereas $A = R$.

Lucas [11] does attribute $actual$ human foibles to "Simpleton" shortcomings: "Our inconsistencies are mistakes rather than set policies. They correspond to the occasional malfunctioning of a machine, not its normal scheme of operations." Along these lines, most discussions exclude option III as irrelevant when considering "ideal" humans.

Consider arguments such as:

- "Perhaps we are sound, but we cannot know unassailably that we are sound." [4]
- "There is an obvious lacuna: the possibility of a program ... which is not 'simple enough to appreciate in a perfectly conscious' way is overlooked." [16]
- "One can show quite rigorously that Penrose's notion of what it is to know oneself to be sound cannot itself be sound." And, "Humans may be $unable$ to know that they are consistent." [10–$emphasis\ mine$]
- "We cannot fully analyze a complicated learning machine, let alone the human mind. Hence, one cannot establish one's own self-consistency." [1–$my\ translation$]

These quotes do not make it clear what the authors believe human mathematicians do in the face of this lack of soundness/consistency. Some are (perhaps) suggesting that R is "inadequate" and need not have an answer to each and every question. Rather, R—in honest ignorance—does not respond at all to the most vexing of questions, C_A, or perhaps reaches his demise without ever having reached a conclusion. Interpreted thus, they are subscribing to Option IV.

Finally, it is engaging to consider the analogous situation where A is an android (Andrea), designed to parrot R when asked whether C (A's alter ego) diverges on C. That places R in a quandary: Any answer will turn out to be wrong. Whenever someone inquires of C, C consults A, who turns the question over to R. If R says "yes" to A, when asked if C will diverge, then A answers "yes" to C, and C converges, instead. If, on the other hand, R predicts that C will respond, then R says "no", and A also says "no", in which case C cycles, contrary to R's assertion. Thus, the only sound alternative for R, in such a circumstance, would be to "take the Fifth" and avoid perjuring himself.

Paraphrasing Turing [23]:

If a machine is intelligent, it must also be fallible.

Acknowledgement

I thank Udi Boker, Yishai Feldman, and referees for their reactions.

References

1. Arnon Avron. *Mishpete Gedel u-ve'ayat ha-yesodot shel ha-matematikah (= Gödel's Theorems and the Problem of the Foundations of Mathematics)*. Broadcast University, Ministry of Defence, Tel Aviv, Israel, 1998. (In Hebrew).
2. Udi Boker and Nachum Dershowitz. Comparing computational power. *Logic Journal of the IGPL*, 2006. To appear; available at: http://www.cs.tau.ac.il/~nachum/papers/ComparingComputationalPower.pdf.
3. David Chalmers, editor. *Symposium on Roger Penrose's Shadows of the Mind*, volume 2. Association for the Scientific Study of Consciousness, 1995. Available at http://psyche.cs.monash.edu.au/psyche-index-v2.html (viewed September 2005).
4. David J. Chalmers. Minds, machines, and mathematics: A review of *Shadows of the Mind* by Roger Penrose. *Psyche: An Interdisciplinary Journal of Research on Consciousness*, 2(9), June 1995. Available at http://psyche.cs.monash.edu.au/v2/psyche-2-09-chalmers.html (viewed September 2005).
5. Martin Davis. *Engines of Logic: Mathematicians and the Origin of the Computer*. W. W. Norton & Company, New York, 2001.
6. Nachum Dershowitz. Orderings for term-rewriting systems. *Theoretical Computer Science*, 17(3):279–301, March 1982.
7. Douglas R. Hofstadter. *Gödel, Escher, Bach: An Eternal Golden Braid*. Basic Books, 1979.
8. Tien D. Kieu. Quantum algorithm for Hilbert's Tenth Problem. *ArXiv Quantum Physics e-prints*, October 2003. Available at arXiv:quant-ph/0110136.
9. Tien D. Kieu. Hypercomputability of quantum adiabatic processes: Fact versus prejudices. *ArXiv Quantum Physics e-prints*, April 2005. Available at arXiv.org:quant-ph/0504101.
10. Geoffrey LaForte, Patrick J. Hayes, and Kenneth M. Ford. Why Gödel's theorem cannot refute computationalism. *Artificial Intelligence*, 104(1–2):265–286, 1998.
11. John R. Lucas. Minds, machines and Gödel. *Philosophy*, XXXVI:112–127, 1961. Reprinted in *The Modeling of Mind*, K. M. Sayre and F. J. Crosson, eds., Notre Dame Press, 1963, pp. 269–270; available at http://users.ox.ac.uk/ jrlucas/mmg.html (viewed September 2005).

12. John McCarthy. Awareness and understanding in computer programs: A review of *Shadows of the Mind* by Roger Penrose. *Psyche: An Interdisciplinary Journal of Research on Consciousness*, 2(11), July 1995. Available at http://psyche.cs.monash.edu.au/v2/psyche-2-11-mccarthy.html (viewed September 2005).

13. Allen Newell and Herbert A. Simon. Computer science as empirical enquiry. *Communications of the ACM*, 19(3):113–126, March 1976.

14. Roger Penrose. *The Emperor's New Mind: Concerning Computers, Minds, and The Laws of Physics*. Oxford University Press, New York, 1989.

15. Roger Penrose. *Shadows of the Mind: A Search for the Missing Science of Consciousness*. Oxford University Press, Oxford, 1994.

16. Hilary Putnam. Book review: *Shadows of the Mind* by Roger Penrose. *Bulletin of the American Mathematical Society*, 32(3):370–373, July 1995. Available at http://www.ams.org/bull/pre-1996-data/199507/199507015.pdf (viewed September 2005).

17. Edward M. Reingold and Xiaojun Shen. More nearly optimal algorithms for unbounded searching, Part II: The transfinite case. *SIAM J. Comput.*, 20(1):184–208, 1991.

18. John Searle. Minds, brains and programs. *Behavioral and Brain Sciences*, 3:417–424, 1980. Available at http://members.aol.com/NeoNoetics/MindsBrainsPrograms.html September 2005).

19. Warren D. Smith. Three counterexamples refuting Kieu's plan for "quantum adiabatic hypercomputation"; and some uncomputable quantum mechanical tasks. *Journal of Applied Mathematics and Computation*, 2006. To appear.

20. Gaisi Takeuti. Ordinal diagrams. II. *J. Math. Soc. Japan*, 12:385–391, 1960.

21. Boris Tsirelson. The quantum algorithm of Kieu does not solve the Hilbert's Tenth Problem. Available at arXiv.org/abs/quant-ph/0111009, November 2001.

22. Alan M. Turing. On computable numbers, with an application to the Entscheidungsproblem. *Proceedings of the London Mathematical Society, Ser. 2*, 42:230–265, November 1936. Correction in vol. 43 (1937), pp. 544-546. Available at http://www.abelard.org/turpap2/tp2-ie.asp (viewed September 2005).

23. Alan M. Turing. Lecture to the London Mathematical Society on 20 February 1947. In B. E. Carpenter and R. W. Doran, editors, *A. M. Turing's ACE Report of 1946 and Other Papers*, volume 10 of *Charles Babbage Institute Reprint Series for the History of Computing*. MIT Press, Cambridge, MA, 1986.

24. Doron Zeilberger. A 2-minute proof of the 2nd most important theorem of the 2nd millennium. Available at http://www.math.rutgers.edu/ zeilberg/mamarim/mamarimhtml/halt.html (viewed September 2005), October 1998.

An Algorithmic Account of Ehrenfeucht Games on Labeled Successor Structures

Angelo Montanari, Alberto Policriti, and Nicola Vitacolonna

University of Udine,
Department of Mathematics and Computer Science,
via delle Scienze 206, 33100 Udine (UD), Italy
{montana, policrit, vitacolo}@dimi.uniud.it

Abstract. Ehrenfeucht-Fraïssé games are commonly used as a method to measure the expressive power of a logic, but they are also a flexible tool to compare structures. To exploit such a comparison power, explicit conditions characterizing the winning strategies for both players must be provided. We give a necessary and sufficient condition for Duplicator to win games played on finite structures with a successor relation and a finite number of unary predicates. This structural characterization suggests an algorithmic approach to the analysis of games, which can be used to compute the "remoteness" of a game and to determine the optimal moves for both players, that is, to derive algorithms for Spoiler and Duplicator that play optimally. We argue that such an algorithmic solution may be used in contexts where the "degree of similarity" between two structures must be measured, such as the comparison of biological sequences.

1 Introduction

The Ehrenfeucht-Fraïssé method was introduced in [6] in its algebraic form, and then interpreted in a game-theoretic framework in [4]. We will refer to the latter as an *EF-game*. The importance of the method rests on its intuitive appeal and its wide applicability: it is one of the few tools in model theory that can still be used when restricting to finite structures, so it is particularly relevant to problems in computer science [16].

EF-games are two-player combinatorial games of perfect information, that is, no chance, probability or information hiding mechanism are involved, which can be used to compare two structures. The first player is called *Spoiler*, the second *Duplicator*. Roughly speaking, *Spoiler* aims at proving that the two structures are "different", while Duplicator wants to show that they are "equivalent". Typically, they must achieve their purpose in a fixed, bounded number of rounds (although infinite variants of the game can be defined). The structures form the *playground* and in each round the players pick elements from them.

The rules of an EF-game usually have a logical counterpart, in a way that the existence of a winning strategy for one of the players relates to the ability of formulas of a suitable logic to distinguish the structures used in the game. As

G. Sutcliffe and A. Voronkov (Eds.): LPAR 2005, LNAI 3835, pp. 139–153, 2005.

a consequence, the main use of EF-games is to prove inexpressibility results: if a property $\mathcal{P}$ of a class of structures is not definable by a given logic, this can be proved by showing that, no matter how many rounds are to be played, there are always two (finite) structures $\mathfrak{A}$ and $\mathfrak{B}$ such that $\mathfrak{A}$ satisfies $\mathcal{P}$, $\mathfrak{B}$ does not satisfy $\mathcal{P}$, and Duplicator has a winning strategy in the game played on $\mathfrak{A}$ and $\mathfrak{B}$ that corresponds to the logic.

In this paper we focus our attention on the *comparison power* of EF-games. As we have just pointed out, EF-games are used to establish whether two structures can be distinguished or not (by a logic), so they are widely recognized as a handy tool to measure the expressive power of a logic. But EF-games also provide information on "how much" and "where" two structures differ. We argue that this feature may be useful in contexts where the *degree of similarity* of structures is relevant, e.g. in the comparison of biological sequences: we will provide a concrete example of such an application at the end of Section 4. EF-games provide a mathematically precise, yet flexible, way to define what similarity is. Besides, they bring in logical languages that can formally describe how the structures look alike. So, instead of using games to study properties of a logic, we tailor our approach towards a use of games for the study of properties of structures.

In order to use games in this way, *structural characterizations* of playgrounds are needed. The existence of a winning strategy for Duplicator implies that the structures involved must share common features, and vice versa. Moreover, the ability to exhibit a winning strategy in an effective way can lead to further insight into the similarities and discrepancies of the two structures. It turns out to be difficult to give such characterizations. In [13] it is shown that the problem of determining the existence of a winning strategy for Duplicator in an m-round EF-game on two finite structures over any vocabulary containing at least a binary and a ternary relation is PSPACE-complete.

In this paper we will consider EF-games adequate for first-order logic. Several general sufficient conditions for Duplicator to be able to win such games have been proposed in the literature [5, 14, 1, 11], but complete knowledge is achieved only in special cases, the simplest being probably unlabeled successor structures and unlabeled linear orderings. We give a necessary and sufficient condition for Duplicator to win games played on finite structures with a successor relation and a finite number of unary predicates (Theorem 5).

In Section 2 we give the necessary definitions needed further. In Section 3 we review a characterization of the languages definable in the first-order logic of one successor. In Section 4, we give an algorithmic characterization of EF-games on labeled sets with a successor relation, and in Section 5 we briefly comment on the algorithmic aspects.

2   Basics

For $m, n \in \mathbb{N}$, let $[m, n] \triangleq \{ i \in \mathbb{N} \mid m \leq i \leq n \}$. Let τ be a finite relational vocabulary. We denote τ-structures with symbols $\mathfrak{A}$, $\mathfrak{B}$, etc... The domain of a structure will be denoted by the corresponding roman letter, e.g. A,

B, and so on. A structure $\mathfrak{A}$ with designated elements $a_1, \ldots, a_k \in A$ is denoted by $(\mathfrak{A}, a_1, \ldots, a_k)$. Two structures $(\mathfrak{A}, a_1, \ldots, a_k)$ and $(\mathfrak{B}, b_1, \ldots, b_k)$, with $k \geq 0$, are *isomorphic*, $(\mathfrak{A}, a_1, \ldots, a_k) \cong (\mathfrak{B}, b_1, \ldots, b_k)$ for short, if there is an isomorphism between $\mathfrak{A}$ and $\mathfrak{B}$ that maps a_j to b_j, for $1 \leq j \leq k$. A *partial isomorphism* p from A to B is an injective function such that $\mathrm{dom}(p) \subseteq A$, $\mathrm{cod}(p) \subseteq B$ and p is an isomorphism between the substructures of $\mathfrak{A}$ and $\mathfrak{B}$ induced by $\mathrm{dom}(p)$ and $\mathrm{cod}(p)$, respectively. For $m \in \mathbb{N}$, two τ-structures $(\mathfrak{A}, a_1, \ldots, a_k)$ and $(\mathfrak{B}, b_1, \ldots, b_k)$ are *m-equivalent*, $(\mathfrak{A}, a_1, \ldots, a_k) \equiv_m (\mathfrak{B}, b_1, \ldots, b_k)$ for short, if, for every first-order formula $\phi(\mathbf{x})$ with quantifier depth at most m and free variables among $\mathbf{x} = x_1, \ldots, x_k$, $(\mathfrak{A}, a_1, \ldots, a_k) \models \phi(\mathbf{x})$ if and only if $(\mathfrak{B}, b_1, \ldots, b_k) \models \phi(\mathbf{x})$. For more detailed definitions, see [3]. In this paper, we restrict our attention to finite structures.

We now give a more precise definition of EF-games for first-order logic. The game is played by two players, called *Spoiler* and *Duplicator*: to help distinguish between the two, we conventionally refer to the former as a male and to the latter as a female player. The playground is made by two τ-structures $\mathfrak{A}$ and $\mathfrak{B}$. The game is divided into n *rounds*, and each round consists of a move by Spoiler followed by a move by Duplicator.

Definition 1. *A* configuration *of an EF-game played on structures $\mathfrak{A}$ and $\mathfrak{B}$ is a relation $p \subseteq A \times B$. Given tuples $\mathbf{a} = a_1, \ldots, a_k$ of elements of A and $\mathbf{b} = b_1, \ldots, b_k$ of elements of B, we write $((\mathfrak{A}, \mathbf{a}), (\mathfrak{B}, \mathbf{b}))$ to denote the configuration $p = \{(a_i, b_i)\}_{1 \leq i \leq k}$.*

A position is a configuration specifying the number of remaining rounds.

Definition 2. *A* position *in an EF-game played on structures $\mathfrak{A}$ and $\mathfrak{B}$ is a triple $((\mathfrak{A}, \mathbf{a}), (\mathfrak{B}, \mathbf{b}), j)$ where $j \in \mathbb{N}$ is the number of rounds yet to be played.*

Thus, in the game-theoretic view, relations are viewed as configurations in a game; a play from an initial position $((\mathfrak{A}, \mathbf{a}), (\mathfrak{B}, \mathbf{b}), m)$, with $m \geq 0$, consists in performing m extensions of the initial configuration according to the following rules:

- Spoiler chooses one of the two structures (say $\mathfrak{A}$) and an element c in it;
- Duplicator replies by choosing an element d in the other structure (say $\mathfrak{B}$);
- the new position becomes $((\mathfrak{A}, \mathbf{a}, c), (\mathfrak{B}, \mathbf{b}, d), m - 1)$.

The game ends at positions of the form $((\mathfrak{A}, \mathbf{a}), (\mathfrak{B}, \mathbf{b}), 0)$.

Definition 3. *An* ending position $((\mathfrak{A}, \mathbf{a}), (\mathfrak{B}, \mathbf{b}), 0)$ *is winning for Duplicator if and only if $((\mathfrak{A}, \mathbf{a}), (\mathfrak{B}, \mathbf{b}))$ is a partial isomorphism. Duplicator has a winning strategy from position $((\mathfrak{A}, \mathbf{a}), (\mathfrak{B}, \mathbf{b}), m)$, written $\mathsf{D}((\mathfrak{A}, \mathbf{a}), (\mathfrak{B}, \mathbf{b}), m)$, if she can reach a winning ending position no matter how Spoiler plays. We write $\mathsf{S}((\mathfrak{A}, \mathbf{a}), (\mathfrak{B}, \mathbf{b}), m)$ to denote that Duplicator does not have a winning strategy.*

As EF-games are finite and do not have draw positions, it is not difficult to prove that they are determined, that is, exactly one of the players has a winning strategy. The relevance of EF-games is tied to the following characterization of m-equivalence.

Theorem 1 (Ehrenfeucht, [4,3]). *For structures* $\mathfrak{A}$ *and* $\mathfrak{B}$, *k-tuples* $\mathbf{a} \in A^k, \mathbf{b} \in B^k$ *and* $m \in \mathbb{N}$,

$$\mathsf{D}((\mathfrak{A}, \mathbf{a}), (\mathfrak{B}, \mathbf{b}), m) \quad \Longleftrightarrow \quad (\mathfrak{A}, \mathbf{a}) \equiv_m (\mathfrak{B}, \mathbf{b}) .$$

Corollary 1. *A class* $\mathcal{K}$ *of τ-structures is first-order definable if and only if there is* $m \in \mathbb{N}$ *such that, whenever* $\mathfrak{A} \in \mathcal{K}$ *and* $\mathfrak{B} \notin \mathcal{K}$, *then* $\mathsf{S}(\mathfrak{A}, \mathfrak{B}, m)$.

Corollary 1 can be used to prove that a property is not first-order definable: it is sufficient to show that Duplicator has a winning strategy in suitable EF-games. Proving this, however, can be very difficult.

In the proof of our results we make use of Fraïssé's characterization of m-equivalence, based on the following notion of m-isomorphism.

Definition 4. *Let* $\mathbf{a} = a_1, \ldots, a_k$ *and* $\mathbf{b} = b_1, \ldots, b_k$. *Two structures* $(\mathfrak{A}, \mathbf{a})$ *and* $(\mathfrak{B}, \mathbf{b})$ *are m-isomorphic, written* $(\mathfrak{A}, \mathbf{a}) \cong_m (\mathfrak{B}, \mathbf{b})$, *if there is a sequence of nonempty sets* $I_0, \ldots, I_m$ *of partial isomorphisms such that* $\{(a_i, b_i)\}_{1 \le i \le k} \in I_m$ *and, for every* $k = 1, \ldots, m$, *the following back-and-forth property holds:*

(forth property) *for every* $p \in I_k$ *and for every* $a \in A$ *there is* $b \in B$ *such that* $p \cup \{(a, b)\} \in I_{k-1}$;
(back property) *for every* $p \in I_k$ *and for every* $b \in B$ *there is* $a \in A$ *such that* $p \cup \{(a, b)\} \in I_{k-1}$.

Theorem 2 (Fraïssé, [6,3]). *For structures* $\mathfrak{A}$ *and* $\mathfrak{B}$, *k-tuples* $\mathbf{a} \in A^k, \mathbf{b} \in B^k$ *and* $m \ge 0$,

$$(\mathfrak{A}, \mathbf{a}) \cong_m (\mathfrak{B}, \mathbf{b}) \quad \Longleftrightarrow \quad (\mathfrak{A}, \mathbf{a}) \equiv_m (\mathfrak{B}, \mathbf{b}) .$$

A logical description of the equivalence classes of the relation $\cong_m$ by formulas of quantifier depth at most m can be given by means of the so-called m-*Hintikka formulas* [10]: for a given structure $(\mathfrak{A}, \mathbf{a})$ and given m there exists a formula $\varphi^m_{(\mathfrak{A}, \mathbf{a})}(\mathbf{x})$ of quantifier depth m that holds exactly in the structures m-isomorphic to $(\mathfrak{A}, \mathbf{a})$ (see [3] for details). Every first-order formula $\varphi(\mathbf{x})$ is equivalent to the disjunction of a finite number of Hintikka formulas, each one describing one $\cong_m$-class.

Another interesting characterization of first-order logic is due to Gaifman [7]: every first-order sentence is equivalent to a boolean combination of "local" sentences. Each local sentence can be evaluated by examining small neighborhoods of a set of elements of the domain far apart from each other, where the distance between two points is the distance in the Gaifman graph associated to the structure [3].

The locality of first-order logic is a well-known fact, which has consequences on the form assumed by the strategies of the corresponding EF-games. The "high-level" strategy of Duplicator in such games prescribes that she "mimicks" Spoiler if he plays in the neighborhoods of already chosen elements; otherwise, Duplicator must find an element with a sufficiently large "equivalent" neighborhood outside all current neighborhoods. The difficult part in characterizing a winning strategy lies in the precise meaning of "mimicking" and finding "equivalent" neighborhoods.

All the sufficient conditions proposed in the literature [5, 1, 14, 11] implement in some way the high-level strategy sketched above. Maybe unsurprisingly, there is a lack of complete structural characterizations of winning strategies, even for restricted classes of structures. The simplest result of this kind is probably the characterization of (unlabeled) linear orderings: $D(([1, n], <), ([1, p], <), m)$ if and only if $n = p$ or $n, p \geq 2^m - 1$. In Section 4 we will characterize games played on labeled successor structures.

3   Definability in the First-Order Logic of One Successor

In [15] the class of languages definable in the first-order logic of one successor (FOL(s) for short) is characterized as the class of the *threshold* (or *generalized*) *locally testable* languages. In this section we review and comment this result, especially from a computational and algorithmic point of view. We first define the relevant structures.

Definition 5. *Let Σ be a finite alphabet, and let $w = w_1 \cdots w_n \in \Sigma^+$ be a nonempty word of length $|w| = n$. The labeled s-structure induced by w is the relational structure $\mathfrak{S}_w = ([1, n], s, \{P_c\}_{c \in \Sigma})$, where s is the successor relation over $[1, n]$, that is, $s(x, y)$ holds if and only if $y = x + 1$, and, for each $c \in \Sigma$, $P_c = \{i \mid i \in [1, n] \wedge w_i = c\}$. The distance $\delta(a, b)$ between two elements of a structure $\mathfrak{S}_w$ is $\delta(a, b) = |a - b|$.*

A word x is a *factor of length l* of a word $w = w_1 \cdots w_n$ if there exists $i \in [1, n - l + 1]$ such that $x = w_i \cdots w_{i+l-1}$. The factor x is a *prefix* (resp., *suffix*) of w if $i = 1$ (resp., $i = n - l + 1$). We denote the prefix (resp., suffix) of w of length l by $pref_l(w)$ (resp., $suff_l(w)$).

Given the above correspondence between words and labeled s-structures, we will freely use words and models interchangeably. For example, we will say that a word w satisfies a formula ϕ, meaning that $\mathfrak{S}_w$ satisfies ϕ, and we will speak of a factor of a labeled s-structure $\mathfrak{S}_w$, meaning the substructure induced by a factor of w.

The *multiplicity* of x in w, denoted by $\begin{bmatrix} w \\ x \end{bmatrix}$, is the number of occurrences of x as a factor of w. Given $t \in \mathbb{N}$, let $=_t$ be an equivalence relation on $\mathbb{N}$ defined as follows: for $m, n \in \mathbb{N}$, $m =_t n$ if $m = n$ or $m, n > t$.

For given $k, t > 0$, let $\sim_{k,t}$ be the congruence defined, for $u, v \in \Sigma^+$, by setting $u \sim_{k,t} v$ if and only if

1. $pref_{k-1}(u) = pref_{k-1}(v)$;
2. $suff_{k-1}(u) = suff_{k-1}(v)$;
3. for every $x \in \Sigma^+$ of length k, $\begin{bmatrix} u \\ x \end{bmatrix} =_t \begin{bmatrix} v \\ x \end{bmatrix}$.

Note that if $u \sim_{k,t} v$ then $u \sim_{k',t'} v$ for all $k' \leq k$ and $t' \leq t$.

Definition 6. *A language $L \subseteq \Sigma^+$ is threshold locally testable if there exist integers $k, t > 0$ such that L is a finite union of $\sim_{k,t}$-classes.*

Theorem 3 (Thomas, [15]). *A language $L \subseteq \Sigma^+$ is definable in $FOL(s)$ if and only if it is threshold locally testable.*

To what extent does this result help characterizing m-equivalence? Since each $\equiv_m$-class can be defined by an m-Hintikka formula [3], each $\equiv_m$-class is a finite union of $\sim_{k,t}$-classes for some k and t; that is, there are k and t, depending on m, such that $\sim_{k,t}$ is a refinement of $\equiv_m$. The proof of Theorem 3, from left to right, makes use of a sufficient condition essentially due to Hanf [9], which guarantees that $u \equiv_m v$ if $u \sim_{3^m,3^m+1} v$. This condition is not necessary, however, and, actually, such values are not tight.

Even if the tightest values for k and t can be provided, given a fixed m, deriving a procedure to test the m-equivalence of two words w and w' from Theorem 3 is not straightforward. If m is part of the input, the procedure becomes even more involved and computationally complex.

It should be clear that, although definability and m-equivalence are strictly related (see also Corollary 1), from an algorithmic point of view the two problems are better tackled independently. Theorem 3 does not provide an explicit way to establish whether two given words are m-equivalent for a given m or to determine the maximum m such that two given words are m-equivalent.

In the next section, we provide an effective characterization of m-equivalence of two labeled s-structures, based on a structural description of two words that guarantees a winning strategy for a player of an EF-game. Our result provides algorithms for determining the winner of an EF-game in m rounds, for determining the least m such that Spoiler has a winning strategy (or, equivalently, the greatest m such that Duplicator has a winning strategy), and for determining the set of optimal moves for each player in a given configuration of a game.

4   EF-Games on Successor Structures

From now on, two expressions will recur very often, namely 2^{m-i-1} and $2^{m-i}-1$ (as we will see, they are the radii of entailing and reachable intervals at round i in an EF-game with m rounds). To make the notation a little more compact, we will give them names. So, let $\mathfrak{e}_i^m \triangleq 2^{m-i-1}$ and $\mathfrak{r}_i^m \triangleq 2^{m-i}-1$. These quantities are related as follows: $\mathfrak{r}_i^m = 2\mathfrak{e}_i^m - 1$ and $\sum_{k=i}^{m-1} \mathfrak{e}_k^m = \mathfrak{r}_i^m$.

Definition 7. *Given a word $w = w_1 \cdots w_n$, $i \in [1, n]$ and $r \in \mathbb{N}$, the factor of w of radius r centered at position i, written $w_r(i)$, is $w_{i-r} \cdots w_i \cdots w_{i+r}$, where we assume, for convenience, that $w_k = \$$, for $k < 1$ or $k > n$, with $\$ \notin \Sigma$. We denote the set of factors of radius r of a word w with $F_r(w)$.*

Note that, by the above definition, the length of $w_r(i)$ is always $2r + 1$, even if $i < r$ or $i > n - r$. Moreover, the multiplicity of a factor $w_r(i)$ containing at least one $\$$ is always 1.

Definition 8. *Given a structure $(\mathfrak{S}_w, \mathbf{a})$, a tuple of elements $\mathbf{b}$, and $r \in \mathbb{N}$, the $(r\text{-})$neighborhood $N_r^{(\mathfrak{S}_w, \mathbf{a})}(\mathbf{b})$ around $\mathbf{b}$ is the substructure of $(\mathfrak{S}_w, \mathbf{a}, \mathbf{b})$ induced by the set of elements whose distance from some element of $\mathbf{b}$ is less than or equal to r.*

We start by analyzing strategies involving moves in the neighborhoods of current configurations. In each round, Spoiler can constrain Duplicator to make a specific move when he plays within certain regions, which we will call "entailing", whose size halves after each round. The move Duplicator is forced to do inside such regions must "mimic" Spoiler's action: she must select an element that has exactly the same distance from close elements as Spoiler's choice, and it lies "on the same side" with respect to them. The following definition formalizes this concept.

Definition 9. *Let $\mathbf{a} = a_1, \ldots, a_k$ and $\mathbf{b} = b_1, \ldots, b_k$, and let $m, i \in \mathbb{N}$, with $i \le m$. A position $((\mathfrak{S}_w, \mathbf{a}), (\mathfrak{S}_{w'}, \mathbf{b}), m - i)$ is* locally safe *for Duplicator if, for all $1 \le j, l \le k$, whenever $\delta(a_j, a_l) \le \mathfrak{e}_{i-1}^m$ or $\delta(b_j, b_l) \le \mathfrak{e}_{i-1}^m$, then $a_j - a_l = b_j - b_l$.*

The following result shows that local safety is a necessary condition for Duplicator to be able to win.

Lemma 1. *Given $w, w' \in \Sigma^*$, let $\mathbf{a} = a_1, \ldots, a_k$ and $\mathbf{b} = b_1, \ldots, b_k$ be tuples of elements in $[1, |w|]$ and in $[1, |w'|]$, respectively, and let $m, i \in \mathbb{N}$ with $i \le m$. If position $((\mathfrak{S}_w, \mathbf{a}), (\mathfrak{S}_{w'}, \mathbf{b}), m - i)$ is not locally safe for Duplicator, then Spoiler has a winning strategy.*

Proof. The proof is by induction on the number of remaining rounds.

Induction base: when $i = m$, the position is an ending position. Suppose that it is not locally safe: then there are j, l such that $a_j - a_l \ne b_j - b_l$. Without loss of generality, we may assume that $0 \le a_j - a_l \le \mathfrak{e}_m^m = 1/2$. So, $a_j = a_l$ and $b_j \ne b_l$, hence the final configuration is not a partial isomorphism.

Induction step: w.l.o.g., suppose that, at position $((\mathfrak{S}_w, \mathbf{a}), (\mathfrak{S}_{w'}, \mathbf{b}), m - i)$, there are j, l such that $0 \le a_l - a_j \le \mathfrak{e}_{i-1}^m = 2\mathfrak{e}_i^m$ and $a_l - a_j \ne b_l - b_j$. Let Spoiler pick a_{k+1} in $\mathfrak{S}_w$ such that $a_{k+1} - a_j \le \mathfrak{e}_i^m$ and $a_l - a_{k+1} \le \mathfrak{e}_i^m$. There is no b_{k+1} in $\mathfrak{S}_{w'}$ such that $b_{k+1} - b_j = a_{k+1} - a_j$ and $b_l - b_{k+1} = a_l - a_{k+1}$ (otherwise, we would get $b_j - b_l = a_j - a_l$, against the hypothesis). So, the new position is not locally safe and, by the inductive hypothesis, it is winning for Spoiler. $\square$

So, positions that are not locally safe for Duplicator are winning for Spoiler. Besides, the winning strategy is independent of the words associated to the two structures. As the game goes on and less rounds are left, Spoiler's ability to force moves exponentially decreases.

The bound $\mathfrak{e}_{i-1}^m$ in Lemma 1 is tight: at round i, Spoiler may not be able to force Duplicator's choice when he picks an element whose distance from previously chosen elements is greater than $\mathfrak{e}_{i-1}^m$. So, we give the following definition.

Definition 10. *Let $\mathfrak{S}_w$ be a labeled s-structure. Let $a \in [1, |w|]$ and $m, i \in \mathbb{N}$, with $i \leq m$. The i/m-entailing interval around a is $N_{\mathfrak{e}_i^m}^{\mathfrak{S}_w}(a)$. For a tuple $\mathbf{a}$, $N_{\mathfrak{e}_i^m}^{\mathfrak{S}_w}(\mathbf{a})$ is called the i/m-entailing region around $\mathbf{a}$.*

In s-structures there is always a unique feasible reply to each Spoiler's move in the entailing region. This is not true for arbitrary structures, but the above rule is valid in general.

Lemma 1 describes which moves Spoiler can force *in the next round*. By applying the lemma iteratively, we can say what Spoiler can force from a position *up to the end of a game*.

Definition 11. *Let $w \in \Sigma^*$, $a \in [1, |w|]$ and $m, i \in \mathbb{N}$, with $i \leq m$. The i/m-reachable interval around a is $N_{\mathfrak{r}_i^m}^{\mathfrak{S}_w}(a)$. For a tuple $\mathbf{a}$, $N_{\mathfrak{r}_i^m}^{\mathfrak{S}_w}(\mathbf{a})$ is called the i/m-reachable region around $\mathbf{a}$.*

Lemma 2. *Necessary condition for Duplicator to be able to win a game from position $((\mathfrak{S}_w, \mathbf{a}), (\mathfrak{S}_{w'}, \mathbf{b}), m - i)$ is that the i/m-reachable interval around a_j is isomorphic to the i/m-reachable interval around b_j, for $1 \leq j \leq k$.*

Proof. If $N_{\mathfrak{r}_i^m}^{(\mathfrak{S}_w, \mathbf{a})}(a_j) \not\cong N_{\mathfrak{r}_i^m}^{(\mathfrak{S}_{w'}, \mathbf{b})}(b_j)$, for some j, then every difference between the two intervals can be found by Spoiler by playing at most $m - i$ entailing moves. $\qquad \square$

Figure 2 shows the reachable interval around a when $m = 4$ and a is picked at the first round.

Corollary 2. *Duplicator can win an EF-game from $((\mathfrak{S}_w, \mathbf{a}), (\mathfrak{S}_{w'}, \mathbf{b}), m)$ only if w and w' have the same factors of length $\mathfrak{r}_0^m$, and the same prefix and suffix of length $\mathfrak{r}_1^m$.*

Lemma 2 suggests the following definition.

Definition 12. *A position $((\mathfrak{S}_w, \mathbf{a}), (\mathfrak{S}_{w'}, \mathbf{b}), m - i)$ is globally safe if it is locally safe and the i/m-reachable interval around a_j is isomorphic to the i/m-reachable interval around b_j, for $1 \leq j \leq k$.*

Note that the $\mathfrak{r}_i^m$-neighborhoods around a_j and b_j may be isomorphic for all j, even if the position is not locally safe. Consider, for example, the unlabeled s-structures $(\{1, 2, 3\}, s)$ and $(\{1, 2, 3, 4\}, s)$: it is easy to check that position $((\{1, 2, 3\}, s, 1, 3), (\{1, 2, 3, 4\}, s, 1, 4), 1)$ is not locally safe, but the corresponding $0/1$-reachable intervals are isomorphic in the two structures. Vice versa, position $((\{1, 2, 3\}, s, 1, 3), (\{1, 2, 3, 4\}, s, 2, 4), 1)$ is locally safe, but the $0/1$-reachable interval around 1 is not isomorphic to the $0/1$-reachable interval around 2.

Global safety characterizes the winning strategies when there are no unary predicates.

Theorem 4. *Let $\mathfrak{S}_n = ([1, n], s)$ and $\mathfrak{S}_p = ([1, p], s)$ be two unlabeled s-structures, and let $\mathbf{a}$ and $\mathbf{b}$ be two nonempty tuples of elements in $[1, n]$ and $[1, p]$, respectively, such that $|\mathbf{a}| = |\mathbf{b}|$. Then,*

$$\mathsf{D}((\mathfrak{S}_n, \mathbf{a}), (\mathfrak{S}_p, \mathbf{b}), m) \quad \Longleftrightarrow \quad ((\mathfrak{S}_n, \mathbf{a}), (\mathfrak{S}_p, \mathbf{b}), m) \text{ is globally safe.}$$

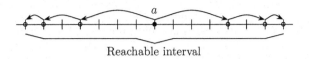

Reachable interval

Fig. 1. Reachable intervals

Proof. ($\Rightarrow$) If $((\mathfrak{S}_n, \mathbf{a}), (\mathfrak{S}_p, \mathbf{b}), m)$ is not globally safe, then Spoiler wins either by Lemma 1 or by Lemma 2.

($\Leftarrow$) (Sketch) Build a sequence of sets of partial isomorphisms having the back-and-forth property, and apply Fraïssé's Theorem. From the game-theoretic standpoint, Duplicator's strategy runs as follows: if Spoiler, at the first round, plays inside an entailing interval, Duplicator will reply with the same (relative) position in the corresponding entailing interval of the other structure. The hypothesis guarantees that this can always be done. If Spoiler plays outside the entailing region, Duplicator must reply with an element outside the entailing region of the other structure, such that the $1/m$-reachable intervals determined by the two elements are isomorphic. Local safety guarantees that Duplicator can always find an element outside the entailing region, and the isomorphisms between reachable intervals ensure that Duplicator can find an isomorphic reachable interval. □

In general, an outline of a winning strategy for Duplicator requires that, in each round, Duplicator be able to find a sufficiently long factor that matches the reachable interval around Spoiler's choice; moreover, if Spoiler plays outside all entailing intervals, Duplicator must be able to do the same in the other structure. To guarantee this, w and w' must have the same factors of suitable lengths and there must be enough copies of such factors (or both words must have the same number of them), distributed in a similar way in both words. We now formalize these concepts.

Definition 13. *Let $A \subseteq \mathbb{N}$. An l-partition of A is a partition of A such that for all $i, j \in A$, if i and j are in the same class, then $|i - j| \leq l + 1$.*

Definition 14. *Let $occ_w(v)$ be the set of starting positions of the occurrences of v in w. The offset-multiplicity $\sigma_w(v)$ of v in w is the minimum cardinality of a $|v|$-partition of $occ_w(v)$.*

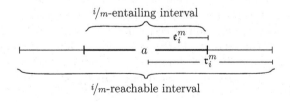

i/m-reachable interval

Fig. 2. Entailing and reachable intervals

The offset-multiplicity corresponds to the maximum "scattering" of the occurrences of a factor v, that is, the maximum number of occurrences of v whose pairwise distance is greater than $|v| + 1$. In Fig. 3, the coarsest offset-partitions of $occ_w(aba)$ are $(\{1, 3, 5\}, \{10, 13\}, \{15\})$ and $(\{1, 3, 5\}, \{10\}, \{13, 15\})$, so the offset-multiplicity of aba in w is 3.

$$
\begin{array}{c}
\overset{1\quad 3\quad 5}{\longmapsto\hspace{-1pt}\llcorner\hspace{-1pt}\dashrightarrow} \qquad \overset{10\quad 13\quad 15}{\longmapsto\hspace{-1pt}\dashrightarrow} \\
w = a\,b\,a\,b\,a\,b\,a\,b\,b\,a\,b\,a\,a\,b\,a\,b\,a
\end{array}
$$

Fig. 3. Offset-multiplicity

Definition 15. *Given a word $w \in \Sigma^*$, $i, j \in [1, |w|]$ and $r \in \mathbb{N}$, we say that $w_r(i)$ falls inside $w_{r'}(j)$ if $|i - j| \leq r'$.*

In Fig. 4, the occurrence around a of radius r *falls inside* the occurrence around b of radius r' (but not vice versa).

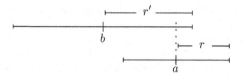

Fig. 4. A factor falling inside another

The following lemma will be used in the proof of Theorem 5.

Lemma 3. *Let $i, m \in \mathbb{N}$ with $i \leq m$. Given a word $w \in \Sigma^*$ and a factor $v \in F_{\mathfrak{r}_{i+1}^m}(w)$, $\sigma_w(v) \leq k$ if and only if there is a tuple of positions $\mathbf{a} = a_1, \ldots, a_k \in [1, |w|]$ such that all occurrences of v fall inside the i/m-entailing region around $\mathbf{a}$.*

Proof. Suppose that all occurrences of v fall inside the i/m-entailing intervals around $a_1, \ldots, a_k$. Define a partition of $occ_w(v)$ such that all occurrences in the same class fall inside a common entailing interval. Then, the distance between two occurrences of v in the same class is at most $2\mathfrak{e}_i^m = \mathfrak{e}_{i-1}^m = (2\mathfrak{r}_{i+1}^m + 1) + 1 = |v| + 1$. So, the partition is a $|v|$-partition with at most k classes.

For the converse, suppose that $\sigma_w(v) \leq k$. Let $\mathcal{P} = \{I_1, \ldots, I_k\}$ be a (not necessarily minimal) $|v|$-partition of $occ_w(v)$. The distance between any two occurrences in the same class is at most $|v| + 1 = 2\mathfrak{e}_i^m$. Then, for every $j = 1, \ldots, k$ there is $a_j \in [1, |w|]$ such that, for all $c \in I_j$, $\delta(a_j, c) \leq \mathfrak{e}_i^m$ (for instance, take $a_j = \lfloor (\max I_j + \min I_j)/2 \rfloor$), so all occurrences in I_j fall inside the i/m-entailing interval around a_j. $\square$

The equivalence relation that characterizes EF-games over labeled s-structures is a refinement of the following.

Definition 16. *Let $\sim_{\mathfrak{r}_i^m}$ be the equivalence relation over Σ^* defined as follows: given two words $w, w' \in \Sigma^*$, $w \sim_{\mathfrak{r}_i^m} w'$ if and only if for every $v \in F_{\mathfrak{r}_i^m}(w) \cup F_{\mathfrak{r}_i^m}(w')$, either $\sigma_w(v), \sigma_{w'}(v) \geq i$ or $(\sigma_w(v) = \sigma_{w'}(v)$ and $\begin{bmatrix} w \\ v \end{bmatrix} = \begin{bmatrix} w' \\ v \end{bmatrix})$.*

Now we are ready to state our main result.

Theorem 5. *Given two words $w, w' \in \Sigma^*$ and $m \in \mathbb{N}$,*

$$D(\mathfrak{S}_w, \mathfrak{S}_{w'}, m) \iff w \sim_{\mathfrak{r}_i^m} w', \text{ for } 1 \leq i \leq m .$$

Proof. ($\Leftarrow$): The proof uses Theorem 2. We define a sequence of sets $I_0, \ldots, I_m$ of partial isomorphisms such that[1] $\{(a_j, b_j)\}_{1 \leq j \leq i}$ is in I_{m-i} if and only if, for every $j = 1, \ldots, i$, $w_{\mathfrak{r}_i^m}(a_j) = w'_{\mathfrak{r}_i^m}(b_j)$ and, for all $1 \leq j, l \leq i$, whenever $\delta(a_j, a_l) \leq \mathfrak{e}_i^m$ or $\delta(b_j, b_l) \leq \mathfrak{e}_i^m$, then $a_j - a_l = b_j - b_l$. By the equivalence of Fraïssé's and Ehrenfeucht's characterization, we only need to prove that such sequence satisfies the back and forth properties of Definition 4.

Let us prove the forth property. Let $a = a_{i+1} \in [1, |w|]$. We distinguish two cases:

1. for some $1 \leq j \leq i$, a is in the i/m-entailing interval around a_j. Then, we may choose $b = b_{i+1} \in [1, |w'|]$ such that $a - a_j = b - b_j$, because in this case $w_{\mathfrak{r}_{i+1}^m}(a)$ is a factor of $w_{\mathfrak{r}_j^m}(a_j)$, and $w_{\mathfrak{r}_j^m}(a_j) = w'_{\mathfrak{r}_j^m}(b_j)$ by the inductive hypothesis.

2. Let $\alpha = w_{\mathfrak{r}_{i+1}^m}(a)$. If a is outside all i/m-entailing intervals, we must choose b outside the entailing region of $\mathfrak{S}_{w'}$ such that $w'_{\mathfrak{r}_{i+1}^m}(b) = \alpha$. For the sake of contradiction, assume that this is not possible, that is, all $b \in [1, |w'|]$ satisfying $w'_{\mathfrak{r}_{i+1}^m}(b) = \alpha$ fall inside the i/m-entailing intervals around $b_1, \ldots, b_i$. Then, by Lemma 3, the offset-multiplicity of α in w' is at most i. So, the hypothesis of the theorem implies that α must have the same multiplicity both in w and in w'.

   Since every $w'_{\mathfrak{r}_{i+1}^m}(b)$ such that $w'_{\mathfrak{r}_{i+1}^m}(b) = \alpha$ falls inside the i/m-entailing interval around some b_j, and $\mathfrak{r}_{i+1}^m < \mathfrak{e}_i^m$, every $w'_{\mathfrak{r}_{i+1}^m}(b)$ is a factor of $w'_{\mathfrak{r}_i^m}(b_j)$. By the inductive hypothesis, $w'_{\mathfrak{r}_i^m}(b_j) = w_{\mathfrak{r}_i^m}(a_j)$, so all such occurrences exist also in w. But, as α is outside the i/m-entailing region of w, it cannot be among such occurrences. Therefore, $\begin{bmatrix} w \\ \alpha \end{bmatrix} > \begin{bmatrix} w' \\ \alpha \end{bmatrix}$, which contradicts the hypothesis of the theorem.

The back property can be proved in a similar way.

($\Rightarrow$): We describe Spoiler's winning strategy when $w \not\sim_{\mathfrak{r}_i^m} w'$ for some i. Without loss of generality, suppose that, for some $1 \leq i + 1 \leq m$, there is $v \in F_{\mathfrak{r}_{i+1}^m}(w)$ having offset-multiplicity $\sigma_1 < i + 1$ in w and offset-multiplicity $\sigma_2 > \sigma_1$ in w'. Then, by Lemma 3, there are positions $\mathbf{a} = a_1, \ldots, a_{\sigma_1}$ in w

---

[1] Note that I_m only contains the empty map.

such that all occurrences of v fall inside the i/m-entailing intervals around $\mathbf{a}$. Let Spoiler pick such elements (possibly repeating moves) in the first i rounds.

At round $(i+1)$, the i/m-entailing region of w covers all occurrences of v, and, since Duplicator must match the reachable intervals, corresponding occurrences are in the entailing region of w'. Since $\sigma_{w'}(v) > \sigma_1$, there must be an occurrence of v in w' outside all entailing intervals. Let Spoiler pick the center of such occurrence. Spoiler wins because Duplicator must reply inside an i/m-entailing interval or choose a non-matching $(i+1)/m$-reachable interval.

As for other case, suppose that, for some $1 \leq i+1 \leq m$, there is $v \in F_{\mathfrak{r}_{i+1}^m}(w)$ such that $\sigma_w(v) = \sigma_{w'}(v) < i + 1$, but $\begin{bmatrix} w \\ v \end{bmatrix} < \begin{bmatrix} w' \\ v \end{bmatrix}$. As before, Spoiler will move in order to make all occurrences of v in w fall inside i/m-entailing intervals after round i, forcing Spoiler to cover the same occurrences and leave out of the i/m-entailing region in w' at least one occurrence of v. This must be possible, otherwise v would have the same multiplicity in w and w'. At round $i + 1$, Spoiler selects the center of an occurrence of v outside all entailing intervals. This will force Duplicator to reply in an entailing interval or choose a non-matching $(i+1)/m$-reachable interval, and lose by Lemma 11.   □

Corollary 3. *Let $\mathfrak{S}_n$ and $\mathfrak{S}_p$ be two unlabeled s-structures, as in Theorem 4, and let $m \geq 2$. Then,*

$$\mathsf{D}(\mathfrak{S}_n, \mathfrak{S}_p, m) \quad \Longleftrightarrow \quad \mathfrak{S}_n \cong \mathfrak{S}_p \vee n, p \geq 2^m .$$

Proof. $\mathfrak{S}_n$ and $\mathfrak{S}_p$ can be thought of as induced by words over $\Sigma = \{a\}$.   □

To be able to describe the optimal strategies in a game between words, we must first extend Theorem 5 to arbitrary configurations.

Theorem 6. *Given two words $w, w' \in \Sigma^*$, and $m \in \mathbb{N}$,*

$$\mathsf{D}((\mathfrak{S}_w, \mathbf{a}), (\mathfrak{S}_{w'}, \mathbf{b}), m) \quad \Longleftrightarrow \quad w \sim_{\mathfrak{r}_i^m} w', \text{ for } 1 \leq i \leq m,$$
$$\text{and } ((\mathfrak{S}_w, \mathbf{a}), (\mathfrak{S}_{w'}, \mathbf{b})) \text{ is globally safe.}$$

Proof. ($\Rightarrow$) By contraposition, using Theorem 5 and Theorem 4.

($\Leftarrow$) The proof goes as in Theorem 5, by considering partial isomorphisms extending $((\mathfrak{S}_w, \mathbf{a}), (\mathfrak{S}_{w'}, \mathbf{b}))$.   □

We conclude the section by giving a hint of how games provide an alternative way of measuring the similarity of two structures, which may be useful in biological sequence comparison, especially when the classical alignment methods, based on dynamic programming [8], turn out to be too rigid. Two facts, in our opinion, are relevant in this context: genomes often contain a high percentage of repeated sequences (up to 80% in some plants), and they undergo different kinds of rearrangements, in particular inversions and transpositions of DNA regions (see, for example, [12] and the references thereby). As a first example, consider the two strings *agggagttttaga* and *agtttagaggga*: a standard alignment algorithm based on the computation of their edit distance may align the two sequences as follows:

$$ag\text{-}ggagttttaga$$
$$agtttag\text{-}\text{-}aggga$$

Such an alignment misses completely the similarity between the prefix of each string with the suffix of the other. On the contrary, by Theorem 5 Duplicator has a winning strategy in a 2-round game played on *agggagttttaga* and *agtttagaggga*. Her winning strategy clearly connects the corresponding substrings *aggga* and *gtt(t)tag*. Note that a game based on the less-than relation would not allow such inversions: biological comparison calls for a "local" notion of similarity, which requires relations of bounded degree.

Successor structures do not need to be mapped at a nucleotide level, though. We may consider a higher level view of a genome, as composed of several successive discrete elements: genes, pseudogenes, transposons, microsatellites, etc... Figure 5 shows parts of two genomes, where segments are classified either as "genes" or "LINE elements" or "SINE elements" (which are two kinds of interspersed repetitions). It is interesting to note that Duplicator can always reply to two moves of Spoiler, unless Spoiler picks an element inside one of the dashed boxes. The fact that the structures are (almost) 2-equivalent allows one to express some very simple properties that hold for both sequences, such as "every gene in the considered region is immediately followed by a LINE".

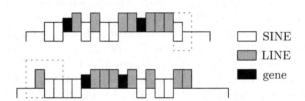

Fig. 5. Duplicator has winning strategy in a 2-round game between the two above successor structures with unary predicates *gene*, *LINE* and *SINE*, when Spoiler is not allowed to pick the elements inside the dashed boxes

We argue that variants of EF-games can be successfully applied to a class of problems of biological significance. The successor relation is not the only relation one may consider and first-order logic is not necessarily the most natural logic for this kind of applications. But the above examples give some hint for further variations that could be developed: in particular, it is apparent that Spoiler's and Duplicator's abilities should be tuned to the "approximate" context that molecular biology introduces, which might result in a new logical formalism with an associated game with completely different rules. A possible extension would consist in letting Duplicator play a limited number of "cheating moves", which would allow her to perform modifications of the structures "on the fly", e.g. substitutions, insertions and deletions of (subsets of) elements. It would be interesting to investigate how winning strategies would be affected by adding such rules.

5   Complexity of the Winning Strategies

Given a configuration $((\mathfrak{S}_w, \mathbf{a}), (\mathfrak{S}_{w'}, \mathbf{b}))$, we want to establish the computational complexity of determining the minimum m such that Spoiler has a winning strategy (or, equivalently, the maximum m such that Duplicator has a winning strategy) in a game from $((\mathfrak{S}_w, \mathbf{a}), (\mathfrak{S}_{w'}, \mathbf{b}), m)$. We call such number the *remoteness* of the given configuration (the remoteness of a game is a standard notion in combinatorial game theory, see [2]). We assume that $(\mathfrak{S}_w, \mathbf{a}) \not\cong (\mathfrak{S}_{w'}, \mathbf{b})$, otherwise Duplicator has a winning strategy for every m.

By Theorem 6, this problem amounts to computing the minimum m such that either global safety fails, or $w \approx_{\mathfrak{r}_i^m} w'$ for some i. Local safety can be checked in $O(|\mathbf{a}|)$ time if we assume that $a_1 \leq \cdots \leq a_k$. The minimum value such that local safety does not hold is $\log_2\left(\min\{\,\delta(a_{j+1}, a_j), \delta(b_{j+1}, b_j) \mid a_{j+1} - a_j \neq b_{j+1} - b_j\,\}\right)$. The isomorphic region around $\mathbf{a}$ and $\mathbf{b}$ can easily be computed in $O(\min(|w|, |w'|))$ time by any linear string matching algorithm.

To examine the equivalence relation $\sim_{\mathfrak{r}_i^m}$, we may concentrate on configurations of the form $(\mathfrak{S}_w, \mathfrak{S}_{w'})$, with $w \neq w'$. By Corollary 3, $\log_2 \min(|w|, |w'|) + 1$ is an upper bound to the number of rounds needed by Spoiler to win a game. A tighter bound can be obtained by Corollary 2: it is sufficient to compare the prefixes and suffixes of w and w' until a mismatch is found. For example, suppose that the prefix of w differs from the prefix of w' at position j: then, $\log_2(j+1) + 1$ is an upper bound to the remoteness. Let U be the tightest upper bound determined in this way. Note that $U = O(\log_2 \min(|w|, |w'|))$.

Then, we enumerate all the factors of length $2^j - 1$, for $1 \leq j \leq U$ occurring in w or w'. There are $O((|w| + |w'|)U)$ such substrings. For each factor, we may compute its multiplicity and offset-multiplicity in $O(|w| + |w'|)$ time by a linear search. Therefore, the remoteness is the minimum among the values m such that

$$\mathfrak{r}_i^m = |v|, \ i = \min(\sigma_w(v), \sigma_{w'}(v)) + 1, \ \text{and either } \sigma_w(v) \neq \sigma_{w'}(v) \text{ or } \begin{bmatrix} w \\ v \end{bmatrix} \neq \begin{bmatrix} w' \\ v \end{bmatrix},$$

where v ranges over the set of the enumerated factors. The overall complexity is therefore $O((|w| + |w'|)^2 \log \min(|w|, |w'|))$.

6   Concluding Remarks

We have given a structural characterization for m-equivalence of labeled successor structures, and we have proved that the complexity of determining the winner of a game played on two words is polynomial in the size of the words. Moreover, the proofs of our results are constructive, that is, algorithms, both for Spoiler and Duplicator, which play optimally can be derived from them. We are investigating whether the computational complexity of the problem can be lowered by building (generalized) suffix trees of the words [8].

References

1. S. Arora and R. Fagin. On winning strategies in Ehrenfeucht-Fraïssé games. *Theoretical Computer Science*, 174:97–121, 1997.
2. E. R. Berlekamp, J. H. Conway, and R. K. Guy. *Winning Ways for Your Mathematical Plays*, volume 2. A K Peters Ltd, second edition, January 2003.
3. H.-D. Ebbinghaus and J. Flum. *Finite Model Theory*. Springer Verlag, 1995.
4. A. Ehrenfeucht. An application of games to the completeness problem for formalized theory. *Fundamenta Mathematicae*, 49:129–141, 1961.
5. R. Fagin, L. Stockmeyer, and M. Y. Vardi. On monadic NP vs. monadic co-NP. *Inform. and Comput.*, 120(1):78–92, 1995.
6. R. Fraïssé. Sur quelques classifications des systèmes de relations. *Publications Scientifiques*, 1:35–182, 1954.
7. H. Gaifman. On local and nonlocal properties. In J. Stern, editor, *Proceedings of the Herbrand Symposium, Logic Colloquium '81*, pages 105–135. North Holland Pub. Co., 1982.
8. D. Gusfield. *Algorithms on Strings, Trees and Sequences: Computer Science and Computational Biology*. Cambridge University Press, New York, 1997.
9. W. Hanf. Model-Theoretic Methods in the Study of Elementary Logic. In J. W. Addison, L. Henkin, and A. Tarski, editors, *The Theory of Models*, pages 132–145. North-Holland, Amsterdam, 1965.
10. J. Hintikka. Distributive normal forms in the calculus of predicates. *Acta Philosofica Fennica*, 6:1–71, 1953.
11. H. J. Keisler and W. B. Lotfallah. Shrinking Games and Local Formulas. *Annals of Pure and Applied Logic*, 128:215–225, 2004.
12. P. Pevzner and G. Tesler. Genome Rearrangements in Mammalian Evolution: Lessons From Human and Mouse Genomes. *Genome Res.*, 13(1):37–45, January 2003.
13. E. Pezzoli. Computational Complexity of Ehrenfeucht-Fraïssé Games on Finite Structures. *Lecture Notes in Computer Science*, 1584:159–170, 1999.
14. T. Schwentick. On winning Ehrenfeucht games and monadic NP. *Annals of Pure and Applied Logic*, 79:61–92, 1996.
15. W. Thomas. Classifying regular events in symbolic logic. *Journal of Computer and System Sciences*, 25(3):360–376, 1982.
16. W. Thomas. On the Ehrenfeucht-Fraïssé Game in Theoretical Computer Science. *Lecture Notes in Computer Science*, 668:559–568, 1993.

Second-Order Principles in Specification Languages for Object-Oriented Programs

Bernhard Beckert[1] and Kerry Trentelman[2]

[1] Department of Computer Science, University of Koblenz-Landau
beckert@uni-koblenz.de
[2] Automated Reasoning Group, Australian National University
Kerry.Trentelman@anu.edu.au

Abstract. Within the setting of object-oriented program specification and verification, pointers and object references can be considered as relations between the elements of a data structure. When we specify properties of these data structures, we often describe properties of relations. Hence it is important to be able to talk about relations and their properties when specifying object-oriented programs or programs with pointers. Many interesting properties of relations such as transitive closure, finiteness, and generatedness are not expressible in first-order logic (FOL); hence neither are they expressible in first-order fragments of specification languages. In this paper we give an overview of the different ways such properties can be expressed in various logics, with a particular emphasis on extensions of FOL, *i.e.* transitive closure logic, fixed-point logic, and first-order dynamic logic. Within the paper we also discuss which of these extensions already are – or in fact should be – implemented within specification languages. We feel that such a discussion is necessary since it is often the case that when an extension of FOL is implemented within a specification language it is done so in an *ad hoc* manner or the underpinning logical concepts are not well documented.

1 Introduction

When it comes to specifying object-oriented programs, we need to be able to: (a) refer to a set of particular objects in an object structure; and (b) talk about the properties of the relation between the objects. As an example, consider the definition of sets of related objects which are used in modifies clauses (a modifies clause allows one to specify those parts of a program state that are exclusively allowed to change [28, 6]). To illustrate, suppose we have a linked list with objects of class `Node` having a `next` field. For a method say, `sortInPlace`, it would be useful to be able to write `list.next*` in the method's modifies clause, where * denotes some form of transitive closure. Its semantic intention would then be that the set of locations that are reachable from `list` using the field `next` may be modified during the method's execution. One may also wish to specify that the list is not cyclic; assuming that this is the case, a field such as `position()` may be introduced such that it returns a reference to a node at a given position. If the position is less than or greater than 1, then the field returns `null`.

G. Sutcliffe and A. Voronkov (Eds.): LPAR 2005, LNAI 3835, pp. 154–168, 2005.
© Springer-Verlag Berlin Heidelberg 2005

All specification languages have some form of modification which allows them to extend beyond the limitations of first-order logic. For example the query language SQL implements fixed-point logic, the Object Constraint Language OCL uses the `iterate` and `let` constructs, the Common Algebraic Specification Language CASL uses the notion of freeness, and the Java Modeling Language, JML, incorporates built-in recursion. However it is often the case that the modifications made to specification languages are done in a "make-do" fashion and their designers are unaware of the logic underpinning their decisions. In this paper we attempt to clarify what is really going on within these specification languages.

Our work is carried out in the framework of the KeY project. The KeY system is a commercial CASE tool augmented with specification and deductive verification functionalities [1] (see website at `www.key-project.org`). KeY uses the Unified Modeling Language UML for visual modelling of designs and specifications, along with OCL for specifying constraints and other expressions attached to the models [29]. The target language for program verification is Java. Both the specification language OCL and the verification language of the KeY tool – namely, dynamic logic – have second-order elements (as described in Section 4). Our case study experience has shown that often there is a need for expressing second-order principles in a more usable and/or flexible way; this need provides the motivation behind our investigations. In particular, a modifies clause has been recently implemented within the KeY system [6]. As the above example demonstrates, it would be advantageous to be able to express transitive closure in OCL in an easier fashion than the current method – which is by using the OCL `iterate` construct – described in Section 4.

The paper is organised as follows: in Section 2 we look at how one goes about expressing properties of relations and composing relations. We discuss various properties which may or may not be expressed in first-order logic. This logic's lack of expressiveness leads us to an examination of a number of extensions of first-order logic in Section 3. In Section 4 we discuss several specification languages and the approaches they take in determining properties of relations. Finally, we draw conclusions in Section 5.

2   Relations and Relational Formulae in a FOL Setting

We are interested in both expressing properties of relations and composing relations in relational formulae. In this section we provide the basic definitions for these notions and briefly discuss relational algebra. We conclude by describing a number of properties which can or cannot be expressed in first-order logic. However, before we begin, we need to stipulate what we mean by a relation within an object-oriented language.

Following [30] we say that a relation expresses (the symmetric form of) those associations which are represented in a programming language as pointers or object references. Hence we model both object references and pointers as first-order functions on objects.

A property P of a relation R (a formula with two free variables) is said to be expressible if there is a closed formula $\phi_P(R)$ such that, for all models M, the interpretation R^M has property P if and only if $\phi_P(R)$ is true in M. Here R^M is the (single) interpretation of relation R in M. The formula $\phi_P(R)$ must be effectively constructible from any given R in a uniform way. This notion is extended to properties of tuples of relations. Formally, a property is a relation on relations.

A composition C of relations $R_1, \ldots, R_k$ is expressible if there is a formula $\psi_P(R_1, \ldots, R_k)(x, y)$ with free variables x and y such that $(\psi_P(R_1, \ldots, R_k))^M$ is the relation composed from $R_1^M, \ldots, R_k^M$. Here $(\psi_P(R_1, \ldots, R_k))^M$ is the (single) interpretation of $\psi_P(R_1, \ldots, R_k)(x, y)$ in M. The formula $\psi_P(R_1, \ldots, R_k)$ must be effectively constructible from any given $R_1, \ldots, R_k$ in a uniform way. Formally, a composition is a function on relations.

Note that the constructibility of ϕ and ψ neither implies the decidability of P, nor respectively the computability of C. This is because the validity of the constructed formula is in general undecidable. Moreover, the composition of relations may be iterated, but the properties themselves cannot be iterated.

Relational algebra is a formal system used for manipulating relations. The set of its operations may vary per definition, but it usually includes set operations – since relations are sets of tuples – and special operators defined for relations such as select, project, and join. The select operator selects tuples from a relation whose attributes meet the selection criteria (which is normally expressed as a predicate). The project operator selects certain attributes from a single relation, discarding the rest. The join operator composes two relations. Relational algebra forms the basis of a multitude of relational query languages; these are used in order to manipulate the data of a relational database. We discuss aspects of one of the standard languages, SQL, in Section 4.

Examples of properties expressible in FOL are reflexivity and transitivity; concatenation is an expressible composition: We say that R is reflexive if $\forall x.\ xRx$ and R is transitive if $\forall x \forall y \forall z.\ (xRy \land yRz \rightarrow xRz)$. The concatenation of two relations R and S is expressible by $R \circ S \equiv \{(x, z) \mid \exists y.\ xRy \land ySz\}$. Note that we use the notation xRy for $(x, y) \in R$ and $R(x, y)$ respectively.

On the other hand, properties that demand the finiteness of certain sets of elements are not expressible. For example: "all elements are at most related to a finite number of other elements". Furthermore, many properties that demand the existence of a finite but unknown number of elements which are related in a certain way are not expressible. For example quantifications such as $\exists n.\ \exists x_1 \ldots x_n$ (which are routinely used in mathematical notation) do not exist in FOL and often cannot be expressed by any other means.

Another typical but important example is transitive closure. The transitive closure of a relation R is the relation $TC(R)$ such that for all elements x and y the relation $TC(R)(x, y)$ holds if and only if there is a finite number of intermediate points $z_0, \ldots, z_n$ where $n \in \mathbb{N}$ with $x = z_0$, $y = z_n$ and $z_{i-1} R z_i$ for $1 \leq i \leq n$. Accordingly, one cannot express in FOL that some point b is R-reachable from some other point a, i.e. $TC(R)(a, b)$. An alternative – yet equivalent – definition of transitive closure $TC(R)$ is: (1) $TC(R)$ is transitive; (2) $R \subseteq TC(R)$ and; (3) if R' is transitive and $R \subseteq R'$ then $TC(R) \subseteq R'$. The latter condition is not expressible in FOL as it implicitly quantifies over R'.

It is important to note, however, that the transitive closure of a structure can be expressed in a FOL setting if the structure is both finite and acyclic (see Section 4).

3   Extensions of FOL

In this section we investigate a number of extensions of first-order logic including transitive closure logic, fixed-point logic, and first-order dynamic logic. These extensions allow us to express various properties and compositions of relations that cannot be expressed using first-order logic alone.

Transitive Closure Logic. First-order logic extended by a transitive closure operator – written $FO(TC)$ and called transitive closure logic – was first introduced by Immerman [16]. If we let the formula $\phi(\bar{x}, \bar{y})$ represent a binary relation on two n-tuples of domain variables – which range over the universe of a Kripke structure – then the reflexive transitive closure of this relation is expressed by $TC_{\bar{x},\bar{y}}\phi(\bar{x}, \bar{y})$, or more succinctly $TC\phi$. Strict transitive closure is denoted $TC^s\phi$. This represents the transitive closure of ϕ as opposed to the reflexive transitive closure of ϕ. The restriction $FO^2(TC)$ is such that only two variables x and y may appear in a formula ϕ. For example, the formula $\exists y.\,((TC_{x,y}R_a(x, y))(x, y) \wedge p(y))$ expresses "there is a path of a-edges from x to a vertex where p holds".

Reachability Logic $\mathcal{RL}$ is a fragment of $FO^2(TC)$ with an unbounded number of boolean variables in addition to the two domain variables x and y [3]. Boolean variables are first-order variables restricted to range over 0 and 1. Formulae of the logic are constructed using an adjacency formula $\delta(x, \bar{b}, y, \bar{b}')$ which is a binary relation between two n-tuples $(x, b_1, \dots, b_{n-1})$ and $(y, b'_1, \dots, b'_{n-1})$. This is in fact a disjunction of conjunctions where each conjunction contains at least one of the following: $x = y$, $R_a(x, y)$, or $R_a(y, x)$ for some binary relation R_a. Hence the adjacency formula necessarily implies that there is an edge from x to y, or an edge from y to x, or that x is equal to y. Conjuncts may also contain expressions of the form $\neg(b_i = b_j)$, $b_i = 0$, or $b_i = 1$. For $\phi \in \mathcal{RL}$ the formulae $NEXT(\delta)\phi$ (denoting $\exists y.\,(\delta(x, \bar{0}, y, \bar{1}) \wedge \phi[y/x])$), $REACH(\delta)\phi$ (*i.e.*, $\exists y.\,(TC\delta)(\delta(x, \bar{0}, y, \bar{1}) \wedge \phi[y/x])$), and $CYCLE(\delta)$ (*i.e.*, $(TC^s\delta)(\delta(x, \bar{0}, x, \bar{0}))$) are also formulae of $\mathcal{RL}$. Hence it is possible to describe in this logic: steps out of the current vertex x, paths out of x, and cycles from x back to itself.

Importantly, the boolean variables allow Propositional Dynamic Logic (PDL) and the variation of Computational Tree Logic, CTL*, to be embedded in $\mathcal{RL}$. Consider the PDL formula $\langle \alpha \rangle p$, which is a true property of a state s whenever there is some state t in which p holds that is reachable from s by execution of α. The regular expression α can be translated into an non-deterministic finite automaton N_α with n states. Within the framework of $\mathcal{RL}$ the adjacency formula of α is a translation of the transition relation of N_α, whereby each state of the automaton is represented by $k \equiv 1 + \log n$ bits with $\bar{0}$ and $\bar{1}$ representing the initial and final states respectively. For example, if α is the sequential composition $\pi_0; \pi_1$ then a transition from state s to state t in $N_{\pi_0;\pi_1}$ is represented by the adjacency formula $R_{\pi_0}(x, y) \wedge b_1 \ldots b_k = s \vee R_{\pi_1}(x, y) \wedge b'_1 \ldots b'_k = t$ where $b_1 \ldots b_k$ is the initial state and $b'_1 \ldots b'_k$ is the final state. Hence an example of a formula in $\mathcal{RL}$ is $REACH(\delta)p$ where $\delta(x, b_1, b_2, y, b'_1, b'_2)$ is $(R_{\pi_0}(x, y) \wedge b_1 b_2 = 00 \wedge b'_1 b'_2 = 01) \vee (R_{\pi_1}(x, y) \wedge b_1 b_2 = 01 \wedge b'_1 b'_2 = 11)$. This has the meaning that it is possible to take the path of a π_0-edge followed by a π_1-edge to a point where p holds; this is just $\langle \pi_0; \pi_1 \rangle p$ in PDL.

Regular Expressions Over Relations. Kleene algebras are algebraic structures that generalise the operations of regular expressions. A Kleene algebra consists of a set K with binary $+$ and $\cdot$ operations, a unary operation *, and constants 0 and 1. In general the algebra's operational semantics depends on the model, but typically * involves some notion of finite iteration. A Kleene algebra gives rise to a relational algebra extended with reflexive transitive closure when the following interpretations of the operations are made: operation $\cdot$ as join; element 0 as the null/empty relation; element 1 as the identity relation; and * as the reflexive transitive closure of a relation.

As mentioned previously, an extension of first-order logic with the ability to write `list.next`* – or even more generally, to be able to use regular expressions to describe terms or term sets – would be very useful. There exist approaches which allow an extended syntax for terms in first-order logic. For example in [10] recursive term definitions are added to first-order logic.

Rather than using regular expressions and Kleene algebras to extend FOL, it is possible to manipulate FOL formulae such that they fulfill a purpose similar to that of regular expressions.

Two ways to define words and/or formal languages are by using: (1) predicate logics, such that each model corresponds to a word in the language; and (2) modal logics, such that each path in a Kripke structure corresponds to a word. There is a large amount of literature on the latter. For (1), we fix a family of signatures Σ_A. They contain the binary relation symbol $<$, a constant symbol first, a unary postfix function $+1$, and for every a in the alphabet A, we have the unary relation symbol Q_a. The set of words over A is denoted A^*. For $w \in A^* \backslash \{\Lambda\}$, where Λ is the empty word, the associated Σ_A-structure is denoted $\mathcal{M}_w$ (the empty model is not possible). The formula $\mathcal{M}_w \models Q_a(\text{first})$ holds true if and only if the first letter of w is a. The formula $\mathcal{M}_w \models Q_b(+1)$ holds true if and only if the second letter of w is b, $etc.$ For (2), we express information about semi-structured data – represented as a graph – by imposing constraints on the possible paths through the graph. Such a constraint might be "all objects reachable by a path p are also reachable via a path q", where p and q are sequences of labels possibly involving regular expressions. In order to check that the constraints hold, we recast them as model or satisfiability checking tasks in some logic (usually modal). For example, see [2] where this is done using propositional dynamic logic, and [12] where this is done using monadic second-order logic.

Fixed-Point Logic. Fixed-point logics are particularly well-suited for modelling recursion and have consequently found applications in various areas of computer science such as database theory, finite model theory and, formal verification. Following [22, 13], for a set A and a function $F : \wp(A) \to \wp(A)$, a fixed-point P of F is any set $P \subseteq A$ such that $F(P) = P$. A fixed point Q is called the least (greatest) fixed-point of F if and only if $Q \subseteq P$ $(P \subseteq Q)$ holds for all fixed points P of F. The function F is said to be monotone if $F(X) \subseteq F(Y)$ for all $X \subseteq Y \subseteq A$. A well-known theorem by Knaster and Tarski states that every monotone function has a least and a greatest fixed-point [33]. For limit ordinals λ and the monotone function F, consider the sequence $(X^\alpha)_{\alpha \in Ord}$ of sets $X^\alpha \subseteq A$ defined by (i) $X^0 = \emptyset$, (ii) $X^{\alpha+1} = F(X^\alpha)$, and (iii) $X^\lambda = \bigcup_{\xi < \lambda} X^\xi$. A fixed-point X^∞ is reached in this sequence whereby $X^\infty = X^\alpha$ for the least ordinal α such that $X^\alpha = X^{\alpha+1}$. This fixed-point X^∞ is called the inductive fixed-point of F. A second theorem by Knaster and Tarski states that the least and inductive fixed-points coincide, hence any least fixed-point of a monotone function can be defined inductively by a sequence of sets as described above. Dually, the greatest fixed-point of a monotone function F can be defined inductively using the sequence $(X^\alpha)_{\alpha \in Ord}$ of sets $X^\alpha \subseteq A$ defined by (i) $X^0 = A$, (ii) $X^{\alpha+1} = F(X^\alpha)$, and (iii) $X^\lambda = \bigcap_{\xi < \lambda} X^\xi$. Note that if F is inflationary (*i.e.* $X \subseteq F(X)$ for all $X \subseteq A$) rather than monotone, then X^∞ is called the inflationary fixed-point of F. Next let τ be a signature, *i.e.* a finite set of relation symbols, and let $\mathcal{A}$ be a structure consisting of a universe A and interpretations for each relation symbol in τ. Consider a first-order formula $\varphi(R, \bar{x})$ with R a k-ary free relation symbol not occurring in τ and $\bar{x}$ a k-tuple of free variables. On $\mathcal{A}$ the formula φ induces a fixed-point operator $F_\varphi : \wp(A^k) \to \wp(A^k)$ such that $F_\varphi(R) = \{\bar{a} \mid (\mathcal{A}, R) \models \varphi(\bar{a})\}$. Here $(\mathcal{A}, R) \models \varphi(\bar{a})$ means that formula φ is satisfied by the interpretation that assigns to each variable x_i of $\bar{x}$ the element a_i of $\bar{a} \in A^k$.

Below we investigate three fundamental fixed-point logics: monotone, least, and inflationary fixed-point logics. First of all we discuss monotone fixed-point logic. Using this logic we can nest inductive definitions; from one fixed-point built-up from a formula we can define another.

Monotone Fixed-Point Logic. Monotone Fixed-Point Logic *MFP* is the extension of FOL by the following rule: if R is a k-ary free relation variable, $\bar{x}$ is a k-tuple of free first-order variables, $\bar{t}$ is a k-tuple of terms and $\varphi(R, \bar{x})$ is a formula such that the corresponding operator F_φ is monotone on all structures, then $[lfp_{R,\bar{x}}\varphi](\bar{t})$ is also a formula. For any structure $\mathcal{A}$ that provides an interpretation of the free variables of φ except for $\bar{x}$, $\mathcal{A} \models [lfp_{R,\bar{x}}\varphi](\bar{t})$ if and only if the interpretation of $\bar{t}$ in $\mathcal{A}$ is in the least fixed-point of the operator defined by $\varphi(R, \bar{x})$. As we have mentioned previously, the least and greatest fixed-point of any monotone operator always exists. However it is undecidable as to whether a formula induces a monotone operator. In order to guarantee monotonicity on the operator one can restrict the formulae such that they are positive in the relation variable R. This leads us to the definition of least fixed-point logic.

Least Fixed-Point Logic. Least Fixed-Point Logic *LFP* is the extension of FOL by the following rule: if R is a k-ary free relation variable, $\bar{x}$ is a k-tuple of free first-order variables, $\bar{t}$ is a k-tuple of terms and $\varphi(R, \bar{x})$ is a formula in which R occurs only positively, then $[lfp_{R,\bar{x}}\varphi](\bar{t})$ is also a formula. For any structure $\mathcal{A}$ that provides an interpretation of the free variables of φ except for $\bar{x}$, $\mathcal{A} \models [lfp_{R,\bar{x}}\varphi](\bar{t})$ if and only if the interpretation of $\bar{t}$ in $\mathcal{A}$ is in the least fixed-point of the operator defined by $\varphi(R, \bar{x})$. Consider, for example, the directed graph (V, E), where V is a set of n vertices and $E \subseteq V \times V$ is a set of ordered pairs, *i.e.* edges. Then the transitive closure of E is defined as $[lfp_{R,x,y}(xEy \lor \exists z. (xRz \land zRy))](x, y)$.

Inflationary Fixed-Point Logic. Inflationary Fixed-Point Logic *IFP* can be considered the simplest non-monotone fixed-point logic. It is the extension of first-order logic by the following rule: if R is a k-ary free relation variable, $\bar{x}$ is a k-tuple of free first order variables, $\bar{t}$ is a k-tuple of terms and $\varphi(R, \bar{x})$ is a formula, then $[ifp_{R,\bar{x}}\varphi](\bar{t})$ is also a formula. Let $\mathcal{A}$ be a structure which provides an interpretation of the free variables of φ except for $\bar{x}$. The operator $I_\varphi(R) = \{\bar{a} \mid \bar{a} \in R \text{ or } (\mathcal{A}, R) \models \varphi(\bar{a})\}$ is inflationary and therefore has an inflationary fixed-point R^∞. Hence $\mathcal{A} \models [ifp_{R,\bar{x}}\varphi](\bar{t})$ if and only if the interpretation of $\bar{t}$ in $\mathcal{A}$ is in the inflationary fixed-point. An interesting result is that both least and inflationary fixed-point logics are equally expressive on arbitrary structures [21].

First-Order Dynamic Logic. The principle of dynamic logic (DL) is to facilitate the formulation of statements about program behaviour by integrating programs and formulas within a single language (see *e.g.* [15, 20] for general expositions of DL). By permitting arbitrary programs α as actions of a labelled multi-modal logic, dynamic logic provides formulas of the form $[\alpha]\phi$ and $\langle\alpha\rangle\phi$.

When considering states during program execution as worlds of modal logic, $[\alpha]\phi$ expresses that all (terminating) executions of program α lead to states in which ϕ holds; whereas $\langle\alpha\rangle\phi$ is a true property of a state s whenever there is some state t reachable from s by execution of program α in which ϕ holds. A Hoare-style specification $\{\phi\}\alpha\{\psi\}$ of partial correctness can be expressed as $\phi \to [\alpha]\psi$. In contrast to Hoare logic and temporal logic approaches to program verification, dynamic logic permits the expression of structural relationships between different programs by using multiple modalities. For example relative correctness statements like $\langle\alpha\rangle\phi \to \langle\alpha'\rangle\phi$ as well as nesting are possible, as in the formula $[\alpha](c \geq 0 \to \langle\alpha'\rangle c \leq d \cdot d)$.

Provided that they are computable, dynamic logic can express properties of relations that are ordinarily not expressible in pure first-order logic. For example to express that y is reachable from x *via* applications of the function *next* (*i.e.* x and y are related in the transitive closure of the relation p defined by $p(u, v)$ iff $v = next(u)$) can be expressed by $\langle$while $(x \neq y)\ x := next(x)\rangle true$.

4   Specification Languages

In this section we look at the approaches that specification languages take in defining transitive closure and similar properties of relations. Most require "hacks" to force a model's finiteness and acyclicity before transitive closure can be determined (an interesting and unique approach is taken by the Java Modeling Language JML).

Alloy. The Alloy Analyzer implements an automatic analysis method for formulae of relational logic [17, 18]. This logic acts as an intermediate language for the object modelling notation Alloy. It is a first-order logic with sets and relations whereby each formula is accompanied by a declaration that associates variables to their types. The combination of formula and declaration is called a problem. There are three kinds of types: set, relation, and function. Scalar variables are treated as singleton sets and sets are encoded as "degenerate" relations. For example, a scalar variable v of set type T can also be represented as the relational type $T \rightarrow Unit$, where $Unit$ is a special type designed for this purpose.

A "navigation" expression $s.r$ denotes the image of a set s under a relation r. The encoding of sets as degenerate relations allows a uniform syntax to be given to such expressions, *i.e.* if p is a person then $p.mother$ will denote p's mother, whereas $p.parents$ will denote the set of p's parents. A transitive closure operator $+$ is also included in Alloy. For example, the formula $(p+) \cap Id = 0$ expresses that p is acyclic. Here Id is the identity relation and 0 is the empty relation.

Because relational logic is undecidable, it is in general impossible to prove that a formula is either consistent or valid. To determine for a given formula whether a model exists (within a particular scope), the Alloy Analyzer places restrictions on the size of the sets of the basic types. A model is said to be within a scope of k if it assigns to each type a set consisting of no more than k elements.

SQL. In order to manipulate the data of a relational database, relational query languages – based on relational algebra – are used. The database query language SQL was adopted as an industry standard in 1986 [32]. Having undergone two major revisions, SQL3 is now the current version.

```
WITH
RECURSIVE AncestorDescendant(ancestor, descendant) AS
    ((SELECT * FROM ParentChild)
    UNION
    (SELECT ad1.ancestor, ad2.descendant
    FROM AncestorDescendant ad1, AncestorDescendant ad2
    WHERE ad1.descendant = ad2.ancestor))
SELECT ancestor FROM AncestorDescendant WHERE descendant = "Mary";
```

Fig. 1. SQL specification

Unlike its predecessors, SQL3 supports linear recursion; a recursive query has the form "WITH RECURSIVE R AS r Q;", where r is the expression that you want to recurse and R is its name that can then be used in the associated query expression Q. If we consider a query as a function on tables, then a recursive query computes the "fixed-point table" [34]. Essentially, we start with R as an empty table. We then evaluate r using the (temporary) contents of R and replace R with this new value. As long as $R^{new} \neq R$, we continue to evaluate r and replace R by its new value. Once $R^{new} = R$, we compute Q using the current contents of R and output the result. The example shown in Figure 1 outlines how we find Mary's ancestors from the schema ParentChild(parent, child). The first part of the recursive definition – utilising * – is the base case. Its meaning is that all "parent/child" pairs are also "ancestor/descendant" pairs. Although initially we know nothing about ancestor-descendant relationships, after the first round we deduce that parents are ancestors and children are descendants. In each subsequent round we use the facts deduced in previous rounds to get more ancestor-descendant relationships. We eventually stop when no new facts can be proven.

When the query Q is non-monotone, *i.e.* adding tuples to R might cause some tuple to be removed from the result of Q, then the fixed-point iteration may not converge. A way to circumvent this is to construct a dependency graph whereby: (1) each table R_i is a node; (2) there is a directed arc from R_i to R_j if R_i is defined in terms of R_j; and (3) the arc is labelled "-" if the query defining R_i is non-monotone with respect to R_j, *i.e.* by adding something to R_j we may cause something to be removed from R_i. The maximum number of - arcs on any path from R in the dependency graph is called the stratum of node R. A recursive query statement is said to be stratified if every node has a finite stratum, *i.e.* there are no cycles containing - arcs. Hence legal SQL3 recursive queries are required to be stratified. Note that this technique can also be used in other languages using fixed-point definitions in order to exclude non-monotonicity cases that lead to fixed-points being undefined.

CASL. The Common Algebraic Specification Language (CASL), has been developed by CoFI, the international Common Framework Initiative for algebraic specification and development (see website at http://www.cofi.info). The algebraic approach to software specification was conceived in the early 1970s, see for example [35]. Programs are considered as algebras consisting of datatypes and operations; the intended behaviour of a program is specified by formulae involving these operations. The development of dozens of languages, all with slight variations in syntax and semantics, demanded the need for a common framework, hence CoFI was formed. The resulting specification language CASL features partial functions, subsorts, sort generation constraints, first-order logic, and structural and architectural specifications [27].

In CASL datatypes are specified using the keyword **type** and are given in terms of sorts (*i.e.* the types of values) and constructors. Datatypes may be declared to be either **generated** or **free**. When a generated datatype is declared, then the corresponding sort is constrained to be generated only by the declared constructors. For example in the specification of GENERATED_CONTAINER taken from the CASL User Manual [7] (see Figure 2), the generatedness constraint is such that any value of sort *Container* is denoted by a term built only with operators *empty*, *insert* and variables of sort *Elem*.

Note that within this specification, the pairs of underscores "_" indicate place-holders for the binary predicate *is_in* and the bulleted list features "axioms" which constrain the predicate. Essentially, the generatedness constraint allows one to prove – by induction on the declared constructors – properties

spec GENERATED_CONTAINER [**sort** *Elem*] =
   generated type *Container* ::= *empty* | *insert*(*Elem*; *Container*)
   pred __*is_in*__ : *Elem* × *Container*
   $\forall e, e'$: *Elem*; *C* : *Container*
   • $\neg$(*e is_in empty*)
   • *e is_in insert*(*e'*, *C*) $\Leftrightarrow$ (*e* = *e'* ∨ *e is_in C*)
end

spec TRANSITIVE_CLOSURE [**sort** *Elem* **pred** __*R*__ : *Elem* × *Elem*] =
   free { **pred** __*R*$^+$__ : *Elem* × *Elem*
       $\forall x, y, z$: *Elem* • $x\,R\,y \rightarrow x\,R^+\,y$
                         • $x\,R^+\,y \wedge y\,R^+\,z \rightarrow x\,R^+\,z$ }
end

Fig. 2. CASL specifications

of values of the sort *Container*. A **free** datatype declaration has the same interpretation as the **generated** datatype declaration with the additional property that all distinct constructor terms of the same sort denote distinct values.

In CASL a "freeness" constraint – using the keyword **free** – can be imposed on a predicate declaration. This has the effect that a predicate that is consistent with the given axioms but not a consequence of the axioms will be false; predicates hold minimally. We can see this in the specification of TRANSITIVE_CLOSURE shown in Figure 2 (also taken from [7]). Here the transitive closure of a binary relation R on some sort *Elem* is specified. Since predicates hold minimally in models of free specifications, R^+ is actually the smallest transitive relation including R.

OCL. The Object Constraint Language (OCL) [19] is a part of the Unified Modeling Language (UML) [14]. Currently the industry standard, UML allows software developers to graphically specify, visualise and document models of software systems. OCL can be used to augment UML object models with additional textual information which cannot otherwise be expressed by UML diagrams. This additional information takes the form of side-effect-free expressions and constraints. An expression is a specification of a value. A constraint is a restriction of one or more values in (part of) the object-oriented model. The semantics of OCL constraints is defined by an evaluation function which maps – in a given object diagram – any constraint to one of the logical constants **true**, **false**, and **undefined**. Admissible diagrams are those whereby all constraints of the corresponding class diagram evaluate to **true**.

The type of an OCL expression is either pre-defined (**Boolean**, **Integer**, *etc.*) or it is the type of a class in the corresponding class diagram. Dot notation is used for accessing the attributes of objects. The basic data structures of OCL are the collections **Set**, **Bag** and **Sequence**.

OCL does not have a primitive operator for transitive closure, but it does allow recursion. Consider the following OCL invariant in the context **Person**, where ancestors are recursively defined in order to represent the transitive closure of the relation defined by parents (note that both ancestors and parents are of type Set(Person)): ancestors = parents -> union(parents.ancestors). The expression parents.ancestors computes the set of all ancestors of a set of parents and returns a value of type Set(Person).

Now suppose A is a parent of B, who in turn is a parent of C. Then the minimal object structure which solves the constraint is such that the parent of B is A and the ancestors of C include both B and A. However, additional solutions involve situations where B and A are both ancestors of each other and themselves. In our case we would prefer to use the minimal solution (corresponding to the minimal fixpoint), but this cannot always be found: there may be more than one equivalent solution, or it may not even exist. A suggestion to uniquely characterise the minimal solution is given in [11]. This paper suggests mimicking induction over a natural number n. This is exhibited in the following OCL specification.

```
ancestors_up_to(n) = if (n==1) then parents
                     else parents -> union(parents.ancestors_up_to(n-1))
Nat -> forall(n | ancestors_up_to(n) = ancestors_up_to(n+1)
                     implies ancestors = ancestors_up_to(n))
```

Of course this makes the assumption that the models are finite. Alternatively, as done in [9], we can use the OCL let construct to stipulate that the inheritance relationship must be acyclic. Note that self refers to any instance of the class in which it is specified.

```
let parents = self.parents
let ancestors = self.parents -> union(self.parents.ancestors)
    in <some_expression_using_definition_of_ancestor>
```

The let construct is a new addition to OCL, introduced in version 2.0. The expression let x = e_1 in e_2 evaluates expression e_2 with each occurrence of x replaced by the value of e_1. Its use avoids evaluating the same expression multiple times. However the construct's semantics within OCL is not entirely clear [9]. Whether arbitrary recursively defined expressions are allowed is uncertain. Thus, using let to define transitive closure is not advised.

In [26] the transitive closure of a relation is computed by coding the well-known Warshall's algorithm in OCL. This coding makes use of the OCL iterate construct which iterates through all items of a collection, verifying a given condition and possibly updating the value of a variable returned at the end of the iteration. The algorithm itself calculates the transitive closure of a directed graph (V, E), where V is a set of n vertices and $E \subseteq V \times V$ is a set of ordered pairs, i.e. edges. A path from vertex v_0 to v_k is denoted $v_0 \xrightarrow{*} v_k$ and is a sequence of edges $(v_0, v_1), (v_1, v_2), \ldots, (v_{k-1}, v_k)$. The intuition behind Warshall's algorithm is this: if the graph contains paths $v \xrightarrow{*} w$ and $w \xrightarrow{*} u$ whose intermediate vertices belong to the set S, then the graph also contain a path $v \xrightarrow{*} u$ such that the intermediate vertices belong to $S \cup \{w\}$. The algorithm iterates from 1 to n. At the kth iteration it selects paths whose intermediate vertices come from $\{v_1, \ldots, v_{k-1}\}$. Unfortunately the resulting OCL code of this algorithm is about one and a half pages in length; it is neither intuitive nor easy to read, and furthermore it requires the directed graph to be finite.

A transitive closure construct for OCL is proposed by Schürr in [31]. This is based on features of the path expression sublanguage – similar to OCL – of PROGRES, a graph transformation language. The transitive closure operator * is implemented to keep track of already visited objects and therefore avoids any cyclic problems. Schürr defines it as follows:

```
self.ancestors* = self.ancestorsClosure(self)
self.ancestorsClosure(visitedObj) =
    let S : ... = self.ancestors -> excludeAll(visitedObj) in
    S -> collect(ancestorsClosure(S -> union(visitedObj))) -> asSet
```

This definition will suffer from the unclear semantics of the `let` construct.

As mentioned in Section 2, it is possible to define the transitive closure of relations known to be finite and acyclic. To illustrate this, Baar [4] defines `ancestors` by $APar(x) = Par(x) \cup \{y \mid \exists z. z \in Par(x) \land y \in APar(z)\}$, where $Par(x)$ and $APar(x)$ are the translations of `x.parents` and `x.ancestors`, respectively. Correspondingly, in first-order logic, this definition can be expressed by the formula $r^*(x, y) \Leftrightarrow (r(x, y) \lor \exists z. r(x, z) \land r^*(z, y))$, where the relation symbols r and r^* are substituted for Par and $APar$, with $r(x, y)$ meaning $y \in Par(x)$ and $r^*(x, y)$ meaning $y \in APar(x)$. This formula is interpreted by the structure (U, R, R^*) where U is a universe of variables, and R and R^* are interpretations of the relations r and r^*, respectively. Countermodels for this formula are presented whereby R^* does not coincide with the transitive closure of R. However if the model (U, R, R^*) is finite and the axiom $\neg r^*(x, x)$ holds – enforcing R^*s acyclicity – then R^* is a correct definition of transitive closure (however, in general finiteness is not expressible).

JML and SPEC#. The Java Modeling Language (JML) was originally designed by Leavens *et al.* at Iowa State University in 1998. Having spawned a much larger community of users and tool developers who are now actively involved in its development, JML has since become the standard specification language used for verification of Java programs. JML is used to specify Java classes and interfaces [23, 24].

The Spec# system [5] has been developed as a specification language for .Net. The recent developments in the JML community have been influenced and some ideas have been adopted that originated from the Spec# project. The treatment of second-order concepts is similar in both languages (we concentrate on JML in the following).

Specifications in JML are formulated by making use of (side-effect-free) boolean Java expressions; they are written as Java comments. The original JML tool is a pre-compiler designed to translate specified programs into Java programs that explicitly monitor assertions at run-time. Specification violations that are found throw Java exceptions. Since JML's conception, many more tools have been developed using JML as an input specification language. For a more extensive overview of JML tools and applications, see [8].

When specifying transitive closure, JML manages to avoid the whole issue of acyclicity by defining recursive datagroups [28]. These have been designed primarily with frame-condition issues in mind. To solve the information hiding problem (*i.e.* that protected or private fields of a class should remain hidden from their clients) the `represents` clause was introduced to JML, allowing one to specify the representation of concrete fields by particular abstract fields. Hence protected or private fields in an implementation can be changed without changing the specification visible to its clients. Unfortunately, the use of abstract fields generated problems with the `modifies` clause. (A method's `modifies` clause specifies those locations that are permitted to be changed by execution of the method.) This was fixed by a `depends` clause which relates those locations used to determine an abstract location's values. A datagroup can be modelled by an abstract location whose value contains no information. By using a `depends` clause, a location can be declared to be in a datagroup, therefore membership in a datagroup allows the locations in the datagroup to be modified whenever the datagroup is mentioned in the `modifies` clause. The license to modify a datagroup implies the license to modify the members of the datagroup as defined by a downward closure rule [25]. For any set of datagroups S, the downward closure of this set is the smallest superset of S such that for any group G in the closure of S, all nested datagroup members of G also belong in the closure of S. For example, consider the following Java linked list with `Node` objects having `next` and `value` fields:

```
class Node { Integer value; Node next; }
```

The datagroups `nodeValues` and `nodeLinks`are are defined recursively using clauses such as "maps next.nodeValues \into nodeValues". Hence the clause "modifies list.nodeLinks;", when it is added to the JML specification of a method `sortInPlace(Node list)`, says that all node objects reachable from `list` may be changed whenever `sortInPlace` is executed.

Such specifications rely on a smallest-fixed-point semantics for recursive definitions built into JML. Gleaned from mailing list discussions, Leavens *et al.* have considered introducing regular expressions, (*i.e.* writing `list.next`* in order to specify the `JMLObjectSet` of all objects reachable from `list` using the field name `next`) but have rejected this as not particularly beneficial since using datagroups seems to be an adequate enough solution.

5   Conclusions

Although important properties of relations are not expressible in classical first-order logic, it is possible to extend first-order logic (*e.g.* with fixed-point and transitive closure operators) in order to describe such properties. We find that all specification languages feature modifications which allow them to extend beyond the limitations of first-order logic. For example SQL implements fixed-point logic, OCL uses the `iterate` and `let` constructs, CASL implements the notion of freeness, whereas JML incorporates built-in recursion. However, the logical concepts underpinning these modifications are often not well documented. This paper has attempted to clarify what is going on regarding these extensions.

Generally we have found that once integers are "available" in a specification language, it is possible to define transitive closure and other properties of relations in the language. Otherwise this is possible only for finite relations (which is mostly adequate). In our opinion the best solution is that which is taken by CASL and JML, namely by building freeness or minimal fixed-points either explicitly or implicitly into the language. It still seems desirable to add regular expressions to specification languages. It is not clear yet how this should be done; this is the subject of future work.

References

1. W. Ahrendt, T. Baar, B. Beckert, R. Bubel, M. Giese, R. Hähnle, W. Menzel, W. Mostowski, A. Roth, S. Schlager, and P. H. Schmitt. The KeY tool. *Software and System Modeling*, 4:32–54, 2005.
2. N. Alechina, S. Demri, and M. de Rijke. A modal perspective on path constraints. *Journal of Logic and Computation*, 13:1–18, 2003.
3. N. Alechina and N. Immerman. Reachability logic: An efficient fragment of transitive closure logic. *Logic Journal of the IGPL*, 8(3):325–337, 2000.
4. T. Baar. The definition of transitive closure with OCL: Limitations and applications. In *Proceedings of the Fifth Andrei Ershov International Conference on Perspectives of System Informatics*, LNCS 2890, pages 358–365. Springer, 2003.
5. M. Barnett, K. R. M. Leino, and W. Schulte. The Spec# programming system: An overview. In *Construction and Analysis of Safe, Secure, and Interoperable Smart Devices, International Workshop, CASSIS 2004, Marseille, France, Revised Selected Papers*, LNCS 3362. Springer, 2005.
6. B. Beckert and P. H. Schmitt. Program verification using change information. In *Proceedings, SEFM 2003*, pages 91–99. IEEE Press, 2003.
7. M. Bidoit and P. Mosses. *CASL User Manual: Introduction to Using the Common Algebraic Specification Language*. LNCS 2900. Springer, 2004.
8. L. Burdy, Y. Cheon, D. Cok, M. Ernst, J. Kiniry, G. Leavens, K. Leino, and E. Poll. An overview of JML tools and applications. In *Formal Methods for Industrial Critical Systems (FMICS 2003)*, volume 80 of *ENTCS*. Elsevier, 2003.
9. M. V. Cengarle and A. Knapp. A formal semantics for OCL 1.4. In *Proceedings, The Unified Modeling Language (UML 2001)*, LNCS 2185. Springer, 2001.
10. H. Chen, J. Hsiang, and H. Kong. On finite representation of infinite sequences of terms. In *Proceedings of 2nd International Workshop on Conditional and Typed Rewriting Systems*, number 516 in LNCS, pages 100–114. Springer, 1990.
11. S. Cook, A. Kleppe, R. Mitchell, B. Rumpe, J. Warmer, and A. Wills. The Amsterdam manifesto on OCL, 1999. Available at `http://www.trireme.com/whitepapers/design/components/OCL_manifesto.PDF`.
12. B. Courcelle. The expression of graph properties and graph transformations in monadic second-order logic. In G. Rozenberg, editor, *Handbook of Graph Grammars and Computing by Graph Transformations*. World Scientific, 1997.

13. A. Dawar and Y. Gurevich. Fixed point logics. In *The Bulletin of Symbolic Logic*, volume 8, pages 65–88. Association for Symbolic Logic, 2002.
14. M. Fowler and K. Scott. *UML Distilled, 2nd ed.* Addison-Wesley, 2000.
15. D. Harel. Dynamic logic. In D. Gabbay and F. Guenthner, editors, *Handbook of Philosophical Logic*, volume II, chapter 10, pages 497–604. Reidel, 1984.
16. N. Immerman. Languages that capture complexity classes. *SIAM Journal of Computing*, 16(4):760–778, 1987.
17. D. Jackson. Automating first-order relational logic. In *Foundations of Software Engineering*, pages 130–139, 2000.
18. D. Jackson, I. Schechter, and I. Shlyakhter. Alcoa: the Alloy constraint analyzer. In *Proceedings,ICSE 2000*, pages 730–733. IEEE, 2000.
19. Klasse Objecten. OCL center, 1999. At `http://www.klasse.nl/ocl`.
20. D. Kozen and J. Tiuryn. Logics of programs. In J. van Leeuwen, editor, *Handbook of Theoretical Computer Science*, volume B, chapter 14. The MIT Press, 1990.
21. S. Kreutzer. Expressive equivalence of least and inflationary fixed-point logic. In *Proceedings, Symposium on Logic in Computer Science (LICS)*. IEEE, 2000.
22. S. Kreutzer. *Pure and Applied Fixed-Point Logics*. PhD thesis, Aachen University of Technology, 2002.
23. G. T. Leavens, A. L. Baker, and C. Ruby. Preliminary design of JML: A behavioral interface specification language for Java. Technical report, Iowa State Univ., 2000. Available at `ftp://ftp.cs.iastate.edu/pub/techreports/TR98-06/TR.ps.gz`.
24. G. T. Leavens, E. Poll, C. Clifton, Y. Cheon, C. Ruby, D. Cok, and J. Kiniry. JML reference manual. At `http://www.cs.iastate.edu/~leavens/JML/jmlrefman`.
25. K. R. M. Leino. Specifying the modification of extended state. Technical Report 1997-026, Digital Systems Research Center, 1997.
26. L. Mandel and M. V. Cengarle. On the expressive power of OCL. In *Proceedings, FM 1999*, LNCS 1708, pages 854–874. Springer, 1999.
27. P. D. Mosses. CASL: A guided tour of its design, 1999. Available at `http://www.brics.dk/Projects/CoFI/Documents/CASL/GuidedTour/index.html`.
28. P. Müller, A. Poetzsch-Heffter, and G. Leavens. Modular specification of frame properties in JML. Technical Report 02-02, Iowa State University, 1997.
29. Object Management Group. UML resource page, 1999. At `http://www.uml.org`.
30. J. Rumbaugh. Relations as semantic constructs in an object-oriented language. In *Proceedings, OOPSLA 1987*, pages 466–481, 1987.
31. A. Schürr. Adding graph transformation concepts to UML's constraint language OCL. In *Proceedings, First Workshop on Language Descriptions, Tools and Applications (LDTA)*, ENTCS 44. Elsevier, 2001.
32. JCC's SQL std. page. At `http://www.jcc.com/SQLPages/jccs_sql.htm`.
33. A. Tarski. A lattice-theoretical fixpoint theorem and its applications. *Pacific Journal of Mathematics*, 5:285–309, 1955.
34. J. Yang. SQL3 recursion. Lecture notes, Stanford University, 1999.
35. S. Zilles. Algebraic specification of data types. Technical Report XI, MIT Laboratory for Computer Science, 1974.

Strong Normalization of the Dual Classical Sequent Calculus

Daniel Dougherty[1], Silvia Ghilezan[2], Pierre Lescanne[3], and Silvia Likavec[2,4]

[1] Worcester Polytechnic Institute, USA
dd@wpi.edu
[2] Faculty of Engineering, University of Novi Sad, Serbia
gsilvia@uns.ns.ac.yu
[3] ENS Lyon, France
pierre.lescanne@ens-lyon.fr
[4] Dipartimento di Informatica, Università di Torino, Italy
likavec@di.unito.it

Abstract. We investigate some syntactic properties of Wadler's dual calculus, a term calculus which corresponds to classical sequent logic in the same way that Parigot's $\lambda\mu$ calculus corresponds to classical natural deduction. Our main result is strong normalization theorem for reduction in the dual calculus; we also prove some confluence results for the typed and untyped versions of the system.

1 Introduction

This paper establishes some of the key properties of reduction underlying Wadler's dual calculus [30, 31]. The basic system, obtained as a term-assignment system for classical sequent calculus, is not confluent, inheriting the well-known anomaly of classical cut-elimination. Wadler recovers confluence by restricting to reduction strategies corresponding to (either of) the call-by-value or call-by-name disciplines, indeed these subcalculi and the duality between them are the main focus of attention in Wadler's work.

In this paper we are less interested in call-by-value and call-by-name *per se* than in the pure combinatorics of reduction itself, consequently we work with as few restrictions as possible on the system. We prove strong normalization (SN) for unrestricted reduction of typed terms, including expansion rules capturing extensionality. We show that once the obvious obstacle to confluence is removed (the "critical pair" in the reduction system) confluence holds in both the typed and untyped versions of the term calculus. This critical pair (see Section 3) can be disambiguated in two ways but the proof we give dualizes to yield confluence results for each system, an example of the "two theorems for the price of one" benefit of duality.

The dual calculus is an embodiment of the "proofs-as-programs" paradigm in the setting of classical logic, as well as being a clear expression of the relationship between call-by-name and call-by-value in functional programming. So the fundamental syntactic results given here should play an important role in the currently active investigations into the relationship between classical logic and computation.

G. Sutcliffe and A. Voronkov (Eds.): LPAR 2005, LNAI 3835, pp. 169–183, 2005.
© Springer-Verlag Berlin Heidelberg 2005

Background. The Curry-Howard correspondence expresses a fundamental connection between logic and computation [18]. In its traditional form, terms in the λ-calculus encode proofs in intuitionistic natural deduction; from another perspective the proofs serve as typing derivations for the terms. Griffin extended the Curry-Howard correspondence to classical logic in his seminal 1990 POPL paper [16], by observing that classical tautologies suggest typings for certain control operators. This initiated a vigorous line of research: on the one hand classical calculi can be seen as pure programming languages with explicit representations of control, while at the same time terms can be tools for extracting the constructive content of classical proofs [21, 3]. In particular the $\lambda\mu$ calculus of Parigot [23] has been the basis of a number of investigations [24, 11, 22, 5, 1] into the relationship between classical logic and theories of control in programming languages.

As early as 1989 Filinsky [14] explored the notion that the reduction strategies call-by-value and call-by-name were dual to each other. Filinski defined a symmetric lambda-calculus in which values and continuations comprised distinct syntactic sorts and whose denotational semantics expressed the call-by-name vs call-by-value duality in a precise categorical sense. Later Selinger [27] modeled the call-by-name and call-by-value variants of the $\lambda\mu$ by dual control and co-control categories.

These two lines of investigation come together nicely in the framework of classical *sequent calculus*. In contrast to natural deduction proof systems (upon which Parigot's $\lambda\mu$, for example, is based) sequent calculi exhibit inherent symmetries not just at the level of terms, but of proof structures as well. There are several term calculi based on sequent calculus. The most relevant to the current study are those in which terms unambiguously encode sequent derivations for which reduction corresponds to cut elimination. See, for example, [29, 9, 19, 2]. Curien and Herbelin [17, 9] defined the system $\overline{\lambda}\mu\tilde{\mu}$, a sequent calculus-inspired calculus exhibiting symmetries in the syntax, whose terms represent derivations in the implicational fragment of Gentzen's system LK [15]. In addition, as described in [9], the sequent calculus basis for $\overline{\lambda}\mu\tilde{\mu}$ supports an interpretation of the reduction rules of the system as operations of an abstract machine. In particular, the right- and left-hand sides of a sequent directly represent the *code* and *environment* components of the machine. This perspective is elaborated more fully in [8]. See [7] for a discussion of the importance of symmetries in computation. In [2], a calculus, which interprets directly the implicational sequent logic, is proposed as a language in which many kinds of other calculi can be implemented, from λ-calculus to $\overline{\lambda}\mu\tilde{\mu}$ through a calculus of explicit substitution and $\lambda\mu$.

The Symmetric Lambda Calculus of Barbanera and Berardi [3], although not based on sequent calculus, belongs in the tradition of exploiting the symmetries found in classical logic, in their case with the goal of extracting constructive content from classical proofs. Barbanera and Berardi [3] proved SN for their calculus using a "symmetric candidates" technique; Urban and Bierman [29] adapted their technique to prove SN for their sequent-based system. Lengrand [19] shows how simply-typed $\overline{\lambda}\mu\tilde{\mu}$ and the calculus of Urban and Bierman [29] are mutually interpretable, so that the strong normalization proof of the latter calculus yields another proof of strong normalization for simply-typed $\overline{\lambda}\mu\tilde{\mu}$. Polonovski [25] presents a proof of SN for $\overline{\lambda}\mu\tilde{\mu}$ with explicit substitutions using the symmetric candidates idea. Pym and Ritter [26] identify two forms of disjunction for Parigot's[23] $\lambda\mu$ calculus; they prove strong normalization for $\lambda\mu\nu$ calculus ($\lambda\mu$ calculus extended with such disjunction). David and Nour [10] give an arithmetical proof of strong normalization for a symmetric $\lambda\mu$ calculus.

The Dual Calculus. Wadler's dual calculus [30] refines and unifies these themes. It is a term-assignment system based on classical sequent calculus, and a key step is that implication is not taken as a primitive connective. It turns out that this permits a very clear expression of the way in which the traditional duality between the left- and right-hand sides of a sequent reflects the duality between call-by-value and call-by-name.

Unfortunately these beautiful symmetries come at the price of some anomalies in the behavior of reduction. The unrestricted reduction relation in the dual calculus (as well as in $\overline{\lambda}\mu\tilde{\mu}$) has a critical pair, and indeed this system is not confluent. In [30] Wadler gives two restricted versions of each reduction rule obtaining subcalculi which naturally correspond to call-by-value and call-by-name, respectively. He then defines translations of these systems into the simply-typed λ-calculus; each translation both preserves and reflects reductions. See Propositions 6.6, 6.9, 6.10 on [30]. (Curien and Herbelin [9] gave a similar encoding of their $\overline{\lambda}\mu\tilde{\mu}$ calculus.)

It was "claimed without proof" in [30], that these call-by-value and call-by-name reductions are confluent and that the call-by-value and call-by-name reduction relations (without expansions) are strongly normalizing. But in fact confluence and strong normalization for each of call-by-value and call-by-name follows from the corresponding results in the λ-calculus by diagram-chasing through the CPS translations into the simply-typed λ-calculus, given the fact that reductions are preserved and reflected by the translations.

In [31] the emphasis is on the equational theory of the dual calculus. The equations of the dual calculus include a group of equations called "η-equations" which express extensionality properties; these equations play an important role in the relationship between the dual calculus and $\lambda\mu$. The relationship with Parigot's $\lambda\mu$ is worked out, the result is a clear notion of duality for $\lambda\mu$.

Summary of Results

We prove that unrestricted reduction of typed expressions in the dual calculus is strongly normalizing. The proof is a variation on the "semantical" method of reducibility, where types are interpreted as *pairs* of sets of terms (observe: yet another symmetry). Our proof technique uses a fixed-point construction similar to that in [3] but the technique is considerably simplified here (Section 6).

In fact our proof technique also shows the strong normalization for the reduction system including the η-expansion rules of the dual calculus. Due to space restrictions we only outline the treatment of the expansions but the machinery is the same as for the core calculus and filling in the missing details should only be an exercise for the reader.

To our knowledge none of the previous treatments of strong normalization for classical calculi has addressed extensionality rules.

We prove that if we disambiguate the single critical pair in the system, by giving priority to either the "left" or to the "right" reductions, the resulting subsystems are confluent. Furthermore reduction is confluent whether terms are typed or untyped. The proof is an application of Takahashi's parallel reductions technique [28]; we prove the result for one system and are able to conclude the result for the other by duality (Section 4).

The relationship between our results and those in [30, 31] is somewhat subtle. Wadler is motivated by programming language concerns and so is led to focus on sub-calculi of the dual calculus corresponding to call-by-name and call-by-value reduction; not only is the critical pair in the system removed but reductions must act on "values" (or "covalues"). In contrast, we are interested in the pure combinatorics of reduction, and so

- in exploring strong normalization we consider unrestricted reduction of typed terms (as well as incorporating expansions), and

- in exploring confluence we consider reduction of untyped terms, and impose only the restriction that the critical pair (which demonstrably destroys confluence) be disambiguated.

2   Syntax

Following Wadler, we distinguish three syntactic categories: *terms*, *coterms*, and *statements*. Terms yield values, while coterms consume values. A statement is a cut of a term against a coterm. We call the expressions in the union of these three categories *D-expressions*.

Let r, q range over the set Λ_R of terms, e, f range over the set Λ_L of coterms, and c ranges over statements. Then the syntax of the dual calculus is given by the following:

Term: $r, q ::= x \mid \langle r, q \rangle \mid \langle r \rangle \text{inl} \mid \langle r \rangle \text{inr} \mid [e]\text{not} \mid \mu\alpha.c$

Coterm: $e, f ::= \alpha \mid [e, f] \mid \text{fst}[e] \mid \text{snd}[e] \mid \text{not}\langle r \rangle \mid \tilde{\mu}x.c$

Statement: $c ::= (\!| r \bullet e |\!)$

where x ranges over a set of term variables Var_R, $\langle r, q \rangle$ is a pair, $\langle r \rangle\text{inl}$ ($\langle r \rangle\text{inr}$) is an injection on the left (right) of the sum, $[e]\text{not}$ is a complement of a coterm, and $\mu\alpha.c$ is a covariable abstraction. Next, α ranges over a set of covariables Var_L, $[e, f]$ is a case, $\text{fst}[e]$ ($\text{snd}[e]$) is a projection from the left (right) of a product, $\text{not}\langle r \rangle$ is a complement of a term, and $\tilde{\mu}x.c$ is a variable abstraction. Finally $(\!| r \bullet e |\!)$ is a cut. The term variables can be bound by μ abstraction, whereas the coterm variables can be bound by $\tilde{\mu}$ abstraction. The sets of free term and coterm variables, Fv_R and Fv_L, are defined as usual, respecting Barendregt's convention [4] that no variable can be both, bound and free, in the expression. As in [30, 31], angle brackets always surround terms and square brackets always surround coterms. Also, curly brackets are used for substitution and to denote holes in contexts.

We decided to slightly alter the notation given by Wadler. First of all, we use $\mu\alpha.c$ and $\tilde{\mu}x.c$ instead of $(S).\alpha$ and $x.(S)$. Furthermore, we use $(\!| r \bullet e |\!)$ for statements, since from our point of view it is easier to read than $r \bullet e$. Finally, the lowercase letters that we use to denote D-expressions should help to distinguish such expressions from types.

3   Reduction Rules

Wadler defines the dual calculus, giving the reductions that respect call-by-value and call-by-name reduction strategies, respectively. We give the reduction rules for an

$(\beta\tilde{\mu})$	$(\!(r \bullet \tilde{\mu}x.c)\!)$	$\rightarrow c\{r/x\}$
$(\beta\mu)$	$(\!(\mu\alpha.c \bullet e)\!)$	$\rightarrow c\{e/\alpha\}$
$(\beta\wedge)$	$(\!(\langle r, q \rangle \bullet \text{fst}[e])\!)$	$\rightarrow (\!(r \bullet e)\!)$
$(\beta\wedge)$	$(\!(\langle r, q \rangle \bullet \text{snd}[e])\!)$	$\rightarrow (\!(q \bullet e)\!)$
$(\beta\vee)$	$(\!(\langle r \rangle \text{inl} \bullet [e, f])\!)$	$\rightarrow (\!(r \bullet e)\!)$
$(\beta\vee)$	$(\!(\langle r \rangle \text{inr} \bullet [e, f])\!)$	$\rightarrow (\!(r \bullet f)\!)$
$(\beta\neg)$	$(\!([e]\text{not} \bullet \text{not}\langle r \rangle)\!)$	$\rightarrow (\!(r \bullet e)\!)$

Fig. 1. Reduction rules for the dual calculus

unrestricted calculus in Figure 1. Of course the notion of reduction is defined on raw expressions, and does not make use of any typing constraints. We use $\twoheadrightarrow$ to denote the reflexive transitive closure of $\rightarrow$ (with a similar convention for other relations denoted by other arrows).

Remark 1. The following observation will be useful later; it is the analogue of the standard λ-calculus trick of "promoting head reductions." Specifically, if a reduction sequence out of a statement ever does a top-level μ-reduction, then we can promote the first such reduction to be the first in the sequence, in the following sense: the reduction sequence $(\!(\mu\alpha.c \bullet e)\!) \twoheadrightarrow (\!(\mu\alpha.c' \bullet e')\!) \longrightarrow c'\{e'/\alpha\}$ can be transformed to the reduction sequence $(\!(\mu\alpha.c \bullet e)\!) \longrightarrow c\{e/\alpha\} \twoheadrightarrow c'\{e'/\alpha\}$.

The calculus has a critical pair $(\!(\mu\alpha.c_1 \bullet \tilde{\mu}x.c_2)\!)$ where both the $(\beta\tilde{\mu})$ and $(\beta\mu)$ rules can be applied ambiguously, producing two different results. For example,

$$(\!(\mu\alpha.(\!(y \bullet \beta)\!) \bullet \tilde{\mu}x.(\!(z \bullet \gamma)\!))\!) \rightarrow (\!(y \bullet \beta)\!), \qquad (\!(\mu\alpha.(\!(y \bullet \beta)\!) \bullet \tilde{\mu}x.(\!(z \bullet \gamma)\!))\!) \rightarrow (\!(z \bullet \gamma)\!)$$

Hence, the calculus is not confluent. But if the priority is given to one of the rules, we obtain two subcalculi Dual_R and Dual_L. Therefore, there are two possible reduction strategies in the dual calculus that depend on the orientation of the critical pair. The system Dual_L with call-by-value reduction is obtained if the priority is given to (μ) redexes, whereas the system Dual_R with call-by-name reduction is obtained by giving the priority to $(\tilde{\mu})$ redexes.

That is, Dual_R is defined by refining the reduction rule $(\beta\mu)$ as follows

$$(\!(\mu\alpha.c \bullet \underline{e})\!) \rightarrow c\{\underline{e}/\alpha\} \qquad \text{provided } \underline{e} \text{ is a coterm not of the form } \tilde{\mu}x.c'$$

and Dual_L is defined similarly by refining the reduction rule $(\beta\tilde{\mu})$ as follows

$$(\!(\underline{r} \bullet \tilde{\mu}x.c)\!) \rightarrow c\{\underline{r}/x\} \qquad \text{provided } \underline{r} \text{ is a term not of the form } \mu\alpha.c'$$

Both systems Dual_R and Dual_L are shown to be confluent in Section 4.

Implication, λ-Terms, and Application

Implication can be defined in terms of other connectives, indeed in two ways:

- under call-by-value $A \supset B \equiv \neg(A \wedge \neg B)$
- under call-by-name $A \supset B \equiv \neg A \vee B$.

Under each of these conventions we can define expressions $\lambda x.r$ and $q@e$ validating the reduction $(\!|\, \lambda x.r \bullet q@e \,|\!) \;\;\rightarrow\;\; (\!|\, q \bullet \tilde{\mu}x.(\!|\, r \bullet e \,|\!) \,|\!)$ in the sense that when $\supset$ is defined by call-by-value and the translation of $(\!|\, \lambda x.r \bullet q@e \,|\!)$ is reduced according to the call-by-value calculus, we get to $(\!|\, q \bullet \tilde{\mu}x.(\!|\, r \bullet e \,|\!) \,|\!)$ after several steps (and the same claim holds for call-by-name).

4   Confluence of the Dual Calculus

To prove the confluence of the dual calculi Dual_R and Dual_L we adopt the technique of parallel reductions given by Takahashi in [28] (see also [20]). This approach consists of simultaneously reducing all the redexes existing in an expression and is simpler than standard Tait-and-Martin-Löf proof of confluence of β-reduction for lambda calculus. We omit the proofs for the lack of space. The detailed proofs of confluence for $\overline{\lambda}\mu\tilde{\mu}$ can be found in [20].

We denote the union of all the reduction relations for Dual_R by $\xrightarrow[R]{}$. Its reflexive transitive closure and closure by congruence is denoted by $\xrightarrow[R]{}\!\!\!\!\rightarrow$.

First, we define the notion of parallel reduction $\Rightarrow_R$ for Dual_R. Since we will show that $\xrightarrow[R]{}\!\!\!\!\rightarrow$ is the reflexive and transitive closure of $\Rightarrow_R$, in order to prove the confluence of $\xrightarrow[R]{}\!\!\!\!\rightarrow$ it is enough to prove the diamond property for $\Rightarrow_R$. The diamond property for $\Rightarrow_R$ follows from the stronger "Star property" for $\Rightarrow_R$ that we prove.

Applying the duality transformations that Wadler gives, reductions dualize as well, and in particular a μ-step is dual to a $\tilde{\mu}$-step. A reduction from s to t under the restriction that μ-steps have priority over $\tilde{\mu}$-steps dualizes to a reduction from the dual of s to the dual of t under the restriction that $\tilde{\mu}$-steps have priority over μ-steps. So if we prove confluence for one of these systems, we get confluence for the other by diagram-chasing a duality argument.

4.1   Parallel Reduction for Dual_R

The notion of parallel reduction is defined directly by induction on the structure of D-expressions, and does not need the notion of residual or any other auxiliary notion.

Definition 2 (Parallel reduction for Dual_R). *The parallel reduction, denoted by $\Rightarrow_R$ is defined inductively in Figure 2, where $\underline{e}$ is a coterm not of the form $\tilde{\mu}x.c'$.*

Lemma 3. *For every D-expression D, $D \Rightarrow_R D$.*

Lemma 4 (Substitution lemma). *If $x \neq y$ and $x \notin Fv_R(r_2)$ then*

1. $D\{r_1/x\}\{r_2/y\} = D\{r_2/y\}\{r_1\{r_2/y\}/x\}$;
2. $D\{e/\alpha\}\{r/x\} = D\{r/x\}\{e\{r/x\}/\alpha\}$;
3. $D\{r/x\}\{e/\alpha\} = D\{e/\alpha\}\{r\{e/\alpha\}/x\}$;
4. $D\{e_1/\alpha\}\{e_2/\beta\} = D\{e_2/\beta\}\{e_1\{e_2/\beta\}/\alpha\}$.

$$\frac{}{x \Rightarrow_R x} \ (pr1_R) \qquad \frac{c \Rightarrow_R c'}{\mu\alpha.c \Rightarrow_R \mu\alpha.c'} \ (pr2_R) \qquad \frac{}{\alpha \Rightarrow_R \alpha} \ (pr3_R) \qquad \frac{c \Rightarrow_R c'}{\widetilde{\mu}x.c \Rightarrow_R \widetilde{\mu}x.c'} \ (pr4_R)$$

$$\frac{r \Rightarrow_R r', q \Rightarrow_R q'}{\langle r, q \rangle \Rightarrow_R \langle r', q' \rangle} \ (pr5_R) \qquad \frac{r \Rightarrow_R r'}{\langle r \rangle \mathrm{inl} \Rightarrow_R \langle r' \rangle \mathrm{inl}} \ (pr6_R) \qquad \frac{r \Rightarrow_R r'}{\langle r \rangle \mathrm{inr} \Rightarrow_R \langle r' \rangle \mathrm{inr}} \ (pr7_R)$$

$$\frac{e \Rightarrow_R e', f \Rightarrow_R f'}{[e, f] \Rightarrow_R [e', f']} \ (pr8_R) \qquad \frac{e \Rightarrow_R e'}{\mathrm{fst}[e] \Rightarrow_R \mathrm{fst}[e']} \ (pr9_R) \qquad \frac{e \Rightarrow_R e'}{\mathrm{snd}[e] \Rightarrow_R \mathrm{snd}[e']} \ (pr10_R)$$

$$\frac{r \Rightarrow_R r'}{\mathrm{not}\langle r \rangle \Rightarrow_R \mathrm{not}\langle r' \rangle} \ (pr11_R) \qquad \frac{e \Rightarrow_R e'}{[e]\mathrm{not} \Rightarrow_R [e']\mathrm{not}} \ (pr12_R) \qquad \frac{r \Rightarrow_R r', e \Rightarrow_R e'}{(\! r \bullet e \!) \Rightarrow_R (\! r' \bullet e' \!)} \ (pr13_R)$$

$$\frac{c \Rightarrow_R c', \underline{e} \Rightarrow_R \underline{e}'}{(\! \mu\alpha.c \bullet \underline{e} \!) \Rightarrow_R c'\{\underline{e}'/\alpha\}} \ (pr14_R) \qquad \frac{r \Rightarrow_R r', c \Rightarrow_R c'}{(\! r \bullet \widetilde{\mu}x.c \!) \Rightarrow_R c'\{r'/x\}} \ (pr15_R)$$

$$\frac{r \Rightarrow_R r', q \Rightarrow_R q', e \Rightarrow_R e'}{(\! \langle r, q \rangle \bullet \mathrm{fst}[e] \!) \Rightarrow_R (\! r' \bullet e' \!)} \ (pr16_R) \qquad \frac{r \Rightarrow_R r', q \Rightarrow_R q', e \Rightarrow_R e'}{(\! \langle r, q \rangle \bullet \mathrm{snd}[e] \!) \Rightarrow_R (\! q' \bullet e' \!)} \ (pr17_R)$$

$$\frac{r \Rightarrow_R r', e \Rightarrow_R e', f \Rightarrow_R f'}{(\! \langle r \rangle \mathrm{inl} \bullet [e, f] \!) \Rightarrow_R (\! r' \bullet e' \!)} \ (pr18_R) \qquad \frac{r \Rightarrow_R r', e \Rightarrow_R e', f \Rightarrow_R f'}{(\! \langle r \rangle \mathrm{inr} \bullet [e, f] \!) \Rightarrow_R (\! r' \bullet f' \!)} \ (pr19_R)$$

$$\frac{r \Rightarrow_R r', e \Rightarrow_R e'}{(\! [e]\mathrm{not} \bullet \mathrm{not}\langle r \rangle \!) \Rightarrow_R (\! r' \bullet e' \!)} \ (pr20_R)$$

Fig. 2. Parallel reduction

Lemma 5.

1. *If* $D \xrightarrow{R} D'$ *then* $D \Rightarrow_R D'$;
2. *If* $D \Rightarrow_R D'$ *then* $D \xrightarrow{\ \ }_R D'$;
3. *If* $D \Rightarrow_R D'$ *and* $H \Rightarrow_R H'$, *then* $D\{H/x\} \Rightarrow_R D'\{H'/x\}$ *and* $D\{H/\alpha\} \Rightarrow_R D'\{H'/\alpha\}$.

From the points 1. and 2. in Lemma 5 we conclude that $\xrightarrow{\ \ }_R$ is the reflexive and transitive closure of $\Rightarrow_R$.

4.2 Confluence of Dual$_R$

Next, we define the D-expression D^* which is obtained from D by simultaneously reducing all the existing redexes of the D-expression D.

Definition 6. *Let D be an arbitrary D-expression of Dual$_R$. The D-expression D^* is defined inductively as follows:*

$$(*1_R) \ x^* \equiv x \quad (*2_R) \ (\mu\alpha.c)^* \equiv \mu\alpha.c^* \quad (*3_R) \ \alpha^* \equiv \alpha \quad (*4_R) \ (\widetilde{\mu}x.c)^* \equiv \widetilde{\mu}x.c^*$$
$$(*5_R) \ \langle r, q \rangle^* \equiv \langle r^*, q^* \rangle \quad (*6_R) \ \langle r \rangle \mathrm{inl}^* \equiv \langle r^* \rangle \mathrm{inl} \quad (*7_R) \ \langle r \rangle \mathrm{inr}^* \equiv \langle r^* \rangle \mathrm{inr}$$
$$(*8_R) \ [e, f]^* \equiv \langle e^*, f^* \rangle \quad (*9_R) \ \mathrm{fst}[e]^* \equiv \mathrm{fst}[e^*] \quad (*10_R) \ \mathrm{snd}[e]^* \equiv \mathrm{snd}[e^*]$$

$(*11_R)$ $\text{not}\langle r\rangle^* \equiv \text{not}\langle r^*\rangle$ $(*12_R)$ $[e]\text{not}^* \equiv [e^*]\text{not}$

$(*13_R)$ $(\!| r \bullet e |\!)^* \equiv (\!| r^* \bullet e^* |\!)$ if $(\!| r \bullet e |\!) \neq (\!| [e']\text{not} \bullet \text{not}\langle r'\rangle |\!)$ and

$\quad\quad (\!| r \bullet e |\!) \neq (\!| \mu\alpha.c \bullet \underline{e} |\!)$ and $(\!| r \bullet e |\!) \neq (\!| r \bullet \tilde{\mu}x.c |\!)$ and

$\quad\quad (\!| r \bullet e |\!) \neq (\!| \langle r', q\rangle \bullet \text{fst}[e'] |\!)$ and $(\!| r \bullet e |\!) \neq (\!| \langle r', q\rangle \bullet \text{snd}[e'] |\!)$ and

$\quad\quad (\!| r \bullet e |\!) \neq (\!| \langle r'\rangle\text{inl} \bullet [e', f] |\!)$ and $(\!| r \bullet e |\!) \neq (\!| \langle r'\rangle\text{inr} \bullet [e', f] |\!)$

$(*14_R)$ $(\!| \mu\alpha.c \bullet \underline{e} |\!)^* \equiv c^*\{\underline{e}^*/\alpha\}$ $\quad\quad$ $(*15_R)$ $(\!| r \bullet \tilde{\mu}x.c |\!)^* \equiv c^*\{r^*/x\}$

$(*16_R)$ $(\!| \langle r, q\rangle \bullet \text{fst}[e] |\!)^* \equiv (\!| r^* \bullet e^* |\!)$ $\quad$ $(*17_R)$ $(\!| \langle r, q\rangle \bullet \text{snd}[e] |\!)^* \equiv (\!| q^* \bullet e^* |\!)$

$(*18_R)$ $(\!| \langle r\rangle\text{inl} \bullet [e, f] |\!)^* \equiv (\!| r^* \bullet e^* |\!)$ $\quad$ $(*19_R)$ $(\!| \langle r\rangle\text{inr} \bullet [e, f] |\!)^* \equiv (\!| r^* \bullet f^* |\!)$

$$(*20_R)\ (\!| [e]\text{not} \bullet \text{not}\langle r\rangle |\!)^* \equiv (\!| r^* \bullet e^* |\!)$$

Theorem 7 (Star property for $\Rightarrow_R$). *If $D \Rightarrow_R D'$ then $D' \Rightarrow_R D^*$.*

Now it is easy to deduce the diamond property for $\Rightarrow_R$.

Theorem 8 (Diamond property for $\Rightarrow_R$).
If $D_1\ {}_R\!\!\Leftarrow D \Rightarrow_R D_2$ then $D_1 \Rightarrow_R D'\ {}_R\!\!\Leftarrow D_2$ for some D'.

Finally, from Lemma 5 and Theorem 8, it follows that Dual_R is confluent.

Theorem 9 (Confluence of Dual_R).
If $D_1 \overset{}{\underset{R}{\twoheadleftarrow}} D \overset{}{\underset{R}{\twoheadrightarrow}} D_2$ then $D_1 \overset{}{\underset{R}{\twoheadrightarrow}} D' \overset{}{\underset{R}{\twoheadleftarrow}} D_2$ for some D'.

5   Type Assignment System

A complementary perspective to that of considering the dual calculus as term-assignment to logic proofs is that of viewing sequent proofs as typing derivations for raw expressions. The set of types corresponds to the logical connectives; for the dual calculus the set of types is given by closing a set of *base types* X under conjunction, disjunction, and negation.

$$\text{Type: } A, B ::= X \mid A \wedge B \mid A \vee B \mid \neg A$$

Type bases have two components, the *antecedent,* a set of bindings of the form $\Gamma = x_1 : A_1, \ldots, x_n : A_n$, and the *succedent* of the form $\Delta = \alpha_1 : B_1, \ldots, \alpha_k : B_k$, where x_i, α_j are distinct for all $i = 1, \ldots, n$ and $j = 1, \ldots, k$.

The judgements of the type system are given by the following:

$$\Gamma \vdash \Delta, \boxed{r : A} \quad\quad \boxed{e : A}, \Gamma \vdash \Delta \quad\quad c : (\Gamma \vdash \Delta)$$

where Γ is the antecedent and Δ is the succedent. The first judgement is the typing for a term, the second is the typing for a coterm and the third one is the typing for a statement. The box denotes a distinguished output or input, i.e. a place where the computation will continue or where it happened before.

The type assignment system for the dual calculus, introduced by Wadler [30, 31], is given in Figure 3.

$$\frac{}{\Gamma, x:A \vdash \Delta, \boxed{x:A}} \; (axR) \qquad\qquad \frac{}{\boxed{\alpha:A}, \Gamma \vdash \alpha:A, \Delta} \; (axL)$$

$$\frac{\boxed{e:A}, \Gamma \vdash \Delta \qquad \boxed{e:B}, \Gamma \vdash \Delta}{\boxed{\mathsf{fst}[e]:A \wedge B}, \Gamma \vdash \Delta \quad \boxed{\mathsf{snd}[e]:A \wedge B}, \Gamma \vdash \Delta} \; (\wedge L) \qquad \frac{\Gamma \vdash \Delta, \boxed{r:A} \qquad \Gamma \vdash \Delta, \boxed{q:B}}{\Gamma \vdash \Delta, \boxed{\langle r, q \rangle:A \wedge B}} \; (\wedge R)$$

$$\frac{\boxed{e:A}, \Gamma \vdash \Delta \qquad \boxed{f:B}, \Gamma \vdash \Delta}{\boxed{[e, f]:A \vee B}, \Gamma \vdash \Delta} \; (\vee L) \qquad \frac{\Gamma \vdash \Delta, \boxed{r:A} \qquad \qquad \Gamma \vdash \Delta, \boxed{r:B}}{\Gamma \vdash \Delta, \boxed{\langle r \rangle \mathsf{inl}:A \vee B} \quad \Gamma \vdash \Delta, \boxed{\langle r \rangle \mathsf{inr}:A \vee B}} \; (\vee R)$$

$$\frac{\boxed{e:A}, \Gamma \vdash \Delta}{\Gamma \vdash \Delta, \boxed{[e]\mathsf{not}:\neg A}} \; (\neg R) \qquad\qquad \frac{\Gamma \vdash \Delta, \boxed{r:A}}{\boxed{\mathsf{not}\langle r \rangle:\neg A}, \Gamma \vdash \Delta} \; (\neg L)$$

$$\frac{c:(\Gamma \vdash \alpha:A, \Delta)}{\Gamma \vdash \Delta, \boxed{\mu\alpha.c:A}} \; (\mu) \qquad\qquad \frac{c:(\Gamma, x:A \vdash \Delta)}{\boxed{\tilde{\mu}x.c:A}, \Gamma \vdash \Delta} \; (\tilde{\mu})$$

$$\frac{\Gamma \vdash \Delta, \boxed{r:A} \qquad \boxed{e:A}, \Gamma \vdash \Delta}{(\!| r \bullet e |\!):(\Gamma \vdash \Delta)} \; (cut)$$

Fig. 3. Type system for the dual calculus

6   Strong Normalization of Typeable D-Expressions

Definition 10. *A pair is given by two sets* $\mathbb{T}$ *and* $\mathbb{C}$ *with* $\mathbb{T} \subseteq \Lambda_R$ *and* $\mathbb{C} \subseteq \Lambda_L$. *If each of the components of a pair is non-empty we refer to it as a* non-trivial *pair.*

The pair $(\mathbb{T}, \mathbb{C})$ *is a* stable *pair if each of* $\mathbb{T}$ *and* $\mathbb{C}$ *is non-empty and for every* $r \in \mathbb{T}$ *and every* $e \in \mathbb{C}$, *the statement* $(\!| r \bullet e |\!)$ *is SN.*

For example, the pair (Var_R, Var_L) is stable. Note that the terms and coterms in any stable pair are themselves SN.

We can use pairs to interpret types; the following technical condition will be crucial.

Definition 11. *A pair* $(\mathbb{T}, \mathbb{C})$ *is* saturated *if*

- $\mathbb{T}$ *contains all term variables and* $\mathbb{C}$ *contains all coterm variables,*
- *whenever* $\mu\alpha.c$ *satisfies* $\forall e \in \mathbb{C}, c\{e/\alpha\}$ *is SN then* $\mu\alpha.c \in \mathbb{T}$, *and*
- *whenever* $\tilde{\mu}x.c$ *satisfies* $\forall r \in \mathbb{T}, c\{r/x\}$ *is SN then* $\tilde{\mu}x.c \in \mathbb{C}$.

A pair $(\mathbb{T}, \mathbb{C})$ *is* simple *if no term in* $\mathbb{T}$ *is of the form* $\mu\alpha.c$ *and no coterm in* $\mathbb{C}$ *is of the form* $\tilde{\mu}x.c$.

We can always expand a pair to be saturated. The next result shows that if the original pair is stable and simple, then we may always arrange that the saturated extension is stable. The technique is similar to the "symmetric candidates" technique as used by Barbanera and Berardi [3] for the Symmetric Lambda Calculus and further adapted by Polonovski [25] in his proof of strong normalization for $\overline{\lambda}\mu\tilde{\mu}$ calculus with explicit substitutions.

Note that the saturation condition on variables is no obstacle to stability: it is easy to see that if $(\mathbb{T}, \mathbb{C})$ is any stable pair, then the pair obtained by adding all term variables to $\mathbb{T}$ and all coterm variables to $\mathbb{C}$ will still be stable.

Lemma 12. *Let* $(\mathbb{T}, \mathbb{C})$ *be a simple stable pair. Then there is an extension of* $(\mathbb{T}, \mathbb{C})$ *which is saturated and stable.*

Proof. As observed above, we may assume without loss of generality that $\mathbb{T}$ already contains all term variables and $\mathbb{C}$ already contains all coterm variables.

Define the maps $\widetilde{\Phi}_{\mathbb{C}} : \Lambda_{\mathrm{R}} \to \Lambda_{\mathrm{L}}$ and $\Phi_{\mathbb{T}} : \Lambda_{\mathrm{L}} \to \Lambda_{\mathrm{R}}$ by

$$\widetilde{\Phi}_{\mathbb{C}}(\mathbb{T}) = \mathbb{C} \cup \{ \widetilde{\mu}x.c \mid \forall r \in \mathbb{T}, c\{r/x\} \text{ is SN} \}$$

$$\Phi_{\mathbb{T}}(\mathbb{C}) = \mathbb{T} \cup \{ \mu\alpha.c \mid \forall e \in \mathbb{C}, c\{e/\alpha\} \text{ is SN} \}$$

Each of $\Phi_{\mathbb{T}}$ and $\widetilde{\Phi}_{\mathbb{C}}$ is antimonotone. So the map $\Phi_{\mathbb{T}} \circ \widetilde{\Phi}_{\mathbb{C}} : \Lambda_{\mathrm{R}} \to \Lambda_{\mathrm{R}}$ is monotone (indeed it is continuous).

Let $\mathbb{T}^*$ be any fixed point of $(\Phi_{\mathbb{T}} \circ \widetilde{\Phi}_{\mathbb{C}})$; then take $\mathbb{C}^*$ to be $\widetilde{\Phi}_{\mathbb{C}}(\mathbb{T}^*)$. Since $\mathbb{T}^* = \Phi_{\mathbb{T}}(\widetilde{\Phi}_{\mathbb{C}}(\mathbb{T}^*))$ we have

$$\mathbb{T}^* = \Phi_{\mathbb{T}}(\mathbb{C}^*) = \mathbb{T} \cup \{ \mu\alpha.c \mid \forall e \in \mathbb{C}^*, c\{e/\alpha\} \text{ is SN} \} \quad \text{and} \tag{1}$$

$$\mathbb{C}^* = \widetilde{\Phi}_{\mathbb{C}}(\mathbb{T}^*) = \mathbb{C} \cup \{ \widetilde{\mu}x.c \mid \forall r \in \mathbb{T}^*, c\{r/x\} \text{ is SN} \} \tag{2}$$

It follows easily that $\mathbb{T} \subseteq \mathbb{T}^*$ and $\mathbb{C} \subseteq \mathbb{C}^*$ and that $(\mathbb{T}^*, \mathbb{C}^*)$ is saturated. It remains to show that $(\mathbb{T}^*, \mathbb{C}^*)$ is stable.

Since $\mathbb{T}$ is a set of SN terms and $\mathbb{C} \neq \emptyset$, $\Phi_{\mathbb{T}}(\mathbb{C})$ is a set of SN terms; similarly $\widetilde{\Phi}_{\mathbb{C}}(\mathbb{T})$ is a set of SN coterms. The key fact is that, since $(\mathbb{T}, \mathbb{C})$ was simple, a term $\mu\alpha.c$ is in $\mathbb{T}^*$ iff $\forall e \in \mathbb{C}^*, c\{e/\alpha\}$ is SN: this is because a μ-term is in $\mathbb{T}^*$ precisely if it is in $\Phi_{\mathbb{T}}(\mathbb{C}^*) \setminus \mathbb{T}$. Similarly a coterm $\widetilde{\mu}x.c$ is in $\mathbb{C}^*$ if and only if $\forall r \in \mathbb{T}^*, c\{r/x\}$ is SN.

So consider any statement $(\!| \, r \bullet e \, |\!)$ with $r \in \mathbb{T}^*$ and $e \in \mathbb{C}^*$; we must show that this statement is SN. If in fact $r \in \mathbb{T}$ and $e \in \mathbb{C}$ then $(\!| \, r \bullet e \, |\!)$ is SN since $(\mathbb{T}, \mathbb{C})$ was stable.

So suppose $r \in (\mathbb{T}^* \setminus \mathbb{T})$ and/or $e \in (\mathbb{C}^* \setminus \mathbb{C})$, and consider any reduction sequence out of $(\!| \, r \bullet e \, |\!)$. If no top-level ($\mu$- or $\widetilde{\mu}$-) reduction is ever done then the reduction must be finite since r and e are individually SN. If a top-level reduction is ever done then (cf Remark 1) we may promote this to be the first step, so that the reduction sequence begins $(\!| \, \mu\alpha.c \bullet e \, |\!) \longrightarrow c\{e/\alpha\}$ or $(\!| \, r \bullet \widetilde{\mu}x.c \, |\!) \longrightarrow c\{r/x\}$. But we observed above that in these cases the reduced D-expression is SN by definition of $(\mathbb{T}^*, \mathbb{C}^*)$ and so our reduction is finite in length. □

6.1 Pairs and Types

As a preliminary step in building pairs to interpret types we define the following constructions on pairs. Script letters will denote pairs, and if $\mathcal{P}$ is a pair, $\mathcal{P}_{\mathrm{R}}$ and $\mathcal{P}_{\mathrm{L}}$ denote its component sets of terms and coterms.

Definition 13. *Let* $\mathcal{P}$ *and* $\mathcal{Q}$ *be pairs.*

- *The pair* $(\mathcal{P} \curlywedge \mathcal{Q})$ *is given by:*
  - $(\mathcal{P} \curlywedge \mathcal{Q})_R = \{\langle r_1, r_2\rangle \mid r_1 \in \mathcal{P}_R, r_2 \in \mathcal{Q}_R\}$
  - $(\mathcal{P} \curlywedge \mathcal{Q})_L = \{\mathrm{fst}[e] \mid e \in \mathcal{P}_L\} \cup \{\mathrm{snd}[e] \mid e \in \mathcal{Q}_L\}.$
- *The pair* $(\mathcal{P} \curlyvee \mathcal{Q})$ *is given by:*
  - $(\mathcal{P} \curlyvee \mathcal{Q})_R = \{\langle r\rangle\mathrm{inl} \mid r \in \mathcal{P}_R\} \cup \{\langle r\rangle\mathrm{inr} \mid r \in \mathcal{Q}_R\}.$
  - $(\mathcal{P} \curlyvee \mathcal{Q})_L = \{[e_1, e_2] \mid e_1 \in \mathcal{P}_L. e_2 \in \mathcal{Q}_L\}$
- *The pair* $\mathcal{P}^{\circ}$ *is given by:*
  - $(\mathcal{P}^{\circ})_R = \{[e]\mathrm{not} \mid e \in \mathcal{P}_L\}$
  - $(\mathcal{P}^{\circ})_L = \{\mathrm{not}\langle r\rangle \mid r \in \mathcal{P}_R\}$

Note that each of $(\mathcal{P} \curlywedge \mathcal{Q})$, $(\mathcal{P} \curlyvee \mathcal{Q})$, and $\mathcal{P}^{\circ}$ is simple.

Lemma 14. *Let* $\mathcal{P}$ *and* $\mathcal{Q}$ *be stable pairs. Then* $(\mathcal{P} \curlywedge \mathcal{Q})$, $(\mathcal{P} \curlyvee \mathcal{Q})$, *and* $\mathcal{P}^{\circ}$ *are each stable.*

Proof. For $(\mathcal{P} \curlywedge \mathcal{Q})$: Let $r \in (\mathcal{P} \curlywedge \mathcal{Q})_R$ and $e \in (\mathcal{P} \curlywedge \mathcal{Q})_L$. We need to show that $(\!| r \bullet e |\!)$ is SN. Since $\mathcal{P}$ and $\mathcal{Q}$ are stable, it is easy to see that each of r and e is SN. So to complete the argument it suffices to show, again by the fact that top-level reductions can be promoted to be the first step in a reduction sequence, that the result of a top-level reduction is SN. Consider, without loss of generality, $(\!| \langle r_1, r_2\rangle \bullet \mathrm{fst}[e] |\!) \rightarrow (\!| r_1 \bullet e |\!)$. Then $r_1 \in \mathcal{P}_R$ and $e \in \mathcal{P}_L$, and since $\mathcal{P}$ is stable $(\!| r_1 \bullet e |\!)$ is SN, as desired.

The arguments for $(\mathcal{P} \curlyvee \mathcal{Q})$ and $\mathcal{P}^{\circ}$ are similar. $\square$

The following is our notion of reducibility candidates for the dual calculus.

Definition 15. *The type-indexed family of pairs* $S = \{S^T \mid T \text{ a type }\}$ *is defined as follows.*

- *When* T *is a base type,* S^T *is any stable saturated extension of* (Var_R, Var_L).
- $S^{A \wedge B}$ *is any stable saturated extension of* $(S^A \curlywedge S^B)$.
- $S^{A \vee B}$ *is any stable saturated extension of* $(S^A \curlyvee S^B)$.
- $S^{\neg A}$ *is any stable saturated extension of* $(S^A)^{\circ}$.

The construction of each pair S^T succeeds by Lemma 12 and Lemma 14. Note that by definition of saturation each S^T contains all term variables and all coterm variables.

6.2 Strong Normalization

Strong normalization of typeable D-expressions will follow if we establish the fact that typeable terms and coterms lie in the candidates S.

Theorem 16. *If term* r *is typeable with type* A *then* r *is in* S_R^A; *if coterm* e *is typeable with type* A *then* e *is in* S_L^A.

Proof. To prove the theorem it is convenient, as usual, to prove a stronger statement. Say that a substitution θ *satisfies* Γ if
$$\forall(x : A) \in \Gamma, \quad \theta x \in S_R^A,$$
and that θ *satisfies* Δ if
$$\forall(\alpha : A) \in \Delta, \quad \theta\alpha \in S_L^A.$$

Then the theorem follows from the assertion

suppose that θ *satisfies* Γ *and* Δ.
- *If* $\Gamma \vdash \boxed{r:A}, \Delta$, *then* $\theta r \in S_R^A$.
- *If* $\Gamma, \boxed{e:A} \vdash \Delta$, *then* $\theta e \in S_L^A$.

since the identity substitution satisfies every Γ and Δ.

Choose a substitution θ which satisfies Γ and Δ, and a typeable term r or a coterm e; we wish to show that $\theta r \in S_R^T$ or $\theta e \in S_L^T$, as appropriate. We prove the statement above by induction on typing derivations, considering the possible forms of the typing in turn. For lack of space we only show a representative sample of cases here.

Case: When the derivation consists of an axiom the result is immediate since θ satisfies Γ and Δ.

Case: Suppose the derivation ends with rule $(\wedge L)$. Without loss of generality we examine fst[ ]:

$$\frac{\boxed{e:A}, \Gamma \vdash \Delta}{\boxed{\text{fst}[e]:A \wedge B}, \Gamma \vdash \Delta}$$

We wish to show that $\theta\text{fst}[e] \equiv \text{fst}[\theta e] \in S_L^{A \wedge B}$. By induction hypothesis $\theta e \in S_L^A$ and so $\text{fst}[\theta e] \in (S^A \curlywedge S^B)_L \subseteq S_L^{A \wedge B}$.

Case: Suppose the derivation ends with rule $(\wedge R)$.

$$\frac{\Gamma \vdash \Delta, \boxed{r:A} \qquad \Gamma \vdash \Delta, \boxed{q:B}}{\Gamma \vdash \Delta, \boxed{\langle r, q \rangle : A \wedge B}} \, (\wedge R)$$

We wish to show that $\theta\langle r, q \rangle \equiv \langle \theta r, \theta q \rangle \in S_R^{A \wedge B}$. By induction hypothesis $\theta r \in S_R^A$ and $\theta q \in S_R^B$, and so $\langle \theta r, \theta q \rangle \in (S^A \curlywedge S^B)_R \subseteq S_R^{A \wedge B}$.

Case: Suppose the derivation ends with rule $(\neg L)$.

$$\frac{\Gamma \vdash \Delta, \boxed{r:A}}{\boxed{\text{not}\langle r \rangle : \neg A}, \Gamma \vdash \Delta} \, (\neg L)$$

We wish to show that $\theta\text{not}\langle r \rangle \equiv \text{not}\langle \theta r \rangle \in S_L^{\neg A}$. By induction hypothesis $\theta r \in S_R^A$, and so $\text{not}\langle \theta r \rangle \in (S^{A^\circ})_L \subseteq S_L^{\neg A}$.

Case: Suppose the derivation ends with rule (μ).

$$\frac{\dfrac{\Gamma \vdash \boxed{r:T}, \alpha:A, \Delta \quad \Gamma, \boxed{e:T} \vdash \alpha:A, \Delta}{(\!| r \bullet e |\!) : (\Gamma \vdash \alpha:A, \Delta)} \, (cut)}{\Gamma \vdash \boxed{\mu\alpha.(\!| r \bullet e |\!) : A}, \Delta} \, (\mu)$$

Note that any application of the typing rule (μ) must indeed immediately follow a cut. We wish to show that $\mu\alpha.(\!| \theta r \bullet \theta e |\!) \in S_R^A$.

Since $\mathcal{S}^A$ is saturated, to show this it suffices to show that for each $e_1 \in \mathcal{S}_L^A$

$$(\theta r \bullet \theta e)\{e_1/\alpha\} \quad \text{is SN.}$$

Letting θ' denote the substitution obtained by augmenting θ with the binding $\alpha \mapsto e_1$, what we want to show is that $(\theta'r \bullet \theta'e)$ is SN.

The substitution θ' satisfies the basis $\alpha : A, \Delta$ by hypothesis and the fact that $e_1 \in \mathcal{S}_L^A$. So $\theta'r \in \mathcal{S}_R^T$ and $\theta'e \in \mathcal{S}_L^T$ by induction hypothesis, so $(\theta'r \bullet \theta'e)$ is SN.

Case: When the derivation ends with rule $(\tilde{\mu})$ the argument is similar to the (μ) case.

The remaining cases are each similar to one of those above.   □

Theorem 17. *Every typeable term, coterm, and statement is SN.*

Proof. If t is a term [respectively, e is a coterm] typeable with type A then by Theorem 16 we have $t \in \mathcal{S}_R^A$ [respectively, $\mathcal{S}_L^A$], and each of these consists of SN expressions. If $t = c$ is a typeable statement then it suffices to observe that, taking α to be any covariable not occurring in c, the term $\mu\alpha.c$ is typeable.   □

6.3 Extensionality and Expansion Rules

The equations of the dual calculus of [31] include a group of equations called "η-equations" which express extensionality properties. A typical equation for a term of type $A \wedge B$ is

$$(\eta\wedge) \qquad r = \langle \mu\alpha.(r \bullet \text{fst}[\alpha]), \mu\beta.(r \bullet \text{snd}[\beta]) \rangle$$

and there are similar equations for the other types. In traditional λ-calculus it has been found convenient to orient such equations from left to right, i.e. as expansions, as a tool for analyzing the equality relation.

As with all expansions there are obvious situations which allow immediate infinite application of the rules (see for example [13] or [6] for a discussion in the setting of the lambda-calculus). For example, we must forbid application of the above expansion rule to a term already of the form $\langle r_1, r_2 \rangle$ to prevent an infinite reduction. Slightly more subtly, if the term r is already part of a statement whose other side is one of the forms $\text{fst}[e]$ or $\text{snd}[e]$ then we can immediately fall into a cycle of $(\eta\wedge);(\beta\wedge)$ reductions.

But if we forbid only those clearly ill-advised situations, the result is a reduction relation with all the nice properties one might want. Lack of space forbids a detailed treatment here but the key points are as follows.

– The constraints on the expansion relation do not change the equalities we can prove, even under restrictions such as call-by-name or call-by-value, in the sense that if a term t can be expanded to term t' by a "forbidden" expansion, then t' can be *reduced* to t by one of the "computational" reductions (i.e., those from Figure 1).
– The resulting reduction relation is SN on typed terms.

It is straightforward to verify the first assertion. The second claim is proved by precisely the same techniques presented in the current section: the notions of saturated stable pair is robust enough so that there are no conceptual difficulties in accommodating expansions. Details will appear in the full version of the paper.

7 Conclusion

We have explored some aspects of the reduction relation on raw expressions of the dual calculus, and proven strong normalization and confluence results for several variations on the basic system.

An interesting open problem is to find a *characterization* of the SN terms, presumably in the form of an extension of the system of simple types studied here. For traditional λ-calculus, system of intersection types have been an invaluable tool in studying reduction properties, characterizing strong-, weak- and head-normalization. As shown in [12], subtle technical problems arise with the interaction between intersection types and symmetric calculi, so this promises to be a challenging line of inquiry.

References

1. Z. M. Ariola and H. Herbelin. Minimal classical logic and control operators. In *ICALP: Annual International Colloquium on Automata, Languages and Programming*, volume 2719 of *LNCS*, pages 871–885. sv, 2003.
2. S. v. Bakel, S. Lengrand, and P. Lescanne. The language *X*: circuits, computations and classical logic. In *ICTCS 2005 Ninth Italian Conference on Theoretical Computer Science, Certosa di Pontignano (Sienna), Italy*, 2005.
3. F. Barbanera and S. Berardi. A symmetric lambda calculus for classical program extraction. *Information and Computation*, 125(2):103–117, 1996.
4. H. P. Barendregt. *The Lambda Calculus: its Syntax and Semantics*. North-Holland, Amsterdam, revised edition, 1984.
5. G. M. Bierman. A computational interpretation of the λμ-calculus. In *Proc. of Symposium on Mathematical Foundations of Computer Science.*, volume 1450 of *LNCS*, pages 336–345. Springer-Verlag, 1998.
6. R. D. Cosmo and D. Kesner. Simulating expansions without expansions. *Mathematical Structures in Computer Science*, 4(3):315–362, 1994.
7. P.-L. Curien. Symmetry and interactivity in programming. *Archive for Mathematical Logic*, 2001. to appear.
8. P.-L. Curien. Abstract machines, control, and sequents. In *Applied Semantics, International Summer School, APPSEM 2000, Advanced Lectures*, volume 2395 of *LNCS*, pages 123–136. Springer-Verlag, 2002.
9. P.-L. Curien and H. Herbelin. The duality of computation. In *Proc. of the 5th ACM SIGPLAN Int. Conference on Functional Programming (ICFP'00)*, Montreal, Canada, 2000. ACM Press.
10. R. David and K. Nour. Arithmetical proofs of strong normalization results for the symmetric λμ-calculus. In *TLCA*, pages 162–178, 2005.
11. P. de Groote. On the relation between the λμ-calculus and the syntactic theory of sequential control. In Springer-Verlag, editor, *LPAR'94*, volume 822 of *LNCS*, pages 31–43, 1994.
12. D. Dougherty, S. Ghilezan, and P. Lescanne. Characterizing strong normalization in a language with control operators. In *Sixth ACM SIGPLAN Conference on Principles and Practice of Declarative Programming PPDP'04*, pages 155–166. ACM Press, 2004.
13. D. J. Dougherty. Some lambda calculi with categorical sums and products. In C. Kirchner, editor, *Proc. 5th International Conference on Rewriting Techniques and Applications (RTA)*, volume 690 of *LNCS*, pages 137–151, Berlin, 1993. Springer-Verlag.
14. A. Filinski. Declarative continuations and categorical duality. Master's thesis, DIKU, Computer Science Department, University of Copenhagen, Aug. 1989. DIKU Rapport 89/11.

15. G. Gentzen. Unterschungen über das logische Schliessen, Math Z. 39 (1935), 176–210. In M. Szabo, editor, *Collected papers of Gerhard Gentzen*, pages 68–131. North-Holland, 1969.
16. T. Griffin. A formulae-as-types notion of control. In *POPL 17*, pages 47–58, 1990.
17. H. Herbelin. *Séquents qu'on calcule : de l'interprétation du calcul des séquents comme calcul de λ-termes et comme calcul de stratégies gagnantes*. Thèse, U. Paris 7, Janvier 1995.
18. W. A. Howard. The formulas-as-types notion of construction. In J. P. Seldin and J. R. Hindley, editors, *To H.B. Curry: Essays on Combinatory Logic, Lambda Calculus and Formalism*, pages 479–490, New York, 1980. Academic Press.
19. S. Lengrand. Call-by-value, call-by-name, and strong normalization for the classical sequent calculus. In B. Gramlich and S. Lucas, editors, *ENTCS*, volume 86. Elsevier, 2003.
20. S. Likavec. *Types for object oriented and functional programming languages*. PhD thesis, Università di Torino, Italy, ENS Lyon, France, 2005.
21. C. R. Murthy. Classical proofs as programs: How, what, and why. In J. P. M. Jr. and M. J. O'Donnell, editors, *Constructivity in Computer Science*, volume 613 of *LNCS*, pages 71–88. Springer, 1991.
22. C.-H. L. Ong and C. A. Stewart. A Curry-Howard foundation for functional computation with control. In *POPL 24*, pages 215–227, 1997.
23. M. Parigot. An algorithmic interpretation of classical natural deduction. In *Proc. of Int. Conf. on Logic Programming and Automated Reasoning, LPAR'92*, volume 624 of *LNCS*, pages 190–201. Springer-Verlag, 1992.
24. M. Parigot. Proofs of strong normalisation for second order classical natural deduction. *The J. of Symbolic Logic*, 62(4):1461–1479, December 1997.
25. E. Polonovski. Strong normalization of $\lambda\mu\bar{\mu}$-calculus with explicit substitutions. In I. Walukiewicz, editor, *Foundations of Software Science and Computation Structures, 7th International Conference, FOSSACS 2004*, volume 2987 of *LNCS*, pages 423–437. Springer, 2004.
26. D. Pym and E. Ritter. On the semantics of classical disjunction. *J. of Pure and Applied Algebra*, 159:315–338, 2001.
27. P. Selinger. Control categories and duality: On the categorical semantics of the lambda-mu calculus. *Mathematical Structures in Computer Science*, 11(2):207–260, 2001.
28. M. Takahashi. Parallel reduction in λ-calculus. *Information and Computation*, 118:120–127, 1995.
29. C. Urban and G. M. Bierman. Strong normalisation of cut-elimination in classical logic. In *Typed Lambda Calculus and Applications*, volume 1581 of *LNCS*, pages 365–380, 1999.
30. P. Wadler. Call-by-value is dual to call-by-name. In *Proc. of the 8th Int. Conference on Functional Programming*, pages 189–201, 2003.
31. P. Wadler. Call-by-value is dual to call-by-name, reloaded. In *Rewriting Technics and Application, RTA'05*, volume 3467 of *LNCS*, pages 185–203, 2005.

Termination of Fair Computations in Term Rewriting

Salvador Lucas[1] and José Meseguer[2]

[1] DSIC, Universidad Politécnica de Valencia, Spain
[2] CS Dept., University of Illinois at Urbana-Champaign, USA

Abstract. The main goal of this paper is to apply rewriting termination technology —enjoying a quite mature set of termination results and tools— to the problem of proving automatically the termination of concurrent systems under fairness assumptions. We adopt the thesis that a concurrent system can be naturally modeled as a rewrite system, and develop a *reductionistic* theoretical approach to systematically transform, under reasonable assumptions, fair-termination problems into ordinary termination problems of associated relations, to which standard rewriting termination techniques and tools can be applied. Our theoretical results are combined into a practical *proof methodology* for proving fair-termination that can be automated and can be supported by current termination tools. We illustrate this methodology with some concrete examples and briefly comment on future extensions.

Keywords: Concurrent programming, fairness, term rewriting, program analysis, termination.

1 Introduction

This paper is about technology transfer. Our goal is to transfer a mature set of termination results and tools developed in recent years for term rewriting systems to prove termination of concurrent systems under fairness assumptions. This requires both adopting a certain theoretical stance about the modeling of concurrent systems, and developing new results and techniques to make the desired technology transfer possible. The theoretical stance in question is the thesis that *a concurrent system can be naturally modeled as a rewrite system*. This has by now been amply demonstrated to hold by theoretical approaches such as reduction semantics [BB92] and rewriting logic [Mes92], and by quite exhaustive studies showing that almost any imaginable concurrent system can be naturally modeled as a rewrite theory (see for example the survey [MM02]).

Once this theoretical stance is adopted, since fairness is a pervasive property of concurrent systems, needed to establish many properties of interest, the first thing required is to correctly express the fairness notion within the rewriting framework. In this regard, the early work of Porat and Francez [PF85, PF86], and the work of Tison for the ground fair termination case [Tis89], complemented by the more recent "localized fairness" notion in [Mes05] offer a good basis. As

G. Sutcliffe and A. Voronkov (Eds.): LPAR 2005, LNAI 3835, pp. 184–198, 2005.
© Springer-Verlag Berlin Heidelberg 2005

we explain in Section 7, other notions of fairness have also been proposed for rewrite systems, with other, quite different, motivations that make such notions inadequate for our purposes, namely, modeling concurrent systems. For concurrent systems, rewrite rules describe system transitions, and the notion of fair computation should require that if the rule is infinitely often enabled, then it is infinitely often taken.

Example 1. Consider the following TRS modeling a *scheduler* which is responsible for the distribution of processing in a concurrent operating system, where a number of processes p run independently.

```
[end]      exec(P) -> stop
[execute]  schedule(cons(p,PS)) -> schedule(shift(exec(p),PS))
[remove]   schedule(cons(stop,PS)) -> schedule(PS)
[round]    schedule(cons(exec(P),PS)) -> schedule(shift(exec(P),PS))
[shift1]   shift(P,nil) -> cons(P,nil)
[shift2]   shift(P,cons(Q,PS)) -> cons(Q,shift(P,PS))
```

Processes are in one of three different states: *ready* (p), *running* (exec(p)), and *finished* (stop). A "round robin" fair scheduling strategy is to give each process a fixed amount of processing time and then shift the activity to the next one in a list of processes. If a process is ready, then it is executed (rule execute). If it is running, then the next one is taken (round). If the process stops, then it is removed from the system (remove). A running process exec(p) finishes when the rule end is applied. Although the system is clearly nonterminating, computations following the previous *fair* strategy will terminate. We will provide a formal proof of this claim later.

The situation in Example 1 cannot be modeled with other notions of fairness like the introduced in [KZ05] where fair rewriting computations can *only* be nonterminating, which makes any discussion of fair termination impossible.

The question that this paper then addresses, and presents partial answers to, is: how can rewriting termination techniques and tools be used to *automatically* prove the fair termination of a concurrent system? To the best of our knowledge, except for the quite restricted case of ground term rewriting systems for which Tison's tree automata techniques provide a decision procedure [Tis89], this precise question has not been previously posed or answered in the literature. Yet, we believe that, given the maturity of methods and tools for termination of rewrite systems, this is an important problem to attack, both theoretically and because of its many potential applications. The related question of finding general methods of proving fair termination of term rewriting systems has indeed been studied before, particularly by Porat and Francez [PF85, PF86]. However, their efforts followed the Floyd's classical approach, which uses predicates on states (in our setting, ground terms) to achieve termination (see [Fra86–Chapter 2] for a general description of this approach, and also [LPS81]). In particular, their characterization of fair termination of a rewrite system in terms of the compatibility of a well-founded ordering with all possible *full derivations* [PF86–Definition 9] does not lend itself to mechanization, since it suffers from the same problems as the Manna and Ness's classical termination criterion [MN70], namely, from the need to check *all* (infinitely many) full derivations, which makes automatic proofs of fair-termination quite hard.

Our approach is quite different. It is *reductionistic*, in the sense that *it seeks reasonable conditions under which fair-termination can be reduced to ordinary termination* of associated relations, for which standard rewriting termination techniques and tools can be applied. In Section 3, we show that the problem of proving (rule) fair-termination of a TRS $\mathcal{R}$ can be treated (without loss of generality) as the problem of proving fair-termination of $\mathcal{R}$ w.r.t. a subTRS $\mathcal{R}_F \subseteq \mathcal{R}$ of $\mathcal{R}$. If we take $\mathcal{S} = \mathcal{R} - \mathcal{R}_F$, we show that fair-termination of $\mathcal{R}$ w.r.t. $\mathcal{R}_F$ can be proved by proving termination of the reduction relations $\rightarrow_{\mathcal{S}}^* \circ \rightarrow_{\mathcal{R}_F}$ and $\rightarrow_{\mathcal{R}_F}^! \circ \rightarrow_{\mathcal{S}}$ (Section 4). We prove that, if $\mathcal{R}_F$ is a single-rule TRS, then this is not only sufficient but also necessary for fair-termination of $\mathcal{R}$ w.r.t. $\mathcal{R}_F$. Then, in Section 5 we show how to translate such requirements into more standard termination problems, namely: proving or disproving termination, innermost termination, and relative termination of TRSs. Fortunately, methods for addressing such termination problems are currently available in existing termination tools like APROVE[1] and TPA[2], among others. Therefore, we get quite a practical approach for proving fair-termination of TRSs which clearly differs from more ad-hoc or restrictive approaches like the ones in [PF85, PF86, Tis89].

The results that we propose in this paper, although open to many extensions and generalizations, do indeed provide a quite practical *proof methodology* for proving fair-termination that can be automated and can be supported by current termination tools. In Section 5.4 we explain how our results can be synergistically combined into such a unified methodology, which offers different proof strategies to tackle a fair-termination problem. We show this methodology in action in proofs of concrete examples in Section 6. We consider the results obtained so far as encouraging, since they can allow proving fair-termination automatically. As we further discuss in Section 7, many extensions remain open as interesting research questions. However, our general methodology of reducing fair-termination to standard termination to try to make such proofs automatic is already a viable new methodology that we have put into practice using existing tools, and that we plan to incorporate into the Maude Termination Tool (MTT) [DLMMU04] and to further perfect as new results become available.

2   Preliminaries

Let $R \subseteq A \times A$ be a binary relation on a set A. We denote by R^+ the transitive closure of R and by R^* its reflexive and transitive closure. An R-sequence is a finite or countably infinite sequence (i.e., either $a_1, a_2, \ldots, a_n$ for some $n \in \mathbb{N}$, or $a_1, a_2, \ldots$) such that for a_i, a_{i+1} two consecutive elements in the sequence, we have $a_i \ R \ a_{i+1}$; we say that such a sequence begins with a_1 (if it is finite, we also say that it *ends* with a_n). An element $a \in A$ is said to be an R-*normal form*

---

[1] Available at http://www-i2.informatik.rwth-aachen.de/AProVE
[2] Available at http://www.win.tue.nl/tpa

if there exists no b such that $a\ R\ b$. The set of all R-normal forms is denoted by NF_R. We say that b is an R-normal form of a (written $aR^!b$) if $b \in \mathsf{NF}_R$ and $a\ R^*b$. We say that R is *terminating* iff there is no infinite sequence $a_1\ R\ a_2\ R\ a_3 \cdots$. Given binary relations R and S (on the same set A), we say that S *preserves* the R-normal forms if for each $a \in \mathsf{NF}_R$ and $b \in A$, $a\ S\ b$ implies that $b \in \mathsf{NF}_R$.

Throughout this paper, $\mathcal{X}$ denotes a countable set of variables, and $\mathcal{F}$ denotes a signature, i.e., a set of function symbols $\{f, g, \ldots\}$, each having a fixed arity given by a mapping $ar : \mathcal{F} \to \mathbb{N}$. The set of terms built from $\mathcal{F}$ and $\mathcal{X}$ is $\mathcal{T}(\mathcal{F}, \mathcal{X})$. Terms are viewed as labelled trees in the usual way. Positions $p, q, \ldots$ are represented by chains of positive natural numbers used to address subterms of t. The set of positions of a term t is $\mathcal{P}os(t)$. The subterm at position p of t is $t|_p$ and $t[s]_p$ is the term t with the subterm at position p replaced by s.

A *rewrite rule* is an ordered pair (l, r), written $l \to r$, with $l, r \in \mathcal{T}(\mathcal{F}, \mathcal{X})$, $l \notin \mathcal{X}$ and $\mathcal{V}ar(r) \subseteq \mathcal{V}ar(l)$. The left-hand side (*lhs*) of the rule is l and r is the right-hand side (*rhs*). A TRS is a pair $\mathcal{R} = (\mathcal{F}, R)$ with R a (possibly infinite) set of rewrite rules. A term $t \in \mathcal{T}(\mathcal{F}, \mathcal{X})$ rewrites to s (at position p), written $t \xrightarrow{p}_{\mathcal{R}} s$ (or just $t \to s$), if $t|_p = \sigma(l)$ and $s = t[\sigma(r)]_p$, for some rule $\rho : l \to r \in R$, $p \in \mathcal{P}os(t)$ and substitution σ. A TRS is *terminating* if $\to$ is terminating. The set of normal forms of $\mathcal{R}$ ($\mathcal{R}$-normal forms) is denoted by $\mathsf{NF}_{\mathcal{R}}$.

Given TRSs $\mathcal{R} = (\mathcal{F}, R)$ and $\mathcal{S} = (\mathcal{F}, S)$, we denote by $\mathcal{R} \cup \mathcal{S}$ the TRS $(\mathcal{F}, R \cup S)$; also, we write $\mathcal{R} \subseteq \mathcal{S}$ to indicate that $R \subseteq S$.

The problem of proving termination of a TRS is equivalent to finding a well-founded, stable, and monotonic (strict) ordering $>$ on terms (i.e., a *reduction ordering*) which is *compatible* with the rules of the TRS, i.e., such that $l > r$ for all rules $l \to r$ of the TRS. Here, *monotonic* means that, for all k-ary symbol f, $i \in \{1, \ldots, k\}$, and $t, s, t_1, \ldots, t_k \in \mathcal{T}(\mathcal{F}, \mathcal{X})$, whenever $t > s$, we have $f(t_1, \ldots, t_{i-1}, t, \ldots, t_k) > f(s_1, \ldots, t_{i-1}, s, \ldots, t_k)$. *Stable* means that, whenever $t > s$, we have $\sigma(t) > \sigma(s)$ for all terms t, s and substitutions σ.

3 Fairness and Fair Termination

The following definition is analogous to [PF85], but our formulation follows [Mes05]. Roughly speaking, an $\mathcal{R}$-sequence is fair (w.r.t. a subset of rules of $\mathcal{R}$) if each rule which is infinitely often enabled during the sequence is infinitely often taken.

Definition 1 (Rule fairness). *Given a TRS $\mathcal{R}$, we say that an $\mathcal{R}$-sequence $A : t_1 \to_{\mathcal{R}} t_2 \to_{\mathcal{R}} \cdots$ is rule fair w.r.t. the rules in $\mathcal{R}_F \subseteq \mathcal{R}$ (abbreviated $\mathcal{R}_F$-fair) if for all rules $\alpha : l \to r \in \mathcal{R}_F$, we have: If the set*

$$I_\alpha^A = \{i \in \mathbb{N} \mid \exists C_i, \sigma_i, p_i, s.t.\ t_i = C_i[\sigma_i(l)]_{p_i}\}$$

is infinite, then there is an infinite set $J_\alpha^A \subseteq I_\alpha^A$ such that, for all $j \in J_\alpha^A$, $t_j \to_{l \to r} t_{j+1}$.

As a simple consequence of Definition 1, finite $\mathcal{R}$-sequences are always fair w.r.t. any $\mathcal{R}_F \subseteq \mathcal{R}$. Also, all $\mathcal{R}$-sequences are fair w.r.t. $\mathcal{R}_F = \varnothing$.

Definition 2 (Rule fair-termination). *A TRS $\mathcal{R}$ is* fairly-terminating *w.r.t.* $\mathcal{R}_F \subseteq \mathcal{R}$ *if there is no infinite $\mathcal{R}_F$-fair $\mathcal{R}$-sequence. A TRS $\mathcal{R}$ is* rule fairly-terminating *if it is fairly-terminating w.r.t. $\mathcal{R}$ itself.*

Rule fair-termination coincides with Porat and Francez's [PF85] and the 'localized' definition w.r.t. a subset of rules $\mathcal{R}_F \subseteq \mathcal{R}$ is equivalent to [PF86–Definition 17]. Note that ordinary termination of TRSs is subsumed by Definition 2: take $\mathcal{R}_F = \varnothing$; then all $\mathcal{R}$-sequences are trivially fair w.r.t. $\mathcal{R}_F$, and $\mathcal{R}$ is fairly-terminating w.r.t. $\mathcal{R}_F$ if and only if $\mathcal{R}$ is terminating. And, clearly, termination of $\mathcal{R}$ impies rule fair-termination of $\mathcal{R}$. However, the opposite is not true: the system {a -> b, a -> a} is rule fairly-terminating but not terminating.

In contrast to ordinary termination, fair-termination is *not* preserved if some of the rules of the TRS are dismissed: there can be TRSs $\mathcal{R}$ which are $\mathcal{R}_F$-fairly-terminating for some $\mathcal{R}_F \subseteq \mathcal{R}$, whereas they are not $\mathcal{R}'_F$-fairly-terminating for a subset $\mathcal{R}'_F \subset \mathcal{R}_F$ of $\mathcal{R}_F$.

Example 2. Consider the following TRS $\mathcal{R}$ [PF85, Tis89]:

    a -> f(a)
    a -> b

As noticed by Tison, $\mathcal{R}$ is rule fairly-terminating (i.e., fairly-terminating w.r.t. $\mathcal{R}$ itself). Let $\mathcal{R}_F$ be the subTRS of $\mathcal{R}$ consisting of the first rule (then take $\mathcal{S} = \mathcal{R} - \mathcal{R}_F$). The following infinite $\mathcal{R}$-sequence (as usual, we underline the contracted redex):

$$\underline{a} \rightarrow_{\mathcal{R}_F} f(\underline{a}) \rightarrow_{\mathcal{R}_F} f(f(\underline{a})) \rightarrow_{\mathcal{R}_F} \cdots$$

is $\mathcal{R}_F$-fair. This shows that $\mathcal{R}$ is not $\mathcal{R}_F$-fairly-terminating.

The key observation is that, given $\mathcal{R}_F, \mathcal{R}'_F \subseteq \mathcal{R}$, the set of $\mathcal{R}_F \cup \mathcal{R}'_F$-fair sequences is the *intersection* of the sets of $\mathcal{R}_F$-fair and $\mathcal{R}'_F$-fair sequences. Therefore, we have the following obvious sufficient condition in the other direction.

Proposition 1. *A TRS $\mathcal{R}$ is fairly-terminating w.r.t. $\mathcal{R}_F \subseteq \mathcal{R}$ if there is a subset $\mathcal{R}'_F \subset \mathcal{R}_F$, such that $\mathcal{R}$ is fairly-terminating w.r.t. $\mathcal{R}'_F$.*

The subset $\mathcal{R}'_F$ in Proposition 1 can be a *single* rule. For instance, Tison observes that $\mathcal{R}$ in Example 2 is rule fairly-terminating thanks to the rule a -> b. As we shall see below, this is a specially interesting case. The system in Example 1, however, is $\mathcal{R}_F$-fairly-terminating provided that $\mathcal{R}_F$ contains all three rules end, execute, and remove. It is easy to see that the absence of one of them destroys fair-termination. Proposition 1 will be used later.

4   Reducing Fair Termination to Termination

Termination analysis has recently experimented a remarkable development in the term rewriting community, leading to the birth of a new generation of promising methods, tools, and technology transfer. An important goal of this paper is giving an appropriate theoretical basis for fair-termination on which machine-implementable fair-termination techniques can be based. In this section, we investigate how to reduce a proof of fair-termination to the problem of proving termination of particular (combinations of) reduction relations.

Intuitively, a sufficient condition for $\mathcal{R}_F$-fair-termination of a TRS $\mathcal{R} = \mathcal{R}_F \cup \mathcal{S}$ is that: (1) there is no infinite $\mathcal{R}$-sequence performing an infinite number of $\mathcal{R}_F$-steps, and (2) every infinite $\mathcal{S}$-sequence contains an $\mathcal{R}_F$-redex. The first condition corresponds to the termination of the relation $\rightarrow^*_\mathcal{S} \circ \rightarrow_{\mathcal{R}_F}$ (which implies termination of $\mathcal{R}_F$). The second condition can be captured as the termination of the relation $\rightarrow^!_{\mathcal{R}_F} \circ \rightarrow_\mathcal{S}$. Note, however, that they are not equivalent. For instance, for $\mathcal{S} = \{a \rightarrow a, b \rightarrow a\}$ and $\mathcal{R}_F = \{a \rightarrow b\}$ we have that $\rightarrow^!_{\mathcal{R}_F} \circ \rightarrow_\mathcal{S}$ is not terminating, but (2) holds. Theorem 1 below formalizes this intuition. In order to prove it, we first need the following.

Proposition 2. *Let $\mathcal{R} = \mathcal{R}_F \cup \mathcal{S}$ be a TRS such that $\mathcal{R}_F$ is finite and $\rightarrow^!_{\mathcal{R}_F} \circ \rightarrow_\mathcal{S}$ is terminating. If $\mathcal{R}$ is not fairly-terminating w.r.t. $\mathcal{R}_F$, then for each infinite $\mathcal{R}_F$-fair $\mathcal{R}$-sequence A there is a rule $\alpha : l \rightarrow r \in \mathcal{R}_F$ for which I^A_α is infinite.*

PROOF. We proceed by contradiction. If $\mathcal{R}$ is not fairly-terminating w.r.t. $\mathcal{R}_F$, then there is an infinite $\mathcal{R}_F$-fair $\mathcal{R}$-sequence A. Assume that there exists one such sequence A such that for all rules $\alpha : l \rightarrow r$ in $\mathcal{R}_F$, I^A_α is finite. Then, since $\mathcal{R}_F$ is finite, A can be written as follows: $A : t_1 \rightarrow^*_\mathcal{R} t_n \rightarrow_\mathcal{S} t_{n+1} \rightarrow_\mathcal{S} \cdots$ where the terms t_i contain no $\mathcal{R}_F$-redex for $i \geq n$. Then, those t_i are $\mathcal{R}_F$-normal forms. Since $t \rightarrow^!_{\mathcal{R}_F} t$ for any $\rightarrow_{\mathcal{R}_F}$-normal form t, we can write the subsequence of A starting from t_n as follows: $t_n \rightarrow^!_{\mathcal{R}_F} \circ \rightarrow_\mathcal{S} t_{n+1} \rightarrow^!_{\mathcal{R}_F} \circ \rightarrow_\mathcal{S} \cdots$ This contradicts the termination of $\rightarrow^!_{\mathcal{R}_F} \circ \rightarrow_\mathcal{S}$. □

Theorem 1. *A TRS $\mathcal{R} = \mathcal{R}_F \cup \mathcal{S}$ with $\mathcal{R}_F$ finite is fairly-terminating w.r.t. $\mathcal{R}_F$ if $\rightarrow^*_\mathcal{S} \circ \rightarrow_{\mathcal{R}_F}$ and $\rightarrow^!_{\mathcal{R}_F} \circ \rightarrow_\mathcal{S}$ are terminating.*

PROOF. Assume that $\rightarrow^*_\mathcal{S} \circ \rightarrow_{\mathcal{R}_F}$ and $\rightarrow^!_{\mathcal{R}_F} \circ \rightarrow_\mathcal{S}$ are terminating, and that $\mathcal{R}$ is not fairly-terminating w.r.t. $\mathcal{R}_F$. Then there is an infinite $\mathcal{R}_F$-fair $\mathcal{R}$-sequence A. By Proposition 2, there is a rule $\alpha : l \rightarrow r \in \mathcal{R}_F$ such that I^A_α is infinite. Since, by $\mathcal{R}_F$-fairness, J^A_α is infinite, A can be written as follows:

$$A : t_1 \rightarrow^*_\mathcal{S} \circ \rightarrow_{\mathcal{R}_F} t_{j_1+1} \rightarrow^*_\mathcal{S} \circ \rightarrow_{\mathcal{R}_F} t_{j_2+1} \rightarrow^*_\mathcal{S} \circ \rightarrow_{\mathcal{R}_F} \cdots$$

which contradicts termination of $\rightarrow^*_\mathcal{S} \circ \rightarrow_{\mathcal{R}_F}$. □

The following example, however, shows that Theorem 1 does *not* provide a complete method for proving rule fair termination.

Example 3. Consider the following TRS $\mathcal{R}$ [PF85]:

a -> f(a)	g(a,b) -> c	a -> g(a,b)

which is rule fairly-terminating. It is not difficult to see that $\mathcal{R}$ is fairly-terminating w.r.t. $\mathcal{R}_F \subset \mathcal{R}$ given by the two rightmost rules above. Since $\mathcal{R}_F$ is *not* terminating, $\to_S^* \circ \to_{\mathcal{R}_F}$ is nonterminating. Therefore, Theorem 1 cannot be used to prove fair termination of $\mathcal{R}$ w.r.t. $\mathcal{R}_F$, even though $\mathcal{R}$ is fairly-terminating w.r.t. $\mathcal{R}_F$ and $\to_{\mathcal{R}_F}^! \circ \to_S$ is terminating.

Hence, termination of $\to_S^* \circ \to_{\mathcal{R}_F}$ (alone) is not a necessary condition for fair-termination of $\mathcal{R}$ w.r.t. $\mathcal{R}_F$. Similarly, one could see that termination of $\to_{\mathcal{R}_F}^! \circ \to_S$ is *not* a necessary condition either. However, when $\mathcal{R}_F$ is a single rule TRS, we have the following characterization.

Theorem 2. *Let $\mathcal{R} = \mathcal{R}_F \cup S$ and $\mathcal{R}_F$ be a single rule TRS. Then, $\mathcal{R}$ is $\mathcal{R}_F$-fairly-terminating if and only if $\to_S^* \circ \to_{\mathcal{R}_F}$ and $\to_{\mathcal{R}_F}^! \circ \to_S$ are terminating.*

PROOF.   The ($\Leftarrow$) part follows by Theorem 1. To prove the ($\Rightarrow$) part, we reason by contradiction and assume that either $\to_S^* \circ \to_{\mathcal{R}_F}$ or $\to_{\mathcal{R}_F}^! \circ \to_S$ are nonterminating. If $\to_S^* \circ \to_{\mathcal{R}_F}$ is nonterminating, then there is an infinite sequence: $A : t_1 \to_S^* t_1' \to_{\mathcal{R}_F} t_2 \to_S^* t_2' \to_{\mathcal{R}_F} \cdots$ which (by $\mathcal{R}_F$ containing only one rule) is $\mathcal{R}_F$-fair, thus contradicting $\mathcal{R}_F$-fair termination of $\mathcal{R}$. If $\to_{\mathcal{R}_F}^! \circ \to_S$ is nonterminating, then there is an infinite sequence $t_1 \to_{\mathcal{R}_F}^! t_1' \to_S t_2 \to_{\mathcal{R}_F}^! t_2' \to_S \cdots$ which, since $\mathcal{R}_F$ contains only one rule, is $\mathcal{R}_F$-fair: note that either t_i contains no $\mathcal{R}_F$-redex (and then $t_i' = t_i$) or t_i is normalized by $\mathcal{R}_F$ (hence all $\mathcal{R}_F$-redexes in t_i are contracted). $\square$

5   Proving Fair-Termination

According to Theorem 1, if we prove termination of both $\to_S^* \circ \to_{\mathcal{R}_F}$ and $\to_{\mathcal{R}_F}^! \circ \to_S$, then fair-termination of $\mathcal{R} = S \cup \mathcal{R}_F$ follows.

Note that given two reduction relations $\to_1$ and $\to_2$, the (non)termination of $\to_2^* \circ \to_1$ and $\to_1^! \circ \to_2$ do not have any (easy) connection: let $\to_1$ and $\to_2$ be relations on $A = \{a, b, c\}$ such that $a \to_1 b$ and $c \to_2 c$ are the only components of the respective relations. Then, $\to_2^* \circ \to_1 = \to_1$ is terminating but $\to_1^! \circ \to_2$ is not terminating: $c \to_1^! c \to_2 c \to_1^! c \to_2 \cdots$. On the other hand, $\to_2^! \circ \to_1$ is terminating (since $\to_2^! = \{(a,a),(b,b)\}$, we have $\to_2^! \circ \to_1 = \to_1$), but $\to_1^* \circ \to_2 \supseteq \to_2$ is not terminating. Thus, in the following, we consider how to address these two (more standard) termination problems in more detail.

5.1   Termination of $\to_S^* \circ \to_{\mathcal{R}_F}$

Given binary relations $\to_1$ and $\to_2$ on an abstract set A, $\to_1$ is called *relatively noetherian* (or better *relatively terminating*) with respect to $\to_2$ if every infinite $\to_1 \cup \to_2$-derivation contains only finitely many $\to_1$-steps (see [Ges90–Section 2.1], although the notion goes back to Klop: see also [Klo92–Exercise 2.0.8(11)]).

In his PhD thesis [Ges90], A. Geser has investigated relative termination. In our setting, this notion is interesting due to the following result.

Proposition 3. *[Ges90] Let $\to_1$ and $\to_2$ be binary relations. Then, $\to_2^* \circ \to_1$ is terminating if and only if $\to_1$ is relatively terminating with respect to $\to_2$.*

Thus, according to this result, termination of $\to_{\mathcal{S}}^* \circ \to_{\mathcal{R}_F}$ can be investigated as the relative termination of $\mathcal{R}_F$ w.r.t. $\mathcal{S}$. Fortunately, there are even automatic tools which can be used to prove relative termination of TRSs.

Example 4. Consider the TRS $\mathcal{R}$ in Example 2. Let $\mathcal{R}_F$ be the subTRS consisting of the rule a -> b and $\mathcal{S} = \mathcal{R} - \mathcal{R}_F$. Now, TPA can be used to prove termination of $\to_{\mathcal{S}}^* \circ \to_{\mathcal{R}_F}$. Consider again the system $\mathcal{R}$ in Example 1 with $\mathcal{R}_F$ consisting of the rules end, execute, and remove and $\mathcal{S} = \mathcal{R} - \mathcal{R}_F$. We have used TPA to obtain an automatic proof of termination of $\to_{\mathcal{S}}^* \circ \to_{\mathcal{R}_F}$.

5.2 Termination of $\to_{\mathcal{R}_F}^! \circ \to_{\mathcal{S}}$

Termination of $\to_2^! \circ \to_1$ for binary relations $\to_1$ and $\to_2$ can also be investigated as *relative* termination of $\to_1$ w.r.t. $\to_2$.

Proposition 4. *Let A be a set and $\to_1, \to_2 \subseteq A \times A$ be binary relations. If $\to_1$ is relatively terminating w.r.t. $\to_2$, then $\to_2^! \circ \to_1$ is terminating.*

PROOF.   Since relative termination of $\to_1$ w.r.t. $\to_2$ is equivalent to termination of $\to_2^* \circ \to_1$ (Proposition 3) and, since $\to^! \subseteq \to^*$ for all binary relation $\to$, termination of $\to_2^* \circ \to_1$ implies termination of $\to_2^! \circ \to_1$. □

Since termination of $\to_{\mathcal{R}_F}^* \circ \to_{\mathcal{S}}$ implies termination of $\mathcal{S}$ and termination of $\to_{\mathcal{S}}^* \circ \to_{\mathcal{R}_F}$ (which is also required) implies termination of $\mathcal{R}_F$, this means that both $\mathcal{R}_F$ and $\mathcal{S}$ must be terminating (at least as separate TRSs) which is quite a restrictive setting. The following results are helpful to prove termination of $\to_{\mathcal{R}_F}^! \circ \to_{\mathcal{S}}$.

Proposition 5. *Let $\mathcal{R}$ and $\mathcal{S}$ be two TRSs. Let $\mathcal{S}' = \{l \to r \in \mathcal{S} \mid l \in \mathrm{NF}_{\mathcal{R}}\}$. Then, $\to_{\mathcal{R}}^! \circ \to_{\mathcal{S}'}$ is terminating if and only if $\to_{\mathcal{R}}^! \circ \to_{\mathcal{S}}$ is terminating.*

PROOF.   By definition of $\mathcal{S}'$ and $\to_{\mathcal{R}}^!$, we have $(\to_{\mathcal{R}}^! \circ \to_{\mathcal{S}}) = (\to_{\mathcal{R}}^! \circ \to_{\mathcal{S}'})$. □

Example 5. Consider the TRS $\mathcal{R}$ in Example 2 with $\mathcal{R} = \mathcal{R}_F \cup \mathcal{S}$ as in Example 4. Since $\mathcal{S}'$ computed as in Proposition 5 is empty, $\to_{\mathcal{R}_F}^! \circ \to_{\mathcal{S}}$ is terminating.

Consider again the TRS in Example 1 with $\mathcal{R}_F$ and $\mathcal{S}$ as in Example 4. The use of Proposition 5 produces a simpler version $\mathcal{S}'$ of $\mathcal{S}$, which consists of the rules shift1 and shift2. Since $\mathcal{R}_F \cup \mathcal{S}'$ can be proved terminating (by using, e.g., APROVE), we have that $\to_{\mathcal{R}_F}^! \circ \to_{\mathcal{S}'}$ is clearly terminating. By Proposition 5, $\to_{\mathcal{R}_F}^! \circ \to_{\mathcal{S}}$ is also terminating.

Proposition 6. *Let A be a set and $\to_1, \to_2 \subseteq A \times A$ be binary relations. If $\to_2$ is terminating and preserves the $\to_1$-normal forms, then $\to_1^! \circ \to_2$ is terminating.*

PROOF.   If $\to_1^! \circ \to_2$ is nonterminating, then there is an infinite sequence

$$t = t_1 \to_1^! t_1' \to_2 t_2 \to_1^! t_2' \to_2 \cdots$$

and since $\to_2$ preserves the $\to_1$-normal forms, we can then extract the infinite sequence $t = t_1' \to_2 t_2 \to_2 \cdots$ which contradicts termination of $\to_2$. □

The following example shows the limitations of this approach.

Example 6. Consider the following TRS $\mathcal{R}$:

```
f(a) -> a
f(X) -> f(a)
```

Let $\mathcal{R}_F$ be the subTRS of $\mathcal{R}$ consisting of the first rule and $\mathcal{S} = \mathcal{R} - \mathcal{R}_F$. It is not possible to apply the results in this section to prove termination of $\to^!_{\mathcal{R}_F} \circ \to_{\mathcal{S}}$ (note that $\mathcal{S}$ is nonterminating and the *lhs* f(X) is an $\mathcal{R}_F$-normal form).

In the following section, we introduce a transformation for proving termination of $\to^!_{\mathcal{R}} \circ \to_{\mathcal{S}}$ for arbitrary TRSs $\mathcal{R}$ and $\mathcal{S}$.

5.3   Termination of $\to^!_{\mathcal{R}_F} \circ \to_{\mathcal{S}}$ by Transformation

Given TRSs $\mathcal{R}_1$ and $\mathcal{R}_2$, our idea here is to implement a 'distributed' computation by performing as many $\to_{\mathcal{R}_1}$-steps as possible (thus obtaining an $\mathcal{R}_1$-normal form) followed by a *single* $\to_{\mathcal{R}_2}$-step. Inspired by the transformations in [GM04] (which have been developed for a completely different purpose), our transformation keeps track of each *single* reduction step issued by $\mathcal{R}_2$. This is achieved by shifting a single symbol active to (non-deterministically) reach the position where a redex is placed. The application of a rewrite rule changes active into mark, which is propagated upwards through the term in order to be replaced by a new symbol active that enables new reduction steps. Given a TRS $\mathcal{R} = (\mathcal{F}, R)$, the TRS $\mathcal{U}_{\mathcal{R}} = (\mathcal{F} \cup \{\text{active}, \text{mark}, \text{top}\}, U)$ consists of the following rules: for all $l \to r \in R$, $f \in \mathcal{F}$ such that $k = ar(f) > 0$, and $i \in \{1, \dots, ar(f)\}$,

$$\text{active}(l) \to \text{mark}(r)$$
$$\text{active}(f(x_1, \dots, x_i, \dots, x_k)) \to f(x_1, \dots, \text{active}(x_i), \dots, x_k)$$
$$f(x_1, \dots, \text{mark}(x_i), \dots, x_k) \to \text{mark}(f(x_1, \dots, x_i, \dots, x_k))$$
$$\text{top}(\text{mark}(x)) \to \text{top}(\text{active}(x))$$

We are actually interested in the *union* $\mathcal{R}_1 \cup \mathcal{U}_{\mathcal{R}_2}$ of $\mathcal{R}_1$ and $\mathcal{U}_{\mathcal{R}_2}$. In order to ensure that before starting the application of a rule marked with active (which belongs to $\mathcal{R}_2$), the argument of mark is in $\mathcal{R}_1$-normal form, we use *innermost* rewriting. We have the following:

Theorem 3. *Let $\mathcal{R}_1 = (\mathcal{F}, R_1)$ be a confluent and innermost terminating TRS and $\mathcal{R}_2 = (\mathcal{F}, R_2)$ be a TRS. If $\mathcal{R}_1 \cup \mathcal{U}_{\mathcal{R}_2}$ is innermost terminating, then $\to^!_{\mathcal{R}_1} \circ \to_{\mathcal{R}_2}$ is terminating.*

PROOF.   By contradiction. Assume that $\to^!_{\mathcal{R}_1} \circ \to_{\mathcal{R}_2}$ is nonterminating. Then, there is an infinite sequence $t = t_1 \to^!_{\mathcal{R}_1} s_1 \to_{\mathcal{R}_2} t_2 \to^!_{\mathcal{R}_1} s_2 \to_{\mathcal{R}_2} \cdots$ starting from a term t. We show that there is an innermost counterpart in $\mathcal{R}_1 \cup \mathcal{U}_{\mathcal{R}_2}$ starting from top(mark(t)):

1. Since $\mathcal{R}_1$ is innermost terminating, there is s_1' such that $t_1 \xrightarrow{i}^!_{\mathcal{R}_1} s_1'$; by confluence, $s_1' = s_1$. Thus, we have top(mark(t_1)) $\xrightarrow{i}^!_{\mathcal{R}_1}$ top(mark(s_1)). Furthermore, top(mark(t_1)) $\xrightarrow{i}^!_{\mathcal{R}_1 \cup \mathcal{U}_{\mathcal{R}_2}}$ top(mark(s_1)).

2. Since s_1 is an $\mathcal{R}_1$-normal form, there is only one reduction step which can be issued on $\texttt{top}(\texttt{mark}(s_1))$, i.e., $\texttt{top}(\texttt{mark}(s_1)) \xrightarrow{i}_{\mathcal{R}_1 \cup \mathcal{U}_{\mathcal{R}_2}} \texttt{top}(\texttt{active}(s_1))$.

3. Finally, we have that $\texttt{top}(\texttt{active}(s_1)) \xrightarrow{i}^{*}_{\mathcal{R}_1 \cup \mathcal{U}_{\mathcal{R}_2}} \texttt{top}(\texttt{mark}(s_2))$. The need of considering the rules in $\mathcal{R}_1$ demands some further explanation. Since s_1 is an $\mathcal{R}_1$-normal form, all steps issued by the group of rules

$$\texttt{active}(f(x_1, \ldots, x_i, \ldots, x_k)) \rightarrow f(x_1, \ldots, \texttt{active}(x_i), \ldots, x_k)$$

which put symbol $\texttt{active}$ deeper and deeper (until reaching the position of the $\mathcal{R}_2$-redex in s_1) are clearly innermost. After issuing the reduction step by using a rule $\texttt{active}(l) \rightarrow \texttt{mark}(r)$ for some $l \rightarrow r \in \mathcal{R}_2$, new $\mathcal{R}_1$-redexes can appear *below* symbol $\texttt{mark}$ which signals the position of the recently contracted redex. The innermost reduction sequence could need to continue, then, by issuing $\mathcal{R}_1$-steps. After this partial innermost $\mathcal{R}_1$-normalization, a rule $f(x_1, \ldots, \texttt{mark}(x_i), \ldots, x_k) \rightarrow \texttt{mark}(f(x_1, \ldots, x_i, \ldots, x_k))$ would eventually apply as the only (innermost!) reduction step, to push up the symbol $\texttt{mark}$. These interleaved process would continue until putting $\texttt{mark}$ immediately below $\texttt{top}$, having s_2 (in $\mathcal{R}_1$-normal form!) as the only argument.

This contradicts innermost termination of $\mathcal{R}_1 \cup \mathcal{U}_{\mathcal{R}_2}$. $\qquad\qquad\square$

In our setting, we use Theorem 3 with $\mathcal{R}_1 = \mathcal{R}_F$ and[3] $\mathcal{R}_2 = \mathcal{S}$. In practice, checking innermost termination of $\mathcal{R}_F$ is not necessary if we have already proved that $\rightarrow^*_{\mathcal{S}} \circ \rightarrow_{\mathcal{R}_F}$ is terminating because this implies termination of $\mathcal{R}_F$.

Example 7. Consider $\mathcal{R}$, $\mathcal{R}_F$ and $\mathcal{S}$ as in Example 6. Termination of $\rightarrow^*_{\mathcal{S}} \circ \rightarrow_{\mathcal{R}_F}$ can be proved with TPA. Regarding termination of $\rightarrow^{!}_{\mathcal{R}_F} \circ \rightarrow_{\mathcal{S}}$, the transformed system TRS $\mathcal{R}_F \cup \mathcal{U}_{\mathcal{S}}$:

```
f(a) -> a
active(f(X)) -> mark(f(a))
active(f(X)) -> f(active(X))
f(mark(X)) -> mark(f(X))
top(mark(X)) -> top(active(X))
```

is innermost terminating (although we were not able to obtain an automatic proof). Note that $\mathcal{R}_F$ is clearly confluent. Therefore, by Theorem 3, we conclude termination of $\rightarrow^{!}_{\mathcal{R}_F} \circ \rightarrow_{\mathcal{S}}$. Thus, the system $\mathcal{R}$ is fairly-terminating.

5.4   A Methodology for Proving Fair-Termination as Termination

PROBLEM 1: Given a TRS $\mathcal{R}$ and a finite subTRS $\mathcal{R}_F \subseteq \mathcal{R}$, is $\mathcal{R}$ fairly-terminating w.r.t. $\mathcal{R}_F$? We have two lines of attack:

---

[3] The tool MU-TERM provides an implementation of Giesl and Middeldorp's transformation from which $\mathcal{U}_{\mathcal{S}'}$ is easily obtained. MU-TERM is available on http://www.dsic.upv.es/~slucas/csr/termination/muterm.

1. *Prove termination of $\mathcal{R}$*: If $\mathcal{R}$ is terminating, then $\mathcal{R}$ is fairly-terminating w.r.t. $\mathcal{R}_F$.
2. If $\mathcal{R}_F$ is not terminating, then *look for a terminating subset* $\mathcal{R}'_F \subset \mathcal{R}_F$ of $\mathcal{R}_F$. By Proposition 1 we can change $\mathcal{R}_F$ be the selected $\mathcal{R}'_F$ and go to Problem 2 below to try to prove the new configuration of the problem.

PROBLEM 2: Given a TRS $\mathcal{R}$ and a finite and terminating subTRS $\mathcal{R}_F \subseteq \mathcal{R}$, is $\mathcal{R}$ fairly-terminating w.r.t. $\mathcal{R}_F$?

With $\mathcal{S} = \mathcal{R} - \mathcal{R}_F$, according to Theorem 1, we try to prove termination of both $\to^*_{\mathcal{S}} \circ \to_{\mathcal{R}_F}$ and $\to^!_{\mathcal{R}_F} \circ \to_{\mathcal{S}}$:

1. Prove the *relative termination of $\mathcal{R}_F$ w.r.t. $\mathcal{S}$* (see Proposition 3). Termination tools like TPA can also be used to obtain an automatic proof.
2. Prove termination of $\to^!_{\mathcal{R}_F} \circ \to_{\mathcal{S}}$: first, restrict the TRS $\mathcal{S}$ to $\mathcal{S}' \subseteq \mathcal{S}$ as indicated in Proposition 5. Now, we can prove termination of $\to^!_{\mathcal{R}_F} \circ \to_{\mathcal{S}'}$ by using one of the following methods:
   (a) If $\mathcal{R}_F \cup \mathcal{S}'$ is terminating, then $(\to_{\mathcal{R}_F} \cup \to_{\mathcal{S}'})^+$ is terminating and therefore $\to^!_{\mathcal{R}_F} \circ \to_{\mathcal{S}'} \subseteq (\to_{\mathcal{R}_F} \cup \to_{\mathcal{S}'})^+$ also is.
   (b) If $\mathcal{S}'$ is terminating, then
       i. If $\mathcal{S}'$ preserves the $\mathcal{R}_F$-normal forms, then by Proposition 6, termination of $\to^!_{\mathcal{R}_F} \circ \to_{\mathcal{S}'}$ follows.
       ii. Prove the relative termination of $\mathcal{S}'$ w.r.t. $\mathcal{R}_F$. By Proposition 4, this implies termination of $\to^!_{\mathcal{R}_F} \circ \to_{\mathcal{S}'}$.
   (c) Otherwise, prove innermost termination of the union of $\mathcal{R}_F$ and the transformed TRS $\mathcal{U}_{\mathcal{S}'}$. If $\mathcal{R}_F$ is confluent, by Theorem 3 termination of $\to^!_{\mathcal{R}_F} \circ \to_{\mathcal{S}'}$ follows.

PROBLEM 3: Is a TRS $\mathcal{R}$ rule fairly-terminating? We have two lines of attack:

1. *Prove termination of $\mathcal{R}$*: If $\mathcal{R}$ is terminating, then $\mathcal{R}$ is rule fairly-terminating.
2. According to Proposition 1, we can look for a subTRS $\mathcal{R}_F$ such that $\mathcal{R}$ is fairly-terminating w.r.t. $\mathcal{R}_F$ (thus reducing to Problems 1 and 2).

Fortunately, the previous termination problems (proving termination, innermost termination, and relative termination of TRSs) are currently supported by existing termination tools like APROVE and TPA, among others.

6   Applications

In this section, we describe two more practical (still simple) examples of nonterminating systems which are fairly-terminating and show how to formally prove this property using our results and the methodology of Section 5.4.

Lottery

Consider the following scenario: a lottery where a finite number of balls are rolling inside a container assumed here to be circular. Eventually, a ball will be removed to pick a number and, of course, the repeated extraction of balls will make the whole process terminating. The following TRS can be used to model this process:

```
[extract]   cons(X,XS) -> XS [shift] cons(X,cons(Y,XS))
-> cons(Y,snoc(XS,X)) [circular1] snoc(nil,X) -> cons(X,nil)
[circular2] snoc(cons(X,XS),Y) -> cons(X,snoc(XS,Y))
```

Here, $\mathcal{R}_F$ consists of the rule extract, which represents the extraction of a ball. The remaining rules (shift, circular1 and circular2) are collected into a nonterminating TRS $\mathcal{S}$ which represents a finite list whose elements are shifted in a circular fashion over and over again.

Let us prove that $\mathcal{R}$ is fairly-terminating w.r.t. $\mathcal{R}_F$. According to Theorem 2, we *have* to prove that both $\to_{\mathcal{S}}^* \circ \to_{\mathcal{R}_F}$ and $\to_{\mathcal{R}_F}^! \circ \to_{\mathcal{S}}$ are terminating. Regarding termination of $\to_{\mathcal{S}}^* \circ \to_{\mathcal{R}_F}$, by Proposition 3 this is equivalent to proving that $\mathcal{R}_F$ is relatively terminating with respect to $\mathcal{S}$. We have used TPA to obtain an automatic proof of this. Regarding termination of $\to_{\mathcal{R}_F}^! \circ \to_{\mathcal{S}}$, we can use Proposition 5 to obtain a subTRS $\mathcal{S}'$ of $\mathcal{S}$ which only contains circular1. By Proposition 5, termination of $\to_{\mathcal{R}_F}^! \circ \to_{\mathcal{S}}$ is equivalent to termination of $\to_{\mathcal{R}_F}^! \circ \to_{\mathcal{S}'}$. The TRS $\mathcal{S}'$ is obviously terminating. Since $\mathcal{R}_F \cup \mathcal{S}'$ is also terminating, $\to_{\mathcal{R}_F}^! \circ \to_{\mathcal{S}'}$ is terminating and $\mathcal{R}$ is fairly-terminating w.r.t. $\mathcal{R}_F$.

Noisy Channel

Consider the following scenario: there are three agents A, B, and C. Agents A and B have to perform tasks a and b (respectively) in a distributed fashion. Agent C receives information about their completion through a two-component channel. Agent A (resp. B), writes "a", (resp. "b") on the corresponding channel to communicate to C that his/her task has been finished. Once the tasks performed by A and B have both terminated, C closes the channel. However, the channel is *noisy* in such a way that, when both values are on it, they can get lost. Thus, both A and B may have to repeat their respective signals before the channel is closed. The following TRS can be used to model this process:

```
[A]     [null,Y] -> [a,Y]
[B]     [X,null] -> [X,b]
[C]     [a,b] -> done
[loss]  [a,b] -> [null,null]
```

The key point here is that if rule C is fair, then the system is terminating. Thus, we consider $\mathcal{R}_F$ consisting of rule C.

Let us prove that $\mathcal{R}$ is fairly-terminating w.r.t. $\mathcal{R}_F$. Let $\mathcal{S} = \mathcal{R} - \mathcal{R}_F$, i.e., $\mathcal{S}$ contains the rules A, B and loss (and it is nonterminating). According to Theorem 2, we have to prove that both $\to_{\mathcal{S}}^* \circ \to_{\mathcal{R}_F}$ and $\to_{\mathcal{R}_F}^! \circ \to_{\mathcal{S}}$ are terminating. Regarding termination of $\to_{\mathcal{S}}^* \circ \to_{\mathcal{R}_F}$, by Proposition 3 this is equivalent to proving that $\mathcal{R}_F$ is relatively terminating with respect to $\mathcal{S}$. Again, we have used

TPA to obtain an automatic proof of this. Regarding termination of $\rightarrow^{!}_{\mathcal{R}_F} \circ \rightarrow_{\mathcal{S}}$, we use Proposition 5 to obtain a simpler version $\mathcal{S}'$ of $\mathcal{S}$, namely, $\mathcal{S}'$ containing rules A and B. Termination of $\rightarrow^{!}_{\mathcal{R}_F} \circ \rightarrow_{\mathcal{S}}$ is equivalent to termination of $\rightarrow^{!}_{\mathcal{R}_F} \circ \rightarrow_{\mathcal{S}'}$. The TRS $\mathcal{S}'$ is easily proved terminating. Since $\mathcal{R}_F \cup \mathcal{S}'$ is also terminating, we can conclude now that $\rightarrow^{!}_{\mathcal{R}_F} \circ \rightarrow_{\mathcal{S}}$ is terminating. Hence, $\mathcal{R}$ is fairly-terminating w.r.t. $\mathcal{R}_F$.

7   Related Work and Conclusions

A number of other approaches to fairness within term rewriting have been developed so far. In particular, the notion of fairness as related to the removal of (residuals) of *redexes* rather than concerning the application of rules is well-known after O'Donnell's work [O'D77] on the so-called *outermost-fair reduction strategy* and the corresponding normalization results [O'D77, HL91]. O'Donnell's notion of fairness was intended to provide a basis for computing the normal form of terms. In those works, a (finite or infinite) reduction sequence $t_1 \rightarrow t_2 \rightarrow \cdots$ is fair if for all $i \geq 1$, and (position of a) redex Δ in t_i, there is $j > i$ such that t_j does not contain any residual of Δ [Ter03–Definition 4.9.10] (see also [Klo92]). It is not difficult to see that this notion of fairness is not comparable to ours.

Following these works, fairness plays a very important role in infinitary rewriting as an essential ingredient of strategies which intend to approximate infinitary normal forms [KKSV95]. The introduced notions, however, follow the previous style and become, then, uncomparable to ours.

Termination techniques have been recently proposed as suitable tools for proving *liveness properties of fair computations* [KZ05]. As in our approach, Koprowski and Zantema define fairness as relative to a given TRS. Their formal notion, however, is quite different: according to [KZ05–Sections 2.2 and 2.3], an infinite reduction in $\mathcal{R}_F \cup \mathcal{S}$ is called *fair* (w.r.t. $\mathcal{R}_F$) if it contains infinitely many $\mathcal{R}_F$-steps. No distinction between enabled and taken steps is made. This, of course, is a clear difference with the notion of fairness we are interested in. Moreover, the authors explicitly remark that *all fair reductions are infinite*. Thus, apart from the fact that this means that there are fair sequences in our sense which are not fair in Koprowski and Zantema's approach (e.g., the finite ones), no discussion about termination of such fair sequences is even possible!

In summary, we have shown that the problem of proving (rule) fair-termination of a TRS $\mathcal{R}$ w.r.t. a subTRS $\mathcal{R}_F$ can be reduced to the problem of proving termination of $\rightarrow^{*}_{\mathcal{S}} \circ \rightarrow_{\mathcal{R}_F}$ and $\rightarrow^{!}_{\mathcal{R}_F} \circ \rightarrow_{\mathcal{S}}$ (where $\mathcal{S} = \mathcal{R} - \mathcal{R}_F$). We have proven that, if $\mathcal{R}_F$ is a single-rule TRS, fair-termination of $\mathcal{R}$ w.r.t. $\mathcal{R}_F$ is equivalent to termination of such relations. We have also investigated how to prove termination of $\rightarrow^{!}_{\mathcal{R}_F} \circ \rightarrow_{\mathcal{S}}$ as ordinary termination of TRSs. We can equivalently consider a subTRS $\mathcal{S}' \subseteq \mathcal{S}$ whose left-hand sides are $\mathcal{R}_F$-normal forms and then either prove termination of $\mathcal{R}_F \cup \mathcal{S}'$ (or even $\mathcal{S}'$ under some additional conditions), or transform $\mathcal{S}'$ into a TRS $\mathcal{U}_{\mathcal{S}'}$ and then prove *innermost* termination of $\mathcal{R}_F \cup \mathcal{U}_{\mathcal{S}'}$. Therefore, we always obtain (more) standard termination problems, namely: proving and disproving termination, innermost termination, and relative termination of TRSs, which can be addressed by existing termination tools. We believe that the results that we propose in this paper, although open to many extensions and generalizations, do indeed provide a quite practical *proof methodology* for proving fair-termination.

A number of interesting issues, however, remain to be investigated. For instance, Example 3 (which we cannot manage with our methodology) shows that a deeper analysis is needed to extend the use of termination techniques (and tools) for proving fair-termination. Regarding future extensions of our techniques, we think the following are interesting to consider:

1. The more general setting of *localized fairness* [Mes05] (also including weaker fairness notions like *justice* [Fra86, LPS81]).
2. The analysis of fair-termination *modulo* a set of equations; this notion has already been investigated by Porat and Francez [PF86].
3. Another important aspect of fairness is that, in many applications, only initial expressions satisfying concrete properties are expected to exhibit a fairly-terminating behavior. Indeed, this can be crucial to achieve fair termination in some cases.
4. The role of typing information in fair-termination. It is well-known that types play an important role in termination. As shown in [DLMMU04], it is possible to deal with termination of sorted TRS by reducing this problem to the problem of proving termination of a TRS (without sorts). We believe that a similar treatment could be useful for fair termination.

Of course, the implementation of our techniques in a system like MTT which is able to use external tools to solve termination problems is also envisaged (together with more experimentation on practical examples).

Acknowledgements. The authors thank the anonymous referees for many suggestions and useful remarks. José Meseguer was partially supported by ONR grant N00014-02-1-0715 and NSF Grant CCR-0234524; Salvador Lucas was partially supported by Spanish MEC grant SELF TIN 2004-07943-C04-02.

References

[BB92]   G. Berry and G. Boudol. The Chemical Abstract Machine. *Theoretical Computer Science* 96(1):217–248, 1992.

[DLMMU04] F. Durán, S. Lucas, J. Meseguer, C. Marché, and X. Urbain. Proving Termination of Membership Equational Programs. In P. Sestoft and N. Heintze, editors, *Proc. of ACM SIGPLAN 2004 Symposium on Partial Evaluation and Program Manipulation, PEPM'04*, pages 147-158, ACM Press, New York, 2004.

[Fra86]   N. Francez. Fairness. Springer-Verlag, Berlin, 1986.

[Ges90]   A. Geser. Relative Termination. PhD Thesis. Fakultät für Mathematik und Informatik. Universität Passau, 1990.

[GM04]   J. Giesl and A. Middeldorp. Transformation techniques for context-sensitive rewrite systems. *Journal of Functional Programming*, 14(4): 379-427, 2004.

[HL91]   G. Huet and J.J. Lévy. Computations in orthogonal term rewriting
             systems I, II. In J.L. Lassez and G. Plotkin, editors, *Computational
             logic: essays in honour of J. Alan Robinson*, pages 395-414 and 415-
             443. The MIT Press, Cambridge, MA, 1991.

[KKSV95]   R. Kennaway, J.W. Klop, M.R. Sleep, and F.-J. de Vries. Transfinite
             Reductions in Orthogonal Term Rewriting Systems. *Information and
             Computation* 119(1):18-38, 1995.

[Klo92]   J.W. Klop. Term Rewriting Systems. In S. Abramsky, D.M. Gabbay,
             and T.S.E. Maibaum. *Handbook of Logic in Computer Science*, volume
             2, pages 1-116. Oxford University Press, 1992.

[KZ05]   A. Koprowski and H. Zantema. Proving Liveness with Fairness using
             Rewriting. In B. Gramlich, editor, *Proc. of the 5th International Work-
             shop on Frontiers of Combining Systems, FroCoS'05*, LNAI 3717:232-
             247, 2005.

[LPS81]   D. Lehmann, A. Pnueli, and J. Stavi. Impartiality, Justice and Fairness:
             the ethics of concurrent termination. In S. Even and O. Kariv, editors,
             *Proc. of the 8th International Colloquium on Automata, Languages, and
             Programming, ICALP'81*, LNCS 115:264-277, Springer-Verlag, Berlin,
             1981.

[Mes92]   J. Meseguer. Conditional Rewriting Logic as a Unified Model of Con-
             currency. *Theoretical Computer Science* 96(1):73-55, 1992.

[Mes05]   J. Meseguer. Localized Fairness: A Rewriting Semantics. In J. Giesl,
             editor, *Proc. of the 16th International Conference on Rewriting Tech-
             niques and Applications, RTA'05*, LNCS 3467:250-263, Springer-Verlag,
             Berlin, 2005.

[MM02]   N. Martí-Oliet and J. Meseguer. Rewriting logic: roadmap and bibliog-
             raphy. *Theoretical Computer Science* 285(2):121–154, 2002.

[MN70]   Z. Manna and S. Ness. On the termination of Markov algorithms. In
             Proc. of the Third Hawaii International Conference on System Science,
             pages 789-792, 1970.

[O'D77]   M.J. O'Donnell. Computing in Systems Described by Equations. LNCS
             58, Springer-Verlag, Berlin, 1977.

[Ohl02]   E. Ohlebusch. *Advanced Topics in Term Rewriting*. Springer-Verlag,
             Berlin, 2002.

[PF85]   S. Porat and N. Francez. Fairness in term rewriting systems. In J.-P.
             Jouannaud, editor, *Proc. of the 1st International Conference on Rewrit-
             ing Techniques and Applications, RTA'85*, LNCS 202:287-300, Springer-
             Verlag, Berlin, 1985.

[PF86]   S. Porat and N. Francez. Full-commutation and fair-termination in
             equational (and combined) term rewriting systems. In J.H. Siekmann,
             editor, *Proc. of the 8th International Conference on Automated Deduc-
             tion, CADE'86*, LNCS 230:21-41, Springer-Verlag, Berlin, 1986.

[Ter03]   TeReSe, editor, *Term Rewriting Systems*, Cambridge University Press,
             2003.

[Tis89]   S. Tison. Fair termination is decidable for ground systems. In N. Der-
             showitz, editor, *Proc. of the 3rd International Conference on Rewrit-
             ing Techniques and Applications, RTA'89*, LNCS 355:462-476, Springer-
             Verlag, Berlin, 1989.

On Confluence of Infinitary Combinatory Reduction Systems

Jeroen Ketema[1] and Jakob Grue Simonsen[2]

[1] Department of Computer Science, Vrije Universiteit Amsterdam,
De Boelelaan 1081a, 1081 HV Amsterdam, The Netherlands
jketema@cs.vu.nl
[2] Department of Computer Science, University of Copenhagen (DIKU),
Universitetsparken 1, DK-2100 Copenhagen Ø, Denmark
simonsen@diku.dk

Abstract. We prove that fully-extended, orthogonal infinitary combinatory reduction systems with finite right-hand sides are confluent modulo identification of hypercollapsing subterms. This provides the first general confluence result for infinitary higher-order rewriting.

1 Introduction

Lazy declarative programming employs several approaches that are well-suited for description by term rewriting. This is of interest when studying basic constructs such as lazy lists:

$$\text{from}(x, y) \leftarrow x' \text{ is } x + 1, \text{from}(x', z), y = [x|z]$$

and (lazy) narrowing or residuation, in conjunction with, say, higher-order functions, e.g. the map functional:

$$\text{map}(f, []) = []$$
$$\text{map}(f, [x|xs]) = [f(x)|\text{map}(f, xs)]$$

Such a combination occurs in several pure functional languages, as well as in functional logic languages such as CURRY [1, 2] and TOY [3].

An extension of term rewriting intended to model lazy computations is *infinitary rewriting*, a formalism allowing for terms and reductions to be infinite [4,5,6]. Technical properties known as *strong convergence* and *compression* furnish the computational intuition for such systems: The limit term of every infinitely long sequence of computations is also the limit of a sequence of *finite* computations. Unfortunately, many desirable properties of ordinary (first-order) term rewriting systems fail to hold when considering infinitary term rewriting systems (iTRSs). Furthermore, substantial care and ingenuity is needed to treat bound variables and applications in the infinitary setting, a fact already evident in infinitary lambda calculus (iλc) [6,7].

While many language features require some sort of extension or restriction on the rewrite relation to model actual computations correctly (e.g. conditional

G. Sutcliffe and A. Voronkov (Eds.): LPAR 2005, LNAI 3835, pp. 199–214, 2005.

rewriting for logic programming [8,9]), any systematic treatment of such variants of *infinitary* rewriting must wait until the basic theory for infinitary higher-order rewriting has been pinned down. The contribution of this paper is to do exactly that by proving a general confluence (or Church-Rosser) theorem for infinitary higher-order rewriting. Our proof follows the general outline of confluence proofs for more restricted kinds of infinitary rewriting [6], but the crucial methods we employ are adapted from van Oostrom's treatment [10] of a method by Sekar and Ramakrishnan [11]. We work with infinitary combinatory reduction systems (iCRSs), as introduced in [12].

The outline of the paper is as follows: Section 2 introduces the basic concepts, Section 3 treats developments of sets of redexes, Section 4 concerns a special class of troublesome terms: the *hypercollapsing* ones, and the proof methods needed to tackle them, while Section 5 provides a proof of the main result.

2   Preliminaries

This section briefly recapitulates basic facts concerning both ordinary and infinitary CRSs; the reader is referred to [13] for an account of CRSs, and to [12] for iCRSs.

Throughout the paper we assume a signature Σ, each element of which has finite arity. We also assume a countably infinite set of variables, and, for each finite arity, a countably infinite set of meta-variables. Countably infinite sets are sufficient, given that we can employ 'Hilbert hotel'-style renaming. We denote the first infinite ordinal by ω, and arbitrary ordinals by $\alpha, \beta, \gamma, \ldots$. We use $\mathbb{N}$ to denote the set of natural numbers, starting at zero.

The standard way of defining infinite terms in infinitary rewriting is by defining a metric on the set of finite terms and letting the set of infinite terms be the completion of the metric space of finite terms [5, 7, 14], an approach also used in [12]; here, we give a shorter, but equivalent, definition using so-called "candidate" meta-terms:

Definition 2.1. *The set of (infinite)* candidate meta-terms *is defined by interpreting the following rules coinductively:*

1. *each variable x is a candidate meta-term,*
2. *$[x]s$ is a candidate meta-term, if x is a variable and s is a candidate meta-term,*
3. *$Z(s_1, \ldots, s_n)$ is a candidate meta-term, if Z is a meta-variable of arity n and $s_1, \ldots, s_n$ are candidate meta-terms, and*
4. *$f(s_1, \ldots, s_n)$ is a candidate meta-term, if $f \in \Sigma$ has arity n and $s_1, \ldots, s_n$ are candidate meta-terms.*

A candidate meta-term of the form $[x]s$ is called an abstraction. *Each occurrence of the variable x in s is* bound *in $[x]s$.*

The set of finite *meta-terms, a subset of the candidate meta-terms, is the set inductively defined by the above rules.*

Thus, $[x]x$, $[x]f(Z(x))$, $Z(Z(Z(\ldots)))$, and $Z([x]Z'([y](Z([x]Z')\ldots)))$ are all candidate meta-terms. Moreover, $[x]x$ and $[x]f(Z(x))$ are also finite meta-terms.

As usual in rewriting, we define the set of positions of candidate meta-terms as a set of *finite* strings over $\mathbb{N}$, with ϵ the empty string, such that each string corresponds to the "location" of subterm. For instance, the position of y in $[x]f(x,y)$ is 01 ('0' to get to $f(x,y)$ and '1' to get to the second argument of f). The set of positions of term s is denoted $\mathcal{P}os(s)$. If $p \in \mathcal{P}os(s)$, then we denote by $s|_p$ the *subterm of s at p* (e.g. $[x]f(x,y)|_{01} = y$). The length of a position p is denoted $|p|$. There is a natural well-founded (but not necessarily total) order $<$ on positions such that $p < q$ iff p is a proper prefix of q. If p and q are incomparable in this order, we write $p \parallel q$ and say that p and q are *parallel*.

A (one-hole) context is a candidate meta-term over $\Sigma \cup \{\Box\}$ where $\Box$ is a fresh constant that occurs at most once in the term.

We next define the set of meta-terms:

Definition 2.2. *Let s be a candidate meta-term. A chain in s is a sequence of (context,position)-pairs $(C_i[\Box], p_i)_{i<n}$ where $n \in \omega + 1$, such that for each $(C_i[\Box], p_i)$ there exists a term t_i with the property that $C_i[t_i] = s|_{p_i}$ and $p_{i+1} = p_i \cdot q$ where q is the position of the hole in $C_i[\Box]$.*

A chain of meta-variables is a chain $(C_i[\Box], p_i)_{i<n}$ such that for each $i < n$ it holds that $C_i[\Box] = Z(t_1, \ldots, t_m)$ with $t_j = \Box$ for at most one $1 \le j \le m$.

A meta-term is a candidate metaterm s such that no infinite chain of meta-variables occurs in s.

Observe that $\Box$ occurs only in $C_i[\Box]$ if $i+1 < n$, otherwise $C_i[\Box] = s|_{p_i}$. Moreover, note that candidate meta-terms such as $Z(Z(Z(\cdots Z(\cdots))))$ are not meta-terms. These terms are rejected as meta-terms as the result of applying substitutions to them is generally not well-defined [12]. Note too that $[x_1]Z_1([x_2]Z_2(\ldots))$ is a meta-term.

We can now define terms:

Definition 2.3. *A term is a meta-term without meta-variables.*

As usual, we consider terms modulo α-equivalence. Note that the definition of meta-terms only restricts meta-terms containing meta-variables, not meta-terms *without* meta-variables, i.e. not *terms*. Substitutions are defined by interpreting the ordinary rules of substitution coinductively, minding α-conversion when applicable. We write $s[\boldsymbol{x} := \boldsymbol{t}]$ for the substitution of a vector $\boldsymbol{t}$ of terms for a vector $\boldsymbol{x}$ of variables (of the same length) in a term s. An n-*ary substitute* is a mapping denoted $\underline{\lambda}x_1, \ldots, x_n.s$ or $\underline{\lambda}\boldsymbol{x}.s$, with s a term, such that:

$$(\underline{\lambda}\boldsymbol{x}.s)(t_1, \ldots, t_n) = s[\boldsymbol{x} := \boldsymbol{t}].$$

A *valuation* $\bar{\sigma}$ is an extension of a function σ which assigns n-ary substitutes to n-ary meta-variables. The extension maps meta-terms to terms. For instance, if $\sigma(Z) = [x]f(x)$, we have $\bar{\sigma}(g(Z,x)) = g([x]f(x),x)$. As above, it is defined by interpreting the usual rules for valuations [13] coinductively.

The following is proved in [12]:

Proposition 2.4. *Let s be a meta-term and $\bar{\sigma}$ a valuation. There exists a unique term that is the result of applying $\bar{\sigma}$ to s.*

2.1 Infinitary Rewriting

Definition 2.5. *A finite meta-term is a* pattern *if each of its meta-variables has distinct bound variables as its arguments. Moreover, a meta-term is* closed *if all its variables occur bound.*

Definition 2.6. *A* rewrite rule *is a pair (l, r), denoted $l \rightarrow r$, where l is a finite meta-term and r is a meta-term, such that:*

1. *l is a pattern and of the form $f(s_1, \ldots, s_n)$ with $f \in \Sigma$ of arity n,*
2. *all meta-variables that occur in r also occur in l, and*
3. *l and r are closed.*

An infinitary combinatory reduction system *(iCRS) is a pair $\mathcal{C} = (\Sigma, R)$ with Σ a signature and R a set of rewrite rules.*

Definition 2.7. *A rewrite rule $l \rightarrow r$ is* left-linear, *respectively* collapsing, *if each meta-variable occurs at most once in l, respectively if r has a meta-variable as root symbol. An iCRS is* left-linear *if all its rewrite rules are left-linear.*

Definition 2.8. *A pattern is* fully-extended *[15, 16], if, for each of its meta-variables Z, and each abstraction $[x]$ having Z in its scope, x is an argument of Z. An iCRS is* fully-extended *if the left-hand sides of all rewrite rules are.*

We now define redexes and rewrite steps.

Definition 2.9. *Let $l \rightarrow r$ be a rewrite rule. Given a valuation $\bar{\sigma}$, the term $\bar{\sigma}(l)$ is called a $l \rightarrow r$-redex. If $s = C[\bar{\sigma}(l)]$ for some context $C[\Box]$ with $\bar{\sigma}(l)$ a $l \rightarrow r$-redex and p the position of the hole in $C[\Box]$, then an $l \rightarrow r$-redex, or simply a redex, occurs at position p and depth $|p|$ in s. Moreover, a position q occurs in the* redex pattern, *if $q \geq p$ and if there does not exist q' such that $q \geq p \cdot q'$ and q' is the position of a meta-variable in l.*

A rewrite step *is a pair (s, t), denoted $s \rightarrow t$, such that an $l \rightarrow r$-redex occurs in $s = C[\bar{\sigma}(l)]$ and such that $t = C[\bar{\sigma}(r)]$. A redex or rewrite step is* collapsing *if the employed rewrite rule is collapsing. It is* root-collapsing *if it is collapsing and if the redex occurs at position ϵ.*

Throughout the paper, sets of redexes are denoted by calligraphic capitals such as $\mathcal{U}$. We can now define what a transfinite reduction sequence is. The definition copies the definition from iTRSs and iλc verbatim [5, 7]:

Definition 2.10. *A* transfinite reduction sequence *of ordinal length α is a sequence of terms $(s_\beta)_{\beta < \alpha+1}$ such that $s_\beta \rightarrow s_{\beta+1}$ for all $\beta < \alpha$. For each rewrite step $s_\beta \rightarrow s_{\beta+1}$, let d_β denote the depth of the contracted redex. The reduction* *sequence is* weakly convergent *or* Cauchy convergent *if for every ordinal* $\gamma \le \alpha$ *the distance between* t_β *and* t_γ *tends to 0 as* β *approaches* γ *from below. The reduction sequence is* strongly convergent *if it is weakly convergent and if* d_β *tends to infinity as* β *approaches* γ *from below.*

Notation 2.11. By $s \twoheadrightarrow^\alpha t$, respectively $s \twoheadrightarrow^{\le \alpha} t$, we denote a *strongly convergent* transfinite reduction sequence of ordinal length α, respectively of ordinal length less than or equal to α. By $s \twoheadrightarrow t$ we denote a *strongly convergent* transfinite reduction sequence of arbitrary ordinal length and by $s \to^* t$ we denote a reduction sequence of finite length. Reduction sequences are usually ranged over by capitals such as D, S, and T. The concatenation of two reduction sequences S and T is denoted by $S; T$. Note that the concatenation of any finite number of strongly convergent reductions is a strongly convergent reduction.

Lemma 2.12 (See [12]). *If* $s \twoheadrightarrow t$, *then the number of steps contracting redexes at depths less than* $d \in \mathbb{N}$ *is finite for any* d.

As in [5, 7, 6], we consider strongly converging reduction sequences. This ensures that we can restrict our attention to reduction sequences of length at most ω by the so-called *compression property*:

Theorem 2.13 (Compression, see [12]). *For every fully-extended, left-linear iCRS, if* $s \twoheadrightarrow^\alpha t$, *then* $s \twoheadrightarrow^{\le \omega} t$.

Left-linearity and fully-extendedness ensure no redex is created by either making two subterms equal or erasing some variable in an infinite number of steps. As shown in [12], they cannot be omitted from the theorem. In the remainder we work exclusively with *orthogonal* systems; these are defined as in the finite case:

Definition 2.14. *Let* $R = \{l_i \to r_i \mid i \in I\}$ *be a set of rewrite rules.*

1. *R is* non-overlapping *if it holds that:*
    - *each* $l_i \to r_i$*-redex that occurs at a position* p *in an* $l_j \to r_j$*-redex with* $i \ne j$ *occurs such that there exists a position* $q \le p$ *with* $q \in \mathcal{P}os(l_j)$ *and* $root(l_j|_p)$ *a meta-variable,*
    - *likewise for* $p \ne \epsilon$ *and* $i = j$.
2. *R is* orthogonal *if it is left-linear and non-overlapping.*
3. *An iCRS is* orthogonal *if its set of rewrite rules is orthogonal.*

As shown in [12], orthogonality suffices for the definition of well-defined *descendant* and *residual relations*, i.e. the relations that describe respectively what "happens to" positions and redexes across reductions.

Notation 2.15. Let s and t be terms such that $s \twoheadrightarrow t$. Assume that $P \subseteq \mathcal{P}os(s)$ and that $\mathcal{U}$ is a set of redexes in s. We denote descendants of P across $s \twoheadrightarrow t$, respectively residuals of $\mathcal{U}$ across $s \twoheadrightarrow t$, by $P/(s \twoheadrightarrow t)$ and $\mathcal{U}/(s \twoheadrightarrow t)$. If $P = \{p\}$ and $\mathcal{U} = \{u\}$ we also write $p/(s \twoheadrightarrow t)$ and $u/(s \twoheadrightarrow t)$.

3 Developments

The results in this section apply to orthogonal iCRSs. Orthogonality is required, as descendants and residuals are only defined in the orthogonal case.

Definition 3.1. *Let $\mathcal{U}$ be a set of redexes in a term s. A development of $\mathcal{U}$ is a strongly convergent reduction sequence such that each step contracts a residual of a redex in $\mathcal{U}$. A development $s \twoheadrightarrow t$ is complete if $\mathcal{U}/(s \twoheadrightarrow t) = \emptyset$.*

Notation 3.2. If $\mathcal{U}$ is a set of redexes in term s and there is some development of $\mathcal{U}$ that results in term t, we write $s \Rightarrow t$, where the arrow is adorned with $\mathcal{U}$ if needed. Observe that there may exist $t' \neq t$ with $s \Rightarrow t'$, as the development $s \Rightarrow t$ need not to be complete.

The following is the main result of [12]:

Theorem 3.3. *Let $\mathcal{U}$ be a set of redexes in a term s. If $\mathcal{U}$ has a complete development then all complete developments of $\mathcal{U}$ end in the same term.*

Lemma 3.4. *If $\mathcal{U}$ has a complete development and if $s \twoheadrightarrow t$ is a development of $\mathcal{U}$ (not necessarily complete), then $\mathcal{U}/(s \twoheadrightarrow t)$ has a complete development.*

Proof. Immediate by inspection of the proof of Theorem 5.12(1) in [12].   □

Lemma 3.5. *Let $\mathcal{U}$ be a set of redexes in a term s, let $\mathcal{U}$ have a complete development, and let u be a redex in s. Then $\mathcal{U} \cup \{u\}$ has a complete development.*

Proof (Sketch). By the finite chain condition on meta-terms and the variable convention, residuals of u can only be nested in "finite chains" across a complete development of $\mathcal{U}$. One can coinductively perform complete developments of these finite chains in a top-down manner, yielding a complete development of $\mathcal{U} \cup \{u\}$.   □

Corollary 3.6. *Let $\mathcal{U}$ be a set of redexes in a term s which has a complete development $s \twoheadrightarrow t$ and let v be a redex of s. The following diagram commutes (where all developments are complete):*

$$
\begin{array}{ccc}
s & \xrightarrow{\;v\;} & t \\[4pt]
\Big\downarrow{\scriptstyle \mathcal{U}} & & \Big\downarrow{\scriptstyle \mathcal{U}/(s\to t')} \\[4pt]
t' & \underset{v/(s\twoheadrightarrow t)}{\Longrightarrow} & s'
\end{array}
$$

Proof. By Lemmas 3.4 and 3.5, Theorem 3.3 and the fact that $(\mathcal{U} \cup \{v\})/(s \to t') = \mathcal{U}/(s \to t')$, respectively $(\mathcal{U} \cup \{v\})/(s \twoheadrightarrow t) = v/(s \twoheadrightarrow t)$.   □

4   Hypercollapsingness and Essentiality

From this section onwards we consider *only* fully-extended, orthogonal iCRSs where each rewrite rule has a *finite* right-hand side. Finiteness of the right-hand sides is essentially used to show that Definition 4.11 is well-defined[1].

In this section, we treat a special kind of troublesome term and reduction:

Definition 4.1. *A* hypercollapsing reduction *is a sequence of terms* $(s_i)_{i<\omega}$ *such that* $s_i \to s_{i+1}$ *for all* $i < \omega$ *and such that an infinite number of these steps are root-collapsing.*

Thus, a hypercollapsing reduction is a transfinite reduction sequence of length ω which is not convergent in any sense and from which the term s_ω is omitted.

Definition 4.2. *A term* s *is said to be* hypercollapsing *if, for all terms* t *with* $s \twoheadrightarrow t$, *there exists a term* t' *with* $t \twoheadrightarrow t'$ *such that* t' *has a collapsing redex at the root.*

The objective of this section is to prove the following lemma:

Lemma 4.3. *Let* s *be a term. If there is a hypercollapsing reduction starting from* s, *then* s *is hypercollapsing.*

This result is key for results concerning confluence modulo in iTRSs and iλc. Alas, the existing proof methods [6] cannot be lifted to the general higher-order case: For iTRSs, the known proofs hinge on the Strip Lemma, and for iλc on head reductions, none of which generalise to iCRSs. Instead, we employ a measure on *finite* reduction sequences and proof technique as developed by Sekar and Ramakrishnan [11] and as extended to higher-order rewriting by Van Oostrom [10].

4.1   Essential Reductions

To define the measure on finite reduction sequences, we first need to define the notions of *contribution* and *essentiality*.

Definition 4.4. *Let* s *and* t *be terms and* $s \to t$ *with an* $l \to r$-*redex contracted at position* p. *If* $q \in \mathcal{P}os(s)$ *and* $P \subseteq \mathcal{P}os(t)$, *then* q contributes *to* P, *whenever:*

- *one or more positions of* $q/(s \to t)$ *are in* P, *or*
- *the position* q *occurs in the redex pattern of the contracted redex and* p *is a prefix of some positions in* P.

Contribution is extended to finite reductions of positive length by transitive closure. If $s \to^= s$, *then every position in* P *contributes only to itself.*

---

[1] The restriction to finite right-hand sides is crucial to the technique of considering *essentiality* that we employ in our proofs. We conjecture that it is possible to lift the restriction.

Observe that several distinct positions in s can contribute to a single position in t. In the case the redex contracted in $s \to t$ occurs at position p, at least all positions in the redex pattern contribute to the position p in t.

Definition 4.5. *Let $s \to^* t$ and let $P \subseteq \mathcal{P}os(t)$. A position in any term along $s \to^* t$ is* essential *for P (usually the explicit mention of P is suppressed) if it contributes to P. A set of positions is essential for P if every position in the set is. A redex is essential for P if its root position contributes to P. A rewrite step is essential for P if its redex is. A finite reduction is essential for P if all of its rewrite steps are. A redex is* inessential *if its root position does not contribute to P. A rewrite step is* inessential *if its redex is.*

Lemma 4.6. *A rewrite step is either essential or inessential.*

Proof. By the fact that all positions in a redex pattern contribute to a redex.   □

Definition 4.7. *A* prefix *of a term s is a finite set $P \subseteq \mathcal{P}os(s)$ such that all prefixes of positions in P are also in P.*

Take heed that prefixes are *finite*.

Lemma 4.8. *Let $s_0 \to^* s_n$ and let P be a prefix of s_n. The positions in s_0 that are essential for P form a prefix of s_0.*

Proof. By induction on n. If $n = 0$, we are done, since the reduction is empty. If $n = n' + 1$, then P consists of a (possibly empty) set of positions P' "created" by the right-hand side of the redex contracted in the step $s'_n \to s_n$ and a (possibly empty) set of positions descending from positions Q in $s_{n'}$. The positions contributing to P' are exactly the positions that occur in the redex pattern of the redex contracted in $s_{n'} \to s_n$, and Q consists of any position above or parallel to the redex, and of positions in arguments of the redex. The union of all these positions clearly constitutes a prefix of $s_{n'}$. The induction hypothesis now furnishes the result.   □

By the above lemma, we may consider $s_0 \to^* s_n$ as a sequence of n prefixes such that each step either is inside the prefix of its term (and is hence essential), or is below the prefix (and is hence inessential).

Lemma 4.9. *Let $s_0 \to^* s_n$ and let P be a prefix of s_n. There exists a reduction $s_0 \to^* s' \twoheadrightarrow s_n$ where $s_1 \to^* s'$ consists of steps essential for P and $s' \twoheadrightarrow s_n$ consists of steps inessential for P (hence the prefix P exists in s').*

Proof. It suffices to show that if $t_i \Rightarrow t'_i \to t_{i+1}$ where $t_i \Rightarrow t'_i$ consists of a complete development of some set of redexes that contracts only inessential steps and $t'_i \to t_{i+1}$ is an essential step, then $t_i \to t''_i \Rightarrow t_{i+1}$ for some term t''_i. Observe that since $t_i \Rightarrow t'_i$ is inessential, the prefix of t_i will not be touched by any step in $t_i \Rightarrow t'_i$. Hence, the redex contracted in $t'_i \to t_{i+1}$ is the unique residual of an essential redex in t_i. By Corollary 3.6 there now exists a term t''_i such that $t_i \to t''_i \Rightarrow t_{i+1}$.   □

Notation 4.10. With the notation of the above lemma, we write $s_0 \to^* s'$ as D_e ('e' for 'essential') and $s' \twoheadrightarrow s_n$ as $D_{\bar{e}}$ ('$\bar{e}$' for 'inessential').

Definition 4.11. *Let* $D : s_0 \Rightarrow^{\mathcal{U}_1} s_1 \Rightarrow^{\mathcal{U}_2} \cdots \Rightarrow^{\mathcal{U}_n} s_n$ *be a reduction consisting of a finite number of developments of finite sets of redexes (with finite right-hand sides). The measure,* $\mu(D)$ *of* D *is the* n-tuple $(l_n, \ldots, l_1)$—*note the reverse ordering!—where* l_i *is the maximal length of a development of* $\mathcal{U}_i$ *that contracts only essential steps. Tuples are compared first by their length and then by their successive elements (in the natural order). This yields a well-founded order* $\prec$.

Note that the Finite Developments Theorem for ordinary CRSs applies: All developments of a finite set of redexes (with finite right-hand sides) are finite and end in the same term, and all maximal developments of such sets are complete [17]. Hence, each l_i in the definition is well-defined.

Remark 4.12. Let $s_0 \Rightarrow s_1 \Rightarrow \cdots \Rightarrow s_n = D_1; D_2; \cdots; D_n$ be a finite reduction consisting of developments of finite sets contracting only redexes *essential* to some prefix P of s_n. In the remainder of this section we will consider a special kind of projection of such a reduction across a step $u : s_0 \to t_0$ contracting a redex u. By applying the Finite Developments Theorem for finite CRSs to each single rewrite step in each D_i, we can erect the following diagram, in which each development is *finite* (but not necessarily complete):

$$
\begin{array}{ccccccc}
s_0 & \overset{D_1}{\Longrightarrow} & s_1 & \overset{D_2}{\Longrightarrow} & \cdots\cdots\cdots & \overset{D_n}{\Longrightarrow} & s_n \\
\big\downarrow{\scriptstyle u} & & \big\downarrow{\scriptstyle u/D_1} & & \big\downarrow{\scriptstyle u/(D_1;D_2)} & & \big\downarrow{\scriptstyle u/(D_1;\ldots;D_n)} \\
t_0 & \underset{D_1/u}{\Longrightarrow} & t_1 & \underset{D_2/(u/D_1)}{\Longrightarrow} & \cdots\cdots\cdots & \Longrightarrow & t_n
\end{array}
$$

If u is inessential, then it is outside the sequence of prefixes in $s_0 \Rightarrow^* s_n$ contributing to P. Therefore, all bottommost steps in the above diagram are essential, and P is a prefix of t_n.

If u is essential *and* some residual of the redex of u occurs in D_i, then some of the steps in the development $D_i/(u/D_1; \ldots; D_{i-1})$ may be *in*essential, since redexes may have been duplicated by u and since not all copies need to be essential. If this is the case, Lemma 4.9 ensures that we can rearrange $t_0 \Rightarrow^* t_n$ an essential initial part $t_0 \to^* q$ and an inessential final part $q \twoheadrightarrow t_n$ (such that P is a prefix of the term q). We can thus "strip away" all inessential steps in the original projection to obtain an "emaciated" projection $t_0 \to^* q$; observe that, in this case, we do not necessarily have $s_n \twoheadrightarrow q$.

The above remark ensures that the following definition is meaningful:

Definition 4.13. *Let* $s_0 \Rightarrow s_1 \Rightarrow \cdots \Rightarrow s_n = D_1; D_2; \cdots; D_n$ *be a finite reduction consisting of developments of finite sets contracting only redexes essential to some prefix* P *for* s_n. *Let* $s_0 \to t_0$ *contract a redex* u. *The emaciated projection of* $D_1; \cdots D_n$ *across* u, *with respect to* P, *written* $D /\!/ u$ *is the usual projection where inessential steps have been stripped out as in Remark 4.12.*

Proposition 4.14. *Let $D : s_0 \Rightarrow^* s_n$, let P be a prefix of s_n and let $s_0 \to t_0$ contract a redex u. Then, in the emaciated projection $D/\!/u : t_0 \Rightarrow^* q$, the term q contains P as a prefix and $D/\!/u$ contains only essential steps for P.*

Proof. This is the content of Remark 4.12.   □

We want to relate the measure of the emaciated projections to the original reductions. The following two lemmas ensure that this can be done:

Lemma 4.15. *If D factors as $D_e; D_{\bar{e}}$ (according to Lemma 4.9), then $\mu(D_e) \preceq \mu(D)$.*

Proof. Inessential steps are not counted by μ. In the proof of Lemma 4.9, the number of essential steps is constant under the permutation, whence the result.   □

Lemma 4.16. *If $D : s_0 \Rightarrow^* s_n$, $\mu(D) = (l_n, \ldots, l_1)$, and $s_0 \to t_0$ contracts an essential redex u, then $\mu(D/\!/u) \prec \mu(D)$.*

Proof. If u is essential, then a residual of u that is essential is contracted in one of the steps $s_i \Rightarrow_i^{\mathcal{U}} s_{i+1}$. Assume that i is the largest index of a set $\mathcal{U}_i$ such that $\mathcal{U}_i$ contains a residual u' of u that is essential. If u' is the sole redex in $\mathcal{U}_i$, then the ith component of D/u becomes empty, and $\mu(D/u)$ will have length at least one less than $\mu(D)$. By Lemma 4.15 we have $\mu(D/\!/u) \preceq \mu(D/u)$. Hence, we obtain $\mu(D/\!/u) \prec \mu(D)$.

If u' is not the sole redex in $\mathcal{U}_i$, then write $\mu(D/\!/u) = (l'_n, \ldots, l'_1)$ and notice that u may duplicate redexes from $\mathcal{U}_1, \ldots, \mathcal{U}_{i-1}$ Hence, increase the maximal length of their essential developments, i.e. we may have $l'_j > l_j$ for $j < i$. However, the maximal length of a partial development of $\mathcal{U}_i$ that contracts only essential steps is now at least one less. Hence, $l'_i < l_i$, and for all l_j with $j > i$ we have $l'_j = l_j$. Thus, $\mu(D/\!/u) \prec \mu(D)$.   □

Lemma 4.17. *Suppose $D : s_0 \to^* s_n$ is a reduction to a root-collapsing term and suppose $s_0 \to t_0$ contracting a redex u is not root-collapsing. Then, t_0 reduces to a root-collapsing term in a finite number of steps.*

Proof. We may assume that $s_0 \to^* s_n$ does not contain any root-collapsing steps (minimality). This implies that the collapsing redex at the root of s_0 is either (1) created along the reduction, or (2) that it was already at the root in s_0 (which implies $n = 0$). If it was already in s_0, but at some other position than the root, then a root-collapsing step must occur in $s_0 \to^* s_n$ (otherwise the root-collapsing redex can never be at the root), which is impossible by minimality.

Let P be the set of positions in the redex pattern of the root-collapsing redex of s_n, and consider the emaciated projection $D/\!/u$. Since u is not root-collapsing, we have in the case of (1) that the final term q in the emaciated projection must also be root-collapsing. In the case of (2) this is also holds, as the redex contracted in $s_0 \to t_0$ must differ from the root-collapsing one in s_0, by the assumption on $s_0 \to t_0$.   □

Lemma 4.18. *If $s \twoheadrightarrow t$ contains no root-collapsing steps and s reduces to a collapsing redex, then so does t.*

Proof. If $s \twoheadrightarrow t$ is finite, the result follows by repeated application of Lemma 4.17.

If $s \twoheadrightarrow t$ is infinite, we may by compression assume that it has length ω and by strong convergence that $s \to^* s_n$ by a finite reduction D where s_n is a collapsing redex. Let P be the set of positions in the redex pattern of the root-collapsing redex in s_n. By Lemma, 4.8, the set of positions in s that contribute to P form a prefix Q of s and by Lemma 4.9 the reduction $s \to^* s_n$ consists solely of essential steps. We write $s \Rightarrow s_1 \Rightarrow \cdots \Rightarrow s_n$, and $\mu(D) = (l_n, \ldots, l_1)$.

Since $s \twoheadrightarrow t$ is infinite, it consists of a first step $s \to t_1$ contracting a redex u and an infinite reduction $t_1 \twoheadrightarrow t$. Taking the emaciated projection of $s \Rightarrow s_1 \Rightarrow \cdots \Rightarrow s_n$ over u yields a reduction $D/\!/u = t_1 \to^* s'_n$ to a collapsing redex. If u is inessential, then $\mu(D/\!/v) \preceq \mu(D)$. Otherwise, by Lemma 4.16, $\mu(D/\!/v) \prec \mu(D)$.

If, from some t_i in $s \twoheadrightarrow t$ onwards, no step is essential, then all steps are outside the prefix Q_i of t_i that contributes to P, hence the final term t contains a prefix that reduces to a collapsing redex in "the same way" as t_i does. Assume, for contradiction, that there are an infinite number of essential steps in $s \twoheadrightarrow t$. Then, Lemma 4.16 furnishes that the measure of the emaciated projected sequence decreases strictly in each of these steps, contradicting well-foundedness of $\prec$. □

4.2 Hypercollapsing Reductions Imply Hypercollapsingness

The following is the iCRS analogue of Lemma 12.8.4 in [6] for iTRSs and strengthening for iλc:

Lemma 4.19. *Let s_0 be a term. If there exists a hypercollapsing reduction starting from s_0, and a rewrite step $s_0 \to t_0$, then there is a hypercollapsing reduction starting from t_0.*

Proof (Sketch). By definition of hypercollapsing reductions we may write:

$$s_0 \to^* s'_0 \to s_1 \to^* s'_1 \to s_2 \to^* \cdots ,$$

with $s_i \to s_{i+1}$ a root-collapsing step and no root-collapsing steps in $s_i \to^* s'_i$, for all $i \in \mathbb{N}$. By repeated application of Corollary 3.6 we can erect the following diagram, where u takes on the rôle of the set $\mathcal{U}$ when the corollary is first applied:

We write S_i for $s_i \twoheadrightarrow s'_i \twoheadrightarrow s_{i+1} \twoheadrightarrow \cdots$ and T_i for $t_i \twoheadrightarrow t'_i \twoheadrightarrow t_{i+1} \twoheadrightarrow \cdots$. Note that T_i may have length greater than ω.

If it holds for each $i \in \mathbb{N}$ that a root-collapsing step occurs in T_i, then an infinite number of root-collapsing steps occurs in T_0. We show this first. Afterwards, we extract a hypercollapsing reduction from T_0 employing this property.

To show the property we distinguish two cases: either (1) a root-collapsing step occurs in S_i that does not contract a residual of u, or (2) all root-collapsing steps contract residuals of u. Careful case analysis shows that in both cases, T_i will contain a root-collapsing step.

To show that a hypercollapsing reduction starting from t_0 exists, one repeatedly applies the case distinction above to T_i for successively larger $i \in \mathbb{N}$.   □

We can now prove Lemma 4.3:

Proof (Lemma 4.3). Let $s \twoheadrightarrow t$ and assume by compression that this reduction has length at most ω. By strong convergence, we can write $s \rightarrow^* t' \twoheadrightarrow t$ such that all root-reductions occur in $s \rightarrow^* t'$. By repeated application of Lemma 4.19, there is a hypercollapsing reduction starting from t', in particular, t' reduces to a collapsing redex. Since $t' \twoheadrightarrow t$ contains no steps at the root, Lemma 4.18 yields that t reduces to a collapsing redex, proving that s is hypercollapsing.   □

5   Confluence Modulo

We use the notion of a *tiling diagram* from [6]:

Definition 5.1. *A* tiling *diagram of two strongly convergent reductions S : $s_{0,0} \rightarrow^\alpha s_{\alpha,0}$ and T : $s_{0,0} \rightarrow^\beta s_{0,\beta}$ is a rectangular arrangement of strongly convergent reductions:*

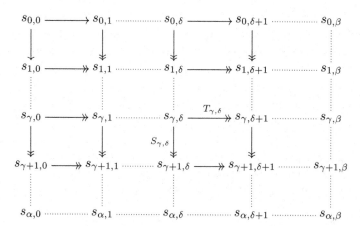

such that (1) each reduction $S_{\gamma,\delta}$: $s_{\gamma,\delta} \twoheadrightarrow s_{\gamma,\delta+1}$ is a complete development of a set of redexes of $s_{\gamma,\delta}$, and conversely with $T_{\gamma,\delta}$: $s_{\gamma,\delta} \twoheadrightarrow s_{\gamma+1,\delta}$, (2) the topmost horizontal reduction is T and the leftmost vertical reduction is S, and (3) for each γ, δ, the set of redexes developed in $T_{\gamma,\delta}$ is the set of residuals of the redex contracted in $s_{0,\delta} \rightarrow s_{0,\delta+1}$ across the (strongly convergent) reduction $S_{[0,\gamma],\delta}$: $s_{0,\delta} \rightarrow s_{1,\delta} \rightarrow \cdots s_{\gamma,\delta}$ (symmetrically for $S_{\gamma,\delta}$).

The below is part of Thm. 12.6.5 in [6]:

Theorem 5.2. *Let S and T be strongly convergent reductions starting from the same term. The following are equivalent:*

1. *The tiling diagram of S and T can be completed, i.e. S/T and T/S are strongly convergent and have the same limit.*
2. *S/T is strongly convergent.*
3. *T/S is strongly convergent.*

Proof. The proof in [6] is independent of the details of rewriting.   □

Notation 5.3. By $s \twoheadrightarrow^{\text{out}} t$ we denote a rewrite step that does not occur inside any hypercollapsing subterm of s.

We now prove the analogue of Lemma 12.8.14 in [6]:

Lemma 5.4. *If $S : s \twoheadrightarrow^{\text{out}} t_0$ and $T : s \twoheadrightarrow^{\text{out}} t_1$, then for some term q, we have $t_0 \twoheadrightarrow q$ and $t_1 \twoheadrightarrow q$.*

Proof. Let $s \twoheadrightarrow^{\text{out}} t_0$ have length α and $s \twoheadrightarrow^{\text{out}} t_1$ have length β, respectively. Assume without loss of generality that $\alpha \leq \beta$, and proceed by induction on β (the "outer" induction). Each case in this induction is in turn performed by induction on α (the "inner" induction). Induction ensures that it suffices to give a proof for $\alpha = \beta = 1$, for $\alpha = 1$ and $\beta = \omega$ (by Compression), and for $\alpha = \beta = \omega$.

- The case $\alpha = \beta = 1$ is covered by Lemma 3.5.
- For the case $\alpha = 1$ and $\beta = \omega$, Theorem 5.2 ensures that we need only prove that S/T is strongly convergent, indeed since S contracts a single redex u we need only prove that the set u/T has a strongly convergent complete development. Assume the contrary. Observe that only residuals of u are contracted in any development of u/T and that the employed rewrite rule is collapsing (otherwise any development u/T is strongly convergent). As contracting residuals of u cannot create further nestings of the residuals that are left, there exists a subterm of t_1 with a hypercollapsing reduction starting from it (obtained by a development of u/T), say at position p. In fact, there must exist an infinite chain of nested residuals of u in the subterm at p. By strong convergence and limit length of T, we can write $T = T''; T'$ where $T' : t \twoheadrightarrow^{\text{out}} t_1$ is a non-empty final segment of T that performs no steps at prefix positions of p. Note that T'' is finite, by strong convergence. Thus, we have $t|_p \twoheadrightarrow^{\text{out}} t_1|_p$. Since there is a hypercollapsing reduction starting from $t_1|_p$, there is also a hypercollapsing reduction starting from $t|_p$ interleaving the steps from $t|_p \twoheadrightarrow^{\text{out}} t_1|_p$ and the hypercollapsing reduction starting from $t_1|_p$. But then by Lemma 4.3 we have that $t|_p$ is hypercollapsing, which implies that $t|_p \twoheadrightarrow^{\text{out}} t_1|_p$ is empty and that $t|_p = t_1|_p$. Thus, $t|_p$ contains a set of descendants of u having no complete development (giving rise to the hypercollapsing reduction from $t|_p$), whence u/T'' has no complete development. Since T'' has length less than ω, this contradicts the (outer) induction hypothesis.

- When $\alpha = \beta = \omega$, the argument from the proof of Lemma 12.8.14 in [6] can be copied verbatim, as it is independent of the details of rewriting.   □

Define $s \sim_{hc} t$ if and only if t can be obtained from s by replacing a number of hypercollapsing subterms of s by other hypercollapsing terms. By orthogonality, $\sim_{hc}$ is an equivalence relation, which is closed under substitution of terms for free variables.

Lemma 5.5. *If $s \twoheadrightarrow t$ and $s \sim_{hc} s'$, then $s' \twoheadrightarrow^{out} t'$ and $t \sim_{hc} t'$.*

Proof. Let $s \twoheadrightarrow^\alpha t$ and $s \sim_{hc} s'$. We prove the result by transfinite induction.

- If $\alpha = 0$, then the result is immediate, as an empty reduction sequence is by definition one that only contracts redexes outside hypercollapsing subterms.
- If $\alpha = \beta + 1$, then assume $s \twoheadrightarrow^\alpha t = s \twoheadrightarrow^\beta q \to t$. By induction hypothesis we have that there exist q' such that $s' \twoheadrightarrow^{out} q'$ and $q \sim_{hc} q'$. There are now two possibilities for $q \to t$, depending on the contracted redex occurring either outside or inside a hypercollapsing subterm:
  - If the redex occurs outside a hypercollapsing subterm, then we have by $q \sim_{hc} q'$ and orthogonality that a redex employing the same rewrite rule occurs at the same position in q' and that this redex occurs outside a hypercollapsing subterm. By definition of $\sim_{hc}$, contracting the redex in q' yields a term t' by a reduction outside a hypercollapsing subterm. That $t \sim_{hc} t'$ follows by the fact that the same rewrite rule is employed in $q \to t$ and $q' \to t'$ and the fact that $q \sim_{hc} q'$: Clearly, t and t' are identical at all positions p that descend from positions not in hypercollapsing subterms of q or q'. If p' is the position of a maximal hypercollapsing subterm of q, it is also the position of a maximal hypercollapsing subterm of q' and vice versa, and p' descends to identical positions in t, respectively t'. Any descendant of the subterm at p' will be a (not necessarily maximal) hypercollapsing subterm, and the result then follows by $q \sim_{hc} q'$ and its closure under substitution.
  - If the redex occurs inside a hypercollapsing subterm, then we have $t \sim_{hc} q$. Hence, by transitivity of $\sim_{hc}$ we have $t \sim_{hc} q'$ and we can define $t' = q'$.
- If $\alpha = \gamma$, with γ a limit ordinal, then the result is immediate by strong convergence and the induction hypothesis.   □

Definition 5.6. *An iCRS is said to be* confluent modulo *an equivalence relation $\sim$ if $s \sim t$, $s \twoheadrightarrow s'$, and $t \twoheadrightarrow t'$ imply existence of terms s'' and t'' such that $s' \twoheadrightarrow s''$, $t' \twoheadrightarrow t''$ and $s'' \sim t''$.*

Theorem 5.7. *Fully-extended, orthogonal iCRSs with finite right-hand sides are confluent modulo $\sim_{hc}$.*

Proof. Let $s \sim_{hc} t$, and assume that $s \twoheadrightarrow s'$ and $t \twoheadrightarrow t'$. Consider the following diagram:

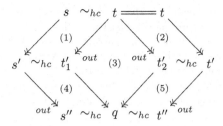

Prisms (1) and (2) follow by Lemma 5.5. Square (3) follows by Lemma 5.4. The diagram is completed by noting that (4) and (5) follow by Lemma 5.5 The result now follows by transitivity of $\sim_{hc}$.   □

References

1. Hanus, M.: A unified computation model for functional and logic programming. In: Proc. of the 24th Annual SIGPLAN-SIGACT Symposium on Principles of Programming Languages (POPL '97), ACM Press (1997) 80–93
2. Albert, E., Hanus, M., Huch, F., Oliver, J., Vidal, G.: An operational semantics for declarative multi-paradigm languages. In: Proc. of the 11th Int. Workshop on Functional and (Constraint) Logic Programming (WFLP '02), Università degli Studi di Udine (2002) 7–20
3. Fernández, A.J., Hortalá-Gonzales, T., Sáenz-Pérez, F.: Solving combinatorial problems with a constraint functional logic language. In: Proc. of the 5th Int. Symposium on Practical Aspects of Declarative Languages (PADL '03). Volume 2562 of LNCS., Springer-Verlag (2003) 320–338
4. Dershowitz, N., Kaplan, S., Plaisted, D.A.: Rewrite, rewrite, rewrite, rewrite, rewrite, ... Theoretical Computer Science **83** (1991) 71–96
5. Kennaway, R., Klop, J.W., Sleep, R., de Vries, F.J.: Transfinite reductions in orthogonal term rewriting systems. Information and Computation **119** (1995) 18–38
6. Terese: Term Rewriting Systems. Cambridge University Press (2003)
7. Kennaway, J.R., Klop, J.W., Sleep, M., de Vries, F.J.: Infinitary lambda calculus. Theoretical Computer Science **175** (1997) 93–125
8. Marchiori, M.: Logic programs as term rewriting systems. In: Proc. of the 4th Int. Conf. on Algebraic and Logic Programming. Volume 850 of LNCS., Springer-Verlag (1994) 223–241
9. van Raamsdonk, F.: Translating logic programs into conditional rewriting systems. In: Proc. of the 14th Int. Conf. on Logic Programming (ICLP '97), MIT Press (1997) 168–182
10. van Oostrom, V.: Normalisation in weakly orthogonal rewriting. In: Proc. of the 10th Int. Conf. on Rewriting Techniques and Applications (RTA '99). Volume 1631 of LNCS., Springer-Verlag (1999) 60–74
11. Sekar, R.C., Ramakrishnan, I.V.: Programming in equational logic: beyond strong sequentiality. Information and Computation **104** (1993) 78–109
12. Ketema, J., Simonsen, J.G.: Infinitary combinatory reduction systems. In: Proc. of the 16th Int. Conf. on Rewriting Techniques and Applications (RTA '05). Volume 3467 of LNCS., Springer-Verlag (2005) 438–452
13. Klop, J.W., van Oostrom, V., van Raamsdonk, F.: Combinatory reduction systems: introduction and survey. Theoretical Computer Science **121** (1993) 279–308

14. Arnold, A., Nivat, M.: The metric space of infinite trees. Algebraic and topological properties. Fundamenta Informaticae **3** (1980) 445–476
15. Hanus, M., Prehofer, C.: Higher-order narrowing with definitional trees. In: Proc. of the 7th Int. Conf. on Rewriting Techniques and Applications (RTA'96). Volume 1103 of LNCS., Springer-Verlag (1996) 138–152
16. van Oostrom, V.: Higher-order families. In: Proc. of the 7th Int. Conf. on Rewriting Techniques and Applications (RTA '96). Volume 1103 of LNCS., Springer-Verlag (1996) 392–407
17. Klop, J.W.: Combinatory Reduction Systems. PhD thesis, Rijksuniversiteit Utrecht (1980)

Matching with Regular Constraints

Temur Kutsia[1,*] and Mircea Marin[2,**]

[1] Research Institute for Symbolic Computation,
Johannes Kepler University, A-4040 Linz, Austria
tkutsia@risc.uni-linz.ac.at
[2] Graduate School of Systems and Information Engineering,
University of Tsukuba, Tsukuba 305-8573, Japan
mmarin@cs.tsukuba.ac.jp

Abstract. We describe a sound, terminating, and complete matching
algorithm for terms built over flexible arity function symbols and context, function, sequence, and individual variables. Context and sequence
variables allow matching to move in term trees to arbitrary depth and
breadth, respectively. The values of variables can be constrained by regular expressions which are not necessarily linear. We describe heuristics
for optimization, and discuss applications.

1 Introduction

We describe an algorithm to solve matching problems for terms built over flexible
arity function symbols and context, function, sequence, and individual variables.
Context and sequence variables can be constrained by regular expressions. These
four kinds of variables, together with regular constraints, make the term tree
traversal and subterm extraction process very flexible: The algorithm can explore
terms in a uniform way in vertical (via function and context variables) and in
horizontal (via individual and sequence variables) directions.

Context variables may be instantiated with a context—a term with a hole,
while function variables match a single function symbol. Hence, context variables support "vertical movement" in the tree in arbitrary depth, and function
variables do the same in one depth level only. Sequence and individual variables
can be seen as the "horizontal counterparts" for context and function variables:
Sequence variables match arbitrarily long sequences of terms, and individual
variables match only a single term.

Sequence variables can be constrained by regular expressions over terms. The
values of constrained variables are required to be elements of the corresponding
regular word language. Context variables are constrained by regular expressions
over contexts. The values of constrained context variables should be elements of

---
* Supported by the Austrian Science Foundation (FWF) under the Project SFB F1302
and F1322.
** Supported by the JSPS Grant-in-Aid no. 17700025 for Scientific Research sponsored
by the Japanese Ministry of Education, Culture, Sports, Science and Technology
(MEXT).

G. Sutcliffe and A. Voronkov (Eds.): LPAR 2005, LNAI 3835, pp. 215–229, 2005.

the corresponding regular tree language (it extends the result from [29] where context variables have been restricted by regular expressions over function symbols). Moreover, regular expressions are not limited to be linear. This gives a powerful data extraction mechanism. On the other hand, we do not allow recursion in constraints. The algorithm with regular constraints is sound, terminating, and complete. We show how to optimize the algorithm by early failure detection and branching reduction heuristics, and discuss possible applications.

The paper is organized as follows: Preliminary notions are introduced in Section 2. In Section 3 we describe the CSM algorithm and its optimizations. CSM with regular expressions is addressed in Section 4. Applications are discussed in Section 5. Related work is reviewed in Section 6. Section 7 concludes.

Due to space limitations, proofs are given in a technical report [30].

2   Preliminaries

We assume the following mutually disjoint sets of symbols fixed: individual variables $\mathcal{V}_{\mathrm{Ind}}$, sequence variables $\mathcal{V}_{\mathrm{Seq}}$, function variables $\mathcal{V}_{\mathrm{Fun}}$, context variables $\mathcal{V}_{\mathrm{Con}}$, and function symbols $\mathcal{F}$. The sets $\mathcal{V}_{\mathrm{Ind}}$, $\mathcal{V}_{\mathrm{Seq}}$, $\mathcal{V}_{\mathrm{Fun}}$, and $\mathcal{V}_{\mathrm{Con}}$ are countable. The set $\mathcal{F}$ is finite or countably infinite. All the symbols in $\mathcal{F}$ except a distinguished constant $\circ$ (called a *hole*) have flexible arity. We will use x, y, z for individual variables, $\overline{x}, \overline{y}, \overline{z}$ for sequence variables, F, G, H for function variables, $\overline{C}, \overline{D}, \overline{E}$ for context variables, and a, b, c, f, g, h for function symbols. We may use these meta-variables with indices as well.

Terms are constructed using the following grammar:

$$t ::= x \mid \overline{x} \mid \circ \mid f(t_1, \dots, t_n) \mid F(t_1, \dots, t_n) \mid \overline{C}(t).$$

In $\overline{C}(t)$ the term t can not be a sequence variable. We will write a for the term $a()$ where $a \in \mathcal{F}$. The meta-variables s, t, r, maybe with indices, will be used for terms. A function symbol f is called the *head* of $f(t_1, \dots, f_n)$. A *ground* term is a term without variables. A *context* is a term with a single occurrence of the hole constant $\circ$. To emphasize that a term t is a context we will write $t[\circ]$. A context $t[\circ]$ may be applied to a term s that is not a sequence variable, written $t[s]$, and the result is the term consisting of t with $\circ$ replaced by s. We will use C and D, with or without indices, for contexts.

A *substitution* is a mapping from individual variables to those terms which are not sequence variables and contain no holes, from sequence variables to finite, possibly empty sequences of terms without holes, from function variables to function variables and symbols, and from context variables to contexts, such that all but finitely many individual and function variables are mapped to themselves, all but finitely many sequence variables are mapped to themselves considered as singleton sequences, and all but finitely many context variables are mapped to themselves applied to the hole. For example, the mapping $\{x \mapsto f(a, \overline{y}), \overline{x} \mapsto \ulcorner \urcorner, \overline{y} \mapsto \ulcorner a, \overline{C}(f(b)), x \urcorner, F \mapsto g, \overline{C} \mapsto g(\circ)\}$ is a substitution.[1] We will use lower

---

[1] To improve readability we write sequences between the symbols $\ulcorner$ and $\urcorner$.

case Greek letters $\sigma, \vartheta, \varphi$, and ε for substitutions, where ε denotes the empty substitution. As usual, indices may be used with the meta-variables.

Substitutions are extended to terms: $v\sigma = \sigma(v)$ for $v \in \mathcal{V}_{\text{Ind}} \cup \mathcal{V}_{\text{Seq}}$, $\overline{C}(t)\sigma = \sigma(\overline{C})[t\sigma]$, $F(t_1, \ldots, t_n)\sigma = \sigma(F)(t_1\sigma, \ldots, t_n\sigma)$, $f(t_1, \ldots, t_n)\sigma = f(t_1\sigma, \ldots, t_n\sigma)$.

A substitution σ is *more general* than ϑ, denoted $\sigma \leq \vartheta$, if there exists a φ such that $\sigma\varphi = \vartheta$. A substitution σ is *more general* than ϑ *on a set of variables* $\mathcal{V}$, denoted $\sigma \leq^{\mathcal{V}} \vartheta$, if there exists a φ such that $v\sigma\varphi = v\vartheta$ for all $v \in \mathcal{V}$. A CSM *problem* is a finite multiset of term pairs (CSM *equations*), written $\{s_1 \ll t_1, \ldots, s_n \ll t_n\}$, where the s's and the t's contain no holes, the s's are not sequence variables, and the t's are ground. We will also call the s's the *query* and the t's the *data*. Substitutions are extended to CSM equations and problems in the usual way. A substitution σ is called a *matcher* of the CSM problem $\{s_1 \ll t_1, \ldots, s_n \ll t_n\}$ if $s_i\sigma = t_i$ for all $1 \leq i \leq n$. We will use Γ and Δ to denote CSM problems. A *complete set of matchers* of a CSM problem Γ is a set of substitutions S such that (i) each element of S is a matcher of Γ, and (ii) for each matcher ϑ of Γ there exist a substitution $\sigma \in S$ such that $\sigma \leq \vartheta$. The set S is a *minimal complete set of matchers* of Γ if it is a complete set and two distinct elements of S are incomparable with respect to $\leq$.

Example 1. The minimal complete set of matchers for the context sequence matching problem $\{\overline{C}(f(\overline{x})) \ll g(f(a, b), h(f(a), f))\}$ consists of three elements: $\{\overline{C} \mapsto g(\circ, h(f(a), f)), \ \overline{x} \mapsto \ulcorner a, b \urcorner\}$, $\{\overline{C} \mapsto g(f(a, b), h(\circ, f)), \ \overline{x} \mapsto a\}$, and $\{\overline{C} \mapsto g(f(a, b), h(f(a), \circ)), \ \overline{x} \mapsto \ulcorner \urcorner\}$.

3 Matching Algorithm

We now present inference rules for deriving solutions for CSM problems. A *system* is either the symbol $\bot$ (failure) or a pair $\Gamma; \sigma$, where Γ is a CSM problem and σ is a substitution. The inference system $\mathfrak{I}$ consists of the transformation rules listed below. The indices n and m are non-negative unless otherwise stated.

T: **Trivial**

$\{t \ll t\} \cup \Gamma; \ \sigma \Longrightarrow \Gamma; \ \sigma.$

IVE: **Individual Variable Elimination**

$\{x \ll t\} \cup \Gamma; \ \sigma \Longrightarrow \Gamma\vartheta; \ \sigma\vartheta, \qquad$ where $\vartheta = \{x \mapsto t\}$.

FVE: **Function Variable Elimination**

$\{F(s_1, \ldots, s_n) \ll f(t_1, \ldots, t_m)\} \cup \Gamma; \ \sigma$
$\Longrightarrow \{f(s_1\vartheta, \ldots, s_n\vartheta) \ll f(t_1, \ldots, t_m)\} \cup \Gamma\vartheta; \ \sigma\vartheta, \quad$ where $\vartheta = \{F \mapsto f\}$.

PD: **Partial Decomposition**

$\{f(s_1, \ldots, s_n) \ll f(t_1, \ldots, t_m)\} \cup \Gamma; \ \sigma$
$\Longrightarrow \{s_1 \ll t_1, \ldots, s_{k-1} \ll t_{k-1}, f(s_k, \ldots, s_n) \ll f(t_k, \ldots, t_m)\} \cup \Gamma; \ \sigma,$

if $f(s_1, \ldots, s_n) \neq f(t_1, \ldots, t_m)$, $s_k \in \mathcal{V}_{\text{Seq}}$ for some $1 < k \leq \min(n, m) + 1$, and $s_i \notin \mathcal{V}_{\text{Seq}}$ for all $1 \leq i < k$.

TD: Total Decomposition

$$\{f(s_1, \ldots, s_n) \ll f(t_1, \ldots, t_n)\} \cup \Gamma;\ \sigma \Longrightarrow \{s_1 \ll t_1, \ldots, s_n \ll t_n\} \cup \Gamma;\ \sigma,$$

if $f(s_1, \ldots, s_n) \neq f(t_1, \ldots, t_n)$ and $s_i \notin \mathcal{V}_{\mathrm{Seq}}$ for all $1 \leq i \leq n$.

SVD: Sequence Variable Deletion

$$\{f(\overline{x}, s_1, \ldots, s_n) \ll t\} \cup \Gamma;\ \sigma \Longrightarrow \{f(s_1\vartheta, \ldots, s_n\vartheta) \ll t\} \cup \Gamma\vartheta;\ \sigma\vartheta,$$

where $\vartheta = \{\overline{x} \mapsto \ulcorner \urcorner\}$.

W: Widening

$$\{f(\overline{x}, s_1, \ldots, s_n) \ll f(t, t_1, \ldots, t_m)\} \cup \Gamma;\ \sigma$$
$$\Longrightarrow \{f(\overline{x}, s_1\vartheta, \ldots, s_n\vartheta) \ll f(t_1, \ldots, t_m)\} \cup \Gamma\vartheta;\ \sigma\vartheta, \text{ where } \vartheta = \{\overline{x} \mapsto \ulcorner t, \overline{x} \urcorner\}.$$

CVD: Context Variable Deletion

$$\{\overline{C}(s) \ll t\} \cup \Gamma;\ \sigma \Longrightarrow \{s\vartheta \ll t\} \cup \Gamma\vartheta;\ \sigma\vartheta, \qquad \text{where } \vartheta = \{\overline{C} \mapsto \circ\}.$$

D: Deepening

$$\{\overline{C}(s) \ll f(t_1, \ldots, t_m)\} \cup \Gamma;\ \sigma \Longrightarrow \{\overline{C}(s\vartheta) \ll t_j\} \cup \Gamma\vartheta;\ \sigma\vartheta,$$

where $\vartheta = \{\overline{C} \mapsto f(t_1, \ldots, t_{j-1}, \overline{C}(\circ), t_{j+1}, \ldots, t_m)\}$ for some $1 \leq j \leq m$, and $m > 0$.

SC: Symbol Clash

$$\{f(s_1, \ldots, s_n) \ll g(t_1, \ldots, t_m)\} \cup \Gamma;\ \sigma \Longrightarrow \bot, \qquad \text{if } f \notin \mathcal{V}_{\mathrm{Con}} \cup \mathcal{V}_{\mathrm{Fun}} \text{ and } f \neq g.$$

AD: Arity Disagreement

$$\{f(s_1, \ldots, s_n) \ll f(t_1, \ldots, t_m)\} \cup \Gamma;\ \sigma \Longrightarrow \bot,$$

if $m \neq n$ and $s_i \notin \mathcal{V}_{\mathrm{Seq}}$ for all $1 \leq i \leq n$, or $m = 0$ and $s_i \notin \mathcal{V}_{\mathrm{Seq}}$ for some $1 < i \leq n$.

We may use the rule name abbreviations as subscripts, e.g. $\Gamma_1; \sigma_1 \Longrightarrow_{\mathrm{T}} \Gamma_2; \sigma_2$ for the Trivial rule. SVD, W, CVD, and D are non-deterministic rules. A *derivation* is a sequence $\Gamma_1; \sigma_1 \Longrightarrow \Gamma_2; \sigma_2 \Longrightarrow \cdots$ of system transformations.

Definition 1. *A* CSM *algorithm* $\mathfrak{M}$ *is any program that takes a system* $\Gamma; \varepsilon$ *as input and uses the rules in* $\mathfrak{I}$ *to generate a complete tree of derivations, called the* matching tree for Γ, *in the following way:*

1. *The root of the tree is labeled with* $\Gamma; \varepsilon$.
2. *Each branch of the tree is a derivation. The nodes in the tree are systems.*
3. *If several transformation rules, or different instances of the same transformation rule are applicable to a node in the tree, they are applied concurrently. No rules are applicable to the leaves.*

The algorithm $\mathfrak{M}$ was first introduced in [29]. The leaves of a matching tree are labeled either with the systems of the form $\emptyset; \sigma$ or with $\bot$. The branches that end with $\emptyset; \sigma$ are *successful branches*, and those that end with $\bot$ are *failed branches*. We denote by $\mathcal{S}ol_{\mathfrak{M}}(\Gamma)$ the solution set of Γ generated by $\mathfrak{M}$, i.e., the set of all σ's such that $\emptyset; \sigma$ is a leaf of the matching tree for Γ.

Theorem 1. *The matching algorithm* $\mathfrak{M}$ *terminates for any input problem* Γ *and generates a minimal complete set of matchers of* Γ.

Moreover, $\mathfrak{M}$ never computes the same matcher twice. If we are not interested in bindings for certain variables, we can replace them with the anonymous variables: "$\_$" for any individual or function variable, and "$\_\_$" for any sequence or context variable. It is straightforward to adapt the rules in $\mathfrak{I}$ to such cases: If an anonymous variable occurs in the rule IVE, FVE, SVD, W, CVD, or D then the substitution ϑ in the same rule is ε. Strictly speaking, if $\{s \ll t\}$ is a CSM problem where s contains anonymous variables and ϑ is a solution computed by the adapted version of the algorithm then $s\vartheta$ is not identical to t (because it still contains anonymous variables) but is embedded in t.

We can use (the adapted form of) $\mathfrak{M}$ for multi-slot information extraction from data by nonlinear queries (cf. e.g. [38]):

Example 2. Solving the CSM problem

$$\{\overline{C}(F(\_\_, \overline{D}(f(x)), \_\_, \overline{E}(f(x)), \_\_)) \ll f(g(b, f(a), f(a)), f(b), f(a))\}$$

by $\mathfrak{M}$ gives three solutions:

$$\{\overline{C} \mapsto \circ, \overline{D} \mapsto g(b, \circ, f(a)), \overline{E} \mapsto \circ, F \mapsto f, x \mapsto a\},$$
$$\{\overline{C} \mapsto \circ, \overline{D} \mapsto g(b, f(a), \circ), \overline{E} \mapsto \circ, F \mapsto f, x \mapsto a\},$$
$$\{\overline{C} \mapsto f(\circ, f(b), f(a)), \overline{D} \mapsto \circ, \overline{E} \mapsto \circ, F \mapsto g, x \mapsto a\}.$$

It extracts contexts under which two equal subtrees of the form $f(x)$ are located. With the help of function variables one can also extract contexts under which two equal leaves lie: $\{\overline{C}(F(\_\_, \overline{D}(G()), \_\_, \overline{E}(G()), \_\_)) \ll f(g(a, b), a)\}$ returns $\{\overline{C} \mapsto \circ, \overline{D} \mapsto g(\circ, b), \overline{E} \mapsto \circ, F \mapsto f, G \mapsto a\}$ (remember that $a() = a$).

The algorithm $\mathfrak{M}$ can be further optimized by detecting failure early and avoiding branching whenever possible. Below we consider some of the methods to achieve this. Let $s \ll t$ be a CSM equation where $s = f(s_1, \ldots, s_n)$ and $t = f(t_1, \ldots, t_m)$. Then $s \ll t$ fails if any of the following matching pretests succeeds:

1. The number of symbol occurrences N different from context and sequence variables in s is greater than that in t. For instance, if $s = f(\overline{C}(a), F(x), \overline{y})$ and $t = f(a, a)$, then $N(s) = 4$, $N(t) = 3$ and, hence, $s \ll t$ fails.
2. If s contains a function symbol that does not occur in t like, for instance, for $s = f(\overline{x}, \overline{C}(a), b)$ and $t = f(c, b)$ where a does not occur in t.
3. If the sequence of heads of s's is not a subsequence of the sequence of heads of t's. This is the case, for instance, for $s = f(\overline{C}(a), g(x), \overline{x}, g(y))$ and $t = f(a, g(a), f(a))$, where the sequence g, g is not a subsequence of a, g, f.
4. If the minimum depth of s is greater than the depth of t. The minimum depth of a term is computed as the depth without context variables. For instance, the minimum depth of $s = f(f(\overline{C}(F(\overline{x}, f(a)))), g(a, f(x)))$ is 4, and s does not match $t = f(f(a, f(a)), g(a, f(b)))$ whose depth is 3.

Various such pretests are known in the term indexing literature; see, e.g. [42].

Branching is caused by context and sequence variables that permit multiple bindings. It happens in the rules SVD, W, CVD, and D. In certain cases backtracking can be avoided if we can detect the right binding early enough. For instance, for the matching equation $f(\overline{x}) \ll f(a, b, c)$ we can compute the solution $\{\overline{x} \mapsto \ulcorner a, b, c \urcorner\}$ immediately instead of applying the rule W three times and then SVD once. Therefore, a good heuristics would be first, to select such equations as early as possible, and second, to facilitate generating such equations. To achieve the latter whenever possible, we introduce the following two rules:

Sp: **Splitting**

$$\{f(\overline{x}, s_1, \ldots, s_i, \ldots, s_n) \ll f(t_1, \ldots, t_j, \ldots, t_m)\} \cup \Gamma; \ \sigma \Longrightarrow$$
$$\{f(\overline{x}, s_1, \ldots, s_{i-1}) \ll f(t_1, \ldots, t_{j-1}), s_i \ll t_j,$$
$$f(s_{i+1}, \ldots, s_n) \ll f(t_{j+1}, \ldots, t_m)\} \cup \Gamma; \ \sigma, \text{ where } head(s_i) = head(t_j).$$

TID: **Tail Decomposition**

$$\{f(\overline{x}, s_1, \ldots, s_{i-1}, \overline{y}, s_{i+1}, \ldots, s_n) \ll f(t_1, \ldots, t_j, \ldots, t_m)\} \cup \Gamma; \ \sigma \Longrightarrow$$
$$\{f(\overline{x}, s_1, \ldots, s_{i-1}, \overline{y}) \ll f(t_1, \ldots, t_j), s_{i+1} \ll t_{j+1}, \ldots, s_n \ll t_m\} \cup \Gamma; \ \sigma,$$

if $s_k \notin \mathcal{V}_{\mathsf{Seq}}$ for all $i < k \leq n$ and $n - i = m - j$.

Note that Sp still introduces branching because there can be several choices of s_i and t_j. (Branching factor can be reduced by tailoring early failure pretests into Sp.) Applying Sp and TID eagerly together with early failure detection tests and the deterministic rules from $\mathfrak{J}$ eventually generates CSM problems where sequence variables occur in the equations like $f(\overline{x}) \ll t$ and $f(\overline{x}, s_1, \ldots, s_n, \overline{y}) \ll t$. Here s's are variables or have function or context variables in the topmost position. The equations of the former type can be solved immediately, while the latter ones can be attacked either by SVD and W rules, or by eliminating sequence variables by Diophantine techniques. It can be done as follows: Let $f(s_1, \ldots, s_n) \ll f(t_1, \ldots, t_m)$ be a CSM problem, where $\overline{x}_1, \ldots, \overline{x}_k$ are all sequence variables among s's, and N_i is the number of occurrences of $\overline{x}_i$ (at the topmost level). We associate a linear Diophantine equation $\sum_{i=1}^{k} N_i X_i = m - n + k$ to each such CSM problem and solve it for X's over naturals. If the equation is unsolvable then the matching attempt fails. Otherwise, a solution l_i for each X_i specifies the length of sequence the variable $\overline{x}_i$ can be bound with. Therefore, we replace $f(s_1, \ldots, s_n) \ll f(t_1, \ldots, t_m)$ with new matching problems $f(s_i) \ll f(t_{j_i}, \ldots, t_{j_i+k_i})$ for each $1 \leq i \leq n$, where $j_1 = 1, j_{i+1} = j_i + k_i + 1, j_n + k_n = m$, $k_i = l_i - 1$ if s_i is a sequence variable, and $k_i = 0$ otherwise. Since linear Diophantine equations can have several solutions, this technique introduces a branching point. For instance, the matching problem $\{f(\overline{x}, \overline{y}) \ll f(a, b)\}$ will lead either to $\{f(\overline{x}) \ll f(), f(\overline{y}) \ll f(a, b)\}$, to $\{f(\overline{x}) \ll f(a), f(\overline{y}) \ll f(b)\}$, or to $\{f(\overline{x}) \ll f(a, b), f(\overline{y}) \ll f()\}$.

Although solving linear Diophantine equations over naturals is NP-complete, in practice it may still be useful to apply this technique for certain problems. Hence, in this way a CSM problem can essentially be reduced to matching with individual, context, and function variables. For such problems we can easily adapt context matching optimization techniques from [41] and add them to $\mathfrak{M}$.

4   Matching Algorithm with Regular Constraints

Regular expressions provide a powerful mechanism for restricting data values. The classical approach to regular expression matching is based on automata. In this section we show that regular expression matching can be easily incorporated into the rule-based framework of CSM.

Regular expressions on terms are defined by the following grammar:

$$R ::= t \mid \ulcorner \urcorner \mid \ulcorner R_1, R_2 \urcorner \mid R_1 | R_2 \mid R^*,$$

where t is a term without holes, $\ulcorner \urcorner$ is the empty sequence, "," is concatenation, "|" is choice, and "*" is repetition (Kleene star). The operators are right-associative; "*" has the highest precedence, followed by "," and "|".

Substitutions are extended to regular expressions on terms in the usual way: $\ulcorner \urcorner \sigma = \ulcorner \urcorner$, $\ulcorner R_1, R_2 \urcorner \sigma = \ulcorner R_1 \sigma, R_2 \sigma \urcorner$, $(R_1 | R_2)\sigma = R_1 \sigma | R_2 \sigma$, and $R^* \sigma = (R\sigma)^*$. Each regular expression on terms R defines the corresponding regular language $L(R)$.

Regular expressions on contexts are defined as follows:

$$Q ::= C \mid \ulcorner Q_1, Q_2 \urcorner \mid Q_1 | Q_2 \mid Q^*.$$

Like for regular expressions on terms, substitutions are extended to regular expressions on contexts in the usual way. Each regular expression on contexts Q defines the corresponding regular tree language $L(Q)$ as follows:

$$L(C) = \{C\}.$$
$$L(\ulcorner Q_1, Q_2 \urcorner) = \{C_1[C_2] \mid C_1 \in L(Q_1) \text{ and } C_2 \in L(Q_2)\}.$$
$$L(Q_1 | Q_2) = L(Q_1) \cup L(Q_2).$$
$$L(Q^*) = \{\circ\} \cup L(\ulcorner Q, Q^* \urcorner).$$

Membership atoms are atoms of the form Ts in R or Cv in Q, where Ts is a finite, possibly empty, sequence of terms, and Cv is either a context or a context variable. *Regular constraints* are pairs (p, f) where p is a membership atom and f is a flag that is a boolean expression (with the possible values 0 or 1). The intuition behind the regular constraint (Ts in R, f) is that $Ts \in L(R) \setminus \{\ulcorner \urcorner\}$ for $f = 1$ and $Ts \in L(R)$ for $f = 0$.[2] Similarly, the intuition behind (Cv in Q, g) is that $Cv \in L(Q) \setminus \{\circ\}$ for $g = 1$ and $Cv \in L(Q)$ for $g = 0$. It will be needed later to guarantee that the regular matching algorithm terminates. Substitutions are extended to regular constraints in the usual way. A *regular* CSM *problem* is a multiset of matching equations and regular constraints of the form:

$$\{s_1 \ll t_1, \ldots, s_n \ll t_n, (\overline{x}_1 \text{ in } R_1, f_1), \ldots, (\overline{x}_m \text{ in } R_m, f_m),$$
$$(\overline{C}_1 \text{ in } Q_1, g_1), \ldots, (\overline{C}_k \text{ in } Q_k, g_k)\},$$

---

[2] Note that (Ts in R^*, 1) does not have the same meaning as (Ts in $\ulcorner R, R^* \urcorner$, 0): Just take a^* as R.

where all $\overline{x}$'s and all $\overline{C}$'s are distinct and do not occur in R's and Q's.[3] We will assume that all $\overline{x}$'s and $\overline{C}$'s occur in the matching equations. A substitution σ is called a *regular matcher* for such a problem if $s_i\sigma = t_i$, $\mathbf{f}_j\sigma \in \{0,1\}$, $\mathbf{Q}_l\sigma \in \{0,1\}$, $\overline{x}_j\sigma \in L(\mathbf{R}_j\sigma)_{\mathbf{f}_j\sigma}$, and $\overline{C}_l\sigma \in L(\mathbf{Q}_l\sigma)_{\mathbf{g}_l\sigma}$ for all $1 \leq i \leq n$, $1 \leq j \leq m$, and $1 \leq l \leq k$, where $L(\mathbf{R})_0 = L(\mathbf{R})$, $L(\mathbf{R})_1 = L(\mathbf{R}) \setminus \{\ulcorner\urcorner\}$, $L(\mathbf{Q})_0 = L(\mathbf{Q})$, and $L(\mathbf{Q})_1 = L(\mathbf{Q}) \setminus \{\circ\}$.

A straightforward way to solve regular CSM problems would be first computing matchers and then testing whether the values of constrained variables satisfy the corresponding constraints. Testing can be done by automata constructed from regular expressions for each computed matcher. (Since regular expressions contain variables that get instantiated during the matching process, the automata would be different for each matcher.) Below we propose a different approach that saves the effort of solution testing. We construct an algorithm that computes the correct answers directly. Another advantage of this approach is that we are not restricted to linear regular expressions.

We define the inference system $\mathfrak{I}_R$ to solve regular CSM problems. It operates on systems $\Gamma; \sigma$ where Γ is a regular CSM problem and σ is a substitution. The system $\mathfrak{I}_R$ includes all the rules from the system $\mathfrak{I}$, but SVD, W, CVD, and D need an extra condition on applicability: For the variables $\overline{x}$ and $\overline{C}$ in those rules there should be no regular constraint ($\overline{x}$ in R, f) and ($\overline{C}$ in Q, g) in the matching problem. There are additional rules in $\mathfrak{I}_R$ for the variables constrained by regular constraints listed below. For the function symbols NonEmptySeq, NonEmptyCtx, and $\oplus$ used in these rules the following equalities hold: NonEmptySeq() $= 0$ and NonEmptySeq($r_1,\ldots,r_n$) $= 1$ if $r_i \notin \mathcal{V}_{\text{Seq}}$ for some $1 \leq i \leq n$; NonEmptyCtx($\circ$) $= 0$ and NonEmptyCtx(C) $= 1$ if the context C contains at least one symbol different from context variables and the hole constant; $0 \oplus 0 = 1 \oplus 1 = 0$ and $1 \oplus 0 = 0 \oplus 1 = 1$.

ESRET: Empty Sequence in a Regular Expression for Terms

$$\{f(\overline{x}, s_1, \ldots, s_n) \ll t, (\overline{x} \text{ in } \ulcorner\urcorner, \mathbf{f})\} \cup \Gamma; \ \sigma$$
$$\Longrightarrow \begin{cases} \{f(\overline{x}, s_1, \ldots, s_n)\vartheta \ll t\} \cup \Gamma\vartheta; \ \sigma\vartheta, \text{ with } \vartheta = \{\overline{x} \mapsto \ulcorner\urcorner\} & \text{if } \mathbf{f} = 0, \\ \bot & \text{if } \mathbf{f} = 1. \end{cases}$$

TRET: Term in a Regular Expression for Terms

$$\{f(\overline{x}, s_1, \ldots, s_n) \ll t, (\overline{x} \text{ in } s, \mathbf{f})\} \cup \Gamma; \ \sigma$$
$$\Longrightarrow \{f(\overline{x}, s_1, \ldots, s_n)\vartheta \ll t\} \cup \Gamma\vartheta; \ \sigma\vartheta, \quad \text{where } \vartheta = \{\overline{x} \mapsto s\} \text{ and } s \notin \mathcal{V}_{\text{Seq}}.$$

SVRET: Sequence Variable in a Regular Expression for Terms

$$\{f(\overline{x}, s_1, \ldots, s_n) \ll t, (\overline{x} \text{ in } \overline{y}, \mathbf{f})\} \cup \Gamma; \ \sigma \Longrightarrow \{f(\overline{x}, s_1, \ldots, s_n)\vartheta \ll t\} \cup \Gamma\vartheta; \ \sigma\vartheta,$$

where $\vartheta = \{\overline{x} \mapsto \overline{y}\}$ if $\mathbf{f} = 0$. If $\mathbf{f} = 1$ then $\vartheta = \{\overline{x} \mapsto \ulcorner y, \overline{y}\urcorner, \ \overline{y} \mapsto \ulcorner y, \overline{y}\urcorner\}$ where y is a fresh variable.

ChRET: Choice in a Regular Expression for Terms

$$\{f(\overline{x}, s_1, \ldots, s_n) \ll t, (\overline{x} \text{ in } \mathbf{R}_1|\mathbf{R}_2, \mathbf{f})\} \cup \Gamma; \ \sigma$$
$$\Longrightarrow \{f(\overline{x}, s_1, \ldots, s_n) \ll t, (\overline{x} \text{ in } \mathbf{R}_i, \mathbf{f})\} \cup \Gamma; \ \sigma, \text{ for } i = 1, 2.$$

---

[3] This restriction can be relaxed allowing occurrences without cycles.

CRET: Concatenation in a Regular Expression for Terms

$$\{f(\overline{x}, s_1, \ldots, s_n) \ll t, \ (\overline{x} \text{ in } \ulcorner R_1, R_2 \urcorner, f)\} \cup \Gamma; \ \sigma$$
$$\implies \{f(\overline{x}, s_1, \ldots, s_n)\vartheta \ll t, \ (\overline{y}_1 \text{ in } R_1, f_1), (\overline{y}_2 \text{ in } R_2, f_2)\} \cup \Gamma\vartheta; \ \sigma\vartheta,$$

where $\overline{y}_1$ and $\overline{y}_2$ are fresh variables, $\vartheta = \{\overline{x} \mapsto \ulcorner \overline{y}_1, \overline{y}_2 \urcorner\}$, and f_1 and f_2 are computed as follows: If $f = 0$ then $f_1 = f_2 = 0$ else $f_1 = 0$ and $f_2 = \text{NonEmptySeq}(\overline{y}_1) \oplus 1$.

RRET1: Repetition in a Regular Expression for Terms 1

$$\{f(\overline{x}, s_1, \ldots, s_n) \ll t, \ (\overline{x} \text{ in } R^*, 0)\} \cup \Gamma; \ \sigma$$
$$\implies \{f(\overline{x}, s_1, \ldots, s_n)\vartheta \ll t\} \cup \Gamma\vartheta; \ \sigma\vartheta, \text{ where } \vartheta = \{\overline{x} \mapsto \ulcorner \urcorner\}.$$

RRET2: Repetition in a Regular Expression for Terms 2

$$\{f(\overline{x}, s_1, \ldots, s_n) \ll t, \ (\overline{x} \text{ in } R^*, f)\} \cup \Gamma; \ \sigma$$
$$\implies \{f(\overline{x}, s_1, \ldots, s_n)\vartheta \ll t, \ (\overline{y} \text{ in } R, 1), \ (\overline{x} \text{ in } R^*, 0)\} \cup \Gamma\vartheta; \ \sigma\vartheta,$$

where y is a fresh variable and $\vartheta = \{\overline{x} \mapsto \ulcorner \overline{y}, \overline{x} \urcorner\}$.

HREC: Hole in a Regular Expression for Contexts

$$\{\overline{C}(s) \ll t, \ (\overline{C} \text{ in } \circ, g)\} \cup \Gamma; \ \sigma$$
$$\implies \begin{cases} \{\overline{C}(s)\vartheta \ll t\} \cup \Gamma\vartheta; \ \sigma\vartheta, \text{ with } \vartheta = \{\overline{C} \mapsto \circ\} & \text{if } g = 0, \\ \bot & \text{if } g = 1. \end{cases}$$

CxREC: Context in a Regular Expression for Contexts

$$\{\overline{C}(s) \ll t, \ (\overline{C} \text{ in } C, g)\} \cup \Gamma; \ \sigma \implies \{\overline{C}(s)\vartheta \ll t\} \cup \Gamma\vartheta; \ \sigma\vartheta,$$

where $C \neq \circ$, $head(C) \notin \mathcal{V}_{\text{Con}}$, and $\vartheta = \{\overline{C} \mapsto C\}$.

CVREC: Context Variable in a Regular Expression for Contexts

$$\{\overline{C}(s) \ll t, \ (\overline{C} \text{ in } \overline{D}(\circ), g)\} \cup \Gamma; \ \sigma \implies \{\overline{C}(s)\vartheta \ll t\} \cup \Gamma\vartheta; \ \sigma\vartheta,$$

where $\vartheta = \{\overline{C} \mapsto \overline{D}(\circ)\}$ if $g = 0$. If $g = 1$ then $\vartheta = \{\overline{C} \mapsto F(\overline{x}, \overline{D}(\circ), \overline{y}), \ \overline{D} \mapsto F(\overline{x}, \overline{D}(\circ), \overline{y})\}$, where $F, \overline{x}$, and $\overline{y}$ are fresh variables.

ChREC: Choice in a Regular Expression for Contexts

$$\{\overline{C}(s) \ll t, \ (\overline{C} \text{ in } Q_1|Q_2, g)\} \cup \Gamma; \ \sigma \implies \{\overline{C}(s) \ll t, \ (\overline{C} \text{ in } Q_i, g)\} \cup \Gamma; \ \sigma,$$

for $i = 1, 2$.

CREC: Concatenation in a Regular Expression for Contexts

$$\{\overline{C}(s) \ll t, \ (\overline{C} \text{ in } \ulcorner Q_1, Q_2 \urcorner, g)\} \cup \Gamma; \ \sigma$$
$$\implies \{\overline{C}(s)\vartheta \ll t, \ (\overline{D}_1 \text{ in } Q_1, g_1), (\overline{D}_2 \text{ in } Q_2, g_2)\} \cup \Gamma\vartheta; \ \sigma\vartheta,$$

where $\overline{D}_1$ and $\overline{D}_2$ are fresh variables, $\vartheta = \{\overline{C} \mapsto \overline{D}_1(\overline{D}_2(\circ))\}$, and g_1 and g_2 are computed as follows: If $g = 0$ then $g_1 = g_2 = 0$ else $g_1 = 0$ and $g_2 = \text{NonEmptyCtx}(\overline{D}_1) \oplus 1$.

RREC1: Repetition in a Regular Expression for Contexts 1

$$\{\overline{C}(s) \ll t, \ (\overline{C} \text{ in } Q^*, 0)\} \cup \Gamma; \ \sigma$$
$$\implies \{\overline{C}(s)\vartheta \ll t\} \cup \Gamma\vartheta; \ \sigma\vartheta, \text{ where } \vartheta = \{\overline{C} \mapsto \circ\}.$$

RREC2: Repetition in a Regular Expression for Contexts 2

$$\{\overline{C}(s) \ll t, \ (\overline{C} \text{ in } Q^*, g)\} \cup \Gamma; \ \sigma$$
$$\implies \{\overline{C}(s)\vartheta \ll t, \ (\overline{D} \text{ in } Q, 1), \ (\overline{C} \text{ in } Q^*, 0)\} \cup \Gamma\vartheta; \ \sigma\vartheta,$$

where $\overline{D}$ is a fresh variable and $\vartheta = \{\overline{C} \mapsto \overline{D}(\overline{C}(\circ))\}$.

A regular CSM algorithm $\mathfrak{M}_R$ is defined in a similar way to the algorithm $\mathfrak{M}$ (Definition 1) with the only difference that the rules of $\mathfrak{I}_R$ are used instead of the rules of $\mathfrak{I}$. From the beginning, each flag in the input problem is set either to 0 or to 1. Note that the rules in $\mathfrak{I}_R$ work either on a selected matching equation, or on a selected pair of a matching equation and a regular constraint. No rule selects a regular constraint alone. We denote by $Sol_{\mathfrak{M}_R}(\Gamma)$ the solution set of Γ generated by $\mathfrak{M}_R$. The following theorems show that $\mathfrak{M}_R$ is sound, terminating, and complete.

Theorem 2 (Soundness of $\mathfrak{M}_R$). *Let Γ be a regular CSM problem. Then every substitution $\sigma \in Sol_{\mathfrak{M}_R}(\Gamma)$ is a regular matcher of Γ.*

Theorem 3 (Termination of $\mathfrak{M}_R$). *$\mathfrak{M}_R$ terminates on any input.*

Theorem 4 (Completeness of $\mathfrak{M}_R$). *Let Γ be a regular CSM problem, ϑ be a regular matcher of Γ, and $\mathcal{V}$ be a variable set of Γ. Then there exists a substitution $\sigma \in Sol_{\mathfrak{M}_R}$ such that $\sigma \leq^{\mathcal{V}} \vartheta$.*

We can adapt $\mathfrak{M}_R$ to anonymous variables like we did for $\mathfrak{M}$. However, a remark has to be made about using anonymous variables in regular expressions with Kleene star. There they behave differently from named singleton variables and play a similar role as, for instance, the pattern Any in [24]. The reason is that the variables that had only one occurrence in the matching problem (in an expression with Kleene star) will have two occurrences after the application of the RRET2 and RREC2 rules, while duplicated anonymous variables are not considered to be the same. It affects solvability. For instance, the regular CSM problem $\{f(\overline{x}) \ll f(g(a), g(b)), (\overline{x} \text{ in } g(\_)^*, 0)\}$ has a solution $\{\overline{x} \mapsto \ulcorner g(a), g(b) \urcorner\}$ while the problem $\{f(\overline{x}) \ll f(g(a), g(b)), (\overline{x} \text{ in } g(x)^*, 0)\}$ is unsolvable because it is reduced to $\{f(\overline{x}) \ll f(g(b)), (\overline{x} \text{ in } g(a)^*, 0)\}$. In general, the notion of a *regular matcher* for regular CSM problems with anonymous variables has to be redefined: First, we write $s \preccurlyeq t$ iff the term s (maybe with holes) whose only variables are anonymous variables can be made identical to the ground term t (maybe with holes) by replacing anonymous variables in s with the corresponding expressions (terms, term sequences, function symbols, contexts) and applying contexts as long as possible. For instance, $f(\_, \_\_(\_(\circ, \_\_, a)), \_\_) \preccurlyeq f(a, f(b, g(\circ, \circ, b, a)), c)$. Next, we write $\ulcorner t_1, \ldots, t_n \urcorner \dot{\in} S$ iff there exists $\ulcorner s_1, \ldots, s_n \urcorner \in S$ such that $s_i \preccurlyeq t_i$ for each $1 \leq i \leq n$. Now, let a regular CSM problem be $\{s_1 \ll t_1, \ldots, s_n \ll t_n, (\overline{x}_1 \text{ in } \mathtt{R}_1, \mathtt{f}_1), \ldots, (\overline{x}_m \text{ in } \mathtt{R}_m, \mathtt{f}_m), (\overline{C}_1 \text{ in } \mathtt{Q}_1, \mathtt{g}_1), \ldots, (\overline{C}_k \text{ in } \mathtt{Q}_k, \mathtt{g}_k)\}$, where s's, $\mathtt{R}$'s, and $\mathtt{Q}$'s may contain anonymous variables. A substitution σ is a regular matcher for such a problem if $s_i\sigma \preccurlyeq t_i$, $\mathtt{f}_j\sigma \in \{0, 1\}$, $\mathtt{Q}_l\sigma \in \{0, 1\}$, $\overline{x}_j\sigma \dot{\in} L(\mathtt{R}_j\sigma)_{\mathtt{f}_j\sigma}$, and $\overline{C}_l\sigma \dot{\in} L(\mathtt{Q}_l\sigma)_{\mathtt{g}_l\sigma}$ for all $1 \leq i \leq n$, $1 \leq j \leq m$, and $1 \leq l \leq k$, where the only variables in $s_i\sigma, \mathtt{R}_j\sigma$, and in $\mathtt{Q}_l\sigma$ are anonymous variables. For instance, $\{\overline{x} \mapsto \ulcorner g(a), g(b) \urcorner, x \mapsto c, \overline{C} \mapsto f(g(\circ))\}$ is a regular matcher for the matching problem $\{f(\overline{x}, \overline{C}(x), \_) \ll f(g(a), g(b), f(g(c)), d), (\overline{x} \text{ in } g(\_)^*, 0), (\overline{C} \text{ in } f(\_, g(\circ), \_), 0)\}$.

Special failure detection tests can be incorporated into $\mathfrak{M}_R$. For instance, we can add the rule $\{f(\overline{x}, s_1, \ldots, s_n) \ll f(), (\overline{x} \text{ in } \mathtt{R}, 1)\} \cup \Gamma; \sigma \Longrightarrow \bot$.

Note that for a problem Γ there might be $\sigma, \vartheta \in \mathcal{S}ol_{\mathfrak{M}_R}(\Gamma)$ such that $v\sigma = v\vartheta$ for all v in the set of variables of Γ. This is the case, for instance, for $\{f(\overline{x}) \ll f(a, b, b, a), (\overline{x} \text{ in } \ulcorner a^*, b^{*\urcorner*}, 0)\}$ and $\{\overline{C}(a) \ll f(g(a), f(a)), (\overline{C} \text{ in } (f(\_, \circ, \_)^* | g(\_, \circ, \_)^*)^*, 0)\}$. It can be avoided by replacing regular expressions with the equivalent "disambiguated" ones like, e.g. star normal forms [5]. Such an equivalent formulation for the matching problems above are $\{f(\overline{x}) \ll f(a, b, b, a), \overline{x} \text{ in } ((a|b)^*, 0)\}$ and $\{\overline{C}(a) \ll f(g(a), f(a)), (\overline{C} \text{ in } (f(\_, \circ, \_)| g(\_, \circ, \_))^*, 0)\}$.

As syntactic sugar for regular context expressions, we let function symbols, function variables, and context variables be used as the basic building blocks for regular expressions. Such regular expressions are understood as abbreviations for the corresponding regular expressions on contexts. For example, $\ulcorner F, f | \ulcorner \overline{C}, g \urcorner^{*\urcorner}$ abbreviates $\ulcorner F(\_, \circ, \_), f(\_, \circ, \_) | \ulcorner \overline{C}(\circ), g(\_, \circ, \_) \urcorner^{*\urcorner}$. Answer substitutions can also be modified correspondingly. In this way $\mathfrak{M}_R$ will understand the regular path expression syntax.

5   Applications

CSM is the main pattern matching mechanism in the rule-based programming system ρLog [33,35]. ρLog supports strategic programming with deterministic (labeled) conditional transformation rules, matching with regular constraints, and is built on top of the Mathematica system. As an example, we show a ρLog clause (in a conventional notation) that implements rewriting: $\overline{C}(x) \rightarrow_{\text{rewrite}(z)} \overline{C}(y) \Leftarrow x \rightarrow_z y$. Assume that we have another clause $a \rightarrow_r b$ that defines the rule labeled by r. Then the query $f(a, a) \rightarrow_{\text{rewrite}(r)} x$ (read: find such an x to which $f(a, a)$ can be rewritten by r) succeeds twice: with $x = f(b, a)$ and $x = f(a, b)$. The order in which these answers are generated (and, hence, the term traversal strategy) is defined by the order of matching rules in CSM that compute bindings for $\overline{C}$.

Another ρLog example is the program that from a given term selects subterms whose nodes are all labeled with a. It consists of the following three clauses $\_\_(x) \rightarrow_{a\text{-subt}} x \Leftarrow x \rightarrow_{\text{NF}[a\text{'s}]} true$, $a \rightarrow_{a\text{'s}} true$, $\overline{C}(a(a, \overline{x})) \rightarrow_{a\text{'s}} \overline{C}(a(\overline{x}))$, where NF is the ρLog strategy for a normal form computation.

CSM can be used to achieve more control on rewriting, to match program schemata with programs (cf. semi-unification [11], see also [9]), in Web site verification (e.g. in a rewriting-based framework similar to [1]), in XML querying, transformation, schema matching, and related areas. For this purpose (especially for XML related applications) we would need to extend our matching algorithm for *orderless* function symbols. (The orderless property generalizes commutativity for flexible arity function symbols.) Such functions are important for XML querying because the users often are not concerned with the actual order of elements in an XML document. A straightforward but inefficient way of dealing with orderless functions is to consider all possible permutations of their arguments and applying the CSM. To achieve a better performance one can carry over some known techniques from AC-matching to CSM with orderless functions.

In our opinion, a (conditional) rewriting-based query language that implements CSM with orderless functions would possess the advantages of both navigational (path-based) and positional (pattern-based) types of XML query languages. (See [18] for a recent survey on this topic.) It would easily support, for instance, a wide range of queries (selection and extraction, reduction, negation, restructuring, combination), parent-child and sibling relations and their closures, access by position, unordered matching, order-preserving result, partial and total queries, multiple results, and other properties. Moreover, the rule-based paradigm would provide a clean declarative semantics. As an example, we show how to express a reduction query. Reduction is one of the query operations described as desiderata for XML query languages in [32] and, according to [4], is a bottleneck for many of them. Let the XML data (translated into our syntax) consist of the elements of the form:

$$manufacturer(mn\text{-}name(Mercury), year(1999),$$
$$model(mo\text{-}name(SLT), front\text{-}rating(3.84), side\text{-}rating(2.14), rank(9)), \ldots).$$

The reduction query operation is formulated as follows: From the *manufacturer* elements drop those *model* sub-elements whose *rank* is greater than 10, and elide the *front-rating* and *side-rating* elements from the remaining models. It can be expressed as a rule $manufacturer(\overline{x}) \to_{\mathrm{NF[Reduce]}} y$ that evaluates as follows: Its left hand side matches the data, the obtained instance is rewritten into the normal form with respect to the rule Reduce, and the result is returned in y. Reduce is defined by two conditional rewrite rules:

$$manufacturer(\overline{x}_1, model(\_\_, rank(x), \_\_), \overline{x}_2)$$
$$\to_{\mathrm{Reduce}} manufacturer(\overline{x}_1, \overline{x}_2) \Leftarrow x > 10.$$
$$manufacturer(\overline{x}_1, model(\overline{y}_1, front\text{-}rating(\_), side\text{-}rating(\_), rank(x), \overline{y}_2), \overline{x}_2)$$
$$\to_{\mathrm{Reduce}} manufacturer(\overline{x}_1, model(\overline{y}_1, rank(x), \overline{y}_2), \overline{x}_2) \Leftarrow x \leq 10.$$

In general, we believe that such a language would be a good candidate to meet many of the requirements for versatile Web query languages [7]. At least, the core principles of referential transparency and answer-closedness, and incomplete queries and answers can be easily supported. As for dealing with nonhierarchical relations provided by, e.g. ID/IDREF links (that naturally asks for the graph data model), one could apply techniques of equational CSM to query such data. As an equational theory we could specify (oriented) equalities between constants representing IDREFs and terms that correspond to IDs. If such a theory can be turned into a convergent rewrite system, it would mean that the data it represents contains no cycles via ID/IDREFs. It would be interesting to study equational CSM in more details. Another interesting and useful future work would be to identify the types of matching problems that CSM can solve efficiently.

6   Related Work

Solving equations with context variables has been intensively investigated in the recent years; see e.g, [13,14,31,39,40,41]. Context matching is NP-complete.

Decidability of context unification is still an open question. Sequence matching and unification was addressed, for instance, in [3,20,23,26,27,28,34]. Sequence unification (and, hence, matching as well) is decidable.

There is a rich literature on matching with regular expressions, especially in the context of general-purpose programming languages and semistructured data querying. Regular expressions are supported in Perl, Emacs-Lisp, XDuce [25], CDuce [2], Xtatic [19], and in the languages based on XPath [12], just to name a few. Various automata-based approaches have been proposed for XML querying; see, e.g. [36,6,37,16,10]. Context matching is closely related to the evaluation of conjunctive queries over trees [22].

Hosoya and Pierce [25] propose regular expression pattern matching for developing convenient programming constructs for tree manipulation in a statically typed setting. Similar in spirit to ML style pattern matching, their algorithm uses regular expression types to dynamically match values. Patterns can be recursive (under certain restrictions that guarantee that the language remains regular). Recursion allows to write patterns that match, for instance, trees whose nodes are labeled with the same label. CSM does not allow recursion in regular constraints. That is why we needed three ρLog clauses above to solve the problem of selecting terms with all a-labeled nodes. Patterns of Hosoya and Pierce are restricted to be linear. We do not have such a restriction. In general, non-linearity is one of the main difficulties for tree automata-based approaches [15]. Niehren et al [38] use tree automata for multi-slot information extraction from semistructured data. The automata are restricted to be unambiguous that limits n-ary queries to finite unions of Cartesian closed queries (Cartesian products of monadic queries), but this restricted case is processed efficiently. For monadic queries an efficient and expressive information extraction approach, monadic Datalog, was proposed by Gottlob and Koch [21].

Simulation unification [8] uses the *descendant* construct that is similar to context variables in the sense that it allows us to descend in terms to arbitrary depth, but it does not allow regular expressions along it. Also, sequence variables are not present there. However, it can process unordered and incomplete queries, and it is a full scale unification, not a matching.

Our technique of using flags in constraints to guarantee termination is similar to that of Frisch and Cardelli [17] for dealing with ambiguity in matching sequences against regular expressions.

7   Conclusions

We described a sound, complete and terminating matching algorithm for terms built over flexible arity function symbols and context, sequence, function, and individual variables. Values of some context and sequence variables can be constrained by regular expressions. The constraints are not restricted to be linear. We discussed ways to optimize the main algorithm as well as some of the possible applications. Interesting future developments would be the complexity analysis of the algorithm and extending CSM for equational case.

References

1. M. Alpuente, D. Ballis, and M. Falaschi. A rewriting-based framework for web sites verification. *Electr. Notes on Theoretical Comp. Science*, 124(1):41–61, 2005.
2. V. Benzaken, G. Castagna, and A. Frisch. CDuce: an XML-centric general-purpose language. In *Proc. of ICFP'03*, pages 51–63. ACM, 2003.
3. H. Boley. *A Tight, Practical Integration of Relations and Functions*, volume 1712 of *LNAI*. Springer, 1999.
4. A. Bonifati and S. Ceri. Comparative analysis of five XML query languages. *ACM SIGMOD Record*, 29(1):68–79, 2000.
5. A. Brüggemann-Klein. Regular expressions into finite automata. *Theoretical Computer Science*, 120(2):197–213, 1993.
6. A. Brüggemann-Klein, M. Murata, and D. Wood. Regular tree and regular hedge languages over unranked alphabets. Technical Report HKUST-TCSC-2001-05, Hong Kong University of Science and Technology, 2001.
7. F. Bry, Ch. Koch, T. Furche, S. Schaffert, L. Badea, and S. Berger. Querying the web reconsidered: Design principles for versatile web query languages. *Int. J. Semantic Web Inf. Syst.*, 1(2):1–21, 2005.
8. F. Bry and S. Schaffert. Towards a declarative query and transformation language for XML and semistructured data: Simulation unification. In *Proc. of ICLP*, number 2401 in LNCS, Copenhagen, Denmark, 2002. Springer.
9. B. Buchberger and A. Crăciun. Algorithm synthesis by Lazy Thinking: Examples and implementation in Theorema. *Electr. Notes Theor. Comput. Sci.*, 93:24–59, 2004.
10. J. Carme, J. Niehren, and M. Tommasi. Querying unranked trees with stepwise tree automata. In V. van Oostrom, editor, *Proc. of RTA'04*, volume 3091 of *LNCS*, pages 105–118. Springer, 2004.
11. E. Chasseur and Y. Deville. Logic program schemas, constraints and semi-unification. In *Proc. of LOPSTR'97*, volume 1463 of *LNCS*, pages 69–89. Springer, 1998.
12. J. Clark and S. DeRose, editors. *XML Path Language (XPath) Version 1.0*. W3C, 1999. Available from: http://www.w3.org/TR/xpath/.
13. H. Comon. Completion of rewrite systems with membership constraints. Part I: Deduction rules. *J. Symbolic Computation*, 25(4):397–419, 1998.
14. H. Comon. Completion of rewrite systems with membership constraints. Part II: Constraint solving. *J. Symbolic Computation*, 25(4):421–453, 1998.
15. H. Comon, M. Dauchet, R. Gilleron, F. Jacquemard, D. Lugiez, S. Tison, and M. Tommasi. Tree automata techniques and applications. Available from: http://www.grappa.univ-lille3.fr/tata, 1997.
16. M. Frick, M. Grohe, and Ch. Koch. Query evaluation on compressed trees. In *Proc. of LICS'03*, pages 188–198. IEEE Computer Society, 2003.
17. A. Frisch and L. Cardelli. Greedy regular expression matching. In *Proc. of ICALP'04*, pages 618–629, 2004.
18. T. Furche, F. Bry, S. Schaffert, R. Orsini, I. Horroks, M. Kraus, and O. Bolzer. Survey over existing query and transformation languages. Available from: http://rewerse.net/deliverables/i4-d1.pdf, 2004.
19. V. Gapeyev and B. C. Pierce. Regular object types. In L. Cardelli, editor, *Proc. of ECOOP'03*, volume 2743 of *LNCS*, pages 151–175. Springer, 2003.
20. M. Ginsberg. The MVL theorem proving system. *SIGART Bull.*, 2(3):57–60, 1991.
21. G. Gottlob and Ch. Koch. Monadic Datalog and the expressive power of languages for web information retrieval. *J. ACM*, 51(1):74–113, 2004.

22. G. Gottlob, Ch. Koch, and K. Schulz. Conjunctive queries over trees. In A. Deutsch, editor, *Proc. of PODS'04*, pages 189–200. ACM, 2004.
23. M. Hamana. Term rewriting with sequences. In: Proc. of the First Int. *Theorema* Workshop. Technical report 97–20, RISC, Johannes Kepler University, Linz, 1997.
24. H. Hosoya. Regular expression pattern matching—a simpler design. Manuscript, 2003.
25. H. Hosoya and B. Pierce. Regular expression pattern matching for XML. *J. Functional Programming*, 13(6):961–1004, 2003.
26. T. Kutsia. *Solving and Proving in Equational Theories with Sequence Variables and Flexible Arity Symbols*. PhD thesis, Johannes Kepler University, Linz, 2002.
27. T. Kutsia. Unification with sequence variables and flexible arity symbols and its extension with pattern-terms. In J. Calmet, B. Benhamou, O. Caprotti, L. Henocque, and V. Sorge, editors, *Proc. of Joint AISC'2002—Calculemus'2002 Conference*, volume 2385 of *LNAI*, pages 290–304. Springer, 2002.
28. T. Kutsia. Solving equations involving sequence variables and sequence functions. In B. Buchberger and J. A. Campbell, editors, *Proc. of AISC'04*, volume 3249 of *LNAI*, pages 157–170. Springer, 2004.
29. T. Kutsia. Context sequence matching for XML. In M. Alpuente, S. Escobar, and M. Falaschi, editors, *Proc. of WWV'05*, pages 103–119, 2005. (Full version to appear in ENTCS).
30. T. Kutsia and M. Marin. Matching with regular constraints. Technical Report 05-05, RISC, Johannes Kepler University, Linz, 2005.
31. J. Levy and M. Villaret. Linear second-order unification and context unification with tree-regular constraints. In L. Bachmair, editor, *Proc. of RTA'2000*, volume 1833 of *LNCS*, pages 156–171. Springer, 2000.
32. D. Maier. Database desiderata for an XML query language. Available from: http://www.w3.org/TandS/QL/QL98/pp/maier.html, 1998.
33. M. Marin. Introducing ρLog. Available from: http://www.score.is.tsukuba.ac.jp/~mmarin/RhoLog/, 2005.
34. M. Marin and D. Ţepeneu. Programming with sequence variables: The *Sequentica* package. In *Proc. of the 5th Int.* Mathematica *Symposium*, pages 17–24, 2003.
35. M. Marin and T. Ida. Progress of ρLog, a rule-based programming system. In *7th Intl. Mathematica Symposium (IMS'05)*, Perth, Australia, 2005. To appear.
36. A. Neumann and H. Seidl. Locating matches of tree patterns in forests. In *Proc. of FSTTCS'98*, volume 1530 of *LNCS*, pages 134–145. Springer, 1998.
37. F. Neven and T. Schwentick. Query automata on finite trees. *Theoretical Computer Science*, 275:633–674, 2002.
38. J. Niehren, L. Planque, J.-M. Talbot, and S. Tison. N-ary queries by tree automata. In *Proc. of DBPL'05*, 2005.
39. M. Schmidt-Schauß. A decision algorithm for stratified context unification. *J. Logic and Computation*, 12(6):929–953, 2002.
40. M. Schmidt-Schauß and K. U. Schulz. Solvability of context equations with two context variables is decidable. *J. Symbolic Computation*, 33(1):77–122, 2002.
41. M. Schmidt-Schauß and J. Stuber. On the complexity of linear and stratified context matching problems. *Theory Comput. Systems*, 37:717–740, 2004.
42. R. C. Sekar, I. V. Ramakrishnan, and A. Voronkov. Term indexing. In J. A. Robinson and A. Voronkov, editors, *Handbook of Automated Reasoning*, pages 1853–1964. Elsevier and MIT Press, 2001.

Recursive Path Orderings
Can Also Be Incremental

Mirtha-Lina Fernández[1], Guillem Godoy[2], and Albert Rubio[2]

[1] Universidad de Oriente,
Santiago de Cuba, Cuba
mirtha@csd.uo.edu.cu
[2] Universitat Politècnica de Catalunya,
Barcelona, España
ggodoy,rubio@lsi.upc.edu

Abstract. In this paper the *Recursive Path Ordering* is adapted for proving termination of rewriting incrementally. The new ordering, called *Recursive Path Ordering with Modules*, has as ingredients not only a precedence but also an underlying ordering $\sqsupseteq_B$. It can be used for incremental (innermost) termination proofs of hierarchical unions by defining $\sqsupseteq_B$ as an extension of the termination proof obtained for the base system. Furthermore, there are practical situations in which such proofs can be done modularly.

1 Introduction

Term rewriting provides a simple (but Turing-complete) model for symbolic computation. A *term rewrite system* (TRS) is just a binary relation over the set of terms of a given signature. The pairs of the relation are used for computing by replacements until an irreducible term is eventually reached. Hence, the absence of infinite sequences of replacements, called *termination*, is a fundamental (though undecidable) property for most applications of rewriting in program verification and automated reasoning. For program verification, the termination of a particular rewriting strategy called innermost termination has special interest. In this strategy the replacements are performed inside-out, i.e. arguments are fully reduced before reducing the function. Therefore, it corresponds to the *"call by value"* computation rule of programming languages. This strategy is also important because for certain classes of TRSs, innermost termination and termination coincide [12].

Term rewrite systems are usually defined in hierarchies. This hierarchical structure is very important when reasoning about TRS properties in an incremental manner. Roughly, a property P is proved incrementally for a hierarchical TRS $\mathcal{R} = \mathcal{R}_0 \cup \mathcal{R}_1$ if we can prove it by using information from the proof of P for the base system $\mathcal{R}_0$. The simplest form of incrementality is modularity, i.e. proving P for $\mathcal{R}$ just by proving P for $\mathcal{R}_0$ and $\mathcal{R}_1$ independently. However, termination is not a modular property even for disjoint unions of TRSs [21]. A stronger form of termination, called $C_\mathcal{E}$-termination, and innermost termination,

G. Sutcliffe and A. Voronkov (Eds.): LPAR 2005, LNAI 3835, pp. 230–245, 2005.

are indeed modular for a restricted class of hierarchical unions [17, 14], but not in general. Therefore, it is of great importance to tackle (innermost) termination of hierarchical systems using an incremental approach.

Regardless the previous facts, the problem of ensuring termination of a hierarchical union without finding (if possible) an alternate proof for the base system has received quite few attention. The first and important step was done by Urbain in [22]. He showed that from the knowledge that a base system is $\mathcal{C}_\varepsilon$-terminating, the conditions for the termination proof of a hierarchical union can be relaxed. In the context of the *Dependency Pair method* (DP) [1] (the most successful for termination of rewriting) this entails a significant reduction in the number and the strictness of the DP-constraints. Very recently, Urbain's contribution was used for improving the application of the *Size-Change Principle* (SCP) [15] to $\mathcal{C}_\varepsilon$-termination of rewriting [10]. In the latter paper it was shown that a termination measure for a base system $\mathcal{R}_0$ can be used for proving size-change termination of a hierarchical extension $\mathcal{R}_1$, and this guarantees $\mathcal{R}_0 \cup \mathcal{R}_1$ is $\mathcal{C}_\varepsilon$-terminating. Using this result, the next TRS is easily (and even modularly) proved simply terminating.

Example 1. The following hierarchical union ($\mathcal{R}_{plus}$ is taken from [19]) can be used for computing Sudan's function[1].

$$\mathcal{R}_{plus} = \begin{cases} plus(s(s(x)), y) & \rightarrow & s(plus(x, s(y))) \\ plus(x, s(s(y))) & \rightarrow & s(plus(s(x), y)) \\ plus(s(0), y) & \rightarrow & s(y) \\ plus(0, y) & \rightarrow & y \end{cases}$$

$$\mathcal{R}_F = \begin{cases} F(0, x, y) & \rightarrow & plus(x, y) \\ F(s(n), x, 0) & \rightarrow & x \\ F(s(n), x, s(y)) & \rightarrow & F(n, F(s(n), x, y), s(plus(F(s(n), x, y), y))) \end{cases}$$

In order to prove termination of $\mathcal{R} = \mathcal{R}_{plus} \cup \mathcal{R}_F$ (when using the DP-approach) the whole union must be included in some (quasi-) ordering. But $\mathcal{R}_{plus}$ requires semantical comparisons while $\mathcal{R}_F$ needs lexicographic ones. Therefore, no (quasi-) ordering traditionally used for automated proofs serves for this purpose. However, simple termination of $\mathcal{R}_{plus}$ is easy to prove e.g. using the *Knuth-Bendix Ordering* (KBO) [3]. Besides, every size-change graph of $\mathcal{R}_F$ decreases w.r.t. the lexicographic extension of KBO. Thus, $\mathcal{R}_F$ is size-change terminating w.r.t. KBO and we conclude $\mathcal{R}$ is simply terminating.

SCP provides a more general comparison than lexicographic and multiset ones. But it has as main drawback that it cannot compare *defined* function symbols (i.e. those appearing as root of left-hand sides) syntactically.

---

[1] Chronologically, Sudan's function [7] is the first example of a recursive but not primitive recursive function. Sudan's function $F(p, m, n)$ is greater than or equal to Ackermann's function $A(p, m, n)$ except at the single point $(2, 0, 0)$. The latter was used in [19] combined with $\mathcal{R}_{plus}$.

Example 2. Let $\mathcal{R}_{F'} = \mathcal{R}_F \cup \{F(s(n), F(s(n), x, y), z) \rightarrow F(s(n), x, F(n, y, z))\}$. The new rule [6][Lemma 6.7, page 47] can be used for computing an upper bound of the left-hand side while decreasing the size of the term. But now SCP fails in proving termination of $\mathcal{R}_{plus} \cup \mathcal{R}_{F'}$. This is due to the new rule which demands a lexicographic comparison determined by a subterm rooted with the defined symbol F.

When dealing with defined symbols, SCP cannot compete with classical syntactical orderings like the *Recursive Path Ordering* [8]. Therefore, it would be nice to adapt RPO in order to prove termination of $\mathcal{R}_{plus} \cup \mathcal{R}_{F'}$ and other hierarchical systems incrementally.

In this paper we present a new RPO-like ordering which can be used for these purposes, called the *Recursive Path Ordering with Modules* (RPOM). It has as ingredients not only a precedence, but also an *underlying ordering* $\sqsupseteq_\mathcal{B}$.

Actually RPOM defines a class of orderings that can be partitioned into three subclasses, RPOM-STAB, RPOM-MON and RPOM-IP-MON, where, under certain conditions, the first one contains stable orderings, the second one contains monotonic orderings (or a weak form of monotonocity related to $\sqsupseteq_\mathcal{B}$), and the third one contains IP-monotonic orderings.

We use these orderings for proving $\mathcal{C}_\mathcal{E}$-termination and innermost termination of a hierarchical union $\mathcal{R} = \mathcal{R}_0 \cup \mathcal{R}_1$ incrementally as follows. The system $\mathcal{R}_0$ is known terminating, and perhaps an ordering $\succ_\mathcal{B}$ including the relation $\rightarrow_{\mathcal{R}_0}$ on terms of $\mathcal{T}(\mathcal{F}_0, \mathcal{X})$ is given. An ordering $\sqsupseteq_\mathcal{B}$ is then constructed, perhaps as an extension of $\succ_\mathcal{B}$ to $\mathcal{T}(\mathcal{F}, \mathcal{X})$, or perhaps independently of the possible $\succ_\mathcal{B}$. Three orderings from RPOM-STAB, RPOM-MON and RPOM-IP-MON are then obtained from $\sqsupseteq_\mathcal{B}$, satisfying that the one in RPOM-STAB is included into the one in RPOM-MON under some conditions on $\sqsupseteq_\mathcal{B}$ and $\mathcal{R}_0$, and into the one in RPOM-IP-MON under weaker conditions. Including $\mathcal{R}_1$ in RPOM-STAB will then allow to prove $\mathcal{C}_\mathcal{E}$-termination or innermost termination of $\mathcal{R}$ depending on the original properties of $\sqsupseteq_\mathcal{B}$ and $\mathcal{R}_0$. Note that, in the case of innermost termination, no condition at all is imposed on $\sqsupseteq_\mathcal{B}$ and $\mathcal{R}_0$.

Our results are a first step towards the definition of a general framework for combining and extending different termination proof methods (this idea of combining ordering methods was early considered in [18]), and thus obtain termination proofs of hierarchical unions of TRS's whose modules have been proved using different techniques. As a first step, since based on RPO, these results are still weak to compete with the recent refinements of the DP method in [16, 20]. However, we believe that the extension of these results to more powerful path orderings, like the *Monotonic Semantic Path Ordering* in [5], will provide fairer comparison.

The remainder of the paper is organized as follows. In Section 2 we review basic notation, terminology and results. In Section 3 we define RPOM and prove its properties, and the ones corresponding to every subclass RPOM-STAB, RPOM-MON and RPOM-IP-MON. In Section 4 (resp. Section 5) we show how to use RPOM for proving $\mathcal{C}_\mathcal{E}$-termination (resp. innermost termination) incrementally. We present some concluding remarks in Section 6.

2   Preliminaries

We assume familiarity with the basics of term rewriting (see e.g. [2]).

The set of terms over a signature $\mathcal{F}$ is denoted as $\mathcal{T}(\mathcal{F}, \mathcal{X})$, where $\mathcal{X}$ represents a set of variables. The symbol labelling the root of a term t is denoted as $root(t)$. The root position is denoted by λ. The set of positions of t is denoted by $\mathcal{P}os(t)$. The *subterm* of t at position p is denoted as $t|_p$ and $t \rhd t|_p$ denotes the *proper subterm relation*. A *context*, i.e. a term with a hole, is denoted as $t[\ ]$. The term t with the hole replaced by s is denoted as $t[s]$, and the term $t[s]_p$ obtained by replacing $t|_p$ by s is defined in the standard way. For example, if t is $f(a, g(b, h(c)), d)$, then $t|_{2.2.1} = c$, and $t[d]_{2.2} = f(a, g(b, d), d)$. We denote $t[s_1]_{p_1}[s_2]_{p_2} \ldots [s_n]_{p_n}$ by $t[s_1, s_2, \ldots, s_n]_{p_1, p_2, \ldots, p_n}$. We write $p_1 > p_2$ (or, $p_2 < p_1$) if p_2 is a proper prefix of p_1. In this case we say that p_2 is *above* p_1, or that p_1 is *below* p_2. We will usually denote a term $f(t_1, \ldots, t_n)$ by the simplified form $f t_1 \ldots t_n$.

The notation $\bar{t}$ is ambiguously used to denote either the tuple $(t_1, \ldots, t_n)$ or the multiset $\{t_1, \ldots, t_n\}$, even in case of $t = f(t_1, \ldots, t_n)$. The number of symbols of t is denoted as $|t|$ while $|\bar{t}|$ denotes the number of elements in $\bar{t}$. Substitutions are denoted with the letter σ. A substitution application is written in postfix notation.

We say that a binary relation $\sqsupset$ on terms is *variable preserving* if $s \sqsupset t$ implies that every variable in t occurs in s. It is said that $\sqsupset$ is *non-duplicating* if $s \sqsupset t$ implies that every variable in t occurs at most as often as in s. If $s \sqsupset t$ implies $s\sigma \sqsupset t\sigma$ then $\sqsupset$ is *stable*. If for every function symbol f, $s \sqsupset t$ implies $f(\ldots s \ldots) \sqsupset f(\ldots t \ldots)$ then $\sqsupset$ is *monotonic*. It is said that a relation $\sqsupset$ is *well-founded* if there is no infinite sequence $s_1 \sqsupset s_2 \sqsupset s_3 \sqsupset \ldots$. The transitive and the reflexive-transitive closure of $\sqsupset$ are denoted as $\sqsupset^+$ and $\sqsupset^*$ resp. The union of $\sqsupset$ and the syntactical equality $\equiv$ is denoted as $\sqsupseteq$. We say that $\sqsupset$ is *compatible* with $\sqsupset'$ if $\sqsupset \circ \sqsupset' \subseteq \sqsupset$ and $\sqsupset' \circ \sqsupset \subseteq \sqsupset$.

A (strict partial) *ordering* on terms is an irreflexive transitive relation. A *reduction ordering* is a monotonic, stable and well-founded ordering. A *simplification ordering* is a reduction ordering including the strict subterm relation. A *precedence* $\succsim_{\mathcal{F}}$ over $\mathcal{F}$ is the union of a well-founded ordering $\succ_{\mathcal{F}}$ and a compatible equivalence relation $\approx_{\mathcal{F}}$. We say that a precedence $\succsim_{\mathcal{F}}$ is compatible with a partition of $\mathcal{F}$ if $f \approx_{\mathcal{F}} g$ implies that f and g belongs to the same part of $\mathcal{F}$.

The *multiset extension* of an ordering $\sqsupset$ on terms to multisets, denoted as $\sqsupset^{mul}$, is defined as $\bar{s} \sqsupset^{mul} \bar{t}$ iff there exists $\bar{u} \subset \bar{s}$ such that $\bar{u} \subseteq \bar{t}$ and for all $t' \in \bar{t} - \bar{u}$ there is some $s' \in \bar{s} - \bar{u}$ s.t. $s' \sqsupset t'$. The *lexicographic extension* of $\sqsupset$ to tuples, denoted as $\sqsupset^{lex}$, is defined as $\bar{s} \sqsupset^{lex} \bar{t}$ iff $s_i \sqsupset t_i$ for some $1 \leq i \leq |\bar{s}|$ and $s_j \equiv t_j$ for all $1 \leq j < i$. These extensions preserve irreflexivity, transitivity, stability and well-foundedness.

If $\sqsupset$ is defined on $\mathcal{T}(\mathcal{F}_0, \mathcal{X})$ and $\mathcal{F}_0 \subset \mathcal{F}$ then $\sqsupset^{\mathcal{F}} = \{(s\sigma, t\sigma) \mid s \sqsupset t, \forall x \in \mathcal{X}, x\sigma \in \mathcal{T}(\mathcal{F}, \mathcal{X})\}$ is called the *stable extension* of $\sqsupset$ to $\mathcal{F}$. The stable extension of a stable (and well-founded) ordering is also a stable (and well-founded) ordering [19].

A *term rewrite system* over $\mathcal{F}$ is denoted as $\mathcal{R}$. Here, we deal with variable preserving TRSs. Regarding termination, this restriction is not a severe one. A *rewriting step* with $\mathcal{R}$ is written as $s \to_{\mathcal{R}} t$. The notation $s \to_{\lambda,\mathcal{R}} t$ is used for a rewriting step at position λ.

A TRS $\mathcal{R}$ is *terminating* iff $\to_{\mathcal{R}}^+$ is well-founded. It is said that $\mathcal{R}$ is *simply terminating* iff $\mathcal{R} \cup \mathcal{E}mb_{\mathcal{F}}$ is terminating where $\mathcal{E}mb_{\mathcal{F}} = (\mathcal{F}, \{f(x_1, \ldots, x_n) \to x_k \mid f \in \mathcal{F}, 1 \le k \le n\})$ and $x_1, \ldots, x_n$ are pairwise distinct variables. It is said that $\mathcal{R}$ is $\mathcal{C}_{\mathcal{E}}$-*terminating* iff $\mathcal{R}_{\mathcal{E}} = \mathcal{R} \cup \mathcal{C}_{\mathcal{E}}$ is terminating, where $\mathcal{C}_{\mathcal{E}} = (\mathcal{G}, \{G(x, y) \to x, G(x, y) \to y\})$ and $\mathcal{G} = \mathcal{F} \uplus \{G\}$.

Given a TRS $\mathcal{R}$, $f(t_1, \ldots, t_n)$ is said to be *argument normalized* if for all $1 \le k \le n$, t_k is a normal form. A substitution σ is said to be *normalized* if $x\sigma$ is a normal form for all $x \in \mathcal{X}$. An *innermost redex* is an argument normalized redex. A term s *rewrites innermost* to t w.r.t. $\mathcal{R}$, written $s \to_i t$, iff $s \to t$ at position p and $s|_p$ is an innermost redex. A term s *rewrites innermost in parallel* to t w.r.t. $\mathcal{R}$, written $s \dashrightarrow_{i,\mathcal{R}} t$, iff $s \to_{i,\mathcal{R}}^+ t$ and either $s \to_{i,\mathcal{R}} t$ at position λ (denoted as $s \to_{i,\lambda,\mathcal{R}}$) or $s = f(\bar{s})$, $t = f(\bar{t})$ and for all $1 \le k \le |\bar{s}|$ either $s_k \dashrightarrow_{i,\mathcal{R}} t_k$ or $s_k = t_k$ is a normal form (denoted as $\bar{s} \dashrightarrow_{i,\mathcal{R}} \bar{t}$). A binary relation $\sqsupset$ is *IP-monotonic* w.r.t. $\mathcal{R}$ iff $\dashrightarrow_{i,\mathcal{R}} \subseteq \sqsupset$ [11].

A TRS $\mathcal{R}$ is *innermost terminating* iff $\to_{i,\mathcal{R}}^+$ is well-founded. Alternatively, we have the following characterization for innermost termination.

Theorem 1. *[11] A TRS $\mathcal{R}$ is innermost terminating iff there exists a well-founded relation which is IP-monotonic w.r.t. $\mathcal{R}$.*

The *defined* symbols of a TRS $\mathcal{R}$ are $\mathcal{D} = \{root(l) \mid l \to r \in \mathcal{R}\}$ and the *constructors* are $\mathcal{C} = \mathcal{F} - \mathcal{D}$. The union $\mathcal{R}_0 \cup \mathcal{R}_1$ is said to be *hierarchical* if $\mathcal{F}_0 \cap \mathcal{D}_1 = \emptyset$.

3   RPOM

In this section we define RPOM in terms of an underlying ordering $\sqsupset_{\mathcal{B}}$ and show that it is an ordering. Moreover, we prove that well-foundedness of $\sqsupset_{\mathcal{B}}$ implies well-foundedness of RPOM.

Actually RPOM defines a class of orderings that depends on three parameters. These are the underlying ordering $\sqsupset_{\mathcal{B}}$, the (usual in RPO and other orderings) statusses of the symbols in the signature, and a last parameter $mc \in \{rmul, mul, set\}$. Due to mc, this class of orderings can be partitioned into three subclasses, RPOM-STAB, RPOM-MON and RPOM-IP-MON, where, under certain conditions, the first one contains stable orderings, the second one contains monotonic orderings (or a weak form of monotonocity related to $\sqsupset_{\mathcal{B}}$), and the third one contains IP-monotonic orderings. At the end of this section we prove the corresponding properties to every subclass.

Before going into the definition of RPOM, we need some additional notation. Apart from the multiset extension $\sqsupset^{mul}$ of an ordering $\sqsupset$ defined in the preliminaries we need two other extensions of orderings to multisets: the *set* extension and the *rmul* extension.

Definition 1. *Let* $\sqsupseteq$ *be an arbitrary ordering. Given two multisets S and T,
$S \sqsupseteq^{set} T$ if $S' \sqsupseteq^{mul} T'$, where S' and T' are obtained from S and T, respectively,
by removing repetitions. $S \sqsupseteq^{rmul} T$ if $S \neq \emptyset$ and for all $t \in T$ there is some
$s \in S$ such that $s \sqsupseteq t$.*

It is easy to see that the relation $\sqsupseteq^{rmul}$ is included into $\sqsupseteq^{mul}$ and $\sqsupseteq^{set}$, and that it
preserves irreflexivity, transitivity, stability and well-foundedness, whereas $\sqsupseteq^{set}$
preserves all these properties except for stability.

We will use the notation $\supseteq_{set}$ and $\supseteq_{mul}$ for denoting the inclusion in the sense
of sets and multisets, respectively, in the cases where $\supseteq$ alone is not clear by the
context. For facility of notations, we identify $\supseteq_{rmul}$ with $\supseteq_{set}$.

The ordering $RPOM$ is defined as the union of the underlying ordering $\sqsupseteq_{\mathcal{B}}$,
and a RPO-like ordering $\succ$. Hence, we need a definition of $\succ$ not in contradiction
(or even more, compatible) with $\sqsupseteq_{\mathcal{B}}$. Since $\sqsupseteq_{\mathcal{B}}$ will be generally obtained as an
extension of an ordering $\succ_{\mathcal{B}}$ on the base signature $\mathcal{B} = \mathcal{F}_0$, it seems natural to
demand this ordering to relate pairs of terms where at least one is rooted by a
base symbol (i.e. a symbol in $\mathcal{B}$), but as we see as follows, a more strict condition
is needed for $\sqsupseteq_{\mathcal{B}}$.

The definition of $s \succ t$ differs depending on if the roots of s and t are or not
in $\mathcal{B}$. If no root is in $\mathcal{B}$, then we use a classical RPO-like recursive definition. If
some root is in $\mathcal{B}$, we eliminate all the context containing symbols of $\mathcal{B}$, resulting
in two multisets, and compare them with the corresponding extension $\succ^{rmul}$,
$\succ^{mul}$ or $\succ^{set}$.

Definition 2. *Given a signature $\mathcal{B}$, we say that p is a* frontier position *and
$t|_p$ is a* frontier term *occurrence of t if $root(t|_p) \notin \mathcal{B}$ and $root(t|_{p'}) \in \mathcal{B}$, for
all $p' < p$. The multiset of all frontier subterm occurrences of t is denoted as
$frt_{\mathcal{B}}(t)$[2].*

For example, if $\mathcal{B} = \{f\}$, then $frt_{\mathcal{B}}(f(g(a), f(g(f(g(a), g(b))), g(a))))$ is $\{g(a),$
$g(f(g(a), g(b))), g(a)\}$.

If we want $frt_{\mathcal{B}}(s) \succ^{rmul} frt_{\mathcal{B}}(t)$ or $frt_{\mathcal{B}}(s) \succ^{mul} frt_{\mathcal{B}}(t)$ or $frt_{\mathcal{B}}(s) \succ^{set}$
$frt_{\mathcal{B}}(t)$ to be not in contradiction with $\sqsupseteq_{\mathcal{B}}$, it is necessary to demand that $s \sqsupseteq_{\mathcal{B}} t$
implies $frt_{\mathcal{B}}(s) \supseteq_{rmul} frt_{\mathcal{B}}(t)$ or $frt_{\mathcal{B}}(s) \supseteq_{mul} frt_{\mathcal{B}}(t)$ or $frt_{\mathcal{B}}(s) \supseteq_{set} frt_{\mathcal{B}}(t)$,
depending on the case. We call frontier preserving (w.r.t. *rmul*, *mul* or *set*) to
this property.

Definition 3. *Let $mc \in \{mul, rmul, set\}$, $\mathcal{B} \subset \mathcal{F}$ and $\succsim_{\mathcal{F}}$ be a precedence over
$\mathcal{F} - \mathcal{B}$ compatible with the partition of $\mathcal{F} - \mathcal{B}$, $\mathcal{F}_{Mul} \uplus \mathcal{F}_{Lex}$. Moreover, let $\sqsupseteq_{\mathcal{B}}$
be an ordering on $\mathcal{T}(\mathcal{F}, \mathcal{X})$ s.t. $s \sqsupseteq_{\mathcal{B}} t$ implies $frt_{\mathcal{B}}(s) \supseteq_{mc} frt_{\mathcal{B}}(t)$. Then, the*
Recursive Path Ordering with Modules *(RPOM) is defined as $\succ_{rpom} = \sqsupseteq_{\mathcal{B}} \cup \succ$
where $s = f(\bar{s}) \succ t$ iff one of the following conditions holds:*

1. *$f, root(t) \notin \mathcal{B}$ and $s' \succeq t$ for some $s \rhd s'$.*
2. *$t = g(\bar{t})$, $f \succ_{\mathcal{F}} g$ and $s \succ t'$, for all $t' \in \bar{t}$.*

---

[2] Note that these multisets include not only maximal subterms of t rooted by non-base
function symbols, but also variables.

3. $t = g(\bar{t})$, $f \approx_{\mathcal{F}} g$, $f \in \mathcal{F}_{\mathcal{M}ul}$ and $\bar{s} \succ_{rpom}^{mul} \bar{t}$.

4. $t = g(\bar{t})$, $f \approx_{\mathcal{F}} g$, $f \in \mathcal{F}_{\mathcal{L}ex}$, $\bar{s} \succ_{rpom}^{lex} \bar{t}$ and $s \succ t'$, for all $t' \in \bar{t}$.

5. $f \in \mathcal{B}$ or $root(t) \in \mathcal{B}$, $s \notin \mathcal{T}(\mathcal{B}, \mathcal{X})$, and $frt_\mathcal{B}(s) \succ^{mc} frt_\mathcal{B}(t)$.

We define $\succ_{rpom-stab}$, $\succ_{rpom-mon}$ and $\succ_{rpom-IP-mon}$ to be $\succ_{rpom}$ in the cases where mc is rmul, mul and set, respectively. Analogously, $\succ_{stab}$, $\succ_{mon}$ and $\succ_{IP-mon}$ refer to $\succ$.

It is not difficult to show (using induction on the size of s and t) that RPOM is well-defined. In order to prove that RPOM is an ordering, first we show that $\succ$ is compatible with $\sqsupseteq_\mathcal{B}$, and then, it suffices to show that $\succ$ is transitive and irreflexive.

Lemma 1. $s \succ t$ iff $s \notin \mathcal{T}(\mathcal{B}, \mathcal{X})$ and $frt_\mathcal{B}(s) \succ^{mc} frt_\mathcal{B}(t)$.

Proof. The result holds by definition if $root(s) \in \mathcal{B}$ or $root(t) \in \mathcal{B}$. Otherwise, $root(s), root(t) \notin \mathcal{B}$ and $\{s\} = frt_\mathcal{B}(s) \succ^{mc} frt_\mathcal{B}(t) = \{t\}$ iff $s \succ t$.   □

Lemma 2. $\succ$ is compatible with $\sqsupseteq_\mathcal{B}$.

Proof. It has to be shown that $u \sqsupseteq_\mathcal{B} s \succ t \sqsupseteq_\mathcal{B} v$ implies $u \succ v$. By the frontier preserving condition of $\sqsupseteq_\mathcal{B}$ and Lemma 1 we have $frt_\mathcal{B}(u) \supseteq_{mc} frt_\mathcal{B}(s) \succ^{mc} frt_\mathcal{B}(t) \supseteq_{mc} frt_\mathcal{B}(v)$. This implies $u \notin \mathcal{T}(\mathcal{B}, \mathcal{X})$ and $frt_\mathcal{B}(u) \succ^{mc} frt_\mathcal{B}(v)$ by definition of $\succ^{mc}$. Therefore, using again Lemma 1, $u \succ v$ holds.   □

Lemma 3. If $root(s) \notin \mathcal{B}$ and $s \rhd t \succeq_{rpom} u$ then $s \succ u$.

Proof. Either $t \sqsupseteq_\mathcal{B} u$ and hence $frt_\mathcal{B}(t) \supseteq_{mc} frt_\mathcal{B}(u)$, or $t \succ u$ and hence, by Lemma 1, $frt_\mathcal{B}(t) \succ^{mc} frt_\mathcal{B}(u)$. In both cases, for all $u' \in frt_\mathcal{B}(u)$, there exists $t' \in frt_\mathcal{B}(t)$ s.t. $s \rhd t' \succeq u'$ holds, and we obtain $s \succ u'$ by case 1. Thereby, $frt_\mathcal{B}(s) = \{s\} \succ^{mc} frt_\mathcal{B}(u)$ and the required result follows by Lemma 1.   □

Lemma 4. $\succ$ is transitive. More generally, $s \succ t(\succ \cup \rhd)u$ implies $s \succ u$.

Proof. Assuming that $s_1 \succ s_2(\succ \cup \rhd)s_3$ we prove that $s_1 \succ s_3$, and we do it by induction on the multiset $\{|s_1|, |s_2|, |s_3|\}$ and the multiset extension of the usual ordering on naturals.

First, note that if $s_2' \rhd s_3$ for some $s_2' \in frt_\mathcal{B}(s_2)$, then, $s_2' \succ s_3$, and hence, by Lemma 1 $frt_\mathcal{B}(s_2) \supseteq_{mc} frt_\mathcal{B}(s_2') \succ^{mc} frt_\mathcal{B}(s_3)$, which implies $frt_\mathcal{B}(s_2) \succ^{mc} frt_\mathcal{B}(s_3)$, and $s_2 \succ s_3$ by Lemma 1 again. Therefore, in general we have that either $s_2 \succ s_3$ or $frt_\mathcal{B}(s_2) \supseteq_{mc} frt_\mathcal{B}(s_3)$.

Assume that some of the symbols $root(s_1)$, $root(s_2)$ or $root(s_3)$ are in $\mathcal{B}$. By Lemma 1 and previous observation, $frt_\mathcal{B}(s_1) \succ^{mc} frt_\mathcal{B}(s_2)(\succ^{mc} \cup \supseteq_{mc})frt_\mathcal{B}(s_3)$. By induction hypothesis, transitivity holds for smaller terms, and since the extension mc preserves transitivity and is compatible with $\supseteq_{mc}$, we can conclude that $frt_\mathcal{B}(s_1) \succ^{mc} frt_\mathcal{B}(s_3)$. Again by Lemma 1, $s_1 \succ s_3$.

Hence, from now on we can assume that all $root(s_1)$, $root(s_2)$ or $root(s_3)$ are not in $\mathcal{B}$, and therefore case 5 of the definition of RPOM does not apply any more and, moreover, by our first observation, $s_2 \succ s_3$.

If $s_1 \succ s_2$ by case 1, then there exists a proper subterm s_1' of s_1 satisfying $s_1' \succeq s_2$. Either because $s_1' \equiv s_2$ or by induction hypothesis, $s_1' \succ s_3$, and $s_1 \succ s_3$ holds by case 1. Hence, from now on assume that $s_1 \succ s_2$ is not due to case 1.

At this point it is easy to show that $s_1 \succ s_2'$ for any proper subterm s_2' of s_2. Note that for such s_2' there is some s_2'' in $\overline{s_2}$ that contains s_2' as subterm. If $s_1 \succ s_2$ is due to case 2 or 4, then $s_1 \succ s_2''$. Otherwise, if it is due to case 3, for some s_1' in $\overline{s_1}$, $s_1' \succeq_{rpom} s_2''$, and by Lemma 3, we obtain $s_1 \succ s_2''$ again. In any case $s_1 \succ s_2''$, and either s_2'' is s_2' and hence $s_1 \succ s_2'$ directly, or $s_2'' \rhd s_2'$ and by induction hypothesis on $s_1 \succ s_2'' \rhd s_2'$ we obtain $s_1 \succ s_2'$ again.

If $s_2 \succ s_3$ by case 1, then there exists a proper subterm s_2' of s_2 satisfying $s_2' \succeq s_3$. By the previous observation, $s_1 \succ s_2'$, and by induction hypothesis, $s_1 \succ s_3$. Hence, from now on we can assume that case 1 does not apply in $s_1 \succ s_2 \succ s_3$.

Reasoning analogously as before, it is easy to show that $s_2 \succ s_3'$ for any proper subterm s_3' of s_3. Moreover, by induction hypothesis on $s_1 \succ s_2 \succ s_3'$, we obtain $s_1 \succ s_3'$ for any of such s_3''s. Hence, if $root(s_1) \succ_{\mathcal{F}} root(s_3)$, then $s_1 \succ s_3$ by case 2. On the other hand $root(s_3) \succ_{\mathcal{F}} root(s_1)$ can not happen since case 1 does not apply in $s_1 \succ s_2$ and $s_2 \succ s_3$. Therefore, from now on we can assume that $root(s_1) \approx_{\mathcal{F}} root(s_3)$. Again since case 1 does not apply, we have $root(s_1) \approx_{\mathcal{F}} root(s_2) \approx_{\mathcal{F}} root(s_3)$.

If such a root symbol is from $\mathcal{F}_{Mul}$ ($\mathcal{F}_{Lex}$) then, since the mul (lex) extension preserves transitivity, $\bar{s}_1 \succ_{rpom}^{mul} \bar{s}_3$ ($\bar{s}_1 \succ_{rpom}^{lex} \bar{s}_3$): note that $\succ_{rpom}$ is transitive on smaller subterms since, by induction hypothesis, $\succ$ is, and, moreover, it is compatible with $\sqsupset_{\mathcal{B}}$, which is transitive too. Hence (using that $s_1 \succ s_3'$ for any proper subterm s_3' of s_3 in the case where the root symbol is from $\mathcal{F}_{Lex}$) we conclude that $s_1 \succ s_3$.   □

Lemma 5. $\succ$ *is irreflexive.*

Proof. Obviously, $s \nsucc s$ for all $s \in \mathcal{X}$. Hence, we proceed by contradiction, using induction on the size of s. Depending on the case $s \succ s$ holds we consider 3 cases. If $s \succ s$ holds by case 1 then, $root(s) \in \mathcal{F} - \mathcal{B}$ and for some $s \rhd s'$, $s' \succ s$ holds. But by Lemma 3, $s \succ s'$, and by transitivity $s' \succ s \succ s'$ implies $s' \succ s'$ contradicting the induction hypothesis. The irreflexivity of $\succ_{\mathcal{F}}$ is contradicted if $s \succ s$ holds by case 2. Finally, $s \succ s$ holding by case 3, 4 or 5 implies either $\bar{s} \succ_{rpom}^{mul} \bar{s}$, $\bar{s} \succ_{rpom}^{lex} \bar{s}$ or $frt_{\mathcal{B}}(s) \succ^{mc} frt_{\mathcal{B}}(s)$. But $\sqsupset_{\mathcal{B}}$ is irreflexive and, by the induction hypothesis, $\succ$ is irreflexive for the subterms of s. Hence, since the multiset and lexicographic extensions preserve irreflexivity we obtain $\bar{s} \nsucc_{rpom}^{mul} \bar{s}$, $\bar{s} \nsucc_{rpom}^{lex} \bar{s}$ or $frt_{\mathcal{B}}(s) \nsucc^{mc} frt_{\mathcal{B}}(s)$ which is a contradiction.   □

Well-foundedness of RPO follows from the fact that it is a monotonic ordering which includes the subterm relation. This is not the case of $\succ$ when $mc \neq mul$: for example, even if $\mathcal{B} = \{f\}$ and $a \succ_{\mathcal{F}} b$, $faab \nsucc fabb$. Therefore, we prove its well-foundedness directly by contradiction.

Lemma 6. *If $\sqsupset_\mathcal{B}$ is well-founded then $\succ$ is well-founded.*

Proof. Proceeding by contradiction, suppose there is an infinite sequence with $\succ$. We choose a minimal one w.r.t. the size of the terms involved; that is, the infinite sequence $S = s_1, s_2, s_3, \ldots$ satisfies that for any other sequence $t_1, t_2, t_3, \ldots$ with different sequence of sizes, i.e. with $|s_1|, |s_2|, |s_3|, \ldots \neq |t_1|, |t_2|, |t_3|, \ldots$, there exists an $i > 0$ such that $|t_i| > |s_i|$ and $|t_j| = |s_j|$ for all $j < i$.

If there exists a step in S s.t. $s_i \succ s_{i+1}$ holds by case 1, then the minimality of S is contradicted. Note that if so, by definition of $\succ$ and Lemma 3 we have $s_i \succ s' \succeq s_{i+1}$ for some $s_i \rhd s'$. Hence, by transitivity we obtain the sequence $S' = s_1, s_2, \ldots, s_{i-1}, s', s_{i+2}, \ldots$, which is smaller than S. This also applies when $s_i \succ s_{i+1}$ holds by case 5 and $root(s_{i+1}) \notin \mathcal{B}$. In this case $s' \succeq s_{i+1}$ holds for some $s' \in frt_\mathcal{B}(s_i)$ and when $i > 1$ by Lemma 4 we have $s_{i-1} \succ s'$. Therefore, there is at most one step in S s.t. $root(s_i) \notin \mathcal{B}$ and $root(s_{i+1}) \in \mathcal{B}$. Thus, any other step in S holding by case 5 involves terms which are both rooted by a base symbol.

By the previous facts and since $\succsim_\mathcal{F}$ is a precedence, we conclude that there is some $i \geq 1$ satisfying that for all $j > i$, $s_j \succ s_{j+1}$ holds by the same case 3, 4 or 5. In cases 3 and 4, by definition of the multiset and lexicographic extensions, from the infinite sequence $\bar{s}_{i+1}, \bar{s}_{i+2}, \bar{s}_{i+3}, \ldots$ with $\succ_{rpom}^{mul}$ or $\succ_{rpom}^{lex}$ we extract another infinite sequence $t_1, t_2, t_3, \ldots$ with $\succ_{rpom}$ with $t_1 \in \bar{s}_{i+1}$. Since $\sqsupset_\mathcal{B}$ is well-founded and $\succ$ is compatible with $\sqsupset_\mathcal{B}$, from the latter sequence we construct another infinite sequence $s'_{i+1}, s'_{i+2}, s'_{i+3}, \ldots$ with $\succ$ and where $s'_{i+1} = t_1$. In case 5, from the infinite sequence $frt_\mathcal{B}(s_{i+1}), frt_\mathcal{B}(s_{i+2}), frt_\mathcal{B}(s_{i+3}), \ldots$ with $\succ^{mc}$ we construct another infinite sequence $s'_{i+1}, s'_{i+2}, s'_{i+3}, \ldots$ with $\succ$ and where $s_{i+1} \in frt_\mathcal{B}(s_{i+1})$. Thus, we have $s_{i+1} \rhd s'_{i+1}$ and $s_i \succ s'_{i+1}$ holds by Lemma 4. Therefore, we construct the infinite sequence $s_1, s_2, \ldots, s_i, s'_{i+1}, s'_{i+2}, s'_{i+3}, \ldots$ with $\succ$ which again contradicts the minimality of S. $\square$

Corollary 1. *$\succ_{rpom}$ is an ordering. If $\sqsupset_\mathcal{B}$ is well-founded then $\succ_{rpom}$ is well-founded.*

3.1 A Stable Subclass of RPOM

In this subsection we show that $\succ_{rpom-stab}$ preserves the stability of $\sqsupset_\mathcal{B}$.

Proposition 1. *If $\sqsupset_\mathcal{B}$ is stable, then $\succ_{rpom-stab}$ is stable.*

Proof. We just need to show that $s \succ_{stab} t$ implies $s\sigma \succ_{stab} t\sigma$ for every substitution σ. We use induction on the size of s and t.

If $s \succ_{stab} t$ holds by a case different from 5 then $s\sigma \succ_{stab} t\sigma$ is easily obtained by the same case using the induction hypothesis and the stability of $\rhd$, $\sqsupset_\mathcal{B}$ and the multiset and lexicographic extensions. In the case where $s \succ_{stab} t$ holds by case 5, note that $s \notin \mathcal{F}(\mathcal{B}, \mathcal{X})$ implies $s\sigma \notin \mathcal{F}(\mathcal{B}, \mathcal{X})$, and hence $frt_\mathcal{B}(s\sigma)$ is not empty. Besides, every term in $frt_\mathcal{B}(t\sigma)$ is either at a position p such that $t|_p$ is in $frt_\mathcal{B}(t)$ and $root(t|_p) \notin \mathcal{B}$, or at a position of the form $p.p'$ such that $t|_p$ is a variable x, and $t\sigma|_{p.p'} \in frt_\mathcal{B}(x\sigma)$. In the first case, there is a term $s' \in frt_\mathcal{B}(s)$

such that $s' \succ t|_p$ and $root(s') \notin \mathcal{B}$. Hence, $s'\sigma \in frt_\mathcal{B}(s\sigma)$ and by induction hypothesis $s'\sigma \succ_{stab} t|_p\sigma$. In the second case, there is a term $s' \in frt_\mathcal{B}(s)$ with $root(s) \notin \mathcal{B}$ that has x as proper subterm, and hence $s'\sigma \in frt_\mathcal{B}(s)$ and $s'\sigma \succ_{stab} t|_{p.p'}\sigma$ by case 1. Altogether shows that $frt_\mathcal{B}(s\sigma) \succ_{stab}^{rmul} frt_\mathcal{B}(t\sigma)$, and hence $s\sigma \succ_{stab} t\sigma$ holds by case 5. $\square$

The orderings $\succ_{rpom-mon}$ and $\succ_{rpom-IP-mon}$ are not stable. This is due to the terms rooted by base function symbols which are compared by using the frontier subterms and the multiset extension. Note that, after applying a substitution, some frontier positions (corresponding to variables) may disappear and thus a strict superset relation (which is included in the multiset extension) may become equality. For example, for $\mathcal{B} = \{g, a\}$, we have $s = g(a, h(x), y) \succ_{mon} g(a, a, h(x)) = t$ but $s\sigma \not\succ_{mon} t\sigma$ if $y\sigma$ is a ground term of $\mathcal{T}(\mathcal{B}, \mathcal{X})$. The same and more complex situations hold for $\succ_{IP-mon}$.

3.2   A Monotonic Subclass of RPOM

In this subsection we show that $\succ_{mon}$ is monotonic, and $\succ_{rpom-mon}$ preserves the monotonicity of $\sqsupseteq_\mathcal{B}$. Moreover, even if $\sqsupseteq_\mathcal{B}$ is not monotonic, there is a monotonic relation between $\succ_{mon}$ and $\sqsupseteq_\mathcal{B}$ that we define as follows.

Definition 4. *A relation $\sqsupseteq$ on terms is monotonic on an other relation $\sqsupseteq'$ w.r.t. a set of symbols $\mathcal{F}_1$ if for all $f \in \mathcal{F}_1$, $s \sqsupseteq t$ implies $f(\ldots, s, \ldots) \sqsupseteq' f(\ldots, t, \ldots)$.*

Proposition 2. $\succ_{mon}$ *is monotonic, and $\sqsupseteq_\mathcal{B}$ is monotonic on $\succ_{mon}$ w.r.t. $\mathcal{F} - \mathcal{B}$.*

Proof. Let $u = f(\ldots, s, \ldots)$, $v = f(\ldots, t, \ldots)$. If $f \in \mathcal{B}$ and $s \succ_{mon} t$, then $frt_\mathcal{B}(s) \succ_{mon}^{mul} frt_\mathcal{B}(t)$ by Lemma 1, and hence $frt_\mathcal{B}(u) \succ_{mon}^{mul} frt_\mathcal{B}(v)$, which implies $u \succ_{mon} v$ by case 5.

If $f \notin \mathcal{B}$ and either $s \succ_{mon} t$ or $s \sqsupseteq_\mathcal{B} t$, then $s \succ_{rpom-mon} t$. Hence $\bar{u} \succ_{rpom-mon}^{mul} \bar{v}$ and $\bar{u} \succ_{rpom-mon}^{lex} \bar{v}$. If $f \in \mathcal{F}_{Mul}$ then $u \succ_{mon} v$ holds by case 3. If $f \in \mathcal{F}_{Lex}$ then $u \succ_{mon} v$ holds by case 4 because by Lemma 3, $u \succ_{mon} v'$ holds for all $v' \in \bar{v}$. $\square$

Corollary 2. *If $\sqsupseteq_\mathcal{B}$ is monotonic then $\succ_{rpom-mon}$ is monotonic.*

3.3   An IP-Monotonic Subclass of RPOM

In this subsection we show that, for a given hierarchical TRS $\mathcal{R} = \mathcal{R}_0 \cup \mathcal{R}_1$ and under certain conditions, IP-monotonicity of $\sqsupseteq_\mathcal{B}$ w.r.t. $\mathcal{R}_0$ (on terms of $\mathcal{T}(\mathcal{F}_0, \mathcal{X})$) implies IP-monotonicity of $\succ_{rpom-IP-mon}$ w.r.t. $\mathcal{R}$ (on terms of $\mathcal{T}(\mathcal{F}, \mathcal{X})$). Since $\sqsupseteq_\mathcal{B}$ will usually be an extension from an ordering orienting $\mathcal{R}_0$, it is not expectable to be IP-monotonic on terms on the extended signature $\mathcal{F} = \mathcal{F}_0 \cup \mathcal{F}_1$. Even more, including $\Longrightarrow_{i,\mathcal{R}_0}$ applied to terms on $\mathcal{T}(\mathcal{F}, \mathcal{X})$ into $\sqsupseteq_\mathcal{B}$ is not possible because then the condition stating that $s \sqsupseteq_\mathcal{B} t$ implies $frt_\mathcal{B}(s) \supseteq_{set} frt_\mathcal{B}(t)$ is violated for terms rooted by $f \notin \mathcal{B}$. Instead of including the whole relation $\Longrightarrow_{i,\mathcal{R}_0}$ in $\sqsupseteq_\mathcal{B}$ we demand a weaker condition based on the following definition.

Definition 5. *Let s and t be terms in $\mathcal{T}(\mathcal{F}, \mathcal{X})$. Then we write $s \mathrel{+\!\!\!+\!\!\!\rightarrow}_{i,\mathcal{R}_0,\mathcal{F}_0} t$ if $s \mathrel{+\!\!\!+\!\!\!\rightarrow}_{i,\mathcal{R}_0} t$ and all innermost redexes in s are at positions p such that for all $p' \leq p$, $root(s|_p) \in \mathcal{F}_0$.*

Proposition 3. *Let $\mathcal{R} = \mathcal{R}_0 \cup \mathcal{R}_1$ be a hierarchical TRS, $\mathcal{B} = \mathcal{F}_0$ and $\sqsupset_\mathcal{B}$ be an ordering on $\mathcal{T}(\mathcal{F}, \mathcal{X})$ s.t. $s \sqsupset_\mathcal{B} t$ implies $frt_\mathcal{B}(s) \sqsupseteq_{set} frt_\mathcal{B}(t)$, and $\mathrel{+\!\!\!+\!\!\!\rightarrow}_{i,\mathcal{R}_0,\mathcal{B}} \subseteq \sqsupset_\mathcal{B}$. Let $\rightarrow_{i,\lambda,\mathcal{R}_1} \subseteq \succ_{IP-mon}$.*
Then $\succ_{rpom-IP-mon}$ is IP-monotonic w.r.t. $\mathcal{R}$.

For proving the previous lemma we need the following basic facts concerning the set extension of any ordering.

Proposition 4. *Let $\sqsupset$ be any ordering.*

- *$S \sqsupset^{set} T$, $S' \sqsupset^{set} T'$ and $S \cap S' = \emptyset$ imply $S \cup S' \sqsupset^{set} T \cup T'$.*
- *$\{s_1\} \sqsupset T_1, \ldots, \{s_n\} \sqsupset T_n$ implies $\{s_1, \ldots, s_n\} \sqsupset^{set} T_1 \cup \ldots \cup T_n$.*

Proof. (of Proposition 3) To prove that $s \mathrel{+\!\!\!+\!\!\!\rightarrow}_{i,\mathcal{R}} t$ implies $s \succ_{rpom-IP-mon} t$, we prove, by induction on term structure, a more general statement: $s \mathrel{+\!\!\!+\!\!\!\rightarrow}_{i,\mathcal{R}} t$ implies $s \succ_{rpom-IP-mon} t$ and if $root(s) \notin \mathcal{B}$ then $s \succ_{IP-mon} t$. We distinguish two cases depending on whether or not $root(s)$ is in $\mathcal{B}$.

Assume that $root(s) \notin \mathcal{B}$. If $s \rightarrow_{i,\lambda,\mathcal{R}_1} t$ then trivially $s \succ_{IP-mon} t$ by the assumptions of the lemma. Otherwise, s and t are of the form $f(s_1 \ldots s_m)$ and $f(t_1 \ldots t_m)$, respectively, every s_j is either an $\mathcal{R}$-normal form or $s_j \mathrel{+\!\!\!+\!\!\!\rightarrow}_{i,\mathcal{R}} t_j$, and for some $j \in \{1 \ldots m\}$, $s_j \mathrel{+\!\!\!+\!\!\!\rightarrow}_{i,\mathcal{R}} t_j$. By induction hypothesis, every s_j is either a normal form or $s_j \succ_{rpom-IP-mon} t_j$, and for some $j \in \{1 \ldots m\}$, $s_j \succ_{rpom-IP-mon} t_j$. If $f \in \mathcal{F}_{\mathcal{M}ul}$, $s \succ_{IP-mon} t$ by case 3. If $f \in \mathcal{F}_{\mathcal{L}ex}$, then $s \succ_{IP-mon} t$ holds by case 4 because by Lemma 3 we have $s \succ_{IP-mon} t_j$ for all $j \in \{1 \ldots m\}$.

Assume now that $root(s) \in \mathcal{B}$. We consider the set containing only the minimal positions from $\{p \mid s|_p \in frt_\mathcal{B}(s)$ or $s|_p$ is an innermost redex$\}$, i.e. the ones in this set such that no other is above them. This set is of the form $\{p_1, \ldots, p_n, p'_1, \ldots, p'_m\}$ where the p_j's are frontier positions without innermost redexes above them, and the p'_j's are redex positions satisfying $root(s|_{p'}) \in \mathcal{B}$ for every $p' \leq p'_j$. Hence, s and t can be written as $s[s_1, \ldots, s_n, s'_1, \ldots, s'_m]_{p_1, \ldots, p_n, p'_1, \ldots, p'_m}$ and $s[t_1, \ldots, t_n, t'_1, \ldots, t'_m]_{p_1, \ldots, p_n, p'_1, \ldots, p'_m}$, respectively, where every s_j satisfies $root(s_j) \notin \mathcal{B}$ and either $s_j \mathrel{+\!\!\!+\!\!\!\rightarrow}_{i,\mathcal{R}} t_j$ or s_j is a normal form and $s_j = t_j$, and every s'_j satisfies $s'_j \rightarrow_{i,\lambda,\mathcal{R}_0} t'_j$. Moreover, $frt_\mathcal{B}(s) = \{s_1, \ldots, s_n\} \cup frt_\mathcal{B}(s'_1) \cup \ldots \cup frt_\mathcal{B}(s'_m)$, and $frt_\mathcal{B}(t) = frt_\mathcal{B}(t_1) \cup \ldots \cup frt_\mathcal{B}(t_n) \cup frt_\mathcal{B}(t'_1) \cup \ldots \cup frt_\mathcal{B}(t'_m)$. If all the s_j's are normal forms, then $s \mathrel{+\!\!\!+\!\!\!\rightarrow}_{i,\mathcal{R}_0,\mathcal{B}} t$, and by our assumptions $s \sqsupset_\mathcal{B} t$, and hence $s \succ_{rpom-IP-mon} t$ holds. Hence, assume that for some $j \in \{1 \ldots n\}$, $s_j \mathrel{+\!\!\!+\!\!\!\rightarrow}_{i,\mathcal{R}} t_j$. By induction hypothesis $s_j \succ_{IP-mon} t_j$, and by Lemma 1, $\{s_j\} \succ^{set}_{IP-mon} frt_\mathcal{B}(t_j)$. Similarly, for the rest of $j \in \{1, \ldots, n\}$ we have that either $\{s_j\} \succ^{set}_{IP-mon} frt_\mathcal{B}(t_j)$ or $s_j = t_j$, depending on whether or not s_j is a normal form. Since every s'_j satisfies $s'_j \rightarrow_{i,\lambda,\mathcal{R}_0} t'_j$, $frt_\mathcal{B}(s'_j) \sqsupseteq_{set} frt_\mathcal{B}(t'_j)$, and hence $frt_\mathcal{B}(s'_j) \succeq^{set}_{IP-mon} frt_\mathcal{B}(t'_j)$. By propositon 4, $\{s_1, \ldots, s_n\} \cup frt_\mathcal{B}(s'_1) \cup \ldots \cup frt_\mathcal{B}(s'_m) \succ^{set}_{IP-mon} frt_\mathcal{B}(t_1) \cup \ldots \cup frt_\mathcal{B}(t_n) \cup frt_\mathcal{B}(t'_1) \cup \ldots \cup frt_\mathcal{B}(t'_m)$, and hence $s \succ_{IP-mon} t$ by case 5, and $s \succ_{rpom-IP-mon} t$.   □

4   Proving $\mathcal{C}_{\mathcal{E}}$-Termination Incrementally with RPOM

Assume we have a hierarchical system $\mathcal{R} = \mathcal{R}_0 \cup \mathcal{R}_1$, and we want to prove it terminating using RPOM. We will usually have a reduction ordering $\succ_B$ defined on $\mathcal{T}(\mathcal{F}_0, \mathcal{X})$ orienting $\mathcal{R}_0$, or more generally, a well founded ordering $\succ_B$ including $\rightarrow_{\mathcal{R}_0}$ on $\mathcal{T}(\mathcal{F}_0, \mathcal{X})$, and we will want to obtain from it an ordering $\succ_{rpom-stab}$ orienting $\mathcal{R}_1$. A first simple idea is to extend $\succ_B$ to some $\sqsupset_B$ for terms on $\mathcal{T}(\mathcal{F}, \mathcal{X})$ including $\rightarrow_{\mathcal{R}_0}$ on $\mathcal{T}(\mathcal{F}, \mathcal{X})$. But this will not be useful with RPOM since rewriting with $\mathcal{R}_0$ on a term rooted by a symbol $f \notin B$ does not preserve the frontier. An alternative idea is then to restrict the extension of $\succ_B$ to rewriting steps with $\mathcal{R}_0$ not below a symbol $f \notin B$. Then, we can take $\sqsupset_B = \succ_B^{\mathcal{F}}$ to this end, which is not monotonic, but preserves well foundedness of $\succ_B$ (recall that $\succ_B^{\mathcal{F}}$ is the stable extension of $\succ_B$ to $\mathcal{F}$).

Definition 6. *Let s and t be terms in $\mathcal{T}(\mathcal{F}, \mathcal{X})$. Then we write $s \rightarrow_{\mathcal{R}_0, \mathcal{F}_0} t$ if $s \rightarrow_{\mathcal{R}_0} t$ and the involved redex is at a position p such that for all $p' \leq p$, $root(s|_p) \in \mathcal{F}_0$.*

The following theorem combines the use of $\succ_{stab}$ and $\succ_{mon}$ constructed from $\sqsupset_B$. The monotonicity of the second requires $\sqsupset_B$ to be frontier preserving in the sense of multisets. Therefore, when $\sqsupset_B$ is defined as $\succ_B^{\mathcal{F}}$, we also need $\succ_B$ to be non-duplicating.

Theorem 2. *Let $\mathcal{R} = \mathcal{R}_0 \cup \mathcal{R}_1$ be a hierarchical union, $B = \mathcal{F}_0$ and $\sqsupset_B$ be a stable, well-founded on $\mathcal{T}(\mathcal{F}, \mathcal{X})$, such that $s \sqsupset_B t$ implies $frt_B(s) \sqsupseteq_{mul} frt_B(t)$, and $\rightarrow_{\mathcal{R}_0, B} \subseteq \sqsupset_B$.*
If $\mathcal{R}_1 \subseteq \succ_{stab}$ then $\mathcal{R}$ is $\mathcal{C}_{\mathcal{E}}$-terminating.

Proof. Recall that $\mathcal{R}_{\mathcal{E}} = \mathcal{R} \cup \mathcal{C}_{\mathcal{E}}$. We prove that $\rightarrow_{\mathcal{R}_{\mathcal{E}}}$ is included in $\succ_{rpom-mon}$ because then the well-foundedness of $\succ_{rpom-mon}$ implies termination of $\mathcal{R}_{\mathcal{E}}$. First note that $\mathcal{R}_1 \cup \mathcal{C}_{\mathcal{E}} \subset \succ_{stab}$, and since $\succ_{stab}$ is stable, $\succ_{stab} \subset \succ_{mon}$ and $\succ_{mon}$ is monotonic we conclude that $\rightarrow_{\mathcal{R}_1 \cup \mathcal{C}_{\mathcal{E}}}$ is included in $\succ_{mon}$. Now, let $s, t \in \mathcal{T}(\mathcal{F}, \mathcal{X})$ be s.t. $s \rightarrow_{\mathcal{R}_0} t$ at position p. If every position above p is rooted by a symbol in $\mathcal{F}_0$ then we have $s \sqsupset_B t$ by the assumptions of the theorem. It remains to see the case where there exist a context $u[\ ]$, a symbol $f \notin \mathcal{F}_0$ and a position $q < p$ s.t. $s = u[f(\ldots, s', \ldots)]_q$, $t = u[f(\ldots, t', \ldots)]_q$ and $s' \rightarrow_{\mathcal{R}_0} t'$ with every position between q and p rooted by a symbol in $\mathcal{F}_0$. In this case $s' \sqsupset_B t'$ holds by the assumptions of the theorem, and $s \succ_{mon} t$ is obtained by Proposition 2. $\square$

Corollary 3. *A hierarchical TRS $\mathcal{R} = \mathcal{R}_0 \cup \mathcal{R}_1$ is $\mathcal{C}_{\mathcal{E}}$-terminating if there is a non-duplicating reduction ordering $\succ_B$ s.t. $\mathcal{R}_0 \subseteq \succ_B$ and $\mathcal{R}_1 \subseteq \succ_{stab}$.*
In addition, if $\succ_B$ is a simplification ordering then $\mathcal{R}$ is simply terminating.

Example 3. Simple termination of $\mathcal{R}_{plus} \cup \mathcal{R}_{F'}$ in Example 2 is easily obtained using RPOM. Since $\mathcal{R}_{plus}$ is simply terminating, $\succ_B$ can be defined as the non-duplicating part of any simplification ordering including $\mathcal{R}_{plus}$. The rules of the extension $\mathcal{R}_{F'}$ (listed below) are oriented using $\succ_{stab}$ with $\mathcal{F}_{Lex} = \{F\}$.

$$\left\{\begin{array}{rcl} F(0,x,y) & \to & plus(x,y) \\ F(s(n),x,0) & \to & x \\ F(s(n),x,s(y)) & \to & F(n,F(s(n),x,y),s(plus(F(s(n),x,y),y))) \\ F(s(n),F(s(n),x,y),z) & \to & F(s(n),x,F(n,y,z)) \end{array}\right.$$

Note that the first rule, here denoted as $l_1 \to r_1$, holds by case 5 of the definition of RPOM. This is because $l_1 \succ_{stab} x$ and $l_1 \succ_{stab} y$ hold by case 1 and therefore we have $frt(l_1) = \{l_1\} \succ^{rmul}_{stab} \{x,y\} = frt(r_1)$. The second rule trivially holds by case 1. The last two hold by case 4. We detail the proof for the third one, denoted as $l_3 \to r_3$. First note that $s(t) \succ_{\mathcal{B}} t$ for every term t. Thereby, we have $\bar{l}_3 \succ^{lex}_{\mathcal{B}} \bar{r}_3$. By the former fact and using case 1 we obtain $l_3 \succ_{stab} F(s(n),x,y)$ by case 4. Finally, $l_3 \succ_{stab} s(plus(F(s(n),x,y),y))$ holds by case 5 since $frt(l_3) = \{l_3\} \succ^{rmul}_{stab} \{F(s(n),x,y),y\} = frt(s(plus(F(s(n),x,y),y)))$.

Analogously to the case of SCP, there are situations where the proofs with RPOM can be done modularly.

Theorem 3. *Let $\mathcal{R} = \mathcal{R}_0 \cup \mathcal{R}_1$ be a hierarchical TRS where $\mathcal{R}_0$ is non-duplicating and terminating. Let $\sqsupset_{\mathcal{B}}$ be $\rhd^{\mathcal{F}}_0$ where $\rhd_0$ is $\rhd$ on $\mathcal{T}(\mathcal{F}_0, \mathcal{X})$, and let $\mathcal{R}_1 \subseteq \succ_{stab}$.*
Then $\mathcal{R}$ is $\mathcal{C}_{\mathcal{E}}$-terminating.

Proof. The result can be obtained by Theorem 2 if we use $\sqsupset'_{\mathcal{B}} = (\to_{\mathcal{R}_0,\mathcal{F}_0} \cup \sqsupset_{\mathcal{B}})^+$ and the corresponding $\succ'_{stab}$ instead of $\sqsupset_{\mathcal{B}}$ and $\succ_{stab}$. Trivially $\mathcal{R}_1 \subseteq \succ'_{stab}$ and $\to_{\mathcal{R}_0,\mathcal{F}_0} \subseteq \sqsupset'_{\mathcal{B}}$. We just need to show that $\sqsupset'_{\mathcal{B}}$ is frontier preserving, stable and well-founded. The first two properties follow from the fact that $\to_{\mathcal{R}_0,\mathcal{F}_0}$ and $\rhd_0$ are non-duplicating and stable, and the stable extension preserves these properties. Well-foundedness of $\sqsupset'_{\mathcal{B}}$ follows from the fact that $\mathcal{R}_0$ is terminating, and that any derivation with $(\to_{\mathcal{R}_0,\mathcal{F}_0} \cup \sqsupset_{\mathcal{B}})$ can be commuted to a derivation with $(\to_{\mathcal{R}_0,\mathcal{F}_0})$ followed by a derivation with $\rhd^{\mathcal{F}}_0$, preserving the number of rewrite steps. $\square$

Example 4. Actually, $\mathcal{R}_{F'}$ in Example 2 is included in $\succ_{stab}$ with $\sqsupset_{\mathcal{B}}$ defined as $\rhd^{\mathcal{F}}_0$. Hence, by Theorem 3, the hierarchical union of $\mathcal{R}_{F'}$ and any non-duplicating base system $\mathcal{R}_{plus}$ is $\mathcal{C}_{\mathcal{E}}$-terminating whenever $\mathcal{R}_{plus}$ is so.

Example 5. Consider the following system which describes some properties of the conditional operator.

$$\mathcal{R}_{if} = \left\{\begin{array}{rcl} if(0,y,z) & \to & z \\ if(s(x),y,z) & \to & y \\ if(x,y,y) & \to & y \\ if(if(x,y,z),x_1,x_2) & \to & if(x,if(y,x_1,x_2),if(z,x_1,x_2)) \\ if(x,if(x,y,x_1),z) & \to & if(x,y,z) \\ if(x,y,if(x,x_1,z)) & \to & if(x,y,z) \\ if(x,plus(y,x_1),plus(z,x_2)) & \to & plus(if(x,y,z),if(x,x_1,x_2)) \end{array}\right.$$

The rules of $\mathcal{R}_{if}$ are included in RPOM with $\mathcal{F}_{\mathcal{L}ex} = \{if\}$ and $\sqsupset_\mathcal{B}$ defined as $\rhd_0^\mathcal{F}$. The first three rules hold by case 1 and the three next by case 4. The last rule holds by case 5. Note that $plus(x, y) \sqsupset_\mathcal{B} x$ and $plus(x, y) \sqsupset_\mathcal{B} y$ hold. Hence, using case 4 we obtain $if(x, plus(y, x_1), plus(z, x_2)) \succ_{stab} if(x, y, z)$ and $if(x, plus(y, x_1), plus(z, x_2)) \succ_{stab} if(x, x_1, x_2)$. Therefore, by Theorem 3 we conclude that the hierarchical union of $\mathcal{R}_{if}$ and any base system $\mathcal{R}_{plus}$ is $\mathcal{C}_\mathcal{E}$-terminating whenever $\mathcal{R}_{plus}$ is non-duplicating and $\mathcal{C}_\mathcal{E}$-terminating.

We stress that $\mathcal{R}_{F'}$ and $\mathcal{R}_{if}$ are hierarchical extensions which are not proper and where SCP cannot be used. Hence, no previous modularity result can be applied to these examples.

5   Proving Innermost Termination Incrementally with RPOM

This section proceeds analogously to the previous one. The main difference is that, for proving innermost termination, $\sqsupset_\mathcal{B}$ needs to be frontier preserving only in the sense of sets. Hence, if $\sqsupset_\mathcal{B}$ is constructed from $\succ_\mathcal{B}$, the non-duplicating requirement on $\succ_\mathcal{B}$ disappears.

Theorem 4. *Let $\mathcal{R} = \mathcal{R}_0 \cup \mathcal{R}_1$ be a hierarchical union, $\mathcal{B} = \mathcal{F}_0$ and $\sqsupset_\mathcal{B}$ be a stable, well-founded on $T(\mathcal{F}, \mathcal{X})$, such that $s \sqsupset_\mathcal{B} t$ implies $frt_\mathcal{B}(s) \sqsupseteq_{set} frt_\mathcal{B}(t)$, and $\longmapsto_{i, \mathcal{R}_0, \mathcal{B}} \subseteq \sqsupset_\mathcal{B}$.*
If $\mathcal{R}_1 \subseteq \succ_{stab}$ then $\mathcal{R}$ is innermost terminating.

Proof. By the assumptions and Proposition 1, $\succ_{rpom-stab}$ is stable. Hence, it includes $\rightarrow_{i, \lambda, \mathcal{R}}$. Since $\succ_{rpom-stab} \subseteq \succ_{rpom-IP-mon}$, it follows that $\rightarrow_{i, \lambda, \mathcal{R}} \subseteq \succ_{rpom-IP-mon}$. By the assumptions and Proposition 3, $\succ_{rpom-IP-mon}$ is IP-monotonic w.r.t. $\mathcal{R}$, and by Lemma 6, it is well-founded. Altogether with Theorem 1 imply that $\mathcal{R}$ is innermost terminating. $\qquad\square$

Theorem 5. *Let $\mathcal{R} = \mathcal{R}_0 \cup \mathcal{R}_1$ be a hierarchical TRS where $\mathcal{R}_0$ is innermost terminating. Let $\sqsupset_\mathcal{B}$ be $\rhd_0^\mathcal{F}$ where $\rhd_0$ is $\rhd$ on $T(\mathcal{F}_0, \mathcal{X})$, and let $\mathcal{R}_1 \subseteq \succ_{stab}$.*
Then $\mathcal{R}$ is innermost terminating.

Proof. We use $\sqsupset'_\mathcal{B} = (\longmapsto_{i, \mathcal{R}_0, \mathcal{F}_0} \cup \sqsupset_\mathcal{B})^+$ and the corresponding $\succ'_{IP-mon}$. Note that $\sqsupset'_\mathcal{B}$ and $\succ'_{stab}$ are not necessarily stable whereas $\sqsupset_\mathcal{B}$ and $\succ_{stab}$ are, the second one by Proposition 1, and hence, $\succ_{stab}$ includes $\rightarrow_{i, \lambda, \mathcal{R}_1}$. Since $\succ_{rpom-stab} \subseteq \succ_{rpom-IP-mon} \subseteq \succ'_{rpom-IP-mon}$, it follows that $\rightarrow_{i, \lambda, \mathcal{R}} \subseteq \succ'_{rpom-IP-mon}$.

By the definition of $\sqsupset'_\mathcal{B}$, it is IP-monotonic w.r.t. $\mathcal{R}_0$ in $T(\mathcal{F}_0, \mathcal{X})$. It is also well-founded since any derivation with $\longmapsto_{i, \mathcal{R}_0, \mathcal{F}_0} \cup \sqsupset_\mathcal{B}$ can be commuted to a derivation with $\longmapsto_{i, \mathcal{R}_0, \mathcal{F}_0}$ followed by a derivation with $\rhd_0^\mathcal{F}$, with the same number of rewrite steps, and the fact that $\mathcal{R}_0$ is innermost terminating.

By the assumptions and Proposition 3, $\succ'_{rpom-IP-mon}$ is IP-monotonic w.r.t. $\mathcal{R}$, and by Lemma 6, it is well-founded. Altogether with Theorem 1 imply that $\mathcal{R}$ is innermost terminating. $\qquad\square$

Example 6. Recall the systems $\mathcal{R}_{F'}$ in Example 2 and $\mathcal{R}_{if}$ in Example 5 are included in $\succ_{stab}$ with $\sqsupset_\mathcal{B}$ defined as $\rhd_0^\mathcal{F}$. Hence, by Theorem 5, the hierarchical union of $\mathcal{R}_{F'} \cup \mathcal{R}_{if}$ and any (possibly duplicating) base system $\mathcal{R}_{plus}$ is innermost terminating whenever $\mathcal{R}_{plus}$ is innermost terminating.

6   Conclusions

The stable subclass of the RPOM is suitable for proving termination automatically. It is more powerful than RPO since it allows the reuse of termination proofs. But at the same time it inherits from its predecessor the simplicity and all the techniques for the automated generation of the precedence. The two main differences between RPO and RPOM-STAB are the use of $\sqsupset_\mathcal{B}$ and the treatment of terms rooted by base function symbols. But these difference can be easily handled: frontier subterms can be computed in linear time and the decision between applying case 5 or $\sqsupset_\mathcal{B}$ is deterministic. Besides, if $\sqsupset_\mathcal{B}$ is defined as $\succ_\mathcal{B}^\mathcal{F}$, we can prove $s \sqsupset_\mathcal{B} t$ just by proving $s_r \succ_\mathcal{B} t_r$, where s_r and t_r are obtained by replacing each occurrence of a frontier subterm of s by the same fresh variable.

As future work we plan to investigate more deeply the use of RPOM for proving innermost termination incrementally, since for this particular case no condition need to be imposed on the base TRS. In particular, we will consider the combination of RPOM with the ideas from [9, 11]. Furthermore, we are interested in extending the given results to the monotonic semantic path ordering [5, 4] which will provide a much more powerful framework for combining orderings and prove termination incrementally.

Finally we are also interested in extending these results to the higher-order recursive path ordering [13], which will provide necessary results for hierarchical unions for the higher-order case.

References

1. T. Arts and J. Giesl. Termination of term rewriting using dependency pairs. *Theoretical Computer Science*, 236(1-2):133–178, 2000.
2. F. Baader and T. Nipkow. *Term Rewriting and All That*. Cambridge University Press, 1998.
3. P. B. Bendix and D. E. Knuth. Simple word problems in universal algebras. In *Computational Problems in Abstract Algebra*, pages 263–297. Pergamon Press, 1970.
4. C. Borralleras. *Ordering-based methods for proving termination automatically*. PhD thesis, Dpto. LSI, Universitat Politècnica de Catalunya, España, 2003.
5. C. Borralleras, M. Ferreira, and A. Rubio. Complete monotonic semantic path orderings. In *Proc. CADE*, volume 1831 of *LNAI*, pages 346–364, 2000.
6. C. Calude. *Theories of Computational Complexity*. North-Holland, 1988.
7. C. Calude, S. Marcus, and I. Tevy. The first example of a recursive function which is not primitive recursive. *Historia Math.*, 9:380–384, 1979.
8. N. Dershowitz. Orderings for term rewriting systems. *Theoretical Computer Science*, 17(3):279–301, 1982.

9. M.L. Fernández. Relaxing monotonicity for innermost termination. *Information Processing Letters*, 93(3):117–123, 2005.
10. M.L. Fernández. On proving $C_\mathcal{E}$-termination of rewriting by size-change termination. *Information Processing Letters*, 93(4):155–162, 2005.
11. M.L. Fernández, G. Godoy, and A. Rubio. Orderings for innermost termination. In *Proc. RTA*, volume 3467 of *LNCS*, pages 17–31, 2005.
12. B. Gramlich. On proving termination by innermost termination. In *Proc. RTA*, volume 1103 of *LNCS*, pages 93–107, 1996.
13. J.P. Jouannaud and A. Rubio. The higher-order recursive path ordering. In *Proc. LICS*, pages 402–411, 1999.
14. M.R.K. Krishna Rao. Modular proofs for completeness of hierarchical term rewriting systems. *Theoretical Computer Science*, 151(2):487–512, 1995.
15. C. S. Lee, N. D. Jones, and A. M. Ben-Amram. The size-change principle for program termination. In *Proc. POPL*, pages 81–92, 2001.
16. N. Hirokawa, and A. Middeldorp. Dependency Pairs Revisited. In *Proc. 15th RTA*, volume 3091 of *LNCS*, pages 249–268, 2004.
17. E. Ohlebusch. Hierarchical termination revisited. *Information Processing Letters*, 84(4):207–214, 2002.
18. A. Rubio. Extension Orderings. In *Proc. ICALP*, volume 944 of *LNCS*, pages 511–522, 1995.
19. R. Thiemann and J. Giesl. Size-change termination for term rewriting. In *Proc. RTA*, volume 2706 of *LNCS*, pages 264–278, 2003.
20. R. Thiemann, J. Giesl, and P. Schneider-Kamp: Improved Modular Termination Proofs Using Dependency Pairs. In *Proc. 2nd IJCAR*, volume 3097 of *LNCS*, pages 75–90, 2004.
21. Y. Toyama. Counterexamples to termination for the direct sum of term rewriting systems. *Information Processing Letters*, 25:141–143, 1987.
22. X. Urbain. Modular and incremental automated termination proofs. *Journal of Automated Reasoning*, 32:315–355, 2004.

Automating Coherent Logic

Marc Bezem[1] and Thierry Coquand[2]

[1] Department of Computer Science, University of Bergen,
P.O. Box 7800, N-5020 Bergen, Norway
bezem@ii.uib.no
[2] Department of Computer Science,
Chalmers University of Technology and Gothenburg University,
SE-412 96 Göteborg, Sweden
coquand@cs.chalmers.se

Abstract. First-order coherent logic (CL) extends resolution logic in that coherent formulas allow certain existential quantifications. A substantial number of reasoning problems (e.g., in confluence theory, lattice theory and projective geometry) can be formulated *directly* in CL without any clausification or Skolemization. CL has a natural proof theory, reasoning is constructive and proof objects can easily be obtained. We prove completeness of the proof theory and give a linear translation from FOL to CL that preserves logical equivalence. These properties make CL well-suited for providing automated reasoning support to logical frameworks. The proof theory has been implemented in Prolog, generating proof objects that can be verified directly in the proof assistant Coq. The prototype has been tested on the proof of Hessenberg's Theorem, which could be automated to a considerable extent. Finally, we compare the prototype to some automated theorem provers on selected problems.

1 Introduction

As far as we know, Skolem [20] was the first who used coherent logic (*avant la lettre*) to solve a decision problem in lattice theory and to prove the independence of Desargues' Axiom from the other axioms of projective plane geometry. Modern coherent logic, also called finitary geometric logic, arose in algebraic geometry, see for example [14–Sect. D.1.1]. Full geometric logic includes infinitary disjunctions and even a certain fragment of higher-order logic, as argued in [5]. In this paper we define coherent logic (abbreviated by CL) as the fragment of first-order logic (FOL) consisting of implicitly universally quantified implications of the following form:

$$A_1 \wedge \cdots \wedge A_n \rightarrow E_1 \vee \cdots \vee E_m$$

Here the A_i are first-order atoms. In contrast to resolution logic [19], where the E_j must also be atoms, they may here be existentially quantified conjunctions of atoms. Thus the general format of a *coherent formula* reads:

$$A_1 \wedge \cdots \wedge A_n \rightarrow \exists \boldsymbol{x}_1.C_1 \vee \cdots \vee \exists \boldsymbol{x}_m.C_m$$

G. Sutcliffe and A. Voronkov (Eds.): LPAR 2005, LNAI 3835, pp. 246–260, 2005.

where the C_j are conjunctions of atoms. The special cases $n = 0$, $m = 0$ and no existential quantification, in all possible combinations, are understood to be included. (If the premiss is empty we leave out the $\rightarrow$ as well.)

One important reason to be interested in CL is a genuine interest in proofs and not only in truth. Let us elaborate this point. In resolution logic one reduces a reasoning problem $T \models \phi$ to $cl(T \land \neg\phi) \models \bot$, where cl stands for a clausification operation. The latter problem is *not* equivalent to the former, but the two problems are 'equisolvable' in the sense that the former is solvable if and only if the latter is refutable by resolution. Though possible in principle (a system called TRAMP [18] supports this), it is rather unattractive to transform one solution to the other. This is caused by the fact that the clausification operation cl relies on classical logic and on some weak instances of the Axiom of Choice called Skolem axioms. The latter axioms change the meaning of the theory and classical logic spoils the possible constructivity of the solution to $T \models \phi$. A proof object for $T \vdash \phi$ can be construed on the basis of a resolution refutation (see [4]), but this is seldom a very appealing one. Even for those who do not care about proof objects or constructive logic, resolution has some disadvantages: intuitions do not easily carry over from $T \models \phi$ to $cl(T \land \neg\phi) \models \bot$ and back. Regrettably, your automated reasoning assistant is working on a different problem than you and you are not able to help when it gets stuck. Moreover you have to truly believe the soundness of your reasoning assistant.

Another interesting issue in connection with CL is efficiency. CL will never for any existential conclusion introduce a new witness if there exists already one. Skolem functions give new witnesses even if there exists already one. As a simple example, consider the coherent axiom $p(x) \rightarrow \exists y.\, p(y)$. This is, of course, an easy tautology. CL will never use it since the conclusion is fulfilled whenever the premiss is true. In clausifying it *without thinking* one starts by partly spoiling the dependence of the conclusion on the premiss: $\exists y.\, (p(x) \rightarrow p(y))$. Then one makes the dependence of y on x explicit by introducing a Skolem function: $p(x) \rightarrow p(f(x))$. This is no longer a tautology, but a clause which makes the Herbrand universe infinite and can play a complicating role in the proof search. Of course, in the case above the tautology could easily be detected and removed at an early stage, but in general this is not possible.

To give a more interesting example, consider a rewrite relation r which is reflexive and satisfies the diamond property:

$$r(x,y) \land r(x,z) \rightarrow \exists u.(r(y,u) \land r(z,u))$$

In CL where we add a witness *only* if there is no one already available, no new facts will be generated from $r(a,a)$. From the set of facts

$$X = \{r(a,a), r(b,b), r(c,c), r(a,b), r(a,c)\}$$

only the two new facts $r(b,d), r(c,d)$, for some fresh constant d, will be generated. In contrast, the Skolemized version:

$$r(x,y) \land r(x,z) \rightarrow r(y, f(x,y,z)) \land r(z, f(x,y,z))$$

would, despite the reflexivity of r, generate $r(a, f(a, a, a))$ from $r(a, a)$, and *infinitely many more* facts from these. From X one would not only get $r(b, f(a, b, c))$, $r(c, f(a, b, c))$, but also facts involving Skolem terms $f(a, c, b)$, $f(a, b, b)$, $f(a, c, c)$, $f(a, a, b)$, $f(a, b, a)$, $f(a, a, c)$, $f(a, c, a)$, $f(a, a, a)$, $f(b, b, b)$, $f(c, c, c)$.

This phenomenon explains why a CL prover in interpreted Prolog can prove the induction step in the proof of Newman's Lemma in 52 steps, orders of magnitude faster than most resolution theorem provers (see [2–readme] and Section 6): the clausal form of this coherent problem contains two ternary and one binary Skolem function. (We do not claim that CL is generally faster than resolution.)

A substantial number of reasoning problems (e.g., in confluence theory, lattice theory and projective geometry) can be formulated *directly* in CL without any clausification or Skolemization. CL has a natural proof theory, reasoning in CL is constructive and proof objects can easily be obtained. In summary, the advantages of this approach are:

- the search space may be smaller in some cases;
- the search for a proof can be guided by intuitions about the problem;
- the proofs are not complicated by a translation of the problem;
- the proof objects can be used in other systems, typically logical frameworks with greater expressivity but less automation than CL;
- the proofs can be verified independently, algorithms could be extracted.

An illustrative example of a coherent formula is the elimination axiom for transitive-reflexive closure:

$$path(x, z) \rightarrow equal(x, z) \lor \exists y.(edge(x, y) \land path(y, z)) \qquad (*)$$

Being (classically) contained in the $\forall\exists$-fragment, there are certainly formulas that cannot be expressed directly in CL, but fewer than is the case in resolution logic. Of course, when a problem doesn't fit into the CL fragment one has to accept a certain reformulation. A simple example is an implication with a universal quantification in the premiss: $(\forall x.\ p(x)) \rightarrow q$. Such formulas can be translated linearly into an equivalent set of coherent formulas, see Section 7.

In the next section we provide formal definitions and prove completeness. Section 3 sketches the easy conversion of proofs in CL to ordinary derivations in natural deduction. In Section 4 we elaborate a small case study taken from rewriting theory. Section 5 discusses strategies for finding proofs in CL. In Section 6 we show how the method scales up with some fully automated medium-scale examples and an interactive large-scale example, Hessenberg's Theorem, which states that Pappus implies Desargues in projective plane geometry.

2   Formal Definition, Proof Theory and Completeness

In order to keep things as simple as possible we restrict attention to one-sorted first-order logic without function symbols. The completeness proof can be generalized to the case with function symbols. Without function symbols, terms are either constants or variables. A special category is formed by the *parameters*, (eigen)variables that are never to be bound. Alternatively, parameters may be viewed as new constants, not appearing in any formula of the theory nor in the formula that is to be proved. Parameters will be used during the inference process as witnesses for existential formulas. A *closed formula* or *sentence* is a formula without free variables, but possibly with constants and parameters.

Definition 1. *A* coherent formula *is a formula of the form $C \to D$, implicitly universally closed, where $C \equiv A_1 \wedge \cdots \wedge A_n$ (with $n \geq 0$ and the subscripted A's first-order atoms) and $D \equiv E_1 \vee \cdots \vee E_m$ ($m \geq 0$). Here $E_i \equiv \exists x_1 \ldots x_k. C_i$ ($k \geq 0$), for every $1 \leq i \leq m$ the formula C_i is a conjunction of atoms. The special cases will be treated as follows: if $n = 0$, then we may leave out $C \to$ altogether; if $m = 0$, then we may write $\perp$ for D; if $k = 0$ in E_i, then we leave out $\exists$ as well. A* fact *is a closed atom. The formulas C, D, $C \to D$ above are also called* coherent conjunction, coherent disjunction *and* coherent implication, *respectively. A* coherent theory *is a set of coherent implications.*

CL extends resolution logic [19] in that coherent formulas allow an existential conclusion. A coherent formula without existential quantifiers reduces to one or more resolution clauses by, first, distributing the disjunctions over the conjunctions in the conclusion and then distributing the implication over the conjunction of disjunctions. An important special case are the so-called *Horn clauses* [13], where the right-hand side D is atomic. If D is a conjunction of atoms, then $C \to D$ is also considered to be a Horn clause, although strictly speaking such a formula reduces to a set of Horn clauses. Coherent formulas containing $\vee$ and/or $\exists$ will be called *disjunctive clauses*.

In this section we prove the completeness of a consequence relation $\Vdash$ which can be viewed as a breadth-first variant of the more usual relation $\vdash$ from [11, 3, 9]. Completeness of the latter follows then easily.

Completeness here means completeness with respect to truth in all Tarskian models, which have non-empty domains. Therefore we assume that the signature contains at least one constant symbol.[1] Note that this assumption is also useful for, e.g., the equivalence of $\exists x.(p(x) \vee q)$ to the coherent formula $(\exists x.p(x)) \vee q$.

Definition 2. *Let X be a set of facts, also called a* state. *A closed coherent conjunction C is* true *in X, denoted by $X \models C$ (or $C \subseteq X$), if all conjuncts in C occur in X. A closed coherent disjunction D is* true *in X, denoted by $X \models D$ if for some disjunct $\exists \boldsymbol{x}.C$ of D there exist parameters $\boldsymbol{a}$ such that $C[\boldsymbol{x} := \boldsymbol{a}] \subseteq X$.*

For any open coherent conjunction C, let $\overline{C}$ denote a closed instance of C with fresh parameters substituted for the free variables. The usual care in avoiding name conflicts should be taken here. For example, in expressions like $\overline{C_1} \wedge \overline{C_2}$ we tacitly assume that the fresh parameters are distinct. Thus, for example, $\overline{C_1} \wedge \overline{C_2}$ can be different from $\overline{C_1 \wedge C_2}$.

Let X and $\{F_1, \ldots, F_m\}$ be finite sets of facts. As usual, we write $X, F_1, \ldots, F_m$ for $X \cup \{F_1, \ldots, F_m\}$ and even X, C for $X, F_1, \ldots, F_m$ when $C = F_1 \wedge \cdots \wedge F_m$.

---

[1] In categorical geometric logic there is no such assumption.

Definition 3. *Let T be a finite coherent theory, X a finite set of facts and D a closed coherent disjunction. We define inductively $X \Vdash^T D$, which expresses that D is a breadth-first consequence in T of the facts in X. Here and below we simply write $\Vdash$ instead of $\Vdash^T$ whenever T is clear from the context.*

- *(base case) $X \Vdash D$ if D is true in X.*
- *(induction step) Consider all closed instances $C_i \to D_i$ of axioms of T such that C_i is true in X but D_i is not. There exist at most finitely many such instances and we may enumerate all their conclusions by $D_0, \ldots, D_n$. Now assume there is at least one such conclusion and let*

$$D_i \equiv \cdots \vee \exists \boldsymbol{x}_{ij}. \, C_{ij} \vee \cdots$$

for all $0 \leq i \leq n$ and $1 \leq j \leq m_i$, where m_i is the length of D_i. In other words, C_{ij} is the conjunction in the j-th disjunct of D_i. The idea is now to consider all possible combinations of selecting one disjunct from each D_i, taking fresh instances of their conjunctions. The induction step is: infer $X \Vdash D$ from

$$\forall j_0 \in \{1, \ldots, m_0\} \, \cdots \, \forall j_n \in \{1, \ldots, m_n\} \, (X, \overline{C_{0j_0}}, \ldots, \overline{C_{nj_n}} \Vdash D)$$

The induction step can be depicted as follows, leading to the usual representation of $\Vdash$-derivations as finite trees.

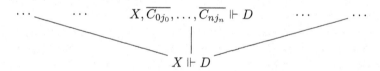

Note that, if some $D_i \equiv \bot$, then $m_i = 0$ and we have $X \Vdash D$ since the domain of quantification of j_i is empty. On the other hand, if there are no conclusions D_i as above, then the induction step doesn't apply and we only have $X \Vdash D$ if D is true in X.

In the next paragraphs we make a number of remarks on this definition.

The finite sets of facts grow along the branches of a derivation tree. This growth is strict since the D_i are false in X. In the leaves of the tree we have either $X, \ldots \models D$, or there exists a closed instance $C \to \bot$ of an axiom in T such that $X, \ldots \models C$.

In the above induction step, every D_i is true in any set $X, \overline{C_{0j_0}}, \ldots, \overline{C_{nj_n}}$. This holds vacuously if some $D_i \equiv \bot$, since then there are no sets $X, \overline{C_{0j_0}}, \ldots, \overline{C_{nj_n}}$. One could consider this as a base case, but it is more systematic to view it as a special case of the induction step.

It is possible that both the base case and the induction step apply. In that case it is normal to cut the detour ('cutting to truth') by applying the base case. The following theorem is in fact a strong but trivial cut-elimination result.

Theorem 1. *A ⊩-derivation is* normal *if the induction step has been applied only if the base case doesn't apply. Any derivation of $X \Vdash D$ can be normalized. Normal derivations of $X \Vdash D$ differ only in the names of the parameters.*

If the induction step doesn't apply, then all closed instances of axioms in T are true in X, so that the set of facts X can be viewed as a Tarskian model M_X of T in the following precise sense. The domain of M_X consists of the constant symbols of T and the parameters occurring in X. The relation symbols are interpreted in M_X such that the facts in X are the only closed atoms that are true in M_X. These models are in fact Herbrand models or term models, with the Herbrand universe extended with the parameters. We will also use this model construction when the set of facts is infinite. Note that the facts may not only contain constants from the fixed signature of T, but also parameters introduced during the derivation.

The same kind of trees, though possibly infinite, can be used to organize the search for a normal derivation of $X \Vdash D$. First we check if $X \models D$. If so, we are done. Otherwise, we try the induction step. If this is not possible since all axioms of T are true in X, then M_X is a countermodel of T against D and there exists no derivation of $X \Vdash D$. If we can apply the induction step, we do so and apply this search procedure recursively to all premises. (If there are no premises, we are done.)

For reasons of computability it is important that X and T are finite. Then all the case distinctions and quantifications in the above procedure are finite. The search procedure itself is semi-computable, since it is not guaranteed to terminate. The search procedure terminates successfully if and only if there exist a normal derivation of $X \Vdash D$.

Actually, the above search procedure terminates successfully if and only if D is true in all Tarskian models of T, X. The only-if part is soundness and is obvious. We prove the if-part by contraposition. If the search procedure doesn't terminate, then the tree is infinite. Since the tree is finitely branching, it must have an infinite branch, say β, by König's Lemma. Starting at the root $X \Vdash D$, the set of facts is strictly increasing along β. We collect all these facts in an infinite set B. In the same way as M_X above we define a Herbrand model M_B based on the set B. Since $X \subseteq B$ we have that M_B is a model of X. We shall argue that M_B is also a model of T. Let $C_i \to D_i$ be a closed instance of an axiom in T such that $C_i \subseteq B$. This means that at some point $Y \Vdash D$ on β we have $C_i \subseteq Y$. We have $Y \subseteq B$ and hence $B \models D_i$ if $Y \models D_i$. We cannot have $D_i \equiv \bot$ since β is infinite. But then, by the remark after Definition 3, we have $Z \models D_i$ for any successor Z of Y, so in particular for $Z \subseteq B$ on β. Hence $B \models D_i$, which completes the proof that M_B is a model of T. It follows that M_B is a model of T, X in which D is false since β is infinite. This completes the proof of the if-part by contraposition and we conclude:

Theorem 2. *The consequence relation ⊩ is complete with respect to Tarskian truth.*

As a corollary we get that in CL classical provability and intuitionistic provability coincide. In other words, we don't miss any classical truths in CL by reasoning intuitionistically. We finish this section with some results relating $\Vdash$ and $\vdash$ from [11, 3, 9]. The consequence relation $\vdash$ has almost the same definition as $\Vdash$ but in the induction step only one closed instance $C_0 \to D_0$ with $C_0 \subseteq X$ is used instead of all invalid ones, see Definition 3.

Lemma 1. *For any T, if $X \Vdash D$, then $X \vdash D$.*

Proof. One step in a $\Vdash$-derivation involving n closed instances of axioms in T corresponds to n steps in the $\vdash$-derivation involving the same closed instances, in any arbitrary order.

Corollary 1. *The consequence relation $\Vdash$ is sound for any semantics for which $\vdash$ is sound.*
The consequence relation $\vdash$ is complete for any semantics for which $\Vdash$ is complete.
The consequence relation $\vdash$ is complete with respect to Tarskian truth.

The main differences between completeness here and in [9] are: the completeness proof here is simple but relies essentially on classical logic; the proof in [9] is constructive but is based on a more complex notion of satisfaction defined as a forcing relation. As a result the respective consequence relations are classically equivalent but not constructively.

3   Natural Deduction Proofs

In this section we show by example how to convert $\vdash$-derivations to ordinary derivations in natural deduction. Relying on the well-known Curry-Howard correspondence, it can easily be imagined how to convert our derivations to lambda terms that can be type checked. This conversion has been implemented for the proof assistant Coq [8] and all proof terms have successfully been type checked. For reasons of space we refer the interested reader to the website [2–files *.v].

Example 1. The derivation of p in the coherent theory $q(x) \to p$, $p \vee \exists x.q(x)$

$$
\cfrac{p \vdash p \quad \cfrac{\cfrac{q(c), p \vdash p}{q(c) \vdash p} \quad q(x) \to p}{\vdash p}}{\vdash p} \; p \vee \exists x.q(x)
$$

can be converted to the following derivation in natural deduction:

$$
\cfrac{[p]^2 \quad \cfrac{[\exists x.q(x)]^2 \quad \cfrac{[q(c)]^1 \quad \cfrac{\forall x\,(q(x) \to p)}{q(c) \to p}\;\forall\text{-el}}{p}\;\to\text{-el}}{p}\;\exists\text{-el}^1 \quad p \vee \exists x.q(x)}{p} \; \vee\text{-el}^2
$$

Note that in principle only elimination rules are involved. However, for reasons of efficiency when scaling up, sharing of identical subderivations requires separate lemmas whose proofs also involve introduction rules.

4   A Small Case Study

The theory of confluence of Abstract Rewriting Systems [22–Sect.1.3.1] provides many simple examples of coherent theories. In order to illustrate the inference procedure from the previous sections we prove a little result from confluence theory: the preservation of the diamond property of a rewriting relation under reflexive closure of the relation. We start by giving the coherent theory which states that rewrite relation r satisfies the diamond property (1) and defines re as the reflexive closure of r (2–4), using e for equality (5–7).

1. $r(x, y) \wedge r(x, z) \rightarrow \exists u.(r(y, u) \wedge r(z, u))$ (diamond property of r)
2. $re(x, y) \rightarrow r(x, y) \vee e(x, y)$ (re-elimination)
3. $r(x, y) \rightarrow re(x, y)$ (re, r-introduction)
4. $e(x, y) \rightarrow re(x, y)$ (re, e-introduction)
5. $e(x, x)$ (reflexivity of e)
6. $e(x, y) \rightarrow e(y, x)$ (symmetry of e)
7. $e(x, y) \wedge re(y, z) \rightarrow re(x, z)$ (left re-congruence of e)

The last axiom expresses a necessary congruence property. Transitivity of equality is not needed.

We wish to prove that re satisfies the diamond property:

8. $re(x, y) \wedge re(x, z) \rightarrow \exists u.(re(y, u) \wedge re(z, u))$ (diamond property of re)

We start by instantiating the axiom (8) by introducing three new parameters, say a, b, c and replacing the universally quantified variables x, y, z by these respective parameters. The goal is then to prove the conclusion

$$D \equiv \exists u.(re(b, u) \wedge re(c, u))$$

using the theory and the two assumptions $re(a, b)$ and $re(a, c)$.

The next step is to identify the closed instances of axioms that are invalid in the initial state consisting of the parameters a, b, c and the facts $re(a, b)$ and $re(a, c)$. This means that we apply the axioms (1–7) in so far they yield new information. Axiom (5) yields three new facts $e(a, a), e(b, b), e(c, c)$ and axiom (2) two disjunctions, $r(a, b) \vee e(a, b)$ and $r(a, c) \vee e(a, c)$. In total we get four new states and we can only conclude to D if we can prove D in all these four states. The four states each contain $e(a, a), e(b, b), e(c, c)$ besides one of the following four combinations of facts from the two disjunctions, in increasing order of difficulty: (i) $e(a, b), e(a, c)$; (ii) $e(a, b), r(a, c)$; (iii) $r(a, b), e(a, c)$; (iv) $r(a, b), r(a, c)$. We elaborate each of these four cases.

(i) In this new state axiom (4) yields the new facts $re(a, a), re(b, b), re(c, c)$ and axiom (6) $e(b, a), e(c, a)$. In the resulting state axiom (4) yields $re(b, a)$, $re(c, a)$ and so a is found as witness for D and we are done.

(ii) Again we get $re(a, a), re(b, b), re(c, c), e(b, a)$, but now, unexpectedly, also axiom (1) has an invalid instance, namely $x = a$ and $y = z = c$, by $r(a, c)$. This means that we also have to add a fact $r(c, d)$ for some new parameter d.

In the new state we have $e(b, a)$ and $re(a, c)$, so axiom (7) yields $re(b, c)$ (in addition to some other facts by other axioms). In combination with $re(c, c)$ this allows us to conclude D with witness c. Note that $r(c, d)$ and many other facts have not been used to obtain the conclusion.

(iii) This case is symmetric to the previous one, with b as witness for D.

(iv) This is the most interesting case, in which $r(a, b), r(a, c)$ have been added besides the equality facts. From the latter we get $re(a, a), re(b, b), re(c, c)$. The only other axiom yielding something new is (1), the diamond property of r. There are in total four (!) instantiations of axiom (1) that are false in the current state, namely all four combinations of $y, z \in \{b, c\}$ in $r(a, y) \wedge r(a, z) \rightarrow \exists u.(r(y, u) \wedge r(z, u))$. These combinations are not disjunctive but conjunctive. Hence we get a lot of new information in the form of the formulas $\exists u.(r(b, u) \wedge r(b, u))$, $\exists u.(r(b, u) \wedge r(c, u))$, $\exists u.(r(c, u) \wedge r(b, u))$, $\exists u.(r(c, u) \wedge r(c, u))$. (Here the second and the third are of course equivalent, and the first and the fourth follow from the second. This actually poses an interesting optimization problem: make all conclusions true with a minimum number of witnesses.) In order to add this partially redundant information to the current state new parameters $d, d', \ldots$ are introduced witnessing the existential formulas above. Instantiating them in due order (and omitting those that have become true already by previous instantiations, as a small optimization of the breadth-first strategy) one adds $r(b, d), r(b, d'), r(c, d')$. Now axiom (4) yields $re(b, d')$, $re(c, d')$ (besides many other facts generated by other axioms) and thus d' is found as witness for the goal D.

As all branches have now been completed, this completes the proof of D.

5 Strategies and Implementation

Already Skolem viewed coherent axioms as generating rules (*Erzeugungsprinzipien*). For resolution logic, that is, without existential quantification, this idea has been applied in the satisfiability checker and model generator SATCHMO [17]. SATCHMO has a very concise Prolog implementation which has inspired our implementation of the proof procedure for coherent theories as described above. The resulting system extends SATCHMO with existential quantifications and with the generation of proof objects. A related extension of SATCHMO are the Extended Positive Tableaux from [6]. However, the latter aims at finding finite models rather than proof objects.

The complete proof procedure described in Definition 3 can be viewed as breadth-first forward reasoning with case distinction. This approach has some well-known disadvantages, notably the generation of too many cases and an astronomical number of irrelevant facts.

In fact ⊩ has only been introduced to simplify the completeness proof. A first step towards a practical proof procedure is to use ⊢ instead of ⊩. This is still complete, but in order to be more efficient than ⊩ one needs to know in which order which instances of the axioms have to be applied.

Another approach is to give up completeness in favour of a faster procedure which, though incomplete, may (dis)prove coherent formulas in a substantial number of practical cases. This is actually also one of the design choices taken in the programming language Prolog [7, 15, 24] where the completeness of breadth-first SLD-resolution has been given up in favour of a generally faster but incomplete depth-first approach. For the moment we are satisfied with this approach, which at the same time makes Prolog into a particular natural choice of an implementation language. In the next section we will touch upon proof scripts to remedy incompleteness.

A depth-first strategy takes the theory as an ordered set of axioms and searches for the first axiom which is invalid in the current state. The state is a list of parameters and facts in order of creation and addition, respectively. The instance that invalidates the axiom is the one using the 'oldest' facts. The depth-first strategy branches on disjunctions immediately after their appearance as conclusion of the invalidated instance.

In the depth-first strategy, like in Prolog, the order of the axioms of the theory becomes of crucial importance. In the example of Section 4, a depth-first strategy would start by applying axiom (2) with $re(a, b)$, inferring $r(a, b) \lor e(a, b)$. Upon examination of the case $r(a, b)$ the behaviour changes dramatically. Then axiom (1) becomes invalidated and starts generating new r-facts. This doesn't stop since axiom (1) is all the time invalidated by the new r-facts generated in previous rounds. This example shows that the depth-first strategy is incomplete.

In order to make the depth-first stategy 'more complete' there is a natural order in which the Horn clauses precede the disjunctive clauses. Of the latter, the clauses without existential quantification should precede those with and it is in many cases advisable to put the clauses that combine existential quantifications with disjunctions last. Then every application of a disjunctive clause is followed by a finite Horn closure, possibly validating disjunctive clauses that would otherwise have contributed to the combinatorial explosion. In the example of Section 4 the depth-first strategy can complete the proof procedure without any problem when we change the order in which the theory has been listed to the natural order as described above. However, there are problems for which the depth-first strategy is incomplete with any order of the axioms (see the second example below).

A typical example where a depth-first strategy is better than the breadth-first strategy is when p has to be proven from $p \lor p$ preceeding lots of other (irrelevant) disjunctions. A typical example where the breadth-first strategy is better than a depth-first strategy, with respect to any possible ordering of the theory, is proving $\exists uv.(r(b, u) \land s(b, v))$ from the facts $r(a, b), s(a, b)$ using two 'co-routining' seriality axioms:

$$r(x, y) \rightarrow \exists u.r(y, u)$$

$$s(x, y) \rightarrow \exists u.s(y, u)$$

Here the breadth-first strategy succeeds in one round where any depth-first strategy fails.

6   Scaling Up

On the website [2–see `readme`] we have collected a number of experiments with a prototype CL prover. The example in Section 4 is very small and can easily be done by any theorem prover. Yet it is useful to have a compact proof object at hand. The relevant files are [2–`dpe.*`].

A more interesting case is the induction step in the proof of Newman's Lemma. This problem has been described at length in [3]. Newman's Lemma states that a rewrite relation is confluent whenever it is locally confluent and terminating. Termination is essentially higher-order but in Huet's inductive formulation the whole proof boils down to an induction step which is first-order and even coherent. Skolemization would involve two ternary Skolem functions (one for the induction hypothesis and one for local confluence) and a binary one (for the elimination axiom for reflexive-transitive closure, see formula (∗), Section 1). In CL existential quantification is demand-driven and Skolemization is avoided. The CL prover promptly finds a proof in 52 steps (0.01 sec.), before E (1.7 sec.), E-SETHEO (30 sec.) and Vampire (44 sec.). The relevant files are [2–`nl.*` and `readme`].

In larger examples it will be necessary to further narrow the proof search by specifying some instances of axioms that have to be used in some specific order. The fact that this is not fully automatic can be regretted, but we did find in this way proofs [2–`pd_hes` and `pd_cro`] where the number of automatic steps is two orders of magnitude larger than the number of specified steps. As the system automatically generates proof objects, these proof objects are thus obtained in a way which requires far less human interaction than normally required in Coq and other proof assistants.

The largest example is the proof of Hessenberg's Theorem that Pappus implies Desargues in projective plane geometry. Let us say a few words on this interesting case. Pappus' Axiom states that for any two lines l and m and points a, b, c on l and d, e, f on m, the intersections $((ae)(bd)), ((af)(cd)), ((bf)(ce))$ are collinear. Here we have used (xy) to denote the line through the points x and y, as well as the intersection of x and y if x and y are lines. In order to be valid, Pappus' Axiom requires some side conditions to exclude degenerate cases in which the intersections are indeterminate. There is some variation in these side conditions. One variation is to require that a, b, c are not on m and d, e, f not on l. Another variation is to require that the intersections are determinate. With $x \mid l$ denoting that the point x lies on the line l, the latter variation of Pappus' Axiom reads:

$$a \mid l \,\wedge\, b \mid l \,\wedge\, c \mid l \,\wedge\, d \mid m \,\wedge\, e \mid m \,\wedge\, f \mid m \,\wedge\,$$
$$a \mid n \,\wedge\, e \mid n \,\wedge\, g \mid n \,\wedge\, b \mid o \,\wedge\, d \mid o \,\wedge\, g \mid o \,\wedge\,$$
$$a \mid p \,\wedge\, f \mid p \,\wedge\, h \mid p \,\wedge\, c \mid q \,\wedge\, d \mid q \,\wedge\, h \mid q \,\wedge\,$$
$$b \mid r \,\wedge\, f \mid r \,\wedge\, i \mid r \,\wedge\, c \mid s \,\wedge\, e \mid s \,\wedge\, i \mid s \qquad\qquad \rightarrow$$

$$n{=}o \,\vee\, p{=}q \,\vee\, r{=}s \,\vee\, \exists t.(g \mid t \,\wedge\, h \mid t \,\wedge\, i \mid t)$$

Thus Pappus' Axiom is clearly coherent, and so are all the other axioms of projective plane geometry. The equivalence of the two variations of Pappus' Axiom is fully automated in [2–p1p2 and p2p1].

Desargues' Axiom states that, under certain conditions excluding degenerate cases, two triangles are perspective from a line, whenever they are perspective from a point. Let the triangles be $a_1b_1c_1$ and $a_2b_2c_2$, then perspectivity from a point o means that there exist lines o_a, o_b, o_c through o, a_1, a_2, o, b_1, b_2 and o, c_1, c_2, respectively. Perspectivity from a line means that the intersections of corresponding edges of the respective triangles, that is, the points $((a_1b_1)(a_2b_2))$, $((a_1c_1)(a_2c_2))$, $((b_1c_1)(b_2c_2))$, are collinear. Desargues' Axiom, including the side conditions, is again coherent.

The proof of Hessenberg's Theorem has an interesting history. The original argument from 1905 contains a gap in that it requires some extra side conditions, which means that it actually leaves open 8 special cases. The gap was closed by Cronheim in [10] who first reduces the 8 special cases to 2 and then solves these.

This history makes it interesting to formally verify the proof. The many auxiliary points and lines involved make a fully automated proof a real challenge. We have been able to reconstruct the whole proof in a semi-automatic way, with the use of proof scripts. These proof scripts are readable and have a size which is a tiny fraction of the whole proof. For example, the essential part of the script for Hessenberg's original argument is a list [line(a1,b2,L0),point(L0,oc,P1), ...,pappus(b2,c2,P5),...] which is to be interpreted as: construct the line through a1 and b2 and call it L0, construct the intersection of this line with oc and call it P1, ..., apply Pappus' Axiom to prove that b2, c2 and P5 are collinear, ... In this way we had to specify 10 steps on a total of around 1000 steps. The other steps settle the many degenerate cases. The relevant files are [2–pd_hes.*].

No automated theorem prover has been able to generate Hessenberg's original argument (in the correct formulation, with the extra side conditions). Cronheim's reduction of 8 special cases to 2 is easier. This argument is independent of Pappus and has been fully automated in [2–cro_8_2.*]. Cronheim's argument solving the remaining cases has been reconstructed in [2–pd_cro.*] with the use of a proof script specifying 6 steps on a total of 723. Again no automated theorem prover has been able to find this proof. The three formal proofs have been assembled together in the Coq vernacular file [2–pdmain.v]. This completes a full formalization of Hessenberg's Theorem, the proof of which has been automated to a considerable extent.

The following table shows the performance of some other theorem provers on problems discussed in this paper. More detailed information can be found in [2–readme]. All problems have been submitted to the TPTP database [23].

7   A General Translation of FOL into CL

We now provide a general way to transform any first-order problem into a coherent problem. More precisely we associate to any first-order formula ϕ a coherent

Table 1. Timings in wall clock seconds, − means: no proof found within 300 sec

system/problem	dpe	nl	p2p1	p1p2	cro_8_2	pd_cro	pd_hes
E 0.82	0.0	1.7	16.4	−	257.8	−	−
Vampire 7.0	0.0	44.6	−	−	8.7	−	−
E-SETHEO csp04	0.5	30.2	46.7	−	1.0	−	−
SPASS 2.1	0.0	−	−	−	3.6	−	−
CL	0.0	0.01	0.27	2.31	0.4	−	−

theory such that ϕ is a tautology if and only if the corresponding theory is inconsistent. The idea is simply to express the method of analytic tableaux [21] as a coherent theory. In the case of resolution logic the method of tableaux to build a set of clauses from a formula has been used in [1]. The idea of introducing new predicates to abbreviate subformulas can be traced further back to Skolem [20], who proved that every theory has a conservative extension which is equivalent to a $\forall\exists$-theory.

For each subformula $\psi(\boldsymbol{x})$ of ϕ we introduce two atomic predicates $T(\psi)(\boldsymbol{x})$ and $F(\psi)(\boldsymbol{x})$ with the following coherent axioms

$$\text{if } \psi(\boldsymbol{x}) \text{ is } \psi_1 \wedge \psi_2 \text{ then } \begin{cases} T(\psi)(\boldsymbol{x}) \to T(\psi_1)(\boldsymbol{x}) \wedge T(\psi_2)(\boldsymbol{x}) \\ F(\psi)(\boldsymbol{x}) \to F(\psi_1)(\boldsymbol{x}) \vee F(\psi_2)(\boldsymbol{x}) \end{cases}$$

$$\text{if } \psi(\boldsymbol{x}) \text{ is } \psi_1 \vee \psi_2 \text{ then } \begin{cases} T(\psi)(\boldsymbol{x}) \to T(\psi_1)(\boldsymbol{x}) \vee T(\psi_2)(\boldsymbol{x}) \\ F(\psi)(\boldsymbol{x}) \to F(\psi_1)(\boldsymbol{x}) \wedge F(\psi_2)(\boldsymbol{x}) \end{cases}$$

$$\text{if } \psi(\boldsymbol{x}) \text{ is } \psi_1 \to \psi_2 \text{ then } \begin{cases} T(\psi)(\boldsymbol{x}) \to F(\psi_1)(\boldsymbol{x}) \vee T(\psi_2)(\boldsymbol{x}) \\ F(\psi)(\boldsymbol{x}) \to T(\psi_1)(\boldsymbol{x}) \wedge F(\psi_2)(\boldsymbol{x}) \end{cases}$$

$$\text{if } \psi(\boldsymbol{x}) \text{ is } \neg\psi_1 \text{ then } \begin{cases} T(\psi)(\boldsymbol{x}) \to F(\psi_1)(\boldsymbol{x}) \\ F(\psi)(\boldsymbol{x}) \to T(\psi_1)(\boldsymbol{x}) \end{cases}$$

$$\text{if } \psi(\boldsymbol{x}) \text{ is } \forall y.\psi_1(\boldsymbol{x}, y) \text{ then } \begin{cases} T(\psi)(\boldsymbol{x}) \to T(\psi_1)(\boldsymbol{x}, y) \\ F(\psi)(\boldsymbol{x}) \to \exists x.F(\psi_1)(\boldsymbol{x}, y) \end{cases}$$

$$\text{if } \psi(\boldsymbol{x}) \text{ is } \exists y.\psi_1(\boldsymbol{x}, y) \text{ then } \begin{cases} T(\psi)(\boldsymbol{x}) \to \exists x.T(\psi_1)(\boldsymbol{x}, y) \\ F(\psi)(\boldsymbol{x}) \to F(\psi_1)(\boldsymbol{x}, y) \end{cases}$$

if $\psi(\boldsymbol{x})$ is atomic then $T(\psi)(\boldsymbol{x}) \to \neg F(\psi)(\boldsymbol{x})$ (or: $T(\psi)(\boldsymbol{x}) \wedge F(\psi)(\boldsymbol{x}) \to \bot$)

It follows from the method of analytic tableaux that ϕ is a tautology if and only if $F(\phi) \to \bot$ is provable in the coherent theory where, for any subformula $\psi(\boldsymbol{x})$ of ϕ, we add the axiom for $F(\psi)(\boldsymbol{x})$ (resp. for $T(\psi)(\boldsymbol{x})$) if $\psi(\boldsymbol{x})$ occurs positively (resp. negatively) in ϕ. Note that the translation is linear.

The surprising fact is that these implications are the only ones needed. For instance, if $\psi = \psi_1 \vee \psi_2$ is at a positive occurrence, we need only to write

$$F(\psi) \to F(\psi_1) \wedge F(\psi_2)$$

and we don't need the converse implication

$$F(\psi_1) \wedge F(\psi_2) \to F(\psi)$$

We give a simple example. The following formula (called the *Drinker Paradox* under the interpretation 'x is drunk' for $d(x)$, see [2–`drinker.in`])

$$\phi = \exists x.(d(x) \rightarrow \forall y.d(y))$$

is a tautology. This means that $F(\phi) \rightarrow \bot$ should be derivable from the following coherent theory, writing ψ for $\forall y.d(y)$:

$$F(\phi) \rightarrow T(d)(x) \wedge F(\psi) \qquad F(\psi) \rightarrow \exists y.F(d)(y) \qquad T(d)(x) \rightarrow \neg F(d)(x)$$

Clearly, if we assume $F(\phi)$ then we can deduce $T(d)(x)$ and $F(\psi)$ for all x (recall that coherent formulas are universally closed). If the domain is non-empty we can infer $F(\psi)$ and hence we have a such that $F(d)(a)$. But then we have $T(d)(a)$ and $F(d)(a)$ and hence a contradiction.

As a corollary of the translation we get that CL is undecidable. In contrast, resolution logic with only constants is decidable.

8   Conclusion and Future Research

We have argued that CL is a fragment of first-order logic which is interesting to consider in relation to (semi-) automated theorem proving. We discussed several examples with a prototype CL prover. Obvious next steps are: extending CL with a native equational logic and developing a notion of relevancy for CL. Relevancy means: if we branch on $p \vee q$ and in case p prove the goal without using p, then we can assume the goal to be proved in case q as well, see [16, 12]. In CL we have in addition: if we prove the goal from $\exists x.p(x)$ without using the new witness, then the goal can be proved without $\exists x.p(x)$. (The latter optimizes the *proof* rather than the *search*.)

Acknowledgements

The authors are indebted to Dimitri Hendriks for useful comments, testing the system and porting it to Coq Version 8. We thank Wolfgang Ahrendt for drawing our attention to SATCHMO. The system has been implemented in SWI-Prolog [24] and all generated proofs have been checked in Coq [8]. We wish to express our appreciation for these excellent examples of Free Software.

References

1. A. Avron, Gentzen-type systems, resolution and tableaux. *Journal of Automated Reasoning* **10**(2):265–281, 1993.
2. M. Bezem, Website for geometric logic: `www.ii.uib.no/~bezem/GL`
3. M. Bezem and T. Coquand. Newman's Lemma – a Case Study in Proof Automation and Geometric Logic. In Y. Gurevich, editor, The Logic in Computer Science Column, *Bulletin of the European Association for Theoretical Computer Science* **79**:86–100, February 2003. Also in G. Paun, G. Rozenberg and A. Salomaa, editors, *Current trends in Theoretical Computer Science*, Volume 2, pp. 267–282, World Scientific, Singapore, 2004.

4. M.A. Bezem, D. Hendriks and H. de Nivelle, Automated proof construction in type theory using resolution. *Journal of Automated Reasoning* **29**(3–4):253–275, 2003.

5. A. Blass, Topoi and computation. *Bulletin of the EATCS* **36**:57–65, October 1998.

6. F. Bry and S. Torge, *Model generation for applications – A tableau method complete for finite satisfiability.* Research Report PMS-FB-1997-15, LMU, 1997.

7. A. Colmerauer e.a., *Un système de communication homme-machine en français.* Technical Report, Université II Aix-Marseille, 1973.

8. The Coq Development Team, *The Coq Proof Assistant Reference Manual, Version 8.0.* Available at: http://coq.inria.fr/

9. T. Coquand. A Completeness Proof for Geometric Logic. To appear in *Proceedings LMPS 2003.*

10. A. Cronheim, A proof of Hessenberg's Theorem. *Proceedings of the AMS* **4**(2):219–221, 1953.

11. M. Coste, H. Lombardi and M.F. Roy, Dynamical methods in algebra: effective Nullstellensätze. *Annals of Pure and Applied Logic* **111**(3):203–256, 2001.

12. L. He, Y. Chao and H. Itoh, R-SATCHMO: Refinements on I-SATCHMO. *Journal of Logic and Computation* **14**(2):117–143, 2004.

13. A. Horn, On sentences which are true of direct unions of algebras. *Journal of Symbolic Logic* **16**(1):14–21, 1951.

14. P. Johnstone, *Sketches of an Elephant: a topos theory compendium,* Volume 2, Oxford Logic Guides 44, OUP, 2002.

15. R.A. Kowalski, Predicate logic as a programming language. *Proceedings IFIP'74,* pp. 569–574, 1974.

16. D. Loveland, D. Reed and D. Wilson, SATCHMORE: SATCHMO with RElevancy, *Journal of Automated Reasoning* **14**:325–351, 1995.

17. R. Manthey and F. Bry, SATCHMO: a theorem prover implemented in Prolog. In E. Lusk and R. Overbeek, editors, *Proceedings of the 9-th Conference on Automated Deduction,* Lecture Notes in Computer Science **310**:415–434, Springer-Verlag, 1988.

18. A. Meier, The proof transformation system TRAMP: http://www.ags.uni-sb.de/~ameier/tramp.html

19. J.A. Robinson, A Machine-Oriented Logic Based on the Resolution Principle. *Journal of the ACM* **12**(1): 23–41, 1965.

20. Th. Skolem, *Logisch-kombinatorische Untersuchungen über die Erfüllbarkeit und Beweisbarkeit mathematischen Sätze nebst einem Theoreme über dichte Mengen,* Skrifter I **4**:1–36, Det Norske Videnskaps-Akademi, 1920. Also in Jens Erik Fenstad, editor, *Selected Works in Logic by Th. Skolem,* pp. 103–136, Universitetsforlaget, Oslo, 1970.

21. R.M. Smullyan. *First-order logic.* Corrected reprint of the 1968 original. Dover Publications Inc., New York, 1995.

22. Terese, *Term Rewriting Systems.* Cambridge University Press, 2003.

23. Thousands of Problems for Theorem Provers, *The TPTP Problem Library for Automated Theorem Proving:* http://www.cs.miami.edu/~tptp.

24. J. Wielemaker, *SWI-Prolog 5.4.1 Reference Manual.* Available at: http://www.swi-prolog.org/

The *Theorema* Environment
for Interactive Proof Development

Florina Piroi[1] and Temur Kutsia[2,*]

[1] Johann Radon Institute for Computational and Applied Mathematics,
Austrian Academy of Sciences, A-4040 Linz, Austria
Florina.Piroi@oeaw.ac.at
[2] Research Institute for Symbolic Computation,
Johannes Kepler University, A-4040 Linz, Austria
Temur.Kutsia@risc.uni-linz.ac.at

Abstract. We describe an environment that allows the users of the *Theorema* system to flexibly control aspects of computer-supported proof development. The environment supports the display and manipulation of proof trees and proof situations, logs the user activities (commands communicated with the system during the proving session), and presents (also unfinished) proofs in a human-oriented style. In particular, the user can navigate through the proof object, expand/remove proof branches, provide witness terms, develop several proofs concurrently, proceed step by step or automatically and so on. The environment enhances the effectiveness and flexibility of the reasoners of the *Theorema* system.

1 Introduction

In general terms, it is agreed that mechanized theorem proving is about using computers to find a formal proof [1]. A rough classification of theorem provers divides them in automatic provers, where close to no human assistance is needed, and interactive provers, which require human assistance in developing the proof [18]. An extensive list of both automatic and interactive provers can be inspected at [3].

The goal of the *Theorema* project [8] is to provide support to the entire process of mathematical theory exploration. By default, *Theorema* tries to solve given reasoning problems automatically. However, since many mathematical theorems are hard to prove completely automatically, it is helpful to have an environment that supports interactive reasoning. This paper describes the current status of an experimental version of such an environment in *Theorema*. Although *Theorema* has support also for computing and solving, the environment is currently used only for proof development. It allows a finer grained interaction between a human user and the system. The environment aims at three groups of users. For the first one the environment has a didactic value: it can be used to train formal

* Temur Kutsia has been supported by the Austrian Science Foundation (FWF) under Project SFB F1302 and F1322.

G. Sutcliffe and A. Voronkov (Eds.): LPAR 2005, LNAI 3835, pp. 261–275, 2005.

proving. In the second group are those users who are already familiar with formal proving techniques and with the details of *Theorema*. For them, the environment enriches the proving power of the system by allowing them to use their creative ideas and intuition (for example, providing witness terms). The third group of users is the *Theorema* developers group, for which the environment is used as a tool for testing the provers that are still in development.

The first attempts to integrate interactivity into *Theorema* are described in [9] and some of those ideas were a starting point for the current interactive environment. Prior to this work, in [27] it is shown how interactive proving was to be integrated in the architecture of *Theorema*, but no implementation was done. Another attempt to provide user-system interaction is described in [17] and [16].

Shortly, our main contribution to the previous implementations are improved proof tree and proof situation management, a schematic representation of the proof tree, and multiple interconnected views of the underlying data structures.

This paper is organized as follows: In Section 2 we discuss general requirements for an interactive proof development environment. Section 3 gives an overview of the *Theorema* system and describes the experimental implementation of the *Theorema* interactive environment. In Section 4 an example of interactive proof development in *Theorema* is given. We overview some related work in Section 5 and we end with conclusions and future work in Section 6.

2   Requirements for an Interactive Environment for Proof Development

Design principles for interfaces to (interactive) provers, as well as the functionalities such interfaces should offer, have already been formulated by a number of authors; see [6, 12, 13, 28]. We do not intend to give yet another set of principles, but we will just gather user actions that correspond to the already formulated principles and classify them into logical and abstract interaction actions.

Our classification is based on the levels of abstraction described in [1]: a logical, an abstract interaction, and a concrete interaction level are considered to be necessary to characterise the interaction with an automated reasoning system. In this paper, we do not consider the actions at the concrete interaction level. We give, however, some considerations in this respect in Section 3.4. (For more usage and implementation details see [21].)

At the logical level the user actions are sketched only in terms of logical concepts [1], like for example the activity of reducing a mathematical expression to its canonical form. Other actions that are to be included in the class of logical level activities are providing witness terms, adding and removing formulae from the list of formulae used during a reasoning session, selecting formulae and/or proof strategies that are to be used in the next reasoning chain. At this level, a mathematician using an automated theorem prover must be given the possibility to save and restore proving sessions, to abandon proof attempts, and to work on several partial proofs at the same time. Additionally, it is also important that the user has quick access to information relevant to the development of the proof and that she is not burdened with unnecessary information. Proof navigation should be available and as simple as possible. A bonus for any interactive system is the presence of a comprehensive help system which gives users hints on how to use the system's commands and answers to their actions.

These activities do not assume having a good knowledge about automated reasoners, but only basic knowledge on doing proofs, which any user with a background in mathematics is supposed to have.

At the abstract interaction level users manipulate visual objects in order to communicate with the system. At this level no implementation details are considered, this is done at the third level, the concrete interaction level (which will not be discussed in this paper).

To realize the logical actions of the interactive reasoning systems, at the abstract interaction level, we have to provide means for structure manipulation and we should make use of objects representing logical knowledge. For example a directed graph structure can be used for visualising and navigating in a proof or for representing hierarchically composed theories of mathematical knowledge. Manipulating such structures requires maintaining connections between objects as data structures and their displays (tree representation or textual, user-friendly proof explanation). In order to facilitate users to store and restore proving sessions, the designer of an interactive proving system will have to provide mechanisms for script management to record, store, and maintain a history of user actions. Commands for developing proofs have to offer default behaviour in case they are incompletely specified. Articulating commands by various means (mouse clicks, typing, etc.) is also a feature which interactive proving systems should supply.

Finally, we remark that an action performed at the logical interaction level can be seen as an explanation and motivation for an action at the abstract level [1].

3   *Theorema*'s Interactive Environment

3.1   An Overview of the *Theorema* System

Theorema[1] is implemented in the programming language of the Mathematica system. The development is carried out since mid nineties under the guidance of Bruno Buchberger. A user exploring theories using *Theorema* interacts (automatically or semiautomatically) with three blocks of system components: reasoners, organizational tools, and libraries of mathematical knowledge [8].

Basic building blocks of the system's reasoners are inference rules that operate on reasoning situations—goals and knowledge bases. The rules are implemented as Mathematica functions. They can be grouped into modules and then combined into reasoners by various strategies. The reasoning process is guided by a *common search procedure*. The output of this procedure is a *global reasoning object* that follows a common structure which allows a homogeneous display of the output independent of which reasoner was used. The object is an AND-OR

---

[1] See www.theorema.org

tree which, during the search procedure, is expanded top-down, and the root contains the original reasoning situation. Terminal nodes on successful or failed branches and non-terminal nodes are labeled by (certain encodings of) the reasoning steps performed. Terminal nodes on the other branches are labeled by reasoning situations.[2]

The language of *Theorema* is an untyped higher order language extended with sequence variables. Type (or sort) information is in general handled by unary predicates or sets (if one decides to work in a set theory). However, particular reasoners may implement rules to deal with such information in a special way.

Theorema advocates efficient reasoning in special theories—like geometry, analysis, combinatorics—using algebraic algorithms as black box inference rules. For this purpose several special reasoners have been developed, e.g. the PCS prover [7] (standing for 'Prove Compute Solve') which implements a heuristics for elementary analysis and uses Collins's Cylindrical Algebraic Decomposition algorithm [10] as a solver. Another example of a special reasoner is the solver and simplifier for two-point linear boundary value problems [22]. *Theorema* currently contains 19 reasoners and is linked to 11 external reasoning systems and to the TPTP library; see [8].

During a *Theorema* session reasoners are accessed by a call of the form

$$Reason[entity, \text{ using } \rightarrow knowledge\text{-}base, \text{ by } \rightarrow reasoner, \text{ options}],$$

where *Reason* is Prove, Compute, or Solve; *entity* is the mathematical entity to which *Reason* applies, e.g. a proposition in the case of proving or an expression in the case of computing; *knowledge-base* is the knowledge with respect to which the reasoning should be performed; *reasoner* is the concrete (internal or external) reasoner we want to use. There are two groups of *options*: those specific to reasoners, which give means to influence their behaviour, and those that control the general search mechanism and the eventual post-processing tools (presentation, simplification, etc.). For convenience default values for each of the options are available. Information and usages of the available *Theorema* reasoners and options can be displayed with the Mathematica '?*symbol*' command.

In the sequel we concentrate on proof development only, i.e., the concrete reasoners are provers. A sample *Theorema* proving session consists of the following steps. First, Mathematica must be started and then *Theorema* loaded. Next, the knowledge the user wants to use (e.g. *formula, knowledge-base*) must be made available to the system. This can be done either by typing it in a Mathematica notebook[3] and evaluating it, or by loading a previously stored file. Finally, the corresponding *Reason* command should be (typed and) evaluated. The output is given in a separate notebook in a pretty-printed, textbook-style syntax.

If the proof does not succeed the user may re-start the proof search process with different premises (additional knowledge, different options of the used

---

[2] Those who are familiar with the NUPRL proof object may notice that the *Theorema* reasoning object and the NUPRL proof object are quite similar.

[3] Notebooks are part of the Mathematica front end. They are complete interactive documents combining text, tables, graphics, calculations, and other elements.

prover, different prover of *Theorema*). However, we would like to have the possibility to guide the proof search routines *during* the proof search. For example, we would like to hint to the prover that it should use certain instances for specific quantified variables at various points in the proof. In the following sections we will describe the tools that support such a user-system interaction.

The components of the *Theorema* interactive interface are working files, windows for displaying messages and logs, and menu-palette windows (toolbars).

The working files are usual Mathematica notebooks in which the users write and store the mathematical knowledge employed in a reasoning session (interactive or not). Special notebooks are The Proof Window, presenting proofs in a user-friendly style, and The Proof Tree Window which shows the tree structure of the proof. These two windows are maintained and updated by the system. By combining selections of cells in The Proof Window, in the working files, selections in The Proof Tree Window, and button clicks on the toolbars users can navigate within the proof, introduce new proof variants, give witness terms, etc.

Whenever an action could not be accomplished, the *Theorema* interactive interface makes use of notification dialogs with short explanation messages on why the action could not be performed. Also, a log window is present, where environment and proof information, actions performed by the user, etc. are displayed. The content of this window can be saved but, at the moment, to restore a proving session the users have to do the actions themselves, as recorded in the stored log, one by one.

The commands that realize the various actions for the interactive proof development can be articulated either with the help of the toolbars or by typing the commands in the working notebooks and sending them to the Mathematica kernel for evaluation.

3.2 Managing the Proof Tree

In the non-interactive mode, the *Theorema* provers apply the inference rules automatically. The inferences are repeatedly applied until either a proof is obtained or no further inferences can be applied. The users only see the final output of this process. In contrast, when searching for proofs in the interactive environment, the system is compelled to stop after each application of an inference rule, to present the proof produced so far, and to wait for a decision from the user.

In the interactive mode, the proofs are gradually developed starting from an initial proof tree: the root node that contains the proof problem as given by the user (goal formula and assumption formulae, if any) and, additionally, internal information specific to the provers and to the proof search routines of *Theorema*. Initially, the root is an unexplored node, or in *Theorema* terminology: a pending node. The information stored in an unexplored node is called a "proof situation".

The node expansion is done by calling a prover to apply one of its inferences to the node's proof situation. An inference rule application will produce none, one, or more proof situations that are inserted into the proof tree as unexplored children of the now expanded node. The proof search mechanism will add to the information stored in the expanded node a trace of the inference rule application.

When a proof under development has more than one unexplored node the user can select which one to expand next. If an expansion action is performed but no prior explicit selection of an unexplored node is made, the system will choose the leftmost unexplored one. Currently we are working on giving users the possibility to see a list of inference rules and proof methods that are applicable to a proof situation, as well as means to choose an inference rule and to select the formulae the rule should be applied on. The proof tree can be displayed in two variants, shown in Fig. 1: an english textual explanation produced from the traces of the inference rule applications, with pretty-printed formulae (in The Proof Window), or a schematic tree representation (in The Proof Tree Window). In both views, users can select nodes in the proof. If the selected node is expanded, the user

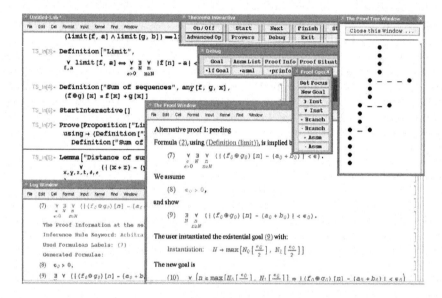

Fig. 1. The *Theorema* interactive environment: the working notebook, the most used menu-palettes, the two proof view windows, and the log window

can choose whether to start a new proof variant by adding a branch to the proof tree at the selection point, or to abandon the reasoning chain below the selection point by removing it. Removing a reasoning chain in the proof and continuing with a different one at the removal point can be seen as an undo operation. Users can also work on different proofs at the same time. The way this can be done in the interactive environment of *Theorema* is the following: For a newly added branch in the proof tree, the user has the possibility to state a different goal that is not necessarily derived from the originally given one. The assumptions available in the prove session when stating the new goal may be used in its proof, but new assumptions can also be added.

At the end of the proof development the proof tree will contain the traces of the user's actions during interactive development of proofs. However, this data structure does not record the order these actions were performed.

3.3 Managing the Proof Situation

In the previous sections we have mentioned that *Theorema* provers' inference rules take as input proof situations, i.e., a goal formula, a list of assumption formulae, and some local context storing facts and additional proof strategy information used by the provers of the system. For example, one such fact is keeping track of which formulae in the list of assumptions were matched against the goal formula. Another example is the storage of the names of the metavariables introduced by certain inference rules and their dependencies.

One of the specific difficulties in algorithmic proof generation is finding appropriate instances (at appropriate moments) for quantified variables. Within the interactive environment of *Theorema* it is possible to give the system witness terms which should be used for certain variables. If the variable is existentially quantified, a user-given instance will be taken into consideration only if the formula in which it occurs is the current goal and the quantifier that binds the variable is the outermost one. For universally quantified variables, a user-given instance is accepted only if the formula occurs in the list of current assumptions and if the quantifier binding the variables is the outermost one.

When we prove a theorem with pen and paper we use, for a start, only few definitions, properties, etc. of the notions occurring in the theorem we try to prove. As we proceed with the proof we usually recall other lemmata, properties, etc. which we use in the attempt to complete the proof. At the same time we may discard some formulae. *Theorema*'s interactive interface does allow users to add and remove formulae from the assumption list of an unexpanded node.

The natural language representation of the proof displays, for each proof step, the result of inference rule applications, namely, which formulae were used, which were generated, the used instantiations (if any), etc. Obviously, this does not reflect all the content of the nodes in the proof. One reason for this is that part of the information stored in the nodes is not relevant for the user, but only for the provers of the system. However, it is often the case that we are interested in the whole content of the proof node. We may want to know, for example, which are the formulae that are or were available when an inference rule was applied. The developers of the *Theorema* system may want to check the prover specific information to help them to develop and improve their provers. For this reasons, the interactive interface to *Theorema* provides access to the additional information stored in a node.

3.4 Comments on Implementation

Until recently, *Theorema* was used mainly in an automated mode and no interaction with the system during the proof search was possible. The first solution chosen to provide interaction was to suspend the execution of the proof search routine after one inference rule application. This was done by starting a Mathematica subprocess that collected the user actions [16].

In the current implementation we have opted for a different, simpler solution. We have introduced a system-global boolean variable which keeps track of the current proving mode (interactive or non-interactive), and a step-counter that controls the number of proof steps to be performed by the proof search routine.

In the non-interactive proving mode, the step-counter variable is ignored and the proof search routine proceeds until either a successful proof is obtained or no inference rule can be applied anymore. In the interactive mode, every time the proof search routine is invoked the step-counter is, first, set to a predefined value. With each inference rule application this value is decreased by one. As soon as the step-counter reaches zero, the proof search routine stops, and returns the proof developed sofar which is, then, presented to the user, in The Proof Window, The Proof Tree Window being also updated. When the user chooses to further expand the proof, the search routine will continue with expanding the left-most unexplored situation in the proof tree, unless otherwise indicated. The default value of the step-counter in the current implementation is set to 1, which means that the proof search stops after one inference rule application.

We mention here two important advantages of this solution. One is that only few modifications of the main proof search routines of the system were necessary: First, a check of the step-counter value was added to the termination conditions of the proof search routine and, second, certain *Theorema* specific variable initialization are by-passed when the proof search is invoked in the interactive mode. (For example, we do not want the proof-tree to be re-initialized, as in the non-interactive mode, but we want to expand it further). The second important advantage of the solution chosen by us is that no alteration of the existing provers of the *Theorema* system had to be done in order to use them for proving in the interactive mode.

Until version 5.1, Mathematica did not have facilities for developing user interfaces. Therefore, with the exception of buttons, the elements of the interactive environment interface do not include drop-down lists, dynamic menus, check boxes, context-sensitive menus, etc. Also, to our knowledge, in Mathematica, we cannot track the mouse actions. In other words, we cannot determine user inputs by tracking the mouse clicks and movements. The solution we have chosen to overcome this difficulty is to (require users to) make selections in notebooks and, on button clicks, manipulate the notebooks in the Mathematica kernel.

Within any open notebook, the front end always maintains a current selection (see [30], Section 2.11.3). Selections can be done by user clicks or by issuing commands from the kernel. Mathematica also provides commands for extracting the content of a selections in a notebook. So we are able to retrieve user input when the user makes selections in notebooks. The retrieved input is passed to the routines implementing the tools of the interactive environment. The routines process the input correspondingly to the tool they implement, e.g. add an assumption to the current proof situation, delete a branch in the proof-tree, provide witness terms, etc.

4   An Example

Assume now that we, as *Theorema* users, want to prove that the limit of the sum of two sequences is the sum of their limits. First, we formalize the proposition and the corresponding definitions in a *Theorema* notebook:

Proposition["Limit of sum",

$$\underset{f,a,g,b}{\forall} \ ((\mathrm{limit}[f,a] \wedge \mathrm{limit}[g,b]) \Rightarrow \mathrm{limit}[f \oplus g, a+b])\ ].$$

Definition["Limit",

$$\underset{f,a}{\forall} \ (\mathrm{limit}[f,a] \Leftrightarrow (\ \underset{\varepsilon>0}{\forall} \ \underset{N}{\exists} \ \underset{n \geq N}{\forall} \ |f[n] - a| < \varepsilon))\ ].$$

Definition["Sum of sequences",

$$\underset{f,g,x}{\forall} \ ((f \oplus g)[x] = f[x] + g[x])\ ].$$

This is exactly how it would look in the notebook: *Theorema* has a human-oriented, two-dimensional syntax. Next, we activate the interactive proving mode by evaluating the command **StartInteractive[]** which will open the necessary menu-palettes (see Fig. 1). We want to prove the proposition by one of the *Theorema* provers (PredicateProver), using the given definitions. For this we type, in a working notebook, the corresponding **Prove** command, as below, select it, and press the **Start** button on the *Theorema* Interactive palette (see Fig. 1).

Prove[Proposition["Limit of sum"],
        using→{Definition["Limit"], Definition["Sum of sequences"]},
        by→PredicateProver]

The system will show the user The Proof Window with the following content, where 'Pending proof of (*formula_label*)' represents an unexpanded node:

Prove:

    (Proposition(Limit of sum))

$$\underset{f,a,g,b}{\forall} \ ((\mathrm{limit}[f,a] \wedge \mathrm{limit}[g,b]) \Rightarrow \mathrm{limit}[f \oplus g, a+b])$$

   under the assumptions:

    (Definition(Limit)) $\underset{f,a}{\forall} \ (\mathrm{limit}[f,a] \Leftrightarrow (\ \underset{\varepsilon>0}{\forall} \ \underset{N}{\exists} \ \underset{n \geq N}{\forall} \ |f[n] - a| < \varepsilon)),$

    (Definition(Sum of sequences)) $\underset{f,g,x}{\forall} \ ((f \oplus g)[x] = f[x] + g[x]).$

Pending proof of (Proposition(Limit of sum)).

Here we can simply proceed by clicking the **Next** button. The prover applies the first rule applicable to the current proof situation ($\forall$-Right rule). In The Proof Window the last line (pending proof) is replaced by the following output:

For proving (Proposition(Limit of sum)) we take all variables arbitrary but fixed and prove:

(1) $\text{limit}[f_0, a_0] \wedge \text{limit}[g_0, b_0] \Rightarrow \text{limit}[f_0 \oplus g_0, a_0 + b_0]$

Pending proof of (1).

After several default steps this proof attempt will fail. The reason the proof fails is manifold. The main one, however is that the knowledge we started with is not sufficient for proving the goal formula. Secondly, the prover we have used is not strong enough and we would like to use a different one that, implicitly, uses some special knowledge on real numbers and, in addition, applies a particular strategy for handling formulae with alternating quantifiers. Therefore, we undo the proof, with the help of the -Branch button, and start again by using the Pcs prover. (We could also have started an alternative proof by adding a branch at a properly chosen point in the proof tree, using the +Branch button, and by selecting another prover to continue with, e.g., Pcs. In this way the previous failed attempt would still be present in the proof tree, giving us the possibility to see how different provers act on the same proof problem.)

From the previous failed proof attempt we, as humans, conclude that additional knowledge about absolute values and distances between points may help:

Lemma["Distance of sum",

$$\underset{x,y,z,t,\delta,\varepsilon}{\forall} \left(|(x+z) - (y+t)| < (\delta + \varepsilon) \right) \Leftrightarrow \left(|x-y| < \delta \wedge |z-t| < \varepsilon \right)].$$

After several proving steps the content of The Proof Window is:

Prove: ... (The initial proof problem is omitted for space reasons.)
We assume

(1) $\text{limit}[f_0, a_0] \wedge \text{limit}[g_0, b_0]$

and show

(2) $\text{limit}[f_0 \oplus g_0, a_0 + b_0]$.

Formula (1.1), by (Definition(Limit)), implies:

(3) $\underset{\substack{\varepsilon \\ \varepsilon > 0}}{\forall} \; \underset{N}{\exists} \; \underset{\substack{n \\ n \geq N}}{\forall} \; |f_0[n] - a_0| < \varepsilon.$

By (3), we can take an appropriate Skolem function such that

(4) $\underset{\substack{\varepsilon \\ \varepsilon > 0}}{\forall} \; \underset{\substack{n \\ n \geq N_1[\varepsilon]}}{\forall} \; |f_0[n] - a_0| < \varepsilon.$

Formula (1.2), by (Definition(Limit)), implies:

(5) $\underset{\substack{\varepsilon \\ \varepsilon > 0}}{\forall} \; \underset{N}{\exists} \; \underset{\substack{n \\ n \geq N}}{\forall} \; |g_0[n] - b_0| < \varepsilon.$

By (5), we can take an appropriate Skolem function such that

(6) $\forall_{\substack{\varepsilon \\ \varepsilon > 0}} \forall_{\substack{n \\ n \geq N_2[\varepsilon]}} |g_0[n] - b_0| < \varepsilon.$

Formula (2), using (Definition(Limit)), is implied by:

(7) $\forall_{\substack{\varepsilon \\ \varepsilon > 0}} \exists_N \forall_{\substack{n \\ n \geq N}} |(f_0 \oplus g_0)[n] - (a_0 + b_0)| < \varepsilon.$

We assume

(8) $\varepsilon_0 > 0$

and show

(9) $\exists_N \forall_{\substack{n \\ n \geq N}} |(f_0 \oplus g_0)[n] - (a_0 + b_0)| < \varepsilon_0.$

At this point we, as users, decide to influence the proof by providing an appropriate witness term for N. Selecting the formula (9) and clicking the button $\exists$ Inst, a dialog window opens where the witness term can be specified. We type in $\max[N_1[\varepsilon_0/2], N_2[\varepsilon_0/2]]$, and the proof proceeds:

Instantiation: $N \rightarrow \max[N_1[\frac{\varepsilon_0}{2}], N_2[\frac{\varepsilon_0}{2}]]$.

The current goal is

(10) $\forall_n ((n \geq \max[N_1[\frac{\varepsilon_0}{2}], N_2[\frac{\varepsilon_0}{2}]]) \Rightarrow |(f_0 \oplus g_0)[n] - (a_0 + b_0)| < \varepsilon_0).$

We assume

(11) $n_0 \geq \max[N_1[\frac{\varepsilon_0}{2}], N_2[\frac{\varepsilon_0}{2}]]$

and show

(12) $|(f_0 \oplus g_0)[n_0] - (a_0 + b_0)| < \varepsilon_0.$

Formula (12), using (Definition(Sum of sequences)), is implied by:

(13) $|(f_0[n_0] + g_0[n_0]) - (a_0 + b_0)| < \varepsilon_0.$

Formula (13), using (Lemma(Distance of sum)), is implied by:

(14) $\exists_{\substack{\delta, \varepsilon \\ \delta + \varepsilon = \varepsilon_0}} (|f_0[n_0] - a_0| < \delta \wedge |g_0[n_0] - b_0| < \varepsilon).$

Here we interact again by instantiating δ and ε with $\varepsilon_0/2$.

Instantiation: $\delta \rightarrow \frac{\varepsilon_0}{2}$, $\varepsilon \rightarrow \frac{\varepsilon_0}{2}$.

The current goal is

(15) $\frac{\varepsilon_0}{2} + \frac{\varepsilon_0}{2} = \varepsilon_0 \wedge |f_0[n_0] - a_0| < \frac{\varepsilon_0}{2} \wedge |g_0[n_0] - b_0| < \frac{\varepsilon_0}{2}.$

Formula (15) is implied by

(16) $|f_0[n_0] - a_0| < \frac{\varepsilon_0}{2} \wedge |g_0[n_0] - b_0| < \frac{\varepsilon_0}{2}.$

Formula (16), by (4) is implied by

(17) $\frac{\varepsilon_0}{2} > 0 \wedge n_0 \geq N_1[\frac{\varepsilon_0}{2}] \wedge |g_0[n_0] - b_0| < \frac{\varepsilon_0}{2}$,

which by (6) is implied by

(18) $\frac{\varepsilon_0}{2} > 0 \wedge n_0 \geq N_1[\frac{\varepsilon_0}{2}] \wedge n_0 \geq N_2[\frac{\varepsilon_0}{2}]$.

Formula (18), by (8), is implied by

(19) $n_0 \geq N_1[\frac{\varepsilon_0}{2}] \wedge n_0 \geq N_2[\frac{\varepsilon_0}{2}]$.

Here we notice that another assumption is needed that we add immediately to the knowledge base used by the proof search routine. To add the assumption we use the +Assm button. The proof proceeds then as follows:

The user added the assumption:

(Lemma(Max))

$$\underset{m,M_1,M_2}{\forall} \; (m \geq \max[M_1, M_2] \Rightarrow (m \geq M_1 \wedge m \geq M_2)).$$

Formula (19), by (Lemma(Max)), is implied by

(20) $n_0 \geq \max[N_1[\frac{\varepsilon_0}{2}], N_2[\frac{\varepsilon_0}{2}]]$.

Formula (20) is proved because it is identical to (11).

To summarize, this example demonstrates various ways of interaction with the system: cutting a branch and backtracking, changing the prover, adding assumptions, and providing witness terms.

5   Related Work

A concise historical overview of interactive systems is given in [19]. Though in most of the cases the design principles listed in [6, 12, 13] or [28] were not specifically followed, many interfaces have common functionalities. We briefly describe some of these systems (mathematical assistants), insisting on those features similar to the ones present in *Theorema*. For more details on the described systems we direct the reader to the literature (e.g. [29], or the forthcoming issue on Mathematics Assistance Systems of the Journal of Applied Logic [4]).

One of the interactive systems with the largest pool of users is the HOL system [14], now at version 4. It is an environment for interactive theorem proving in higher-order logic and has a wide variety of uses from formalizing mathematics (see for example [15]) to verification of industrial hardware. It has high degree of programmability through the meta language ML which allows extending the system to provide more functionality. Thus, packages for proof tree administration, goal tracking, script save and replay, etc. are available within HOL. As a theorem proving system, HOL has a command-line interface. As in *Theorema*, the system permits adding assumptions to a proof in development, but no removing of formulae is possible. The proofs are done in a goal directed style but tacticals that do forward inferencing are also present in the system. If users decide that wrong proof steps were done, they can undo to the previous proof state. There is also a restart possibility by backtracking to the root. Switching between goals is possible both in HOL and in *Theorema*. Several graphical interfaces were implemented for the system, like Tk-HOL [26], `xhol` [23], and Emacs modes are widely used. The interfaces provide theory browsing and searching, graphical views of the proof state (similar to the schematic proof tree representation in *Theorema*'s interactive environment), etc.

The Isabelle system [20] is a generic proof assistant which allows defining different logical calculi and using them for proving. It is closely integrated with the Proof General [2] for editing and developing proofs and, similar to the HOL system, allows proof storage and replay, undo and revert operations, proof states display, etc. (Proof General [2] is a generic tool for proof development that provides a uniform interface and interaction mechanism not only for Isabelle but for other proof assistants as well, like Coq, LEGO, and, experimentally, with HOL, ACL2 and λClam.) However, the system does not maintain a proof object and only one view of the proof is available (the one shown in the Proof General window). In its latest version, Isabelle provides a tool for searching theorems in the system's library of theories by simple patterns.

Coq [5], another logical framework system, is a proof assistant for the Calculus of Inductive Constructions. It allows the interactive construction of formal proofs, and also the manipulation of functional programs. A variety of user interfaces are provided for it. For example CoqIde is a graphical user interface based on gtk which allows proof tree navigation, structural editing of formulae and commands, and has an autocomplete facility for command articulation. Pcoq, CtCoq, and Proof General are other interfaces for Coq. Lately, an integration of Coq into TeXmacs is also available.

Ωmega [24] is an interactive proof development system. The system has two main components: a proof planner, and an integrated collection of tools for formulating problems, proving subproblems, and proof presentation. LΩui is an interface for Ωmega which combines features for graphical display of proofs as a graph, hypertext facilities for term browsing, proof and proof plan presentation in natural language. It also has an editor for adding and maintaining the knowledge base, and a command suggestion mechanism; see [25].

NuPRL [11] supports the interactive creation of proofs, formulas, and terms. Based on Martin-Löf type theory, it is a system for implementing mathematics. NuPRL has a multi-window graphical environment and a keyboard-based proof navigation tools.

6 Future Work and Conclusions

The current status of the *Theorema* interactive environment allows users to select a proof situation in the proof; inspect the content of a selected proof situation; add or remove assumptions in a selected proof situation; suggest witness terms; add or remove branches in the proof tree; model concurrent proof development; select one from several provers to continue the proof, eventually change its options; make the system expand the proof by one inference rule application; ask the system to automatically complete the proof.

In future versions of the environment we plan to include a tool for inference rule selection. Namely, for a selected proof situation, the tool should present, on request, a list of applicable inference rules. The user can select one or more inferences to be applied in the next step. Selecting more than one inference from the list means that the user intends to investigate several proof alternatives for the given proof situation, one alternative for each inference rule selected. However, to implement such a inference selection tool, important modifications of the *Theorema* system are necessary. For example, inference rules need to be uniquely identifiable among all the inferences of the system. We also plan to include facilities for specifying tactics.

Other tools we plan to include in the environment are possibilities to store and load proof sessions, extracting proof strategies from a proof session. A variant of the latter tool can be used to help the developers of the Theorema provers compose new provers based on the sequence of inferences used in an interactive proof session. To achieve this, we will have to analyze the proofs obtained in the interactive mode, in order to extract the relevant proof steps and inference rules.

References

1. J. S. Aitken, P. D. Gray, T. F. Melham, and M. Thomas. Interactive theorem proving: An empirical study of user activity. *J. Symb. Comp.*, 25(2):263–284, 1998.
2. D. Aspinall. Proof general: A generic tool for proof development. In *Proc. TACAS'2000*, volume 1785 of *LNCS*, pages 38–42. Springer, 2000.
3. A database of mechanized reasoning systems. `http://www-formal.stanford.edu/clt/ARS/systems.html`.
4. C. Benzmüller, editor. *Mathematics Assistance Systems*. Special Issue of J. Applied Logic. Elsevier, 2005. To appear.
5. Y. Bertot and P. Castèran. *Interactive Theorem Proving and Program Development: Coq'Art: The Calculus of Inductive Constructions*. Texts in Theoretical Computer Science. An EATCS Series. Springer, 2004.
6. R. Bornat and B. Sufrin. Jape's quiet interface. In *Proc. Second Workshop on User Interfaces for Theorem Provers (UITP'96)*, 1996.
7. B. Buchberger. The PCS prover in Theorema. In R. Moreno-Díaz, B. Buchberger, and J. Luis Freire, editors, *EUROCAST'01*, volume 2178 of *LNCS*, pages 469–478. Springer, 2001.
8. B. Buchberger, A. Crăciun, T. Jebelean, L. Kovács, T. Kutsia, K. Nakagawa, F. Piroi, N. Popov, J. Robu, M. Rosenkranz, and W. Windsteiger. *Theorema*: Towards computer-aided mathematical theory exploration. *J. Applied Logic*, 2005. To appear in [4].
9. B. Buchberger, T. Jebelean, and D. Văsaru. Theorema: A system for formal scientific training in natural language presentation. In T. Ottmann and I. Tomek, editors, *Proc. ED-MEDIA/ED-TELECOM'98*, pages 174–179, 1998.
10. G. E. Collins. Quantifier elimination for real closed fields by cylindrical algebraic decomposition. In *Second GI Conference on Authomata Theory and Formal Languages*, volume 33 of *LNCS*, pages 134–183. Springer, 1975.

11. R. Constable. *Implementing Mathematics Using the Nuprl Proof Development System.* Prentice Hall, 1986.
12. K. Eastaughffe. Support for interactive theorem proving: Some design principles and their application. In *Proc. 4th Workshop on User Interfaces for Theorem Provers (UITP'98)*, 1998.
13. J. A. Goguen. Social and semiotic analyses for theorem prover user interface design. *Formal Aspects of Computing*, 11(3):272–301, 1999.
14. M. Gordon and T. Melham. *Introduction to HOL: A Theorem Proving Environment for Higher-Order Logic.* Cambridge University Press, 1993.
15. T. C. Hales. A computer verification of the Kepler conjecture. In *Proceedings of the ICM*, volume 3, pages 795–804, Beijing, China, 2002.
16. F. Kossak. An interface for interactive proving with the mathematical software system Theorema. Technical Report 99–19, RISC, University of Linz, 1999.
17. F. Kossak and K. Nakagawa. User–System Interaction within Theorema. Technical Report 99-37, RISC, University of Linz, 1999.
18. R. Moten. Just the facts, Jack: Truths and myths of automated theorem provers. *Contemporary Mathematics*, 252:31–48, 1999.
19. T. Nipkow and W. Reif. An introduction to interactive theorem proving. In W. Bibel and P. Schmitt, editors, *Automated Deduction—A Basis for Applications.* Kluwer Academic Publishers, 1998.
20. L. Paulson. Isabelle: the next 700 theorem provers. In P. Odifreddi, editor, *Logic and Computer Science*, pages 361–386. Academic Press, 1990.
21. F. Piroi. *Tools for Using Automated Provers in Mathematical Theory Exploration.* PhD thesis, RISC, Johannes Kepler University, Linz, Austria, August 2004.
22. M. Rosenkranz. A new symbolic method for solving linear two-point boundary value problems on the level of operators. *J. Symb. Comp.*, 39(2):171–199, 2005.
23. T. Schubert and J. Biggs. A tree-based, graphical interface for large proof development. In *HOL Theorem Proving and Its Applications, 7th Int. Workshop*, 1994.
24. J. Siekmann, C. Benzmüller, and S. Autexier. Computer Supported Mathematics with ΩMEGA. *J. Applied Logic*, 2005. To appear in [4].
25. J. Siekmann, S. Hess, C. Benzmüller, L. Cheikhrouhou, A. Fiedler, H. Horacek, M. Kohlhase, K. Konrad, A. Meier, E. Melis, M. Pollet, and V. Sorge. LΩUI: Lovely Ωmega User Interface. *Formal Aspects of Computing*, 11(3):326–342, 1999.
26. D. Syme. A new interface for HOL—ideas, issues and implementation. In E. T. Schubert, P. J. Windley, and J. Alves-Foss, editors, *HOL Theorem Proving and Its Applications, 8th Int. Workshop*, number 971 in LNCS, pages 324–339. Springer, 1995.
27. E. Tomuţa. *An Architecture for Combining Provers and its Applications in the Theorema System.* PhD thesis, Johannes Kepler University, Linz, July 1998.
28. N. Völker. Thoughts on requirements and design issues of user interfaces for proof assistants. *Electronic Notes in Theoretical Computer Science*, 103:139–159, 2004.
29. F. Wiedijk. Comparing mathematical provers. In A. Asperti, B. Buchberger, and J. H. Davenport, editors, *Proc. MKM'03*, volume 2594 of *LNCS*, pages 188–202. Springer, 2003.
30. S. Wolfram. *The Mathematica Book.* Wolfram Media Inc., 5th edition, 2003.

A First Order Extension of Stålmarck's Method

Magnus Björk

Department of Computing Science,
Chalmers University of Technology,
Gothenburg, Sweden

Abstract. We describe an extension of Stålmarck's method in First Order Logic. Stålmarck's method is a tableaux-like theorem proving method for propositional logic, that uses a branch-and-merge rule known as the dilemma rule. This rule opens two branches and later merges them, by retaining their common consequences. The propositional version does this with normal set intersection, while the FOL version searches for pairwise unifiable formulae from the two branches. The proof procedure attempts to find proofs with as few simultaneously open branches as possible. We present the proof system and a proof procedure, and show soundness and completeness. We also present benchmarks for an implementation of the proof procedure.

1 Introduction

Stålmarck's method [9] is a method for tautology checking in propositional logic, that has been successful in many real world verification problems. Its most distinguishing feature is the *dilemma rule*, which is a branch-and-merge rule. Similarly to the analytic cut rule, it creates two branches, and assumes that a formula (called the *dilemma formula*) is true in one branch, and false in the other one. If a contradiction is found in one of the branches, the proof method continues in the other one as usual. The difference from other tableaux calculi is that if none of the branches leads to a contradiction, then they are merged into one branch, consisting of the *intersection* of the two branches. Thereby, all the facts that were derived in *both* branches are retained after the merge.

Stålmarck's method is only complete if we allow arbitrary nesting of dilemmas. However, it has turned out that many interesting verification problems only require one or two simultaneous dilemmas. The proof procedure initially searches for proofs without dilemmas. Thereafter, it searches for proofs with at most one simultaneously open dilemma, and then two dilemmas, and so on.

In a privately circulated draft, Stålmarck sketched a first order extension of the proof method. Since then it has been refined several times [7, 2, 3, 4]. Lundgren and Björk have made implementations of different versions of the proof method.

---

[1] Proofs to some of the theorems in this paper can be found in an appendix, available at http://www.cs.chalmers.se/~mab/LPAR05.

G. Sutcliffe and A. Voronkov (Eds.): LPAR 2005, LNAI 3835, pp. 276–291, 2005.

Figure 1 contains an example proof. The formulae labelled 1 through 3 are the axioms that we start from. These axioms are consistent, so we will not be able to derive a contradiction in the example, but it is enough to show how the dilemma rule works. The numbers within square brackets show the premises for each derived formula. Formulae 4 to 6 are derived from the axioms, by eliminating the quantifiers, and replacing the quantified variables with fresh ones. These variables are *universal*, and may be unified with anything.

After formula 6, it is not possible to derive anything else with non-branching rules. Therefore we pick a dilemma formula ($P(X, Y)$ in this example), create two branches, and assume that the dilemma formula is true in one branch, and false in the other one. While the variables in formulae 4 to 6 are universal, the variables in the dilemma formula are *rigid*. That means that they cannot be substituted. They denote arbitrary but fixed values, and must be treated as the same values in both branches.

The two branches contain relatively simple derivations. Note that we can introduce more complex formulae from simpler ones (see formula 1.3) if the resulting formula is an instance of a subformula of an existing formula (in this case formula 5).

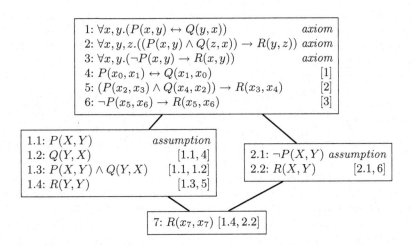

$$1: \forall x, y.(P(x, y) \leftrightarrow Q(y, x)) \qquad axiom$$
$$2: \forall x, y, z.((P(x, y) \wedge Q(z, x)) \rightarrow R(y, z)) \; axiom$$
$$3: \forall x, y.(\neg P(x, y) \rightarrow R(x, y)) \qquad axiom$$
$$4: P(x_0, x_1) \leftrightarrow Q(x_1, x_0) \qquad [1]$$
$$5: (P(x_2, x_3) \wedge Q(x_4, x_2)) \rightarrow R(x_3, x_4) \quad [2]$$
$$6: \neg P(x_5, x_6) \rightarrow R(x_5, x_6) \qquad [3]$$

1.1: $P(X, Y)$	*assumption*
1.2: $Q(Y, X)$	[1.1, 4]
1.3: $P(X, Y) \wedge Q(Y, X)$	[1.1, 1.2]
1.4: $R(Y, Y)$	[1.3, 5]

2.1: $\neg P(X, Y)$	*assumption*
2.2: $R(X, Y)$	[2.1, 6]

$$7: R(x_7, x_7) \; [1.4, 2.2]$$

Fig. 1. One application of the dilemma rule

When it is time to merge the branches, we are allowed to do more with the rigid variables. Here, we can substitute them, and in this case it is useful to unify X and Y, since then both branches contain $R(Y, Y)$. Furthermore, we can replace the rigid variables with universal variables, so after the branches are merged, x_7 may be unified with any terms. Note that the rigid variables weren't destructively instantiated in the branches, so if it had been possible to substitute them in other ways to create other conclusions, we could have done that too: Say, for instance, that the left branch had contained the formula

$R(c, d)$. Then we could have added $R(c, d)$ to the merged branch, together with $R(x_7, x_7)$.

No destructive instantiations are ever performed. If we find that instantiating a rigid variable may lead further, we memorize that instantiation, and later repeat the same dilemma, but with the more specific instance. In this way, we can easily find good candidates for future dilemma formulae.

The rest of this paper is organized as follows: Section 2 describes the proof system and states the soundness theorem. Section 3 describes two versions of the proof procedure (one simplified and one efficient), states the completeness theorems, and outlines the proofs thereof. Section 4 presents benchmarks of an implementation of the proof method.

The main contributions of this paper, that are previously unpublished, are the completeness proof, the benchmarks, and some notation that makes the proof system more readable.

2   The Proof System and Soundness

2.1   A Logic with Universal and Rigid Variables

We define a logic that has two syntactic categories for variables: *universal variables* (denoted by x, y, z) and *rigid variables* (denoted X, Y, Z). In short, we define the semantics by introducing *models* (usually denoted by M), that are pairs $\langle D, I \rangle$ consisting of a *domain*, which is a non-empty set, and an *interpretation*, which is a function that assigns domain elements to all constant symbols and rigid variable symbols, n-ary functions to all n-ary function symbols, and n-ary relations to all n-ary predicate symbols. In addition, we use *variable assignments* (denoted β), which are functions that assign domain elements to universal variable symbols. We say that two interpretations I and I' are V-variants if they assign the same values to all symbols, except the ones occurring in the set V (and similarly for variable assignments).

Given a model $M = \langle D, I \rangle$ and a variable assignment β we define the value of terms and formulae in a standard way. For instance, $f(t_1, \ldots, t_n)^{I, \beta} = (f^I)(t_1^{I, \beta}, \ldots, t_n^{I, \beta})$ and $X^{I, \beta} = X^I$. The value of a formula is either $\mathbf{t}$ or $\mathbf{f}$. For instance we define $[A \wedge B]^{I, \beta} = \mathbf{t}$ iff $A^{I, \beta} = B^{I, \beta} = \mathbf{t}$. We say that a model $M = \langle D, I \rangle$ *satisfies* a set of formulae Δ (denoted $M \models \Delta$) if for all variable assignments β and all formulae $A \in \Delta$, $A^{I, \beta} = \mathbf{t}$. A set of formulae Δ' is a *logical consequence* of another set of formulae Δ (denoted $\Delta \models \Delta'$) if all models that satisfy Δ also satisfy Δ'.

So, in the semantics of the logic, the rigid variables and the constants have similar roles. The difference arises when we define *substitutions*, which are finite mappings from both universal and rigid variable symbols to terms. Single substitutions usually only substitute one kind of variables. We denote substitutions with only universal variables in their support by σ, and substitutions of rigid variables with τ. We say that a substitution is *universal with respect to a set of formulae* Δ if its support only contains universal variables, and it does not introduce any variables that occur bound in formulae in Δ. It is straightforward to show lemmas such as $\Delta \models \Delta \cup \Delta\sigma$ for any given Δ and σ which is universal w.r.t. Δ.

We say that a set of formulae Δ is *contradictory* if there are formulae $A \in \Delta$ and $\neg B \in \Delta$, and a universal substitution σ, such that $A\sigma = B\sigma$. Although all contradictory sets are unsatisfiable, the two concepts are not identical: contradiction is a syntactically decidable property, which is an approximation of the semantical property of undecidability.

We define an operation *refresh*, which given a set of formulae returns virtually the same set of formulae, except that some of the free universal variables occurring in formulae in Δ have been replaced by fresh variables, in such a way that no universal variable symbol occurs free in more than one formula in the new set. It is straightforward to show that $\Delta \models \mathit{refresh}(\Delta)$.

An important lemma states that if a set of formulae holds for all possible valuations of some specific rigid variables, then these rigid variables can be replaced by universal ones. The lemma is formulated as follows:

Lemma 1. *Given a model $\langle D, I \rangle$, a set of rigid variable symbols V, a set of formulae Δ, a substitution $\tau = \{X_1 \mapsto x_1, \ldots, X_n \mapsto x_n\}$, where $X_1, \ldots, X_n$ are the elements of V, and $x_1, \ldots, x_n$ are universal variable symbols not occurring in formulae in Δ, then if $\langle D, I' \rangle \models \Delta$ for all V-variants I' of I, then $\langle D, I \rangle \models \Delta\tau$.*

2.2   Logical Intersections

As we mentioned before, Stålmarck's method in propositional logic allows two branches to be merged, retaining the intersection of the consequences of the two branches. For soundness and completeness it would be enough to use ordinary set intersection in the first order version as well. However, it is possible to do a bit better than that. Consider, for instance, the two sets of formulae $\{P(x)\}$ and $\{P(c_0), \neg P(c_1)\}$. Clearly, $P(c_0)$ is a logical consequence of both the sets, but the intersection of the two sets is empty. We introduce the notion of *logical intersections* of sets of formulae, which are sets consisting of formulae that come from unifications of formulae in the original sets.

Definition 1. *Given three sets of logical formulae Δ_1, Δ_2, and Δ, we say that Δ is a logical intersection of Δ_1 and Δ_2 if for all $A \in \Delta$ there are formulae $A_1 \in \Delta_1$ and $A_2 \in \Delta_2$, and a substitution σ which is universal w.r.t. $\Delta_1 \cup \Delta_2$, such that $A = A_1\sigma = A_2\sigma$.*

As an example, the set $\{P(g(y)), Q(c, d)\}$ is a logical intersection of the two sets $\{P(x), Q(c, z), \neg Q(d, d)\}$ and $\{P(f(x)), P(g(y)), Q(x, d)\}$. $P(f(x))$ is not in the intersection, since that would require unifying x and $f(x)$. We unify $P(x)$ and $P(g(y))$ to yield $P(g(y))$, and $Q(c, z)$ and $Q(x, d)$ to yield $Q(c, d)$. We cannot unify $\neg Q(d, d)$ with anything, so it does not give rise to any of the formulae in the intersection.

2.3 Derivations

We now define *derivations*, which essentially are sequences of rule applications. Derivations and rules are defined in terms of each other, and we chose to begin with the definition of derivations. Rules will be defined immediately afterwards.

Derivations always have a *source* and a *sink*, both of which are sets of formulae. We denote that Π is a derivation with source Δ and sink Δ' by $\Pi : \Delta \vdash \Delta'$. In contrast to usual sequent and tableaux calculi, dilemma derivations are always linear, in the sense that they have one entry point and one exit point. Internally, they may have several branches though.

Definition 2 (Derivations).

- *For any set of formulae Δ, $\Delta : \Delta \vdash \Delta$. Such derivations are called* empty.
- *For any two sets of formulae Δ and Δ', $\Delta/\Delta' : \Delta \vdash \Delta'$ if Δ/Δ' is an instance of a simple rule*
- *For any two sets of formulae Δ and Δ', and any derivations Π_1 and Π_2,*

$$\frac{\Delta}{\dfrac{\Pi_1 \quad \Pi_2}{\Delta'}} : \Delta \vdash \Delta' \text{ if } \frac{\Delta}{\dfrac{\Pi_1 \quad \Pi_2}{\Delta'}} \text{ is an instance of the dilemma rule.}$$

- *For any sets of formulae Δ_1, Δ_2, and Δ_3, and derivations Π_1 and Π_2 such that $\Pi_1 : \Delta_1 \vdash \Delta_2$ and $\Pi_2 : \Delta_2 \vdash \Delta_3$, $\Pi_1/\Pi_2 : \Delta_1 \vdash \Delta_3$.*

Derivations are always finite.

2.4 Rules

The proof system consists of a number of non-branching rules (called *simple rules*), and a branch-and-merge rule (called *the dilemma rule*).

The Propositional Propagation Rule. This rule allows us to propagate information through propositional connectives. If more than one premise is involved, we may need to unify them. This is done with the help of the substitution σ.

Given two sets of formulae Δ and Δ', Δ/Δ' is an instance of the propositional propagation rule *if there are $n + 1$ formulae $A_1, \ldots, A_n, A$ for some positive n, and a substitution σ such that:*

- $A_1 \ldots A_n \in \Delta$
- σ *is universal w.r.t.* Δ
- $A_1\sigma, \ldots, A_n\sigma/A\sigma$ *is an instance of a propositional propagation condition (see below).*
- $\Delta' = \Delta \cup \{A\sigma\}$

Example:

$$\frac{\{\neg(P(x) \wedge Q(x,y)), P(c)\}}{\{\ldots, \neg Q(c,y)\}}$$

Below are all propositional propagation conditions[1]. A, A_1 and A_2 are meta-variables denoting arbitrary formulae, $i, j \in \{1, 2\}$, and $i \neq j$.

$$\neg\neg A/A \qquad A_1 \wedge A_2/A_i \qquad\qquad A_1, A_2/A_1 \wedge A_2$$
$$A/\neg\neg A \qquad \neg(A_1 \wedge A_2), A_i/\neg A_j \qquad \neg A_i/\neg(A_1 \wedge A_2)$$

The $\forall$-introduction rule. Universal variables are implicitly universally quantified. The $\forall$-introduction rule allows us to make them explicitly quantified. This rule, and all other introduction rules, may only be used if the introduced formula is an instance of a subformula of the original axioms. The expression σ_x denotes the same substitution as σ, except that it does not substitute x.

Given two sets of formulae Δ and Δ', Δ/Δ' is an instance of the $\forall$-introduction rule if there is a formula A, two universal variable symbols x and x_0, and a substitution σ such that:

- $A \in \Delta$
- No quantifier in A binds the variable x
- $x_0 \mapsto x \in \sigma$ and σ_{x_0} is universal w.r.t. Δ
- $\Delta' = \Delta \cup \{\forall x.A\sigma\}$

Example:

$$\frac{\{P(f(x_0))\}}{\{P(f(x_0)), \forall x.P(f(x))\}}$$

The $\forall$-elimination rule. Just as we can turn free variables into quantified ones, we can do the opposite, and make universally quantified variables free.

Given two sets of formulae Δ and Δ', Δ/Δ' is an instance of the $\forall$-elimination rule iff there is a formula A, a universal variable symbol x, and a substitution σ such that $\forall x.A \in \Delta$, σ is universal w.r.t. Δ, and $\Delta' = \Delta \cup \{A\sigma\}$.

The $\neg\forall$-introduction rule. If we know a formula to be false, we can replace any of its subterms with a variable, and state that the formula is not true for all values of that variable.

Given two sets of formulae Δ and Δ', Δ/Δ' is an instance of the $\neg\forall$-introduction rule if there is a formula A, a universal variable symbol x, a term t, and a substitution σ, such that:

- $\neg A\{x \mapsto t\} \in \Delta$
- $\{x \mapsto t\}$ is universal w.r.t. Δ
- σ is universal w.r.t. Δ
- $\Delta' = \Delta \cup \{(\neg\forall x.A)\sigma\}$

Example:

$$\frac{\{\neg P(f(x_0, c))\}}{\{\neg P(f(x_0, c)), \neg\forall x.P(x)\}}$$

The $\neg\forall$-elimination rule. If we know that a formula of the shape $\neg\forall x.A$ is true, then A is false for some value of x. We call such a value a *witness*. To eliminate the quantifier, we can give a name to a witness, even if we do not

---

[1] We use a logic that only contains the connectives $\wedge$ and $\neg$, since all other connectives can be expressed in terms of these two. It is straightforward to extend the proof system and the related theorems to also include other connectives. In figure 1, we assume that these extensions has been made.

know what value the witness has. If A contains free variables, then the witness may depend on the value of these variables, so we have to introduce a function that takes them as argument. This technique is usually called *skolemization*.

Given two sets of formulae Δ and Δ', Δ/Δ' is an instance of the $\neg\forall$-elimination rule if there is a formula A, a universal variable symbol x, a substitution σ, and a term t such that:

- $\neg\forall x.A \in \Delta$
- σ is universal w.r.t. Δ
- t is a fresh constant symbol if $freevars(\neg\forall x.A) \cup rigid(\neg\forall x.A) = \emptyset$, otherwise $t = f(x_1,\ldots,x_n,X_1,\ldots,X_m)$, where f is a fresh function symbol, $freevars(\neg\forall x.A) = \{x_1,\ldots,x_n\}$ and $rigid(\neg\forall x.A) = \{X_1,\ldots,X_m\}$.
- $\Delta' = \Delta \cup \{\neg A\{x \mapsto t\}\sigma\}$

Example:

$$\frac{\{\neg(\forall x.P(x,x_0))\}}{\{\ldots,\neg P(f_0(x_0),x_0)\}}$$

The Dilemma Rule. The dilemma rule has a different shape than the rules we have seen so far. It introduces a formula A (called *the dilemma formula*), that must not contain any free universal variables, but may contain rigid variables. We let V denote the set of rigid variables occurring in A, but not in Δ. Each application of the dilemma rule contains two subderivations Π_1 and Π_2, that are the two branches. At the end of the dilemma rule, all rigid variables that were introduced in the dilemma formula are turned into fresh universal variables by the substitution τ.

Given sets of formulae Δ, Δ_1, Δ_2, and Δ', a formula A, and derivations

$\Pi_1 : \Delta \cup \{A\} \vdash \Delta_1$ *and* $\Pi_2 : \Delta \cup \{\neg A\} \vdash \Delta_2$, *then* $\dfrac{\Delta}{\dfrac{\Pi_1 \quad \Pi_2}{\Delta'}}$ *is an instance of*

the dilemma rule, if there is a set of rigid variable symbols V, and a substitution τ such that:

- $freevars(A) = \emptyset$
- $V = rigid(A) \setminus rigid(\Delta)$
- $\tau = \{X_1 \mapsto x_1,\ldots,X_n \mapsto x_n\}$, where $X_1\ldots X_n$ are the elements of V, and $x_1,\ldots,x_n$ are fresh universal variables.
- Δ' is any set of formulae if both Δ_1 and Δ_2 are contradictory.
- $\Delta' = refresh(\Delta_2\tau)$ if only Δ_1 is contradictory
- $\Delta' = refresh(\Delta_1\tau)$ if only Δ_2 is contradictory
- $\Delta' = refresh(\Delta_\cap)$, where $\Delta_\cap$ is a logical intersection of $\Delta_1\tau$ and $\Delta_2\tau$ if neither Δ_1 nor Δ_2 is contradictory

2.5   Soundness

Basically, the soundness theorem states that if $\Pi : \Delta \vdash \Delta'$ then $\Delta \models \Delta'$. But since the system includes skolemization (the $\neg\forall$-elimination rule), this notion of soundness does not hold. Instead, the soundness theorem is formulated as:

Theorem 1 (Soundness). *Given two sets of formulae Δ and Δ', a derivation $\Pi : \Delta \vdash \Delta'$, and a model $M = \langle D, I \rangle$ (for some D and I), such that $M \models \Delta$. Then there exists a model $M^\Pi = \langle D, I^\Pi \rangle$ such that $M^\Pi \models \Delta'$. We call M^Π the* canonical model of M for Π.

The proof of the soundness theorem can be found in the appendix of this paper (see footnote on title page). It goes through all forms of derivations, and describes how to construct the canonical model in each case.

The most interesting part is proving the soundness of the dilemma rule when neither of the branches is contradictory. In essence, we pick an arbitrary formula B in the logical intersection, and note by the definition of logical intersections that then there are formulae B_1 and B_2 in the respective branches, and a substitution σ s.t. $B = B_1\sigma = B_2\sigma$. We then prove that for any interpretation I and assignment β, $B_1^{I,\beta} = \mathbf{t}$ or $B_2^{I,\beta} = \mathbf{t}$ (this follows by induction). This, in turn, means that $(B_1 \vee B_2)^{I,\beta} = \mathbf{t}$. Applying σ to this formula preserves its truth, and since $B_1\sigma \vee B_2\sigma = B \vee B$, we see that $B^{I,\beta} = \mathbf{t}$ for all I and β.

3 Proof Procedures and Completeness

We now define a proof procedure that applies simple rules as far as possible. When it cannot do that any more, it applies dilemmas with only simple rules in the branches. The procedure increases the nesting level of the dilemmas, until a contradiction has been found. The completeness of the procedure relies on the fact that the set of derived formulae meets a notion of saturation after each new nesting level. It can be shown that if a set of formulae has a KE-refutation [5] of a finite size, then when the set of consequences has reached a certain (finite) saturation level, it must be contradictory. Since KE is complete, it follows that our proof procedure is complete.

The first problem is how to define saturated sets. In propositional logic, we say that a set of formulae is n-saturated if no new consequences can be derived using simple rules and dilemma rules that are nested at most n levels. A finite set of propositional formulae always has a finite n-saturated superset, for each n. That is not the case in FOL; for instance, the smallest 0-saturated superset of $\{P(c), P(x) \to P(f(x))\}$ contains all formulae $P(f^i(c))$, for all i. To remedy this problem, we introduce a notion of term rank, which measures how complex terms are (and thereby how complex formulae are). There are several possible ways of defining rank, and we will not present any of them in this paper. The important thing is that the notion of rank limits the size of the formulae, and that if we can derive a formula B from the premises A_0 and A_1, then the rank of B must be larger than that of A_0 as well as of A_1.

During proof search, we only use formulae whose rank is less than some preselected maximal rank. The proof procedure is only complete if we select a maximal rank that is large enough. One could imagine a proof procedure that applies iterative deepening to find a sufficiently large rank. However, benchmarks suggest that it is better to fix a rather large maximal rank from the beginning.

3.1   Preliminaries

Given a set of formulae Γ (typically the set of user supplied formulae that the proof procedure attempts to refute) and natural number r, we denote by $instances(\Gamma, r)$ the set of all formulae $A\sigma$ or $\neg A\sigma$, where A is a subformula of a formula in Γ, and σ is a substitution (that is universal w.r.t. Γ), that instantiates the free variables of A with terms consisting only of the function- and constant symbols found in formulae in Γ, and any rigid and universal variable symbols, in such a way that the rank of $A\sigma$ and $\neg A\sigma$ does not exceed r. Similarly, we denote by $gInstances(\Gamma, r)$ the set of all ground formulae in $instances(\Gamma, r)$.

Given a finite set of formulae Γ, and a natural r, the set $gInstances(\Gamma, r)$ is finite. The proof of this relies on the observation that $gInstances(\Gamma, r)$ is a set of strings that are bounded in size (due to the bounded rank), with symbols from a finite alphabet (namely the symbols occurring in Γ). The set $instances(\Gamma, r)$ may be infinite, but any variant free subset of it is finite, for similar reasons.

A set of formulae Δ is a *context* for another set of formulae Γ if Δ is a subset of $instances(\Gamma, r)$ for some r. Contexts are used to keep a record of formulae that are known to be true. The goal is to find a contradictory context.

We say that a formula A is a *generalization* of a formula B if $B = A\sigma$ for some substitution σ that is universal w.r.t. A. In particular, any formula is a generalization of itself. If A is a generalization of B, then $\{A\} \models \{B\}$.

We say that a formula A is an *immediate consequence* of a set of formulae Δ, if it possible to derive A with only one application of a single rule, and only formulae from Δ as premises. We call these formulae premises of A. If A is an immediate consequence of Δ, but there is no generalization of A in Δ, we say that A is a *locally unsaturated point of* Δ.

3.2   A Simplified Proof Procedure

We now present a simplified proof procedure, and show that it is complete. The first simplification is how it selects dilemma formulae. The procedure we present here simply enumerates all ground formulae with low enough rank. Later in the paper, we describe a more efficient strategy. The second simplification we have done is to exclude all introduction rules. We do this since the proof procedure is complete without them, and it makes the completeness proof simpler.

The proof procedure consists of three parts: *propagation*, *0-saturation*, and *n-saturation*. The propagation procedure (below) takes as arguments a context and a specific formula in the context, and returns all immediate consequences of the context, that have the specific formula as a premise. The $parentsOf(A, context)$ operation used on line 3 returns all subformulae of instances of formulae in *context*, that have A as an immediate subformula. It also returns the substitutions that creates the right instance. For example, if $(P(x) \wedge Q(y)) \wedge R \in context$, then $(P(x) \wedge Q(y), \sigma) \in parentsOf(P(f(z)), context)$, where $\sigma = \{x \mapsto f(z)\}$, since $(P(x) \wedge Q(y))\sigma$ is a parent of $P(f(z))$. The operation $findAllUnif(\Delta, A)$ returns the set of substitutions σ, such that σ is a most general unifier for A and some formula in Δ.

The propagate procedure mainly consists of two parts. The loop on lines 3 to 12 tries to find instances of the propagation condition $\neg(A_1 \wedge A_2), A_i/\neg A_j$, where our A corresponds to A_i in the condition. It does so by first checking if there is a parent of A that is a conjunction, and then checking if there are instances of the conjunction that are known to be false. The second part (lines 13-27) finds all applicable elimination rules, that have A as a premise. It does this by pattern matching on the shape of A.

```
1.   propagate(A, context) =
2.     new ← ∅
3.     for each (B, σ) ∈ parentsOf(A, context) do
4.       switch B
5.         case b₀ ∧ b₁ :
6.           for each σ' ∈ findAllUnif(context, ¬Bσ) do
7.             if b₀σ = A then
8.               new ← new ∪ {¬b₁σσ'}
9.             else
10.              new ← new ∪ {¬b₀σσ'}
11.        case default:
12.          skip
13.    switch A
14.      case B ∧ C :
15.        new ← new ∪ {refresh(B), refresh(C)}
16.      case ¬(B ∧ C) :
17.        for each σ ∈ findAllUnif(context, B) do
18.          new ← new ∪ {refresh(¬Cσ)}
19.        for each σ ∈ findAllUnif(context, C) do
20.          new ← new ∪ {refresh(¬Bσ)}
21.      case ∀x.B :
22.        new ← new ∪ {refresh(B)}
23.      case ¬∀x.B :
24.        if findAllUnif(context, ¬B) = ∅ then
25.          new ← new ∪ {refresh(skolemize(¬B, x))}
26.      case ¬¬B :
27.        new ← new ∪ {refresh(B)}
28.    return new
```

The 0-saturation procedure repeatedly calls the propagation procedure, until no more facts can be derived using simple rules (or all such facts have too high rank). It maintains a queue, *unprocessed*, which contains all new consequences that have been added to the context, and that may themselves lead to new consequences. The caller of *saturate* must provide the initial state of the queue (usually all new assumptions). The procedure does not modify the context passed in the argument (*gcontext*); it maintains a local context (*lcontext*), that contains all new consequences.

```
1.   saturate(0, gcontext, start, maxRank) =
2.     lcontext ← ∅
3.     unprocessed ← start
4.     while hasElement(unprocessed) do
5.       A ← dequeue(unprocessed)
6.       new ← propagate(A, gcontext ∪ lcontext)
7.       for each B ∈ new do
8.         if findGenOf(gcontext ∪ lcontext, B) = nothing then
9.           if findUnif(gcontext ∪ lcontext, B̄) ≠ nothing then
10.            return contradiction
11.          lcontext ← lcontext ∪ {B}
12.          if rank(B) < maxRank then
13.            enqueue(B, unprocessed)
14.    return lcontext
```

The n-saturation procedure iterates through all ground formulae smaller than the maximal rank, creates two branches for each formula (one where the formula is assumed to be true, and one where it is false), and recursively calls $n-1$-saturation on the branches. The branches are thereafter combined according to the dilemma rule. As already mentioned, we later describe a more efficient way to find dilemma formulae.

```
1.  saturate(n, gcontext, start, maxRank) =
2.     candidates ← gInstances(gcontext, maxRank)
3.     lcontext ← saturate(n − 1, gcontext, start, maxRank)
4.     if gcontext ∪ lcontext = contradiction then
5.        return contradiction
6.     while hasElement(candidates) do
7.        A ← dequeue(candidates)
8.        if findGenOf(gcontext ∪ lcontext, A) = nothing and
              findGenOf(gcontext ∪ lcontext, Ā) = nothing then
9.           switch(saturate(n − 1, gcontext ∪ lcontext ∪ {A}, {A}, maxRank)
                 , saturate(n − 1, gcontext ∪ lcontext ∪ {Ā}, {Ā}, maxRank))
10.             case (contradiction, contradiction) :
11.                return contradiction
12.             case (context1, contradiction) :
13.                lcontext ← lcontext ∪ context1
14.             case (contradiction, context1) :
15.                lcontext ← lcontext ∪ context1
16.             case (context1, context2) :
17.                lcontext ← lcontext ∪ intersect(context1, context2)
18.     return lcontext
```
The main

loop of the proof procedure simply applies n-saturation for an increasing value of n, starting with 0.

```
1. main(problem, maxRank) =
2.    context ← saturate(0, problem, problem, maxRank)
3.    level ← 1
4.    while not contradictory(context) do
5.       context ← context ∪ saturate(level, context, ∅, maxRank)
6.       level ← level + 1
7.    return contradiction
```

3.3   Completeness

We now state some important lemmas for the code presented above, and outline their proofs. The first lemma is about the *propagate* procedure.

Lemma 2. *Given a context Δ for a finite set of formulae Γ, and a formula $A \in \Delta$, then propagate(A, Δ) terminates and returns a finite context for Γ that contains a generalization of each immediate consequence[2] of Δ that has A as premise.*

A proof of this lemma essentially matches the cases in the *propagate* procedure with all simple rules. The termination of *propagate* relies on that *parentsOf* and *findAllUnif* returns finite sets.

---

[2] This is a slightly simplified version of the lemma. A full version must state an exception: an immediate consequence of Δ, with a premise of the shape $\neg\forall x.A'$ is only required to be present if there are no witnesses of $\neg\forall x.A'$ already in Δ. Some of the following definitions and lemmas are simplified in the same way.

We now define what it means for a set of first order formulae to be saturated. The notion of saturation has three parameters: n, r, and Θ. The parameter n corresponds to the nesting level of dilemma rules, r to the maximal rank of formulae, and Θ to the set of formulae that are used as dilemma formulae. It may be surprising that the definition of saturated sets does not contain a case corresponding to the fourth case of the dilemma rule, the one where the branches are merged using the logical intersection. However, even though this case makes the proof system more powerful, it is not needed for completeness. The proof procedure would still be complete, although very inefficient, if it never calculated the intersection of any branches, and only relied on finding contradictions.

Definition 3. *Given two sets of formulae Δ and Θ and a natural number r, we say that Δ is $(0, r, \Theta)$-saturated if each immediate consequence of Δ with rank less than r has a generalization in Δ.*

Given two sets of formulae Δ and Θ and two natural numbers $n > 0$ and r, we say that Δ is (n, r, Θ)-saturated if Δ is $(n - 1, r, \Theta)$-saturated, and for all formulae $A \in \Theta$:

- *If all $(n - 1, r, \Theta)$-saturated supersets of $\Delta \cup \{A\}$ as well as of $\Delta \cup \{\neg A\}$ are contradictory, then Δ is contradictory too.*
- *If all $(n - 1, r, \Theta)$-saturated supersets of $\Delta \cup \{A\}$ are contradictory, but there are non-contradictory $(n - 1, r, \Theta)$-saturated supersets of $\Delta \cup \{\neg A\}$, then $\neg A \in \Delta$.*
- *If all $(n - 1, r, \Theta)$-saturated supersets of $\Delta \cup \{\neg A\}$ are contradictory, but there are non-contradictory $(n - 1, r, \Theta)$-saturated supersets of $\Delta \cup \{A\}$, then $A \in \Delta$.*

Any contradictory set is (n, r, Θ)-saturated for all n, r, and Θ.

There is a correspondence between locally unsaturated points and saturated sets: a (n, r, Θ)-saturated set can only have locally unsaturated points of which the rank is larger than r. This proposition is related to the following lemma:

Lemma 3. *Given a natural number r, a set of formulae Δ that is $(0, r, \Theta)$-saturated (for some Θ), and another set of formulae Δ', then any locally unsaturated point of $\Delta \cup \Delta'$ either has a formula in Δ' as premise, or has a rank larger then r.*

We now come to the most important part of the completeness proof, where we show that the saturate procedure produces saturated sets. One of the arguments to the saturate procedure is a queue, *start*, that must contain at least one premise of each unsaturated point. Using lemma 3, we can do this by dividing the context into two parts, where one part is previously saturated. The proof procedure maintains a saturated context, and calls the saturate procedure after adding assumptions, so this is in line with how the procedure is used.

Lemma 4. *Given a finite queue Q, three finite sets of formulae Δ, Δ', and Γ, and two natural numbers n and r, such that $\Delta \cup \Delta'$ is a context for Γ, Δ is*

$(n-1, r, gInstances(\Gamma, r))$-*saturated, and all the elements of Δ' are in Q. Then* *saturate$(n, \Delta \cup \Delta', Q)$ terminates and returns a finite set $\Delta^\star$ such that $\Delta \cup \Delta' \cup \Delta^\star$* *is a $(n, r, gInstances(\Gamma, r))$-saturated context for Γ.*

Proof. We prove this lemma by induction over n. This comes naturally, since both the definition of saturated sets and of the *saturate* procedure are recursive. We will only outline the proof here.

Base case: For the base case, we assume that $n = 0$, and look at the code for 0-saturation, which mainly consists of a loop. We show that the loop has the following invariant: any locally unsaturated point of the set $\Delta \cup \Delta' \cup$ *lcontext* either has a premise in *unprocessed* or has a rank larger than r. Initially, *lcontext* is empty, so the invariant follows from lemma 3. When the loop terminates, *unprocessed* is empty, so then the whole base case follows from the invariant. The termination of the loop follows from the fact that no element can be added to *unprocessed* twice, and there are only finitely many possible elements to add.

Step: We assume that $n > 0$ and that the theorem holds for $n - 1$. Once again, the main effort goes into proving a loop invariant: that $\Delta \cup \Delta' \cup$ *lcontext* is $(n, r, gInstances(\Gamma, r) \setminus candidates)$-saturated. This invariant holds initially, since the set $gInstances(\Gamma, r) \setminus candidates$ is empty. After the loop terminates, it implies the entire step, since *candidates* is empty. Termination follows since *candidates* is finite, and no elements are ever added to it after initialization.

It is easy to show that in the nth iteration, the loop in the main procedure produces an $(n, r, gInstances(\Gamma, r))$-saturated superset of the problem formulation Γ. It is also possible to show that any $(n, r, gInstances(\Gamma, r))$-saturated superset of Γ is contradictory, if there is a KE refutation of Γ with depth n, and r is chosen large enough. However, that proof is beyond the scope of this paper. The completeness of our proof procedure follows from the completeness of KE:

Theorem 2. *Given any unsatisfiable set of first order formulae, Γ, $main(\Gamma, r)$* *terminates and returns a contradiction, provided r is large enough.*

3.4   A More Efficient Proof Procedure

Although this strategy is complete, it is very inefficient due to its naive way of selecting dilemma formulae. We now describe a more efficient strategy, and briefly argue for its completeness.

The simplified procedure initializes *candidates* with all ground formulae up to a certain rank (see line 2 of the n-saturation procedure). The efficient version only adds the subformulae of formulae of Γ, with all variables replaced by fresh rigid variables. This allows us to introduce universal variables, since the dilemma rule lets us turn rigid variables into universal ones when we merge branches. Therefore, we may derive more general conclusions early in the proof with this approach. But that is not the main benefit.

The proof system does not allow any unification of rigid variables — all substitutions are universal, except when dilemma branches are merged. But what we are interested in is finding the instances of the rigid variables that can help us get further. The way this is done, for instance in Fitting tableaux [6] is to let the unification algorithms detect when instantiating a variable can allow two formulae to be unified, and then destructively perform the instantiation in the whole proof. Our proof procedure detects possible instances of rigid variables in a similar way, but never performs any destructive updates. Instead of instantiating a variable before the branch ends, the saturate procedure enqueues a new dilemma formula in the *candidates* queue. This new dilemma formula is the same as the one currently used, except that the rigid variables are instantiated the way the unification algorithm suggested.

In this way, the current dilemma will be finished without any instantiations being made. Later in the proof, the more specialized version of the same dilemma will be dequeued and carried out, and will now lead to more conclusions. This approach also solves the fairness problem in many tableaux calculi; since we can enqueue several instances of the same dilemma formula, we do not need to select only one of them. The proof procedure memorizes all dilemma formulae that have been used in the current branch, so that the identical dilemmas are not repeated. It is also necessary to limit the rank of the dilemma formulae, or else we can run into non-termination.

The most important difference in the completeness proof is the new loop invariant for the n-saturation procedure. It now states that $\Delta \cup \Delta' \cup lcontext$ is $(n, r, gInstances(\Gamma, r) \setminus gInstances([candidates]\tau, r))$-saturated, where τ is a substitution that replaces the rigid variables introduced in the dilemma formula with universal ones. While the previous version ignores all formulae still in the *candidates* queue, this version ignores *all instances* of the formulae in the queue.

Termination is motivated as follows: in the previous version we relied on the fact that no new formulae were added to the *candidates* queue. Now, termination follows from the observation that the same formula can only be enqueued once, and the number of possible formulae are bounded by a finite rank.

4 Benchmarks

In 2004, the theorem prover *Dilemma* was implemented. It implements the more efficient proof procedure, described in the last section. The implementation is quite straightforward, and leaves many opportunities for optimizations. It first ran in late June, and made it first public appearance a couple of weeks later, when it participated in the FOF division of CASC-J2 [10]. Lacking equality handling, it performed poorly in the division — 65 of the 88 selected problems required equality reasoning. Out of the 23 remaining problems, it proved 9. As a comparison, E-SETHEO proved all 23, while Otter proved 4. However, given the immature state of Dilemma, we believe the results aren't too bad. Both Otter and Dilemma are quite simple implementations of their respective calculi, and with the right optimizations it would probably be possible to increase the efficiency of both substantially.

Benchmarks have been performed on large parts of the TPTP library [11]. We ran the tests on AMD XP 2800+ machines with 1GB RAM and Linux, and set the timeout to ten minutes. Of the problems in TPTP 2.7.0, Dilemma proves 192 of the 305 equality free theorems encoded as formulae, 120 of the 974 theorems with equality encoded as formulae, and 733 of the 1290 theorems without equality encoded as clauses (by parsing the clause sets as formulae).

The TPTP library assigns a rating between 0 and 1 for each problem, where 0 means that all current theorem provers can solve it, and 1 means that no known theorem prover has managed to prove the problem so far. Out of the 1045 solved problems, 205 have a non-zero rating, and 20 are rated 0.5 or higher. The four highest rated problems that dilemma solves have rating 0.78.

5 Future Work

As the benchmarks and results from CASC suggest, the proof procedure could really benefit from having support for equality. Perhaps the main ideas behind paramodulation [8] can be incorporated into our proof procedure?

The propositional version of Stålmarck's method is usually defined using partial equivalence relations (PER) instead of contexts. Instead of just keeping track of formulae that are known to be true, a PER keeps track of formulae that are known to be equivalent. This is powerful in combination with the dilemma rule; complementary conclusions often arise in the two branches, and the fact that these formulae are equivalent to the dilemma formula holds in both branches. We want something similar in FOL. Attempts have been made [4], but the problem is a lot more complex than in propositional logic. Maybe it is only possible to come up with an approximate solution - perhaps inspired by equality reasoning.

Another highly interesting topic for future work is to find conditions for when the proof procedure can safely stop, and conclude that no contradiction can be found, and perhaps even produce a counter example. Such techniques exist for similar calculi, such as Model Evolution [1].

References

1. Baumgartner, P., Tinelli, C.: The Model Evolution Calculus. CADE 19, LNAI 2741, Springer, 2003
2. Björk, M.: Extending Stålmarck's Method to First Order Logic. TABLEAUX 2003 Position Papers and Tutorials. (2003) 23–36
3. Björk, M.: Stålmarck's Method for Automated Theorem Proving in First Order Logic. Licentiate Thesis, (2003) http://www.cs.chalmers.se/~mab
4. Björk, M: Adding Equivalence Classes to Stålmarck's Method in First Order Logic. Doctoral Programme of IJCAR 04, CEUR workshop proc., ISSN 1613-0073, Vol 106
5. D'Agostino, M., Mondadori, M.: The Taming of the Cut. Journal of Logic and Computation, Nr 3, Vol 4, 1994, 285–319
6. Fitting, M.C.: First-Order Logic and Automated Theorem Proving. Springer-Verlag, New York (1996), 2nd ed

7. Lundgren, L.: Stålmarck's Method in FOL. Master's th., Chalmers University, 1999
8. G. Robinson and L. Wos: Paramodulation and theorem-proving in first-order theories with equality. In Machine Intelligence 4, Vol. Edinburgh U. Press, 1969.
9. Sheeran, M., Stålmarck, G.: A Tutorial On Stålmarck's Proof Procedure for Propositional Logic, Formal Methods in System Design, 16:1, 2000, 23-58.
10. CADE ATP System Competition 2004 (CASC), organized by Geoff Sutcliffe. http://www.cs.miami.edu/~tptp/CASC/J2
11. Thousands of Problems for Theorem Provers, http://www.cs.miami.edu/~tptp/

Regular Derivations in Basic Superposition-Based Calculi

Vladimir Aleksić and Anatoli Degtyarev

Department of Computer Science, King's College,
Strand, London WC2R 2LS, U.K.
{vladimir, anatoli}@dcs.kcl.ac.uk

Abstract. We prove the completeness of the regular strategy of derivations for superposition-based calculi. The regular strategy was pioneered by Kanger in [Kan63], who proposed that all equality inferences take place before all other steps in the proof. We show that the strategy is complete with the elimination of tautologies. The implication of our result is the completeness of non-standard selection functions by which in non-relational clauses only equality literals (and all of them) are selected.

1 Introduction

In this work we prove the completeness of *regular* strategy in derivations in superposition-based calculi. Introducing the concept of regular derivation for sequent calculus with equality, Kanger [Kan63] proposed that all equality inferences take place at the beginning of the derivation, so that they precede all other steps in the proof.

In the case of clause calculi, the possibility to regularize derivations was formulated and proved by Robinson and Wos [RW69b], as a result about the completeness of paramodulation:

If a functionally reflexive set of clauses S is closed under paramodulation and factoring, and if S is E-unsatisfiable, then S is unsatisfiable.

This work analyzes regular derivation strategy in clause calculi. Proving completeness of regular derivations turns out not to be a trivial problem, especially with showing compatibility with a set of redundancy criteria. The goal is to prove the following conjecture from [DV01]:

Let S be a set of Horn clauses with respect to equality literals, with the following property: the arguments of every non-equality atom in S are variables. Then there exists a refutation of S with redundancy criteria C in which applications of superposition precede applications of all other rules [1] (resolution, equality solution and factoring).

---

[1] We try to prove the existence of a more constrained form of derivations, in which both superposition and equality solution precede all other inferences.

G. Sutcliffe and A. Voronkov (Eds.): LPAR 2005, LNAI 3835, pp. 292–306, 2005.
© Springer-Verlag Berlin Heidelberg 2005

The statement of the conjecture addresses clauses in which the arguments of non-equality literals are variables. Even though this may sound as a restriction, the reason behind is that this way we can eliminate tautologies from derivations. Focus on the example by Lynch [Ly97].

Example 1. Consider the following set of clauses

$$\to P(c, b, b)$$
$$P(c, c, b), P(c, b, c) \to b \approx c$$
$$P(x, y, y) \to P(x, y, x)$$
$$P(x, y, y) \to P(x, x, y)$$
$$P(c, c, c) \to$$

and assume an ordering such that $b \succ c$. If an equality literal is selected in each clause, it is possible to make exactly two superposition inferences, which both derive a tautology.

However, this set of clauses can be transformed to a logically equivalent set of *flat clauses*, which have the property that all arguments of predicate literals are variables.

1. $\quad\quad\quad\quad\quad\quad\quad\quad x \approx c, y \approx b \to P(x, y, y)$
2. $x \approx c, y \approx b, P(x, x, y), P(x, y, x) \to b \approx c$
3. $\quad\quad\quad\quad\quad\quad\quad\quad\quad P(x, y, y) \to P(x, y, x)$
4. $\quad\quad\quad\quad\quad\quad\quad\quad\quad P(x, y, y) \to P(x, x, y)$
5. $\quad\quad\quad\quad\quad\quad\quad\quad x \approx c, P(x, x, x) \to$

Let selection be the same as in the original set of clauses. Inferences that previously led to tautologies can not be preformed anymore since paramodualtions into variables are forbidden. As a result, there is a regular derivation without tautologies.

6. $\quad\quad\quad\quad\quad\quad\quad\quad\quad y \approx b \to P(c, y, y)$ [es 1]
7. $y \approx b, P(c, c, y), P(c, y, c) \to b \approx c \quad$ [es 2]
8. $\quad\quad\quad\quad P(c, c, b), P(c, b, c) \to b \approx c \quad$ [es 7]
9. $y \approx c, P(c, c, b), P(c, b, c) \to P(c, y, y) \quad$ [s 8, 6]
10. $\quad\quad P(c, c, b), P(c, b, c) \to P(c, c, c) \quad$ [es 9]
11. $\quad\quad\quad\quad\quad\quad\quad\quad P(c, c, c) \to \quad$ [es 5]
12. $\quad\quad\quad\quad\quad\quad\quad\quad \to P(c, b, b) \quad$ [es 6]

The Horn subset consisting of the "relational" clauses 3, 4, 10, 11 and 12 is unsatisfiable, i.e. is refuted by resolution without tautologies under arbitrary selection function.

Recall the conjecture from [DV01], quoted earlier in this chapter. We prove, motivated by the previous example, that the statement of the conjecture holds taken that the set C contains only one redundancy criterion – tautology elimination.

In case of superposition calculi like basic superposition (see [BGLS92], [NR92a]) and strict basic superposition (see [BG97]), it turns out that the conjecture holds only if inference rules are applied on clauses that are *Horn with respect to equality literals* (for general clauses, it is obvious that some factoring inferences must precede superposition). This, however, is not a restriction, since any set of general (w.r.t. equality literals) clauses can, by renaming equality literals using new predicate symbols, be translated into a satisfiability equivalent set of clauses which are Horn with respect to equality literals.

Example 2. For the following unsatisfiable set of clauses, it is obvious that factoring has to take place before superposition.

$$\to a \approx b, a \approx b$$
$$\to a \approx c, a \approx c$$
$$b \approx c \to$$

This set of clauses can be modified to a satisfiability equivalent set of clauses that is Horn with respect to equality literals. For example, it can be done in the following way.

$$\to P, a \approx b$$
$$\to Q, a \approx c$$
$$P \to a \approx b$$
$$Q \to a \approx c$$
$$b \approx c \to$$

It is easy to check that using only equality inferences the unsatisfiable set of "relational" clauses $\{P \to Q,\ Q \to P,\ P, Q \to,\ \to P, Q\}$ can be derived without applying factorisation on equality literals.

In terms of the latest results in paramodulation-based theorem proving, our result can be formulated in a few different ways, as a theorem about the completeness of a superposition-based calculus which:

– employs a special selection strategy by which all equality literals and only they are selected in non relational clauses;
– employs an ordinary selection strategy, but imposes the order by which equality literals are always greater then relational literals, i.e. admits $t \succ P(t)$, where t is a term, P is a predicate symbol, and hence, dismissing the subterm property.

Referring to the items listed above, there have been some results in the direction of refining superposition-based systems either by weakening term and literal orderings or by allowing arbitrary selection strategies. However, none of them is wide enough to cover our result. Here we outline such attempts.

Trying to weaken term ordering constraints, Bofill and Rubio (see [BR02]) proved the completeness of ordered paramodulation for Horn clauses that is based on orderings without the sub-term property. Since their result does not implement basic strategies, and being restricted to ordered paramodulation (not superposition), it can not be used to prove our claim. Moreover, it is not certain if their result can be extended to employ redundancy notions like simplification and tautology elimination.

Regarding arbitrary selection strategies, the latest result has been presented by Aleksić and Degtyarev in [AD05], where they extend the results on the completeness of arbitrary selection strategies for basic paramodulation on Horn clauses of Bofill and Godoy given in [BG01]. The result presented in [AD05] is about the completeness of arbitrary selection strategies for basic superposition on general constrained clauses, provided there exists a refutation with no factoring inferences. Our consideration, in strictly equational setting, also addresses derivations from general clauses but does not require the existence of a factoring free refutation. For this reason, and for the reason that it does not support standard redundancy elimination techniques, the result of [AD05] on arbitrary selection can not be used to cover our claim either.

Overall, the regular derivation strategy defines a framework for some refinements of the state-of-art superposition-based inference systems, which can be considered non-standard because of the following reasons:

- Superposition-based systems are normally based on reduction orderings. Regular strategy addresses weakened versions, in particular the orderings without the sub-term property in the sense given below.
- Classical selection strategies for superposition-based proving are parametrized by a given ordering on ground terms. Namely, if a positive atom is selected it has to be maximal in the clause, with respect to the given ordering. Regular strategy means a refinement of this, since it allows literals to be selected regardless of their maximality.
- Normally, the application of superposition rules is restricted to the maximal literals of the premises. Regular strategy enables dropping the literal ordering constraints in order to postpone the applications of the inferences on predicate literals (i.e. resolution and factoring) till the end of the derivation.

Even though our proof is based on transformations of derivation trees, it is essentially different to the one given by Bofil and Godoy in [BG01], because:

- Their transformation method assumes that the initial derivation employs eager selection of negative literals, which is not a requirement in our transformations.
- The calculi they use are on Horn clauses. Having to deal with multiple positive literals in our case produces a plenty of difficult cases in our transformations.

2   Preliminaries

Here we present only notions and definitions necessary for understanding the paper. For a more thorough overview, see [NR99]. It is assumed that the reader has a basic knowledge in substitution and unification.

All formulae are constructed over a fixed signature Σ containing at least one constant and a binary predicate symbol $\approx$. In order to distinguish equality from identity, we use $=$ to denote the latter. By X we denote a set of variables. The set of all *terms* over the signature Σ with variables from X is denoted by $T_\Sigma(X)$ and the set of *ground terms* $T_\Sigma(\emptyset)$ by T_Σ.

An *equation* is an expression denoted by $t_1 \approx t_2$ or equivalently $t_2 \approx t_1$. For dealing with non-equality predicates, atoms $P(t_1, \ldots, t_n)$, where P is a predicate symbol of arity n and $t_1, \ldots, t_n$ are terms, can be expressed by equations $P(t_1, \ldots, t_n) \approx true$, where $true$ is a new symbol. In order for this encoding to be sound, we use a two-sorted logic, in which the sort of predicate symbols and the symbol $true$ is different from the sort of the function symbols. A *literal* is a positive or a negative equation.

The expression $A[s]_p$ indicates that an expression A contains s as a sub-expression at a position p. $A[t]_p$ is a result of replacing the occurrence of s in A at the position p by t. We assume that the position of t in A is always the same as the position of s. Therefore we will not explicitly mention positions of sub-terms within terms, and will write $A[s]$ and $A[t]$ meaning $A[s]_p$ and $A[t]_p$. An *instance* $A\sigma$ of A is the result of applying the substitution σ to A.

A *clause* is a disjunction of literals, denoted by a formula $L_1, L_2, \ldots, L_m$. This definition allows for multiple occurences of identical literals, i.e. for treating clauses as multiset of literals. Sometimes, especially in examples to improve readability, we use the sequent notation by which a clause $\neg A_1, \ldots, \neg A_k, B_1, \ldots B_l$ is represented as $A_1, \ldots, A_k \to B_1, \ldots, B_l$.

A *constraint* is a possibly empty conjunction of *atomic equality constraints* $s = t$ or *atomic ordering constraints* $s \succ t$ or $s \succeq t$. The empty constraint is denoted by $\top$.

A *constrained clause* is a pair consisting of a clause C and a constraint T, written as $C \mid T$. The part C will be referred to as the *clause part* and T the *constraint part* of $C \mid T$. A constrained clause $C \mid \top$ will be identified with the unconstrained clause C.

A substitution σ is said to be a *solution of an atomic equality constraint* $s = t$, if $s\sigma$ and $t\sigma$ are syntactically equivalent. It is a *solution of an ordering constraint* $s \succ t$ (with respect to a reduction ordering $>$ which is total on ground terms), if $s\sigma > t\sigma$, and a solution of $s \succeq t$ if it is a solution of $s \succ t$ or $s = t$. Generally, a substitution σ is a solution of a constraint T, if it is a simultaneous solution to all its atomic constraints. A constraint is satisfiable if it has a solution.

A *ground instance* of a constrained clause $C \mid T$ is any ground clause $C\sigma$, such that σ is a ground substitution and σ is a solution to T.

A *tautology* is a constrained clause whose all ground instances are tautologies. There are two forms of tautologies:

$$C, l \approx r \mid T \quad \text{where } \sigma \text{ is a solution to } T \text{ and } l\sigma = r\sigma$$

and

$$C, s \not\approx t, l \approx r \mid T \quad \text{where } \sigma \text{ is a solution to } T \text{ and } l\sigma = s\sigma \text{ and } r\sigma = t\sigma.$$

A *contradiction* is a constrained clause $\square \mid T$, with an empty clause part such that the constraint T is satisfiable. A constrained clause is called *void* if its constraint is unsatisfiable. Void clauses have no ground instances and therefore are redundant.

A set of constrained clauses is *satisfiable* if the set of all its ground instances is satisfiable.

A *derivation* is a possibly infinite ordered sequence of sets of clauses, where each set is obtained from the previous one either by adding a clause (conclusion of an inference) or by deleting a clause by using deletion rules. Further in the paper, we define a set of inference and deletion rules relevant for this work. A derivation of the empty clause is differently called a *refutation*.

Throughout the paper we assume that derivations are in tree-like form, with constrained clauses as nodes. In the tree representation, premisses of inferences are children nodes of their conclusions. In a derivation tree, a node can not have more than one parent. Therefore, if a clause takes part in more than one inference, the derivation tree contains as many copies of the clause (with the whole sub-derivation it is a conclusion of). The constrained clause which is the root of the tree will be referred to as the *root* of the derivation. Similarly, the inference with the root clause as its consequence will be called the *root inference* of the derivation.

A derivation is *regular*, if all applications of superposition and equality solution rules in the derivation precede all other inferences. Otherwise, a derivation is *irregular*.

A *selection strategy* is a function from a set of clauses, that maps each clause to its sub-multiset. If a clause is non-empty, then the selected sub-multiset is non-empty too. A derivation is *compatible* with a selection strategy if all the inferences are performed on the selected literals, i.e. all the literals involved in the inferences are selected.

3   Regular Transformations

We prove the completeness with tautology elimination of regular derivations in basic setting by transforming derivation trees, where a transformation step is an application of a *permutation rule*, which we define in a later chapter. A similar approach is used in [dN96], but for derivations by resolution. For paramodulation-based calculi, in [BG01] the authors use a transformation method to prove their result on arbitrary selection on Horn clauses. However, our transformation method is essentially different, for two reasons. First, we address derivations on general clauses, whereas they restrict themselves to the Horn case. Secondly, opposite to our transformation method, the application of their method may cause the appereance of tautologies in the derivations.

The starting point of our transformations is a refutation by $\mathcal{BFP}$ (see [Ly95]). This is the calculus of choice because, appart from being complete, it is basic, does not contain a factoring rule and allows for tautology elimination. The absence of a factoring rule is essential for our result. The transformations method that we present is based on permuting two consecutive inferences, which is not always possible in the presence of factoring.

Assume, for a moment, that our calculus of choice contains *equality factoring* inference (for example, see [BGLS92], [NR92a]). Consider the following derivation sequence:

$$\frac{a \not\approx b, a \approx c, a \approx d}{c \approx d \quad \dfrac{a \not\approx b, c \not\approx d, a \approx d}{a \not\approx b, d \not\approx d, a \approx d}} \ (eq\ fac)$$
(sup)

and assume that $a \succ b \succ c \succ d$. Here an application of equality factoring precedes a superposition inference. Effectively, the application of factoring produces the literal $c \not\approx d$, which is made up of the smaller terms of the literals $a \approx c$ and $a \approx d$. To regularize this fragment of derivation, it is necessary to transform the derivation in a way that superposition precedes factoring. If the two inferences were to swap positions, it would mean that superposition takes place into the smallest term of the literal $a \approx c$, which is never possible by the definition of superposition.

The situation is somewhat different if the calculus contains *positive factoring*, like it is the case with $\mathcal{SBS}$ of [BG97]. Positive factoring does not produce fresh literals, it removes literals that are sintacticly equivalent. Hence, it is possible to permute every application of positive factoring with a superposition inference. As for equality solution inferences, it is also always possible to permute them with applications of positive factoring rule. This, however, may result in the appearance of tautologies that did not exist in the original derivation. More precisely, we can not prove using transformations of derivations, that the calculus $\mathcal{SBS}$ allows for the elimination of tautologies.

3.1   The Calculus $\mathcal{EBFP}$

The calculus $\mathcal{EBFP}$ (extended $\mathcal{BFP}$) of constrained clauses consists of the rules:

Factored (positive and negative) overlap

$$\frac{l_1 \approx r_1, \ldots, l_n \approx r_n, \Gamma_1 \mid T_1 \quad s[l] \doteq t, \Gamma_2 \mid T_2}{s[r_1] \doteq t, \ldots, s[r_n] \doteq t, \Gamma_1, \Gamma_2 \mid T_1 \wedge T_2 \wedge \delta}$$

where δ is a shortcut for $(l_1 \succ r_1 \wedge \ldots \wedge l_n \succ r_n \wedge s \succ t \wedge l_1 = l \wedge \ldots \wedge l_n = l)$ and $\doteq\, \in \{\approx, \not\approx\}$.

Equality solution[2]

$$\frac{s \not\approx t, \Gamma \mid T}{\Gamma \mid T \wedge s = t}$$

Relational resolution

$$\frac{\Gamma_1, P \mid T_1 \quad \Gamma_2, \neg Q \mid T_2}{\Gamma_1, \Gamma_2 \mid T_1 \wedge T_2 \wedge P = Q}$$

---

[2] In [Ly95] that introduced the calculus $\mathcal{BFP}$, this inference is called "reflection". We use the terminology from the papers which present the results that our work is a continuation of, like [DV01].

Relational factoring (positive and negative)

$$\frac{\Gamma, L_1, L_2 \mid T}{\Gamma, L_1 \mid T \wedge L_1 = L_2}$$

where
- L_1 and L_2 are either both positive or both negative literals;
- L_1 and L_2 are identical up to variable renaming.

It is assumed that the premises of the above rules have disjoint variables, which can always be achieved by their renaming.

The calculus $\mathcal{EBFP}$ consists of the rules of the calculus $\mathcal{BFP}$ (see [Ly95]), with the addition of the explicitly stated resolution inference rule and relational factoring (positive and negative). Note that $\mathcal{BFP}$ is defined on purely equational clauses, in which case resolution is expressed by a sequence of steps in which factored overlap is followed by reflection. Reflection and factored (positive and negative) overlap inferences will be referred to as equational inferences, while the ones that take place with predicate literals will be called relational.

The reason for introducing negative relational factoring rule is of a technical nature – it is only used in the proof of regular transformations and its existence does not affect the completeness of the calculus. In other words, the calculus $\mathcal{EBFP}$ without the negative factoring rule is complete.

3.2   Permutation Rules

As it has already been mentioned in the introduction, we work with the clauses that have only variables as arguments of predicate literals (*flat* clauses). This property of clauses prevents superposition inferences into arguments of the predicate literals (into variables), which furthermore makes it possible to characterize the superposition inferences as strictly equational inferences, which proves essential in the definition of the below permutation rules.

The permutation rules are applied to derivation trees, and their effect is inverting the order of two consecutive inferences, whenever a relational inference precedes an equality inference. In the definitions below, wherever the symbol $\backsimeq$ is used, it can represent either $\approx$ or $\not\approx$.

res-es rule – Resolution precedes equality solution

$$\frac{\dfrac{\Gamma_1, s \not\approx t, \neg Q \mid T_1 \quad \Gamma_2, P \mid T_2}{\Gamma_1, \Gamma_2, s \not\approx t \mid T_1 \wedge T_2 \wedge P = Q} \; (res)}{\Gamma_1, \Gamma_2 \mid T_1 \wedge T_2 \wedge s = t \wedge P = Q} \; (sup)$$

This sequence transforms to:

$$\frac{\dfrac{\Gamma_1, \neg Q, s \not\approx t \mid T_1}{\Gamma_1, \neg Q \mid T_1 \wedge s = t} \; (sup) \quad \Gamma_2, P \mid T_2}{\Gamma_1, \Gamma_2 \mid T_1 \wedge T_2 \wedge s = t \wedge P = Q} \; (res)$$

fac-es rule – Relational factoring precedes equality solution

$$\frac{\dfrac{\Gamma, s \not\approx t, L_1, L_2 \mid T}{\Gamma, s \not\approx t, L_1 \mid T \wedge L_1 = L_2}\ (fac)}{\Gamma, L_1 \mid T \wedge s = t \wedge L_1 = L_2}\ (es)$$

where L_1 and L_2 are either both positive or both negative predicate literals. Similarly to the previous rule, this sequence transforms to:

$$\frac{\dfrac{\Gamma, L_1, L_2, s \not\approx t \mid T}{\Gamma, L_1, L_2 \mid T \wedge s = t}\ (es)}{\Gamma, L_1 \mid T \wedge s = t \wedge L_1 = L_2}\ (fac)$$

This permutation, as well as the previous one, is always possible to make, since predicate inferences always take place on predicate literals, while equality solutions are always preformed on equality literals.

res-sup rule – Resolution followed by superposition

$$\frac{\dfrac{\Gamma_{11}, l_1 \approx r_1, \ldots, l_n \approx r_n, \neg Q \mid T_1 \quad \Gamma_{12}, P \mid T_2}{\Gamma_{11}, \Gamma_{12}, l_1 \approx r_1, \ldots, l_n \approx r_n \mid T_1 \wedge T_2 \wedge P = Q}\ (res) \quad \Gamma_2, u[l] \leftrightsquigarrow v \mid T}{\Gamma_{11}, \Gamma_{12}, \Gamma_2, u[r_1] \leftrightsquigarrow v, \ldots, u[r_n] \leftrightsquigarrow v \mid T_1 \wedge T_2 \wedge T \wedge P = Q \wedge T_4}\ (sup)$$

where T_4 stands for $(l_1 \succ r_1 \wedge \ldots \wedge l_n \succ r_n \wedge s \succ t \wedge l_1 = l \wedge \ldots \wedge l_n = l)$, and $\leftrightsquigarrow \in \{\approx, \not\approx\}$. In this case, the sequence transforms to:

$$\frac{\dfrac{\Gamma_{11}, l_1 \approx r_1, \ldots, l_n \approx r_n, \neg Q \mid T_1 \quad \Gamma_2, u[l] \leftrightsquigarrow v \mid T}{\Gamma_{11}, \Gamma_2, u[r_1] \leftrightsquigarrow v, \ldots, u[r_n] \leftrightsquigarrow v, \neg Q \mid T \wedge T_1 \wedge T_4}\ (sup) \quad \Gamma_{12}, P \mid T_2}{\Gamma_{11}, \Gamma_{12}, \Gamma_2, u[r_1] \leftrightsquigarrow v, \ldots, u[r_n] \leftrightsquigarrow v \mid T \wedge T_1 \wedge T_2 \wedge P = Q \wedge T_4}\ (res)$$

fac-sup rule – Relational factoring followed by superposition

$$\frac{\dfrac{\Gamma_1, l_1 \approx r_1, \ldots, l_n \approx r_n, L_1, L_2 \mid T_1}{\Gamma_1, l_1 \approx r_1, \ldots, l_n \approx r_n \mid T_1 \wedge L_1 = L_2}\ (fac) \quad \Gamma_2, u[l] \leftrightsquigarrow v \mid T}{\Gamma_1, \Gamma_2, u[r_1] \leftrightsquigarrow v, \ldots, u[r_n] \leftrightsquigarrow v \mid T_1 \wedge T_2 \wedge T \wedge L_1 = L_2 \wedge T_3}\ (sup)$$

where T_3 stands for $(l_1 \succ r_1 \wedge \ldots \wedge l_n \succ r_n \wedge s \succ t \wedge l_1 = l \wedge \ldots \wedge l_n = l)$ and $\leftrightsquigarrow \in \{\approx, \not\approx\}$. L_1 and L_2 are either both positive or both negative literals. In this case, the sequence transforms to:

$$\frac{\dfrac{\Gamma_1, l_1 \approx r_1, \ldots, l_n \approx r_n, L_1, L_2 \mid T_1 \quad \Gamma_2, u[l] \leftrightsquigarrow v \mid T}{\Gamma_1, \Gamma_2, u[r_1] \leftrightsquigarrow v, \ldots, u[r_n] \leftrightsquigarrow v, L_1, L_2 \mid T_1 \wedge T \wedge T_3}\ (sup)}{\Gamma_1, \Gamma_2, u[r_1] \leftrightsquigarrow v, \ldots, u[r_n] \leftrightsquigarrow v \mid T_1 \wedge T_2 \wedge T \wedge L_1 = L_2 \wedge T_3}\ (fac)$$

By analyzing the permutation rules **res-sup** and **fac-sup**, one can easily notice that, once applied to derivation trees, they can introduce some tautologies. In the case of the rule **res-sup**, this is due to the fact that, different to what it is in the original derivation, the literal $\neg Q$, after the transformation, appears in the same clause with Γ_2 (which may contain a literal Q). It is important, at this point, to note that tautologies introduced this way can only be tautologies with respect to predicate literals.

Lemma 1. *The above permutation rules modify BFP derivations into BFP derivations.*

Proof. Every permutation rule defines a way of inverting the order of two adjacent inference rules in a derivation tree. After changing positions, the inferences still take place with the same literals at the same positions in terms as it was in the original derivation. Also, all ordering constraints are kept. Therefore, the resulting derivation is a valid BFP derivation.

3.3   A Proof by Transformation

In order to prove the completeness of the regular strategy for basic superposition, we start with a refutation by BFP of an unsatisfiable set of clauses S. Assume that the root of the refutation is $\Box \mid T$, where T is a satisfiable constraint. Since the calculus employs constraint inheritance, we can find a solution to T, and apply it to the whole refutation. Having that our transformations do not introduce inferences "from" and "to" some fresh literals, and that they they do not change the positions at which the inferences take place, we can consider only ground instances of the refutation. Further in this work, all the transformations will be assumed to take place on ground derivations.

A quick word on notation. The compound

$$\frac{\Omega}{C}$$

denotes a derivation (derivation tree) Ω which is rooted by a clause C. The clause C is a part of Ω. When it is not important which clause roots a derivation, we will use only Ω.

Lemma 2. *Any derivation by BFP can be transformed to a derivation by EBFP without introducing new tautologies.*

Proof. The statement of the lemma talks about the treatment of predicate literals. We can chose to treat them as predicate literals or equality atoms. The calculus BFP treats predicates as equality atoms. On the other hand, to make our transformations easier we need treat them as predicate literals.

Every factored overlap with a literal of the form $P(\mathbf{t}) \approx true$ (where P is a predicate symbol of arity n and $\mathbf{t}$ is an n-tuple of terms) and can be turned into a sequence of inferences that consists of a number of positive factoring steps followed by an application of resolution. It is clear that this transformation does not introduce new literals to clauses, it may only take some duplicate positive literals away. It follows that the transformation does not cause apperance of new tautologies. Therefore, if there were no tautologies in the original derivation, there will be no tautologies after the transformation has taken place.

Lemma 3. *Any $\mathcal{E}\mathcal{B}\mathcal{F}\mathcal{P}$ derivation Ω of the form:*

$$\frac{\dfrac{\Pi_1 \qquad \Pi_2}{\neg P, C_1 \quad P, C_2} \, (res) \qquad \Pi_3}{C_1, C_2} \; (sup)$$
$$\begin{array}{c} E \\ \vdots \;\; (eq \; infs) \\ F \end{array}$$

where the inferences that follow res *are all equality inferences, can be split into two derivations Ω_1 and Ω_2 with conclusions F_1 and F_2 for which:*

- *The clause F_1 contains the literal P (can be written as F_1^*, P) and F_2 contains the literal $\neg P$ (can be written as $F_2^*, \neg P$).*
- *The union of the literals from F_1^* and F_2^* contains all the literals that appear in F and only those literals, with possible duplicates.*

Proof. The induction is on the number of (equality) inferences in Ω that take place after the inference res. Let Ω' with a conclusion F' be a derivation that is obtained from Ω by cutting off its last inference. By the induction hypothesis, Ω' can be split into Ω_1' and Ω_2', rooted by F_1' and F_2' respectively.

Focus to the final inference of Ω. It involves one or more literals from the clause F'. Let the final inference of Ω, without a loss of generality, be a positive superposition inference with F' as the "from" clause. Note that the conclusion of this inference is in fact the clause F.

$$\frac{\Gamma_1, l \approx r_1, \ldots, l \approx r_m \qquad \Gamma_2, u[l] \approx v}{\Gamma_1, \Gamma_2, u[r_1] \approx v, \ldots, u[r_m] \approx v}$$

In case all the literals $l \approx r_1, \ldots, l \approx r_m$ belong to (w.l.o.g.) F_1', we add the following derivation to Ω_1', thus defining the final form of Ω_1. The added inference has F_1' as the "from" premise:

$$\frac{F_1'^*, l \approx r_1, \ldots, l \approx r_m \qquad \Gamma_2, u[l] \approx v}{\Gamma_2, F_1'^*, u[r_1] \approx v, \ldots, u[r_m] \approx v}$$

There are no added inferences to Ω_2', which is then the same as Ω_2. By the induction hypothesis, the clauses F_1' and F_2' contain all the literals form Γ_1. Besides, F_1' contains the literal P and F_2' the literal $\neg P$. Therefore, the conclusion F_1 of Ω_1 inherits the literal P from the F_1', and similarly F_2 inherits $\neg P$ from F_2', and the union of the literals from F_1 and F_2 contains only (and all of them) the literals from Γ_1, Γ_2.

Otherwise, assume that the literals $l \approx r_1, \ldots, l \approx r_k$ appear in F_1', while the literals $l \approx r_{k+1}, \ldots l \approx r_m$ appear in F_2'. It is easy to see that, in order to obtain all the literals that appear in Ω, both F_1' and F_2' should paramodulate into the negative premise of the last inference of Ω. We therefore produce Ω_1 and Ω_2 by adding an inference to both Ω_1' and Ω_2'. These inferences have the clauses F_1' and F_2' as positive premises.

$$\frac{F_1'^*, l \approx r_1, \ldots, l \approx r_k \quad \Gamma_2, u[l] \approx v}{\Gamma_2, F_1'^*, u[r_1] \approx v, \ldots, u[r_k] \approx v}$$

and

$$\frac{F_2'^*, l \approx r_{k+1}, \ldots, l \approx r_m \quad \Gamma_2, u[l] \approx v}{\Gamma_2, F_2'^*, u[r_{k+1}] \approx v, \ldots, u[r_m] \approx v}$$

Similarly to the previous case, the statement of the lemma holds. It is worth pointing out that this case produces duplicate literals in the union of the literals from the clauses F_1 and F_2. It due to the fact that the "to" clause of the final inference of Ω appears as the "to" clause of the final inferences of both Ω_1 and Ω_2, and therefore the literals from Γ_2 are inherited to both F_1 and F_2.

Note that the same reasoning applies when the last inference of Ω is equality solution. The consideration then forks in two sub-cases, determined by whether the literal inferenced upon in Ω appears in both F_1' and F_2' or just in one of them.

It can be seen, from the proof of the previous lemma, that every clause in the two newly obtained derivations is a clause that contains no other literals than some clause of the original derivations. Thus, if there are no tautologies in the original derivation, there will be no tautologies after the transformation has taken place.

Definition 1. *A clause is* e-empty *if it contains no equality literals (and zero or more predicate literals). A derivation of an e-empty clause from a set of clauses which contain both predicate and equality literals is called* e-refutation. *An e-refutation that ends with equality inferences is called* s-e-refutation *(from short e-refutation). Note that the empty clause is also e-empty. Similarly, every refutation is also an e-refutation.*

Lemma 4. *An e-refutation by $\mathcal{EBFP}$ can be transformed into a regular $\mathcal{EBFP}$ e-refutation with the same conclusion.*

Proof. In a derivation tree, a predicate inference for which there is an equality inference following it is called a non-terminating predicate inference. Let Ω be an e-refutation by $\mathcal{EBFP}$ with a conclusion R. Without a loss of generality, we assume that the final inference of Ω is an equality inference. Otherwise, we can always neglect the predicate inferences at the end of the derivation tree, and apply the lemma on the sub-derivation obtained this way. Let n be the number of non-terminating predicate inferences in Ω. Among all the predicate inferences in the derivation that are not followed by other predicate inferences, pick the one that is followed by the least number of inferences and call it `inf`. If the number of the inferences that follow `inf` is m, the induction is on the regularity pair (n, m), where:

$$(n_1, m_1) > (n_2, m_2) \quad if \quad \begin{matrix} n_1 > n_2 \ or \\ n_1 = n_2 \ and \ m_1 > m_2 \end{matrix}$$

A regular derivation is assigned the pair $(0, 0)$.

Assume that `inf` is a resolution inference. In case of factoring, the discussion is similar (the difference is in the permutation rules applied) and less complex. The inference that follows `inf` can be equality solution. In this case, the rule **res–es** applies, which modifies the Ω to a derivation Ω', which at least has the second member of the regularity pair lesser than m. This transformation does not change the conclusion of Ω'. The induction hypothesis applies to the sub-derivation of Ω' without the trailing resolution inferences.

Alternatively, the derivation Ω is of the form:

$$\dfrac{\dfrac{\Pi_1 \quad \Pi_2}{C_1 \quad C_2}}{\Gamma_1, l \approx r_1, \ldots l \approx r_k} (inf) \quad \dfrac{}{\Gamma_3, u[l] \approx v} \Pi_3$$
$$\overline{\Gamma_1, \Gamma_2, u[r_1] \approx v, u[r_2] \approx v, \ldots u[r_k] \approx v}$$

If all the literals $l \approx r_1, \ldots, l \approx r_k$ belong to either C_1 or C_2, then similarly to the previous case, the permutation **res–sup** can be applied, which also results in obtaining a derivation with a smaller regularity pair.

If neither of the previous two scenarios apply, then some of the literals $l \approx r_1, \ldots, l \approx r_k$ appear in C_1, while the others are inherited from C_2. In other words,

$$C_1 = P, \Gamma_1, l \approx r_1, \ldots, l \approx r_l \quad \text{and} \quad C_2 = \neg P, \Gamma_2, l \approx r_{l+1}, \ldots l, \approx r_m.$$

By the previous lemma, the derivation can be split into two e-regular derivations Ω_1 and Ω_2. They can be transformed, by the induction hypothesis, to regular e-refutations Ω_1' and Ω_2' with the conclusions F_1' and F_2'. The previous lemma states that the clauses F_1' and F_2' contain the literals P and $\neg P$. This means that, by performing a resolution inference on F_1' ($= F_1'*, P$) and F_2' ($= F_2'^*, \neg P$), the derivations Ω_1' and Ω_2' can be joined to a derivation with the conclusion $F_1'^*, F_2'^*$ that contains all the literals that appear in the conclusion of Ω, with possible duplicates. However, the duplicates problem can be solved by applying positive and negative factoring inference rules.

The base of the induction is a derivation with the regularity pair $(1, k)$ where $k \geq 1$. More precisely, in case the previous lemma applies to a derivation with only one non-terminating predicate inference, k is allowed to be greater than 1. This is because the previous lemma makes it possible to push all predicate inferences down, below all equality inferences that follow. Otherwise, the base of the induction is any derivation which can be assigned the pair $(1, 1)$. By applying a suitable permutation rule, such derivation can be made regular.

Lemma 5. *Any set of unsatisfiable clauses has a regular refutation in which tautologies are redundant.*

Proof. Because of its completeness property and compatibility with tautology elimination, there is always a tautology-free $\mathcal{BFP}$ refutation from a set of unsatisfiable clauses. Every such refutation is also an e-refutation, and by the previous lemma, it can be transformed to a regular $\mathcal{EBFP}$ refutation. As it has been already stated, the preformed transformation does not cause the appearance of tautologies w.r.t. equality literals. Having a regular derivation means that there can be derived a set of purely predicate clauses from which the empty clause can be derived by resolution. Each of those purely predicate clauses is actually the root of a regular derivation. If there are tautologies w.r.t. predicate clauses in such regular derivations, the corresponding root will be a tautology, too. As such, it is not needed in the further refutation by resolution, and can be discarded. By discarding this clause, we discard the whole sub-derivation where tautologies appeared. This proves that even tautologies w.r.t. predicate literals can be eliminated.

The following is an instance of the conjecture from [DV01], and is a straight forward consequence of the previous lemma.

Theorem 1. *Let S be a set of Horn with respect to equality literals with the following property: the arguments of every non-equality atom in S are variables. Then there exists a refutation of S with tautology elimination in which applications of superposition precede applications of all other rules (resolution, equality solution and factoring).*

4   Future Work

A topic for further research is whether regular derivations are compatible with other redundancy elimination techniques, such as simplification. It would be interesting (and challenging) to implement a theorem prover based on equality elimination [DV01] (which is based on regular derivations), which would be competitive with resolution-based provers.

Acknowledgements

We thank the anonymous referees for helpful comments and suggestions. Our work is supported by EPSRC research grants GR/S61973/01 and GR/S63175/01.

References

[AD05]   V. Aleksić, A. Degtyarev. On arbitrary selection strategies for superposition. *Proceedings of FTP, Technical Report of the University of Koblenz,* September 2005.

[BGLS92] L. Bachmair, H. Ganzinger, C. Lynch, and W. Snyder. Basic paramodulation and superposition. In D. Kapur, editor, *11th International Conference on Automated Deduction,* volume 607 of *Lecture Notes in Artificial Intelligence,* pages 462–476, Saratoga Springs, NY, USA, June 1992. Springer Verlag.

[BG97]   L. Bachmair and H. Ganzinger. Strict basic superposition and chaining. Research report MPI-I-97-2-011, Max-Planck-Institut für Informatic, Saarbrücken.

[BG01]   L. Bofill, G. Godoy. On the completeness of arbitrary selection strategies for paramoduletion. In *Proceedings of ICALP 2001,* pages 951–962, 2001.

[BR02]   L. Bofill, A. Rubio. Well-foundedness is sufficient for completeness of ordered paramodulation. In *Proceedings of CADE'18*, volume 2392 of *LNCS*, pages 456–470. Springer, 2001.

[DV01]   A. Degtyarev and A. Voronkov. Equality reasoning in sequent-based calculi. In A. Robinson, A. Voronkov, editors, *Handbook of Automated Reasoning*, pages 613–706, Elsevier Science Publishers B.V., 2001.

[DV96a]   A. Degtyarev and A. Voronkov. Handling equality in logic programs via basic folding. In R. Dyckhoff, H. Herre, and P. Schroeder-Heister, editors, *Extensions of Logic Programming (5th International Workshop, ELP'96)*, volume 1050 of *Lecture Notes in Computer Science*, pages 119–136, Leipzig, Germany, March 1996.

[Kan63]   S. Kanger. A simplified proof method for elementary logic. In J. Siekmann and G. Wrightson, editors, *Automation of Reasoning. Classical Papers on Computational Logic*, volume 1, pages 364–371. Springer Verlag, 1983. Originally appeared in 1963.

[Ly95]   M. Moser, C. Lynch and J. Steinbach. Model Elimination with Basic Ordered Paramodulation.

[Ly97]   C. Lynch. Oriented Equational Logic is Complete. *Journal of Symbolic Computations*, 23(1):23–45, 1997. Technical Report AR-95-11, TU München, 1995.

[NR92a]   R. Nieuwenhuis and A. Rubio. Basic superposition is complete. In *ESOP'92*, volume 582 of *Lecture Notes in Computer Science*, pages 371–389. Springer Verlag, 1992.

[NR99]   R. Nieuwenhuis and A. Rubio. Paramodulation-based theorem proving. In A. Robinson and A. Voronkov, editors, *Handbook of Automated Reasoning*, pages 3–73, 1999. Elsevier Science Publishers B.V.

[dN96]   H. de Nivelle. Ordering refinements of resolution. *Dissertation, Technische Universiteit Delft, Delft*, 1996.

[RW69b]   G. Robinson and L. Wos. Completeness of paramodulation. *Journal of Symbolic Logic*, 34(1):159–160, 1969.

On the Finite Satisfiability Problem for the Guarded Fragment with Transitivity

Wiesław Szwast and Lidia Tendera

Institute of Mathematics and Informatics, Opole University, Poland
{szwast, tendera}@math.uni.opole.pl

Abstract. We study the finite satisfiability problem for the guarded fragment with transitivity. We prove that in case of one transitive predicate the problem is decidable and its complexity is the same as the general satisfiability problem, i.e. 2EXPTIME-complete. We also show that finite models for sentences of GF with more transitive predicate letters used only in guards have essentially different properties than infinite ones.

Keywords: finite model, guarded fragment, transitivity, decision problem, computational complexity.

1 Introduction

In this paper we study the finite satisfiability problem for the extension of the guarded fragment of first-order logic with transitivity statements.

The *satisfiability problem* for a given logic $\mathcal{L}$, Sat($\mathcal{L}$), is the problem of deciding, for a given sentence ϕ of the logic, whether ϕ has a model; the *finite satisfiability problem* for $\mathcal{L}$, FinSat($\mathcal{L}$), is the problem of deciding, for a given sentence ϕ, whether ϕ has a finite model. A logic $\mathcal{L}$ enjoys the *finite model property*, if every satisfiable sentence of $\mathcal{L}$ has a finite model.

The guarded fragment, GF, introduced by H. Andréka, J. van Benthem and I. Németi [1], has appeared to be a successful attempt to transfer good properties of modal and temporal logics to a naturally defined fragment of predicate logic. In the guarded fragment formulas are built as in first-order logic with the only restriction that quantifiers are appropriately relativized by atoms, i.e. neither the pattern of alternations of quantifiers nor the number of variables is restricted.

Andréka et al. showed that modal logic can be embedded in GF and that GF inherits the nice properties of modal logic. E. Grädel [2] proved that Sat(GF) is complete for double exponential time and complete for exponential time, when the number of variables is bounded. Moreover, he showed that GF has the finite model property; hence Sat(GF) and FinSat(GF) coincide.

GF was generalized by van Benthem [3] to the *loosely guarded fragment*, LGF, by M. Marx [4] to the *packed fragment*, PF, and by Grädel [5] to the *clique guarded fragment*, CGF, where all quantifiers are relativized by more general formulas, preserving the idea of quantification only over elements that are close

G. Sutcliffe and A. Voronkov (Eds.): LPAR 2005, LNAI 3835, pp. 307–321, 2005.

together in the model. Most of the properties of GF generalize to LGF, PF and CGF. In particular, I. Hodkinson [6] showed that they all enjoy the finite model property (see also [7] for a simpler and nicer proof of the result).

Two notable extensions of GF that are decidable for satisfiability but do not enjoy the finite model property are studied in the literature. One is the extension of GF with *fixed point operators*, GF+FP, investigated by E. Grädel and I. Walukiewicz [8]. This fragment captures the modal μ-calculus and has the same complexity for deciding satisfiability as pure GF.

The second important fragment is the extension of GF with *transitive guards*, GF+TG, motivated by the paper [9] by H. Ganzinger, C. Meyer and M. Veanes, and studied by Szwast and Tendera [10]. In GF+TG some binary predicate letters are declared to be transitive, so that their interpretation is required to be transitive, but these *transitive* predicate letters appear only in guards. This extension captures many expressive modal and description logics and is decidable for satisfiability in double exponential time. Surprisingly, the complexity stays the same even for the monadic two-variable fragment with one transitive predicate letter as it was proved by E. Kieroński in [11].

The lack of the finite model property for the above mentioned fragments naturally leads to the question, whether their FinSat problems are decidable. This question is particularly important, if one would like to use these formalism for automatic reasoners in practical applications, where the structures investigated are essentially finite.

A partial answer about the complexity of FinSat for GF+FP is given by M. Bojańczyk [12], who has shown decidability of the FinSat problem for the modal μ-calculus with backwards modalities. To the best of our knowledge, the nice alternating automata on finite graphs introduced in his paper have not yet been generalized to answer the open question of the decidability of FinSat for full GF with fixed points.

In our paper we attack the FinSat problem for GF with transitive guards. The main result is that the problem is decidable if there is one transitive predicate letter in the signature. In the proof we observe that to check existence of a finite model it suffices to check existence of an appropriate regular, possibly infinite, tree-like model. This observation leads to a decision procedure working in double exponential time.

We also show that we cannot generalize the technique developed for the one transitive predicate case in a straightforward way. Namely, we show that if we have more transitive predicate letters, we can describe models that cannot be obtained from their tree-unravelling in an easy way. In particular, we give an example of a finitely satisfiable sentence ϕ that has infinite tree-like models with transitive cliques of cardinality at most exponential w.r.t. the length of ϕ, but whose each finite model contains a transitive clique of double exponential size.

The above observation leads to a conjecture that FinSat(GF+TG)in case of more transitive predicate letters can be essentially harder than the corresponding satisfiability problem. It is perhaps worth mentioning that if this conjecture is true, we would probably have the first natural logic for which the complexity of the satisfiability problem and of the finite satisfiability problem do not coincide. So far, we know examples of decidable logics without the finite model property for which both Sat and FinSat are of the same complexity; take the description logic $\mathcal{ALCQI}$, i.e. the $\mathcal{ALC}$ augmented with qualifying number restrictions, inverse roles, and general TBoxes (see [13] for general reasoning and [14] for the finite case), or the two-variable first-order logic with counting quantifiers (see [15] for satisfiability and [16] for finite satisfiability) as two remarkable examples.

2   Guarded Fragments

The *guarded fragment*, GF, of first-order logic with no function symbols is defined as the least set of formulas such that

1. every atomic formula belongs to GF,
2. GF is closed under logical connectives $\neg, \vee, \wedge, \rightarrow$,
3. if $\mathbf{x}, \mathbf{y}$ are tuples of variables, $\alpha(\mathbf{x}, \mathbf{y})$ is an atomic formula containing all the variables of $\{\mathbf{x}, \mathbf{y}\}$ and $\psi(\mathbf{x}, \mathbf{y})$ is a formula of GF with free variables contained in $\{\mathbf{x}, \mathbf{y}\}$, then the formulas

$$\forall \mathbf{y}(\alpha(\mathbf{x}, \mathbf{y}) \rightarrow \psi(\mathbf{x}, \mathbf{y})) \quad \text{and} \quad \exists \mathbf{y}(\alpha(\mathbf{x}, \mathbf{y}) \wedge \psi(\mathbf{x}, \mathbf{y}))$$

belong to GF.

The atom $\alpha(\mathbf{x}, \mathbf{y})$ in the above formulas is called the *guard* of the quantifier. A guard that is a P-atom, where P is a predicate letter from the signature, is called a P-guard.

We denote by FO^k the class of first-order sentences with k variables over a relational signature. By GF^k we denote the fragment $\mathrm{GF} \cap \mathrm{FO}^k$.

By a *transitivity statement* we mean an assertion $Trans[P]$, saying that the binary relation P is a transitive relation. A binary predicate letter P is called *transitive* if $Trans[P]$ holds.

By GF+TG we denote the guarded fragment with *transitive guards* that is the restriction of GF with transitivity statements where all transitive predicate letters appear in guards only and where the equality symbol can appear everywhere. By GF^2+TG we denote the restriction of GF+TG to two variables.

3   Preliminaries

In this paper by σ we denote a signature without function symbols.

Let $\mathbf{x} = (x_1, \ldots, x_l)$ be a sequence of variables. An l-*type* $t(\mathbf{x})$ is a maximal consistent set of atomic and negated atomic formulas over σ in the variables of $\mathbf{x}$. A type t is often identified with the conjunction of formulas in t. In this paper we need 1- and 2-types that, if not stated otherwise, will be types of the variable x and of the variables x and y, respectively. A 2-type t is *proper* if t contains the formula $x \neq y$. If $t(x, y)$ is a proper 2-type such that $t(x, y) \models T(x, y) \wedge T(y, x)$, then we say that t is T-*symmetric*.

Let $\psi(\mathbf{x})$ be a quantifier-free formula in the variables of $\mathbf{x}$. We say that a type t *satisfies* ψ, $t \models \psi$, if ψ is true under the truth assignment that assigns true to an atomic formula precisely when it is a member of t.

We denote σ-structures by Gothic capital letters and their universes by Latin capitals. If $\mathfrak{A}$ is a σ-structure with the universe A, and if $\mathbf{a}$ is an l-tuple of elements of A, then we denote by $tp^{\mathfrak{A}}(\mathbf{a})$ the unique l-type $t(\mathbf{x})$ realized by $\mathbf{a}$ in $\mathfrak{A}$. If $B \subseteq A$ then $\mathfrak{A}{\restriction}B$ denotes the substructure of $\mathfrak{A}$ induced on B.

Let $\mathfrak{A}$ be a σ-structure, P a binary predicate letter in σ and $\mathfrak{C}$ a substructure of $\mathfrak{A}$. We say that $\mathfrak{C}$ is a P-*clique* if C is a one-element set, or for every $a, b \in C$ we have $\mathfrak{A} \models P(a, b)$. If a predicate letter T has transitive interpretation in a structure $\mathfrak{A}$ and $a \in A$, then we denote by $[a]_T^{\mathfrak{A}}$ the maximal T-clique containing a. Where the structure $\mathfrak{A}$ (or a predicate letter T) is understood or not important, we sometimes omit the letter $\mathfrak{A}$ (or a predicate letter T) and write $[a]$.

Let γ be a σ-sentence of the form $\forall x\, \alpha(x) \to \exists y\, \phi(x, y)$, $\mathfrak{A}$ be a σ-structure and $a \in A$. We say that an element $b \in A$ is a *witness of* γ for a in $\mathfrak{A}$ if $\mathfrak{A} \models \alpha(a) \to \phi(a, b)$. Note that if $\mathfrak{A} \not\models \alpha(a)$, then any element $b \in A$ is a witness of γ for a in $\mathfrak{A}$. Similarly, we say that $a \in A$ is a *witness of* γ of the form $\exists x \phi(x)$ in $\mathfrak{A}$ if $\mathfrak{A} \models \phi(a)$.

Definition 1. *A GF+TG-sentence is in* normal form *if it is a conjunction of sentences of the following forms:*

$$\exists \mathbf{x}\, (\alpha(\mathbf{x}) \wedge \psi(\mathbf{x})), \tag{1}$$

$$\forall \mathbf{x}\, (\alpha(\mathbf{x}) \to \exists y\, (\beta(\mathbf{x}, y) \wedge \psi(\mathbf{x}, y))), \tag{2}$$

$$\forall \mathbf{x} \forall y\, (\alpha(\mathbf{x}, y) \to \psi(\mathbf{x}, y)), \tag{3}$$

where $y \notin \mathbf{x}$, α, β *are atomic formulas,* ψ *is quantifier-free and contains no transitive predicate letter.*

The following lemma can be proved in the same way as in [17].

Lemma 1. *With every GF+TG-sentence Γ of length n over a signature τ one can effectively associate a set Δ of GF+TG-sentences in normal form over an extended signature σ, $\Delta = \{\Delta_1, \ldots, \Delta_d\}$, such that*

1. *Γ is (finitely)satisfiable if and only if $\bigvee_{i \leq d} \Delta_i$ is (finitely) satisfiable,*
2. *$d \leq O(2^n)$, $card(\sigma) \leq n$ and for every $i \leq d$, $|\Delta_i| = O(n \log n)$,*
3. *Δ can be computed deterministically in exponential time and every sentence Δ_i can be computed in time polynomial with respect to n.*

In [10] it was shown that every satisfiable GF+TG-sentence has a regular model called a *ramified model*. We recall the definition here.

Definition 2. *Let $\mathfrak{R}$ be a model for a GF+TG-sentence Φ over σ.*

- *$\mathfrak{R}$ is* singular, *if for every $a, b \in R$ such that $a \neq b$, there is at most one transitive predicate letter T such that $\mathfrak{R} \models T(a, b) \vee T(b, a)$.*

- $\mathfrak{R}$ *has a* clique-bound *r, for an integer r, if for every $a \in R$, the cardinality of $[a]_T^{\mathfrak{R}}$ is bounded by r.*
- $\mathfrak{R}$ *is* forest-like, *if for every transitive predicate letters T, T' such that $T \neq T'$, for every $a, b, c \in R$, $b \neq a, c \neq a$, if $b \in [a]_T^{\mathfrak{R}}$ and $c \in [a]_{T'}^{\mathfrak{R}}$ then for every binary predicate letter $P \in \sigma$ we have $\mathfrak{R} \not\models P(b, c)$.*
- $\mathfrak{R}$ *is* ramified, *if $\mathfrak{R}$ is singular, forest-like and has a clique-bound.*

Theorem 1 (Szwast, Tendera [10]). *Every satisfiable GF+TG-sentence Φ in normal form has a ramified model with a clique-bound $r = 3 \cdot |\Phi| \cdot 2^{card(\sigma)}$.*

We emphasize that a ramified model is usually an infinite structure. So, for the purpose of this paper, we have only the following corollary.

Corollary 1. *Every (finitely) satisfiable GF+TG-sentence in normal form has an (infinite) ramified model with exponential cliques.*

4   Finite Models. One Transitive Predicate

In this section we prove that the finite satisfiability problem for the two-variable guarded fragment with one transitive predicate letter is decidable in double exponential time. We assume that we have a signature σ that contains unary and binary predicate letters and that T is the only transitive predicate letter in σ. In this case a $GF^2 + TG$ normal form sentence is a conjunction of sentences of the following forms:

$$\exists x \, (\alpha(x) \wedge \psi(x)), \tag{1}$$

$$\forall x \, (\alpha(x) \rightarrow \exists y \, (\beta(x, y) \wedge \psi(x, y))), \tag{2}$$

$$\forall x \forall y \, (\alpha(x, y) \rightarrow \psi(x, y)). \tag{3}$$

We additionally assume that any normal form sentence contains exactly one conjunct of the form (1) (conjuncts of the form (1) can be replaced by sentences of the form (2)).

The main idea of the proof is to give up working with complicated finite models and to deal with a special kind of tree-unravellings of finite models in which every node is a clique of elements. This requires some care since tree-unravellings are generally infinite.

In the following Definition we emphasize the simple notion of a node.

Definition 3. *Let $\mathfrak{A}$ be a σ-structure in which the interpretation of T is transitive. Every maximal T-clique in $\mathfrak{A}$ is called an $\mathfrak{A}$-node. Denote the set of $\mathfrak{A}$-nodes by $\mathbf{N}(\mathfrak{A}) : \mathbf{N}(\mathfrak{A}) = \{[a] : a \in A\}$.*

Every σ-structure $\mathfrak{A}$ with transitive T is partitioned into $\mathfrak{A}$-nodes.

In the first step (Lemma 2), given a finite model $\mathfrak{A}$ of a normal form $GF^2 + TG$-sentence Φ over σ, we build a tree-like σ-structure $\mathfrak{R}$ such that $\mathfrak{R} \models \Phi$. The tree-like structure $\mathfrak{R}$ can be seen as an edge-labelled tree $\mathbf{T}(\mathfrak{R})$, whose nodes are copies of T-cliques from $\mathfrak{A}$ and where the root contains a witness for the conjunct of Φ of the form (1). Moreover, for every node $\mathfrak{B}$ of the tree $\mathbf{T}(\mathfrak{R})$, for every $b \in B$ and for every conjunct ϕ of Φ of the form (2), there is a son $\mathfrak{C}$ of the node $\mathfrak{B}$ and an element $c \in C$ such that c is a witness of b for ϕ in $\mathfrak{R}$; the label of the edge from $\mathfrak{B}$ to $\mathfrak{C}$ is the pair (b, c).

In our technique cliques are treated in a special way: we consider them only once when we create a node of a tree, and hence we do not have to consider symmetric 2-types between elements from distinct nodes later, in particular, when we define types between elements from nodes of one tree path.

The tree-like models, although they are usually infinite and have arbitrarily large nodes, have also one good feature: every T-path is finite.

In the next step (Lemma 3 and Theorem 2) we show that in a tree-like model of a finitely satisfiable sentence Φ we can bound both, the cardinality of nodes and the length of T-paths, by respectively, exponential and double exponential numbers (with respect to the length of Φ). This leads to an alternating exponential space decision procedure for $\mathrm{FinSat}(\mathrm{GF}^2 + \mathrm{TG})$.

In this section we usually omit the letter T in the notions, and where the structure $\mathfrak{A}$ is understood or not important, we sometimes omit the letter $\mathfrak{A}$ and speak about *nodes*.

In the following definition, we introduce tree-like structures formally and recall a few notions for trees.

Definition 4. *Let $\mathfrak{R}$ be σ-structure in which the interpretation of T is transitive and let $l : \mathbf{N}(\mathfrak{R}) \mapsto R \times R$ be a function such that $\mathrm{tp}^{\mathfrak{R}}(l(\mathfrak{D}))$ is not T-symmetric, for every $\mathfrak{D} \in \mathbf{N}(\mathfrak{R})$. The structure $\mathfrak{R}$ is an l-tree-like structure if the pair $\mathbf{T}(\mathfrak{R}) = (\mathbf{N}(\mathfrak{R}), \{(\mathfrak{B}, \mathfrak{C}) : l(\mathfrak{C}) = (b, c)\}, [b] = \mathfrak{B}, [c] = \mathfrak{C}\}$ is a tree (with the edge labelling l).*

- *A tree-path in $\mathbf{T}(\mathfrak{R})$ is a sequence of pairwise distinct nodes $\mathfrak{C}_0, \mathfrak{C}_1, \ldots$ such that for every i, $\mathfrak{C}_i$ is either a son or a father of $\mathfrak{C}_{i-1}$.*
- *A T-path in $\mathbf{T}(\mathfrak{R})$ is a tree-path $\mathfrak{C}_0, \mathfrak{C}_1, \ldots$ such that for every i, if $\mathfrak{C}_i$ is a son of $\mathfrak{C}_{i-1}$, then $\mathrm{tp}^{\mathfrak{R}}(l(\mathfrak{C}_i)) \models T(x, y)$, otherwise $\mathrm{tp}^{\mathfrak{R}}(l(\mathfrak{C}_{i-1})) \models T(y, x)$.*
- *A T-path from $\mathfrak{C}$ to $\mathfrak{C}'$ is a finite T-path $\mathfrak{C} = \mathfrak{C}_0, \mathfrak{C}_1, \ldots \mathfrak{C}_m = \mathfrak{C}'$.*
- *An ancestor of a node $\mathfrak{C}$ is a node $\mathfrak{C}_i \neq \mathfrak{C}$ of the tree-path $\mathfrak{C}_0, \mathfrak{C}_1, \ldots, \mathfrak{C}_i, \ldots, \mathfrak{C}$, where $\mathfrak{C}_0$ is the root of $\mathbf{T}(\mathfrak{R})$.*
- *For $\mathfrak{C} \in \mathbf{N}(\mathfrak{R})$, $\mathrm{tree}(\mathfrak{C})$ is the subtree of $\mathbf{T}(\mathfrak{R})$ rooted at the node $\mathfrak{C}$.*
- *For $\mathfrak{C}, \mathfrak{D} \in \mathbf{N}(\mathfrak{R})$, $\mathrm{tree}(\mathfrak{C}) \cong \mathrm{tree}(\mathfrak{D})$ if there exists an isomorphism function i_1 between $\mathrm{tree}(\mathfrak{C})$ and $\mathrm{tree}(\mathfrak{D})$ and an isomorphism function i_2, $i_2 : \mathfrak{R}{\restriction}\{c : c \in \mathfrak{C}', \mathfrak{C}' \in \mathrm{tree}(\mathfrak{C})\} \mapsto \mathfrak{R}{\restriction}\{d : d \in \mathfrak{D}', \mathfrak{D}' \in \mathrm{tree}(\mathfrak{D})\}$, such that for every $\mathfrak{C}' \in \mathrm{tree}(\mathfrak{C})$, $i_1(\mathfrak{C}') = i_2(\mathfrak{C}')$ and for every $\mathfrak{C}' \in \mathrm{tree}(\mathfrak{C})$, $\mathfrak{C}' \neq \mathfrak{C}$, if $l(\mathfrak{C}') = (b, c)$ then $l(i_1(\mathfrak{C}')) = (i_2(b), i_2(c))$.*

Definition 5. *Let $\mathfrak{R}$ be a model for a normal form sentence Φ. $\mathfrak{R}$ is a tree-like model for Φ if there exists a function l such that $\mathfrak{R}$ in an l-tree-like structure and:*

1. *the number of sons of any node $\mathfrak{C}$ is not bigger than $n_2(\Phi) \cdot \mathrm{card}(C)$, where $n_2(\Phi)$ is the number of conjuncts of Φ of the form (2);*

2. *there is a witness of the conjunct of the form (1) in the root;*
3. *for every conjunct $\phi = \forall x \, (\alpha(x) \to \exists y \, (\beta(x, y) \wedge \psi(x, y)))$ of the form (2) and every element $a \in R$, if there is no witness of ϕ for a in $[a]$, then there is a witness b of ϕ for a in $\Re$ such that $l([b]) = (a, b)$ ($[b]$ is a son of $[a]$);*
4. *for every two elements $a, b \in R$, $\Re \models T(a, b) \wedge \neg T(b, a)$ iff there is a T-path from $[a]$ to $[b]$;*
5. *every T-path in $\mathbf{T}(\Re)$ is finite.*

Lemma 2. *Every finitely satisfiable sentence Φ in normal form has a tree-like model.*

Proof. Assume $\mathfrak{A} \models \Phi$, A is finite. We construct a tree-like model $\Re$ for Φ such that every node of $\Re$ is isomorphic to an $\mathfrak{A}$-node and the isomorphism is given by a global function $h : R \mapsto A$. Additionally, for every $a, b \in R$ it is ensured that if any of the following cases holds

- $[b]$ is a son of $[a]$ or $[a]$ is a son of $[b]$ in $\mathbf{T}(\Re)$,
- there is a T-path from $[a]$ to $[b]$ or from $[b]$ to $[a]$ in $\mathbf{T}(\Re)$,

then $tp^{\Re}(a, b) = tp^{\mathfrak{A}}(h(a), h(b))$.

We start with finding a witness $b \in A$ of the conjunct of Φ of the form (1) $\phi = \exists x \, (\alpha(x) \wedge \psi(x))$. Let $\mathfrak{B} \cong [b]^{\mathfrak{A}}$ be an isomorphic structure to the node $[b]^{\mathfrak{A}}$ such that $B \cap A = \emptyset$. Define the root of $\mathbf{T}(\Re)$ as $\mathfrak{B}$ and $h : \Re \mapsto A$ as the isomorphism function of $\mathfrak{B}$ and $[b]^{\mathfrak{A}}$.

Now, assume that we have already defined i levels of the tree $\mathbf{T}(\Re)$. To construct the $i + 1$-th level, L_{i+1}, for every node $\mathfrak{B} \in L_i$, for every conjunct of the form (2) $\phi = \forall x \, (\alpha(x) \to \exists y \, (\beta(x, y) \wedge \psi(x, y)))$ for every $b \in \mathfrak{B}$, if there is no witness of ϕ for b in $[b]$ then

1. find $c' \in A$ such that c' is a witness of ϕ for $h(b)$ in $\mathfrak{A}$,
2. define $\mathfrak{C} \cong [c']^{\mathfrak{A}}$ such that $C \cap R = \emptyset, C \cap A = \emptyset$,
3. extend the structures $\Re$ and $\mathbf{T}(\Re)$ by $\mathfrak{C}$ in the following way:
   (a) extend the function h by the isomorphism function of $\mathfrak{C}$ and $[c']^{\mathfrak{A}}$,
   (b) define $l(\mathfrak{C}) = (b, h^{-1}(c'))$ and $tp^{\Re}(b, c) = tp^{\mathfrak{A}}(h(b), h(c))$,
   (c) complete $\Re$: for every $e \in C, f \in R \setminus C$, such that $tp^{\Re}(e, f)$ is not defined, if there exists a T-path in $\mathbf{T}(\Re)$ from $\mathfrak{C}$ to $[f]^{\Re}$ or from $[f]^{\Re}$ to $\mathfrak{C}$, then define $tp^{\Re}(e, f) = tp^{\mathfrak{A}}(h(e), h(f))$, otherwise define $\Re \models \bigwedge_{P \in \sigma} \neg P(e, f) \wedge \neg P(f, e)$.

It is easy to see, that after possibly infinite number of steps, we obtain a tree-like model $\Re$ for Φ. In particular, condition 5 of definition 5 is ensured; otherwise there would exist an infinite T-path in $\mathbf{T}(\Re)$ and then there would exist a sequence of nodes of $\mathbf{N}(\mathfrak{A})$ connected by a T-loop, and this is impossible, when T is transitive. □

Notation. For a sentence Φ in normal form we define the numbers $r(\Phi) = 3 \cdot |\Phi| \cdot 2^{card(\sigma)}$, $K(\Phi) = 2^{2card(\sigma)(2r^2(\Phi)+1)}$ and $G(\Phi) = K^2(\Phi) \cdot 2^{4card(\sigma)}$.

We point out that $r(\Phi)$ is exponential w.r.t. $|\Phi|$, whereas $K(\Phi)$ and $G(\Phi)$ are double exponential. We use the numbers in the following definition of *special* tree-like models that have a node bound $r(\Phi)$, that have bounded length of T-paths (by $2K(\Phi)$), and can be constructed recursively from an initial part of height at most $G(\Phi)$. We should note that $r(\Phi)$ coincides with the clique bound that already appeared in Theorem 1. The exact values of $K(\Phi)$ and $G(\Phi)$ will become important in the proof of Theorem 2.

Definition 6. *We say that a tree-like model $\mathfrak{R}$ for Φ is* special, *if the following conditions hold:*

1. $\mathfrak{R}$ *has* node-bound $r(\Phi)$, *that is for every node* $\mathfrak{C} \in \mathbf{N}(\mathfrak{R}), card(C) \leq r(\Phi)$,
2. *every T-path in $\mathbf{T}(\mathfrak{R})$ is not longer than $2K(\Phi)$,*
3. *for every node $\mathfrak{D}$ at a level L_p, where $p > G(\Phi)$, there is an ancestor node $\mathfrak{C}$ such that $tree(\mathfrak{D}) \cong tree(\mathfrak{C})$.*

Lemma 3. *Every finitely satisfiable sentence Φ in normal form has a tree-like model with node-bound $r(\Phi)$.*

Proof. Assume Φ is a finitely satisfiable sentence in normal form, $\mathfrak{A}$ is a tree-like model for Φ and l is an edge labelling in $\mathbf{T}(\mathfrak{R})$ (they exist by Lemma 2). In the proof we use a technique introduced in [10].

Definition 7. *We say that a clique $\mathfrak{C}$ is a* petal *of a $\mathfrak{A}$-node $\mathfrak{C}'$ if*

1. $card(C) \leq r(\Phi)$,
2. *the set of 1-types realized in $\mathfrak{C}$ coincides with the set of 1-types realized in $\mathfrak{C}'$,*
3. *the set of 2-types realized in $\mathfrak{C}$ is a subset of the set of 2-types realized in $\mathfrak{C}'$,*
4. *for every element $a' \in C'$ and for every conjunct ϕ of Φ of the form (2), if there is a witness for a' of ϕ in $\mathfrak{C}'$, then there is a witness for a of ϕ in $\mathfrak{C}$.*

By Lemma 17 of [10], every $\mathfrak{A}$-node has a petal.

Assume $\mathfrak{R}$ is a structure isomorphic to $\mathfrak{A}$ with an isomorphism function $h : R \mapsto A$. To construct a tree-like model for Φ with node-bound $r(\Phi)$ assume that $\mathfrak{C}' \in \mathbf{N}(\mathfrak{R})$ is a node of cardinality bigger then $r(\Phi)$. We replace $\mathfrak{C}'$ in $\mathfrak{R}$ by its petal and appropriately modify $\mathfrak{R}$ in the following way:

1. let $\mathfrak{B}$ be the father of $\mathfrak{C}'$ in $\mathbf{T}(\mathfrak{R})$, and $l(\mathfrak{C}') = (b, c')$, where $b \in B$, $c' \in C'$;
2. define $\mathfrak{R}' = \mathfrak{R}\!\restriction\! tree(\mathfrak{C}')$ and cut off the subtree $tree(\mathfrak{C}')$ from $\mathbf{T}(\mathfrak{R})$: define $\mathfrak{R} = \mathfrak{R}\!\restriction\!(R \setminus R')$;
3. take a petal $\mathfrak{C}$ of $\mathfrak{C}'$ such that $C \cap R = \emptyset, C \cap A = \emptyset$ and connect $\mathfrak{C}$ to $\mathfrak{B}$ in the following way:
   find an element $c \in C$ such that $tp^{\mathfrak{C}'}(c') = tp^{\mathfrak{C}}(c)$,
   put $tp^{\mathfrak{R}}(b, c) = tp^{\mathfrak{A}}(h(b), h(c'))$ and define $l(\mathfrak{C}) = (b, c)$ in $\mathbf{T}(\mathfrak{R})$;
4. for every $a \in C$:
   find an element $a' \in C'$ (given by condition 4 of Definition 7) such that $tp^{\mathfrak{C}}(a) = tp^{\mathfrak{C}'}(a')$ and for every conjunct ϕ of Φ of the form (2), if there is a witness for a' of ϕ in $\mathfrak{C}'$, then there is a witness for a of ϕ in $\mathfrak{C}$,
   and extend $\mathfrak{R}$ by connecting to $\mathfrak{C}$ every necessary subtree:
   for every $d \in R'$ such that $l([d]) = (a', d)$ in $\mathbf{T}(\mathfrak{R}')$ define in $\mathbf{T}(\mathfrak{R})$ $l([d]) = (a, d)$ and define $tp^{\mathfrak{R}}(a, d) = tp^{\mathfrak{R}'}(a', d)$;

5. complete $\mathfrak{R}$ according to the following cases:
   - for elements $e, f \in R \setminus C$, define $tp^{\mathfrak{R}}(e, f) = tp^{\mathfrak{A}}(h(e), h(f))$,
   - for elements $e \in R \setminus C$, $f \in C$, find $f' \in C'$ such that $tp^{\mathfrak{C}}(f) = tp^{\mathfrak{C}'}(f')$ and define $tp^{\mathfrak{R}}(e, f) = tp^{\mathfrak{A}}(h(e), h(f'))$.

One can check that $\mathfrak{R}$ is a tree-like model for Φ. Now it suffices to repeat the above procedure to get a model for Φ in which every node is not bigger than $r(\Phi)$.   □

Definition 8. *Let $\mathfrak{R}$ be a tree-like model for a normal-form sentence Φ. A node-type of an $\mathfrak{R}$-node $\mathfrak{C}$, denoted by $\overline{\mathfrak{C}}$, is the pair $(ism(\mathfrak{C}), In(\mathfrak{C}))$, where $ism(\mathfrak{C})$ is the isomorphism type of $\mathfrak{C}$ and $In(\mathfrak{C})$ is the set of 1-types realized in $\mathfrak{R}$ by elements appearing in nodes on any T-path from a node of $\mathbf{T}(\mathfrak{R})$ to $\mathfrak{C}$.*

Notice that if $\mathfrak{R}$ has a node-bound $r(\Phi)$, then $card(\{\overline{\mathfrak{C}} : \mathfrak{C} \in \mathbf{N}(\mathfrak{R})\}) \leq K(\Phi)$.

Theorem 2. *For every normal form Φ, Φ is finitely satisfiable if and only if Φ has a special tree-like model.*

Proof. ($\Rightarrow$) Assume $\mathfrak{A}$ is a tree-like model for Φ with node-bound $r(\Phi)$ that exists by Lemma 3. Then, the number of distinct node-types realized in $\mathfrak{A}$ is bounded by $K(\Phi)$.

We show how to construct a special tree-like model for Φ from $\mathfrak{A}$. Let $\mathfrak{R}$ be a structure isomorphic to $\mathfrak{A}$ with an isomorphism function $h : R \mapsto A$

First, distinguish in $\mathfrak{R}$ the set R' consisting of all elements c of R such that there is a T-path from $[c]$ to the root or there is a T-path from the root to $[c]$. Since $\mathfrak{A}$ is a tree-like model, condition 5 of Definition 5 ensures that $\mathfrak{R}'$ is finite.

Note that for every $\mathfrak{R}'$-node $\mathfrak{C}$ that is not a leaf in $\mathbf{T}(\mathfrak{R}')$, the node-type of $\mathfrak{C}$ in $\mathfrak{R}'$ is the same as its node-type in $\mathfrak{R}$.

We modify $\mathfrak{R}$ in a finite number of steps $i = 1, \ldots, height(\mathfrak{R}')$. At every step i we modify the structure $\mathfrak{R}'$ obtained in the previous step.

Step i. For every node $\mathfrak{C} \in L_i$-level of $\mathbf{T}(\mathfrak{R}')$:

1. assume $\mathfrak{B}$ is a father of $\mathfrak{C}$ and $l(\mathfrak{C}) = (b, c)$;
2. find in $\mathfrak{R}'$ a node $\mathfrak{D}$ of $tree(\mathfrak{C})$ such that $\overline{\mathfrak{D}} = \overline{\mathfrak{C}}$ and no other node in $tree(\mathfrak{D})$ of $\mathbf{T}(\mathfrak{R}')$ has a node-type $\overline{\mathfrak{D}}$;
3. cut off the subtree $tree(\mathfrak{C})$ from $\mathbf{T}(\mathfrak{R})$: define $\mathfrak{R} = \mathfrak{R}{\restriction}(R \setminus \{a : a \in \mathfrak{C}, \mathfrak{C} \in tree(\mathfrak{C})\}$
4. connect $tree(\mathfrak{D})$ to $\mathfrak{B}$: find $d \in \mathfrak{D}$ such that $tp^{\mathfrak{D}}(d) = tp^{\mathfrak{C}}(c)$, define in $\mathbf{T}(\mathfrak{R})$ $l([\mathfrak{D}]) = (b, d)$ and define $tp^{\mathfrak{R}}(b, d) = tp^{\mathfrak{A}}(h(b), h(c))$;
5. Complete $\mathfrak{R}$ according to the following cases:
   - for every $e, f \in R'$, $e \in tree(\mathfrak{D})$, $f \notin tree(\mathfrak{D})$, if there is a T-path from $[e]$ to $[f]$ in $\mathbf{T}(R')$ then find an element $\mathfrak{E}$ in $tree([h(c)]$ in $\mathbf{T}(\mathfrak{A})$ and $e' \in E$ such that $tp^{\mathfrak{A}}(e') = tp^{\mathfrak{R}}(e)$ and there is a T-path from $[e']$ to $[h(f)]$ in $\mathbf{T}(\mathfrak{A})$ (such an element e' exists since $tp(e') = tp(e) \in In(\mathfrak{D}) = In(\mathfrak{C}) = In([h(c)]) \subseteq In([h(f)]))$ and define $tp^{\mathfrak{R}}(e, f) = tp^{\mathfrak{A}}(e', h(f))$;

- for every $e, f \in R'$, $e \in tree(\mathfrak{D})$, $f \notin tree(\mathfrak{D})$, if there is a T-path from $[f]$ to $[e]$ in $\mathbf{T}(R')$ then find an element $\mathfrak{E}$ in $tree([h(c)]$ in $\mathbf{T}(\mathfrak{A})$ and $e' \in E$ such that $tp^{\mathfrak{A}}(e') = tp^{\mathfrak{R}}(e)$ and there is a T-path from $[h(f)]$ to $[e']$ in $\mathbf{T}(\mathfrak{A})$ (such an element e' exists since $h(f) \in In([h(c)]) = In(\mathfrak{E}) = In(\mathfrak{D}) \subseteq In([e])$) and define $tp^{\mathfrak{R}}(e, f) = tp^{\mathfrak{A}}(e', h(f))$;
- for every $e, f \in \mathfrak{R}$ such that $tp^{\mathfrak{R}}(e, f)$ has not been defined, put $\mathfrak{R} \models \bigwedge_{P \in \sigma} \neg P(e, f) \wedge \neg P(f, e)$.

Observe that $height(\mathfrak{R}') \leq K(\Phi)$ and every T-path in $\mathbf{T}(\mathfrak{R})$ starting or ending at the root is not longer than $K(\Phi)$.

We repeat the above construction for every $tree(\mathfrak{C})$ of $\mathbf{T}(\mathfrak{R}')$, where $\mathfrak{C}$ is at level L_i, starting with $i = 1$.

To show that condition 3 holds, note that $G(\Phi)$ is big enough to ensure that on every tree-path starting at the root that is longer than $G(\Phi)$, there are two distinct nodes, $\mathfrak{D}$ and its ancestor $\mathfrak{C}$, such that $\overline{\mathfrak{C}} = \overline{\mathfrak{D}}$ and $tp^{\mathfrak{R}}(l(\mathfrak{C})) = tp^{\mathfrak{R}}(l(\mathfrak{D}))$ and there is no T-path either from $\mathfrak{C}$ to $\mathfrak{D}$ or from $\mathfrak{D}$ to $\mathfrak{C}$ in $\mathbf{T}(\mathfrak{R})$. So, it suffices to construct $tree(\mathfrak{D})$ as $tree(\mathfrak{C})$. □

$(\Leftarrow)$ Assume $\mathfrak{A}$ is a special tree-like model. For $\mathcal{X} \subseteq \mathbf{N}(\mathfrak{A})$ define $\mathcal{T}(\mathcal{X}) = \{\overline{\mathfrak{C}} : \mathfrak{C} \in \mathcal{X}\}$. Denote by $\mathcal{L}_i = L_i \cup \ldots \cup L_{i+G(\Phi)}$ the *layer* of $\mathfrak{A}$ (a fragment of $\mathfrak{A}$ starting at level i of $\mathbf{T}(\mathfrak{A})$ of width $G(\Phi)$).

Observe that for every $i > G(\Phi)$, $\mathcal{T}(\mathcal{L}_i) = \mathcal{T}(\bigcup_{j=i}^{\infty} L_j)$. Moreover, for every i, there is no T-path starting above the layer $\mathcal{L}_i$ and ending below the layer.

Due to technical reasons, we assume there is a fixed (usual) ordering on nodes of $\mathfrak{A}$ such that the root is the first element, sons of every $\mathfrak{A}$-node are consecutive elements of the ordering and for $\mathfrak{C}, \mathfrak{C}' \in L_i$ and their sons $\mathfrak{D}, \mathfrak{D}'$: if $\mathfrak{C} < \mathfrak{C}'$ then $\mathfrak{D} < \mathfrak{D}'$.

Let p be a fixed big enough number and $\mathfrak{C}, \mathfrak{C}'$ be two nodes of $\mathfrak{A}$ at level p such that $\mathfrak{C}$ is the m-th element of the ordering and $\mathfrak{C}'$ is $m + s + 1$-th element of the ordering, where $s = n_2(\Phi)r(\Phi)^{2K(\Phi)}$ is the maximal number of leaves of a tree of degree $n_2(\Phi)r(\Phi)$ of height $2K(\Phi)$. Then there is no T-path between $\mathfrak{C}$ and $\mathfrak{C}'$. To construct the finite model of Φ take the substructure $\mathfrak{R}$ of $\mathfrak{A}$ consisting of the first $p = G(\Phi) + 2s \cdot G(\Phi) + 1$ levels of $\mathbf{T}(\mathfrak{A})$. Note that $\mathfrak{R}$ consists of the initial part of $\mathfrak{A}$ of height $G(\Phi)$ and $2s$ consecutive layers of $\mathfrak{A}$, say $\mathcal{L}^0, \mathcal{L}^{0'}, \mathcal{L}^1, \mathcal{L}^{1'}, \ldots, \mathcal{L}^{G(\Phi)-1}, \mathcal{L}^{G(\Phi)-1'}$.

To complete the structure $\mathfrak{R}$ we bend the edges leading from the nodes from level p to other elements in $\mathfrak{A}$. Assume, $\mathfrak{C}_0, \mathfrak{C}_1, \ldots$ is the finite sequence of consecutive nodes (in fixed ordering) of level $p + 1$. For every node $\mathfrak{C}_i$ at level $p + 1$, where $i = 0, 1, 2, \ldots$, find a node $\mathfrak{D}_i \in \mathcal{L}^{i \mod s}$ such that $\overline{\mathfrak{C}} = \overline{\mathfrak{D}}$ and $tp^{\mathfrak{R}}(l(\mathfrak{C}_i)) = tp^{\mathfrak{R}}(l(\mathfrak{D}_i))$ (such a node exists by condition 3 of Definition 6, since the number of nodes with different node-types and different labels is not bigger than $G(\Phi)$). Note that there is no T-path between $\mathfrak{C}_i$ and $\mathfrak{D}_i$. Let h be the isomorphism function such that $h : C_i \mapsto D_i$. For every $a \in R$, if there is a T-path between $[a]$ and $\mathfrak{C}_i$, then for every $c \in \mathfrak{C}_i$ define $tp^{\mathfrak{R}}(a, h(c)) = tp^{\mathfrak{R}}(a, c)$ (note that before $tp^{\mathfrak{R}}(a, h(c)) \models \bigwedge_{P \in \sigma} \neg P(x, y) \wedge \neg P(y, x)$). □

Theorem 3. *The finite satisfiability problem for* $GF^2 + TG$ *with one transitive predicate letter is* 2EXPTIME-*complete.*

Proof. (Sketch) To check if a GF^2+TG-sentence Φ in normal form is satisfiable we need to check if an initial part of height $G(\Phi)$ of a special tree-like model can be constructed. This can be done using an alternating procedure working in exponential space. In fact we build a single path of a tree that either ends at an node not needing new witnesses, or is infinite but does not contain any T-path longer than $2K(\Phi)$. During the construction it suffices to keep node-types of two consecutive nodes and two counters to count up to $G(\Phi)$ and $K(\Phi)$, respectively. This information can be written using exponential space. Details are similar to the alternating exponential space algorithm for Sat(GF+TG) given in [17].

2EXPTIME-hardness of the FinSat problem can be shown in a similar way as done by Kieroński in [11] for the satisfiability problem. $\qquad\qquad\square$

The same methods can be used to prove the analogous results for the guarded fragment with unbounded number of variables.

5   Finite Models. More Transitive Relations

In this section we discuss main similarities and differences between finite and general reasoning for our logic in case we have more transitive predicate letters in the signature.

First, we give an example of a satisfiable sentence Φ over a signature with a few transitive predicate letters, such that every finite model of Φ has at least one clique of double exponential size. This result is rather surprising since by Corollary 1, Φ has an infinite model with exponential cliques. prove decidability of FinSat(GF^2+TG) with more than one transitive predicate letter, one needs to use essentially different techniques than for the satisfiability problem in general and for the one transitive predicate case.

In this section we also note that every finitely satisfiable sentence has a finite singular model of polynomial size with respect to the original model. We believe that this is a key observation for an efficient decision procedure for FinSat(GF+TG) with more transitive predicate letters.

Example 1. We write a sentence Φ describing a model consisting of a full binary tree of height 2^n that is mapped onto a double exponential T-clique that is disjoint with the tree. The size of the tree enforces the size of the T-clique. In fact, we cannot ensure that every model of Φ contains exactly one tree or one clique but, as we will see, in any finite model for Φ at least one T-clique has to be of double exponential size.

We assume that T, T_1, T_2, T_3, F are transitive predicate letters in the signature. We also use additional unary predicate letters. In particular, we assume that there are n unary predicate letters $L_1, \ldots, L_n$ that are used to encode in every element a of the structure a number $L(a)$ from 0 to $2^n - 1$, defined by taking the k-th bit of $L(a)$ set to 1, if $L_i(a)$ is true. It is easy to express the following properties with formulas of our logic of polynomial length: $L(x) = L(y)$, $L(x) = L(y) + 1$, $L(x) = k$ and $L(x) \leq k$, for fixed k with $0 \leq k < 2^n$.

We define Φ to be the conjunction of the following sentences.

First, we say that the universe of the model contains two disjoint sets C and D, each of them containing a distinguished element (root in D, and R in C).

$$\exists x\, R(x) \wedge \exists x\, Root(x) \tag{4}$$

$$\forall x\, R(x) \rightarrow (Cx \wedge L(x) = 0) \wedge \forall x\, Root(x) \rightarrow (Dx \wedge L(x) = 0) \tag{5}$$

$$\forall x\, Cx \rightarrow \neg Dx \wedge \forall x\, Dx \rightarrow \neg Cx \tag{6}$$

We use F to define a bijection from C to D (here transitivity of F is essential).

$$\forall x\, Cx \rightarrow (\exists y\, (Fxy \wedge Dy) \wedge \exists y\, (Fyx \wedge Dy)) \tag{7}$$

$$\forall x\, Dx \rightarrow (\exists y\, (Fxy \wedge Cy) \wedge \exists y\, (Fyx \wedge Cy)) \tag{8}$$

$$\forall xy\, Fxy \rightarrow ((Cx \wedge Dy \vee Dx \wedge Cy \vee x = y) \wedge L(x) = L(y)) \tag{9}$$

Elements in C are partitioned into T-cliques, each of them containing exactly one element in R (by transitivity of T).

$$\forall x\, Cx \rightarrow (\exists y\, (Txy \wedge Ry) \wedge \exists y\, (Tyx \wedge Ry)) \tag{10}$$

$$\forall xy\, Txy \rightarrow (\neg(Rx \wedge Ry) \vee x = y) \tag{11}$$

Elements in D constitute trees of exponential height, each of them starting at a root node. The edges in the trees are either T_1-, T_2- or T_3-edges.

We ensure that distinct elements connected by each T_i are located on consecutive levels of D.

$$\bigwedge_{i=1,2,3} (\forall xy\, T_i xy \rightarrow (Dx \wedge Dy \wedge (L(x) = L(y) + 1 \vee L(y) = L(x) + 1 \vee x = y))) \tag{12}$$

To shorten the further formulas we define the following abbreviations:

$$Father(x, T_i) \equiv \exists y\, (T_i xy \wedge L(y) + 1 = L(x)) \wedge \exists y\, (T_i yx \wedge L(y) + 1 = L(x))$$
$$Son(x, T_i) \equiv \exists y\, (T_i xy \wedge \neg Root(y) \wedge L(y) = L(x) + 1) \wedge$$
$$\exists y\, (T_i xy \wedge \neg Root(y) \wedge L(y) = L(x) + 1)$$

Note that for any element a in a structure satisfying (12), if $Father(a, T_i)$ is true then, by transitivity of T_i, there is a unique element $b \neq a$ such that $T_i ba$ is true. The same holds for $Son(a, T_i)$.

Finally, we add to Φ conjuncts describing the sons of elements in the trees.

$$\forall x\, Root(x) \rightarrow (Son(x, T_2) \wedge Son(x, T_3)) \tag{13}$$

$$\forall x\, Dx \rightarrow ((L(x) \geq 1) \wedge (L(x) < 2^n) \rightarrow$$
$$((Father(x, T_1) \rightarrow (Son(x, T_2) \wedge Son(x, T_3))) \wedge$$
$$(Father(x, T_2) \rightarrow (Son(x, T_1) \wedge Son(x, T_3))) \wedge \tag{14}$$
$$(Father(x, T_3) \rightarrow (Son(x, T_1) \wedge Son(x, T_2)))))$$

Note that the last formula in the given form is not guarded but can easily be written as a guarded one.

One can check that Φ has a model in which D constitutes a full binary tree of height 2^n and C is a T-clique of cardinality equal cardinality of the set D, that is double exponential. Additionally, we can prove the following claim.

Claim. Every finite model of Φ has a T-clique of cardinality at least double exponential w.r.t. the length of Φ.

Proof (of claim). Let $\mathfrak{A}$ be a finite model of Φ. Obviously, A contains two nonempty disjoint sets C and D of the same cardinality. However, there might be more roots (i.e. elements for which $Root(a)$ is true) and more than one non-trivial (i.e. of size bigger than one) T-cliques.

Let r be a root in D. Define $D(r)$ as the subset of D consisting of those elements that are reachable from r by any T_1, T_2, T_3-path.

Observe that for any two roots $r_1, r_2 \in D$ such that $r_1 \neq r_2$, we have $D(r_1) \cap D(r_2) = \emptyset$. For, assume $a \in D(r_1) \cap D(r_2)$ and $L(a) = k$. Then, there is a unique path from a to r_1 in $D(r_1)$ and a unique path from a to r_2 in $D(r_2)$. One can prove that the two paths must have the same length. By (14), the predicates T_1, T_2, T_3 behave as functions, so the two paths coincide. Hence, $r_1 = r_2$ - a contradiction.

Now, let k be the number of elements of A that are roots in D. Then k is also the number of non-trivial T-cliques in $\mathfrak{A}$. The cardinality of every set $D(r)$, where r is a root is at least double exponential. Hence, since all elements of $D(r)$ are mapped in a 1-1 way to elements of non-trivial T-cliques, at least one of the cliques must be of double exponential size. $\qquad\square$

We note that the number of transitive predicate letters used in the above example could be easily reduced to three. To save space and simplify presentation we used more of them. At the moment it is not clear whether two transitive predicate letters would also suffice.

From the above Example, in contrast to Corollary 1, we get the following corollary in the finite model case.

Corollary 2. *Not every finitely satisfiable $GF^2 + TG$-sentence in normal form has a finite ramified model with exponential cliques.*

In the last part of this section, if not stated otherwise, we assume that Φ is a GF^2+TG-sentence in normal form over a signature σ with p transitive predicate letters $T_0, \ldots, T_{p-1}$.

As the last observation in this paper we formulate the following lemma.

Lemma 4. *If Φ has a finite model of cardinality n, then Φ has a finite singular model of cardinality n^p.*

We believe that FinSat(GF+TG) is decidable for any number of transitive predicate letters and that the above Lemma will be a key tool for the proof. Since this claim might not be motivated strongly enough, we prove only a weaker version of the lemma.

First define the following operations. If $t(x, y)$ is a 2-type, then $t \uparrow T$ is the unique 2-type obtained from t by replacing every two-variable T'-atom, where T' is a transitive predicate letter, $T' \neq T$, by its negation.

Assume that $\mathfrak{A} \models \Phi$, $A = \{a_0, a_1, \dots a_{n-1}\}$ and denote by $\mathfrak{A} \uparrow T$ the structure with the universe $\{b_0, b_1, \dots b_{n-1}\}$ such that $tp^{\mathfrak{A} \uparrow T}(b_i, b_j) = tp^{\mathfrak{A}}(a_i, a_j) \uparrow T$.

We have the following easy observation.

Proposition 1. *Let $t(x, y)$ be a proper 2-type.*

1. *For every conjunct ϕ of Φ of the form (2): $\forall x \, (\alpha(x) \rightarrow \exists y \, (\beta(x, y) \wedge \psi(x, y)))$, if $t \models \alpha(x) \wedge \beta(x, y) \wedge \psi(x, y)$, where $\beta(x, y)$ is a T-guard or a P-guard with not transitive P, then $t \uparrow T \models \alpha(x) \wedge \beta(x, y) \wedge \psi(x, y)$.*
2. *For every conjunct ϕ of Φ of the form (3): $\forall x \forall y \, (\alpha(x, y) \rightarrow \psi(x, y))$ if $t \models \alpha(x, y) \rightarrow \psi(x, y)$, then $t \uparrow T \models \alpha(x, y) \rightarrow \psi(x, y)$.*
3. *For every conjunct ϕ of Φ of the form (3), if t contains no two-variable atoms, then $t \models \alpha(x, y) \rightarrow \psi(x, y)$.*
4. *If $\mathfrak{A} \models \Phi$, then for the conjunct ϕ of Φ of the form (1): $\exists x \, (\alpha(x) \wedge \psi(x))$, for every conjunct ϕ of the form (2): $\forall x \, (\alpha(x) \rightarrow \exists y \, (\beta(x, y) \wedge \psi(x, y)))$, where $\beta(x, y)$ is a T-guard or a P-guard with not transitive P and for every conjunct ϕ of Φ of the form (3), $\mathfrak{A} \uparrow T \models \phi$.*

Example 2. Let $p = 2$, i.e. σ contains exactly two transitive predicate letters T_0 and T_1 and let $\mathfrak{A}'$ be a finite model for Φ such that $card(A) = n$. We will construct a singular model $\mathfrak{A}$ for Φ of cardinality n^2.

Assume $A' = \{a_0, a_1, \dots a_{n-1}\}$ and define the universe of the structure $\mathfrak{A}$ as a union of pairwise disjoint sets, $A = \bigcup_{k=0}^{n-1} A_k$, where $A_k = \{a_{0k}, a_{1k}, \dots, a_{n-1,k}\}$. To define $\mathfrak{A}$, for $k = 0, 1, \dots, n-1$ put

1. $tp^{\mathfrak{A}}(a_{ik}, a_{jk}) = tp^{\mathfrak{A}'}(a_i, a_j) \uparrow T_0$,
2. $tp^{\mathfrak{A}}(a_{ik}, a_{j,(k+j-i) \mod n}) = tp^{\mathfrak{A}'}(a_i, a_j) \uparrow T_1$,

where $i = 0, 1, \dots, n-2$, $j = i+1, \dots, n-1$. The partially defined structure is completed using 2-types containing no two-variable atoms.

Notice that $\mathfrak{A}$ is singular. To show that $\mathfrak{A} \models \Phi$, for $k = 0, 1, \dots, n-1$ define

$$C_k = \{a_{0k}, a_{1,(k+1) \mod n}, \dots, a_{n-1,(k+n-1) \mod n}\}.$$

Each set C_k contains exactly n elements of $\mathfrak{A}$ and the family $\mathcal{P}^1 = \{C_0, C_1, \dots, C_{n-1}\}$ constitutes a partition of the set A. Moreover, we have $card(A_k \cap C_l) \leq 1$, for every $k, l = 0, 1, \dots, n-1$, $k \neq l$. Since 2-types of the form 1 appear inside each subset A_k and 2-types of the form 2 - inside each subset C_k, the structure $\mathfrak{A}$ is well-defined (every 2-type was defined once only).

Now observe that for every $k = 0, 1, \dots, n-1$ we have

1. $tp^{\mathfrak{A}}(a_{ik}, a_{jk}) = tp^{\mathfrak{A}_k}(a_{ik}, a_{jk})$,
2. $tp^{\mathfrak{A}}(a_{ik}, a_{j,(k+j-i) \mod n}) = tp^{\mathfrak{C}_{(k-i) \mod n}}(a_{ik}, a_{j,(k+j-i) \mod n})$, where $i = 0, 1, \dots, n-2$, $j = i, i+1, \dots, n-1$.

Hence, $\mathfrak{A} \restriction A_k \cong \mathfrak{A}' \uparrow T_0$ and $\mathfrak{A} \restriction C_k \cong \mathfrak{A}' \uparrow T_1$, for $k = 0, 1, \ldots, n - 1$. So, by Proposition 1, $\mathfrak{A} \models \Phi$.

In case when the signature σ contains $p > 2$ transitive predicate letters, one can simply iterate the above procedure to obtain the following corollary.

Corollary 3. *If Φ has a finite model of cardinality n, then Φ has a finite singular model of cardinality $n^{2^{p-1}}$.*

References

1. H. Andréka, J. van Benthem, I. Németi, Modal languages and bounded fragments of predicate logic, ILLC Research Report ML-1996-03 University of Amsterdam, journal version in: *J. Philos. Logic*, 27 (1998), no. 3, 217-274.
2. E. Grädel, On the restraining power of guards, J. Symbolic Logic 64 (1999) 1719–1742.
3. J. van Benthem, Dynamics bits and pieces, ILLC Research Report LP-97-01 University of Amsterdam.
4. M. Marx, Tolerance logic, Journal of Logic, Language and Information 10:3 (2001) 353–374.
5. E. Grädel, Decision procedures for guarded logics, in: 16th International Conference in Artificial Intelligence, Vol. LNCS 1932, Springer, 1999, pp. 31–51.
6. I. Hodkinson, Loosely guarded fragment of first-order logic has the finite model property, Studia Logica 70 (2002) 205–240.
7. I. Hodkinson, M. Otto, Finite conformal hypergraph covers, with two applications, Bull. Symbolic Logic 9 (2003) 387–405.
8. E. Grädel, I. Walukiewicz, Guarded fixed point logic, in: Fourteenth Annual IEEE Symposium on Logic in Computer Science, 1999, pp. 45–54.
9. H. Ganzinger, C. Meyer, M. Veanes, The two-variable guarded fragment with transitive relations, in: Fourteenth Annual IEEE Symposium on Logic in Computer Science, 1999, pp. 24–34.
10. W. Szwast, L. Tendera, On the decision problem for the guarded fragment with transitivity, in: Proc. 16th IEEE Symposium on Logic in Computer Science, 2001, pp. 147–156.
11. E. Kieroński, The two-variable guarded fragment with transitive guards is 2EXPTIME-Hard, in: Proc. Foundations of Software Science and Computational Structures, 6th International Conference, FOSSACS, Vol. LNCS 2620, Springer Verlag, 2003, pp. 299–312.
12. M. Bojańczyk, Two-way alternating automata and finite models, in: Proceedings of the 29th International Colloquium on Automata, Languages, and Programming, Vol. LNCS 2380, Springer, 2002, pp. 833–844.
13. G. De Giacomo, M. Lenzerini, Tbox and Abox reasoning in expressive description logics, in: Proc. of KR-96, Morgan Kaufmann, 1996, pp. 316–327.
14. C. Lutz, U. Sattler, L. Tendera, The complexity of finite model reasoning in description logics, in: Proc. of CADE-19, Vol. 2741 of LNAI, Springer-Verlag, 2003, pp. 60–74.
15. L. Pacholski, W. Szwast, L. Tendera, Complexity results for first-order two-variable logic with counting, SIAM J. of Computing 25 (2000) 1083–1117.
16. I. Pratt-Hartmann, Complexity of the two-variable fragment with (binary-coded) counting quantifiers, Journal of Logic, Language and Information, to appear.
17. W. Szwast, L. Tendera, The guarded fragment with transitive guards, Annals of Pure and Applied Logic 128 (2004) 227–276.

Deciding Separation Logic Formulae by SAT and Incremental Negative Cycle Elimination

Chao Wang, Franjo Ivančić, Malay Ganai, and Aarti Gupta

NEC Laboratories America,
4 Independence Way, Princeton, NJ 08540, USA

Abstract. Separation logic is a subset of the quantifier-free first order logic. It has been successfully used in the automated verification of systems that have large (or unbounded) integer-valued state variables, such as pipelined processor designs and timed systems. In this paper, we present a fast decision procedure for separation logic, which combines Boolean satisfiability (SAT) with a graph based incremental negative cycle elimination algorithm. Our solver abstracts a separation logic formula into a Boolean formula by replacing each predicate with a Boolean variable. Transitivity constraints over predicates are detected from the constraint graph and added on a need-to basis. Our solver handles Boolean and theory conflicts uniformly at the Boolean level. The graph based algorithm supports not only incremental theory propagation, but also constant time theory backtracking without using a cumbersome history stack. Experimental results on a large set of benchmarks show that our new decision procedure is scalable, and outperforms existing techniques for this logic.

1 Introduction

Separation logic (also called difference logic) is a subset of the quantifier-free first order logic for which efficient decision procedures exist. It has been successfully used in the automated verification of systems that have large (or unbounded) integer-valued state variables, such as pipelined processor designs and timed systems. Since integer variables and arithmetic operators are not flattened into the bit vector format, separation logic can model and verify systems at a higher abstraction level than Boolean logic. The UCLID verifier [4], for instance, relies on the decision procedure for separation logic as its back-end engine.

A separation logic formula contains the standard Boolean connectives as well as separation predicates of the form $(v_i - v_j \leq c)$ where v_i, v_j are integer variables and c is an integer constant. The validity of a separation logic formula can be checked by translating it to an equi-satisfiable Boolean formula, which in turn is checked by a Boolean SAT solver. Many existing techniques took this approach to leverage the recent advances of Boolean SAT algorithms, with differences only in the timing of the transformation and in the Boolean encoding methods. In particular, they can be classified as either *eager* or *lazy* depending on when the transformation happens.

In the eager approaches [4, 18, 16, 19], separation logic formulae are converted to equi-satisfiable Boolean formulae in a single step. The two existing encoding methods used during the transformation are *small domain encoding* and *per constraint encoding*.

G. Sutcliffe and A. Voronkov (Eds.): LPAR 2005, LNAI 3835, pp. 322–336, 2005.

In small domain encoding, integer variables and arithmetic operators are bit-blasted with a sufficiently large vector size. In per constraint encoding, the formula is abstracted by replacing each predicate with a Boolean variable, and then augmented by adding all possible transitivity constraints over predicates. In addition, a hybrid method can be used to combine the strength of these two encoding schemes. A previous experimental study [16] showed that per constraint encoding based approach is often faster than small domain encoding. However, the complete set of transitivity constraints is added in one shot regardless of whether they are needed or not.

In the lazy approaches [2, 1, 8, 9, 3], transitivity constraints are added only dynamically on a "need-to" basis to augment the Boolean skeleton. Whenever the assignment to the Boolean skeleton is not consistent with the separation predicates, a transitivity constraint is added to eliminate the inconsistency before SAT search is resumed. Lazy approaches exploit the fact that transitivity constraints are often highly redundant and some of them may never be needed in solving the validity problem.

Deciding separation logic is an NP-complete problem [13]. However, experience with Boolean SAT solvers shows that practically efficient search heuristics often exist even for NP-complete problems. For example, the recent advances of DPLL SAT solvers (Davis-Putnam-Logemann-Loveland [7]) have led to their widespread application in industry settings, e.g. in verification of pipelined microprocessors. The two technical breakthroughs responsible for much of the performance improvement are (1) conflict analysis based learning and non-chronological backtracking [17] and (2) watched literal based fast Boolean Constraint Propagation (BCP) [11, 10]. These two parts, however, remain the weak links in separation logic solvers based on the lazy approach.

In this paper, we propose a procedure for lazily deciding separation logic by combining a DPLL Boolean SAT procedure with an efficient graph algorithm in the style of recent SAT Modulo Theory (SMT) solvers. Our emphasis is on the efficient implementation of conflict analysis (for both Boolean and theory conflicts) and on the data structure that supports fast theory backtracking. Our method maintains and incrementally updates a constraint subgraph for all active separation constraints. The theory part only receives assignments from the Boolean part and detects conflicts; it does not perform exhaustive theory propagation nor feed back implications. Theory conflicts are removed by augmenting the Boolean formula with conflicting clauses. Our procedure is both sound and complete; it terminates as soon as a consistent assignment is found or all possible cases are explored.

A major contribution of this paper is our fast theory propagation and backtracking algorithm, which not only prunes theory constraints incrementally, but also performs constant time backtracking. Unlike the existing techniques in [2, 9, 3, 6], we do not need expensive book-keeping on the constraint graph for (non-chronological) backtracking, nor do we need a history stack to store any of its previous states. In fact an analogy exists between our graph-based constraint propagation (GCP) algorithm and the watched literal based Boolean constraint propagation (BCP) in Chaff [11], in that both have constant time backtracking.

In [3], an incremental and layered procedure for deciding linear arithmetic logic was proposed for the MathSat solver. It includes a separation logic solver based on incremental Bellman-Ford algorithm for detecting theory conflicts, but no further details of the algorithm are available in [3] or related papers. In particular, it is not clear how their theory backtracking is implemented and what the backtracking cost is.

The more recent work by Cotton [6] also has an incremental negative cycle detection algorithm, but is significantly different from ours in backtracking. In the broader area, the work by Ramalingam *et al.* [15] is the first dynamic algorithm for arbitrary edge weighted graphs that has a per edge complexity bound better than that of Bellman-Ford. The cycle detection algorithm in our approach has the same complexity bound as [15]. In addition to incremental cycle elimination, we propose several optimizations for its tighter integration with the Boolean SAT solver and for fast backtracking.

In [9], a DPLL(T) framework was proposed for SAT modulo theories, but including only EUF logic. Recently, the DPLL(T) approach has been extended to separation logic [12]. They perform exhaustive theory propagation, making the algorithm quite different from ours. We have implemented a variant of [12] on top of our own solver; our experiments show that this addition can further improve the performance of our solver on examples where theory conflicts play a larger role.

We also provide in this paper experimental comparisons of our solver with the latest versions of both DPLL(T) and MathSAT, as well as other solvers including ICS [8], UCLID [4], and TSAT++ [1]. The results show that our new algorithm outperforms these existing techniques, particularly on harder test cases.

The rest of the paper is organized as follows. We give technical background in Section 2, describing separation logic, the transformation to SAT, and the constraint subgraph. We then give the overall algorithm in Section 3. Our fast GCP and incremental negative-cycle detection algorithms are described in Section 4. We give experimental results in Section 6, and then conclude in Section 7.

2 Separation Logic

Definition 1. *A separation logic formula consists of the standard propositional connectives and predicates of the form $v_i - v_j \leq c$, where v_i and v_j are integer variables and c is a constant.*

To canonize the individual predicates, we impose an order on the integer variables such that $i \leq j$ for all constraints of the form $v_i - v_j \leq c$. Input formulae that do not meet this above requirement are normalized through rewriting, before they are given to the solver. For example, $(x - y > 5)$ is equivalent to $\neg(x - y \leq 5)$, while $(x - y < 5)$ is equivalent to $(x - y \leq 4)$. For predicates in the form of $x \leq c$, a common integer variable $ZERO$ can be added to encode the predicates into $(x - ZERO \leq c)$. Note that with the implicit order on all integer variables, predicates $(x - y \leq 5)$ and $(y - x \leq -6)$ are mapped to the same Boolean variable (P and $\neg P$) instead of two.

The validity of a separation formula can be checked by a Boolean SAT solver via transformation. The first step is to abstract the original formula ϕ into a Boolean skeleton ϕ_{bool}, by replacing separation predicates with fresh Boolean variables. Since transitivity constraints among predicates are removed, ϕ_{bool} has all the possible satisfying assignments of ϕ, and possibly more. Formula ϕ_{bool} is put into the Conjunctive Normal Form (CNF) before it is given to the SAT solver. A CNF formula is a conjunction of *clauses*, each of which is a disjunction of *literals*. A literal is a Boolean variable or its negation.

An example of a separation logic formula is given as follows,

$$(x - y \leq 2 \vee x - z \leq 6) \wedge (x - y \leq 2 \vee \neg(x - z \leq 6)) \wedge$$
$$(\neg(x - y \leq 2) \vee y - z \leq 3) \wedge (\neg(x - y \leq 2) \vee \neg(y - z \leq 3) \vee w - y \leq 10)$$
$$(\neg(x - y \leq 2) \vee w - y \leq 10) \ ,$$

where w, x, y and z are all integer variables. Note that this formula is already in the CNF format. After replacing the predicates by Boolean variables as follows,

$$A : (x - y \leq 2), B : (x - z \leq 6), C : (y - z \leq 3), D : (w - y \leq 10)$$

ϕ is abstracted into ϕ_{bool}:

$$(A \vee B) \wedge (A \vee \neg B) \wedge (\neg A \vee C) \wedge (\neg A \vee \neg C \vee D) \wedge (\neg A \vee D) \ .$$

Although the Boolean assignment $(A, \neg B, C, D)$ satisfies ϕ_{bool}, the set of corresponding separation constraints do not have a solution. In fact, $(x - y \leq 2 \wedge y - z \leq 3) \rightarrow (x - z \leq 5)$. To make the Boolean formula equi-satisfiable to ϕ, one must augment ϕ_{bool} with transitivity constraints among separation predicates to rule out inconsistent assignments. In the above example, we can derive the constraint $A \wedge C \rightarrow B$ to augment the Boolean skeleton.

A set of separation predicates can be mapped to a weighted directed graph, called the *constraint graph*. Every negative weight cycle in this graph represents a transitivity constraint.

Definition 2. *The constraint graph G of a set of separation predicates is a weighted directed graph whose vertices correspond to integer variables and whose edges correspond to predicates and their negations. In particular, $(v_i - v_j \leq c)$ corresponds to the edge (v_j, v_i) with weight c, and $\neg(v_i - v_j \leq c)$ corresponds to (v_i, v_j) with weight $(-c - 1)$.*

A *constraint subgraph* contains all the vertices but a subset of the edges of a constraint graph. A full or partial assignment to ϕ_{bool} induces a constraint subgraph, which has only those edges corresponding to the active constraints.

Theorem 1. *Let G_s be the constraint subgraph induced by a (partial) assignment to ϕ_{bool}. The assignment is consistent with the set of separation predicates if and only if G_s does not have a negative weight cycle.*

As an example, the constraint graph for the set of predicates $\{A, B, C, D\}$ is given in Figure 1. The positive and negative phases of each predicate are mapped to two different edges. Such a graph implicitly encodes all the possible transitivity constraints. The constraint subgraph corresponding to the assignment $(A, \neg B, C, D)$ is given in Figure 2, which has a negative weight cycle $(x \rightarrow z \rightarrow y \rightarrow x)$.

In the lazy approaches, transitivity constraints in G_s are added dynamically whenever they are needed. However, this requires a call to the negative cycle detection algorithm every time a full or partial assignment is found. A standard graph-based approach

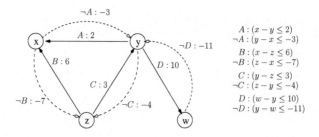

Fig. 1. Constraint graph for the predicate set $\{A, B, C, D\}$

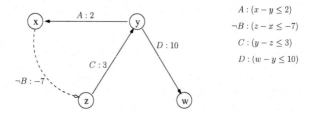

Fig. 2. Constraint subgraph induced by the assignment $(A, \neg B, C, D)$

for detecting negative cycles is the Bellman-Ford shortest path algorithm, which gives negative cycles as a by-product. In practice, the number of calls to a negative cycle detection procedure can be extremely large, therefore making it a potential bottleneck for lazy separation logic solvers.

3   SLICE: The New Solver

We present a new solver called SLICE (for Separation Logic solver with Incremental Cycle Elimination), which tightly integrates a DPLL style SAT procedure with a fast graph-based constraint propagation algorithm. The theory part in SLICE is kept quite passive. It only reports conflicts, but does not propagate implications back as in [12]. However, it is equipped with new data structures that support efficient propagation and constant time backtracking.

3.1   The Overall Algorithm

The overall algorithm of SLICE can be viewed as a modification of the DPLL procedure (Figure 3). It takes the Boolean skeleton ϕ_{bool} as input, and initializes the constraint subgraph G_s with all the vertices – one for each integer variable – but no edges. Procedure *decide()* picks one Boolean variable at a time and assigns it either true or false. When all Boolean variables are assigned and there is no conflict, it returns with SAT; if a conflict appears before any decision is made (i.e. the decision level is 0), we declare the formula UNSAT.

```
slice_sat() {
  while (1) {
    if (decide()) {
      while (slice_cp()==CONFLICT) {
        level = conflict_analysis();
        if (level < 0)
          return UNSAT;
        else
          back_track(level);
      }
    }else
      return SAT;
  }
}

slice_cp() {
  if (bcp()==CONFLICT)
    return CONFLICT;
  else if (gcp()==CONFLICT)) { //propagate constraints on graph
    add_conflicting_clause(); //add new constraints on Boolean formula
    return CONFLICT;
  }else
    return NO_CONFLICT;
}
```

Fig. 3. SLICE: The new decision procedure for separation logic

SLICE only makes Boolean decisions. Implications of these decisions are propagated first by *bcp()* among Boolean clauses, then by *gcp()* in the constraint subgraph. Note that the passing of implications from Boolean to theory part is one-way; there is no feedback from *gcp()* to *bcp()*. BCP is based on unit implication, i.e. when all the other literals are set to false in a clause, the only remaining one must evaluate to true. GCP is based on the incremental negative cycle detection algorithm (details in Section 4). If either of them detects a conflict, we perform conflict analysis to locate the decision level at which the conflict is triggered. After adding a conflict clause to rule out the same assignment in the future, the procedure backtracks non-chronologically to the appropriate decision level and resumes the search. Procedure *slice_sat()* terminates as soon as a valid assignment is found or all possible cases have been explored.

3.2 Handling Conflicts

Conflicts from BCP and GCP are both handled at the Boolean level, by the same conflict analysis procedure. Our Boolean SAT solver is based on Chaff [11], which maintains an *implication graph* by recording the clause responsible for each implication (called the *antecedent*) and associating it with the implied variable. BCP detects a conflict when it finds a conflicting clause. During conflict analysis, we start from the conflicting clause and trace backward in the implication graph, to locate a proper cut-set (e.g. the 1st UIP in Chaff) between the decision nodes and the conflict. A *conflict clause* is then derived and added to the clause database, after which the procedure backtracks non-chronologically to the decision level where the conflict is triggered.

In GCP, we maintain a constraint subgraph to store all the active predicates, but do not maintain any data structure to store the implication relation. Every time a predicate is assigned at the Boolean level, its corresponding edge is scheduled to be added to the constraint subgraph. GCP starts adding and propagating edges only after BCP finishes, in order to amortize the cost of GCP (other heuristically driven schemes are also possible to change the ratio of calls to BCP and GCP). For each negative cycle detected during the propagation, it adds a conflicting clause whose literals are the negation of the edges on the negative cycle. Note that this particular call sequence guarantees that the added conflicting clause is always irredundant—otherwise, BCP would have detected the conflict. When we jump back to the Boolean level, the added conflicting clause enables us to perform conflict analysis and non-chronological backtracking using the same procedure, as if the conflict is detected during BCP.

We use the example in Section 2 to illustrate how conflicts are handled. Here we use $\neg D@L1$ to denote that Variable D is set to false at decision level 1.

- Assume that the SAT procedure makes the following decisions/implications,

$$
\begin{array}{lll}
\neg D@L1; & & \text{decision} \\
& \neg A@L1; & \text{due to } (\neg A \vee D) \\
& \neg B@L1; & \text{due to } (A \vee \neg B) \\
& (A \vee B) = false; & \text{conflict!}
\end{array}
$$

Note that the first line is decision and the rest are implications. By tracing back from $(A \vee B)$, we find the 1st UIP $(\neg A@L1)$, add the conflict clause (A), and backtrack to decision level 0. Backtracking restores all the assignments made to D, A and B.

- The added clause (A) forces the SAT procedure to flip the value of A,

$$
\begin{array}{ll}
A@L0; & \text{due to } (A) \\
D@L0; & \text{due to } (\neg A \vee D) \\
C@L0; & \text{due to } (\neg A \vee C) \\
\neg B@L1; & \text{satisfiable assignment!}
\end{array}
$$

At this point, BCP finishes without detecting any conflict. This Boolean assignment induces the constraint subgraph in Figure 2. However, GCP finds a negative weight cycle due to $\{A, \neg B, C\}$, and adds a conflicting clause $(\neg A \vee B \vee \neg C)$. The added clause itself represents a conflict in the Boolean part, therefore triggers the 1st UIP conflict analysis. After adding a conflict clause (B), we backtrack again to decision level 0.

- The added clause (B) forces the SAT procedure to flip the value of B.

$$
\begin{array}{ll}
A@L0; & \text{due to } (\neg A); \\
D@L0; & \text{due to } (\neg A \vee D); \\
C@L0; & \text{due to } (\neg A \vee C); \\
B@L0; & \text{due to } (B);
\end{array}
$$

Another call to GCP confirms that this is a consistent assignment; therefore, the separation logic formula is satisfiable.

We should note that both the conflicting clauses added for negative cycles and the conflict clauses learned from conflict analysis can be made *volatile*; that is, they are allowed to be deleted. In many modern SAT solvers, periodically deleting redundant clauses has been helpful in solving hard SAT problems. The removal of conflict clauses does not affect the completeness of the SAT algorithm (for proof, please refer to [20]).

In practice, however, we choose to make the conflicting clauses added for negative cycles *non-volatile*, since they represent the constraints not yet contained in the original Boolean formula ϕ_{bool}. On the other hand, we make conflict clauses *volatile* since they are always redundant (though their existence may help prune the search space).

4 Negative Cycle Elimination

Let the constraint subgraph $G_s = (V, E)$ be a weighted directed graph, $w[u, v]$ be the weight of edge (u, v), and $d[v]$ be the cost of node v. The following statements are equivalent: (1) The set of separation constraints has a valid solution $\{d[v]\}$; and (2) there is no negative weight cycle in the corresponding constraint subgraph.

Bellman-Ford solves the single-source shortest-paths problem in graphs where edge weights can be negative; as a by-product, it also detects negative-weight cycles that are reachable from the source (cf. [5]). Although several separation logic solvers use Bellman-Ford to detect theory conflicts, it is not very suitable for a tight on-line integration with the Boolean SAT solver. This is especially true when the cycle detection algorithm must be called every time a predicate is assigned. In such a case, even making Bellman-Ford incremental is not very effective. However, studying Bellman-Ford does shed some light on how an efficient theory solver can be implemented.

The basic operation in searching for a solution is **relax**, which operates on edges as shown below. Here $pi[v]$ represents the edge responsible for the last change to $d[v]$; it can be used to retrieve the negative weight cycles.

```
relax (u,v) {
    if (d[v] > d[u] + w[u,v]) {
        d[v]  = d[u] + w[u,v];
        pi[v] = (u,v);
    }
}
```

An edge is *stable* if relax does not change the cost of its sink node. A solution is found when all edges are stable. Each solution $\{d[v]\}$ represents a class of solutions $\{d[v] + c\}$, since $(d[v] \leq d[u] + w[u, v])$ implies $(d[v] + c \leq d[u] + c + w[u, v])$. If a solution exists, all edges will become stable after a bounded number of relaxing operations. When there is no solution (i.e. some negative cycles exist), some edges can never become stable. This is the basis of many existing negative cycle detection algorithms, including Bellman-Ford.

However, the original Bellman-Ford algorithm runs $n \times m$ relax operations (where n and m are the number of nodes and edges, respectively) before checking whether all edges are stable. The first optimization is to stop relaxing as soon as all edges are stable, or to stop as soon as possible in the presence of negative cycles.

Bellman-Ford returns more information than needed for negative cycle detection or finding an arbitrary solution. Assume that $Ax \leq b$ is a system of m separation constraints in n integer variables, Bellman-Ford algorithm gives a solution that maximizes $\sum_{i=1}^{n} x_i$ subject to $Ax \leq b$ and $x_i \leq 0$ for all x_i ([5]). We recognize and exploit the fact that if the purpose is to search for an arbitrary solution or simply to detect negative cycles, we can use an arbitrary set of initial node values as the starting point. Note that the proof follows Pratt's theorem in [14] (and also in [5]).

Proposition 1. *For the purpose of detecting negative weight cycles, Bellman-Ford is sound and complete by starting with an arbitrary set of initial node values (instead of initializing d[v] to ∞).*

Although the initial node values do not affect the correctness of the algorithm, they do affect the run-time in practice. Typically, the closer $\{d[v]\}$ is to a solution, the less effort is needed for the relaxing phase to converge. For example, if the current $\{d[v]\}$ is already a solution, then no edge needs to be relaxed. Our new GCP algorithm exploits this fact by updating the subgraph incrementally.

Let the set $\{d_i[v]\}$ be the stable node values after adding the i-th edge. The key invariant to our negative cycle detection algorithm is given as follows:

Theorem 2. *If no conflict is detected by the previous call to negative cycle detection, all edges in the subgraph must have been stable. Therefore, the set $\{d_i[v]\}$ of node values is always a valid solution to the current set of separation constraints.*

Since there is no negative cycle in the subgraph, if adding a new edge creates one, the cycle must go through the new edge. In the relaxing phase, if the new edge is relaxed more than once, we declare it as a conflict.

The algorithm is given in Figure 4. Initially, the constraint subgraph contains all the nodes but no edge. Each time a separation predicate is assigned a value, the corresponding edge is scheduled to be added. After each SAT decision (and after BCP finishes), we search for negative weight cycles in the subgraph. Starting from the newly added edge (u, v), we propagate the value of the separation predicate. If all edges eventually

```
gcp()
{
  for each predicate assigned at current level {
    added edge (u,v);
    if (detect_negative_cycle(u,v))
        return CONFLICT;
  }
  return NO_CONFLICT;
}

detect_negative_cycle(u,v)
{
  if (d[v]>d[u]+w[u,v]) {
    relax (u,v);
    enqueue(v);
  }
  while ((x=dequeue())!=NULL) {
    for each edge (x,y) {          // sequenced with priority queue
      if (d[y]>d[x]+w[x,y]) {
        if (u==x && v==y)
          return TRUE;
        else {
          relax (x,y);
          enqueue(y);
        }
      }
    }
  }
  return FALSE;
}
```

Fig. 4. Incremental negative cycle detection algorithm

become stable, the FIFO queue becomes empty, meaning that there is no negative cycle. If there exists a negative cycle, the cycle must go through edge (u, v); therefore we can detect it when node v is visited again during the constraint propagation. The cycle can be retrieved by following $pi[v]$ all the way back to edge (u, v).

Given a constraint subgraph with n nodes and k edges, the detection algorithm can run in $O(n \log n + k)$ time per added separation predicate. Since all edges are stable before adding (u, v), we can sequence our relaxation operations with a Fibonacci heap based priority queue ordering nodes according to their maximal node value changes [15] and [6]. If there is no negative weight cycle even after adding (u, v), relaxing will converge after going through those nodes exactly once. However, it is worth pointing out that this worst-case complexity bound seldom reflects the performance of the algorithm in practice.

Unlike Bellman-Ford which recomputes node values each time from scratch, our new algorithm propagates the constraints incrementally. Since all existing edges are already stable before the addition of the new edge, the number of edges that need to be relaxed is often significantly reduced. For example, if the new edge is already stable under the previous $\{d_j[v]\}$ (i.e. node values at the j-th decision level), then no propagation is needed; if the new edge is not stable but $\{d_j[v]\}$ is already very close to a solution, then not many edges need to be relaxed. Data in Section 6 show that the reduction in the number of relax operations can be several orders of magnitude.

5   Efficient Backtracking

Efficient implementation of backtracking on the theory part is important since in practice the number of backtracks is often very large. This imposes two constraints on designing a backtracking algorithm: First, it should have low runtime overhead; second, it should be scalable in terms of memory usage. For instance, the approach of storing the theory solver's states at all previous decision levels in a history stack does not scale well in practice. In SLICE, we do not need such a history stack, and we do not need to restore the theory solver's state either, even during non-chronological backtracking.

Indeed, the invariant maintained by our algorithm makes a constant-time backtracking possible. Note that in Chaff's two-literal watch list based BCP, backtracking in the Boolean part has already been made a constant time operation – Chaff does not update during backtracking any of the affected clauses and their watched literals. Similarly, in SLICE we do not need to update (or restore) any of the node values; the procedure remains sound and complete as long as all existing edges are stable before every call to negative cycle detection. We shall show in the following that this invariant is maintained throughout the solving process.

First, the invariant always holds when we add edges to the subgraph and there is no conflict in either BCP or GCP. Let $\{d_j[v]\}$ be the node values at the j-th decision level. If no conflict is detected, $\{d_j[v]\}$ is a solution to the set of separation constraints after the call to negative cycle detection. Furthermore,

Theorem 3. $\{d_j[v]\}$ *is also a solution for the set of separation constraints at any previous decision level i such that $i \leq j$.*

This is because constraint subgraphs at previous levels contain subsets of these edges—a solution remains valid when some constraints are dropped. We should note that multiple edges can be added at each decision level, and a conflict detected in GCP is guaranteed to involve at least one assignment at the current decision level.

Second, if backtracking from decision level j to i is triggered by a conflict in BCP, the node values right before backtracking are $\{d_{j-1}[v]\}$ (since GCP has not been performed yet). The only thing we need to do is to delete edges added after decision level i. However, we *do not have to* restore the node values from $\{d_{j-1}[v]\}$ back to $\{d_i[v]\}$. More often than not, $\{d_{j-1}[v]\}$ is a better solution than $\{d_i[v]\}$ since it satisfies more separation constraints. In practice, relaxation of edges will be avoided later if some of the deleted edges are added back.

Third, if backtracking from decision level j to i is triggered by a conflict in GCP, by the time we detect the negative cycle (i.e. edge (u, v) is revisited), $\{d_j[v]\}$ may no longer be a valid solution (because some edges may still need to be relaxed). We have two choices in restoring the invariant. If we keep relaxing the edges other than (u, v) until convergence, we will get a set $\{d_j[v]\}$ that is a solution at the previous level. However, if we want to stop the propagation as soon as the first conflict is detected, backtracking is no longer constant-time since we need to restore a valid solution. We can record the node value changes during the current cycle detection call and restore them as soon as we detect the first negative cycle. Note that only local changes in the current call need to be recorded (as opposed to all the solver states between level i and level j), even when the backtracking is non-chronological. Finally, none of these two choices affects the worst-case complexity of negative cycle detection.

The Working Example. Figure 5 shows the constraint subgraphs at different stages of applying our GCP algorithm. We use the same separation logic formula (from Section 2) as an example. The initial subgraph is given at the left top, in which all node are initialized to 0. The subgraph at the right top is after the partial assignment $(\neg D, \neg A, B)$; note that no constraint propagation is needed when the edges (z, x) and (x, y) are added, because they are already stable under the existing node values after (w, y) is added. When backtracking from this partial assignment, we only delete the three edges while leaving the node values unchanged. The right bottom subgraph is under the assignment $(A, \neg B, C, D)$, which has a negative weight cycle. After backtracking and setting B true, the subgraph is shown at the left bottom. At this point, all Boolean variables are assigned and there is no conflict, the separation formula is proved to be satisfiable. Note that the set of $\{d[v]\}$ values is a solution to the current set of separation constraints.

6   Experiments

We have implemented our new decision procedure on top of the zChaff SAT solver, by integrating the incremental negative cycle elimination algorithm with the DPLL based SAT search. During the implementation of our graph algorithm, effort has been made to make sure that both adding and deleting an edge take constant time.

We have conducted experiments with a set of 385 public benchmark formulae generated from verification problems and scheduling problems. It includes 159 formulae of the MathSAT suite, 99 of the SAL suite, 31 of the DLSAT suite, 60 DTP formulae, and 36 *diamonds* formulae. All the experiments were run on a workstation with 3.0 GHz Intel Pentium 4 processor and 2 GB of RAM running Red Hat Linux 7.2. We set the time limit to 3600 seconds and the memory limit to 1 GB.

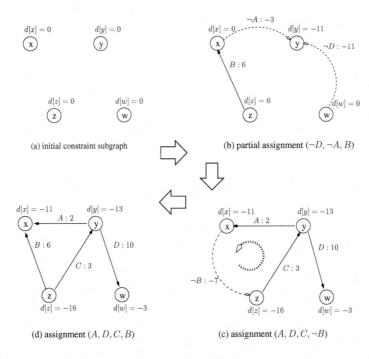

Fig. 5. Applying the graph based constraint propagation

Table 1 compares SLICE's Incremental Negative Cycle Detection with Bellman-Ford. Columns 1-3 show for each set of formulae the suite name, the category and the number of formulae. Column 4 gives the average percentage of non-Boolean variables (or separation predicates). Columns 5-8 are from SLICE runs with incremental cycle detection, which include the average percentage of GCP generated conflicts, the ratio of BCP calls to GCP calls, the percentage of CPU time spent in GCP, and the average number of relaxed nodes per negative cycle detection call. Columns 9-10 are from solver runs with Bellman-Ford, which include the information on CPU time and the number of relaxed nodes per call to Bellman-Ford. Note that only two columns are presented for Bellman-Ford, because the percentage of GCP conflicts and the BCP/GCP ratio stay roughly unchanged with both cycle detection algorithms.

The data show that our incremental graph algorithm significantly reduces the overhead of GCP. Compared to Bellman-Ford, the reduction in the number of relax operations can be several orders of magnitude. In fact, except for *diamonds*, the number of nodes relaxed per call have been reduced to single digit or less. The hand-made *diamonds* formulae [18] are known to have exponential number of negative cycles, each of which contains half of the separation constraints in the formulae.

Table 1. Comparison of Incremental Negative Cycle Detection and Bellman-Ford

Benchmarks				Data from SLICE runs					
				Incremental cycle detection				Bellman-Ford	
suite	name	num. of formulae	non-Boolean vars (%)	conflicts in GCP (%)	num. of BCP/GCP	time in GCP (%)	num. of relax	time in GCP (%)	num. of relax
mathsat	FISCHER	119	30	1	20	8	2	46	17
	PO2	7	40	2	16	0	1	14	13
	PO3	9	30	1	14	16	0.4	25	9
	PO4	11	20	1	13	9	0.3	46	5
	PO5	13	13	1	13	4	0.2	57	4
sal	lpsat	20	13	1	10	10	2	62	49
	inf-bak	20	50	32	7	30	3	70	294
	fischer	59	60	12	21	18	7	80	1186
DLSAT	abz5	12	100	32	12	55	7	49	1152
	ba-max	19	13	22	8	25	4	84	233
DTP		60	100	62	8	47	0.4	89	205
diamonds		36	100	3	2	66	79	89	1101

We have also conducted experimental comparison of our new algorithm with other state-of-the-art tools, including UCLID, MathSAT, ICS, TSAT++, and DPLL(T). For all tools, their latest public available released versions were used. For DPLL(T), it includes their latest development as described in [12]. For UCLID we used the default "hybrid method" which combines the strengths of per constraint and small-domain encoding. The overall result is given in scatter plots in Figure 6. Here the x-axis is the CPU time of SLICE, while the y-axis is the CPU time for other solvers. For DPLL(T), which is the closest competitor on this set of benchmarks, we also give the scatter plot in linear scale.

The result shows that SLICE performs significantly better than UCLID, MathSAT, and ICS on the majority of the benchmarks. The only cases on which UCLID runs faster are some smaller *diamonds* formulae. However, SLICE finishes all the 36 *diamonds* formulae within 1 hour, but UCLID times out on 8 larger ones. ICS 2.0 runs faster than SLICE on several formulae from the MathSAT suite, although overall ICS 2.0 is much less robust. The comparison with TSAT++ shows that SLICE performs significantly better on most cases. DPLL(T) is the closest competitor to SLICE on this set of benchmarks. However, as is shown by the last scatter plot, SLICE tends to do better on harder cases, therefore seems to be more robust and scalable.

Note that in most of these benchmark examples the percentage of GCP conflicts is very low, which indicates that computing all theory consequences as in [12] will not pay off. We have also implemented in our solver a variant of the exhaustive theory propagation technique of [12], which spends a limited (but not exhaustive) amount of effort in deriving theory implications. We then conducted controlled experiments on a set of randomly generated DTP formulae; in these formulae, the number of integer variables and separation constraints can be carefully controlled. (Due to space limit, we omit the result table.) Our experiments show that on examples in which GCP conflicts play a larger role, spending a limited amount of effort in deriving theory implications can significantly improve the performance of SLICE.

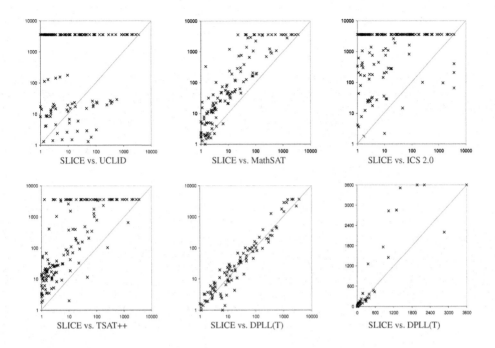

Fig. 6. Performance comparison in scatter plots: The CPU time is in seconds. The x-axis is for SLICE. Comparison with DPLL(T) is also shown in the linear scale.

7 Conclusions

We have presented a fast decision procedure for separation logic, which has an efficient theory engine for incremental conflict detection and constant time backtracking. The graph based theory solver allows fast backtracking without any additional bookkeeping. Controlled experiments indicate that the incremental algorithm is superior to the naive approach of Bellman-Ford; it significantly reduces the overhead of graph based constraint propagation. Performance evaluation on a set of public benchmarks shows that our new solver significantly outperforms leading separation logic solvers. For future work, we want to investigate more efficient ways of handling equality and inequality relations than translating them into separation predicates.

References

[1] A. Armando, C. Castellini, E. Giunchiglia, M. Idini, and M. Maratea. TSAT++: an open platform for satisfiability modulo theories. In *Workshop on Pragmatics of Decision Procedures in Automated Reasoning*, 2004.

[2] C. Barrett, D. L. Dill, and J. Levitt. Validity checking for combinations of theories with equality. In *Formal Methods in Computer Aided Design*, November 1996. LNCS 1166.

[3]   M. Bozzano, R. Bruttomesso, A. Cimatti, T. Junttila, P. Rossum, S. Schulz, and R. Sebastiani. An incremental and layered procedure for the satisfiability of linear arithmetic logic. In *Tools and Algorithms for the Construction and Analysis of Systems*, pages 317–333, 2005. LNCS 3440.

[4]   R. E. Bryant, S. K. Lahiri, and S. A. Seshia. Modeling and verifying systems using a logic of counter arithmetic with lambda expressions and uninterpreted functions. In *Computer Aided Verification*, July 2002. LNCS 2404.

[5]   T. H. Cormen, C. E. Leiserson, and R. L. Rivest. *Introduction to Algorithms*. The MIT Press, Cambridge, MA, 1990.

[6]   S. Cotton. Satisfiability checking with difference constraints. Msc thesis, IMPRS Computer Science, Saarbrucken, 2005.

[7]   M. Davis, G. Logemann, and D. Loveland. A machine program for theorem proving. *Communications of the ACM*, 5:394–397, 1962.

[8]   J.-C. Filliâtre, S. Owre, H. Rueß, and N. Shankar. ICS: integrated canonizer and solver. In *Computer Aided Verification*, pages 246–249, July 2001. LNCS 2102.

[9]   H. Ganzinger, G. Hagen, R. Nieuwenhuis, A. Oliveras, and C. Tinelli. DPLL(T): Fast decision procedures. In *Computer Aided Verification*, pages 175–188, July 2004. LNCS 3114.

[10] E. Goldberg and Y. Novikov. BerkMin: A fast and robust SAT-solver. In *Design, Automation and Test in Europe (DATE'03)*, pages 142–149, March 2002.

[11] M. Moskewicz, C. F. Madigan, Y. Zhao, L. Zhang, and S. Malik. Chaff: Engineering an efficient SAT solver. In *Proceedings of the Design Automation Conference*, pages 530–535, June 2001.

[12] R. Nieuwenhuis and A. Oliveras. DPLL(T) with exhaustive theory propagation and its application to difference logic. In *Computer Aided Verification*, pages 321–334, July 2005. LNCS 3576.

[13] A. Pnueli, Y. Rodeh, O. Shtrichman, and M. Siegel. The small model property: How small can it be? *Information and Computation*, 178(1):275–293, October 2002.

[14] V.R. Pratt. Two easy theories whose combination is hard. Technical report, Massachusetts Institute of Technology, 1977.

[15] G. Ramalingam, J. Song, L. Joscovicz, and R.E. Miller. Solving difference constraints incrementally. *Algorithmica*, 23(3):261–275, 1999.

[16] S. A. Seshia, S. K. Lahiri, and R. E. Bryant. A hybrid SAT-based decision procedure for separation logic with uninterpreted functions. In *Proceedings of the Design Automation Conference*, pages 425–430, June 2003.

[17] J. P. M. Silva and K. A. Sakallah. Grasp—a new search algorithm for satisfiability. In *International Conference on Computer-Aided Design*, pages 220–227, November 1996.

[18] O. Strichman, S. A. Seshia, and R. E. Bryant. Deciding separation formulas with SAT. In *Computer Aided Verification*, pages 209–222, July 2002. LNCS 2404.

[19] M. Talupur, N. Sinha, O. Strichman, and A. Pnueli. Range allocation for separation logic. In *Computer Aided Verification*, pages 148–161, July 2004. LNCS 3114.

[20] L. Zhang and S. Malik. Validating SAT solvers using an independent resolution-based checker: Practical implementations and other applications. In *Design, Automation and Test in Europe (DATE'03)*, pages 880–885, March 2003.

Monotone AC-Tree Automata

Hitoshi Ohsaki[1], Jean-Marc Talbot[2], Sophie Tison[2], and Yves Roos[2]

[1] National Institute of Advanced Industrial Science and Technology,
PRESTO, Japan Science and Technology Agency
ohsaki@ni.aist.go.jp
[2] Laboratoire d'Informatique Fondamentale de Lille,
Université des Sciences et Technologies de Lille, France
{talbot, tison, yroos}@lifl.fr

Abstract. We consider several questions about *monotone AC-tree automata*, a class of equational tree automata whose transition rules correspond to rules in Kuroda normal form of context-sensitive grammars. Whereas it has been proved that this class has a decision procedure to determine if, given a monotone AC-tree automaton, it accepts no terms, other important decidability or complexity results have not been well-investigated yet. In the paper, we prove that the membership problem for monotone AC-tree automata is *PSPACE-complete*. We then study the expressiveness of monotone AC-tree automata: precisely, we prove that the family of AC-*regular* tree languages is strictly subsumed in that of AC-monotone tree languages. The proof technique used in obtaining the above result yields the answers to two different questions, specifically that the family of monotone AC-tree languages is *not* closed under complementation, and that the inclusion problem for monotone AC-tree automata is undecidable.

Keywords: equational tree automata, closure properties, decidability, complexity.

1 Introduction

Tree automata [5] have been applied successfully in many areas of computer science, such as protocol verification [1, 12], type inference [7, 11], checking the sufficient completeness of algebraic specifications [3, 16], and checking the consistency of semi-structured documents [17]. This widespread use is due to good closure properties of tree automata, such as the (effective) closedness under Boolean operations and rewrite descendant computation, as well as efficient decision procedures. However, the standard framework of tree automata is not powerful when some algebraic laws such as associativity and commutativity have to be taken into account. In particular, it is known that the regularity of tree languages is not preserved for the congruence closure with respect to an equational theory. To overcome this problem, Ohsaki [23] in 2001 and Goubault-Larrecq and Verma [14] in 2002 independently proposed extensions of tree automata. Their ideas in new frameworks are to combine tree automata with equational theories, and each of their studies considers by coincidence the case in particular where some of the function symbols have associative (A), commutative (C), and/or some other equational properties like the identity (I) and nilpotent (U) axioms. The notion of accepted languages may differ for these two approaches, however, they coincide in the regular case for any combination of the axioms A, C, I and U.

G. Sutcliffe and A. Voronkov (Eds.): LPAR 2005, LNAI 3835, pp. 337–351, 2005.

The AC case is of particular interest since this kind of automata which are able to deal with AC symbols are closely related to tree automata with arithmetical constraints, such as multitree automata [21] and Presburger tree automata [29]. Further discussion on this relationship can be found in our recent paper [2]. It has been shown that for AC-tree automata good properties of "classical" tree automata remain: the membership and emptiness are decidable and the closure of automata by Boolean operations can be computed [23, 30, 31].

Motivated by cryptographic protocol verification, Goubault-Larrecq and Verma proposed to extend AC-tree automata by considering two-way and/or alternating computations [14]. They proved on one hand that two-way AC-tree automata are not more powerful than (one-way) AC-tree automata. On the other hand, the alternation strictly increases the expressiveness of AC-tree automata while the emptiness problem is undecidable.

Inspired by commutative grammars [13, 27] (alternatively, called multiset grammars [19]) Ohsaki proposed another extension of AC-tree automata [23], called monotone AC-tree automata; he proved that both emptiness and membership remain decidable for monotone AC-tree automata and that the languages defined by these automata are closed under union and intersection [23, 25]. Furthermore, Ohsaki and Takai develop the automated system, called ACTAS, manipulating AC-tree automata computation by using the exact and approximation algorithms [26].

In this paper, we further investigate monotone AC-tree automata. First, we prove that the membership problem of deciding, "given a term t and an automaton $\mathcal{A}/\mathrm{AC}$, whether t belongs to the language defined by $\mathcal{A}/\mathrm{AC}$" is PSPACE-complete: we give a non-deterministic algorithm running in polynomial space with respect to the size of the input tree and automaton. For the lower bound, we reduce the validity problem of quantified Boolean formulas to the membership problem. Then we show that the class of monotone AC-tree automata is strictly wider than the class of regular AC-tree automata by exhibiting a tree language accepted by a monotone AC-tree automaton but that cannot be defined by any regular AC-tree automaton. Following the same ideas, we prove that the family of AC-monotone tree languages is *not* closed under complement while this class is closed under union and intersection. Finally, using similar techniques, we show that the inclusion problem for monotone AC-tree automata is not decidable.

The paper is organized as follows. Definitions and terminologies concerning equational tree language theory are introduced in Section 2. The closure properties and the decidability of equational tree automata are also summarized. In Section 3, we discuss the complexity of the membership problem for monotone AC-tree automata, proving that the problem is PSPACE-complete. Section 4 is devoted to the study of the relative expressiveness of AC-tree automata. Using the proof technique introduced in the previous section, we show in Section 5 that AC-monotone tree languages are not closed under complementation. Section 6 contains the proof for the undecidability of the inclusion problem. Finally, we conclude by summarizing the results obtained in the paper that give us the solutions to open questions in [6].

2   Preliminaries

A *signature* is a finite set $\mathcal{F}$ of function symbols together with natural numbers n. A natural number n associated with f, denoted by $\mathsf{arity}(f) = n$, is the *arity* of f. Function symbols of arity 0 are called *constants*. We assume the existence of a countable set $\mathcal{V}$ of variables. The set $\mathcal{T}(\mathcal{F}, \mathcal{V})$ of terms over $\mathcal{F}$ with $\mathcal{V}$ is inductively defined as follows: $\mathcal{V} \subseteq \mathcal{T}(\mathcal{F}, \mathcal{V})$; $f(t_1, \ldots, t_n) \in \mathcal{T}(\mathcal{F}, \mathcal{V})$ if arity$(f) = n$ and $t_i \in \mathcal{T}(\mathcal{F}, \mathcal{V})$ for all $1 \leqslant i \leqslant n$. Elements in the set $\mathcal{T}(\mathcal{F}, \varnothing)$ are called *ground* terms. In the paper, we write $\mathcal{T}(\mathcal{F})$ for $\mathcal{T}(\mathcal{F}, \varnothing)$.

Let $\square$ be a fresh constant, named a *hole*. Elements in the set $\mathcal{T}(\mathcal{F} \cup \{\square\}, \mathcal{V})$ of terms, denoted by $\mathcal{C}(\mathcal{F}, \mathcal{V})$, are *contexts*. The *empty* context is the hole $\square$. If C is a context with n holes and $t_1, \ldots, t_n$ are terms, then $C[t_1, \ldots, t_n]$ represents the term from $\mathcal{T}(\mathcal{F}, \mathcal{V})$ obtained from C by replacing the holes from left to right by $t_1, \ldots, t_n$. Terms $t_1, \ldots, t_n$ are *subterms* of $C[t_1, \ldots, t_n]$.

A *tree automaton* (TA for short) $\mathcal{A}$ is a 4-tuple $(\mathcal{F}, \mathcal{Q}, \mathcal{Q}_{fin}, \Delta)$, whose components are the signature $\mathcal{F}$, a finite set $\mathcal{Q}$ of states such that $\mathcal{F} \cap \mathcal{Q} = \varnothing$, a subset $\mathcal{Q}_{fin}$ of $\mathcal{Q}$ consisting of *final states*, and a finite set Δ of transition rules whose shapes are in one of the following types:

$$(\text{TYPE 1}) \quad f(p_1, \ldots, p_n) \to q \qquad (\text{TYPE 2}) \quad f(p_1, \ldots, p_n) \to f(q_1, \ldots, q_n)$$

for some $f \in \mathcal{F}$ with arity$(f) = n$ and $p_1, \ldots, p_n, q, q_1, \ldots, q_n \in \mathcal{Q}$.

An *equational system* (ES for short) $\mathcal{E}$ is a set of equations $s = t$, where s, t are terms over the signature $\mathcal{F}$ with the set $\mathcal{V}$ of variables. For two terms s, t, we write $s =_{\mathcal{E}} t$ whenever s, t are equivalent modulo the equational system $\mathcal{E}$, i.e. s, t are the elements in the same equivalence class of the quotient term model $\mathcal{T}(\mathcal{F}, \mathcal{V})/{=_{\mathcal{E}}}$. The *associativity* and *commutativity* axioms for a binary function symbol f in $\mathcal{F}$ are the equations

$$f(f(x, y), z) = f(x, f(y, z)) \qquad\qquad f(x, y) = f(y, x),$$

respectively, where x, y, z are variables in $\mathcal{V}$. In the paper, we write $\mathcal{F}_A$ for the set of binary function symbols with associativity laws *only*, and $\mathcal{F}_{AC}$ for the set of binary symbols equipped with *both* associativity and commutativity. The ES A consists of the associativity axioms for each $f \in \mathcal{F}_A$, and AC is the ES consisting of the associativity and commutativity axioms for each $f \in \mathcal{F}_{AC}$.

An *equational tree automaton* (ETA for short) $\mathcal{A}/\mathcal{E}$ is a pair of a TA $\mathcal{A}$ and an ES $\mathcal{E}$ over the same signature $\mathcal{F}$. An ETA $\mathcal{A}/\mathcal{E}$ is called

- *regular* if it has only rules of TYPE 1,
- *monotone* if it has rules of TYPE 1 and/or TYPE 2.

We say $\mathcal{A}/\mathcal{E}$ is a AC-TA (A-TA) if $\mathcal{E} = \text{AC}$ (resp. $\mathcal{E} = \text{A}$). Besides, in the following discussion, we suppose $\mathcal{F}_A = \varnothing$ when considering $\mathcal{A}/\text{AC}$; likewise, $\mathcal{F}_{AC} = \varnothing$ for $\mathcal{A}/\text{A}$. The readers are recommended to consult [23] for a more detailed presentation.

We write $s \to_{\mathcal{A}/\mathcal{E}} t$ if there exist s', t' such that $s =_{\mathcal{E}} s'$, $s' = C[l]$, $t =_{\mathcal{E}} t'$ and $t' = C[r]$ for some transition rule $l \to r \in \Delta$ and context $C \in \mathcal{C}(\mathcal{F} \cup \mathcal{Q})$. This relation $\to_{\mathcal{A}/\mathcal{E}}$ on $\mathcal{T}(\mathcal{F} \cup \mathcal{Q})$ is called a *move relation* of $\mathcal{A}/\mathcal{E}$. The transitive closure and reflexive-transitive closure of $\to_{\mathcal{A}/\mathcal{E}}$ are denoted by $\to_{\mathcal{A}/\mathcal{E}}^{+}$ and $\to_{\mathcal{A}/\mathcal{E}}^{*}$, respectively. For an ETA $\mathcal{A}/\mathcal{E}$ with $\mathcal{E} = \varnothing$, we simply write $\to_{\mathcal{A}}$, $\to_{\mathcal{A}}^{+}$ and $\to_{\mathcal{A}}^{*}$, instead.

A term t is *accepted* by $\mathcal{A}/\mathcal{E}$ if $t \in \mathcal{T}(\mathcal{F})$ and $t \to_{\mathcal{A}/\mathcal{E}}^{*} q$ for some $q \in \mathcal{Q}_{fin}$. Elements in the set $\mathcal{L}(\mathcal{A}/\mathcal{E})$ are ground terms accepted by $\mathcal{A}/\mathcal{E}$. A *tree language* L

	regular AC-TA	monotone A-TA	monotone AC-TA
closure under union, intersection	Yes [4]	Yes	Yes
closure under complement	Yes [4]	Yes	?
decidability of emptiness	Linear	No	Yes
decidability of membership	NP-complete	PSPACE-complete	?
decidability of inclusion	Yes	No	?

Fig. 1. Some closure properties and decidability results

over $\mathcal{F}$ is a subset of $\mathcal{T}(\mathcal{F})$. A tree language L is $\mathcal{E}$-*regular* ($\mathcal{E}$-*monotone*) if there exists some regular (resp. monotone) $\mathcal{E}$-tree automaton $\mathcal{A}/\mathcal{E}$ such that $L = \mathcal{L}(\mathcal{A}/\mathcal{E})$. If L is $\mathcal{E}$-regular with $\mathcal{E} = \varnothing$, we say L is regular. Likewise, we say L is monotone if L is $\varnothing$-monotone.

Let op be an n-ary mapping from $\wp(\mathcal{T}(\mathcal{F}))^n \mapsto \wp(\mathcal{T}(\mathcal{F}))$. The family of $\mathcal{E}$-regular (resp. $\mathcal{E}$-monotone) languages is *closed under* op if whenever $L_1, \ldots, L_n$ are $\mathcal{E}$-regular (resp. $\mathcal{E}$-monotone) languages then so is $\text{op}(L_1, \ldots, L_n)$. We say that the family of $\mathcal{E}$-regular (resp. $\mathcal{E}$-monotone) languages is *effectively closed under* op if there exists an algorithm which, given regular (resp. monotone) ETA $\mathcal{A}_1/\mathcal{E}, \ldots, \mathcal{A}_n/\mathcal{E}$, computes a regular (resp. monotone) ETA $\mathcal{A}/\mathcal{E}$ such that $\mathcal{L}(\mathcal{A}/\mathcal{E}) = \text{op}(\mathcal{L}(\mathcal{A}_1/\mathcal{E}), \ldots, \mathcal{L}(\mathcal{A}_n/\mathcal{E}))$. One should note that non-regular and equational tree automata defined in [23] are in the above monotone case. It is folklore that whenever $\mathcal{E} = \varnothing$ then $\varnothing$-regular and $\varnothing$-monotone languages coincide. Things are different when some equational theory is taken into account. For instance, it has been shown in [24] that monotone A-TA are strictly more expressive than regular A-TA. But the question remained open in the case of AC.

We sum up in the table of Fig. 1 some known results concerning respectively regular AC-TA, monotone A-TA and monotone AC-TA. The positive results are marked with "Yes", and the negative cases are marked with "No". In case the results are proved in our previous work, the references are omitted. The complexity of the emptiness for regular AC-TA is a direct consequence of Lemma 2 in [23] and the result of regular TA [5]. Question marks "?" in the three columns denote open problems registered in [6].

For most of the results described in the present paper, we will consider a rather simple signature consisting of finitely many constant symbols and a single AC symbol f. In this case, the *regular* transition rules $f(p_1, p_2) \rightarrow q$ and $a \rightarrow q$ correspond to the production rules $q \rightarrow p_1 p_2$ and $q \rightarrow a$ of context-free grammars in Chomsky normal form. In case of monotone TA, the additional form $f(p_1, p_2) \rightarrow f(q_1, q_2)$ together with the previous two forms corresponds to context-sensitive grammar in Kuroda normal form [20]. Following the same approach for monotone AC-TA, the transition rules correspond to the production rules of some commutative context-sensitive grammar. The commutative context-sensitive grammars are known to be close to Petri nets [10]. Therefore, most of our developments are related to Petri nets. For this reason, on the other hand, the complexity of the emptiness problem for monotone AC-TA is unclear and may correspond to the reachability problem for Petri nets [8].

3   The Complexity of the Membership Problem

In this section, we investigate the complexity of the membership problem for monotone AC-tree automata. To show in particular the PSPACE-hardness, we use a proof technique proposed by Esparza [9] where he shows that the reachability problem for one-safe Petri nets is PSPACE-hard. Note that Petri nets corresponding to monotone AC-tree automata are not in general one-safe.

Theorem 1. *Given a monotone AC-tree automaton $\mathcal{A}/AC$ and a term t, the problem whether $t \in \mathcal{L}(\mathcal{A}/AC)$ is PSPACE-complete.*   □

To show that the membership problem for monotone AC-TA is in PSPACE, it suffices to prove that the size of any ground term t reachable from an initial term t_0 by the move relation of $\mathcal{A}/AC$ is polynomial relative to the size of t_0 and $\mathcal{A}/AC$. This allows us to prove that the existence of a successful run for t_0 implies that there exists a "short" successful run at most exponential with respect to the size of t_0 and $\mathcal{A}/AC$. We use this property to devise a non-deterministic polynomial space algorithm for the membership problem using that the execution of the move relation can be done in polynomial time. We appeal to Savitch's theorem [28] stating that NPSPACE = PSPACE to conclude.

Let us define the special notation of terms. We assume that a term t in this section is represented by the following grammar:

$$t ::= f\langle t_1, \ldots, t_n \rangle \mid a$$

where f is a function symbol in $\mathcal{F}$ with $\mathsf{arity}(f) > 0$, and a is a constant. Moreover, $\langle t_1, \ldots, t_n \rangle$ is a non-empty sequence of terms $t_1, \ldots, t_n$ such that:

1. if f is a non-AC symbol, then n is the arity of f,
2. if f is an AC symbol, then $n \geqslant 2$ and the root symbol of t_i is not f.

Given a subterm position and a rule to be applied at the subterm position, the corresponding transition step by $\mathcal{A}/AC$ can be performed on the above term representation in linear time with respect to the size of a term. In the transition steps, there are two non-standard cases, that are done by the transitions rules of the form $f(p_1, p_2) \to q$ and $f(p_1, p_2) \to f(q_1, q_2)$ with f an AC symbol. In both of the two cases, instead of the standard pattern matching, we find p_1, p_2 among subterms $t_1, \ldots, t_n$ of $f\langle t_1, \ldots, t_n \rangle$.

By definition of monotone AC-TA, if a term s is reachable from t by $\to_{\mathcal{A}/AC}$, the size $|s|$ is less than or equal to $|t| * \log(|\mathcal{A}/AC|)$, where $|\mathcal{A}/AC|$ is the number of state symbols of $\mathcal{A}/AC$. Then we can show that for any tree t admitting a successful run $r : t \to^*_{\mathcal{A}/AC} q$ with q a final state of $\mathcal{A}/AC$, there exists a successful run $r' : t \to^*_{\mathcal{A}/AC} q$ reaching the same state q of length at most $2^{|t| * \log(|\mathcal{A}/AC|)}$. In fact, for the proof by contradiction, we suppose that $t \to^*_{\mathcal{A}/AC} q$ is the shortest successful run whose length is strictly greater than $2^{|t| * \log(|\mathcal{A}/AC|)}$. Then terms reachable from t by $\to_{\mathcal{A}/AC}$ can be described using a space relative to the size at most $|t| * \log(|\mathcal{A}/AC|)$. This implies that the previous shortest run $t \to^*_{\mathcal{A}/AC} q$ can be represented as $t \to^*_{\mathcal{A}/AC} u \to^+_{\mathcal{A}/AC} u \to^*_{\mathcal{A}/AC} q$. By shrinking this run by chopping off the loop of u, one can obtain a successful run strictly shorter than the original, leading to the contradiction with respect to the minimality assumption.

Based on the above observation, let us define (non-deterministic) algorithm to solve the question if $t \in \mathcal{L}(\mathcal{A}/\text{AC})$. We write in the algorithm $\text{apply}(u, u', r)$ for denoting to "apply the transition rule r at the position of a subterm u' of u." This algorithm needs for the computation a polynomially bounded space with respect to the size $|t| * \log(|\mathcal{A}/\text{AC}|)$: let t be a term over the signature $\mathcal{F}$ and $\mathcal{A}/\text{AC}$ a monotone AC-TA with $\mathcal{A} = (\mathcal{F}, \mathcal{Q}, \mathcal{Q}_{fin}, \Delta)$.

```
membership( t , A/AC ) {
    c := 1 ; u := t ;
    while ( c ⩽ 2^(|t|*log(|A/AC|)) ) {
        if ( u ∈ Q_fin ) then { return true }
        else {
            guess  r : transition rule in Δ,  u' : subterm of u to which r is applied at the root ;
            nu := apply(u, u', r) ; u := nu }
        c := c + 1 }
    return false }
```

Let us estimate the space complexity of this algorithm. One can see that apply runs in polynomial time, and thus, in polynomial space. For membership we observe that this procedure requires the space for the counter c and the terms u, u' and nu. Obviously this space can be bounded linearly in $|t| * \log(|\mathcal{A}/\text{AC}|)$. So, membership can be executed by a non-deterministic machine using polynomial space.

Next, to show that the membership problem is PSPACE-hard, we consider the validity problem for closed *quantified Boolean formulas* (QBF). This problem is known to be PSPACE-complete. Every formula φ can be represented by the following grammar:

$$\varphi ::= x \mid \neg\varphi \mid \varphi \wedge \varphi \mid \exists x. \varphi \qquad (x: \text{ a proposition variable})$$

This assumption is justified by the fact that any quantified Boolean formula can be translated into a formula of the above form in linear time. We assume also that each variable x in the formula occurs in the scope of some quantifier $\exists x$ or $\forall x$ and that each variable is bounded exactly once in the formula.

We suppose that $x_1, \ldots, x_k$ are variables bounded in φ. We show in the following that we can build from a closed formula φ a monotone AC-tree automaton $\mathcal{A}_\varphi/\text{AC}$ and a term t_φ in polynomial time relative to the size of φ such that t_φ is accepted by $\mathcal{A}_\varphi/\text{AC}$ if and only if φ is valid. For this construction, we take the signature $\{\oplus, \mathsf{i}, \mathsf{v}, \mathsf{e}\}$, where $\oplus$ is an AC symbol and $\mathsf{i}, \mathsf{v}, \mathsf{e}$ are constants. We denote by t_φ a term consisting of exactly k constants of v, a constant of i, and a constant of e. For each subformula ψ of φ, we define the state symbols $q_{(\psi,?)}$, $q_{(\psi,T)}$, and $q_{(\psi,F)}$. In case of $\psi \equiv \exists x. x \wedge x$, the two subformulas x's are distinguished in this construction. For each variable x_i ($1 \leqslant i \leqslant k$), we take the two states q_{true/x_i} and q_{false/x_i}. The state q_{fin} is the final state. Let us describe the intended meaning of each state symbol. The truth value of the formula φ is computed recursively in our encoding. Along this idea, the state $q_{(\psi,?)}$ means that the subformula ψ can be taken into consideration. When the computation for ψ is performed, the state $q_{(\psi,?)}$ is "transformed" to either $q_{(\psi,T)}$ or $q_{(\psi,F)}$, depending on the truth value of ψ. The state $q_{(\psi,T)}$ means that ψ is true, and $q_{(\psi,F)}$ means that ψ

is false. The two states q_{true/x_i} and q_{false/x_i} are the environment to store the information for the valuation to x_i.

Using the above state symbols, next we define the transition rules. For the constants i, v, e, we take the following transition rules: $\text{i} \to q_{(\varphi,?)}$, $\text{v} \to q_v$, $\text{e} \to q_e$.

The first rule is used to initiate the computation. We define the transition rules for instantiating a variable x_i $(1 \leq i \leq k)$ to true or false:

$$q_{(x_i,?)} \oplus q_{\text{true}/x_i} \to q_{(x_i,T)} \oplus q_{\text{true}/x_i} \qquad q_{(x_i,?)} \oplus q_{\text{false}/x_i} \to q_{(x_i,F)} \oplus q_{\text{false}/x_i}$$

The rules for negation are defined as follows: for a subformula $\neg\psi$ of the formula φ,

$$q_{(\neg\psi,?)} \oplus q_e \to q_{(\psi,?)} \oplus q_e$$

$$q_{(\psi,T)} \oplus q_e \to q_{(\neg\psi,F)} \oplus q_e \qquad q_{(\psi,F)} \oplus q_e \to q_{(\neg\psi,T)} \oplus q_e.$$

The first rule decomposes $\neg\psi$ and the last two rules re-construct $\neg\psi$ with the truth value by using ψ with the truth value. Similarly, the rules for the conjunction can be defined. For any subformula $\psi \wedge \psi'$ of the formula φ,

$$q_{(\psi\wedge\psi',?)} \oplus q_e \to q_{(\psi,?)} \oplus q_e$$

$$q_{(\psi,F)} \oplus q_e \to q_{(\psi\wedge\psi',F)} \oplus q_e \qquad q_{(\psi,T)} \oplus q_e \to q_{(\psi',?)} \oplus q_e$$

$$q_{(\psi',F)} \oplus q_e \to q_{(\psi\wedge\psi',F)} \oplus q_e \qquad q_{(\psi',T)} \oplus q_e \to q_{(\psi\wedge\psi',T)} \oplus q_e.$$

In the above definition, $\psi \wedge \psi'$ is evaluated in a sequential manner: first we consider the subformula ψ and evaluate it, and then we take the remaining subformula ψ'. For the existential quantification $\exists x_i.\psi$, we need to consider both valuations for the bound variable x_i and the computation for ψ:

$$q_{(\exists x_i.\psi,?)} \oplus q_v \to q_{\text{true}/x_i} \oplus q_{(\psi,?)}$$

$$q_{\text{true}/x_i} \oplus q_{(\psi,T)} \to q_{(\exists x_i.\psi,T)} \oplus q_{\text{true}/x_i} \qquad q_{\text{true}/x_i} \oplus q_{(\psi,F)} \to q_{\text{false}/x_i} \oplus q_{(\psi,?)}$$

$$q_{\text{false}/x_i} \oplus q_{(\psi,T)} \to q_{(\exists x_i.\psi,T)} \oplus q_{\text{false}/x_i} \qquad q_{\text{false}/x_i} \oplus q_{(\psi,F)} \to q_{(\exists x_i.\psi,F)} \oplus q_{\text{false}/x_i}$$

In the above definition, we start with the valuation associating the Boolean value true with x_i. If ψ turns out to be true under this valuation, $\exists x.\psi$ is also true; otherwise, the valuation associating the Boolean value false with x_i is tried. The following rules are used to finalize the computation:

$$\oplus(q_{(\varphi,T)}, q_e) \to q_{\text{fin}} \qquad \oplus(q_{\text{true}/x_i}, q_{\text{fin}}) \to q_{\text{fin}} \qquad \oplus(q_{\text{false}/x_i}, q_{\text{fin}}) \to q_{\text{fin}}$$

We can show that the previous encoding is correct, by using the induction over the structure of the formula ψ. The remainder of the proof is obtained from the following observation: Let $t_{(\psi,?)}$ be a term that contains exactly a $q_{(\psi,?)}$, a q_e, and n_v occurrences of c_v (c_v being either the constant v or the state q_v, and n_v being the number of variables that do not freely occur in ψ) and for each free variable $x_{i_1}, \ldots, x_{i_\ell}$, either $q_{\text{true}/x_{i_j}}$ or $q_{\text{false}/x_{i_j}}$. Suppose δ is the Boolean valuation defined for $x_{i_1}, \ldots, x_{i_\ell}$ such that δ associates with x_{i_j} the value true if $q_{\text{true}/x_{i_j}}$ appears in $t_{(\psi,?)}$, and false otherwise. Then we have:

- $t_{(\psi,?)} \to^*_{\mathcal{A}_\varphi/\mathsf{AC}} t_{(\psi,T)}$ iff ψ is valid under δ, $t_{(\psi,T)}$ being the same as $t_{(\psi,?)}$ except
  1. $q_{(\psi,?)}$ in $t_{(\psi,?)}$ is replaced by $q_{(\psi,T)}$,
  2. if $x_{i_{l+1}}, \ldots, x_{i_{l+m}}$ are bound variables in ψ, then m occurrences of v and q_v in $t_{(\psi,?)}$ are replaced by $q_{b_1/x_{i_{\ell+1}}}, \ldots, q_{b_m/x_{i_{\ell+m}}}$ with $b_1, \ldots, b_m \in \{\mathsf{true}, \mathsf{false}\}$.
- $t_{(\psi,?)} \to^*_{\mathcal{A}_\varphi/\mathsf{AC}} t_{(\psi,F)}$ iff ψ is not valid under δ, $t_{(\psi,F)}$ being the same as $t_{(\psi,?)}$ except
  1. $q_{(\psi,?)}$ in $t_{(\psi,?)}$ is replaced by $q_{(\psi,F)}$,
  2. if $x_{i_{l+1}}, \ldots, x_{i_{l+m}}$ are bound variables in ψ, then m occurrences of v and q_v in $t_{(\psi,?)}$ are replaced by $q_{b_1/x_{i_{\ell+1}}}, \ldots, q_{b_m/x_{i_{\ell+m}}}$ with $b_1, \ldots, b_m \in \{\mathsf{true}, \mathsf{false}\}$.

As is suggested by one of the referees, the proof of PSPACE-hardness for the membership problem could have been obtained by reduction from the reachability problem of 1-conservative Petri nets. In this kind of Petri nets, transition does not change the total number of tokens in the net. We recall that the reachability problem is to decide for a Petri net N and two configurations m, m' whether m' is reachable from m in N. The reachability problem for 1-conservative Petri nets is PSPACE-complete, and moreover, this result holds even for nets in which each transition consumes two tokens [18].

Therefore, given a Petri net N in this type, it is encoded in linear time using transitions in (TYPE 2) of a monotone AC-tree automaton. The initial configuration m is encoded as an input term t_m of the membership problem. Transition rules in (TYPE 1) of the same automaton verify that m in N reaches the goal m', by replacing all constants in t_m by corresponding states, and by reducing a term corresponding to m' to a final state.

4 Expressiveness: Regular vs. Monotone AC-Tree Automata

Obviously, by definition, monotone AC-tree automata are at least as expressive as regular AC-tree automata. We show in this section that monotone AC-tree automata are strictly more expressive than regular AC-tree automata. In other words, we are going to present a monotone AC-tree automaton whose accepted language can not be defined by any regular AC-tree automaton.

To construct such a tree language, we consider in particular the signature $\mathcal{F}_\oplus = \{\oplus\} \cup \mathcal{F}_0$ consisting of a single AC symbol $\oplus$ and constant symbols $a_1, \ldots, a_n$ ($n \geqslant 1$). We then define the Parikh mapping π ([27]) associated with the signature $\mathcal{F}_\oplus$ as follows. For a term t in $\mathcal{T}(\mathcal{F}_\oplus)$, $\pi(t)$ is a vector v in $\mathbb{N}^n$ such that the i-th component $v(i)$ is the number of occurrences of a_i in t. For instance, $\pi(\oplus(a_1, \oplus(a_3, a_1))) = (2, 0, 1, 0, \ldots, 0)$. The Parikh mapping π is homomorphically extended to tree languages: for a tree language L over $\mathcal{F}_\oplus$, $\pi(L)$ is the set of vectors in $\mathbb{N}^n$ defined as $\pi(L) = \{\pi(t) \mid t \in L\}$.

Proposition 1 ([4]). *Given an AC-regular tree language L over $\mathcal{F}_\oplus$, the set $\pi(L)$ is a semi-linear set over $\mathbb{N}^n$.* □

The reverse of the above property also holds; for a semi-linear set S, there effectively exists an AC-regular tree language L with $\pi(L) = S$. We recall that a subset S of $\mathbb{N}^n$

is called a *linear set* if $S = \mathrm{Lin}(b, p_1, \ldots, p_k)$, where b is a vector, called *base*, in $\mathbb{N}^n$ and $p_1, \ldots, p_k$ are a finite number k of vectors, called *periods*, such that

$$\mathrm{Lin}(b, p_1, \ldots, p_k) = \{\, b + \sum_{i=1}^{k} (\lambda_i \times p_i) \mid \lambda_1, \ldots, \lambda_k \in \mathbb{N} \,\}.$$

A finite union of such linear sets is called a *semi-linear set*.

Lemma 1. *Suppose* $\mathcal{F}_\oplus$ *is defined with 5 constants. There exists a monotone AC-tree automaton* $\mathcal{A}_\leqslant / \mathrm{AC}$ *over* $\mathcal{F}_\oplus$ *defining a tree language* $L_\leqslant$ *such that*

$$\pi(L_\leqslant) = \{\, (k_1, k_2, k_3, 1, 2) \mid k_3 \leqslant k_1 \times k_2 \ \text{for} \ k_1, k_2, k_3 \in \mathbb{N} \,\}.$$

Proof. We take $\mathsf{a}, \mathsf{b}, \mathsf{c}, \#, \mathsf{s}$ for the constants of $\mathcal{F}_\oplus$. The corresponding Parikh images are the numbers of these constants in the above order. We define the tree automaton $\mathcal{A}_\leqslant = (\mathcal{F}_\oplus, \mathcal{Q}, \mathcal{Q}_{fin}, \Delta_\leqslant)$ over $\mathcal{F}_\oplus$ where $\mathcal{Q} = \{p_\mathsf{a}, p_\mathsf{b}, p_\mathsf{c}, p_\#, p_\mathsf{s}, p_{fin}, q_\mathsf{a}, q_\#, q_\mathsf{s}, r_\#\}$, $\mathcal{Q}_{fin} = \{p_{fin}\}$ and

$$\Delta_\leqslant: \quad \mathsf{a} \ \to \ p_\mathsf{a} \quad \mathsf{b} \ \to \ p_\mathsf{b} \quad \mathsf{c} \ \to \ p_\mathsf{c} \quad \# \ \to \ p_\# \quad \mathsf{s} \ \to \ q_\mathsf{s} \quad q_\mathsf{s} \oplus q_\mathsf{s} \ \to \ p_\mathsf{s}$$

$$p_\# \oplus p_\mathsf{a} \ \to \ p_\# \qquad\qquad p_\# \oplus p_\mathsf{a} \ \to \ q_\# \oplus q_\mathsf{a}$$

$$q_\# \oplus p_\mathsf{c} \ \to \ p_\# \qquad\qquad p_\# \oplus p_\mathsf{b} \ \to \ r_\#$$

$$r_\# \oplus q_\mathsf{a} \ \to \ r_\# \oplus p_\mathsf{a} \qquad r_\# \oplus p_\mathsf{s} \ \to \ p_\# \oplus p_\mathsf{s} \qquad p_\# \oplus p_\mathsf{s} \ \to \ p_{fin}$$

We denote by $|t|_\alpha$ the number of occurrences of a constant α ($\in \mathcal{F}_0 \cup \mathcal{Q}$) in a term t over $\mathcal{F}_\oplus \cup \mathcal{Q}$. We observe that for any term t over $\mathcal{F}_\oplus$ such that $|t|_\# = 1$ and $|t|_\mathsf{s} = 2$ and $|t|_\mathsf{c} \leqslant |t|_\mathsf{a} \times |t|_\mathsf{b}$, there exists a derivation $t \to^*_{\mathcal{A}_\leqslant / \mathrm{AC}} p_{fin}$ from t to p_{fin}. In order to prove this observation, let us define the assertions and the algorithm in Fig.2. The function apply in the algorithm corresponds to a single application of its argument to a term in consideration. The derivation of t is the sequence of terms obtained during the computation. Proofs of correctness and termination easily follow from the annotations.

Conversely, for any term t_0 over $\mathcal{F}_\oplus$ and t over $\mathcal{F}_\oplus \cup \mathcal{Q}$, if $t_0 \to^*_{\mathcal{A}_\leqslant / \mathrm{AC}} t$, it holds that:

$$|t_0|_\mathsf{s} = (|t|_\mathsf{s} + |t|_{q_\mathsf{s}}) + 2 \times (|t|_{p_{fin}} + |t|_{p_\mathsf{s}}) \qquad (\textsc{Inv}\ 1)$$

$$|t_0|_\# = |t|_\# + |t|_{p_\#} + |t|_{q_\#} + |t|_{r_\#} + |t|_{p_{fin}} \qquad (\textsc{Inv}\ 2)$$

$$|t_0|_\mathsf{a} \geqslant |t|_\mathsf{a} + |t|_{p_\mathsf{a}} + |t|_{q_\mathsf{a}} \qquad (\textsc{Inv}\ 3)$$

Moreover, if $t_0 \to^*_{\mathcal{A}_\leqslant / \mathrm{AC}} p_{fin}$, then by (\textsc{Inv}\ 1), $|t_0|_\mathsf{s} = 2$ and by (\textsc{Inv}\ 2), $|t_0|_\# = 1$. Now we suppose $|t_0|_\# = 1$. Due to (\textsc{Inv}\ 3), we have

$$|t_0|_\mathsf{c} - (|t|_\mathsf{c} + |t|_{p_\mathsf{c}}) \leqslant |t_0|_\mathsf{a} \times (|t_0|_\mathsf{b} - (|t|_\mathsf{b} + |t|_{p_\mathsf{b}})) + |t|_{q_\mathsf{a}} \times (1 - |t|_{r_\#}) - |t|_{q_\#}.$$

Accordingly, if $t_0 \to^*_{\mathcal{A}_\leqslant / \mathrm{AC}} p_{fin}$, then $|t_0|_\mathsf{c} \leqslant |t_0|_\mathsf{a} \times |t_0|_\mathsf{b}$. Therefore, $t_0 \in L_\leqslant$ if and only if $\pi(t_0) = (k_1, k_2, k_3, 1, 2)$ with $k_3 \leqslant k_1 \times k_2$. $\qquad\square$

Theorem 2. *The family of AC-regular tree languages is properly included in the family of AC-monotone tree languages.*

Proof. Straightforward from Proposition 1 and Lemma 1, because the Parikh image of $L_\leqslant$ is not semi-linear. $\qquad\square$

/* Given t in $\mathcal{T}(\mathcal{F}_\oplus)$ such that $|t|_\# = 1$ and $|t|_s = 2$ and $|t|_c \leqslant |t|_a \times |t|_b$ */
while ($|t|_a + |t|_b + |t|_c + |t|_\# + |t|_s > 0$) {
    apply $a \to p_a$, $b \to p_b$, $c \to p_c$, $\# \to p_\#$, $s \to q_s$ }

/* INVARIANT:

$$|t|_{p_c} + |t|_{qa} + (|t|_{pa} \times |t|_{r_\#}) \leqslant (|t|_{pa} + |t|_{qa}) \times (|t|_{p_b} + |t|_{r_\#}) + |t|_{q_\#}$$

$$|t|_{p_\#} + |t|_{q_\#} + |t|_{r_\#} = |t|_{ps} = 1$$

$$|t|_a + |t|_b + |t|_c = 0 \qquad\qquad\qquad */$$

apply $q_s \oplus q_s \to p_s$; /* INVARIANT & $|t|_{p_\#} = 1$ & $|t|_{qa} = 0$ */
while ($|t|_{p_b} > 0$) {   /* INVARIANT & $|t|_{p_\#} = 1$ & $|t|_{qa} = 0$ */
    while ($|t|_{pa} > 0$ & $|t|_{pc} > 0$) {
        apply $p_\# \oplus p_a \to q_\# \oplus q_a$; apply $q_\# \oplus p_c \to p_\#$ }
    /* INVARIANT & $|t|_{p_\#} = 1$ */
    apply $p_\# \oplus p_b \to r_\#$;
    /* INVARIANT & $|t|_{r_\#} = 1$ */
    while ($|t|_{q_a} > 0$) {
        apply $r_\# \oplus q_a \to r_\# \oplus p_a$ }
    /* INVARIANT & $|t|_{r_\#} = 1$ & $|t|_{q_a} = 0$ */
    apply $r_\# \oplus p_s \to p_\# \oplus p_s$
    /* INVARIANT & $|t|_{p_\#} = 1$ & $|t|_{q_a} = 0$ */
}
/* $|t|_{p_\#} = 1$ & $|t|_{q_a} = |t|_{p_b} = |t|_{p_c} = 0$ */
while ($|t|_{p_a} > 0$) {
    apply $p_\# \oplus p_a \to p_\#$ }
/* $t = p_\# \oplus p_s$ */
apply $p_\# \oplus p_s \to p_{fin}$
/* $t = p_{fin}$ */

Fig. 2. Reduction strategy and the assertions

5   Complementation of AC-Monotone Tree Languages

As is explained in the introduction, *monotone* rules in tree case correspond to context-sensitive grammars in word case. In fact, based on this observation, we proved in a previous paper [24] that A-monotone tree languages are closed under Boolean operations by reduction from the fact that context-sensitive languages are closed under complementation. In this section, however, we show that AC-monotone tree languages are *not* closed under complementation.

Theorem 3. *There exists an AC-monotone tree language whose complement is not an AC-monotone tree language.*

In the remaining part of this section, we devote to show the proof of Theorem 3. Our proof proceeds in the way of proof by contradiction.

Lemma 2. *Suppose $\mathcal{F}_\oplus$ is defined with 5 constants. There exists an AC-tree automaton $\mathcal{A}_</\mathrm{AC}$ over $\mathcal{F}_\oplus$ defining a tree language $L_<$ such that*

$$L_< = \{\, (k_1, k_2, k_3, 1, 2) \mid k_3 < k_1 \times k_2 \text{ for } k_1, k_2, k_3 \in \mathbb{N} \,\}.$$

Proof. We define the automaton $\mathcal{A}_</\mathrm{AC}$ exactly as is the monotone AC-tree automaton $\mathcal{A}_\leqslant/\mathrm{AC}$ in Lemma 1 *except* that the rule $q_\mathsf{s} \oplus q_\mathsf{s} \to p_\mathsf{s}$ is replaced by the rule $q_\mathsf{s} \oplus q_\mathsf{s} \to p_\mathsf{s} \oplus p_\mathsf{c}$. One can show as we have done for $\mathcal{A}_\leqslant/\mathrm{AC}$, that for any term t_0 in $\mathcal{T}(\mathcal{F}_\oplus)$, $t_0 \to^*_{\mathcal{A}_</\mathrm{AC}} p_{fin}$ if and only if $\pi(t_0) = (k_1, k_2, k_3, 1, 2)$ with $k_3 < k_1 \times k_2$. □

Let us consider the tree language $L_\geqslant$ defined below over the above signature $\mathcal{F}_\oplus = \{\oplus\} \cup \{\mathsf{a}, \mathsf{b}, \mathsf{c}, \#, \mathsf{s}\}$:

$$L_\geqslant = \{\, (k_1, k_2, k_3, 1, 2) \mid k_3 \geqslant k_1 \times k_2 \text{ for } k_1, k_2, k_3 \in \mathbb{N} \,\},$$

and we take the hypothesis

$\mathcal{H}$: $L_\geqslant$ is an AC-monotone tree language.

We then state the following property associated to $\mathcal{H}$.

Lemma 3. *If $\mathcal{H}$ holds, there exists a monotone AC-tree automaton that accepts $L_=$ over $\mathcal{F}_\oplus$ such that $\pi(L_=) = \{(k_1, k_2, k_3, 1, 2) \mid k_3 = k_1 \times k_2 \text{ for } k_1, k_2, k_3 \in \mathbb{N}\}$.*

Proof. Due to the hypothesis $\mathcal{H}$, there exists a monotone AC-tree automaton $\mathcal{A}_\geqslant/\mathrm{AC}$ with $\mathcal{L}(\mathcal{A}_\geqslant/\mathrm{AC}) = L_\geqslant$. It is known that the class of monotone AC-tree automata is effectively closed under intersection (Thm. 3, [23]). Then we let $\mathcal{B}/\mathrm{AC}$ be the intersection of $\mathcal{A}_\leqslant/\mathrm{AC}$ in the previous section and $\mathcal{A}_\geqslant/\mathrm{AC}$. Trivially as $(n_1 \geqslant n_2) \wedge (n_1 \leqslant n_2)$ if and only if $n_1 = n_2$, $\mathcal{B}/\mathrm{AC}$ accepts $L_\geqslant \cap L_\leqslant$, and therefore, $\mathcal{B}/\mathrm{AC}$ accepts $L_=$. □

Lemma 4. *If $\mathcal{H}$ holds, there exists an algorithm that takes as an input $\mathcal{D}$ a diophantine equation and returns as an output "yes" if $\mathcal{D}$ admits a non-negative solution; otherwise, "no".*

Proof. Let us assume a finite set of variables $x_1, \ldots, x_n$ ranging over the natural numbers $\mathbb{N}$. We consider a *system of numerical equations* $\mathcal{S} = \{\mathsf{Eq}_1, \ldots, \mathsf{Eq}_m\}$, where each Eq_ℓ $(1 \leqslant \ell \leqslant m)$ in $\mathcal{S}$ is in one of the following forms:

$$x_i = c \quad (c: \text{ a fixed natural number}) \qquad x_i = x_j + x_k \qquad x_i = x_j \times x_k$$

Here i must be different from j and k, i.e. x_i does not occur in the right-hand side of the same equation. But a variable x_i may occur in the left hand-sides of different equations. A solution σ for an equation Eq_ℓ is a mapping from $\{x_1, \ldots, x_n\}$ to $\mathbb{N}$, such that the structure $(\mathbb{N}, +, *, =)$ is a model of Eq_ℓ under the valuation σ. A solution σ for a system $\mathcal{S}$ is a solution for every equation in $\mathcal{S}$.

It is well-known that from any diophantine equation $\mathcal{D}$, one can compute a system of numerical equations $\mathcal{S}$ such that $\mathcal{D}$ admits a solution if and only if $\mathcal{S}$ admits a solution. Now, for each equation Eq_ℓ in $\mathcal{S}$, we define a monotone AC-TA $\mathcal{A}_{\mathsf{Eq}_\ell}/\mathsf{AC}$ over the signature $\mathcal{F}_\oplus = \{\oplus\} \cup \{\mathsf{a}_1, \ldots, \mathsf{a}_n, \#, \mathsf{s}\}$, such that for any term t in $\mathcal{T}(\mathcal{F}_\oplus)$, $t \in \mathcal{L}(\mathcal{A}_{\mathsf{Eq}_\ell}/\mathsf{AC})$ if and only if $|t|_\# = 1$, $|t|_s = 2$ and the valuation σ defined as $\sigma(x_i) = |t|_{\mathsf{a}_i}$ (for $1 \leqslant i \leqslant n$) is a solution for Eq_ℓ. For each kind of numerical equations, we define the transition rules of the automaton assuming that p_{fin} is the unique final state:

– For the constraint equation $x_i = 0$ we define the tree automaton $\mathcal{A}_{x_i=0}$ equipped with the transition rules

$$\{\, p_\mathsf{s} \oplus p_\mathsf{s} \to q_\mathsf{s}, \; q_\mathsf{s} \oplus p_\# \to p_{fin} \,\} \cup$$
$$\{\, p_{\mathsf{a}_j} \oplus p_{fin} \to p_{fin} \mid j \neq i \text{ and } 1 \leqslant j \leqslant n \,\}$$

with the rules for constants $\{\, \mathsf{a}_j \to p_{\mathsf{a}_j} \mid 1 \leqslant j \leqslant n \,\} \cup \{\, \# \to p_\#, \; \mathsf{s} \to p_\mathsf{s} \,\}$. For $x_i = c$ $(c > 0)$ we additionally take the transition rules

$$\{\, p_{\mathsf{a}_i} \oplus p_{fin} \to p_1 \,\} \cup \{\, p_{\mathsf{a}_i} \oplus p_j \to p_{j+1} \mid 1 \leqslant j \leqslant c - 2 \,\} \cup$$
$$\{\, p_{\mathsf{a}_i} \oplus p_{c-1} \to p_{fin} \,\}.$$

– For the linear equation $x_i + x_j = x_k$ we define the tree automaton $\mathcal{A}_{x_i+x_j=x_k}$ equipped with the transition rules

$$\{\, p_\mathsf{s} \oplus p_\mathsf{s} \to q_\mathsf{s}, \; q_\mathsf{s} \oplus p_\# \to p_{fin} \,\} \cup \{\, p_{\mathsf{a}_i} \oplus p_{\mathsf{a}_k} \to p, \; p_{\mathsf{a}_j} \oplus p_{\mathsf{a}_k} \to p \,\} \cup$$
$$\{\, p_{\mathsf{a}_\ell} \oplus p_{fin} \to p_{fin} \mid \ell \neq i \text{ and } \ell \neq j \text{ and } \ell \neq k \,\} \cup$$
$$\{\, p \oplus p \to p, \; p \oplus p_{fin} \to p_{fin} \,\}$$

with the rules for constants $\{\, \mathsf{a}_\ell \to p_{\mathsf{a}_\ell} \mid 1 \leqslant \ell \leqslant n \,\} \cup \{\, \# \to p_\#, \; \mathsf{s} \to p_\mathsf{s} \,\}$.

– Finally, for a numerical equation $x_i = x_j \times x_k$, we build the automaton $\mathcal{A}_{x_i=x_j \times x_k}$; let $\mathcal{B}/\mathsf{AC}$ the automaton defined in the proof of Lemma 3. We assume without loss of generality that p_{fin} is the unique final state of $\mathcal{B}/\mathsf{AC}$. We then define $\mathcal{A}_{x_i=x_j \times x_k}$ by relabeling c by a_i, a by a_j and b by a_k and by adding the transition rules

$$\{\, p_{\mathsf{a}_\ell} \oplus p_{fin} \to p_{fin} \mid \ell \neq i \text{ and } \ell \neq j \text{ and } \ell \neq k \,\} \cup$$
$$\{\, \mathsf{a}_\ell \to p_{\mathsf{a}_\ell} \mid 1 \leqslant \ell \leqslant n \,\}.$$

One should note that for the first two cases, transition rules for $\#$ and s are not essential, but they must be included under our construction if a system $\mathcal{S}$ contains an equation Eq_k of the multiplication $x_i = x_j \times x_k$.

Accordingly, for the system $\mathcal{S} = \{\, \mathsf{Eq}_1, \ldots, \mathsf{Eq}_m \,\}$ of numerical equations, we can construct a monotone AC-TA $\mathcal{A}_\mathcal{S}/\mathsf{AC}$ such that

$$\mathcal{L}(\mathcal{A}_\mathcal{S}/\mathsf{AC}) = \bigcap_{1 \leqslant \ell \leqslant m} \mathcal{L}(\mathcal{A}_{\mathsf{Eq}_\ell}/\mathsf{AC})$$

whose accepted language is non-empty if and only if $\mathcal{S}$ admits a solution. Since the emptiness problem for monotone AC-TA is decidable, there exists an algorithm under the hypothesis $\mathcal{H}$ that takes as an input a diophantine equation $\mathcal{D}$ and returns "yes" if there is a non-negative solution; otherwise, "no". $\qquad\square$

It is well-known that Hilbert's 10th problem is undecidable [22], even only in the case of non-negative solutions to be considered. Thus we obtain the next theorem.

Theorem 4. *There is no monotone AC-tree automaton that accepts $L_{\geqslant}$ over the signature $\mathcal{F}_{\oplus}$.*

Corollary 1. *The class of AC-monotone tree languages is not closed under complementation.*

Proof. Straightforward from Theorem 4, as AC-monotone tree languages are closed under intersection and $L_{\geqslant} = (L_<)^c \cap \{ t \in \mathcal{T}(\mathcal{F}_{\oplus}) \mid |t|_{\#} = 1 \ \& \ |t|_s = 2 \}$, where $L_<$ and $\{ t \in \mathcal{T}(\mathcal{F}_{\oplus}) \mid |t|_{\#} = 1 \ \& \ |t|_s = 2 \}$ are AC-monotone tree languages. $\square$

6 The Inclusion Problem for Monotone AC-Tree Automata

Using the previous tree automata construction, we show in this section that the inclusion problem for AC-monotone tree languages is undecidable. The remainder of this section is devoted to the proof of the following undecidability result.

Theorem 5. *Given two monotone AC-tree automata $\mathcal{A}_1/\mathsf{AC}$ and $\mathcal{A}_2/\mathsf{AC}$ over the same signature, the problem whether $\mathcal{L}(\mathcal{A}_1/\mathsf{AC}) \subseteq \mathcal{L}(\mathcal{A}_2/\mathsf{AC})$ is not decidable.*

As we did in the previous section, we consider a system $\mathcal{S} = \{ \mathsf{Eq}_1, \ldots, \mathsf{Eq}_m \}$ of numerical equations defined over a finite set of variables $\{ x_1, \ldots, x_n \}$. One should note that according to the syntax, Eq_i is an equation in the form of $x_j = e$, where e is either a fixed natural number c, the addition $x_k + x_\ell$, or the multiplication $x_k \times x_\ell$, such that $x_j \neq x_k$ and $x_j \neq x_\ell$.

We then define the system $\mathcal{S}_{\leqslant}$ of *inequations* obtained by replacing each equation $x_i = e$ by the inequation $x_i \leqslant e$. Namely, $\mathcal{S}_{\leqslant} = \{ x_i \leqslant e \mid x_i = e \in \mathcal{S} \}$.

Finally we define, for each k with $1 \leqslant k \leqslant m$, $\mathcal{S}_k$ a system of inequations obtained from $\mathcal{S}_{\leqslant}$ by replacing only the k-th inequation $x_i \leqslant e_k$ by the strict inequation $x_i < e_k$.

From previous sections, we know that one can effectively associate with each inequation Ineq_k (being either $x_j \leqslant e_k$ or $x_j < e_k$) a monotone AC-tree automaton $\mathcal{A}_{\mathsf{Ineq}_k}$ such that a term t from $\mathcal{T}(\mathcal{F}_{\oplus})$ is accepted by an automaton $\mathcal{A}_{\mathsf{Ineq}_k}/\mathsf{AC}$ if and only if $|t|_{\#} = 1$, $|t|_s = 2$ and either Ineq_k is of the form

- $x_i \leqslant c$ and $|t|_{a_i} \leqslant c$ (resp. $x_i < c$ and $|t|_{a_i} < c$),
- $x_i \leqslant x_v + x_w$ and $|t|_{a_i} \leqslant |t|_{a_v} + |t|_{a_w}$ (resp. $x_i < x_v + x_w$ and $|t|_{a_i} < |t|_{a_v} + |t|_{a_w}$), or
- $x_i \leqslant x_v * x_w$ and $|t|_{a_i} \leqslant |t|_{a_v} * |t|_{a_w}$ (resp. $x_i < x_v * x_w$ and $|t|_{a_i} < |t|_{a_v} * |t|_{a_w}$).

Moreover, we let for all $1 \leqslant k \leqslant m$,

$$\mathcal{A}_{\mathcal{S}_{\leqslant}}/\mathsf{AC} = \bigcap_{\mathsf{Ineq} \in \mathcal{S}_{\leqslant}} \mathcal{A}_{\mathsf{Ineq}}/\mathsf{AC}, \qquad \mathcal{A}_{\mathcal{S}_k}/\mathsf{AC} = \bigcap_{\mathsf{Ineq} \in \mathcal{S}_k} \mathcal{A}_{\mathsf{Ineq}}/\mathsf{AC}$$

In the above definition, $\bigcap_{\mathsf{Ineq} \in \mathcal{S}_{\leqslant}} \mathcal{A}_{\mathsf{Ineq}}/\mathsf{AC}$ represents an AC-TA that accepts the tree language accepted by $\mathcal{A}_{\mathsf{Ineq}}/\mathsf{AC}$ for all $\mathsf{Ineq} \in \mathcal{S}$.

Lemma 5. $\mathcal{L}(\mathcal{A}_{\mathcal{S}_{\leqslant}}/\mathsf{AC}) \not\subseteq \mathcal{L}(\bigcup_{1 \leqslant i \leqslant m} \mathcal{A}_{\mathcal{S}_i}/\mathsf{AC})$ *if and only if $\mathcal{S}$ admits a solution.* $\square$

Theorem 5 follows easily from the above Lemma 5 together with the effective closedness under union and intersection of monotone AC-tree automata and the undecidability of Hilbert's 10th problem [22].

7 Concluding Remarks

In this paper, we have shown the 4 new results (Theorems 1, 2, 5 and Corollary 1) for the class of monotone AC-tree automata. Our proof technique used for showing the expressiveness of AC-monotone tree languages explains also a new idea of how to interpret by AC-tree automata the *arithmetic constraints* over the natural numbers, while an observation obtained from this tree automata construction gives rise to the negative closure property of the complementation and the undecidability of the inclusion problem.

For further research along monotone AC-tree automata, it might be interesting to consider the question about decision problems concerning regularity, called the *regularity* problem; it is not clear how to determine, given a monotone AC-tree automaton, whether the accepted tree language can also be accepted by some regular AC-tree automaton. Useful ideas to solve this decision problem are found in the study about Petri nets. In fact, it is known that the *semi-linearity* problem for Petri nets is decidable [15]. The regularity problem for AC-monotone tree languages can be regarded in some sense as an generalization of the above semi-linearity problem.

Another interesting question about monotone AC-tree automata is the universality problem [6]; this problem is known to be decidable for regular AC-tree automata and it is undecidable for monotone A-tree automata.

Acknowledgments. The authors thank anonymous referees for their detailed comments and suggestions to improve the early version of the paper.

References

1. A. Armando, D. Basin, M. Bouallagui, Y. Chevalier, L. Compagna, S. Mödersheim, M. Rusinowitch, M. Turuani, L. Viganò, and L. Vigneron. The AVISS Security Protocol Analysis Tool. In *Proc. of 14th CAV,* Copenhagen (Denmark), volume 2404 of *LNCS,* pages 349–353. Springer, 2002.
2. I. Boneva and J.-M. Talbot. Automata and Logics for Unranked and Unordered Trees. In *Proc. of 16th RTA,* Nara (Japan), volume 3467 of *LNCS,* pages 500–515. Springer, 2005.
3. A. Bouhoula, J. P. Jouannaud, and J. Meseguer. Specification and Proof in Membership Equational Logic. *TCS,* 236:35–132, 2000.
4. T. Colcombet. Rewriting in the Partial Algebra of Typed Terms Modulo AC. In *Proc. of 4th INFINITY,* Brno (Czech Republic), volume 68(6) of *ENTCS.* Elsevier, 2002.
5. H. Comon, M. Dauchet, R. Gilleron, F. Jacquemard, D. Lugiez, S. Tison, and M. Tommasi. *Tree Automata Techniques and Applications,* 2002. (http://www.grappa.univ-lille3.fr/tata).
6. N. Dershowitz and R. Treinen. Problem #101. *The RTA List of Open Problems.* Available at http://www.lsv.ens-cachan.fr/rtaloop/.
7. P. Devienne, J.-M. Talbot, and S. Tison. Set-Based Analysis for Logic Programming and Tree Automata. In *Proc. of 4th SAS,* volume 1302 of *LNCS,* pages 127–140. Springer, 1997.
8. J. Esparza. Decidability and Complexity of Petri Net Problems – An Introduction. In *Petri Nets,* Dagstuhl (Germany), volume 1491 of *LNCS,* pages 374–428. Springer, 1996.
9. J. Esparza. Decidability of Model-Checking for Infinite-State Concurrent Systems. *Acta Informatica,* 34:85–107, 1997.
10. J. Esparza. Grammars as Processes. In *Formal and Natural Computing – Essays Dedicated to Grzegorz Rozenberg,* volume 2300 of *LNCS,* pages 277–297. Springer, 2002.

11. J. P. Gallagher and G. Puebla. Abstract Interpretation over Non-Deterministic Finite Tree Automata for Set-Based Analysis of Logic Programs. In *Proc. of 4th PADL,* Portland (USA), volume 2257 of *LNCS,* pages 243–261. Springer, 2002.

12. T. Genet and F. Klay. Rewriting for Cryptographic Protocol Verification. In *Proc. of 17th CADE,* Pittsburgh (USA), volume 1831 of *LNCS,* pages 271–290. Springer, 2000.

13. S. Ginsburg. *The Mathematical Theory of Context-Free Languages.* McGraw-Hill, 1966.

14. J. Goubault-Larrecq and K. N. Verma. *Alternating Two-way AC-Tree Automata.* Technical Report LSV-02-11, Laboratoire Spécification et Vérification, 2002.

15. D. Hauschildt. *Semilinearity of the Reachability Set is Decidable for Petri Nets.* Technical Report FBI-HH-B-146/90, Universität Hamburg, 1990.

16. J. Hendrix, H. Ohsaki, and J. Meseguer. *Sufficient Completeness Checking with Propositional Tree Automata.* Technical Report AIST-PS-2005-013, National Institute of Advanced Industrial Science and Technology, 2005. (http://staff.aist.go.jp/ hitoshi.ohsaki/).

17. H. Hosoya, J. Vouillon, and B. C. Pierce. Regular Expression Types for XML. In *Proc. of 5th ICFP,* Montreal (Canada), volume 35(9) of *SIGPLAN Notices,* pages 11–22. ACM, 2000.

18. N. D. Jones, L. H. Landweber, and Y. E. Lien. Complexity of Some Problems in Petri Nets. *TCS,* 4(3):277–299, 1977.

19. M. Kudlek and V. Mitrana. Normal Forms of Grammars, Finite Automata, Abstract Families, and Closure Properties of Multiset Languages. In *Multiset Processing,* volume 2235 of *LNCS,* pages 135–146. Springer, 2001.

20. S. Y. Kuroda. Classes of Languages and Linear Bounded Automata. *Information and Control,* 7(2):207–223, 1964.

21. D. Lugiez. Counting and Equality Corstraints for Multitree Automata. In *Proc. of 6th FOSSACS,* Warsaw (Poland), volume 2620 of *LNCS,* pages 328–342. Springer, 2003.

22. Y. Matiyasevich. Enumerable Sets are Diophantine. *Doklady Akademii Nauk SSSR,* 191(2):279–282, 1970 (in Russian). Improved and English translation in *Soviet Mathematics Doklady,* 11:354–357.

23. H. Ohsaki. Beyond Regularity: Equational Tree Automata for Associative and Commutative Theories. In *Proc. of 15th CSL,* volume 2142 of *LNCS,* pages 539–553. Springer, 2001.

24. H. Ohsaki, H. Seki, and T. Takai. Recognizing Boolean Closed A-Tree Languages with Membership Conditional Rewriting Mechanism. In *Proc. of 14th RTA,* Valencia (Spain), volume 2706 of *LNCS,* pages 483–498. Springer, 2003.

25. H. Ohsaki and T. Takai. Decidability and Closure Properties of Equational Tree Languages. In *Proc. of 13th RTA,* Copenhagen (Denmark), volume 2378 of *LNCS,* pages 114–128. Springer, 2002.

26. H. Ohsaki and T. Takai. ACTAS: A System Design for Associative and Commutative Tree Automata Theory. In *Proc. of 5th RULE,* Aachen (Germany), volume 124(1) of *ENTCS,* pages 97–111. Elsevier, 2005.

27. R. J. Parikh. On Context-Free Languages. *JACM,* 13(4):570–581, 1966.

28. W. Savitch. Relationships between Nondeterministic and Deterministic Tape Complexities. *Journal of Computer and Systems Sciences,* 4(2):177–192, 1970.

29. H. Seidl, T. Schwentick, and A. Muscholl. Numerical Document Queries. In *Proc. of 22nd PODS,* San Diego (USA), pages 155–166. ACM, 2003.

30. K. N. Verma. On Closure under Complementation of Equational Tree Automata for Theories Extending AC. In *Proc. of 10th LPAR,* volume 2850 of *LNCS,* pages 183–197. Springer, 2003.

31. K. N. Verma. Two-Way Equational Tree Automata for AC-like Theories: Decidability and Closure Properties. In *Proc. of 14th RTA,* Valencia (Spain), volume 2706 of *LNCS,* pages 180–197. Springer, 2003.

On the Specification of Sequent Systems

Elaine Pimentel[1] and Dale Miller[2],[*]

[1] Departamento de Matemática,
Universidade Federal de Minas Gerais, Belo Horizonte, M.G. Brasil
[2] INRIA-Futurs & Laboratoire d'Informatique (LIX),
École Polytechnique, France

Abstract. Recently, linear Logic has been used to specify sequent calculus proof systems in such a way that the proof search in linear logic can yield proof search in the specified logic. Furthermore, the meta-theory of linear logic can be used to draw conclusions about the specified sequent calculus. For example, derivability of one proof system from another can be decided by a simple procedure that is implemented via bounded logic programming-style search. Also, simple and decidable conditions on the linear logic presentation of inference rules, called *homogeneous* and *coherence*, can be used to infer that the initial rules can be restricted to atoms and that cuts can be eliminated. In the present paper we introduce *Llinda*, a logical framework based on linear logic augmented with inference rules for definition (fixed points) and induction. In this way, the above properties can be proved entirely inside the framework. To further illustrate the power of *Llinda*, we extend the definition of coherence and provide a new, semi-automated proof of cut-elimination for Girard's Logic of Unicity (LU).

1 Introduction

Logics and type systems have been exploited in recent years as frameworks for the specification of deduction in a number of logics. Such *meta-logics* or *logical frameworks* have been mostly based on intuitionistic logic (see, for example, [FM88, NM88, Har93]) or dependent types (see [Pfn89]) in which quantification at (non-predicate) higher-order types is available. These computer systems have been used as meta-languages to automate various aspects of different logics.

Features of a meta-logic are often directly inherited by any object-logic. This inheritance can be, at times, a great asset: for example, the meta-logic treatment of binding and substitution can be exploited directly in specifying the object-logic. On the other hand, features of the meta-logic can limit the kinds of object-logics that can be directly and naturally encoded. For example, the structural rules of an intuitionistic meta-logic (weakening and contraction) are also inherited and make it difficult to have natural encodings of logics for which these structural rules are not intended. Also, intuitionistic logic does not have

---

[*] This work has been supported in part by the ACI grants Geocal and Rossignol and the INRIA "Equipes Associées" Slimmer.

G. Sutcliffe and A. Voronkov (Eds.): LPAR 2005, LNAI 3835, pp. 352–366, 2005.
© Springer-Verlag Berlin Heidelberg 2005

an involutive negation and this makes it difficult to address directly dualities in object-logic proof systems. This lack of dualities is particularly unfortunate when specifying sequent calculus [Gen69] since they play a central role in the theory of such proof systems.

Pfenning in [Pfn95, Pfn00] used the logical framework LF to give new proofs of cut elimination for intuitionistic and classical sequent calculi. His approach is elegant since many technical details of the cut-elimination proof were aborbed by the LF. That approach, however, is based on an intuitionistic meta-logic and is not so suitable for handling the dualities of the sequent calculus.

In [Mil96, MP04, MP02], classical linear logic was used as a meta-logic in order to specify and reason about a variety of proof systems. Since the encodings of such logical systems are natural and direct, the meta-theory of linear logic can be used to draw conclusions about the object-level proof systems. More specifically, in [MP02], the authors present a decision procedure for determining if one encoded proof system is derivable from another. In the same paper, necessary conditions were presented (together with a decision procedure) for assuring that an encoded proof system satisfies cut-elimination. This last result used linear logic's dualities to formalize the fact that if the left and right introduction rules are suitable duals of each other then non-atomic cuts can be eliminated.

In the present paper, we go a step further and introduce *Llinda*, a logical framework based on linear logic augmented with inference rules for definition (fixed points) and induction. In this stronger logic, such properties on an object-logic as the elimination of non-atomic cuts can be proved entirely inside the logical framework. In particular, much of the meta-reasoning that appears in [MP02] can be internalized in *Llinda*. We also use *Llinda* to give sufficient and decidable conditions that guarantee the completeness of the atomic initial rule. Many consider, as Girard [Gir99], that such a property is a crucial condition when designing a "good sequent system". To further illustrate the power of *Llinda* as a framework for specifying and reasoning about sequent systems, we extend the definition of coherence [MP02] and provide a new, semi-automated proof of cut-elimination for LU, Girard's Logic of Unicity [Gir93].

The rest of the paper is organized as follows. Section 2 introduces the notion of flat linear logic and Section 3 extends linear logic with definitions and induction. Section 4 presents a method for encoding logical rules and Section 5 represents introduction rules as definitions. Section 6 highlights the role of bipolar formulas in the specification of sequent systems. Section 7 presents a necessary condition for characterizing systems having the cut-elimination property while in Section 8 a necessary condition is given that guarantees that initial rules can be restricted to atomic formulas. Finally, Section 9 presents a semi-automated proof of cut-elimination for LU.

2   Flat Linear Logic

The connectives of linear logic [Gir87] can be classified as *synchronous* and *asynchronous* [And92]: the asynchronous connectives have right-introduction rules that are invertible while the right-introduction rules of *synchronous* connective are not generally invertible and they usually require "synchronization" between the introduced formula and its context within a sequent. The de Morgan dual of a connective in one class yields a connective in the other class.

Although full linear logic is important in this work, we need to consider certain formulas of rather restricted nesting of synchronous and asynchronous connectives. These restricted formulas will carry the adjective "flat".

Definition 1. *A flat goal is a linear logic formula that contains only occurrences of the asynchronous connectives (namely $\otimes, \&, \perp, \top, \forall$) together with the modal ? which can only have atomic scope. A flat clause is a linear logic formula of the form:*

$$\forall \bar{y}(G_1 \hookrightarrow \cdots \hookrightarrow G_m \hookrightarrow A_1 \otimes \cdots \otimes A_n), \quad (m, n \geq 0)$$

where $G_1, \ldots, G_m$ are flat goals, $A_1, \ldots, A_n$ are atomic formulas and occurrences of $\hookrightarrow$ represent either $\multimap$ or $\Rightarrow$. The formula $A_1 \otimes \cdots \otimes A_n$ is the head *of such a clause, while for each $i = 1, \ldots, m$, the formula G_i is a* body *of this clause. If $n = 0$, then we write the head simply as $\perp$ and say that the head is* empty.

A flat clause is logically equivalent to a formula in *uncurried* form, namely, a formula of the form

$$\forall \bar{y}(B \multimap A_1 \otimes \cdots \otimes A_n)$$

where $n \geq 0$, $\bar{y}$ is the list of variables free in the head $A_1 \otimes \cdots \otimes A_n$, all free variables of B are also free in the head, and B may have outermost occurrences of the synchronous connectives: 1, $\oplus$, $\otimes$, $\exists$ and !. We will call B an *uncurried flat body*.

A formula that is either a flat goal or a uncurried flat body is an example of a *bipolar* formula, namely, a formula in which no synchronous connective is in the scope of an asynchronous connective.

As in Church's Simple Theory of Types [Chu40], types for both terms and formulas are built using a simply typed λ-calculus. Variables are simply typed that do not contain the type o, which is reserved for the type of formulas. We will call types which do not contain the type o *object types*, and variables and constants of object types are named object variables and object constant, respectively. Otherwise types will be referred as *meta-level types* and formulas will be called meta-level formulas. We assume the usual rules of α, β, and η-conversion and we identify terms and formulas up to α-conversion. A term is λ-normal if it contains no β and no η redexes. All terms are λ-convertible to a term in λ-normal form, and such a term is unique up to α-conversion. The substitution notation $B[t/x]$ denotes the λ-normal form of the β-redex $(\lambda x.B)t$.

3   *Llinda:* **Linear Logic with Definition and Induction**

Following the lines described by McDowell and Miller [MM00] and Tiu [Tiu04] on the proof theoretic notion of definitions, we will extend linear logic by allowing the definition of atomic formulas.

Definition 2. *A definition $\mathcal{D}$ is a finite set of* definition clauses, *which are expressions of the form $\forall \bar{x}[p\bar{x} \triangleq B\bar{x}]$, where p is a predicate constant. The formula $B\bar{x}$ is the* body *and the atomic formula $p\bar{x}$ is the* head *of that clause. A predicate may occur at most once in the heads of the clauses of a definition.*

The symbol $\triangleq$ is not a logical connective: it simply marks a definition clause.

Linear logic augmented with such *definitions* is not consistent if these definitions are not restricted. For instance, if negative occurrences of the exponential ! are allowed in the body of definitions, inconsistencies can be easily constructed. In order to avoid such inconsistencies, we introduce the notion of level of a formula to define a proper stratification on definitions, as done in [MM00, Tiu04]. To each predicate p we associate a natural number $lvl(p)$, the level of p. The notion of level is then extended to formulas.

Definition 3. *Given a formula B, its level $lvl(B)$ is defined as follows:*

1. $lvl(p\bar{t}) = lvl(p)$
2. $lvl(\bot) = lvl(\top) = lvl(1) = lvl(0) = 0$
3. $lvl(!\,A) = lvl(?\,A) = lvl(A)$
4. $lvl(B \oplus C) = lvl(B \otimes C) = lvl(B \,\&\, C) = lvl(B \otimes C) = max(lvl(B); lvl(C))$
5. $lvl(\forall x.A) = lvl(\exists x.A) = lvl(A)$
6. $lvl(A_1 \multimap A_2) = max(lvl(A_1) + 1; lvl(A_2))$.

Definition 4. *A definition clause $\forall \bar{x}.[p\bar{x} \triangleq B]$ is* stratified *if $lvl(B) \leq lvl(p)$. A definition is* stratified *if all its definition clauses are stratified. An occurrence of a formula A in a formula C is* strictly positive *if that particular occurrence of A is not to the left of any implication in C. In this way, the stratification of definitions implies that for every definition clause all occurrences of the head predicate in the body are strictly positive.*

Observe that stratification excludes the possibility of circular calling through implications (negations). Since all occurrences of p in B are *positive*, the existence of fixed points is always guaranteed. Thus the provability of pt means that t is in a solution of the corresponding fixed point equation.

Note also that a flat clause that is written in its uncurried form can be seen as a definition clause since uncurried bodies are uncurried flat goals (and hence do not contain implications).

Definition 5. *A definition clause $\forall \bar{x}.[p\bar{x} \triangleq B]$ is* flat *if B is an uncurried flat body. A definition is* flat *if all its definition clauses are flat.*

Given a definition clause $\forall \bar{x}[p\bar{x} \triangleq B\bar{x}]$, the left and right rules for atoms are

$$\frac{B\bar{t}, \Delta \longrightarrow \Gamma}{p\bar{t}, \Delta \longrightarrow \Gamma} \; def\mathcal{L} \qquad \frac{\Delta \longrightarrow B\bar{t}, \Gamma}{\Delta \longrightarrow p\bar{t}, \Gamma} \; def\mathcal{R}.$$

The rules above show that an atom can be substituted by its definition during a proof. This means that a defined atom can be seen as a generalized connective, whose behavior is determined by its defining clause.

Since a predicate may occur at most once in the heads of definitions, explicit equality must appear as part of the syntax. The rules for the equality predicate makes use of (the standard notion of) substitutions. The left and right introduction rules for equality are:

$$\frac{\{\Gamma\theta \longrightarrow \Delta\theta \mid s\theta =_{\beta,\eta} t\theta, \ \theta \in CSU(s,t)\}}{(s = t), \Gamma \longrightarrow \Delta} \ eq\mathcal{L} \qquad \frac{}{\longrightarrow t = t} \ eq\mathcal{R}.$$

The set $CSU(s,t)$ is a *complete set of unifiers* for s and t. In general, $CSU(s,t)$ can be empty (for non-unifiability), finite, or infinite. Thus the set of sequents as the premise in the $eq\mathcal{L}$ rule should be understood to mean that each sequent in the set is a premise of the rule. Notice that in the $eq\mathcal{L}$ rule, the free variables of the conclusion can be instantiated in the premises. In the examples in this paper, the set $CSU(s,t)$ can be taken as being either empty or a singleton, containing the most general unifier of s and t.

As observed before, a definition $\forall x.px \triangleq Bx$ can be seen as a fixed point equation, but that fixed point is not necessarily the least or the greatest one. We now add extra rules for capturing the least fixed point via *induction*.

Let $\forall\bar{x}[p\bar{x} \triangleq B\bar{x}]$ be a stratified definitional clause and let S be a closed term of the same type as p. The left introduction rule for an atom with predicate p can be strengthed to be

$$\frac{(B\bar{x})[S/p] \longrightarrow S\bar{x} \quad \Delta, S\bar{t} \longrightarrow \Gamma}{\Delta, p\bar{t} \longrightarrow \Gamma} \ ind\mathcal{L}.$$

The formula S is an invariant of the induction and it is called the *inductive predicate*. The variables $\bar{x}$ are new eigenvariables. The expression $(B\bar{x})[S/p]$ denotes the result of replacing the predicate p in $B\bar{x}$ with S (and λ-normalizing).

Definition 6. *Llinda is linear logic with stratified definition and induction.*[1]

A sequent in *Llinda* will be represented as $\mathcal{D} \parallel \Delta \longrightarrow \Gamma$, meaning the linear sequent with the set of definitions $\mathcal{D}$. If the definition is empty or when it is clear from the context, we will write the sequent above as the usual linear sequent $\Delta \longrightarrow \Gamma$.

We introduce the natural numbers via the type nt, the constants $z : nt$ for zero and $s : nt \to nt$ for successor function and the inductive predicate $nat : nt \to o$, with the following definition clause:

$$nat\ x \triangleq [x = z] \oplus \exists y.[x = sy \otimes nat\ y].$$

Proposition 1. *The following rules can be derived in Llinda:*

$$\frac{\longrightarrow B\,z \quad B\,i \longrightarrow B\,(s\,i) \quad B\,I, \Delta \longrightarrow \Gamma}{nat\ I, \Delta \longrightarrow \Gamma} \ nat\mathcal{L}$$

---

[1] The word *"linda"*, in Portuguese, means "extremely beautiful."

$$\frac{!\varDelta \longrightarrow B\,z,?\,\varGamma \quad !\varDelta, B\,j \longrightarrow B\,(s\,j),?\,\varGamma \quad B\,I,!\varDelta,\varDelta' \longrightarrow \varGamma',?\,\varGamma}{\mathrm{nat}\,I,!\varDelta,\varDelta' \longrightarrow \varGamma',?\,\varGamma}$$

$$\frac{\longrightarrow B \quad B,\varDelta \longrightarrow \varGamma}{\mathrm{nat}\,I,\varDelta \longrightarrow \varGamma} \qquad \frac{\varDelta \longrightarrow \varGamma}{\mathrm{nat}\,I,\varDelta \longrightarrow \varGamma} \qquad \forall n[\mathrm{nat}\,n \equiv\, !\,\mathrm{nat}\,n]$$

For an example of specifying an object-logic, consider intuitionistic logic over the following logical connectives: $\cap$, $\cup$, f_i, and t_i for conjunction, disjunction, false, and true; $\supset$ for implication, and $\forall_i$ and $\exists_i$ for universal and existential quantification. Now introduce the type *bool* of intuitionistic formulas and the inductive predicate $form_i(\cdot) : bool \to o$ with the following defined clause:

$$
\begin{aligned}
form_i(x) \triangleq\ & [x = t_i] && \oplus \\
& [x = f_i] && \oplus \\
& atomic(x) && \oplus \\
& \exists y, w.[(x = y \cap w) \otimes form_i(y) \otimes form_i(w)] && \oplus \\
& \exists y, w.[(x = y \cup w) \otimes form_i(y) \otimes form_i(w)] && \oplus \\
& \exists y, w.[(x = y \supset w) \otimes form_i(y) \otimes form_i(w)] && \oplus \\
& \exists X.[(x = \forall_i u.X\,u) \otimes (\forall u.form_i(X\,u))] && \oplus \\
& \exists X.[(x = \exists_i u.X\,u) \otimes (\forall u.form_i(X\,u))]
\end{aligned}
$$

The predicate *atomic* is given elsewhere as a definition. The *ind$\mathcal{L}$* rule applied to this definition yields an induction principle for object-level formulas. Following the same arguments used above for natural numbers, it is possible to derive the following, more intuitive rule for structural induction.

Proposition 2. *The following rule can be derived in Llinda*

$$
\frac{
\begin{array}{c}
\longrightarrow B\,t_i \qquad \longrightarrow B\,f_i \qquad atomic(x) \longrightarrow B\,x \\
B\,x, B\,y \longrightarrow B\,(x \cap y) \qquad B\,x, B\,y \longrightarrow B\,(x \cup y) \qquad B\,x, B\,y \longrightarrow B\,(x \supset y) \\
\forall u[B\,(X\,u)] \longrightarrow B\,(\forall_i u.Xu) \qquad \forall u[B\,(X\,u)] \longrightarrow B\,(\exists_i u.Xu) \\
B\,I,\varDelta \longrightarrow C
\end{array}
}{form_i(I),\varDelta \longrightarrow C} \ form_i\mathcal{L}.
$$

In fact, we can consider a more general version of this rule, where classical contexts can be added on both sides of the sequent, like in Proposition 1.

In general, given an object logic L with j connectives $\diamond_j$ of arity greater or equal to zero and a first order quantifier *quant*, the predicate $form_L(\cdot) : bool \to o$ is defined as follows:

$$
\begin{aligned}
form_L(x) \triangleq\ & atomic(x) && \oplus \\
& \{\exists y_1 \ldots y_n.[x = \diamond_j(y_1, \ldots, y_n) \otimes form_L(y_1) \otimes \ldots \otimes form_L(y_n)]\}_j && \oplus \\
& \exists X.[(x = quant\,u.X\,u) \otimes (\forall u.form_L(X\,u))]
\end{aligned}
$$

It is well known that proving cut-elimination for a logic with definitions *and* induction is not easy [MM00]. The method developed for cut-elimination of *Llinda* (see [Pim05]) is based on some of the ideas present in [Tiu04] and uses a particular notion of *rank* of cut formulas that depends on the level of the formula and on the shape of the derivation itself.

4   Encoding Sequent Systems

Let *bool* be the type of object-level propositional formulas and let $\lfloor \cdot \rfloor$ and $\lceil \cdot \rceil$ be two meta-level predicates, both of type $bool \to o$.

We shall encode the object-level sequent $B_1, \ldots, B_n \longrightarrow C_1, \ldots, C_m$ $(n, m \geq 0)$ as the linear logic formula $\lfloor B_1 \rfloor \,\mathbin{\bindnasrepma}\cdots\mathbin{\bindnasrepma} \lfloor B_n \rfloor \mathbin{\bindnasrepma} \lceil C_1 \rceil \mathbin{\bindnasrepma} \cdots \mathbin{\bindnasrepma} \lceil C_m \rceil$. The $\lfloor \cdot \rfloor$ and $\lceil \cdot \rceil$ predicates are used in order to identify which object-level formulas appear on which side of the sequent arrow.

Encoding structural rules. The structural rules *weakening* and *contraction* are encoded using the ? of linear logic together by the clauses:

$$\forall B(\lceil B \rceil \mathbin{\circ\!\!-} ?\lceil B \rceil) \quad (Neg) \qquad\qquad \forall B(\lfloor B \rfloor \mathbin{\circ\!\!-} ?\lfloor B \rfloor) \quad (Pos).$$

Neg and *Pos* will be called *structural clauses*. All object-level two-sided sequents $\Delta \longrightarrow \Gamma$ considered here will be restricted so that Δ and Γ are either multisets or sets of formulas. Sets are used if the structural rules are implicit; multisets are used if no structural rule is implicit. We will assume that exchange is always implicit.

The initial and cut rules. The initial rule, which asserts that the sequent $B \longrightarrow B$ is provable, is represented by the following clause, which has a head with two atoms and no body.

$$\forall B(\lfloor B \rfloor \mathbin{\bindnasrepma} \lceil B \rceil) \qquad\qquad\qquad (Init)$$

The cut rule can be specified as following clause with an empty head and two atomic bodies.

$$\forall B(\lceil B \rceil \mathbin{-\!\!\circ} \lfloor B \rfloor \mathbin{-\!\!\circ} \bot) \qquad\qquad\qquad (Cut)$$

Other variations on the cut rule appear in the literature and many of these can be encoded by changing one or both of the $\mathbin{-\!\!\circ}$ to $\Rightarrow$. Since the formula *Cut* entails these other variations, so we shall not consider them further.

The *Init* and *Cut* clauses together proves that $\lfloor \cdot \rfloor$ and $\lceil \cdot \rceil$ are duals of each other: that is, they entail the equivalence $\forall B(\lfloor B \rfloor^{\perp} \equiv \lceil B \rceil)$. Notice that this duality of the object-level sequent system becomes a concise equivalence in classical linear logic via negation.

Encoding inference rules. Let $\mathcal{Q}$ be a fixed a set of unary meta-level predicates all of type $bool \to o$. Object-level logical constants will also be assumed to be fixed. These constants will have types of order 0, 1, or 2 and all will build terms of type *bool*. Object-level quantification is first-order and over one domain, denoted at the meta-level by i.

Definition 7. *An* introduction clause *is an uncurried closed flat formula of the form*

$$\forall x_1 \ldots \forall x_n [q(\diamond(x_1, \ldots, x_n)) \mathbin{\circ\!\!-} B]$$

where $\diamond$ is an object-level connective of arity n $(n \geq 0)$ and q is a meta-level predicate. Furthermore, an atom occurring in B is either of the form $p(x_i)$ or

$p(x_i(y))$ *where p is a meta-level predicate and* $1 \leq i \leq n$. *In the first case,* x_i *has a type of order 0 while in the second case* x_i *has a type of order 1 and y is a variable quantified (universally or existentially) in B (in particular, y is not in* $\{x_1, \ldots, x_n\}$).

In the inference systems we shall consider now, the set of meta-level predicates $\mathcal{Q}$ is exactly the set $\{\lfloor \cdot \rfloor, \lceil \cdot \rceil\}$. In Section 9, we will consider Girard's **LU** proof system [Gir93] and there we will use some additional meta-level predicates. See [MP04] for other examples of encodings of sequent systems.

5   Introduction Clauses as Definitions

Given an encoded sequent system $\mathcal{P}$ and an object-level connective $\diamond$ of arity $n \geq 0$, list all the formulas in $\mathcal{P}$ that specify a left-introduction rule for $\diamond$ as:

$$\forall \bar{x}(\lfloor \diamond(x_1, \ldots, x_i) \rfloor \circ\!\!-\, L_1) \quad \cdots \quad \forall \bar{x}(\lfloor \diamond(x_1, \ldots, x_i) \rfloor \circ\!\!-\, L_p) \quad (p \geq 0).$$

Similarly, list all the formulas in $\mathcal{P}$ that specify a right-introduction rule for $\diamond$:

$$\forall \bar{x}(\lceil \diamond(x_1, \ldots, x_i) \rceil \circ\!\!-\, R_1) \quad \cdots \quad \forall \bar{x}(\lceil \diamond(x_1, \ldots, x_i) \rceil \circ\!\!-\, R_q) \quad (q \geq 0)$$

All of these $p+q$ displayed formulas can be replaced by the following two clauses

$$\forall \bar{x}(\lfloor \diamond(x_1, \ldots, x_i) \rfloor \circ\!\!-\, L_1 \oplus \cdots \oplus L_p) \text{ and } \forall \bar{x}(\lceil \diamond(x_1, \ldots, x_i) \rceil \circ\!\!-\, R_1 \oplus \cdots \oplus R_q)$$

(An empty $\oplus$ is written as the linear logic additive false 0.)

Definition 8. *The formulas*

$$\forall \bar{x}(\lfloor \diamond(x_1, \ldots, x_i) \rfloor \overset{\triangle}{=} L_1 \oplus \cdots \oplus L_p) \text{ and } \forall \bar{x}(\lceil \diamond(x_1, \ldots, x_i) \rceil \overset{\triangle}{=} R_1 \oplus \cdots \oplus R_q)$$

are said to represent the introduction rules for the object level connective $\diamond$ *in their* definition form.

Hence introduction clauses of encoded sequent systems form a *flat definition*. As an example, Figures 1 and 2 present the definitions $\mathcal{LK}$ and $\mathcal{LJ}$, respectively. Notice that these specifications are identical except for a systematic renaming of logical constants. To state the formal difference between these two formalisms, we first introduce the named formulas in Figure 3. Notice that the *Cut* and *Init* rules are encoded not as definitions but as formulas.

The following correctness of the LJ and LK encoding is proved in [MP04– Prop 4.2]: The definition $\mathcal{LJ}$ along with the formulas $\{Cut, Init, Pos\}$ correctly represents the provability in LJ, while the definition $\mathcal{LK}$ along with the formulas $\{Cut, Init, Pos, Neg\}$ correctly represents the provability in LK. Thus, LK and LJ are distinquished by specifying whether or not structural rules can be applied to formulas on the right.

An interesting question regarding the formulas appearing in Figure 3 is whether or not the atom-restricted version of each formula entails its general

$(\Rightarrow L)$ $\lfloor A \Rightarrow B \rfloor \triangleq \lceil A \rceil \multimap \lfloor B \rfloor.$ $(\Rightarrow R)$ $\lceil A \Rightarrow B \rceil \triangleq \lfloor A \rfloor \,\invamp\, \lceil B \rceil.$

$(\wedge L)$ $\lfloor A \wedge B \rfloor \triangleq \lfloor A \rfloor \oplus \lfloor B \rfloor.$ $(\wedge R)$ $\lceil A \wedge B \rceil \triangleq \lceil A \rceil \,\&\, \lceil B \rceil.$

$(\vee R)$ $\lceil A \vee B \rceil \triangleq \lceil A \rceil \oplus \lceil B \rceil.$ $(\vee L)$ $\lfloor A \vee B \rfloor \triangleq \lfloor A \rfloor \,\&\, \lfloor B \rfloor.$

$(\forall_c L)$ $\lfloor \forall_c B \rfloor \triangleq \lfloor Bx \rfloor.$ $(\forall_c R)$ $\lceil \forall_c B \rceil \triangleq \forall x \lceil Bx \rceil.$

$(\exists_c L)$ $\lfloor \exists_c B \rfloor \triangleq \forall x \lfloor Bx \rfloor.$ $(\exists_c R)$ $\lceil \exists_c B \rceil \triangleq \lceil Bx \rceil.$

$(f_c L)$ $\lfloor f_c \rfloor \triangleq \top.$ $(t_c R)$ $\lceil t_c \rceil \triangleq \top.$

Fig. 1. Definition $\mathcal{LK}$

$(\supset L)$ $\lfloor A \supset B \rfloor \triangleq \lceil A \rceil \multimap \lfloor B \rfloor.$ $(\supset R)$ $\lceil A \supset B \rceil \triangleq \lfloor A \rfloor \,\invamp\, \lceil B \rceil.$

$(\cap L)$ $\lfloor A \cap B \rfloor \triangleq \lfloor A \rfloor \oplus \lfloor B \rfloor.$ $(\cap R)$ $\lceil A \cap B \rceil \triangleq \lceil A \rceil \,\&\, \lceil B \rceil.$

$(\cup R)$ $\lceil A \cup B \rceil \triangleq \lceil A \rceil \oplus \lceil B \rceil.$ $(\cup L)$ $\lfloor A \cup B \rfloor \triangleq \lfloor A \rfloor \,\&\, \lfloor B \rfloor.$

$(\forall_i L)$ $\lfloor \forall_i B \rfloor \triangleq \lfloor Bx \rfloor.$ $(\forall_i R)$ $\lceil \forall_i B \rceil \triangleq \forall x \lceil Bx \rceil.$

$(\exists_i L)$ $\lfloor \exists_i B \rfloor \triangleq \forall x \lfloor Bx \rfloor.$ $(\exists_i R)$ $\lceil \exists_i B \rceil \triangleq \lceil Bx \rceil.$

$(f_i L)$ $\lfloor f_i \rfloor \triangleq \top.$ $(t_i R)$ $\lceil t_i \rceil \triangleq \top.$

Fig. 2. Definition $\mathcal{LJ}$

$APos = \forall A(\lfloor A \rfloor \multimap ?\lfloor A \rfloor \multimap atomic(A)).$ $Pos = \forall B(\lfloor B \rfloor \multimap ?\lfloor B \rfloor).$

$ANeg = \forall A(\lceil A \rceil \multimap ?\lceil A \rceil \multimap atomic(A)).$ $Neg = \forall B(\lceil B \rceil \multimap ?\lceil B \rceil).$

$AInit = \forall A(\lfloor A \rfloor \,\invamp\, \lceil A \rceil \multimap atomic(A)).$ $Init = \forall B(\lfloor B \rfloor \,\invamp\, \lceil B \rceil).$

$ACut = \forall A(\bot \multimap \lfloor A \rfloor \multimap \lceil A \rceil \multimap atomic(A)).$ $Cut = \forall B(\bot \multimap \lfloor B \rfloor \multimap \lceil B \rceil)$

Fig. 3. Some formulas named

version. Proving the entailment $ACut \vdash Cut$ allows us to conclude that non-atomic cuts can always be reduced to the atomic case. A full cut-elimination proof then only needs to deal with eliminating atomic cuts. Section 7 provides conditions on inference rule encodings that ensures that this entailment can be proved. Dually, the entailment $AInit \vdash Init$ allows us to eliminate non-atomic initial rules, a property that helps can be used to judge the design of a good proof system, especially when using *synthetic connectives* (see [Gir99]). Elimination of non-atomic initial rules is discussed further in Section 8. Finally, it is worthy to say that restricting logical rules and axioms to the atomic case also plays a central role in *Calculus of Structures* [Gug05].

6   Bipolar Clauses

In this section we shall clarify better the role of bipolar clauses in the specification of sequent systems.

Since introduction clauses are defined as flat clauses, they are bipolar. It is interesting to ask, however, if there exist sequent calculus inference rules that can be encoded in linear logic by a formula that is not necessarily bipolar.

Suppose that c is the introduction clause $\forall \bar{x}.[q(\diamond(x_1, \ldots, x_n)) \triangleq B]$ corresponds to a sequent calculus specification. This means that, when doing some meta-level reasoning, backchaining over c:

$$\frac{\begin{array}{c} \Pi' \\ \Delta \longrightarrow \Gamma, B\bar{t} \end{array}}{\Delta \longrightarrow q(\diamond(t_1, \ldots, t_n)), \Gamma} \; defR$$

must mimic exactly the behavior of the inference rule for $\diamond$. Hence the body B *must be* decomposed at once before some other meta level action can be done. That is, B cannot interact with any possible context in Π'. The *focussing* property of linear logic guarantees this only if no synchronous connective is in the scope of an asynchronous connective; that is, if c is bipolar.

Example 1. Consider the following clauses:

$$\lceil \diamond(A, B, C) \rceil \circ\!\!-\ \lceil A \rceil \, \& \, (\lceil B \rceil \otimes \lceil C \rceil) \qquad \lfloor \diamond(A, B, C) \rfloor \circ\!\!-\ \lfloor A \rfloor \oplus (\lfloor B \rfloor \, \otimes \, \lfloor C \rfloor)$$

Note that the first clause is not bipolar. If they are to correspond to the encoding of sequent inference rules, the *natural* candidates would be

$$\frac{\Gamma_1, \Gamma_2 \vdash \Delta_1, \Delta_2, A \quad \Gamma_1 \vdash \Delta_1, B \quad \Gamma_2 \vdash \Delta_2, C}{\Gamma_1, \Gamma_2 \vdash \Delta_1, \Delta_2, \diamond(A, B, C)}$$

$$\frac{\Gamma, A \vdash \Delta}{\Gamma, \diamond(A, B, C) \vdash \Delta} \qquad \frac{\Gamma, B, C \vdash \Delta}{\Gamma, \diamond(A, B, C) \vdash \Delta}$$

But it turns out that while at the meta level it is possible to prove the sequent $!\,Init \vdash \lceil A \rceil \, \& \, (\lceil B \rceil \otimes \lceil C \rceil), \lfloor A \rfloor \oplus (\lfloor B \rfloor \, \otimes \, \lfloor C \rfloor)$ at the object level the two sequent rules listed above cannot be used to prove $\diamond(A, B, C) \vdash \diamond(A, B, C)$. That is, this object-logic sequent can be proved only a non-atomic instance of the initial rule. Hence, *provability* is not the same and the flat clauses above are not *adequate* for representing the inference figures.

Once we know that introduction clauses must necessarily be bipolar, the next question that arises is if every introduction clause is a meta-level representation of a sequent inference rule. This can be shown by a straightforward case analysis.

Proposition 3. *Every introduction clause corresponds to a specification of a sequent calculus introduction rule.*

7 Canonical and Coherent Proof Systems

The purpose of strengthening linear logic with definitions and induction is to enhance the number of properties about encoded proof systems that can be formally proved inside the framework. In this section we will present a necessary condition for characterizing systems having the cut-elimination property.

Definition 9. *A* canonical proof system *is a set $\mathcal{P}$ of flat clauses such that (i) the initial clause is a member of $\mathcal{P}$, (ii) the cut clause is a member of $\mathcal{P}$, (iii) structural clauses (Pos and Neg) may be members of $\mathcal{P}$, and (iv) all other clauses in $\mathcal{P}$ are introduction clauses with the additional restriction that, for every pair of atoms of the form $\lfloor T \rfloor$ and $\lceil S \rceil$ in a body, the head variable of T differs from head variable of S. A formula that satisfies condition (iv) is also called a* canonical clause.

Definition 10. *Consider a canonical proof system $\mathcal{P}$ and an object-level connective, say, $\diamond$ of arity $n \geq 0$. Let the formulas*

$$\forall \bar{x}(\lfloor \diamond(x_1, \ldots, x_n) \rfloor) \triangleq B_l) \quad and \quad \forall \bar{x}(\lceil \diamond(x_1, \ldots, x_n) \rceil) \triangleq B_r)$$

be the definition form for the left and right introduction rules for $\diamond$. The object-level connective $\diamond$ has dual *left and right introduction rules if* $!\, Cut \vdash \forall \bar{x}(B_l \multimap B_r \multimap \bot)$ *in linear logic.*

Definition 11. *A canonical system is called* coherent *if the left and right introduction rules for each object-level connective are duals.*

The cut-elimination theorem for a particular logic can often be divided into two parts. The first part shows that a cut involving a non-atomic formula can be replaced by possibly multiple cuts involving subformulas of the original cut formula. This process stop when cut formulas are atoms. This part of the proof works because left and right introduction rules for each logical connective are duals (formalized here in Definition 10). The second part of the proof argues how cuts with atomic formulas can be removed. Cut-elimination for coherent proof systems is proved similarly: Theorem 1 shows that non-atomic cuts can be reduced to atomic. The remarkable aspect about this is that this part of the cut-elimination process is done *entirely* inside the logical framework *Llinda*.

Proving that atomic cuts can be eliminated requires induction over proofs, hence the reasoning cannot be done inside *Llinda*. This was done in [MP02], where it was also shown that "being coherent" is a general and decidable characterization. Since all the reasoning is done using linear logic, the essence of cut-elimination can be captured totally at the meta-level. Hence it is, in fact, independent of the object logic analyzed.

Theorem 1. *Let $\mathcal{P}$ be a coherent system and let* form$(\cdot)$ *be the inductive predicate defining object-level formulas. The sequent*

$$\mathcal{P} \parallel !\, Init, !\, ACut, \mathrm{form}(B) \longrightarrow Cut(B)$$

is provable in Llinda.

Proof. The proof is by induction where the invariance is $\lambda x.\, !\, Cut(x)$. Consider the following derivation

$$
\cfrac{
  \cfrac{
    !\, Cut(x_1), \ldots, !\, Cut(x_n), B_r, B_l \longrightarrow \bot
  }{
    !\, Cut(x_1), \ldots, !\, Cut(x_n), \lfloor \diamond(x_1, \ldots, x_n) \rfloor, \lceil \diamond(x_1, \ldots, x_n) \rceil \longrightarrow \bot
  }\ def\mathcal{L}
}{
  !\, Cut(x_1), \ldots, !\, Cut(x_n) \longrightarrow !\, Cut(\diamond(x_1, \ldots, x_n))
}\ !\, R, \multimap R
$$

By definition of coherent systems, the sequent

$$!\,Cut(x_1), \ldots, !\,Cut(x_n), B_r, B_l \longrightarrow \perp$$

is provable. The second part is trivial and consists on proving the sequent $\lambda x.\,!\,Cut(x), !\,ACut, atomic(B) \longrightarrow Cut(B)$. ∎

8   Homogeneous Systems

Theorem 1 shows that, for coherent systems, the cut rule can be restricted to the atomic case. A similar problem is that of analyzing when the initial rule can be also restricted to the atomic case. It turns out that duality is not enough for this case.

Example 2. Consider the connective $\diamond(A, B, C)$ with associated rules:

$$\frac{\Gamma \vdash \Delta, A}{\Gamma \vdash \Delta, \diamond(A, B, C)} \;(\diamond R_1) \qquad \frac{\Gamma \vdash \Delta, B \quad \Gamma \vdash \Delta, C}{\Gamma \vdash \diamond(A, B, C)} \;(\diamond R_2)$$

$$\frac{\Gamma, A \vdash \Delta \quad \Gamma, B \vdash \Delta}{\Gamma, \diamond(A, B, C) \vdash \Delta} \;(\diamond L_1) \qquad \frac{\Gamma, A \vdash \Delta \quad \Gamma, C \vdash \Delta}{\Gamma, \diamond(A, B, C) \vdash \Delta} \;(\diamond L_2)$$

These rules can be specified in *Llinda* as:

$$\lceil \diamond(A, B, C) \rceil \triangleq \lceil A \rceil \oplus (\lceil B \rceil \,\&\, \lceil C \rceil) \qquad \lfloor \diamond(A, B, C) \rfloor \triangleq (\lfloor A \rfloor \,\&\, \lfloor B \rfloor) \oplus (\lfloor A \rfloor \,\&\, \lfloor C \rfloor)$$

It is easy to see that $!\,Cut, \lceil A \rceil \oplus (\lceil B \rceil \,\&\, \lceil C \rceil), (\lfloor A \rfloor \,\&\, \lfloor B \rfloor) \oplus (\lfloor A \rfloor \,\&\, \lfloor C \rfloor) \vdash \perp$ holds and hence a system formed with these two defined rules plus *initial* and *cut* is coherent.

However, the sequent $!\,Init \vdash \lceil A \rceil \oplus (\lceil B \rceil \,\&\, \lceil C \rceil), (\lfloor A \rfloor \,\&\, \lfloor B \rfloor) \oplus (\lfloor A \rfloor \,\&\, \lfloor C \rfloor)$ is not provable. This reflects the fact that, at the object-level, the sequent $\diamond(A, B, C) \longrightarrow \diamond(A, B, C)$ has only the trivial proof: the one where the only rule applied is the initial rule. The formula $\diamond(A, B, C)$, hence, cannot be decomposed.

The problem with the system above is that the introduction rules for the connective $\diamond$ are not *homogeneous*, in the sense that their meta-level behavior is captured using connectives of different polarities[2] (see [Gir99] for an object-level discussion on *syntectic connectives*).

Definition 12. *A coherent system is* homogeneous *if all connectives appearing in a body of a defined rule have the same polarity.*

Theorem 2. *Let $\mathcal{P}$ be a coherent system and let* form$(\cdot)$ *be the inductive predicate for object-level formulas. If $\mathcal{P}$ is homogeneous then the following is provable.*

$$\mathcal{P} \;\|\; !\,AInit, form(B) \longrightarrow Init(B)$$

Proof. Let $\mathcal{P}$ be a homogeneous system. Since $\mathcal{P}$ is coherent, it is easy to see that all left and right bodies of defined clauses are dual linear logic formulas. Hence the result follows by structural induction (invariant $\lambda x.\,!\,Init(x)$). ∎

---

[2] Note that, as Example 2 shows, at the meta-level the encoding of dual rules may not be dual linear logic formulas.

9 LU

In [Gir93], Girard introduced the sequent system **LU** (logic of unity) in which classical, intuitionistic, and linear logics appear as fragments. In this logic, all three of these logics keep their own characteristics but they can also communicate via formulas containing connectives mixing these logics. The key to allowing these logics to share one proof system lies in using *polarities*. In terms of the encoding we have presented here, polarities allow the meta-level atom $\lfloor B \rfloor$ be replaced by $?\lfloor B \rfloor$ if B is positive and the meta-level atom $\lceil B \rceil$ be replaced by $?\lceil B \rceil$ if B is negative. This possibility of replacement is in contrast to the examples of classical and intuitionistic sequent proof systems presented earlier where $\lfloor \cdot \rfloor$ and $\lceil \cdot \rceil$ atoms are either all preceded by the ? modal or all are not so prefixed. The neutral polarity is also available and corresponds to the case where this replacement with a ? modal is not allowed. Many of the **LU** inference rules for classical and intuitionistic connectives are specified in Figure 4. The definition of the predicates $pos(\cdot)$, $neg(\cdot)$, and $neu(\cdot)$ can be directly obtained from the various polarity tables given in [Gir93]. These definitions, together with the ones in Figure 5 will be denoted by $\mathcal{P}$.

Proving cut-elimination for **LU** is not at all easy: there are some rules concerning polarities that have an empty head and bodies with an erase function. In this particular case, moving the cut up is not possible for some proofs, and the usual cut-elimination proof doesn't work.

LU is not canonical since the side conditions in its rules require meta-level predicates other than simply $\lfloor \cdot \rfloor$ and $\lceil \cdot \rceil$. On proving cut-elimination for coherent systems, it was essential to restrict the predicates to left and right since the cut rule is a rule about duality of these two predicates. In the case of allowing some other predicates one have to be careful on reasoning about proofs where rules concerning these predicates are applied.

Proposition 4. *The following clauses can be proved in* Llinda

$$\forall B.(pos(B) \Rightarrow neg(B) \Rightarrow 0). \quad \forall B.(pos(B) \Rightarrow neu(B) \Rightarrow 0).$$
$$\forall B.(neg(B) \Rightarrow neu(B) \Rightarrow 0).$$

These clauses play the role of the *Cut* rule on determining the dual predicates for polarities. Let $\mathcal{L}$ be the set of clauses above. The following is easily proved (the proof can be automated in the same way as described in [MP02]).

Proposition 5. *For every connective $\diamond$ of **LU**, if the left and right introduction clauses for $\diamond$ in their definition form are $\forall \bar{x}(\lfloor \diamond(x_1, \ldots, x_i) \rfloor \circ\!\!-\ B_l)$ and $\forall \bar{x}(\lceil \diamond(x_1, \ldots, x_i) \rceil \circ\!\!-\ B_r)$ then*

$$\mathcal{P} \parallel \,! \mathcal{L}, ! \, Init, ! \, Cut, ! \, Pos, ! \, Neg \vdash \forall \bar{x}(B_l \multimap B_r \multimap \bot) \qquad (1)$$

in linear logic, where Neg is the third and Pos the fourth clause in Figure 4.

This suggests that such an entailment might be used as a natural generalization of coherence to this setting. In fact, we have the following results:

$$\text{Identity and structure}$$
$$\lfloor B \rfloor \,\invamp\, \lceil B \rceil. \qquad\qquad \bot \multimap \lfloor B \rfloor \multimap \lceil B \rceil.$$
$$\lceil N \rceil \multimap ?\lceil N \rceil \Leftarrow neg(N). \qquad \lfloor P \rfloor \multimap ?\lfloor P \rfloor \Leftarrow pos(P).$$

Conjunction
$$\lceil A \wedge B \rceil \triangleq\, !\lceil A \rceil \otimes\, !\lceil B \rceil \otimes\, !(pos(A) \oplus pos(B)). \qquad \lceil A \wedge B \rceil \triangleq \lceil A \rceil \,\&\, \lceil B \rceil \otimes\, !(notpos(A) \,\&\, notpos(B)).$$
$$\lfloor A \wedge B \rfloor \triangleq\, ?\lfloor A \rfloor \,\invamp\, ?\lfloor B \rfloor \otimes\, !(pos(A) \oplus pos(B)). \qquad \lfloor A \wedge B \rfloor \triangleq \lfloor A \rfloor \oplus \lfloor B \rfloor \otimes\, !(notpos(A) \,\&\, notpos(B)).$$

$$\text{Intuitionistic implication}$$
$$\lceil A \supset B \rceil \triangleq\, ?\lfloor A \rfloor \,\invamp\, \lceil B \rceil. \qquad\qquad \lfloor A \supset B \rfloor \triangleq\, !\lceil A \rceil \otimes \lfloor B \rfloor.$$

Quantifiers
$$\lceil \forall A \rceil \triangleq \forall x\, ?\lceil Ax \rceil. \qquad\qquad \lfloor \forall A \rfloor \triangleq\, !\lfloor Ax \rfloor.$$
$$\lceil \exists A \rceil \triangleq\, !\lceil Ax \rceil. \qquad\qquad \lfloor \exists A \rfloor \triangleq \forall x\, ?\lfloor Ax \rfloor.$$

Disjunction
$$\lceil A \vee B \rceil \triangleq\, !\lceil A \rceil \oplus\, !\lceil B \rceil \quad \otimes\, !(notneg(A) \,\&\, notneg(B)).$$
$$\lceil A \vee B \rceil \triangleq\, ?\lceil A \rceil \invamp\, ?\lceil B \rceil \quad \otimes\, !((pos(A) \,\&\, neg(B)) \oplus (neg(A) \,\&\, notneu(B))).$$
$$\lceil A \vee B \rceil \triangleq \lceil A \rceil \invamp\, ?\,!\lceil B \rceil \quad \otimes\, !(neg(A) \,\&\, neu(B)).$$
$$\lceil A \vee B \rceil \triangleq\, ?\,!\lceil A \rceil \invamp \lceil B \rceil \quad \otimes\, !(neu(A) \,\&\, neg(B)).$$
$$\lfloor A \vee B \rfloor \triangleq\, ?\lfloor A \rfloor \,\&\, ?\lfloor B \rfloor \quad \otimes\, !(notneg(A) \,\&\, notneg(B)).$$
$$\lfloor A \vee B \rfloor \triangleq\, !\lfloor A \rfloor \otimes\, !\lfloor B \rfloor \quad \otimes\, !((pos(A) \,\&\, neg(B)) \oplus (neg(A) \,\&\, notneu(B))).$$
$$\lfloor A \vee B \rfloor \triangleq \lfloor A \rfloor \otimes\, !\,?\lfloor B \rfloor \quad \otimes\, !(neg(A) \,\&\, neu(B)).$$
$$\lfloor A \vee B \rfloor \triangleq\, !\,?\lfloor A \rfloor \otimes \lfloor B \rfloor \quad \otimes\, !(neu(A) \,\&\, neg(B)).$$

Classical implication
$$\lceil A \Rightarrow B \rceil \triangleq\, ?\lfloor A \rfloor \invamp\, ?\lceil B \rceil \quad \otimes\, !((neg(A) \,\&\, neg(B)) \oplus (pos(A) \,\&\, notneu(B))).$$
$$\lceil A \Rightarrow B \rceil \triangleq \lceil B \rceil \oplus \lfloor A \rfloor \quad \otimes\, !(neg(A) \,\&\, pos(B)).$$
$$\lfloor A \Rightarrow B \rfloor \triangleq \lceil A \rceil \,\&\, \lfloor B \rfloor \quad \otimes\, !(neg(A) \,\&\, pos(B)).$$
$$\lfloor A \Rightarrow B \rfloor \triangleq\, !\lceil A \rceil \otimes\, !\lfloor B \rfloor \quad \otimes\, !((neg(A) \,\&\, neg(B)) \oplus (pos(A) \,\&\, notneu(B))).$$

Fig. 4. LU rules

$$notpos(A) \triangleq (neu(A) \oplus neg(A)). \qquad notneg(A) \triangleq (neu(A) \oplus pos(A)).$$
$$notneu(A) \triangleq (neg(A) \oplus pos(A)).$$

Fig. 5. Polarities

Theorem 3. *Let* **LU** *be the encoding for LU (including the polarity table and definitions in Figure 5). The following is provable in Llinda:*

$$\textbf{LU} \,\|\, !\mathcal{L}, !\,Init, !\,APos, !\,ANeg, !\,ACut \rightarrow Pos \otimes Neg \otimes Cut.$$

Theorem 4. *Let B be the encoding of an object-level LU formula. If*

$$\textbf{LU} \,\|\, !\mathcal{L}, !\,Init, !\,Cut, !\,Pos, !\,Neg \rightarrow B$$

is provable then there is a proof of the same sequent without backchaining over the Cut clause.

10   Conclusion

We have illustrated how object-level sequent calculus proof systems can be encoded into linear logic in such a way that the meta-theory of linear logic helps to establish formal meta-theoretic properties of the object-logic proof system. By strengthening linear logic with a form of induction, much of this meta-theory can be captured entirely in the meta-logic. We illustrated our approach by showing how such a meta-level approach can be used to establish cut-elimination for LU.

References

[And92] J.-M. Andreoli. Logic programming with focusing proofs in linear logic. *Journal of Logic and Computation*, 2(3):297–347, 1992.

[Chu40] A. Church. A formulation of the simple theory of types. *Journal of Symbolic Logic*, 5:56–68, 1940.

[FM88]   A. Felty and D. Miller Specifying theorem provers in a higher-order logic programming language, *Ninth International Conference on Automated Deduction*, 1988.

[Gen69] G. Gentzen. Investigations into logical deductions. In M. E. Szabo, editor, *The Collected Papers of Gerhard Gentzen*, pp. 68–131. North-Holland Publishing Co., Amsterdam, 1969.

[Gir87] J.-Y. Girard. Linear logic. *Theoretical Computer Science*, vol. 50, pp. 1-102, 1987.

[Gir93] J.-Y. Girard. On the unity of logic. *Ann. of Pure and Applied Logic*, 59:201–217, 1993.

[Gir99] J.-Y. Girard. On the meaning of logical rules I: syntax vs. semantics. *Computational Logic*, eds Berger and Schwichtenberg, pp. 215-272, SV, 1999.

[Gug05] A. Guglielmi A system of Interaction and Structure. *ACM Transactions in Computational Logic*, to appear, 2005.

[Har93] R. Harper, F. Honsell, and G. Plotkin A framework for defining logics, *Journal of the ACM*, vol.40(1), pp. 143-184, 1993.

[Mil96] Dale Miller. Forum: A multiple-conclusion specification language. *Theoretical Computer Science*, 165(1):201–232, September 1996.

[MM00]   R. McDowell and D. Miller. Cut-elimination for a logic with definitions and induction. *Theoretical Computer Science*, 232:91–119, 2000.

[MP04]   D. Miller and E. Pimentel. Linear logic as a framework for specifying sequent calculus. *Lecture Notes in Logic 17, Logic Colloquium'99*, 2004.

[MP02]   D. Miller and E. Pimentel. Using linear logic to reason about sequent systems. *Proceedings of Tableaux 2002*, LNAI 2381, 2002.

[NM88]   G. Nadathur and D. Miller. An Overview of λProlog. In *Fifth International Logic Programming Conference*, pp. 810–827, August 1988. MIT Press.

[Pfn89] F. Pfenning. Elf: A Language for Logic Definition and Verified Metaprogramming. *Fourth Annual Symposium on Logic in Computer Science*, 1989.

[Pfn95] F. Pfenning. Structural Cut Elimination. *Proceedings, Tenth Annual IEEE Symposium on Logic in Computer Science*, 1995.

[Pfn00] F. Pfenning. Structural Cut Elimination: I. Intuitionistic and Classical Logic. *Information and Computation*, 157(1-2) pp. 84-141, 2000.

[Pim01] E. G. Pimentel. *Lógica linear e a especificação de sistemas computacionais*. PhD thesis, Universidade Federal de Minas Gerais, Belo Horizonte, M.G., Brasil, December 2001. (written in English).

[Pim05] E. G. Pimentel. *Cut elimination for Llinda*, 2005. Draft available from http://www.mat.ufmg.br/~elaine

[Tiu04] A. Tiu. *A Logical Framework for Reasoning about Logical Specifications*. PhD thesis, Penn State University, 2004.

Verifying and Reflecting Quantifier Elimination for Presburger Arithmetic

Amine Chaieb and Tobias Nipkow

Institut für Informatik,
Technische Universität München

Abstract. We present an implementation and verification in higher-order logic of Cooper's quantifier elimination for Presburger arithmetic. Reflection, i.e. the direct execution in ML, yields a speed-up of a factor of 200 over an LCF-style implementation and performs as well as a decision procedure hand-coded in ML.

1 Introduction

This paper presents a formally verified quantifier elimination procedure for Presburger arithmetic ($\mathcal{P\!A}$) in higher-order logic. There are three approaches to decision procedures in theorem provers: unverified code (which we ignore), *LCF-style* proof procedures programmed in a meta-language (ML) that invoke the inference rules of the kernel, and *reflection*, where the decision procedure is formalized and proved correct inside the system and is executed not by inference but by direct computation.

The LCF-style requires no formalization of the meta-theory but has a number of disadvantages: (a) it requires intimate knowledge of the internals of the underlying theorem prover (which makes it very unportable); (b) there is no way to check at compile type if the proofs will really compose (which easily leads to run time failure and thus incompleteness); (c) it is inefficient because one has to go through the inference rules in the kernel; (d) if the prover is based on proof objects this can lead to excessive space consumption (proofs for $\mathcal{P\!A}$ may require super exponential space [7, 16]).

For all these reasons we have formalized and verified Cooper's quantifier elimination procedure for $\mathcal{P\!A}$ [5]. Our development environment is Isabelle/HOL [14]. An experimental feature allows reflective extensions of the kernel: computations of ML code generated from HOL functions [3] are accepted as equality proofs. Such extensions are sound provided the code generator is correct. Coq uses a fast internal λ-calculus evaluator for the same purpose [8].

We found that reflection leads to a substantial performance improvement. This is especially marked when proof objects [2] are involved: reflective subproofs are of constant size, which is particularly important for proof carrying code applications, where the size of full $\mathcal{P\!A}$ proofs is prohibitive.

The main contributions of our work are: (a) the first-time formalization and verification of Cooper's decision procedure in a theorem prover; (b) the most

G. Sutcliffe and A. Voronkov (Eds.): LPAR 2005, LNAI 3835, pp. 367–380, 2005.

substantial (5000 lines) application of reflection in any theorem prover to date (as far as we are aware); (c) a formalization that is easily portable to other theorem provers supporting reflection (in contrast to LCF-tactics); (d) performance figures that show a speed-up of up to 200 w.r.t. a comparable LCF-style implementation; (e) a first demonstration of reflection in Isabelle/HOL. We also provide a nice example of how reflection allows to formalize duality/symmetry arguments based on syntax (function mirror in 4.2).

Related Work. $\mathcal{PA}$ has first been proven decidable by Presburger [17] whose (inefficient) algorithm was improved by Cooper [5]. Harrison [12] implemented Cooper's procedure as an oracle as well as partially reflected in HOL Light. In [4] we presented an LCF-style implementation of Cooper's algorithm for $\mathcal{PA}$, which is our point of reference. Harrison [10] has also studied the general issue of reflection in LCF-like theorem provers and bemoans the lack of a natural example where reflection yields a speed-up of more than a constant factor. This is true for $\mathcal{PA}$ as well, but a constant factor of 200 over an LCF-style tactic is worth it. Norrish [15] discusses implementations for both Cooper's algorithm (in tatic style) and Omega [18] (checking a reflected "proof trace"). Pierre Crgut [6] presents a reflective version of the Omega test written for Coq, where an optimized proof trace is interpreted to solve the goal. Unlike the other references his implementation only deals with quantifier-free $\mathcal{PA}$ and is incomplete. Presburger's original algorithm has been formalized in Coq by Laurent Thry and is available on the Coq web site.

The problem of programming errors in decision procedures has recently been addressed by several authors using dependent types [13, 1]. But it seems unlikely that anything as complex as $\mathcal{PA}$ can be dealt with automatically in such a framework. Nor does this approach guarantee completeness: missing cases and local proofs that fail are not detected.

Notation. Datatypes are declared using datatype. Lists are built up from the empty list [] and consing ·; the infix @ appends two lists. For a list l, $\{l\}$ denotes the set of elements of l, and $l!n$ denotes its nth element. The data type α option with the constructors $\perp : \alpha$ option and $\lfloor . \rfloor : \alpha \to \alpha$ option models computations that can fail.

The rest of this paper is structured as follows. In 2 we give a brief overview of reflection. The actual decision procedure and its verification is presented in 3 and 4. In 5 we discuss some design decisions and alternatives. Performance results are shown in 6.

2 Reflection

2.1 An Informal Introduction

Reflection means to perform a proof step by computation inside the logic. However, inside the logic it is not possible to write functions by pattern matching over the syntax of terms or formulae because two syntactically distinct formulae may be logically equivalent. Hence the relevant fragment of formulae must be represented (*reflected*) inside the logic as a datatype, sometimes also called the *shadow syntax* [11]. Let us call this type *rep*, the representation.

Then there are two functions: *interp*, a function in the logic, maps an element of *rep* to the formula it represents; *convert*, an ML function, maps a formula to its representation. The two functions should be inverses of each other: taking the ML representation of a formula P and applying *convert* to it yields an ML representation of a term p of type *rep* such that the theorem *interp* $p = P$ can be proved by by rewriting with the equations for *interp*.

Typically, the formalized proof step is some equivalence $P = P'$ where P is given and P' is some simplified version of P (e.g. the elimination of a quantifier). This transformation is now expressed as a recursive function *simp* of type $rep \to rep$ and it is proved (typically by induction on *rep*) that *simp* preserves the interpretation:

$$interp\ p = interp(simp\ p).$$

To apply this theorem to a given formula P we compute (in ML) $p = convert\ P$, substitute it into our theorem, and compute the value P' of $interp(simp\ p)$. The latter step should be done as efficiently as possibly. In our case it is performed by an ML computation using the code automatically generated from the defining equations for *simp* and *interp*. This yields the theorem $interp(simp\ p) = P'$. Combining it (by symmetry and transitivity) with *interp* $p = P$ and $interp\ p = interp(simp\ p)$ we obtain the theorem $P = P'$.

2.2   Reflection of $\mathcal{PA}$

$\mathcal{PA}$ is reflected as follows. The syntax is represented by the data types ι for integer expressions and ϕ for formulae.

$$\text{datatype } \iota = \widehat{int} \mid v_{nat} \mid -\iota \mid \iota + \iota \mid \iota - \iota \mid \iota * \iota$$
$$\text{datatype } \phi = \iota < \iota \mid \iota > \iota \mid \iota \leq \iota \mid \iota \geq \iota \mid \iota = \iota \mid \iota \text{ } \mathbf{dvd} \text{ } \iota$$
$$\mid \mathbf{T} \mid \mathbf{F} \mid \neg\ \phi \mid \phi \wedge \phi \mid \phi \vee \phi \mid \phi \to \phi \mid \phi = \phi \mid \exists\ \phi \mid \forall\ \phi$$

The bold symbols $\mathbf{+}$, $\mathbf{\leq}$, $\mathbf{\wedge}$ etc are constructors and reflect their counterparts $+$, $\leq$, $\wedge$ etc in the logic. The integer constant i in the logic is represented by the term $\hat{\imath}$. Bound variables are represented by de Bruijn indices: v_n represents the bound variable with index n (a natural number). Hence quantifiers need not carry variable names.

Throughout the paper p and q are of type ϕ.

The interpretation functions ($[\![.]\!]_\iota$ and $[\![.]\!]^{\cdot}$) in Fig. 1 map the representations back into logic. They are parameterized by an environment *is* which is a list of integer expressions. The de Bruijn index v_n picks out the nth element from that list.

The definition of ι-terms is too liberal since it allows to express nonlinear terms. Hence we will impose conditions during verification which guarantee that terms have certain syntactic shapes.

$$
\begin{aligned}
[\![i]\!]_\iota^{is} &= i \\
[\![v_n]\!]_\iota^{is} &= is!n \\
[\![-a]\!]_\iota^{is} &= -[\![a]\!]_\iota^{is} \\
[\![a+b]\!]_\iota^{is} &= [\![a]\!]_\iota^{is} + [\![b]\!]_\iota^{is} \\
[\![a-b]\!]_\iota^{is} &= [\![a]\!]_\iota^{is} - [\![b]\!]_\iota^{is} \\
[\![a*b]\!]_\iota^{is} &= [\![a]\!]_\iota^{is} \cdot [\![b]\!]_\iota^{is}
\end{aligned}
\qquad
\begin{aligned}
[\![\boldsymbol{T}]\!]^{is} &= True \\
[\![\boldsymbol{F}]\!]^{is} &= False \\
[\![a < b]\!]^{is} &= ([\![a]\!]_\iota^{is} < [\![b]\!]_\iota^{is}) \\
[\![a > b]\!]^{is} &= ([\![a]\!]_\iota^{is} > [\![b]\!]_\iota^{is}) \\
[\![a \le b]\!]^{is} &= ([\![a]\!]_\iota^{is} \le [\![b]\!]_\iota^{is}) \\
[\![a \ge b]\!]^{is} &= ([\![a]\!]_\iota^{is} \ge [\![b]\!]_\iota^{is}) \\
[\![a = b]\!]^{is} &= ([\![a]\!]_\iota^{is} = [\![b]\!]_\iota^{is})
\end{aligned}
\qquad
\begin{aligned}
[\![\neg p]\!]^{is} &= (\neg [\![p]\!]^{is}) \\
[\![p \wedge q]\!]^{is} &= ([\![p]\!]^{is} \wedge [\![q]\!]^{is}) \\
[\![p \vee q]\!]^{is} &= ([\![p]\!]^{is} \vee [\![q]\!]^{is}) \\
[\![p \to q]\!]^{is} &= ([\![p]\!]^{is} \to [\![q]\!]^{is}) \\
[\![p = q]\!]^{is} &= ([\![p]\!]^{is} = [\![q]\!]^{is}) \\
[\![\exists\, p]\!]^{is} &= (\exists x.[\![p]\!]^{x \cdot is}) \\
[\![\forall\, p]\!]^{is} &= (\forall x.[\![p]\!]^{x \cdot is})
\end{aligned}
$$

Fig. 1. Semantics of the shadow syntax

3 Quantifier Elimination

A generic quantifier elimination function is implemented by qelim_ϕ (Fig. 2). Its parameter qe is supposed to eliminate a single $\exists$ and qelim_ϕ applies qe to all quantified subformulae in a bottom-up fashion. We allow quantifier elimination to fail, i.e. return $\bot$. This is necessary in case the input formula is not linear, i.e. involves multiplication by more than just a constant. To deal with failure we define two combinators for lifting arbitrary $n$ary functions f to $f^\bot$ and $f_\bot$:

$$
\begin{aligned}
f^\bot \lfloor x_1 \rfloor \ \dots \ \lfloor x_n \rfloor &= f\, x_1 \ \dots \ x_n \\
f_\bot \lfloor x_1 \rfloor \ \dots \ \lfloor x_n \rfloor &= \lfloor f\, x_1 \ \dots \ x_n \rfloor
\end{aligned}
$$

If any of the arguments are $\bot$, $f^\bot$ and $f_\bot$ return $\bot$.

Let $\mathsf{qfree}\, p$ (not shown) formalize that p is quantifier-free. We can prove by structural induction that if qe takes a quantifier-free formula q and returns a quantifier-free formula q' equivalent to $\exists\, q$, then $\mathsf{qelim}_\phi\, qe$ is a quantifier-elimination procedure:

$$
\begin{aligned}
(\forall q, q', is.\ \mathsf{qfree}\, q \wedge qe\, q = \lfloor q' \rfloor \to \mathsf{qfree}\, q' \wedge [\![\exists\, q]\!]^{is} = [\![q']\!]^{is}) \\
\to \mathsf{qelim}_\phi\, qe\, p = \lfloor p' \rfloor \to \mathsf{qfree}\, p' \wedge [\![p]\!]^{is} = [\![p']\!]^{is}.
\end{aligned}
\tag{1}
$$

Note that qe must eliminate the innermost bound variable v_0, otherwise $[\![\exists\, q]\!]^{is} = [\![q']\!]^{is}$ will not hold.

The goal of 4 is to present cooper, an instance of qe fulfilling the premise of (1).

$$
\begin{aligned}
\mathsf{qelim}_\phi\, qe\, (\forall\, p) &= \neg_\bot(qe^\bot(\neg_\bot(\mathsf{qelim}_\phi\, qe\, p))) \\
\mathsf{qelim}_\phi\, qe\, (\exists\, p) &= qe^\bot(\mathsf{qelim}_\phi\, qe\, p) \\
\mathsf{qelim}_\phi\, qe\, (p \wedge q) &= (\mathsf{qelim}_\phi\, qe\, p) \wedge_\bot (\mathsf{qelim}_\phi\, qe\, p) \\
\mathsf{qelim}_\phi\, qe\, (p \vee q) &= (\mathsf{qelim}_\phi\, qe\, p) \vee_\bot (\mathsf{qelim}_\phi\, qe\, p) \\
\mathsf{qelim}_\phi\, qe\, (p \to q) &= (\mathsf{qelim}_\phi\, qe\, p) \to_\bot (\mathsf{qelim}_\phi\, qe\, p) \\
\mathsf{qelim}_\phi\, qe\, (p = q) &= (\mathsf{qelim}_\phi\, qe\, p) =_\bot (\mathsf{qelim}_\phi\, qe\, p) \\
\mathsf{qelim}_\phi\, qe\, p &= \lfloor p \rfloor
\end{aligned}
$$

Fig. 2. Quantifier elimination for ϕ-formulae

4   Cooper's Algorithm

Like many decision procedures, Cooper's algorithm [5] for eliminating one $\exists$ follows a simple scheme:

- Normalization of input formula (4.1).
- Calculation of some characteristic data from the formula (4.2).
- Correctness theorem proving that $\exists\, p$ is semantically equivalent to a simpler formula p' involving the data from the previous step (Cooper's theorem in 4.3).
- Construction of p' (4.4).

4.1   Normalization

Normalization goes trough three steps: the N-step puts the formula into NNF (negation normal form), the L-step linearizes the formula and the U-step sets the coefficients of v_0 to $\widehat{1}$ or $\widehat{-1}$.

The N-Step. We omit the straightforward implementation of nnf : $\phi \to \phi$ and isnnf : $\phi \to bool$. Property isnnf p expresses that p is in NNF and that all atoms are among $\leq$, $=$ and **dvd** and that negations only occur in front of **dvd** or $=$. We prove that nnf is correct and that it implies quantifier-freedom:

$$\llbracket p \rrbracket^{is} = \llbracket \text{nnf } p \rrbracket^{is} \qquad \text{isnnf(nnf } p) \qquad \text{isnnf } p \to \text{qfree } p$$

The L-Step. An ι-term t is *linear* if it has the form

$$\widehat{c_1} * v_{i_1} + \cdots + \widehat{c_n} * v_{i_n} + \widehat{c_{n+1}}$$

where $n \in \mathbb{N}, i_1 < \cdots < i_n$ and $\forall j \leq n.c_j \neq 0$. Note that $\widehat{c_{n+1}}$ is always present even if $c_{n+1} = 0$. The implementation is easy:

$$
\begin{array}{lll}
\text{islinn}_\iota\ n_0\ \widehat{i} & = & True \\
\text{islinn}_\iota\ n_0\ (\widehat{i} * v_n + r) & = & i \neq 0 \wedge n_0 \leq n \wedge \text{islinn}_\iota\ (n+1)\ r \\
\text{islinn}_\iota\ n_0\ t & = & False \\
\text{islin}_\iota\ t & = & \text{islinn}_\iota\ 0\ t
\end{array}
$$

A formula p is *linear* (islin$_\phi$ p) if it is in NNF, all ι-terms occurring in it are linear, and its atoms are of the form $t \leq \widehat{0}$, $t = \widehat{0}$ or $\widehat{d}$ **dvd** t where $d \neq 0$. The formal definition is omitted.

The goal of the L-step is to transform a formula into an equivalent linear one. Due to the unrestricted use of $*$ in the input syntax ι this may fail. Function lin$_\iota$ (Fig. 3) tries to linearize an ι-term using lin$_+$, lin$_*$ and lin$_-$. These operate on linear ι-terms, preserve linearity and behave semantically like addition, multiplication by a constant integer and multiplication by -1, respectively. This is expressed by the following theorems provable by induction:

$\mathsf{lin}_+ \ (\widehat{k} * v_n + r) \ (\widehat{l} * v_m + s) =$
if $n = m$ **then**
   if $k + l = 0$ **then** $\mathsf{lin}_+ \ r \ s$ **else** $\widehat{k+l} * v_n + \mathsf{lin}_+ \ r \ s$
  else if $n \leq m$ **then** $\widehat{k} * v_n + \mathsf{lin}_+ \ r \ (\widehat{l} * v_m + s)$
   else $\widehat{l} * v_m + \mathsf{lin}_+ \ (\widehat{k} * v_n + r) \ s$
$\mathsf{lin}_+ \ (\widehat{k} * v_n + r) \ \widehat{b} = \widehat{k} * v_n + \mathsf{lin}_+ \ r \ \widehat{b}$
$\mathsf{lin}_+ \ \widehat{a} \ (\widehat{l} * v_n + s) = \widehat{l} * v_n + \mathsf{lin}_+ \ s \ \widehat{a}$
$\mathsf{lin}_+ \ \widehat{k} \ \widehat{l} = \widehat{k+l}$

$\mathsf{lin}_\iota \ \widehat{c} = \lfloor \widehat{c} \rfloor$
$\mathsf{lin}_\iota \ v_n = \lfloor (\widehat{1} * v_n + \widehat{0}) \rfloor$
$\mathsf{lin}_\iota \ (-\ a) = \mathsf{lin}_{-\perp}(\mathsf{lin}_\iota \ a)$
$\mathsf{lin}_\iota \ (a + b) = \mathsf{lin}_{+\perp}(\mathsf{lin}_\iota \ a) \ (\mathsf{lin}_\iota \ b)$
$\mathsf{lin}_\iota \ (a - b) = \mathsf{lin}_{+\perp}(\mathsf{lin}_\iota \ a) \ (\mathsf{lin}_\iota \ (-\ b))$
$\mathsf{lin}_\iota \ (a * b) =$
case $(\mathsf{lin}_\iota \ a, \mathsf{lin}_\iota \ b)$ **of**
  $(\lfloor \widehat{c} \rfloor, \lfloor b' \rfloor) \Rightarrow \lfloor \mathsf{lin}_* \ c \ b' \rfloor$
  $(\lfloor a' \rfloor, \lfloor \widehat{c} \rfloor) \Rightarrow \lfloor \mathsf{lin}_* \ c \ a' \rfloor$
  $(x, y) \Rightarrow \perp$

Fig. 3. linearization of ι-terms

$$\mathsf{islin}_\iota \ a \wedge \mathsf{islin}_\iota \ b \rightarrow \mathsf{islin}_\iota(\mathsf{lin}_+ \ a \ b) \wedge ([\![\mathsf{lin}_+ \ a \ b]\!]_\iota^{is} = [\![a + b]\!]_\iota^{is})$$
$$\mathsf{islin}_\iota \ a \rightarrow \mathsf{islin}_\iota(\mathsf{lin}_* \ i \ a) \wedge ([\![\mathsf{lin}_* \ i \ a]\!]_\iota^{is} = [\![\widehat{i} * a]\!]_\iota^{is})$$
$$\mathsf{islin}_\iota \ a \rightarrow \mathsf{islin}_\iota(\mathsf{lin}_- \ a) \wedge ([\![\mathsf{lin}_- \ a]\!]_\iota^{is} = [\![-\ a]\!]_\iota^{is})$$

The implementations of lin_* and lin_- are omitted for space limitations.

Linearization of ϕ-formulae (lin_ϕ, not shown) lifts lin_ι. We have proved that it also preserves semantics and linearizes its input:

$$\mathsf{isnnf} \ p \wedge \mathsf{lin}_\phi \ p = \lfloor p' \rfloor \ \rightarrow \ [\![p]\!]^{is} = [\![p']\!]^{is} \wedge \mathsf{islin}_\phi \ p'$$

Since full linearization is not really part of Presburger arithmetic, we keep matters simple and do not try to cancel arbitrary monomials: $\mathsf{lin}_\iota(v_0 * v_0 - v_0 * v_0) = \perp$ although one could also return $\lfloor \widehat{0} \rfloor$. Such simplifications could be performed by a specialized algebraic preprocessor.

The U-Step. The key idea in this step is to multiply the terms occurring in atoms by appropriate constants such that the (absolute values of) coefficients of v_0 are the same everywhere, e.g. the *lcm* of all coefficients of v_0. The equivalence

$$(\exists x. \ P(l \cdot x)) = (\exists x. \ l \ \mathsf{dvd} \ x \wedge P(x)). \tag{2}$$

will allow us to obtain a formula where all coefficients of v_0 are $\widehat{1}$ or $\widehat{-1}$. Function lcm_ϕ takes a formula p and computes $lcm\{c \mid \widehat{c} * v_0 \text{ occurs in } p\}$. Predicate $\mathsf{alldvd} \ l \ p$ checks if all coefficients of v_0 in p divide l. Both functions are defined in the following table where lcm computes the positive least common multiple of two integers.

p	$\mathsf{lcm}_\phi\ p$	$\mathsf{alldvd}\ l\ p$
$\widehat{c} * v_0 + r \leq \widehat{z}$	$\lvert c \rvert$	$c\ \mathbf{dvd}\ l$
$\widehat{c} * v_0 + r = \widehat{z}$	$\lvert c \rvert$	$c\ \mathbf{dvd}\ l$
$\widehat{d}\ \mathbf{dvd}\ \widehat{c} * v_0 + r$	$\lvert c \rvert$	$c\ \mathbf{dvd}\ l$
$\neg p$	$\mathsf{lcm}_\phi\ p$	$\mathsf{alldvd}\ l\ p$
$p \wedge q$	$\mathsf{lcm}\ (\mathsf{lcm}_\phi\ p)\ (\mathsf{lcm}_\phi\ q)$	$(\mathsf{alldvd}\ l\ p) \wedge (\mathsf{alldvd}\ l\ q)$
$p \vee q$	$\mathsf{lcm}\ (\mathsf{lcm}_\phi\ p)\ (\mathsf{lcm}_\phi\ q)$	$(\mathsf{alldvd}\ l\ p) \wedge (\mathsf{alldvd}\ l\ q)$
$-$	1	$True$

The correctness of these functions is expressed by the following theorem:

$$\mathsf{islin}_\phi\ p \;\rightarrow\; \mathsf{alldvd}\ (\mathsf{lcm}_\phi\ p)\ p \wedge \mathsf{lcm}_\phi\ p > 0$$

The main part of the U-step is done by the function adjust. It takes a positive integer l and a linear formula p (assuming that $\mathsf{alldvd}\ l\ p$ holds) and produces a linear formula p' s.t. the coefficients of v_0 are set to either $\widehat{1}$ or $\widehat{-1}$. Function unity performs the U-step:

> unity $p =$
> **let** $l = \mathsf{lcm}_\phi\ p$; $p' = \mathsf{adjust}\ l\ p$ **in**
> **if** $l = 1$ **then** p' **else** $(\widehat{l}\ \mathbf{dvd}\ \widehat{1} * v_0 + \widehat{0}) \wedge p'$

The resulting formula is said to be unified (unified p'). We omit the definition of adjust and unified. Note that unified $p \rightarrow \mathsf{islin}_\phi\ p$. We can prove that adjust preserves semantics and its result is unified

$$\mathsf{islin}_\phi\ p \wedge \mathsf{alldvd}\ l\ p \wedge l > 0 \rightarrow$$
$$[\![p]\!]^{i \cdot is} = [\![\mathsf{adjust}\ l\ p]\!]^{(l \cdot i) \cdot is} \wedge \mathsf{unified}(\mathsf{adjust}\ l\ p)$$

and with (2) the correctness of unity follows:

$$\mathsf{islin}_\phi\ p \;\rightarrow\; [\![\exists\ p]\!]^{is} = [\![\exists\ (\mathsf{unity}\ p)]\!]^{is} \wedge \mathsf{unified}(\mathsf{unity}\ p) \qquad (3)$$

4.2   Calculation

In the next subsection we need to compute for a given p a pair of a set (represented as a list) of coeffcients in p and a modified version of p. More precisely, we need to compute $(\mathsf{bset}\ p, p_-)$ or $(\mathsf{aset}\ p, p_+)$, which are dual to each other. Fig. 4 shows how to perform these computations recursively and it should be seen as the definition of four functions bset, aset, minusinf and plusinf. We use p_- and p_+ as shorthands for minusinf p and plusinf p. Before we start proving properties about bset and minusinf we formalize the duality between $(\mathsf{bset}\ p, p_-)$ and $(\mathsf{aset}\ p, p_+)$. Theorems about bset and minusinf will then yield theorems about aset and plusinf. Syntactically the duality is expressed by the function mirror (Fig. 5) which negates all coefficients of v_0. The following intuitive relationships between a formula and its mirrored version can be proved:

$$\mathsf{unified}\ p \;\rightarrow\; [\![p]\!]^{i \cdot is} = [\![\mathsf{mirror}\ p]\!]^{(-i) \cdot is} \wedge \mathsf{unified}\ (\mathsf{mirror}\ p)$$
$$[\![\exists\ p]\!]^{is} = [\![\exists\ (\mathsf{mirror}\ p)]\!]^{is} \qquad (4)$$

p	aset p	bset p	p_-	p_+
$q \wedge r$	aset q @ aset r	bset q @ bset r	$q_- \wedge r_-$	$q_+ \wedge r_+$
$q \vee r$	aset q @ aset r	bset q @ bset r	$q_- \vee r_-$	$q_+ \vee r_+$
$\widehat{1} * v_0 + a \leq \widehat{0}$	$[-a, -a+\widehat{1}]$	$[-a-\widehat{1}]$	F	T
$\widehat{-1} * v_0 + a \leq \widehat{0}$	$[a - \widehat{1}]$	$[a, a - \widehat{1}]$	T	F
$\widehat{1} * v_0 + a = \widehat{0}$	$[-a+\widehat{1}]$	$[-a-\widehat{1}]$	F	F
$\widehat{-1} * v_0 + a = \widehat{0}$	$[a+\widehat{1}]$	$[a-\widehat{1}]$	F	F
$\neg\,\widehat{1} * v_0 + a = \widehat{0}$	$[-a]$	$[-a]$	T	T
$\neg\,\widehat{-1} * v_0 + a = \widehat{0}$	$[a]$	$[a]$	T	T
$-$	$[]$	$[]$	p	p

Fig. 4. Definition of aset p, bset p, p_- and p_+

$$\text{mirror } (\widehat{c} * v_0 + r \leq \widehat{z}) \quad = \quad (\widehat{-c} * v_0 + r \leq \widehat{z})$$
$$\text{mirror } (\widehat{c} * v_0 + r = \widehat{z}) \quad = \quad (\widehat{-c} * v_0 + r = \widehat{z})$$
$$\text{mirror } (\widehat{d} \text{ dvd } \widehat{c} * v_0 + r) \quad = \quad (\widehat{d} \text{ dvd } \widehat{-c} * v_0 + r)$$
$$\text{mirror } (\neg\widehat{d} \text{ dvd } \widehat{c} * v_0 + r) \quad = \quad (\neg\widehat{d} \text{ dvd } \widehat{-c} * v_0 + r)$$
$$\text{mirror } (\neg\widehat{c} * v_0 + r = \widehat{z}) \quad = \quad (\neg\widehat{-c} * v_0 + r \leq \widehat{z})$$
$$\text{mirror } (p \wedge q) \quad = \quad (\text{mirror } l\ p) \wedge (\text{mirror } l\ q)$$
$$\text{mirror } (p \vee q) \quad = \quad (\text{mirror } l\ p) \wedge (\text{mirror } l\ q)$$
$$\text{mirror } p \quad = \quad p$$

Fig. 5. Mirroring a formula

Furthermore we have the following dualities:

$$\text{islin}_\phi\ p \to [\![\text{plusinf } p]\!]^{i \cdot is} = [\![\text{minusinf}(\text{mirror } p)]\!]^{(-i) \cdot is}$$
$$\text{unified } p \to \text{aset } p = \text{map lin}_-\ (\text{bset (mirror } p)) \tag{5}$$

We will also need to compute $\delta_p = lcm\{d \mid \widehat{d} \text{ dvd } \widehat{c} * v_0 + r$ occurs in $p\}$. Its definition is very similar to that of $lcm_\phi\ p$. Finally let the predicate $\text{alldvd}_{\textbf{dvd}}\ l\ p$ be the analogue of alldvd $l\ p$ which ensures $\text{islin}_\phi\ p \to \text{alldvd}_{\textbf{dvd}}\ \delta_p\ p$. The definition of both functions is obvious and omitted.

4.3 Cooper's Theorem

Our proof sketch of Cooper's theorem (10) follows [15]. The conclusion of Cooper's theorem is of the form $A = (B \vee C)$ and we prove $B \to A$, $C \to A$ and $A \wedge B \to C$. We first prove (by induction on p) that any unified p behaves exactly like minusinf p for values that are small enough, cf. (6), and that this behaviour is periodic, cf. (7).

$$\text{unified } p \to \exists z. \forall x. x < z \to ([\![p]\!]^{x \cdot is} = [\![\text{minusinf } p]\!]^{x \cdot is}) \tag{6}$$
$$\text{unified } p \to \forall x, k. [\![\text{minusinf } p]\!]^{x \cdot is} = [\![\text{minusinf } p]\!]^{(x - k \cdot \delta_p) \cdot is} \tag{7}$$

Using (6) and (7) we can prove the first implication (8), i.e. any witness j for p_- provides a witness for p. According to (7) we can keep on decreasing j by δ until we reach the limit z of (6). This proof is based on induction over integers bounded from above. Note also that (8) holds for all d.

$$\text{unified } p \wedge (\exists j \in \{1..d\}.\llbracket \text{minusinf } p \rrbracket^{j \cdot js}) \rightarrow \llbracket \exists\, p \rrbracket^{js} \tag{8}$$

The second implication is trivial: given $b \in \{\!\{\text{bset } p\}\!\}$ and $j \in \{1..\delta_p\}$ such that $\llbracket p \rrbracket^{\llbracket i \cdot is \rrbracket_\iota^b + j}$ we have a witness for p. If there is no such b and j then p behaves periodically and hence any witness for p must be a witness for p_-. Hence (9) proves with (6) and (7) the last implication and Cooper's theorem (10) follows directly using (8).

$$\begin{aligned}\text{unified } p \rightarrow \forall x.(\exists j \in \{\!\{1..\delta_p\}\!\}.\exists b \in \{\!\{\text{bset } p\}\!\}.\llbracket p \rrbracket^{(\llbracket b \rrbracket_\iota^{i \cdot is} + j) \cdot is}) \\ \rightarrow \llbracket p \rrbracket^{x \cdot is} \rightarrow \llbracket p \rrbracket^{(x - \delta_p) \cdot is}\end{aligned} \tag{9}$$

$$\begin{aligned}\text{unified } p \rightarrow (\llbracket \exists\, p \rrbracket^{is} = ((\exists j \in \{1..\delta_p\}.\llbracket \text{minusinf } p \rrbracket^{j \cdot is}) \vee \\ (\exists j \in \{1..\delta_p\}.\exists b \in \{\!\{\text{bset } p\}\!\}.\llbracket p \rrbracket^{(\llbracket b \rrbracket_\iota^{i \cdot is} + j) \cdot is})))\end{aligned} \tag{10}$$

This expresses that an existential quantifier is equivalent with a finite disjunction. The latter is still expressed with existential quantifiers, but we will now replace them by executable functions.

4.4   The Decision Procedure

In order to compute the rhs of Cooper's theorem (10) we need substitution for v_0 in ι-terms (subst_ι) and ϕ-formulae (subst_ϕ) such that

$$\llbracket \text{subst}_\iota\ r\ t \rrbracket_\iota^{i \cdot is} = \llbracket t \rrbracket_\iota^{\llbracket r \rrbracket_\iota^{i \cdot is} \cdot is}$$
$$\llbracket \text{subst}_\phi\ r\ p \rrbracket^{i \cdot is} = \llbracket p \rrbracket^{\llbracket r \rrbracket_\iota^{i \cdot is} \cdot is}$$

Let $\text{nov0}_\iota\ t$ and $\text{nov0}_\phi\ p$ express that v_0 does not occur in t and p, and let $\text{decr}_\iota\ t$ and $\text{decr}_\phi\ p$ denote t and p where all variable indices are decremented by one. The implementation of subst_ι, subst_ϕ, nov0_ι, nov0_ϕ, decr_ι and decr_ϕ is simple and omitted. The following properties are easy:

$$\text{nov0}_\iota\ t \rightarrow \text{nov0}_\iota\ (\text{subst}_\iota\ t\ r) \wedge \text{nov0}_\phi\ (\text{subst}_\phi\ t\ p)$$
$$\text{nov0}_\iota\ t \rightarrow \llbracket t \rrbracket_\iota^{i \cdot is} = \llbracket \text{decr}_\iota\ t \rrbracket_\iota^{is}$$
$$\text{nov0}_\phi\ p \rightarrow \llbracket p \rrbracket^{i \cdot is} = \llbracket \text{decr}_\phi\ p \rrbracket^{is}$$

To generate the disjunction $\bigvee_{t \in \{\!\{ts\}\!\}} \text{subst}_\phi\ t\ p$ we use $\text{explode}_\vee\ ts\ p$ (Fig. 6). Function simp evaluates ground atoms and performs simple propositionsal simplifications. We prove

$$\begin{aligned}\text{qfree } p \wedge (\forall t \in \{\!\{ts\}\!\}.\text{nov0}_\iota\ t) \rightarrow \\ \text{nov0}_\phi(\text{explode}_\vee\ ts\ p) \wedge (\exists t \in \{\!\{ts\}\!\}.\llbracket \text{subst}_\phi\ t\ p \rrbracket^{i \cdot is} = \llbracket \text{explode}_\vee\ ts\ p \rrbracket^{i \cdot is})\end{aligned}$$

$\mathsf{explode}_\lor\ [] \ p = \pmb{F}$
$\mathsf{explode}_\lor\ (i \cdot is)\ p =$
$\mathbf{case}\ (\mathsf{simp}\ (\mathsf{subst}_\phi\ i\ p), \mathsf{explode}_\lor\ is\ p)\ \mathbf{of}$
$\quad (\pmb{T}, \_) \Rightarrow \pmb{T}$
$\quad (\pmb{F}, p_{is}) \Rightarrow p_{is}$
$\quad (\_, \pmb{T}) \Rightarrow \pmb{T}$
$\quad (p_i, \pmb{F}) \Rightarrow p_i$
$\quad (p_i, p_{is}) \Rightarrow p_i \lor p_{is}$

Fig. 6. Generate disjunctions

$\mathsf{explode}_{-\infty}\ (p, B) =$
$\mathbf{case}\ (\mathsf{explode}_\lor\ [\widehat{1} .. \widehat{\delta_p}]\ p_-, \mathsf{explode}_\lor\ (\mathsf{all}_+\ \delta_p\ B)\ p)\ \mathbf{of}$
$\quad (\pmb{T}, \_) \Rightarrow \pmb{T}$
$\quad (\pmb{F}, r_2) \Rightarrow r_2$
$\quad (r_1, \pmb{T}) \Rightarrow \pmb{T}$
$\quad (r_1, \pmb{F}) \Rightarrow r_1$
$\quad (r_1, r_2) \Rightarrow r_1 \lor r_2$

$\mathsf{all}_+\ d\ [] = []$
$\mathsf{all}_+\ d\ (i \cdot is) = (\mathsf{map}\ (\mathsf{lin}_+\ i)\ [\widehat{1} .. \widehat{d}])\ @\ (\mathsf{all}_+\ d\ is)$

Fig. 7. The rhs of Cooper's theorem

$\mathsf{unify}\ p =$
$\mathbf{let}\ q = \mathsf{unity}\ p\ ;\ (A, B) = (\mathsf{remdups}\ \mathsf{aset}\ q, \mathsf{remdups}\ \mathsf{bset}\ q)$
$\mathbf{in\ if}\ |B| \leq |A|\ \mathbf{then}\ (q, B)\ \mathbf{else}\ (\mathsf{mirror}\ q, A)$

$\mathsf{cooper}\ p = (\lambda f.\mathsf{decr}_\phi(\mathsf{explode}_{-\infty}\ (\mathsf{unify}\ f)))_\perp\ (\mathsf{lin}_\phi\ (\mathsf{nnf}\ p))$

$\mathsf{pa} = \mathsf{qelim}_\phi\ \mathsf{cooper}$

Fig. 8. The decision procedure for linearizable ϕ-formulae

We implement $\mathsf{explode}_{-\infty}$ (Fig. 7) and prove that it computes the right hand side of Cooper's theorem, cf. (11). It uses $\mathsf{all}_+\ d\ ts$ to generate all the sums of an element of $\{\!\{ts\}\!\}$ and of some $\widehat{i}$ where $1 \leq i \leq d$, cf. (12).

$$\mathsf{unified}\ p \land \{\!\{B\}\!\} = \{\!\{\mathsf{bset}\ p\}\!\}$$
$$\rightarrow ([\![\exists\ p]\!]^{is} = [\![\mathsf{decr}_\phi(\mathsf{explode}_{-\infty}\ (p, B))]\!]^{is}) \tag{11}$$
$$\exists i \in \{1..d\}.\exists b \in \{\!\{ts\}\!\}.P(\mathsf{lin}_+\ b\ \widehat{i}) = \exists t \in \{\!\{\mathsf{all}_+\ d\ ts\}\!\}.P\ t \tag{12}$$

Let us now look at the implementation of the decision procedure in Fig. 8. Function unify performs the U-step but also prepares the application of Cooper's theorem. For efficiency, both aset and bset are computed. Depending on their size, either the unified term and its bset or the mirrored version and its aset are passed to $\text{explode}_{-\infty}$ to compute the rhs of Cooper's theorem. Function cooper composes all the normalization steps, the elimination of v_0 by unify, and the decrementation of the remaining de Bruijn indices. Function pa applies generic quantifier elimination to Cooper's algorithm.

Using (3), (4) and (5) we can prove

$$\text{islin}_\phi\ p \wedge \text{unify}\ p = (q, B) \rightarrow$$
$$[\![\exists\ p]\!]^{is} = [\![\exists\ q]\!]^{is} \wedge \text{unified}\ q \wedge \{\!\{B\}\!\} = \{\!\{\text{bset}\ q\}\!\} \tag{13}$$

and with (11) this implies

$$\text{islin}_\phi\ p\ \rightarrow\ [\![\exists\ p]\!]^{is} = [\![\text{decr}_\phi(\text{explode}_{-\infty}(\text{unify}\ p))]\!]^{is}$$

which implies the correctness of cooper directly

$$\text{qfree}\ q \wedge \text{cooper}\ q = \lfloor q' \rfloor\ \rightarrow\ \text{qfree}\ q' \wedge [\![\exists\ q]\!]^{is} = [\![q']\!]^{is}$$

and hence, using (1), the correctness of the whole decision procedure pa:

$$\text{pa}\ p = \lfloor p' \rfloor\ \rightarrow\ [\![p]\!]^{is} = [\![p']\!]^{is} \wedge \text{qfree}\ p'.$$

5   Formalization Issues

Normal Forms. Cooper's decision procedure transforms the input formula into successively more specialized normal forms, which is typical for many decision procedures. In our formalization these different normal forms are specified by predicates on the input languages ϕ and ι. This has the advantage that we do not need to define new languages and translations between languages. Instead we need to add preconditions to our theorems (e.g. $\text{islin}_\iota\ a$) and end up with more complicated function definitions (see below). Highly tuned code may require special representations of certain normal forms even using special data structures for efficiency. (e.g. [9]). For Cooper's algorithm such optimizations do not promise substantial gains.

Recursive Functions. The advantages of defining recursive functions by pattern matching are well known and it is used extensively in our work. Isabelle/HOL supports such definitions [19] by lists of equations. However, it is not always possible to turn each equation directly into a theorem because an equation is only applicable if all earlier equations are inapplicable. Hence Isabelle instantiates and possibly duplicates equations to make them non-overlapping. In the case of function mirror, the given list of 8 equations leads to 144 equations after disambiguation. This blow-up is the result of working with the full language ϕ even when a function operates only on a certain normal form. These non-overlapping theorems are later exported to ML, which may influence the quality of the code generated by the ML compiler.

Tailored Induction. Isabelle/HOL derives a tailored induction rule [19] from a recursive function definition which simplifies proofs enormously. This may seem surprising since the induction rule for mirror has 144 cases. However, most of the cases are irrelevant if the argument is assumed to be linear. These irrelevant cases disappear by simplification.

6   Performance

We tested three implementations on a batch of 64 theorems, where the distribution of quantifiers is illustrated by Fig. 9. The 64 formulae contain up to five quantifiers and three quantifier alternations. The number n_q in Fig. 9 represents the number of formulae with q quantifiers. The number of quantifier alternations is also given by the n_{qi}'s. We have $n_q = n_{q0} + n_{q1} + n_{q2} + n_{q3}$, where n_{qi} is the number of formulae containing q quantifiers and i quantifier alternation. The column $\widehat{c}_{max}$ gives the maximal constant occurring in the given set of formulae. Finally the last column gives the speed up factor achieved.

The adaptation of Harrison's implementation [12] (the current oracle in Isabelle/HOL) took 3.91 seconds to solve all goals. Our adaptation of this implementation to produce full proofs based on inference rules [4] took 703.08 seconds. The ML implementation obtained by Isabelle's code generator from the formally verified procedure presented above took 3.48 seconds, a speed-up of a factor of 200. All timings were carried out on a PowerBook G4 with a 1.67 GHz processor running OSX. The reason why the hand coded version is slightly slower than the generated one is that it operates on a symbolic binary representation of integers whereas the generated one uses (arbitrary precision!) ML-integers.

q	n_q	n_{q0}	n_{q1}	n_{q2}	n_{q3}	$\widehat{c}_{max}$	speedup
1	3	3	0	0	0	24	10
2	27	20	7	0	0	13	101
3	21	2	19	0	0	129	420
4	6	1	0	0	5	6	99
5	5	3	0	5	0	12	103

Fig. 9. Number of quantifiers ans speedup in the test-formulae

7   Conclusion

We presented a formally verified procedure for quantifier elimination in $\mathcal{PA}$. Generating ML code from it we achieved substantial performance improvements over an LCF-style implementation. Decision procedures developed this way are much easier to maintain and especially to share. Other systems supporting reflection should be able to import our work fairly directly, especially if they are of the HOL family as well.

References

1. Andrew W. Appel and Amy P. Felty. Dependent types ensure partial correctness of theorem provers. *J. Funct. Program.*, 14(1):3–19, 2004.
2. Stefan Berghofer and Tobias Nipkow. Proof terms for simply typed higher order logic. In J. Harrison and M. Aagaard, editors, *Theorem Proving in Higher Order Logics*, volume 1869 of *LNCS*, pages 38–52. Springer-Verlag, 2000.
3. Stefan Berghofer and Tobias Nipkow. Executing higher order logic. In *In Types for Proofs and Programs (TYPES 2000)*, volume 2277 of *LNCS*, pages 24–40. Springer-Verlag, 2002.
4. A. Chaieb and T. Nipkow. Generic proof synthesis for presburger arithmetic. Technical report, TU München, 2003. `http://www4.in.tum.de/~nipkow/pubs/presburger.pdf`.
5. D.C. Cooper. Theorem proving in arithmetic without multiplication. In B. Meltzer and D. Michie, editors, *Machine Intelligence*, volume 7, pages 91–100. Edinburgh University Press, 1972.
6. Pierre Crégut. Une procédure de décision réflexive pour un fragment de l'arithmétique de Presburger. In *Informal proceedings of the 15th journées francophones des langages applicatifs*, 2004.
7. Fischer and Rabin. Super-exponential complexity of presburger arithmetic. In *SIAMAMS: Complexity of Computation: Proceedings of a Symposium in Applied Mathematics of the American Mathematical Society and the Society for Industrial and Applied Mathematics*, 1974.
8. Benjamin Grégoire and Xavier Leroy. A compiled implementation of strong reduction. In *Int. Conf. Functional Programming*, pages 235–246. ACM Press, 2002.
9. Benjamin Grégoire and Assia Mahboubi. Proving equalities in a commutative ring done right in Coq. In J. Hurd, editor, *Theorem Proving in Higher Order Logics, TPHOLs 2005*, volume ? of *LNCS*, page ? Springer-Verlag, 2005.
10. John Harrison. Metatheory and reflection in theorem proving: A survey and critique. Technical Report CRC-053, SRI Cambridge, Millers Yard, Cambridge, UK, 1995. `http://www.cl.cam.ac.uk/users/jrh/papers/reflect.dvi.gz`.
11. John Harrison. *Theorem proving with the real numbers*. PhD thesis, University of Cambridge, Computer Laboratory, 1996.
12. John Harrison's home page. `http://www.cl.cam.ac.uk/users/jrh/atp/OCaml/cooper.ml`.
13. Robert Klapper and Aaron Stump. Validated Proof-Producing Decision Procedures. In C. Tinelli and S. Ranise, editors, *2nd Int. Workshop Pragmatics of Decision Procedures in Automated Reasoning*, 2004.
14. Tobias Nipkow, Lawrence Paulson, and Markus Wenzel. *Isabelle/HOL — A Proof Assistant for Higher-Order Logic*, volume 2283 of *LNCS*. Springer-Verlag, 2002. `http://www.in.tum.de/~nipkow/LNCS2283/`.
15. Michael Norrish. Complete integer decision procedures as derived rules in HOL. In D.A. Basin and B. Wolff, editors, *Theorem Proving in Higher Order Logics, TPHOLs 2003*, volume 2758 of *LNCS*, pages 71–86. Springer-Verlag, 2003.
16. Derek C. Oppen. Elementary bounds for presburger arithmetic. In *STOC '73: Proceedings of the fifth annual ACM symposium on Theory of computing*, pages 34–37, New York, NY, USA, 1973. ACM Press.

17. Mojzesz Presburger. Über die Vollständigkeit eines gewissen Systems der Arithmetik ganzer Zahlen, in welchem die Addition als einzige Operation hervortritt. In *Comptes Rendus du I Congrès de Mathématiciens des Pays Slaves*, pages 92–101, 1929.
18. William Pugh. The Omega test: a fast and practical integer programming algorithm for dependence analysis. In *Proceedings of the 1991 ACM/IEEE conference on Supercomputing*, pages 4–13. ACM Press, 1991.
19. Konrad Slind. Derivation and use of induction schemes in higher-order logic. In *TPHOLs '97: Proceedings of the 10th International Conference on Theorem Proving in Higher Order Logics*, pages 275–290, London, UK, 1997. Springer-Verlag.

Integration of a Software Model Checker into Isabelle*

Matthias Daum[1], Stefan Maus[2], Norbert Schirmer[3], and M. Nassim Seghir[2]

[1] Universität des Saarlandes, Saarbrücken, Germany
[2] Max-Planck Institut für Informatik, Saarbrücken
[3] Technische Universität München, Germany

Abstract. The paper presents a combination of interactive and automatic tools in the area of software verification. We have integrated a newly developed software model checker into an interactive verification environment for imperative programming languages. Although the problems in software verification are mostly too hard for full automation, we could increase the level of automated assistance by discharging less interesting side conditions. That allows the verification engineer to focus on the abstract algorithm, safely assuming unbounded arithmetic and unlimited buffers.

1   Introduction

Our work is part of the Verisoft project.[1] This large, coordinated project aims at the pervasive formal verification of entire computer systems consisting of hardware, compiler, operating system, communication system, and applications. To the best of our knowledge, the last attempt to deal with such an ambitious topic has been the famous CLI stack [5] back in 1989—even though the principal researcher of the famous CLI stack project, J. S. Moore [8], declared that the formal verification of a system 'from transistor to software level' is a grand-challenge problem. However, basic research in the area of formal verification has greatly evolved during the last 15 years. A major goal of the Verisoft project is to solve that challenge by integrating and improving the existing technology.

Like in the CLI-stack project, we have several layers of abstraction. However, for the vast majority of our software, we employ a single verification environment. It was implemented on top of the general-purpose theorem prover Isabelle as an instance of the well-known Hoare calculus. Within this environment, we plan to verify the different software layers, starting from considerable parts of the micro kernel, via the operating system, up to the application level.

An interesting observation is that, by far, most of the problems of today's software are not caused by a malicious algorithm but by overlooked corner cases in

---

* Work partially funded by the German Federal Ministry of Education and Research (BMBF) in the Verisoft project under grant 01 IS C38.
[1] More information on the Verisoft project can be found at http://www.verisoft.de/

G. Sutcliffe and A. Voronkov (Eds.): LPAR 2005, LNAI 3835, pp. 381–395, 2005.

the specific implementation: Bounded arithmetic and limited buffers lead to unintended over- or underflows. Hence we conclude that programmers—and quite likely verification engineers—focus primarily on the abstract algorithm when implementing, respectively verifying, software and tend to neglect the machine dependent limitations.

Of course, the verification engineer has to address these issues at some point. Our experience in the Verisoft project is, however, that the corner cases are usually perceived as distraction from the "real"—the functional—verification goal and addressed at last.

Furthermore, a maximum degree of automation is crucial for such an ambitious project as Verisoft. However, our verification environment yet provided an interactive-only user interface. Hence we have integrated a model checker for the automatic pre-verification of side conditions as they arise due to the finiteness of the underlying machine. This integration allows verification engineers to concentrate on the abstract problem with virtually unbounded arithmetic and unlimited buffers.

The rest of the paper is organized as follows: Section 2 presents related work in this area. Section 3 introduces Isabelle and the Hoare Logic module. Furthermore, it gives an idea of the checked side conditions and illustrates our verification environment by a small example. In Section 4, we present our newly developed software model checker for reachability analysis in C programs. Section 5 reports on the integration of this model checker into our verification environment. We describe certain aspects of the novel *swmc-guards* tactic, which implements the user interface to our model checker. Moreover, we discuss some enhancements of the model checker to simultaneously test the reachability of multiple locations. In Section 6, we give an estimation of the speed-up to expect from the use of our tool. Finally, Section 7 concludes the paper.

2   Related Work

Several works for combining verification techniques have been proposed in the literature, including different ways of integrating automatic approaches into interactive theorem proving. Pisini *et al* [4] integrated the MDG tool, which supports model checking and equivalence checking, into the HOL system, a theorem prover for higher order logic, for the verification of hardware. They introduced two tactics, MDG_COMB_TAC and MDG_SEQ_TAC, to generate the adequate input files so that the MDG system can complete the proof.

Similarly in the context of hardware verification, Joyce and Seger [7] proposed a link between symbolic trajectory evaluation and interactive theorem proving. Their technique consists in introducing a new proof procedure, called VOSS_TAC, through which the Voss system is invoked for checking the validity of assertions, and returning the result to the theorem prover.

Rajan *et al* [10] described an approach where a BDD-based model checker for the propositional mu-calculus was used as a decision procedure within the framework of the PVS proof checker.

Our integration approach is quite similar to the one proposed by Pisini *et al* [4]. However, while all systems mentioned above aim at hardware verification, our integration approach concerns software verification. Software is more complex than hardware in the sense that it includes more language constructs and a larger variety of data types.

3   Verification Environment

Isabelle is a generic proof assistant. It provides a framework to declare deductive systems, rather than to implement them from scratch. Currently the best developed object logic is HOL [9], higher order logic, including an extensive library of (concrete) mathematics, as well as various packages for advanced definitional concepts like (co-)inductive sets and types, primitive and well-founded recursion etc. To define an object logic, the user has to declare the syntax and the inference rules of the object logic. By employing the built-in mechanisms of Isabelle/Pure, higher-order unification and resolution in particular, one already gets a decent deductive system. Moreover, Isabelle follows the well-known *LCF system approach*, which allows us to write arbitrary proof procedures in ML without breaking system soundness since all those procedures are expanded into primitive inferences of the logical kernel. To integrate trusted external programs, the mechanism of *oracles* can be employed. An oracle produces a theorem without breaking its proof down to primitive inferences. The software model checker is integrated as such an oracle into a Hoare Logic module of Isabelle/HOL.

The Hoare Logic module [11] is built on top of Isabelle/HOL. An imperative programming language is defined as HOL data-type together with an operational semantics and a Hoare calculus for partial and total correctness. Programs are specified as Hoare triples and verified using a verification condition generator. A Hoare triple has the format $\Gamma \vdash P\ c\ Q$ where Γ is the procedure environment that maps procedure names to their bodies, c is a code fragment and P and Q are assertions. Intuitively, the formula states that if P holds before the execution of c then Q will hold afterwards. In this paper we only focus on partial correctness. For total correctness, we are about to integrate a termination checker in a similar fashion.

Runtime faults are modeled as explicit *guards* within the program c. Such a guard formulates constraints on the current program state. The semantics of the Hoare Logic ensures that every such guard must hold under the precondition P. Formally assertions and guards are sets of program states. The states are represented as records in HOL. As example, the assertion $\{\!|\ \acute{i} \leq N\ |\!\}$ abbreviates the set comprehension $\{s.\ i\ s \leq N\}$, where i is a record selector. The abstraction on state s is hidden in assertions, and the application to s is abbreviated by the prefixed acute symbol ($'$).

Many runtime errors can occur during the execution of a program due to the violation of some constraints imposed by the definition of the data types used in the program. Examples of errors are overflow and underflow exceptions and array out-of-bound access. The programming language used in the Verisoft project is called C0. It is a type-safe subset of C with an exact specified semantics, which is also formalized in Isabelle/HOL. Numeric expressions in C0 are evaluated using bounded modulo arithmetic with silent over- and underflows. However for specifying and reasoning about programs, we want to "think unbounded". Therefore we regard over- and underflows as runtime errors on the level of the Hoare Logic and use ordinary unbounded arithmetic.

To prove the absence of such runtime errors, we have to identify which expressions can potentially cause which errors. We have formalized the error conditions. Table 1 shows a non-exhaustive list of expressions that might cause runtime errors. For each of these expressions, the table lists a set of guards. The evaluation of an expression causes a runtime error if and only if the conjunction of its guards evaluates to false. The guards are automatically generated by Isabelle through the parsing process of the program code.

Table 1. The table shows some expressions causing runtime errors together with their respective guards (top) and the ranges for the basic integer types (bottom)

expression e	guards	runtime error
$e_1 + e_2$		
$e_1 - e_2$	$e \leq (max_{type(e)})$	overflow
$- e_1$	$e \geq (min_{type(e)})$	underflow
$e_1 * e_2$		
e_1 / e_2	$e_2 \neq 0$	division by zero
	$e \leq (max_{type(e)})$	overflow
	$e \geq (min_{type(e)})$	underflow
$e_1 [e_2]$	$e_2 < size(e_1)$	above bounds of e_1
	$e_2 \geq 0$	below bounds of e_1

type T	min_T	max_T
`int`	-2^{31}	$2^{31} - 1$
`unsigned`	0	$2^{32} - 1$
`char`	-2^7	$2^7 - 1$

Figure 1 on the next page illustrates the program representation in our verification environment. It shows the proof goal for the correctness theorem of a bubble-sort implementation. The code fragment sorts the first ´array-size values contained in an array variable named ´array.

4   The Model Checker ACSAR

ACSAR (Automatic Checker of Safety properties based on Abstraction Refinement) is a software model checker for C programs that we developed in the spirit of Magic [1] and Blast [2,3]. Most data types of the C language are handled by

$\bigwedge \sigma.\ \Gamma \vdash \{\!|\sigma.\ 0\ <\ 'array\text{-}size\ \wedge\ 'array\text{-}size\ \leq\ length\ 'array|\!\}$
$\qquad \{\!|1\ \leq\ 'array\text{-}size|\!\} \mapsto\ 'i\ :=\ 'array\text{-}size\ -\ 1;$
$\qquad WHILE\ 0\ <\ 'i$
$\qquad DO\ 'j\ :=\ 0;$
$\qquad\qquad WHILE\ 'j\ <\ 'i$
$\qquad\qquad DO\ \{\!|'j\ +\ 1\ \leq\ max\text{-}nat\ \wedge$
$\qquad\qquad\qquad 'j\ +\ 1\ <\ length\ 'array\ \wedge\ 'j\ <\ length\ 'array|\!\}$
$\qquad\qquad\qquad \mapsto\ IF\ 'array['j\ +\ 1]\ <\ 'array['j]$
$\qquad\qquad\qquad\qquad THEN\ \{\!|'j\ <\ length\ 'array|\!\} \mapsto\ 'temp\ :=\ 'array['j];$
$\qquad\qquad\qquad\qquad\quad \{\!|'j\ <\ length\ 'array\ \wedge$
$\qquad\qquad\qquad\qquad\qquad 'j\ +\ 1\ \leq\ max\text{-}nat\ \wedge\ 'j\ +\ 1\ <\ length\ 'array|\!\}$
$\qquad\qquad\qquad\qquad\quad \mapsto\ 'array['j]\ :=\ 'array['j\ +\ 1];$
$\qquad\qquad\qquad\qquad\quad \{\!|'j\ +\ 1\ \leq\ max\text{-}nat\ \wedge\ 'j\ +\ 1\ <\ length\ 'array|\!\}$
$\qquad\qquad\qquad\qquad\quad \mapsto\ 'array['j\ +\ 1]\ :=\ 'temp$
$\qquad\qquad\qquad\qquad FI;$
$\qquad\qquad\qquad\quad \{\!|'j\ +\ 1\ \leq\ max\text{-}nat|\!\} \mapsto\ 'j\ :=\ 'j\ +\ 1$
$\qquad\qquad OD;$
$\qquad\qquad\quad \{\!|1\ \leq\ 'i|\!\} \mapsto\ 'i\ :=\ 'i\ -\ 1$
$\qquad OD;$
$\qquad 'res\ :=\ 0$
$\qquad \{\!|\forall j\ <\ {}^{\sigma}array\text{-}size.\ \forall i\ <\ j.\ 'array[i]\ \leq\ 'array[j]|\!\}$

Fig. 1. An external representation of code with guarded commands within our verification environment. A guarded command consists of a list of guard conditions and the affected command. The conditions are enclosed in braces: $\{\!|\ |\!\}$. The guard conditions are separated from the command by $\mapsto$. The term ${}^{\sigma}array\text{-}size$ refers to the old value of *array-size* before the execution of the program fragment.

ACSAR, including integer types, arrays and structs. Furthermore, ACSAR supports all control structures of the C language. Function calls are handled by inlining the body of each function into the corresponding call site. Local variables are renamed to avoid name conflicts. Thus, after inlining all the functions, we obtain a unique global control-flow graph. The obtained control flow graph contains only two types of nodes: branches and updates. In the following, we explain the basic verification algorithm of ACSAR.

4.1   Translating Programs to Transition Constraints

A transition constraint tc is a tuple (l, g, u, d) where l and d are the values of the program counter before and after performing the transition, g is the transition condition and u is the variable update. Consecutive assignments are considered as one simultaneous update. We illustrate the translation procedure considering the function *three_times* as example:

Example 1.

```
1   void three_times(int n)
2   {
3       int s = 0, i=0, result;
4       while (i != n) {
5           s = s + 3;
6           i = i + 1;
7       }
8       result  = s;
9   }
```

Function *three_times* can be represented by the following system of transition constraints:

$$(1, \; True, \; [s \leftarrow 0, \; i \leftarrow 0], \; 4) \qquad (1)$$
$$(4, \; i \neq n, \; [i \leftarrow i + 1, \; s \leftarrow s + 3], \; 4) \qquad (2)$$
$$(4, \; i = n, \; [result \leftarrow s], \; 10) \qquad (3)$$

Upon translation, lines 1-3 are merged into transition constraint (1). Transition constraint (2) models the case where the control enters the loop (lines 4-8) and transition (3) represents the case where the control proceeds with the instruction after the loop (line 9) because the loop condition does not hold.

4.2   Abstraction

ACSAR uses the predicate abstraction technique [6] to automatically abstract an infinite system by a finite one. The idea of predicate abstraction is to represent a set of states by a logical formula built from a set of predicates. This logical formula represents an abstract state. ACSAR uses a backward search to explore the set of abstract states. Formally, we introduce:

- The set of program states S, the set of error states S_{err}, the set of predicates P (initially empty) and the set of transition constraints Tc. A state s is provided as a logical formula $s = (x_1 = v_1 \wedge x_2 = v_2 \wedge \cdots \wedge x_n = v_n)$, where x_i are program variables and v_i their values ($i \in [1, n]$).
- the abstraction function $\alpha : L \rightarrow L$ with $\alpha(s) = \bigwedge p$ such that ($p \in P \wedge s \Rightarrow p$), where L is the set of quantifier-free first-order logic formulas restricted to program variables.
- the operator $Pre^{\#}$ that returns the previous abstract state: $Pre^{\#}(a, tc) = \alpha(wp(a, tc))$, where a is an abstract state provided as a logical formula, $tc \in Tc$ is some transition constraint, and $wp(a, tc)$ is the exact weakest precondition of a with respect to tc. Intuitively, the $Pre^{\#}$ operator provides the abstract state that reaches the state a after performing the transition tc.

Now, we can build the abstract system. We start with the abstract error state $\alpha(S_{err})$ and try to compute the least fixpoint of $Pre^{\#}$. Either we find the least fixpoint or a counter example. If we find a counter example, we have to test its validity using a SAT solver. In case of a spurious counter example, our abstraction has been too coarse, and we have to refine it.

4.3 Refinement

When an abstraction is too coarse, i. e. we have found a spurious counter example, ACSAR rebuilds a more precise abstraction by inferring new predicates. It increases only the relevant part of the abstract system. This concept of *laziness* is inspired by the work of Henzinger *et al* [2]. If the backward search reaches the initial state S_I, the path leading from S_{err} to S_I is analyzed by using the exact weakest precondition wp to check the validity of transitions that constitute the path. If the analysis indicates that this path is a real counter example, the path is returned as witness to the user. Otherwise, we obtain a formula showing the invalidity of the path. Predicates appearing in this formula are used to refine the system.

5 Integrating ACSAR into the Verification Environment

As shown in Table 1 on page 384, the guards are expressed as assertions in quantifier-free first-order logic. Software model checkers deal efficiently with such properties. In order to take advantage of the efficiency and automation of model checking, we integrated our tool ACSAR into Isabelle.

In Figure 1 on page 385, we have already seen the external representation of a bubble-sort implementation. At that point, we would like to discharge the guards automatically with ACSAR. We have integrated the model checker via a new tactic, called *swmc-guards*. To deal with multiple guards, we have extended the verification procedure of ACSAR.

When the verification engineer applies *swmc-guards*, the current proof goal is converted into a reachability problem and presented to ACSAR. The model checker generates a reachability check report. The tactic evaluates this report and forms a new proof goal from the old one and the new results from the model checker. In the next sections, we describe this process in detail.

5.1 Conversion of the Original Proof Goal

In Isabelle, the proof goal is basically a Hoare triple with a code fragment that contains guards. The model checker, however, expects a C program with labelled error locations. Hence we have to convert the original problem. For the check against runtime faults, only the precondition and the actual code fragment with the guard conditions are of interest. Quantifier-free conditions can easily be formulated as C expressions, and the conversion of the basic commands like *WHILE* or *IF* is straightforward.

The conversion of the code fragment is primarily a syntax transformation. However, the internal representation in Isabelle is quite opulent. Hence we decided to introduce an intermediate language and implemented the transformation in two stages. This intermediate language is much more compact and was tailormade to represent usual imperative programming languages. We expect that this approach will simplify the integration of similar tools.

The conceptual core of the conversion is the representation of precondition and guards. The precondition is an assumption, hence the guard conditions have only to be checked if the precondition holds. We represent this fact by enclosing the whole code fragment in an **if** command that has the precondition as branch condition. For each guard condition g, we introduce a distinct error location r and generate a conditional jump to this error location for the case that the condition does not hold. Consequently, r is reachable if and only if g is satisfiable.

5.2   Checking Reachability of Multiple Error Locations

Initially, ACSAR was designed to check the reachability of only one error location at a time. To deal with multiple error locations, one has the choice between two options. The first option is to invoke ACSAR several times from Isabelle. This approach is simple in the sense that no major changes are needed. Its drawback is the time consumed by communications between the theorem prover and the model checker. The second option, that we adopted, is to extend the checking algorithm of ACSAR to deal with multiple error locations. All guards are transmitted at once to the model checker rather than transmitting one guard at a time.

Therefore we have to extend the translation algorithm above. We assume a finite set G of guards and a finite set L of control locations. Furthermore there should be a control location $l_i \in L$ associated to each guard $g_i \in G$. Now we introduce a new error location r_i for each guard such that the set of error locations R will be distinct from the control locations and from each other, i. e.

$$L \cap R = \emptyset \quad \wedge \quad \forall g_i, g_j.\ r_i = r_j \longrightarrow g_i = g_j$$

Finally, we have to introduce a transition constraint $tc_i = (l_i, \neg g_i, -, r_i)$ for each guard $g_i \in G$, and can state:

$$\forall g \in G.\ \exists! r \in R \text{ such that } (r \text{ is reachable}) \longleftrightarrow (\neg g \text{ can hold})$$

Figure 2 on the facing page illustrates the resulting C code of the previous bubble-sort example after its translation into a reachability problem and adding the necessary error locations.

Verification Approach. In the verification phase, we check the validity of each guard in isolation. With this approach, the verification engineer might be able to find several bugs at a time. In order to avoid the influence between guards, we have to disable all but the currently processed guard. Consider the following example:

```
     int array [10];
     unsigned int i, j, array_size ;
     int temp, res;

 5   int main () {
        if (((0 < array_size) && (array_size <= 10))) {
           if (!(1 <= array_size )) goto ERROR_1;
           i = (array_size − 1);
           while (0 < i) {
10            j = 0;
              while (j < i) {
                 if (!((j + 1) <= max_nat)) goto ERROR_2;
                 if (!((j + 1) < 10)) goto ERROR_3;
                 if (!(j < 10)) goto ERROR_4;
15               if ((array [(j + 1)] < array [j ])) {
                    if (!(j < 10)) goto ERROR_5;
                    temp = array[j];
                    if (!(j < 10)) goto ERROR_6;
                    if (!((j + 1) <= max_nat)) goto ERROR_7;
20                  if (!((j + 1) < 10)) goto ERROR_8;
                    array[j] = array [(j + 1)];
                    if (!((j + 1) <= max_nat)) goto ERROR_9;
                    if (!((j + 1) < 10)) goto ERROR_10;
                    array [(j + 1)] = temp;
25               }
                 if (!((j + 1) <= max_nat)) goto ERROR_11;
                 j = (j + 1);
              }
              if (!(1 <= i)) goto ERROR_12;
30            i = (i − 1);
           }
           res = 0;
        }
        goto end;
35
     ERROR_12:       goto end;
     ERROR_11:       goto end;
     ERROR_10:       goto end;
        /* ... */
40   ERROR_1:        goto end;

     end:            ;
     }
```

Fig. 2. Result of the translation (input to ACSAR). Note: For better readability, we have replaced the numerical upper limit of unsigneds with *max_nat*.

Example 2.

```
    int a [6], b [4], i ,j ,k;
    i = 5;
    j = i − 1;
4   if (j+2 > 5) goto ERROR_1;
    a[j+2] = 3;
    k = j + 1;
    if (k > 4) goto ERROR_2;
8   b[k] = 1;
    goto end;
    ERROR_1:    goto end;
    ERROR_2:    goto end;
12  end:        ;
```

If the guard leading to label ERROR_1 is not disabled when checking the next guard, we can not find out whether label ERROR_2 is reachable because the expression (j+2 > 5) at line 4 is always true.

Let us now consider a program in terms of a set of transition constraints Tc. We introduce the subset Tc_{err} containing the transition constraints tc_i that lead to error locations. For each transition constraint $tc_i = (l_i, \neg g_i, -, r_i) \in Tc_{err}$, there exists a transition constraint $tc'_i = (l_i, g_i, u_i, k_i) \in Tc$ corresponding to the case that guard g_i holds.

We disable all currently not concerned guards g_j in the following way: We build a transition constraint tc''_j from tc'_j by removing the guard condition g_j and keeping all other fields unchanged: $tc''_j = (l_j, True, u_j, k_j)$. Now, we remove the transition constraints tc_j and tc'_j from the set of transition constraints Tc, and add tc''_j to Tc.

Introducing Assumptions. In the previously described approach, each guard is checked in isolation from the other guards. This is equivalent to having each time a program P_i containing only the guard g_i that we want to prove. This approach can be improved by exploiting results for previous guards in the verification of the actual guard. When a guard is proven to hold, we use it as an assumption for the verification of other guards. Formally, we remove tc'_i for each proven guard g_i and keep tc_i as we know that the error location r_i is never reachable. This approach is described in Figure 3 on the next page.

Table 2 on the facing page presents a performance comparison between the approach when we use valid guards as assumptions and the approach without assumptions. We have measured the execution times of the software model checker for the already presented *bubble-sort* example and an implementation of the more naive *selection-sort* algorithm. In both cases, the execution time is substancially shorter if we keep proven guards as assumptions.

5.3   Returning the Results to Isabelle

Our interface is implemented as a so called *oracle*. In this way, we can introduce a theorem into the verification process without giving a proof for it. In our case,

Input:

  - the set Tc of all transition constraints
  - the set Tc_{err} of transition constraints leading to error locations
  - the set G of guards

Output:

  - a report rep specifying for each guard whether it is *valid, invalid* or *unknown*.

begin
$Tc'_{err} = \bigcup \{tc'_i$ such that $tc_i \in Tc_{err}\}$;
$Tc''_{err} = \bigcup \{tc''_i$ such that $tc_i \in Tc_{err}\}$;
$Tc = (Tc - (Tc_{err} \cup Tc'_{err})) \cup Tc''_{err}$;
for each guard g_i such that $g_i \in G$ **do**
$\quad Tc = (Tc - \{tc''_i\}) \cup \{tc_i, tc'_i\}$;
$\quad res = check\_reach(err\_loc(g_i), Tc)$;
$\quad$ **switch** (res)
$\quad\quad$ **case** *unreachable:*
$\quad\quad\quad store\_in\_report(rep, g_i, valid); \; Tc = Tc - tc'_i$;
$\quad\quad$ **case** *reachable:*
$\quad\quad\quad store\_in\_report(rep, g_i, invalid); \; Tc = (Tc - \{tc_i, tc'_i\}) \cup tc''_i$;
$\quad\quad$ **otherwise:**
$\quad\quad\quad store\_in\_report(rep, g_i, unknown); \; Tc = (Tc - \{tc_i, tc'_i\}) \cup tc''_i$;
$\quad init()$;
return(rep);
end

Legend:

  - The function *err_loc* takes a guard as argument and returns the corresponding error location.
  - The function *check_reach* returns either (a) *unreachable* if the guard is valid, (b) *reachable* if the guard is invalid, or (c) *unknown* if no definite decision on the validity of the guard can be made.
  - The function *init* reinitializes the system by erasing states generated so far.
  - The function *store_in_report* stores the result of the verification concerning the guard in a report file. The report is returned to the theorem prover.

Fig. 3. Multiple error verification by exploiting assumptions

Table 2. Model checking time of programs with and without using assumptions

Program	number of guards	verification time (in seconds)	
		without assumptions	with assumptions
selection-sort	14	5.918	2.729
bubble-sort	12	140.189	29.622

a Hoare triple with annotated guard conditions is returned as theorem. The annotation expresses whether guards will not fail. This Hoare triple is used as premise of an Hoare rule that allows us to regard the proven guards as granted for the remaining verification.

In this section we discuss how this rule is formally justified within the Hoare calculus. Within our verification environment, validated guards are decorated with $\sqrt{}$ as shown in Figure 4.

$\bigwedge \sigma. \; \Gamma \vdash /\{ \text{True} \}$ $\{\!|\sigma. \; 0 < \text{'array-size} \wedge \text{'array-size} \leq \text{length 'array}|\!\}$
$\{\!|1 \leq \text{'array-size}|\!\}\sqrt{} \mapsto \text{'}i := \text{'array-size} - 1;$
$WHILE \; 0 < \text{'}i$
$DO \; \text{'}j := 0;$
$\qquad WHILE \; \text{'}j < \text{'}i$
$\qquad DO \; \{\!|\text{'}j + 1 \leq \text{max-nat}|\!\}\sqrt{}, \; \{\!|\text{'}j + 1 < \text{length 'array}|\!\}\sqrt{},$
$\qquad\qquad \{\!|\text{'}j < \text{length 'array}|\!\}\sqrt{}$
$\qquad\qquad \mapsto IF \; \text{'array}[\text{'}j + 1] < \text{'array}[\text{'}j]$
$\qquad\qquad\qquad THEN \; \{\!|\text{'}j < \text{length 'array}|\!\}\sqrt{} \mapsto \text{'temp} := \text{'array}[\text{'}j];$
$\qquad\qquad\qquad\qquad \{\!|\text{'}j < \text{length 'array}|\!\}\sqrt{}, \; \{\!|\text{'}j + 1 \leq \text{max-nat}|\!\}\sqrt{},$
$\qquad\qquad\qquad\qquad \{\!|\text{'}j + 1 < \text{length 'array}|\!\}\sqrt{}$
$\qquad\qquad\qquad\qquad \mapsto \text{'array}[\text{'}j] := \text{'array}[\text{'}j + 1];$
$\qquad\qquad\qquad\qquad \{\!|\text{'}j + 1 \leq \text{max-nat}|\!\}\sqrt{}, \; \{\!|\text{'}j + 1 < \text{length 'array}|\!\}\sqrt{}$
$\qquad\qquad\qquad\qquad \mapsto \text{'array}[\text{'}j + 1] := \text{'temp}$
$\qquad\qquad\qquad FI;$
$\qquad\qquad \{\!|\text{'}j + 1 \leq \text{max-nat}|\!\}\sqrt{} \mapsto \text{'}j := \text{'}j + 1$
$\qquad OD;$
$\qquad \{\!|1 \leq \text{'}i|\!\}\sqrt{} \mapsto \text{'}i := \text{'}i - 1$
$OD;$
$\text{'res} := 0$
$\{\!|\forall j < {}^{\sigma}\text{array-size}. \; \forall i < j. \; \text{'array}[i] \leq \text{'array}[j]|\!\}$

Fig. 4. The bubble-sort example after calling the software model checker. All validated guard conditions are decorated with $\sqrt{}$.

To integrate the notion of discharging a guard into the Hoare calculus, the guarded command of the programming-language model described by Schirmer [11] is augmented with a flag: *Guard f g c*, where *f* is the kind of fault that the guarded command will raise if the guard condition *g* for command *c* fails. The syntax in the examples $g \mapsto c$ is an abbreviation for *Guard False g c*, and $g\sqrt{} \mapsto c$ for *Guard True g c*. A comma-separated list of guard conditions before the $\mapsto$ abbreviates nested guarded commands. The state of the programming language is a polymorphic HOL data-type with two constructors:

$$\textbf{datatype} \; (\text{'f,'s}) \; state = Normal \; \text{'s} \mid Fault \; \text{'f},$$

where 's is a type variable for the raw state and 'f for the faults. The operational big-step semantics has the format $\Gamma \vdash \langle c, s \rangle \Rightarrow t$, where Γ is the procedure environment that maps procedure names to their bodies. The meaning is that execution of command c in the initial state s ends in final state t. The big-step semantic rules for guarded commands are the following:

$$\frac{s \in g \qquad \Gamma\vdash \langle c, \textit{Normal } s\rangle \Rightarrow t}{\Gamma\vdash \langle \textit{Guard } f \text{ } g \text{ } c, \textit{Normal } s\rangle \Rightarrow t} \qquad\qquad \frac{s \notin g}{\Gamma\vdash \langle \textit{Guard } f \text{ } g \text{ } c, \textit{Normal } s\rangle \Rightarrow \textit{Fault } f}$$

The guard condition g is modeled as a set of states. If it holds, execution is continued otherwise the error is signaled. For the integration of the software model checker, the flag f is Boolean. The flag $\textit{True}$ indicates that the guard is proven. But as the semantic rules above indicate, the value of the flag is not considered to decide whether the guard holds or not. It is only used in the Hoare calculus. The Hoare triples are extended with a set of faults F that are regarded as proven. Validity of a Hoare triple $\Gamma\models_{/F} P \text{ } c \text{ } Q$ is defined as partial correctness modulo faults in F:

$$\Gamma\models_{/F} P \text{ } c \text{ } Q \equiv \Gamma\vdash \langle c, \textit{Normal } s\rangle \Rightarrow t \longrightarrow s \in P \longrightarrow t \notin \textit{Fault } ` F \longrightarrow \\ t \in \textit{Normal } ` Q$$

Here $`$ denotes the set image operation, e.g. $f ` M$ can be rewritten as set comprehension: $\{f \text{ } s. \text{ } s \in M\}$. Given an execution of command c from an initial state s satisfying the precondition P, provided that the final state t is not a fault in set F, then the final state will satisfy postcondition Q. An empty set of faults F can be omitted, since this is the ordinary case. It ensures that no runtime faults will occur. The Hoare calculus is proven sound with respect to this notion of validity [12].

Theorem 1. $\Gamma\vdash_{/F} P \text{ } c \text{ } Q \longrightarrow \Gamma\models_{/F} P \text{ } c \text{ } Q$

To integrate the results of the software model checker, we derive a rule that allows us to switch from an empty set F to the set $\{\textit{True}\}$, which means that all guards marked with $\textit{True}$ can be assumed as correct. Here are the Hoare Logic rules for guards:

$$\frac{\Gamma\vdash_{/F} P \text{ } c \text{ } Q}{\Gamma\vdash_{/F} (g \cap P) \text{ } (\textit{Guard } f \text{ } g \text{ } c) \text{ } Q} \qquad\qquad \frac{f \in F \qquad \Gamma\vdash_{/F} P \text{ } c \text{ } Q}{\Gamma\vdash_{/F} \{s. \text{ } s \in g \longrightarrow s \in P\} \text{ } (\textit{Guard } f \text{ } g \text{ } c) \text{ } Q}$$

The left rule is the ordinary rule for guarded commands. The guard g has to hold in the precondition. On the right hand side, however, the guard can be taken as assumption for the precondition P, since validity of Hoare triples assumes that no fault in F can occur. For interactive verification this means that guards marked with a fault in F can be taken as assumptions whereas the other ones have to be proven. To illustrate the integration of the software model checker, consider the following situation. The current proof goal is a Hoare triple of the form $\Gamma\vdash_{/\{\}} P \text{ } c \text{ } Q$, where all guards in c are marked with $\textit{False}$. The goal is to reduce this to a new proof state $\Gamma\vdash_{/\{\textit{True}\}} P \text{ } c'' \text{ } Q$, where c'' contains the same guards as c, but some may be marked as $\textit{True}$. The software model checker has to prove that those guards that are marked with $\textit{True}$ actually hold. Formally the oracle returns a Hoare triple of the form $\Gamma\vdash_{/\{\}} P \text{ } c' \text{ } \textit{UNIV}$, where UNIV is the universal set that denotes the trivial postcondition, and c' only contains the guards of c'' that are marked with *True*. The guards marked with *False* are missing, since those are the guards that are not provable by the model checker. Referring to the semantics of Hoare triples, the result of the oracle describes that no guard in c' will fail. This is exactly what the model checker claims. The following rule implements this strategy:

$$\frac{\Gamma\vdash_{/\{True\}} P\ c''\ Q \qquad \Gamma\vdash_{/\{\}} P\ c'\ UNIV}{c' = strip\text{-}guards\ \{False\}\ c'' \qquad c = mark\text{-}guards\ False\ c''}$$
$$\Gamma\vdash_{/\{\}} P\ c\ Q$$

The conclusion is the current Hoare triple that is verified (e.g. Figure 1 on page 385). The first premise is the subgoal that remains for verification after the tactic *swmc-guards* is finished (e.g. Figure 4 on page 392). The second assumption denotes the result of the software model checker and is the only part that is provided as an oracle. The effect of the model checker is clearly integrated into the Hoare Logic proof. The side-conditions on c, c' and c'' are solved by Isabelles simplifier. The auxiliary HOL functions *mark-guards* and *strip-guards* are defined recursively on the HOL data-type of commands. The relevant equations for *Guard f g c* are:

$$
\begin{aligned}
mark\text{-}guards\ f'\ (Guard\ f\ g\ c) &= \ Guard\ f'\ g\ (mark\text{-}guards\ c) \\
strip\text{-}guards\ F\ (Guard\ f\ g\ c) &= \ if\ f \in F\ then\ strip\text{-}guards\ F\ c \\
&\quad\ else\ Guard\ f\ g\ (strip\text{-}guards\ F\ c)
\end{aligned}
$$

In the context of total correctness the tactic *swmc-guards* basically works the same. The Hoare triple returned by the oracle is of course still an partial correctness one. Hence the termination proof is left to the user.

6   Evaluation

It is hard to give a general measure of the speed-up that verification engineers gain by the use of the integrated model checker because it depends on the considered problem. For the shown bubble-sort implementation, for example, our verification condition generator could subsume all but two guard conditions. It took just 5 tactics to verify these conditions by hand.

However, our example is very light-weight: The interesting part of the proof consists of just about 40 tactics. Nevertheless, when employing the software model checker, we could use a simpler invariant for the while loop. Finding a suitable invariant is usually one of the most time consuming tasks during the verification process. This does especially apply to nested while loops.

7   Conclusion and Future Work

We have developed the new software model checker ACSAR, which is—in our application field—more powerful than competing tools. For example, if the code of our bubble-sort example is presented to the model checker Blast, it only reports that the first and the last error location are not reachable. Presently we are tackling aliasing problems in order to deal with pointer dereferencing. We expect to essentially improve the treatment of pointers in the near future.

We have integrated the model checker into our verification environment. It turned out to be very helpful that we have developed our own model checker instead of integrating a standard tool. So we were able to adopt ACSAR to check multiple error locations at a time.

The translation mechanism implemented by the *swmc-guards* tactic works in two stages in order to facilitate the integration of similar automatic tools. One such tool is a termination checker, which is already integrated; other tools might follow.

Furthermore, we plan to translate properties with quantifiers. Though the side conditions in guards are always quantifier-free, quantifiers might occur in preconditions. Currently, these preconditions are not transferred to the model checker. Moreover, we examine how the integration can be improved in order to enable the model checker to reason about simple proof goals.

References

1. Sagar Chaki et al. Modular verification of software components in C. In *ICSE*, pages 385–395. IEEE Computer Society, 2003.
2. Thomas A. Henzinger et al. Lazy abstraction. In *POPL*, pages 58–70, 2002.
3. Thomas A. Henzinger et al. Software verification with BLAST. In Thomas Ball and Sriram K. Rajamani, editors, *SPIN*, volume 2648 of *LNCS*, pages 235–239. Springer, 2003.
4. V. K. Pisini et al. Formal hardware verification by integrating HOL and MDG. In M. Sarrafzadeh, P. Banerjee, and K. Roy, editors, *ACM Great Lakes Symposium on VLSI*, pages 23–28. ACM, 2000.
5. William R. Bevier et al. An approach to systems verification. *J. Autom. Reasoning*, 5(4):411–428, 1989.
6. Susanne Graf and Hassen Saïdi. Construction of abstract state graphs with PVS. In O. Grumberg, editor, *CAV*, volume 1254 of *LNCS*, pages 72–83. Springer, 1997.
7. Jeffrey J. Joyce and Carl-Johan H. Seger. Linking BDD-based symbolic evaluation to interactive theorem-proving. In *DAC*, pages 469–474, 1993.
8. J. Strother Moore. A grand challenge proposal for formal methods: A verified stack. In Bernhard K. Aichernig and T. S. E. Maibaum, editors, *10th Anniversary Colloquium of UNU/IIST*, volume 2757 of *LNCS*, pages 161–172. Springer, 2002.
9. Tobias Nipkow, Lawrence C. Paulson, and Markus Wenzel. *Isabelle/HOL — A Proof Assistant for Higher-Order Logic*, volume 2283 of *LNCS*. Springer, 2002.
10. S. Rajan, Natarajan Shankar, and Mandayam K. Srivas. An integration of model checking with automated proof checking. In Pierre Wolper, editor, *CAV*, volume 939 of *LNCS*, pages 84–97. Springer, 1995.
11. Norbert Schirmer. A verification environment for sequential imperative programs in Isabelle/HOL. In F. Baader and A. Voronkov, editors, *LPAR*, volume 3452 of *LNCS*, pages 398–414. Springer, 2004.
12. Norbert Schirmer. *Verification of Sequential Imperative Programs in Isabelle/HOL*. PhD thesis, TU-München, 2005. to appear.

Experimental Evaluation of Classical Automata Constructions*

Deian Tabakov and Moshe Y. Vardi

Department of Computer Science, Rice University, Houston, TX
{dtabakov, vardi}@cs.rice.edu

Abstract. There are several algorithms for producing the canonical DFA from a given NFA. While the theoretical complexities of these algorithms are known, there has not been a systematic empirical comparison between them. In this work we propose a probabilistic framework for testing the performance of automata-theoretic algorithms. We conduct a direct experimental comparison between Hopcroft's and Brzozowski's algorithms. We show that while Hopcroft's algorithm has better overall performance, Brzozowski's algorithm performs better for "high-density" NFA. We also consider the universality problem, which is traditionally solved explicitly via the subset construction. We propose an encoding that allows this problem to be solved symbolically via a model-checker. We compare the performance of this approach to that of the standard explicit algorithm, and show that the explicit approach performs significantly better.

1 Introduction

Over the last 20 years automata-theoretic techniques have emerged as a major paradigm in automated reasoning, cf. [39]. The most fundamental automata-theoretic model is that of non-deterministic finite automata (NFA) [24]. (While the focus in automated reasoning is often on automata on infinite objects, automata on finite words do play a major role, cf. [28].) There are two basic problems related to NFA: finding the canonical minimal deterministic finite automaton (DFA) that accepts the same language as the original automaton (cf. [1] for an application in verification), and checking whether a given automaton is universal (i.e., accepts all words, corresponding to logical validity). Both problems have been studied extensively (eg. [40, 41]) and several algorithms for their solution have been proposed. For the canonization problem, two classical algorithms are by Hopcroft [23], which has the best asymptotic worst-case complexity for the minimization step, and by Brzozowski [10], which is quite different than most canonization algorithms. The standard way to check for universality is to determinize the automaton explicitly using the subset construction, and check if a rejecting set is reachable from the initial state. We call this the *explicit* approach. In addition to the explicit approach, we introduce in this paper a novel method, which reduces the universality problem to model checking [17], enabling us to apply *symbolic* model checking

---

* Work supported in part by NSF grants CCR-9988322, CCR-0124077, CCR-0311326, IIS-9908435, IIS-9978135, EIA-0086264, and ANI-0216467, by BSF grant 9800096, by Texas ATP grant 003604-0058-2003, and by a grant from the Intel Corporation.

G. Sutcliffe and A. Voronkov (Eds.): LPAR 2005, LNAI 3835, pp. 396–411, 2005.
© Springer-Verlag Berlin Heidelberg 2005

algorithms [12]. These algorithms use Binary Decision Diagrams (BDDs) [8], which offer compact encoding of Boolean functions.

The complexities of Brzozowski's and Hopcroft's algorithms are known [40], but there has not been a systematic empirical comparison between them. (A superficial evaluation in [20] claimed superiority of Hopcroft's algorithm.) Similarly, the universality problem is known to be PSPACE-complete [35], but a symbolic approach to universality has not been pursued. The comparison is complicated by the fact that there are no really good benchmarks for automata-theoretic algorithms and it is not even clear what types of automata should be included in such benchmarks.

We propose here evaluating automata-theoretic algorithms based on their performance on randomly generated NFA. This is inspired by recent work on randomly generated problem instances [14], for example random 3-SAT [37]. We can vary the hardness of the instances by controlling their density. In the case of NFA, there are two densities to control: the density of the accepting states (i.e., ratio of accepting states to total states) and the density of transitions (i.e., density of transitions per input letter to total states). For both densities we are interested in constant ratios, which yields linear densities. This is analogous to the model used in random 3-SAT problems [37]. (For simplicity here we assume a unique initial state.)

It is not a priori clear that the linear-density model is an interesting model for studying automata-theoretic algorithms. We show empirically that this probability model does yield an interesting problem space. On one hand, the probability of universality does increase from 0 to 1 with both acceptance density and transition density. (Unlike the situation with random 3-SAT, the probability here changes in a smooth way and no sharp transition is observed.) On the other hand, the size of the canonical DFA does exhibit a (coarse) phase transition with respect to the transition density of the initial NFA, peaking at density 1.25. (It is interesting to note that random directed graphs with linear density are known to have a sharp phase transition with respect to connectivity at density 1.0 [26].) The scaling of the size of the canonical DFA depends on the transition density, showing polynomial behavior for high densities, but super-polynomial but subexponential behavior for low densities.

Once we have established that the linear-density model is an interesting model for studying automata-theoretic algorithms, we go on to study the canonization and universality problems for that model. We first compare Hopcroft's and Brzozowski's canonization algorithms. Both algorithms' running times display coarse phase transitions that are similar to that for the size of the canonical DFA. Interestingly, however, while Brzozowski's algorithm peaks at transition density 1.25, Hopcroft's algorithm peaks an density 1.5. We show empirically that while Hopcroft's algorithm generally performs better than Brzozowski's, the latter does perform better at high transition densities.

The universality problem can be solved both explicitly and symbolically. The explicit approach applies the classical subset construction (determinization) and after that searches for a rejecting reachable set, i.e. a reachable set that doesn't contain an accepting state [35]. To solve universality symbolically, we observe that the determinized automaton can be viewed as a synchronous sequential circuit. The reachability-of-rejecting-set condition can be expressed as a temporal property of this digital system. Thus, the universality problem can be reduced to a model-checking problem and solved by a symbolic model checker; we used two versions of SMV–Cadence SMV [13] and NuSMV [15]. To get the best possible performance from the model checker, we considered several optimization techniques, including the encoding of the determinized automata as a digital system, the representation of the transition relation, and the order of the BDD variables. In our experiments we used the configuration that led to the best performance.

The conventional wisdom in the field of model checking is that symbolic algorithms typically outperform explicit algorithms on synchronous systems, while the latter outperform on asynchronous systems. In view of that, we expected our optimized symbolic approach to outperforms the explicit, rather straightforward approach. Surprisingly, our empirical results show that the conventional wisdom does not apply to the universality problem, as the explicit algorithm dramatically outperformed the symbolic one.

The paper is organized as follows. In Section 2 we describe the random model and examine its properties. In Section 3 we compare the performance of Hopcroft's and Brzozowski's algorithms for the canonization problem. In Section 4 we compare the performance of the explicit and symbolic algorithms for the universality problems. Our conclusions are in Section 5.

2   The Random Model

We briefly introduce the notation used throughout this paper. Let $A = (\Sigma, S, S^0, \rho, F)$ be a finite nondeterministic automaton, where Σ is a finite nonempty alphabet, S is a finite nonempty set of states, $S^0 \subseteq S$ is a non-empty set of initial states, $F \subseteq S$ is the set of accepting states, and $\rho \subseteq S \times \Sigma \times S$ is a transition relation. Recall that A has a canonical, minimal DFA that accepts the same language [24]. The *canonization* problem is to generate this DFA. A is said to be universal if it accepts Σ^*. The *universality* problem is to check if A is universal.

In our model the set of initial states S^0 is the singleton $\{s_0\}$ and the alphabet Σ is the set $\{0, 1\}$. For each letter $\sigma \in \Sigma$ we generate a random directed graph D_σ on S with k edges, corresponding to transitions (s, σ, s'). Hereafter, we refer to the ratio $r = \frac{k}{|S|}$ as the *transition density for σ* (intuitively, r represents the expected outdegree of each node for σ). In our model the transition density of D_0 and D_1 is the same, and we refer to it as the transition density of A. The idea of using a linear density of some structural parameter to induce different behaviors has been quite popular lately, most notably in the context of random 3-SAT [37].

Our model for D_σ is closely related to Karp's model of random directed graphs [26]; for each positive integer n and each p with $0 < p < 1$, the sample space consists of all labeled directed graphs $D_{n,p}$ with n vertices and edge probability p. Karp shows that when n is large and np is equal to a constant greater than 1, it is very likely that the graph contains one large strongly connected component and several very small components. When $np < 1$, the expected size of the set of reachable nodes is very small.

It is known that random graphs defined as in [26] in terms of their edge probability or defined as here in terms of the number of edges display essentially the same behavior [7]. Thus, Karp's $np = 1$ corresponds to density 1 in our model. While Karp's considers reachability, which would correspond to non-emptiness [24], we consider here canonization and universality. Karp's phase transition at density 1 seems to have no effect on either canonization or universality. The density of the directed graphs underlying our automata is $2r$, but we see no interesting phenomenon at $r = 0.5$.

In our model the number of final states m is also a linear function of the total number of states, and it is given by a *final state density* $f = \frac{m}{|S|}$. The final states themselves are selected randomly, except for the initial state, which is always chosen to be an accepting state[1]. This additional restriction avoids the cases when an automaton is trivially non-universal because the initial state is not accepting. (One may also consider a model with a fixed number of accepting states rather than with a linear density; we found that such a model behaves similarly to the one we consider here).

In Figure 1[2] we present the probability of universality as a function of r and f. To generate each data point we checked the universality of 200 random automata with $|S| = 30$. The behavior here is quite intuitive. As transition and acceptance densities increase, the automaton has more accepting runs and is therefore more likely to be universal. Note that even if all states are accepting ($f = 1$), the automaton is still not guaranteed to be universal. This follows from the fact that the transition relation is not necessarily total, and the missing transitions are replaced by an implicit transition to a rejecting sink state.

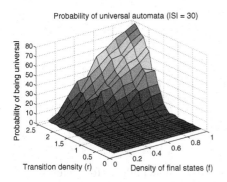

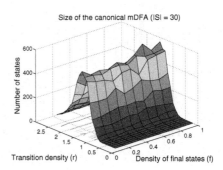

Fig. 1. Probability of universal automata ($|S| = 30$)

Fig. 2. Median number of states in the mDFA ($|S| = 30$)

A completely different pattern emerges when we look at the size of canonical minimized DFA (mDFA) corresponding to the input NFA A (Figure 2). For each data point on the graph we determinized and minimized 200 random automata and took the median of the size of the minimized DFA (we chose to report the median rather than the mean because the median is less affected by outlying points). We refer to the latter as the *canonical size*. While the effect of the acceptance density on the canonical size is not too dramatic, transition density does have a dramatic effect on canonical size. The latter rises and then falls with tradition density, peaking at $r = 1.25$. We see that the canonical size has a coarse phase transition at that density.

---

[1] We thank Ken McMillan for this suggestion.

[2] We recommend viewing the figures in this paper online: www.cs.rice.edu/~vardi/papers/

Finally, we investigated how the canonical size *scales* with respect to the size of the input NFA A. Since the values of f do not have a large effect on the canonical size, we fixed $f = 0.5$ here. Figure 3 shows that canonical size scales differently at different transition densities. The scaling curves exhibit a range of behaviors. For $r \leq 1.25$ they grow super-polynomially but subexponentially (in fact, a function of type $ab^{\sqrt{|S|}}$ provides a very good approximation), for $r = 1.5$ the growth is polynomial, and for higher transition densities they remain almost constant. Interestingly, though in the worst case the canonical size may scale exponentially [34], we do not observe such exponential scaling in our probabilistic model.

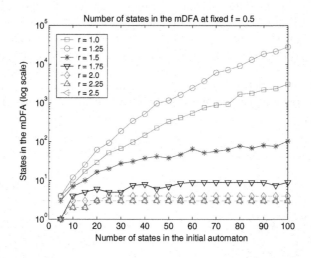

Fig. 3. Scaling of canonical size at different transition densities (log scale)

Based on these results we argue that our proposed model allows for "interesting" behavior as we vary r, f, and the size of the input NFA. In the next sections we use this model to study the performance of algorithms for canonization and universality.

3   Canonization

The *canonization* problem consists of constructing the minimal DFA that accepts the same language as a given (possibly non-deterministic) finite automaton. In addition to its theoretical appeal, this problem has an array of applications, from compilers to hardware circuit design to verification [40].

There are two different approaches to canonization. The first approach involves a two-step process: first, determinize the NFA, and second, minimize the resulting DFA. To complete the first step, we use the *subset construction*, which we present briefly here (see eg. [31] for a detailed description). Let $A = (\Sigma, S, S^0, \rho, F)$ be an NFA. We construct $A_d = (\Sigma, 2^S, \{S^0\}, \rho_d, F_d)$, where $F_d = \{T \in 2^S : T \cap F \neq \emptyset\}$ and $\rho_d(T_1, a, T_2) \iff T_2 = \{t_2 \in S : \rho(t1, a, t_2) \text{ for some } t_1 \in T_1\}$. The subset construction can be applied on the fly: starting with the initial state S^0, we determine the "next" state for each letter, and then recur. The automaton A_d is deterministic and accepts exactly the same language as A. For the second step, Watson [40] presents 15 algorithms that can be used to minimize a DFA, including one of the simplest (Huffman's [25]), and the one with the best known worst-case complexity (Hopcroft's [23]). The second approach to canonization, due to Brzozowski [10], avoids the minimization step, but applies the determinization step twice. In our study we compare the two approaches by evaluating the performance of Hopcroft's and Brzozowski's algorithms on randomly generated automata.

We present briefly the idea of the two algorithms. Let $L(A^{(p)})$ be the language accepted by the automaton A starting from the state p. Given a DFA, Huffman's and Hopcroft's algorithms construct an equivalence relation $E \subseteq S \times S$ with the following property: $(p, q) \in E \Leftrightarrow L(A^{(p)}) = L(A^{(q)})$. The equivalence relation E is computed as the greatest fixed point of the equation

$$(p, q) \in E \Leftrightarrow (p \in F \Leftrightarrow q \in F) \wedge (\forall a \in \Sigma, (p, a, p') \in \rho, (q, a, q') \in \rho : (p', q') \in E).$$

In Huffman's algorithm all states are assumed equivalent until proven otherwise. Equivalence classes are split repeatedly until a fixpoint is reached. The algorithm runs in asymptotic time $O(|S|^2)$. Hopcroft made several clever optimizations in the way equivalence classes are split, which allowed him to achieve the lowest known running time $O(|S| \log |S|)$ [21, 23]. Hopcroft's algorithm also significantly outperforms Huffman's algorithm in practice, so we can ignore Huffman's algorithm from this point on. Strictly speaking, Hopcroft's algorithm is just the DFA minimization algorithm, but we take it here to refer to the canonization algorithm, with determinization in the first step and minimization in the second step. Because the subset construction is applied in the first step, the worst-case complexity of this approach is exponential.

Brzozowski's algorithm is a direct canonization algorithm, and it does not use minimization, but, rather, two determinization steps. To describe the algorithm, we introduce some notation. If A is an automaton $(\Sigma, S, S^0, \rho, F)$, then $reverse(A)$ is the automaton $A^R = (\Sigma, S, F, \rho^R, S^0)$, where $\rho^R \subseteq S \times \Sigma \times S$ and $(s_2, a, s_1) \in \rho^R \Leftrightarrow (s_1, a, s_2) \in \rho$. Intuitively, $reverse$ switches the accepting and the initial states, and changes the direction of the transitions. Let $determinize(A)$ be the deterministic automaton obtained from A using the subset construction, and let $reachable(A)$ be the automaton A with all states not reachable from the initial states removed.

Theorem 1 (Brzozowski). *Let A be an NFA. Then*

$$A' = [reachable \circ determinize \circ reverse]^2(A)$$

is the minimal DFA accepting the same language as A.

It is not immediately obvious what the complexity of Brzozowski's algorithm is. The key to the correctness of the algorithm is, however, the following lemma.

Lemma 1. *Let $A = (\Sigma, S, \{s_0\}, \rho, F)$ be a DFA with the property that all states in S are reachable from s_0. Then $reachable(determinize(reverse(A)))$ is a minimal-state DFA.*

Since the canonical size is at most exponential in the size of the input automaton and since *reachable* and *determinize* can be combined to generate only reachable sets (which is exactly what we do in Hopcroft's algorithm), it follows that the worst-case complexity of Brzozowski's algorithm is also exponential.

For our experimental study we used the tool dk.brics.automaton [32], developed by Anders Møller. All experiments were performed on the Rice Terascale Cluster[3], which is a large Linux cluster of Itanium II processors with 4 GB of memory each.

We first study performance on fixed-size automata. Again, our sample contains 200 random automata per (r, f) pair, and median time is reported (as we mentioned earlier, median time is less affected by outlying points than the mean. These, and all subsequent timing data, refer to the median). To generate each data point in Figure 4, we determinized and then minimized with Hopcroft's algorithm each automaton; we measured combined running time for both steps. Note that Figure 4 is similar to Figure 2, but the two peaks occur in different densities ($r = 1.5$ and $r = 1.25$, respectively). As in Figure 2, for a fixed transition density, the impact of acceptance density on running time is not large.

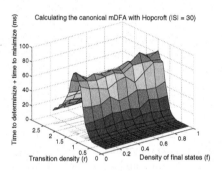

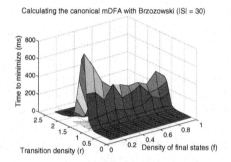

Fig. 4. Canonization using Hopcroft   **Fig. 5.** Canonization using Brzozowski

For Brzozowski's algorithm, we measured the total time to perform the two *reachable* ∘ *determinize* ∘ *reverse* steps. The results are presented in Figure 5. The peak for Brzozowski's algorithm coincides with the peak of Figure 2 ($r = 1.25$). For a fixed transition density, the impact of acceptance density on running time is much more pronounced that in Hopcroft's algorithm.

Our experiments indicate that neither Hopcroft's nor Brzozowski's algorithm dominates the other across the whole density landscape. In Figure 6 we show the running times of both algorithms for fixed $f = 0.5$. In Figure 6(a) the areas under both curves are 691 for Hopcroft and 995.5 for Brzozowski, and in Figure 6(b) the areas are 1900 for Hopcroft and 5866 for Brzozowski, so Hopcroft's algorithm has a better overall performance, but for $r > 1.5$ Brzozowski's algorithm is consistently faster. The conclusion is that Hopcroft's algorithm is faster for low-density automata, while Brzozowski's algorithm is better for high-density automata. It remains to be seen if this conclusion applies also for automata that arise in practical applications, e.g, [1].

---

[3] http://support.rtc.rice.edu/

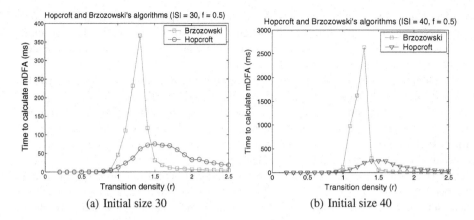

Fig. 6. Comparison between Hopcroft's and Brzozowski's algorithms for fixed $f = 0.5$

Similar to the approach of [36], we also investigated how Hopcroft's and Brzozow-ski's algorithms scale with automaton size. We fixed the acceptance density at $f = 0.5$, because its effect on the running time is less dramatic than that of the transition density. The results (Figure 7) indicate that none of the algorithms scales better than the other over the whole landscape. Brzozowski's algorithm has an edge over Hopcroft's for $r \geq 1.5$, and the opposite is true for the lower densities. At the peak, Hopcroft's algorithm scales exponentially, but generally the algorithms scale subexponentially. Again we see that Hopcroft's algorithm is better at low densities, while Brzozowski's algorithm is better at high densities.

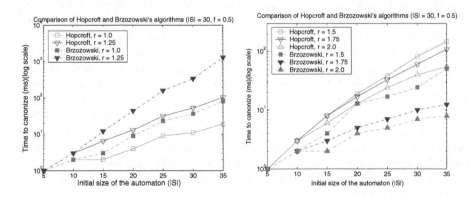

Fig. 7. Scaling comparison of Hopcroft and Brzozowski's algorithms

4   Universality

The straightforward way to check for universality of an NFA $A = (\Sigma, S, S^0, \rho, F)$ is to determinize it, using the subset construction, and then verify that every reachable state is accepting and that the transition relation is total. We optimize this by modifying the subset construction algorithm slightly. When a "next" state is generated, the algorithm first checks whether it is accepting, and if this is not the case the algorithm terminates early, indicating that the automaton is not universal.

An alternative approach is to view the determinized automaton $A_d = (\Sigma, 2^S, \{S^0\}, \rho_d, F_d)$, with $F_d = \{T \in 2^S : T \cap F \neq \emptyset\}$ and $\rho_d(T_1, a, T_2) \iff T_2 = \{t_2 \in S : \rho(t1, a, t_2)$ for some $t_1 \in T_1\}$, as a *sequential circuit* (SC). An SC [22] is a tuple (I, L, δ, α) where I is a set of input signals, L is a set of registers, $\delta : 2^L \times 2^I \to 2^L$ is the next-state function, describing the next assignment of the of the registers given their current assignment and an input assignment, and $\alpha \in 2^L$ is an initial assignment to the registers. (Usually we also have output signals and an output function, but this is not needed here.) The alphabet $\Sigma = \{0, 1\}$ corresponds here to a single input signal. The state set S can be viewed as the register set L; a set in 2^S can be viewed as a Boolean assignment to the state in S, using the duality between sets and their characteristic functions. The intuition is that every state in S can be viewed as a register that is either "active" or "inactive". The initial state s_0 correspond to an initial assignment, assigning 1 to s_0 and 0 to all other registers, as only s_0 is active, initially. Finally, the transition relation ρ_d, which is really a function, correspond to the next-state function, where $\delta(P, \sigma) = Q$ when $\rho_d(P, a, Q)$ holds (note that we view here subsets of S as Boolean assignments to S). Universality of A now correspond to an invariance property of A_d, expressed in CTL as $AG(\bigvee_{s \in F} s)$. Thus, we can check universality using a model checker.

In our evaluation we used two symbolic model checkers, both referred to as SMV: Cadence SMV [33] and NuSMV [15]. SMV is based on binary decision diagrams (BDDs) [8, 9], which provide a canonical representation for Boolean functions. A BDD is a rooted, directed acyclic graph with one or two terminal nodes labeled **0** or **1**, and a set of variable nodes of out-degree two. The variables respect a given linear order on all paths from the root to a leaf. Each path represents an assignment to each of the variables on the path. Since there can be exponentially more paths than vertices and edges, BDDs are often substantially more compact explicit representations, and have been used successfully in the verification of complex circuits [12]. To encode the SC for A_d in SMV, we use the states in S as state variables, corresponding to the registers. The SC is defined via the *init* and *next* statements: $init(s) = 1$ iff $s = s_0$, and $next(s) = 1$ iff $\bigvee_{\rho(t, \sigma, s)} t$, when the input is σ; we provide an example in Figure 8. We use a Boolean array to encode the registers, and a variable *input* to encode the input symbol. The specification in the example is the universality property. The NFA A is universal iff the sequential circuit corresponding to A_d satisfies the specification.

In order to improve the running time of the model checkers we considered several optimization techniques.

Sloppy vs. Fussy Encoding. Actually, to check universality we need not determinize A. Instead, we can construct the non-deterministic automaton $A_n = (\Sigma, 2^S, \{S^0\}, \rho_n, F_d)$, with $F_d = \{T \in 2^S : T \cap F \neq \emptyset\}$ and $\rho_n(T_1, a, T_2) \iff T_2 \subseteq \{t_2 \in S : \rho(t1, a, t_2)$ for some $t_1 \in T_1\}$. It is easy to see that A is universal iff every reachable state in A_n is accepting. Intuitively, A_n allows more states to be active in the subset construction. Unlike A_d, we cannot view A_n as an SC, since it is not

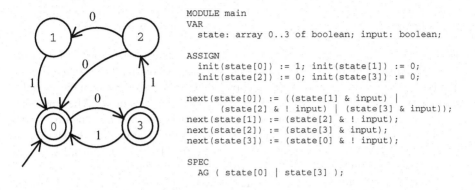

```
MODULE main
VAR
   state: array 0..3 of boolean; input: boolean;

ASSIGN
   init(state[0]) := 1; init(state[1]) := 0;
   init(state[2]) := 0; init(state[3]) := 0;

next(state[0]) := ((state[1] & input) |
         (state[2] & ! input) | (state[3] & input));
next(state[1]) := (state[2] & ! input);
next(state[2]) := (state[3] & input);
next(state[3]) := (state[0] & ! input);

SPEC
   AG ( state[0] | state[3] );
```

Fig. 8. A simple automaton and its encoding in SMV

deterministic. SMV, however, can also model non-deterministic systems. Rather than require that $next(s) = 1$ iff $\bigvee_{\rho(t,\sigma,s)} t$, when the input is σ, we requite that $next(s) = 1$ if $\bigvee_{\rho(t,\sigma,s)} t$, when the input is σ (the "iff" is replaced by "if"). We refer to the initial encoding as *fussy* and to this encoding as *sloppy*. In an explicit construction the sloppy approach would generate more subsets, but in a symbolic approach the sloppy approach uses "looser" logical constraints (trans, rather than assign), which might result in smaller BDDs. See Figure 9 for a sloppy encoding of the previous example.

```
...
TRANS
   ((state[1] & input) | (state[2] & (! input)) |
                    (state[3] & input)) -> next(state[0]);
   (state[2] & (! input)) -> next(state[1]);

   (state[3] & input) -> next(state[2]);

   (state[0] & (! input)) -> next(state[3]);
```

Fig. 9. Sloppy encoding of the automaton in Figure 8

Monolithic vs. Conjunctive Partitioning. In [11] Burch, Clarke and Long suggest an optimization of the representation of the transition relation of a sequential circuit. They note that the transition relation is the conjunction of several small relations, and the size of the BDD representing the entire transition relation may grow as the product of the sizes of the individual parts. This encoding is called *monolithic*. The method that Burch *et al.* suggest represents the transition relation by a list of the parts, which are implicitly conjuncted. Burch *et al.* call their method *conjunctive partitioning*, which has since then become the default encoding in NuSMV and Cadence SMV.

Conjunctive partitioning introduces an overhead when calculating the set of states reachable in the next step. The set of transitions has to be considered in some order, and choosing a good order is non-trivial, because each individual transition may depend on many variables. In large systems the overhead is negligible compared to the advantage of using small BDDs [11]. However, in our models the transitions are fairly simple, and it is not immediately clear whether monolithic encoding is a better choice.

Variable Ordering. When using BDDs, it is crucial to select a good order of the variables. Finding an optimal order is itself a hard problem, so one has to resort to different heuristics. The default order in NuSMV corresponds to the order in which the variables are first declared; in Cadence SMV it is based on some internal heuristic. The orders that we considered included the default order, and the orders given by three heuristics that are studied with respect to tree decompositions: Maximum Cardinality Search (MCS), LEXP and LEXM [27]. In our experiments MCS proved to be better than LEXP and LEXM, so we will only report the results for MCS and the default order.

In order to apply MCS we view the automaton as a graph whose nodes are the states, and in which two nodes are connected iff there is a transition between them. MCS orders [38] the vertices from 1 to $|S|$ according to the following rule: The first node is chosen arbitrarily. From this point on, a node that is adjacent to a maximal number of already selected vertices is selected next, and so on. Ties can be broken in various ways (eg. minimize the degree to unselected nodes [3] or maximize it [5], or select one at random), but none leads to a significant speedup. For our experiments, when we used MCS we broke ties by minimizing the degree to the unselected nodes.

Traversal. In our model the safety condition is of the form $\mathbf{AG}\alpha$: i.e. α is a property that we want to hold in all reachable states. CTL formulas are normally evaluated backwards in NuSMV [16], via the greatest fixpoint characterization:

$$\mathbf{AG}\alpha = \mathbf{gfp}_Z[\alpha \wedge \mathbf{AX}Z]$$

This approach ("backwards traversal") can be sometimes quite inefficient. As an optimization (only for $\mathbf{AG}\alpha$ formulas), NuSMV supports another strategy: calculate the set of reachable states, and verify that they satisfy the property α ("forward traversal"). In Cadence SMV, forward traversal is the default mode, but backwards traversal is also available. We considered forward and backwards traversal for both tools.

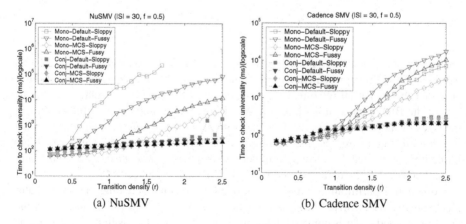

(a) NuSMV   (b) Cadence SMV

Fig. 10. Optimizing the running times of NuSMV and Cadence SMV

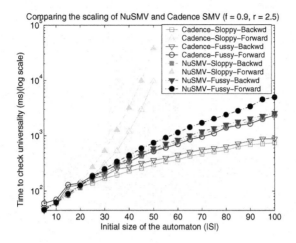

Fig. 11. Optimizing NuSMV and Cadence SMV (scaling)

Evaluating The Symbolic Approach. Generally, running times of the various symbolic approaches increase with both transition density and acceptance density. In Figure 10 we present the effect of the first three optimizations (for this set of experiments forward traversal direction was used) to the running times of NuSMV and Cadence SMV for fixed size automata. No single configuration gives the best performance throughout the range of transition density. Nevertheless, we can make several conclusions about the individual optimizations. Ordering the variables with MCS is always better than using the default ordering. Monolithic encoding is better than conjunctive partitioning for low transition density; the threshold varies depending on the tool and the choices for the other optimizations. Sloppy encoding is better than fussy when used together with monolithic encoding; the opposite is true when using conjunctive partitioning. The only exception to the latter is sloppy monolithic encoding in NuSMV, which gives the worst performance. Overall, for both tools, the best performance is achieved by using *monolithic-MCS-sloppy* up to $r = 1.3$, and *conjunctive-MCS-⋆* thereafter (the results for sloppy and fussy are too close to call here).

In order to fine-tune the two tools we next looked at their scaling performance (Figure 11). We considered automata with $f = 0.9$ and $r = 2.5$ (our choice is explained later). We fixed the transition encoding to conjunctive and variable order to MCS, and varied traversal direction and sloppy vs. fussy encoding. For both tools backwards traversal is the better choice, not surprisingly, since 90% of the states are accepting and a fixed point is achieved very quickly. When using backwards traversal, sloppy encoding gives better performance, and the opposite is true when using forward traversal. Overall, the best scaling is achieved by Cadence SMV with backwards traversal and sloppy encoding, and this is what we used for comparison with the explicit approach.

Comparing The Explicit and Symbolic Approaches. We compared the performance of the explicit and the symbolic approaches on a set of random automata with a fixed initial size. For each data point we took the median of all execution times (200 sample points).

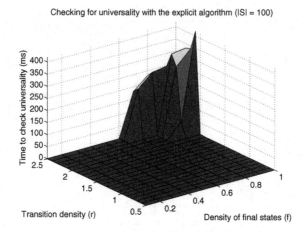

Fig. 12. Median time to check for universality with the explicit algorithm

Our results indicate that for small automata the explicit algorithm is much faster than the symbolic. In fact, even when using automata with initial size $|S| = 100$, the median of the execution time is 0 almost everywhere on the landscape (see Figure 12). In contrast, even for automata with $|S| = 30$ the symbolic algorithm takes non-negligible time (Figure 10).

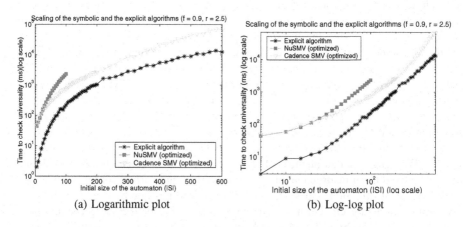

| (a) Logarithmic plot | (b) Log-log plot |

Fig. 13. Scaling comparison of the symbolic and the explicit algorithms

As before, we also investigated which algorithm scales better as we increase the initial size of the automata. For this set of experiments, we fixed the densities of the final states and the transitions at $f = 0.9$ and $r = 2.5$ (i.e. on of the furthest edge of the landscape). We chose this point because almost everywhere else the median execution time of the explicit algorithm is 0 for small automata. We varied the initial size of the automata between 5 and 600. The results are presented on Figure 13. The symbolic algorithm (Cadence SMV) is quite slower than the explicit throughout the whole range. All algorithms scale sub-exponentially; however, the symbolic algorithm scales $2^{O(\sqrt{|S|})}$ worse than the explicit one (Figure 13(b)). We also present data for NuSMV, which scales the worst of the three algorithms and is the slowest for $|S| > 20$. We note that at lower transition and/or acceptance density, the advantage of the explicit approach over the symbolic approach is much more pronounced.

5   Discussion

In this paper we proposed a probabilistic benchmark for testing automata-theoretic algorithms. We showed that in this model Hopcroft's and Brzozowski's canonization algorithms are incomparable, each having an advantage in a certain region of the model. In contrast, the advantage of the explicit approach to universality over the symbolic approach is quite clear.

An obvious question to raise is how "realistic" our probabilistic model is. There is no obvious answer to this question; partly because we lack realistic benchmarks of finite automata. Since automata represent finite-state control, it is hard to see why random directed graphs with linear density do not provide a realistic model. Hopefully, with the recent increase in popularity of finite-state formalisms in industrial temporal property specification languages (c.f., [4, 6]), such benchmarks will become available in the not-too-far future, enabling us to evaluate our findings on such benchmarks. While our results are purely empirical, as the lack of success with fully analyzing related probabilistic models indicates (cf. [19, 18, 2]), providing rigorous proof for our qualitative observations may be a very challenging task. At any rate, gaining a deeper understanding why one method is better than another method is an important challenge. Another research direction is to consider minimization on the fly, as, for example, in [30].

Our most surprising result, we think, is the superiority of the explicit approach to universality over the symbolic approach. This runs against the conventional wisdom in verification [12]. One may wonder whether the reason for this is the fact that our sequential circuits can be viewed as consisting of "pure control", with no data component, unlike typical hardware designs, which combine control and data. This suggests that perhaps in model checking such designs, control and data ought to be handled by different techniques. Another possible explanation is that the sequential circuits corresponding to the determinized NFA have registers with large fan-in, while realistic circuits typically have small-fan-in registers. We believe that these point deserve further study.

In future work we plan to extend the comparison between the explicit and symbolic approaches to universality to automata on infinite words, a problem of very direct relevance to computer-aided verification [29]. It is known that complementation of such automata is quite intricate [29], challenging both explicit and symbolic implementation.

Acknowledgments. We are grateful to Andreas Podelski for raising the question of comparing Hopcroft's and Brzozowski's algorithms.

References

1. Y. Abarbanel, I. Beer, L. Gluhovsky, S. Keidar, and Y. Wolfstal. FoCs - automatic generation of simulation checkers from formal specifications. In *CAV, Proc. 12th International Conference*, volume 1855 of *LNCS*, pages 538–542. Springer-Verlag, 2000.
2. D. Achlioptas. Setting two variables at a time yields a new lower bound for random 3-SAT. In *Proc. of 32nd Annual ACM Symposium on Theory of Computing*, 2000.
3. A. San Miguel Aguirre and M. Y. Vardi. Random 3-SAT and BDDs: The plot thickens further. In *Principles and Practice of Constraint Programming*, pages 121–136, 2001.
4. R. Armoni, L. Fix, A. Flaisher, R. Gerth, B. Ginsburg, T. Kanza, A. Landver, S. Mador-Haim, E. Singerman, A. Tiemeyer, M.Y. Vardi, and Y. Zbar. The ForSpec temporal logic: A new temporal property-specification logic. In *Proc. 8th International Conference on Tools and Algorithms for the Construction and Analysis of Systems*, volume 2280 of *LNCS*, pages 296–211, Grenoble, France, April 2002. Springer-Verlag.
5. D. Beatty and R. Bryant. Formally verifying a microprocessor using a simulation methodology. In *Proc. 31st Design Automation Conference*, pages 596–602. IEEE Computer Society, 1994.
6. I. Beer, S. Ben-David, C. Eisner, D. Fisman, A. Gringauze, and Y. Rodeh. The temporal logic sugar. In *Proc. 13th International Conference on Computer Aided Verification*, volume 2102 of *LNCS*, pages 363–367, Paris, France, July 2001. Springer-Verlag.
7. B. Bollobas. *Random Graphs*. Cambridge University Press, January 2001.
8. R.E. Bryant. Graph-based algorithms for boolean-function manipulation. *IEEE Trans. on Computers*, C-35(8), 1986.
9. R.E. Bryant. Symbolic boolean manipulation with ordered binary-decision diagrams. *ACM Computing Surveys*, 24(3):293–318, 1992.
10. J. A. Brzozowski. Canonical regular expressions and minimal state graphs for definite events. In *Mathematical theory of Automata*, pages 529–561. Polytechnic Press, Polytechnic Institute of Brooklyn, N.Y., 1962. Volume 12 of MRI Symposia Series.
11. J. R. Burch, E. M. Clarke, and D. E. Long. Symbolic model checking with partitioned transition relations. In *Proc. IFIP TC10/WG 10.5 International Conference on Very Large Scale Integration*, pages 49–58, 1991.
12. J.R. Burch, E.M. Clarke, K.L. McMillan, D.L. Dill, and L.J. Hwang. Symbolic model checking: 10^{20} states and beyond. *Information and Computation*, 98(2):142–170, June 1992.
13. Cadence. SMV. http://www.cadence.com/company/cadence_labs_research.html.
14. P. Cheeseman, B. Kanefsky, and W. M. Taylor. Where the really hard problems are. In *IJCAI '91*, pages 331–337, 1991.
15. A. Cimatti, E. Clarke, E. Giunchiglia, F. Giunchiglia, M. Pistore, M. Roveri, R. Sebastiani, and A. Tacchella. NuSMV Version 2: An OpenSource Tool for Symbolic Model Checking. In *Proc. International Conference on Computer-Aided Verification (CAV 2002)*, volume 2404 of *LNCS*, Copenhagen, Denmark, July 2002. Springer.
16. A. Cimatti, E. M. Clarke, F. Giunchiglia, and M. Roveri. NUSMV: A new symbolic model checker. *International Journal on Software Tools for Technology Transfer*, 2(4):410–425, 2000.
17. E.M. Clarke, O. Grumberg, and D. Peled. *Model Checking*. MIT Press, 1999.
18. Olivier Dubois, Yacine Boufkhad, and Jacques Mandler. Typical random 3-SAT formulae and the satisfiability threshold. In *SODA*, pages 126–127, 2000.
19. E. Friedgut. Necessary and sufficient conditions for sharp thresholds of graph properties, and the k-SAT problem. *Journal of the A.M.S.*, 12:1017–1054, 1999.
20. James Glenn and William I. Gasarch. Implementing WS1S via finite automata: Performance issues. In *Workshop on Implementing Automata*, pages 75–86, 1997.

21. D. Gries. Describing an algorithm by Hopcroft. *Acta Informatica*, 2:97–109, 1973.
22. G.D. Hachtel and F. Somenzi. *Logic Synthesis and Verification Algorithms*. Kluwer Academic Publishers, Norwell, Massachusetts, 1996.
23. J. E. Hopcroft. An n log n algorithm for minimizing the states in a finite automaton. In Z. Kohavi, editor, *The Theory of Machines and Computations*, pages 189–196. Academic Press, 1971.
24. J.E. Hopcroft and J.D. Ullman. *Introduction to Automata Theory, Languages, and Computation*. Addison-Wesley, 1979.
25. D. A. Huffman. The synthesis of sequential switching circuits. In E. F. Moore, editor, *Sequential Machines: Selected Papers*. Addison-Wesley, 1964.
26. R. M. Karp. The transitive closure of a random digraph. *Random Struct. Algorithms*, 1(1):73–94, 1990.
27. A. M. C. A. Koster, H. L. Bodlaender, and C. P. M. van Hoesel. Treewidth: Computational experiments. ZIB-Report 01–38, Konrad-Zuse-Zentrum für Informationstechnik Berlin, Berlin, Germany, 2001. Also available as technical report UU-CS-2001-49 (Utrecht University) and research memorandum 02/001 (Universiteit Maastricht).
28. O. Kupferman and M.Y. Vardi. Model checking of safety properties. *Formal methods in System Design*, 19(3):291–314, November 2001.
29. O. Kupferman and M.Y. Vardi. Weak alternating automata are not that weak. *ACM Trans. on Computational Logic*, 2001(2):408–429, July 2001.
30. D. Lee and M. Yannakakis. Online minimization of transition systems. In *Proc. 24th ACM Symp. on Theory of Computing*, pages 264–274, Victoria, May 1992.
31. P. Linz. *An introduction to formal languages and automata*. D. C. Heath and Company, Lexington, MA, USA, 1990.
32. A. Møller. dk.brics.automaton. http://www.brics.dk/automaton/, 2004.
33. K.L. McMillan. *Symbolic Model Checking*. Kluwer Academic Publishers, 1993.
34. A.R. Meyer and M.J. Fischer. Economy of description by automata, grammars, and formal systems. In *Proc. 12th IEEE Symp. on Switching and Automata Theory*, pages 188–191, 1971.
35. A.R. Meyer and L.J. Stockmeyer. The equivalence problem for regular expressions with squaring requires exponential time. In *Proc. 13th IEEE Symp. on Switching and Automata Theory*, pages 125–129, 1972.
36. G. Pan and M.Y. Vardi. Search vs. symbolic techniques in satisfiability solving. In *SAT 2004*, LNCS, Aalborg, May 2004. Springer-Verlag.
37. Bart Selman, David G. Mitchell, and Hector J. Levesque. Generating hard satisfiability problems. *Artificial Intelligence*, 81(1-2):17–29, 1996.
38. R. E. Tarjan and M. Yannakakis. Simple linear-time algorithms to test chordality of graphs, test acyclicity of hypergraphs, and selectively reduce acyclic hypergraphs. *SIAM J. Comput.*, 13(3):566–579, 1984.
39. M.Y. Vardi and P. Wolper. An automata-theoretic approach to automatic program verification. In *Proc. 1st Symp. on Logic in Computer Science*, pages 332–344, Cambridge, June 1986.
40. B. W. Watson. A taxonomy of finite automata minimization algorithmes. Computing Science Note 93/44, Eindhoven University of Technology, The Netherlands, 1993.
41. B. W. Watson. *Taxonomies and Toolkits of Regular Language Algorithms*. PhD thesis, Eindhoven University of Technology, the Netherlands, 1995.

Automatic Validation of Transformation Rules for Java Verification Against a Rewriting Semantics*

Wolfgang Ahrendt[1], Andreas Roth[2], and Ralf Sasse[3]

[1] Chalmers University of Technology, Göteborg, Sweden
ahrendt@cs.chalmers.se
[2] Universität Karlsruhe, Germany
aroth@ira.uka.de
[3] University of Illinois at Urbana-Champaign, USA
rsasse@uiuc.edu

Abstract. This paper presents a methodology for automatically validating program transformation rules that are part of a calculus for Java source code verification. We target the Java Dynamic Logic calculus which is implemented in the interactive prover of the KeY system. As a basis for validation, we take an existing SOS style rewriting logic semantics for Java, formalized in the input language of the Maude system. That semantics is 'lifted' to cope with schematic programs like the ones appearing in program transformation rules. The rewriting theory is further extended to generate valid initial states for involved program fragments, and to check the final states for equivalence. The result is used in frequent validation runs over the relevant fragment of the calculus in the KeY system.

1 Introduction

In our work we relate two formal artifacts dealing with the programming language Java. The first is a *sequent calculus* for *Java Dynamic Logic* (JavaDL), a program logic for Java source code. This calculus [2] is implemented in the interactive prover of the KeY system [1]. The other artifact is a rewriting logic semantics [11, 10] for Java, written as a rewrite theory $\mathcal{R}_{Java}$ in the input language of the Maude system [5]. The objective of the work is to achieve an *automatic validation* of certain parts of the JavaDL calculus with respect to $\mathcal{R}_{Java}$, taking advantage of the executability of $\mathcal{R}_{Java}$.

The particular calculus rules we want to validate with this approach are *program transformation rules* of the form (cf. Sect. 2)

$$\frac{\Gamma \vdash \langle \Pi' \text{ rs} \rangle \ \phi, \Delta}{\Gamma \vdash \langle \Pi \text{ rs} \rangle \ \phi, \Delta} \tag{1}$$

* This research has been partly supported by STINT (The Swedish Foundation for International Cooperation in Research and Higher Education) and by the ONR Grant N00014-02-1-0715.

G. Sutcliffe and A. Voronkov (Eds.): LPAR 2005, LNAI 3835, pp. 412–426, 2005.

Roughly speaking, this proof rule replaces, in the beginning of a list of Java statements, a match of Π by the corresponding instance of Π'. (rs stands for the list of remaining statements.) Even if this appears as a very special case, a large and important part of the Java related rules of the JavaDL calculus (about 45%) is of exactly that kind! Note that the applicability of rules of this particular shape does not depend on the logical context, as Γ, Δ, and ϕ match arbitrary (lists of) formulae. Neither is the context affected by the rule application. The soundness of such a rule only depends on Π and Π'. Therefore, validating the rule reduces to showing *semantical equivalence* of Π and Π'.

It is important to note that one cannot simply 'run' $\mathcal{R}_{Java}$, in spite of its executability, on Π and Π'. The reason is that the statements in Π and Π' are not in plain Java syntax, but *schemata* for Java code. An example for a program transformation rule is

$$\frac{\Gamma \vdash \langle \mathsf{typeof(e)}\ \mathsf{v}_1 = \mathsf{e};\ \mathsf{typeof(n)}\ \mathsf{v}_2 = \mathsf{n};\ \mathsf{l} = \mathsf{v}_1 * \mathsf{v}_2;\ \mathsf{rs} \rangle\ \phi, \Delta}{\Gamma \vdash \langle \mathsf{l} = \mathsf{e} * \mathsf{n};\ \mathsf{rs} \rangle\ \phi, \Delta} \qquad (2)$$

Here, l, e, n, rs, v_1, and v_2 are *schema variables*, matching certain syntactical categories (Sect. 2), and typeof delivers the static type of its argument. Comparing such schematic program fragments raises several issues.

First of all, $\mathcal{R}_{Java}$ is made for computing with *concrete* entities, like concrete memory locations, concrete (primitive) values, concrete object references, and so forth. It is an essential part of this work to have extended $\mathcal{R}_{Java}$ to a *lifted* Java semantics, $\mathcal{R}_{Java^{lift}}$, executing also *schematic*, i.e. *abstract*, Java code. Some central ingredients are the storage of *conditional values* in the memory, and parameterizing the values of abstract expressions by *snapshots* of the dynamic parts of the execution state. One can easily imagine that such an abstract execution would explode beyond feasibility if applied to longer program schemata. However, the pragmatics of program transformation rules (used for verification) make the considered program fragments short enough to keep the execution by $\mathcal{R}_{Java^{lift}}$ feasible.

Another issue is that the syntactical categories of schema variables, while sufficient for the proof rule, are not detailed enough to induce a unique execution by $\mathcal{R}_{Java}$, which for instance would need to distinguish between local variables and object fields as instances of l. This problem is addressed by the generation of all possible (and often very many) combinations.

One of the potential errors in a transformation rule is that certain instantiations are forgotten, namely those in which the instance of *different* schema variables *coincide*. The validation takes care of this by creating all possible unifying combinations of variables before checking for equivalence.

Besides our restriction to transformation rules, we are further constrained by the fact that $\mathcal{R}_{Java}$, in its current form, does not support all features of sequential Java. In spite of those restrictions, we could apply the automated validation to 56 rules, three of which turned out to be incorrect. We also discovered some errors in the semantics. As noted in [10], the whole process can be understood as a *mutual debugging*, which we consider very natural in a context where the ultimate reference (here the Java language specification [7]) is informal.

In general, what we needed for our purpose was a semantic formalism which is executable yet *abstract*. Rewriting logic, with its special support for associativity and commutativity, suited this purpose well. For instance, we need to represent a memory and all we know is that it maps a location L to a value V. The memory can be represented by [L,V] rm, with rm being a *constant* representing the arbitrary rest of the memory, and the juxtaposition with empty syntax being the *associative and commutative multiset union*, allowing us to abstract away from the concrete position of the location L in the memory. Such abstractions are heavily used in semantics formulated in a rewriting logic framework [10], where states are concrete but left hand sides of rewrite rules are abstract. We need abstraction even more, as in our *lifted* semantics even the states are abstract.

The paper is structured as follows. In the next two sections we present the two formalisms which we are concerned with: the program transformation rules of the JavaDL calculus (Sect. 2) and the rewriting logic which we use as basis for the validation (Sect. 3). Our approach to validate program transformation rules is then described in Sect. 4. In Sect. 5 we explain our lifting of the semantics. In Sect. 6, our implementation and experiences are sketched, before we conclude in Sect. 7 with a comparison to other approaches.

2   A Calculus for Java Source Code Verification

The KeY system aims at the deductive verification of sequential Java programs. The verification is based on a sequent calculus for JavaDL, which covers, among the propositional and first-order rules, full sequential Java[1].

Java Dynamic Logic (JavaDL) is a multi-modal logic, described in detail in [2]. For the purpose of this paper it is sufficient to state roughly that sub-formulae can be of the shapes $[\pi]\phi$ and $\langle\pi\rangle\phi$, where π is a sequence of Java statements and ϕ is again a formula. The intuitive meaning of $[\pi]\phi$ is that, if π terminates normally ϕ holds in the final state; $\langle\pi\rangle\phi$ means that π must terminate and afterwards ϕ must hold. The logic is closed under the usual first-order quantifiers and junctors, so the typical Hoare triple $\{\psi\}\pi\{\phi\}$ is formalized as $\psi \rightarrow [\pi]\phi$. In the following we only consider formulae with modality $\langle\cdot\rangle$, the other modality is treated exactly the same way.

Example 1. For local variables i and j of type int, the following JavaDL formula, which is valid in all states, says that after executing the piece of Java code in angled brackets j * j equals i:

$$\langle \texttt{i=(j=i)*(i++);} \rangle \; \texttt{j} * \texttt{j} \doteq \texttt{i} \tag{3}$$

The JavaDL calculus rules that work on sequents consisting of JavaDL formulae can be divided into the following categories:

---

[1] More precisely, the target language is JavaCard, but the calculus covers a larger fragment of Java which can be characterized as Java with exactly one thread and without garbage collection.

1. axiomatic program transformation rules,
2. axiomatic rules connecting the program and first order logic,
3. axiomatic first-order or theory specific rules,
4. derived rules, i.e. rules whose application could be simulated by applying a series of axiomatic rules,
5. axiomatic rules that apply state changes (*updates*) on first order formulae.

The basic concept behind the JavaDL calculus is the paradigm of *symbolic execution*. In order to resolve a formula $\langle \pi_1 \ldots \pi_n \rangle \phi$ (with statements $\pi_1, \ldots, \pi_n$), π_1 is taken into focus first. If it contains complex expressions, like `i=(j=i)*(i++);`, rules of group 1 transform it into less complex expressions, in our example to `int eval1=(j=i); int eval2=i++; i=eval1*eval2;`. Otherwise the state change of the first statement is, by applying rules of group 2, memorized as an *update* written in front of the modality. E.g., (3) is transformed—by several rule applications—into the equivalent formula $\mathcal{U} \langle \rangle \, j * j \doteq i$ where $\mathcal{U} = \{i := i * i, j := i\}$ is an update capturing the effect of the considered code as a *parallel* assignment to `i` and `j`. When code in a modality is completely worked off, rules of group 5 make the formula pure first order, by simplifying and executing the accumulated updates.

All of the rules from the groups 1 to 4 are implemented as *taclets* [3]. Taclets are representations of traditional rule schemes, but additionally have an operational meaning. Also, they embody a precise notion of schematic expressions. *This work is only concerned with taclets of group 1.* These taclets are mostly concerned with correctly reflecting the sophisticated evaluation order of complex Java expressions. Due to this non-trivial task and the sheer number (see Sect. 6) of rules of this kind, correctness checks are highly desired. In the sequel, we will detail only those parts of taclets which are relevant for this work.

A program transformation rule is written as a taclet as follows:

$$\mathsf{find}(\langle \varPi \, \mathsf{rs} \rangle \, b) \quad \mathsf{varcond}(\mathsf{new} \, T_1 v_1, \ldots, T_n v_n) \quad \mathsf{replacewith}(\langle \varPi' \, \mathsf{rs} \rangle \, b) \qquad (4)$$

where $\varPi, \varPi'$ are (schematic) sequences of Java statements. We call taclets which comply with this shape *program transformation taclets (PTT)*. Intuitively, such taclets implement the concept of rewrite rules: when they are applied during proof construction, an occurrence of a formula $\langle \varPi \, \mathsf{rs} \rangle \phi$ is rewritten to $\langle \varPi' \, \mathsf{rs} \rangle \phi$. $\varPi'$ may contain new program variables declared in the **varcond** section.

Example 2. This is a PTT:

$$\begin{aligned} &\mathsf{find}(\langle \mathsf{l} = \mathsf{e} * \mathsf{n}; \mathsf{rs} \rangle \, b) \\ &\mathsf{varcond}(\mathsf{new} \, \mathsf{typeof}(\mathsf{e}) \, v_1, \mathsf{typeof}(\mathsf{n}) \, v_2) \\ &\mathsf{replacewith}(\langle \mathsf{typeof}(\mathsf{e}) \, v_1 = \mathsf{e}; \, \mathsf{typeof}(\mathsf{n}) \, v_2 = \mathsf{n}; \, \mathsf{l} = v_1 * v_2; \mathsf{rs} \rangle \, b) \end{aligned} \qquad (5)$$

Traditionally, one would denote the represented sequent rule as (2). Note however, that—in contrast to that rule—the taclet is applicable on both sides of the sequent, and even on *sub*-formulae of sequent formulae. Most importantly however, side conditions on the instantiations of the rule schema are explicitly defined with taclets.

Table 1. Schema variable sorts and instantiations for *Example 3*

Schema variable sort	Conditions on instantiations ι	Schema var. in (5)	ι in (3)
Formula	ι is a formula	b	$j * j \doteq i$
Expression	ι is an expression	e	(j=i)
Lefthandside	ι is a local variable *or* a field with either no prefix or a prefix not possibly causing side-effects	l v_1 v_2	i eval1 eval2
NonSimpleExpression	ι is an expression but does not satisfy the *Lefthandside* condition and is not a (possibly negated) literal	n	i++
RemainingStatements	arbitrary sequence of statements	rs	(empty)

Clearly, a taclet must be interpreted as a *pattern*: For instance, (5) should be applicable *for all* formulae b, *for all* Java expressions l, e, n, v_1, v_2 which satisfy certain criteria, and *for all* sequences of Java statements rs. Expressions in taclets usually contain *schema variables* (printed in sans-serif here) to capture this need for genericity. When a taclet is applied, schema variables are *instantiated* with concrete expressions. Schema variables are assigned *conditions* and, in a special declaration section, *sorts*. Conditions and sorts determine which concrete expressions are legal instantiations for the schema variable. A taclet is *applicable* if there are legal and consistent instantiations of all the schema variables of the taclet. Table 1 gives an overview of the most important schema variable sorts. All terminology in this table refers to [7]. For PTTs, there is only the condition varcond(new $T_1 v_1, \ldots, T_n v_n$), which requires instances of $v_1, \ldots, v_n$ to be fresh and of the (Java) types $T_1, \ldots, T_n$.

Example 3. Consider Table 1. Let the schema variables of the taclet (5) be declared as shown in the third column. The instantiations in the last column satisfy the conditions imposed by the second column *and* by the varcond condition of (5). Thus, taclet (5) is applicable to formula (3).

Taclets can be applied in a proof through either user interaction or the automated deduction engine. The effect of an application of a PTT is quite intuitive: the occurrence in the formula matching the find part of the taclet is replaced by the instantiated version of the replacewith part.

There is another bit to make the description of PTTs complete: The typeof($\cdot$) construct provides taclets with the static types of (instantiated schematic) expressions. This *meta construct* [3] allows for introducing declarations into the results of taclet applications as the following example demonstrates.

Example 4. When the taclet (5) is applied to (3) the following formula results:

$$\langle \text{int eval1=(j=i); int eval2=i++; i=eval1*eval2;} \rangle \; j * j \doteq i$$

Because of the variable condition in (5) two new variables of type int have been introduced since the expressions j=i and i++ are both of that type.

3   The Rewriting Logic Semantics of Java

In this section, we introduce the semantics we validate against, and the framework in which it is formalized.

3.1   Rewriting Logic and Maude

Rewriting logic [9] is the logical framework in which the semantics of Java we want to use is given. A (simplified) rewrite theory is a triple $(\Sigma, E, \mathcal{R})$ where (Σ, E) is an equational theory with the signature Σ of operations and sorts and the set E of equations, and $\mathcal{R}$ is a set of rewrite rules. The equations and rewrite rules can also be conditional. The rewrite rules are always used modulo the equations. A rewrite rule $t \Rightarrow t'$, with t and t' terms over the signature Σ, is an inference from a logical point of view while from a computational point of view it is a concurrent transition of states.

Maude [5] is a high performance implementation of rewriting logic. Equations in Maude theories are directed, have to be terminating and need to have the Church-Rosser property. In Maude we mostly work on multisets as data structures due to the possibility of using the internal associativity, commutativity and identity axioms which are declared as attributes for an operator.

3.2   The Maude Rewriting Semantics of Java $\mathcal{R}_{Java}$

The rewrite theory for Java semantics[2], called $\mathcal{R}_{Java}$ in the sequel, was developed by Feng Chen at the University of Illinois at Urbana-Champaign and presented in the paper [6]. This rewriting logic theory is given as an executable specification in Maude, thus it gives us a Java interpreter for free. The semantics uses continuation-passing style (CPS) to keep track of the code which is to be executed. Continuations can roughly be seen as an executable stack of statements which can be restored anytime. The semantics uses an explicit environment and memory model, i.e. variables are mapped to locations inside the environments and those locations are mapped to values in the memory. We call the whole state information, including the memory and environments, *configuration* from now on. As is usual within such rewriting logic specifications most rewrite rules and equations can be used locally and do not need to specify precisely the rest of the state in which they can be used. There is no documentation by the developers of this Java semantics but to get an impression on how it is structured we recommend the paper [11] where a (simpler) semantics for a CaML-like language has been developed in great detail. For a more general account of the design of such semantics, and on Maude as a semantic framework, see [10].

In Fig. 1 we present the configuration parts of $\mathcal{R}_{Java}$ in Maude-style notation. With code1 and code2 being code pieces which shall be executed sequentially, the continuation looks like (a): k wraps a continuation so it can later be used inside a multiset. The environment (b), wrapped by e, maps variable names Xi to locations Li. The continuation, environment, and additionally the current

---

[2] This Maude theory can be downloaded from http://fsl.cs.uiuc.edu/javafan/

object currObj, constitute one part of the overall configuration, the context (c). Moreover, explicit memory (d) is needed, mapping locations Li to values Vi. The next free location in the memory is denoted by an integer I. Other parts of the configuration are the static environment staticEnv and the list listOfClasses of all classes, used for instance in method lookups.

(a) Continuation: k(code1 −> code2 −> ...)
(b) Environment: e([X1, L1] [X2, L2] ...)
(c) Context: c(k(code1 −> code2 −> ...), e([X1,L1] [X2, L2] ...), o(currObj))
(d) Memory: m([L1, V1] [L2, V2] ...), n(I)
(e) Static env.: s(staticEnv)
(f) List of classes: cl(listOfClasses)

Fig. 1. Important parts of an $\mathcal{R}_{Java}$ configuration

These items (and a few more which we omit here) are put together under the run operator. Any such configuration can be executed by $\mathcal{R}_{Java}$.

run(c(k (...), e (...), o (...)), m (...), n (...), s (...), cl (...))

Note that the comma ',' here is a multiset-union operator, both inside run and inside c. As an example of a rewrite rule operating on such a configuration, we show the rule for writing to the memory:

      c(k(change(V, L) −> K), Cnt),
      m([L, V'] M)
 => c(k(K), Cnt),
      m([L, V] M)

In this rule the actual Java code has been evaluated long enough to have been reduced to change(V, L). K matches the rest of the continuation. The context Cnt matches the subset of all other components wrapped inside c, apart from the explicitly given k. In the memory at location L there is a value V' which is overwritten. The rest M of the memory remains unchanged and the change code has disappeared from the continuation after its execution.

3.3   Limitations of $\mathcal{R}_{Java}$ and Improvements

$\mathcal{R}_{Java}$ is a prototypic formalization of the Java semantics, and therefore has a couple of limitations, which restrict the number of transformation rules to which we can apply our approach (see Sect. 6). Some interesting Java features are not modeled, such as abrupt termination, switch, conditional expressions, method overloading, and static class initialization. Some other features were realized in an incomplete or faulty manner. During the realization of our approach, we fixed several of these shortcomings. Finally, we have added additional features to $\mathcal{R}_{Java}$ by introducing type checks for assignments and type casts. More on the improvements to the original $\mathcal{R}_{Java}$ can be found in [12].

4   Validating Program Transformation Rules

The style of semantics formalized in the rewriting logic framework partly builds on the tradition of *structural operational semantics* (SOS)[3]. One central paradigm is to include a 'still-to-be-executed' program in the *state* of execution which is modified as execution proceeds. In SOS, one notationally separates the program π from the rest of the state, by writing (π, s). Correspondingly, by $(\pi_0, s_0) \to (\pi_1, s_1)$ we mean that there is a number of steps after which the execution of the program π_0, when started in s_0, results in the program π_1 to be executed from state s_1.[4] A special case is $(\pi\pi_{rs}, s_0) \to (\pi_{rs}, s_1)$, where the second program π_{rs} (remaining statements) is a suffix of the first, and a certain number of execution steps will resolve π completely, while π_{rs} is still untouched.

Now, a transformation rule of the shape (1) (or a corresponding PTT (4)) is sound if the following holds for all programs π matching the schema Π, all programs π' matching the schema Π', all *arbitrary* programs π_{rs}, and all states s_0 being 'admissible' w.r.t. $\pi\pi_{rs}$ and $\pi'\pi_{rs}$: If $(\pi\pi_{rs}, s_0) \to (\pi_{rs}, s_1)$ and $(\pi'\pi_{rs}, s_0) \to (\pi_{rs}, s_1')$, then s_1 and s_1' are 'equivalent'. We defer a discussion of state equivalence to Sect. 5.3. A state is called *admissible* w.r.t. some programs if those programs can possibly be executed starting from this state. For instance, the state must, in its environment, map all variables in π to some locations, and in its memory, map all those locations to values.

The above statement is quantified over infinitely many programs π, π', π_{rs} and states s_0. The goal is, however, to have an *executable* criteria for the statement. In short, the idea is to define a *lifted* semantics, executing the *schematic* programs Π and Π' *directly*, working on *generic* states. With such a semantics at hand, the 'universally quantified' soundness criteria given above reduces to showing: If $(\Pi\, \mathbf{rs},\ \mathbf{s}_{\Pi,\Pi'}) \to (\mathbf{rs}, s)$ and $(\Pi'\, \mathbf{rs},\ \mathbf{s}_{\Pi,\Pi'}) \to (\mathbf{rs}, s')$, then s and s' are equivalent, where $\mathbf{s}_{\Pi,\Pi'}$ is the generic state being admissible w.r.t. Π and Π', and $\mathbf{rs}$ is a generic constant representing the 'remaining statements', not being executed. For instance, validating the PTT (5) (or equivalent the rule (2)) amounts to executing both

- l = e * n;   and
- typeof(e) v_1 = e; typeof(n) v_2 = n; l = v_1 * v_2;

from the generic state admissible for both, and comparing the results.

The realization of this approach is elaborated in the next section.

5   Lifting the Semantics

In order to enable the execution of schematic code, we can first of all turn several less problematic schema variables into generic constants, allowing the rewrite rules to perform symbolic computation. This, together with the complication of meaningful typing, is discussed in Sect. 5.1. *Schematic expressions*, however,

---

[3] See [10] for the similarities and differences.

[4] The usage of $\to$ instead of $\overset{*}{\to}$ conforms with rewriting logic rather than with SOS.

require some extra effort. Instances of schematic expressions might have arbitrary side effects on the state, but we do not know which. Moreover, the same schematic expression can appear more than once in schematic code, with the different appearances having *different results* and *different side effects*. Therefore, evaluating schematic expressions requires extra constructs, which we introduce in Sect. 5.2. Problems concerning fresh variables introduced by PTTs are solved in Sect. 5.3, and in Sect. 5.4 we refine our analysis by nondeterministically *identifying different* schema variables.

5.1   Schema Variables Versus Generic Constants

When preparing a piece of schematic code (like l = e * n;) for execution, we model *side-effect free schema variables* as *generic constants*, with the effect that the rules of the rewriting semantics will perform symbolic computation. Such a generic constant is a true constant only to rewriting logic, i.e. on a technical level. Intuitively, however, it acts as a representative of *any* fitting expression. By side-effect free schema variables, we mean those where instantiations are restricted to expressions which, by their syntactic nature, cannot possibly have a side-effect. Luckily, the taclet language provides this information, among other things, by *sorts* (which we have not spelled out in taclet (5), but indicated in the first column of Table 1). It is actually the very purpose of sorts in the taclet language, to *constrain* the *applicability* of taclets during proof construction. It is not surprising that, for the sound application of certain rules, it matters a lot whether or not side-effects can arise. Here, the needs of theorem proving match well with the needs of symbolic computation, where side-effects matter even more. In the example, l is of sort *Lefthandside*, a sort which happens to embody side-effect freeness. Therefore, l can in principle be turned into a generic constant.

Unfortunately, we also have to deal with a certain mismatch between program logic rules and symbolic computation via a rewrite semantics. The latter is, even if symbolic, yet more concrete. For instance, a schema variable of type *Lefthandside* can be instantiated with either of: a local variable, a static field, or a field of the current object. As the rewriting semantics executes these different possibilities each in a different way, our approach requires to test out all of them. As we usually have several schema variables in a taclet, all possible combinations must be checked in the validation. This leads to an explosion of combinations. Fortunately, programs in PTTs are by their very nature quite small, containing usually at most five schema variables, which is why this approach is feasible.

5.2   Computing with the Unknown

Even with the help of generic constants, $\mathcal{R}_{Java}$ per se does not provide means to 'execute' arbitrary unknown expressions possibly having side-effects, like those matching the sorts *Expression* or *NonSimpleExpression*. To be able to treat those, we lift $\mathcal{R}_{Java}$ to a *rewrite theory for schematic Java* ($\mathcal{R}_{Java^{lift}}$) as described in this section. First of all, we note that the same expression, when executed twice in different states, can have different side-effects and results. On the other hand, when executed twice but starting in the same state, side-effects and result will be identical. Therefore we introduce *snapshots* of the state capturing those parts of the configuration which both side-effects and result can depend on. This allows to compare two states in which such an expression is executed, and to decide whether the side-effects and results of two evaluations are the same.

We demonstrate the concept of snapshots by an example configuration in Fig. 2.a. All the sans-serif typed elements are operators of the semantics whereas the others represent elements of the appropriate types.

(a) run(c(k(*Code*), e(*Localenv*),
         o(*Currentobject*)),
      m(*Memory*), n(*Nextfreememcounter*),
      s(*Staticenv*), cl(*Listofclasses*),
      nextSnapshot(*Natnextsnapcounter*),
      snapshots(*Snapshotlist*), ...)

(b) (snap(*Natnextsnapcounter*),
      c(e(*Localenv*), o(*Currentobject*)),
      m(*Memory*))

Fig. 2. An example configuration (a) and a fitting snapshot (b)

Fig. 2.a shows that we extend the structure of configurations by a *Snapshotlist* and a *Natnextsnapcounter* (syntactically wrapped by snapshots or nextSnapshot, respectively). The snapshot taken for this very configuration is depicted in Fig. 2.b. Its first element (snap(*Natnextsnapcounter*) in this case) acts as a name for the snapshot, to be used as a parameter elsewhere (see below). After such a snapshot is taken, it is added to the *Snapshotlist*, and the *Natnextsnapcounter* is incremented. Using snapshots, we can now represent the state-dependent evaluation of unknown expressions. For that, what remains is to model the effect of an arbitrary side-effect on the memory.

The side-effects of any expression can be viewed in the following way: a number n of memory locations $L_1, \ldots, L_n$ is updated with certain values $V_1, \ldots, V_n$. We however do not know any of $L_1, \ldots, L_n$ or $V_1, \ldots, V_n$, nor even the number n of affected memory locations. Therefore, when modeling the side-effects of a symbolic expression e, to be evaluated in a symbolic state s, we represent $L_1, \ldots, L_n$ by the *symbolic location list* LI(e, s), parameterized over e and s. Accordingly, $V_1, \ldots, V_n$ is represented by the *symbolic value list* VI(e, s). Furthermore, we actually do not use the full (symbolic) state for s, but only the name of the state's snapshot.

Now, when executing the so represented symbolic side-effects on the memory, we replace the value of *each* memory location with a 'kind of' conditional term, called *extended conditional value*. (Simple conditional terms are insufficient for this task.) Suppose that, before executing e, some particular symbolic memory location L holds the particular value V. The execution of e triggers that V is rewritten to the extended conditional value

L in LI(e, s) ?? VI(e, s) :: V

This construct represents the new value and has the following meaning: if L is a member of the list $\mathsf{Ll}(e, s)$ then the resulting value is the corresponding element in the list $\mathsf{Vl}(e, s)$. Otherwise the result is V, which was the old value. Note that this replacement is performed at *each* location/value pair in the memory, but everywhere using the according L and V.

Extended conditional values cannot be further evaluated (since expressions e are symbolic) but instead remain in the memory as they are, which is fine since we just aim at comparing two resulting states.

We illustrate the lifted semantics with the help of the following example:

Example 5. The following taclet is a slight variation of (5) but it is unsound since the order of evaluation is wrongly simulated:

$$\mathsf{find}(\langle\, \mathsf{l} = \mathsf{e} * \mathsf{n}; \rangle\ \mathsf{b})$$
$$\mathsf{varcond}(\mathsf{new}\ \mathsf{typeof}(\mathsf{e})\ \mathsf{v_1}, \mathsf{typeof}(\mathsf{n})\ \mathsf{v_2})$$
$$\mathsf{replacewith}(\langle\mathsf{typeof}(\mathsf{n})\ \mathsf{v_2} = \mathsf{n}; \mathsf{typeof}(\mathsf{e})\ \mathsf{v_1} = \mathsf{e}; \mathsf{l} = \mathsf{v_1} * \mathsf{v_2}; \mathsf{rs}\rangle\ \mathsf{b})$$

After processing both programs as described above, we end up with the following two values as memory contents at the location that l is mapped to. To simplify the presentation, we omit certain complications of purely syntactical kind here. i stands for the initial snapshot counter.

- $(\ \mathsf{resultof}\ \mathsf{e}\ \mathsf{in}\ \mathsf{snap}(\mathsf{i})\ ) * (\ \mathsf{resultof}\ \mathsf{n}\ \mathsf{in}\ \mathsf{snap}(\mathsf{i}{+}1)\ )$
- $(\ \mathsf{resultof}\ \mathsf{e}\ \mathsf{in}\ \mathsf{snap}(\mathsf{i}{+}1)\ ) * (\ \mathsf{resultof}\ \mathsf{n}\ \mathsf{in}\ \mathsf{snap}(\mathsf{i})\ )$

A further analysis of the snapshots with names $\mathsf{snap}(\mathsf{i})$ and $\mathsf{snap}(\mathsf{i}{+}1)$, which could in principle be equal but are different in this case, finally reveals that the two considered programs are in fact different in result and side-effects. To better understand the actual side-effects, just imagine we had in our memory any other location, say, $\mathsf{l1}$, with value $\mathsf{v1}$. Executing both programs would then lead to replacing $\mathsf{v1}$ by one of the following new values, respectively:

- $\mathsf{l1}\ \mathsf{in}\ \mathsf{Ll}(\mathsf{n}, \mathsf{snap}(\mathsf{i}{+}1))\ ??\ \mathsf{Vl}(\mathsf{n}, \mathsf{snap}(\mathsf{i}{+}1))\ ::$
  $(\mathsf{l1}\ \mathsf{in}\ \mathsf{Ll}(\mathsf{e}, \mathsf{snap}(\mathsf{i}))\ ??\ \mathsf{Vl}(\mathsf{e}, \mathsf{snap}(\mathsf{i}))\ ::\ \mathsf{v1})$
- $\mathsf{l1}\ \mathsf{in}\ \mathsf{Ll}(\mathsf{e}, \mathsf{snap}(\mathsf{i}{+}1))\ ??\ \mathsf{Vl}(\mathsf{e}, \mathsf{snap}(\mathsf{i}{+}1))\ ::$
  $(\mathsf{l1}\ \mathsf{in}\ \mathsf{Ll}(\mathsf{n}, \mathsf{snap}(\mathsf{i}))\ ??\ \mathsf{Vl}(\mathsf{n}, \mathsf{snap}(\mathsf{i}))\ ::\ \mathsf{v1})$

5.3   State Equivalence

Recall that, after 'running' $(\Pi\,\mathsf{rs},\ \mathsf{s}_{\Pi,\Pi'}) \rightarrow (\mathsf{rs}, s)$ and $(\Pi'\,\mathsf{rs},\ \mathsf{s}_{\Pi,\Pi'}) \rightarrow (\mathsf{rs}, s')$, we require s and s' to be *equivalent*. We now explain what we mean by that. The states s and s' are considered equivalent if they are *equal modulo new variables*. A variable is called *new* if it is introduced by the transformation, and thus *only* appears in Π', and is freshly declared therein. Examples of such new variables are $\mathsf{v_1}$ and $\mathsf{v_2}$ in rule (2) and PTT (5).

The need for an extended notion of equivalence is obvious: variables newly introduced in Π' appear in the configuration representing s', but not in the configuration representing s, which is why these configurations cannot possibly be entirely equal. However since new variables cannot appear in the remaining code rs, they *could* just as well *be removed* before executing rs. This is however not what the semantics does, as it is not designed for being aware of variables appearing anymore or not. Instead, we realize a certain removal of new variables within the *'comparison modulo'* of resulting states. This is part of the *rewrite theory for validating transformation rules*, $\mathcal{R}_{Java^{valTransf}}$ [5], which further extends $\mathcal{R}_{Java^{lift}}$.

To get a handle on when to perform the *comparison modulo* we use a new *marker*, the pause operator, to indicate where the 'interesting' part of the program (either of Π or Π') is over, with only some 'uninteresting' rest rs left. Note that the following rewriting logic rule, which triggers the comparison modulo, only matches continuations starting with pause:

compareResultsModNewVars(run(c(k(pause $->$ K), context), state),
 run(c(k(pause $->$ K), context'), state'))
= compareResult(removeNewVarsLocs(run(c(k(pause $->$ K), context), state)),
 removeNewVarsLocs(run(c(k(pause $->$ K), context'), state')))

compareResult(run(c(k(pause $->$ K), context), state) ,
 run(c(k(pause $->$ K), context'), state'))
= run(c(k(pause $->$ K), context), state)
== run(c(k(pause $->$ K), context'), state')

First, the new variables are removed from environments and memories in the actual state and in the snapshots. The 'cleaned' resulting states are then compared using Maude's default equality check ==.

5.4 Identical Instantiation of Different Schema Variables

As mentioned in Sect. 1, it can easily be forgotten that, in situations where a PTT applies, different schema variables can match the same instantiation.

Stenzel [13] remarks that a transformation x=y++; $\rightsquigarrow$ x=y; y=y+1; is wrong since an assignment x=x++; leaves x unchanged, while x=x; x=x+1; increments x (according to [7]). Stenzel discovered the erroneous transformation, which was part of his calculus, by an 'on paper' verification of the rules. Remarkably, the calculus we investigate here carried the same error, in the form of the taclet:

find($\langle l_1 = l_2 ++; \ rs \rangle$ b) replacewith($\langle l_1 = l_2; \ l_2 = l_2 + 1; \ rs \rangle$ b)

Our automatic validation detects errors of this kind by means of nondeterministic rewrite rules for the generation of configurations, and using the Maude support for exhaustively trying out all branches. In our example, l_1 and l_2 are identified on the one branch, and distinguished on the other. Note that the whole idea of 'running' a schema Π instead of its instances π (Sect. 4) would be unsound if we forced constants representing unknowns to be different.

---

[5] Available at http://i12www.ira.uka.de/~aroth/download/maude/.

6   Automated Validation and Results

Our approach to validate the PTTs of KeY is implemented as a completely automated process. It consists of two steps: (1) Using the taclet infrastructure of KeY, the code transformation of each PTT is extracted and Maude code is generated which triggers the generation of start configurations and (2) Maude builds the actual start configurations and executes them as input to $\mathcal{R}_{Java^{valTransf}}$.

In the first step two tasks are accomplished: The Java syntax of the PTTs is transformed to that used by $\mathcal{R}_{Java}$ (and $\mathcal{R}_{Java^{valTransf}}$), which slightly differs from the standard syntax. More importantly, schema variables are replaced by concrete generic constants as described in Sect. 5.1. Depending on the schema variable sort *several* start configurations are generated, each containing another generic constant. If there is more than one schema variable in the considered programs, *all combinations* of their generic instantiations are generated.

KeY currently contains around 210 PTTs (of around 480 Java related rules). We could not check all of them mainly because of the prototypic nature of the Maude Java semantics $\mathcal{R}_{Java}$ (Sect. 3.3) and because some (37) contain advanced meta constructs which capture program transformations not expressible by pure schematic means. Despite these restrictions, 56 PTTs are currently treatable.

Our checker identified three unsound taclets, one as reported in Sect. 5.4, one for the analog case of the decrement operation, and one which was caused by evaluating a side-effect twice. With the help of logging output, one could quite easily find out in which cases problems occurred. After correcting the three rules, we were able to validate all of the 56 PTTs. The runs are sufficiently fast (around 3 minutes), thus confirming our estimations from Sect. 5.1 that the combinatorial explosion of cases is irrelevant for our purposes. Our implementation is now already used in practice within the KeY project. Nightly runs ensure that accidentally introduced mistakes in the rules are detected as soon as possible.

7   Conclusions and Related Work

The described approach achieves a completely automated validation of program transformation rules of the JavaDL calculus against a semantics in rewriting logic, a high level declarative formalism. The validation machinery is almost entirely defined in rewriting logic itself. For the purpose of validating transformations, we exploited (a) the precise formalization of the JavaDL rule schemas as taclets and (b) the executability of the rewrite semantics. As a major contribution, we lifted the Java rewrite semantics to deal with schematic programs. Moreover, we solved the issues arising from a certain mismatch in the typing systems of both formalisms, from newly introduced variables, and from potentially identical instantiations of different schema variables.

There is extensive literature relating program logic calculi and language semantics. We restrict ourselves to works targeted at similarly complete calculi over similarly complex languages (which actually happens to further narrow down to calculi over Java only).

We start with work targeting the *same* calculus. [4] describes how a taclet-specific mechanism ensures the soundness of *derived* rules (group 4 in Sect. 2). It creates correctness proof obligations from taclets, rendered in the object logic. In contrast to our work on axiomatic transformation rules, the justification of derived rules does not involve a definition of the (Java) semantics. In that respect, what comes closer is the work of K. Trentelman [14] on three JavaDL rules of group 2 (which connect the program and the logic part of sequents). Those taclets are proven correct w.r.t. a formalization of Java in Isabelle/HOL, called *Bali*. The whole metatheory for relating both formalisms is explicitly formalized within Isabelle/HOL. The correctness proofs of the taclets are therefore completely formal, and machine checked, but require non-trivial interaction.

In the LOOP project [8], a denotational semantics of Java is formalized as a PVS theory. Java programs are compiled into semantical objects, and proofs are performed in the PVS theory directly. On top of that, a Hoare-style and a *wp* style calculus are formalized as a PVS theory, and verified against the semantics within PVS. As opposed to 'usual' Hoare-style or *wp* calculi, these ones work on the *semantical* objects, not on the syntax of Java.

In [13], K. Stenzel reports on an 'on paper' verification of his dynamic logic calculus for Java against a big-step semantics for Java he developed as well. He found three mistakes in the calculus, one of which was also present in two rules of the calculus we consider here (see Sect. 5.4). We profitted from that work in the sense that it made us aware of the identical-schema-variable-instantiations problem. As a result, our mechanism can (and did) detect mistakes which are of this nature.

Except from [4], all these approaches have in common that the rule verification is performed by interacting with a proof system, or even by hand. In contrast to this, our approach is *much more lightweight*, as the 'mental reasoning' which determines for instance our lifting of the semantics, is *not* captured by a *formal meta theory* of any kind, thereby gaining a lower level of certainty. On the other hand, we achieve a *fully automatic* validation of more than 50 rules though the used semantics does not cover all features of (sequential) Java yet. We will however need to investigate whether our 'lifting features' are already sufficient or need further extension when the coverage is extended.

Another future work is to weaken the now very restrictive form of transformation rules, to also cope with simple dependencies from the logical context of the programs. This would allow for handling certain *branching* rules as well.

We consider it a strength of the approach (and the same holds for [14]) that the two artifacts, calculus and semantics, are defined in very different formalisms, by different people, for different purposes. We believe that some of the certainty which we lose by not performing formal meta reasoning is regained by the different origins of the formalisms we use for cross-validation.

Acknowledgments

We would like to thank Richard Bubel for many discussions and valuable feedback throughout this work. Many thanks go to Wojciech Mostowski for several valuable hints and to Steffen Schlager for commenting on an earlier version of this paper. We also would like to thank José Meseguer for inspiring discussions about our work, and putting it in a bigger context [10]. Finally, we thank the anonymous referees for very valuable feedback.

References

1. W. Ahrendt, T. Baar, B. Beckert, R. Bubel, M. Giese, R. Hähnle, W. Menzel, W. Mostowski, A. Roth, S. Schlager, and P. H. Schmitt. The KeY tool. *Software and System Modeling*, 4:32–54, 2005.
2. B. Beckert. A dynamic logic for the formal verification of Java Card programs. In I. Attali and T. P. Jensen, editors, *Java Card Workshop*, volume 2041 of *Lecture Notes in Computer Science*, pages 6–24. Springer, 2000.
3. B. Beckert, M. Giese, E. Habermalz, R. Hähnle, A. Roth, P. Rümmer, and S. Schlager. Taclets: A new paradigm for constructing interactive theorem provers. *Revista de la Real Academia de Ciencias Exactas, Físicas y Naturales, Serie A: Matemáticas (RACSAM)*, 98(1), 2004. Special Issue on Symbolic Computation in Logic and Artificial Intelligence.
4. R. Bubel, A. Roth, and P. Rümmer. Ensuring correctness of lightweight tactics for Java Card Dynamic Logic. In *Proceedings of Workshop on Logical Frameworks and Meta-Languages (LFM) at Second International Joint Conference on Automated Reasoning 2004*, pages 84–105, 2004.
5. M. Clavel, F. Durán, S. Eker, P. Lincoln, N. Martí-Oliet, J. Meseguer, and C. Talcott. *Maude Manual*, April 2005. Available from http://maude.cs.uiuc.edu.
6. A. Farzan, F. Chen, J. Meseguer, and G. Roşu. Formal analysis of Java programs in JavaFAN. In R. Alur and D. Peled, editors, *CAV*, volume 3114 of *Lecture Notes in Computer Science*, pages 501–505. Springer, 2004.
7. J. Gosling, B. Joy, G. Steele, and G. Bracha. *The Java Language Specification Second Edition*. Addison-Wesley, Boston, Mass., 2000.
8. B. Jacobs and E. Poll. Java program verification at Nijmegen: Developments and perspective. In K. Futatsugi, F. Mizoguchi, and N. Yonezaki, editors, *Software Security – Theories and Systems*, LNCS 3233, pages 134–153. Springer, 2004.
9. N. Martí-Oliet and J. Meseguer. Rewriting logic: roadmap and bibliography. *Theor. Comput. Sci.*, 285(2):121–154, 2002.
10. J. Meseguer and G. Roşu. The Rewriting Logic semantics project. In *Structural Operational Semantics, Proceedings of the SOS Workshop, Lisbon, Portugal, 2005*, ENTCS. Elsevier, 2005. to appear.
11. J. Meseguer and G. Roşu. Rewriting Logic semantics: From language specifications to formal analysis tools. In *Proceedings of the IJCAR'04, Cork, Ireland*, volume 3097, pages 1–44. Springer-Verlag LNCS, July 2004.
12. R. Sasse. Taclets vs. rewriting logic - relating semantics of Java. Technical Report in Computing Science No. 2005-16, Fakultät für Informatik, Universität Karlsruhe, Germany, May 2005.
13. K. Stenzel. A formally verified calculus for full Java Card. In C. Rattray, S. Maharaj, and C. Shankland, editors, *AMAST*, volume 3116 of *Lecture Notes in Computer Science*, pages 491–505. Springer, 2004.
14. K. Trentelman. Proving correctness of JavaCard DL taclets using Bali. In B. Aichernig and B. Beckert, editors, *Software Engineering and Formal Methods. 3rd IEEE International Conference, SEFM 2005, Koblenz, Germany, September 7-9, 2005, Proceedings*. IEEE Press, 2005.

Reasoning About Incompletely Defined Programs

Christoph Walther and Stephan Schweitzer

Fachgebiet Programmiermethodik,
Technische Universität Darmstadt
chr.walther@informatik.tu-darmstadt.de, stephan.schweitzer@sdm.de

Abstract. We consider automated reasoning about recursive partial functions with decidable domain, i.e. functions computed by incompletely defined but terminating functional programs. Incomplete definitions provide an elegant and easy way to write and to reason about programs which may halt with a run time error by throwing an exception or printing an error message, e.g. when attempting to divide by zero. We investigate the semantics of incompletely defined programs, define an interpreter for those programs and discuss the termination of incompletely defined procedures. We then analyze which problems need to be solved if a theorem prover designed for verification of completely defined programs is modified to work for incompletely defined programs as well. We also discuss how to reason about stuck computations which arise when calling incompletely defined procedures with invalid arguments. Our method of automated reasoning about incompletely defined programs has been implemented in the verification tool √eriFun. We conclude by discussing experiences obtained in several case studies with this implementation and also compare and relate our proposal to other work.

1 Introduction

Programs which halt with a run time error by throwing an exception or printing an error message are ubiquitous in the use of computers. Division by zero is a common example of such a fault that programming beginners soon become familiar with. Formally, the program computes a *partial* function, where the argument causing the failure is not in the domain of that function. For other arguments not in the domain, the program may even run forever, for example if an interpreter is called with a non-terminating program.

But there is an important difference between these two cases of partiality: In the former case, the domain of the computed function is *decidable*. Therefore a program may check whether an argument is not in the domain and then react appropriately. In the latter case, however, the domain may be *undecidable*, and then there is no cure to prevent looping.

If the domain of a function computed by some procedure is decidable, a procedure can be "completed" by returning arbitrary results for *stuck arguments*, i.e. arguments not in the original domain. However, stipulating artificial results

G. Sutcliffe and A. Voronkov (Eds.): LPAR 2005, LNAI 3835, pp. 427–442, 2005.

for a procedure applied to stuck arguments spoils the readability of programs. One immediately starts to think about whether the program's author had a specific reason to define the result in the way he did, or just gave some arbitrary return value (as the result does not matter at all). Also statements which obviously are senseless may become true and can be proved. E.g., one may prove $hd(empty)=last(empty)$ if hd maps a non-empty list $\langle n_1, \ldots, n_k \rangle$ of numbers to the leftmost list element n_1, $last$ maps such a list to the rightmost list element n_k and $hd(empty) := last(empty) := 0$. Finally, problems arise if *polymorphic data types* are used. E.g., we cannot complete the definition of hd and $last$ applied to *empty* if hd and $last$ map lists $list[\tau]$ of any type τ to elements of τ.

A remedy to these problems is the use of *partially determined* functions, i.e. functions with *indetermined* results if applied to stuck arguments. For example, we may have a *total* but only *partially determined* function *last*, such that the value of $last(empty)$ is *defined*, because *last* is *total*, but is *indetermined*, because *last* is only *partially determined*. Hence *(1)* $\forall l{:}list \; \exists n{:}nat. \; last(l){=}n$ is a true statement about *last* from which we soundly conclude *(2)* $\exists n{:}nat. \; last(empty){=}n$. But we cannot give a number N such that $last(empty){=}$N holds.

2   Completely Defined Programs

Syntax. We use a programming language in which data structures are defined in the spirit of (free) algebraic data types. A data structure s is defined by stipulating the *constructors* of the data structure as well as a *selector* for each argument position of a constructor. The set of all *constructor ground terms* built with the constructors of s then defines the elements of the data structure s. For example, truth values are represented by the set $\mathcal{T}(\{true, false\}) = \{true, false\}$ and the set of natural numbers is represented by the set $\mathcal{T}(\{0, succ\}) = \{0, succ(0), succ(succ(0)), \ldots\}$, both given by data structures bool and nat of Fig. 1.[1] Likewise, the data structure list of Fig. 1 represents the set of linear lists of natural numbers, with e.g. $add(succ(0), add(0, empty)) \in \mathcal{T}(\{0, succ, empty, add\})$. The *selectors* act as inverses to their constructors, since e.g. $hd(add(n, k)) = n$ and $tl(add(n, k)) = k$ is demanded. Each definition of a data structure s implicitly introduces an equality symbol $=_s : s \times s \to bool$ (where $s \neq bool$) and a function symbol $if_s : bool \times s \times s \to s$ for conditionals.

A procedure, which operates on these data structures, is defined by giving the procedure name, say f, the formal parameters and the result type in the *procedure head*. The *procedure body* is given as a first-order term over the set of formal parameters, the function symbols already introduced by some data structures and other procedures plus the function symbol f to allow recursive definitions, cf. Fig. 1 where "|| *" in the procedure bodies should be ignored.

A finite list P of data structure and procedure definitions—always beginning with the data structure definitions of bool and nat as given in Fig. 1—is called a

---

[1] $\mathcal{T}(\Sigma, \mathcal{V})_s$ denotes the set of *terms* of type s over a signature Σ for function symbols and a set $\mathcal{V}$ of variable symbols, $\mathcal{T}(\Sigma)_s$ is the set of *ground* terms of type s over Σ, and $\mathcal{F}(\Sigma, \mathcal{V})$ is the set of all *closed* first-order formulas over Σ and $\mathcal{V}$.

```
structure bool  <=  true, false
structure nat   <=  0, succ(pred:nat)
structure list  <=  empty, add(hd:nat,tl:list)
```

```
function minus(x,y:nat):nat <=        function remainder(x,y:nat):nat <=
if y=0                                if y=0
  then x                                then 0 || *
  else if x=0                           else if y>x
        then 0 || *                           then x
        else minus(pred(x),pred(y))           else remainder(minus(x,y),y)
      end                                   end
end                                   end
```

Fig. 1. Data structures and completely || incompletely defined procedures

completely defined functional program. We define $\Sigma(P)$ as the set of all function symbols of the data structures and procedures of P, and $\Sigma(P)^c \subset \Sigma(P)$ is the set of all constructor function symbols given by the data structures of P.

Computation. An interpreter $eval_P$ for a (completely defined functional) program P evaluates terms of $\mathcal{T}(\Sigma(P))$ to "values", i.e. terms of $\mathcal{T}(\Sigma(P)^c)$. The interpreter computes calls $f(t_1, \ldots, t_n)$ of a procedure $\texttt{function } f(x_1:s_1, \ldots, x_n:s_n):s \ <= R_f$ *call-by-value*, i.e. by replacing each formal parameter x_i in the procedure body R_f by the computation t_i' of the actual parameter t_i, and then continuing with the computation of the instantiated procedure body obtained, cf. Fig. 2 where all expressions in $\boxed{\cdots}$ should be ignored. The interpreter also respects the definitions of the data structures by computing, for instance, *false* for $0=succ(t)$ and q for $pred(succ(t))$, provided $eval_P(t) = q$ for some $q \in \mathcal{T}(\Sigma(P)^c)$. For selectors $sel : s \to s'$ applied to constructors *cons* to which they do not belong, so-called *witness terms* $\omega_{sel}[x] \in \mathcal{T}(\Sigma(P), \{x\})_{s'}$ with $x \in \mathcal{V}_s$ are assigned in P to sel, and then we define $eval_P(sel(cons(q_1, \ldots, q_n))) :=$ $eval_P(\omega_{sel}[cons(q_1, \ldots, q_n)])$. Hence, for example, $eval_P(hd(empty)) = 0$ and $eval_P(tl(empty)) = empty$ if $\omega_{hd}[x] := 0$ and $\omega_{tl}[x] := x$ for the selectors of data structure $\texttt{list}$, cf. Fig. 1.

Termination and Semantics. Since P may contain non-terminating procedures, $eval_P$ is a *partial* mapping only, i.e. $eval_P : \mathcal{T}(\Sigma(P)) \mapsto \mathcal{T}(\Sigma(P)^c)$.

Definition 1. (Termination) *A procedure* $\texttt{function } f(x_1:s_1, \ldots, x_n:s_n):s \ <=$ *... of a completely defined program P terminates in P iff $eval_P(f(q_1, \ldots, q_n)) \in \mathcal{T}(\Sigma(P)^c)$ for all $q_i \in \mathcal{T}(\Sigma(P)^c)_{s_i}$. P terminates iff (i) each procedure of P terminates in P and (ii) $eval_P(\omega_{sel}[q]) \in \mathcal{T}(\Sigma(P)^c)_{s'}$ for each selector $sel : s \to s'$ and for all $q \in \mathcal{T}(\Sigma(P)^c)_s$.*

If a completely defined program P terminates, then $eval_P$ is a *total* mapping, i.e. $eval_P : \mathcal{T}(\Sigma(P)) \to \mathcal{T}(\Sigma(P)^c)$. The semantics of terminating functional programs is now defined by:

Definition 2. (Standard Model $\mathcal{M}_P$, Theory Th_P) *Let P be a completely defined and terminating program. Then the* standard model $\mathcal{M}_P$ *of P is a $\Sigma(P)$-algebra $\mathcal{M}_P = (\mathcal{T}(\Sigma(P)^c), \phi)$ such that $\phi_f(q_1, \ldots, q_n) = eval_P(f(q_1, \ldots, q_n))$ for all $f \in \Sigma(P)_{s_1,\ldots,s_n,s}$ and all $q_i \in \mathcal{T}(\Sigma(P)^c)_{s_i}$.*

The theory Th_P *of P is defined as $\{\varphi \in \mathcal{F}(\Sigma(P), \mathcal{V}) \mid \mathcal{M}_P \vDash \varphi\}$. A verification system for P is* sound *iff $\varphi \in Th_P$ for each $\varphi \in \mathcal{F}(\Sigma(P), \mathcal{V})$ verified by the system.*

Theorem 1. *Let P be a completely defined and terminating program, $t_1, t_2 \in \mathcal{T}(\Sigma(P))$ and $b \in \mathcal{T}(\Sigma(P), \{x_1, \ldots, x_n\})_{bool}$. Then*

1. *$eval_P(t_1)=eval_P(t_2) \Rightarrow [t_1{=}t_2] \in Th_P$,*   3. *$P$ has exactly one standard model,*
2. *$[t_1{=}t_2] \in Th_P \Rightarrow eval_P(t_1)=eval_P(t_2)$,*   4. *$Th_P$ is complete, and*
5. *$[\forall x_1{:}s_1, \ldots, x_n{:}s_n.\ b] \in Th_P \Leftrightarrow eval_P(\theta(b))=true$ for each θ with $\theta(x_i) \in \mathcal{T}(\Sigma(P)^c)_{s_i}$.[2]*

When we formulate proof obligations of the form "$\varphi \in Th_P$" for completely defined programs P, we assume the availability of some "sound verification system for P", cf. e.g. [3],[4],[5],[17],[18],[23], to compute a proof for φ. Such a system is also used to verify the termination of procedures, cf. [25],[27].

3   Incompletely Defined Programs

Syntax. Partially determined (recursive) functions are computed by *incompletely defined* programs, also called *loose specifications* [19] or *underspecifications* [11]. A data structure s is incompletely defined by not stipulating witness terms for the selectors of s. For defining a procedure f incompletely, we use a wildcard $*$ to stipulate the result when calling f with a stuck argument. E.g., procedure minus of Fig. 1 is incompletely defined if "0 $\parallel$" is ignored in the procedure body, and the value of $minus(n, m)$ is only determined if $n \geq m$. Also procedure remainder of Fig. 1 is incompletely defined when ignoring "0 $\parallel$", and the value of $remainder(n, m)$ is determined iff $m \neq 0$.

Formally, we assume a constant symbol $*_s \notin \Sigma(P)$ for each data structure s in a functional program P, and we demand upon the extension of P by a new procedure function $f(x_1{:}s_1, \ldots, x_n{:}s_n){:}s \mathrel{<=} R_f$, that $R_f \in \mathcal{T}(\Sigma(P) \cup \{f, *_s\}, \{x_1, \ldots, x_n\})$ be $*$-*correct*, i.e. $R_f = *$ or $*$ is only used as a (direct) argument in the *alternatives* of an *if*-conditional.

Termination and Semantics. For defining the termination of incompletely defined programs, the notion of a *fair completion* is needed:

Definition 3. (Fair Completions) *Let P be an incompletely defined program. Then $\widehat{P}$ denotes the set of all* fair completions *P' of P, where each $P' \in \widehat{P}$ is a completely defined* program *satisfying*

---

[2] We refer to [25] for omitted proofs.

1. *for each definition D_s of a data structure s in P, P' contains a data structure definition obtained from D_s by stipulating a witness term $\omega_{sel}[x] \in T(\Sigma(P), \{x\})_{s'}$ for each selector $sel : s \to s'$ in D_s such that (i) $eval_P(\omega_{sel}[q]) \in T(\Sigma(P)^c)_{s'}$ for all $q \in T(\Sigma(P)^c)_s$, and*

2. *for each procedure* function $f(x_1{:}s_1, \ldots, x_n{:}s_n){:}s \mathrel{<=} R_f$ *in P, there is some procedure* function $f(x_1{:}s_1, \ldots, x_n{:}s_n){:}s \mathrel{<=} R'_f$ *in P' such that*
   (i) *$R_f = R'_f [\pi_1 \leftarrow *, \ldots, \pi_k \leftarrow *]$ where $Occ^*(R_f) = \{\pi_1, \ldots, \pi_k\}$,[3] and*
   (ii) *$eval_{P'}(\theta(\mathtt{AND}(C_f^\pi))) = true \Rightarrow eval_{P'}(f(q_1, \ldots, q_n)) \in T(\Sigma(P)^c)_s$ for all $\pi \in Occ^*(R_f)$ and all $q_i \in T(\Sigma(P)^c)_{s_i}$, where C_f^π is the clause under which $R_{f|\pi}$ appears in R_f and $\theta = \{x_1/q_1, \ldots, x_n/q_n\}$.[4]*

Each procedure function $f(x_1{:}s_1, \ldots, x_n{:}s_n){:}s \mathrel{<=} R_f$ of an incompletely defined program P coincides with a procedure function $f(x_1{:}s_1, \ldots, x_n{:}s_n){:}s \mathrel{<=} R'_f$ of any fair completion P' of P except for the indetermined $*$-cases, cf. 2(i) of Definition 3. Almost any result may be stipulated for those cases in a fair completion P', however the *fairness requirements* 1(i) and 2(ii) of Definition 3 demand that the termination of procedure f in P' not be spoiled *just because* procedure f was completed by a non-terminating result in a $*$-case or a non-terminating witness term was assigned to a selector.

For the procedures minus of Fig. 1, for example, a fair completion of a program containing the incompletely defined minus may contain the completely defined minus. Also the occurrence of $*$ in the incompletely defined procedure minus may be replaced by $succ(y)$ or 13 or $minus(x, pred(y))$ etc. in a fair completion P' of P. But we may not replace $*$ by $minus(x, y)$ or by $loop(y)$, where function loop(x:nat):nat $\mathrel{<=}$ succ(loop(x)) is a procedure of P', as this violates the fairness requirement 2(ii) of Definition 3.

Using the notion of a fair completion, termination of incompletely defined programs and in turn the semantics of those programs now can be defined:

Definition 4. (Termination) *A procedure* function $f(x_1{:}s_1, \ldots, x_n{:}s_n){:}s \mathrel{<=} R_f$ *of an incompletely defined program P terminates in P iff for each $P' \in \widehat{P}$ procedure* function $f(x_1{:}s_1, \ldots, x_n{:}s_n){:}s \mathrel{<=} R'_f$ *of P' terminates in P'. P terminates iff each procedure of P terminates in P.*

Definition 5. (Standard Model $\mathcal{M}_P$, Theory Th_P) *Let P be an incompletely defined and terminating program. Then a standard model $\mathcal{M}_P$ of P is a $\Sigma(P)$-algebra $\mathcal{M}_P = (T(\Sigma(P)^c), \phi)$ such that some $P' \in \widehat{P}$ exists with $\phi_f(q_1, \ldots, q_n) = eval_{P'}(f(q_1, \ldots, q_n))$ for all $f \in \Sigma(P)_{s_1, \ldots, s_n, s}$ and all $q_i \in T(\Sigma(P)^c)_{s_i}$.[5]*

The theory Th_P of P is defined as $\{\varphi \in \mathcal{F}(\Sigma(P), \mathcal{V}) \mid \mathcal{M}_P \models \varphi$ for each standard model $\mathcal{M}_P$ of $P\}$. A verification system for P is sound iff $\varphi \in Th_P$ for each $\varphi \in \mathcal{F}(\Sigma(P), \mathcal{V})$ verified by the system.

---

[3] $t[\pi_1 \leftarrow r_1, \ldots, \pi_k \leftarrow r_k]$ originates from t by replacing each subterm $t_{|\pi_i}$ of t at position $\pi_i \in Occ(t)$ by r_i, and $Occ^*(t) := \{\pi \in Occ(t) \mid t_{|\pi} = *\}$.

[4] $\mathtt{AND}(C)$ denotes the conjunction and $\mathtt{OR}(C)$ denotes the disjunction of the elements in C represented by *if*-conditionals.

[5] We cannot use $\mathcal{M}_{P'}$ since termination of P does not entail termination of $P' \in \widehat{P}$.

Theorem 2. *Let P be an incompletely defined and terminating program and $t_1, t_2 \in \mathcal{T}(\Sigma(P))$. Then*

1. *P has infinitely many standard models,*   2. *Th_P is not complete, and*
3. *$[t_1{=}t_2] \in Th_P \Leftrightarrow eval_{P'}(t_1) = eval_{P'}(t_2)$ for each $P' \in \widehat{P}$.*

By Definition 5, incompletely defined procedures (and selectors) are understood as *loose specifications* [19] of *total* functions. The standard models for incompletely defined (and terminating) programs differ only in the interpretation of functions applied to stuck arguments, but coincide for all other function applications. So, for instance, if P contains the incompletely defined procedure minus of Fig. 1, one standard model $\mathcal{M}_P^1$ of P may assign 25 to $minus(2,4)$ whereas another standard model $\mathcal{M}_P^2$ of P may yield 0. However, $\mathcal{M}_P(minus(0,n)) = \mathcal{M}_P(minus(succ(m), succ^{(m+1)}(n)))$ and $\mathcal{M}_P(minus(succ^{(m+1)}(n), succ(m))) = n$ for each standard model $\mathcal{M}_P$ of P, hence

- $[\, minus(2,4){=}25 \,] \notin Th_P$,
- $[\, minus(2,4){\neq}25 \,] \notin Th_P$,
- $[\, \forall n,m{:}nat.\ minus(0,n){=}minus(succ(m), succ^{(m+1)}(n)) \,] \in Th_P$, and
- $[\, \forall n,m{:}nat.\ minus(succ^{(m+1)}(n), succ(m)){=}n \,] \in Th_P$.

Computation. When defining an interpreter $eval_P$ for computing P-expressions of an incompletely defined program P, we demand that $eval_P$ return its argument if applied to a procedure which is called with a stuck argument, but computation of this procedure call does not result in a recursive call. For instance, $eval_P$ simply returns $remainder(3,0)$ upon computation of $remainder(3,0)$. Upon computation of $minus(2,4)$, $minus(1,3)$ is obtained in an intermediate step, yielding $minus(0,2)$ as the final result of the computation, cf. Fig. 1.

For recognizing stuck arguments in procedure calls, a so-called *exception guard* is associated with each procedure:

Definition 6. (Exception Guard) *Let* function $f(x_1{:}s_1, \ldots, x_n{:}s_n){:}s \mathrel{<=} R_f$ *be a procedure of an incompletely defined program, and let C_f^π be the clause under which $R_{f|\pi}$ appears in R_f.*
Then procedure f is assigned the exception guard

$$except_f[x_1, \ldots, x_n] := \texttt{OR}(\bigcup_{\pi \in Occ^*(R_f)}\texttt{AND}(C_f^\pi)) \ .$$

An exception guard $except_f$ represents all conditions which trigger the throwing of an exception upon computation of a procedure call $f(\ldots)$. For example, $except_{minus}[x,y] = if(y{=}0, false, x{=}0)$ for the incompletely defined procedure minus of Fig. 1 and $except_{log}[x] = if(x{=}0, true, if(pred(x){=}0, false, if(even(x), false, true)))$ for procedure log of Fig. 5. Now we demand that the computation of a call $f(t_1, \ldots, t_n)$ of procedure function $f(x_1{:}s_1, \ldots, x_n{:}s_n){:}s \mathrel{<=} R_f$ by $eval_P$ simply stop—yielding a *stuck computation*—if $except_f[t_1, \ldots, t_n]$ is *not* falsified by $eval_P$. In this way, a stuck computation is the formal representation of an exceptional event caused by applying a procedure to a stuck argument, for example upon division by zero.

The computation of procedure calls is formally defined by the computation rules *(a)*, *(b.1)*–*(b.3)* of Fig. 2. Computation rule *(a)* implements the *call-by-value* parameter passing discipline, hence this rule is the same as for the computation of procedure calls in completely defined programs. Also computation rule *(b.1)* coincides with the computation in completely defined programs, but with the additional requirement that no exception is raised. Otherwise a stuck computation is obtained by computation rule *(b.2)*, and a stuck computation results too if *(b.3)* the computation of some actual parameter gets stuck. Computation rule *(b.3)* guarantees that the computation of procedure calls is *strict* wrt. stuck arguments, which has to be demanded, because one cannot conclude that a term t *denotes a value* from a *halting* computation of t, cf. Example 1.

$$(a) \quad eval_P(f(t_1,\ldots,t_n)) := eval_P(f(t_1,\ldots,t_{j-1},eval_P(t_j),t_{j+1},\ldots,t_n)) \ ,$$
$$\text{if } \bigwedge_{i=1}^{j-1} eval_P(t_i) = t_i \wedge eval_P(t_j) \neq t_j \ ;$$

$$(b.1) \ eval_P(f(t_1,\ldots,t_n)) := eval_P(\sigma(R_f)) \ \text{(with } \sigma = \{x_1/t_1,\ldots,x_n/t_n\})$$
$$\text{if } \bigwedge_{i=1}^{n} eval_P(t_i) = t_i \in T(\Sigma(P)^c) \boxed{\wedge eval_P(except_f[t_1,\ldots,t_n]) = false} \ ;$$

$$\boxed{\begin{array}{l}(b.2) \ eval_P(f(t_1,\ldots,t_n)) := f(t_1,\ldots,t_n) \ ,\\ \quad \text{if } \bigwedge_{i=1}^{n} eval_P(t_i) = t_i \in T(\Sigma(P)^c) \wedge eval_P(except_f[t_1,\ldots,t_n]) \neq false \ ;\end{array}}$$

$$\boxed{\begin{array}{l}(b.3) \ eval_P(f(t_1,\ldots,t_n)) := f(t_1,\ldots,t_n) \ ,\\ \quad \text{if } \bigwedge_{i=1}^{n} eval_P(t_i) = t_i \wedge t_j \notin T(\Sigma(P)^c) \ \text{for some } j \ .\end{array}}$$

Fig. 2. Computation of procedure calls in [in]completely defined programs

Upon computation of *selector* calls, we consider each term t with $eval_P(t) = t$ as a stuck argument for each selector *sel*, i.e. $eval_P(sel(t)) := sel(t)$, if *(i)* t is a non-constructor ground term or *(ii)* t is a constructor ground term of form $cons(\ldots)$ such that *sel* does not belong to *cons*. Hence $eval_P(t)$ returns t if e.g. $t = hd(empty)$, $t = tl(empty)$, $t = pred(hd(empty))$ or $t = hd(tl(empty))$. The computation of *equality* and *conditionals* is modified by stipulating $eval_P(t) = t$ if $t = r{=}r'$, $t = r'{=}r$ or $t = if(r,\ldots,\ldots)$ and $eval_P(r) = r \notin T(\Sigma(P)^c)$.

Formally, $eval_P$ is a *partial* mapping $eval_P : T(\Sigma(P)) \mapsto T(\Sigma(P))$. If an incompletely defined program P terminates, then $eval_{P'} : T(\Sigma(P)) \to T(\Sigma(P)^c)$ for each $P' \in \widehat{P}$, and $eval_P$ is a *total* mapping, i.e. $eval_P : T(\Sigma(P)) \to T(\Sigma(P))$.

Theorem 3. *If P is an incompletely defined program, $t,t_1,t_2 \in T(\Sigma(P))$ and $b \in T(\Sigma(P),\{x_1,\ldots,x_n\})_{bool}$, then*

1. P *terminates* $\Rightarrow \big(eval_P(t_1) = eval_P(t_2) \Rightarrow [t_1{=}t_2] \in Th_P\big)$,
2. $eval_P(t) \in T(\Sigma(P)^c) \Leftrightarrow \big(eval_P(t) = eval_{P'}(t) \text{ for each } P' \in \widehat{P}\big)$, *and*
3. P *terminates* $\Rightarrow \big(eval_{P'}(\theta(b)) = true \text{ for each } \theta \text{ with } \theta(x_i) \in T(\Sigma(P)^c)_{s_i}$
   and each $P' \in \widehat{P} \Leftrightarrow [\forall x_1{:}s_1,\ldots,x_n{:}s_n. \ b] \in Th_P\big)$.

As for completely defined programs P, $eval_P$ is also *sound* for incompletely defined functional programs P, cf. Theorems 1(1) and 3(1). But $eval_P$ is *complete* only for completely defined programs P, cf. Theorem 1(2), and only the weaker properties (3) of Theorems 2 and 3 hold for incompletely defined programs, compare with Theorem 1(5) and see Section 5 for further discussions.

Termination and Semantics (cont.) For completely defined programs P', termination is defined in terms of halting $eval_{P'}$ computations, which entails that each terminating procedure computes a *total* function, cf. Definitions 1 and 2. But by the presence of *stuck computations* in incompletely defined programs P, one cannot conclude that a procedure of P computes a total function from the fact that all $eval_P$ computations halt.

```
function unknown(x:nat):nat <= *

function zero(x:nat):nat <=
if unknown(x)=unknown(x)
  then 0
  else zero(x)
end
```

```
function undef(x:nat):nat <=
if unknown(x)=succ(unknown(x))
  then 0
  else succ(undef(x))
end
```

```
function null(x:nat):nat <=
if x=0
  then *
  else null(null(pred(x)))
end
```

```
function times(x,y:nat):nat <=
if x=0
  then 0
  else plus(times(pred(x),y),y)
end
```

Fig. 3. Terminating and non-terminating incompletely defined procedures

Example 1. For the procedures of Fig. 3, we find for each $q \in \mathcal{T}(\Sigma(P)^c)_{nat}$
- $eval_P(unknown(q)) = unknown(q)$,
- $eval_P(zero(q)) = if(unknown(q)=unknown(q), 0, zero(q))$,
- $eval_P(null(q)) \in \{null(0), null^{(q+q)}(0)\}$, and
- $eval_P(undef(q)) = if(unknown(q)=succ(unknown(q)), 0, succ(undef(q)))$,

where unknown and zero are *terminating* but null and undef are *non-terminating* procedures.[6] In particular, although computation of $undef(q)$ halts for each $q \in \mathcal{T}(\Sigma(P)^c)_{nat}$, there is no *total* function satisfying the definition of undef. □

Example 1 reveals in particular that one cannot conclude anything about whether total functions satisfying the definitions of an incompletely defined procedure f (as well as the procedures called in the body of f) exist from the fact that $eval_P(f(q_1, \ldots, q_n)) \in \mathcal{T}(\Sigma(P))$ for all $q_i \in \mathcal{T}(\Sigma(P)^c)$. This observation motivates our Definition 4 for the termination of incompletely defined programs. But as a consequence, $eval_P$ is *incomplete* because e.g. $[times(0, unknown(0))=0]$

---

[6] Consider any fair completion of procedure null with $null(0) > 0$ for justifying non-termination of procedure null, and a fair completion of procedure unknown with $unknown(q) = q$ for justifying non-termination of procedure undef.

(a) $\text{s-eval}_P(f(t_1,\dots,t_n)) := \text{s-eval}_P(f(t_1,\dots,t_{j-1},\text{s-eval}_P(t_j),t_{j+1},\dots,t_n))$,
  if $\bigwedge_{i=1}^{j-1} \text{s-eval}_P(t_i) = t_i \wedge \text{s-eval}_P(t_j) \neq t_j$;

(b.1) $\text{s-eval}_P(f(t_1,\dots,t_n)) := \text{s-eval}_P(\sigma(R_f))$ (with $\sigma = \{x_1/t_1,\dots,x_n/t_n\}$)
  if $\bigwedge_{i=1}^{n} \text{s-eval}_P(t_i) = t_i \wedge \text{EXECUTE?}[f(t_1,\dots,t_n)]$
  $\boxed{\wedge\ \text{s-eval}_P(except_f[t_1,\dots,t_n]) \neq true}$;

(b.2) $\text{s-eval}_P(f(t_1,\dots,t_n)) := f(t_1,\dots,t_n)$,
  if $\bigwedge_{i=1}^{n} \text{s-eval}_P(t_i) = t_i \wedge \neg\text{EXECUTE?}[f(t_1,\dots,t_n)]$;

(b.3) $\boxed{\begin{array}{l}\text{s-eval}_P(f(t_1,\dots,t_n)) := f(t_1,\dots,t_n) \\ \text{if } \bigwedge_{i=1}^{n} \text{s-eval}_P(t_i) = t_i \wedge \text{s-eval}_P(except_f[t_1,\dots,t_n]) = true \ .\end{array}}$

Fig. 4. Symbolic evaluation of procedure calls in [in]completely defined programs

$\in Th_P$, but $eval_P(times(0,unknown(0))) = times(0,unknown(0)) \neq 0$, cf. Figs. 2 and 3 as well as Example 1.[7]

But despite these different definitions of termination, termination of procedures in incompletely defined programs can be proved like for procedures of completely defined programs, cf. [25]. This means in particular that one need not consider *all fair completions* when proving termination of an incompletely defined procedure (see also [27] for a method to prove termination of incompletely defined procedures by machine).

4   Verification

We briefly illustrate those parts of the **✔eriFun**system [1] that have to be modified to be prepared for reasoning about incompletely defined programs, and we refer to [23],[26] for a sketch and a more detailed account of the system.

Theorems are proved in **✔eriFun** using a sequent calculus, called the *HPL-calculus* (abbreviating *Hypotheses*, *Programs* and *Lemmas*). Some of the HPL-proof rules, called *computed proof rules*, invoke the *symbolic evaluator*. This is a first-order theorem prover—implementing the system's main inference engine—which proves statements about programs or simplifies them at least. Symbolic execution of a call of procedure `function` $f(x_1{:}s_1,\dots,x_n{:}s_n){:}s <= R_f$ in some proof obligation is controlled in the symbolic evaluator by the evaluation rules of Fig. 4 (ignoring all expressions in $\boxed{\cdots}$). Here EXECUTE? denotes a system routine deciding whether it is *heuristically* meaningful to "open up" the procedure call $f(t_1,\dots,t_n)$. Like in the non-symbolic case of Fig. 2, *(a)* all actual parameters must be evaluated—where differently to non-symbolic evaluation, $\text{s-eval}_P(t) = t$ does *not* entail $t \in \mathcal{T}(\Sigma(P)^c)$—before the procedure is "opened up" by *(b.1)* or symbolic evaluation stops by *(b.2)*, because the EXECUTE?-heuristic refuses the symbolic execution of the procedure call.

---

[7] Computation of $times(0,unknown(0))$ gets stuck by the strictness requirement *(b.3)* of Fig. 2. If requirement *(b.3)* was removed, then $eval_P(times(0,unknown(0))) = 0$ but $eval_P(times(0,undef(0))) = 0$ as well.

```
function half(x:nat):nat <=
if x=0
  then 0
  else if pred(x)=0 then * else succ(half(pred(pred(x)))) end
end

function log(x:nat):nat <=
if x=0
  then *
  else if pred(x)=0
         then 0
         else if even(x) then succ(log(half(x))) else * end
       end
end
```

Fig. 5. Incompletely defined procedures (cont.)

Similarly, symbolic execution of procedure calls in incompletely defined programs is implemented by the evaluation rules of Fig. 4, obtained from the computation rules given in Fig. 2. Also here, *(a)* all actual parameters must be evaluated before the procedure either is "opened up" by *(b.1)*, or symbolic evaluation stops by *(b.2)*, because the EXECUTE?-heuristic refuses symbolic execution of the procedure call, or gets stuck by *(b.3)*, because the presence of a stuck argument can be proved. Compared with non-symbolic evaluation, the strictness requirement *(b.3)* of Fig. 2 has no symbolic counterpart. This is because strictness is not required upon *symbolic* evaluation, as only *terminating* programs are considered, and therefore each term denotes.

These moderate modifications are enough to upgrade the system to reasoning about incompletely defined programs. We believe that only similar slight changes are needed to adapt (almost) any verifier to work for incompletely defined programs too. The only exception from this claim we can think of relates to reasoning methods which for some reasons presume that the procedures of a program compute totally determined functions, as e.g. reasoning based on *implicit induction* [6],[15],[16]. In case of √eriFun, the system's routine for automated termination analysis fails to work soundly, and has to be modified as well [27].

5   Reasoning About Stuck Computations

Reasoning about partial functions has a long history in the fields of programming methodology, formal logic and automated reasoning. A lot of proposals for modelling partial functions exist, and various logics have been developed to capture this notion adequately, see [2],[7],[8],[9],[11],[12],[13],[14],[15],[16],[17],[20],[21],[25] for a discussion of various logics and further references.

As observable from the literature, logics coping with partial functions cannot be obtained without accepting certain disadvantages. Hence it seems appropriate to check what our proposal yields in this respect and what we can do about it.

By Definition of Th_P and $eval_P$, we find e.g. for procedures `times` and `log` of Figs. 3 and 5

1. $[times(1, log(1))=log(1)] \in Th_P$ 3. $eval_P(times(1, log(1))) = eval_P(log(1))$,
2. $[times(1, log(0))=log(0)] \in Th_P$ 4. $eval_P(times(1, log(0))) \neq eval_P(log(0))$,

because $eval_P(times(1, log(1))) = 0 = eval_P(log(1))$ but $eval_P(log(0)) = log(0)$, hence $eval_P(times(1, log(0))) = times(1, log(0))$. So obviously, the problem with statement (2.) is that a system user could *erroneously conclude* $eval_P(t) = eval_P(r)$ if the verifier comes up with a proof of $t=r$. However, this is a misinterpretation because *stuck computations* are *not reflected* by *theory membership*.

While the interpreter $eval_{P'}$ of a completely defined program P' is *complete* in the sense that *identical values* from $T(\Sigma(P)^c)$ are computed for expressions from $T(\Sigma(P))$ *denoting* identical values, cf. Theorem 1(2), the interpreter of an incompletely defined program P is *incomplete*, i.e. $eval_P$ may compute *different expressions* for expressions *denoting* identical values, cf. (2.) and (4.) above. For incompletely defined programs P, only a weaker completeness result holds, viz. that identical values are computed for expressions denoting identical values by the interpreter $eval_{P'}$ of *any fair completion* $P' \in \widehat{P}$, cf. Theorem 2(3).

As a consequence, a system user must be aware of this incompleteness when drawing conclusions about the results *computed* by $eval_P$ from the fact that a statement is *verified*. We therefore synthesize so-called *domain procedures* ∇_f for procedures f to provide machine support for *reasoning about stuck-freeness*:

Definition 7. (Determination guard ∇t, Domain procedures ∇_f) *Let P be an incompletely defined program and assume $\nabla_f \in \Sigma(P)_{s_1,\ldots,s_n,bool}$ for each $f \in \Sigma(P)_{s_1,\ldots,s_n,s}$. Then the determination guard $\nabla t \in T(\Sigma(P), \mathcal{V})_{bool}$ of a $*$-correct term $t \in T(\Sigma(P) \cup \{*\}, \mathcal{V})$ is defined (assuming $f \neq if$ and $v \in \mathcal{V}$) by*

1. $\nabla *:= false$,   3. $\nabla f(t_1, \ldots, t_n) := if(\text{AND}(\nabla t_1, \ldots, \nabla t_n), \nabla_f(t_1, \ldots, t_n), false)$,
2. $\nabla v:= true$,   4. $\nabla if(t_1, t_2, t_3) := if(\nabla t_1, if(t_1, \nabla t_2, \nabla t_3), false)$.

We assign each procedure `function` $f(x_1{:}s_1, \ldots, x_n{:}s_n){:}s <= R_f$ *in P the domain procedure* `function` $\nabla_f(x_1{:}s_1, \ldots, x_n{:}s_n){:}bool <= \nabla R_f$. *Further on, we assign each selector sel_i of a data structure definition* `structure` $s <= \ldots$ $cons(sel_1{:}s_1, \ldots, sel_n{:}s_n) \ldots$ *the domain procedure* `function` $\nabla_{sel_i}(x{:}s){:}bool <= ?cons(x)$, *where $?cons(x)$ abbreviates $x{=}cons(sel_1(x), \ldots, sel_n(x))$. All other function symbols are assigned a domain procedure with body "true".*

Theorem 4. *Let P be an incompletely defined program and let $f \in \Sigma(P)_{s_1,\ldots,s_n,s}$. Then for all $t \in T(\Sigma(P))$ and for all $q_i \in T(\Sigma(P)^c)_{s_i}$*

1. *procedure f terminates $\Leftrightarrow$ procedure ∇_f terminates,*
2. $eval_P(\nabla t){=}true \Leftrightarrow eval_P(t) \in T(\Sigma(P)^c)$,
3. $eval_P(\nabla t) \in T(\Sigma(P)) \Leftrightarrow eval_P(\nabla t) \in \{true, false\}$,
4. $eval_P(\nabla_f(q_1, \ldots, q_n)) \in T(\Sigma(P)) \Leftrightarrow eval_P(\nabla_f(q_1, \ldots, q_n)) \in \{true, false\}$,
5. $eval_P(\nabla_f(q_1, \ldots, q_n)){=}true \Leftrightarrow eval_P(f(q_1, \ldots, q_n)) \in T(\Sigma(P)^c)$.

By Theorem 4(1), each domain procedure ∇_f terminates iff its "mother" procedure f terminates. By proposition (2), the determination guard ∇t provides an equivalent requirement that the computation of t does not get stuck. By proposition (3), the computation of the determination guard ∇t yields a truth value whenever the computation of ∇t succeeds. Consequently, (4) each domain procedure computes a totally determined function, and (5) equivalently characterizes whether the computation of a procedure call results in a stuck computation.

Since domain procedures are tail recursive and compute a truth value, the optimization techniques developed in [22] (for so-called *difference procedures*) apply to domain procedures as well: Having generated a domain procedure ∇_f, the body of ∇_f is *simplified* in a first optimization step, and then it is tried to *eliminate recursive calls* in the simplified procedure body. Recursion elimination is particularly important, because proofs are more easily obtained if the procedures "called" in a proof obligation have no unnecessary recursive calls.

Example 2.
(i)
```
function ∇minus(x,y:nat):bool <=
  if y=0
    then true
    else if x=0 then false else ∇minus(pred(x),pred(y)) end
  end
```
is computed as the optimized domain procedure for the incompletely defined procedure minus from Fig. 1, and we find $\nabla_{\mathtt{minus}}(n,m) = true$ iff $n \geq m$.

(ii)
```
function ∇remainder(x,y:nat):bool <=
  if y=0 then false else true end
```
is computed as the optimized domain procedure for the incompletely defined procedure remainder from Fig. 1, and $\nabla_{\mathtt{remainder}}(n,m) = true$ iff $m \neq 0$.

(iii)
```
function ∇log(x:nat):bool <=
  if x=0
    then false
    else if pred(x)=0
            then true
            else if even(x) then ∇log(half(x)) else false end
         end
  end
```
is computed as the optimized domain procedure for procedure log from Fig. 5, and we find $\nabla_{\mathtt{log}}(n) = true$ iff $n = 2^k$ for some $k \in \mathbb{N}$.

(iv)
```
function ∇half(x:nat):bool <=
  if x=0
    then true
    else if pred(x)=0 then false else ∇half(pred(pred(x))) end
  end
```
is computed as the optimized domain procedure for procedure half from Fig. 5, and we find $\nabla_{\mathtt{half}}(n) = true$ iff n is even. $\square$

Domain procedures are used for reasoning about stuck-freeness in the following way: If $[t=r] \in Th_P$, then (*) $eval_{P'}(t) = eval_{P'}(r)$ for any fair completion

$P' \in \widehat{P}$ by Theorem 2(3). Now assume that $[\nabla(t{=}r)] \in Th_P$ holds as well. Then $eval_P(t) = eval_{P'}(t)$ as well as $eval_P(r) = eval_{P'}(r)$ for any fair completion $P' \in \widehat{P}$ by Definition 7, Theorems 3(2,3) and Theorems 4(2,3), and consequently $eval_P(t) = eval_P(r)$ by (*). Hence we obtain

Theorem 5. *Let P be an incompletely defined and terminating program, and let $t, r \in \mathcal{T}(\Sigma(P))$. Then $[t{=}r] \in Th_P \Rightarrow (\, [\nabla(t{=}r)] \in Th_P \Rightarrow eval_P(t) = eval_P(r))$.*

So $[\forall \ldots \nabla\varphi] \in Th_P$ has to be verified additionally for guaranteeing stuck-freeness for each constructor ground instance of a verified statement $[\forall \ldots \varphi]$.

For example, for statements (1.) and (2.) from the beginning of this section, $\nabla(times(1, log(1)){=}log(1))$ is obtained as $\nabla_{log}(1)$, which is trivially verified, whereas $\nabla(times(1, log(0)){=}log(0))$ is obtained as $\nabla_{log}(0)$, which is trivially falsified, cf. Example 2(iii). Hence statement (3.) has been proved by Theorem 5 without running $eval_P$, and the presence of a stuck computation in statement (2.) has been verified by (contraposition of) Theorem 4(2).

As a more general example, consider statement $\varphi = [l{\neq}empty \to hd(rev(l)){=}last(l)]$ for which $\nabla\varphi = [l{\neq}empty \to \nabla_{hd}(rev(l))]$ is generated (after optimization), expressing that the reversal of a non-empty list is not empty. Having verified $[\forall l{:}list.\ \varphi]$ as well as $[\forall l{:}list.\ \nabla\varphi]$, Theorem 5 guarantees that $eval_P$ yields *true* for each constructor ground instance of φ, i.e. $eval_P(hd(rev(q))) = eval_P(last(q)) \in \mathcal{T}(\Sigma(P)^c)_{\mathrm{nat}}$ must hold for all $q \in \mathcal{T}(\Sigma(P)^c)_{\mathrm{list}} \setminus \{empty\}$.

In conclusion, the problem of misinterpretations raised by incompleteness of $eval_P$ is the price we have to pay for keeping our reasoning method as simple as possible. But fortunately, using domain procedures we can cope with this problem by verifying the absence of stuck computations explicitly.[8]

6   Experiences and Conclusion

There is no royal road to reasoning about partial functions, as each proposal bringing strength in one respect shows weakness in another. The literature, see Section 5, provides a lot of challenges for a naïve logic user, e.g. *different forms of equality in the same logic, strong and weak forms of relational operators, non-standard interpretations for logical operators, invalidity of the law of excluded middle, non-associativity of equivalence, "unusual" theorems and non-theorems, non-compositional computation, notationally awkward languages and calculi, user-provided witness procedures* etc., and we added to this list (while avoiding these problems) *proving termination*, thus *excluding reasoning about functions with undecidable domain*, as well as *incompleteness of the interpreter*, raising the need for *proving the absence of stuck computations*.

Generally, logics for verification of programs computing partial functions are more complicated than logics for verification of programs computing total functions only. However, if only the "harmless" cases of partiality have to be dealt

---

[8] Domain procedures are also used for *program* [25] and *termination analysis* [27] and for reasoning about *partial termination* of *completely defined* procedures [9],[10],[24].

with, i.e. all functions computed by a program have a decidable domain, logics for verification of programs computing total functions can be used also in this case. Our proposal allows to avoid overspecifications by not forcing a programmer to stipulate results for don't care arguments, e.g. when dividing by zero or computing the minimum of an empty list, and supports the use of polymorphic data types. It has been integrated and proved successful in √eriFun, a semi-automated verifier for functional programs [23],[26] which is obtainable from the web [1]. Several case studies reveal that the system's reasoning performance is not spoiled by upgrading the system for incompletely defined programs. Of course, rather than proving more statements than before, the system proves less as senseless statements like $hd(empty)=last(empty)$ do not hold in an incompletely defined program.

However, we observed that generally proofs become more complicated if incompletely defined procedures f having a *recursively defined* domain procedure ∇_f are involved in a statement. This is because verifying the absence of stuck computations may add some burden to the verifier in those cases. Therefore one should use e.g. the incompletely defined procedure **minus** of Fig. 1 instead of its completely defined counterpart only if there is a specific reason in a case study to have the incompletely defined version. Also the induction schemes suggested by procedures may become more specific which may complicate proofs too. For instance, procedure **remainder** of Fig. 1 (being it completely or incompletely defined) suggests an induction with a step case of form $\forall x, y{:}nat.\ y \neq 0 \wedge x \neq 0 \wedge \forall y^*{:}nat.\ \phi\,[minus(x,y),y^*] \rightarrow \phi\,[x,y]$ if procedure **minus** is completely defined, whereas the *weaker* step formula $\forall x, y{:}nat.$ $y \neq 0 \wedge x \geq y \wedge \forall y^*{:}nat.\ \phi\,[minus(x,y),y^*] \rightarrow \phi\,[x,y]$ results for the incompletely defined version of **minus**. So also here, an incomplete definition should be used only if it is explicitly required by a specification. Finally, recursion elimination of domain procedures may become quite expensive in realistic case studies although there are some optimizations that reduce costs.[9] However, we do not consider these problems as a lack of our proposal, but as the price which has to be paid when reasoning about partial functions.

Acknowledgement. We are grateful to Markus Aderhold and Andreas Schlosser for useful comments as well as to Jürgen Giesl for thorough and fruitful discussions and for constructive criticism on a draft of this paper.

References

[1] http://www.verifun.org.
[2] R. D. Arthan. Undefinedness in Z: Issues for Specification and Proof. In *Proc. CADE 13 Workshop on Mechanization of Partial Functions*, available from http://www.cs.bham.ac.uk/~mmk/cade96-partiality/. New Brunswick, NJ, 1996.

---

[9] Incompletely defined procedures f having a *non*-recursively defined domain procedure ∇_f (like **remainder** as compared to **minus**, **half** and **log**) do not cause any of these problems.

[3] S. Autexier, D. Hutter, H. Mantel, and A. Schairer. inka 5.0 - A Logic Voyager. In H. Ganzinger, editor, *Proc. 16th Inter. Conf. on Autom. Deduction (CADE-16)*, volume 1632 of *Lect. Notes in Artif. Intell.*, pages 207–211, Trento, 1999. Springer.

[4] R. S. Boyer and J. S. Moore. *A Computational Logic*. Acad. Press, NY, 1979.

[5] A. Bundy, F. van Harmelen, C. Horn, and A. Smaill. The Oyster-Clam System. In M. Stickel, editor, *Proc. of the 10th Inter. Conf. on Autom. Deduction*, volume 449 of *Lect. Notes in Artif. Intell.*, pages 647–648, Kaiserslautern, 1990. Springer.

[6] H. Comon. Inductionless Induction. In A. Robinson and A. Voronkov, editors, *Handb. of Autom. Reasoning.*, volume I, chapter 14, pages 913–962. Elsevier, 2001.

[7] W. M. Farmer. Mechanizing the Traditional Approach to Partial Functions. In *Proc. CADE 13 Workshop on Mechanization of Partial Functions*, available from http://www.cs.bham.ac.uk/~mmk/cade96-partiality/. New Brunswick, NJ, 1996.

[8] S. Finn, M. P. Fourmann, and J. Longley. Partial Functions in a Total Setting. *Journal of Automated Reasoning*, 18:85–104, 1997.

[9] J. Giesl. Induction Proofs with Partial Functions. *J. Aut. Reason.*, 26:1–49, 2001.

[10] J. Giesl, C. Walther, and J. Brauburger. Termination Analysis for Functional Programs. In W. Bibel and P. Schmitt, editors, *Automated Deduction - A Basis for Applications*, volume 3, pages 135–164. Kluwer Acad. Publ., Dordrecht, 1998.

[11] D. Gries and F. B. Schneider. Avoiding the Undefined by Underspecification. In J. van Leeuwen, editor, *Computer Science Today: Recent Trends and Developments*, volume 1000 of *Lecture Notes in Computer Science*, pages 366–373. Springer, 1995.

[12] C. B. Jones. Partial functions and logics: A warning. *Information Processing Letters*, 54(2), 1995.

[13] C. B. Jones. TANSTAAFL (with partial functions). In *Proc. Workshop on Mechanization of Partial Functions, CADE 13*, available from http://www.cs.bham.ac.uk/~mmk/cade96-partiality/. New Brunswick, NJ, 1996.

[14] D. Kapur. Constructors Can Be Partial, Too. In R. Veroff, editor, *Automated Reasoning and Its Applications – Essays in Honor of Larry Wos*, pages 177–210. The MIT Press, Cambridge,MA, 1997.

[15] D. Kapur and D. R. Musser. Inductive Reasoning with Incomplete Specifications. In *Symposium on Logic in Computer Science*, volume 720, pages 367–377, Cambridge, MA, 1986. IEEE Computer Society.

[16] D. Kapur and D. R. Musser. Proof by Consistency. *Artificial Intelligence*, 31(2):125–157, 1987.

[17] D. Kapur and M. Subramaniam. New Uses of Linear Arithmetic in Automated Theorem Proving by Induction. *J. Automated Reasoning*, 16(1-2):39–78, 1996.

[18] M. Kaufmann and J. S. Moore. ACL2: An Industrial Strength Version of NQTHM. In *Compass'96: 11th Annual Conf. on Computer Assurance*, Gaithersburg, Maryland, 1996. National Institute of Standards and Technology.

[19] J. Loeckx, H.-D. Ehrich, and M. Wolf. *Specification of Abstract Data Types*. Wiley-Teubner, New York, Stuttgart, 1996.

[20] P. Manolios and J. S. Moore. Partial Functions in ACL2. *Journal of Automated Reasoning*, 31:107–127, 2003.

[21] B. Schieder and M. Broy. Adapting Calculational Logic to the Undefined. *The Computer Journal*, 42(2):73–81, 1999.

[22] C. Walther. On Proving the Termination of Algorithms by Machine. *Artificial Intelligence*, 71(1):101–157, 1994.

[23] C. Walther and S. Schweitzer. About √eriFun. In F. Baader, editor, *Proc. of the 19th Inter. Conf. on Automated Deduction (CADE-19)*, volume 2741 of *Lecture Notes in Artifical Intelligence*, pages 322–327, Miami Beach, 2003. Springer.

[24] C. Walther and S. Schweitzer. Automated Termination Analysis for Incompletely Defined Programs. Technical Report VFR 04/03, Programmiermethodik, Technische Universität Darmstadt, 2004.

[25] C. Walther and S. Schweitzer. Reasoning about Incompletely Defined Programs. Technical Report VFR 04/02, Programmiermethodik, Technische Universität Darmstadt, 2004.

[26] C. Walther and S. Schweitzer. Verification in the Classroom. *Journal of Automated Reasoning - Special Issue on Automated Reasoning and Theorem Proving in Education*, 32(1):35–73, 2004.

[27] C. Walther and S. Schweitzer. Automated Termination Analysis for Incompletely Defined Programs. In F. Baader and A. Voronkov, editors, *Proc. of the 11th Inter. Conf. on Logic for Progr., Artif. Intell. and Reasoning (LPAR-11)*, volume 3452 of *Lect. Notes in Artif. Intell.*, pages 332–346, Montevideo, Uruguay, 2005. Springer.

Model Checking Abstract State Machines
with Answer Set Programming

Calvin Kai Fan Tang and Eugenia Ternovska

School of Computing Science, Simon Fraser University, Burnaby, BC, Canada
{ctang, ter}@cs.sfu.ca

Abstract. Answer Set Programming (ASP) has been demonstrated as
an effective tool in various application areas, including formal verification. In this paper we present Bounded Model Checking (BMC) of Abstract State Machines (ASMs) based on ASP. We show how to succinctly
translate an ASM and a temporal property into a logic program and
solve the BMC problem for the ASM by computing an answer set for the
corresponding program. Experimental results for our method using the
answer set solvers SMODELS and CMODELS are also given.

1 Introduction

Answer Set Programming (ASP) (see e.g., [11]) is a declarative logic programming paradigm for solving combinatorial search problems. In ASP, a problem
is represented as a logic program whose answer sets stand for the solutions to
the problem. A solution is determined by computing an answer set for the logic
program using an answer set solver.

Model Checking [4] is a highly effective approach to formal verification of
finite systems. It is mainly used to detect errors that are difficult to uncover
through testing and simulation. The first widely used method of model checking
is *symbolic model checking* [12], in which states and transitions are represented as
boolean functions using Ordered Binary Decision Diagrams (BDDs). However,
some operations cannot be represented compactly as BDDs, and the size of the
BDD representation of a boolean function is sensitive to the variable ordering.
As a result, methods based on propositional satisfiability (SAT) emerged due to
the better space efficiency of SAT procedures. In particular, SAT-based *Bounded
Model Checking* (BMC) [2] is regarded as a complement to BDD-based model
checking. The idea of BMC is to search for a *counterexample* for a property
whose length is bounded by an integer. A BMC problem can be translated into
a SAT problem and solved with SAT checking techniques.

The motivation to achieve a succinct encoding of BMC brought the development of ASP-based BMC. Its idea is to describe models and properties in logic
programs and reduce BMC problems to finding answer sets for logic programs.
This approach realizes a linear encoding in the size of the model, the property
and the bound. In [9], it was shown to be competitive to the SAT-based BMC
with the well-known model checker NuSMV.

G. Sutcliffe and A. Voronkov (Eds.): LPAR 2005, LNAI 3835, pp. 443–458, 2005.
© Springer-Verlag Berlin Heidelberg 2005

In this paper we present a method of applying answer set programming to the bounded model checking of *Abstract State Machines* (ASMs) [3]. The language of ASMs is a high-level formal specification tool that is used in both industrial and academic settings and in various application domains. It enables designers to precisely capture system requirements and facilitates modelling on different levels of abstraction. Since the language of ASMs is popular for system modelling, and verification is important as it focuses on ensuring system quality, it is worthwhile to develop an efficient method of checking ASM models. Our contribution lies in combining the notions of ASP, BMC and ASMs to develop a novel verification approach.

The rest of this paper is organized as follows. In Section 2 we provide the necessary mathematical background for answer set programming. In Section 3 we introduce bounded model checking as well as temporal logic. In Section 4 we introduce abstract state machines. In Section 5 we explain in detail our ASP-based BMC of ASMs. Section 6 reports our experimental results. We discuss related work in Section 7 and finish with our conclusions in Section 8.

2   Answer Set Programming

In ASP, a *normal logic program* consists of a set of *normal logic rules* which have the form

$$a \leftarrow a_1, ..., a_m, not\ a_{m+1}, ..., not\ a_n \tag{1}$$

where a is called the *head* of the rule, and $a_1, ..., a_m, not\ a_{m+1}, ..., not\ a_n$ is called the *body* of the rule. The symbols $a, a_1, ...,$ and a_n are propositional atoms. A *literal* is an atom or its negation. A set of atoms X satisfies an atom a if $a \in X$ and a negative literal *not* a if $a \notin X$. X satisfies a rule of the form (1) if it satisfies the head a whenever it satisfies the body (i.e., all of $a_1, ..., a_m, not\ a_{m+1}, ...,$ and $not\ a_n$). X satisfies a program Π if it satisfies every rule of Π.

The *reduct* of a program Π with respect to a set of atoms X is the program Π^X derived from Π by removing every rule with a literal *not* a in its body if $a \in X$ and removing all negative literals from the bodies of the remaining rules. The program Π^X contains no negation, which implies that there exists a unique minimal set of atoms that satisfies it [7]. A set of atoms X is an *answer set* of a program Π if it is the unique minimal set of atoms that satisfies Π^X.

We employ two extensions to normal logic rules. A *constraint* is a rule without the head. A set of atoms X satisfies a constraint iff X does not satisfy the body. A *cardinality expression* has the form

$$l\ \{\ a_1, ..., a_m, not\ a_{m+1}, ..., not\ a_n\ \}\ u. \tag{2}$$

The symbols l and u are integers called the lower and upper bound. Cardinality expressions can be placed in the head and the body of a rule, just like literals. They are useful for expressing choices. Intuitively, a set of atoms X satisfies a cardinality expression of the form (2) iff the number of literals satisfied by X is between l and u inclusive.

3   Bounded Model Checking

In model checking, a model is described as a *Kripke structure* $M=(S,I,T,L)$. S is the set of states, $I \subseteq S$ is the set of initial states, $T \subseteq S \times S$ is the transition relation (assumed to be total), and L: $S \rightarrow 2^A$ is the labelling function, where A is the set of atomic propositions and $L(s)$ is the set of those that are true in state s. A *path* π of M is a finite or infinite state sequence $(s_0, s_1, ...)$, where $T(s_i, s_{i+1})$ holds for all $0 \le i < |\pi|$-1 with $|\pi|$ denoting the length of π. The symbol $\pi(i)$ stands for the i-th state s_i of the path, and π_i represents the suffix of π starting at s_i. If $\pi(0) \in I$, π is called an *initialized* path.

In model checking, properties are specified in *temporal logic*. We concentrate on *Linear Temporal Logic* (LTL). The syntax of LTL formulas is given as follows:

$$\psi ::= p \in A \mid \neg \psi \mid \psi_1 \wedge \psi_2 \mid \psi_1 \vee \psi_2 \mid \mathbf{G}\psi \mid \mathbf{F}\psi \mid \mathbf{X}\psi.$$

We omit binary temporal operators such as $\mathbf{U}$ and refer readers to [4] for details. The relation that a path π satisfies an LTL formula ψ ($\pi \models \psi$) is defined below:

$\pi \models p$ iff $p \in L(\pi(0))$. $\pi \models \neg \psi$ iff $\pi \not\models \psi$.

$\pi \models \psi_1 \wedge \psi_2$ iff $\pi \models \psi_1$ and $\pi \models \psi_2$. $\pi \models \psi_1 \vee \psi_2$ iff $\pi \models \psi_1$ or $\pi \models \psi_2$.

$\pi \models \mathbf{G}\psi$ iff π is infinite and $\pi_i \models \psi$ for all $0 \le i < |\pi|$.

$\pi \models \mathbf{F}\psi$ iff $\pi_i \models \psi$ for some $0 \le i < |\pi|$.

$\pi \models \mathbf{X}\psi$ iff $\pi(1)$ exists and $\pi_1 \models \psi$.

A Kripke structure M satisfies ψ iff all its initialized paths satisfy ψ. Our definition of the semantics of LTL is somewhat different from the traditional version, such as the one in [4], in which paths are defined to be infinite. Here we take finite paths into account. As explained below, we consider finite prefixes of paths in bounded model checking, and such a prefix can be a finite or infinite path.

The idea of bounded LTL model checking is as follows. Given a Kripke structure M, an LTL formula ψ and a bound k, we search in M for a finite prefix $(s_0, s_1, ..., s_k)$ of an initialized path that satisfies $\neg \psi$. Such a prefix is a counterexample for ψ. In practice, we start with a small value for k and increase it until a counterexample is found, a pre-determined upper bound is reached, or the problem becomes intractable.

A finite prefix $(s_0, ..., s_k)$ corresponds to an infinite path if it contains a *loop* transition from state s_{k-1} to a state s_i, where $0 \le i \le k$-1 (i.e., s_k is equivalent to s_i). In some cases, a loop is necessary for a prefix to be a counterexample. For example, for the formula $\mathbf{F}p$, even if p does not hold in any state from s_0 to s_k, without a loop, it is unknown whether p actually holds in any state beyond s_k. Consequently, the prefix is not sufficient to be a counterexample for $\mathbf{F}p$.

4   Abstract State Machines

An abstract state machine is defined over a *signature* Σ, which consists of a set of *sorts* and a set of *functions* [14]. Each function can be classified as a *static* function which has a fixed interpretation, a *controlled* function whose interpretation can only be changed by the ASM, or a *monitored* function whose interpretation can only be modified by the environment. A *constant* is a static nullary function. A signature also has the sort *Boolean*, the constants *true, false* and *undef*, and the operators $=, \neg, \wedge$ and $\vee$. The constant *undef* represents an undetermined element that is the default interpretation of a function.

A *state s* of a signature Σ is a set of *universes* and the *interpretations* of the functions in Σ over the universes. Each universe D_i^s is associated with a sort D_i in Σ. The interpretation of each function $f: D_1 \times ... \times D_n \rightarrow D_p$ is given by a function $f^s: D_1^s \times ... \times D_n^s \rightarrow D_p^s$. The *super-universe* D^s of s is the union of all universes, $\{undef\}$ and the *reserve*, which has the infinite set of new elements that can be dynamically imported to extend universes.

A signature has a collection of *variables V*. A *variable assignment* over a state s is a function $\zeta: V \rightarrow D^s$ such that a variable of sort D_i is mapped to an element in the universe D_i^s. We denote with $\zeta(v \mapsto a)$ the assignment that is identical to ζ except that it maps the variable v to the element a.

A *term* is a syntactic expression which has a value given a state s and a variable assignment ζ. We define a term t and its value $Val_{s,\zeta}(t)$ as follows:

- A variable is a term. If t is a variable v, then $Val_{s,\zeta}(t) = \zeta(v)$.
- If $f: D_1 \times ... \times D_n \rightarrow D_p$ is a function, and $t_1, ...,$ and t_n are terms of sorts D_1, ..., and D_n, respectively, then $f(t_1,...,t_n)$ is a term of D_p. If t is $f(t_1,...,t_n)$, then $Val_{s,\zeta}(t) = f^s(Val_{s,\zeta}(t_1),...,Val_{s,\zeta}(t_n))$.
- If v is a variable of sort D_i, and $g(v)$ and $s(v)$ are boolean terms, then $(\forall v : g(v))\ s(v)$ and $(\exists v : g(v))\ s(v)$ are *first-order terms* with *head variable v*, *guard g(v)* and *body s(v)*. The *range* of the guard $g(v)$ in a state s consists of all elements a in D_i^s such that $Val_{s,\zeta(v \mapsto a)}(g(v)) = true$.

    If t is $(\forall v : g(v))\ s(v)$, then $Val_{s,\zeta}(t) = true$ iff $Val_{s,\zeta(v \mapsto a)}(s(v)) = true$ for all a in the range of $g(v)$. If t is $(\exists v : g(v))\ s(v)$, then $Val_{s,\zeta}(t) = true$ iff $Val_{s,\zeta(v \mapsto a)}(s(v)) = true$ for some a in the range of $g(v)$.

A *location* of a state s is a pair $(f, \bar{a})$, where $f: D_1 \times ... \times D_n \rightarrow D_p$ is a controlled or monitored function and $\bar{a}$ is an n-tuple in $D_1^s \times ... \times D_n^s$. The value of $(f, \bar{a})$ is $f^s(\bar{a})$. An *update* of s is a pair (loc, val), where loc is a location of a sort D_i and val is an element in D_i^s or $undef$. The value of loc is set to val when the update is *fired*. An *update set* is fired when all its updates are fired simultaneously.

The behaviour of an ASM is defined by *transition rules*. The semantics of a transition rule R is given by its update set $\Delta_{s,\zeta}(R)$. We focus on *skip, update, block, conditional* and *do-forall* rules, whose semantics is defined as follows:

$$\Delta_{s,\zeta}(\texttt{skip}) = \emptyset.$$
$$\Delta_{s,\zeta}(f(t_1,...,t_n) := t_p) = \{ ((f, (Val_{s,\zeta}(t_1),...,Val_{s,\zeta}(t_n))), Val_{s,\zeta}(t_p)) \}.$$
$$\Delta_{s,\zeta}(\texttt{block } R_1 ... R_n \texttt{ endblock}) = \Delta_{s,\zeta}(R_1) \cup ... \cup \Delta_{s,\zeta}(R_n).$$
$$\Delta_{s,\zeta}(\texttt{if } g \texttt{ then } R_1 \texttt{ else } R_2 \texttt{ endif}) = \Delta_{s,\zeta}(R_1) \text{ if } Val_{s,\zeta}(g) = true.$$
$$\Delta_{s,\zeta}(\texttt{if } g \texttt{ then } R_1 \texttt{ else } R_2 \texttt{ endif}) = \Delta_{s,\zeta}(R_2) \text{ if } Val_{s,\zeta}(g) = false.$$
$$\Delta_{s,\zeta}(\texttt{do forall } v : g(v)\ R(v) \texttt{ enddo}) =$$
$$\bigcup_{a \in Ran} \Delta_{s,\zeta(v \mapsto a)}(R(v)), \text{ where } Ran \text{ is the range of } g(v) \text{ in } s.$$

The keywords **block** and **endblock** in a block rule can be omitted, and the else-part in a conditional rule is optional. The evaluation of the transition rules in a state s results in the update set of s. An execution of an ASM is called a *run*, which is a state sequence $(s_0, s_1, ...)$ such that s_0 is an initial state and s_{i+1} is obtained by firing the update set of s_i for all $i \geq 0$.

We give an ASM for the dining-philosophers problem[1]. Its signature has the sorts *Philosopher* associated with the set of constants $\{p_1, p_2, p_3\}$, *Chopstick* with $\{c_1, c_2, c_3\}$, and *Boolean*. The static functions are *leftchop: Philosopher→Chopstick* and *rightchop: Philosopher→Chopstick*, the controlled functions are *eating: Philosopher→Boolean* and *free: Chopstick→Boolean*, and the monitored functions are *me: →Philosopher* and *hungry: Philosopher→Boolean*. The behaviour of the ASM is defined by the following two conditional rules:

```
if hungry(me)=true ∧                    if eating(me)=true ∧
   free(leftchop(me))=true ∧               hungry(me)=false then
   free(rightchop(me))=true then           free(leftchop(me))  := true
   free(leftchop(me))  := false            free(rightchop(me)) := true
   free(rightchop(me)) := false            eating(me) := false
   eating(me) := true                   endif
endif
```

5 Mapping BMC to ASP

Given an ASM M, an LTL formula ψ and a bound k, we encode the behaviour of M up to k steps as a logic program $\Pi(M,k)$ and the negation of ψ as $\Pi(\neg\psi,k)$. We look for a counterexample for ψ by computing an answer set for the program $\Pi(M,k) \cup \Pi(\neg\psi,k)$. We let DP be the name of the ASM for the dining-philosophers problem in the previous section and use it to illustrate our method.

We first introduce two predicates that will be used extensively in the rest of this section: *valid_state*, which is true for the states up to k transitions away from an initial state, and *has_next_state*, which is true for the states that have a successor in a prefix. For each $0 \leq i \leq k$, add the rule *valid_state(i)* ←. If $k > 0$, then for each $0 \leq j \leq k\text{-}1$, include the rule *has_next_state(j)* ←.

5.1 Constructing Program $\Pi(M,k)$

Let the signature of M be Σ_M. We assume that each sort in Σ_M is associated with a fixed universe and dynamic extension of universes is not allowed. We divide the task of constructing the program $\Pi(M,k)$ into four parts: sorts, functions, terms and transition rules.

---

[1] A dining-philosophers problem describes a multi-processing environment with shared resources. There are N philosophers sitting at a round table and sharing N chopsticks. One chopstick is placed between two philosophers. A philosopher needs both chopsticks on his sides to eat, and thus no two adjacent philosophers can be eating at the same time. We assume that exactly one philosopher is active at any time.

Sorts. Each sort D_p in Σ_M is associated with a universe U_p. Let $\{c_{p1},...,c_{pm}\}$ be a set of constants such that each element in U_p is the interpretation of exactly one c_{pj}, where $1 \leq j \leq m$. For each c_{pj}, add the rule $d_p(c_{pj}) \leftarrow$. The predicate d_p stands for the sort D_p. Consider the sort *Philosopher* in *DP*, for which we add the rules

$$philosopher(p_1) \leftarrow \qquad philosopher(p_2) \leftarrow \qquad philosopher(p_3) \leftarrow.$$

Functions. Each function $f\colon D_1 \times ... \times D_n \rightarrow D_p$ in Σ_M is static, controlled or monitored. We differentiate the three cases as follows:

- If f is static, and $Val_{s,\zeta}(f(c_1,...,c_n)) = Val_{s,\zeta}(c_{pj})$ for every state s and variable assignment ζ, where each c_i is a constant of sort D_i for $1 \leq i \leq n$ and c_{pj} is a constant of sort D_p, add the rule $f(c_1,...,c_n,c_{pj}) \leftarrow$. The arity of the predicate f is $n+1$, as opposed to n for the function f, because of the extra parameter for the value of $f(c_1,...,c_n)$. In *DP*, if the chopstick on the left of philosopher p_1 is c_1 and the one on the right is c_2 (i.e., $Val_{s,\zeta}(leftchop(p_1)) = Val_{s,\zeta}(c_1)$ and $Val_{s,\zeta}(rightchop(p_1)) = Val_{s,\zeta}(c_2)$), we include the rules

  $$leftchop(p_1,c_1) \leftarrow \qquad rightchop(p_1,c_2) \leftarrow.$$

- If f is controlled, and $Val_{s_0,\zeta}(f(c_1,...,c_n)) = Val_{s_0,\zeta}(c_{pj})$ in every initial state s_0 of M, add the rule $f(c_1,...,c_n,c_{pj},0) \leftarrow$. The last parameter '0' indicates the state, and thus the arity of the predicate f is $n+2$. In *DP*, suppose all philosophers are not eating initially (i.e., $Val_{s_0,\zeta}(eating(p)) = false$ for all philosophers p). Then we add the rules

  $$eating(p_1,0,0) \leftarrow \qquad eating(p_2,0,0) \leftarrow \qquad eating(p_3,0,0) \leftarrow.$$

  Note that we use '1' and '0' for *true* and *false*, respectively.

  If no fixed initial value is given to $f(c_1,...,c_n)$, add the following rule which chooses one constant of sort D_p to be equal to $f(c_1,...,c_n)$ in an initial state:

  $$1 \; \{ \; f(c_1,...,c_n,c_{p1},0), \; ..., \; f(c_1,...,c_n,c_{pm},0) \; \} \; 1 \leftarrow$$

  where c_{pj} is a constant of D_p for $1 \leq j \leq m$.

  If the value of a location of f is not updated in state s_i, it remains unchanged for state s_{i+1}, where $0 \leq i \leq k\text{-}1$. For each constant c_{pj} of D_p, where $1 \leq j \leq m$, include the rule

  $$\begin{aligned} f(X_1,...,X_n,c_{pj},I+1) \leftarrow \\ not \; f(X_1,...,X_n,c_{p1},I+1), \; ..., \; not \; f(X_1,...,X_n,c_{pj-1},I+1), \\ not \; f(X_1,...,X_n,c_{pj+1},I+1), \; ..., \; not \; f(X_1,...,X_n,c_{pm},I+1), \\ f(X_1,...,X_n,c_{pj},I), \; d_1(X_1), \; ..., \; d_n(X_n), \; has\_next\_state(I). \end{aligned}$$

Therefore, for the function *eating* in *DP*, we add the rules

$$\begin{aligned} eating(X_1,1,I+1) \leftarrow not \; eating(X_1,0,I+1), \; eating(X_1,1,I), \\ philosopher(X_1), \; has\_next\_state(I) \\ eating(X_1,0,I+1) \leftarrow not \; eating(X_1,1,I+1), \; eating(X_1,0,I), \\ philosopher(X_1), \; has\_next\_state(I). \end{aligned}$$

The symbols X_1, ..., X_n and I are *variables*, which must be capital, while d_1, ..., d_n and *has_next_state* are called *domain predicates*. A domain predicate restricts the range of values that a variable can take. Before answer sets are computed, all variables are substituted by the values given by the corresponding domain predicates. This process is called *grounding*.

– If f is monitored, the initial value of $f(c_1,...,c_n)$ is handled in the same way as a controlled function. A monitored function changes non-deterministically. To encode this behaviour, add the rule

$$1 \ \{ \ f(X_1,...,X_n,c_{p1},I+1), \ ..., \ f(X_1,...,X_n,c_{pm},I+1) \ \} \ 1 \ \leftarrow$$
$$d_1(X_1), \ ..., \ d_n(X_n), \ has\_next\_state(I).$$

For example, for the function *me* in *DP*, we introduce the rule

$$1 \ \{ \ me(p_1,I+1), \ me(p_2,I+1), \ me(p_3,I+1) \ \} \ 1 \ \leftarrow \ has\_next\_state(I).$$

Terms. Let the transformation of terms be a function E_t, which takes two parameters: a term t and an integer i identifying a state that is i transitions away from an initial state.

– A variable v of sort D_p is transformed into a logic program variable:

$$E_t(v,i) = X \text{ for all } i,$$

where X acts as a placeholder for the value of v. The transformation also creates the atom $d_p(X)$. We refer to the atoms introduced during the transformation of a term as 'side atoms'. If a logic program variable which represents the value of a term appears in a logic rule, the side atoms for the term must be present in the body of the rule.

The choice of the name for the logic program variable is not unrestricted. If two distinct terms are translated into variables that appear in the same logic rule, then they must have different names.

– For a function application $f(t_1,...,t_n)$, if f is a static nullary function, i.e. a constant c, then $f(t_1,...,t_n)$ is not affected by the transformation:

$$E_t(c,i) = c \text{ for all } i.$$

If $f: D_1 \times ... \times D_n \rightarrow D_p$ is not a constant, $f(t_1,...,t_n)$ is transformed into a logic program variable:

$$E_t(f(t_1,...,t_n),i) = X \text{ for all } i,$$

where X holds the value of $f(t_1,...,t_n)$. If f is static, the side atoms are $f(E_t(t_1,i),...,E_t(t_n,i),X)$ and $d_p(X)$. If f is controlled or monitored, the side atoms are $f(E_t(t_1,i),...,E_t(t_n,i),X,i)$ and $d_p(X)$.

For example, the transformation of the term *eating(me)* results in a variable X as well as the side atoms $eating(E_t(me,i),X,i)$ and $boolean(X)$. $E_t(me,i)$ produces a variable Y with the side atoms $me(Y,i)$ and *philosopher(Y)*.

- An application of a function that is supported by the chosen answer set tool should be transformed into the appropriate syntax of the tool. These functions, which we call built-in functions, include the operators $=$, $\wedge$, $\vee$ and $\neg$. For instance, to translate the guard $eating(me)=true \wedge hungry(me)=false$ in the second conditional rule in DP, we first introduce two atoms $q_1(i)$ and $q_2(i)$, which are defined by the rules:

$$q_1(i) \leftarrow E_t(eating(me)=true,i), <side\ atoms>$$
$$q_2(i) \leftarrow E_t(hungry(me)=false,i), <side\ atoms>.$$

The symbol $<side\ atoms>$ stands for the set of side atoms created during the transformation of the terms in a rule, and thus its two occurrences above refer to the side atoms from $E_t(eating(me)=true,i)$ and $E_t(hungry(me)=false,i)$, respectively. We assume that '$==$' is the equality operator in the chosen answer set tool. Then the two rules above become

$$q_1(i) \leftarrow X==1,\ eating(Y,X,i),\ boolean(X),\ me(Y,i),\ philosopher(Y)$$
$$q_2(i) \leftarrow X==0,\ hungry(Y,X,i),\ boolean(X),\ me(Y,i),\ philosopher(Y).$$

The result of the transformation is an atom $q(i)$, supported by the rule

$$q(i) \leftarrow q_1(i),\ q_2(i).$$

We generalize the transformation of a term t which is $t_1=t_2$, $t_1 \wedge t_2$, $t_1 \vee t_2$ or $\neg t_1$. In $t_1=t_2$, t_1 and t_2 are variables, constants or function applications that are transformed into logic program variables. In $t_1 \wedge t_2$, $t_1 \vee t_2$ and $\neg t_1$, t_1 and t_2 are equalities, conjunctions, disjunctions, negations or first-order terms. Then $E_t(t,i)$ returns an atom $q(i)$ with the following auxiliary rule(s):

$$q(i) \leftarrow E_t(t_1,i)==E_t(t_2,i), <side\ atoms> \quad \text{if } t \text{ is } t_1=t_2,$$
$$q(i) \leftarrow E_t(t_1,i),\ E_t(t_2,i) \qquad\qquad \text{if } t \text{ is } t_1 \wedge t_2,$$
$$q(i) \leftarrow E_t(t_1,i) \text{ and } q(i) \leftarrow E_t(t_2,i) \quad \text{if } t \text{ is } t_1 \vee t_2, \text{ and}$$
$$q(i) \leftarrow not\ E_t(t_1,i) \qquad\qquad\qquad \text{if } t \text{ is } \neg t_1.$$

- A first-order term $(\exists v:g(v))\ s(v)$ is transformed as follows. We say that a first-order term t_f 'encloses' another one $t_{f'}$ if $t_{f'}$ appears in the guard or the body of t_f. Let v_1, ..., and v_n be the head variables of the first-order terms enclosing $(\exists v:g(v))\ s(v)$. The variables v_1, ..., v_n and v range over sorts D_1, ..., D_n and D_p and are transformed into logic program variables X_1, ..., X_n and X_p, respectively.

We assume that each of the guard $g(v)$ and the body $s(v)$ is an equality, conjunction, disjunction, negation or first-order term, and thus $E_t(g(v),i)$ and $E_t(s(v),i)$ are atoms $q_g(i)$ and $q_s(i)$, respectively. We add X_1, ..., X_n and X_p to $q_g(i)$ and $q_s(i)$ as parameters and also add them to the head of each auxiliary rule created by $E_t(g(v),i)$ and $E_t(s(v),i)$ as parameters.

The term $(\exists v:g(v))\ s(v)$ is represented by an atom $q(X_1,...,X_n,i)$, which is true if both $q_g(X_1,...,X_n,X_p,i)$ and $q_s(X_1,...,X_n,X_p,i)$ are true:

$$q(X_1,...,X_n,i) \leftarrow q_g(X_1,...,X_n,X_p,i),\ q_s(X_1,...,X_n,X_p,i),$$
$$d_1(X_1),\ ...,\ d_n(X_n),\ d_p(X_p).$$

A first-order term $(\forall v{:}g(v))\ s(v)$ is handled by first converting it into its equivalence $\neg((\exists v{:}g(v))\ \neg s(v))$.

Transition Rules. Let the transformation of transition rules be a function E_r, which takes a transition rule as a parameter and returns a set of logic rules.

- A skip rule does nothing, so $E_r(\texttt{skip})$ is the empty set.
- An update rule is translated into the logic rule:

$$E_r(f(t_1,...,t_n) := t_p) =$$
$$f(E_t(t_1,I),...,E_t(t_n,I),E_t(t_p,I),I{+}1) \leftarrow <side\ atoms>,$$
$$has\_next\_state(I).$$

In this case, $<side\ atoms>$ contains all side atoms from $E_t(t_1,I)$, ..., $E_t(t_n,I)$ and $E_t(t_p,I)$. For example,

$$E_r(eating(me) := false) =$$
$$eating(E_t(me,I),E_t(false,I),I{+}1) \leftarrow <side\ atoms>,$$
$$has\_next\_state(I).$$

The rule eventually becomes

$$eating(X,0,I{+}1) \leftarrow me(X,I),\ philosopher(X),\ has\_next\_state(I).$$

- A block rule is transformed into the union of the sets of logic rules for all the sub-rules:

$$E_r(\texttt{block}\ R_1\ ...\ R_n\ \texttt{endblock}) = E_r(R_1)\ \cup\ ...\ \cup\ E_r(R_n).$$

- For a conditional rule with guard g, suppose that $E_t(g,I)$ is an atom $q(I)$. We add $q(I)$ to the body of each rule in $E_r(R_1)$ (then-part) and $not\ q(I)$ to the body of each rule in $E_r(R_2)$ (else-part). In the following, the notation $E_r(R)[+lit]$ denotes the set of rules obtained by adding the literal lit to the body of each rule in $E_r(R)$:

$$E_r(\texttt{if}\ g\ \texttt{then}\ R_1\ \texttt{else}\ R_2\ \texttt{endif}) = E_r(R_1)[+q(I)]\ \cup\ E_r(R_2)[+not\ q(I)].$$

Consider the second conditional rule in DP. We have translated the guard $eating(me) \wedge hungry(me)$ for some i into an atom $q(i)$. To do it for all $0 \le i \le k{-}1$, we replace i by I in the rules that define q, q_1 and q_2 and add $has\_next\_state(I)$ to their bodies. The update rule $eating(me) := false$ is in the then-part of the conditional rule. Therefore, we add $q(I)$ to the body of the rule resulting from the transformation of $eating(me) := false$:

$$eating(X,0,I{+}1) \leftarrow q(I),\ me(X,I),\ philosopher(X),\ has\_next\_state(I).$$

- A do-forall rule is treated as follows. We assume that its head variable v is of sort D_p and is transformed into a logic program variable X. The guard $g(v)$ is translated by $E_t(g(v),I)$ into an atom $q(I)$. We add X as a parameter to $q(I)$ and the head of each auxiliary rule from $E_t(g(v),I)$. Then we include the atoms $q(X,I)$ and $d_p(X)$ in the body of each rule in $E_r(R(v))$, where $R(v)$ is the sub-rule of the do-forall rule:

$$E_r(\texttt{do forall}\ v\ :\ g(v)\ R(v)\ \texttt{enddo}) = (E_r(R(v))[+q(X,I)])[+d_p(X)].$$

5.2 Constructing Program $\Pi(\neg\psi,k)$

Recall that a prefix $(s_0,s_1,...,s_k)$ of a path may have a loop. The existence of a loop is indicated by the equivalence between the last state s_k in the prefix and some previous state s_i, where $0 \le i \le k\text{-}1$. Two state s_1 and s_2 of M are equivalent iff for each location, its values in s_1 and s_2 are equal.

Let h be a formula obtained by converting $\neg\psi$ into negation normal form in which negations only appear in front of atomic propositions. The method to construct the program $\Pi(\neg\psi,k)$, which is partly derived from [9][2], is as follows:

- Let the atom $el(i)$ represent the equivalence between states s_k and s_i, where $0 \le i \le k\text{-}1$. There is at most one i such that $el(i)$ can be true because a prefix has at most one loop. Therefore, we add the rule

$$0 \ \{ \ el(0), \ ..., \ el(k\text{-}1) \ \} \ 1 \leftarrow .$$

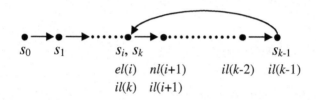

Fig. 1. Loop-related atoms

- For each controlled or monitored function $f: D_1 \times ... \times D_n \rightarrow D_p$ in Σ_M, include the constraint

$$\leftarrow el(I), \ f(X_1,...,X_n,X_p,I), \ not \ f(X_1,...,X_n,X_p,k),$$
$$d_1(X_1), \ ..., \ d_n(X_n), \ d_p(X_p), \ has\_next\_state(I).$$

The idea is that if s_k is equivalent to s_i, and $Val_{s_i,\varsigma}(f(c_1,...,c_n))$ is equal to $Val_{s_i,\varsigma}(c_p)$, where each c_j is a constant of sort D_j for $j=1, ..., n$ and p, then $Val_{s_k,\varsigma}(f(c_1,...,c_n))$ must also be equal to $Val_{s_k,\varsigma}(c_p)$.
- Define the atoms le, $nl(i)$ and $il(i)$. A loop exists if le is true. The state s_i is the 'next state' of the last state s_k if $nl(i)$ is true, and it is inside the loop if $il(i)$ is true (see Fig. 1 for an example). Add the rules

$le \leftarrow el(I), \ has\_next\_state(I)$ $\qquad$ $nl(I{+}1) \leftarrow el(I), \ has\_next\_state(I)$
$il(I{+}1) \leftarrow el(I), \ has\_next\_state(I)$ $\qquad$ $il(I{+}1) \leftarrow il(I), \ has\_next\_state(I).$

- Recursively translate the formula h by adding the rules in Table 1. In the end, we require that a prefix of a run in M satisfy h by including the constraint

$$\leftarrow not \ h(0).$$

---

[2] The temporal operator **X** is not treated in [9].

Table 1. Translation of an LTL formula

Formula h	Translation	
atomic proposition	$h(I) \leftarrow f(c_1,...,c_n,c_p),\ valid\_state(I)$	if f is static
$f(c_1,...,c_n)=c_p$	$h(I) \leftarrow f(c_1,...,c_n,c_p,I),\ valid\_state(I)$	otherwise
$\neg(f(c_1,...,c_n)=c_p)$	$h(I) \leftarrow not\ f(c_1,...,c_n,c_p),\ valid\_state(I)$	if f is static
	$h(I) \leftarrow not\ f(c_1,...,c_n,c_p,I),\ valid\_state(I)$	otherwise
$h_1 \wedge h_2$	$h(I) \leftarrow h_1(I),\ h_2(I),\ valid\_state(I)$	
$h_1 \vee h_2$	$h(I) \leftarrow h_1(I),\ valid\_state(I)$	
	$h(I) \leftarrow h_2(I),\ valid\_state(I)$	
$\mathbf{G}h_1$	$h(I) \leftarrow h_1(I),\ h(I+1),\ valid\_state(I)$	
	$h(k+1) \leftarrow le,\ not\ q$	
	$q \leftarrow il(I),\ not\ h_1(I),\ valid\_state(I)$	
$\mathbf{F}h_1$	$h(I) \leftarrow h_1(I),\ valid\_state(I)$	
	$h(I) \leftarrow h(I+1),\ valid\_state(I)$	
	$h(k+1) \leftarrow nl(I),\ h(I),\ valid\_state(I)$	
$\mathbf{X}h_1$	$h(I) \leftarrow h_1(I+1),\ has\_next\_state(I)$	
	$h(k) \leftarrow nl(I),\ h_1(I),\ valid\_state(I)$	

5.3   Correctness of Method

Given an ASM M, an LTL formula ψ and a bound k, we have the following soundness and completeness results for the program $\Pi(M,k)\cup\Pi(\neg\psi,k)$[3]:

Theorem 1 (Soundness). If $\Pi(M,k)\cup\Pi(\neg\psi,k)$ has an answer set, then there exists a run $(s_0,...,s_k)$ of M which satisfies $\neg\psi$.

Theorem 2 (Completeness). If there exists a run $(s_0,...,s_k)$ of M which satisfies $\neg\psi$, then $\Pi(M,k)\cup\Pi(\neg\psi,k)$ has an answer set.

6   Experiments

We have implemented a bounded model checker for ASMs based on the method described in the previous section. It accepts an ASM written in ASM-SL [5]. The choice of ASM-SL makes it easier for us to compare our approach to the one based on NuSMV, since it is the input language of the ASM-to-SMV translator developed by Winter [14], and NuSMV is a reimplementation and extension of the BDD-based model checker SMV.

We compared the ASP solvers SMODELS 2.28[4] and CMODELS 3.54[5] to the SAT-based bounded model checker (NuSMV/BMC) and the BDD-based checker (NuSMV/BDD) in NuSMV 2.3.0[6]. SMODELS computes the answer sets of a program

---

[3] An extended version of this paper with proofs of the theorems is available at http://www.sfu.ca/~ctang/LPAR-05-extended.pdf.
[4] http://www.tcs.hut.fi/Software/smodels/
[5] http://www.cs.utexas.edu/users/tag/cmodels.html
[6] http://nusmv.irst.itc.it/

as its stable models [13], while CMODELS is based on the relationship between answer set semantics and completion semantics [1] and uses a SAT solver to find answer sets. Both ASP solvers require the preprocessor LPARSE 1.0.15[7], whose primary task is grounding. The SAT solver invoked by both CMODELS and NuSMV/BMC was zChaff 2004.11.15[8]. We set a limit of 3600 seconds for each tool. For BMC, we initialized the bound to 10 and increased it by 5 when no counterexample was found. All experiments were conducted on a Linux PC with a 2.8GHz CPU and 1024MB RAM.

For the first batch of our experiments, we chose the FLASH Cache Coherence Protocol used by Winter as a case study in [14]. The protocol supports sharing of memory among interconnected processors. Memory is divided into lines, each of which is associated with a host processor. A processor that wants to access a line sends a request to its host. We modified Winter's correct ASM to reproduce some of the errors she detected and formulated the following properties in LTL:

- P1: No two processors have exclusive access to the same line at any time.
- P2: Every request will eventually be acknowledged.
- P3: Whenever a processor obtains shared access to a line, it will be marked as a sharer of the line.

The experimental results are shown in Table 2. The first column gives the model parameters: the number of processors (P), the number of lines (L), and the size of the message queue of each processor (Q). In the columns SMODELS, CMODELS and NuSMV/BMC, '$k=n$, t' reports the time t in seconds taken for the corresponding tool to find a counterexample within the bound n. For SMODELS and CMODELS, the time for grounding is included. If no counterexample was found, '$k>n$, t' reports the time taken to prove the absence of counterexamples within the largest bound n before the time limit was exceeded. The question mark '?' means that the tool did not terminate within the time limit for the initial bound 10. The last column reports the time taken for NuSMV/BDD to complete, with '?' indicating that it failed to finish within the time limit.

In the second batch of experiments, we tried to detect the 'livelock error' in an early version of the i-Protocol. The i-Protocol is an optimized sliding window protocol and has been used as a benchmark for various model checkers in [6]. We modelled the erroneous version of the i-Protocol as an ASM. Based on the error scenario described in [6], we specified the following property in LTL:

- P4: If a data packet from the sender has been accepted by the receiver, and eventually no packets will be dropped or corrupted, then the next data packet from the sender will eventually be accepted by the receiver.

This property will be violated if the livelock error is present. The model parameter is the window size (W). The experimental results are given in Table 3. In the

---

[7] http://www.tcs.hut.fi/Software/smodels/

[8] http://www.princeton.edu/~chaff/zchaff.html

Table 2. LTL Model Checking Experiments for FLASH Cache Coherence Protocol

Model Parameters	Property	SMODELS	CMODELS	NuSMV/BMC	NuSMV/BDD
P=2, L=1, Q=1	P1	k=20, 43.7	k=20, 3.8	k=20, 1007.6	?
	P2	k=15, 10.8	k=15, 9.1	k=15, 266.6	?
	P3	k>20, 248.2	k>50, 1341.2	k>20, 1153.1	?
P=2, L=2, Q=1	P1	k=20, 620.1	k=20, 13.3	k>10, 470.3	?
	P2	k=15, 7.2	k=15, 8.7	k>10, 375.6	?
	P3	k>15, 404.6	k>40, 1745.6	k>10, 118.9	?
P=3, L=1, Q=2	P1	k=20, 619.4	k=20, 17.5	?	?
	P2	k>15, 140.1	k=25, 2675.2	?	?
	P3	k>20, 2441.8	k>45, 2429.1	?	?

table, '×' indicates the lack of result because Winter's ASM-to-SMV translator failed to produce an NuSMV model due to a run-time error.

Both SMODELS and CMODELS outperformed NuSMV. In each case, they found a counterexample faster or reached a higher bound without exceeding the time limit. Both CMODELS and NuSMV converted their inputs into propositional formulas in conjunctive normal form (CNF). We noticed that the CNF formulas generated by CMODELS were much smaller. For example, at bound 20 for property P1 with parameters P=2, L=1 and Q=1, the CNF formula created by CMODELS had 14379 atoms and 47601 clauses, compared to 176566 atoms and 655268 clauses in the one by NuSMV. The difference can be partly attributed to the fact that the NuSMV models from the ASM-to-SMV translator were unnecessarily large and consequently affected the performance of NuSMV.

Table 3. LTL Model Checking Experiments for i-Protocol

Model Parameter	Property	SMODELS	CMODELS	NuSMV/BMC	NuSMV/BDD
W=1	P4	k=15, 7.0	k=15, 1.9	k=15, 310.0	?
W=2	P4	k=15, 12.0	k=15, 2.8	×	×
W=4	P4	k=20, 1362.0	k=20, 39.6	×	×

One benefit of using ASP in the model checking of ASMs is the ease of transforming ASMs into logic programs. Easier transformation of the given model can certainly lower the overall model checking effort. In our ASP-based approach, no 'location unfolding' is needed during the transformation. To see what location unfolding is, consider the update rule *InMess(Self)* := *noMess* in the ASM for the FLASH Cache Coherence Protocol, where *InMess*: *AGENT→TYPE* is a controlled function, *Self*: *→AGENT* is a monitored function, and *noMess* is a constant of sort *TYPE*. In order to use NuSMV, the parameter *Self* has to be 'unfolded' into every value it can have, and the update rule is unfolded into a set of conditional rules:

$InMess(Self) := noMess \Rightarrow$ if $Self=a_1$ then $InMess\_a_1 := noMess$ endif

$\qquad\qquad\qquad\qquad\qquad ...$

$\qquad\qquad\qquad\qquad$ if $Self=a_n$ then $InMess\_a_n := noMess$ endif

where a_1, ..., and a_n are constants of sort $AGENT$. The unnecessarily large NuSMV models in our experiments were caused by redundant location unfolding. With ASP, the translation of the update rule always produces one logic rule:

$inmess(X,noMess,I+1) \leftarrow self(X,I), agent(X), has\_next\_state(I).$

In general, to translate an ASM into the language of a model checker with no support for parameterized functions, every location that occurs as a parameter of a non-built-in function must be unfolded into every possible value. In ASP, parameterized functions can easily be handled with parameterized atoms and variables. Note that location unfolding is not totally eliminated, since variables in a logic program must still be replaced by their possible values during grounding. Rather, it is taken out of the transformation algorithm and handled by an efficient grounding program like LPARSE. The result is a more compact and natural encoding of an ASM that requires less effort to produce.

As for the comparison between the two ASP solvers, CMODELS outperformed SMODELS in all but one case. The former appears to be more scalable in the size of the model and the bound. The superior results by CMODELS largely coincide with other experimental results which compare the solvers on computing one answer set, such as those in [10]. In our experiments, they were configured to compute one answer set which would suffice to show the violation of a property.

The ASM models, LTL formulas, logic programs and NuSMV models used in all experiments are available at http://www.sfu.ca/~ctang/experiments.html.

7   Related Work

Answer set programming has been applied to model checking before. Heljanko and Niemelä introduced in [9] bounded LTL model checking of 1-safe Petri nets with ASP. Their approach is similar to ours in that 1-safe Petri nets and LTL formulas are translated into logic programs such that BMC problems become tasks of finding answer sets. A notable difference between the two approaches is that ours requires a much more extensive use of variables in logic programs in order to encode terms in ASMs.

Several ASM model checking methods based on existing model checkers are available in the literature. In [14], Winter showed how to transform ASMs into SMV code. She also proposed a way to verify ASMs using the model checker MDG. MDG is based on Multiway Decision Graphs and supports abstract data types and uninterpreted functions. The transformations into SMV and MDG both require location unfolding so that the given ASM is unfolded into a set of conditional rules with only nullary functions. In [8], the authors presented a way to encode an ASM in the language of Spin, which is an LTL model checker in which reachable states are represented as enumerable elements. However, they did not address non-nullary functions, first-order terms and do-forall rules.

8   Conclusions

We present the application of answer set programming to bounded LTL model checking of abstract state machines. We introduce a mapping from a BMC problem to a problem of answer set computation through a compact encoding of the given ASM and LTL formula in a logic program. The compact encoding is realized by the power of logic rules to succinctly represent the transition behaviour of ASMs and the recursive evaluation of LTL formulas. Our experimental results show that the application of ASP is promising in BMC of ASMs. As ASP is a research area of high interest, we believe that better answer set solving and grounding techniques will emerge. Our future directions include exploring ways to optimize our logic program encoding and studying the possibility of applying ASP to unbounded model checking.

References

1. Yu. Babovich, E. Erdem, and V. Lifschitz. Fages' theorem and answer set programming. In *Proceedings of the 8th International Workshop on Non-Monotonic Reasoning*, 2000.
2. A. Biere, A. Cimatti, E. M. Clarke, O. Strichman, and Y. Zhu. *Bounded Model Checking*, volume 58 of *Advances In Computers*. Elsevier, 2003.
3. E. Börger and R. Stärk. *Abstract State Machines: A Method for High-Level System Design and Analysis*. Springer, New York, NY, USA, 2003.
4. E. M. Clarke, O. Grumberg, and D. Peled. *Model Checking*. MIT Press, Cambridge, MA, USA, 1999.
5. G. Del Castillo. *ASM-SL, a Specification Language based on Gurevich's Abstract State Machines: Introduction and Language Definition*. Heinz Nixdorf Institut Paderborn, Germany, 1999.
6. Y. Dong, X. Du, Y. S. Ramakrishna, C. R. Ramakrishnan, I. V. Ramakrishnan, S. A. Smolka, O. Sokolsky, E. W. Stark, and D. S. Warren. Fighting livelock in the i-Protocol: A comparative study of verification tools. In *Proceedings of the 5th International Conference on Tools and Algorithms*, pages 74–88, 1999.
7. M. H. Van Emden and R. A. Kowalski. The semantics of predicate logic as a programming language. *Journal of the ACM*, 23(4):733–742, 1976.
8. A. Gargantini, E. Riccobene, and S. Rinzivillo. Using Spin to generate tests from ASM specifications. *Lecture Notes in Computer Science*, 2589:263–277, 2003.
9. K. Heljanko and I. Niemelä. Bounded LTL model checking with stable models. *Theory and Practice of Logic Programming*, 3(4&5):519–550, 2003.
10. Yu. Lierler and M. Maratea. Cmodels-2: SAT-based answer set solver enhanced to non-tight programs. In *Proceedings of the 7th Conference on Logic Programming and Non-monotonic Reasoning*, pages 346–350, 2004.
11. V. Lifschitz. Introduction to answer set programming, 2004. Introductory course at the 16th European Summer School in Logic, Language and Information.

12. K. L. McMillan. *Symbolic Model Checking*. Kluwer Academic Publishers, Norwell, MA, USA, 1993.
13. P. Simons. *Extending and Implementing the Stable Model Semantics*. PhD thesis, Helsinki University of Technology, 2000.
14. K. Winter. *Model Checking Abstract State Machines*. PhD thesis, Technical University of Berlin, 2001.

Characterizing Provability in BI's Pointer Logic Through Resource Graphs

Didier Galmiche and Daniel Méry

LORIA - Université Henri Poincaré,
Campus Scientifique, BP 239,
Vandœuvre-lès-Nancy, France

Abstract. We propose a characterization of provability in BI's Pointer Logic (PL) that is based on semantic structures called resource graphs. This logic has been defined for reasoning about mutable data structures and results about models and verification have been already provided. Here, we define resource graphs that capture PL models by considering heaps as resources and by using a labelling process. We study provability in PL from a new calculus that builds such graphs from which proofs or countermodels can be generated. Properties of soundness and completeness are proved and the countermodel generation is studied.

1 Introduction

Separation logics are logics for reasoning about mutable data structures in which the pre- and postconditions are written in a logic enriched with specific forms of conjunction or implication. In this context, Reynolds has proposed an intuitionistic logic extended with a separation connective $*$ [12] and Ishtiaq and O'Hearn have investigated the same approach from the point of view of the logic of Bunched Implications (BI) [10]. A key point of BI logic is its joint treatment of intuitionistic implication $\rightarrow$ and conjunction $\wedge$ (additive connectives) and linear implication $-\!\!*$ and conjunction $*$ (multiplicative connectives). BI's semantics allows statements to be made using standard connectives and then to combine them in a modular way using $-\!\!*$ and $*$. The resource interpretation of the connectives, where $*$ decomposes the current resource into pieces and $-\!\!*$ talks about new and fresh resource, is central. BI's pointer logic (PL) provides a concrete way of understanding the connectives in the context of program verification apart from logical concerns [6] . It is a possible worlds model of Boolean BI (BBI) where additives are classical that validates the axioms for Hoare triples. PL being used as an assertion language for mutable data structures, it appears essential to provide a proof theory and related proof search methods in order to check PL assertions.

In this paper we propose a characterization of provability in PL that is based on semantic structures, called resource graphs, and a new labelled calculus that builds such graphs from which proofs or countermodels can be generated. A similar approach has been developed for BI with intuitionistic additives [3, 4] but it cannot be directly applied to BBI and its classical additives. The key point consists in defining resource graphs that capture PL models by considering heaps as resources and by using an appropriate labelling process. Such graphs allow to capture semantic information essential for the

G. Sutcliffe and A. Voronkov (Eds.): LPAR 2005, LNAI 3835, pp. 459–473, 2005.

provability analysis [5]. Having defined PL resource graphs, we propose a calculus with labels and constraints for a propositional fragment of PL, called PL$^{\rightharpoonup}$, in a tableau style that is adapted to countermodel extraction. Soundness and completeness of the related proof search method are proved and countermodel generation from resource graphs is analyzed. Finally, extensions of the calculus and results to PL can be developed.

2   BI's Pointer Logic

BI's Pointer Logic (PL) is a logic for reasoning about mutable data structures [6]. Some problems about pointer management, including aliasing, are difficult to deal with. Recent works have provided logics with a spatial form of conjunction $*$ that splits the heap into distinct subheaps and with a form of assertion, the points-to relation $\mapsto$, to make statements about the contents of heap cells [9, 12]. It leads to simple axioms and captures the intuitive operational locality of assignment. They are based on BI logic that includes two implication connectives $\rightarrow$ and $-\!\!*$ with two conjunction connectives $\wedge$ and $*$ [10]. BI's semantics allow statements to be made using standard (additive) connectives and then to combine them using the (multiplicative) connectives.

Here, we consider PL that is a model of Boolean BI (with classical additives) [6] and summarize its key notions and results. First, we have a set of values Val that can be integers or locations, a set of variables Var and a countable set of locations Loc. A stack $s : Var \rightharpoonup_{fin} Val$ is a finite partially defined function that associates values to variables and a heap $h : Loc \rightharpoonup_{fin} Val \times Val$ is a finite partially defined function that associates pairs of values to locations. An expression E can represent a variable, called a stack variable, an integer or a constant that is interpreted w.r.t. a stack s as a value ($[\![E]\!]s \in Val$).

Definition 2.1. *The language of* PL *consists of the predicates* $\mapsto$ *and* $=$, *the connectives of* BI, *the existential quantifier and two countable sets of variables of stacks and values. The set of formulae is inductively defined as follows:*

- $At ::= (E \mapsto E_1, E_2) \mid E_1 = E_2$ *where* E, E_1 *and* E_2 *are expressions,*
- $\phi ::= At \mid I \mid \phi * \phi \mid \phi -\!\!* \phi \mid \top \mid \bot \mid \phi \wedge \phi \mid \phi \rightarrow \phi \mid \phi \vee \phi \mid \exists x. \phi.$

Moreover, we can define $\neg\phi$ by $\neg\phi \equiv \phi \rightarrow \bot$ and use it to define connectives rather than taking them as primitives. The predicate $(x \mapsto a, b)$ allows to represent the state of the memory: there exists a variable x in a stack s such that there exists a location l in a heap h such that $[\![E]\!]s = l$ and $h(l) = \langle a, b \rangle$. The actual use of PL consists in describing states about resources with the language and in proving properties about these resources with the logic. The semantics of the formulae is given by a satisfaction relation of the form $s, h \models \phi$ that asserts that ϕ is true in stack $s \in S$ and heap $h \in H$. It is required that the free variables of ϕ are included in the domain of s.

Definition 2.2. *The semantics of the formulae is defined as follows:*

- $s, h \models E_1 = E_2$ *iff* $[\![E_1]\!]s = [\![E_2]\!]s$
- $s, h \models (E \mapsto E_1, E_2)$ *iff* $dom(h) = \{[\![E]\!]s\}$ *and* $h([\![E]\!]s) = \langle [\![E_1]\!]s, [\![E_2]\!]s \rangle$
- $s, h \models \top$ *always*

- $s,h \models \bot$ *never*
- $s,h \models \phi \wedge \psi$ *iff* $s,h \models \phi$ *and* $s,h \models \psi$
- $s,h \models \phi \vee \psi$ *iff* $s,h \models \phi$ *or* $s,h \models \psi$
- $s,h \models \phi \rightarrow \psi$ *iff* *if* $s,h \models \phi$ *then* $s,h \models \psi$
- $s,h \models I$ *iff* h *is the empty heap*
- $s,h \models \phi * \psi$ *iff* $\exists h_1, h_2. \; h_1 \# h_2, \; h_1 \cdot h_2 = h, \; s,h_1 \models \phi$ *and* $s,h_2 \models \psi$
- $s,h \models \phi \mathbin{-\!\!*} \psi$ *iff* $\forall h_1. \; if \; h_1 \# h$ *and* $s,h_1 \models \phi$ *then* $s,h_1 \cdot h \models \psi$
- $s,h \models \exists x.\phi$ *iff* $\exists v \in Val. \; [s|x \mapsto v], h \models \phi$

In the previous definition, $h_1 \# h_2$ means that the domains of heaps h_1 and h_2 are disjoint and $h_1 \cdot h_2$ denotes the union of disjoint heaps (union of functions with disjoint domains). Composition of non-disjoint heaps is undefined so that heap composition is only partial. Moreover, the semantic consequence relation $\phi \models \psi$ between formulae holds if and only if for all s,h, if $s,h \models \phi$ then $s,h \models \psi$.

In this model, the worlds are heaps (collections of cons cells in storage) and the conjunction $\phi * \psi$ is true just when the current heap can be split into two components, one of which makes ϕ true and the other which makes ψ true. The implication $\phi \mathbin{-\!\!*} \psi$ talks about new or fresh pieces of heap, disjoint from the current heap. It says that, whenever we have a new heap that makes ϕ true, the combined new and current heap will make ψ true. The other connectives are interpreted pointwise. For instance, the formula $(x \mapsto 3,5) * ((x \mapsto 7,5) \mathbin{-\!\!*} P)$ says that x denotes a cell which holds $(3,5)$ in the current heap and that if we update the car to 7 then P will be true. The semantics of $*$ splits the heap into two parts, one where $(x \mapsto 3,5)$ holds and another where the location x is dangling. Then the semantics of $\mathbin{-\!\!*}$ and $\mapsto$ ensures that P must be true when the second heap is extended by binding x's location to $(7,5)$.

Main concepts and results about the use of PL as an assertion language are given in [6]. As an interesting result, we can mention an operation that disposes of memory, by creating dangling pointers, through the command $dispose(E)$ which deallocates a location. From a semantic point of view, it removes a location from the heap and is defined by the following axiom: $\{P * \exists a \, b.(E \mapsto a,b)\} \; dispose(E) \; \{P\}$, where a,b are not free in E. Reasoning backwards from $\top$ we can find cases under which a program is safe to execute. With a double dispose we obtain $\bot$ for the precondition as expected, indicating that the program is not safe to execute for any start state:

$$\{\bot\}$$
$$\{\top * \exists a \, b.(x \mapsto a,b) * \exists c \, d.(x \mapsto c,d)\}$$
$$dispose(x)$$
$$\{\top * \exists a \, b.(x \mapsto a,b)\}$$
$$dispose(x)$$
$$\{\top\}$$

We first study a propositional fragment of PL, denoted $\text{PL}^{\mapsto}$, restricted to atomic formulae $(l \mapsto a,b)$ in which l,a,b are constants, meaning that at location l there is a cell containing (a,b). Then, we can forget the stack variables in the semantic clauses corresponding to this fragment.

3 Heaps, Labels and Resource Graphs

Purely syntactic proof methods (in sequent or natural deduction style) usually deal with a great amount of operational overhead (structural rules, permutabilities of inferences) which is mainly irrelevant w.r.t. the provability of a formula. On the other hand, purely semantic methods often abstract away too much of the operational aspects to be significant and helpful for countermodel construction. In the case of PL, we have a complete semantics based on partial monoids of heaps, and then syntactic and semantic consequence relations (provability and validity) coincide [1]. Therefore, the main properties of heap composition and of PL semantic consequence relation can be reflected at a syntactic level using labels, constraints and a specific closure operator [5] in order to define a resource driven proof method for PL.

3.1 Labels and Constraints

Definition 3.1 (labels). *The labelling language consists of a countable set of constant symbols $c_0, c_1, \cdots$ and a binary symbol $\circ$. The set $\mathcal{L}$ of labels is the smallest set which contains constants c_i $(i \in \mathbb{N})$ (atomic labels) and such that $x \circ y$ is a (compound) label whenever x, y are labels which do not share any constant symbol.*

The constants are intended to reflect heaps, while $\circ$ is intended to reflect heap composition. We view labels as unordered sequences of symbols, *i.e.*, $\circ$ is interpreted as an associative and commutative operation on labels. For example, we consider the two labels $c_1 \circ (c_2 \circ (c_3 \circ c_4))$ and $(c_2 \circ c_1) \circ (c_4 \circ c_3)$ as equal and we do not distinguish between the two of them. Since order and association are irrelevant, we frequently omit the symbol $\circ$ and simply write xyz instead of $x \circ y \circ z$.

More formally, we first say that a label x is a *sublabel* of a label y if any constant occuring in x also occurs in y, *i.e.*, $x \leq y$ iff $(\forall c_i \in x)(c_i \in y)$. Then, we define $x = y$ iff $x \leq y$ and $y \leq x$. The length $|x|$ of a label x is the number of constants it contains. Moreover, we define $x - y$ as the label z obtained from x by discarding all the constants in y that also occur in x, eventually setting z to c_0 if there is no constant left in x. We then define label constraints as expressions of the form $yz \lhd x$, Zx, Ux, Ax that respectively reflect that a heap can be decomposed into two sub-heaps, may contain *no* cell (Zero), may contain *exactly one* cell (Unit) and may contain *at least one* cell (Aggregate).

Definition 3.2 (constraints). *A label constraint is an expression of the form $x \lhd y$ or of the form $\mathrm{T}x$, where x and y are labels and $\mathrm{T} \in \{Z, U, A\}$.*

Moreover we need to capture the various resource interactions that occur in PL models and we do it through a closure operator $(\cdot)^\dagger$ on sets of labels and constraints. Let us note that when we write $x \in X^\dagger$, x being a label, we do not intend x to be a member of $X^\dagger$ explicitly, we only require that $X^\dagger$ contains some label y such that $y = x$, *i.e.*, we slightly abuse our notations to work with equivalence classes of labels modulo the equality $=$ induced by the associativity and commutativity of label composition. Given a constraint k ($y \lhd x$, Zx, Ux or Ax), we say that k *holds in* X, written $X \vdash k$, if $k \in X^\dagger$. The domain $\mathcal{D}(X)$ of a set X of labels and constraints is defined as the restriction of $X^\dagger$ to its labels.

---

[1] This is not the case for Boolean BI, for which there is currently no known complete monoid-based semantics.

Definition 3.3 $((\cdot)^\dagger$**-closure**). *Let X be set of labels and label constraints. We define $X^\dagger$ as the smallest set containing $X \cup \{c_0, Zc_0\}$ such that*

- $x \in X^\dagger$ *and* $y \leq x \Rightarrow y \in X^\dagger$ *(saturation),*
- $x \lhd y \in X^\dagger \Rightarrow x, y \in X^\dagger$ *($\lhd$-completion),*
- $Zx \in X^\dagger$ *or* $Ux \in X^\dagger \Rightarrow x \in X^\dagger$ *(ZU-completion),*
- $x \in X^\dagger \Rightarrow x \lhd x \in X^\dagger$ *(reflexivity),*
- $x \lhd y \in X^\dagger$ *and* $y \lhd z \in X^\dagger \Rightarrow x \lhd z \in X^\dagger$ *(transitivity),*
- $x \lhd y \in X^\dagger$ *and* $yz \in X^\dagger \Rightarrow xz \lhd yz \in X^\dagger$ *($\lhd$-propagation),*
- $Zx \in X^\dagger$ *and* $y \leq x \Rightarrow Zy \in X^\dagger$ *(Z-decomposition),*
- $Ux \in X^\dagger$ *and* $y \leq x$ *and* $Uy \in X^\dagger \Rightarrow Z(x - y) \in X^\dagger$ *(U-decomposition),*
- $Tx \in X^\dagger$ *and* $(y \lhd x$ *or* $x \lhd y) \in X^\dagger \Rightarrow Ty \in X^\dagger$ *(T-propagation).*

The reflexivity, transitivity and $\lhd$-propagation conditions simply capture the fact that in PL, the validity relation satisfies $\phi \models \phi$, $\phi \models \psi$ and $\psi \models \chi$ imply $\phi \models \chi$, and $\phi \models \psi$ implies $\phi * \chi \models \psi * \chi$. The Z-decomposition condition reflects that all sub-heaps of an empty heap are empty. The U-decomposition condition reflects that if x stands for a heap having exactly one location and if y represents a sub-heap with only one location also, then any sub-heap of x disjoint from y must be empty. Finally, the T-propagation condition simply explains how the properties of being an empty heap, a one-location heap, or an aggregate heap are propagated through heap composition. For example, let us set $T = Z$, $x = c_1$ and $y = c_2c_3$, then, the condition means that if c_1 represents an empty heap (Zc_1) which may be obtained by composition of the two heaps c_2 and c_3 ($c_2c_3 \lhd c_1$), then c_2c_3 also represents an empty heap (Zc_2c_3).

3.2 Resource Graphs

In this subsection, we explain how labels and constraints give rise to a specific semantic structure, called a *resource graph*, which is a graphical representation of the $(\cdot)^\dagger$-closure operator.

Definition 3.4. *Let X be set of labels and constraints, the resource graph associated to X and denoted $\mathcal{G}(X)$ is a directed graph $[N, E]$.*
The set of nodes N is derived from the labels occurring in $X^\dagger$ (the domain of X) by decorating each label x with a tag Γ which is a (possibly empty) subset of $\{Z, U, A\}$ such that, for any $T \in \{Z, U, A\}$, if $X \vdash Tx$ then $T \in \Gamma$.
The set of arrows E is such that there is an arrow $\Gamma x \twoheadrightarrow \Delta y$ from the node Γx to the node Δy iff the constraint $x \lhd y$ holds in X, i.e., $X \vdash x \lhd y$.

Let us illustrate the previous definition with some examples. Firstly, we consider the set $X = \{Zc_0, c_2c_3 \lhd c_1, Uc_2, Uc_2c_3\}$. In order to obtain $X^\dagger$, we must add the constraint Zc_3 to satisfy the *(U-decomposition)* of Definition 3.3 since we have Uc_2, Uc_2c_3 and $c_3 \leq c_2c_3$. Furthermore, due to the presence of $c_2c_3 \lhd c_1$ and Uc_2c_3, *(U-propagation)* leads to the addition of Uc_1 so that $X^\dagger = \{Zc_0, c_2c_3 \lhd c_1, Uc_2, Uc_2c_3, Zc_3, Uc_1\}$.

Secondly, beginning with the set $Y = \{Zc_0, c_2c_3 \lhd c_1, Uc_2, Uc_3, Zc_1\}$, the application of *(Z-propagation)* and *(Z-decomposition)* on the constraints $c_2c_3 \lhd c_1$ and Zc_1 lead to $Y^{\dagger} = \{Zc_0, c_2c_3 \lhd c_1, Uc_2, Uc_3, Zc_1, Zc_2c_3, Zc_2, Zc_3\}$. The resource graphs $\mathcal{G}_0(X)$ and $\mathcal{G}_0(Y)$, respectively associated to X and Y, then look as follows [2]:

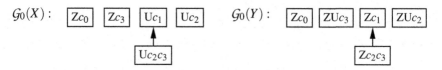

3.3 Normalizing Resource Graphs

In order to reduce the size of the resource graphs, we need to remove nodes that are semantically redundant. For that, we define a normalization process on resource graphs that takes into account that there is only one empty heap which is moreover the unit of heap composition. Therefore, we only keep the node Zc_0 to represent the empty heap and discard all other nodes of the form Zx. Let $\mathcal{G}(X) = [N, E]$ be the resource graph associated with a set X of labels and constraints. Labels $x \in \mathcal{D}(X)$ such that $X \vdash Zx$ are called Z-labels, or Z-constants when x is a constant symbol. Since such labels are assumed to behave as units w.r.t. label composition $\circ$, we define an equivalence relation $\simeq$ on X such that $x \simeq y$ iff $(\forall c_i)(X \not\vdash Zc_i \Rightarrow (c_i \in y \leftrightarrow c_i \in x))$, *i.e.*, the labels x and y are equivalent upto $\simeq$ if they have the same non-zero constants. We write $X \vdash x \simeq y$ to mean that $x \simeq y$ holds in X. In terms of the resource graph $\mathcal{G}(X)$, $\Gamma x \simeq \Delta y$ holds in $\mathcal{G}(X)$, written $\mathcal{G}(X) \vdash \Gamma x \simeq \Delta y$, iff $x \simeq y$ holds in X[3]. For example, $Uc_2c_3 \simeq Uc_2$ holds in $\mathcal{G}_0(X)$ because Zc_3 holds in $\mathcal{G}_0(X)$.

In order to put a resource graph $\mathcal{G}(X) = [N, E]$ in normal form, the first step is to gather all labels that are equivalent upto $\simeq$, *i.e.*, for all labels x, its equivalence class modulo $\simeq$ is given by $\bar{x} = \{y \mid X \vdash x \simeq y\}$. For the equivalence classes of labels modulo $\simeq$ to give rise to the nodes $\bar{N}$ of a resource graph in normal form, we need to decorate them with appropriate tags. Therefore, the second step of the normalization process is to merge the tags associated to the labels populating an equivalence class using set union. Thus, for all classes $\bar{x}$, we compute the set $\varphi = \bigcup_{\Delta y \in N, y \in \bar{x}} \Delta$. The tag associated to $\bar{x}$, denoted Φ, is then obtained from φ by discarding the A letter whenever the U letter is already a member of φ, *i.e.*, $\Phi = \varphi - \{A\}$ if $\{U, A\} \subseteq \phi$ and $\Phi = \varphi$ otherwise [4]. Finally, in order to give rise to the edges $\bar{E}$ of the normal resource graph associated to $\mathcal{G}(X)[N, E]$, we add an arrow $\Phi \bar{x} \dashrightarrow \Psi \bar{y}$ going from a node $\Phi \bar{x}$ to a node $\Psi \bar{y}$ iff $\Gamma u \dashrightarrow \Delta v \in E$ for some $u \in \bar{x}$ and $v \in \bar{y}$. Keeping the label with a minimum length as the witness for its equivalence class modulo $\simeq$, the previous examples lead to the following normal resource graphs:

----

[2] For simplicity, we do not explicitly represent reflexive and transitive arrows.

[3] In the rest of the paper, we define relations α either in terms of labels, or in terms of nodes, the link between the two forms is such that $X \vdash x \alpha y$ iff $\mathcal{G}(X) \vdash \Gamma x \alpha \Delta y$.

[4] This is semantically justified by the fact that it is no use knowing that a heap contains at least one cell when one already knows it contains exactly one.

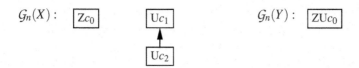

3.4 Points-to Predicate Distributions

Given a resource graph $G(X) = [N,E]$, we consider distributions of points-to predicates over nodes of the form Ux. For example, in the previous resource graph $G_n(X)$, we associate $(l \mapsto a,b)$ and $(k \mapsto c,d)$ to the node Uc_2. Such a distribution is denoted as follows: $Pto(Uc_2) = \{(l \mapsto a,b),(k \mapsto c,d)\}$.

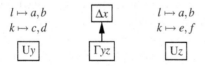

Let us define the new relation $\approx$ as the smallest equivalence on X generated by $(\lhd \cup \simeq)$. Then, in order to keep track of which locations are defined in a given heap, we associate *multisets* of points-to predicates called *loc-sets* to the nodes of a resource graph. The loc-set $Loc(\Gamma x)$ associated to a node Γx is such that $Pto(\Gamma x) \subseteq Loc(\Gamma x)$ and if $G(X) \vdash \Gamma x \approx \Delta yz$ for some $\Sigma_1 y, \Sigma_2 z \in N$, then $Loc(\Sigma_1 y) \cup Loc(\Sigma_2 z) \subseteq Loc(\Gamma x)$. In other words, loc-sets inherit points-to predicates via label composition and arrows of the resource graphs. Finally, we say that $Loc(\Gamma x)$ and $Loc(\Delta y)$ are *compatible*, denoted $Loc(\Gamma x) \# Loc(\Delta y)$, or more shortly $x \# y$, if they share no location l.

Let us illustrate the previous notions with the following resource graph:

$$
\begin{array}{ccc}
\begin{array}{l} l \mapsto a,b \\ k \mapsto c,d \end{array} & \boxed{\Delta x} & \begin{array}{l} l \mapsto a,b \\ k \mapsto e,f \end{array} \\[1em]
\boxed{Uy} & \boxed{\Gamma yz} & \boxed{Uz}
\end{array}
$$

Here, the points-to distribution is such that $Pto(Uy) = \{(l \mapsto a,b),(k \mapsto c,d)\}$ and $Pto(Uz) = \{(l \mapsto a,b),(k \mapsto e,f)\}$. The loc-set associated with the node Δx is such that $Loc(\Delta x) = \{(l \mapsto a,b),(l \mapsto a,b),(k \mapsto c,d),(k \mapsto e,f)\}$. Notice that $(l \mapsto a,b)$ occurs twice in $Loc(\Delta x)$, the first occurence coming from $Pto(Uy)$ and the second coming from $Pto(Uz)$. Therefore $Loc(Uy)$ and $Loc(Uz)$ are not compatible since they share the location l (and the location k too).

3.5 Structural Consistency

Let us define the notion of a structural consistency for (normal) resource graphs, which intuitively means that a resource graph indeed represents a "real" model of PL. We first introduce the notion of *well-formed* resource graphs.

Definition 3.5. *A normal resource graph* $G(X) = [N,E]$ *is* well-formed *iff for all* $\Gamma x \in N$, *the set* Γ *contains at most one element.*

Then, we introduce the notion of *complexity measure* on the nodes of a resource graph. The role of such a notion is to unambiguously determine how many cells are assumed to be in the heap represented by a given node. The information conveyed by the constraints of type Ax is only a rough abstraction (at least one cell) that needs to be completed if we have to extract countermodels from resource graphs as explained later in Section 5.

Definition 3.6. *Given a well-formed normal resource graph* $G(X) = [N, E]$, *a complexity measure on* $G(X)$ *is a total function* $Comp : N \rightarrow \mathbb{N}$ *such that*

- $Comp(Zx) = 0$, $Comp(Ux) = 1$, $Comp(Ax) \geq 1$,
- $Comp(\Gamma xy) = Comp(\Delta x) + Comp(\Sigma y)$,
- $G(X) \vdash \Gamma x \approx \Delta y \Rightarrow Comp(\Gamma x) = Comp(\Delta y)$.

Definition 3.7. *Given a measure of complexity Comp on a well-formed resource graph* $G(X)$ *and a distribution Pto,* $G(X)$ *is* structurally consistent *w.r.t.* $(Pto, Comp)$ *iff:*

- $\forall Zx \in N$, $Loc(Zx)$ *is the empty set (SC1)*,
- $\forall Ux \in N$, $Loc(Ux)$ *is a singleton set (SC2)*,
- $\forall \Gamma x, \Delta y \in N$, $\Sigma xy \in N \Rightarrow Loc(\Gamma x) \# Loc(\Delta y)$ *(SC3)*,
- $\forall \Gamma x$, $Cardinal(Loc(\Gamma x)) \leq Comp(\Gamma x)$ *(SC4)*.

$G(X)$ *is structurally consistent w.r.t. a distribution Pto iff there exists some complexity measure Comp for which it is structurally consistent w.r.t.* $(Pto, Comp)$.

The previous conditions simply reflect that a heap with no cell should have no location, that a heap with one cell should have exactly one location, that heaps must not share locations if they are to be composed and that there should not be more locations in a heap than there are cells. In the rest of the paper, since a label x uniquely determines a node Γx in a resource graph, we shall sometimes write $Loc(x)$ and $Comp(x)$ instead of $Loc(\Gamma x)$ and $Comp(\Gamma x)$.

4   Resource Graphs and Provability

In this section, we propose a tableau-based calculus for PL that builds resource graphs. The choice of a tableau proof-search method is motivated by its well-known ability to propose countermodel extraction facilities [2], but our notions of labels, constraints and resource graphs can be integrated to connection-based, or sequent-based calculi [3], in order to characterize provability in PL.

Definition 4.1. *A signed formula is an expression* $S\phi : x$, *where* $S \in \{F, T\}$ *is a sign,* ϕ *is a* $PL^{\hookrightarrow}$ *formula and x is a label.*

Definition 4.2. *Let χ be a formula in* $PL^{\hookrightarrow}$. *A tableau for χ is a binary tree $\mathcal{T}$ whose root node is labelled with the signed formula* $F\chi : c_0$, *all other nodes being either labelled with a signed formula, or with a constraint, and which is built (respecting the structure of χ) according to the rules depicted on Figure 1.*

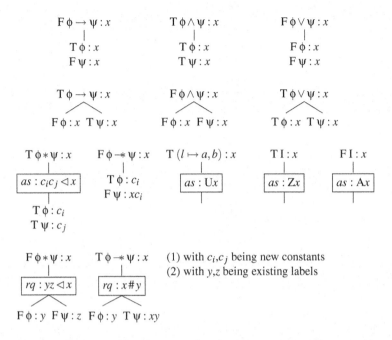

Fig. 1. Tableaux rules for TPL$^{\hookrightarrow}$

Given a branch $\mathcal{B}$, $As(\mathcal{B})$ is the set of its *assertions* and $Rq(\mathcal{B})$ the set of its *requirements*. The domain of a branch $\mathcal{B}$, denoted $\mathcal{D}(\mathcal{B})$, is the restriction of the set $As(\mathcal{B})^{\dagger}$ to its labels. We shall see that assertions behave as known facts while requirements behave as goals that must be achieved using assertions. The application of expansion rules of Figure 1 leads to the (incremental) construction of a resource graph, denoted $\mathcal{G}(\mathcal{B})$, that is induced by the $(\cdot)^{\dagger}$-closure of the assertions occuring in $\mathcal{B}$. Moreover, the points-to predicate distribution is given by the signed formulae of the branch with sign T, *i.e.*, $\mathcal{G}(\mathcal{B})$ is the resource graph $\mathcal{G}(As(\mathcal{B})^{\dagger})[N, E]$ such that, for all nodes $\mathrm{U}x \in N$, $Pto(\mathrm{U}x) = \{\, (l \mapsto a, b) \mid \mathrm{T}\,(l \mapsto a, b) : x \in \mathcal{B} \,\}$.

Having resource graphs associated to tableau branches and built from the assertions we relate them to the requirements generated by the $\mathrm{F}\,\phi * \psi : x$ and $\mathrm{T}\,\phi \mathbin{-\!\!*} \psi : x$ signed formulae. This leads to the notion of *admissible tableau*.

Definition 4.3. *A requirement is* admissible *in a branch $\mathcal{B}$ of a tableau $\mathcal{T}$ if it holds in the $((\cdot)^{\dagger}$-closure of the) assertions that occur (in $\mathcal{B}$) closer to the root of $\mathcal{T}$ than this requirement. A branch $\mathcal{B}$ is* admissible *if all its requirements are admissible in $\mathcal{B}$ and a tableau $\mathcal{T}$ is* admissible *if all its branches are admissible.*

Before we proceed with the notion of *logical consistency*, which intuitively means that a formula of PL$^{\hookrightarrow}$ can be falsified, we need to introduce an equivalence relation on the nodes of a resource graph. Given a complexity measure $Comp$ on the resource graph $\mathcal{G}(\mathcal{B})$ of a branch $\mathcal{B}$, we say that the relation $\Gamma x \sim \Delta y$ holds in $\mathcal{G}(\mathcal{B})$, written $\mathcal{G}(\mathcal{B}) \vdash \Gamma x \sim \Delta y$ (or more shortly $\mathcal{B} \vdash x \sim y$), iff either $\mathcal{G}(\mathcal{B}) \vdash \Gamma x \approx \Delta y$ or $Comp(\Gamma x) =$

$$\sqrt{}_1 \; F\,(((l \mapsto a,b) * ((l \mapsto a,b) \rightarrow\!\!* (k \mapsto c,d))) \rightarrow\!\!* (h \mapsto e,f) : c_0$$

$$\sqrt{}_2 \; T\,((l \mapsto a,b) * ((l \mapsto a,b) \rightarrow\!\!* (k \mapsto c,d)) : c_1$$
$$F\,(h \mapsto e,f) : c_1 (= c_0 c_1)$$

$$\boxed{as_1 : c_2 c_3 \lhd c_1}$$

$$T\,(l \mapsto a,b) : c_2$$
$$\sqrt{}_3 \; T\,(l \mapsto a,b) \rightarrow\!\!* (k \mapsto c,d) : c_3$$

$$F\,(l \mapsto a,b) : c_2 \qquad T\,(k \mapsto c,d) : c_2 c_3$$
$$\times \qquad\qquad\qquad \times$$

Fig. 2. Tableau for $((l \mapsto a,b) * ((l \mapsto a,b) \rightarrow\!\!* (k \mapsto c,d))) \rightarrow\!\!* (h \mapsto e,f)$

$Comp(\Delta y)$, $Loc(\Gamma x) = Loc(\Delta y)$ and $Cardinal(Loc(\Gamma x)) = Comp(\Gamma x)$. In other words, two nodes are equivalent upto $\sim$ if they represent heaps having the same cells (with the same content) and the same locations.

Definition 4.4. *A branch $\mathcal{B}$ is* logically inconsistent *w.r.t. to a complexity measure Comp on $\mathcal{G}(\mathcal{B})$ if it satisfies one of the following conditions:*

- $T\,(l \mapsto a,b) : x$, $F\,(l \mapsto a,b) : y \in \mathcal{B}$ *and* $\mathcal{B} \vdash x \sim y$ *(CL1)*;
- $F\,I : x \in \mathcal{B}$ *and* $Comp(\Gamma x) = 0$ *(CL2)*;
- $F\,\top : x \in \mathcal{B}$ *(CL3)*;
- $T\,\bot : x \in \mathcal{B}$ *(CL4)*.

A tableau is logically inconsistent *w.r.t. Comp if it has a branch that is logically inconsistent w.r.t. Comp.*

Definition 4.5. *A branch $\mathcal{B}$ is* open *if it is logically consistent and if its resource graph $\mathcal{G}(\mathcal{B})$ is structurally consistent w.r.t. some complexity measure Comp on $\mathcal{G}(\mathcal{B})$, otherwise it is* closed. *A tableau $\mathcal{T}$ is* open *if it has an open branch.*

Definition 4.6. *Let ϕ be a formula of* PL$^{\mapsto}$*, a tableau $\mathcal{T}$ is a* TPL-*proof of ϕ if there is a sequence of tableaux $(\mathcal{T}_i)_{1 \leq i \leq n}$ such that*
1. $\mathcal{T}_1$ is the one-node tableau the root of which is labelled with $F\,\phi : c_0$,
2. $\mathcal{T}_{i+1}$ is obtained from $\mathcal{T}_i$ by a decomposition rule of Figure 1,
3. $\mathcal{T}_n = \mathcal{T}$, $\mathcal{T}$ is closed and admissible.
A formula ϕ is provable *in* TPL *if there exists a* TPL-*proof of ϕ.*

Let us illustrate these closure conditions. The tableau of Figure 2 has a left branch which is not logically consistent (condition *(CL1)* on $(l \mapsto a,b)$ and c_2). In the right branch, we have to capture the semantics of $\mapsto$. For instance, if a heap forces $(l \mapsto a,b)$ then this heap has only one cell that is at location l and contains the values $\langle a,b \rangle$. The resource graph associated to this branch is $\mathcal{G}_0(X)$, given in subsection 3.2, that after normalization is not structurally consistent because the loc-set $Loc(Uc_2) =$

$\{(l \mapsto a,b),(k \mapsto c,d)\}$ is not a singleton set as required by condition *(SC2)* of Definition 3.7. Then this branch is closed (marked with a $\times$).

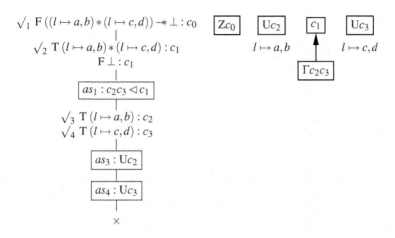

Fig. 3. Tableau for $((l \mapsto a,b) * (l \mapsto c,d)) \twoheadrightarrow \bot$.

Figure 3 gives a tableau for the formula $((l \mapsto a,b) * (l \mapsto c,d)) \twoheadrightarrow \bot$ that means that we cannot have two cells in a heap that are at the same location. We could deduce the existence of two heaps (represented by c_2 and c_3) that respectively force $(l \mapsto a,b)$ and $(l \mapsto c,d)$, but then their composition (represented by $c_2 c_3$) is not defined since they are not disjoint and thus cannot force $(l \mapsto a,b) * (l \mapsto c,d)$. We observe that the associated resource graph in normalized form is not structurally consistent since $Loc(Uc_2) = \{(l \mapsto a,b)\}$ and $Loc(Uc_3) = \{(l \mapsto c,d)\}$, so that $Loc(c_2 c_3) = Loc(c_1) = \{(l \mapsto a,b),(l \mapsto c,d)\}$, which contradicts condition *(SC3)* of Definition 3.7 because the loc-sets $Loc(Uc_2)$ and $Loc(Uc_3)$ are not compatible (they share location l). Then this branch is closed.

5   Countermodel Construction and Completeness

Before we study the completeness we prove the soundness of TPL by introducing the size of a heap h, denoted $Size(h)$, that is the number of locations it contains.

Definition 5.1 (realization). *Let $\mathcal{B}$ be a branch. A* realization *of $\mathcal{B}$ is a mapping $\|-\|$: $\mathcal{D}(\mathcal{B}) \rightarrow Heaps$ that satisfies:*

- *$\|x \circ y\| = \|x\| \cdot \|y\|$, $\mathcal{B} \vdash Zx \Rightarrow \|x\| = e$,*
- *$\mathcal{B} \vdash Ux \Rightarrow Size(\|x\|) = 1$, $\mathcal{B} \vdash Ax \Rightarrow Size(\|x\|) \geq 1$,*
- *$yz \triangleleft x \in As(\mathcal{B}) \Rightarrow \|x\| \cdot \|y\| = \|z\|$, $\mathcal{B} \vdash x \approx y \Rightarrow \|x\| = \|y\|$,*
- *$T \phi : x \in \mathcal{B} \Rightarrow \|x\| \models \phi$ and $F \phi : x \in \mathcal{B} \Rightarrow \|x\| \not\models \phi$.*

A branch $\mathcal{B}$ is realizable *if there exists a realization of $\mathcal{B}$. A tableau $\mathcal{T}$ is* realizable *if it contains a realizable branch.*

Lemma 5.1. *A closed tableau is not realizable.*

Proof. By analysis of the $(\cdot)^{\dagger}$-closure rules.

Lemma 5.2. *The rules of* TPL *preserve realizability.*

Proof. We show that, for all realizable tableaux $\mathcal{T}$, if $\mathcal{T}'$ is a tableau obtained from $\mathcal{T}$ by application of a TPL rule, then $\mathcal{T}'$ is realizable.

Theorem 5.1 (soundness). *Let ϕ be a formula of* PL$^{\mapsto}$. *If there exists a* TPL*-proof of ϕ then ϕ is valid in* PL$^{\mapsto}$ *semantics.*

Proof. Let $(\mathcal{T}_i)_{1 \leq i \leq n}$ be a TPL-proof of ϕ. Suppose that ϕ does not hold in PL$^{\mapsto}$ semantics, then $e \not\models \phi$. Consequently, $\|c_0\| = e$ is a trivial realization of $\mathcal{T}_0$. Lemma 5.2 then entails that all tableaux in $(\mathcal{T}_i)_{1 \leq i \leq n}$ are realizable. This is a contradiction because, by definition of a TPL-proof, $\mathcal{T}_n$ is closed, which implies, by Lemma 5.1, that $\mathcal{T}_n$ is not realizable.

Definition 5.2. *A signed formula* S $\phi : x$ *is analyzed in a branch $\mathcal{B}$, denoted $\mathcal{B} \succ$ S $\phi : x$, iff* S $\phi : y \in \mathcal{B}$ *for some label y such that $\mathcal{B} \vdash x \approx y$.*

Definition 5.3. *A signed formula* S $\phi : x$ *is completely analyzed or fulfilled in a branch $\mathcal{B}$, denoted $\mathcal{B} \Vdash$ S $\phi : x$, if it matches one of the following cases:*

- *$\mathcal{B} \Vdash$ T I $: x$ iff $\mathcal{B} \succ$ T I $: x$ and $\mathcal{B} \vdash Zx$,*
- *$\mathcal{B} \Vdash$ F I $: x$ iff $\mathcal{B} \succ$ F I $: x$ and $\mathcal{B} \vdash Ax$,*
- *$\mathcal{B} \Vdash$ T $(l \mapsto a, b) : x$ iff $\mathcal{B} \vdash Ux$,*
- *$\mathcal{B} \Vdash$ F $\psi \wedge \chi : x$ iff $\mathcal{B} \succ$ F $\psi : x$ or $\mathcal{B} \succ$ F $\chi : x$,*
- *$\mathcal{B} \Vdash$ T $\psi \wedge \chi : x$ iff $\mathcal{B} \succ$ T $\psi : x$ and $\mathcal{B} \succ$ T $\chi : x$,*
- *$\mathcal{B} \Vdash$ F $\psi \vee \chi : x$ iff $\mathcal{B} \succ$ F $\psi : x$ and $\mathcal{B} \succ$ F $\chi : x$,*
- *$\mathcal{B} \Vdash$ T $\psi \vee \chi : x$ iff $\mathcal{B} \succ$ T $\psi : x$ or $\mathcal{B} \succ$ T $\chi : x$,*
- *$\mathcal{B} \Vdash$ F $\psi \rightarrow \chi : x$ iff $\mathcal{B} \succ$ T $\psi : x$ and $\mathcal{B} \succ$ F $\chi : x$,*
- *$\mathcal{B} \Vdash$ T $\psi \rightarrow \chi : x$ iff $\mathcal{B} \succ$ F $\psi : x$ or $\mathcal{B} \succ$ T $\chi : x$,*
- *$\mathcal{B} \Vdash$ F $\psi * \chi : x$ iff $(\forall y, z \in \mathcal{D}(\mathcal{B}))(\mathcal{B} \vdash yz \approx x \Rightarrow (\mathcal{B} \succ$ F $\psi : y$ or $\mathcal{B} \succ$ F $\chi : z))$,*
- *$\mathcal{B} \Vdash$ T $\psi * \chi : x$ iff $(\exists y, z \in \mathcal{D}(\mathcal{B}))(\mathcal{B} \vdash yz \approx x$ and $\mathcal{B} \succ$ T $\psi : y$ and $\mathcal{B} \succ$ T $\chi : z)$,*
- *$\mathcal{B} \Vdash$ F $\psi \multimap \chi : x$ iff $(\exists y \in \mathcal{D}(\mathcal{B}))(xy \in \mathcal{D}(\mathcal{B})$ and $\mathcal{B} \succ$ T $\psi : y$ and $\mathcal{B} \succ$ F $\chi : xy)$,*
- *$\mathcal{B} \Vdash$ T $\psi \multimap \chi : x$ iff $(\forall y \in \mathcal{D}(\mathcal{B}))(xy \in \mathcal{D}(\mathcal{B}) \Rightarrow (\mathcal{B} \succ$ F $\psi : y$ or $\mathcal{B} \succ$ T $\chi : xy))$.*
- *for all other cases, $\mathcal{B} \Vdash$ S $\phi : x$ iff $\mathcal{B} \succ$ S $\phi : x$.*

Definition 5.4. *A branch $\mathcal{B}$ is complete iff it is open and all signed formulae in $\mathcal{B}$ are fulfilled. A tableau $\mathcal{T}$ is complete iff it contains a complete branch.*

It is standard to define a tableau construction procedure that builds either a closed tableau or a complete tableau [2]. Let us now explain how to construct a countermodel from an complete branch using the tableau depicted on Figure 4. In this example, the resource graph induces a complexity mesure such that $Comp(Uc_3) = Comp(Uc_5) = 1$. On the other hand, we have $Loc(c_1) = Loc(c_2c_3) = Loc(c_4c_5) = \{(l \mapsto a, b), (k \mapsto a, b)\}$, which implies $Comp(c_1) = Comp(c_2c_3) = Comp(c_4c_5) \geq 2$.

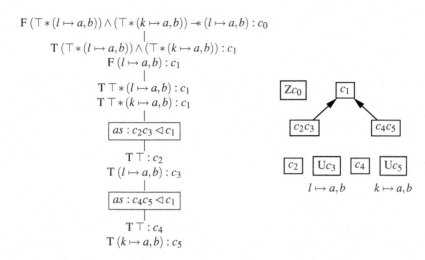

$$F\left(\top * (l \mapsto a,b)\right) \wedge \left(\top * (k \mapsto a,b)\right) \mathbin{-\!\!*} (l \mapsto a,b) : c_0$$

$$\top\left(\top * (l \mapsto a,b)\right) \wedge \left(\top * (k \mapsto a,b)\right) : c_1$$

$$F\,(l \mapsto a,b) : c_1$$

$$\top\top * (l \mapsto a,b) : c_1$$
$$\top\top * (k \mapsto a,b) : c_1$$

$$\boxed{as : c_2 c_3 \vartriangleleft c_1}$$

$$\top\top : c_2$$
$$\top\,(l \mapsto a,b) : c_3$$

$$\boxed{as : c_4 c_5 \vartriangleleft c_1}$$

$$\top\top : c_4$$
$$\top\,(k \mapsto a,b) : c_5$$

Fig. 4. Open tableau for $\left(\top * (l \mapsto a,b)\right) \wedge \left(\top * (k \mapsto a,b)\right) \mathbin{-\!\!*} (l \mapsto a,b)$

After having solved the linear system of equations induced by the definition of a complexity measure, we can deduce $Comp(c_2) = Comp(c_4) = 1$. Moreover, we have $Loc(c_2) = Loc(c_4) = \emptyset$, so that $Cardinal(Loc(c_2)) = Cardinal(Loc(c_4)) = 0$. Then the branch is logically and structurally consistent. However, condition *(SC4)* of Definition 3.7 only requires $Cardinal(Loc(\Gamma x)) \leq Comp(\Gamma x)$ for all nodes Γx. Therefore, in order to obtain a countermodel, we need to find a completion of all loc-sets such that for all nodes Γx, $Cardinal(Loc(\Gamma x)) = Comp(\Gamma x)$.

A completion of all loc-sets can be achieved using set unification on the equations induced by the resource graph and the definition of *Loc*. Here, we obtain four equations:

- $Loc(c_2) \cup Loc(Uc_3) = Loc(c_2 c_3) = \{(l \mapsto a,b), (k \mapsto a,b)\}$,
- $Loc(c_4) \cup Loc(Uc_5) = Loc(c_4 c_5) = \{(l \mapsto a,b), (k \mapsto a,b)\}$,
- $Loc(Uc_3) = \{(l \mapsto a,b)\}$,
- $Loc(Uc_5) = \{(k \mapsto a,b)\}$.

From this, we get $Loc(c_2) = \{(k \mapsto a,b)\}$ and $Loc(c_4) = \{(l \mapsto a,b)\}$, so that all locations in $Loc(c_2)$ and $Loc(c_4)$ are fully determined by the system of *Loc* equations, but in the general case it is sometimes necessary to add special locations, not occurring in the resource graph and pointing to any content. For example, if we replace $(k \mapsto a,b)$ by $(l \mapsto a,b)$ in the formula of Figure 4, then we must complete $Loc(c_2)$ and $Loc(c_4)$ with a location that does not occur in the heap, for instance, $Loc(c_2) = Loc(c_4) = \{(m \mapsto ?,?)\}$. The question marks mean that the content of the cell associated to the additional location does not matter.

The last step of the countermodel construction process is to derive a partial monoid of heaps from the labels in the resource graph. We proceed as follows: for all nodes Γx, we define a heap $h_x : Loc \to Val \times Val$ such that $h_x(l) = \langle a,b \rangle$ iff $(l \mapsto a,b) \in Loc(\Gamma x)$. Then, we define $\mathcal{H} = (H, \cdot, h_{c_0})$ as the structure such that $H = \{h_x \mid \Gamma x \in \mathcal{G}(\mathcal{B})\}$, knowing that heap composition is given by the union of disjoint partial functions.

Lemma 5.3. *If $\mathcal{B}$ is a complete branch then $\mathcal{H} = (H, \cdot, h_{c_0})$ is a PL$^{\hookrightarrow}$-model such that a) if $\mathcal{B} \succ T \phi : x$, then $(\exists \Gamma z \in \mathcal{G}(\mathcal{B}))(\mathcal{B} \vdash z \sim x$ and $h_z \models \phi)$ and b) if $\mathcal{B} \succ F \phi : x$, then $(\exists \Gamma z \in \mathcal{G}(\mathcal{B}))(\mathcal{B} \vdash z \sim x$ and $h_z \not\models \phi)$.*

Proof. We show that condition *(SC1)* of Definition 3.7 implies that h_{c_0} is the empty heap and that condition *(SC3)* implies that whenever there exists Δz in the resource graph such that $\mathcal{B} \vdash z \sim xy$ then $h_x \cdot h_y = h_z$. The two properties a) and b) are deduced by induction on ϕ w.r.t. conditions of Definition 5.3.

Theorem 5.2 (completeness). *Let ϕ be a formula of PL$^{\hookrightarrow}$. If ϕ is valid in PL$^{\hookrightarrow}$ semantics, then there exists a TPL-proof of ϕ.*

Proof. Let ϕ be a valid PL$^{\hookrightarrow}$ formula. Suppose that ϕ has no TPL-proof, then, there exists no sequence of tableaux $(\mathcal{T}_i)_{1 \leq i \leq n}$ such that $\mathcal{T}_n$ is closed. Therefore, any (fair) tableau construction procedure results in a tableau containing a complete branch $\mathcal{B}$ from which we can build the structure $\mathcal{H} = (H, \cdot, h_{c_0})$. Since $\mathcal{B} \succ F \phi : c_0$, Lemma 5.3 entails that $\mathcal{H}$ is a PL$^{\hookrightarrow}$-model such that $h_{c_0} \not\models \phi$, which contradicts the validity of ϕ.

6   Extension to PL

We can extend these results for PL$^{\hookrightarrow}$ in order to deal with the predicate $E_1 = E_2$ and the formula $\exists x.\phi$. Here, $\hookrightarrow$ associates a cell to a stack variable and such variables are in the scope of quantifiers and then the formulae are closed.

In order to deal with $\exists$, we can use a standard technique that eliminates existential quantifiers by instantiating the variables with constants depending on the sign of the signed formulae [2]. When the sign is T one generates a new constant and when it is F we reuse a constant already generated. Here, the constants are locations and we need to memorize the variable instantiations for countermodel construction. The corresponding expansion rules look as follows:

$$* \, T\, \exists x.\phi(x) : y \qquad F\, \exists x.\phi(v) : y$$
$$\mid \qquad\qquad\qquad \mid$$
$$T\, \phi(c) : y \qquad\quad F\, \phi(l) : y$$

$*$:c is a new constant.

Notice that the previous expansion rules do not concern labels because, from the semantics, we observe that we consider stack variables and not heaps that are the actual resources. Coming back to the example about double dispose in Section 2, we can use the tableau method to prove that $\bot \leftrightarrow \top * \exists a \, b.(x \mapsto a,b) * \exists c \, d.(x \mapsto c,d)$ and then to conclude that the program is not safe to execute for any start state.

Finally, in order to deal with the predicate $=$ we have the same rules but need to extend the tableau closure conditions. Having a signed formula $T\, X = Y : x$ with constants X and Y syntactically equal, because of semantics S $(X \mapsto a,b) : x$ is duplicated as S $(Y \mapsto a,b) : x$. For $F\, X = Y : x$, we need to check if constants X and Y are syntactically equal. In this case we have a contradiction with the semantics since the formula is signed by F.

7   Conclusions and Perspectives

Separation logics provide verification formalisms for pointer programs and allow to express properties about data structures with shared mutable state [6, 12]. We study proof-theoretic foundations for such logics, by focusing first on PL, the BI's pointer logic [6]. We mainly define a characterization of provability in PL through so-called resource graphs and provide a new calculus with labels and constraints that builds resource graphs from which countermodels can be extracted. We expect to develop the same approach for the affine variant of PL [6] with intuitionistic additives that allows to prove interesting properties about sharing. Some spatial logics for trees or graphs [1] are related to PL as extensions of Boolean BI and we aim to study these logics from our proof-theoretic perspective. Moreover, comparisons with existing works on theorem proving dedicated to pointer programs [7, 8, 11] could be fruitful for some refinements.

References

1. L. Cardelli, P. Gardner, and G. Ghelli. A spatial logic for querying graphs. In *Int. Conference on Automata, Langages and Programming, ICALP'02, LNCS 2380*, pages 597–610, 2002.
2. M. Fitting. *First-Order Logic and Automated Theorem Proving*. Texts and Monographs in Computer Science. Springer Verlag, 1990.
3. D. Galmiche and D. Méry. Connection-based proof search in propositional BI logic. In *18th Int. Conference on Automated Deduction, CADE-18, LNAI 2392*, pages 111–128, 2002. Copenhagen, Danemark.
4. D. Galmiche and D. Méry. Semantic labelled tableaux for propositional BI without bottom. *Journal of Logic and Computation*, 13(5):707–753, 2003.
5. D. Galmiche and D. Méry. Resource graphs and countermodels in resource logics. *Electronic Notes in Theoretical Computer Science*, 125(3):117–135, 2005.
6. S. Ishtiaq and P. O'Hearn. BI as an assertion language for mutable data structures. In *28th ACM Symposium on Principles of Programming Languages, POPL 2001*, pages 14–26, London, UK, 2001.
7. J. Jenson, M. Jorgensen, N. Klarkund, and M. Schwartzback. Automatic verification of pointer programs using monadic second-order logic. In *Conf. on Programming Language Design and Implementation, PLDI'97*, pages 225–236, 1997.
8. F. Mehta and T. Nipkow. Proving pointer programs in higher-order logic. In *Int. Conference on Automated Deduction, CADE-19, LNCS 2741*, pages 121–135, Miami, USA, July 2003.
9. P. O'Hearn, J. Reynolds, and H. Yang. Local reasoning about programs that alter data structures. In *15th Int. Workshop on Computer Science Logic, CSL 2001, LNCS 2142*, pages 1–19, Paris, France, 2001.
10. P.W. O'Hearn and D. Pym. The Logic of Bunched Implications. *Bulletin of Symbolic Logic*, 5(2):215–244, 1999.
11. S. Ranise and D. Deharbe. Applying light-weight theorem proving to debugging and verifying pointer programs. *Electronic Notes in Theoretical Computer Science*, 86(1), 2003.
12. J. Reynolds. Separation logic: A logic for shared mutable data structures. In *IEEE Symposium on Logic in Computer Science*, pages 55–74, Copenhagen, Danemark, July 2002.

A Unified Memory Model for Pointers

Harvey Tuch and Gerwin Klein

National ICT Australia[*], Sydney, Australia
School of Computer Science and Engineering, UNSW, Sydney, Australia
{harvey.tuch, gerwin.klein}@nicta.com.au

Abstract. One of the challenges in verifying systems level code is the low-level, untyped view of the machine state that operating systems have. We describe a way to faithfully formalise this view while at the same time providing an easy-to-use, abstract and typed view of memory where possible. We have used this formal memory model to verify parts of the virtual memory subsystem of the L4 high-performance microkernel. All formalisations and proofs have been carried out in the theorem prover Isabelle and the verified code has been integrated into the current implementation of L4.

1 Introduction

L4 is a second generation, general purpose microkernel [13] that provides the traditional advantages of microkernels while overcoming the performance limitations of previous generations. With implementations in the order of 10,000 lines of C++/assembler it is an order of magnitude smaller than Mach and two orders of magnitude smaller than Linux. The small size and minimalistic design bring L4 into the reach of formal specification and verification and lead to the unique opportunity of bringing the rigour and trustworthiness of formal verification to the very foundation of practical systems that are in current, industrial use. In this paper, we give an overview of a pilot project testing the feasibility of this idea and present a general solution to the problem of verifying low level pointer modifications in system level code.

During this pilot project we encountered a number of OS code specific verification problems. Among them is the question of how to deal with pointer arithmetic and low level memory modifications, as they are common in system level code. Verifying high-level imperative pointer programs is already considered a hard problem. Recent case studies like Mehta and Nipkow's formalisation of the Schorr-Waite graph marking algorithm [14] show that the complexity of the problem can be reduced to an acceptable level for interactive verification if the right abstractions are used. They exploit the idea that in a type safe language a write to memory position of type S cannot influence another memory position of a different type T (ignoring subtypes for the moment), thus drastically reducing

[*] National ICT Australia is funded through the Australian Government's *Backing Australia's Ability* initiative, in part through the Australian Research Council.

the number of cases that need to be considered for each write. Unfortunately, the implementation language of operating systems (C/C++/assembler) usually is not type safe, and despite a plethora of available safe subsets of C, none of them have caught on in the OS community. This is not entirely for the sake of convenience; there are often good reasons to deliberately break the type safety of the implementation language, among them performance and hardware prescribed data structures. Performance enjoys an especially high priority in the microkernel area: a few cache misses and some hundred processor cycles can make the difference between a practical and impractical system. On the other hand, not all OS code is deliberately type unsafe, in fact the vast majority of it is perfectly fine. The approach presented in this paper enables us to achieve a level of abstraction similar to the one of Mehta and Nipkow for these parts, and at the same time (in the background) to use a very detailed memory model that can faithfully formalise the few occasions of indispensable bit-level operations and pointer arithmetic expressions. The formalisation itself is relatively straightforward (with a twist) — the contribution is that it can conveniently describe both levels of abstraction at the same time and do so with minimal overhead for concrete program verification, exploiting Isabelle/HOL's automatic type inference to avoid reasoning about explicit typing predicates for pointers. As mentioned above the approach is not merely academic, but has been tried out in a larger verification project.

After reviewing related work in section 2 and introducing notation in section 3, we present our formalisation of a typed memory abstraction of untyped memory in section 4 together with a small example. In section 5 we give a rough overview of the verification project in which the technique was used to formally verify parts of the L4 microkernel.

2 Related Work

Earlier work on OS verification includes PSOS [16] and UCLA Secure Unix [24]. Later, KIT [2] describes verification of process isolation properties down to object code level, but for an idealised kernel with far simpler and less general abstractions than modern microkernels. A number of case studies [6, 5, 23] describe the IPC and scheduling subsystems of microkernels in PROMELA and verify them with the SPIN model checker. Manually constructed, these abstractions are not necessarily sound, and so while useful for discovering concurrency bugs, they cannot provide guarantees of correctness. The VeriSoft project [8] is attempting to verify a whole system stack, including hardware, compiler, applications, and a simplified microkernel called VAMOS that is inspired by, but not very close to, L4. While the simplifications are appropriate for the goals of VeriSoft, it is doubtful that the VAMOS kernel will show the necessary performance to be relevant for industrial use.

The idea to use separate heaps for separate pointer types and structure fields goes back to Burstall [4]. On the abstract level, our formalisation is most closely related to Bornat [3] and Mehta and Nipkow's [14] work in Isabelle, although we exploit Isabelle's type inference in a different way. The Caduceus tool [7] supports Hoare logic verification of C programs, including the type safe part of pointer arithmetic. Like all of the above, we do not use any special purpose logics [19, 10], but stay with standard Hoare logic, in our case Schirmer's flexible Hoare logic implementation in Isabelle/HOL [20]. On the concrete level, Norrish [18] presents a very thorough and detailed memory model of C. Our formalisation has similarities to exploratory work on C++ in the VFiasco project [9]. The latter two provide a more precise machine model, while the former allows for more convenient and efficient reasoning. Our model provides both.

Type-safe C variants like CCured [15] also take a dual approach to memory type-safety, by statically detecting safe pointer usage and adding runtime checks for those cases where this cannot be verified. Our approach is oriented towards interactive theorem proving, and does not require any change in language semantics or runtime behavior.

3   Notation

Our meta-language Isabelle/HOL conforms largely to everyday mathematical notation. This section introduces further non-standard notation and in particular a few basic data types along with their primitive operations.

The space of total functions is denoted by $\Rightarrow$. Type variables are written $'a$, $'b$, etc. The notation $t :: \tau$ means that HOL term t has HOL type τ.

$$\textbf{datatype } 'a \text{ } option = None \mid Some \text{ } 'a$$

adjoins a new element $None$ to a type $'a$. We use $'a$ $option$ to model partial functions in the setting of HOL. For succinctness we write $\lfloor a \rfloor$ instead of $Some$ a. The underspecified inverse the of $Some$ satisfies the $\lfloor x \rfloor = x$. Function update is written $f(x := y)$ where $f :: 'a \Rightarrow 'b$, $x :: 'a$ and $y :: 'b$. Implication is denoted by $\Longrightarrow$ and $[\![A_1; \ldots; A_n]\!] \Longrightarrow A$ abbreviates $A_1 \Longrightarrow (\ldots \Longrightarrow (A_n \Longrightarrow A)\ldots)$. Isabelle theories can be augmented with LATEX text which may contain references to Isabelle theorems (by name — see chapter 4 of [17]). We use this presentation mechanism to generate the text for most of the definitions and all of the theorems in this paper directly from the Isabelle proofs.

4   A Typed Heap on Untyped Memory

There are a number of approaches to describing the state space of a program embedded in a theorem prover. In the simple case, without pointers, one most commonly either treats variable names as first-class HOL values, in which case the state may be a function $name \Rightarrow value$, or treats the state as a tuple or record type $var_a\text{-}typ \times var_b\text{-}typ \times var_c\text{-}typ\ldots$ When embedding pointer programs it is convenient to use a model similar to the first for memory addressable by pointers. Introducing pointers however also introduces the problem of *aliasing* [3]. Consider a C program fragment with a **long** pointer **foo** and a

bool pointer **bar** where you want to show *foo = 1 after the program fragment
*foo = 1; *bar = true. The most basic approach is to model the pointers as
values of type *addr* and the heap[1] as a function *addr* $\Rightarrow$ *value*, where *value* is
a datatype with alternatives for long, bool, etc. Ignoring fancy syntax, this formally equates to something like *hp foo := Long* 1; *hp bar := Bool True*, where
hp is a heap function. If we evaluate this in standard Hoare logic, we need the
precondition *foo $\neq$ bar* to show that *hp foo = Long* 1 in the end.

In a type safe language, on the other hand, this precondition is an unnecessary overhead. We already know implicitly that *foo $\neq$ bar*, because they have
different types. In the literature [3, 14], this is modelled by a state space in which
each language type has its own heap. For the example above, that means we now
have functions *bool_h :: addr $\Rightarrow$ bool* and *long_h :: addr $\Rightarrow$ long* and we can show
the Hoare triple $\{$*True*$\}$ *long_h foo := 1; bool_h bar := True* $\{$*long_h foo = 1*$\}$ automatically and without preconditions. The example is simplified, of course. In
a more realistic setting we would still have preconditions and invariants about
heap layout and pointers being not **null**. The key point, however, is that there
is no need to state pair-wise aliasing conditions on all pointers anymore.

As argued in the introduction, OS code does not normally use a type safe
language and does not restrict itself to a type safe subset, so we are forced to
use a model of the state space close to that of the underlying hardware memory
model if we want to preserve soundness. One such extreme treatment of the heap
would be to consider it simply as a function mapping addresses to bits, bytes
or words. This has the significant advantage that the hardware abstraction step
is very small and the model is amenable to reasoning about the type unsafe
operations sometimes present in low-level systems code. On the other hand, this
complicates the aliasing problem even further, because the pointers could also
alias by pointing into the middle of an encoding. Hohmuth et al [9] provide a
semantics for C++ types in such a setting.

What we want to achieve is a low-level heap view when necessary, and the
more convenient abstraction of multiple typed heaps when possible. Following
the reasoning that different types mean unaliased pointers in the type-safe fragment, we require several things. First we need to know which memory locations
should correspond to which types. We then need to know that the memory layout provides a disjoint layout of values. Finally, we need a means of using this
information to transform the untyped heap into multiple typed heaps, one for
each language type, together with rules to reason about updates of the heap
when they conform to the state's type information. All this should be provided
in such a way that the complexity of encoding, decoding, typing etc, stays under
the hood at least for the common case of safe operations. The rest of this section
presents our formalisation of such a model together with a mechanisation that
aids in proofs about pointer programs when they can be shown to be type-safe,
while still allowing us to break type safety when necessary.

---

[1] In this section we refer to a heap model since this is where valid pointers are restricted
to in the rest of our work, but the setting should be generalisable to a model for the
entire memory, including local variables.

4.1   The Model

We begin with Hohmuth et al's [9] treatment of C++ types and extend it to work with a heap abstraction that allows for effective reasoning about both typed and untyped views of the heap and the effects of updates on the heap. The emphasis is on mechanising the proof process, for example taking advantage of the rewriting support in Isabelle and existing record update rules provided for Isabelle record types, to reduce the proof burden on the program verifier. In this discussion we avoid talking about a specific language embedding with the goal of generality, however our main application is clearly C or a C-like language.

The following type synonyms describe the heap state:

$$addr = word32$$
$$heap\text{-}mem = addr \Rightarrow word32$$
$$heap\text{-}typ\text{-}desc = addr \Rightarrow typ\text{-}tag \; option$$
$$heap\text{-}state = heap\text{-}mem \times heap\text{-}typ\text{-}desc$$

where $word32$ is a type representing 32-bit words[2] imported from the HOL4 system and $typ\text{-}tag$ is a type with a value for each language type[3] used by the program. For example, a program operating only on boolean, integer and pointer types would have:

$$\textbf{datatype} \; typ\text{-}tag = BoolTag \mid IntTag \mid PtrTag \; typ\text{-}tag$$

Each language type has both a distinct Isabelle type and a distinct $typ\text{-}tag$ value, which we refer to as its type tag below. A good reason for doing things this way is that in a shallow embedding we can avoid reasoning about possibly ill-typed expressions, e.g. `3.14 / &foo`. Instead, Isabelle's type checker and type inference can prevent us from even writing down such invalid expressions. The tag value allows for explicit referencing of language types in Isabelle terms, and is bound to its corresponding Isabelle type later, as described below. We require this to maintain an explicit record of the type of each value stored in memory. Every language type has a fixed size, given by the function $typ\text{-}size :: typ\text{-}tag \Rightarrow nat$.

The $heap\text{-}typ\text{-}desc$ component of the heap state is a partial function that describes the memory layout. We call it the *heap type description*. A tag t at address a indicates that a is the base of the memory footprint for a value of type t. Type safe programs respect the program's memory layout in both read and write operations. The heap type description is purely a proof convenience, a history variable, and while it may be affected by, does not itself affect the semantics of successful heap operations and should not be confused with hardware support for tagged memory. The heap type description may be updated anywhere in the program, for example by calls to *malloc* or *free*, or if we were to model local and global variables in the program's initial conditions on function call and return.

---

[2] In this work we use 32-bit addresses and words but this could be generalised to n-bit address spaces or finer/coarser granularity of addressing fairly easily.

[3] We distinguish between *language* types of the programming language and *Isabelle* types.

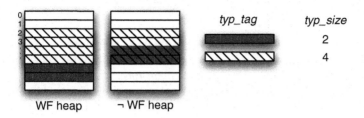

Fig. 1. Well-formed heap layout

The predicate *wf-heap* :: *heap-typ-desc* $\Rightarrow$ *bool* states the well-formedness invariant on the heap type description that is required to establish non-interference of heap updates:

wf-heap d $\equiv$
$\forall x\ y\ t.\ d\ x = \lfloor t \rfloor \wedge 0 < y \wedge y < typ\text{-}size\ t \longrightarrow d\ (n2w\ (w2n\ x + y)) = None$

The type conversions *w2n* and *n2w* transform from *word32* to *nat* and vice versa. Examples of well-formed and not well-formed heap layouts are illustrated in Figure 1.

Each Isabelle type associated with a language type must be an instance of the type class *'a::c-type*. The class declares three new constants:

$$to\text{-}word :: \text{ }'a::c\text{-}type \Rightarrow word32\ list$$
$$from\text{-}word :: \text{ }word32\ list \Rightarrow \text{ }'a::c\text{-}type\ option$$
$$typ\text{-}tag :: \text{ }'a::c\text{-}type\ itself \Rightarrow typ\text{-}tag$$

The functions *to-word* and *from-word* convert between Isabelle values and lists of words suitable for writing to or reading from the raw heap state. The function *typ-tag* associates a type tag with each *'a::c-type*. The type *'a itself* consists of a single element denoted by $TYPE('a)$. This sounds unusual at first, but is easily achieved and part of the Isabelle standard library: since HOL types are non-empty, we can create a polymorphic *'a itself* by taking any element of the type parameter *'a* as the single occupant of *'a itself*. For each fixed *'a*, any constant of type *'a itself*, say *TYPE*, then refers to this one element. The term *TYPE(bool)* is merely another way of writing the type restriction *TYPE::bool*.

The size of the memory footprint of values of a *'a::c-type* is given by *size-of* :: *'a::c-type itself* $\Rightarrow$ *nat*:

$$size\text{-}of\ t \equiv typ\text{-}size\ (typ\text{-}tag\ t)$$

The following conditions, captured in the axiomatic type class *'a::mem-type*, must hold for any *'a::c-type* we want to use in our heap abstraction below.

$$from\text{-}word\ (to\text{-}word\ (x::'a)) = \lfloor x \rfloor$$
$$|to\text{-}word\ (x::'a)| = size\text{-}of\ TYPE('a)$$

Finally, we introduce a distinct Isabelle pointer type for each Isabelle type.

$$\textbf{datatype } 'a\ ptr = PtrVal\ addr$$

The additional $'a$ on the left-hand side can now be used to associate the pointer type information with pointer values in Isabelle's type system. The destructor *ptr-val* retrieves the address from a pointer value. The pointer types themselves can again be shown to be instances of $'a{::}mem\text{-}type$.

We now come to the typed heap abstraction as used by embedded programs. The function $lift :: heap\text{-}mem \Rightarrow 'a{::}c\text{-}type\ ptr \Rightarrow 'a$ turns the raw heap into multiple typed heaps — one for each $'a$.

$heap\text{-}list :: heap\text{-}mem \Rightarrow addr \Rightarrow nat \Rightarrow word32\ list$
$heap\text{-}list\ h\ p\ 0 = []$
$heap\text{-}list\ h\ p\ (Suc\ n) = h\ p\ \#\ heap\text{-}list\ h\ (p + 1)\ n$

$h\text{-}val :: heap\text{-}mem \Rightarrow 'a{::}c\text{-}type\ ptr \Rightarrow 'a\ option$
$h\text{-}val\ h\ p \equiv from\text{-}word\ (heap\text{-}list\ h\ (ptr\text{-}val\ p)\ (size\text{-}of\ TYPE('a)))$

$lift :: heap\text{-}mem \Rightarrow 'a{::}c\text{-}type\ ptr \Rightarrow 'a$
$lift\ h \equiv \lambda p.\ the\ (h\text{-}val\ h\ p)$

As stated earlier, program expressions operate on the raw heap, ignoring the type tags. This on its own may not be sufficient to faithfully express a language's semantics; *lift h p* will give the value at p where the semantics say a heap access is valid, but we need to establish this validity first. This will usually require a guard or precondition on the statement containing the expression. For example, in C, we would need to know that the memory location had a value of the type in consideration written to it at some earlier point, and that the pointer is correctly aligned. This of course is not limited to this model and also applies to even a simple standard model with multiple typed heaps.

Heap updates are performed with $heap\text{-}update :: heap\text{-}mem \Rightarrow 'a{::}c\text{-}type\ ptr \Rightarrow 'a \Rightarrow heap\text{-}mem$:

$heap\text{-}update\text{-}list\ h\ p\ [] = h$
$heap\text{-}update\text{-}list\ h\ p\ (x\ \#\ xs) = heap\text{-}update\text{-}list\ (h(p := x))\ (p + 1)\ xs$

$heap\text{-}update\ h\ p\ v \equiv heap\text{-}update\text{-}list\ h\ (ptr\text{-}val\ p)\ (to\text{-}word\ v)$

Again, heap update statements should be suitably guarded.

We exploit the polymorphism in Isabelle's type system here to avoid explicit definitions of heap abstraction functions for each language type. This may seem a slight gain, but it also enables the simplification rules presented below to be stated once for all types, instead of being reproved for each pair of types.

4.2   The Typed View

So far we are able to dereference pointers in our embedded programs, and may be able to do first simple proofs. However, proofs will still have to consider unnecessary aliasing concerns on lifted heaps if we do not know which pointers respect the heap type description. For example, pointers of different types may still be aliasing the same location, or pointers of the same type may have overlapping memory footprints. The standard way of ruling out these possibilities is an invariant, or ad hoc history variables indicating what the valid pointers of different types are.

Even if we know which pointers are valid, the effect of updates on the lifted heap can only be expressed point-wise: we can determine that pointer p is not affected by an update of pointer q if both are valid. We cannot determine that if the *bool* incarnation of the lifted heap changes, the whole *long* incarnation, as a function, is unaffected.

This means, that if we had, for instance, a heap invariant or abstraction function for a linked list structure that only uses the *long* incarnation of the lifted heap, we would need to prove a separate rule for that abstraction function to show that it remains unchanged under *bool* updates — even if the abstraction function explicitly states that all its pointers are valid.

Utilising the heap type description information we can provide a typed heap abstraction for use in proofs that only depends on the values of the heap at locations valid for the type. We can then prove simplification rules for reasoning about updates to typed heaps once for all language types.

First we introduce the notion of pointer validity. A pointer p of type $'a\ ptr$ is said to be valid under a heap type description d according to the following definition:

$$d \vdash_t p \equiv d\ (ptr\text{-}val\ p) = \lfloor typ\text{-}tag\ TYPE('a) \rfloor$$

It should be noted that this predicate does not explicitly mention the language type, instead the type is determined automatically by Isabelle's type inference. We found this greatly enhancing the clarity of specifications and proofs.

The heap abstraction function $lift_c$ hides updates to heap locations not corresponding to the valid pointers for a particular typed heap:

$$lift_c :: heap\text{-}state \Rightarrow 'a::c\text{-}type\ ptr \Rightarrow 'a\ option$$
$$lift_c\ (h,\ d) \equiv \lambda p.\ if\ d \vdash_t p\ then\ h\text{-}val\ h\ p\ else\ None$$

Like *lift h*, $lift_c\ h$ is polymorphic and returns a heap abstraction of type $'a\ typ\text{-}heap = 'a\ ptr \Rightarrow 'a\ option$. The program text itself can continue to use the functions *lift* and *heap-update*, while pre/post conditions and invariants use the stronger $lift_c$ to make more precise statements. The following conditional rewrite connects the two levels.

$$lift_c\ (h,\ d)\ p = \lfloor x \rfloor \implies lift\ h\ p = x$$

We have proved two further significant rewrite rules that support reasoning about the effects of heap updates on $lift_c$. The first rule states how an $'a\ ptr$ update affects an $'a\ typ\text{-}heap$, the second rule shows that an $'a\ ptr$ update does not affect a $'b\ typ\text{-}heap$ if $'a$ is different from $'b$.

$$\llbracket wf\text{-}heap\ d;\ d \vdash_t p \rrbracket \implies lift_c\ (heap\text{-}update\ h\ p\ v,\ d) = lift_c\ (h,\ d)(p \mapsto v)$$
$$\llbracket wf\text{-}heap\ d;\ d \vdash_t p;\ typ\text{-}tag\ TYPE('a) \neq typ\text{-}tag\ TYPE('b) \rrbracket$$
$$\implies lift_c\ (heap\text{-}update\ h\ p\ v,\ d) = lift_c\ (h,\ d)$$

These are added to a simplification set, with other heap related lemmas, in our work, and do not require manual application. Isabelle's simplifier can resolve the *typ-tag* $TYPE('a) \neq typ\text{-}tag\ TYPE('b)$ condition automatically, as long as the type tag definitions for language types are also in the default simplification set. The heap type description changes relatively infrequently and therefore the proof overhead in showing *wf-heap d* is low.

For any program that respects the heap type description, we can thus automatically simplify away the fact that the heap is shared and pretend to work on multiple typed heaps. At the same time, we can still capture the semantics of type unsafe operations. In this case things are no longer automatic, and we are required to provide rules for how the lifted heaps changed during the operation. This is a small price to pay for the flexibility and convenience gained on the abstract level. It may even be possible to derive a set of rules that capture common type unsafe operations, for example physical subtyping, although we have not done so in our application.

We can also use type tags to write Isabelle expressions over language types. For example, one might want to express in a specification that only heaps of certain types can change during execution. For this we define the predicate *h-id-except* :: *typ-tag set* $\Rightarrow$ *heap-state* $\Rightarrow$ *heap-state* $\Rightarrow$ *bool* which satisfies the following lemma for lifted heaps of type $'a\ typ\text{-}heap$:

$$[\![h\text{-}id\text{-}except\ ts\ s\ s';\ typ\text{-}tag\ TYPE('a) \notin ts]\!] \Longrightarrow lift_c\ s = lift_c\ s'$$

4.3   Example

Picking up the example from the introduction to this section, we show below how it is expressed in our setting.

The state space is now a global program heap of type *heap-state* with two pointers *foo* :: *long ptr* and *bar* :: *bool ptr*. It is easy to show that *long* and *bool* are instances of the type class *mem-type* by defining the constants *to-word*, *from-word* and *typ-tag* and proving that they satisfy the axioms stated in section 4.1. Using Isabelle's syntax mechanisms to abbreviate $lift_c\ (h,d)\ p = \lfloor v \rfloor$ to $*p = v$ and $h := heap\text{-}update\ h\ p\ v$ to $*p := v$, the Hoare triple we can then state and prove automatically, is the following:

$$\{\![wf\text{-}heap\ d \wedge d \vdash_t foo \wedge d \vdash_t bar]\!\}\ *foo := 1;\ *bar := True\ \{\![*foo = 1]\!\}$$

The three preconditions in this statement present only a very small overhead. As long as the program stays in a safe fragment of the language, e.g., when pointers are used like Java references without pointer arithmetic, there is never need to unfold their definition. They can also easily be propagated by the verification condition generator. In contrast to explicit statements of pointer aliasing, they also only talk about one pointer at a time, not pairwise distinctness or, as it would be applicable in this more detailed setting, distinctness of encoding regions.

While structures can be treated like any other language type in this setting, the formalisation presented here does not yet provide a separate heap for each field of each structure as Bornat does. It is possible to achieve this by another, analogous lifting step on top of *lift$_c$* that takes field names into account. We have recently formalised this in Isabelle, but have not used it in our case study yet.

5   The L4 Virtual Memory Manager

In this section we describe the case study which motivated the development of this memory model: the virtual memory (VM) management system, one of the three main abstractions L4 provides. Our approach is a classic and pragmatic refinement methodology. We start out from an abstract model of the kernel that we then formally refine towards an implementation. The last step consists of generating C code that implements the same functionality as the original OS code. We based our formalisation on the L4 X.2 API [12] and used the L4Ka::Pistachio [21] implementation on the ARM architecture to resolve ambiguities in addition to discussions with the developers on the *pistachio-core* mailing list.

5.1   The Abstract Model

The VM subsystem of L4 provides a flexible, hierarchical way of manipulating the mapping from virtual to physical memory pages at user-level. Below we sketch our formalisation and show the definition of *unmap*, one of the VM operations.

This model is still a simplification of the current L4 API because the API stipulates two regions per address space (the kernel interface page and user thread control blocks) that we have not modelled, and because the mapping operations in L4 can work on regions of the address space rather than individual pages.

Fig. 2 illustrates the concept of hierarchical mappings. The example maps virtual page v_1 in space n_1, as well as v_2 in n_2, and v_4 in n_4 to the physical page r_1. Formally, we use the types R for the physical pages, V for virtual pages, and N for names of address spaces.

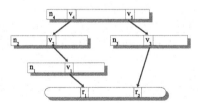

Fig. 2. Address Spaces

Mappings M, i.e. positions in this picture, are uniquely determined either by a page V in a virtual address space N, or by a physical page. An address space is a function from pages V to mappings together with a set of access rights, determining how the mapped page may be used from inside the address space. On a concrete architecture, these will be rights like read/write/execute — here we use the abstract type AR. The machine state is then a partial map from address space names to address spaces.

$$\textbf{datatype} \quad M = \textit{Virtual } N \, V \mid \textit{Real } R$$
$$\textbf{types} \quad \textit{space} = V \Rightarrow M \times AR \textit{ set}$$
$$\textit{state} = N \Rightarrow \textit{space option}$$

The concept of *paths* relates these functions to the arrows in Fig. 2: $s \vdash x \rightsquigarrow^1 y$ means that in state s there is a direct path from x to y. For this to be true, x must be of the form *Virtual n v*, the address space n must be defined in state s and it must map the virtual page v to y:

$$s \vdash x \rightsquigarrow^1 y = (\exists \, n \, v \, ar \, \sigma. \; x = \textit{Virtual } n \, v \wedge s \, n = \lfloor \sigma \rfloor \wedge \sigma \, v = (y, \, ar))$$

We write $\_ \vdash \_ \rightsquigarrow^* \_$ for the reflexive, transitive closure of the direct path relation.

The operation *unmap n v ar* reduces the access rights of all pages leading to *Virtual n v* by ar (a set of access rights). If ar happens to be $\mathcal{U}$ (the universal set) the operation makes these pages inaccessible. In the definition we use a function *clear* that, given a name n, a page v, a set of access rights ar and an address space σ in state s, returns σ where the access rights of all v' leading to *Virtual n v* have been reduced by ar.

unmap $:: N \Rightarrow V \Rightarrow AR$ *set* $\Rightarrow$ *state* $\Rightarrow$ *state*
unmap n v ar s $\equiv \lambda n'.$ **case** *s n'* **of** *None* $\Rightarrow$ *None* $\mid \lfloor \sigma \rfloor \Rightarrow \lfloor clear \, n \, v \, ar \, s \, \sigma \rfloor$

clear n v ar s $\sigma \equiv$
$\lambda v'.$ **let** $(m, ar') = \sigma \, v'$ **in** **if** $s \vdash m \rightsquigarrow^* \textit{Virtual } n \, v$ **then** $(m, ar' - ar)$ **else** (m, ar')

The other operations of the VM subsystem (flush, map, grant, create, and memory lookup) are modelled in a similar way, modifying paths and access rights accordingly. See our earlier work [11, 22] for details on the same formalisation which we have extended with access rights here.

We have shown a number of properties about the reachable states of the VM system, among them that access rights can never increase when a page is mapped to another address space, that there are no loops in the path structure, and that address lookup is a total function. The latter is quite literally an important safety property. Overheating and physical damage may result if two conflicting TLB entries are present for the same virtual address [1–p. B3-26].

5.2   The Concrete Model

The concrete implementation of the address spaces abstraction in L4 is based on two data structures, the *page tables* and the *mapping database* (MDB), as well as the algorithms for their traversal and manipulation. This is because performance, and in the case of ARM, the hardware, dictates that an efficient translation from virtual to physical addresses and corresponding access rights be available. The page tables are used to achieve the translation, while the MDB keeps track of the mapping relation for the purpose of revocations like the unmap operation shown in the previous section.

The state space consists of the *heap-state* together with some local and static global variables. The page table and MDB data structure abstractions are inductively defined on this raw state, i.e. they are a function and relation that take a *'a typ-heap* as a parameter and when used in pre/post-conditions and invariants this takes on a value of *lift$_c$* in the current state. A complete description of the semantics of the concrete operations, specifications and proofs is well beyond the scope of this paper, with the raw theory files alone consisting of over 5000 lines of Isabelle/HOL definitions and proofs. Instead we present the MDB definitions and one example operation here to provide a flavour of the level of detail in the model.

The MDB is a doubly linked list representing the pre-order traversal of a mapping tree, which is essentially the tree described in the abstract model with the arrow directions reversed. Nodes in the MDB are of type *map-node*:

$$\textbf{record } \textit{map-node} = \textit{map-next} :: \textit{word32}$$
$$\textit{map-prev} :: \textit{word32}$$
$$\textit{map-pte} :: \textit{pte ptr}$$
$$\textit{map-depth} :: \textit{word32}$$

We use the integer representation of pointer addresses for next and previous pointers as the type *map-node ptr* is not available until after this declaration. The *map-pte* field stores a pointer to the corresponding page table entry and *map-depth* contains the depth of the node in the tree for the pre-order tree representation.

A subtree relation is defined on a typed heap *s* :: *map-node typ-heap*. The term $s \vdash a \leadsto^T b$ states that b is in a's subtree. This is defined as:

$$s \vdash x \mapsto y = (\exists m.\ s\ x = \lfloor m \rfloor \wedge \textit{get-next}'\ m = \lfloor y \rfloor)$$
$$[\![s \vdash m \mapsto m';\ \textit{get-depth}'\ (s\ m) < \textit{get-depth}'\ (s\ m')]\!] \implies s \vdash m \leadsto^T m'$$
$$[\![s \vdash m \leadsto^T m';\ s \vdash m' \mapsto ma;\ \textit{get-depth}'\ (s\ m) < \textit{get-depth}'\ (s\ ma)]\!]$$
$$\implies s \vdash m \leadsto^T ma$$

where *get-next'* m and *get-depth'* m act as expected, returning the next pointer and depth respectively for a given *map-node*.

It should be clear that proofs about the MDB are localised to just the *map-node typ-heap* and procedures operating on just the MDB can be easily shown not to affect other typed heaps using the previous section's lemmas. *wf-heap* is part of the global invariant in our model.

An example of a procedure in our concrete model's MDB is *map-unlink* used during unmapping to remove a node from the linked list:

```
procedures map-unlink(m,mq) =
      nm := cast TYPE(map-node ptr) (lift h mq·map-next);
      h := heap-struct-update h m map-next-update (cast TYPE(word32) nm);
      IF nm ≠ Null THEN
          h := heap-struct-update h nm map-prev-update (cast TYPE(word32) m)
      FI;
      CALL map-free(mq)
```

where

$$heap\text{-}struct\text{-}update\ h\ p\ f\ v \equiv heap\text{-}update\ h\ p\ (f\ v\ (lift\ h\ p))$$

An abstraction relation that relates the state spaces of the abstract and concrete models is defined based on the page table and MDB abstractions. We have done most of the simulation proofs to show refinement between these levels in other work, but we still have a small gap to fill prior to having the proofs integrated and completed for the models described here.

5.3   Generating High Performance C Code

On a semantic level our concrete model is intended to be faithful to the semantics of C as understood by our compiler, but we require a simple translation step to turn these Isabelle/HOL definitions into C source code suitable for compilation. This involves traversing the abstract syntax tree of the Isabelle/HOL terms for procedures, generating real C syntax and is fairly straightforward. The number of lines of ML code required to do this is less than 400; hence we have reasonable confidence in this step, which might otherwise be seen as a source of soundness concerns. The generated C source for the *map-unlink* example is:

```
extern "C" inline void
map_unlink(struct map_node* m, struct map_node* mq) {
  struct map_node* nm;
  nm = (map_node *)((*(mq)).map_next);
  (*(m)).map_next = (word32)(nm);
  if ((nm) != (NULL)) {
    (*(nm)).map_prev = (word32)(m);
  }
  map_free(mq);
}
```

The generated code is suitable for passing to *gcc* and with the addition of stub code in the existing L4Ka::Pistachio kernel has been linked to the kernel and can replace the modelled part of the VM subsystem.

The investment for the virtual memory part of this verification pilot project was about 1.5 person years. All specifications and proofs together run to about 14,000 lines. This is significantly more than the effort invested in the VM subsystem in the first place, but it includes exploration of alternatives, determining the right methodology, etc. Our final goal is a verified, high performance implementation of L4, and the results so far have been encouraging.

6   Conclusion

We have presented a novel way of modelling memory for imperative pointer programs that allows us to reason abstractly and conveniently about those parts of the program that are type safe and at the same time correctly and precisely about those parts that are not. Both kinds of reasoning can be freely intermixed, using a standard Hoare logic framework.

On the abstract level we can directly express language types inside Isabelle's type system and can therefore enjoy the advantages of type inference as well as avoid explicit type information in specifications and invariants. While we think our model is complete on the low level, we only have shown basic types, pointers and structs on the abstract level. We expect more language features like tagged unions to be expressable.

The model introduces a slight overhead for reasoning about type unsafe operations. Our experience so far in applying the technique to OS kernel verification suggests that this is the right trade-off to make — especially since a model with only low-level reasoning usually very quickly introduces invariants similar to our well-formedness condition.

We showed some important aspects of verifying the VM subsystem of the L4 microkernel in which this technique was applied. We have sketched our abstract model of address spaces with access right restrictions and shown some aspects of refining these operations down to directly executable, high performance C code.

A nice side effect of our memory model is that reasoning about the `malloc` and `free` library functions in C becomes possible. In an abstract setting, their specification is easy: pointers become valid or invalid. Proving their implementation correct, however, is impossible, because they necessarily break the abstraction barrier. In our setting, the specification remains simple, but we are now able to prove in the same framework that their often considerably complex implementation satisfies this specification. We have not done so yet, but are looking forward to taking this on as future work.

Acknowledgements. We thank Rafal Kolanski, Nicolas Magaude, Michael Norrish, Norbert Schirmer, and Simon Winwood for discussing drafts of this paper.

References

1. ARM Limited. *ARM Architecture Reference Manual*, June 2000.
2. W. R. Bevier. Kit: A study in operating system verification. *IEEE Transactions on Software Engineering*, 15(11):1382–1396, 1989.
3. R. Bornat. Proving pointer programs in Hoare Logic. In R. Backhouse and J. Oliveira, editors, *Mathematics of Program Construction (MPC 2000)*, volume 1837 of *LNCS*, pages 102–126. Springer, 2000.
4. R. Burstall. Some techniques for proving correctness of programs which alter data structures. In B. Meltzer and D. Michie, editors, *Machine Intelligence 7*, pages 23–50. Edinburgh University Press, 1972.
5. T. Cattel. Modelization and verification of a multiprocessor realtime OS kernel. In *Proceedings of FORTE '94, Bern, Switzerland*, October 1994.
6. G. Duval and J. Julliand. Modelling and verification of the RUBIS μ-kernel with SPIN. In *SPIN95 Workshop Proceedings*, 1995.
7. J.-C. Filliâtre and C. Marché. Multi-prover verification of C programs. In *Formal Methods and Software Engineering, 6th International Conference on Formal Engineering Methods, ICFEM 2004, Seattle, USA*, volume 3308 of *LNCS*, pages 15–29. Springer, 2004.

8. M. Gargano, M. Hillebrand, D. Leinenbach, and W. Paul. On the correctness of operating system kernels. In *Proc. 18th International Conference on Theorem Proving in Higher Order Logics (TPHOLs 2005)*, Oxford, UK, 2005. to appear.

9. M. Hohmuth, H. Tews, and S. G. Stephens. Applying source-code verification to a microkernel — the VFiasco project. Technical Report TUD-FI02-03-März, TU Dresden, 2002.

10. J. Jensen, M. Joergensen, N. Klarlund, and M. Schwartzbach. Automatic verification of pointer programs using monadic second-order logic. In *PLDI '97*, 1997.

11. G. Klein and H. Tuch. Towards verified virtual memory in L4. In K. Slind, editor, *TPHOLs Emerging Trends '04*, Park City, Utah, USA, 2004.

12. *L4 eXperimental Kernel Reference Manual Version X.2*, 2004. http://l4hq.org/docs/manuals/.

13. J. Liedtke. On μ-kernel construction. In *15th ACM Symposium on Operating System Principles (SOSP)*, December 1995.

14. F. Mehta and T. Nipkow. Proving pointer programs in higher-order logic. *Information and Computation*, 2005. To appear.

15. G. Necula, J. Condit, M. Harren, S. McPeak, and W. Weimer. Ccured: type-safe retrofitting of legacy software. *ACM Trans. Prog. Lang. Syst.*, 27(3):477–526, 2005.

16. P. G. Neumann, R. S. Boyer, R. J. Feiertag, K. N. Levitt, and L. Robinson. A provably secure operating system: The system, its applications, and proofs. Technical Report CSL-116, SRI International, 1980.

17. T. Nipkow, L. Paulson, and M. Wenzel. *Isabelle/HOL — A Proof Assistant for Higher-Order Logic*, volume 2283 of *LNCS*. Springer, 2002.

18. M. Norrish. *C formalised in HOL*. PhD thesis, Computer Laboratory, University of Cambridge, 1998.

19. J. C. Reynolds. Separation logic: A logic for shared mutable data structures. In *Proc. 17th IEEE Symposium on Logic in Computer Science*, pages 55–74, 2002.

20. N. Schirmer. A verification environment for sequential imperative programs in Isabelle/HOL. In F. Baader and A. Voronkov, editors, *Logic for Programming, AI, and Reasoning*, volume 3452 of *LNAI*, pages 398–414. Springer, 2005.

21. System Architecture Group. The L4Ka::Pistachio microkernel. White paper, University of Karlsruhe, May 2003.

22. H. Tuch and G. Klein. Verifying the L4 virtual memory subsystem. In *Proc. NICTA FM Workshop on OS Verification*, pages 73–97. Technical Report 0401005T-1, National ICT Australia, 2004.

23. P. Tullmann, J. Turner, J. McCorquodale, J. Lepreau, A. Chitturi, and G. Back. Formal methods: a practical tool for OS implementors. In *Proceedings of the Sixth Workshop on Hot Topics in Operating Systems*, pages 20–25, 1997.

24. B. Walker, R. Kemmerer, and G. Popek. Specification and verification of the UCLA Unix security kernel. *Communications of the ACM*, 23(2):118–131, 1980.

Treewidth in Verification: Local vs. Global*

Andrea Ferrara[1], Guoqiang Pan[2], and Moshe Y. Vardi[2]

[1] DIS - Università di Roma "La Sapienza",
Via Salaria 113, 00198 Roma, Italy
ferrara@dis.uniroma1.it
[2] Dept. of CS, MS 132, Rice University,
6100 Main St., Houston TX 77005, USA
{gqpan, vardi}@cs.rice.edu

The *treewidth* of a graph measures how close the graph is to a tree. Many problems that are intractable for general graphs, are tractable when the graph has bounded treewidth. Recent works study the complexity of model checking for state transition systems of bounded treewidth. There is little reason to believe, however, that the treewidth of the state transition graphs of real systems, which we refer to as *global* treewidth, is bounded. In contrast, we consider in this paper *concurrent* transition systems, where communication between concurrent components is modeled explicitly. Assuming boundedness of the treewidth of the communication graph, which we refer to as *local* treewidth, is reasonable, since the topology of communication in concurrent systems is often constrained physically.

In this work we study the impact of local treewidth boundedness on the complexity of verification problems. We first present a positive result, proving that a CNF formula of bounded treewidth can be represented by an OBDD of polynomial size. We show, however, that the nice properties of treewidth-bounded CNF formulas are not preserved under existential quantification or unrolling. Finally, we show that the complexity of various verification problems is high even under the assumption of local treewidth boundedness. In summary, while global treewidth boundedness does have computational advantages, it is not a realistic assumption; in contrast, local treewidth boundedness is a realistic assumption, but its computational advantages are rather meager.

1   Introduction

The *treewidth* of a graph measures how close the graph is to a tree (trees have treewidth 1). Many problems that are intractable (e.g. NP-hard, PSPACE-hard) for general graphs, are polynomial or linear-time solvable when the graph has bounded treewidth (see [5–7] for an overview). For example, constraint-satisfaction problems, which are NP-complete, are PTIME-solvable when the variable-relatedness graph has bounded treewidth [11, 14].

In [15, 22] the complexity of the model-checking problem is studied under the hypothesis of bounded treewidth; that is, it is assumed that the model is a state transition

---

* Work supported in part by NSF grants CCR-9988322, CCR-0124077, CCR-0311326, IIS-9908435, IIS-9978135, EIA-0086264, and ANI-0216467, by BSF grant 9800096, by Texas ATP grant 003604-0058-2003, and by a grant from the Intel Corporation.

G. Sutcliffe and A. Voronkov (Eds.): LPAR 2005, LNAI 3835, pp. 489–503, 2005.
© Springer-Verlag Berlin Heidelberg 2005

system, whose underlying graph has bounded treewidth. Bounding treewidth yields a large class of tractable model-checking problems. For example, while it is not known whether model checking μ-calculus formulas is in PTIME [18], it is in PTIME under the bounded treewidth assumption [22].

We refer to the treewidth of the state transition graphs of transition systems as the *global treewidth*. The global treewidth-boundedness assumption used in [15, 22] is not, in our opinion, useful to describe real-world verification problems. There is little reason to believe that the global treewidth of real-world systems is bounded. For example, it is easy to see that the graphs underlying systems with two counters are essentially grids, which are known to have high treewidth [26]. In verification practice, real-world systems are often modeled as *concurrent* transition systems, where communication between concurrent components is modeled explicitly. When we consider the communication graph between the concurrent components (the component are the nodes, and an edge exists between each pair of communicating nodes), assuming treewidth boundedness is not unreasonable. Indeed, the topology of communication in concurrent systems is often constrained physically; for example, by the need to layout a circuit in silicon. Such topological constraints are studied, for example, in [20, 23]. In [20] the width of a Boolean circuit is related to the size of its corresponding OBDD, while in [23] bounded cutwidth is used to explain why ATPG, an NP-complete verification problem, is so easy in practice. Cutwidth boundedness is used also to improve symbolic simulation and Boolean satisfiability in [4, 29]. These various notions of bounded width are assumed because of the constrained topology of communication in concurrent systems.

In this paper, we refer to treewidth of the component communication graph as *local* treewidth and study the impact of local-treewidth boundedness on the complexity of verification problems. We believe that because the component communication graph is often constrained physically, as noted above, assuming local treewidth boundedness is natural and realistic. (In fact, the assumption of treewidth boundedness is less severe than related assumption that are often made, such as *pathwidth* boundedness or *cutwidth* boundedness [5–7]).

We first present a positive result. We prove that a CNF formula of bounded treewidth can be represented by an OBDD of polynomial size (treewidth here is defined on the primal graph of the formula, where vertices represent variables and edges represent the co-occurance of the variables in the same clause). Thus, if a transition relation of a concurrent transition system is specified by a CNF formula with bounded treewidth, then there is an OBDD of polynomial size representing it. In contrast, the OBDD of transition relations often blow up, requiring symbolic model-checking techniques that avoid building these OBDDs [2].

We then show that bounded local treewidth offers little computational advantage for verification in general. First, we show that the small-OBDD property of bounded treewidth CNF formulas is destroyed as soon as we apply existential quantification, which is a basic operation in symbolic model checking, since the image operations involves existential quantification [20]. We then show that treewidth boundedness of a transition relation is not preserved under unrolling, which is a basic operation in SAT-based bounded model checking (BMC) [3]. (Note that while satisfiability of CNF formulas is NP-complete, satisfiability of bounded-treewidth CNF formulas can be solved in polynomial time, cf. [1]).

Finally, we show that the complexity of various verification problems are high even under the assumption of local treewidth boundedness. We review several verification problem for concurrent systems, including model checking, simulation, and containment, and show that the known lower bounds (PSPACE-complete, EXPTIME-complete, and EXPSPACE-complete, respectively [16, 19]) hold also under the assumption of local treewidth boundedness. (Our results are robust: the lower bound apply even under pathwidth boundedness or cutwidth boundedness.)

In summary, while global treewidth boundedness does have computational advantages, it is not a realistic assumption. In contrast, local treewidth boundedness is a realistic assumption, but its computational advantages are rather meager.

The paper is organized as follows: In Section 2 we prove the small-OBDD property for transition relations of bounded treewidth, but then show that this property does not help in symbolic model checking and in bounded model checking. Finally, in Section 3 we show that lower bound for model checking, simulation, and containment hold also under the assumption of local treewidth boundedness.

2   Transition Relation: OBDDs Size and BMC

The notions of treewidth and pathwidth were introduced in [25, 26].

Definition 2.1. *A tree decomposition of a graph $G = (V, E)$ is a pair (T, X), where $T = (I, F)$ is a tree whose node set is I and edge set is F, and $X = \{X_i | i \in I\}$ is a family of subsets of V, one for each node of T, such that:*

- $\bigcup_{i \in I} X_i = V$.
- *for every edges $(v, w) \in E$, there exists an $i \in I$ with $\{v, w\} \subseteq X_i$.*
- *for all $i, j, k \in I$: if j is on the path from i to k in T, then $X_i \cap X_k \subseteq X_j$.*

The *width* of a tree decomposition (T, X) is $max_{i \in I} |X_i| - 1$. The *treewidth* of a graph G is the minimum width over all possible tree decompositions of G. The notions of path decomposition and pathwidth are defined analogously, with the tree T in the tree decomposition restricted to be a path. By Corollary 24 in [7], we know that for a graph G with n vertices we have that $pathwidth(G) = O(treewidth(G) \cdot \log n)$. Clearly, $treewidth(G) \leq pathwidth(G)$.

Definition 2.2. *The Gaifman graph of a CNF formula is a graph having one vertex for each variable and an edge (v_1, v_2) if the variables v_1 and v_2 occur in the same clause of the formula. By treewidth (pathwidth) of a CNF formula we refer to the treewidth (pathwidth) of its Gaifman graph.*

Ordered Boolean decision diagrams (OBDDs) [8] are a canonical form representation for Boolean formulas. An OBDD is a rooted, directed acyclic graph with one or two terminal nodes labeled 0 or 1, and a set of variable nodes of out-degree two. The variables respect a given linear order on all paths from the root to a leaf. Each path represents an assignment to each of the variables on the path. Since there can be exponentially more paths than vertices and edges, OBDDs can be substantially more compact than traditional representations like CNF. In many case, however, going from CNF representation to OBDD representation may cause an exponential blow-up [2]. We now show that this is not the case when the CNF formula has bounded treewidth.

Theorem 2.1. *A CNF formula C with n variables and pathwidth q has an OBDD of size $O(n2^q)$.*

Proof. Let the path decomposition of C be (P, L). Assume without loss of generality that $P = \{1, \ldots, k\}$. We construct a variable order from the path decomposition as follows: Define $First(x) = \min(\{p \in P \mid v \in L(p)\})$ and $Last(x) = \max(\{p \in P \mid v \in L(p)\})$. Now sort the variables in increasing lexicographic order according to $(First(x), Last(x))$; that is, define the variable order so that if $x < y$, then either $First(x) < First(y)$ or $First(x) = First(y)$ and $Last(x) < Last(y)$. We show that, using this variable order, there are at most 2^q nodes per level. The claim then follows.

For each clause c, we define $\min(c)$ as the index of the lowest ordered variable in c and correspondingly for $\max(c)$. Consider level i of the OBDD, corresponding to the variable x_i. The clause set C can be partitioned into three classes with respect to level i, $C_{ended} = \{c \mid \max(c) < i\}$, $C_{cur} = \{c \mid \min(c) \leq i < \max(c)\}$, and $C_{untouched} = \{c \mid i < \min(c)\}$.

A node u at level i corresponds to a set A_u of partial assignments to variables, where each partial assignment $a \in A_u$ is an element in $2^{\{x_1 \ldots x_{i-1}\}}$. For a partial assignment a and a clause set D, we write $a \models D$ if a is a model of D, i.e, for each clause $c \in D$, a satisfies some literal in c. From the semantics of OBDDs, we know that all partial assignments a in A_u are equivalent with respect to extensions, i.e., given $a' \in 2^{\{x_i, \ldots, x_n\}}$ and $a \in A_u$, we have that $a \cup a' \models C$ iff for every $a'' \in A_u$, $a'' \cup a' \models C$. If for $a \in A_u$, $a \not\models C_{ended}$, then we know that for every extension $a \cup a'$ of a we have that $a \cup a' \not\models C_{ended}$, so $a \cup a' \not\models C$. Thus, the node u is identical to Boolean 0 and should not exist at level i. It follows that for every $a \in A_u$, $a \models C_{ended}$. We also know that all clauses in $C_{untouched}$ have none of their variables assigned by $a \in A_u$.

Each partial assignment a at level i can be associated with a subset $M_a \subseteq C_{cur}$ where $M_a = \{c \mid c \in C_{cur}, a \models c\}$, i.e., the clauses in C_{cur} that are already satisfied by a before reading the variable x_i. We know that none of the clauses in C_{cur} have failed (all literals assigned to false) so far, since by definition of C_{cur} all such clauses have literals with variables beyond x_{i-1}. Suppose that for two distinct nodes u and v at level i there exists $a_u \in A_u$ and $a_v \in A_v$ such that $M_{a_u} = M_{a_v}$. Since u and v are distinct, there is a partial assignment $a \in 2^{\{x_i, \ldots, x_n\}}$ that distinguishes between u and v; say, $a_u \cup a \models C$ and $a_v \cup a \not\models C$. Since a_u and a_v, however, both satisfy C_{ended}, both are undefined on the variables of $C_{untouched}$, and we also have, by assumption, that $M_{a_u} = M_{a_v}$, we must have that $a_u \cup a \models C$ iff $a_v \cup a \models C$ – a contradiction. It follows that $M_{a_u} \neq M_{a_v}$.

Let $j = First(x_i)$. We know that $L(j)$ contains at most $q + 1$ variables, including x_i. Let $Var_i = L(j) \cap \{x_1, \ldots, x_{i-1}\}$, then Var_i has at most q variables. Suppose that u and v are two nodes at level i such that there exists $a_u \in A_u$ and $a_v \in A_v$ where a_u and a_v agree on Var_i. We show then $M_{a_u} = M_{a_v}$. Consider a clause $c \in C_{cur}$.

We know that all the variables of c occur in $L(k)$ for some k. We cannot have $k < j$, since then we'd have $c \in C_{ended}$, so $k \geq j$. If x_h occurs in c for some $h < i$, then by construction $x_h \in L(j')$ for some $j' \leq j$. By the property of path decompositions it follows that $x_h \in L(j)$. Since a_u and a_v agree on Var_i, it follows that they agree on c. We showed that if u and v are distinct, then for every $a_u \in A_u$ and $a_v \in A_v$, $M_{a_u} \neq M_{a_v}$. It follows that a_u and a_v cannot agree on Var_i. Since Var_i has at most q variables, there can be at most 2^q nodes at level i. The claim follows since the OBDD as n levels.   □

The relationship described in Theorem 2.1 between pathwidth and OBDD size was first shown in [17]. The proof there goes via a variant of a DPLL-based satisfiability algorithm. Our argument here is direct and show how to obtain an OBDD variable order from a path decomposition.

Recall that we know that for a graph G that contains n vertices we have that $pathwidth(G) = O(treewidth(G) \cdot \log n)$.

Corollary 2.1. *A CNF formula C with n variables and treewidth width q has an OBDD of size polynomial in n and exponential in q.*

While Theorem 2.1 suggests that OBDD-based algorithms are tractable on bounded width problems, typical model-checking algorithms do more than just build OBDDs that correspond to CNF formulas. OBDDs are often used to perform symbolic image operations, which requires applying existential quantification to OBDDs [20]. While it is often claimed that fixed-parameter tractability implies tractability for the bounded-parameter case, the constant factor resulting from the blowup of the parameter needs to be considered on a case-by-case basis. Often, super-exponential blowups in the parameter indicates that the problem is not practically tractable. The following theorem shows that Theorem 2.1 is not likely to be useful in model checking, since using quantification on bounded-width formulas leads to such a super-exponential blowup on the constant factor that is based on the parameter.

Theorem 2.2. *There exists a formula C in CNF with n variables and pathwidth q, and a subset of variables X such that $(\exists X)C$ under every variable order does not have a OBDD of size $n2^{f(q)}$, for a sub-exponential function f.*

Proof. We consider the hidden-weighted bit (HWB) function, which is shown in [9] to have a OBDD size of $\Omega(1.14^m)$ under arbitrary variable order, where m is the number of input bits. The HWB function is a Boolean function $2^m \rightarrow \{0,1\}$, where for an m-bit input vector A, the output is the wth bit of A, w being the number of 1s in A (the *bit count* of A). The OBDD is defined on the set of variables $A[0]$ to $A[m-1]$.

We consider the case where $m = 2^k$, $k > 3$, and use a CNF formula to represent the HWB function. Clearly, from the upper bounds shown in Corollary 2.1, a direct translation can not result in bounded pathwidth; we use $(m+1)k+1$ additional existentially quantified variables to facilitate the CNF encoding. In the additional variables, there are $m+1$ counters (at k bits each), which we call $X_0, \ldots X_m$, and a single bit witness w. Each X_i is used to guess the number of 1s occurring after $A[i]$. The bit witness w guesses the value of $A[X_0]$. We use CNF constraints to check the correctness of our guesses. The CNF formula C is the conjunction of all the following constraints. ($=$ and $+$ are short hand defined on bit vectors of size k):

- For each $0 \leq i < m$, we define $C_i^1 := (A[i] \rightarrow X_i = X_{i+1} + 1) \wedge (\neg A[i] \rightarrow X_i = X_{i+1})$. This asserts that if X_i is a correct guess iff X_{i+1} is a correct guess.
- For each $0 \leq i < m$, we define $C_i^2 := (X_0 = i) \rightarrow (A[i] \leftrightarrow w)$. This asserts that w is a correct guess if X_0 is a correct guess.
- $C^g := w$. Since we are building the OBDD representing inputs where the HWB function returns 1, w is asserted to true.
- The well-formedness constraint is $C^{wf} := X_m = 0$. This asserts that X_m is a correct guess. Combined with the C_i^1s, they assert that all X_is are correct guesses.

The only shorthand we used above is $=$ and $+$ on bit vectors of length k, both of which can be written out in CNF with no additional variables and $O(k^2)$ clauses. Now, $(\exists X_0) \ldots (\exists X_m)(\exists w)C$ characterizes the HWB function.

Next we show there is a path decomposition of C of width $3k + 1$. There is one node per bit in A, ordered from 0 to $m - 1$. Each node contains the support for the constraints C_i^1 and C_i^2 (the last node also contains C^g and C^{wf} with no additional variables). In turn, each node i contains the variables $A[i]$, w, X_0, X_i, and X_{i+1}, giving a pathwidth of $3k + 1$.

Consider the relationship between the size of the OBDD and the pathwidth. Assume we have a BDD of size $n2^{f(q)}$, where the pathwidth is q and the number of variables is n, and f is a sub-exponential function. Here, $q = 3k + 1$ and $n = (m + 1)k + 1 + m = (2^k + 1)(k + 1)$. The size of the OBDD S is then $((2^k + 1)(k + 1))2^{f(3k+1)} < 2^{(k+3)}2^{f(3k+1)} = 2^{f(3k+1)+k+3} = 2^{g(k)}$. Since f is sub-exponential, g is sub-exponential as well. But from [9], the lower bound for the size of such OBDDs is $\Omega(1.14^m) = \Omega(2^{\log 1.14 \times 2^k})$, which contradicts with g being sub-exponential. So such small OBDDs cannot exist. $\qquad\square$

Next we show that our construction is almost worst case, i.e., there is a closely related upper-bound.

Theorem 2.3. *For a CNF formula $C = \bigwedge c$ on n variables with pathwidth q and a subset of variables X, the formula $(\exists X)C$ has an OBDD of size $O((n - |X|)2^{2^q})$.*

Proof. To get the upper bound, we use the same approach as the Theorem 2.1, i.e., we show an upper bound of 2^{2^q} nodes for nodes at each level i by counting the number of equivalence classes.

We use $supp(C)$ to denote the set of variables that occur in C, and define $Y = supp(C) - X$ as the set of *free* variables in $(\exists X)C$. We use the same variable order as Theorem 2.1, and name the variables in Y as $y_1, y_2 \ldots y_m$ according to the variable order. For a set $Z \subseteq supp(C)$, we use $Z_{<i}$ to denote the subset that appears before y_i in the variable order. Also, Z_j is used to denote the subset of Z that occurs in path-decomposition node j. Each node u corresponding to a variable y_i represents a set of assignments A_u to $Y_{<i}$, encoded by the paths to the node from the root of the OBDD. Consider an assignment $a \in A_u$. For each assignment $b \in 2^{X_{<i}}$ to the quantified variables occurring before y_i, we have a corresponding set of clauses in C that are satisfied by $a \cup b$. Assume that y_i occurs in node k of the path decomposition of C. Recall that C can be partitioned into C_{ended}, C_{cur}, and $C_{untouched}$ based on the variable y_i.

Define the function $F_a : 2^{X_{k,<i}} \rightarrow \{\perp\} \cup 2^{C_{cur}}$ such that for each assignment b to $X_{k,<i}$, $F_a(b) = \perp$ if there is no extension b' (on $X_{<i}$) of b such that $a \cup b' \models C_{ended}$; otherwise, $F_a(b) = S$ where $S \subseteq C_{cur}$ is the clauses in C_{cur} satisfied by $a \cup b$. Now, we show that two distinct nodes u and v corresponding to y_i do not contain assignments a_u in A_u and a_v in A_v such that $F_{a_u} = F_{a_v}$. Assume the contrary. Since u and v are distinct, w.l.o.g., there is an assignment a to $Y_{\geq i}$ such that $a_u \cup a \models (\exists X)C$ and $a_v \cup a \not\models (\exists X)C$. Take an assignment b on X where $a_u \cup a \cup b \models C$. Let b' be a restriction of b to the variables in $X_k \cup X_{>i}$, and let b'' be a restriction of b to the variables in $X_{k,<i}$. It is clear that $a \cup b' \models C_{untouched}$. We know that $F_{a_u}(b'') \neq \perp$, since b restricted to $X_{<i}$, which we call b_{a_u}, satisfies $a_u \cup b_{a_u} \models C_{ended}$. Since $F_{a_u} = F_{a_v}$, $F_{a_v}(b'') = F_{a_u}(b'') \neq \perp$. Again, we have an extension b_{a_v} (from the definition of F_{a_v}) of b'' to $X_{<i}$ where $a_v \cup b_{a_v} \models C_{ended}$. For a clause $c \in C_{cur}$, if $c \in F_{a_v}(b'')$, then $c \in F_{a_u}(b'')$, so $a_u \cup b_{a_u} \models c$. Otherwise, $a \cup b' \models c$, since $a_u \cup a \cup b \models c$ and $a_u \cup b'' \not\models c$. So, $a_v \cup b_{a_v} \cup a \cup b' \models C_{cur}$. In summary, $a_v \cup a \cup b_{a_v} \cup b' \models C$, which contradicts with $a_v \cup a \not\models (\exists X)C$.

Now we count the number of possible functions for F_a. For each $b \in 2^{X_{k,<i}}$, the number of possible choices of $F_a(b)$ is $1 + 2^{|Y_{k,<i}|}$ since the satisfaction of clauses in C_{cur} depends only on b and assignments to $Y_{k,<i}$. Thus, the number of possible such F_as is $(1 + 2^{|Y_{k,<i}|})^{2^{|X_{k,<i}|}} \leq (2^{|Y_{k,<i}|+1})^{2^{|X_{k,<i}|}} = 2^{(|Y_{k,<i}|+1)2^{|X_{k,<i}|}} \leq 2^{2^q}$ since $q \geq |X_{k,<i}| + |Y_{k,<i}|$.

The combination of the possible count of F_as and the fact that distinct nodes induce distinct F_as gives us a bound of 2^{2^q} nodes at each level, i.e., a size bound of $(n-|X|)2^{2^q}$ for the whole OBDD. $\qquad\square$

The double exponential blowup for the OBDD size of quantified bounded pathwidth formulas on the pathwidth prevents us from using the property $pathwidth(G) = O(treewidth(G)\log n)$ to achieve a polynomial size OBDD for quantified bounded treewidth formulas. Whether a non-polynomial lower bound exists for the OBDD size of quantified bounded treewidth formulas is left for future research.

Let us now consider the effect of the local bounded treewidth on the complexity of Bounded Model Checking (BMC). In bounded model checking, variable substitutions are used to create distinct copies of the system. Given a formula f with support set $V = \{v_1, v_2, \ldots v_n\}$, and a substitution variable set $V' = \{v'_1, v'_2, \ldots v'_n\}$, we write $f[V/V']$ to represent a copy of f where each v_i in f is replaced with v'_i. To unroll a system to k iterations, we create $k + 1$ copies of the state variable set V, which we call $V^0, V^1, \ldots V^k$. The transition relation is a formula over $V \cup V'$, where V is the current state variables and V' is the next state variables. The BMC $unrolling$ would contain $\bigwedge_{0 \leq i \leq k-1} TR[V/V^i, V'/V^{i+1}]$, in addition to initial and property constraints. In the following theorem, we show that BMC unrolling does not preserve the bounded treewidth.

Theorem 2.4. *Even though the transition relation of a concurrent transition system, represented by a CNF $TR(V, V')$, has bounded treewidth, its unrolling can have unbounded treewidth.*

Proof. As an example, we take the case where the state variable set V is $\{x_1, x_2, \ldots x_w\}$ and the transition function is defined by $x'_i := (x_{i-1} \leftrightarrow x_i) \leftrightarrow x_{i+1}$. The CNF for transition relation $TR(V, V')$ clearly has bounded pathwidth (where each path decomposition node consists of the variables $x_i, x_{i+1}, x'_i, x'_{i+1}$), and, in turn, bounded treewidth.

Now we considering Gaifman graph of the unrolling. An example where two copies are unrolled is shown in Figure 1. The state variable for x_i at iteration j is denoted as x_i^j. We can see clearly that if we unroll, say, $w + 2$ copies, the Gaifman graph will have a $w \times w$ grid as a minor, which implies unbounded pathwidth (and treewidth) [12]. $\square$

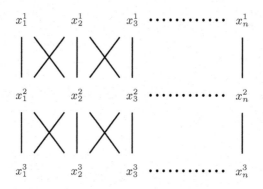

Fig. 1. The $TR(k)$ in Theorem 2.4, for $k = 3$

3   Model Checking, Containment, Simulation

We now introduce definitions of non-deterministic transition systems with bounded concurrency [16]. A non-deterministic transition system with bounded concurrency (*concurrent transition system* for short) is a tuple $P = \langle O, P_1, \ldots, P_n \rangle$ consisting of a finite set O of *observable events* and n components $P_1, \ldots, P_n$ for some $n \geq 1$. Each component P_i is a tuple $\langle O_i, W_i, W_i^0, \delta_i, L_i \rangle$, where:

- $O_i \subseteq O$ is a set of local observable events. The O_j are not necessarily pairwise disjoint; hence, observable events may be shared by several components. We require that $\bigcup_{j \in I}^n O_j = O$.
- W_i is a finite set of states, and we require that the W_j be pairwise disjoint. Also we let $W = \bigcup_{j \in I}^n W_j$.
- $W_i^0 \subseteq W_i$ is the set of initial states.
- $\delta_i \subseteq W_i \times \beta(W) \times W_i$ is a transition relation, where $\beta(W)$ denotes the set of all Boolean propositional formulae over W.
- $L_i : W_i \to 2^{O_i}$ is a labeling function that labels each state with a set of local observable events. The intuition is that $L_i(w)$ are the events that occur, or hold, in w.

Since states are labeled with sets of elements from O, we refer to $\Sigma = 2^O$ as the *alphabet* of P. While each component of P has its local observable events and its own states and transitions, these transitions depend not only on the component's current state but also on the current states of the other components. Also, as we shall now see, the labels of the components are required to agree on shared observable events.

A *configuration* of P is a tuple $c = \langle w_1, w_2, \ldots, w_n, \sigma \rangle \in W_1 \times W_2 \times \cdots \times W_n \times \Sigma$, satisfying $L_i(w_i) = \sigma \cap O_i$ for all $1 \leq i \leq n$. Thus, a configuration describes the current state of each of the components, as well as the set of observable events labeling these states. The requirement on σ implies that these labels are *consistent*, i.e., for any P_i and P_j, and for each $o \in O_i \cap O_j$, either $o \in L_i(w_i) \cap L_j(w_j)$ (in which case, $o \in \sigma$), or $o \notin L_i(w_i) \cup L_j(w_j)$ (in which case, $o \notin \sigma$). For a configuration $c = \langle w_1, w_2, \ldots, w_n, \sigma \rangle$, we term $\langle w_1, w_2, \ldots, w_n \rangle$ the *global state* of c, and we term σ the *label* of c, and denote it by $L(c)$. A configuration is *initial* if for all $1 \leq i \leq n$, we have $w_i \in W_i^0$. We use C to denote the set of all configurations of a given system P, and C_0 to denote the set of all its initial configurations. We also use $c[i]$ to refer to P_i's state in c.

For a propositional formula θ in $\mathcal{B}(W)$ and a global state $p = \langle w_1, w_2, \ldots, w_n \rangle$, we say that p *satisfies* θ if assigning **true** to states in p and **false** to states not in p makes θ true. For example, $s_1 \wedge (t_1 \vee t_2)$, with $s_1 \in W_1$ and $\{t_1, t_2\} \subseteq W_2$, is satisfied by every global state in which P_1 is in state s_1 and P_2 is in either t_1 or t_2. We shall sometimes write disjunctions as sets, so that the above formula can be written $\{s_1\} \wedge \{t_1, t_2\}$. Formulas in $\mathcal{B}(W)$ that appear in transitions are called *conditions*.

Given two configurations $c = \langle w_1, w_2, \ldots, w_n, \sigma \rangle$ and $c' = \langle w_1', w_2', \ldots, w_n', \sigma' \rangle$, we say that c' is a *successor of c in P*, and write $succ_P(c, c')$, if for all $1 \leq i \leq n$ there is $\langle w_i, \theta_i, w_i' \rangle \in \delta_i$ such that $\langle w_1, w_2, \ldots, w_n \rangle$ satisfies θ_i. In other words, a successor configuration is obtained by simultaneously applying to all the components a transition that is enabled in the current configuration. Note that by requiring that successors are indeed configurations, we are saying that transitions can only lead to states satisfying the consistency criterion, to the effect that they agree on the labels for shared observable events.[1]

Given a configuration c, a *c-computation* of P is an infinite sequence $\pi = c_0, c_1, \ldots$ of configurations, such that $c_0 = c$ and for all $i \geq 0$ we have $succ_P(c_i, c_{i+1})$. A *computation* of P is a c-computation for some $c \in C_0$. The computation $c_0, c_1, \ldots$ *generates* the infinite *trace* $\rho \in \Sigma^\omega$, defined by $\rho = L(c_0) \cdot L(c_1) \cdots$. We use $\mathcal{T}(P^c)$ to denote the set of all traces generated by c-computations, and the *trace set* $\mathcal{T}(P)$ of P is then defined as $\bigcup_{c \in C_0} \mathcal{T}(P^c)$. In this way, each concurrent transition system P defines a subset of Σ^ω. We say that P *accepts* a trace ρ if $\rho \in \mathcal{T}(P)$. Also, we say that P is *empty* if $\mathcal{T}(P) = \emptyset$; i.e., P has no computation, and that P is *universal* if $\mathcal{T}(P) = \Sigma^\omega$; i.e., every trace in Σ^ω is generated by some fair computation of P.

The *size* of a concurrent transition system P is the sum of the sizes of its components. Symbolically, $|P| = |P_1| + \cdots + |P_n|$. Here, for a component $P_i = \langle O_i, W_i, W_i^0, \delta_i, L_i, \alpha_i \rangle$, we define $|P_i| = |O_i| + |W_i| + |\delta_i| + |L_i| + |\alpha_i|$, where $|\delta_i| = \sum_{\langle w, \theta, w' \rangle \in \delta_i} |\theta|$, $|L_i| = |O_i| \cdot |W_i|$, and $|\alpha_i|$ is the sum of the cardinalities of the sets in α_i. Clearly, P can be stored in space $O(|P|)$.

When P has a single component, we say that it is a *sequential transition system*. Note that the transition relation of a sequential transition system can be really viewed as a subset of $W \times W$, and that a configuration of a sequential transition system is simply a labeled state.

Now, we introduce the definitions about the *local* and *global* treewidth, and the degree of a graph.

---

[1] This requirement could obviously have been imposed implicitly in the transition relation.

Definition 3.1. *The communication graph of a concurrent transition system P is a graph having one vertex for each component and an edge (v_i, v_j) if either the component for v_i and the component for v_j share observable events or if the transition relation of one of the components for v_i or v_j refer to the variables of the other.*

Definition 3.2. *The local treewidth of the concurrent transition system P is the tree-width of its communication graph.*

By the Theorem 2.2 in [16], every concurrent transition system P can be translated into a sequential transition system of size $2^{O(|P|)}$.

Definition 3.3. *The global treewidth of the concurrent transition system P is the tree-width of its equivalent sequential transition system.*

Definition 3.4. *The degree of a graph the maximum vertex degree, in other words, the maximum count of arcs connected to a single vertex in the graph.*

A graph with bounded pathwidth and bounded degree has bounded cutwidth [28]. The pathwidth bound implies many other structural restrictions [27].

Example 3.1. We construct a concurrent transition system P to encode a (ripple-carry) binary counter; it can count up to 2^n using n components. Each component P_i is used to store the i-th bit (the bit with weight 2^{i-1}), so P_1 is the least significant bit and P_n is the most significant bit. The observable events are the bit-values stored by each component, and the counter works by ripple-carry propagation.

Formally, given the number n of bits, P is $\langle\{bit_1, \ldots, bit_n\}, P_1, \ldots, P_n\rangle$, where $P_i = \langle\{bit_i\}, \{s_{00}^i, s_{01}^i, s_{10}^i\}, \{I^i\}, \delta_i, L_i\rangle$. For each state s_{jk}^i, the subscript j represent the carry status, and the subscript k represent the bit state; for example, the state s_{10}^i represents the case where the value of bit i is 0 and a carry is propagated toward bit $i+1$. I^i is an initial state, described below.

In Figure 2 we show the process P_i. The edges are labeled by the condition of the transition relation: c_{i-1} means that the carry of the process P_{i-1} is 1, and it corresponds to s_{10}^{i-1}, $\neg c_{i-1}$ means that the carry of P_i is 0 and it corresponds to $s_{00}^{i-1} \vee s_{01}^{i-1}$.

We remark that P_1 corresponds to the least significant bit of the counter, and the c_0 is always 1. We define δ_i and L_i as follows:

- $\delta_i = \{\langle s_{00}^i, \neg c_{i-1}, s_{00}^i\rangle, \langle s_{00}^i, c_{i-1}, s_{01}^i\rangle, \langle s_{01}^i, \neg c_{i-1}, s_{01}^i\rangle, \langle s_{01}^i, c_{i-1}, s_{10}^i\rangle, \langle s_{10}^i, \neg c_{i-1}, s_{00}^i\rangle, \langle s_{10}^i, c_{i-1}, s_{01}^i\rangle, \}.$
- $L_i(s_{00}^i) = L_i(s_{10}^i) = \emptyset, L_i(s_{01}^i) = \{bit_i\}.$

Note if we start with s_{00}^i for all states, the ripple-carry nature of the counter would take $2^n + n - 1$ cycles to flip the carry state of the most significant bit, so we initialize the counter with the binary representation of $n-1$ to ensure the carry on the most significant bit will happen after exactly 2^n cycles. The communication graph of this counter have constant pathwidth, since each component P_i interacts only with the components P_{i-1} and P_{i+1}, thus forming a path.

In the following, we introduce the definitions for the verification problems that we consider here: model checking, containment, simulation.

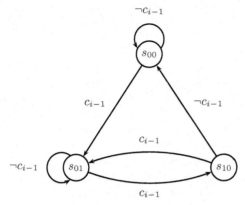

Fig. 2. A cell of the counter

The temporal logics [24] often used in the model checking are *CTL* and *LTL*, which are fragments of *CTL**. The logic *CTL** combines both branching-time and linear-time operators [13]. For the sake of simplicity, we consider LTL (Linear-Time Temporal Logic). It has three unary modal operators (X, G, and F) and one binary modal operator (U). Their meaning is: $X\phi$ is true in particular state if and only if the formula ϕ is true in the next state; $G\phi$ is true if and only ϕ is true from now on; $F\phi$ is true if ϕ will become true at some time in the future; $\phi U \psi$ is true if ψ will eventually become true and ϕ stays true until then. The semantics of LTL is based on computations of transition systems. Intuitively, $F\phi$ is true in a state of a transition system if ϕ is true in some following state, that is the transition system reaches a state in which ϕ is true. In modal logic literature, transition systems are called Kripke structure, and computations of Kripke structure are called Kripke models [10]. The model checking problem is to decide if all runs of a transition system satisfy the LTL formula. In formal verification, we encode the behavior of a system as a concurrent transition system, and a property we want to check as an LTL formula.

The problems that formalize correct trace-based and tree-based implementations of a system are *containment* and *simulation*, respectively. These problems are defined below with respect to two concurrent transition systems $P = \langle O, P_1, \ldots, P_n \rangle$ and $P' = \langle O', P'_1, \ldots, P'_m \rangle$ with $O \supseteq O'$, and with possibly different numbers of components. For technical convenience, we assume that $O = O'$. The *containment problem* for P and P' is to determine whether $T(P) \subseteq T(P')$. That is, whether every trace accepted by P is also accepted by P'. If $T(P) \subseteq T(P')$, we say that P' *contains* P and we write $P \subseteq P'$. While containment refers only to the set of computations of P and P', simulation refers also to the branching structure of the systems. Let c and c' be configurations of P and P', respectively. A relation $H \subseteq C \times C'$ is a *simulation relation* from $\langle P, c \rangle$ to $\langle P', c' \rangle$ iff the following conditions hold [21].

1. $H(c, c')$.
2. For all configurations $a \in C$ and $a' \in C'$ with $H(a, a')$, we have $L(a) = L(a')$.
3. For all configurations $a \in C$ and $a' \in C'$ with $H(a, a')$ and for every configuration $b \in C$ such that $succ_P(a, b)$, there exists a configuration $b' \in C'$ such that $succ_{P'}(a', b')$ and $H(b, b')$.

A simulation relation H is a *simulation from P to P'* iff for every $c \in C_0$ there exists $c' \in C_0'$ such that $H(c, c')$. If there exists a simulation from P to P', we say that P *simulates P'* and we write $S \preceq S'$. Intuitively, it means that the system P' has more behaviors than the system P. In fact, every tree embodied in P is also embodied in P'. The *simulation problem* is, given P and P', to determine whether $S \preceq S'$.

In this section we consider the complexity of the reachability, containment and simulation problems for concurrent transition systems, under the hypothesis of bounded treewidth both in the communication graph and in each component. The complexity of these problems has been studied in [16, 19]. We show that these problems have the same complexity of the general case, even if each component has constant size (and thus bounded treewidth and degree) and the communication graph has bounded pathwidth and degree (and hence bounded treewidth). Our results are then robust; in fact a bounded pathwidth implies many other structural restrictions [27].

In [19], the model-checking problem for temporal logics (e.g. CTL, LTL, CTL*) is shown to be PSPACE-hard, also in the reachability case. The reachability case is when the formula specifies an event that the transition system has to reach. For example in LTL, it is simply $F\psi$, where ψ is a Boolean formula. From the characteristic of the concurrent transition system used in the proof, the following theorem holds.

Theorem 3.1. *The CTL, LTL, and CTL* model checking for concurrent transition systems is PSPACE-hard also in the reachability case, and remains PSPACE-hard even if each component is fixed and the communication graph has bounded pathwidth and bounded degree.*

In [16] the simulation problem is shown to be EXPTIME-complete; from the characteristic of the concurrent transition systems used in the proof, the following theorem holds.

Theorem 3.2. *The simulation problem for concurrent transition systems is EXPTIME-hard, and remains EXPTIME-hard even if each component is fixed and the communication graph has bounded pathwidth and bounded degree.*

In [16] the containment problem is shown to be EXPSPACE-complete, but the concurrent transition systems used in the proofs have communication graphs with unbounded pathwidth and unbounded degree.

Theorem 3.3. *The containment problem for concurrent transition systems is EXPSPACE-hard, and remains EXPSPACE-hard even if each component has fixed size and the communication graph has bounded pathwidth and bounded degree.*

Proof. To prove hardness, we carry out a reduction from deterministic exponential-space-bounded Turing machines. Given a Turing machine T and input u of length n, we want to check whether T accepts the word u in space 2^n. we denote by Σ an alphabet for encoding runs of T (the alphabet Σ and the encoding are defined later). We write u' to represent the initial tape-encoding of u, i.e., if u is $u_1 u_2 \ldots u_n$, u' is $(q_0, u_1) u_2 \ldots u_n$. We then construct a transition system P_T over the alphabet $\Sigma \cup \{\$\}$, for some $\$ \notin \Sigma$, such that (i) the size of P_T is polynomial in $|T|$ and linear in n, and (ii) $\#u(\Sigma^\omega + (\Sigma^* \cdot \$^\omega)) \subseteq \mathcal{T}(P_T)$ iff T does not accept the word u. The crucial point is that using bounded concurrency, we can handle the exponential size of the tape by n components that count to 2^n.

We assume, without loss of generality, that once T reaches a final state it loops there forever. The transition system P_T accepts all traces in Σ^ω, and accepts a trace $w \cdot \$^\omega \in \Sigma^* \cdot \$^\omega$ if either

1. w is not an encoding of a prefix of a legal computation of T,
2. w is an encoding of a prefix of a legal computation of T, but, within this prefix, the computation still has not reached a final state, or
3. w is an encoding of a prefix of a legal, but rejecting, computation of T over any input.

Thus, P_T rejects a trace $w \cdot \$^\omega$ iff w encodes a prefix of a legal accepting computation of T and the computation has already reached a final state. Hence, P_T accepts all traces in $\#u(\Sigma^\omega + \Sigma^* \cdot \$^\omega)$ iff T does not accept the word u.

Now to the details of the construction. Let $T = \langle \Gamma, Q, \mapsto, q_0, F_{acc}, F_{rej} \rangle$, where Γ is the alphabet, Q is the set of states, and $\mapsto : (Q \times \Gamma) \to (Q \times \Gamma \times \{L, R\})$ is the transition function. We write $(q, a) \mapsto (q', b, \delta)$ for $\mapsto (q, a) = (q', b, \delta)$, with the meaning that when in state q and reading a in the current tape cell, T moves to state q', writes b in the current tape cell and moves its head one cell to the left or right, depending on δ. Finally, q_0 is T's initial state, $F_{acc} \subseteq Q$ is the set of final accepting states, and $F_{rej} \subseteq Q$ is the set of final rejecting states.

We encode a configuration of T by a string in $\#\Gamma^*(Q \times \Gamma)\Gamma^*$, of the form $\#\gamma_1\gamma_2 \ldots (q, \gamma_i) \ldots \gamma_{2^n})$. The meaning of this is that the j'th cell, for $1 \leq j \leq 2^n$, is labeled γ_j, T is in state q and its head points to the i'th cell.

We encode a computation of T by a sequence of configurations, which is a word over $\Sigma = \{\#\} \cup \Gamma \cup (Q \times \Gamma)$. Let $\#\sigma_1 \ldots \sigma_{2^n} \#\sigma_1' \ldots \sigma_{2^n}'$ be two successive configurations of T in such a sequence. (Here, each σ_i is in Σ.) If we set $\sigma_0 = \sigma_{2^n+1} = \#$ and consider a triple $\langle \sigma_{i-1}, \sigma_i, \sigma_{i+1} \rangle$, for $1 \leq i \leq 2^n$, it is clear that the transition function of T prescribes σ_i'. In addition, along the encoding of the entire computation, $\#$ must repeat exactly every $2^n + 1$ letters. Let $next(\sigma_{i-1}, \sigma_i, \sigma_{i+1})$ denote our expectation for σ_i'. That is, with the γ's denoting elements of Γ, we have:

- $next(\gamma_{i-1}, \gamma_i, \gamma_{i+1}) = next(\#, \gamma_i, \gamma_{i+1}) = next(\gamma_{i-1}, \gamma_i, \#) = \gamma_i$.
- $next((q, \gamma_{i-1}), \gamma_i, \gamma_{i+1}) = next((q, \gamma_{i-1}), \gamma_i, \#) = \begin{cases} \gamma_i & \text{if } (q, \gamma_{i-1}) \mapsto (q', \gamma_{i-1}', L) \\ (q', \gamma_i) & \text{if } (q, \gamma_{i-1}) \mapsto (q', \gamma_{i-1}', R) \end{cases}$
- $next(\gamma_{i-1}, (q, \gamma_i), \gamma_{i+1}) = next(\#, (q, \gamma_i), \gamma_{i+1}) = next(\gamma_{i-1}, (q, \gamma_i), \#) = \gamma_i'$, where $(q, \gamma_i) \mapsto (q', \gamma_i', \delta)$. [2]
- $next(\gamma_{i-1}, \gamma_i, (q, \gamma_{i+1})) = next(\#, \gamma_i, (q, \gamma_{i+1})) = \begin{cases} \gamma_i & \text{if } (q, \gamma_{i+1}) \mapsto (q', \gamma_{i+1}', R) \\ (q', \gamma_i) & \text{if } (q, \gamma_{i+1}) \mapsto (q', \gamma_{i+1}', L) \end{cases}$
- $next(\sigma_{2^n}, \#, \sigma_1') = \#$.

A necessary and sufficient condition for a trace to encode a legal computation of T on the word u is that consecutive configurations are compatible with $next$.

Now for the construction of P_T. P_T is a concurrent process with $n + 1$ components. The first component, P_M is the master process that accept all the traces Σ^ω, and accept

---

[2] We assume that T's head does not "fall" from the right or the left boundaries of the tape. Thus, the case where $i = 1$ and $(q, \gamma_i) \mapsto (q', \gamma_i', L)$ and the dual case where $i = 2^n$ and $(q, \gamma_i) \mapsto (q', \gamma_i', R)$ are not possible.

all non-accepting traces in $\Sigma^* \cdot \$^\omega$. The other components $P_1, \cdots, P_n$, are used by P_M and their only task is perform the count as in Example 3.1; each of these processes is associated with a bit (P_1 with the least significant, P_n the most significant).

Let us describe the process P_M. In spirit, P_M follows the outline of the master process in [16]. In the construction of P_M, we use the following block of states G_{Σ^3}, which is used to generate sequences of triples $(\sigma_{i-1}, \sigma_i, \sigma_{i+1}) \in \Sigma^3$. G_{Σ^3} have $|\Sigma^3|$ states, each representing a triple, and labeled by the middle state. For two triples (u, u', u'') and (v, v', v''), there is an transition from the first to the second iff $u' = v$ and $u'' = v'$. P_M can either start in a clique of Σ states to generate Σ^ω, or it can start in a block of states (which we call $Init$) to generate non-accepting traces. All edges in $Init$ have condition $true$. From a state s in $Init$, we can reach a corresponding successor state, which represents the same triple as the successors of s in $Init$, in a new block of states B_s, of which every state asserts c_0 to start the count in the component P_1. In other words, $c_0 = \bigvee_{t \in B_s | s \in Init} t$. All edges into states in B_s have condition $true$, except those that go into states with label $next(s)$. As P_M progresses in B_s, the counter is counting to 2^n. The edges into the state labeled with $next(s)$ have condition $\neg s_{10}^n$, and from every state in B_s, we can move to a state which is a self loop labeled $\$$ with condition s_{10}^n. This asserts that the trace we are generating is not a prefix of a legal computation over T. Alternatively, P_M can also start in a clique of size $|\Sigma'|$ where $\Sigma' = \{\#\} \cup \Gamma \cup \{(Q - F_{acc}) \times \Gamma\}$, i.e., all the non-accepting symbols in Σ. Each edge in the clique have condition $true$, and each state in the clique can go to the self loop on $\$$ on condition $true$. This captures all the (legal or illegal) non-accepting traces on T.

It is easy to see that $|P_T|$ is polynomial in $|T|$ and linear in n. The processes $P_M, P_1, \cdots, P_n$ have constant size. P_M interacts only with P_1 and with P_n, the generic P_i interacts only with P_{i-1} and P_{i+1}: the communication graph is a ring and then it has bounded pathwidth and degree.

Now, given the word $u = u_1 u_2 \ldots u_n$, we construct P to be a concurrent transition system that generates the language $\#(q_0, u_1)u_2 \ldots u_n(\Sigma^\omega + (\Sigma^* \cdot \$^\omega))$. In fact, P can be easily taken to be a concurrent transition system with $n + 1$ components, each with $|\Sigma| + 1$ states, implemented as a shifter. In other words, the next state of component i is the current state of component $i + 1$, and component $n + 1$ can non-deterministically generate $\Sigma^\omega + (\Sigma^* \cdot \$^\omega)$. Obviously, each component is of constant size, and the concurrent transition system is of bounded pathwidth and bounded degree. It follows that T does not accept the word u iff $P \subseteq P_T$. By taking T to be an universal Turing machine, we showed that the containment problem for concurrent transition systems is EXPSPACE-hard even if each component has fixed size and the communication graph has bounded pathwidth and bounded degree.   □

References

1. A. Atserias, P.G. Kolaitis, and Moshe Y. Vardi. Constraint propagation as a proof system. In *CP 2004*, pages 77–91, 2004.
2. I. Beer, S. Ben-David, D. Geist, R. Gewirtzman, and M. Yoeli. Methodology and system for practical formal verification of reactive hardware. In *Proc. 6th Conf. on Computer Aided Verification*, pages 182–193, Stanford, June 1994.

3. A. Biere, A. Cimatti, E.M. Clarke, M. Fujita, and Y. Zhu. Symbolic model checking using SAT procedures instead of BDDs. In *DAC 1999*, pages 317–320, 1999.
4. P. Bjesse, J.H. Kukula, R.F. Damiano, T. Stanion, and Y. Zhu. Guiding sat diagnosis with tree decompositions. In *SAT 2003*, volume 2919 of *LNCS*, pages 315–329. Springer, 2004.
5. H.L. Bodlaender. A tourist guide through treewidth. *Acta Cybernetica*, 11:1–23, 1993.
6. H.L. Bodlaender. Treewidth: Algorithmic techniques and results. In Igor Prívara and Peter Ruzicka, editors, *Proc. 22nd Int. Symp. MFCS, LNCS 1295*. Springer, 1997.
7. H.L. Bodlaender. A partial k-arboretum of graphs with bounded treewidth. Technical report, Universiteit Utrecht, 1998.
8. R.E. Bryant. Graph-based algorithms for boolean-function manipulation. *IEEE Trans. on Computers*, C-35(8), 1986.
9. R.E. Bryant. On the complexity of VLSI implementations and graph representations of Boolean functions with application to integer multiplication. *IEEE Transaction on Computers*, 40(2):205–213, February 1991.
10. E.M. Clarke, O. Grumberg, and D.A. Peled. *Model Checking*. MIT Press, 2000.
11. R. Dechter and J. Pearl. Network-based heuristics for constraint-satisfaction problems. *Artificial Intelligence*, 34:1–38, 1987.
12. R. Diestel. *Graph Theory*. Number 173 in Graduate Texts in Mathematics. Springer, 2000.
13. E.A. Emerson and J.Y. Halpern. Sometimes and not never revisited: On the branching versus linear time. *Journal of the ACM*, 33(1):151–178, 1986.
14. E.C Freuder. Complexity of k-tree structured constraint satisfaction problems. In *Proc. AAAI-90*, pages 4–9, 1990.
15. G. Gottlob and R. Pichler. Hypergraphs in model checking: Acyclicity and hypertree-width versus clique-width. *SIAM Journal on Computing*, 33(2):351–378, 2004.
16. D. Harel, O. Kupferman, and M.Y. Vardi. On the complexity of verifying concurrent transition systems. *Information and Computation*, 173(2):143–161, 2002.
17. J. Huang and A. Darwiche. Using DPLL for efficient OBDD construction. In *Proc. 7th Int. Conf. on Theory and Applications of Satisfiability Testing (SAT 2004)*, 2004.
18. M. Jurdziński. Deciding the winner in partity games is in UP ∩ co-UP. *Information Processing Letters*, 68:119–124, 1998.
19. O. Kupferman, M.Y. Vardi, and P. Wolper. An automata-theoretic approach to branching-time model checking. *Journal of ACM*, 47(2):312–360, 2000.
20. K.L. McMillan. *Symbolic Model Checking*. Kluwer Academic Publishers, 1993.
21. R. Milner. An algebraic definition of simulation between programs. In *Proc. 2nd Int. Joint Conf. on Artif. Int.*, pages 481–489. British Computer Society, September 1971.
22. J. Obdržálek. Fast mu-calculus model checking when tree-width is bounded. In *CAV'03*, volume 2725 of *LNCS*, pages 80–92. Springer, 2003.
23. M.R. Prasad, P. Chong, and K. Keutzer. Why is ATPG easy? In *Proc. of 36th ACM/IEEE conference on Design automation*, pages 22–28. ACM Press, 1999.
24. A.N. Prior. *Past, Present, and Future*. Clarendon Press, Oxford, 1967.
25. N. Robertson and P.D. Seymour. Graph minors. i. excluding a forest. *Journal of Combinatorial Theory Series B*, 35:39–61, 1983.
26. N. Robertson and P.D. Seymour. Graph minors. ii. algorithmic aspects of treewidth. *Journal of Algorithms*, 7:309–322, 1986.
27. T. Schiex. A note on CSP graph parameters. Technical Report 1999/03, INRIA, 1999.
28. D.M. Thilikos, M.J. Serna, and H.L. Bodlaender. A polynomial time algorithm for the cutwidth of bounded degree graphs with small treewidth. In *ESA'01*, volume 2161 of *LNCS*, pages 380–390. Springer, 2001.
29. D. Wang, E.M. Clarke, Y. Zhu, and J. Kukula. Using cutwidth to improve symbolic simulation and boolean satisfiability. In *IEEE International High Level Design Validation and Test Workshop (HLDVT 2001)*, page 6, 2001.

Pushdown Module Checking

Laura Bozzelli, Aniello Murano, and Adriano Peron

Università di Napoli Federico II, Via Cintia, 80126 - Napoli, Italy

Abstract. *Model checking* is a useful method to verify automatically the correctness of a system with respect to a desired behavior, by checking whether a mathematical model of the system satisfies a formal specification of this behavior. Many systems of interest are open, in the sense that their behavior depends on the interaction with their environment. The model checking problem for finite–state open systems (called *module checking*) has been intensively studied in the literature. In this paper, we focus on *open pushdown systems* and we study the related model–checking problem (*pushdown module checking*, for short) with respect to properties expressed by *CTL* and *CTL** formulas. We show that pushdown module checking against *CTL* (resp., *CTL**) is 2EXPTIME-complete (resp., 3EXPTIME-complete). Moreover, we prove that for a fixed *CTL** formula, the problem is EXPTIME-complete.

1 Introduction

In the last decades significant results have been achieved in the area of formal design verification of reactive systems. In particular, a meaningful contribution has been given by algorithmic methods developed in the context of *model-checking* ([CE81, QS81, VW86]). In this verification method, the behaviour of a system, formally described by a mathematical model, is checked against a behavioural constraint specified by a formula in a suitable temporal logic, which enforces either a linear model of time (formulas are interpreted over linear sequences corresponding to single computations of the system) or a branching model of time (formulas are interpreted over infinite trees, which describe all the possible computations of the system). Traditionally, model checking is applied to finite-state systems, typically modelled by labelled state-transition graphs.

In system modelling, we distinguish between *closed* and *open* systems. For a closed system, the behavior is completely determined by the state of the system. For an open system, the behaviour is affected both by its internal state and by the ongoing interaction with its environment. Thus, while in a closed system all the nondeterministic choices are internal, and resolved by the system, in an open system there are also external nondeterministic choices, which are resolved by the environment [Hoa85]. Model checking algorithms used for the verification of closed systems are not appropriate for the verification of open systems. In the latter case, we should check the system with respect to arbitrary environments and should take into account uncertainty regarding the environment.

In [KVW01], Kupferman, Vardi, and Wolper extend model checking from closed finite–state systems to open finite-state systems. In such a framework, the

G. Sutcliffe and A. Voronkov (Eds.): LPAR 2005, LNAI 3835, pp. 504–518, 2005.

open finite-state system is described by a labelled state-transition graph called *module* whose set of states is partitioned into a set of *system states* (where the system makes a transition) and a set of *environment states* (where the environment makes a transition). The problem of model checking a module (called *module checking*) has two inputs: a module M and a temporal formula ψ. The idea is that an open system should satisfy a specification ψ no matter how the environment behaves. Let us consider the unwinding of M into an infinite tree, say T_M. Checking whether T_M satisfies ψ is the usual *model-checking problem* [CE81, QS81]. On the other hand, for an open system, T_M describes the interaction of the system with a maximal environment, i.e. an environment that enables all the external nondeterministic choices. In order to take into account all the possible behaviours of the environment, we have to consider all the trees T obtained from T_M by pruning subtrees whose root is a successor of an environment state (pruning these subtrees correspond to disable possible environment choices). Therefore, a module M satisfies ψ if all these trees T satisfy ψ.

Note that for the linear-time paradigm, module checking coincides with the usual model checking, since for linear temporal formulas ψ we require that all the possible interactions of the system with its environment (corresponding to all computations of M, i.e. to all possible full-paths in T_M) have to satisfy ψ. Therefore, while the complexity of model checking for closed and open finite–state systems coincide using linear time logics, when using branching time logics, model checking for open finite–state systems is much harder than model checking for closed finite–state systems. In particular, it is proved in [KVW01], that the problem is EXPTIME–complete for specifications in *CTL* and 2EXPTIME–complete for specifications in *CTL**. Moreover, the complexity of this problem in terms of the size of the module is PTIME-complete.

Recently, the investigation of model-checking techniques has been extended to infinite-state systems. An active field of research is model-checking of closed infinite-state sequential systems. These are systems in which each state carries a finite, but unbounded, amount of information e.g. a pushdown store. The origin of this research is the result of Muller and Schupp that the monadic second-order theory of *context-free graphs* is decidable [MS85]. Concerning *pushdown systems*, Walukiewicz [Wal96] has shown that model checking these systems with respect to *modal μ-calculus* is EXPTIME-complete. Even for a fixed formula in the *alternation-free* modal μ-calculus, the problem is EXPTIME-hard in the size of the pushdown system. The problem remains EXPTIME-complete also for the logic *CTL* [Wal00], which corresponds to a fragment of the alternation-free modal μ-calculus. However, the exact complexity in the size of the system (for a fixed *CTL* formula) is an open problem: it lies somewhere between PSPACE and EXPTIME [BEM97]. To the best of our knowledge, the pushdown model checking problem for *CTL** has not been investigated so far. However, since *CTL** formulas can be translated to modal μ-calculus with an exponential blow-up [BC96], we obtain that the problem is, at worst, in 2EXPTIME. The situation is quite different for linear-time logics. Model-checking with *LTL* and the *linear-time μ-calculus* is

EXPTIME-complete [BEM97]. However, the problem is polynomial in the size of the pushdown system.

In the literature, verification of open systems has been also formulated as two-players games. For pushdown systems, games with parity winning conditions are known to be decidable [Wal96]. More recently, in [LMS04], it is shown that pushdown games against *LTL* specifications are 3EXPTIME-complete.

This paper contributes to the investigation of model checking of open infinite-state systems by introducing *Open Pushdown systems (OPD)* and considering model checking with respect to *CTL* and *CTL**. An *OPD* is a pushdown system augmented with finite information that allow to partition the set of configurations (in accordance with the control state and the symbol on the top of the stack) into a set of *system configurations* and a set of *environment configurations*.

As an example of closed and open pushdown systems, we can consider two drink-dispensing machines (obtained as an extension of the machines defined in [Hoa85]). The first machine repeatedly boils water for a while, makes an internal nondeterministic choice and serves either tea or coffee, with the additional constraint that coffee can be served only if the number of coffees served up to that time is smaller than that of teas served. Such a machine can be modelled as a closed pushdown system (the stack is used to guarantee the inequality between served coffees and teas). The second machine repeatedly boils water for a while, asks the environment to make a choice between coffee and tea, and *deterministically* serves a drink according to the external choice, with the additional constraint that coffee can be served only if the number of coffees served up to that time is smaller than that of teas served. Such a machine can be modelled as an open pushdown system. Both machines can be represented by a pushdown system that induces the same infinite tree of possible executions, nevertheless, while the behavior of the first machine depends on internal choices solely, the behavior of the second machine depends also on the interaction with its environment. Thus, for instance, for the first machine, it is always possible to eventually serve coffee. On the contrary, for the second machine, this does not hold. Indeed, if the environment always chooses tea, the second machine will never serve coffee.

We study module checking of (infinite–state) modules induced by *OPD* w.r.t. the branching-time logics *CTL* and *CTL**. As in the case of finite-state systems, pushdown module checking is much harder than pushdown model checking for both *CTL* and *CTL**. Indeed, we show that pushdown module checking is 2EXPTIME-complete for *CTL* and 3EXPTIME-complete for *CTL**. We also show that for *CTL**, the complexity of pushdown module checking in terms of the size of the given *OPD* is EXPTIME-complete. For the upper bounds of the complexity results, we exploit the standard automata-theoretic approach. In particular, for *CTL* (resp., *CTL**) we propose an exponential time (resp., a double-exponential time) reduction to the emptiness problem of nondeterministic pushdown tree automata with parity acceptance conditions. The latter problem is known to be decidable in exponential time [KPV02]. Finally, the lower bound for *CTL* (resp., *CTL**) is shown by a technically non-trivial reduction from the word problem for EXPSPACE–bounded (resp., 2EXPSPACE–bounded) alternating Turing Machines.

2   Preliminaries

2.1   Module Checking for Branching Temporal Logics

In this subsection we define the module checking problem for *CTL* and *CTL**
[KVW01]. First, we recall syntax and semantics of *CTL* and *CTL**.

Let $\mathbb{N}$ be the set of positive integers. A *tree* T is a prefix closed subset of $\mathbb{N}^*$.
The elements of T are called *nodes* and the empty word ε is the *root* of T. For
$x \in T$, the set of *children* of x (in T) is $children(T, x) = \{x \cdot i \in T \mid i \in \mathbb{N}\}$.
For $k \geq 1$, the (complete) k-ary tree is the tree $\{1, \ldots, k\}^*$. For $x, y \in \mathbb{N}^*$,
we write $x \prec y$ to mean that x is a proper prefix of y. For $x \in T$, a (full)
path π of T from x is a *minimal* set $\pi \subseteq T$ such that $x \in \pi$ and for each
$y \in \pi$ such that $children(T, y) \neq \emptyset$, there is exactly one node in $children(T, y)$
belonging to π. For $y \in \pi$, we denote by π^y the (suffix) path of T from y given
by $\{z \in \pi \mid y \preceq z\}$. For an alphabet Σ, a Σ-*labelled tree* is a pair $\langle T, V \rangle$ where
T is a tree and $V : T \to \Sigma$ maps each node of T to a symbol in Σ.

The logic *CTL** is a branching–time temporal logic [EH86], where a path
quantifier, E ("for some path") or A ("for all paths"), can be followed by an
arbitrary linear-time formula, allowing boolean combinations and nesting, over
the usual linear temporal operators X ("next"), $\mathcal{U}$ ("until"), F ("eventually"),
and G ("always"). There are two types of formulas in *CTL**: *state formulas*,
whose satisfaction is related to a specific state (or node of a labelled tree), and
path formulas, whose satisfaction is related to a specific path. Formally, for a
finite set AP of proposition names, the class of state formulas φ and the class
of path formulas θ are defined by the following syntax:

$$\varphi := p \mid \neg \varphi \mid \varphi \wedge \varphi \mid A\,\theta \mid E\,\theta$$
$$\theta := \varphi \mid \neg \theta \mid \theta \wedge \theta \mid X\theta \mid \theta\,\mathcal{U}\,\theta$$

where $p \in AP$. The set of state formulas φ forms the language *CTL**. The other
operators can be introduced as abbreviations in the usual way: for instance, $F\theta$
abbreviates $true\,\mathcal{U}\,\theta$ and $G\theta$ abbreviates $\neg F \neg \theta$.

The *Computation Tree Logic CTL* [CE81] is a restricted subset of *CTL**,
obtained restricting the syntax of path formulas θ as follows: $\theta := X\varphi \mid \varphi\,\mathcal{U}\,\varphi$.
This means that X and $\mathcal{U}$ must be immediately preceded by a path quantifier.

We define the semantics of *CTL** (and its fragment *CTL*) with respect to
2^{AP}-labelled trees $\langle T, V \rangle$. Let $x \in T$ and $\pi \subseteq T$ be a path from x. For a state
(resp., path) formula φ (resp., θ), the satisfaction relation $(\langle T, V \rangle, x) \models \varphi$ (resp.,
$(\langle T, V \rangle, \pi) \models \theta$), meaning that φ (resp., θ) holds at node x (resp., holds along
path π) in $\langle T, V \rangle$, is defined by induction. The clauses for proposition letters,
negation, and conjunction are standard. For the other constructs we have:

- $(\langle T, V \rangle, x) \models A\,\theta$ iff for each path π in T from x, $(\langle T, V \rangle, \pi) \models \theta$;
- $(\langle T, V \rangle, x) \models E\,\theta$ iff there exists a path π from x such that $(\langle T, V \rangle, \pi) \models \theta$;
- $(\langle T, V \rangle, \pi) \models \varphi$ (where π is a path from x) iff $(\langle T, V \rangle, x) \models \varphi$;
- $(\langle T, V \rangle, \pi) \models X\theta$ iff $\pi \setminus \{x\} \neq \emptyset$ and $(\langle T, V \rangle, \pi \setminus \{x\}) \models \theta$;[1]

---

[1] Note that $\pi \setminus \{x\}$ is a path starting from the unique child of x in π.

- $(\langle T, V \rangle, \pi) \models \theta_1 \, \mathcal{U} \, \theta_2$ iff there exists $y \in \pi$ such that $(\langle T, V \rangle, \pi^y) \models \theta_2$ and $(\langle T, V \rangle, \pi^z) \models \theta_1$ for all $z \in \pi$ such that $z \prec y$.

Given a CTL^* (state) formula φ, we say that $\langle T, V \rangle$ satisfies φ if $(\langle T, V \rangle, \varepsilon) \models \varphi$.

In this paper we consider open systems, i.e. systems that interact with their environment and whose behavior depends on this interaction. The (global) behavior of such a system is described by an *open* Kripke structure (called also *module* [KVW01]) $M = \langle AP, W_s, W_e, R, w_0, \mu \rangle$ where AP is a finite set of atomic propositions, $W_s \cup W_e$ is a countable set of (global) states partitioned into a set W_s of *system* states and a set W_e of *environment* states (we use W to denote $W_s \cup W_e$), $R \subseteq W \times W$ is a (global) transition relation, $w_0 \in W$ is an initial state, and $\mu : W \to 2^{AP}$ maps each state w to the set of atomic propositions that hold in w. For $(w, w') \in R$, we say that w' is a successor of w. We assume that the states in M are ordered and the number of successors of each state w, denoted by $bd(w)$, is finite. For each state $w \in W$, we denote by $succ(w)$ the ordered tuple (possibly empty) of w's successors. We say that a state w is *terminal* if it has no successor. When the module M is in a non-terminal system state w_s, then all the states in $succ(w_s)$ are possible next states. On the other hand, when M is in a non-terminal environment state w_e, then the possible next states (that are in $succ(w_e)$) depend on the current environment. Since the behavior of the environment is not predictable, we have to consider all the possible sub-tuples of $succ(w_e)$. The only constraint, since we consider environments that cannot block the system, is that not all the transitions from w_e are disabled.

The set of all (maximal) computations of M starting from the initial state w_0 is described by a W-labelled tree $\langle T_M, V_M \rangle$, called *computation tree*, which is obtained by unwinding M in the usual way. The problem of deciding, for a given branching-time formula ψ over AP, whether $\langle T_M, \mu \circ V_M \rangle$ satisfies ψ, denoted $M \models \psi$, is the usual *model-checking problem* [CE81, QS81]. On the other hand, for an open system, $\langle T_M, V_M \rangle$ corresponds to a very specific environment, i.e. a maximal environment that never restricts the set of its next states. Therefore, when we examine a branching-time specification ψ w.r.t. a module M, ψ should hold not only in $\langle T_M, V_M \rangle$, but in all the trees obtained by pruning from $\langle T_M, V_M \rangle$ subtrees whose root is a child (successor) of a node corresponding to an environment state. The set of these trees is denoted by $exec(M)$, and is formally defined as follows. $\langle T, V \rangle \in exec(M)$ iff $V(\varepsilon) = w_0$ and the following holds:

- For $x \in T$ with $V(x) = w \in W_s$ and $succ(w) = \langle w_1, \ldots, w_n \rangle$, it holds that $children(T, x) = \{x \cdot 1, \ldots, x \cdot n\}$ and for $1 \leq i \leq n$, $V(x \cdot i) = w_i$.
- For $x \in T$ with $V(x) = w \in W_e$ and $succ(w) = \langle w_1, \ldots, w_n \rangle$, there exists a sub-tuple $\langle w_{i_1}, \ldots, w_{i_p} \rangle$ of $succ(w)$ such that $p \geq 1$ if $succ(w)$ is not empty, $children(T, x) = \{x \cdot i_1, \ldots, x \cdot i_p\}$ and for $1 \leq j \leq p$, $V(x \cdot i_j) = w_{i_j}$.

Intuitively, each tree in $exec(M)$ corresponds to a different behavior of the environment. In the following, we consider the trees in $exec(M)$ as 2^{AP}-labelled trees, i.e. taking the label of a node x to be $\mu(V(x))$.

For a module M and a CTL^* (resp., CTL) formula ψ, we say that M satisfies ψ, denoted $M \models_r \psi$, if all the trees in $exec(M)$ satisfy ψ. The problem of deciding whether M satisfies ψ is called *module checking* [KVW01]. Note that $M \models_r \psi$ implies $M \models \psi$ (since $\langle T_M, V_M \rangle \in exec(M)$), but the converse in general does not hold. Also, note that $M \not\models_r \psi$ is *not* equivalent to $M \models_r \neg\psi$. Indeed, $M \not\models_r \psi$ just states that there is some tree $\langle T, V \rangle \in exec(M)$ satisfying $\neg\psi$.

2.2 Pushdown Module Checking

In this paper we consider Modules induced by *Open Pushdown Systems* (*OPD*, for short), i.e., Pushdown systems where the set of configurations is partitioned (in accordance with the control state and the symbol on the top of the stack) in a set of *environment* configurations and a set of *system* configurations.

An *OPD* is a tuple $\mathcal{S} = \langle AP, \Gamma, P, p_0, \alpha_0, \Delta, L, Env \rangle$, where AP is a finite set of propositions, Γ is a finite stack alphabet, P is a finite set of (control) states, $p_0 \in P$ is an initial state, $\alpha_0 \in \Gamma^* \cdot \gamma_0$ is an initial stack content (where $\gamma_0 \notin \Gamma$ is the *stack bottom symbol*), $\Delta \subseteq (P \times (\Gamma \cup \{\gamma_0\})) \times (P \times \Gamma^*)$ is a finite set of transitions, $L : P \times (\Gamma \cup \{\gamma_0\}) \to 2^{AP}$ is a labelling function, and $Env \subseteq P \times (\Gamma \cup \{\gamma_0\})$ is used to specify the set of *environment configurations*. A *configuration* is a pair (p, α) where $p \in P$ is a control state and $\alpha \in \Gamma^* \cdot \gamma_0$ is a stack content. We assume that the set $P \times \Gamma^*$ is ordered and for each $(p, A) \in P \times (\Gamma \cup \{\gamma_0\})$, we denote by $next_\mathcal{S}(p, A)$ the ordered tuple (possibly empty) of the pairs (q, β) such that $((p, A), (q, \beta)) \in \Delta$.

The size $|\mathcal{S}|$ of $\mathcal{S}$ is $|P| + |\Gamma| + |\alpha_0| + |\Delta|$, with $|\Delta| = \sum_{((p,A),(q,\beta)) \in \Delta} |\beta|$.

An *OPD* $\mathcal{S}$ induces a module $M_\mathcal{S} = \langle AP, W_s, W_e, R, w_0, \mu \rangle$, where:

- $W_s \cup W_e = P \times \Gamma^* \cdot \gamma_0$ is the set of pushdown configurations;
- W_e is the set of configurations $(p, A \cdot \alpha)$ such that $(p, A) \in Env$;
- $w_0 = (p_0, \alpha_0)$;
- $((p, A \cdot \alpha), (q, \beta)) \in R$ iff there is $((p, A), (q, \beta')) \in \Delta$ such that either $A \in \Gamma$ and $\beta = \beta' \cdot \alpha$, or $A = \gamma_0$ (in this case $\alpha = \varepsilon$) and $\beta = \beta' \cdot \gamma_0$ (note that every transition that removes the bottom symbol γ_0 also pushes it back);
- For all $(p, A \cdot \beta) \in W_s \cup W_e$, $\mu(p, A \cdot \beta) = L(p, A)$.

The *pushdown module checking* problem for *CTL* (resp., *CTL**) is to decide, for a given *OPD* S and a *CTL* (resp., *CTL**) formula ψ, whether $M_\mathcal{S} \models_r \psi$.

3 Tree Automata

In order to solve the pushdown module checking problem for *CTL* and *CTL**, we use an automata theoretic approach; in particular, we exploit the formalisms of *Nondeterministic (finite–state) Tree Automata* (*NTA* for short) [Buc62] and *Nondeterministic Pushdown Tree Automata* (*PD-NTA* for short) [KPV02].

Nondeterministic (finite–state) Tree Automata (*NTA*). Here we describe *NTA* over (complete) k-ary trees for a given $k \geq 1$. Formally, an *NTA* is a tuple $\mathcal{A} = \langle \Sigma, Q, q_0, \delta, F \rangle$, where Σ is a finite input alphabet, Q is a finite set of states, $q_0 \in Q$ is an initial state, $\delta : Q \times \Sigma \to 2^{Q^k}$ is a transition function, and F is an acceptance condition. We consider here *Büchi* and *parity* acceptance conditions [Buc62, EJ91]. In the case of a parity condition, $F = \{F_1, \ldots, F_m\}$ is a finite sequence of subsets of Q, where $F_1 \subseteq F_2 \subseteq \ldots \subseteq F_m = Q$ (m is called the index of $\mathcal{A}$). In the case of a Büchi condition, $F \subseteq Q$.

A run of $\mathcal{A}$ on a Σ-labelled k-ary tree $\langle T, V \rangle$ (where $T = \{1, \ldots, k\}^*$) is a Q-labelled tree $\langle T, r \rangle$ such that $r(\varepsilon) = q_0$ and for each $x \in T$, we have that $\langle r(x \cdot 1), \ldots, r(x \cdot k) \rangle \in \delta(r(x), V(x))$. For a path $\pi \subseteq T$, let $inf_r(\pi) \subseteq Q$ be the set of states that appear as the labels of infinitely many nodes in π. For a parity acceptance condition $F = \{F_1, \ldots, F_m\}$, π is *accepting* if there is an *even* $1 \leq i \leq m$ such that $inf_r(\pi) \cap F_i \neq \emptyset$ and for all $j < i$, $inf_r(\pi) \cap F_j = \emptyset$. For a Büchi condition $F \subseteq Q$, π is *accepting* if $inf_r(\pi) \cap F \neq \emptyset$. A run $\langle T, r \rangle$ is *accepting* if all its paths are accepting. The automaton $\mathcal{A}$ accepts an input tree $\langle T, V \rangle$ iff there is an accepting run of $\mathcal{A}$ over $\langle T, V \rangle$. The language of $\mathcal{A}$, denoted $\mathcal{L}(\mathcal{A})$, is the set of Σ-labelled (complete) k-ary trees accepted by $\mathcal{A}$.

The *size* $|\mathcal{A}|$ of an *NTA* $\mathcal{A}$ is $|Q| + |\delta| + |F|$ with $|\delta| = \sum_{(q,\sigma) \in Q \times \Sigma} |\delta(q, \sigma)|$.

It is well-known that formulas of *CTL* and *CTL** can be translated to tree automata (accepting the models of the given formula). In particular, we are interested in optimal translations to parity *NTA*. Concerning a *CTL* (resp., *CTL**) formula ψ, given $k \geq 1$, first we build according to [KVW00] a Büchi (resp., parity[2]) *alternating* tree automata $\mathcal{A}$ with $O(|\psi|)$ (resp., $O(2^{|\psi|})$) states and size $O(k \cdot |\psi|)$ (resp., size $O(k \cdot 2^{|\psi|})$ and index $O(|\psi|)$) accepting exactly the complete k-ary trees satisfying ψ. Then, according to [Var98], we can translate $\mathcal{A}$ into an equivalent parity *NTA* whose size is $O(k \cdot 2^{O(|\psi| \log |\psi|)})$ (resp., $O(k \cdot 2^{2^{O(|\psi|)}})$) and whose index is $O(|\psi|)$ (resp., $O(2^{|\psi|})$).

Lemma 1 ([KVW00, Var98]). *Given a CTL (resp., CTL^*) formula ψ over AP and $k \geq 1$, we can construct a parity NTA of size $O(k \cdot 2^{O(|\psi| \log |\psi|)})$ (resp., $O(k \cdot 2^{2^{O(|\psi|)}})$) and index $O(|\psi|)$ (resp., $O(2^{|\psi|})$) that accepts exactly the set of 2^{AP}-labelled complete k-ary trees that satisfy ψ.*

Remark 1. *Vardi in [Var98] gives a translation from* (two-way) *alternating parity tree automata $\mathcal{A}$ to parity NTA $\mathcal{A}'$. Note that the size of the parity NTA $\mathcal{A}'$ is exponential in k. This depends on the fact that Vardi considers arbitrary memoryless strategies of the form $\tau : \{1, \ldots, k\}^* \to 2^{Q \times \{1, \ldots, k\} \times Q}$ where Q is the set of states of $\mathcal{A}$. On the other hand, if $\mathcal{A}$ corresponds to a CTL or CTL* formula, then any formula of $\mathcal{B}^+(\{1, \ldots, k\} \times Q)$ occurring in the transition function of $\mathcal{A}$ (see [KVW00, Var98] for the definition of the transition function of an alternating tree automata) is a positive boolean combination of sub-formulas either of the form $\bigwedge_{i=1}^{i=k}(i, q)$ or of the form $\bigvee_{i=1}^{i=k}(i, q)$ for some $q \in Q$. This means that we can limit ourselves to consider strategies τ such that the following holds for each $x \in \{1, \ldots, k\}^*$ and $(q, i, p) \in \tau(x)$: either $(q, j, p) \notin \tau(x)$ for each $j \neq i$ or $(q, j, p) \in \tau(x)$ for each $1 \leq j \leq k$. This simple observation applied to the algorithm in [Var98] provides the desired complexity linear in k. This is important, since, as we will see in the next section, k depends on the size of the given*

---

[2] [KVW00] gives a translation from CTL^* to *Hesitant alternating tree automata* which are a special case of parity alternating tree automata.

pushdown system. Moreover, note that classical translations [VW86, EJ88] from CTL and CTL* to NTA lead to NTA whose sizes are exponential in k.

Nondeterministic Pushdown Tree Automata (*PD-NTA*). Here we describe *PD-NTA* (without ε-transitions) over complete k-ary labelled trees. Formally, an *PD-NTA* is a tuple $\mathcal{P} = \langle \Sigma, \Gamma, P, p_0, \alpha_0, \rho, F \rangle$, where Σ is a finite input alphabet, Γ is a finite stack alphabet, P is a finite set of (control) states, $p_0 \in P$ is an initial state, $\alpha_0 \in \Gamma^* \cdot \gamma_0$ is an initial stack content, $\rho : P \times \Sigma \times (\Gamma \cup \{\gamma_0\}) \rightarrow 2^{(P \times \Gamma^*)^k}$ is a transition function, and F is an acceptance condition over P. Intuitively, when the automaton is in state p, reading an input node x labelled by $\sigma \in \Sigma$, and the stack contains a word $A \cdot \alpha$ in $\Gamma^*.\gamma_0$, then the automaton chooses a tuple $\langle (p_1, \beta_1), \ldots, (p_k, \beta_k) \rangle \in \rho(p, \sigma, A)$ and splits in k copies such that for each $1 \leq i \leq k$, a copy in state p_i, and stack content obtained by removing A and pushing β_i, is sent to the node $x \cdot i$ in the input tree.

A run of the *PD-NTA* $\mathcal{P}$ on a Σ-labelled k-ary tree $\langle T, V \rangle$ (with $T = \{1, \ldots, k\}^*$) is a $(P \times \Gamma^*.\gamma_0)$-labelled tree $\langle T, r \rangle$ such that $r(\varepsilon) = (p_0, \alpha_0)$ and for each $x \in T$ with $r(x) = (p, A \cdot \alpha)$, there is $\langle (p_1, \beta_1), \ldots, (p_k, \beta_k) \rangle \in \rho(p, V(x), A)$ such that for all $1 \leq i \leq k$, $r(x \cdot i) = (p_i, \beta_i \cdot \alpha)$ if $A \neq \gamma_0$, and $r(x \cdot i) = (p_i, \beta_i \cdot \gamma_0)$ otherwise (note that in this case $\alpha = \varepsilon$).

As with *NTA*, we consider *Büchi* and *parity* acceptance conditions over P. The notion of *accepting* path π is defined as for *NTA* with $inf_r(\pi)$ defined as follows: $inf_r(\pi) \subseteq P$ is the set such that $p \in inf_r(\pi)$ iff there are infinitely many $x \in \pi$ for which $r(x) \in \{p\} \times \Gamma^* \cdot \gamma_0$. A run $\langle T, r \rangle$ is *accepting* if every path $\pi \subseteq T$ is accepting. The *PD-NTA* $\mathcal{P}$ accepts an input tree $\langle T, V \rangle$ iff there is an accepting run of $\mathcal{P}$ over $\langle T, V \rangle$. The language of $\mathcal{P}$, denoted $\mathcal{L}(\mathcal{P})$, contains all trees accepted by $\mathcal{P}$. The *emptiness* problem for *PD-NTA* is to decide, for a given *PD-NTA* $\mathcal{P}$, whether $\mathcal{L}(\mathcal{P}) = \emptyset$.

Proposition 1 ([KPV02]). *The emptiness problem for a parity PD-NTA of index m with n states, and transition function ρ can be solved in time exponential in $n \cdot m \cdot |\rho|$ with $|\rho| = \sum_{\langle (p_1, \beta_1), \ldots, (p_k, \beta_k) \rangle \in \rho(p, \sigma, A)} |\beta_1| + \ldots + |\beta_k|$.*

PD-NTA are closed under intersection with *NTA*.

Proposition 2. *For a Büchi PD-NTA $\mathcal{P} = \langle \Sigma, \Gamma, P, p_0, \alpha_0, \rho, F \rangle$ with $F = P$ and a parity NTA $\mathcal{A} = \langle \Sigma, Q, q_0, \delta, F' \rangle$, there is a parity PD-NTA $\mathcal{P}'$ such that $\mathcal{L}(\mathcal{P}') = \mathcal{L}(\mathcal{P}) \cap \mathcal{L}(\mathcal{A})$. Moreover, $\mathcal{P}'$ has $|P| \cdot |Q|$ states, the same index of $\mathcal{A}$, and the size of the transition relation is bounded by $|\rho| \cdot |\delta|$.*

4 Deciding Pushdown Module Checking

In this section we solve Pushdown Module Checking for *CTL* and *CTL**.

4.1 Upper Bounds

We fix an *OPD* $\mathcal{S} = \langle AP, \Gamma, P, p_0, \alpha_0, \Delta, L, Env \rangle$ and a formula ψ. We decide pushdown module-checking for $\mathcal{S}$ against ψ using an automata-theoretic approach: we construct a parity *PD-NTA* $\mathcal{P}_{\mathcal{S} \times \neg \psi}$ as the intersection of two tree automata. Essentially, the first automaton, denoted by $\mathcal{P}_S$, is a Büchi *PD-NTA* that accepts the trees in $exec(M_S)$, and the second automaton is a parity *NTA* that accepts the set of trees that do not satisfy ψ. Thus, $M_S \models_r \psi$ iff $\mathcal{L}(\mathcal{P}_{S \times \neg \psi})$ is empty. The construction proposed here follows (and extends) that given in [KVW01] for solving the module-checking problem for finite-state open systems. The extensions concern the handling of terminal states and the use of pushdown tree automata.

In order to define $\mathcal{P}_S$, we consider an equivalent representation of $exec(M_S)$ by complete k-ary trees with $k = max\{bd(w) \mid w \in W_s \cup W_e\}$ (note that for a pushdown system $\mathcal{S}$, k is finite and can be trivially computed from the transition relation Δ of $\mathcal{S}$). Recall that each tree in $exec(M_S)$ is a 2^{AP}-labelled tree that is obtained from $\langle T_{M_S}, V_{M_S} \rangle$ by suitably pruning some of its subtrees. We can encode the tree $\langle T_{M_S}, V_{M_S} \rangle$ as a $2^{AP \cup \{t\}} \cup \{\bot\}$-labelled complete k-ary tree (where $\bot$ and t are fresh proposition names not belonging to AP) in the following way: first, we add the proposition t to the label of all leaf nodes (corresponding to terminal global states) of the tree T_{M_S}; second, for each node $x \in T_{M_S}$ with p children $x \cdot 1, \ldots, x \cdot p$ (note that $0 \leq p \leq k$), we add the children $x \cdot (p+1), \ldots, x \cdot k$ and label these new nodes with $\bot$; finally, for each node x labelled by $\bot$ we add recursively k-children labelled by $\bot$. Let $\langle \{1, \ldots, k\}^*, V' \rangle$ be the tree thus obtained. Then, we can encode a tree $\langle T, V \rangle \in exec(M_S)$ as the $2^{AP \cup \{t\}} \cup \{\bot\}$-labelled complete k-ary tree obtained from $\langle \{1, \ldots, k\}^*, V' \rangle$ preserving all the labels of nodes of $\langle \{1, \ldots, k\}^*, V' \rangle$ that either are labelled by $\bot$ or belong to T, and replacing all the labels of nodes (together with the labels of the corresponding subtrees) pruned in $\langle T, V \rangle$ with the label $\bot$. In this way, all the trees in $exec(M_S)$ have the same structure (they all coincide with $\{1, \ldots, k\}^*$), and they differ only in their labelling. Thus, the proposition $\bot$ is used to denote both "disabled" states and "completion" states. Moreover, since we consider environments that do not block the system, for each node associated with an enabled non-terminal environment state, at least one successor is not labelled by $\bot$. Let us denote by $\widehat{exec}(M_S)$ the set of all $2^{AP \cup \{t\}} \cup \{\bot\}$-labelled k-ary trees obtained from $\langle \{1, \ldots, k\}^*, V' \rangle$ in the above described manner. The Büchi *PD-NTA* $\mathcal{P}_S = \langle \Sigma, \Gamma, P', (p_0, \top), \alpha_0, \rho, P' \rangle$, which accepts all and only the trees in $\widehat{exec}(M_S)$, is defined as follows:

- $\Sigma = 2^{AP \cup \{t\}} \cup \{\bot\}$;
- $P' = P \times \{\bot, \top, \vdash\}$. From (control) states of the form $(p, \bot)$, $\mathcal{P}_S$ can read only the letter $\bot$, from states of the form $(p, \top)$, it can read only letters in $2^{AP \cup \{t\}}$. Finally, when $\mathcal{P}_S$ is in state $(p, \vdash)$, then it can read both letters in $2^{AP \cup \{t\}}$ and the letter $\bot$. In this last case, it is left to the environment to decide whether the transition to a configuration of the form $((p, \vdash), \alpha)$ is enabled. The three types of (control) states are used to ensure that the environment enables all transitions from enabled system configurations, enables at least one transition from each enabled non-terminal environment configuration, and disables transitions from disabled configurations.
- The transition function $\rho : P' \times \Sigma \times (\Gamma \cup \{\gamma_0\}) \to 2^{(P' \times \Gamma)^k}$ is defined as follows. Let $p \in P$ and $A \in \Gamma \cup \{\gamma_0\}$ with $next_S(p, A) = \langle (p_1, \beta_1), \ldots, (p_d, \beta_d) \rangle$

(where $0 \le d \le k$). Then, for $m \in \{\top, \vdash, \bot\}$ and $\sigma \in \Sigma$, $\rho((p,m), \sigma, A) \ne \emptyset$ *iff* one of the following holds (where $\alpha = A$ if $A \in \Gamma$, and $\alpha = \varepsilon$ otherwise):

- $\sigma = \bot$ and $m \in \{\vdash, \bot\}$. In this case we have

$$\rho((p,m), \bot, A) = \{\langle \underbrace{((p,\bot), \alpha), \ldots, ((p,\bot), \alpha)}_{k \ pairs} \rangle\}$$

That is, $\rho((p,m), \bot, A)$ contains exactly one k-tuple. In this case all the successors of the current configuration are disabled.

- $\sigma \ne \bot$, $m \in \{\vdash, \top\}$, and $next_S(p, A)$ is empty (i.e., $d = 0$). In this case $\sigma = L(p, A) \cup \{t\}$ (i.e., the current configuration is terminal) and

$$\rho((p,m), L(p, A) \cup \{t\}, A) = \{\langle ((p,\bot), \alpha), \ldots, ((p,\bot), \alpha) \rangle\}$$

- $\sigma \ne \bot$, $(p, A) \notin Env$, $m \in \{\vdash, \top\}$, and $next_S(p, A)$ is *not* empty (i.e., $d \ge 1$). In this case $\sigma = L(p, A)$ and $\rho((p,m), L(p, A), A)$ is given by

$$\{\langle ((p_1, \top), \beta_1), \ldots, ((p_d, \top), \beta_d), \underbrace{((p,\bot), \alpha), \ldots, ((p,\bot), \alpha)}_{k-d \ pairs} \rangle\}$$

- $\sigma \ne \bot$, $(p, A) \in Env$, $m \in \{\vdash, \top\}$, and $next_S(p, A)$ is *not* empty (i.e., $d \ge 1$). In this case $\sigma = L(p, A)$ and $\rho((p,m), L(p, A), A)$ is given by

$$\{ \langle ((p_1, \top), \beta_1), ((p_2, \vdash), \beta_1), \ldots, ((p_d, \vdash), \beta_d), ((p,\bot), \alpha), \ldots, ((p,\bot), \alpha) \rangle,$$
$$\langle ((p_1, \vdash), \beta_1), ((p_2, \top), \beta_1), \ldots, ((p_d, \vdash), \beta_d), ((p,\bot), \alpha), \ldots, ((p,\bot), \alpha) \rangle,$$
$$\vdots$$
$$\langle ((p_1, \vdash), \beta_1), ((p_2, \vdash), \beta_1), \ldots, ((p_d, \top), \beta_d), ((p,\bot), \alpha), \ldots, ((p,\bot), \alpha) \rangle \}.$$

That is, $\rho((p,m), L(p, A), A)$ contains d k-tuples. When the automaton proceeds according to the ith tuple, the environment can disable the transitions to all successors of the current configuration, except the transition associated with the pair (p_i, β_i), which must be enabled.

Note that $\mathcal{P}_S$ has $3 \cdot |P|$ states, and $|\rho|$ is bounded by $k(|P| \cdot |\Gamma| + |\Delta|)$. Assuming that $|P| \cdot |\Gamma| \le |\Delta|$, we have that $|\rho| \le k \cdot |\Delta|$.

We recall that a node labelled by $\bot$ stands for a node that actually does not exist. Thus, we have to take this into account when we interpret CTL^* or CTL formulas over trees $\langle T, V \rangle \in \widehat{exec}(M_S)$ (where $T = \{1, \ldots, k\}^*$). This means that we have to consider only the paths in $\langle T, V \rangle$ (that we call "legal" paths) that either never visit a node labelled by $\bot$ or contain a *terminal* node (i.e. a node labelled by t). Note that a path is *not* "legal" iff it satisfies the formula $\neg t \, \mathcal{U} \, \bot$. In order to achieve this, as in [KVW01] we define a function $f : CTL^*$ formulas $\rightarrow CTL^*$ formulas such that $f(\varphi)$ restricts path quantification to only "legal" paths (the function f we consider extends that given in [KVW01], since we have to consider also paths that lead to terminal configurations). The function f is inductively defined as follows:

- $f(p) = p$ for any proposition $p \in AP$;
- $f(\neg \varphi) = \neg f(\varphi)$;
- $f(\varphi_1 \wedge \varphi_2) = f(\varphi_1) \wedge f(\varphi_2)$;

- $f(E\varphi) = E((G\neg\bot) \wedge f(\varphi)) \vee E((F\ t) \wedge f(\varphi));$
- $f(A\varphi) = A((\neg t\ \mathcal{U}\ \bot) \vee f(\varphi));$
- $f(X\varphi) = X(f(\varphi) \wedge \neg\bot);$
- $f(\varphi_1\ \mathcal{U}\ \varphi_2) = (f(\varphi_1) \wedge \neg\bot)\ \mathcal{U}\ (f(\varphi_2) \wedge \neg\bot).$

When φ is a *CTL* formula, the formula $f(\varphi)$ is not necessarily a *CTL* formula, but it has a restricted syntax: its path formulas have either a single linear-time operator or two linear-time operators connected by a Boolean operator. By [KG96], such formulas have a linear translation to *CTL*.

By definition of f, it follows that for each formula φ and $\langle T, V\rangle \in \widehat{exec}(M_S)$, $\langle T, V\rangle$ satisfies $f(\varphi)$ *iff* the 2^{AP}-labelled tree obtained from $\langle T, V\rangle$ removing all the nodes labelled by $\bot$ (and removing the label t) satisfies φ. Therefore, module–checking S against formula ψ is reduced to check the existence of a tree $\langle T, V\rangle \in \widehat{exec}(M_S) = \mathcal{L}(\mathcal{P}_S)$ satisfying $f(\neg\psi)$ (note that $|f(\neg\psi)| = O(|\neg\psi|)$). We reduce the latter to check the emptiness of a parity *PD-NTA* $\mathcal{P}_{S\times\neg\psi}$ that is defined as the intersection of the Büchi *PD-NTA* $\mathcal{P}_S$ with a parity *NTA* $\mathcal{A}_{\neg\psi} = \langle \Sigma, Q, q_0, \delta, F\rangle$ accepting exactly the Σ-labelled complete k-ary trees that are models of $f(\neg\psi)$ (recall that $\Sigma = 2^{AP\cup\{t\}} \cup \{\bot\}$). By Lemma 1, if ψ is a *CTL* (resp., *CTL**) formula, then $\mathcal{A}_{\neg\psi}$ has size $O(k\cdot 2^{O(|\psi|\log|\psi|)})$ (resp., $O(k\cdot 2^{2^{O(|\psi|)}})$) and index $O(|\psi|)$ (resp., $O(2^{|\psi|})$). Therefore, by Proposition 2 the following holds:

- If ψ is a *CTL* formula, then $\mathcal{P}_{S\times\neg\psi}$ has $O(k \cdot |P| \cdot 2^{O(|\psi|\log|\psi|)})$ states, index $O(|\psi|)$, and transition relation bounded by $O(k^2 \cdot |\Delta| \cdot 2^{O(|\psi|\log|\psi|)})$.
- If ψ is a *CTL** formula, then $\mathcal{P}_{S\times\neg\psi}$ has $O(k \cdot |P| \cdot 2^{2^{O(|\psi|)}})$ states, index $O(2^{|\psi|})$, and transition relation bounded by $O(k^2 \cdot |\Delta| \cdot 2^{2^{O(|\psi|)}})$.

Therefore, by Proposition 1 we obtain the main result of this subsection.

Theorem 1.
(1) *The pushdown module-checking problem for* CTL *is in* 2EXPTIME.
(2) *The pushdown module-checking problem for* CTL* *is in* 3EXPTIME.
(3) *For a fixed* CTL *or* CTL* *formula, the pushdown module-checking problem is in* EXPTIME.

4.2 Lower Bounds

In this section we give lower bounds for the considered problems that match the upper bounds of the algorithm proposed in the previous subsection. The lower bound for *CTL* (resp., *CTL**) is shown by a reduction from the word problem for EXPSPACE–bounded (resp., 2EXPSPACE–bounded) alternating Turing Machines. Without loss of generality, we consider a model of alternation with a binary branching degree. Formally, an alternating Turing Machine (TM, for short) is a tuple $\mathcal{M} = \langle \Sigma, Q, Q_\forall, Q_\exists, q_0, \delta, F\rangle$, where Σ is the input alphabet, which contains the blank symbol #, Q is the finite set of states, which is partitioned into $Q = Q_\forall \cup Q_\exists$, $Q_\exists$ (resp., $Q_\forall$) is the set of existential (resp., universal) states, q_0 is the initial state, $F \subseteq Q$ is the set of accepting states, and the transition function δ is a mapping $\delta : Q \times \Sigma \to (Q \times \Sigma \times \{L, R\})^2$.

Configurations of $\mathcal{M}$ are words in $\Sigma^* \cdot (Q \times \Sigma) \cdot \Sigma^*$. A configuration $\eta \cdot (q, \sigma) \cdot \eta'$ denotes that the tape content is $\eta \sigma \eta'$, the current state is q, and the reading head is at position $|\eta| + 1$. When $\mathcal{M}$ is in state q and reads an input $\sigma \in \Sigma$ in the current tape cell, then it nondeterministically chooses a triple (q', σ', dir) in $\delta(q, \sigma) = \langle (q_l, \sigma_l, dir_l), (q_r, \sigma_r, dir_r) \rangle$, and then moves to state q', writes σ' in the current tape cell, and its reading head moves one cell to the left or to the right, according to dir. For a configuration c, we denote by $succ_l(c)$ and $succ_r(c)$ the successors of c obtained choosing respectively the left and the right triple in $\langle (q_l, \sigma_l, dir_l), (q_r, \sigma_r, dir_r) \rangle$. The configuration c is *accepting* if the associated state q belongs to F. Given an input $x \in \Sigma^*$, a computation tree of $\mathcal{M}$ on x is a tree in which each node corresponds to a configuration. The root of the tree corresponds to the initial configuration associated with x. A node that corresponds to a universal configuration (i.e. the associated state is in $Q_\forall$) has two successors, corresponding to $succ_l(c)$ and $succ_r(c)$, while a node that corresponds to an existential configuration (i.e. the associated state is in $Q_\exists$) has a single successor, corresponding to either $succ_l(c)$ or $succ_r(c)$. The tree is accepting iff all its paths (from the root) reach an accepting configuration. An input $x \in \Sigma^*$ is *accepted* by $\mathcal{M}$ iff there exists an accepting computation tree of $\mathcal{M}$ on x.

If $\mathcal{M}$ is EXPSPACE–bounded (resp., 2EXPSPACE–bounded), then there is a constant $k \geq 1$ such that for each $x \in \Sigma^*$, the space needed by $\mathcal{M}$ on input x is bounded by $2^{k \cdot |x|}$ (resp., $2^{2^{k \cdot |x|}}$). It is well-known [CKS81] that 2EXPTIME (resp., 3EXPTIME) coincides with the class of all languages accepted by EXPSPACE–bounded (resp., 2EXPSPACE–bounded) alternating Turing Machines.

In the following we fix an input word x and let $n = k \cdot |x|$.

Theorem 2.
(1) *The pushdown module checking problem for* CTL *is* 2EXPTIME*–hard.*
(2) *The pushdown module checking problem for* CTL* *is* 3EXPTIME*–hard.*

Proof. Here we sketch the proof for *CTL*. Given the EXPSPACE–bounded alternating Turing Machine $\mathcal{M} = \langle \Sigma, Q, Q_\forall, Q_\exists, q_0, \delta, F \rangle$ and the input x, we build an *OPD* $\mathcal{S}$ and a *CTL* formula φ whose sizes are *polynomial* in n and in $|\mathcal{M}|$ such that $\mathcal{M}$ accepts x *iff* there is a tree $\langle T, V \rangle \in exec(M_\mathcal{S})$ such that $\langle T, V \rangle$ satisfies φ, i.e. iff $M_\mathcal{S} \not\models_r \neg\varphi$. Some ideas in the proposed reduction are taken from [KTMV00], where there are given lower bounds for the satisfiability of extensions of *CTL* and *CTL**.

Note that any reachable configuration of $\mathcal{M}$ over x can be seen as a word in $\Sigma^* \cdot (Q \times \Sigma) \cdot \Sigma^*$ of length exactly 2^n. If $x = \sigma_1 \ldots \sigma_r$ (where $r = |x|$), then the initial configuration is given by $(q_0, \sigma_1)\sigma_2 \ldots \sigma_r \underbrace{\#\# \ldots \#}_{2^n - r}$.

Each cell of a TM configuration is coded using a block of n symbols of the stack alphabet of $\mathcal{S}$. The whole block is used to encode both the content of the cell and the location (the number of cell) on the TM tape (note that the number of cell is in the range $[0, 2^n - 1]$ and can be encoded using n bits). The stack alphabet is given by $(\Sigma \cup (Q \times \Sigma)) \times 2^{\{b, fc, e, cn, l\}}$ where b is used to mark the first element of a TM block, fc to mark the initial TM configuration, e to mark the first element of the first block of a TM configuration, cn to encode the number of cell, and l to mark a left TM successor. Moreover, $\Sigma \cup (Q \times \Sigma)$ is used to encode the cell content. The pushdown system $\mathcal{S}$ proceeds in two phases.

Phase 1. Starting from the initial configuration (with empty stack content), $\mathcal{S}$ generates nondeterministically by push transitions a sequence of TM configurations on the stack. $\mathcal{S}$ ensures that the first TM configuration is the initial TM configuration (corresponding to the input x). Moreover, the following conditions are satisfied for any generated TM configuration c:

– $\mathcal{S}$ ensures that the symbols b, fc, and e are used properly. Moreover, $\mathcal{S}$ ensures that the last block of c is the unique block in c that has number of cell $2^n - 1$ (i.e, all its elements are marked by the proposition cn).
– All global states of $\mathcal{S}$ associated with all elements of c except the last element are *environment states*. $\mathcal{S}$ keeps track of the TM state q associated with c by its finite control. If c is not accepting (i.e., $q \notin F$), then the global state s associated with the last element of c is a *system state* if c is a TM universal configuration (i.e., $q \in Q_\forall$), and it is an *environment state* otherwise. In such a state s, $\mathcal{S}$ without modifying the stack content chooses a letter $0/1$ to encode the choice of the transition. According to such a choice all elements of the next TM configuration will be marked by the corresponding choice symbol. In particular, we use the proposition l to mark all elements of a TM left successor (this means that $\neg l$ is associated with right TM successors).

Note that $\mathcal{S}$ does *not* ensure that the number of blocks of any generated TM configuration is exactly 2^n, that the cell numbers are updated correctly, and the generated configuration sequence is consistent with the transition function of $\mathcal{M}$.

Phase 2. When $\mathcal{S}$ finishes to generate an accepting configuration, it reaches a *system global state* in which chooses between two possible options opt_1 and opt_2 (without changing the stack content). When $\mathcal{S}$ selects opt_1, then it simply empties deterministically the stack by a sequence of pop transitions. The corresponding subtree of the computation tree of $M_\mathcal{S}$ reduces to a finite linear path that corresponds to the sequence ν of "pseudo" TM configurations generated in the first phase in reversed order. We use this subtree together with a *CTL* formula φ_{opt_1} to check that the cell numbers of the sequence ν are encoded correctly (this also implies that each configuration of ν has exactly length 2^n).

When $\mathcal{S}$ selects opt_2, then it empties the stack by a sequence of pop transitions with the additional ability to generate at most at one block (corresponding to a TM cell) the symbol $check_1$ and successively at most at one block the symbol $check_2$. Therefore, a computation in this phase corresponds to the sequence ν of "pseudo" TM configurations generated in the first phase in *reversed order* with at most one block marked by $check_1$ and with at most one block marked by $check_2$. Any global state of $\mathcal{S}$ in this phase is an *environment state* and has at most two successors. Let $\langle T, V \rangle$ be the corresponding subtree of the computation tree of $M_\mathcal{S}$. We use this subtree $\langle T, V \rangle$ together with a *CTL* formula φ_{opt_2} in order to check that ν is faithful to the evolution of $\mathcal{M}$.

In order to understand how this can be done, let $c = a_1 \ldots a_{2^n}$ be a TM configuration. For any $1 \leq i \leq 2^n$, the value a'_i of the i-th cell of $succ_l(c)$ (resp.,

$succ_r(c))$ is completely determined by the values a_{i-1}, a_i and a_{i+1} (taking a_{2^n+1} for $i = 2^n$ and a_0 for $i = 1$ to be some special symbol). As in [KTMV00], we denote by $next_l(a_{i-1}, a_i, a_{i+1})$ (resp., $next_r(a_{i-1}, a_i, a_{i+1})$) our expectation for a'_i (these functions can be trivially obtained from the transition function of $\mathcal{M}$).

Let $exec(\langle T, V \rangle)$ be the set of the trees obtained by pruning from $\langle T, V \rangle$ subtrees whose root is a child of a node corresponding to an environment state. Then, φ_{opt_2} will capture all trees $\langle T', V' \rangle \in exec(\langle T, V \rangle)$ satisfying the following:

– For each block bl of ν, there is a path in T' (from the root) such that the sequence of nodes associated with bl is labelled by $check_1$.
– For each $u \in T'$ labelled by $check_1$, there is exactly one path in T' from u.
– Each path π of T' from a node u labelled by $check_1$ (and such that u corresponds to some element of a block bl_1 of ν not belonging to the first TM configuration) contains a block bl_2 marked by $check_2$ having the same number of cell of bl_1 and belonging to the previous TM configuration w.r.t. ν (we use the proposition e that marks the first element of the first block of a TM configuration to check this last condition). Moreover, denoting by $\sigma(bl)$ the $\Sigma \cup (Q \times \Sigma)$-value of a block bl, φ_{opt_2} will check that $\sigma(bl_1)$ is consistent with $next_s(\sigma(bl_{succ}), \sigma(bl_2), \sigma(bl_{prec}))$, where $s \in \{l, r\}$, bl_{succ} and bl_{prec} represent the blocks soon after and soon before bl_2 along π, and $s = l$ iff the TM configuration associated with bl_1 is a left successor (i.e. all nodes of bl_1 are labelled by proposition l).

It is clear that assuming that the cell numbers of ν are encoded correctly (this is guaranteed by formula φ_{opt_1}), then ν is a legal sequence of TM configurations iff there is $\langle T', V' \rangle \in exec(\langle T, V \rangle)$ satisfying φ_{opt_2}.

By considerations above, it is clear that $\mathcal{M}$ accepts x iff there is $\langle T, V \rangle \in exec(M_S)$ such that each path of T (from the root) reaches a node u corresponding to the last element of an accepting TM configuration and the following holds: the subtree associated with the opt_1-child (resp., opt_2-child) of u satisfies formula φ_{opt_1} (resp., φ_{opt_2}). Therefore, formula φ is defined as follows:

$$AF\big(EX(opt_1 \wedge \varphi_{opt_1}) \wedge EX(opt_2 \wedge \varphi_{opt_2})\big) \qquad \square$$

Now, we can prove the main result of this paper.

Theorem 3.
(1) *The pushdown module-checking problem for* CTL *is* 2EXPTIME-*complete.*
(2) *The pushdown module-checking problem for* CTL* *is* 3EXPTIME-*complete.*
(3) *The pushdown module-checking problem for* CTL* *is* EXPTIME-*complete in the size of the given* OPD.

Proof. Claims 1 and 2 directly follow from Theorems 1 and 2. Now, let us consider Claim 3. First, we note that model checking pushdown systems corresponds to module checking the class of *OPD* in which there are not environment configurations. Moreover, pushdown model checking against *alternation-free μ-calculus* is known to be EXPTIME-complete also for a fixed formula [Wal96]. Since *CTL** subsumes the alternation-free mu-calculus, Claim 3 follows from Theorem 1.

References

[BC96]   E. Bhat and R. Cleaveland. Efficient model checking via the equational
            μ-calculus. In *LICS'96*, pages 304–312, 1996.
[BEM97]   A. Bouajjani, J. Esparza, and O. Maler. Reachability Analysis of Push-
            down Automata: Application to Model-Checking. In *CONCUR'97*, LNCS
            1243, pages 135–150. Springer-Verlag, 1997.
[Buc62]   J.R. Buchi. On a decision method in restricted second order arithmetic. In
            Proc. Internat. Congr. Logic, Method. and Philos. Sci. 1960, pages 1–12,
            Stanford, 1962.
[CE81]   E.M. Clarke and E.A. Emerson. Design and verification of synchronization
            skeletons using branching time temporal logic. In *Proceedings of Workshop
            on Logic of Programs*, LNCS 131, pages 52–71. Springer-Verlag, 1981.
[CKS81]   A.K. Chandra, D.C. Kozen, and L.J. Stockmeyer. Alternation. *Journal
            of the ACM*, 28(1):114–133, 1981.
[EH86]   E.A. Emerson and J.Y. Halpern. Sometimes and not never revisited: On
            branching versus linear time. *Journal of the ACM*, 33(1):151–178, 1986.
[EJ88]   E.A. Emerson and C.S. Jutla. The complexity of tree automata and logics
            of programs. In *FOCS'88*, pages 328–337, 1988.
[EJ91]   E.A. Emerson and C.S. Jutla. Tree automata, μ-calculus and determinacy.
            In *FOCS'91*, pages 368–377, 1991.
[Hoa85]   C.A.R. Hoare. *Communicating Sequential Processes*. Prentice-Hall, 1985.
[KG96]   O. Kupferman and O. Grumberg. Buy one, get one free!!! *Journal of
            Logic and Computation*, 6(4):523–539, 1996.
[KPV02]   O. Kupferman, N. Piterman, and M.Y. Vardi. Pushdown specifications.
            In *LPAR'02*, LNCS 2514, pages 262–277. Springer-Verlag, 2002.
[KTMV00]   O. Kupferman, P.S. Thiagarajan, P. Madhusudan, and M.Y. Vardi. Open
            systems in reactive environments: Control and Synthesis. In *CONCUR'00*,
            LNCS 1877, pages 92–107. Springer-Verlag, 2000.
[KVW00]   O. Kupferman, M.Y. Vardi, and P. Wolper. An Automata-Theoretic
            Approach to Branching-Time Model Checking. *Journal of the ACM*,
            47(2):312–360, 2000.
[KVW01]   O. Kupferman, M.Y. Vardi, and P. Wolper. Module Checking. *Informa-
            tion and Computation*, 164(2):322–344, 2001.
[LMS04]   C. Loding, P. Madhusudan, and O. Serre. Visibly pushdown games. In
            FSTTCS'04, pages 408–420. Springer-Verlag, 2004.
[MS85]   D.E. Muller and P.E. Shupp. The theory of ends, pushdown automata,
            and second-order logic. *Theoretical Computer Science*, 37:51–75, 1985.
[QS81]   J.P. Queille and J. Sifakis. Specification and verification of concurrent
            programs in Cesar. In *Proceedings of the Fifth International Symposium
            on Programming*, LNCS 137, pages 337–351. Springer-Verlag, 1981.
[Var98]   M.Y. Vardi. Reasoning about the past with two-way automata. In
            ICALP'98, LNCS 1443, pages 628–641. Springer-Verlag, 1998.
[VW86]   M.Y. Vardi and P. Wolper. Automata-theoretic techniques for modal
            logics of programs. *J. of Computer and System Sciences*, 32(2):182–221,
            1986.
[Wal96]   I. Walukiewicz. Pushdown processes: Games and Model Checking. In
            CAV'96, LNCS 1102, pages 62–74. Springer-Verlag, 1996.
[Wal00]   I. Walukiewicz. Model checking CTL properties of pushdown systems. In
            FSTTCS'00, LNCS 1974, pages 127–138. Springer-Verlag, 2000.

Functional Correctness Proofs
of Encryption Algorithms

Jianjun Duan[1], Joe Hurd[2], Guodong Li[1],
Scott Owens[1], Konrad Slind[1], and Junxing Zhang[1]

[1] School of Computing, University of Utah
[2] Oxford University Computer Lab

Abstract. We discuss a collection of mechanized formal proofs of symmetric key block encryption algorithms (AES, MARS, Twofish, RC6, Serpent, IDEA, and TEA), performed in an implementation of higher order logic. For each algorithm, functional correctness, namely that decryption inverts encryption, is formally proved by a simple but effective proof methodology involving application of invertibility lemmas in the course of symbolic evaluation. Block ciphers are then lifted to the encryption of arbitrary datatypes by using modes of operation to encrypt lists of bits produced by a polytypic encoding method.

1   Introduction

Symmetric-key block ciphers represent an important part of today's security infrastructure. Besides their main application, information hiding, block ciphers are also used in the implementation of pseudo-random number generators, message authentication protocols, stream ciphers, and hash functions. There are two main properties that a cipher should have: first, *Functional Correctness*, namely that decryption should invert encryption; second, *Security*, namely that the cipher should be hard to break. In this paper, we focus solely on the first property.

The formal methods community has, to date, paid surprisingly little attention to the functional correctness of block ciphers. This is a pity, since these algorithms provide an application area in which the algorithms are heavily used, security-critical, often well-specified, and well within the scope of theorem proving methods. In this paper, we formalize seven block ciphers and prove their functional correctness.

We have undertaken our proofs in a theorem proving environment: we wanted to see if the seemingly impossible task of brute force analysis of cipher correctness (there would be 2^{128} cases to consider for most of the ciphers we consider) could be avoided by a symbolic analysis. Indeed, it can; we found that the proofs are often quite simple. A major side benefit—which may outweigh the assurance provided by the proofs—is that descriptions of ciphers in higher order logic are elegant and unambiguous. The descriptions are also mathematical and executable. Thus in this work higher order logic is used as a specification language

G. Sutcliffe and A. Voronkov (Eds.): LPAR 2005, LNAI 3835, pp. 519–533, 2005.

for ciphers and its implementation provides a symbolic execution and theorem proving environment. That has two benefits: when prototyping the ciphers, we can use deductive steps to evaluate ciphers on test cases and check results; and we re-use those definitions in the correctness proofs.

In practice, ciphers are used to encrypt compound user-defined data such as numbers, lists, trees, and records. *Modes of operation* [6] can be used to apply a block cipher to the task of encrypting a list of blocks; however, there still remains the issue of how to encrypt higher level datatypes. Often support for this is provided by language-specific libraries. In our work, we have used *polytypism* [11] to implement datatype encryption: elements of datatypes are reduced by polytypic encoders to lists of bits which are then encrypted by a mode of operation instantiated with a particular block cipher. The correctness proofs of block ciphers can be combined with the correctness of encoders to obtain the correctness of data encryption.

This work was initiated in 2002 [17] with a verification of the functional correctness of the then-recent AES standard. We subsequently extended the work to modes of operation, padding, and user-defined datatypes. After that, we were left wondering if the (relative) ease with which AES was verified also held for other block ciphers. Case studies with the other block ciphers mentioned above do seem to indicate that the proof methodology used on AES is widely applicable. The approach (discussed more fully in the sequel) amounts to symbolic evaluation of the formula

$$\forall key\ plaintext.\ \mathsf{decrypt}\ key\ (\mathsf{encrypt}\ key\ plaintext) = plaintext$$

coupled with simplification by *inversion lemmas*, which show that round operations performed during encryption are inverted by their counterparts in decryption. This methodology worked successfully on all our verifications. However, it seems not to be generally automatable: at times, the verification of inversion lemmas can be quite difficult. For example, our proof of invertibility of the column-mixing operation in AES is based on a collection of *ad hoc*, user-specified, lemmas, each proved by brute force. Another example is the verification of IDEA, in which Euclid's extended algorithm needed to be formalized and applied in order to prove invertibility of a special-purpose multiplication operation.

Our verifications[1] have been carried out in HOL-4,[2] an implementation of higher order logic [12]. We have made heavy use of Anthony Fox's HOL-4 library for generating theories and proof tools for fixed-width n-bit words. We use an ML-like functional programming notation to present algorithms in this paper.

2   Encryption Algorithms

Block ciphers usually operate on a fixed, small, amount of data called a *block* which is repeatedly transformed for a number of *rounds*. For example, a block in

---

[1] Accessible at the webpage http://www.cs.utah.edu/~slind/papers/lpar05.

[2] Accessible at the webpage http://hol.sourceforge.net.

AES is a 16-tuple of word8 (8 bit bytes) and each block undergoes ten rounds of transformation. Conceptually, decryption is just 'running encryption in reverse', but often that is not obvious, since decryption round operations can seem quite unrelated to encryption round operations. Although ciphers can have quite complex mathematical underpinnings, their implementations usually require only the most primitive computational objects, found in most machine instruction sets: namely, boolean and arithmetic operations on machine words.

A block cipher takes two inputs: the plaintext and a key. In many cases, before encryption starts, the key is used to generate a *key schedule*, which may be thought of as a list of keys, which get used as encryption proceeds. It is interesting to note that, in many cases, the key schedule calculation is more complex than the actual encryption. We have formalized the computation of key schedules, but have noticed that the actual values in the key schedule are not relevant to functional correctness, at least for the ciphers we have examined. In other words, the key schedule seems to be important for security, and not for functional correctness.

The block ciphers we will examine are *symmetric* key ciphers, which means that the key used for encryption must be used in decryption. Many, but not all, symmetric key ciphers are based on the notion of a *Feistel* network, which divides the plaintext into two halves and repeatedly applies the round function for a number of rounds. In each round, the left half of the plaintext is transformed based on the right half, and then the right half is transformed based on the transformed left half. The round function usually applies several basic linear and non-linear operations: boolean operations such as exclusive-or, substitution (via so-called *S-boxes*), permutation, and modular arithmetic. An S-box is often implemented by an array, but is mathematically just a total function.

In the years previous to 2001, the United States National Institute of Standards (NIST) held a competition to select a successor to the aging DES (Digital Encryption Standard). Among a number of entries, five (MARS, Rijndael, Twofish, Serpent, and RC6) were chosen as finalists, and Rijndael was the eventual winner. Rijndael has since been named AES (Advanced Encryption Standard) and should become widely used in the years ahead.

We have formalized all of the AES finalists, plus a few more ciphers, and proved their functional correctness. In the following, we will introduce each algorithm and discuss any interesting aspects of the correctness proof. Further details on the algorithms can be found in the cited literature.

2.1   AES

The AES block cipher is described in the NIST standards document [13] and in a book [5] by the authors of the cipher. AES is defined for three keylengths: 128, 192, and 256 bits. Our verification is for a keylength of 128, but changing to the other keylengths would be straightforward and involve no changes to the proofs. In the formalization, the original imperative pseudo-code for describing the cipher was converted to a purely functional form which served as an executable model, and also as the code verified in the correctness proof. We followed this practice for the other ciphers as well. We can define the encryption (AES) and decryption (AES_INV) functions using function composition as follows:

```
AES keys = from_state o Round 9 (TL keys)
                     o AddRoundKey (HD keys) o to_state

AES_INV keys = from_state o InvRound 9 (TL keys)
                         o AddRoundKey (HD keys) o to_state
```

AES takes a key schedule (a list of keys) and AES_INV takes the reversed key schedule. The encryptor works by copying the input block into the state, 'xors' the state with the first key, then performs 10 rounds of processing. In each round, one key from the key schedule is consumed. After the rounds of processing are finished, the state is copied to the output. This is formalized as follows: blocks, states, and keys are each represented by 16-tuples of word8. The processing of an arbitrary number of rounds is defined by a recursive function named Round:

```
(Round 0 [key] state = AddRoundKey key (ShiftRows (SubBytes state))) ∧
(Round (n+1) (key::keys) state =
   Round n keys
    (AddRoundKey key
      (MixColumns
        (ShiftRows (SubBytes state)))))
```

AddRoundKey (the names are taken from the original Rijndael documentation) is just pairwise exclusive-or; SubBytes applies an S-box to each element of the state; and ShiftRows performs a simple permutation on the block. The most complex operation is MixColumns; it treats the state as a 4×4 matrix and applies a specialized transformation on each column of the matrix. Mathematically, each column in the state is treated as a four-term polynomial over $\mathbf{GF}(2^8)$ and multiplied modulo $x^4 + 1$ with a fixed polynomial. When encrypting, the fixed polynomial is $a(x) = \mathbf{03}x^3 + \mathbf{01}x^2 + \mathbf{01}x + \mathbf{02}$, while decryption uses the polynomial $a^{-1}(x) = \mathbf{0B}x^3 + \mathbf{0D}x^2 + \mathbf{09}x + \mathbf{0E}$. In the implementation, column multiplication during encryption is implemented by

```
MultCol (a,b,c,d) =
   ((02 • a) ⊕ (03 • b) ⊕ c ⊕ d,      (* F1 *)
     a ⊕ (02 • b) ⊕ (03 • c) ⊕ d,      (* F2 *)
     a ⊕ b  ⊕ (02 • c) ⊕ (03 • d),     (* F3 *)
    (03 • a) ⊕ b ⊕ c ⊕ (02 • d))       (* F4 *)
```

where $(- \bullet -)$ is the finite field multiplication and $\oplus$ is exclusive-or. The actual appplication of MultCol to the block is by the following function (where we have arranged the state tuple so as to suggest a matrix):

```
MixColumns (b1, b2, b3, b4,
            b5, b6, b7, b8,
            b9, b10,b11,b12,
            b13,b14,b15,b16) =
  let (b1',b5',b9',b13') = MultCol (b1,b5,b9,b13)
  and (b2',b6',b10',b14') = MultCol (b2,b6,b10,b14)
  and (b3',b7',b11',b15') = MultCol (b3,b7,b11,b15)
```

```
and (b4',b8',b12',b16') = MultCol (b4,b8,b12,b16)
in
   (b1',b2', b3',b4',b5',b6',b7',b8',
    b9',b10',b11',b12',b13',b14',b15',b16')
```

Decryption also uses `MixColumns`, except that `MultCol` has been replaced by `InvMultCol`:

```
InvMultCol (a,b,c,d) =
  ((0E • a) ⊕ (0B • b) ⊕ (0D • c) ⊕ (09 • d),    (* G1 *)
   (09 • a) ⊕ (0E • b) ⊕ (0B • c) ⊕ (0D • d),    (* G2 *)
   (0D • a) ⊕ (09 • b) ⊕ (0E • c) ⊕ (0B • d),    (* G3 *)
   (0B • a) ⊕ (0D • b) ⊕ (09 • c) ⊕ (0E • d))    (* G4 *)
```

Verification. Functional correctness, namely

```
∀keys block. INV_AES (reverse keys) (AES keys block) = block
```

is proved as follows: the variable `block` is split into a 16-tuple of `word8` variables. Then all the definitions used to define `AES` and `AES_INV` are expanded by symbolic evaluation. This results in (conceptually) a long string of function compositions:

```
from_state ○ .... ○ to_state ○ from_state ○ ... ○ to_state
```

and then we need merely simplify with inversion lemmas, showing that each operation used in encryption inverts its counterpart in decryption. Most of the inversion lemmas for AES are quite easy to prove: `from_state` inverts `to_state` (and *vice versa*), ⊕ inverts itself, the S-boxes are inverses, when regarded as functions, and so on. However, the inversion lemma for column mixing

```
InvMixColumns (MixColumns s) = s
```

is difficult to prove. Naive attempts at this led to overly large goals, and we were forced to much more basic steps. To see the problem, let us consider the action on a column (a, b, c, d). In the forward direction, `MixColumns` applies transformations $F_1 \cdots F_4$ to the column

$$a' = F_1(a, b, c, d)$$
$$b' = F_2(a, b, c, d)$$
$$c' = F_3(a, b, c, d)$$
$$d' = F_4(a, b, c, d)$$

and in the reverse `InvMixColumns` applies transformations $G_1 \cdots G_4$ to the resulting column

$$a'' = G_1(a', b', c', d')$$
$$b'' = G_2(a', b', c', d')$$
$$c'' = G_3(a', b', c', d')$$
$$d'' = G_4(a', b', c', d')$$

and we then wish to show that $a = a'', b = b'', c = c'', d = d''$. Consideration of a should illustrate the strategy.

$$a' = (\mathbf{02} \bullet a) \oplus (\mathbf{3} \bullet b) \oplus c \oplus d$$
$$b' = a \oplus (\mathbf{02} \bullet b) \oplus (\mathbf{03} \bullet c) \oplus d$$
$$c' = a \oplus b \oplus (\mathbf{02} \bullet c) \oplus (\mathbf{03} \bullet d)$$
$$d' = (\mathbf{03} \bullet a) \oplus b \oplus c \oplus (\mathbf{02} \bullet d)$$

Thus a'' is

$$(\mathbf{0E} \bullet a') \oplus (\mathbf{0B} \bullet b') \oplus (\mathbf{0D} \bullet c') \oplus (\mathbf{09} \bullet d')$$

which expands to

$$(\mathbf{0E} \bullet ((\mathbf{02} \bullet a) \oplus (\mathbf{03} \bullet b) \oplus c \oplus d)) \oplus$$
$$(\mathbf{0B} \bullet (a \oplus (\mathbf{02} \bullet b) \oplus (\mathbf{03} \bullet c) \oplus d)) \oplus$$
$$(\mathbf{0D} \bullet (a \oplus b \oplus (\mathbf{02} \bullet c) \oplus (\mathbf{03} \bullet d))) \oplus$$
$$(\mathbf{09} \bullet ((\mathbf{03} \bullet a) \oplus b \oplus c \oplus (\mathbf{02} \bullet d)))$$

By use of associativity and commutativity of $\oplus$ and distribution of $\bullet$ over $\oplus$, we can separate the expression into four subexpressions each involving only one variable. Each subexpression is then simplified by case analysis on the 256 ways of forming a word8 quantity. The subexpression involving a is simplified to a, and the subexpressions for b, c, d all simplify to $\mathbf{0}$, leading to the conclusion $a'' = a$. Such a proof was carried out for each of a, b, c, d. The potential tedium of this was eased by HOL's rewriter, which can perform permutative rewriting (in this case using the associativity and commutativity of $\oplus$).

Enhancements and Optimizations. Working in a theorem prover means that program transformations and optimizations can be easily applied, once proved. For example, in [17], an optimization to the decryption process is verified, and the resulting decryptor is proved to be mathematically equal to the original. As another example, the multiplication used in AES may be specified recursively, iteratively, or as a lookup table (feasible since all multiplications have one argument fixed to one of a small set of constants). In our development, we prove the iterative and recursive functions equal, and generate the tables by proof from the recursive algorithm, achieving high assurance. Thus multiple implementations can be spawned, by proof, from a single source.

In summary, the functional correctness of AES was straightforward, except for one lemma, which required ingenuity in the decomposition. One question we have is whether the difficulty of the proof of invertibility of column mixing is instrinsic, or whether it would be easier as a general argument at the level of finite fields and polynomials. It may also be a good challenge for SAT methods.

2.2   Verifying the Other Ciphers

We now discuss the other ciphers, omitting much detail since the basic ideas have been established in the discussion of AES.

MARS. [4] was IBM's candidate in the AES competition. It has 128 bit blocks (a 4-tuple of word32) and a variable keysize ranging from 128 to 448 bits (we chose 128). The key schedule is a 40-tuple of word32s. Encryption in MARS takes place in three phases: eight rounds of forward mixing, sixteen rounds in the *cryptographic core*, and eight rounds of backwards mixing. Decryption applies counterparts of these three phases. MARS uses a 512 element S-box. Although the formalization of MARS is quite complex, the basic operations are simple boolean operations and addition plus application of the S-boxes. Inversion lemmas for mixing and the cryptographic core are quite easy; again symbolic evaluation plus rewriting with inversion lemmas and some basic word identities (algebraic properties of exclusive-or, for example) sufficed for the final theorem.

Twofish. [16] was also an AES competitor. It has a block size of 128 bits and key sizes up to 256 bits. Twofish's distinctive features are the use of pre-computed key-dependent S-boxes, and a relatively complex key schedule. Twofish is a 16-round Feistel network. We used word4, word8, and word32 in the formalization. A block is a 4-tuple of word32, and the key schedule is a 40-tuple of word32, computed from 32 word8s. Twofish uses several multiplication operations, which are similar to that of AES. It uses these in column multiplication, also much like that of AES. However, unlike AES, the correctness proof for Twofish is almost comically easy.

RC6. [15] is a block cipher based on RC5 and designed by Rivest, Sidney, and Yin for RSA Security. RC6 is a parameterized algorithm where the block size, the key size, and the number of rounds are variable; the upper limit on the key size is 2040 bits. In our formalization, we have fixed on a internal block size of 176 bits (a 6-tuple of word32), a key size of 64 (a pair of word32), and twenty rounds. RC6 uses integer multiplication to increase the diffusion achieved per round so that fewer rounds are needed and the speed of the cipher can be increased. The algorithm also wraps the round computations in 'pre-whitening' and 'post-whitening' steps. RC6 does not use S-boxes. In spite of the fact that multiplication is used, the verification of RC6 was extremely simple, reducing to simple identities on words.

TEA. (Tiny Encryption Algorithm) [22] is a very compact cipher designed by David Wheeler and Roger Needham. TEA operates on 64-bit blocks and uses a 128-bit key. TEA has has a trivial key schedule (the same four keys are used throughout); it also does not use an S-box. It has Feistel structure, using addition and subtraction as the reversible operators rather than exclusive-or. A dual shift causes all bits of the key and data to be mixed repeatedly. The number of rounds before a single bit change of the data or key has spread very close to 32 is at most six, so that sixteen cycles may suffice and the authors suggest 32 (we implemented 32 rounds). The verification of **TEA** was again an easy application of our methodology.

Serpent. [1] is a 128-bit block cipher designed by Ross Anderson, Eli Biham and Lars Knudsen. It placed second in the AES competition. The authors designed Serpent to provide users with the highest practical level of assurance that no shortcut attack will be found. To achieve this, the cipher uses twice as many rounds (32) as are sufficient to block all currently known shortcut attacks. Despite this intentional 'overdesign', Serpent supports a very efficient bitslice implementation. We have verified both the bitslice implementation and a more conventional reference implementation. Perhaps surprisingly, the bitslice implementation was far easier to verify than the reference version! The reference implementation of Serpent uses tables for S-boxes, linear transformations, and permutations. The specification used lists of indices, and we had to derive functions, which were more tractable in later proofs, from them. Several transcription errors were caught in the later invertibility proofs.

IDEA. [8] is used in the popular PGP (Pretty Good Privacy) package. IDEA operates on 64-bit blocks using a 128-bit key, and consists of seventeen rounds. The processes for encryption and decryption are similar. IDEA derives much of its security by interleaving operations from different algebraic groups: exclusive-or, addition modulo 2^{16}, and multiplication modulo $2^{16} + 1$ (a prime), where 0 is treated as 2^{16}. The internal operations of IDEA use `word16`, so the state is a 4-tuple of `word16` and the input key is treated as an 8-tuple of `word16`. The key schedule is a 52-tuple of `word16`.

The verification of IDEA is straightforward, much like the others, except for proving the invertibility of the multiplication. The difficulty comes from the fact that the native multiplication in `word16` is modulo 2^{16}, and not modulo $2^{16} + 1$. So we had to define our own multiplication and give an implementation for its inverse. This required some new formalization work: we had to define the generalized Euclid's algorithm, develop relevant properties, and show that the algorithm does find multiplicative inverses modulo 65537 for all numbers from 1 to 65536 inclusive. A further complication is that, since 65537 can not be represented in 16 bits, we had to map multiplications out to a larger type, and then map back. A full account is given in [23].

In summary, the verification of IDEA has much in similarity with that of AES: mostly the proof was easy, except for one complex operation.

3   Data Encryption

We now turn from block ciphers to techniques for encrypting data. The first step is to formalize so-called modes of operation. A *mode of operation* extends a cipher from single blocks to arbitrary block sequences. Some acronyms of the commonly used modes are ECB, CBC, CFB, OFB, and CTR [6]. In this paper, we chose to work with CBC (Cipher Block Chaining). In CBC, the previous ciphertext block is 'xor'ed with the current plaintext before encryption. We formalize CBC (see Fig. 1) as a pair of recursive functions being parameterized by block encryptors and decryptors *enc* and *dec*. The parameter *xor* represents an 'xor' function: since we do not know *a priori* what the actual type of blocks will be (different ciphers have different representations for blocks), we simply fill *xor* in later.[3] In the actual formalization, block is just a type variable in the HOL logic, to be instantiated to the block type of a particular cipher.

---

[3] A logic with dependent types could avoid this extra parameterization.

$$
\begin{aligned}
&\text{CBC } xor \ enc \ \_ \ [] &&= [] : \text{block list} \\
&\text{CBC } xor \ enc \ v \ (h :: t) &&= \texttt{let } x = enc \ (xor \ h \ v) \ \texttt{in } x :: \text{CBC } xor \ enc \ x \ t \\[6pt]
&\text{CBC}^{-1} \ xor \ dec \ \_ \ [] &&= [] : \text{block list} \\
&\text{CBC}^{-1} \ xor \ dec \ v \ (h :: t) &&= xor \ (dec \ h) \ v :: \text{CBC}^{-1} \ xor \ dec \ h \ t
\end{aligned}
$$

Fig. 1. Cipher Block Chaining

Both CBC and CBC^{-1} have the type

$$
(\text{block} \rightarrow \text{block} \rightarrow \text{block}) \rightarrow (\text{block} \rightarrow \text{block}) \rightarrow \text{block} \rightarrow \text{block list} \rightarrow \text{block list} .
$$

The correctness of CBC using arbitrary inverting encryptors and decryptors

$$
\begin{aligned}
\vdash \forall \ell \ xor \ v \ &encrypt \ decrypt. \\
&(decrypt \circ encrypt) = \mathsf{I} \ \wedge \\
&(\forall x \ y. \ (x \ xor \ y) \ xor \ y = x) \\
&\Rightarrow \\
&\forall k. \ \text{CBC}^{-1} \ (xor) \ (decrypt \ k) \ v \ (\text{CBC} \ (xor) \ (encrypt \ k) \ v \ \ell) = \ell
\end{aligned}
$$

is proved very easily by induction on ℓ. From there, support for data encryption is provided by adding in functions for encoding and decoding arbitrary data, as can be seen in the following trivial consequence:

$$
\begin{aligned}
\vdash \forall (encode : \alpha &\rightarrow \text{bool list}) \ (decode : \text{bool list} \rightarrow \alpha) \\
(block : &\text{bool list} \rightarrow \text{block list}) \ (unblock : \text{block list} \rightarrow \text{bool list}) \\
(encrypt : &\text{block} \rightarrow \text{block}) \ (decrypt : \text{block} \rightarrow \text{block}) \ xor. \\
&(decode \circ encode = \mathsf{I}) \ \wedge \\
&(\forall k. \ decrypt \ k \circ encrypt \ k = \mathsf{I}) \ \wedge \\
&(unblock \circ block = \mathsf{I}) \ \wedge \\
&(\forall x \ y. \ (x \ xor \ y) \ xor \ y = x) \\
\Rightarrow \forall v \ key. \\
&(decode \circ unblock \circ (\text{CBC}^{-1} \ (xor) \ (decrypt \ key) \ v)) \circ \\
&(\text{CBC} \ (xor) \ (encrypt \ key) \ v \circ block \circ encode) = \mathsf{I}
\end{aligned}
\qquad (1)
$$

In other words, provided that inverting encoder/decoder, blocker/unblocker, and encryptor/decryptor are provided, then (a) encoding the data to a list of bits then (b) chunking the list into blocks then (c) using CBC to encrypt the blocks can be inverted by applying the inverse operations in the correct order. Note that there is a hidden complexity, in that the action of turning a list of bits into a list of fixed length blocks requires *padding* the bits to get a list the length of which is a multiple of the block size. Moreover, padding must be implemented in such a way that the extra padding can be dropped off when mapping back from a block to a list of bits.

We have now finished the abstract development. To see how it may be instantiated, we turn our attention to type-directed construction of encoders and decoders.

3.1   Encoding and Decoding Datatypes

A common task in computer science is to package up high-level data as flat strings of bits, and correspondingly, to unpack strings of bits in order to recover the high-level data. When this is done to send data over a communication network, it is called marshalling or serialization but we will use *encoding/decoding* or simply *coding*. A type-directed approach to coding, based on an interpretation of higher order logic types into higher order logic terms, is given in [18]. An encoding function can be thought of simply as an injective function of type $\tau \to$ bool list mapping elements of type τ to lists of booleans. The injectivity condition prevents two elements of τ being encoded as the same list of booleans, and so guarantees that if a list can be decoded then the decoding will be unique.

Encoding functions can be automatically defined when a new datatype is declared; the interpretation is used to calculate the form of the encoder from the declaration of the type. Mutually recursive datatypes and datatypes with recursion under existing type operators (so-called *nested* datatypes) are cleanly handled. Encoding and decoding of polymorphic types is dealt with by abstraction: an encoder for a polymorphic type is parameterized by encoders for types that may be substituted for the type variables.

Without going into the details of encoding, which may be found in [18], each constructor for a datatype is assigned a *marker list*, which serves to distinguish it from other constructors for the type. Lists have two constructors, and so the marker lists have length one. A datatype with eight constructors would need marker lists of length three.

For example, the encoding function for the datatype α list of polymorphic lists is the following:

$$\text{encode\_list } f \; [] \equiv [\mathsf{F}] \; \wedge$$
$$\text{encode\_list } f \; (h :: t) \equiv \mathsf{T} :: f \; h \; @ \; \text{encode\_list } f \; t$$

where $f : \alpha \to$ bool list is the parameter encoder. Lists have two constructors, which are distinguished by the prepending of marker lists [F] and [T].

Although encoders are automatically defined for every datatype declared in HOL, a user may wish to override the automatic definition with an alternative version, or to provide an encoder for a non-datatype *e.g.*, for finite sets. A custom encoder for natural numbers[4] is the following:

$$\text{encode\_num } n \equiv \texttt{if } n = 0 \texttt{ then } [\mathsf{T}; \mathsf{T}]$$
$$\texttt{else if even } n \texttt{ then } \mathsf{F} :: \text{encode\_num } ((n-2) \text{ div } 2)$$
$$\texttt{else } \mathsf{T} :: \mathsf{F} :: \text{encode\_num } ((n-1) \text{ div } 2)$$

A typical environment for encoding functions would include at least the following bindings:

---

[4] Built up from 0 using two successor functions: $2n + 1$ and $2n + 2$.

type	encoder
$\tau_1 * \tau_2$	encode_prod f g $(x, y) \equiv f$ x @ g y
$\tau_1 + \tau_2$	encode_sum f g (INL x) $\equiv$ F :: f x
	encode_sum f g (INR y) $\equiv$ T :: g y
bool	encode_bool $x \equiv [x]$
option	encode_option f NONE $\equiv$ [F]
	encode_option f (SOME x) $\equiv$ T :: f x
num	encode_num (defined above)
τ list	encode_list (defined above)

Encrypting Data. For an example, we will see how to synthesize encryption routines for the type (num*bool option)list. Given a typical encoder environment, traversing the type structure and emitting the corresponding encoders yields the following function in the HOL logic:

```
encode_list (encode_prod encode_num (encode_option encode_bool))
```

Applying it to the list [(1,NONE); (13,SOME T); (257,SOME F)] yields the theorem

```
|- encode_list (encode_prod encode_num (encode_option encode_bool))
       [(1,NONE); (13,SOME T); (257,SOME F)]
   = [T; T; F; T; T; F; T; T; F; F; F; T; T; T; T; T; T; F;
       F; T; F; T; F; T; F; T; F; T; F; T; F; T; T; T; F; F]
```

If we instantiate CBC with the TEA block cipher, the key (1w,2w,3w,4w) and the initial value (5w,10w) for v, and prepend encoding, padding, and blocking, we can deductively evaluate the expression to obtain a theorem giving the result of encrypting our specific input list:

```
|- (CBC XORB (TEAEncrypt (1w,2w,3w,4w)) (5w,10w) o BLOCK o PAD o
       encode_list (encode_prod encode_num (encode_option encode_bool)))
       [(1,NONE); (13,SOME T); (257,SOME F)]
   = [(3008902428w,1274536877w)]
```

Decrypting Data. A decoder for type τ is an algorithm that takes as input a list of booleans and returns an element of type τ. It is also possible to build and compose decoders in a type-directed way. The key is to think of a decoder for type τ as a monadic parser [21] :

$$\text{decode\_}\tau : \text{bool list} \rightarrow (\tau \times \text{bool list}) \text{ option}$$

Such a function tries to parse an input list of booleans into an element of type τ, and if it succeeds then it returns the element of type τ, together with the list of booleans that were left over. If it fails to parse the input list, it signals this by returning NONE. (A decoding function of the expected type bool list $\rightarrow \tau$ can be easily recovered when decoding is expected to succeed.) As an example, the following is the decoding function for lists:

```
wf_decoder d ⇒
  (decode_list d [] = NONE)  ∧
  (decode_list d (F::t) = SOME ([],t))   ∧
  (decode_list d (T::t) =
    case d t
      of NONE -> NONE
      || SOME (x, t') ->
            case decode_list d t'
            of NONE -> NONE
            || SOME (xs, t'') -> SOME (h::xs, t''))
```

Thus, given a parameter decoder d, one decodes to an empty list, provided the marker at the head of the bits list is F; otherwise, the marker must be T, and we expect to be able to use d to deliver the head of the original list x and remaining bits t'. We then recurse to get the rest of the original list xs, and the remaining bits t''. As HOL is a logic of total functions, this function is only well-defined if d does not increase the length of the list of bits; this is enforced by the constraint wf_decoder d.

In our current formalization, a decoding function also has an attached *domain predicate*, in order to deal with subsets of types. We have omitted the domain predicates since they hamper readability, and are not actually used in a significant way in our experiments so far.

Returning to our example, suppose we have a decoder context containing at least decoders for the types num, list, option, and bool, then a type-directed traversal of (num ∗ bool option) list yields the following decoding function.

```
decode_list (decode_prod (decode_num (decode_option decode_bool)))
```

In order to formally apply the abstract inversion theorem (1) for data encryption, we need to show that the synthesized decoder inverts the synthesized encoder. This is relatively easy to automate by backchaining with pre-proved theorems relating basic coders/decoders already in the coder and decoder contexts. Thus we ultimately have that

```
(decode_list (decode_prod (decode_num (decode_option decode_bool)))) o
  UNPAD o UNBLOCK o CBC_DEC XORB (TEADecrypt (1w,2w,3w,4w)) (5w,10w))
o
(CBC XORB (TEAEncrypt (1w,2w,3w,4w)) (5w,10w) o BLOCK o PAD o
  encode_list (encode_prod encode_num (encode_option encode_bool)))
```

is the identity function. In summary, compound encoders and decoders can be formally synthesized and their invertibility property proved in the theorem prover; this property can then be used to show that data encryption for the specified type is invertible.

4 Related Work

Probably the earliest application of a proof assistant to cryptography is the use of Boyer and Moore's Nqthm to verify the invertibilty of encryption in the

RSA public-key algorithm [14]. Whereas their goal seemed to be to check an interesting piece of (then) recently-announced mathematics, we have been more interested in getting an overview of how hard proofs are for a gamut of algorithms in this area.

In [17] we verified the functional correctness of Rijndael, and in [23] we provide further detail on the functional correctness of the IDEA cipher. Toma and Borrione report on an ACL2 verification of an implementation of the SHA-1 hash algorithm in [20]. Higher level security protocol specification and verification has received much more attention than ciphers, and this work is starting to mature: see [2] for example. It would be interesting to explore links between our correctness proofs and that body of work. Finally, the Cryptol language [9] is a domain-specific language, based on functional programming principles, aimed at cryptographers. Cryptol provides a uniform stream-based view of all the data involving in encryption, and supports that view with an interesting type system reflecting how functions manipulate streams. C code can be generated from Cryptol programs, and there is also a path to FPGAs.

5   Conclusions and Further Work

This paper summarizes some case studies in the verification of block ciphers formalized in higher order logic. A simple proof methodology successfully supports functional correctness proofs of these algorithms. Although some ciphers are formulated in terms of concepts from abstract algebra and number theory, we found that in most cases (IDEA was the sole exception) higher mathematics could be avoided in the proofs. We also showed how ciphers can be lifted from blocks to arbitrary user-defined datatypes by use of modes of operation and polytypic encoding techniques.

This activity takes place inside the theorem prover, and although it is encouraging to see that bespoke data encryption can be supported in such an environment, it would be a useful next step to *generate* executable models in real programming languages from our formal models. In fact, we can already do that in HOL-4, generating standalone ML code from the formal specifications. In principle, the generated code could be compiled in with other code to build an application with a formally-justified security component. It would also be useful to input or output code in mainstream languages such as C or Java, as a way of developing a path from verification environments to security applications development. The paper [3] appears to provide an interesting framework in which to work.

We have also been investigating the automatic synthesis of hardware from our specifications using a prototype deduction-based compiler [7]. At present, we are able to generate netlists from the HOL-4 specification of AES, and we plan to further develop and test our prototype on the other ciphers presented here.

Invertibility proofs, as we have seen, are in many cases quite straightforward. It would therefore be interesting to see how much of these proofs could be automated. However, as in AES and IDEA, there can be round operations that have hard to prove inversion lemmas, but that itself is interesting information about a cipher.

An interesting point is that key schedule generation algorithms can be more difficult than the actual encryption core. This means that mistakes can be more easily made when implementing them. In our work, we formalized these algorithms, but proved little about them, other than a few facts about how long the resulting schedule would be, for example. Therefore, correctness properties of key schedules, if such exist and are amenable to mechanized formal proof, could lead to even higher levels of assurance.

We are currently investigating links between HOL-4 and Cryptol. Since Cryptol is a stream-processing language, and its semantics document is not yet in the public domain, we are basing the work on a HOL theory of lazy lists, due to Michael Norrish (based on original work by John Matthews [10]). Several of the ciphers have been ported to work over the new type, and we have been encouraged, since the functional correctness proof of the new algorithm can be reduced with a few simple lemmas to that of the old. A longer-term goal would be to provide a HOL shallow embedding of an interesting subset of Cryptol.

Another operation sometimes used with encryption is compression. It would be interesting to incorporate a formally verified compression algorithm. Since compression, being invertible, is similar to encryption, there may be commonalities in the two formal exercises. A verification of Huffman's algorithm has recently been carried out in the Coq system [19], and there are many other important compression algorithms that could be tackled.

Finally, the investigation of security properties of block ciphers in theorem provers seems to be an obvious area for future work.

References

1. R. Anderson, E. Biham, and L. Knudsen, *Serpent: A proposal for the advanced encryption standard*, Available at http://www.cl.cam.ac.uk/~rja4/serpent.html, August 1998.
2. A. Armando, D. Basin, Y. Boichut, Y. Chevalier, L. Compagna, J. Cuellar, P. Hankes Drielsma, P.C. He, M. Rusinowitch, J. Santiago, M. Turuani, L. Vigano, and L. Vigneron, *The Avispa tool for the automated validation of internet security protocols and applications*, Proceedings of Computer Aided Verification (CAV), Springer LNCS, no. 3576, 2005.
3. Michael Backes, Birgit Pfitzmann, and Michael Waidner, *Symmetric authentication in a simulatable Dolev-Yao style cryptographic library*, Journal of Information Security **4** (2005), no. 3, 135–154.
4. C. Burwick, D. Coppersmith, E. D'Avignon, R. Gennaro, S. Halevi, C. Jutla, S. Mathas Jr., L. O'Connor, M. Peyravian, D. Safford, and N. Zunic, *MARS - a candidate cipher for AES*, Available at http://www.research.ibm.com/security/mars.pdf, September 1999.
5. Joan Daemen and Vincent Rijmen, *The design of Rijndael: AES - the Advanced Encryption Standard*, Information Security and Cryptography, no. 17, Springer-Verlag, 2002.

6. Morris Dworkin, *Recommendation for block cipher modes of operation: Methods and techniques*, Tech. Report SP 800-38A, National Institute of Standards and Technology, 2001.

7. M. Gordon, J. Iyoda, S. Owens, and K. Slind, *Automatic formal synthesis of hardware from higher order logic*, Proceedings of Fifth International Workshop on Automated Verification of Critical Systems (AVoCS), ENTCS, 2005, to appear.

8. X. Lai, J.L. Massey, and S. Murphy, *Markov ciphers and differential cryptanalysis*, Advances in Cryptology - Eurocrypt '91 (Donald W. Davies, ed.), LNCS, vol. 547, Springer Verlag, 1991, pp. 17–38.

9. Jeff Lewis, *Cryptol, a domain specific language for cryptography*, Tech. report, Galois Connections Inc., 2002, URL—http://www.cryptol.net/docs/CryptolPaper.pdf.

10. John Matthews, *Recursive definition over coinductive types*, Proceedings of the 12th International Conference on Theorem Proving in Higher Order Logics (TPHOLs'99) (Nice) (Y. Bertot, G. Dowek, A. Hirschowitz, C. Paulin, and L. Thery, eds.), LNCS, no. 1690, Springer-Verlag, 1999.

11. Lambert Meertens, *Calculate polytypically!*, Proc. 8th Int. Symp. on Programming Languages: Implementations, Logics, and Programs, PLILP'96 (H. Kuchen and S.D. Swiestra, eds.), vol. 1140, Springer-Verlag, Berlin, 1996, pp. 1–16.

12. Michael Norrish and Konrad Slind, *HOL-4 manuals*, 1998-2005, Available at http://hol.sourceforge.net/.

13. United States National Institute of Standards and Technology, *Advanced Encryption Standard*, Web: http://csrc.nist.gov/encryption/aes/, 2001.

14. R.Boyer and J Moore, *Proof checking the RSA public key encryption algorithm*, American Mathematical Monthly **91** (1984), no. 3, 181–189.

15. R. Rivest, M. Robshae, R. Sidney, and Y.L. Yin, *The RC6 block cipher*, Available at http://www.rsasecurity.com/rsalabs/rc6, August 1998.

16. B. Schneier, J. Kelsey, D. Whiting, D. Wagner, C. Hall, and N. Ferguson, *The Twofish encryption algorithm*, John Wiley and Sons, 2003.

17. Konrad Slind, *A verification of Rijndael in HOL*, Supplementary Proceedings of TPHOLs 2002 (V. A Carreno, C. A. Munoz, and S. Tahar, eds.), NASA Conference Proceedings, no. CP-2002-211736, August 2002.

18. Konrad Slind and Joe Hurd, *Applications of polytypism in theorem proving*, Theorem Proving in Higher Order Logics, 16th International Conference, TPHOLs 2003, Rome, Italy, Proceedings (D. Basin and B. Wolff, eds.), Lecture Notes in Computer Science, vol. 2758, Springer, September 2003, pp. 103–119.

19. Laurent Thery, *Formalizing Huffman's algorithm*, Tech. Report TRCS 034/2004, Department of Informatics, University of Acquila, 2004.

20. Diana Toma and Dominique Borrione, *Formal verification of a SHA-1 circuit core using ACL2*, Theorem Proving in Higher Order Logics, 18th International Conference, TPHOLs'05 (Joe Hurd and Tom Melham, eds.), Lecture Notes in Computer Science, vol. 3603, Springer-Verlag, August 2005, pp. 326–341.

21. Phil Wadler, *Monads for functional programming*, Marktoberdorf Summer School on Progam Design Calculi (M. Broy, ed.), NATO ASI Series F: Computer and Systems Sciences, vol. 118, Springer-Verlag, 1992.

22. David Wheeler and Roger Needham, *TEA, a tiny encryption algorithm*, Fast Software Encryption: Second International Workshop, Lecture Notes in Computer Science, vol. 1008, Springer Verlag, 1999, pp. 363–366.

23. Junxing Zhang and Konrad Slind, *Verification of Euclid's algorithm for finding multiplicative inverses*, Emerging Trends: Theorem Proving in Higher Order Logics: 18th International Conference, TPHOLs 2005 (Joe Hurd, ed.), 2005.

Towards Automated Proof Support for Probabilistic Distributed Systems

Annabelle K. McIver[1] and Tjark Weber[2]

[1] Dept. Computer Science, Macquarie University, NSW 2109, Australia
anabel@ics.mq.edu.au
[2] Dept. Computer Science, Technische Universität München, Germany
webertj@in.tum.de

Abstract. The mechanisation of proofs for probabilistic systems is particularly challenging due to the verification of real-valued properties that probability entails: experience indicates [12, 4, 11] that there are many difficulties in automating real-number arithmetic in the context of other program features.

In this paper we propose a framework for verification of probabilistic distributed systems based on the generalisation of Kleene algebra with tests that has been used as a basis for development of concurrency control in standard programming [7]. We show that verification of real-valued properties in these systems can be considerably simplified, and moreover that there is an interpretation which is susceptible to counterexample search via state exploration, despite the underlying real-number domain.

1 Introduction

Recent developments in mechanised theorem-proving approaches to the verification of probabilistic programs [12, 4, 11] have highlighted at once both the benefits and drawbacks of proof-based techniques. On the plus side, we see clearly that proofs provide more general solutions (which can be re-used and easily checked) than do other forms of automated verification such as probabilistic model checking [17] (which, unlike standard model checking, does not compute counterexamples). On the minus side, however, experience has shown that there remain difficulties in automating real arithmetic in the context of other program features, a necessity whenever typical properties are quantitative such as "the probability that the program terminates is at least 0.7".

The infinite domain (of reals) needed for quantitative analysis also implies other limitations when compared to qualitative analysis. For example, it prevents the provision of counterexample search via state exploration [28]. Counterexample search is an effective technique in the activity of mathematical proof, as it leads to the debugging of conjectures, often by directing the prover to strengthen the hypotheses under which the consequent should follow. In program verification this debugging process corresponds to reformulations of specifications under which a proposed refinement is valid, or to the redesign of a suggested implementation. Such debugging strategies have been employed to great effect in tools

G. Sutcliffe and A. Voronkov (Eds.): LPAR 2005, LNAI 3835, pp. 534–548, 2005.

such as Alloy [13]. Given the above however, it appears at first sight that the task of quantitative verification cannot be enhanced straightforwardly by counterexample search.

Nevertheless, the benefits of mechanised proof provide a strong motivation to look for methods that will alleviate the drawbacks. In this paper we present a proof system which reduces the overhead of arithmetic in automated proof, as well as supporting counterexample search. As far as we are aware, this is the first proof system for probabilistic programs to do so.

As our principal context we take probabilistic distributed systems — such systems are particularly difficult to verify, as the interaction of probability with other system features can lead to unexpected behaviour [26, 2]. In these cases, much of the verification is devoted to showing that, under certain simple hypotheses, a highly distributed architecture is equivalent to a serialised one. In fact a proof of such an equivalence can often be done without appeal to probability at all, even though the systems and their correctness depend on explicit quantitative properties. This has the effect of reducing any quantitative reasoning to validation of the hypotheses for a particular concrete system, in general a significantly simpler problem than analysing the two architectures directly. Cohen's work [7, 6] on the practical use of *Kleene algebra* for verification in loosely-coupled (but non-probabilistic) systems provides ample evidence that a Kleene-style algebra is a good candidate for this kind of reasoning, and the evidence applies even when probability is introduced.

Our first contribution is to show how a model for probabilistic systems $\mathcal{LS}$ (for given state space S) [10, 23] can be interpreted over a Kleene-style program algebra [16], so that explicit probabilistic reasoning is significantly reduced.

Next we turn to the feasibility of counterexample search in probabilistic Kleene algebra. For this we propose an abstraction of the probabilistic model that preserves the important limiting features of standard probability, and at the same time yields genuinely finite models which are thus amenable to state exploration techniques similar to those for non-probabilistic systems [28].

Our second contribution is a model of abstract probabilities $\mathcal{KS}$ that is susceptible to complete semantic exploration, yielding counterexamples even for the probabilistic model $\mathcal{LS}$. This appears to be the first facility for counterexample search for probabilistic systems.

In Sec. 2 we set out the probabilistic model $\mathcal{LS}$, together with, in Sec. 2.1, an interpretation in the Kleene-style algebra. Next, in Sec. 3 we set out the abstract model $\mathcal{KS}$ and show that the the interpretation in Kleene algebra is a homomorphic image of the interpretation in $\mathcal{LS}$, and in particular that equalities over Kleene algebra expressions are preserved. Finally in Sec. 4 we show how state exploration techniques within $\mathcal{KS}$ can be used to generate counterexamples even within $\mathcal{LS}$. In Sec. 5 we summarise other research in this area and suggest further topics for investigation.

The notational conventions used are as follows. Function application is represented by a dot, as in $f.x$. If K is a set then $\overline{K}$ is the set of discrete probability distributions over K, that is the normalised functions from K into the real interval $[0, 1]$ (*i.e.* function f is normalised if $\sum_{s:K} f.s = 1$). A point distribution centered at a point k is denoted by δ_k. The $(p, 1-p)$-weighted average of distributions d and d' is denoted $d_p \oplus d'$; more generally we write $p_1 d^1 + \ldots + p_n d^n$ for the $(p_1, \ldots, p_n)$ weighted average over distributions $d^1, \ldots, d^n$. If K is a subset, and d a distribution, we write $d.K$ for $\sum_{s:K} d.s$. The power set of K is denoted $\wp K$.

2   Probabilistic Systems

Given a (discrete) state space S, the set of functions $S \to \wp \overline{S}$, from (initial) states to subsets of distributions over (final) states, is the basis for the transition-system style model now generally accepted for probabilistic systems [19] though, depending on the particular application, the conditions imposed on the subsets of (final) probability distributions can vary [23, 10]. Briefly the idea is that probabilistic systems comprise both *quantifiable* arbitrary behaviour (such as the chance of winning an automated lottery) together with *un*quantifiable arbitrary behaviour (such as the precise order of concurrent events). The functions $S \to \wp \overline{S}$ model the quantifiable events as probability distributions — effectively probabilistic transitions (hence the range of semantic functions includes distributions in $\overline{S}$). On the other hand, the unquantifiable events are modelled as a subset of distributions (hence the range of semantic functions can be a subset of distributions).

For example, a program that simulates a fair coin is modelled by a function that maps an arbitrary state s to the distribution weighted evenly between the point distributions representing heads and tails (but see below):

$$s \mapsto \{\delta_{\mathsf{head}} \, {}_{1/2} \oplus \, \delta_{\mathsf{tail}}\} \ . \tag{1}$$

In contrast a program that simulates a possible bias favouring heads of at most $2/3$, is modelled by a function which takes an arbitrary state to a subset of distributions specifying the precise limits on the bias:

$$s \mapsto \{\delta_{\mathsf{head}} \, {}_{1/2} \oplus \, \delta_{\mathsf{tail}} \, , \delta_{\mathsf{head}} \, {}_{2/3} \oplus \, \delta_{\mathsf{tail}}\} \ . \tag{2}$$

In setting up the details, we follow Morgan *et al.*[23] and take a domain theoretical approach, restricting the result sets of the semantic functions according to an underlying order on the state space. An innovation, however, is to distinguish specially "miraculous" or infeasible behaviour from ordinary behaviour — miracles are used in program semantics to simplify calculations [21, 20], to model "tests" [16] and, here, they will work well with our simple algebra of programs to come. In the semantics, miracles will be associated with a special introduced state $\top$, and our program model is defined over the *probabilistic power domain* [14] based on the underlying (flat) domain $(S^\top, \sqsubseteq)$, where $S^\top$ is S conjoined with the special state $\top$, and the order $\sqsubseteq$ is constructed so that $\top$ dominates all (proper) states in S, which are otherwise unrelated.

Definition 1. *A probabilistic power domain is a pair* $(\overline{S^{\top}}, \sqsubseteq_{\mathcal{D}})$, *where* $\overline{S^{\top}}$ *is the set of normalised functions from* $S^{\top}$ *into the real interval* $[0, 1]$, *and* $\sqsubseteq_{\mathcal{D}}$ *is induced from* $\sqsubseteq$ *on* $S^{\top}$ *so that*

$$d \sqsubseteq_{\mathcal{D}} d' \quad \textit{iff} \quad (\forall K \subseteq S \cdot d.K + d.\top \ \leq \ d'.K + d'.\top) \ .$$

Probabilistic programs (with miracles) are now modelled as the set of functions from initial $S^{\top}$ to sets of final distributions over $S^{\top}$, where the result sets are restricted by so-called *healthiness conditions* characterising viable probabilistic behaviour, and motivated in detail elsewhere [19]. By doing so the semantics accounts for specific features of probabilistic programs. In this case (again following Morgan) we impose *up-closure* (the inclusion of all $\sqsubseteq_{\mathcal{D}}$-dominating distributions), *convex closure* (the inclusion of all convex combinations of distributions), and *Cauchy closure* (the inclusion of all limits of distributions according to the standard Cauchy metric on real-valued functions [23]). Thus, by construction, viable computations are those in which miracles dominate (refine) all other behaviours (implied by up-closure), nondeterministic choice is refined by probabilistic choice (implied by convex closure), and classic limiting behaviour of probabilistic events (such as so-called "zero-one laws" [1]) is also accounted for (implied by Cauchy closure). An additional bonus is that program refinement is simply defined as reverse set-inclusion. We observe that probabilistic properties are preserved with increasing order.

Definition 2. *The space of probabilistic programs [2] is given by* $(\mathcal{LS}, \sqsubseteq_{\mathcal{L}})$ *where* $\mathcal{LS}$ *is the set of functions from* $S^{\top}$ *to the power set of* $\overline{S^{\top}}$, *restricted to subsets which are* Cauchy- , convex- *and* up *closed with respect to* $\sqsubseteq_{\mathcal{D}}$. *All programs are* $\top$*-preserving (mapping* $\top$ *to* $\{\delta_{\top}\}$*). The order between programs is defined*

$$P \sqsubseteq_{\mathcal{L}} P' \quad \textit{iff} \quad (\forall s \colon S \cdot P.s \supseteq P'.s) \ .$$

Thus in the examples above, taking the closure conditions into account, we see that up-closure implies that the result set at (1) would also contain the distributions $a\delta_{\mathsf{head}} + b\delta_{\mathsf{tail}} + c\delta_{\top}$ for a, b, c satisfying the conditions $1/2 \leq a + c$, and $1/2 \leq b + c$. Similarly convex-closure implies that the result set at (2) should also include all $(p, 1 - p)$-weighted distributions of the form $(\delta_{\mathsf{head}\ 2/3} \oplus \delta_{\mathsf{tail}}/3)_{p} \oplus (\delta_{\mathsf{head}\ 1/2} \oplus \delta_{\mathsf{tail}})$, for any $0 \leq p \leq 1$.

In Fig. 1 we define some mathematical operators on the space of programs, which will be used to interpret our language. Informally composition $P; P'$ corresponds to a program P being executed followed by P', so that from initial state s, any result distribution d of $P.s$ can be followed by an arbitrary distribution of $P'.$[3] The probabilistic operator takes the weighted average of the distributions of its operands, and the nondeterminism operator takes their union. To illustrate,

---

[1] An easy consequence of a zero-one law is that if a fair coin is flipped repeatedly, then with probability 1 a head is observed eventually. See the program 'coin' inside an iteration, which is discussed below.

[2] This particular "Lamington" model was first suggested by Carroll Morgan [22].

[3] Compare composition in Markov Decision Processes [9].

Identity	$Id.s$	$\hat{=}$	$\lceil\{\delta_s\}\rceil$,
top	$\top.s$	$\hat{=}$	$\{\delta_\top\}$,
composition	$(P;P').s$	$\hat{=}$	$\{\sum_{u:S\top}(d.u)\times d'_u \mid d\in P.s; d'_u\in P'.u\}$,
choice	$(if\ B\ then\ P\ else\ P').s$	$\hat{=}$	$if\ B.s,\ then\ P.s,\ otherwise\ P'.s$
probability	$(P\ _p\oplus P').s$	$\hat{=}$	$\lceil\{d\ _p\oplus d' \mid d\in r.s; d'\in r'.s\}\rceil$,
nondeterminism	$(P\sqcap P').s$	$\hat{=}$	$\lceil\{d \mid d\in(P.s\cup P'.s)\}\rceil$,
iteration	P^*	$\hat{=}$	$(\nu X\cdot P; X\sqcap Id)$.

In the above definitions s is a state in S and $\lceil K\rceil$ is the smallest up-, convex- and Cauchy-closed subset of distributions containing K. Programs are denoted by P and P', and the expression $(\nu X\cdot f.X)$ denotes the greatest fixed point of the function f — in the case of iteration the function is the monotone $\sqsubseteq_{\mathcal{L}}$-program-to-program function $\lambda X\cdot(P; X\sqcap Id)$. All programs map $\top$ to $\{\delta_\top\}$.

Fig. 1. Mathematical operators on the space of programs [19]

let S be the set of integers, and consider the following transition $\pi_k.s\hat{=}\{\delta_{s+k}\}$. Thus $\pi_k.s$ is the transition that adds k to s. Next we can define more complicated transitions using the operators, for example

$$\Pi.s\quad\hat{=}\quad if\ (s\geq0)\ then\ (\pi_{-1}\ _{\frac{1}{2}}\oplus(Id\ _{\frac{1}{2}}\oplus\pi_{-2})).s\ \ else\ Id.s \qquad (3)$$

The transition at (3) essentially maps initial states with value at least 0 to the weighted sum of point distributions, namely $\frac{1}{2}\times\delta_{s-1}+\frac{1}{4}\times\delta_s+\frac{1}{4}\times\delta_{s-2}$, and otherwise leaves the state alone.

Iteration is the most intricate of the operations — operationally P^* represents the program that can execute P an arbitrary number of finite times. In the probabilistic context, as well as generating the results of all "finite iterations" of $(P\sqcap Id)$ (*viz*, a finite number of compositions of $(P\sqcap Id)$), imposition of Cauchy closure acts as expected on metric spaces, in that it generates all *limiting* distributions as well — *i.e.* if $d_0, d_1, \ldots$ are distributions contained in a result set M which converge to d, then d is contained in M as well. To illustrate, consider the transition at (3) inside an iteration Π^* corresponding to a transition system which can (but does not have to) reduce s indefinitely until its value falls below zero. For states with value less than zero the iteration does nothing to the state (*i.e.* we are considering "skipping forever" to be the the same as terminating). Now it is easy to see that from initial $s=0$, after n iterations of the program at (3) the distribution over the results $s=0, -1$ or -2 is $p_n\delta_0+q_n\delta_{-1}+r_n\delta_{-2}$, where $p_n=1/(4^n)$, $q_n=2(1-p_n)/3$ and $r_n=(1-p_n)/3$. But observe now the limits $\lim_{n\to\infty}p_n=0$, $\lim_{n\to\infty}q_n=2/3$, and $\lim_{n\to\infty}r_n=1/3$, and that Cauchy closure implies the limit distribution $2\delta_{-1}/3+\delta_{-2}/3$ is contained in the result set of the iteration Π^* as well.

More generally we will need to characterise the limiting distributions in terms of distributions contained in the result sets of *finite iterations*. (Recall that a finite iteration of program Q is of the form Q^n for some n, where $Q^0\hat{=}Id$, and $Q^{n+1}\hat{=}Q;Q^n$.) The following lemma provides conditions, in the context of finite state spaces, that a distribution be generated by an iteration. For any distribution d, let supp.d be the smallest subset $K \subseteq S^\top$ with $d.K = 1$, and for iteration (P^*) let $P^\mathcal{N}$ be the set of distributions generated by finite iterations of $(Id \sqcap P)$. Further, we say that "subset K can be reached with probability 1 from state s via executions of program Q" if there exists a sequence (possibly finite) of distributions d_i with each $d_i \in Q^i.s$, such that $\lim_{i \geq 0} d_i.K = 1$. (Note that distributions contained in finite executions are a special case.)

Lemma 1. *Let P be a program in $\mathcal{LS}$, and let S be finite. If distribution d is in $P^*.s$, then supp.d can be reached from s with probability 1 via executions of $(Id \sqcap P)$. Alternatively if K is a subset of supp.d' for some d' in $P^*.s$, and can be reached with probability 1 via executions of $(Id \sqcap P)$ from all s in supp.d', then there is some d in $P^*.s$ with supp.$d = K$.*

Proof. By the greatest fixed point definition, $P^* = \lceil \lim_{n \geq 0} (Id \sqcap P)^n \rceil$, thus the first condition follows. Alternatively if distribution d' is in the result set of $P^*.s$, then the nondeterminism in subsequent executions of $(Id \sqcap P)$ can be exploited to produce a distribution with support K, since if $s' \notin K$, the branch P can be selected until K is established with probability 1, which (if P itself has no non-determinsim) yields an appropriate distribution d. The case that P is nondeterministic reduces to the latter case since it has been shown elsewhere [19, 8] that $P^* = \sqcap_{i:I} P_i^*$, where we are using $\sqcap_{i:I} P_i^*$ to mean the nondeterministic choice over the programs in the index set I, which in this case ranges over all deterministic refinements of P. The result now follows since d is a convex combination of distributions within the $P_i^*.s$.

Now we have introduced a model for general probabilistic contexts, our next task is to investigate its program algebra. That is the topic of the next section.

2.1 Kleene Algebra for Probabilistic Systems

Kleene algebra consists of a sequential composition operator (with a distinguished identity (1) and zero (0)); a binary plus ($+$) and unary star ($*$). Terms are ordered by $\leq$ defined by $+$ (see Fig. 2), and both binary as well as the unary operators are monotone with respect to it. Sequential composition is indicated by the sequencing of terms in an expression so that ab means the program denoted by a is executed first, and then b. The expression $a + b$ means that either a or b is executed, and the Kleene star a^* represents an arbitrary number of executions of the program a. In Fig. 2 we set out the rules for the *probabilistic Kleene algebra, pKA*. We use early letters (a, b, c) to denote expressions (constructed from application of the operators) and late letters (x, y, z) to denote variables (within expressions). In an interpretation of a *pKA* expression the variables are mapped to specific (probabilistic) programs. The next definition sets out the details.

Definition 3. *The semantic mapping from pKA expressions to $\mathcal{LS}$ is given by*

$$[\![1]\!]_\rho \;\hat{=}\; Id \,, \quad [\![0]\!]_\rho \;\hat{=}\; \top$$
$$[\![ab]\!]_\rho \;\hat{=}\; [\![a]\!]_\rho ; [\![b]\!]_\rho \,, \quad [\![a+b]\!]_\rho \;\hat{=}\; [\![a]\!]_\rho \sqcap [\![b]\!]_\rho \,, \quad [\![a^*]\!]_\rho \;\hat{=}\; [\![a]\!]_\rho^*$$

$$
\begin{aligned}
&(i)\ 0 + a = a & &(viii)\ ab + ac \le a(b+c)\ \ (\dagger) \\
&(ii)\ a + b = b + a & &(ix)\ (a+b)c = ac + bc \\
&(iii)\ a + a = a & &(x)\ a \le b \quad \text{iff} \quad a + b = b \\
&(iv)\ a + (b+c) = (a+b) + c & & \\
&(v)\ a(bc) = (ab)c & &(xi)\ a^* = 1 + aa^* \\
&(vi)\ 0a = a0 = 0 & &(xii)\ a(b+1) \le a \quad \Rightarrow \quad ab^* = a \\
&(vii)\ 1a = a1 = a & &(xiii)\ ab \le b \quad \Rightarrow \quad a^*b = b
\end{aligned}
$$

Programs are denoted by a, b and c. Note that the rule ($\dagger$) is weaker than the corresponding rule in standard Kleene algebra [7]; this is because of the well-documented [19, 27] interaction of probability and nondeterminism.

Fig. 2. Rules of Probabilistic Kleene algebra, pKA

Here ρ gives the precise interpretation corresponding to the variables in the expressions a and b, so that for variable x, we have $[\![x]\!]_\rho$ is a specific (fixed) probabilistic program $\rho.x$ in $\mathcal{LS}$.

We use $\ge$ for the order in pKA, which we identify with $\sqsubseteq_{\mathcal{L}}$ from Def. 2; the next result shows that Def. 3 is a valid interpretation for the rules in Fig. 1, in that theorems in pKA apply in general to probabilistic programs.

Theorem 1. *Let ρ be an interpretation as set out at Def. 3. The rules at Fig. 2 are all satisfied, namely if $a \le b$ is a theorem of pKA set out at Fig. 2, then $[\![b]\!]_\rho \sqsubseteq_{\mathcal{L}} [\![a]\!]_\rho$.*

Proof. Follows from Def. 3, and the fact that $P^* = \lceil \bigcup_{n \ge 0} (Id \sqcap P)^n \rceil$.

Next in Lem. 2 we illustrate some proofs within Kleene algebra of some simple properties of programs. The first two theorems are basic technical equalities; the third equality, on the other hand, is of independent interest as it forms the basis for many "separation"-style theorems common in distributed systems [7], and indeed generalises similar theorems to the probabilistic context.

Lemma 2.

$$
\begin{aligned}
a^* a^* &= a^* & (4) \\
a^*(b+c) &= a^*(a^*b + a^*c) & (5) \\
a(b+1) \le ca + d &\Rightarrow ab^* \le c^*(a + db^*) & (6)
\end{aligned}
$$

Proof. For (4) we observe from (xi) that $a^* = 1 + aa^*$, thus $aa^* \le a^*$, and the result follows from ($xiii$).

For (5) we reason as follows:

$$
a^*(a^*b + a^*c) \ \ge \ a^*(b+c) \ = \ a^*a^*(b+c) \ \ge \ a^*(a^*b + a^*c)\,,
$$

where the first inequality follows since $1 \le a^*$; the inequality from (4), and the final inequality from ($viii$).

Finally for (6) we show first that

$$c^*(a + db^*)(b + 1) \leq c^*(a + db^*) ,$$

reasoning as follows.

$$
\begin{array}{llr}
& c^*(a + db^*)(b + 1) & \\
= & c^*(a(b + 1) + db^*(b + 1)) & (ix) \\
\leq & c^*(ca + d + db^*(b + 1)) & hypothesis \\
\leq & c^*(ca + db^* + db^*) & 1, (b + 1) \leq b^*; \ (4) \\
= & c^*(ca + db^*) & (iii) \\
\leq & c^*(c^*a + c^*db^*) & 1, c \leq c^* \\
= & c^*(a + db^*) \ . & (5)
\end{array}
$$

From this inequality we now appeal to the induction rule at (xii) to deduce that $c^*(a+db^*)b^* \leq c^*(a+db^*)$, *and the result now follows since* $ab^* \leq c^*(a+db^*)b^*$.

The rules in Fig. 2 purposefully treat probabilistic choice implicitly, and it is only the failure of the equality at *(viii)* which implies that probability may be present in an interpretation $[\![a]\!]_\rho$: in fact it is this property that characterises probabilistic-like models, separating them from those which contain only pure demonic nondeterminism. [4] The use of implicit probabilities fits in well with our applications, where probability is usually confined to statements within a distributed protocol and nondeterminism refers to the arbitrary sequencing of actions that is controlled by a so-called *adversarial scheduler* [27]. For example, if a and b correspond to atomic program fragments (containing probability), then the expression $(a+b)^*$ means that either a or b (possibly containing probability) is executed an arbitrary number of times (according to the scheduler), in any order — in other words it corresponds to the concurrent execution of a and b. Typically a verification of a distributed protocol might involve transformation of a simple, serialised specification architecture, such as a^*b^* (first a executes for an arbitrary number of times, and then b does), into a distributed implementation architecture, such as $(a+b)^*$ using general hypotheses, such as $ab = ba$ (program fragments a and b commute). For instance a typical conjecture might be the following transformation

$$ab \leq ca \quad \Rightarrow \quad ab^* \leq c^*a , \tag{7}$$

which says that if a and b are programs such that running a followed by b is a refinement of c followed by a, then it should be the case that a followed by running b for an arbitrary number of times is a refinement of running c similarly for an arbitrary number of times followed by a. Were this result to be proved generally within the proof system then for a particular example where a, b and c were specific programs typically containing precise probabilistic choices,

---

[4] Programming models that include *angelic nondeterminism* as well as demonic non-determinism satisfy *(viii)*, and not the stronger equality [3]; however those models do not satisfy the special limiting properties of probabilistic programs.

only the simple hypothesis $ab \leq ca$ *would need to be checked* (*i.e.* that $[\![ca]\!]_\rho \sqsubseteq_{\mathcal{L}}$ $[\![ab]\!]_\rho$) instead of constructing brute force the concrete model for the whole of the (iterative) programs $[\![ab^*]\!]_\rho$ and $[\![c^*a]\!]_\rho$ and then comparing the results explicitly.

Though plausible, unfortunately the particular conjecture at (7) turns out to be invalid in the probabilistic model (though it is valid in the standard model) and so any attempt to prove otherwise using pKA is bound to fail. To see that let ρ be the interpretation such that

$$[\![a]\!]_\rho \quad = \quad [\![b]\!]_\rho \quad = \quad [\![c]\!]_\rho \quad = \quad x := 0 \; {}_{\frac{1}{2}}\!\oplus x := 1 \tag{8}$$

so that $[\![ab^*]\!]_\rho = x := 0 \sqcap x := 1$ and $[\![c^*a]\!]_\rho = x := 0 \; {}_{\frac{1}{2}}\!\oplus x := 1$. Were (7) to be true generally, it would assert (in this case, since $x := 0 \sqcap x := 1 \sqsubseteq_{\mathcal{L}} x := 0 \; {}_{\frac{1}{2}}\!\oplus x := 1$ is generally true) the equality of the programs $x := 0 \sqcap x := 1$ and $x := 0 \; {}_{\frac{1}{2}}\!\oplus x := 1$. But the result set of the latter program does not contain the point distributions δ_0 and δ_1, whereas the result set of the former does.

Such false conjectures are a common pitfall in the activity of proof, and can be seen as intermediate stages of a validation. Once the error is discovered, the solution is usually clear, and in the case of (7) is fixed by strengthening the hypothesis to $a(b+1) \leq ca$ so that the correct theorem becomes

$$a(b+1) \leq ca \quad \Rightarrow \quad ab^* \leq c^*a \; , \tag{9}$$

which can indeed be verified within the proof system. [5] And the above interpretation at (8) is no longer a counterexample for (9) since the new hypothesis now fails to hold.

Determining which conjectures are false can however be a very time consuming and ad hoc process, thus any automated tool to prompt the user with a counterexample is an invaluable resource. Unfortunately automated counterexample searchers normally use some kind of exhaustive search through models of finite size, but this is not possible for the real-number domain needed to model probability distributions. In the next section we consider an abstraction which, overcomes this problem.

3   Abstract Probabilistic Systems

In this section we propose an abstraction of $\mathcal{LS}$ which yields genuinely finite models. The basic idea is to replace a probability distribution d by a simple set, in fact its support supp.d, which contains only the information of which transitions are probabilistic, and the range over which each probabilistic transition extends. We call such a subset the *abstract distribution* associated with d. This abstraction (mapping distributions to their abstract counterparts) induces an order on subsets of $S^\top$: two subsets (abstract distributions) are defined to be comparable only if there exist corresponding probability distributions which are comparable under $\sqsubseteq_{\mathcal{D}}$. The next definition reformulates that idea without referring to distributions at all.

---

[5] Indeed it is a special case of (6) at Lem. 2 above with d set to 0.

Definition 4. *Given a distribution d, its associated* abstract distribution *is defined to be* supp.d. *Abstract distributions K and K' are ordered as follows* [6]

$$K \sqsubseteq_{\mathcal{A}} K' \quad \textit{iff} \quad (K = K') \vee ((\top \in K') \Rightarrow K' \subseteq K).$$

The space of abstract programs now uses abstract distributions. The closure conditions are suitable abstractions of those used in Def. 2; in particular union-closure is an abstraction of convex closure.

Definition 5. *The space of* abstract probabilistic programs *is the pair* $(\mathcal{K}S, \sqsubseteq_{\mathcal{K}})$ *where* $\mathcal{K}S$ *is the set of functions* $S^\top \to \wp \wp S^\top$, *restricted to subsets which are* union- *and up* closed *with respect to* $\sqsubseteq_{\mathcal{A}}$. *The order between programs is defined*

$$U \sqsubseteq_{\mathcal{K}} U' \quad \textit{iff} \quad (\forall s: S \cdot U.s \supseteq U'.s) .$$

Next we define a projection which maps probabilistic programs to abstract probabilistic programs, so that it preserves order.

Definition 6. *The* abstraction projection $\epsilon : \mathcal{L}S \to \mathcal{K}S$ *is defined* $\epsilon.P.s \mathbin{\hat{=}}$ $\{\text{supp.d} \mid d \in P.s\}$.

Lemma 3. *For probabilistic programs* $P, P': \mathcal{L}S$, *if* $P \sqsubseteq_{\mathcal{L}} P'$ *then* $\epsilon.P \sqsubseteq_{\mathcal{K}} \epsilon.P'$.

Proof. Follows from the definitions of ϵ, $\sqsubseteq_{\mathcal{D}}$ *and* $\sqsubseteq_{\mathcal{A}}$.

In Fig. 3 we define some mathematical operators over the space of abstract probabilistic programs — they have been chosen so that they correspond via ϵ to the operators for the probabilistic model given at Fig. 1. We say that if K is a subset of abstract distributions then $\|\lceil K \rceil\|$ is the smallest $\sqsubseteq_{\mathcal{A}}$-up- and union-closed containing K.

Identity	Id.s	$\mathbin{\hat{=}} \|\lceil \{\{s\}\} \rceil\|$,
top	$\top$.s	$\mathbin{\hat{=}} \{\{\top\}\}$,
composition	$(U \mathbin{;} U').s$	$\mathbin{\hat{=}} \{\bigcup_{u:K} K'_u \mid K: U.s;\ K'_u: U'.u\}$,
probability	$(U \oplus U').s$	$\mathbin{\hat{=}} \|\lceil \{K \cup K' \mid K: U.s; K': U'.s\} \rceil\|$,
nondeterminism	$(U \| U').s$	$\mathbin{\hat{=}} \|\lceil \{K \mid K: (U.s \cup U'.s)\} \rceil\|$,

Here s is a state in S, and U , U' are programs, and if K is a subset of abstract distributions then $\|\lceil K \rceil\|$ is the smallest $\sqsubseteq_{\mathcal{A}}$-up- and union-closed subset containing K. We deal with iteration below.

Fig. 3. Mathematical operators on abstract probabilistic programs

By construction the abstraction projection preserves (homomorphically) composition and nondeterminism. In particular it is easy to see that $\epsilon.(P; P') \equiv_{\mathcal{K}}$ $\epsilon.P \mathbin{;} \epsilon.P'$ and that $\epsilon.(P \sqcap P') \equiv_{\mathcal{K}} \epsilon.P \| \epsilon.P'$. Our next task is to do the same for

---

[6] This is actually the well-known Hoare order on subsets based on $\sqsubseteq$ for $S^\top$.

iteration — here, as for composition and nondeterminism, our goal is to define the abstract version so that the abstract distributions in the result set of the iteration can be determined by those in the underlying abstract program — even when they correspond to limit distibutions. For example, a probabilistic program modelling of a fair coin, say $\text{coin} \mathrel{\hat{=}} \text{head} \; {}_{\frac{1}{2}}\oplus \text{tail}$, has the result that its iteration (coin^*) includes both output distributions δ_{head} and δ_{tail} though neither point distribution is a result of any finite number of iterations of coin — it is Cauchy closure that guarantees their inclusion. To see that, we imagine that the implicit "⊓" inside of the definition of coin^* acts like a "demon" which can see the value established by the flipped coin after every execution of coin, and can terminate the iteration at any moment — since the laws of probability assert that a fair coin flipped for an arbitrary number of times must *with probability 1* flip a head eventually, the demon can use this to his advantage to wait only long enough until that head appears. The overall effect is that the iteration can terminate with probability 1 in the state head, which is the same as saying that coin^* outputs the point distribution δ_{head}. A similar argument holds for tail.

Thus we need to define the abstract iteration so that $\epsilon.(\text{coin}^*)$ contains the corresponding abstract distributions $\{\text{head}\}$ and $\{\text{tail}\}$.

Definition 7. *For abstract program A in $\mathcal{K}S$, we define A^* as follows. Subset $K \subseteq A^*.s$ if there exists a probabilistic program P in $\mathcal{L}S$ such that $\epsilon.P = A$ and $K = \text{supp}.d$ for some distribution d in $P^*.s$.*

Our next task is to reformulate Def. 7 so that A^* can be determined without referring to any probabilities at all (in an underlying probabilistic program, P say). Fortunately, for finite state spaces S, Lem. 1 implies that the images in ϵ of limit distributions can be characterised in terms of abstract probabilistic properties alone, which is precisely what we need. The next two lemmas set out the details.

Lemma 4. *For any program P in $\mathcal{L}S$, with S finite, we have the equality $\epsilon.(P^*) = (\epsilon.P)^*$.*

Proof. Follows immediately from Lem. 1 which implies that supports of distributions in iterations are independent of the probabilistic weights of the transitions.

Whilst Lem. 4 implies that the actual numeric values of underlying programs P are irrelevant for determining A^* (provided that they are non zero), the next result shows how to compute A^* without referring to the underlying probabilistic programs at all, but only their abstractions. We say that K is *reachable with probability 1 via executions of A* if K is reachable with probability 1 for some program P in $\mathcal{L}S$ such that $\epsilon.P = A$. It is well-known that in finite state spaces there exist algorithms to compute such *probability 1 reachability sets* using only the information provided by the abstract transitions; for example de Alfaro *et al.* provide such an algorithm [8] with complexity quadratic in the size of the underlying transition system, and we discuss its relevance in the next section.

Lemma 5. *Given abstract program A in $\mathcal{K}S$, where S is a finite state space we can compute A^* as follows. Subset K is in $A^*.s$ if*

1. $K \subseteq (Id \parallel A)^n$ for some $n \geq 0$;
2. or there is some $K' \subseteq A^*.s$ such that $K \subseteq K'$ and for all $k \in K'$ it is possible to reach K with probability 1 from k via executions of $(Id \parallel A)$.

Proof. Let P be any program in $\mathcal{LS}$ such that $\epsilon.P = A$. The result now follows from Lem. 1.

Finally we can define an interpretation of pKA over abstract probabilistic programs so that the two interpretations correspond homomorphically.

Definition 8. *The semantic mapping from pKA terms to the abstract probabilistic semantics is given by* [7]

$$(\! | 1 | \!)_\rho \mathrel{\hat{=}} \mathsf{Id} \ , \quad (\! | 0 | \!)_\rho \mathrel{\hat{=}} \top$$
$$(\! | ab | \!)_\rho \mathrel{\hat{=}} (\! | a | \!)_\rho \ \text{\Large;}\ (\! | b | \!)_\rho \ , \quad (\! | a + b | \!)_\rho \mathrel{\hat{=}} (\! | a | \!)_\rho \parallel (\! | b | \!)_\rho \ , \quad (\! | a^* | \!)_\rho \mathrel{\hat{=}} (\! | a | \!)_\rho^*$$

Here ρ gives the precise interpretation corresponding to the variables in the expressions a and b, so that for variable x, we have $(\! | x | \!)_\rho$ is a specific (fixed) abstract probabilistic program $\rho.x$ in $\mathcal{KS}$.

The next lemma gives states the relationship between interpretations in $\mathcal{LS}$ and in $\mathcal{KS}$.

Lemma 6. *Let e be any expression in pKA, and let ρ be an interpretation in $\mathcal{LS}$, so that all variables are mapped to programs in $\mathcal{LS}$, and Def. 3 is used to interpret the operators. The equality $\epsilon.[\![e]\!]_\rho = (\! | e | \!)_{\epsilon.\rho}$ holds, where $\epsilon.\rho$ denotes the interpretation in $\mathcal{KS}$ where all variables are mapped to the images under ϵ of the programs defined by ρ, and Def. 8 is used to interpret the operators.*

Proof. Structural induction, Def. 8 and Lem. 5.

In this section we have set up a model for abstract probabilistic programs in which the precise weights attached to the probabilistic transitions have been suppressed, whilst retaining the limiting properties of probability theory.

4   Towards a Framework for Counterexample Search

In this next section we show how $\mathcal{KS}$ can be used to find counterexamples in $\mathcal{LS}$ using a strategy based on state exploration over finite abstract models.

Lemma 7. *Let e and f be expressions in the Kleene algebra. If $e \neq f$ is satisfiable within $\mathcal{KS}$ then it is also satisfiable within $\mathcal{LS}$.*

---

[7] Note that we do not claim that the Kleene rules are satisfied by this definition; indeed $(xiii)$ fails to hold. The abstract program $s_0 \mapsto \{\{s_0, s_1\}\}$; $s_1 \mapsto \{\{s_1\}\}$ denoting both a and b is a counterexample.

Proof. Let the variables in e and f be $x_1, \ldots x_n$. Let ρ be an interpretation which maps each x_i to abstract program A_i within $\mathcal{KS}$ so that $(\!|e|\!)_\rho \neq (\!|f|\!)_\rho$ — this is possible since, by assumption, the inequality is satisfiable in $\mathcal{KS}$. We note that for each A_i there is a corresponding probabilistic model A_i' such that $\epsilon.A_i' = A_i$ (let each abstract distribution K in $A_i.s$ be replaced by the uniform distribution over K). It now follows immediately from Lem. 3 and Lem. 6 that the interpretation defined by the A_i' demonstrates that the inequality is satisfiable in $\mathcal{LS}$ as well.

Finally we have our main result — that if a counterexample exists in $\mathcal{KS}$ to a conjectured equality, it is not provable in pKA.

Corollary 1. *Let e and f be expressions in the Kleene algebra. If $e \neq f$ is satisfiable within $\mathcal{KS}$ then the equality $e = f$ it is not provable by probabilistic Kleene algebra rules.*

Proof. By Lem. 7, the inequality $e \neq f$ is satisfiable within $\mathcal{LS}$, and by Thm. 1 interpretations in $\mathcal{LS}$ satisfy the probabilistic Kleene rules.

To see Lem. 7 in action, consider the assertion at (7). In a two state-space $\{s_0, s_1\}$, we define $A_i.s \mathrel{\hat{=}} \|\lceil \{\{s_0, s_1\}\}\rceil\|$ for $i = 1, 2, 3$; the resulting interpretation with a, b, c mapped to A_1, A_2, A_3 respectively show that the negation of (7) is satisfiable in $\mathcal{KS}$. And indeed the construction described in the proof of Lem. 7 shows that it is not satisfiable in $\mathcal{LS}$ either, recovering the counterexample in $\mathcal{LS}$ given at (8).

4.1 Mechanisation of Counterexample Search

Lem. 7 implies that automated counterexample search for equalities within $\mathcal{LS}$ can be based on state exploration of finite models in $\mathcal{KS}$, and Lem. 5 implies that we can use existing reachability algorithms for finite probabilistic systems to compute (within $\mathcal{KS}$) all instances of a^*.

Based on the model $\mathcal{KS}$ we have implemented a counterexample search using the SAT solving facility [29] of the Isabelle theorem proving environment [25], by translating the pKA expressions into CNF. For very small state spaces, the translation into propositional logic creates an explicit representation of the $*$ operator, where a^* is precomputed for every abstract program a. Due to the number of possible models, this approach is infeasible for larger state spaces, though, fortunately, in practice, counterexamples do appear to be exhibited within very small state spaces. Here however partial evaluation is employed instead to compute a^* symbolically, using an appropriate version of de Alfaro's algorithm applied to the propositional representation of the abstract program a under consideration. Still the size of the resulting CNF formula limits the size of the models that can be handled. On-the-fly simplification can be used to reduce the size of the formula when a partially known program is considered. Consequently a hybrid approach, where enumeration of models is performed partially by the SAT solver (to reduce the search space) and partially before translation to SAT (to simplify the translation) might prove to be even more efficient.

The fact that the implementation of $*$ is challenging seems to be the case in other systems using SAT solving in the context of $*$-like operators [13].

Finally we note that the proposed procedure for discovering counterexamples outlined above does not, in general, work well for theorems with hypotheses. That is because the abstraction function does not preserve *inequalities*. However, experience with the Kleene algebra has shown that many universal equalities are needed within any proof, thus automated support extending only to equalities is still an important resource.

That said, there are some interesting special cases for which this approach still applies such as hypotheses of the form $p = 0$ [5].

5   Conclusions and Comparisons with Other Approaches

This work represents the first step towards automated reasoning tools for probabilistic distributions systems. Future work will also explore the use of optimisations and heuristics for mechanised search within $\mathcal{KS}$, other strategies to treat hypotheses, and the use of other generalisations of Kleene algebra, to include *termination* properties [7].

Other techniques for verifying probabilistic systems separate probabilistic from standard reasoning [27], but unlike our algebraic approach the standard reasoning only includes properties that are insensitive to the underlying probabilities, and thus only weak properties (typically non probabilistic) can be verified in this way. Other approaches that combine model checking and reasoning to yield parametrised properties include that of Pnueli *et al.* [1]. There is an extensive literature on probabilistic semantics, for example, [18, 27, 15] but as far as we are aware none of this work can support automated counterexample search.

References

1. T. Arons, A. Pnueli, and L. Zuck. Parameterized verification by probabilistic abstraction. In *Proceedings of FOSSACS*, number 2620 in LNCS, April 2003.
2. James Aspnes and M. Herlihy. Fast randomized consensus using shared memory. *J. Algorithms*, 11(3):441–61, 1990.
3. R.-J.R. Back and J. von Wright. *The Refinement Calculus: A Systematic Introduction.* Springer Verlag, 1998.
4. O. Celiku and A. McIver. Cost-based analysis of probabilistic programs mechanised in HOL. *Nordic Journal of Computing*, 2004.
5. E. Cohen. Hypotheses in Kleene Algebra. Bellcore technical report, 1994.
6. E. Cohen. Lazy caching. Bellcore technical report, 1994.
7. E. Cohen. Separation and reduction. In *Mathematics of Program Construction, 5th International Conference*, volume 1837 of *LNCS*, pages 45–59. Springer, 2000.
8. Luca de Alfaro and T. Henzinger. Concurrent ω-regular games. In *Proc. 15th IEEE Symp. Logic in Computer Science*. IEEE, 2000.
9. C. Derman. *Finite State Markov Decision Processes.* Academic Press, 1970.

10. Jifeng He, K. Seidel, and A.K. McIver. Probabilistic models for the guarded command language. *Science of Computer Programming*, 28:171–192, 1997.
11. Thai Son Huang. *The Development of a Probabilistic B Method and a Supporting Toolkit*. PhD thesis, Dept. Engineering and Computer Science. In draft.
12. Joe Hurd, A.K. McIver, and C.C. Morgan. Probabilistic guarded commands mechanised in HOL. *Proc. QAPL '04 (ETAPS)*, 2004.
13. D. Jackson. Alloy:A lightweight object modelling notation. *ACM Transactions on Software Engineering and Methodology (TOSEM)*, 11:256–290, 2002.
14. C. Jones and G. Plotkin. A probabilistic powerdomain of evaluations. In *Proceedings of the IEEE 4th Annual Symposium on Logic in Computer Science*, pages 186–195, Los Alamitos, Calif., 1989. Computer Society Press.
15. B. Jonsson and K.G. Larsen. Specification and refinement of probabilistic processes. In *Proc. 6th Conf. LICS*, 1991.
16. D. Kozen. Kleene algebra with tests and commutativity conditions. In *Proceedings of TACAS*, 1996.
17. M. Kwiatkowska, G. Norman, and D.Parker. Probabilistic symbolic model checking with PRISM: A hybrid approach. *Proceedings of TACAS, 2002*.
18. G. Lowe. Probabilities and priorities in timed CSP. Technical Monograph PRG-111, Oxford University Computing Laboratory, 1993. (DPhil Thesis).
19. A.K. McIver and C.C. Morgan. *Abstraction, Refinement and Proof for Probabilistic Programs*. Springer, 2005.
20. C.C. Morgan. The specification statement. *ACM Transactions on Programming Languages and Systems*, 10(3), July 1988. Reprinted in [24].
21. C.C. Morgan. *Programming from Specifications*. Prentice-Hall, 1994.
22. C.C. Morgan. Private communication. 2004.
23. C.C. Morgan, A.K. McIver, and K. Seidel. Probabilistic predicate transformers. *ACM Transactions on Programming Languages and Systems*, 18(3):325–353, 1996.
24. C.C. Morgan and T.N. Vickers, editors. *On the Refinement Calculus*. FACIT Series in Computer Science. Springer Verlag, Berlin, 1994.
25. Tobias Nipkow, Lawrence C. Paulson, and Markus Wenzel. *Isabelle/HOL – A Proof Assistant for Higher-Order Logic*, volume 2283 of *LNCS*. Springer, 2002.
26. M.O. Rabin. N-process mutual exclusion with bounded waiting by $4 \log 2n$-valued shared variable. *Journal of Computer and System Sciences*, 25(1):66–75, 1982.
27. Roberto Segala. *Modeling and Verification of Randomized Distributed Real-Time Systems*. PhD thesis, MIT, 1995.
28. N. Shankar. Automated verification using deduction, exploration and abstraction. In A.K. McIver and C.C. Morgan, editors, *Programming Methodology*. Springer, 2003.
29. Tjark Weber. Bounded model generation for Isabelle/HOL. In Wolfgang Ahrendt, Peter Baumgartner, Hans de Nivelle, Silvio Ranise, and Cesare Tinelli, editors, *Selected Papers from the Workshops on Disproving and the Second International Workshop on Pragmatics of Decision Procedures (PDPAR 2004)*, volume 125 of *ENTCS*, pages 103–116. Elsevier, July 2005.

Algebraic Intruder Deductions*

David Basin, Sebastian Mödersheim, and Luca Viganò

Information Security Group, Dep. of Computer Science, ETH Zurich, Switzerland
www.infsec.ethz.ch/~{basin, moedersheim, vigano}

Abstract. Many security protocols fundamentally depend on the algebraic properties of cryptographic operators. It is however difficult to handle these properties when formally analyzing protocols, since basic problems like the equality of terms that represent cryptographic messages are undecidable, even for relatively simple algebraic theories. We present a framework for security protocol analysis that can handle algebraic properties of cryptographic operators in a uniform and modular way. Our framework is based on two ideas: the use of modular rewriting to formalize a generalized equational deduction problem for the Dolev-Yao intruder, and the introduction of two parameters that control the complexity of the equational unification problems that arise during protocol analysis by bounding the depth of message terms and the operations that the intruder can perform when analyzing messages. We motivate the different restrictions made in our model by highlighting different ways in which undecidability arises when incorporating algebraic properties of cryptographic operators into formal protocol analysis.

1 Introduction

Motivation. Many security protocols fundamentally depend on the algebraic properties of cryptographic operators [17]. For example, protocols based on the Diffie-Hellman key-exchange, such as the Station-to-Station, IKE, and JFK protocols, exploit the property of modular exponentiation that $(g^x)^y \bmod p = (g^y)^x \bmod p$. Without this property, these protocols could not even be executed.

A number of approaches have been proposed for formally analyzing security protocols in the presence of an active intruder. Independent of which formalism is adopted, one of the core problems is the *intruder deduction problem*: given a state of the protocol execution, can the intruder derive a given message M? Derivation here is relative to the terms the intruder currently knows, i.e. relative to the closure under a set of deduction rules of his initial knowledge augmented with the messages that he has observed. The intruder deduction problem provides the basis for solving a number of practically relevant protocol analysis problems. We can, for instance, use it to determine whether the intruder is able to construct a

---

* This work was partially supported by the FET Open Project IST-2001-39252 and the BBW Project 02.0431, "AVISPA: Automated Validation of Internet Security Protocols and Applications", and by the Zurich Information Security Center. This work represents the views of the authors.

G. Sutcliffe and A. Voronkov (Eds.): LPAR 2005, LNAI 3835, pp. 549–564, 2005.

message of the form that some honest agent is expecting to receive, or whether he is able to obtain a message that is intended to be a secret, e.g. a key shared by two honest agents.

In this paper, we focus on the intruder deduction problem in the presence of algebraic equations that express properties of cryptographic operators. The underlying intruder model we employ is that of Dolev and Yao [19], in which the intruder observes all network traffic and can generate new messages, impersonating other agents, but cannot break cryptography. Although the Dolev-Yao intruder model is very commonly used, most analysis approaches based on this model are also based on the *free algebra assumption*. Under this assumption, two terms are equal if and only if they are syntactically equal. But, as we noted above, this is inappropriate for protocols that rely on algebraic properties.

Relaxing the free algebra assumption is however nontrivial: even for relatively simple sets of equations, the most basic problem, the *unifiability problem* (i.e. the equality of terms under substitutions for their variables), is only semi-decidable [4, 6, 23]. Moreover, even for those theories where unification is decidable, the intruder deduction problem may still be undecidable [1, 2].

Solutions for the intruder deduction problem have been given for individual algebraic theories of cryptographic operators, such as those formalizing different properties of modular exponentiation or bitwise exclusive or [12, 13, 27]. However, even though these approaches are specialized to particular algebraic properties, the algorithms and correctness proofs are quite complex and usually must be revised or completely re-designed when new properties are added. More general approaches have been recently proposed [14, 24, 26] and we compare our work with them in the concluding section §5.

Contributions. Our principal contribution in this paper is a framework for protocol analysis that is general and can handle algebraic properties of cryptographic operators in a uniform and modular way. In doing so, we pave the way for implementing analysis tools that are not specialized to particular algebraic theories and thereby allow users to declare new operators and properties as part of the protocol specifications. Of course, given the undecidability of the relevant problems, this goal cannot be achieved in full, without any restrictions. We now briefly describe the main ideas and restrictions of our proposed approach.

Our framework is based on two ideas. The first idea is to use *modular rewriting* to formalize a generalized equational deduction problem for the Dolev-Yao intruder. In doing so, we exploit the fact that we can distinguish two kinds of equational theories associated with security protocols: *cancellation theories* (where equations express that certain operations cancel each other out, such as encryption and decryption with the same symmetric key) and *finite equivalence class theories* (which are theories that induce finite equivalence classes for all terms). We show how our use of modular rewriting leads to efficient solutions to the intruder deduction problem.

The second idea is to introduce two "depth parameters" that bound the depth of message terms and the operations that the intruder can use to analyze messages (i.e. decompose messages based on his current knowledge, under perfect

cryptography). These bounds control the complexity of the equational unification problems that arise, transforming undecidable problems into decidable ones.
Moreover, these bounds effectively serve as search parameters that can be used
to control the search over the space of messages.

Our framework is thus parameterized by algebraic theories of the two kinds
above and provides a general algorithm for the algebraic intruder deduction
problem when the depth of message terms and the analysis operations of the
intruder are bounded. Our framework allows us to identify several sub-problems
of the intruder deduction problem (e.g. the reduction of terms to their normal
forms) and provide general algorithms for them. Along the way, we also show
that the problems considered become undecidable when any of the restrictions
made in our framework are removed.

Two remarks are in order to help put into context our use of depth parameters. First, rather than considering specialized theories of algebraic properties
of cryptographic operators, the focus of our work is to provide a general and
flexible framework that supports a large class of such theories. However, in this
generality, many problems are undecidable unless we introduce some restrictions. Our work shows that bounding the term depth and the message analysis
by the intruder simplifies many of the problems that arise and turns undecidable
problems into decidable ones. Moreover, many protocol analysis methods require
bounds on messages in the first place, e.g. methods based on typed models.

Second, our algorithms are less efficient than those algorithms, when they
exist, that are specialized to particular algebraic theories, e.g. [12, 13, 27], which
usually work without bounds. Our framework is open to the integration of such
specialized algorithms, albeit under the restriction of bounded message depth.
In this way, we can benefit from research advances for specialized theories, while
being able to fall back on general algorithms when specialized ones are not
available.

Finally, we note that our framework is not biased towards a particular protocol
analysis method. It can be used as a basis for handling algebraic equations when
employing different types of formalisms (such as strand spaces, process calculi,
or rewriting) or techniques (such as abstractions or the symbolic *lazy intruder*
technique employed in our protocol model-checker OFMC [8, 10]).

Organization. We proceed as follows. In §2 we provide background for our approach. In §3 we introduce a concrete equational theory as a running example
and give an overview of our framework, presenting the central definitions and
theorems. In §4 we focus on how the intruder can analyze messages. In §5 we
compare with related work and draw conclusions.

Due to lack of space, discussions, examples, and proofs have been shortened
or omitted; details can be found in the extended version of this paper [9].

2   Background

Messages and Cryptography. As is standard, we represent protocol messages as
terms built over a finite signature Σ. We write Σ^n, for $n \geq 0$, to denote function

symbols of arity n. Terms in Σ^0 are *constants* (i.e. nullary function symbols) and represent *atomic messages* like agent names or nonces. We define the *depth* of a term t as the number of nodes in the longest path from the root to a leaf in its tree representation, and the *size* of t as the number of nodes (both inner nodes and leaves). We write $\mathcal{T}(\Sigma, V)$ to denote the set of terms that can be generated using symbols of Σ and variables from a set V, and we write $\mathcal{T}(\Sigma)$ for the set of *ground* terms.

Algebraic Properties of Cryptographic Operators. Most approaches to protocol analysis follow the *free algebra assumption*, under which two ground terms are equal iff they are syntactically equal. Many protocols, however, do actually depend on algebraic properties of cryptographic operators, in the sense that the properties are required for the agents to carry out the steps prescribed by their protocol roles. Hence, unlike the practice of abstracting from the concrete behavior of cryptography, we cannot ignore the algebraic properties on which the protocol to be analyzed is based. For example, as we noted above, protocols based on the Diffie-Hellman key-exchange, such as the Station-to-Station, IKE, and JFK protocols (see the web-page of the IETF [21]), exploit the property of modular exponentiation that $(g^x)^y \bmod p = (g^y)^x \bmod p$. As another example, note that many protocols combine two secrets into one using *associative* and *commutative (AC) operators* like *bitwise exclusive or (xor)* $\cdot \oplus \cdot$. Given such a composed secret, every agent who knows one of the two secrets can also find out the other one, but no other agent can. For instance, if an agent knows $x \oplus y$ and x, then he can exploit the properties of $\oplus$ to compute y as $(x \oplus y) \oplus x$.

Equational Theories. The formal analysis of protocols like those above requires explicitly reasoning about the relevant properties of the cryptographic operators employed. We address in this paper those properties that are formalizable by finite sets of equations of the form $t \approx s$, where $t, s \in \mathcal{T}(\Sigma, V)$. For example, the property required for the Diffie-Hellman key-exchange is that $exp(exp(g, x), y) \bmod p \approx exp(exp(g, y), x) \bmod p$.

We assume that notions like *substitution, matching, unification,* and *unifiability* are defined as standard, e.g. as in [4, 6]. *Term positions* are represented as sequences of natural numbers, which are partially ordered by the prefix ordering. We define the *equational theory* $\approx_E$ *induced by a set E of equations* to be the least congruence on the term algebra that is closed under substitution and contains E. We define the *equivalence class* $[t]_{\approx_E}$ of a term t as $\{s \mid t \approx_E s\}$. Given a set E of equations, we interpret terms of $\mathcal{T}(\Sigma, V)$ in the *quotient algebra* of the term algebra with the congruence on terms, written $\mathcal{T}(\Sigma, V)/_{\approx_E}$. In this algebra, two terms are equal iff they are equivalent due to $\approx_E$. The *ground word problem* for a theory E is the problem of deciding $s \approx_E t$ for arbitrary $s, t \in \mathcal{T}(\Sigma)$. Note that, for brevity, we often refer to a set E of equations as a "theory", meaning the equational theory $\approx_E$ induced by E.

We say that a substitution σ is an *instance* of a substitution θ modulo E, and write $\sigma \succsim_E \theta$, iff there is a substitution λ such that $x\sigma \approx_E x\theta\lambda$ for all $x \in domain(\theta)$. Given a set $\mathcal{S}$ of substitutions, $\mathcal{S}_0$ is a *complete set of substitutions of $\mathcal{S}$ under E* iff for all $\sigma \in \mathcal{S}$ there is a $\theta \in \mathcal{S}_0$ with $\sigma \succsim_E \theta$.

Definition 1. *Let* vars(t) *denote the variables of a term t. A* rewrite rule *is an equation $l \approx r$, where l is not a variable and* vars(l) $\supseteq$ vars(r). *In this case, we may write $l \rightarrow r$ instead of $l \approx r$. A* term-rewriting system (TRS) *is a set of rewrite rules. A TRS C and an equational theory E induce a* modular rewriting *relation on E-equivalence classes of terms as follows: $[t]_{\approx_E} \rightarrow_{C/E} [s]_{\approx_E}$ iff there are terms t' and s' such that $t \approx_E t'$, $t' \rightarrow_C s'$, and $s' \approx_E s$.*

Let $\rightarrow^+$ *and $\rightarrow^*$ denote the transitive and the transitive-reflexive closure of a binary relation $\rightarrow$. Given $\rightarrow$, we say that t is* reducible *(and we call t a redex) iff $t \rightarrow s$ for some s. t_1 and t_2 are* joinable, *denoted by $t_1 \downarrow t_2$, iff there is some s such that $t_1 \rightarrow^* s$ and $t_2 \rightarrow^* s$. t is a* normal form *iff it is not reducible, and s is a* normal form of t *iff $t \rightarrow^* s$ and s is a normal form. We denote the normal form of t by $t\downarrow$, when it is unique. We say that $\rightarrow$ is* confluent *iff $t \rightarrow^* t_1$ and $t \rightarrow^* t_2$ implies that $t_1 \downarrow t_2$. Finally, $\rightarrow$ is* convergent *iff it is confluent and terminating.*

Although $\rightarrow_{C/E}$ is defined on equivalence classes of terms, for notational simplicity we will also write $t \rightarrow_{C/E} s$, for terms s and t, rather than $[t]_{\approx_E} \rightarrow_{C/E} [s]_{\approx_E}$. Employing the same convention, we will also write $t\downarrow_{C/E}$ for $[t]_{\approx_E}\downarrow_{C/E}$. Note that for a convergent relation $\rightarrow$, every term has a unique normal form, and hence $t\downarrow_{C/E}$ is always defined.

The definition of modular rewriting works directly on E-equivalence classes, rather than defining a special notion of convergence modulo E. However, while theoretically appealing, this definition is algorithmically difficult to work with. Therefore many approaches to modular rewriting employ a weaker but more tractable variant $\rightarrow_{C,E}$ of the relation $\rightarrow_{C/E}$, namely $s \rightarrow_{C,E} t$ iff $\exists (u \rightarrow v) \in C. \exists \sigma. s \approx_E u\sigma \wedge t = v\sigma$. For $\rightarrow_{C,E}$, there is a completion method [7, 22], and it is not necessary to explore the entire E-equivalence class of a term t in order to determine if t is a redex. While we consider here the relation $\rightarrow_{C/E}$, we remark that all constructions and algorithms in this paper can be adapted to $\rightarrow_{C,E}$ as well.

A standard result tells us that we can solve the ground word problem for terms in the theory $C \cup E$ by normalizing the terms under C and checking the results for equality modulo E. Formally, if $\rightarrow_{C/E}$ is convergent and t_1 and t_2 are ground terms, then $t_1 \approx_{C \cup E} t_2$ iff $[t_1]_{\approx_E}\downarrow_{C/E} = [t_2]_{\approx_E}\downarrow_{C/E}$.

The Dolev-Yao Intruder. The standard Dolev-Yao model [19] formalizes the abilities of an intruder who controls the communication network. The intruder can analyze messages, decomposing them into submessages, and synthesize new messages from their subparts. In our formalization of this, we assume we are given a set of function symbols $\mathcal{O} \subset \Sigma$ that describe the ways of constructing messages (e.g. pairing or cryptographic operations like encryption or hashing). We also call the set $\mathcal{O}$ the set of *intruder-accessible operators*. For readability, we will however avoid displaying the set $\mathcal{O}$ as an explicit parameter of the intruder deduction problem.

Definition 2. *Given a finite set of ground terms IK (for "intruder knowledge") and an equational theory E, we define $\mathcal{DY}_E(IK)$ (for "Dolev-Yao") as the least set that is closed under the rules*

$$\frac{}{t \in \mathcal{DY}_E(IK)} \text{ AX } (t \in IK), \qquad \frac{t_1 \in \mathcal{DY}_E(IK)}{t_2 \in \mathcal{DY}_E(IK)} \text{ EQ } (t_1 \approx_E t_2),$$

$$\frac{t_1 \in \mathcal{DY}_E(IK) \quad \cdots \quad t_n \in \mathcal{DY}_E(IK)}{op(t_1, \ldots, t_n) \in \mathcal{DY}_E(IK)} \text{ OP } (op \in \mathcal{O}).$$

The (Dolev-Yao) intruder deduction problem with respect to the equational theory E *is the problem of deciding whether* $t \in \mathcal{DY}_E(IK)$ *for ground terms* t *and finite sets of ground terms* IK.

Note that in this formalization we do not have analysis rules for decomposing terms. For example, the decryption rule for symmetric encryption

$$\frac{\{\!|m|\!\}_k \in \mathcal{DY}_E(IK) \quad k \in \mathcal{DY}_E(IK)}{m \in \mathcal{DY}_E(IK)}$$

is subsumed by the equation $\{\!|\{\!|m|\!\}_k|\!\}_k \approx m$: whenever the intruder has $\{\!|m|\!\}_k$ and k, he can compose them to construct $\{\!|\{\!|m|\!\}_k|\!\}_k$, which is equal under $\approx_E$ to m.

The intruder deduction problem is the core deduction problem in protocol analysis. Consider a trace of messages exchanged between honest agents and an intruder. For each message m that is sent by the intruder in this trace, the intruder must be able to derive m, i.e. $m \in \mathcal{DY}_E(IK)$, where E is the equational theory considered and IK is the intruder knowledge consisting of the initial intruder knowledge and all messages the intruder has observed so far. Note that in many state-of-the-art approaches to protocol analysis (see [15] for an overview), the term m may contain variables and the resulting symbolic trace represents the set of traces that are obtained by substituting for the variables arbitrary terms from $\mathcal{DY}_E(IK)$. The use of symbolic terms avoids the naïve enumeration of all terms that the intruder can generate from his knowledge.

3   A Framework for Algebraic Properties

While equational reasoning is a general paradigm, our focus in this paper is on its application to security protocol analysis. Let us begin with a concrete example: an algebraic theory formalizing relevant properties used in many protocols, including those based on the Diffie-Hellman key-exchange.

Example 1. Let $\Sigma_{ex} = (\Sigma_{ex}^0, \Sigma_{ex}^1, \Sigma_{ex}^2)$, where Σ_{ex}^0 is a countable set of constants; $\Sigma_{ex}^1 = \{inv(\cdot), \cdot^{-1}\}$, where $inv(t)$ and t^{-1} are the inverses of a message term t for asymmetric encryption and exponentiation, respectively, and the symbols in $\Sigma_{ex}^2 = \{\{\cdot\}., \{\!|\cdot|\!\}., \langle\cdot,\cdot\rangle, exp(\cdot,\cdot), \cdot \oplus \cdot\}$ denote *asymmetric encryption* $\{t_2\}_{t_1}$ and *symmetric encryption* $\{\!|t_2|\!\}_{t_1}$ of a message t_2 with a message t_1, *concatenation* $\langle t_1,t_2 \rangle$ of two messages t_1 and t_2, *modular exponentiation* $exp(t_1,t_2)$ of a message t_1 with a message t_2, and *bitwise xor* $t_1 \oplus t_2$ of a message t_1 with a message t_2 (with identity element e). Our example theory E_{ex} is induced by the following equations over Σ_{ex} (where the x_i are variables from a set disjoint from Σ_{ex}):

$$x_1 \oplus x_2 \approx x_2 \oplus x_1 \qquad (1)$$
$$(x_1 \oplus x_2) \oplus x_3 \approx x_1 \oplus (x_2 \oplus x_3) \qquad (2)$$
$$exp(exp(x_1, x_2), x_3) \approx exp(exp(x_1, x_3), x_2) \qquad (3)$$
$$exp(exp(x_1, x_2), x_2^{-1}) \approx x_1 \qquad (4)$$
$$inv(inv(x_1)) \approx x_1 \qquad (5)$$
$$\left(x_1^{-1}\right)^{-1} \approx x_1 \qquad (6)$$

$$\{\{x_2\}_{x_1}\}_{inv(x_1)} \approx x_2 \quad (7)$$
$$\{\{x_2\}_{inv(x_1)}\}_{x_1} \approx x_2 \quad (8)$$
$$\{\!|\{\!|x_2|\!\}_{x_1}|\!\}_{x_1} \approx x_2 \quad (9)$$
$$x_1 \oplus x_1 \approx \mathsf{e} \quad (10)$$
$$x_1 \oplus \mathsf{e} \approx x_1 \quad (11)$$

We split E_{ex} into two subtheories: F_{ex} is induced by the equations (1)–(3), and C_{ex} is induced by the equations (4)–(11).   □

Note that, as is often done, we leave implicit the modulus of exponentiation in E_{ex}: instead of $g^x \bmod p$ (i.e. $exp(g,x) \bmod p$) we write simply g^x (i.e. $exp(g,x)$), assuming that exponentiation is always performed using the same (publicly known) modulus. Note also that E_{ex} does not contain redundant equations (which are entailed by the given equations) such as $\mathsf{e} \oplus x_1 \approx x_1$.

3.1   Two Kinds of Theories

Our framework is based on *modular rewriting* and exploits the fact that we can distinguish two kinds of equational theories associated with security protocols: cancellation theories and modulo theories. C_{ex} is an example of a *cancellation theory*, which is a theory whose equations express that certain operations (such as encryption followed by decryption with the same key) cancel each other out. Such equations can usually be described by a convergent TRS and we can thus apply these equations to rewrite all terms into normal form. The advantage of separating out a convergent subtheory is that we can then neglect its equations during subsequent equality reasoning when all terms are normalized.

Definition 3. *A* cancellation theory *is a theory induced by* cancellation rules *of the form* $op(t_1, \ldots, t_n) \approx s$, *with s a constant or a subterm of one of the t_i.*

F_{ex} is an example of a *modulo theory*, which is a theory that comprises equations that cannot be oriented into terminating rewrite rules; the standard examples from rewriting are the equations for properties like associativity and/or commutativity. It is common for these equations to form a "background theory" used when applying other rewrite rules (such as the cancellation equations); that is, one performs rewriting modulo the equations of a modulo theory.

Here we will not restrict ourselves to a particular modulo theory, like AC, but rather work with a class of theories, namely *finite equivalence class theories*.

Definition 4. *An equational theory E is a* finite equivalence class (FEC) theory *if the equivalence class $[t]_{\approx_E} = \{t' \mid t' \approx_E t\}$ is finite for all terms $t \in T(\Sigma, V)$.*

We can then, for example, prove that F_{ex} is an FEC theory and C_{ex} is a cancellation theory. In the following, we will use C and F to denote cancellation and FEC theories, respectively. Note also that FEC and cancellation theories are disjoint theory classes as for a cancellation theory, there are always terms with an infinite equivalence class.

As is standard, the *equational matching problem* for a theory E is the question of whether, given a ground term t and a term s with variables, there is a substitution σ such that $t \approx_E s\sigma$. From the definition of FEC theories, we have:

Theorem 1. *The equational matching problem for an FEC theory F is decidable. In particular, there is a terminating algorithm that returns a complete set of matches modulo F for a given instance of the problem.*

A special case of equational matching is the ground word problem (when s is also ground), and hence this problem is also decidable for FEC theories.

As we will see below, our framework relies on the decidability of matching for FEC theories. In contrast, the unification problem (where both terms may contain variables) for FEC theories is undecidable. Consider the theory of distributivity and associativity $D_{\star+}A_+ = \{x \star (y+z) \approx (x \star y)+(x \star z), \ x+(y+z) \approx (x+y)+z\}$. Unifiability in this theory is undecidable as shown in [28]. As equivalence classes in $D_{\star+}A_+$ are finite, we thus have that unifiability modulo an FEC theory is in general undecidable.

In §4 we will use the following important property of FEC theories, namely that they cannot contain equations that introduce new variables:

Lemma 1. *If $l \approx r$ is an equation of an FEC theory, then* $\mathrm{vars}(l) = \mathrm{vars}(r)$.

Hence, $l \in \mathcal{V}$ implies $l = r$, so that such trivial equations can be safely omitted.

We conclude this subsection by observing the relevance of these two kinds of theories to security protocol analysis. As we will see, cancellation rules are closely related to the analysis (e.g. decryption) of terms by the intruder and honest agents, and therefore have a distinguished role in deductions. We will namely define a normal form of the intruder knowledge as a state where the applications of cancellation rules do not give him any "new" terms (in a sense to be precisely defined later).

3.2   Restriction to a Bounded Variable Depth Model

As unifiability modulo an FEC theory is undecidable, we must introduce a restriction under which unification becomes decidable. We achieve this by introducing bounds on messages. There are several ways to do this, e.g. by bounding the number of operations that the intruder can perform to synthesize new messages from his knowledge, or by limiting the depth of terms that may be substituted for variables in the rules formalizing the steps of a protocol execution. We take the second approach here and bound the depth of message terms. To this end, we first define a subset of the variable symbols with an associated depth bound, and we then define which substitutions are permissible for these variables.

Definition 5. *We call a* bounded variable *a variable for which only terms with bounded depth can be substituted. Let $\mathcal{VB} \subseteq \mathcal{V}$ be the* set of bounded variables *such that every variable v has an associated depth bound $\mathrm{depth}(v) \in \mathbb{N}$. We* *extend the function depth($\cdot$) to arbitrary terms as follows: depth(v) = ∞ for $v \in \mathcal{V} \backslash \mathcal{VB}$, depth($c$) = 0 for $c \in \Sigma^0$, depth($op(t_1, \ldots, t_n)$) = $1 + max_{i=1}^n$ depth(t_i) for $op \in \Sigma^n$, with $n > 0$. We say that* a substitution σ respects the depth restrictions of the variables in a term t, *and write* respect_depth(σ, t), *iff depth($v\sigma$) $\leq$ depth(v) for all $v \in$ vars(t).*

We call the *bounded variable depth model (BVDM)* the restricted protocol analysis model in which only substitutions are allowed that respect the depth of variables.

The following lemma tells us that any computable function on ground terms can be extended to a computable function on terms with bounded variables. This will allow us, in the rest of this paper, to restrict ourselves to the ground case while all results can be carried over to terms with bounded variables.

Lemma 2. *Let f be a computable function that takes as input n terms that may contain variables and m ground terms, and which returns a finite set of terms. Then the following function f' is also computable. f' takes as input n terms that may contain (arbitrary) variables and m terms that may contain only bounded variables, and returns a finite set of terms and substitutions such that:*

$$\forall s_1, \ldots, s_n \in \mathcal{T}(\Sigma, \mathcal{V}). \ \forall t_1, \ldots, t_m \in \mathcal{T}(\Sigma, \mathcal{VB}). \ \forall \sigma.$$
$$[ground(t_1\sigma) \wedge \ldots \wedge ground(t_m\sigma) \wedge domain(\sigma) \subseteq \mathcal{VB} \wedge$$
$$respect\_depth(\langle s_1, \ldots, s_n, t_1, \ldots, t_m \rangle, \sigma)] \implies$$
$$[(r, \sigma) \in f'(s_1, \ldots, s_n, t_1, \ldots, t_m) \iff r\sigma \in f(s_1\sigma, \ldots, s_n\sigma, t_1\sigma, \ldots, t_m\sigma)].$$

Lemma 2 allows us, for instance, to easily lift the matching algorithm for FEC theories F to a unification algorithm where one of the two input terms contains only bounded variables.

Note that the depth of messages is often bounded in protocol analysis. For instance, many model-checking approaches bound terms to obtain a finite-state system, e.g. [3, 25]. Moreover, when other parameters of the model are unbounded, like the number of sessions, then restricting the message depth is essential for decidability [20]. Note also that [11] presents an approach that similarly bounds the depth of message terms in order to tackle the problem of algebraic properties in intruder deductions; the approach of [11] is however specialized to a particular algebraic theory.

3.3   Matching and Unification in FEC Theories in the BVDM

We have shown that for every FEC theory F, we can decide the matching problem. By Lemma 2, when the variables are bounded on one side, we can reduce an F-unification problem to a finite number of F-matching problems, which we can solve by Theorem 1. The algorithms that we can obtain from the constructive proof of Theorem 1 however have poor complexity. Moreover, there exist more efficient, specialized algorithms for some of the theories that are relevant for the analysis of security protocols, e.g. [12, 13, 27].

We give a solution to handle F-unification efficiently in the bounded case and which allows for the straightforward integration of existing unification algorithms for disjoint subtheories of F. Due to lack of space, we briefly sketch this solution here and refer to [9] for details. The basic idea is the following. In a free algebra, every term $op(t_1, \ldots, t_n)$ can be decomposed into an operator and its arguments in only one way. Modulo a theory E, however, there may be other ways to decompose a term. For instance, in our example theory E_{ex}, $exp(exp(g, x), y)$ may be decomposed into the exponentiation of $exp(g, x)$ with y or the exponentiation of $exp(g, y)$ with x as these two terms are equal modulo E_{ex}.

For FEC theories, there are only finitely many ways to decompose a ground term, since its equivalence class is finite. For the BVDM, in [9] we show that given a complete decomposition algorithm for an FEC theory F, we can construct a complete one-side-bounded F-unification algorithm. The advantage of this unification algorithm is that it does not explore the entire equivalence class of terms, but rather just what different decompositions are possible at the topmost level of the term.

Moreover, we can show that FEC-decomposition has a nice compositionality property in the BVDM.[1] Let the FEC theory F be composed from disjoint subtheories F_1 and F_2 (i.e. subtheories that have no constant or function symbols in common). Consider F-unifying the two terms $t = op(t_1, \ldots, t_n)$ and $s = op'(s_1, \ldots, s_m)$. For the unification to succeed, op and op' must belong to the same subtheory, say F_1. Then, the unification problem $t \approx_F s$ can be broken into the "smaller" unification problems $t \approx_{F_1} op'(s'_1, \ldots, s'_m)$ and $s'_j \approx_F s_j$ for $1 \leq j \leq m$. That is, $t \approx_F s$ can be reduced to an F_1-problem together with F-problems for the subterms (which may belong to different subtheories). This allows us to construct an F-unification algorithm from the F_i-unification algorithms for the disjoint subtheories F_i.

3.4 Intruder Deduction Modulo F

So far we have considered the problem of unification and matching modulo an FEC theory F. We now turn to the intruder deduction problem modulo F, i.e. whether $t \in \mathcal{DY}_F(IK)$ holds for a ground term t and a set of ground terms IK.

Lemma 3. *If F is an FEC theory, then the problem $t \in \mathcal{DY}_F(IK)$ is decidable for a term t and a set of terms IK.*

In the following, we will consider the generalization of the problem $t \in \mathcal{DY}_F(IK)$, where the term t may contain variables. This is an important question even for a model with only ground terms, since we will later consider intruder derivations modulo $F \cup C$. In particular, given a set IK of ground terms, we must decide whether there is some ground instance $t\sigma$ of the left-hand-side t of a cancellation rule of C such that $t\sigma$ can be derived modulo F from IK (note that t is here a term with unbounded variables). As shown in [9]:

---

[1] Note that, as we discuss in more detail in [9], standard compositionality results for disjoint theories, e.g. [5], are not applicable in the BVDM since that would give rise to unbounded unification problems.

Lemma 4. *There is an FEC theory F such that it is undecidable for a term t and a set of ground terms IK, whether there exists a substitution σ such that $t\sigma$ is ground and $t\sigma \in \mathcal{DY}_F(IK)$.*

Hence, to decide the intruder deduction problem for terms with variables, we must make further restrictions. By Lemma 2, the problem is decidable if t contains only bounded variables.

4   Cancellation Equations

We now turn to the cancellation equations such as $\{\!\{\{\!\{x_2\}\!\}_{x_1}\}\!\}_{x_1} \approx x_2$. Such an equation cannot be formalized as part of an FEC theory like F_{ex} since all equivalence classes are infinite. As introduced in §2, we will now consider rewriting for cancellation theories C modulo an FEC theory F. Note that every cancellation theory is a rewrite theory as every cancellation equation $l \approx r$ has the property that vars(l) $\supseteq$ vars(r).

The principal property that we require is that the modular rewriting relation $\rightarrow_{C/F}$ is convergent, which is the case for our example $\rightarrow_{C_{ex}/F_{ex}}$, as we show in [9]. As a direct consequence of our assumption that $\rightarrow_{C/F}$ is convergent and since we can decide matchability modulo an FEC theory F by Theorem 1, we have that the ground word problem modulo $F \cup C$ is decidable in our framework:

Theorem 2. *Let F be an FEC theory and C a cancellation theory, and let $\rightarrow_{C/F}$ be convergent. Then the ground word problem for $F \cup C$ is decidable.*

By Lemma 2, it follows that we can construct a unification algorithm modulo $F \cup C$ for terms with bounded variables. In particular, this implies that the unifiability problem modulo $F \cup C$ for terms with bounded variables is decidable.

4.1   Cancellation as Analysis

The results that we have presented so far allow us to decide, for ground terms or terms with bounded variables, the equality of terms modulo an FEC theory F and a cancellation theory C, as well as the intruder deduction problem in the theory F. We now consider how to solve the intruder deduction problem in the theory $F \cup C$. In §4.2, we will see that this problem is in general undecidable, so to obtain a decidable problem we must further restrict our model: we bound the number of operations that the intruder can perform.

The idea that we put forth here to solve the intruder deduction problem with respect to $F \cup C$ is to distinguish synthesis (or composition) and analysis (or decomposition) of messages by the intruder. Observe that these two aspects of intruder deduction are not completely independent; for instance, if the intruder knows the messages $\{\!\{m\}\!\}_{\langle k_1, k_2 \rangle}$ and k_1 and k_2, then he can analyze the encrypted message, but only after synthesizing the key $\langle k_1, k_2 \rangle$. We now define a general notion of analysis based on an arbitrary cancellation theory C.

Intuitively, we speak of *synthesis* when the intruder applies the OP rule to compose terms, excluding the case when the resulting composed term is a redex according to the cancellation theory C (as we can then reduce it to a simpler term). We speak of *analysis* when the intruder applies the OP rule to obtain a redex whose normal form cannot be composed from his current knowledge. We can then formalize the notion of the intruder knowledge being completely analyzed based on the notion of cancellation rules present in our framework: we say that the intruder has analyzed his knowledge as far as possible if, by applying the cancellation rules, the intruder can only derive messages (except redices in C) that he can also derive without cancellation rules. Formally:

Definition 6. *Let C be a cancellation theory convergent modulo an FEC theory F. We say that a finite set of ground terms IK is analyzed with respect to C modulo F if $t{\downarrow}_{C/F} \subseteq \mathcal{DY}_F(IK)$ for each $t \in \mathcal{DY}_F(IK)$.*

As an example, consider again F_{ex} and C_{ex}. The set $IK = \{\{|m|\}_k, k\}$ is not analyzed with respect to C_{ex} modulo F_{ex} as the intruder can generate $t = \{|\{|m|\}_k|\}_k \in \mathcal{DY}_{F_{ex}}(IK)$, and $t{\downarrow}_{C_{ex}/F_{ex}} = [m]_{\approx_{F_{ex}}}$, but $m \notin \mathcal{DY}_{F_{ex}}(IK)$. However, $IK' = IK \cup \{m\}$ is analyzed since all messages that can be obtained only by normalizing terms in $\mathcal{DY}_{F_{ex}}(IK')$ are already contained in $\mathcal{DY}_{F_{ex}}(IK')$.

We thus have a characterization of analyzed intruder knowledge as a set that contains all messages that can be derived under $\mathcal{DY}_{F\cup C}(\cdot)$ but not under $\mathcal{DY}_F(\cdot)$. The idea is that when the set of messages known by the intruder is analyzed, then there is no need to consider the cancellation theory in the derivations of the intruder. Hence we can decide the intruder deduction problem $\mathcal{DY}_{F\cup C}(\cdot)$ when the intruder knowledge is analyzed:

Theorem 3. *Let F be an FEC theory and C a cancellation theory, and let $\rightarrow_{C/F}$ be convergent. Further, let t be a ground term and IK be a finite set of ground terms analyzed with respect to C modulo F. Then it is decidable whether $t \in \mathcal{DY}_{F\cup C}(IK)$.*

By Lemma 2, it follows that the intruder deduction problem is decidable for terms with bounded variables when the intruder knowledge is analyzed.

4.2 Undecidability of Analysis

The previous method for solving the intruder deduction problem is restricted to the case where the intruder knowledge is analyzed. The central question thus is how to transform an arbitrary intruder knowledge into an analyzed one. As we show in [9], based on the fact that unification modulo an FEC theory is undecidable in general, it follows that it is undecidable whether a given intruder knowledge is analyzed or not:

Theorem 4. *There is an FEC theory F and a cancellation theory C, where $\rightarrow_{C/F}$ is convergent, such that it is undecidable whether a finite set of ground terms IK is analyzed with respect to C modulo F. Moreover, the intruder deduction problem $t \in \mathcal{DY}_{F\cup C}(IK)$ is also undecidable.*

Note that [1, 2] have shown that the intruder deduction problem in a theory E can be undecidable even if unification in E is decidable. Our theorem is incomparable to this result as it does not require E to be decidable.

We thus need to make further restrictions to obtain a general procedure for analyzing the intruder knowledge. We proceed by limiting the operations that the intruder can perform when analyzing a single message (i.e. the number of steps before he obtains a new redex). We define a bounded derivation of the intruder as follows:

Definition 7. *Given a finite set IK of ground terms and an algebraic theory E, we define the k-bounded intruder model as the least set $\mathcal{DY}_E^k(IK)$ that is closed under the rules*

$$\frac{}{t \in \mathcal{DY}_E^k(IK)} \text{ AX}^k \ (t \in IK \ , \ k \geq 0), \qquad \frac{t_1 \in \mathcal{DY}_E^k(IK)}{t_2 \in \mathcal{DY}_E^k(IK)} \text{ EQ}^k \ (t_1 \approx_E t_2),$$

$$\frac{t_1 \in \mathcal{DY}_E^k(IK) \ \cdots \ t_n \in \mathcal{DY}_E^k(IK)}{op(t_1, \ldots, t_n) \in \mathcal{DY}_E^{k+1}(IK)} \text{ OP}^k \ (op \in \Sigma^n).$$

Note that, under the EQ^k rule, the use of an equivalence from E does not count as a step, i.e. it does not increase the counter k.

Definition 8. *Let F be an FEC theory and C a cancellation theory, and let $\rightarrow_{C/F}$ be convergent. Given a constant $k \in \mathbb{N}$, we say that the intruder knowledge IK, which is a finite set of ground terms, is k-analyzed (with respect to C modulo F) iff $t{\downarrow}_{C/F} \subseteq \mathcal{DY}_F^k(IK)$ for each $t \in \mathcal{DY}_F^k(IK)$.*

Theorem 5. *Let F be an FEC theory and C a cancellation theory, let $\rightarrow_{C/F}$ be convergent, and let $k \in \mathbb{N}$. Then it is decidable if a finite set of ground terms IK is k-analyzed (with respect to C modulo F).*

Note, however, that given a finite set of ground terms IK, there does not always exist a finite superset IK' of ground terms that is $(k$-$)$analyzed. Consider, for example, the theories $F = \{f(x) = g(h(x))\}$ and $C = \{g(X) = X\}$. Clearly, F is a FEC theory, C is a cancellation theory, and $\rightarrow_{C/F}$ is convergent. Furthermore, let $\mathcal{O} = \{f\}$ be the set of functions that the intruder can access, and let IK be a finite set of ground terms that contains a constant c. We then, for instance, have that $h(c), h(h(c)), \ldots \in \mathcal{DY}_{F \cup C}(IK)$. Thus, there is no finite set $IK' \supseteq IK$ such that IK' is analyzed. For the bounded case, observe that $g(t) \in \mathcal{DY}_{F \cup C}^k(IK \cup t)$ for any ground term t, $k \geq 1$, and $n \in \mathbb{N}$. Thus, any k-analyzed superset of IK must also contain $g^n(c)$ for any $n \in \mathbb{N}$, so it must be infinite. Hence, to complete our framework, we must be able to check bounded derivability without first computing an analyzed intruder knowledge. The following theorem tells us that this is possible:

Theorem 6. *Let F be an FEC theory and C a cancellation theory, let $\rightarrow_{C/F}$ be convergent, and let $k \in \mathbb{N}$. Then it is decidable if a ground term t can be derived from a finite set of ground terms IK, i.e. whether $t \in \mathcal{DY}_{F \cup C}^k(IK)$.*

Together with the fact that, by Lemma 2, all problems over terms with bounded variables can be reduced to problems over ground terms, we have now the basis for protocol analysis modulo algebraic theories. Namely, we can check whether a term with bounded variables — representing the set of messages that some agent in its current state can receive as a valid protocol message — can be derived from a ground intruder knowledge under the bounds that we have introduced.

5   Related Work and Concluding Remarks

We have presented a framework for security protocol analysis that can handle algebraic properties in a uniform and modular way. It is not specialized to any particular algebraic theory and thereby allows users to declare new operators and properties as part of the protocol specification. Our framework is based on the use of modular rewriting to formalize a generalized equational deduction problem for the Dolev-Yao intruder, and on bounding the depth of message terms and the analysis operations of the intruder to control the complexity of the equational unification problems that arise. These bounds allow us to give general algorithms for the equational unification and intruder deduction problems. Moreover, under these bounds, our framework is also open to the integration of more efficient algorithms that are specialized to particular algebraic theories (and which usually work without such bounds), e.g. [12, 13, 27].

The idea of providing a general approach for integrating equational properties into security protocol analysis has recently attracted considerable attention. [18] presents an approach based on standard rewriting that supports the specification of properties like the cancellation theories of our framework. However it does not allow for properties like AC, which are handled by our FEC theories. The approach of [14] has aims similar to ours: to provide a general framework that is open to the integration of existing algorithms. This approach, however, is based on a different idea, namely ordered rewriting, and is therefore applicable to classes of theories that are incomparable to the ones that are supported by our framework. The approaches of [2, 16, 24, 26] are the most closely related to ours as they also employ modular rewriting. They differ from our work in that they are more restrictive in terms of the kinds of modulo theories that can be considered; namely they consider a fixed modulo theory (or, similarly, assume given a unification procedure for the modulo theory), or they require that the unification problems are finitary. These restrictions, however, allow them to work without the bounds required by our approach.

Our framework is not biased towards a particular analysis method, and thus can be used as a basis for handling algebraic equations when employing different types of formalisms or techniques for protocol analysis. As a concrete example, we have begun integrating our framework into our protocol model-checker OFMC [8, 10]. In this integration, the message and analysis bounds become parameters of the protocol analysis problem, along with other parameters like the number of sessions. We can then use different search techniques (like iterative deepening) to effectively search the resulting multi-dimensional search space.

The equational reasoning problems that we considered in this paper are in general undecidable and hence one must introduce restrictions to regain decidability. The restrictions that we have introduced are motivated by the practical problems in security protocol analysis and we have begun investigating whether and how they can be applied to other equational reasoning problems.

References

1. M. Abadi and V. Cortier. Deciding knowledge in security protocols under equational theories. In *Proceedings of ICALP'2004*, LNCS 3142, pp. 46–58. Springer, 2004.
2. M. Abadi and V. Cortier. Deciding knowledge in security protocols under (many more) equational theories. In *Proceedings of CSFW'05*, pp. 62–76. IEEE Computer Society Press, 2005.
3. A. Armando and L. Compagna. Automatic SAT-Compilation of Protocol Insecurity Problems via Reduction to Planning. In *Proceedings of FORTE 2002*, LNCS 2529, pp. 210–225. Springer, 2002.
4. F. Baader and T. Nipkow. *Term Rewriting and All That*. Cambridge University Press, 1998.
5. F. Baader and K.U. Schulz. Unification in the union of disjoint equational theories: Combining decision procedures. *Journal of Symbolic Computation*, 21:211-243, 1996.
6. F. Baader and W. Snyder. Unification theory. In *Handbook of Automated Reasoning*, volume I, pp. 445–532. Elsevier Science, 2001.
7. L. Bachmair and N. Dershowitz. Completion for rewriting modulo a congruence. *Theoretical Computer Science*, 67:173–201, 1989.
8. D. Basin, S. Mödersheim, and L. Viganò. Constraint Differentiation: A New Reduction Technique for Constraint-Based Analysis of Security Protocols. In *Proceedings of CCS'03*, pp. 335–344. ACM Press, 2003.
9. D. Basin, S. Mödersheim, and L. Viganò. Algebraic Intruder Deductions (Extended Version). Technical Report 485, Dep. of Computer Science, ETH Zurich, 2005. Available at www.infsec.ethz.ch.
10. D. Basin, S. Mödersheim, and L. Viganò. OFMC: A symbolic model checker for security protocols. *International Journal of Information Security*, 4(3):181–208, 2005.
11. M. Boreale and M. G. Buscemi. A framework for the analysis of security protocols. In *Proceedings of CONCUR 2002*, LNCS 2421, pp. 483–498. Springer, 2002.
12. Y. Chevalier, R. Küsters, M. Rusinowitch, and M. Turuani. An NP Decision Procedure for Protocol Insecurity with XOR. In *Proceedings of LICS'03*, pp. 261–270. IEEE Computer Society Press, 2003.
13. Y. Chevalier, R. Küsters, M. Rusinowitch, and M. Turuani. Deciding the Security of Protocols with Diffie-Hellman Exponentiation and Products in Exponents. In *Proceedings of FST TCS'03*, LNCS 2914, pp. 124–135. Springer, 2003.
14. Y. Chevalier and M. Rusinowitch. Combining Intruder Theories. In *Proceedings of ICALP 2005*, LNCS 3580, pp. 639–651, 2005.
15. H. Comon and V. Shmatikov. Is It Possible to Decide Whether a Cryptographic Protocol Is Secure Or Not? *Journal of Telecommunications and Information Technology*, 4:5–15, 2002.

16. H. Comon-Lundh and S. Delaune. The finite variant property: How to get rid of some algebraic properties. In *Proceedings of RTA'05*, LNCS 3467, pp. 294–307. Springer, 2005.

17. V. Cortier, S. Delaune, and P. Lafourcade. A survey of algebraic properties used in cryptographic protocols. *Journal of Computer Security*, to appear.

18. S. Delaune and F. Jacquemard. A decision procedure for the verification of security protocols with explicit destructors. In *Proceedings of CCS'04*, pp. 278–287. ACM Press, 2004.

19. D. Dolev and A. Yao. On the Security of Public-Key Protocols. *IEEE Transactions on Information Theory*, 2(29), 1983.

20. N. Durgin, P. D. Lincoln, J. C. Mitchell, and A. Scedrov. Undecidability of Bounded Security Protocols. In *Proceedings of the FLOC'99 Workshop on Formal Methods and Security Protocols (FMSP'99)*, 1999.

21. IETF: The Internet Engineering Task Force. http://www.ietf.org.

22. J.-P. Jouannaud and H. Kirchner. Completion of a set of rules modulo a set of equations. *SIAM Journal of Computing*, 15(4):1155–1194, 1986.

23. D. Kapur, P. Narendran, and L. Wang. An E-unification algorithm for analyzing protocols that use modular exponentiation. In *Proceedings of RTA'03*, LNCS 2706, pp. 165–179. Springer, 2003.

24. P. Lafourcade, D. Lugiez, and R. Treinen. Intruder deduction for AC-like equational theories with homomorphisms. In *Proceedings of RTA'05*, LNCS 3467, pp. 308–322. Springer, 2005.

25. G. Lowe. Casper: a Compiler for the Analysis of Security Protocols. *Journal of Computer Security*, 6(1):53–84, 1998.

26. J. Meseguer and P. Thati. Symbolic reachability analysis using narrowing and its application to verification of cryptographic protocols. *Journal of Higher-Order and Symbolic Computation*, to appear.

27. J. K. Millen and V. Shmatikov. Symbolic protocol analysis with products and Diffie-Hellman exponentiation. In *Proceedings of CSFW'03*, pp. 47–61. IEEE Computer Society Press, 2003.

28. J. Siekmann and P. Szabó. The undecidability of the D_A unification problem. *Journal of Symbolic Computation*, 54(2):402–414, 1989.

Satisfiability Checking for PC(ID)*

Maarten Mariën, Rudradeb Mitra, Marc Denecker, and Maurice Bruynooghe

Department of Computer Science, Katholieke Universiteit Leuven, Belgium
{maartenm, mitra, marcd, maurice}@cs.kuleuven.be

Abstract. The logic FO(ID) extends classical first order logic with inductive definitions. This paper studies the satisifiability problem for PC(ID), its propositional fragment. We develop a framework for model generation in this logic, present an algorithm and prove its correctness. As FO(ID) is an integration of classical logic and logic programming, our algorithm integrates techniques from SAT and ASP. We report on a prototype system, called MIDL, experimentally validating our approach.

1 Introduction

The logic FO(ID), or Inductive Definition Logic (ID-logic) [7], extends classical first order logic (FO) with a language primitive that allows a uniform representation of inductive definitions. In general, inductive definitions cannot be represented in first order logic (FO). The semantics of this primitive is based on the well-founded semantics of logic programming [28]; indeed, as argued in [6, 8], it correctly formalizes the semantics of inductive definitions.

While definitions are common in mathematics, they are also crucial in declarative Knowledge Representation. Not only non-inductive definitions are frequent in common-sense reasoning as argued in the seminal paper [2], also inductive definitions are. In [10], the *situation calculus* is given a very natural and general representation as an iterated inductive definition in the well-ordered set of situations and [16] observes that inductive definitions are present in many applications of Answer Set Programming (ASP) [12]. In short, definitions are a distinctive and important form of knowledge that can be naturally represented in FO(ID).

The goal of this paper is to present algorithms to solve SAT(PC(ID)), the satisfiability problem for PC(ID)[1], the propositional fragment of FO(ID), or equivalently, generate models for theories in this fragment. This problem is an extension of SAT, the satisfiability problem of propositional CNF formulas. Current SAT solvers exhibit impressive performance on many industrial instances. Unfortunately, SAT is a rather poor modeling language, and substantial effort is often required to encode a problem. PC(ID) is a major enhancement of the expressivity [19]. Solvers for SAT(PC(ID)) are also strongly related to ASP solvers

---

* Works supported by FWO-Vlaanderen, IWT-Vlaanderen, European Framework 5 Project WASP, and by GOA/2003/08.

[1] PC(ID) stands for "Propositional Calculus, extended with Inductive Definitions".

such as Smodels [21] and DLV [4]. These solvers use the fixpoint operator of the well-founded semantics as a boolean propagation mechanism for rule sets.

Viable approaches for building a solver for SAT(PC(ID)) are:

1. A native approach that integrates inference techniques for inductive definitions with SAT inference techniques.
2. Mapping PC(ID) theories to CNF theories and applying off-the-shelf SAT solvers as in [23].
3. Mapping PC(ID) theories to equivalent general logic programs and then applying off-the-shelf ASP solvers. Using results from [16], it is easy to accomplish, but it completely bypasses PC(ID)'s relation with SAT.

The first approach, explored in this paper, is the most promising in the long run. It will improve our understanding of how to compute with inductive definitions and is best suited to integrate language extensions such as aggregates, constraints and open functions.

Despite the semantical differences, the computational tasks of our algorithm are very similar to those of algorithms like Smodels' Expand [21] and DLV's DetCons [4]. Its novelty lies in the use of justification semantics [9], which offers a different view on the computational task involved:

- One can locally test whether the well-founded operator is required.
- One can use a watched literal technique for propagations, very similar to the Two Watched Literal technique used in SAT [20].

We introduce PC(ID) in Section 2 and the semantic foundations of our algorithm in Section 3. We present the algorithm and argue its correctness in Section 4. Its implementation, MIDL, and a comparison with other approaches are described in Section 5. We finish with conclusions and related work.

2   Preliminaries

2.1   PC(ID)

The semantics of FO(ID) ([7]) is here redefined for the propositional fragment PC(ID). A vocabulary Σ is a set of atom symbols. A definition D is a set of rules of the form $(P \leftarrow \varphi)$, where $P \in \Sigma$ is called the head of the rule, and the body of the rule, φ, is a propositional formula in Σ. We denote by $Def(D)$ the set of atoms that appear in the heads of the rules of D. The set $\Sigma \setminus Def(D)$ is called the set of open symbols of D and is denoted by $Open(D)$. A literal is an atom P or its negation $\neg P$; it is *defined* if $P \in Def(D)$, otherwise it is *open*. A PC(ID) theory T in Σ is a set of propositional formulas and definitions in Σ.

A three-valued Σ-interpretation I is a function from Σ to the set $\{f, u, t\}$ of truth values; a two-valued interpretation maps to $\{f, t\}$ instead. Truth values are ordered by the truth order, defined as $f < u < t$, and the precision order, given by $u <_p t$ and $u <_p f$. We also have $f^{-1} = t$, $u^{-1} = u$ and $t^{-1} = f$. We denote the projection of I on the atoms in a set S by $I|_S$.

The semantics can be defined by means of the well-founded semantics [28]: Given a definition D and an interpretation $I|_{Open(D)}$ of the open atoms of D, there is a unique well-founded model of D extending $I|_{Open(D)}$, which we denote by $\text{wfm}_D(I|_{Open(D)})$. An interpretation I is a model of definition D, denoted $I \models D$, iff I is two-valued and $I = \text{wfm}_D(I|_{Open(D)})$; I is a model of a PC(ID) theory T iff I is two-valued and is a model of every definition and every propositional formula in T. An equivalent characterisation is provided by Corollary 1 below.

Example 1. Consider the definition $D_1 = \{P \leftarrow Q\}$. Then $P \in Def(D_1), Q \in Open(D_1)$. The models of D_1 are $\{P, Q\}$ and $\emptyset$. They are also the models of $D_2 = \{Q \leftarrow P\}$. Hence, $T_1 = \{\{P \leftarrow Q\}, \{Q \leftarrow P\}\}$ which consists of two definitions has models $\{P, Q\}$ and $\emptyset$. However, $T_2 = \{\{P \leftarrow Q, Q \leftarrow P\}\}$ consists of a single definition and has only $\emptyset$ as model.

The theory $T_3 = \{\{P \leftarrow Q\}, \{P \leftarrow\}, \neg Q \vee R\}$ has two definitions for P and one propositional formula; the first definition has two models (as D_1), while the second one has only $\{P\}$ as its model and $\{P, Q, R\}$ is the only model of T_3.

2.2 MIDL Normal Form

Definition 1 (MIDL normal form). *A PC(ID) theory T is in MIDL normal form iff $T = C \cup \{D\} \cup E$ where C is a set of clauses without defined literals, E is a set of equivalences $P \equiv Q$ where P is an open and Q a defined atom, and D is a definition (a set of rules), with for each atom Q in $Def(D)$ exactly one rule with Q in the head. Moreover for all rules R in D, R is in the form $Q \leftarrow L_1 \wedge \ldots \wedge L_n$ or $Q \leftarrow L_1 \vee \ldots \vee L_n$, where $n \geq 1$ and L_i are literals.*

Example 2. $T_3^{MidL} = \{\{P^{D_A} \leftarrow Q, P^{D_B} \leftarrow\}, \neg Q \vee R, P \equiv P^{D_A}, P \equiv P^{D_B}\}$ is the MIDL normal form equivalent to T_3 in Example 1: the models of T_3^{MidL}, restricted to T_3's vocabulary, are the models of T_3.

Defined atoms whose body is a disjunction respectively conjunction are called *disjunctive* respectively *conjunctive* atoms. Let S be a set of literals; then we abbreviate $\bigwedge_{L \in S} L$ by $\bigwedge S$ and $\bigvee_{L \in S} L$ by $\bigvee S$.

A straightforward transformation (time linear in the size of the input) that maps a PC(ID) theory T to an equivalent theory in MIDL normal form by introducing new atoms, is given in [17]. As the above example shows, the head of a definition $P \leftarrow \ldots$ becomes a defined atom P^D which is linked to the original atom P through an equivalence.

3 Semantic Background

This section introduces semantical concepts borrowed from [9].

Definition 2 (Direct justification). *Let D be a definition in MIDL normal form and J_d a set of literals. J_d is a direct justification for a defined atom P iff:*

- *either $P \leftarrow L_1 \wedge \ldots \wedge L_n \in D$ and $J_d = \{L_1, \ldots, L_n\}$;*
- *or $P \leftarrow L_1 \vee \ldots \vee L_n \in D$ and $J_d = \{L_i\}$ for some $i \in 1 \ldots n$.*

J_d *is a* direct justification *for a defined literal* $\neg P$ *iff:*

- *either* $P \leftarrow L_1 \wedge \ldots \wedge L_n \in D$ *and* $J_d = \{\neg L_i\}$ *for some* $i \in 1 \ldots n;$
- *or* $P \leftarrow L_1 \vee \ldots \vee L_n \in D$ *and* $J_d = \{\neg L_1, \ldots, \neg L_n\}.$

Example 3. Consider $D_1 = \{P \leftarrow Q \wedge \neg R, Q \leftarrow \neg P \vee R\}$. The set $\{Q, \neg R\}$ is a direct justification for P and $\{P, \neg R\}$ for $\neg Q$; both $\{\neg P\}$ and $\{R\}$ are direct justifications for Q and both $\{\neg Q\}$ and $\{R\}$ for $\neg P$.

Consider $D_2 = \{P \leftarrow Q, Q \leftarrow P \vee R, R \leftarrow \neg P \wedge S\}$. Though $\{Q\}$ is a direct justification for P and $\{P\}$ for Q, the truth of P doesn't justify the truth of Q or vice versa, as illustrated by the model $\text{wfm}_D(\{S^f\}) = \{P^f, Q^f, R^f, S^f\}$.

A direct justification is insufficient to infer the truth of a literal in the well-founded model. We need to consider graphs of direct justifications. A *leaf* of a graph is a node without outgoing edges.

Definition 3 (Justification). *A justification J of a definition in MIDL normal form is a directed graph where the nodes are literals, such that for each internal node L, L is a defined literal and the set of its children, $Ch_J(L)$, is a direct justification for L. A justification is total if none of its leaves are defined literals.*

Example 4. D_2 from Example 3 has many justifications. Examples are:

$$J_0 = \emptyset, \ J_1 = \begin{bmatrix} P \\ \uparrow\ \downarrow \\ Q \end{bmatrix}, \ J_2 = \begin{bmatrix} P \longrightarrow Q \longrightarrow R \longrightarrow S \\ \uparrow \qquad\qquad\qquad \downarrow \\ \neg R \longleftarrow \neg Q \rightleftarrows \neg P \end{bmatrix}, \ J_3 = \begin{bmatrix} \neg P \\ \uparrow\ \downarrow \\ \neg Q \longrightarrow \neg R \end{bmatrix}.$$

Here J_0, J_1 and J_2 are total, but J_3 is not since $\neg R$ is a defined leaf.

As the example shows, justifications can contain cycles. We distinguish between *positive*, *negative* and *mixed* cycles. They consist of repectively only positive (as in J_1), only negative (as in J_3) and both kind of literals (as in J_2).

A justification is an argument for the truth value of its literals. Its *value* depends on the structure of the justification and the truth value of its leaves.

Definition 4 ($\mathcal{V}_I(J)$, the value of a justification). *Let J be a justification, and I an interpretation.*

- $\mathcal{V}_I(J) = \boldsymbol{f}$ *if J contains either a leaf L with $I(L) = \boldsymbol{f}$ or a positive cycle.*
- $\mathcal{V}_I(J) = \boldsymbol{u}$ *if $\mathcal{V}_I(J) \neq \boldsymbol{f}$ and J contains either a leaf L with $I(L) = \boldsymbol{u}$ or a mixed cycle (or both).*
- $\mathcal{V}_I(J) = \boldsymbol{t}$ *otherwise (all leaves are $\boldsymbol{t}$ and cycles, if any, are negative).*

Example 5. Continuing Example 4. Independent of I, $\mathcal{V}_I(J_0) = \boldsymbol{t}$ and, because J_1 has a positive cycle, $\mathcal{V}_I(J_1) = \boldsymbol{f}$. Now, let $I = \{P^t, Q^t, R^f, S^t\}$. $\mathcal{V}_I(J_2) = \boldsymbol{u}$, indeed, although the only leaf (S) is $\boldsymbol{t}$, J_2 contains a mixed cycle; and finally $\mathcal{V}_I(J_3) = \boldsymbol{t}$, because the only leaf is $\boldsymbol{t}$ and the only cycle is negative.

The value of a total justification J depends only on its cycles and the interpretation of its open symbols. J_L, the *restriction of J to L*, denotes the subgraph with L as root. A defined literal L is *justified* in a justification J if J_L is non-empty and total. The *supported value* $SV_I(L)$ of a defined literal L in an interpretation I is the maximal value in the truth order of its justifications i.e., $SV_I(L) = \max_\leq\{V_I(J)|J$ is a justification and L is justified in $J\}$.

It was proven in [9] that in the well-founded model M, the interpretation of defined literals agrees with the supported values, i.e., $M(L) = SV_M(L)$. Furthermore, [5] proved that $SV_M(L) = SV_M(\neg L)^{-1}$ for any defined literal L.

Example 6. Continuing from Example 4, let I' be an interpretation with $I'(S) = f$. Then $SV_{I'}(P) = f$, since for any justification J in which P is justified, either S is a leaf in J_P, or $J_P = J_1$. And indeed, let J' be the total justification obtained from J_3 by adding the edge $(\neg R, \neg S)$; then $SV_{I'}(\neg P) \geq V_{I'}(J'_{\neg P}) = V_{I'}(J') = t$.

Hence one can compute the well-founded model by computing for each literal its supported value. However, searching over all justifications for the best one is infeasible. Fortunately, attention can be restricted to a subclass of justifications.

Definition 5 ((strict) support, positive residue). *Let J be a justification and I an interpretation. J supports I if $I(L) \leq_p I(\bigwedge Ch_J(L))$ and J strictly supports I if $I(L) = I(\bigwedge Ch_J(L))$ for each internal node L of J.*

The positive residue *of J in I consists of the atoms that would be strictly supported if true but are undefined, i.e., $I(L) = u$ and $I(\bigwedge Ch_J(L)) = t$.*

Definition 6 (Cycle-safe). *Let J be a justification and I an interpretation. J is cycle-safe in I if J contains neither mixed cycles with literals that are true in I nor positive cycles.*

Definition 7 (v-total). *Let J be a justification, I an interpretation, and v a truth value, i.e., $v \in \{f, u, t\}$. Then J is v-total in I if for each defined literal L such that $I(L) = v$, L is justified in J.*

Note that if a justification J is f-, u- and t-total w.r.t. an interpretation I, then J is total, but a total justification might not be f-, u- or t-total w.r.t. any interpretation, because not every literal occurs in J.

Theorem 1. *Let I be an interpretation and J a justification. If the following conditions hold:*

(i1) J strictly supports I;
(i2) J is cycle-safe in I;
(i3) J is t-total in I;
(i4) J is u-total in I,

then for every defined literal L it holds that $I(L) = SV_I(L)$.

Corollary 1. *Let I and J satisfy (i1)-(i4). Then* $\mathrm{wfm}_D(I|_{Open(D)}) = I$.

In the next section we introduce an algorithm that incrementally constructs and maintains a 3-valued interpretation I and a justification J that satisfy the conditions (i1)-(i4).

1 Initialize I and J (see Section 4.4);
2 **while** *there is an open atom A with $I(A) = u$* **do**
3   Select open atom A with $I(A) = u$;
4   **Choose** $S := \{A\}$ or $S := \{\neg A\}$;
    % Boolean Propagation:
5   **while** *true* **do**
6   **if** $S \neq \emptyset$ **then**
7   Direct_Propagation(I, J, S); % Can initiate backtracking
8   **if** *there is an L with $I(L) = u$ and $Ch_J(L) = \emptyset$* **then** select such a L;
9   **else** Break;
10         $S := $ Justify(I, J, L);

11 **if** *I is 2-valued* **then** Return SATISFIABLE;
12 **else Backtrack;**

Algorithm 1. MIDL(T)

4 Algorithm

4.1 Structure of the Algorithm

The progenitor of our algorithm is the DLL algorithm [3], which is also the basis of most of today's SAT solvers. The DLL algorithm incrementally constructs an interpretation I that satisfies an input CNF theory T. In each stage, a choice literal is selected and is made true, after which *boolean propagation* is applied on the current assignment to infer other true literals. In particular, *unit propagation* makes the last non-false literal of a clause true. In case of conflict, backtracking returns to the last choice point. There, the alternative choice is made.[2]

Algorithm 1, the backbone of our algorithm is similar to the DLL algorithm. The input is a PC(ID) theory in MIDL normal form. However, the choice literal is an open one and boolean propagation is extended to include propagations according to the well-founded semantics by maintaining a 3-valued assignment I and a justification J. The aim of Steps 1 and 1 is to establish the conditions (i1)-(i4), as well as the following invariant:

(i5) For each clause $C \in T$, $I(C) \geq u$;

If so, obviously, I is a model when Step 1 returns SATISFIABLE. The "Boolean Propagation" (Step 1) is the core of the algorithm; it consists of two components:

Direct Propagation. The input consists of I and J, the current interpretation and justification and the set of literals S to be made true. The latter are made true, unit propagation on the clauses and propagation from body to head in the rules of the definitions are applied. This establishes the invariants (i1)-(i3) and (i5) unless a conflict is detected and backtracking is initiated.

---

[2] UNSATISFIABLE is returned when no more backtrackings are possible.

Justify. The input consists of the current I and J, and a literal L that violates invariant (i4) (u-totality) (L is a unknown defined literal that has no justification). The procedure tries to adjust J into a justification J' in which all literals of J'_L are strictly supported. In case this fails, an *unfounded set* [28] is found. The involved atoms must become false, their negation is returned in the set S for processing by the direct propagation.

The u-totality invariant is satisfied when the while loop exits in Step 1. It terminates because Direct_Propagation extends the interpretation I and Justify either reduces the number of unknown defined literals without justification or finds a unfounded set that leads to an extension of I in the next iteration. Hence:

Theorem 2. *Steps 1-1 of Algorithm 1 terminate; when they do via Step 1 then invariants (i1)-(i5) are satisfied.*

4.2   Direct Propagation (Algorithm 2)

The Direct_Propagation algorithm uses the following data structures:

- A data structure dj which associates with each defined literal L a direct justification of L. While $dj(L)$ is constant for conjunctive atoms and the negation of disjunctive atom, it consists of a selected literal (the *watched* literal) in the other cases.
- A boolean data structure *just* over defined literals, indicating whether or not the literal's direct justification belongs to the current justification[3].

The data structures dj and *just* together determine a justification J in the following way: if $just(L)$, then $Ch_J(L) = dj(L)$; otherwise, $Ch_J(L) = \emptyset$.

Making a literal in S true (Step 2) invalidates invariant (i1); however, the following weaker invariants are maintained:

(i6) J supports I;
(i7) the positive residue of J in I is a subset of S; for all defined literals $L \in S$: $\mathcal{V}_{J_L}(I) = t$; i.e., there exists a justification for making L true.

From invariant (i7), it follows that there is no positive residue when S becomes empty, hence (i1) is restored. Also (i2) and (i3) are preserved:

t-totality (i3): A defined literal can only be made true in step Step 2 of Algorithm 2.[4] Therefore, if a defined literal L has $I(L) = t$, we know by (i6) that it has children in J that are all also true. By induction over all literals in J_L, J_L must be total and invariant (i3) holds.

---

[3] Hence L is justified if $just(L)$ and the literals in $Ch_J(L)$ are justified.

[4] This explains both the restriction in Step 1 of Algorithm 1 to *open* literals, and the requirement in Definition 1 that the CNF formula cannot contain defined literals.

```
     Assert: (i1), (i2), (i3) and (i5)
 1  repeat
 2  |   Pop L from S;
 3  |   if I(L) = f then backtrack (to choice point in Alg. 1);
 4  |   if I(L) ≠ t then
 5  |   |   I(L) := t;
 6  |   |   if L is defined then Push its original on S (using the equivalences);
 7  |   |   if L is open then for every clause c of T containing ¬L do
 8  |   |   |   if c has exactly one non-false literal L' then Push L' on S;
 9  |   |   for every unknown literal L' for which {L} is a direct justification do
10  |   |   |   just(L') := t; dj(L') := {L}; Push L' on S ;
11  |   |   for every unknown literal L' such that ¬L ∈ dj(L') do
12  |   |   |   case L' = P with P ← ¬L ∧ ··· ∈ T, or L' = ¬P with
        |   |   |   P ← L ∨ ··· ∈ T
13  |   |   |   |   dj(¬L') := {L}; just(¬L) := t; Push ¬L' on S;
14  |   |   |   case L' = ¬P with P ← L ∧ ··· ∈ T
15  |   |   |   |   if P has no unknown body literals left then Push P on S;
16  |   |   |   |   else
17  |   |   |   |   |   Select an unknown body literal L'' of P; dj(L') := {¬L''};
        |   |   |   |   |   just(L') := t ;
18  |   |   |   case L' = P with P ← ¬L ∨ ··· ∈ T
19  |   |   |   |   if P has no unknown body literals left then Push ¬P on S;
20  |   |   |   |   else
21  |   |   |   |   |   if P has unknown open or negative body literal L'' then
22  |   |   |   |   |   |   dj(L') := {L''}; just(L') := t;
23  |   |   |   |   |   else
24  |   |   |   |   |   |   Select an unknown defined body atom Q;
25  |   |   |   |   |   |   dj(L') := {Q}; just(L') := f;

26  until S = ∅;
```

Algorithm 2. Direct Propagation(I, J, S)

Cycle-safeness (i2): By (i3) and (i6), true literals are justified, hence taking a true literal as the direct justiciation of a unknown literal cannot create a mixed cycle containing true literals. We must also verify that none of the steps in Algorithm 2 creates a positive cycle in J. Steps 2-2 don't change J. In the case of Step 2 $Ch_J(L')$ is only changed for a *negative* literal L', in the case of Step 2 J is either not changed, or only for a negative literal. Finally, in the case of Step 2 a positive cycle might be created in J when the direct justification of the atom P is changed to a positive defined atom. This is prevented by removing it from J ($just(L') := f$ implies $Ch_J(L') := \emptyset$). Consequently, u-totality, invariant (i4), is violated.

Making an unknown literal true can violate invariant (i5) on the clauses. Step 2 not only performs unit propagation (not all clauses containing $¬L$ are inspected but the Two Watched Literal technique is used) but also restoration of the invariant. By pushing the last non-false literal on the stack, a violation of the invariant will finally result in the uncovering of a conflict in Step 2.

Example 7. Let $T = \{\{P^D \leftarrow Q^D \vee A, \; Q^D \leftarrow P^D \wedge R^D \wedge \neg B, \; R^D \leftarrow C\},$ $P^D \equiv P, \; Q^D \equiv Q, \; R^D \equiv R\}, I = \emptyset,$ and

$$J = \begin{bmatrix} P^D \leftarrow Q^D \rightarrow R^D & \neg P^D \overset{\rightarrow}{\underset{\leftarrow}{}} \neg Q^D & \neg R \\ \downarrow \quad\;\; \downarrow \quad\;\; \downarrow & \downarrow & \downarrow \\ A \quad \neg B \quad\; C & \neg A & \neg C \end{bmatrix}.$$ Suppose Step 1 in Al-

gorithm 1 chooses $\mathcal{S} := \{B\}$. Then Step 2 makes B true; subsequently Step 2 changes $Ch_J(\neg Q^D)$ from $\neg P^D$ to B, and pushes $\neg Q^D$ on $\mathcal{S}$. In a next iteration of the repeat loop, $\neg Q^D$ is made true, and $\neg Q$ is pushed on $\mathcal{S}$ in Step 2.

Suppose that orginally $\mathcal{S} := \{\neg A\}$ is chosen. After making A false, the algorithm ends up in Step 2. $dj(P^D)$ is changed from A to Q^D. In addition $just(P^D)$ is set to $\boldsymbol{f}$. Note that otherwise a positive cycle $P^D \leftrightarrow Q^D$ would have been created.

The Direct_Propagation algorithm can be understood as performing a watched literal technique for rules, similar to the Two Watched Literals (2WL) technique in SAT [20]. Every literal in a singleton direct justification (i.e., of a positive disjunctive atom, or of a negative conjunctive atom) is "watched": when the literal becomes false, the corresponding rule has to be visited. When any other literal in that body becomes false, we don't need to visit the rule yet, since the "watched literal" is still unknown and thus might still justify the head.

Interpreting the head of each rule as a second watched literal, it can be seen that the Direct_Propagation algorithm actually has the same behaviour as the 2WL scheme has on the completion of the definition.

4.3   Justify (Algorithm 3)

Algorithm 3 tries to adjust J so that J_P is a total justification for the unknown atom P. If $dj(P)$, the direct justification of P, can be added to the current justification J (by setting $Just(P)$ to $\boldsymbol{t}$) without creating a positive cycle (involving P) then we are done. This is tested in Step 3. This is a fairly simple test; however, if it fails, we will have to adjust the direct justification of P to construct a total justification.

The next step then is to find an overestimation of all unknown defined atoms that can potentially contribute to some J_P that is a total justification of P. Note that the unknown open literals and unknown negative literals can be used as valid leaves in a total justification, so they need not be included. This overestimation is computed in Step 3 and stored in $\mathcal{E}$. It consists of all atoms *reachable from* P in the dynamic positive dependency graph. The latter is defined as follows:

Definition 8 (dynamic positive dependency graph). *Let D be a definition in MiDL normal form, I a partial interpretation. The dynamic positive dependency graph of D in I is a directed graph (V, E) of atoms. $P \in V$ iff P is defined in D and $I(P) = \boldsymbol{u}$. $(P, Q) \in E$ iff $\{P, Q\} \subseteq V$ and P is the head of a rule and the atom Q occurs in its body.*

Assert: (i1), (i2), (i3) and $Ch_J(P) = \emptyset$
Result: a set of negative literals $\mathcal{S}$;
1 **if** $IsCycleSafe(P, dj)$ **then** $just(P) := t$; Return $\emptyset$;
2 $\mathcal{E} :=$ FindSet(I, P);
3 $\mathcal{B} :=$ FindBottomSeeds$(I, \mathcal{E})$; $\mathcal{E} := \mathcal{E} \setminus \mathcal{B}$;
4 **while** $\mathcal{B} \neq \emptyset$ **do**
5 $\quad$ Select Q from $\mathcal{B}$; $\mathcal{B} := \mathcal{B} \setminus \{Q\}$;
6 $\quad$ **for** *disjunctive atoms* $Q' \in \mathcal{E}$ *such that* Q *occurs in the body of* Q' **do**
7 $\quad\quad$ $dj(Q') := \{Q\}$; $just(Q') := t$; Move Q' from $\mathcal{E}$ to $\mathcal{B}$;
8 $\quad$ **for** *conjunctive atoms* $Q' \in \mathcal{E}$ *such that* $dj(\neg Q') = \{\neg Q\}$ **do**
9 $\quad\quad$ **if** *there exists a* $Q'' \in \mathcal{E}$ *in the rule of* Q' **then** $dj(\neg Q') := \{\neg Q''\}$;
10 $\quad\quad$ **else** $just(Q') := t$; Move Q' from $\mathcal{E}$ to $\mathcal{B}$;

11 Return $\{\neg Q | Q \in \mathcal{E}\}$;

Algorithm 3. Justify(I, J, P)

Observe that $\mathcal{E}$ not only includes atoms without direct justification such as P itself, but also atoms with direct justification. In order to justify P, however, it may be necessary to update the direct justification of such atoms.In other words, $\mathcal{E}$ is the set of *endangered atoms*: atoms, whose direct justification may have to be revised.

In the following steps, the algorithm tries to construct justifications for elements in $\mathcal{E}$. In Step 3, it collects in $\mathcal{B}$ elements from $\mathcal{E}$ that have a trivial justification:

- conjunctive atoms $C \in \mathcal{E}$ which have no elements from $\mathcal{E}$ in their body (the unknown literals in their body are either open or negative)
- disjunctive atoms $D \in \mathcal{E}$ which have an unknown open or negative literal L in their body (their direct justification is set to that literal).

In the while loop, elements from $\mathcal{B}$ are used one by one as seeds to construct justifications for other elements in $\mathcal{E}$. In Step 3, the direct justification of a disjunctive atom is set to the seed and in Step 3, a conjunctive atom is justified and removed from $\mathcal{E}$ once it has no other body atoms in $\mathcal{E}$. In both steps, the newly justified atoms are added to the seeds. Observe that negative literals returned in Step 3 are justified; their direct justifications have been set in Step 3.

When exiting the while loop, all seeds have been used and what remains is an unfounded set of atoms. They have to be made false, hence their negation is returned by Justify.

This algorithm is an adaptation from [15] to the context of justifications.

Example 8. Continuing from Example 7, where we initially chose $\mathcal{S} := \{\neg A\}$. In Step 1 of Algorithm 1, Justify(I, J, Q^D) will be called. Since $dj(Q^D) = \{P^D\}$ and $dj(P^D) = \{Q^D\}$, $IsCycleSafe(Q^D, dj)$ fails. $\mathcal{E} = \{P^D, Q^D, R^D\}$ is computed in Step 3. In the next step we find $\mathcal{B} = \{R^D\}$ and therefore $\mathcal{E} = \{P^D, Q^D\}$, meaning that R^D might still justify P^D and/or Q^D becoming true.

Since R^D only occurs in a conjunctive body (Q^D), but $dj(\neg Q^D) \neq \{\neg R^D\}$, R^D cannot justify anything, and the while-loop stops. Finally Justify returns $\{\neg P^D, \neg Q^D\}$ which are the negated literals from the unfounded set $\{P^D, Q^D\}$.

Let J be a justification, then we define T_J as the set $\{L | L \in J \land Ch_J(L) = \emptyset \land L$ is defined$\}$, i.e. the defined leaves of J.

Proposition 1. *Let I, J and P satisfy the requirements in Algorithm 3. Let J' be the justification after termination of Algorithm 3 and S the resulting set. Then either S is empty and $T_{J'} \subseteq T_J \setminus \{P\}$, or S is not empty and contains the negated literals from an unfounded set: for each $\neg Q \in S$, $\neg Q$ is justified and $\mathcal{V}_{J_{\neg Q}}(I) = t$.*

Proposition 2. *Algorithm 3 preserves invariants (i1), (i2), (i3) and (i5).*

These propositions formalize our claim in Section 4.1 that after each call to Justify either I is constant and the number of unknown defined leaves of J decreases, or I can be extended by the set returned by Justify.

4.4 Correctness, Initialization and Optimization Issues

Soundness and Completeness. Soundness has been argued in Section 4.1: I is a model when Algorithm 1 returns SATISFIABLE. Completeness follows from the completeness of the DLL algorithm and the observation that our Boolean Propagation extends unit propagation of DLL and computes after each choice point the well-founded model extending the interpretation of the open literals.

Initialization. Step 1 of Algorithm 1 should initialize an interpretation I and a partial justification J such that invariants (i1)-(i5) are satisfied. To do this, we initialize I to the empty interpretation and $dj(L)$ to an arbitrary direct justification of L, for every defined literal. To avoid positive cycles, we set $just(P) := f$ for every defined atom P. Then the set of unit clauses is collected in S, and the initialisation executes the same while loop as described in Step 1 of Algorithm 1.

Backtracking. Backtracking restores I and J to some old value, say I_b and J_b. The invariants (i1)-(i5) hold for I_b and J_b. In fact, with exception of (i4), they also hold for I_b and J. Indeed, a conflict arises at a moment when (i2), (i3) and (i6) all hold. After restoring I to a previous level, for every defined literal L it holds that $I(L) = I(\bigwedge dj(L))$, and hence (i6) still holds, i.e., J supports I. Since (i1)-(i3), (i5) are sufficient pre-conditions for Boolean Propagation, the justification need not be restored upon backtracking.

Endangered Atoms. After an unsuccessful cycle-safety check (which is in fact optional), the first step of Justify is a call to FindSet to produce $\mathcal{E}$, the set of atoms endangered by the modified direct justification of P. There are a number of alternative possibilities. For example, the algorithm would remain correct if FindSet would return all unknown atoms in $Def(D)$ instead. However, one could also compute a smaller set of endangered atoms: Those in the strongly connected component (SCC) of P in the dynamic positive dependency graph. An SCC is a set S of atoms, such that every element of S can reach every other element of S via the directed edges. Tarjan's algorithm searches for strongly connected components in time linear in the size of the graph [26, 22]. Also the SCC of the static positive dependency graph, which we define as the dynamic positive dependency graph after the initialization (Step 1 in Algorithm 1), could be used. The smaller the set of endangered atoms, the faster it is processed. However, there is a trade-off between the work spent to compute the endangered atoms and that spent on processing them.

5   Experimental Results

We have made a prototype implementation, called MIDL, of the algorithm described in the previous section. We have compared MIDL to Smodels [21] and idsat(zChaff) [23, 29]. We have thus a representative for each of the three approaches mentioned in Section 1. Note that the input to Smodels is handcoded and hence behaves possibly better than what one would obtain by an automatic mapping from PC(ID) to ASP. We used two classes of problems: N-queens and Hamiltonian cycles[5]. All the experiments were run on 863 MHz P-III with 254 MB of RAM. In Table 1 timings to find the first model (averaged over 5 runs) are given in seconds.

Since MIDL doesn't enjoy the fine-tuned optimizations of a state of the art SAT or ASP solver, we don't expect comparable effiencies. Most notably, MIDL's data structures are not yet minimized, which can be expected to lead to serious losses in cache usage. Also its heuristics are very crude.

Indeed, the results show poor scaling. However, observe that MIDL outperforms the other solvers on some of the smaller problems. Remarkably, zChaff cannot cope with several Hamiltonian cycle problems; as they contain a lot of induction, idsat increased the size of these problems 20-fold. This confirms the usefulness of our native approach with respect to a translation to SAT. For an important class of problems, MIDL is currently the best PC(ID) model generator.

In Table 2 we compare timings[6], the total number of atoms found to be in an unfounded set (U) and the total number of endangered atoms considered (E) for some variants of MIDL: in MIDL- and MIDL SCC-, the optional Step 1 of Algorithm 3 is disabled, in MIDL SCC and MIDL SCC- the FindSet procedure returns the SCC of the dynamic positive dependency graph, as described in Section 4.4. The first important observation is that the cycle-safety check almost consistently yields faster results. A second observation is that MIDL SCC is doing more intelligent work: it uses less endangered atoms, and it also finds

---

[5] We denote the Hamiltonian cycle problems by "H-*#vertices-#nodes*". Encodings are taken from http://asparagus.cs.uni-potsdam.de/; randomly generated graphs were used.

[6] To save space, we've selected but a few example problems; other problems exhibit the same behaviour.

Table 1. Timings (*sec*) of MIDL, idsat using zChaff, and Smodels. # = >10min.

	MIDL	idsat+zCh	Smod.
9-queens	0.08	0.56+0.02	**0.05**
11-queens	1.49	0.79+0.21	**0.18**
13-queens	10.77	1.18+0.13	**0.43**
15-queens	296.91	**1.67+0.16**	1.85
H-20-200	0.32	61.19+7.62	**0.10**
H-25-200	**0.06**	96.5+82.2	0.10
H-30-200	1.97	98.5+137	**0.13**
H-35-200	3.65	#+#	**0.18**
H-20-400	**0.12**	72.87+#	0.35
H-25-400	**0.20**	128.0+#	0.55
H-30-400	**0.18**	209.2+#	0.56
H-35-400	#	#+#	**0.87**

Table 2. Comparison of unfounded set sizes (U) vs. number of "endangered atoms" (E) and timings (*sec*) for different variants of MIDL

		MIDL	MIDL-	MIDL SCC	MIDL SCC-
H-20-200	U	1427	1461	1022	1433
	E	4570	20327	2535	11363
	time	**0.32**	0.34	3.52	1.57
H-30-200	U	1933	2013	474	1976
	E	10567	116186	2708	62460
	time	1.97	2.87	**1.20**	3.62
H-20-400	U	248	283	112	179
	E	1112	6573	785	4435
	time	**0.12**	0.17	0.25	0.24
H-30-400	U	209	231	85	180
	E	2002	31618	2031	22975
	time	**0.18**	1.70	0.32	1.77

much less unfounded sets, i.e., finds falsity of atoms through Direct Propagation more often. Still, MIDL outperforms MIDL SCC, suggesting that a more careful implementation that removes some overhead of the SCC computation might be beneficial.

6   Conclusions, Related and Future Work

This work is one of the first attempts to build a SAT(PC(ID)) system. We have chosen for a direct implementation, in contrast to a mapping to ASP, or to propositional logic, as was done in [23]. The latter approach is similar to ASP systems such as ASSAT [14] and Cmodels [13].

Despite semantical differences between PC(ID) and ASP, the algorithms presented here share a lot of structure with those of Smodels and DLV. The main novelties of our approach come through the use of justifications:

- this enables us to do the beneficial cycle-safety check;
- it integrates nicely with a watched literal technique for rules;
- the justification graph can be seen as a straightforward extension of the implication graph, which is used for Clause Learning [18]. In the near future, we intend to include this important SAT technique in MIDL.

Another strongly related system is dcs [11]. This system can be viewed as a model generator for a fragment of FO(ID). The system takes as input a function free FO theory and an inductive definition consisting of Horn rules, and computes Herbrand models of this theory.

In future work, we plan to re-implement MIDL, investigating a variety of techniques from SAT, logic programming and ASP. Interesting recent optimizations to SAT solvers are described in [20, 24, 18, 29]. Potentially relevant techniques for computing the well-founded semantics are described in [27, 1, 15, 25].

Finally, we mention some issues that will be investigated in the near future:

- The current solver uses rules only in a bottom up propagation. In some situations it is definitely worthwhile to also exploit proagation from head to body.
- As shown in [20, 24], the quality of the search algorithm strongly depends on the heuristics. Now that our search algorithm is more or less fixed, we should start to evaluate different heuristics for the system.
- A major task in the project is to build an efficient grounder which reduces a FO(ID) theory to a propositional theory by grounding it with respect to the Herbrand universe.

References

1. K.A. Berman, J.S. Schlipf, and J.V. Franco. Computing the well-founded semantics faster. In V. Marek and A. Nerode, editors, *LPNMR*, volume 928 of *Lecture Notes in Computer Science*, pages 113–126. Springer, 1995.
2. R.J. Brachman and H.J. Levesque. Competence in knowledge representation. In *Proc. of the National Conference on Artificial Intelligence*, pages 189–192, 1982.
3. M. Davis, G. Longemann, and D. Loveland. A machine program for theorem proving. *Communications of the ACM*, 5:394–397, 1962.
4. T. Dell'Armi, W. Faber, G. Ielpa, C. Koch, N. Leone, S. Perri, and G. Pfeifer. System description: DLV. In T. Eiter, W. Faber, and M. Truszczyński, editors, *LPNMR*, volume 2173 of *LNCS*, pages 424–428. Springer, 2001.
5. M. Denecker. *Knowledge Representation and Reasoning in Incomplete Logic Programming*. PhD thesis, Department of Computer Science, K.U.Leuven, 1993.
6. M. Denecker. The well-founded semantics is the principle of inductive definition. In J. Dix, L. Fariñas del Cerro, and U. Furbach, editors, *Logics in Artificial Intelligence*, volume 1489 of *LNAI*, pages 1–16. Springer-Verlag, 1998.
7. M. Denecker. Extending classical logic with inductive definitions. In J. Lloyd et al., editor, *CL*, volume 1861 of *LNAI*, pages 703–717. Springer, 2000.
8. M. Denecker, M. Bruynooghe, and V. Marek. Logic programming revisited: logic programs as inductive definitions. *ACM Transactions on Computational Logic*, 2(4):623–654, 2001.
9. M. Denecker and D. De Schreye. Justification semantics: a unifying framework for the semantics of logic programs. In *LPNMR*, pages 365–379. MIT Press, 1993.
10. M. Denecker and E. Ternovska. Inductive situation calculus. In D. Dubois, C.A. Welty, and M. Williams, editors, *KR*, pages 545–553. AAAI Press, 2004.
11. D. East and M. Truszczyński. dcs: An implementation of datalog with constraints. *CoRR*, cs.AI/0003061, 2000.
12. M. Gelfond and V. Lifschitz. Classical negation in logic programs and disjunctive databases. *New Generation Computing*, 9:365–387, 1991.
13. Y. Lierler and M. Maratea. Cmodels-2: SAT-based answer set solver enhanced to non-tight programs. In V. Lifschitz and I. Niemelä, editors, *LPNMR*, volume 2923 of *LNCS*, pages 346–350. Springer, 2004.
14. F. Lin and Y. Zhao. ASSAT: computing answer sets of a logic program by sat solvers. *Artif. Intell.*, 157(1-2):115–137, 2004.

15. Z. Lonc and M. Truszczyński. On the problem of computing the well-founded semantics. In J.W. Lloyd, V. Dahl, U. Furbach, M. Kerber, K. Lau, C. Palamidessi, L.M. Pereira, Y. Sagiv, and P.J. Stuckey, editors, *Computational Logic*, volume 1861 of *LNCS*, pages 673–687. Springer, 2000.

16. M. Mariën, D. Gilis, and M. Denecker. On the relation between ID-logic and answer set programming. In J.J. Alferes and J.A. Leite, editors, *JELIA*, volume 3229 of *LNCS*, pages 108–120. Springer, 2004.

17. M. Mariën, R. Mitra, M. Denecker, and M. Bruynooghe. Satisfiability checking for PC(ID). Technical Report CW426, K.U. Leuven, 2005.

18. J.P. Marques-Silva and K.A. Sakallah. GRASP: A search algorithm for propositional satisfiability. *IEEE Trans. Computers*, 48(5):506–521, 1999.

19. D.G. Mitchell and E. Ternovska. A framework for representing and solving NP search problems. In AAAI Press/MIT Press, editor, *Twentieth National Conf. on Artificial Intelligence (AAAI-05)*, 2005.

20. M.W. Moskewicz, C.F. Madigan, Y. Zhao, L. Zhang, and S. Malik. Chaff: Engineering an efficient SAT solver. In *DAC*, pages 530–535. ACM, 2001.

21. I. Niemelä, P. Simons, and T. Syrjänen. Smodels: a system for answer set programming. In *NMR*, 2000.

22. E. Nuutila and E. Soisalon-Soininen. On finding the strongly connected components in a directed graph. *Inf. Process. Lett.*, 49(1):9–14, 1994.

23. N. Pelov and E. Ternovska. Reducing inductive definitions to propositional satisfiability. In *ICLP*, LNCS, 2005.

24. L. Ryan. Efficient algorithms for clause-learning SAT solvers. Master's thesis, Simon Fraser University, 2004.

25. K.F. Sagonas, T. Swift, and D.S. Warren. XSB as an efficient deductive database engine. In R.T. Snodgrass and M. Winslett, editors, *SIGMOD Conference*, pages 442–453. ACM Press, 1994.

26. R.E. Tarjan. Depth-first search and linear graph algorithms. *SIAM J. Comput.*, 1(2):146–160, 1972.

27. A. Van Gelder. The alternating fixpoint of logic programs with negation. *Journal of Computer and System Sciences*, 47(1):185–221, 1993.

28. A. Van Gelder, K.A. Ross, and J.S. Schlipf. The well-founded semantics for general logic programs. *Journal of the ACM*, 38(3):620–650, 1991.

29. L. Zhang, C.F. Madigan, M.W. Moskewicz, and S. Malik. Efficient conflict driven learning in a boolean satisfiability solver. In *ICCAD*, pages 279–285. ACM, 2001.

Pool Resolution and Its Relation to Regular Resolution and DPLL with Clause Learning

Allen Van Gelder

University of California, Santa Cruz, CA 95060, USA
http://www.cse.ucsc.edu/~avg

Abstract. Pool Resolution for propositional CNF formulas is introduced. Its relationship to state-of-the-art satisfiability solvers is explained. Every regular-resolution derivation is also a pool-resolution derivation. It is shown that a certain family of formulas, called $NT^{**}(n)$ has polynomial sized pool-resolution refutations, whereas the shortest regular refutations have an exponential lower bound. This family is a variant of the $GT(n)$ family analyzed by Bonet and Galesi (FOCS 1999), and the $GT'(n)$ family shown to require exponential-length regular-resolution refutations by Alekhnovitch, Johannsen, Pitassi and Urquhart (STOC 2002). Thus, Pool Resolution is exponentially stronger than Regular Resolution. Roughly speaking a general-resolution derivation is a pool-resolution derivation if its directed acyclic graph (DAG) has a depth-first search tree that satisfies the regularity restriction: on any path in this tree no resolution variable is repeated. In other words, once a clause is derived at a node and used by its tree parent, its derivation is forgotten, and subsequent uses of that clause treat it as though it were an input clause. This policy is closely related to DPLL search with recording of so-called conflict clauses. Variations of DPLL plus conflict analysis currently dominate the field of high-performance satisfiability solving. The power of Pool Resolution might provide some theoretical explanation for their success.

1   Introduction

The reader is assumed to be generally familiar with the propositional satisfiability problem, CNF formulas, and resolution derivations. Some definitions are briefly reviewed in Section 2, but are not comprehensive.

The history of propositional resolution is interesting. In 1960, Davis and Putnam published an algorithm for deciding whether a propositional CNF formula is unsatisfiable [11]. They did not use the term "resolution" but after Robinson introduced the term in 1965, subsequent literature recognized that what Davis and Putnam were doing was a particular policy for propositional resolution. In 1962, Davis, Logemann and Loveland published the search algorithm that is well known today [10]. Interestingly, they described it as an *optimization* of the 1960 algorithm to conserve memory.

It appears to have been "folklore" in the theory community that it is possible to extract a resolution refutation from the 1962 search algorithm of Davis,

G. Sutcliffe and A. Voronkov (Eds.): LPAR 2005, LNAI 3835, pp. 580–594, 2005.

Logemann and Loveland. This fact was probably known to Tseitin in 1968 and to Galil soon after, although we are not able to pinpoint any published statement. About this time, the 1962 search algorithm began to be referred to as the "Davis-Putnam algorithm" or simply "DP" in the literature. This must have been rather irritating to Logemann and Loveland, particularly since the wrong 1960 paper was consistently cited as the source. This misnomer was not discovered until the 1990s, when the 1962 paper was rediscovered and the acronym DPLL was proposed for the search algorithm "to recognize the contributions of all four authors."

In any case, Tseitin introduced the *regularity* restriction on resolution derivations, that no variable may be resolved upon more than once on any path in the derivation, and demonstrated a super-polynomial lower bound for *regular resolution* [23]. Both DP (resolution) and DPLL (search with resolution extracted) fell under the umbrella of *regular resolution*.

In the 1980's practical experience emerged that showed that DPLL (then called DP) performed unexpectedly well *as a propositional decision procedure* in comparison to known published strategies for resolution [20, 21]. In the 1990's further practical experience showed that DPLL performed poorly when used "as is" but could be greatly enhanced with additional "preorder" reasoning [14]. Meanwhile, it was recalled or rediscovered that DPLL was able to extract a resolution refutation from its search [16].

The last decade has apparently seen theory and practice marching in opposite directions. DPLL produces a resolution derivation that is tree-like, whereas DP produces a resolution derivation that is a directed acyclic graph (DAG) and also is *ordered* (i.e., clashing variables appear in the same order along every DAG path). Although DP has achieved very little practical success [12], DPLL has been the work-horse for high performance satisfiability solvers [24, 3, 18, 19, 25, 13]. Yet theory has shown that the best tree-like resolution derivation may be exponential in length when a DAG resolution derivation is polynomial in length [5, 6]; indeed the separation holds even when the DAG resolution derivation is required to be *ordered* or *regular* [7, 8].

1.1 Summary of Results

The purpose of this paper is to show that the *practice* of satisfiability solving has unknowingly been moving in the direction indicated by *proof complexity theory*, away from the limitations of tree-like computations.

We introduce and formalize a new resolution strategy, called *Pool Resolution*. We show that pool resolution is "exponentially stronger" than regular resolution. Specifically, we show that pool resolution can linearly simulate regular resolution on all formulas. Then we exhibit a family of formulas for which there are polynomial-length pool refutations, but only exponential-length regular refutations. The exponential lower bound for regular refutations on this family was already shown by Alekhnovitch, Johannsen, Pitassi and Urquhart [1]; this paper demonstrates the existence of polynomial-length pool refutations. Beame, Kautz, and Sabharwal provide an excellent discussion on comparing reasoning systems through proof complexity and how it applies to DPLL with "clause learning" [4].

Based on proof-complexity comparisons, it was known that exponential separations supported the following strict order: tree-like < regular < general resolution. This paper shows that regular < pool ≤ general resolution. Finally, we show that pool resolution provides a framework that encompasses most, if not all, of the well-known satisfiability solvers based on DPLL and some form of conflict analysis, also known as "clause learning," "clause recording," "nonchronological backtracking," "postorder lemmas," and similar terms. The main difference is that pure pool resolution remembers all derived clauses so they are available for re-use, whereas implemented satisfiability solvers only remember some of their derived clauses. A longer version of this paper, with proofs, is available at `ftp://ftp.cse.ucsc.edu/pub/avg/lpar12long.pdf`.

2 Preliminaries

2.1 Notation

This section collects notations and definitions used throughout the paper. Standard terminology for conjunctive normal form (CNF) formulas is used. Notations are summarized in Table 1. Although the general ideas of resolution and derivations are well known, there is no standard notation for many of the technical aspects, so it is necessary to specify our notation in detail. As usual, a finite set of *propositional variables* is assumed (*variables* for short) and a *literal* is either a variable or a negated variable.

Definition 2.1. (clause, formula, *Lits*, mention) A *clause* is either a *regular clause* or the unique *tautologous clause*, denoted by $\top$. A *regular clause* is a (possibly empty) consistent set of literals, which are logically connected disjunctively. A regular clause C is said to *mention* a literal q if either $q \in C$ or $\neg q \in C$. A *CNF formula* (*formula* for short) is a finite (possibly empty) sequence of clauses, which are logically connected conjunctively. The set of all literals that can be constructed from the variables in formula $\mathcal{F}$ is denoted by $Lits(\mathcal{F})$. This set is assumed to have some fixed linear order. $\qquad\square$

There are technical reasons for defining a formula as a sequence, rather than a set, of clauses. First, this permits duplicate clauses. Second, when a procedure derives clauses sequentially, some or all of the derived clauses can be appended to the input formula, the structure remains a *formula*, and the order of derivation is preserved.

Definition 2.2. (assignment, satisfaction, model) A partial assignment is a partial function from the set of variables into {*false*, *true*}. This partial function is extended to literals, clauses, and formulas in the standard way. If the partial assignment is a total function, it is called a *total assignment*, or simply an *assignment*.

A clause or formula is *satisfied* by a partial assignment if it is mapped to *true*; A partial assignment that satisfies a formula is called a *model* of that formula. $\qquad\square$

Table 1. Summary of notations

$a, \ldots, z$	Literal; i.e., propositional variable or negated propositional variable.
$\neg x$	Complement of literal x; $\neg\neg x$ is not distinguished from x.
$|x|$	The propositional variable in literal x; i.e., if a is a variable, $|a| = |\neg a| = a$.
$A, \ldots, Z$	Disjunctive clause, or set of literals, depending on context.
$\mathcal{A}, \ldots, \mathcal{H}$	CNF formula, or set of literals, depending on context.
π	Resolution derivation DAG.
σ	Total assignment, represented as the set of true literals.
$[p_1, \ldots, p_k]$	Clause consisting of literals $p_1, \ldots, p_k$.
$\perp$	The *empty clause*, which represents *false*.
$\top$	The *tautologous clause*, which represents *true*; (see Definition 2.3).
$\alpha, \ldots, \delta$	Subclause, in the notation $[p, q, \alpha]$, denoting a clause with literals p, q, and possibly other literals, α.
C^-	Read as "C, or some clause that subsumes C".
p	Where context makes it clear, $[p]$ may be abbreviated to p.
C, p	In a context where a formula is expected, $\{C\}$ may be abbreviated to C and $\{[p]\}$ may be abbreviated to p.
$\mathbf{res}(q, C, D)$	Resolvent of C and D, where q and $\neg q$ are the clashing literals (see Definition 2.3).

A partial assignment is conventionally represented by the (necessarily consistent) set of *unit clauses* that are mapped into *true* by the partial assignment. Note that this representation is a very simple formula.

2.2 Resolution as a Total Function

The standard definition of *resolution* is a binary operation on two clauses that contain a distinguished pair of *clashing literals*; i.e., one clause contains x and the other contains $\neg x$. It is convenient to extend the definition to *all* pairs of clauses and all literals, making resolution a total function. Recall that all tautologous clauses are considered to be indistinguishable and are denoted by $\top$.

Definition 2.3. (resolution, subsumption, useless clause) *Resolution* is an operation that takes as parameters a literal, called the *clashing literal*, and two clauses; it produces a clause as its result, called the *resolvent*. In all cases, the *resolvent* is independent of the order of the clause operands C and D, and is independent of the polarity of the clashing literal q:

$$\mathbf{res}(q, C, D) = \mathbf{res}(q, D, C) = \mathbf{res}(\neg q, C, D) = \mathbf{res}(\neg q, D, C).$$

The variable $|q|$ is called the *clashing variable* and $\neg q$ is also called the clashing literal.

If $C=[q, \alpha]$ and $D=[\neg q, \beta]$ are two regular clauses (α and β are subclauses), then

$$\mathbf{res}(q, C, D) = \begin{cases} [\alpha \cup \beta] & \text{if } \alpha \cup \beta \text{ is consistent;} \\ \top & \text{otherwise.} \end{cases}$$

This defines the standard *resolution* operation.

Resolution is extended to include ⊤ as an identity element:

$$\mathbf{res}(q, C, \top) = C.$$

Resolution is further extended to apply to any two regular clauses and any literals, as follows. Fix a total order on the clauses definable with the current set of propositional variables such that ⊥ is smallest, ⊤ is largest, and wider clauses are "bigger" than narrower clauses. The smaller of two equally wide clauses is the one whose literals are lexicographically smaller in the fixed literal ordering (recall Definition 2.1).

If $C = [\alpha]$ does not contain q and does not contain $\neg q$, and $D = [\neg q, \beta]$ or $D = [q, \beta]$, then

$$\mathbf{res}(q, C, D) = [\alpha].$$

If $C = [\alpha]$ and $D = [\beta]$ and neither contains q or $\neg q$, then

$$\mathbf{res}(q, C, D) = \text{the smaller of } C \text{ and } D.$$

If clause $C \subset D$, we say C *properly subsumes* D; if $C \subseteq D$, we say C *subsumes* D. Also, any regular clause properly subsumes ⊤. Notation D^- is read as "D, or some clause that subsumes D". Alternatively, D^- may be read as "some clause that logically implies D".

A clause is said to be *useless* for formula $\mathcal{F}$ if it is subsumed by a clause in $\mathcal{F}$; ⊤ is always useless. (Normally, tautologous resolvents are discarded.)   □

Definition 2.4. (derivation,   refutation)   A   *derivation*   (short   for *propositional resolution derivation*) from formula $\mathcal{F}$ is a directed acyclic graph (DAG) in which each vertex is labeled with a clause and possibly with a clashing literal. Let D be the clause label of vertex v. If $D = C \in \mathcal{F}$, then v has no out-edges and no clashing literal, and is called a *leaf*. Otherwise v is called a *resolution vertex*, has two out-edges, say to vertices with clause labels D_0 and D_1. The edge to D_1 is labeled with some literal, say q, and the edge to D_0 is labeled with $\neg q$. The vertex v is also labeled with the clashing literal q and the clause D such that

$$D = \mathbf{res}(q, D_0, D_1),$$

where **res** is the total function defined in Definition 2.3. When the derivation contains ⊥, it is called a *refutation*.   □

In most analyses a derivation is a *rooted* DAG, and a derivation is said to derive its root clause. In actual computation, some clauses might be derived that turn out to be useless, yet remain in the DAG. In much of the discussion, vertices are referred to by their clause labels. However, it is possible for the same clause to label several vertices and in such cases further specification of the vertex is needed.

3   The Pool Resolution Procedure

In its general form, pool resolution can be regarded as a procedure **PoolRes** that takes a clause P, called the current *pool*, and an input formula $\mathcal{F}$ as parameters, and determines whether $\mathcal{F} \models P$ ($\mathcal{F}$ logically implies P). Of course, $\mathcal{F} \models \bot$ means that $\mathcal{F}$ is unsatisfiable.

For simplicity of description, **PoolRes**$(P, \mathcal{F})$ operates on a global proof structure G. If $\mathcal{F} \models P$, **PoolRes** modifies G to be a derivation of some clause $D \subseteq P$ and returns D. Otherwise, **PoolRes** creates a (global) partial assignment $\mathcal{A}$ that demonstrates that P is not logically implied by $\mathcal{F}$ and returns the special value **SAT** that is not a clause. Note that **PoolRes** might not be able to derive P exactly, but can derive P^- whenever $\mathcal{F} \models P$.

The global proof structure G is a resolution DAG (Definition 2.4) that initially consists of one vertex C_i for each clause in $\mathcal{F}$ and no edges. This is the state of G when the top-level call **PoolRes**$(P, \mathcal{F})$ occurs. To produce a refutation, the top-level call is **PoolRes**$(\bot, \mathcal{F})$. The procedure modifies G as the computation proceeds. Pseudocode for a recursive implementation of **PoolRes** is shown in Figure 1.

PoolRes$(P, \mathcal{F})$

---

1) If $\mathcal{F}$ has no *eligible* clauses:
2)   construct partial assignment $\mathcal{A} = \neg(P)$;
3)   return **SAT**.
4) If G contains an *acceptable* clause $D \subseteq P$:
5)   return *some such* clause D.

6) // (If no base case applies, expand the pool P.)
7) *Choose* a clashing literal q not *mentioned* in P.

8) $D_0 = $ **PoolRes**$([P, \neg q], \mathcal{F})$.
9) If $D_0 = $ **SAT**, return **SAT**.
10) If $\neg q \notin D_0$, return D_0.

11) $D_1 = $ **PoolRes**$([P, q], \mathcal{F})$.
12) If $D_1 = $ **SAT**, return **SAT**.
13) // (If $q \notin D_1$, **res**$(q, D_0, D_1) = D_1$.)

14) Create a new vertex for G labeled with $D = $ **res**(q, D_0, D_1).
     Create an edge labeled $\neg q$ from D to D_0 and an edge labeled q from D to D_1.
15) Return D.

Fig. 1. Pseudocode for the general version of **PoolRes**. To produce a refutation, the top-level call is **PoolRes**$(\bot, \mathcal{F})$. A clause C is *eligible* with respect to pool P if $C \cup P$ is consistent. For "pure" **PoolRes** all clauses are *acceptable*; other options are discussed in the text.

Several remarks about **PoolRes** may be made before analyzing its completeness and performance.

1. An arbitrary clause C is said to be *eligible* with respect to pool P if $C \cup P$ is consistent; otherwise, it is *ineligible* with respect to P. The idea is that only eligible clauses might be useful to **PoolRes** for deriving P^-. For a clause C to be useful to **PoolRes** for deriving P^-, it must eventually play the role of D on line 4 in the current procedure invocation or in some recursive invocation. The first parameter of **PoolRes** is called the *pool parameter*. But all pool parameters for these invocations are consistent supersets of P (possibly P itself), so no clause containing a literal that is complementary to some literal of P can be a subset of P or the pool parameter of any recursive invocation.

   Note that the set of eligible clauses shrinks as recursion depth increases. For example, when $\neg q$ is added to the pool at line 8, all clauses containing q become ineligible in that recursive call.

2. At line 1, suppose there are no eligible clauses in $\mathcal{F}$. Then $\mathcal{A} = \neg(P)$ satisfies all clauses of $\mathcal{F}$. By the soundness of resolution $\mathcal{A}$ must satisfy all clauses in G, so every clause in G has some literal that is complementary to some literal of P, and there are no eligible clauses in G, either.

3. There are many possible policies for what is an *acceptable* clause on line 4. Bookkeeping not shown in the pseudocode might be needed to decide whether a clause is "acceptable" under a particular policy. As discussed above, $D \subseteq P$ is possible only if D is *eligible* with respect to P, so it does not matter whether ineligible clauses are "acceptable." For "pure" **PoolRes**, all clauses in G are "acceptable." To force tree-like derivations to be produced, make all *derived* clauses unacceptable.

   The only restriction on acceptable-clause policies needed to ensure completeness is that, if all variables are mentioned in P and there are any eligible clauses, then *some* eligible clause must be acceptable.

   By formulating **PoolRes** to allow an arbitrary policy for "acceptable" clauses, it is easier to show that some instantiation of **PoolRes** is able to simulate, or imitate, other reasoning systems. With this flexibility, **PoolRes** is able to reject clauses that would generate a base case, and continue to line 7 to derive a better clause.

4. Line 10 is an optimization. Due to resolution being a total function, line 14 would define D to be either D_0 or D_1 if line 10 were omitted.

5. At line 14, if $q \notin D_1$, then D is in a separate vertex from the vertex of D_1, even though D and D_1 are the same clause. In this case, the vertex containing D has an edge to the vertex containing D_0. This technicality ensures that the final G is rooted (unless **SAT** is returned).

6. At line 5, there might be several clauses that could be returned. The selection could greatly influence the future course of the computation.

7. At line 7, there are normally many variables to choose among, then two polarities for the literal to be called q. The policy for this choice is the major determinant of the procedure's practical ability to construct small

derivations. The theoretical (non-deterministic) power of pool resolution is determined (in part) by assuming this choice is always made optimally.

It is quite straightforward to show that **PoolRes** behaves "correctly"; that is, it is sound and complete.

Theorem 3.1. Let $\mathcal{F}$ be a formula; let G be a resolution DAG with the clauses of $\mathcal{F}$ as leaves; let P be a regular clause, $P \subset \mathit{Lits}(\mathcal{F})$. Then **PoolRes**$(P, \mathcal{F})$ as given in Figure 1 returns a clause P^- if and only if $\mathcal{F} \models P$.   □

4   Pool Resolution Graphs

By the time the pool resolution procedure **PoolRes** given in Figure 1 has exited at top level, assuming it did not return **SAT**, it has produced a *rooted* resolution DAG G. Essentially, all rooted resolution DAGs can be characterized according to whether some instantiation of a pool resolution procedure could produce them. For analysis, we are only concerned with *refutation* DAGS, i.e., those whose root is $\bot$. This section shows that there is a close connection, and an important difference, between refutation DAGs produced by regular resolution and those produced by pool resolution.

Definition 4.1. A rooted resolution DAG based on input formula $\mathcal{F}$ is called a *pool resolution DAG* if it can be produced by some sequence of choices in the pool resolution procedure **PoolRes** given in Figure 1. These choices include:

1. Which clauses are "acceptable" at line 4 (without loss of generality, we can assume at most one clause is deemed "acceptable" each time line 4 is executed);
2. Which literal to choose as q at line 7.

   □

Definition 4.2. Let G be a subgraph of a resolution DAG (but not necessarily a resolution DAG in its own right). A path in G is a *regular path* if no clashing variable occurs twice among the vertices of the path. The subgraph G is said to be a *regular DAG* if every path in G is regular.   □

As defined by Tseitin [23], *regular resolution* is the resolution system that produces resolution DAGs that are regular DAGs, in accordance with Definition 4.2. Our use of the term *regular* is simply extended to include DAGs that are not resolution derivations.

Theorem 4.3. If a rooted resolution refutation DAG G (based on input formula $\mathcal{F}$) is a pool resolution DAG, then there is some depth-first search of G (beginning at its root) whose depth-first search tree (DFST) is a regular DAG.   □

Theorem 4.4. Let G be a rooted resolution refutation DAG (based on input formula $\mathcal{F}$) that contains only standard resolution operations (i.e., the clashing literal q is present in one operand and $\neg q$ is present in the other operand and

⊤ never occurs). If there is some depth-first search of G (beginning at its root) whose depth-first search tree (DFST) is a regular DAG, then G is a pool resolution DAG.   □

Corollary 4.5. Let G be a rooted resolution refutation DAG (based on input formula $\mathcal{F}$) that contains only standard resolution operations (i.e., the clashing literal q is present in one operand and $\neg q$ is present in the other operand and ⊤ never occurs). If G was produced by regular resolution, then G is a pool resolution DAG.   □

5   Exponential Separation of Pool Resolution from Regular Resolution

In this section we consider a family of graphs $NT^*(n)$, which has $N = n(n-1)$ variables. It is known that there is a positive constant α such that any regular refutation DAG for $NT^*(n)$ has more than $2^{\alpha n}$ vertices, for large enough n, whereas general refutations of length $\Theta(n^3)$ are known (see discussion of Theorem 5.7 below). An empirical test indicates that zChaff [25] takes time proportional to $e^{0.75\,n}$ on this family, although it is not limited by the regularity restriction. We introduce a related family $NT^{**}(n)$ whose regular refutations are at least as long, but has a pool refutation DAG with $O(n^3)$ vertices. The name NT is an abbreviation for "no triangles."

5.1   The Family $NT^*(n)$ and Related Formulas

The definition of the family $NT^*(n)$ is facilitated by some terminology. For all of the formulas considered, there is an underlying semantic interpretation that guides our understanding. We suppose there is a set W whose elements are denoted w_i, $1 \leq i \leq n$. The propositional variables of $NT^*(n)$ and related formulas correspond to possible directed edges between distinct elements of this set. A variable is true if the edge is present.

Definition 5.1. Let $\langle i, j \rangle$, where i and j are distinct integers in the range $[1, n]$ (1 through n) denote a propositional variable (the semantic interpretation is $w_i \rightarrow w_j$). Define $V = \{\langle i, j \rangle\}$.   □

Definition 5.2. A *qualifying triple* is an ordered triple of distinct positive integers (i, j, k) in the range 1 through n, such that i is the maximum of the three; i.e., $1 \leq j < i \leq n$, $1 \leq k < i$, and $j \neq k$. The set of all qualifying triples is denoted by Q. There are $n(n-1)(n-2)/3$ qualifying triples.

An integer-valued function $f(i, j, k) : Q \rightarrow [0, N-1]$ is called β-*fair* if it maps at least βn qualifying triples into each value in its range.   □

Definition 5.3. Let $\pi : V \rightarrow [0, N-1]$ be the permutation of V that arranges its elements in lexicographical order. Define $s : [0, N-1] \rightarrow V$ by the equation $s(x) = \pi^{-1}(x)$. For example, $s(0) = \langle 1, 2 \rangle$, $s(2n) = \langle 3, 4 \rangle$, etc. (The results hold for $\pi(\langle i, j \rangle)$ being *any* permutation of V, but this degree of generality is not important.)   □

Definition 5.4. Clauses are named as follows for indexes indicated. In clause types A_0 and A_1 $r(i, j, k)$ is some function whose range is $[0, N-1]$ (see Definition 5.2 and (8) for particulars).

$$C(j) \equiv [\langle 1, j \rangle, \dots, \langle j-1, j \rangle, \langle j+1, , j \rangle, \dots, \langle n, j \rangle] \qquad 1 \le j \le n \tag{1}$$

$$B(i, j) \equiv [\neg \langle i, j \rangle, \neg \langle j, i \rangle] \qquad 1 \le i < j \le n \tag{2}$$

$$B^+(i, j) \equiv [\langle i, j \rangle, \langle j, i \rangle] \qquad 1 \le i < j \le n \tag{3}$$

$$A_0(i, j, k) \equiv [\neg \langle i, j \rangle, \neg \langle j, k \rangle, \neg \langle k, i \rangle, \neg s(r(i, j, k))] \qquad (i, j, k) \in Q \tag{4}$$

$$A_1(i, j, k) \equiv [\neg \langle i, j \rangle, \neg \langle j, k \rangle, \neg \langle k, i \rangle, s(r(i, j, k))] \qquad (i, j, k) \in Q \tag{5}$$

$$A(i, j, k) \equiv [\neg \langle i, j \rangle, \neg \langle j, k \rangle, \neg \langle k, i \rangle] \qquad (i, j, k) \in Q \tag{6}$$

$$T(i, j, k) \equiv [\neg \langle i, j \rangle, \neg \langle j, k \rangle, \neg \langle k, i \rangle] \qquad 1 \le i, j, k \le n \text{ and } i, j, k \text{ distinct.} \tag{7}$$

The $C(j)$ are called *long clauses*; the others are *short clauses*. $\square$

Definition 5.5. Formulas are named as follows:

Formula name	Clauses included
$NT^*(n)$	$C(j)$, $B(i, j)$, $B^+(i, j)$, $A_0(i, j, k)$, $A_1(i, j, k)$
$NT(n)$	$C(j)$, $B(i, j)$, $B^+(i, j)$, $A(i, j, k)$
$GT(n)$	$C(j)$, $B(i, j)$, $T(i, j, k)$

$\square$

Note that $A_0(i, j, k)$ and $A_1(i, j, k)$ can be resolved to produce $A(i, j, k)$, after which $A_0(i, j, k)$ and $A_1(i, j, k)$ are subsumed and can be discarded. Further resolutions with B^+ clauses produce *transitivity* clauses $T(i, j, k)$ for all distinct (i, j, k) triples. Thus any model of the short clauses of $NT^*(n)$ must be a complete linear order, where $x \to y$ is interpreted as $x > y$. The same holds for the short clauses of $NT(n)$ and the short clauses of $GT(n)$. But with this interpretation, $C(j)$ states that w_j is not a maximal element. Thus $NT^*(n)$, $NT(n)$ and $GT(n)$ are unsatisfiable. The earlier work on the proof complexity of these families is reviewed here.

Theorem 5.6. ([22, 8, 1]) The families $GT(n)$ and $NT(n)$ have regular refutations of length $O(n^3)$. $\square$

The family $NT^*(n)$ is a variant of the family $GT'(n)$ invented by Alekhnovitch, Johannsen, Pitassi and Urquhart [1]; the modifications are introduced to avoid some possible minor technical problems with the original definitions. They prove very ingeniously that if $r(i, j, k)$ is β-fair, then any regular refutation of $NT^*(n)$ requires at least $2^{0.1 \beta n}$ resolution steps. They define (in effect—their notation is different) a particular $r(i, j, k)$ and claim that it is 1-fair; but the claim was not proved and turns out to be incorrect.[1] However, the idea of the proof is perfectly sound and only needs to be adjusted for an achievable value of β.

---

[1] Their function was actually 0-fair, as it did not map *any* distinct triples to n or $2n + 1$, among other values.

Theorem 5.7. ([1]) Any regular refutation of $NT^*(n)$ requires at least $2^{0.02\,\beta\,n}$ resolution steps.

Proof. (Sketch) The following function can be shown to be β-fair for $\beta = 0.2$ and $n \geq 50$:

$$r(i, j, k) = ((n + 1)\,i + 2\,n\,j + k) \bmod N \tag{8}$$

To show that any x in the range $[0, N-1]$ is mapped to by at least $\beta\,n$ qualifying triples, it is convenient to consider four cases according to whether $\lfloor x/n \rfloor < n/2$ and whether $x \bmod n < n/2$. Then the analysis of each case is straightforward. The rest of the proof is the same as in the cited paper [1].   □

5.2   The Family $NT^{**}(n)$

To demonstrate an exponential separation between regular resolution and pool resolution, we introduce the family of formulas $NT^{**}(n)$, inspired by Beame *et al.* [4]. The formula $NT^{**}(n)$ contains all variables in $NT^*(n)$, plus the variables $x_{i,j,k}$ and $y_{i,j,k}$ for each qualifying triple $(i, j, k) \in Q$. The formula $NT^{**}(n)$ consists of all clauses in $NT^*(n)$, plus the following

$$[x_{i,j,k}, \neg y_{i,j,k}]\,;\ [\neg x_{i,j,k}, y_{i,j,k}]\,;$$
$$[x_{i,j,k}, \langle i, j \rangle]\,;\ [x_{i,j,k}, \langle j, k \rangle]\,;\ [x_{i,j,k}, \langle k, i \rangle]\,;\qquad (i, j, k) \in Q \tag{9}$$

The variables $x_{i,j,k}$ are called *proof-trace* variables [4]. The clauses containing $y_{i,j,k}$ are added so that the $x_{i,j,k}$ are not pure literals.

Theorem 5.8. Any regular refutation of $NT^{**}(n)$ requires at least $2^{0.02\,\beta\,n}$ resolution steps.   □

The idea for the polynomial-length pool refutation of $NT^{**}(n)$ is to use the proof-trace variables $x_{i,j,k}$ to derive $A(i, j, k)$ from $A_0(i, j, k)$ and $A_1(i, j, k)$ for all $(i, j, k) \in Q$ without leaving any variables of $NT(n)$ in the pool. Then the pool refutation can proceed as it would for $NT(n)$ (no asterisks), treating $A(i, j, k)$ as input clauses. The resulting entire refutation is not regular because some non-tree paths leading to $A(i, j, k)$ have $r(s(i, j, k))$ or $\neg r(s(i, j, k))$ as a clashing literal.

Theorem 5.9. The formula $NT^{**}(n)$ has a pool refutation with $O(n^3)$ steps.
                                □

6   Relation of Pool Resolution to DPLL with Clause Learning

Recall the pseudocode of **PoolRes** in Figure 1. Any execution of a DPLL-style search, including popular methods of "clause learning," can be simulated by **PoolRes** by following two basic principles:

1. True assigned literals in DPLL are the *negations* of pool literals in **PoolRes**.
2. "Learned clauses" in the DPLL version are *the same as* (a subset of) clauses derived by **PoolRes**.

Assignment of a literal $q = 1$ as a "decision" (backtrackable "guess," use of splitting rule) in DPLL corresponds to adding $\neg q$ to the pool at line 8. Backtracking to the assignment $q = 0$ in DPLL corresponds to adding q to the pool at line 11.

When DPLL deletes clauses that are satisfied, this corresponds to such clauses becoming ineligible in **PoolRes**. When DPLL shortens clauses due to complements of true literals, the remaining literals are just the nonpool literals in **PoolRes**.

Unit clause propagation in DPLL, say assigning $x = 1$, following a "guess" or "backtrack" assignment to q is simulated in **PoolRes** by adding x to the pool at line 8 and adding $\neg x$ to the pool at line 11. See Section 6.1.

Several clause learning schemes have been analyzed by Zhang *et al.* [25], and more formally by Beame *et al.* [4]. They are primarily outgrowths of the GRASP scheme [18], and much of the terminology originates from that paper. Please see these papers for details. We show how pool resolution can simulate them.

6.1   Unit Nonpool Clauses

Recall the pseudocode of **PoolRes** in Figure 1. As mentioned, the policy for choosing q at line 7 is crucial for both theoretical and practical performance. It is useful, at least in practice, to define the *nonpool literals* in an eligible clause C to be those literals in C that are not in the pool P. The *nonpool count* for C is the number of such nonpool literals, i.e., $|C - P|$. If the nonpool count is 0 (and C is "acceptable"), the base case of lines 4 and 5 applies.

If the nonpool count is 1, C is analogous to a unit clause in DPLL. In this case, let $\neg q$ be the sole nonpool literal of C and choose q as the clashing literal at line 7. The recursive call at line 8 returns immediately. Then for the second recursive call, at line 11, the set of eligible clauses is reduced by discarding all clauses containing $\neg q$. Thus the problem has been simplified without branching. A similar practical strategy is analogous to the pure literal rule of DPLL.

6.2   Correspondence with RelSat Learning

The learning procedure of RelSat [3] has the simplest correspondence with **PoolRes**. Say $q = 1$ was a "decision" assignment and $\perp$ was derived, possibly after some additional assignments by unit-clause propagation. RelSat "learns" a clause of the form $[\neg q, \alpha]$ where the subclause α consists of complements of (some of the) literals that were assigned true before the $q = 1$ "decision." Using the straightforward simulation described above, **PoolRes** derives the same clause in the procedure invocation where q was chosen as the clashing literal at line 7.

6.3   Correspondence with GRASP, First UIP

Marques-Silva and Sakallah [18] introduced the term *unique implication point* (UIP) to refer to a vertex, say x, in their implication graph such that all paths from the decision literal, say q, to $\perp$ pass through x.

If x is a UIP, then a clause $[\neg x, \alpha]$ can be inferred from the implication graph, where subclause α consists of complements of (some of the) literals that were assigned true before the $q = 1$ "decision." This clause is called the *UIP clause*. The decision literal is always a UIP and gives rise to the RelSat clause, as in Section 6.2.

Marques-Silva and Sakallah studied the scheme consisting of learning the UIP clause of the *first UIP*, i.e., the one closest to $\perp$ in the implication graph. Suppose $q = 1$ is the decision literal, $x \neq q$ is the first UIP, and $[\neg x, \alpha]$ is the UIP clause. Using the straightforward simulation described above, **PoolRes** derives the same clause in the procedure invocation that chooses $\neg x$ as the clashing literal at line 7, to simulate the unit-clause propagation assignment $x = 1$ in DPLL. The call at line 8 returns the same D_0 that was used for the antecedent edges of x in the implication graph; this applies to all literals that DPLL assigns through unit-clause propagation. Then $\neg x$ is added to the pool and $D_1 = [\neg x, \alpha]$ is derived and returned at line 11.

However, GRASP and some other search engines have an option to learn *only* the first UIP clause. When $x \neq q$, this means they do not backtrack to the assignment $q = 0$. Instead, they erase all assignments at the current "decision level," i.e., those at and after $q = 1$, then they learn (assert) the first UIP clause, $[\neg x, \alpha]$. At this point all literals of α are false, so $\neg x$ becomes a *failure driven assertion*.

For **PoolRes** to simulate first UIP, it needs to "look ahead" at the point where $q = 1$ is the "decision" and anticipate that x will become the first UIP. So **PoolRes** skips choosing q as the clashing literal, and skips subsequent steps until $x = 1$ is assigned by unit-clause propagation. At this point it chooses x as the clashing literal. That is, $\neg x$ is added to the pool at line 8 as though x were a decision variable in DPLL. Next it "plugs in" the same derivation that occurred in the RelSat style simulation, except that $\neg x$ was added to the pool at line 11 in that simulation, as described a few paragraphs above. Thus $D_0 = [\neg x, \alpha]$ is derived and returned. Then it adds x to the pool at line 11, which simulates GRASP's failure-driven assertion of $\neg x$.

6.4   Correspondence with Decision Learning

The *decision learning* strategy requires the learned clause to contain only the negations of "decision" literals. For **PoolRes** to simulate this strategy, it only simulates "decision" assignments, and defers all unit-clause propagations until a decision assignment has been made that allows unit-clause propagation to derive $\perp$. Suppose that decision is $q = 1$. The decision-literal UIP clause can be derived, and contains only decision literals. All derived clause are available for later use, so those that depend only on decision literals at early levels can potentially be used in many branches.

6.5   Correspondence with FirstNewCut

The *First New Cut strategy* was proposed recently by Beame *et al.* [4]. We refer the reader to that paper for details. Relying on their Proposition 4, the clause specified as First New Cut, can be derived by what they define as a *trivial resolution*. This involves a series of resolution steps in a chain each one with a different clashing literal.

Such a *trivial resolution* is easy to simulate with pool resolution: just add the clashing literals to the pool in the reverse order of the trivial resolution, and derive the clauses on the way back out of the recursions.

The idea to simulate the *First New Cut strategy* is to simulate only the decision assignments. The pool P contains their complements. When a contradiction can be derived, say after the decision $q = 1$, let the pool be $[P, \neg q]$. Simulate the implication graph by adding literals to the pool in a topological order consistent with the implication graph, such that all literals on the *opposite* side of the cut from the empty clause are added before any on the same side. This policy derives the First New Cut clause.

7   Conclusion

We introduce a system called *pool resolution* and show that it simulates regular resolution linearly and has exponentially shorter refutations on at least one family of formulas. This paper draws heavily on earlier work in proof complexity [1, 4]. Thus pool resolution is one of the strongest known refinements of general resolution. Whether it has the full power of general resolution (within a polynomial factor) is unknown, but seems unlikely.

We also show that pool resolution is able to simulate several strategies for clause learning within DPLL. These simulations are natural enough that they provide some hope that most of the power of pool resolution can be realized, at least on practical problems, by some form of DPLL with clause learning. Beame *et al.* have obtained related results for their *First New Cut* learning strategy [4].

References

1. Alekhnovich, M., Johannsen, J., Pitassi, T., Urquhart, A.: An exponential separation between regular and unrestricted resolution. In: Proc. 34th ACM Symposium on Theory of Computing. (2002) 448–456
2. Anderson, R., Bledsoe, W.W.: A linear format for resolution with merging and a new technique for establishing completeness. Journal of the ACM **17** (1970) 525–534
3. Bayardo, Jr., R.J., Schrag, R.C.: Using CSP look-back techniques to solve real-world SAT instances. In: Proc. AAAI. (1997) 203–208
4. Beame, P., Kautz, H., Sabharwal, A.: Towards understanding and harnessing the potential of clause learning. Journal of Artificial Intelligence Research **22** (2004) 319–351

5. Beame, P., Pitassi, T.: Simplified and improved resolution lower bounds. In: Proc. 28th ACM Symposium on Theory of Computing. (1996)
6. Ben-Sasson, E., Wigderson, A.: Short proofs are narrow — resolution made simple. JACM **48** (2001) 149–168
7. Bonet, M., Galesi, N.: A study of proof search algorithms for resolution and polynomial calculus. In: Proc. 40th Symposium on Foundations of Computer Science. (1999) 422–432
8. Bonet, M., Galesi, N.: Optimality of size-width tradeoffs for resolution. Computational Complexity **10** (2001) 261–276
9. Clegg, M., Edmonds, J., Impagliazzo, R.: Using the Groebner basis algorithm to find proofs of unsatisfiability. In: Proc. 28th ACM Symposium on Theory of Computing. (1996) 174–183
10. Davis, M., Logemann, G., Loveland, D.: A machine program for theorem-proving. Communications of the ACM **5** (1962) 394–397
11. Davis, M., Putnam, H.: A computing procedure for quantification theory. Journal of the Association for Computing Machinery **7** (1960) 201–215
12. Dechter, R., Rish, I.: Directional resolution: the davis-putnam procedure, revisited. In: Proc. 4th Int'l Conf. on Principles of Knowledge Representation and Reasoning (KR'94), Morgan Kaufmann, San Francisco (1994) 134–145
13. Goldberg, E., Novikov, Y.: Berkmin: a fast and robust sat-solver. In: Proc. Design, Automation and Test in Europe. (2002) 142–149
14. Johnson, D.S., Trick, M.A., eds.: Cliques, Coloring, and Satisfiability: Second DIMACS Implementation Challenge. Volume 26 of DIMACS Series in Discrete Mathematics and Theoretical Computer Science. American Mathematical Society (1996)
15. Krishnamurthy, B.: Short proofs for tricky formulas. Acta Informatica **22** (1985) 253–274
16. Lee, S.J., Plaisted, D.A.: Eliminating duplication with the hyper-linking strategy. Journal of Automated Reasoning **9** (1992) 25–42
17. Letz, R., Mayr, K., Goller, C.: Controlled integration of the cut rule into connection tableau calculi. Journal of Automated Reasoning **13** (1994) 297–337
18. Marques-Silva, J.P., Sakallah, K.A.: GRASP–a search algorithm for propositional satisfiability. IEEE Transactions on Computers **48** (1999) 506–521
19. Moskewicz, M., Madigan, C., Zhao, Y., Zhang, L., Malik, S.: Chaff: Engineering an efficient SAT solver. In: 39th Design Automation Conference. (2001)
20. Plaisted, D.A. (private communication) (1984)
21. Plaisted, D.A.: The search efficiency of theorem proving strategies. In: 12th International Conference on Automated Deduction, Springer-Verlag (1994) 57–71
22. Stålmarck, G.: Short resolution proofs for a sequence of tricky formulas. Acta Informatica **33** (1996) 277–280
23. Tseitin, G.S.: On the complexity of derivation in propositional calculus. In Slisenko, A.O., ed.: Seminars in Mathematics v. 8: Studies in Constructive Mathematics and Mathematical Logic, Part II. Steklov Math. Inst., Leningrad (1968) 115–125 (English trans., 1970, Plenum.).
24. Zhang, H., Stickel, M.E.: Implementing the davis-putnam method. Journal of Automated Reasoning **24** (2000) 277–296
25. Zhang, L., Madigan, C., Moskewicz, M., Malik, S.: Efficient conflict driven learning in a boolean satisfiability solver. In: ICCAD. (2001)

Another Complete Local Search Method for SAT*

Haiou Shen and Hantao Zhang

Department of Computer Science,
University of Iowa,
Iowa City, IA 52242, U.S.A.
{hzhang, hshen}@cs.uiowa.edu

Abstract. Local search algorithms are one of the effective methods for solving hard combinatorial problems. However, a serious problem of this approach is that the search often traps at local optima. At AAAI 2004, Fang and Ruml proposed a novel approach which makes local optima disappeared. The basic idea is that, at each local optimal point during the search, the value of the objective function (a local gradient function) at that point is changed by adding some information into the database. Once no more local optima exist, the local search can always find a global optimal. In this paper, along the same approach of Fang and Ruml, we propose a different objective function based on an ordering of propositional variables. Based on this ordering, ordered resolution is performed at each local optimal point and the resolvent is added into the database. This resolvent always increases the value of the objective function so that the local optimal point disappears after a finite number of steps. Preliminary experimental results show that our method and Fang and Ruml's method have better performances in different areas.

1   Introduction

Local search algorithms are one of the standard methods for solving hard combinatorial problems. The general idea is to examine the search space by starting from a solution candidate and iteratively move from one point to a neighboring position where the decision on each step is based on a local gradient (or objective) function. For some large propositional satisfiability problems (SAT), local search algorithms are very effective in practice. Another category of algorithms for SAT is based on a systematic search, which explores a tree containing all possible variable assignments. The systematic search is complete because it can implicitly prove that a problem is unsatisfiable by traversing the entire tree without finding a solution. Local search methods are incomplete: They are not guaranteed to find a satisfying assignment, if one exists, in finite time. They will fail to terminate on unsatisfiable problems and are not guaranteed to solve a satisfiable problem. There is great interest in understanding how systematic search and local search methods can be hybridized and whether it might be possible to design a complete local search algorithm [SKM1995, KS2003]. Fang and Ruml [FR2004] showed a basic complete local search framework and applied it to propositional satisfiability problem. Their approach is based on using a novel objective function to compute the

---

* Supported in part by NSF under grant CCR-0098093.

G. Sutcliffe and A. Voronkov (Eds.): LPAR 2005, LNAI 3835, pp. 595–605, 2005.

local gradient. When a local minimum is reached, they generate new implied clauses from the current point. The addition of the new clauses dynamically increases the value of the objective function at that point and the current local optimal point will disappear. A new neighbor assignment may become a local optimal. However, after several steps, this process will incrementally smooth the search space and local optimal points will disappear. They proved that their schema is complete [FR2004].

Clause learning is a very effective technique for popular SAT solvers. For complete SAT solvers based on the DPLL method [DP1960, DLL1962], clause learning becomes an indispensable technique for modern SAT solvers (see [MS1999, Z1997] and [M2001]). For local search, some researchers tried to increase the weights of clauses to escape local minima [M1993, SW1997]. Cha and Iwama [CI1996] and Yokoo [Y1997] suggested that adding implied clauses explicitly is better than adding duplicate clauses. Morris [M1993] also pointed out that explicitly recording and increasing the cost of visited local minimum can force the search to eventually solve a satisfiable instance, but cannot easily detect unsatisfiable instance. It is Fang and Ruml [FR2004] who firstly showed the local search can become complete without embedding it in a tree-like framework.

In this paper, we will take the same approach of Fang and Ruml by using a new objective function and a new clause generation schema. Comparing to Fang and Ruml's objective function, our objective function is easier to compute. Moreover, our clause generation schema will never generate duplicate clauses as the schema in [FR2004] may generate duplicate clauses.

Our new objective function is based on a well-founded ordering on propositional variables and our clause generation schema is a special case of ordered resolution [BG2002]. It is well-known that ordered resolution is a very effective method for first-order theorem proving [BG2002]. However, for propositional satisfiability, ordered resolution still suffers the same problem as general resolution does by generating too many new clauses. While the soundness of our clause generation schema comes from that of ordered resolution, the completeness of our method implies that a very restricted use of ordered resolution can generate the empty clause when the input clauses are unsatisfiable.

After presenting our algorithm for complete local search, we will compare our approach and experimental results with [FR2004]. Then we will discuss the implementation issues for performance improvement.

2   Preliminary

We assume that the reader is familiar with the standard definitions of propositional satisfiability, such as *variable, literal, clause, CNF*, etc. For every literal x, we use variable(x) to denote the variable appearing in x. That is, variable$(x) = x$ for positive literal x and variable$(\overline{x}) = x$ for negative literal $\overline{x}$. If c is a clause, then variable$(c) = \{$variable$(x) \mid x$ is a literal in $c\}$. Let F be a formula in CNF with n variables $V = \{x_1, ..., x_n\}$ and m clauses, then F can be written as $c_1 \wedge ... \wedge c_m$, where $c_1, ..., c_m$ are clauses. An *assignment* is a mapping σ from V to $\{0, 1\}$, where 0 means false and 1 means true, and may be represented by a set of literals such that each variable appearing exactly once and each literal in the set is assigned to be true. A *model* for F is an assignment σ such that $\sigma(F) = 1$. A propositional satisfiability problem (SAT) is concerned with finding a model of F or proving that the formula has no model.

Given a one-to-one mapping π from V to $\{1, 2, ..., |V|\}$, an *ordering* $<_\pi$ over V is defined as follows: for any $x, y \in V$, $x <_\pi y$ if and only if $\pi(x) < \pi(y)$, where $\pi(x)$ is said to be the *order number* of x under π. Obviously, $<_\pi$ is a well-found, total order on V. We then extend π to be a mapping from literals (clauses, sets of clauses) to $\{0, 1, 2, ..., |V|, \infty\}$ as follows:

- For any literal x, $\pi(x) = \pi(\text{variable}(x))$.
- If a clause c is empty, then let $\pi(c) = \infty$; otherwise, $\pi(c) = \min\{\pi(x) \mid x \in c\}$.
- If a set S of clauses is empty, then $\pi(S) = 0$; otherwise $\pi(S) = \max\{\pi(c) \mid c \in S\}$.

For example, if $S = \{x_1 \vee x_2, \overline{x_2} \vee x_3, \overline{x_3} \vee x_4\}$, and $\pi(x_i) = i$, then $\pi(x_1 \vee x_2) = 1$, $\pi(\overline{x_3} \vee x_4) = 3$ and $\pi(S) = 3$.

Accordingly, the ordering $<_\pi$ can be extended to be an ordering over literals and clauses: For any clauses c, c', $c <_\pi c'$ iff $\pi(c) < \pi(c')$, where $\pi(c)$ is the *order number* of c under π.

In a typical local search algorithm for SAT, a *neighbor* of an assignment σ is another assignment which flips the value of a single variable of σ. Typically, local search algorithms make use of an objective function mapping each search space position onto a real or integer number in such a way, that the global optima of the objective function correspond to the solutions. For SAT, the situation is a little bit different, since some SAT problems are unsatisfiable, in other word, there is no solution for those problems. For most local search algorithms for SAT, the global optima correspond to assignments satisfied most clauses. Only when the global optima are equal to a particular value (in most case it is 0), the global optima can correspond to the solutions.

3 A Complete Local Search Algorithm

The outline of our approach is very similar to the one in [FR2004], shown in Figure 1. As in most local search algorithms for SAT, the search procedure starts from an initial (random) assignment σ (step 1). If σ is a model, we will end the while loop and return σ, otherwise we will continue the while loop. If there is a neighboring assignment σ' which is better than σ according to the objective function (step 4), then move to σ'. Any neighboring assignment which yields a better objective value can be chosen. In our implementation, we choose the first one we meet along the search. If there is no such adjacent assignment, we have reached a local minimum. A new implied clause γ is then derived from the current local minimum (step 6). If the newly added clause is an empty clause, the instance is unsatisfiable (step 8); otherwise add the new clause into the current formula F (step 10). The newly added clause will change the result of the objective function and force the search algorithm move out of the current local minimum.

The parameters of function Utility1(F, σ) are the input formula F and the current assignment σ, and it will return an integer. Formally, let Utility1$(F, \sigma) = \pi(False(F, \sigma))$,

function Utility1(F, σ)
  return $\pi(False(F, \sigma))$
end function

function GenerateClause1(F, σ)
  Let $c_1 \in core(F, \sigma)$
  Let $c_2 \in \overline{core}(F, \sigma)$
  $c' := resolution(c_1, c_2)$
  return c'
end function

function CompleteLocalSearch(F)
1 $\sigma :=$ InitialAssignment(F);
2 **while** σ does not satisfy F **do**
3   **if** $\exists \sigma' \in$ Neighbor(σ), Utility1$(F, \sigma') <$ Utility1(F, σ)
4      $\sigma := \sigma'$;
5   **else**
6      $\gamma :=$ GenerateClause1(F, σ)
7   **if** γ is an empty clause
8   **return** unsatisfiable
9   **else**
10        $F := F \wedge \gamma$
11   **end if**
12   **end if**
13 **end while**
14 **return** σ
end function

Fig. 1. A complete local search algorithm

where $False(F, \sigma)$ is the set of false clauses in F under the assignment σ and π is a mapping from V to $\{1, \ldots, |V|\}$ and is extended to be a mapping from set of clauses to $\{0, 1, \ldots, n, \infty\}$ as said in the previous section.

Lemma 1. *The objective function Utility1(F, σ) returns 0 if and only if σ is a model of formula F; and it returns ∞ if and only if F has an empty clause.*

The empty clause in F may come from GenerateClause1(F, σ) and is a witness to show that the input clauses are unsatisfiable as long as GenerateClause1(F, σ) is sound in the sense that if $c =$ GenerateClause1(F, σ) then c is a logical consequence of F. Since in our approach GenerateClause1(F, σ) is based on resolution, its soundness is obvious.

Assuming the empty clause is not in $False(F, \sigma)$, let $frontier(F, \sigma)$ be the literal y in $False(F, \sigma)$ such that $\pi(y) = \pi(False(F, \sigma))$. Let

$$core(F, \sigma) = \{c \in False(F, \sigma) \mid \pi(c) = \pi(frontier(F, \sigma))\}$$
$$\overline{core}(F, \sigma) = \{\overline{y} \vee c' \in F \mid y = frontier(F, \sigma), \pi(y) = \pi(y \vee c'), \sigma(c') = 0\}.$$

For example, assume we have clauses $F = (1 \vee 2 \vee 3) \wedge (\overline{2} \vee 6) \wedge (3 \vee 5) \wedge (\overline{3} \vee 4) \wedge (\overline{3} \vee 6) \wedge (\overline{5} \vee 6)$, and the current assignment $\sigma = \{\overline{1}, \overline{2}, \overline{3}, \overline{4}, \overline{5}, \overline{6}\}$. Clauses $(1 \vee 2 \vee 3)$ and $(3 \vee 5)$ are false under σ. So $False(F, \sigma)$ contains these two clauses, $frontier(F, \sigma) = 3$, $core(F, \sigma) = \{(3 \vee 5)\}$ and $\overline{core}(F, \sigma) = \{(\overline{3} \vee 4), (\overline{3} \vee 6)\}$. σ is a local minimum.

Lemma 2. *The clause generated by GenerateClause1(F, σ) is a logical consequence of F.*

In resolution, clauses such as $x \vee c_1'$ and $\overline{x} \vee c_2'$ are combined to yield a new clause $c' = c_1' \vee c_2'$. The particular variable and clauses that are selected can be decided in many ways. For ordered resolution, the selected variables must be maximum under a partial ordering (in our case, the resolution is done actually on minimum variables). In the algorithm GenerateClause1(F, σ), however, we may have multiple choices for c_1 and c_2, but only one resolution is possible between c_1 and c_2 because of the definitions of $core(F, \sigma)$ and $\overline{core}(F, \sigma)$.

We select one clause c_1 in $core(F, \sigma)$ and one clause c_2 in $\overline{core}(F, \sigma)$. Since $c_1 = y \vee c_1'$ and $c_2 = \overline{y} \vee c_2'$, where $\pi(y) = \pi(False(F, \sigma))$, we can generate a new clause $c' = c_1' \vee c_2'$. To be able to generate this new clause, the set $core(F, \sigma)$ and the set $\overline{core}(F, \sigma)$ cannot be empty. Theorem 1 shows that both $core(F, \sigma)$ and $\overline{core}(F, \sigma)$ must contain some clauses while σ is a local minimum. Theorem 2 shows that the resolvent clause c' is always a new clause and $\pi(c') > \pi(False(F, \sigma))$. Hence, the current objective value will increase if c' is added into F. Since the objective value cannot be greater than $|V|$ unless an empty clause is generated, the current local minimum will disappear eventually. The theorems thus show that we can always smooth the search space by adding a new clause at a local minimum.

Theorem 1. *If σ is a local minimum with respect to Utility1(F, σ) and $0 <$ Utility1 $(F, \sigma) < \infty$, then $core(F, \sigma) \neq \emptyset$ and $\overline{core}(F, \sigma) \neq \emptyset$.*

Proof. When we call function GenerateClause1(F, σ), we are at a local minimum and the current assignment σ is not a model yet. There are some unsatisfied clauses, i.e., the set $False(F, \sigma)$ is not empty. From the definition of $core(F, \sigma) = \{c \in False(F, \sigma) \mid \pi(c) = \pi(False(F, \sigma))\}$, $core(F, \sigma)$ is not empty.

Assume $\overline{core}(F, \sigma)$ is empty. Let $\pi(x) =$ Utility1(F, σ), where the literal x appears in F. If we flip the value of literal x, then the clauses in $core(F, \sigma)$ will become true, and since the set $\overline{core}(F, \sigma)$ is empty, all clauses whose least literal is x will become true. Moreover, there is no clause c' in $False(F, \sigma)$ such that $\pi(c') > \pi(x) = \pi(False(F, \sigma))$. That means we can always flip the value of x in σ to obtain σ' such that Utility1$(F, \sigma') <$ Utility1(F, σ). This contradicts with the local minimum precondition. Now, we can say that $\overline{core}(F, \sigma) \neq \emptyset$ if σ is a local minimum. $\square$

Theorem 2. *If σ is a local minimum with respect to Utility1(F, σ). The clause c' generated by function GenerateClause1(F, σ) is a new clause, $\sigma(c') = 0$ and $\pi(c') > \pi(False(F, \sigma))$.*

Proof. From Theorem 1, we know $core(F, \sigma)$ and $\overline{core}(F, \sigma)$ are not empty. Let $y = frontier(F, \sigma)$ such that $\pi(y) = \pi(False(F, \sigma))$, $c_1 \in core(F, \sigma)$ is of the form:

$y \vee c'_1$, $\pi(c'_1) > \pi(y)$, and $\sigma(c'_1) = 0$. $c_2 \in \overline{core}(F, \sigma)$ is of the form: $\overline{y} \vee c'_2$, $\pi(c'_2) > \pi(y)$, and $\sigma(c'_2) = 0$. Now apply resolution rule to c_1 and c_2, we get $c' = c'_1 \vee c'_2$. Since $\sigma(c'_1) = \sigma(c'_2) = 0$, we have $\sigma(c') = 0$, and since $\pi(c'_1) > \pi(y)$ and $\pi(c'_2) > \pi(y)$, we get $\pi(c') > \pi(y) = \pi(False(F, \sigma))$. Since $\sigma(c') = 0$ and $\pi(c') > \pi(False(F, \sigma))$, c' must be a new clause, otherwise $frontier(F, \sigma)$ could not be y. □

Theorem 3. *For any one-to-one mapping π from V to $\{1, 2, ..., |V|\}$, the algorithm represented by CompleteLocalSearch(F) is sound and complete for the satisfiability of F.*

Proof. The soundness comes from Lemmas 1 and 2. There are two cases for the completeness.

First case: the formula F is unsatisfiable. Since every time when the algorithm moves to a local minimum it will generate a new clause, the algorithm will generate the empty clause because the number of distinct clauses generated by resolution is finite.

Second case: the formula F is satisfiable. To show the algorithm is complete, we need only consider the situation in which all possible implied clauses have already been generated. Assume we are at a local minimum, then the algorithm will call function GenerateClause1(F, σ). From Theorem 2 this function will return a new clause. Since all possible clauses are already added, the assumption is not correct, hence there are only global minima and the algorithm will always give a model. □

4 Comparison with Fang and Ruml's Approach

As said earlier, we take the same approach of [FR2004] as illustrated in Figure 1. The major difference lies on objective functions. Let Utility0(F, σ) be the objective function used in [FR2004]. Instead of returning a single integer, Utility0(F, σ) returns a tuple $\langle d_n, ..., d_0 \rangle$ of integers, where d_i is the number of clauses in $False(F, \sigma)$ of length i. An assignment σ' is better than another assignment σ if and only if Utility0(F, σ') is lexicographically smaller than Utility0(F, σ). That is, Utility0(F, σ') must have a smaller entry at the leftmost position where the two tuples differ.

Another difference is about the way to generate new clauses. For the completeness of Fang and Ruml's algorithm, a new clause must be always added at line 10. However, since there is no way to tell how a resolvent is new, Fang and Ruml's algorithm may have to try many possible resolutions in order to generate a new clause. In the exceedingly rare case in which a new resolvent cannot be generated, a long clause of length $|V|$ (i.e., the clause corresponding to the negation of the current assignment) is added instead.

Because of these differences, our algorithm is different from Fang and Ruml's algorithm in the following ways.

1. It is easier to compute Utility1(F, σ) than to compute Utility0(F, σ). The number of distinct values for Utility1(F, σ) is $|V|$ while the number of distinct values for Utility0(F, σ) is $O(2^{|F|})$.
2. Adding (or deleting) duplicate clauses into F will cause the change in value of Utility0(F, σ), but not Utility1(F, σ). If both c and c' are in $False(F, \sigma)$ and c

subsumes c', then Utility1(F, σ) = Utility1$(F - \{c'\}, \sigma)$. In other words, our algorithm allows the use of popular simplification rules such as subsumption without compromising the completeness of our algorithm.

3. Our algorithm always generates new clauses by resolution while Fang and Ruml's algorithm may generate duplicate clauses at a local minimum and needs extra effort to obtain a new clause: In case no new resolvents can be generated, a long clause from the negation of the current assignment is added.

In [FR2004], Fang and Ruml showed that their implementation compares competitively with the prize winners from 2003 and 2002 SAT competition, including both complete and incomplete systems. Their implementation surpasses all of the local search-based solvers from the 2003 competition on the primary competition measure, number of series solved, both overall and in each category, as well as on the number of instances solved overall. These results show convincingly that this complete local search approach is of practical interest. We have implemented our algorithm in C++ and the preliminary results look promising. The test bed is a Pentium 4 2.4GHz linux machine with 1GB memory. Table 1 presents the performance of [FR2004]'s complete local search together with our new algorithm on some SATLIB [HS2000] problems. From the table, we can see that our algorithm performs better on several classes of problems while Fang and Ruml's algorithm works better on other problems.

Table 1. Experimental results on SAT problem. FR denotes [FR2004]'s complete local search algorithm, NEW denotes our new algorithm. #Inst denotes the number of instances in the category. #TOut denotes the number of unsolved instances after 600 seconds. sec denotes the average running time in second.

Problem	#Inst	FR		NEW	
		#TOut	sec	#TOut	sec
DIMACS/AIM	72	0	< 0.1	0	0.15
DIMACS/BF	4	0	11	1	0.2
DIMACS/II	41	0	0.16	6	32
DIMACS/JNH	50	2	18	0	3.15
DIMACS/PARITY	30	20	0.02	20	0.05
DIMACS/PHOLE	5	5	N/A	2	15
DIMACS/PRET	8	0	2.7	0	0.4
DIMACS/SSA	8	0	1.53	0	24
AIS	4	1	31	0	32
BMC	13	10	79	10	87
PLANNING	11	0	1.3	2	5.2
QG	22	18	25	16	43

5   Implementation Issues

The framework of our CompleteLocalSearch algorithm is very simple. While the performance of our algorithm is orthogonal to that of Fang and Ruml's, we expect that

additional techniques can be incorporated into the algorithm to improve the performance. In this section, we will address these issues by considering different objective
functions and resolution schema. We also notice that random restart is a very important
technique.

5.1 Utility Function

The objective function we used in the algorithm is Utility1$(F, \sigma) = \pi(False(F, \sigma))$. To
speedup the computation of this objective function, we can compute it incrementally.
After getting the initial assignment and compute the first objective value, each time
when we flip one variable's value, we use a tuple to compute it incrementally. Let $\mathcal{D}$ be
a tuple $\langle d_n, ..., d_1 \rangle$, where d_i is the number of clauses whose $\pi(c) = i$. By monitoring
the false clauses while flipping value, we can compute the tuple incrementally. Given
two tuples $\mathcal{D} = \langle d_n, ..., d_k, ..., d_1 \rangle$ and $\mathcal{D}' = \langle d'_n, ..., d'_j, ..., d'_1 \rangle$, assume d_k is the
leftmost nonzero element of $\mathcal{D}$ and d'_j is the leftmost nonzero element of $\mathcal{D}'$, then $\mathcal{D}$
is bigger than $\mathcal{D}'$ if $k > j$. Tuple $\mathcal{D}'$ is better than tuple $\mathcal{D}$ if $\mathcal{D}' < \mathcal{D}$. This objective
function also help to limit our choice of candidates for flipping variables. A variable
not appearing in $core(F, \sigma)$ will not improve the value of objective function. Only the
variables that appear in every clause of $core(F, \sigma)$ can improve the value of objective
function. So we can limit our selection to the set

$$\{x \mid \forall c \in core(F, \sigma), x \in \text{variable}(c)\}.$$

Using the tuple $\mathcal{D}$, we can define a more fine-grain objective function named Utility2
for comparing assignments: σ is better (smaller) than σ' if and only if $\mathcal{D}$ is lexicographically (from left to right) smaller than $\mathcal{D}'$. That is to say $\mathcal{D}$ must have a smaller entry
at the leftmost position where the two tuples differ. The new objective function will not
change the completeness of our algorithm. We will exam the performance of this new
objective function in future experiments.

5.2 Learning Schema

The function GenerateClause1 in the figure 1 returns one clause. Let $CoreGenerate(F,
\sigma)$ be the set of all clauses which can be generated from $core(F, \sigma)$ and $\overline{core}(F, \sigma)$.
We can use any one of the clauses in $CoreGenerate(F, \sigma)$. In our implementation,
we tested many different schema. We can add the shortest clause, or the clause c with
the smallest $\pi(c)$ value, or all the clauses in $CoreGenerate(F, \sigma)$. Our experimental
result shows that the adding shortest clause schema is the best overall because adding
shortest clause has better chance to generate unit clauses or the empty clause. The last
schema, i.e., computing all the new clauses in $CoreGenerate(F, \sigma)$, sometimes can
give a better result. To add all the clauses, one thing needs a notice: we may generate a
new clause more than once. For example, $a \lor b$, $a \lor c$, $\overline{a} \lor b$, and $\overline{a} \lor c$ can generate four
clauses: b, c, $b \lor c$, and $c \lor b$. The last two new clauses are duplicate clauses.

There is another clause generation method GenerateClause2, which is much more
aggressive. Before presenting this schema, let's define the set $Critical(a)$ for literal a.
Assume σ is the current assignment, and we are at a local minimum, $frontier(F, \sigma) =
y$. For a literal a, $\pi(a) \geq y$, let

$$Critical(a) = \{c \in F \mid c = \overline{a} \vee c', \sigma(\overline{a}) = 1, \sigma(c') = 0, \pi(c) \geq \pi(y)\}.$$

This means $\overline{a}$ is the only true literal in the clauses of $Critical(a)$.

This schema will add one clause to the current formula. First we select a shortest clause c in $core(F, \sigma)$. For a literal a in the clause c, $Critical(a)$ is not empty, since if it is empty, we can always improve the current assignment by flipping the value of a. Select one shortest clause in $Critical(a)$ for each literal a in clause C, and store them in a set $R = \{c_1, \ldots, c_k\}$. Now we can do resolution between these clauses. The resolution schema is similar with hyper-resolution [BG2002]. First doing resolution between c and c_1, we can get c'_1. Then doing resolution between c'_1 and c_2 get c'_2, and so on. Finally we can get c'_k.

The second clause generation method is more powerful. In many cases, when we at a local minimum, using the first schema will only move the assignment from one local minimum to another local minimum. Sometimes we need several steps to move out a trap. The proposed aggressive learning method can speedup this procedure.

There is a possible extension of GenerateClause2a, which is more aggressive. First we select a shortest clause c in $core(F, \sigma)$. Select a literal a in c such that $Critical(a)$ is not empty. Select a shortest clause c' in $Critical(a)$ and let $c_r = resolution(c, c')$. Let $c = c_r$, if there is a literal a in c such that $Critical$ is not empty, then go back to the previous resolution step and do resolution, otherwise stop and return c.

While using Utility2, we can have a variation version of GenerateClause2, called GenerateClause3. let's define the set $Critical1(a)$ for literal a.

$$Critical1(a) = \{c \in F \mid c = \overline{a} \vee c', \sigma(\overline{a}) = 1, \sigma(c') = 0, \pi(c) \geq \pi(a)\}.$$

All literals in $Critical(a)$ are bigger than $y = frontier(F, \sigma)$, while in $Critical1(a)$ these literals are bigger than a. The selection of false clauses are not limited to those in $core(F, \sigma)$; any false clause in $False(F, \sigma)$ can be chosen. We can select the shortest false clause or using some other heuristic technique to do the selecting. By using $Critical1(a)$ to replace $Critical(a)$, the rest part is similar with GenerateClause2.

5.3 Restart and Ordering

To overcome or avoid search stagnation, many DPLL based solvers and local search based solvers make use of a restart mechanism that re-initializes the search process whenever a restart condition is satisfied. For example, all GSAT and WalkSAT algorithm restart the search periodically [HS2005]. And for DPLL based algorithm like Chaff [M2001], SATO [], BerkMin [GN2002], and Jerusat [N2002], they restart the search periodically or restart after some steps which determined by a heuristic method.

In our complete local search algorithm, we also employ a restart technique which is different from others. In our algorithm, after each restart, we first reorder the order of variables by doing an random renaming. For example, for variables 1, 2, 3, we may rename them by mapping $1 \rightarrow 3, 2 \rightarrow 1, 3 \rightarrow 2$. After that, we will generate a random assignment and do the search. We also tried a restart schema without random reordering, but the performance is not as good as the one with random reordering. The reason is that while the algorithm is complete with any variable ordering, the ordering plays an important role in the performance of the algorithm. Random ordering reduces the effect of poor choice of an ordering. In fact, we have tried several ordering techniques. For instance, we have tried the ordering of variables according to their occurrences in F (either from big to small or from small to big). While testing various ordering techniques, we could not find a superior ordering technique. Now in our implementation, we first use the nature ordering (variable n is before variable $n + 1$). When restarting, we change the ordering by randomly renaming the variables.

6 Conclusion

Following Fang and Ruml's approach of complete local search, we proposed to use a different objective function which is based on a variable ordering and has different features than Fang and Ruml's objective function. The implied clause generation in our algorithm is a special case of ordered resolution and guarantees that only new clauses will be generated. A preliminary experimental result shows that the two algorithms work orthogonally on benchmark problems. There are many issues in how to implement our algorithm efficiently and we will investigate them in the future study.

References

[BG2002]   Bachmair, L., Ganzinger, H.: Resolution theorem proving, in A. Robinson, and A. Voronkov, editors, *The Hanfbook of Automated Reasoning*, chapter 2, volume I, 19-99. Elsevier Science Pub, 2001.

[B2003]   Beame, P., Kautz, H., Sabharwal, A.: Understanding the power of clause learning. In *Proceedings of IJCAI-03*, pages 1194-1201, 2003.

[CI1996]   Cha, B., Iwama, K.: Adding new clauses for faster local search. In *Proceedings of AAAI-96*, pages 332-337, 1996.

[DP1960]   Davis, M., Putnam, H. A computing procedure for quantification theory. *Journal of the ACM*, **7**, 201–215, 1960.

[DLL1962]   Davis, M., Logemann, G., Loveland, D.: A machine program for theorem proving. Journal of the ACM, 5(7): 394-397, 1962.

[FR2004]   Fang, H., Ruml, W.: Complete Local Search for Propositional Satisfiability. *Proc. of 19th National Conference on Artificial Intelligence*, 2004, pages 161-166.

[GN2002]   Boldberg, E., Novikov, Y.: BerkMin: a Fast and Robust SAT-Solver. *Proc. of DATE2002*, 2002, pages 142-149.

[HS2000]   Hoos, H.H., Stützle, T.: SATLIB: An Online Resource for Research on SAT. In: I.P. Gent, H.V. Maaren, T. Walsh, editor, SAT 2000, pages 283-292, IOS Press. SATLIB is available online at www.satlib.org.

[HS2005]   Hoos, H.H., Stützle, T.: Stochastic Local Search: Foundations and Applications. Morgan Kaufmann Publishers, San Francisco, CA, USA, 2005.

[KS2003]   Kautz, H., Selman, B.: Ten challenges redux: Recent progress in propositional reasoning and search. *Proc. of CP03*, pages 1-18, 2003.

[MS1999]   J.P. Marques-Silva and K.A. Sakallah, GRASP: A search algorithm for propositional satisfiability, IEEE Trans. Comput. 48(5):506-520, May 1999.

[M1993]   Morris, P.: The breakout method for escaping from local minima. In *Proceedings of AAAI-93*, pages 40-45, 1993.

[M2001]   Moskewicz, M., Madigan, C., Zhao, Y., Zhang, L., Malik, S.: Chaff: Engineering an Efficient SAT Solver. *Proc. of Design Automation Conference*, pages 530-535, 2001.

[N2002]   Nadel, A.: Backtrack Search Algorithms for Propositional Logic Satisfiability:
            Review and Innovations. Thesis of Nadel, A. 2002.
[SKM1995]   Selman, B., Kautz, H., McAllester, D.: Ten challenges in propositional reasoning
            and search. *Proc. of IJCAI-95*, pages 50-54, 1995.
[SW1997]   Shang, Y., Wah, B.W.: A discrete Lagrangian-based global-search method for
            solving satisfiability problems. *Journal of Global Optimization* 10:1-40 1997
[WW2000]   Wu, Z., Wah, B.W.: An efficient global-search strategy in discrete Lagrangian
            methods for solving hard satisfiability problems. In *Proceedings of AAAI-00*, 310-
            315, 2000.
[Y1997]   Yokoo, M.: Why adding more constraints makes a problem easier for hill-climbing
            algorithms: Analyzing landscapes of CSPs. In *Proceedings of CP-97*, pages 356-
            370, 1997.
[Z1997]   Zhang, H.: SATO: An efficient propositional prover, Proc. of International Con-
            ference on Automated Deduction (CADE-97). pages 308–312, Lecture Notes in
            Artificial Intelligence 1104, Springer-Verlag, 1997.

Inference from Controversial Arguments

Sylvie Coste-Marquis, Caroline Devred, and Pierre Marquis*

CRIL-CNRS/Université d'Artois,
rue Jean Souvraz - S.P. 16,
F-62307 Lens Cedex - France
{coste, devred, marquis}@cril.univ-artois.fr

Abstract. We present new careful semantics within Dung's theory of argumentation. Under such careful semantics, two arguments cannot belong to the same extension whenever one of them indirectly attacks a third argument while the other one indirectly defends the third. We argue that our semantics lead to a better handling of controversial arguments than Dung's ones in some settings. We compare the careful inference relations induced by our semantics w.r.t. cautiousness; we also compare them with the inference relations induced by Dung's semantics.

1   Introduction

Argumentation is a general approach to model defeasible reasoning, in which the two main issues are the generation of arguments and their exploitation so as to draw some conclusions based on the way arguments interact (see e.g., [1–4]).

Among the various theories of argumentation pointed out so far (see e.g., [5–16]) is Dung's theory [5]. Dung's theory is quite influential since it encompasses many approaches to nonmonotonic reasoning and logic programming as special cases; as such, it has been refined and extended by several authors, including [17–21] In Dung's approach, no assumption is made about the nature of an argument. Dung's theory of argumentation is not concerned with the generation of arguments; arguments and the way they interact w.r.t. the attack relation are considered as initial data of any argumentation framework, which can thus be viewed as a labeled digraph.

Several inference relations can be defined within Dung's theory. Usually, inference is defined at the argument level: an argument is considered derivable from an argumentation framework AF when it belongs to one (credulous consequence) (resp. all (skeptical consequence)) extensions of AF under some semantics, where an extension of AF is an admissible set of arguments (i.e., a conflict-free and self-defending set) that is maximal for a given criterion (made precise by the semantics under consideration). While skeptical derivability can be safely extended to the level of sets of arguments, this is not the case for credulous derivability. Indeed, it can be the case that arguments a and b are (individually) derivable from an argumentation framework AF while the set $\{a, b\}$ is not included in any extension of AF. Now, defining derivability for sets

---

* Many thanks to the anonymous reviewers for their helpful comments. The authors have been partly supported by the IUT de Lens, the Université d'Artois, the Région Nord/Pas-de-Calais through the IRCICA Consortium, and by the European Community FEDER Program.

G. Sutcliffe and A. Voronkov (Eds.): LPAR 2005, LNAI 3835, pp. 606–620, 2005.
© Springer-Verlag Berlin Heidelberg 2005

of arguments as inclusion into some (resp. all) extensions under Dung's semantics does not always lead to expected conclusions.

Consider the following scenario: in a public meeting, a political activist presents the motivations of her policy using arguments and counter-arguments: *"One should really decrease taxes (a); of course, this requires to cut staff in public services (b), but that is not so dramatic: privatizing some activities will lead to better services since free trading is good for it (c); furthermore, I am confident that we should reduce our economical exchanges with other foreign countries (d); this is antagonistic to promoting free trading, but, anyway, the productivity of our public services is definitely bad (e)"*. This sounds quite strange as a political speech since the speaker admits that she is in favour of conflicting arguments; a political opponent could easily point out the presence of such a conflict and concludes that such a policy is just non-sense; in order to convince the audience that a, d and e should be accepted, a more skillful speech would be: *"One should really decrease taxes (a); of course, this requires to cut staff in public services (b), but the productivity of our public services is definitely bad (e); furthermore, I'm confident that we should reduce our economical exchanges with other foreign countries (d)"*.

From an abstract point of view, the scenario can be encoded in Dung's setting using the following argumentation framework:

Example 1. Let $AF_1 = \langle A, R \rangle$ with $A = \{a, b, c, d, e\}$ and $R = \{(b, a), (e, b), (c, b), (d, c)\}$. The digraph for AF_1 is depicted on Figure 1.

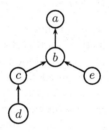

Fig. 1. The digraph for AF_1

If our clumsy political activist adheres to Dung's semantics, she cannot realize that her first speech must be avoided; indeed, AF_1 has a single extension $\{a, d, e\}$ whatever the semantics among Dung's ones, hence a, d and e are considered jointly derivable, which is just what she wants.

One way to cope with this problem is to ask for more demanding notions of absence of conflicts than the one considered in Dung's theory. In this paper, we define and study new semantics for Dung's framework based on the idea that an admissible set S of arguments should not include controversies, i.e. it should not be the case that an element s_1 of S indirectly attacks another argument s whenever a second element s_2 of S indirectly defends s. On Example 1, this prevents from deriving the set of arguments $\{a, d, e\}$ as a whole; nevertheless, $\{d\}$ and $\{a, e\}$ remain derivable separately.

The specific case when $s_1 = s_2$ corresponds to the notion of controversial arguments, as introduced by Dung. While some controversial arguments can be inferred using Dung's standard semantics, they are systematically rejected when our careful semantics are considered.

We believe that such prudent semantics can prove helpful to reason with arguments from domains like politics or justice, where a strong notion of "coherence" on the sets of arguments pointed out makes sense.

In the following, we compare the inference relations induced by our new semantics with Dung's ones and show that in many cases one obtains more cautious notions of derivability.

The rest of this paper is organized as follows. We first recall the main definitions and results pertaining to Dung's theory of argumentation. Then, we present our new, careful semantics for argumentation frameworks. In a third section, a comparison of the various notions of acceptability (including Dung's ones) is provided. A final section concludes the paper and gives a few perspectives.

2   Dung's Theory of Argumentation

Let us present some basic definitions at work in Dung's theory of argumentation [5]. We restrict them to finite argumentation frameworks.

Definition 1 (finite argumentation frameworks). *A finite argumentation framework is a pair $AF = \langle A, R \rangle$ where A is a finite set of so-called arguments and R is a binary relation over A (a subset of $A \times A$), the attacks relation.*

Clearly enough, the set of finite argumentation frameworks is a proper subset of the set of Dung's finitary argumentation frameworks, where every argument must be attacked by finitely many arguments. The definition above clearly shows that a finite argumentation framework is nothing but a finite, labeled digraph.

The main issue is the inference one, i.e., charactering the sets of arguments which could be reasonably derived from a given argumentation framework. Formally, we shall note $AF \mathrel{\vdash\mkern-9mu\sim} S$ where $AF = \langle A, R \rangle$ is a finite argumentation framework and $S \subseteq A$, to state that S is a consequence of AF under $\mathrel{\vdash\mkern-9mu\sim}$. An inference relation $\mathrel{\vdash\mkern-9mu\sim}$ is typically based on a notion of extension, and an inference principle (credulous or skeptical), so that $AF \mathrel{\vdash\mkern-9mu\sim} S$ holds if and only if S is included in all (skeptical) or at least one (credulous) extension of AF.

In order to define a notion of extension, a first important notion is the notion of acceptability: an argument a is acceptable w.r.t. a set of arguments whenever it is defended by the set, i.e., every argument which attacks a is attacked by an element of the set.

Definition 2 (acceptable sets). *Let $AF = \langle A, R \rangle$ be a finite argumentation framework. An argument $a \in A$ is acceptable w.r.t. a subset S of A if and only if for every $b \in A$ s.t. $(b, a) \in R$, there exists $c \in S$ s.t. $(c, b) \in R$. A set of arguments is acceptable w.r.t. S when each of its elements is acceptable w.r.t. S.*

A second important notion is the notion of absence of conflicts. Intuitively, two arguments should not be considered together whenever one of them attacks the other one.

Definition 3 (conflict-free sets). *Let* $AF = \langle A, R \rangle$ *be a finite argumentation framework. A subset* S *of* A *is* conflict-free *if and only if for every* $a, b \in S$, *we have* $(a, b) \notin R$.

Requiring the absence of conflicts and the form of autonomy captured by self-acceptability leads to the notion of admissible set.

Definition 4 (admissible sets). *Let* $AF = \langle A, R \rangle$ *be a finite argumentation framework. A subset* S *of* A *is* admissible *if and only if* S *is conflict-free and acceptable w.r.t.* S.

The significance of the concept of admissible sets is reflected by the fact that every extension of an argumentation framework under the standard semantics introduced by Dung (preferred, stable, complete and grounded extensions) is an admissible set, satisfying some form of optimality:

Definition 5 (extensions). *Let* $AF = \langle A, R \rangle$ *be a finite argumentation framework.*

- *A subset* S *of* A *is a preferred extension of* AF *if and only if it is maximal w.r.t.* $\subseteq$ *among the set of admissible sets for* AF.
- *A subset* S *of* A *is a stable extension of* AF *if and only if it is conflict-free and for every argument* a *from* $A \setminus S$, *there exists* $b \in S$ *s.t.* $(b, a) \in R$.
- *A subset* S *of* A *is a complete extension of* AF *if and only if it is admissible and it coincides with the set of arguments acceptable w.r.t. itself.*
- *A subset* S *of* A *is the grounded extension of* AF *if and only if it is the least element w.r.t.* $\subseteq$ *among the complete extensions of* AF.

Dunne and Bench-Capon gave a sufficient condition for the unicity of preferred extensions:

Proposition 1. *Cor. 9 in [22]*
Let $AF = \langle A, R \rangle$ *be a finite argumentation framework. If* AF *has no even-length cycle, then* AF *has a unique preferred extension.*

Example 1 (cont'ed). Let $E = \{a, d, e\}$. E is the grounded extension of AF_1, the unique preferred extension of AF_1, the unique stable extension of AF_1 and the unique complete extension of AF_1.

Formally, complete extensions of AF can be characterized as the fixed points of its characteristic function $\mathcal{F}_{AF}$:

Definition 6 (characteristic functions). *The* characteristic function $\mathcal{F}_{AF}$ *of an argumentation framework* $AF = \langle A, R \rangle$ *is defined as follows:*

$$\mathcal{F}_{AF} : 2^A \longrightarrow 2^A$$
$$\mathcal{F}_{AF}(S) = \{a \mid a \text{ is acceptable w.r.t. } S\}.$$

Among the complete extensions of AF, the grounded extension of AF is the least element w.r.t. set inclusion [5].

Dung has shown that every argumentation framework AF has a (unique) grounded extension and at least one preferred extension, while it may have zero, one or many stable extensions. These extensions are linked up as follows:

Proposition 2. *Theorem 25 in [5]*
Let AF be an argumentation framework.

1. *Every preferred (resp. stable, complete) extension of AF contains the grounded extension of AF.*
2. *The grounded extension of AF is included in the intersection of all the complete extensions of AF.*

The purest argumentation frameworks AF in Dung's theory are those for which all the notions of acceptability coincide. Dung has provided a sufficient condition for an argumentation framework AF to satisfy this requirement, called the well-foundation of AF; in the finite case, it can be stated as follows:

Definition 7 (well-foundation). *Let $AF = \langle A, R \rangle$ be a finite argumentation framework. AF is well-founded if and only if there is no cycle in the digraph $\langle A, R \rangle$.*

Proposition 3. *Theorem 30 in [5]*
A well-founded argumentation framework AF has exactly one complete extension, which is also the unique preferred extension, the unique stable extension and the grounded extension of AF.

Example 1 (cont'ed). AF_1 has no cycle. Hence AF_1 is well-founded.

Dung has also shown that every stable extension is preferred and every preferred extension is complete; however, none of the converse inclusions holds. When all the preferred extensions of an argumentation framework are stable ones, the framework is said to be coherent:

Definition 8 (coherence). *Let $AF = \langle A, R \rangle$ be an argumentation framework. AF is coherent if and only if every preferred extension of AF is also stable.*

Coherence is a desirable property. Dung gave a sufficient condition for it based on the notion of controversial argument:

Definition 9 (controversial arguments).
Let $AF = \langle A, R \rangle$ be an argumentation framework.

- *Let $a, b \in A$. a indirectly attacks b if and only if there exists an odd-length path from a to b in the digraph for AF.*
- *Let $a, b \in A$. a indirectly defends b if and only if there exists an even-length path from a to b in the digraph for AF. The length of this path is not zero.*
- *Let $a, b \in A$. a is controversial w.r.t. b if and only if a indirectly attacks b and a indirectly defends b.*
- *AF is uncontroversial if and only if there is no pair a, b of arguments of A such that a is controversial w.r.t. b.*
- *AF is limited controversial if and only if there is no infinite sequence of arguments $a_0, \ldots, a_n, \ldots$ of A s.t. a_{i+1} is controversial w.r.t. a_i.*

Dung has shown the following theorem:

Proposition 4. *Theorem 33 in [5]*
Every uncontroversial or limited controversial argumentation framework is coherent.

3 Careful Extensions

Let us now present our new semantics for Dung's argumentation frameworks. They are based on the notion of super-controversial pair of arguments:

Definition 10 (super-controversial arguments). *Let $AF = \langle A, R \rangle$ be a finite argumentation framework and let $a, b, c \in A$. (a, b) is* super-controversial *w.r.t. c if and only if a indirectly attacks c and b indirectly defends c.*

Example 1 (cont'ed). In AF_l, (d, e) is super-controversial w.r.t. a.

Obviously enough, the notion of super-controversial pair of arguments extends the notion of controversial arguments since a is controversial w.r.t. c if and only if (a, a) is super-controversial w.r.t. c.

In order to address Example 1 in a more satisfying way, we need to reinforce Dung's notion of conflict-free set of arguments; we consider in addition the notion of *controversial-free* set of arguments:

Definition 11 (controversial-free sets). *Let $AF = \langle A, R \rangle$ be a finite argumentation framework. $S \subseteq A$ is* controversial-free *for AF if and only if for every $a, b \in S$ and every $c \in A$, (a, b) is not super-controversial w.r.t. c.*

Definition 12 (c-admissible sets). *Let $AF = \langle A, R \rangle$ be a finite argumentation framework. $S \subseteq A$ is* c(areful)-admissible *for AF if and only if every $a \in S$ is acceptable w.r.t. S and S is conflict-free and controversial-free for AF.*

Example 1 (cont'ed). $\{d\}$, and $\{a, e\}$ and its subsets except $\{a\}$ are the c-admissible sets for AF_1.

From Definition 12, the next lemma follows immmediately:

Lemma 1. *Let a, b be two arguments of a finite argumentation framework AF. If a is controversial w.r.t. b, then $\{a\}$ cannot be included in a c-admissible set for AF.*

Obviously, the absence of controversial arguments within a set is only necessary to ensure that the set is controversial-free, hence potentially c-admissible (as Example 1 shows, this is not a sufficient condition). Since every argument belonging to an odd-length cycle of AF is controversial w.r.t. any argument of the cycle [23], no such argument can belong to a c-admissible set. In this respect, our approach departs from [18, 19] who consider that odd-length and even-length cycles in an argumentation framework should be handled in the same way.

On this ground, one can define several notions of *careful extensions*, echoing Dung's ones. Let us start with *preferred c-extensions*:

Definition 13 (preferred c-extensions). *Let $AF = \langle A, R \rangle$ be a finite argumentation framework. A c-admissible set $S \subseteq A$ for AF is a* preferred c-extension *of AF if and only if $\nexists S' \subseteq A$ s.t. $S \subset S'$ and S' is c-admissible for AF.*

Example 1 (cont'ed). $\{a, e\}$ and $\{d\}$ are the preferred c-extensions of AF_1.

We have the following easy proposition:

Proposition 5. *Let $AF = \langle A, R \rangle$ be a finite argumentation framework. For every c-admissible set $S \subseteq A$ for AF, there exists at least one preferred c-extension $E \subseteq A$ of AF s.t. $S \subseteq E$.*

Since $\emptyset$ is c-admissible for any AF, we obtain as a corollary:

Corollary 1. *Every finite argumentation framework $AF = \langle A, R \rangle$ has a preferred c-extension.*

What can be found in preferred c-extensions? Though every argument which is not attacked belongs to at least one preferred c-extension of AF, it is not the case (in general) that it belongs to every preferred c-extension of AF (see Example 1). In this respect, c-preferred extensions hardly contrast with preferred extensions.

Let us now consider the notion of *stable c-extension*:

Definition 14 (stable c-extensions).

Let $AF = \langle A, R \rangle$ be a finite argumentation framework. A conflict-free and controversial-free subset S of A is a stable c-extension of AF if and only if S attacks (in a direct way) every argument from $A \setminus S$.

Example 1 (cont'ed). AF_1 has no stable c-extension.

Every finite argumentation framework has at least one preferred c-extension, and zero, one or many stable c-extensions.

Finally, as for Dung's extensions, we have:

Lemma 2. *Every stable c-extension of a finite argumentation framework AF also is a preferred c-extension of AF. The converse does not hold.*

Here is a more complex example for illustrating those notions:

Example 2. Let $AF_2 = \langle A, R \rangle$ with $A = \{a, b, c, d, i, n\}$ and $R = \{(i, n), (n, a), (b, a), (c, a), (d, c), (b, d), (d, b)\}$. The digraph for AF_2 is depicted on Figure 2.

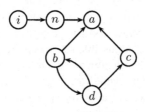

Fig. 2. The digraph for AF_2

$E_1 = \{i, a, d\}$ and $E_2 = \{i, b, c\}$ are the two preferred (and stable) extensions of AF_2. E_1 is the unique stable c-extension of AF_2. E_1 and $E_3 = \{b, c\}$ are the two preferred c-extensions of AF_2.

Let us now explain how c-extensions can be characterized using some fixed point construction:

Definition 15 (c-characteristic functions). *The* c-characteristic function $\mathcal{F}^c_{AF}$ *of a finite argumentation framework* $AF = \langle A, R \rangle$ *is defined as follows:*

$$\mathcal{F}^c_{AF} : 2^A \longrightarrow 2^A$$
$$\mathcal{F}^c_{AF}(S) = \{a \mid a \text{ is acceptable w.r.t. } S \text{ and } S \cup \{a\} \text{ is conflict-free}$$
$$\text{and controversial-free for } AF\}.$$

We immediately get that:

Lemma 3. *Let* $AF = \langle A, R \rangle$ *be a finite argumentation framework and let* $S \subseteq A$ *be a conflict-free and controversial-free set for* AF. S *is c-admissible for* AF *if and only if* $S \subseteq \mathcal{F}^c_{AF}(S)$.

Contrariwise to the characteristic function of an argumentation framework, $\mathcal{F}^c_{AF}$ is in general nonmonotonic w.r.t. $\subseteq$ (and this is also the case for its restriction to the set of all c-admissible subsets of A). Accordingly, we cannot define a notion of c-grounded extension corresponding to the grounded one.

Let us now introduce a notion of *complete c-extension*:

Definition 16 (complete c-extensions). *Let* $AF = \langle A, R \rangle$ *be a finite argumentation framework and let* S *be a c-admissible set for* AF. S *is a* complete c-extension *of* AF *if and only if every argument* a *which is acceptable w.r.t.* S *and such that* $S \cup \{a\}$ *is conflict-free and controversial-free for* AF *belongs to* S.

Example 1 (cont'ed). $\{a, e\}$ is a complete c-extension of AF_1.

From the definition, it comes immediately that:

Lemma 4. *A conflict-free and controversial-free set of arguments* S *is a complete c-extension of* AF *if and only if* $\mathcal{F}^c_{AF}(S) = S$.

Let us now define several inference relations based on our careful semantics for argumentation frameworks:

Definition 17 (careful inference relations). $\sim^{q,s}_c$ *denotes the* careful inference relation *obtained by considering a careful semantics* s *(where* $s = P(referred)$, $s = S(table)$) *and* q *is an inference principle, either credulous* ($q = \exists$) *or skeptical* ($q = \forall$).

For instance, $S \subseteq A$ is a consequence of AF w.r.t. $\sim^{\forall,P}_c$, noted $AF \sim^{\forall,P}_c S$, indicates that S is included in every preferred c-extension of AF.

We have compared all the careful inference relations induced by the different semantics w.r.t. cautiousness. We have focused on the case of finite argumentation frameworks with a stable c-extension (otherwise, both $\sim^{\forall,S}_c$ and $\sim^{\exists,S}_c$ trivialize). We have obtained the following results:

Proposition 6. *The cautiousness relations reported in Table 1 hold for every finite argumentation framework which has a stable c-extension (Each time a cell contains a* $\subseteq$, *it means that for every* $AF = \langle A, R \rangle$ *and every* $S \subseteq A$, *if* S *is a consequence of* AF *w.r.t. the inference relation indexing the row, then* S *is a consequence of* AF *w.r.t. the inference relation indexing the column).*

Table 1. Cautiousness links between careful inference relations for AFs with a stable c-extension

	$\vert\!\sim_c^{\exists,P}$	$\vert\!\sim_c^{\exists,S}$	$\vert\!\sim_c^{\forall,P}$	$\vert\!\sim_c^{\forall,S}$
$\vert\!\sim_c^{\exists,P}$	$=$	$\not\subseteq$	$\not\subseteq$	$\not\subseteq$
$\vert\!\sim_c^{\exists,S}$	$\subseteq$	$=$	$\not\subseteq$	$\not\subseteq$
$\vert\!\sim_c^{\forall,P}$	$\subseteq$	$\subseteq$	$=$	$\subseteq$
$\vert\!\sim_c^{\forall,S}$	$\subseteq$	$\subseteq$	$\not\subseteq$	$=$

One can note that the cautiousness picture for careful inference relations is similar to the one for the inference relations induced from Dung's semantics (assuming that the argumentation frameworks under consideration have stable extension(s)):

$$\vert\!\sim_c^{\forall,P} \subset \vert\!\sim_c^{\forall,S} \subset \vert\!\sim_c^{\exists,S} \subset \vert\!\sim_c^{\exists,P} .$$

4   Comparisons with Dung's Framework

Let us now compare our careful semantics with Dung's ones. Let us start with a comparison in terms of extensions.

4.1   Comparing Extensions

First of all, we immediately obtain the following easy result:

Proposition 7. *Every c-admissible set for a finite argumentation framework AF is also admissible for AF. The converse does not hold.*

Clearly, this does not imply that every preferred c-extension is a preferred extension which is conflict-free and controversial-free since maximality w.r.t. set inclusion is required among c-admissible sets. Nevertheless, as a consequence of Proposition 7, we have:

Corollary 2. *Let $AF = \langle A, R \rangle$ be a finite argumentation framework. For every preferred c-extension E_c of AF, there exists at least one preferred extension E of AF s.t. $E_c \subseteq E$.*

Example 2 (cont'ed). In AF_2, $E_3 \subset E_2$.

This corollary shows in particular that when AF has a unique preferred extension E (especially, when AF is well-founded or without even-length cycle, or *trivial* – i.e., when the unique preferred extension of it is empty), E includes every preferred c-extension of AF.

However, unlike preferred extensions, a well-founded argumentation framework AF can have more than one preferred c-extension (see Example 1).

It can also be the case that a preferred extension of AF does not include any of the preferred c-extensions of AF. Furthermore, the presence of even-length cycles in AF does not prevent it from having a unique preferred c-extension. Those two points are illustrated by the following example:

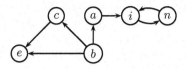

Fig. 3. The digraph for AF_3

Example 3. Let $AF_3 = \langle A, R \rangle$ with $A = \{a, b, c, e, n, i\}$ and $R = \{(b, e), (b, c), (c, e), (b, a), (a, i), (n, i), (i, n)\}$. The digraph for AF_3 is depicted on Figure 3.

$E_1 = \{b, n\}$ and $E_2 = \{b, i\}$ are the preferred (and stable) extensions of AF_3. $E_3 = \{n\}$ is the unique preferred c-extension of AF_3. We have $E_3 \not\subseteq E_2$. Observe that though the digraph for AF_3 has an even-length cycle, AF_3 has a unique preferred c-extension.

Another easy consequence of Proposition 7 is:

Corollary 3. *Let $AF = \langle A, R \rangle$ be a finite argumentation framework. If AF is trivial, then AF is c-trivial, i.e., the unique preferred c-extension of AF is empty. The converse does not hold.*

Let us now turn to stable c-extensions:

Lemma 5. *Every stable c-extension of a finite argumentation framework AF also is a stable extension of AF. The converse does not hold.*

As a direct consequence, we obtain that every stable c-extension of a finite argumentation framework AF also is a preferred extension of AF. However, the converse does not hold.

While every well-founded argumentation framework has a stable extension, it is not the case that every well-founded argumentation framework has a stable c-extension; furthermore, it is also not the case that every argumentation framework which is uncontroversial has a stable c-extension. Example 1 is a counter-example for both cases. In the same vein, a finite argumentation framework AF that is both well-founded and uncontroversial is not always c-coherent (i.e., such that every preferred c-extension of AF is a stable c-extension of AF). In particular, it is not the case that a coherent finite argumentation framework AF is always c-coherent as well (see Example 1).

It turns out that argumentation frameworks AF with a stable c-extension are particularly interesting. Indeed, whenever AF has a stable c-extension, we have:

Proposition 8. *Let $AF = \langle A, R \rangle$ be a finite argumentation framework. If AF has a stable c-extension, the grounded extension of AF and the intersection of all preferred extensions of AF coincide (i.e., AF is relatively grounded).*

Proposition 9. *Let $AF = \langle A, R \rangle$ be a finite argumentation framework. If AF has a stable c-extension, the intersection of all preferred c-extensions of AF is included in the grounded extension of AF.*

Subsequently, if AF has a stable c-extension, the intersection of all preferred c-extensions of AF is included in the intersection of all preferred extensions of AF; hence, it is also included in the intersection of all stable extensions of AF.

Now, what's about controversies? We have the two following lemmata:

Lemma 6. *Let $AF = \langle A, R \rangle$ be a finite argumentation framework. AF is limited controversial if and only if AF has no odd-length cycle.*

Lemma 7. *Let $AF = \langle A, R \rangle$ be a finite argumentation framework. If AF has a stable c-extension, then AF is limited controversial.*

Thanks to Proposition 4, we obtain the following corollary:

Lemma 8. *Let $AF = \langle A, R \rangle$ be a finite argumentation framework. If AF has a stable c-extension, then AF is coherent.*

We also have:

Proposition 10. *Let $AF = \langle A, R \rangle$ be a finite argumentation framework s.t. AF has a stable c-extension. For every preferred c-extension E_c of AF, there exists at least one stable extension S of AF s.t. $E_c \subseteq S$.*

Finally, we can show that the set of complete extensions of AF and the set of complete c-extensions of AF are not comparable w.r.t. $\subseteq$.

4.2 Comparing Inference Relations

We have compared our careful inference relations with the ones induced by Dung's semantics w.r.t. cautiousness. Let $\vdash^{q,s}$ denote the inference relation obtained by considering Dung's semantics s (where $s = P(referred)$, $s = S(table)$ or $s = G(rounded)$) and q is an inference principle, either credulous ($q = \exists$) or skeptical ($q = \forall$).

Since the presence of a stable c-extension changes the picture, we have first considered this specific case, then the general case. We have obtained the following results:

Proposition 11. *The cautiousness relations reported in Table 2 hold for every finite argumentation framework which has a stable c-extension.*

Table 2. Cautiousness links between careful relations and Dung's ones for AFs with a stable c-extension

	$\vdash_c^{\exists,P}$	$\vdash_c^{\exists,S}$	$\vdash_c^{\forall,P}$	$\vdash_c^{\forall,S}$
$\vdash^{\exists,P}$	$\not\subseteq, \supseteq$	$\not\subseteq, \supseteq$	$\not\subseteq, \supseteq$	$\not\subseteq, \supseteq$
$\vdash^{\exists,S}$	$\not\subseteq, \supseteq$	$\not\subseteq, \supseteq$	$\not\subseteq, \supseteq$	$\not\subseteq, \supseteq$
$\vdash^{\forall,P}$	$\subseteq, \not\supseteq$	$\subseteq, \not\supseteq$	$\not\subseteq, \supseteq$	$\subseteq, \not\supseteq$
$\vdash^{\forall,S}$	$\subseteq, \not\supseteq$	$\subseteq, \not\supseteq$	$\not\subseteq, \supseteq$	$\subseteq, \not\supseteq$
$\vdash^{\cdot,G}$	$\subseteq, \not\supseteq$	$\subseteq, \not\supseteq$	$\not\subseteq, \supseteq$	$\subseteq, \not\supseteq$

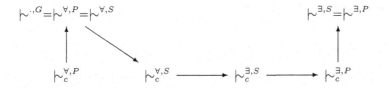

Fig. 4. Cautiousness links between inference relations for AF's with a stable c-extension

$$\vdash\!\!\sim^{.,G} \longrightarrow \vdash\!\!\sim^{\forall,P} \longrightarrow \vdash\!\!\sim^{\exists,P} \longleftarrow \vdash\!\!\sim_c^{\exists,P} \longleftarrow \vdash\!\!\sim_c^{\forall,P}$$

Fig. 5. Cautiousness links between inference relations

Tables 1 and 2 are summarized on Figure 4 (Each arrow can be read as "strictly more cautious than").

In the light of Figure 4, one can observe that the most cautious inference relation among those considered here is $\vdash\!\!\sim_c^{\forall,P}$ and the least cautious ones are $\vdash\!\!\sim^{\exists,S}=\vdash\!\!\sim^{\exists,P}$. Furthermore, strict cautiousness is a complete ordering over the set of inference relations considered in this paper.

Let us now turn to the general case, i.e., argumentation frameworks which do not have necessarily a stable c-extension, or even a stable extension. We do not put potentially trivial relations into the picture (i.e., $\vdash\!\!\sim_c^{\forall,S}$, $\vdash\!\!\sim_c^{\exists,S}$, $\vdash\!\!\sim^{\forall,S}$, $\vdash\!\!\sim^{\exists,S}$ are not considered hereafter):

Proposition 12. *The cautiousness relations reported in Tables 3 and 4 hold for every finite argumentation framework.*

Tables 3 and 4 are summarized on Figure 5.

Proposition 12 shows that the lack of a stable c-extension does not question the way $\vdash\!\!\sim_c^{\exists,P}$ and $\vdash\!\!\sim_c^{\forall,P}$ are linked up (see Proposition 6). Contrastingly, when the existence of a stable c-extension is not guaranteed, the cautiousness links between our careful relations and Dung's ones are heavily modified. Compared with the results reported on Figure 4, one can observe that in the general case, it is not guaranteed that $\vdash\!\!\sim^{.,G}$ and $\vdash\!\!\sim^{\forall,P}$ coincide, that $\vdash\!\!\sim_c^{\forall,P}$ is more cautious than $\vdash\!\!\sim^{.,G}$ and that $\vdash\!\!\sim^{\forall,P}$ is more cautious than $\vdash\!\!\sim_c^{\exists,P}$.

Table 3. Cautiousness links between careful relations

	$\vdash\!\!\sim_c^{\exists,P}$	$\vdash\!\!\sim_c^{\forall,P}$
$\vdash\!\!\sim_c^{\exists,P}$	$=$	$\not\subseteq$
$\vdash\!\!\sim_c^{\forall,P}$	$\subseteq$	$=$

Table 4. Cautiousness links between careful relations and Dung's ones

	$\vdash\!\!\sim_c^{\exists,P}$	$\vdash\!\!\sim_c^{\forall,P}$
$\vdash\!\!\sim^{\exists,P}$	$\not\subseteq, \supseteq$	$\not\subseteq, \supseteq$
$\vdash\!\!\sim^{\forall,P}$	$\not\subseteq, \not\supseteq$	$\not\subseteq, \not\supseteq$
$\vdash\!\!\sim^{.,G}$	$\not\subseteq, \not\supseteq$	$\not\subseteq, \not\supseteq$

5   Some Complexity Issues

Before concluding the paper, let us consider some complexity issues. Indeed, in an AI perspective, it is important to determine how hard are the new inference relations we pointed out w.r.t. the computational point of view. We assume the reader acquainted with basic notions of complexity theory, especially the complexity classes P, NP, coNP and the polynomial hierarchy (see e.g. [24]).

We have shown in a previous paper [25] that considering sets of arguments (instead of single arguments) as input queries for the inference problem does not lead to a complexity shift when Dung's inference relations are considered (the purpose is to determine whether such sets are derivable from a given finite argumentation framework AF). As to the careful inference relations, the same conclusion can be drawn.

First of all, it is easy to show that, given a finite argumentation framework AF, deciding whether a given argument indirectly attacks (resp. indirectly defends) a given argument is in P, and deciding whether a set of arguments is controversial-free is in P. Accordingly, deciding whether a given set of arguments is c-admissible for AF is in P. As a consequence, deciding whether a given set of arguments is a stable c-extension of AF is in P as well. Therefore, deciding whether a given set of arguments S is included in every stable c-extension of AF is in coNP (in order to show that the complementary problem is in NP, it is sufficient to guess a set $E \subseteq A$ and to check in polynomial time that E is a stable c-extension of AF and that S is not included in E).

Besides, deciding whether a set of arguments S is a preferred c-extension of AF is in coNP (in order to show that the complementary problem is in NP, it is sufficient to guess a proper superset S' of S and to check in polynomial time that S' is c-admissible for AF). As a consequence, deciding whether a given set of arguments S is included in every preferred c-extension of AF is in Π_2^p (in order to show that the complementary problem is in Σ_2^p, it is sufficient to guess a set $E \subseteq A$ and to check in polynomial time using an NP oracle that E is a preferred c-extension of AF and that S is not included in E).

Finally, deciding whether a given set of arguments is included in a preferred c-extension (resp. a stable c-extension) of AF is in NP. To be more precise:

Definition 18. C-CA(AF, S) *is defined as follows:*
    ⋆ **Input** $AF = \langle A, R \rangle$ *a finite argumentation framework, and* $S \subseteq A$.
    ⋆ **Quest** *Is* S *included in a preferred c-extension of AF?*

Proposition 13. C-CA(AF, S) *is* NP-*complete.*

Definition 19. IN-C-STAB(AF, S) *is defined as follows:*
    ⋆ **Input** $AF = \langle A, R \rangle$ *a finite argumentation framework, and* $S \subseteq A$.
    ⋆ **Quest** *Is* S *included in a stable c-extension of AF?*

Proposition 14. IN-C-STAB(AF, S) *is* NP-*complete.*

Accordingly, our careful inference relations are not computationally more complex that the corresponding ones based on Dung's semantics (see [26, 27]).

6   Conclusion

We have presented new careful semantics within Dung's theory of argumentation. Under such careful semantics, two arguments cannot belong to the same extension whenever one of them indirectly attacks a third argument, while the second one indirectly defends it. In particular, controversial arguments are always rejected. This seems to be highly desirable in domains where controversies can be interpreted as contradictions, as we exemplified it. We have also compared our careful inference relations with Dung's ones and considered some complexity issues, showing that our inference relations are not more complex than the corresponding ones based on Dung's semantics.

Our work calls for some perspectives. A first perspective consists in developing specific algorithms for computing careful extensions, based on algorithms for computing extensions like those described in [28, 29, 30]. A second perspective consists in combining the notion of safe extension introduced recently [31] with the notion of careful extension.

References

1. Toulmin, S.: The Uses of Argument. Cambridge University Press (1958)
2. Prakken, A., Vreeswijk, G.: Logics for defeasible argumentation. Volume 4 of Handbook of Philosophical Logic, 2nd edition. Kluwer Academic Publishers (2002) 219–318
3. Bondarenko, A., Dung, P.M., Kowalski, R., Toni, F.: An abstract, argumentation-theoretic approach to default reasoning. Art. Intelligence 93 (1997) 63–101
4. Kakas, A., Toni, F.: Computing argumentation in logic programming. J. of Logic and Computation 9 (1999) 515–562
5. Dung, P.M.: On the acceptability of arguments and its fundamental role in nonmonotonic reasoning, logic programming and n-person games. Art. Intelligence 77 (1995) 321–358
6. Pollock, J.: How to reason defeasibly. Art. Intelligence 57 (1992) 1–42
7. Simari, G., Loui, R.: A mathematical treatment of defeasible reasoning and its implementation. Art. Intelligence 53 (1992) 125–157
8. Elvang-Gøransson, M., Fox, J., Krause, P.: Acceptability of arguments as logical uncertainty. In: ECSQARU'93. Volume 747 of LNCS. (1993) 85–90
9. Elvang-Gøransson, M., Fox, J., Krause, P.: Dialectic reasoning with inconsistent information. In: UAI'93. (1993) 114–121
10. Elvang-Gøransson, M., Hunter, A.: Argumentative logics: Reasoning with classically inconsistent information. Data and Knowledge Engineering 16 (1995) 125–145
11. Vreeswijk, G.: Abstract argumentation systems. Art. Intelligence 90 (1997) 225–279
12. Besnard, P., Hunter, A.: A logic-based theory of deductive arguments. Art. Intelligence 128 (2001) 203–235
13. Amgoud, L., Cayrol, C.: Inferring from inconsistency in preference-based argumentation frameworks. J. of Automated Reasoning 29 (2002) 125–169
14. Amgoud, L., Cayrol, C.: A reasoning model based on the production of acceptable arguments. Ann. of Mathematics and Artificial Intelligence 34 (2002) 197–215
15. Cayrol, C.: From non-monotonic syntax-based entailment to preference-based argumentation. In: ECSQARU'95. Volume 946 of LNAI. (1995)
16. Dimopoulos, Y., Nebel, B., Toni, F.: On the computional complexity of assumption-based argumentation for default reasoning. Art. Intelligence 141 (2002) 57–78

17. Baroni, P., Giacomin, M., G.Guida: Extending abstract argumentation systems theory. Art. Intelligence **120** (2000) 251–270
18. Baroni, P., Giacomin, M.: Solving semantic problems with odd-length cycles in argumentation. In: ECSQARU'03. Volume 2711 of LNAI. (2003) 440–451
19. Baroni, P., Giacomin, M.: A recursive approach to argumentation: motivation and perspectives. In: NMR'04. (2004) 50–58
20. Cayrol, C., Doutre, S., Lagasquie-Schiex, M.C., Mengin, J.: Minimal defence: a refinement of the preferred semantics for argumentation frameworks. In: NMR'02. (2002) 408–415
21. Cayrol, C., Lagasquie-Schiex, M.C.: Gradual handling of contradiction in argumentation frameworks. In: IPMU'02. (2002) 83–90
22. Dunne, P., Bench-Capon, T.: Complexity and combinatorial properties of argument systems. Technical report, Dept. of Computer Science, Univ. of Liverpool (2001)
23. Doutre, S.: Autour de la sémantique préférée des systèmes d'argumentation. Thèse de doctorat d'université, Université Paul Sabatier, Toulouse (2002)
24. Papadimitriou, C.: Computational complexity. Addison-Wesley (1994)
25. Coste-Marquis, S., Devred, C., Marquis, P.: Symmetric argumentation frameworks. In: ECSQARU'05. Volume 3571 of LNCS. (2005) 317–328
26. Dimopoulos, Y., Torres, A.: Graph theoretical structures in logic programs and default theories. Theoretical Computer Science **170** (1996) 209–244
27. Dunne, P., Bench-Capon, T.: Coherence in finite argument system. Art. Intelligence **141** (2002) 187–203
28. Vreeswijk, G., Prakken, H.: Credulous and sceptical argument games for preferred semantics. In: JELIA'00. (2000) 224–238
29. Cayrol, C., Doutre, S., Mengin, J.: On decision problems related to the preferred semantics for argumentation frameworks. J. of Logic and Computation **13** (2003) 377–403
30. Doutre, S., Mengin, J.: On sceptical vs credulous acceptance for abstract argument systems. In: NMR'04. (2004) 134–139
31. Cayrol, C., Lagasquie-Schiex, M.: On the acceptability of arguments in bipolar argumentation framework. In: ECSQARU'05. Volume 3571 of LNCS. (2005) 378–389

Programming Cognitive Agents in Defeasible Logic

Mehdi Dastani[1], Guido Governatori[2], Antonino Rotolo[3], and Leendert van der Torre[4]

[1] Intelligent Systems Group, Utrecht University
mehdi@cs.uu.nl
[2] School of ITEE, University of Queensland
guido@itee.uq.edu.au
[3] CIRSFID, University of Bologna
rotolo@cirsfid.unibo.it
[4] CWI, Amsterdam, and Delft University of Technology
torre@cwi.nl

Abstract. Defeasible Logic is extended to programming languages for cognitive agents with preferences and actions for planning. We define rule-based agent theories that contain preferences and actions, together with inference procedures. We discuss patterns of agent types in this setting. Finally, we illustrate the language by an example of an agent reasoning about web-services.

1 Introduction

This paper combines two perspectives: (a) a cognitive account of agents that specifies their mental attitudes; (b) modelling agents' behaviour by means of normative concepts. For the first approach, our background is the belief-desire-intention (BDI) architecture, where mental attitudes are taken as primitives to give rise to a set of Intentional Agent Systems [16, 3]. This view is interesting especially when the behaviour of agents is the outcome of a rational balance among their (possibly conflicting) mental states. The normative aspect is rather based on the assumption that normative concepts play a role to characterize the idea of social co-ordination of autonomous agents [15]. The combination of these perspectives leads to an account of agents' deliberation and behaviour in terms of the interplay between mental attitudes and normative (external) factors such as obligations.

Given this background, several rule-based approaches are available for programming cognitive agents [5, 9, 4]. In this paper we extend the Defeasible Logic (DL) approach. As is well-known, DL is based on a logic programming-like language and it is a simple, efficient but flexible non-monotonic formalism able to deal with many different intuitions of non-monotonic reasoning and recently applied in many fields. In addition, several efficient implementations have been developed [14, 2]. Here we propose a non-monotonic logic of agency, based on the framework of [1], which extends the preliminary work we presented in [7]. Indeed, DL is one of the most expressive languages that allows for the definition of large sets of patterns called agent types. Moreover, it is flexible to incorporate ideas from other languages, such as extension generation and selection from BOID [5], or deliberation languages from 3APL [9, 6].

However, as we argued in [7], it has two limits. First, DL, as well as its rival rule based programming languages, is based on a uniform representation of rules, whereas

G. Sutcliffe and A. Voronkov (Eds.): LPAR 2005, LNAI 3835, pp. 621–636, 2005.

in artificial intelligence and in practical reasoning other complex structures have been proposed. Most importantly, rule-based approaches are based on conditionals, whereas an alternative approach is based on comparative notions. Examples are preference logics and CP nets instead of logics of desires and goals, ordered disjunctions instead of default logics, betterness logics instead of logics of ideality, logics of sub-ideality in deontic logic, etc. Second, it is not immediate how DL can deal with complex actions discussed in action languages such as 3APL [9] and in recent incarnations of the BOID architecture [8].

Some issues on agent programming languages should be addressed: how to detect and resolve conflicts that include such preferences, and which kind of agent types can be introduced to deal with preferences. We contribute to cognitive agent programming languages by addressing the following question: How to use DL extended with actions and graded preferences? This question breaks down in the following sub-questions: (a) How to introduce preferences and actions for planning in DL? (b) How to detect and resolve conflicts using preferences and actions? (c) How to define agent types based on preferences and actions?

We provided in [7] some first intuitions on the question which kind of preferences can be introduced in DL. In particular, we reconsidered the introduction of the $\otimes$ operator of [11] in DL, given its advantages over other comparative notions. First, we argued that it can be integrated with a rule based formalism (see also [10]). Second, it has been applied to complicated problems in deontic logic [11]. Third, it allows to clearly distinguish between conflicts and violations [10, 11]. In fact, though these notions may conflate, conflicts and violations have in general to be kept separate. Suppose you have an agent doing B while an obligation states OBL$\neg B$. Since the logic for OBL is usually not reflexive[1], the scenario does not lead necessarily to a logical conflict but a violation: conflict-resolution strategies may require that OBL$\neg B$ is not overridden. This paper provides a further step as it provides a more extensive treatment of conflict-detection and -resolution strategies. In addition, it discusses a more comprehensive classification of agent types.

A second substantial step of this work is that it shows how DL can embed a machinery for dealing with planning agents. In this regard, to attack the questions with respect to complex actions in BOID, [8] separate conflict-detection from -resolution. They ask the question whether two plans are conflicting or not, and they ask the question how to resolve conflicts between plans. Analogously, we use the distinction between conflict-detection and -resolution for the $\otimes$ constructions too. This asks for another way to deal with the notion of conflict.

We will distinguish between goal (desires, intentions, obligations) generation and plan generation. The goal generation generates goals based on existing beliefs, desires, intentions and obligations, and the plan generation generates sequences of actions based on these goals. As for the first aspect, rules will allow the derivation of new motivational factors of an agent. We will divide the rules into rules for beliefs, desires, intentions, and obligations. Provability for beliefs will not generate goals, since in our view they concern the knowledge an agent has about the world: beliefs may contribute to derive

---

[1] As is well-known, in a non-reflexive modal logic A does not follow from XA, where X is a modal operator.

goals (desires, intentions, and obligations), but they are not in themselves motivations for action. As for the second aspect, the inference mechanism will be used to deduce sequences of actions (plans) to achieve goals.

The layout of this paper is as follows. In Section 2 we introduce agents with preferences and actions in DL, and in Section 3 we show how to infer goal conclusions from rules with preferences. In Section 4 we discuss how to integrate the previous framework to reason about plans in DL. Finally, in Section 5 we extensively discuss conflicts among rules and patterns called agent types.

2   Agents in Defeasible Logic

We focus on how mental attitudes and obligations jointly interplay in modelling agent's deliberation and behaviour.

Accordingly the formal language contains modal literals, preferences, and actions, and is defined as follows:

Definition 1 (Language). *Let* $M = \{\text{BEL}, \text{DES}, \text{INT}, \text{OBL}\}$ *be a set of modal operators,* P *a set of propositional atoms, and* $Act = \{\alpha, \beta, \dots\}$ *a set of basic actions. The set of literals is defined as* $L = P \cup \{\neg p | p \in P\}$. *If* q *is a literal,* $\sim q$ *denotes the complementary literal (if* q *is a positive literal* p *then* $\sim q$ *is* $\neg p$; *and if* q *is* $\neg p$, *then* $\sim q$ *is* p).

- *The goal language* L_{goal} *is the smallest set containing modal literals* Xl *and* $\neg Xl$ *when* $l \in L$ *is a literal and* $X \in M$ *is a modal operator, and* $\otimes$*-expressions* $l_1 \otimes \dots \otimes l_n$ *when* $l_1, \dots, l_n \subseteq L$ *are* $n \geq 1$ *literals.*
- *The plan language* L_{plan} *is the smallest set containing* Act *(basic action plan),* $l?$ *for all literals* l *(test action plan),* $Achieve(\psi)$ *for* $\psi \in L$ *(abstract action plan),* ε *(empty plan), and if* $\pi, \pi' \in L_{plan}$, *then* $\pi; \pi'$ *(first do* π *then* π'), $\pi | \pi'$ *(choose either* π *or* π'), $\pi \parallel \pi'$ *(do* π *and* π' *simultaneously),* π^* *(repeat doing* π) *are in* L_{plan} *(composite plans). As usual we assume* $\forall \pi \in L_{plan} : \varepsilon; \pi = \pi; \varepsilon = \pi.$

An abstract action plan, $Achieve(\psi)$, can be considered as the representation of a plan which will achieve the goal ψ when it is executed. Moreover, we call a plan π a partial plan if an abstract action occurs in π. A plan in which no abstract action occurs is called a total plan. When the difference is irrelevant, we use the term *plan* to indicate either a partial or a total plan.

For $X \in \{\text{BEL}, \text{INT}, \text{DES}, \text{OBL}\}$, we have that $\phi_1, \dots, \phi_n \rightarrow_X \psi$ is a *strict rule* such that whenever the premises $\phi_1, \dots, \phi_n$ are indisputable so is the conclusion ψ. $\phi_1, \dots,$ $\phi_n \Rightarrow_{X \cup \{p\}} \psi$ is a *defeasible rule* that can be defeated by contrary evidence. A rule $\phi_1, \dots, \phi_n \rightsquigarrow_X \psi$ is a *defeater* that is used to defeat some defeasible rules by supporting evidence to the contrary.

Definition 2 (Rules). *A rule* r *consists of its* antecedent *(or body)* $A(r)$ *(*$A(r)$ *may be omitted if it is the empty set), an arrow (*$\rightarrow$ *for a strict rule,* $\Rightarrow$ *for a defeasible rule, and* $\rightsquigarrow$ *for a defeater), and its* consequent $C(r)$ *(or head). In addition the arrow is labelled either with a modal operator* $X \in \{\text{BEL}, \text{DES}, \text{INT}, \text{OBL}\}$ *or* p *(only for defeasible* rules[2]). *If the arrow is labelled with* BEL *the rule is for belief, and similarly for the other modal operators; if it is labelled with p, then the rule is a planning rule.*

- *A goal rule is a rule r, where $A(r)$ is a set of literals or modal literals, and $C(r)$ is a literal for strict rules, and an $\otimes$-expression for defeasible rules and defeaters.*
- *A planning rule is a defeasible rule of the form $\phi_1, \ldots, \phi_n : \psi \Rightarrow_p \pi$ where $\pi \in L_{plan}$, and $\phi_1, \ldots, \phi_n, \psi \in L_{goal}$ are literals or modal literals.*
- *Given a set R of rules, we denote the set of all strict rules in R by R_s, the set of strict and defeasible rules in R by R_{sd}, the set of defeasible rules in R by R_d, and the set of defeaters in R by R_{dft}. $R[q]$ denotes the set of rules in R with consequent q. For some i, $1 \leq i \leq n$, such that $c_i = q$, $R[c_i = q]$ and $r_d^X[c_i = q]$ denote, respectively, the set of rules and a defeasible rule of type X with the head $\otimes_{i=1}^n c_i$.*

The purpose of goal generation is to derive modalised literals (with the exception of rules for beliefs, which are meant to constitute the reasoning core of the system). For example, the application of $p \Rightarrow_{INT} q$ permits to infer $INTq$.

Accordingly, modalities will not occur in the consequents of rules to keep the system manageable. We also impose that action symbols may occur only in planning rules.

Definition 3 (Defeasible agent theory). *A defeasible agent theory is a structure $D = (F, R^{BEL}, R^{DES}, R^{INT}, R^{OBL}, R^p, >)$ where F is a finite set of facts, R^{BEL} is a finite set of rules for belief, R^{DES} is a finite set of rules for desire, R^{INT} is a finite set of rules for intention, R^{OBL} is a finite set of rules for obligation, R^p is a set of planning rules, and $>$, the superiority relation, is a binary relation over the set of rules.*

The *superiority relation* $>$ says when one rule may override the conclusion of another rule. *Facts* are indisputable statements.

Beside the superiority relation, which is used when we have contradictory or conflicting conclusions, we can establish a preference over and within complex conclusions by using the operator $\otimes$.

In fact, the intuitive reading of a sequence like $a \otimes b \otimes c$ is that a is preferred, but if $\neg a$ is the case, then b is preferred; if $\neg b$ is the case, given $\neg a$, then the third choice is c.

Definition 4 (Preference operator). *A preference operator $\otimes$ is a binary operator satisfying the following properties: (1) $a \otimes (b \otimes c) = (a \otimes b) \otimes c$ (associativity); (2)*

---

[2] We assume that planning rules are only defeasible. Since their intuitive role is to infer the plans that allow the achievement of the goals of their antecedents, it may seem odd that planning rules may be defeaters, e.g., rules that only block inferences. Indeed, it could be argued that a defeater $\phi_1, \ldots, \phi_n : \psi \rightsquigarrow \pi$ intuitively can be just used to prevent the conclusion of a plan π' that is is incoherent with regard to another plan which would lead to ψ. But the conceptual plausibility of this reading strongly depends on the precise account we provide for the notion of coherence of plans. Since we do not not commit ourselves to any specific interpretation of this notion, we prefer not to consider this case here. We also assumed that planning rules cannot be strict. Suppose to have two planning rules with the same antecedent a but with consequents α and β. Intuitively, we could expect that these rules generate a new rule with the antecedent a and with the consequent $\alpha|\beta$. However, we will not discuss these cases to keep the system manageable.

$\bigotimes_{i=1}^{n} a_i = (\bigotimes_{i=1}^{k-1} a_i) \otimes (\bigotimes_{i=k+1}^{n} a_i)$ *where exists j such that $a_j = a_k$ and $j < k$ (duplication and contraction on the right).*

The general idea of degree of preferences and $\otimes$ formulas are interpreted as preference formulas like in [11] and are here extended to cover all motivational components (but $\otimes$-expressions will not occur in planning rules). Let us see some examples to see the intuitive meaning of such extension:

For beliefs, rule $\neg SunShining \Rightarrow_{BEL} Raining \otimes Snowing$ says that the agent believes that it is raining, but if it is not raining then it is snowing as the sun is not shining;

For desires, rule $TimeForHoliday \Rightarrow_{DES} GoToAustralia \otimes GoToSpain$ means that, if it is time for holiday, the agent has the primary desire to go to Australia, but, if this is not the case, her desire is to go to Spain;

For intentions, rule $SunShining \Rightarrow_{INT} Jogging \otimes Walking$ says that the agent intends to do jogging if the sun is shining, but, if, for some other reasons, this is not the case, then she will have the intention to have a walk;

For obligations, rule $Order \Rightarrow_{OBL} Pay \otimes PayInterest$ says that, if the agent sends a purchase order, then she will be obliged to pay, but, in the event this is not done, she will have to pay interest.

According to the reading proposed for $\otimes$, suppose we have a rule for obligation such as $a \Rightarrow_{OBL} b \otimes c$: if a is given, it says that b is obligatory; but, if $\neg b$, then c is obligatory. A similar intuition applies to the other types of rules.

Example 1. (Running example) Suppose an agent desires an application server. She can buy two products from X or Y. She prefers X but, for working with Linux, she does not intend to order X's product. X requires a payment, within 2 days, of 300\$, otherwise X forbids to download the software. Y requires a payment of 600\$ within 1 day, or, as a second choice, a payment of 660\$. The agent does not intend to pay to Y 660\$. Agent's financial resources amount to 700\$, which are available in 4 days. We also know that the agent is a Linux user, and has a credit card and a bank account. With $X \in \{BEL, DES, INT, OBL\}$, this piece of theory is used to derive goals.

$F = \{BAccount, CCard, 700\$In4days, UseLinux, DESApplserver\}$

$R_X = \{r_1 : 700\$In4days \Rightarrow_{BEL} \neg PayY600\$1days, \ r_2 : 700\$In4days \Rightarrow_{BEL} \neg PayX300\$2days,$

$\quad r_3 : DESApplserver \Rightarrow_{INT} OrderX \otimes OrderY, \ r_4 : UseLinux \Rightarrow_{INT} \neg OrderX$

$\quad r_5 : INTOrderY \Rightarrow_{INT} \neg PayY660\$, \ r_6 : INTOrderY \Rightarrow_{OBL} PayY600\$1days \otimes PayY660\$,$

$\quad r_7 : INTOrderX \Rightarrow_{OBL} PayX300\$2days \otimes \neg DownloadApplserverX\}$

$>= \{r_4 > r_3\}$

Making an order requires to send the order. However, the plan theory does not specify how to achieve this goal with X. On the other hand, sending an order to Y requires to provide agent's data and send them. Y allows to pay either by bank transfer, which requires to provide a digital signature, bank data of Y and to specify the amount of 660\$, or by credit card, which requires to send credit card data and specify the amount. It is not possible to pay by a bank transfer *and* by credit card. The following piece of theory is considered for generating agent's plans (bold symbols denote actions):

$R^P = \{r_8 : \top : OrderX \Rightarrow_p Achieve(SendOrderX), \ r_9 : \top : OrderY \Rightarrow_p Achieve(SendOrderY)$

$\qquad r_{10} : \top : SendOrderY \Rightarrow_p \mathbf{ProvData; SendDataToY}$

$\qquad r_{11} : BAccount : PayY660\$ \Rightarrow_p Achieve(TransferY660\$) \parallel \neg Achieve(Pay660\$CCard)$

$\qquad r_{12} : CCard : PayY660\$ \Rightarrow_p \neg Achieve(TransferY660\$) \parallel Achieve(Pay660\$CCard)$

$\qquad r_{13} : \top : TransferY660\$ \Rightarrow_p \mathbf{DigitalSign; ProvBankDataY; Spec660\$}$

$\qquad r_{14} : \top : Pay660\$CCard \Rightarrow_p \mathbf{SendToYCreditCardData} \parallel \mathbf{Spec660\$}\}$

$\quad >= \{r_{11} > r_{12}\}$

3   Goal Generation: Inference with Preferences

Definition 5 (Proofs). *Given an agent theory D, a proof in D is a linear derivation, i.e, a sequence of labelled formulas of the type* $+\Delta_X q$, $-\Delta_X q$, $+\partial_X q$ *and* $-\partial_X q$, *where the proof conditions defined in the rest of this section hold.*

The meaning of the proof tags $+\Delta$, $-\Delta$, $+\partial$ and $-\partial$ is as follows: $+\Delta_X q$ means that q is provable using only facts and strict rules for X, $-\Delta_X q$ means that it has been proved that q is not definitely provable, $+\partial_X q$ that q is defeasibly provable in D and $-\partial_X q$ that q is not defeasibly provable.

We start with some terminology. As explained in the previous section, the following definition states the special status of belief rules, and that an introduction of a modal operator corresponds to being able to derive the associated literal using the rules for the modal operator.

Definition 6. *Let* $\# \in \{\Delta, \partial\}$, *and* $P = (P(1), \ldots, P(n))$ *be a proof in D. A literal q is* #-*provable in P if there is a line* $P(m)$ *of P such that either*

1. *q is a literal and* $P(m) = +\#_{\mathrm{BEL}} q$ *or*
2. *q is a modal literal* $X p$ *and* $P(m) = +\#_X p$ *or*
3. *q is a modal literal* $\neg X p$ *and* $P(m) = -\#_X p$.

A literal q is #-*rejected in P if there is a line* $P(m)$ *of P such that either*

1. *q is a literal and* $P(m) = -\#_{\mathrm{BEL}} q$ *or*
2. *q is a modal literal* $X p$ *and* $P(m) = -\#_X p$ *or*
3. *q is a modal literal* $\neg X p$ *and* $P(m) = +\#_X p$.

The first type of tagged literals, denoted by Δ_X, correspond to strict rules. The definition of Δ_X describes just forward chaining of strict rules:

$+\Delta_X$: If $P(i+1) = +\Delta_X q$ then $-\Delta_X$: If $P(i+1) = -\Delta_X q$ then
(1) $q \in F$ or   (1) $q \notin F$ and
(2) $\exists r \in R_s^X[q] \ \forall a \in A(r) \ a$ is Δ-provable or   (2) $\forall r \in R_s^X[q] \ \exists a \in A(r) : a$ is Δ-rejected and
(3) $\exists r \in R_s^{\mathrm{BEL}}[q] \ \forall a \in A(r) \ Xa$ is Δ-provable.   (3) $\forall r \in R_s^{\mathrm{BEL}}[q] \ \exists a \in A(r) \ Xa$ is Δ-rejected.

For a literal q to be definitely provable we need to find a strict rule with head q, whose antecedents have all been definitely proved previously. And to establish that q cannot be proven definitely we must establish that for every strict rule with head q there is at least one of antecedent which has been shown to be non-provable. Condition (3) says that a belief rule can be used as a rule for a different modal operator in case all literals in the body of the rules are modalised with the modal operator we want to prove. Thus, for example, given the rule $p, q \rightarrow_{\text{BEL}} s$, we can derive $+\Delta_Y s$ if we have $+\Delta_Y p$ and $+\Delta_Y q$.

Conditions for ∂_X are more complicated since we have to consider $\otimes$-expressions. We define when a rule is applicable or discarded. A rule for a belief is applicable if all the literals in the antecedent of the rule are provable with the appropriate modalities, while the rule is discarded if at least one the literals in the antecedent is not provable. For the other types of rules we have to take complex derivations into account called conversions [12]. In this paper we say there is a conversion from X to Y if a X rule can also be used as a Y rule. We have thus to determine conditions under which a rule for X can be used to directly derive a literal q modalised by Y. Roughly, the condition is that all the antecedents a of the rule are such that $+\partial_Y a$. We represent all allowed conversions by a conversion relation c (see also Section 5).

Definition 7. *Let a conversion relation c be a binary relation between* $\{\text{BEL}, \text{INT}, \text{DES}, \text{OBL}\}$, *such that $c(X, Y)$ stands for the conversion of X rules into Y rules.*

- *A rule r in R^{BEL} is applicable iff $\forall a \in A(r)$, $+\partial_{\text{BEL}} a \in P(1..n)$ and $\forall X a \in A(r)$, where X is a modal operator, $+\partial_X a \in P(1..n)$.*
- *A rule $r \in R_{sd}[c_i = q]$ is applicable in the condition for $\pm\partial_X$ iff*

  1. $r \in R^X$ and $\forall a \in A(r)$, $+\partial a \in P(1..n)$ and $\forall Y a \in A(r)$ $+\partial_Y a \in P(1..n)$, or
  2. $r \in R^Y$ and $\forall a \in A(r)$, $+\partial_X a \in P(1..n)$.

- *A rule r is discarded if we prove either $-\partial_{\text{BEL}} a$ or $-\partial_X a$ for some $a \in A(r)$.*

Example 2. Rule $a, \text{INT} b \Rightarrow_{\text{BEL}} c$ is applicable if we can prove $+\partial_{\text{BEL}} a$ and $+\partial_{\text{INT}} b$.

Remark 1. The notion of conversion is not strange. In many formalisms we can convert from one type of conclusion into a different one. Take for example the right weakening rule of non-monotonic consequence relations, where it is possible to combine non-monotonic consequence with classical consequences: $B \vdash C$ and $A \hspace{0.5mm}\vert\hspace{-1mm}\sim B$ imply $A \hspace{0.5mm}\vert\hspace{-1mm}\sim C$ [13]. Here, conversions will simply allow to obtain conclusions modalised by a certain X through the application of rules which are not modalised by X.

Example 3. If we have a type of agent that allows a deontic rule to be converted into a rule for intention, $c(\text{OBL}, \text{INT})$, then the definition of applicable in the condition for $\pm\partial_{\text{INT}}$ is as follows: a rule $r \in R_{sd}[c_i = q]$ is applicable iff (1) $r \in R^{\text{INT}}$ and $\forall a \in A(r)$, $+\partial a \in P(1..n)$ and $\forall X a \in A(r)$, $+\partial_X a \in P(1..n)$, (2) or $r \in R^O$ and $\forall a \in A(r)$, $+\partial_{\text{INT}} a \in P(1..n)$. In this second case, for example, given the rule $p, q \Rightarrow_{\text{OBL}} s$, we can derive $+\partial_{\text{INT}} s$ if we have $+\partial_{\text{INT}} p$ and $+\partial_{\text{INT}} q$.

Proof conditions for $\pm\partial_X$ are thus as follows:

$+\partial_X$: If $P(n+1) = +\partial_X q$ then
(1) $+\Delta_X q \in P(1..n)$ or
    (2.1) $-\Delta_X {\sim} q \in P(1..n)$ and
    (2.2) $\exists r \in R_{sd}[c_i = q]$ such that r is applicable, and $\forall i' < i, -\partial_{BEL} c_{i'} \in P(1..n)$; and
    (2.3) $\forall s \in R[c_j = {\sim} q]$, either s is discarded, or $\exists j' < j$ such that $+\partial_X c_{j'} \in P(1..n)$, or
    (2.3.1) $\exists t \in R[c_k = q]$ s.t. r is applicable and
             $\forall k' < k, -\partial_{BEL} c_{k'} \in P(1..n)$ and $t > s$

$-\partial_X$: If $P(n+1) = -\partial_X q$ then
(1) $-\Delta_X q \in P(1..n)$) and either
    (2.1) $+\Delta_X {\sim} q \in P(1..n)$ or
    (2.2) $\forall r \in R_{sd}[c_i = q]$, either r is discarded or $\exists i' < i$ such that $+\partial_{BEL} c_{i'} \in P(1..n)$, or
    (2.3) $\exists s \in R[c_j = {\sim} q]$, such that s is applicable and $\forall j' < j, -\partial_X c_{j'} \in P(1..n)$ and
    (2.3.1) $\forall t \in R[c_k = q]$ either t is discarded, or
             $\exists k' < k$ such that $+\partial_{BEL} c_{k'} \in P(1..n)$ or $t \not> s$

For defeasible rules we deal with $\otimes$ formulas. To show that q is provable defeasibly we have two choices: (1) We show that q is already definitely provable; or (2) we need to argue using the defeasible part of a theory D. For this second case, three (sub)conditions must be satisfied. First, we require that there must be a strict or defeasible rule for q which can be applied (2.1). Second, we need to consider possible reasoning chains in support of ${\sim} q$, and show that ${\sim} q$ is not definitely provable (2.2). Third, we must consider the set of all rules which are not known to be inapplicable and which permit to get ${\sim} q$ (2.3). Essentially each such a rule s attacks the conclusion q. For q to be provable, s must be counterattacked by a rule t for q with the following properties: (i) t must be applicable, and (ii) t must be stronger than s. Thus each attack on the conclusion q must be counterattacked by a stronger rule. In other words, r and the rules t form a team (for q) that defeats the rules s. $-\partial_X q$ is defined in an analogous manner.

Goals are obtained as $+\partial_G$ or $+\Delta_G$, $G \in \{DES, INT, OBL\}$. As it was said, provability for beliefs does not directly generate goals.

Example 4 (Running example; continued). Let us assume that the agent is realistic, namely that beliefs override all motivational components (see Section 5). Below is the set C of all conclusions we get using the rules in R^X:

$$C = \{\neg PayY600\$1days, \ \neg PayX300\$2days, \ INT\,OrderY,$$
$$INT\neg OrderX, \ INT\neg PayY660\$\}$$

Since the agent desires an application server, from r_3, $r_4, r_4 > r_3$ and $\otimes$-elimination, we have $+\partial_{INT} OrderY$. This makes r_6 and r_5 applicable, while r_7 is not. However, the agent will have 700 \$ available within 4 days and so, since the agent is realistic, from r_1 we get $+\partial_{BEL} \neg PayY600\$1days$, which is a violation of the primary obligation in r_6. We would obtain $+\partial_{OBL} PayY660\$$, but this not the case since the theory does not provide criteria for resolving the conflict between this conclusion and that of r_5.

4   Plan Generation

A planning rule $\phi_1, \ldots, \phi_n : \psi \Rightarrow_p \pi$ may be intuitively read as a rule that allows for the derivation of a plan π that permits to achieve a single goal ψ, given the beliefs $\phi_1, \ldots, \phi_n$. In other words, such a rule can be applied if $\phi_1, \ldots, \phi_n$ are believed, i.e. if they are derivable from the agent's beliefs, and ψ should be achieved, i.e. if ψ is derivable from the agent's goals. This implies that we will have various conclusions for goal formulae and thus the following tagged literals: $+\Delta_G p, -\Delta_G p, +\partial_G p, -\partial_G p$ where $G \in \{\text{DES}, \text{INT}, \text{OBL}\}$. Similar to the definition of derivations of tagged literals, we define the notion of provability of plans. In the following, we use $A^B(r)$ to denote the belief conditions of the planning rule r, and $A^G(r)$ to denote its goal condition. For example, for the planning rule $r = \phi : \psi \Rightarrow_p \pi$, we have $\phi \in A^B(r)$ and $A^G(r) = \psi$. A plan π is derivable if no plan π' is derivable which is incoherent with π. The notion of coherence of plans is the counterpart of the notion of consistency of logical formulae which is used for the provability of literals. The notion of coherence can be defined, for example, in terms of resource conflicts or possibility of plan execution. We will not enter here into a detailed discussion of this issue. However, we can formulate a very minimal condition for compatible plans in terms of the belief and goal conditions of rules that generate them. In particular, two plans are compatible iff the belief and goal conditions of the rules applied to their derivations are consistent. This fact is already embedded in our framework because the goal generation phase described in this paper provides criteria for deriving consistent goals. The only exceptions are when facts (not derived goals) are inconsistent or, we will see in Section 5, when the agent type adopted permits to obtain, for example, that $+\partial_{\text{OBL}} a$ and $+\partial_{\text{INT}} \neg a$. In these cases, the superiority relation that may apply specifically to planning rules can be decisive. In fact, given the possibility to obtain $+\partial_{\text{OBL}} a$ and $+\partial_{\text{INT}} \neg a$, two planning rules $\top : a \Rightarrow_p \pi$ and $\top : \neg a \Rightarrow_p \pi'$ turn out to be both applicable. However, although for certain agent types $+\partial_{\text{OBL}} a$ and $+\partial_{\text{INT}} \neg a$ do not correspond to a conflict (OBLa and INT$\neg a$ are not necessarily in contradiction), it may be argued that the plans leading to achieve a and $\neg a$ are incoherent (intuitively incompatible). Notice also that the plan language introduced in Section 2 does not admit the negation of action symbols. So, in theory, logical inconsistency is not relevant as regards the derivation of plans (the consequents of planning rules). However, we may also have partial plans that include special abstract actions to achieve goals. In this case, logical consistency of derived plans and the corresponding conflict resolution may play a role as in the phase of goal generation.

Let us see first the basic proof conditions for the generation of total plans, i.e., plans in which no abstract actions occur.

$+\Pi$: If $P(i+1) = +\Pi\pi$ then
(1) $\exists r \in R^p[\pi]$ such that
   (1.1) $\phi_1, \ldots, \phi_n \in A^B(r)$ and $A^G(r) = \psi$, and
   (1.2) $\forall k, 1 \leq k \leq n, +\partial_{\text{BEL}}\phi_k \in P(1..i)$ and $+\partial_G \psi \in P(1..i)$, and
(2) $\forall s \in R^p[\pi']$ such that incoherent(π, π') either
   (2.1) $\exists \phi' \in A^B(s) : -\partial_{\text{BEL}}\phi' \in P(1..i)$ or
   (2.2) $\psi' \in A^G(s) : -\partial_G \psi' \in P(1..i)$ or
   (2.3) $\exists t \in R^p[\pi]$ such that $t > s$ and $\forall \phi'' \in A^B(t) : +\partial_{\text{BEL}}\phi'' \in P(1..i)$ and
       $\psi'' \in A^G(t) : +\partial_G \psi'' \in P(1..i)$.

Thus, a total plan is defeasibly derivable if the conditions (1) and (2) hold. Condition (1) states that a total plan π is defeasibly derivable at derivation step $P(i+1)$ if there exists a planning rule with π as its consequent such that its belief and goal conditions are defeasibly provable at derivations $P(1..i)$. Condition (2) states that if there exists a planning rule s such that its consequent is the total plan π' which is incoherent with plan π, then either the belief and goal conditions of rule s are not defeasibly derivable or there exists a preferred planning rule t with plan π as its consequent for which its beliefs and goals are defeasibly derivable. Note that we assume that a planning rule is applicable if its belief and goal conditions are defeasibly provable. We may also consider the case where the belief and goal conditions are definitely provable.

Analogously, we define the non-provability of total plans $-\Pi\pi$ as follows:

$-\Pi$: If $P(i+1) = -\Pi\pi$ then
(1) $\forall r \in R^p[\pi]$ either
   (1.1) $\exists\phi \in A^B(r)$ and $-\partial_{\text{BEL}}\phi \in P(1..i)$ or
   (1.2) $A^G(r) = \psi$ and $-\partial_G\psi \in P(1..i)$, or
(2) $\exists s \in R^p[\pi']$ such that incoherent(π,π') and
   (2.1) $\forall\phi' \in A^B(s) : +\partial_{\text{BEL}}\phi' \in P(1..i)$ and
   (2.2) $\psi' \in A^G(s) : +\partial_G\psi' \in P(1..i)$ and
   (2.3) $\forall t \in R^p[\pi]$ either $t \not\succ s$ or $\exists\phi'' \in A^B(t) : -\partial_{\text{BEL}}\phi'' \in P(1..i)$ or
      $\psi'' \in A^G(t) : -\partial_G\psi'' \in P(1..i)$.

Thus, a total plan is not defeasibly provable if one of the conditions (1) or (2) holds. Condition (1) states that a total plan π is not defeasibly derivable at derivation step $P(i+1)$ if the belief or goal conditions of all planning rules with π as its consequent are not defeasibly provable at derivations $P(1..i)$. Condition (2) states that if there exists a planning rule (s) such that its consequent is the total plan π' which is incoherent with plan π, then its belief and goal conditions are defeasibly derivable and, moreover, for all more preferred planning rules t with the total plan π as its consequent it is the case that their beliefs or goals are not defeasibly derivable.

This definition of plan provability should be modified to allow the derivation of plans that are obtained from the application of planning rules to refine an existing partial plan. In order to define this notion of plan provability, we first assume the function $occurs(\psi,\pi)$, which returns true if the abstract action $Achieve(\psi)$ occurs in the partial plan π, and the function $sub(\psi,\pi',\pi'')$, which returns a plan by substituting the abstract action $Achieve(\psi)$ in π' with plan π''. For example, consider the partial plan $\pi = \alpha;Achieve(\psi);\beta$. Then, $occur(\psi,\pi) = true$ and $sub(\psi,\pi,\gamma|\delta) = \alpha;(\gamma|\delta);\beta$. The definition of defeasible provability of plans which involve abstract actions, indicated by $+\Omega\pi$, can be defined as follows:

$+\Omega$: If $P(i+1) = +\Omega\pi$ then either
(1) $+\Pi\pi \in P(1..i)$, or
(2) $+\Omega\pi' \in P(1..i)$ such that
   (2.1) $\exists r \in R^p[\pi'']$ and
   (2.2) $\phi_1,\ldots,\phi_n \in A^B(r)$ and $A^G(r) = \psi$, and
   (2.3) $\forall k, 1 \leq k \leq n, +\partial_{\text{BEL}}\phi_k \in P(1..i)$ and $+\partial_G\psi \in P(1..i)$ and
   (2.4) $occurs(\psi,\pi')$ and $sub(\psi,\pi',\pi'') = \pi$.

Thus, a plan is defeasibly provable if one of the conditions (1) or (2) holds. Condition (1) states that a plan is provable if it is provable directly by applying planning rules. Condition (2) states that a plan is derivable if there exists a partial plan which can be refined by applying a rule.

Analogously, for plans that involve abstract actions we define the non-provability of plans $-\Omega\pi$ as follows:

$-\Omega$: If $P(i+1) = -\Omega\pi$ then
(1) $-\Pi\pi \in P(1..i)$, and
(2) $+\Omega\pi' \in P(1..i)$ such that
   (2.1) $occurs(\psi, \pi')$ and $sub(\psi, \pi', \pi'') = \pi$ and
   (2.2) $\forall r \in R^p[\pi'']$:
      (2.2.1) $\phi_1, \ldots, \phi_n \in A^B(r)$ and $\exists k, 1 \le k \le n, -\partial_{BEL}\phi_k \in P(1..i)$ or
      (2.2.2) $A^G(r) = \psi$ and $-\partial_G\psi \in P(1..i)$.

Thus, a plan is not defeasibly provable if the conditions (1) or (2) hold. Condition (1) states that a plan is not provable if it is not directly provable and condition (2) states that the plan is not provable through applications of planning rules to partial plans.

Example 5 (Running example; continued). Given the conclusions derived in Section 3, let us consider the only positive goal, namely $+\partial_{INT}OrderY$. However, assume, as we will do in Example 6, to have also $+\partial_{OBL}PayY660\$$ and $+\partial_{INT}PayY660\$$. These goals make planning rules r_9, r_{11} and r_{12} applicable, whereas $INT\neg OrderX$ makes r_8 non-applicable. r_9 includes an abstract plan to be specified. This is possible via r_{10}. On the other hand, the agent has to pay 660$ to Y, but has to choose between two incompatible plans: paying using the credit card of by bank transfer. Here r_{11} and r_{12} provide each simultaneous partial plans that dictate to make a bank transfer and not paying by credit card or the opposite. Since $r_{11} > r_{12}$, the agent prefers the latter option. The derived total plans are then

$$\{\textbf{ProvData}; \textbf{SendDataToY}, \textbf{DigitalSign}; \textbf{ProvBankDataY}; \textbf{Spec660\$}\}$$

Finer criteria for dealing with provability in plans may be introduced when finer criteria are used in the goal generation. If the agent is realistic and 1-stable, as we will see in Section 5, then $-\partial_{INT}OrderY$; thus we cannot derive, too, any plan.

5   Conflict Resolution and Agent Types

At which phase do agent types intervene in the treatment of conflicts, and how can they be generalised to incorporate $\otimes$ formulas? Classically, agent types are characterised by stating conflict resolution types in terms of orders of overruling between rules [5, 12]. For example, an agent is *realistic* when rules for beliefs override all other components; she is *social* when obligations are stronger than the other motivational components with the exception of beliefs. Agent types can be characterised by stating that, for any types of rules X and Y, for every r and r' such that $r \in R^X[c_i = q]$ and $r' \in R^Y[d_i = \sim q]$, we have that $r > r'$.

Let us assume to work with realistic agents, namely, with agents for which, for every r and r', $r \in R^{BEL}[c_i = q]$ and $r' \in R^Y[d_i = \sim q]$, $Y \in \{DES, INT, OBL\}$ we have that $r > r'$. Then let us see the agent types that can be identified in the framework we have defined so far. Table 1 shows all possible cases and, for each kind of rule, indicates all attacks on it. It should be read as follows. Each of the three main columns identifies a possible kind of conflict between two types X, Y of applicable rules that would permit to infer the literals p and $\sim p$ labelled by X and Y respectively. The first two sub-columns in each main column indicate whether both literals are derived (i.e., there is no real conflict, which is indeed a logical possibility since we are dealing with modalities which do not enjoy reflexivity), or whether we have conflict where one rule prevails over the other, or where the two rules defeat each other. Finally, the third sub-column defines the agent type for which each conflict-detection and -resolution policy is appropriate. Since we have to consider three kinds of rules for generating goals, we have to analyse twelve combinations. (To save space, in Table 1 "s-" is an abbreviation for "strongly-"; "indep." abbreviates "independent".)

Table 1. Agent Types: Basic Attacks

$r_d^{OBL}[c_i = p]/ r_d^{INT}[c_j = \sim p]$			$r_d^{OBL}[c_i = p]/ r_d^{DES}[c_j = \sim p]$			$r_d^{INT}[c_i = p]/ r_d^{DES}[c_j = \sim p]$		
$+\partial_{OBL}p$	$+\partial_{INT}\sim p$	s-indep.	$+\partial_{OBL}p$	$+\partial_{DES}\sim p$	indep.	$+\partial_{INT}p$	$+\partial_{DES}\sim p$	unstable
$+\partial_{OBL}p$	$-\partial_{INT}\sim p$	s-social	$+\partial_{OBL}p$	$-\partial_{DES}\sim p$	social	$+\partial_{INT}p$	$-\partial_{DES}p$	stable
$-\partial_{OBL}p$	$+\partial_{INT}\sim p$	s-deviant	$-\partial_{OBL}p$	$+\partial_{DES}\sim p$	deviant	$-\partial_{INT}p$	$+\partial_{DES}\sim p$	selfish
$-\partial_{OBL}p$	$-\partial_{INT}\sim p$	s-pragmatic	$-\partial_{OBL}p$	$-\partial_{DES}\sim p$	pragmatic	$-\partial_{INT}p$	$-\partial_{DES}\sim p$	slothful

Independent and strongly-independent agents are free respectively to adopt desires and intentions in conflict with obligations. As expected, for social and strongly-social agents obligations override desires and intention. For pragmatic and strongly-pragmatic, no derivation is possible and so the agent's generation of goals is open to any other course of action other than those specified in the rules considered. Stable and selfish agents are those for which, respectively, intentions override desires or the opposite. Unstable agents are free to adopt desires in conflict with intentions, while, for slothful agents, conflicting desires and intentions override each other.

Table 1 does not cover all possible types of agent. In fact, the table focuses on possible attacks that involve only two rules; in addition we will assume that belief rules are always stronger than intentions, desires and obligations. This is motivated by the intuition that belief rules describe specification of the environment where the agent is situated. Table 2 completes the scenario and provides all possible combinations when we deal with three rules, in particular, we consider all possible relationships between obligation rules on one side and intention and desire rules on the other side. For example we consider agent types where an obligation rule can be defeated by an intention rule and, at the same time, it can defeat a desire rule (social-strongly social). This allows for the specification of new agent types based on the basic types defined in Table 1.

However, this taxonomy can be enriched thanks to the role that may be played by $\otimes$-expressions. In fact, in traditional rules-based systems, conflict-detection returns a boolean: either there is a conflict, or there is not. For $\otimes$ constructs, it seems that we may need a finer distinction. For example, we can have degrees of violation. Of course, if we define a conflict detection function that returns no longer booleans but a more complex structure (e.g., an integer that returns 0 if no violation, 1 if violation of primary

Table 2. Agent Types: Other Attacks

$r_d^{OBL}[c_i = p]$	$/r_d^{INT}[c_j = \sim p]$	$/r_d^{DES}[c_k = \sim p]$	
$+\partial_{OBL}p$	$+\partial_{INT}\sim p$	$+\partial_{DES}\sim p$	hyper-independent
$+\partial_{OBL}p$	$+\partial_{INT}\sim p$	$-\partial_{DES}\sim p$	social-strongly-independent
$+\partial_{OBL}p$	$-\partial_{INT}\sim p$	$+\partial_{DES}\sim p$	social-independent
$+\partial_{OBL}p$	$-\partial_{INT}\sim p$	$-\partial_{DES}\sim p$	hyper-social
$-\partial_{OBL}p$	$+\partial_{INT}\sim p$	$+\partial_{DES}\sim p$	hyper-deviant
$-\partial_{OBL}p$	$+\partial_{INT}\sim p$	$-\partial_{DES}\sim p$	social-strongly-deviant
$-\partial_{OBL}p$	$-\partial_{INT}\sim p$	$+\partial_{DES}\sim p$	social-deviant
$-\partial_{OBL}p$	$-\partial_{INT}\sim p$	$-\partial_{DES}\sim p$	hyper-pragmatic

obligation, 2 if violation of secondary obligation), then we have to write conflict resolution methods which can somehow deal with this. Section 3 provides criteria to solve conflict between rules including $\otimes$ constructions. In this perspective, the role of $\otimes$ can be made fruitful. In particular, the introduction of $\otimes$ is crucial if we want to impose some constraints on the number of violations in deriving a goals. Goal generation can be constrained, so that provability of a goal g is permitted only if getting g does not require more than m violations for each rule with g in the head:

Definition 8 (Violation constraint on goals). *Let m and X be an integer and a type of rule, respectively. A theory D will be m-X-constrained iff, given the definition of $+\partial$, for all literals q, $+\partial_X q$ iff (1) $i' \leq m$; and (2) if $1 \leq j' \leq j$ and $s \in R^X$, then $j' \leq m$; and (3) $k' \leq m$. Otherwise, $-\partial_X q$.*

Similar intuitions are applicable to directly constraint agent types, thus introducing graded agent types: e.g., for any two rules $r_1 : r_d^{OBL}[c_i = p]$ and $r_2 : r_d^{DES}[c_j = \sim p]$ we may reframe the type "social" of Table 1 stating that an m-social agent is such that

$$+\partial_{OBL}p/-\partial_{DES}\sim p \text{ iff } i \leq m$$

Thus the idea of agent type can also be generalised taking into account $\otimes$ constructs.

It is possible to integrate the above classifications by referring to the notion of conversion [12]. Conversions do not have a direct relation with conflict resolution because they simply affect the condition of applicability of rules. However, they indeed contribute to define the cognitive profile of agents because they allow to obtain conclusions modalised by a certain X through the application of rules which are not modalised by X. According to this view, for example, we may have agent types for which, given $p \Rightarrow_{OBL} q$ and $+\partial_{INT}p$ we can obtain $+\partial_{INT}q$. Of course, this is possible only if we assume a kind of norm regimentation, by which we impose that all agents intend what is prescribed by deontic rules. This conversion, in particular, seems appropriate to characterize some kinds of social agent. Other conversions, which, on the contrary, should hold for all realistic agents are, for example, those that permit to obtain $+\partial_X q$, $X \in \{DES, INT, OBL\}$, from $p \Rightarrow_{BEL} q$ and $+\partial_X p$ [12]. Table 3 shows the conversions and specify the agent types with respect to which each conversion seems to be appropriate. We assume to work at least with realistic agents. Since conversions are used only indirectly for conflict resolution but are conceptually decisive for characterising agents,

Table 3. Conversions

$c(\text{BEL},\text{OBL})$	realistic	$c(\text{BEL},\text{INT})$	realistic	$c(\text{BEL},\text{DES})$	realistic
$c(\text{OBL},\text{DES})$	c-social	$c(\text{OBL},\text{INT})$	c-strongly-social	$c(\text{DES},\text{OBL})$	c-deviant
$c(\text{INT},\text{DES})$	c-stable	$c(\text{DES},\text{INT})$	c-selfish	$c(\text{INT},\text{OBL})$	c-strongly-deviant

they provide criteria to specify new agent types. Not all conversion types make sense and so we consider only 9 cases out of 12 possible combinations.

At which phase do agent types intervene in the treatment of conflicts? Classic agent types, violation constraints and conversions play their role mainly in the goal generation phase, because all these features mainly contribute to characterize the motivational profile of the agent. Notice, however, that we could also introduce $\otimes$ in plans. With plans, in fact, we would need as well a finer distinction than just assuming that either two plans conflict or they do not; for example, in [8] no finer distinction was made. In particular, $\otimes$ in planning rules could express non-deterministic effects of actions. However, we prefer here not to do this, to keep the system manageable. This does not mean that we cannot introduce finer criteria for dealing with provability in plans, but this can be simply made just referring to derivation of the goals that occur, as results, in the planning rules. As we have seen, a planning rule $\phi_1, \ldots, \phi_n : \psi \Rightarrow_p \pi$ permits to infer plan π, a plan that is meant to produce the goal ψ given beliefs $\phi_1, \ldots, \phi_n$. Plan π is conceptually the condition for obtaining ψ. Thus, Definition 8 will allow the agent to obtain π only if ψ or $\phi_1, \ldots, \phi_n$ do not require more than m violations for each X rule.

Example 6 (Running example; continued). Suppose the agent be strongly-social and c-strongly-social, namely, that obligations override intentions and that we accept conversion $c(\text{OBL}, \text{INT})$. So, we obtain the following additional goals:

$$\{\text{OBL}PayY660\$, \text{INT}PayY660\$\}$$

Since r_6 is now stronger than r_5, we obtain $\text{OBL}PayY660\$$, while the second goal is derived via r_6 and conversion $c(\text{OBL}, \text{INT})$. This second means that we drop the previous conclusion obtained in Example 4, i.e. that the agent intends the opposite.

Assume now that the theory is also 0-X-constrained, for $X \in \{\text{INT}, \text{OBL}\}$. This means that no violation is permitted. If so, no new intention or obligation can be derived.

Finally, suppose the agent is realistic and 1-stable. Let us add to R^X the rule r' : $a \Rightarrow_{\text{DES}} \neg OrderY$, and to F the fact a. Thus we would obtain $\text{DES}\neg OrderY$, which is in conflict with the conclusion that can be obtained from r_3. Indeed this is the case since an intention overrides a conflicting desire only if the former is a primary intention.

6   Conclusions

In this paper we extend DL with preferences and actions. We show how to detect and resolve conflicts using preferences and actions. Rule based languages follow the tradition of production rules in knowledge based systems and logic programming. The extension of production rules is based on the use of rule based systems in cognitive attitudes in practical reasoning. Indeed, the new issue is the interaction among mental attitudes. Examples are Thomason's BDP, programming languages based on the BOID architecture, 3APL, etc. In general, conditional approaches and preference based approaches have been traditionally defined in terms of each other. For example, "if A then B" has been defined as "A and B is preferred to A without B", and "A is preferred to B" has been defined as "if A or B, then A". However, it may be unnatural to define preferences in terms of conditionals, and it is more natural to define them directly. Moreover, special preference-based formalisms may be more efficient, such as CP nets. Finally, the kind of preferences which can be expressed in terms of conditionals is only limited to special kinds. This explains why comparative notions are now a major topic of concern in artificial intelligence and practical reasoning.

Let us summarise some requirements for programming cognitive agents. First, the interaction among mental attitudes needs fine-grained mechanisms to represent and resolve conflicts among rules. Second, the programming language has to distinguish between an abstract language that deals with interaction among mental attitudes, called a deliberation language, and low level procedures to deal with definitions of conflicts based on temporal and causal reasoning, resources, scheduling, and the like. Third, ways to resolve conflicts must be described abstractly. Fourth, patterns of ways to deal with conflicts and more generally patterns of agent behaviour must be described. Such patterns have been called agent types. Fifth, the interaction between mental attitudes and semantics of MAS communication—as defined e.g. by FIPA—should be realised.

In this paper we assumed that we can use the same deliberation language with preferences as has been used by Dastani and van der Torre [8]. Moreover, we did not address the issue of MAS communication, because the mental attitudes approach to communication has been attacked recently by social commitment approaches; a careful reconsideration of this issue is beyond the scope of this paper [17] and is left for future research.

References

1. G. Antoniou, D. Billington, G. Governatori, and M.J. Maher. A flexible framework for defeasible logics. In *Proc. AAAI-2000*. AAAI/MIT Press, 2000.
2. N. Bassiliades, G. Antoniou, and I. Vlahavas. DR-DEVICE: A defeasible logic system for the Semantic Web. In *Proc. PPSWR 2004*. Springer, 2004.
3. M. Bratman, D. Israel, and M. Pollack. Plans and resource-bounded practical reasoning. *Computational Intelligence*, 1988.
4. F.M.T. Brazier, B. Dunin Keplicz, N. Jennings, and J. Treur. Desire: Modelling multi-agent systems in a compositional formal framework. *Int. J. Coop. Inf. Syst.*, 1997.
5. J. Broersen, M. Dastani, J. Hulstijn, and L. van der Torre. Goal generation in the BOID architecture. *Cog. Sc. Quart.*, 2002.
6. M. Dastani, F. de Boer, F. Dignum, and J.-J. Meyer. Programming agent deliberation. In *Proc. AAMAS'03*. 2003.
7. M. Dastani, G. Governatori, A. Rotolo, and L. van der Torre. Preferences of agents in defeasible logic. In *Proc. AI05*. Springer, 2005.
8. M. Dastani and L.W.N. van der Torre. Programming BOID-plan agents: Deliberating about conflicts among defeasible mental attitudes and plans. In *Proc. AAMAS 2004*. ACM, 2004.
9. M. Dastani, B. van Riemsdijk, F. Dignum, and J.-J. Meyer. A programming language for cognitive agents: Goal directed 3APL. In *Proc. ProMAS'03*. 2003.

10. G. Governatori. Representing business contracts in RuleML. *Int. J. Coop. Inf. Syst.*, 2005.
11. G. Governatori and A. Rotolo. A Gentzen system for reasoning with contrary-to-duty obligations. In *Proc. Δeon'02*. Imperial College, 2002.
12. G. Governatori and A. Rotolo. Defeasible logic: Agency, intention and obligation. In *Proc. Δeon'04*. Springer, 2004.
13. S. Kraus, D. Lehmann, and M. Magidor. Nonmonotonic reasoning, preferential models and cumulative logics. *Artificial Intelligence*, 1990.
14. M.J. Maher, A. Rock, G. Antoniou, D. Billignton, and T. Miller. Efficient defeasible reasoning systems. *Int. J. Art. Int. Tools*, 2001.
15. J. Pitt, editor. *Open Agent Societies*. Wiley, Chichester, 2004.
16. A. Rao and M. Georgeff. Modelling rational agents within a BDI-architecture. In *KR'91*. Morgan Kaufmann, 1991.
17. M.P. Singh. A social semantics for agent communication languages. In *Issues in Agent Communication*. Springer, 2000.

The Relationship Between Reasoning About Privacy and Default Logics

Jürgen Dix[1,*], Wolfgang Faber[2,**], and V.S. Subrahmanian[3]

[1] Institut für Informatik,
TU Clausthal, 38678 Clausthal, Germany
dix@tu-clausthal.de
[2] Department of Mathematics,
University of Calabria, 87030 Rende (CS), Italy
wf@wfaber.com
[3] Department of Computer Science,
University of Maryland, College Park, MD 20742
vs@cs.umd.edu

Abstract. There is now an incredible wealth of data about individuals, businesses and organisations. This data is freely available over the Internet to almost anyone willing to pay for it, independently of whether they are identity thieves or credit card scam artists or legitimate users. This has led to a growing need for privacy. In this paper, we first present a simple logical model of privacy. We then show that the problem of privacy may be reduced to that of brave reasoning in default logic theories, thus reducing this important problem to a well understood reasoning paradigm. By leveraging this reduction, we are able to develop an efficient privacy preservation algorithm and a set of complexity results for privacy preservation. Efficient systems based on answer set programming are available to implement our algorithm.

1 Introduction

The privacy of individuals is under attack as never before. In the wake of recent terrorist events, various government agencies worldwide are seeking to acquire all kinds of private information about individuals in an effort to preserve national security. Another area where potential privacy disasters loom is in the area of medical data—many hospitals post some seemingly innocuous data on web sites (e.g. about births) but it is often possible to infer private health information about individuals. A third need for privacy mechanisms is because of poor access control and network security mechanisms that may allow outsiders to get into supposedly secure networks. In this case, there is a need to maintain privacy of data even from insiders (both genuine insiders and hackers).

---

* Partially funded by the Information Society Technologies programme of the European Commission, Future and Emerging Technologies under the IST-2001-37004 WASP project.
** Funded by an APART grant of the Austrian Academy of Sciences.

G. Sutcliffe and A. Voronkov (Eds.): LPAR 2005, LNAI 3835, pp. 637–650, 2005.

Most databases have only weak privacy mechanisms—these mechanisms by and large boil down to saying certain columns of the database are hidden from certain types of users. However, the reality of life is that many users can infer information designated private by asking queries that do not involve private information and then making common sense inferences from the answers to infer private information.

The primary goal of this paper is to show that there is a close connection between the problem of providing privacy preserving answers to queries and the problem of computing extensions of certain kinds of default theories. In particular, we define a linear time and linear space transformation **trans** of the privacy preservation problem to the problem of computing extensions of default logic theories. We prove that there is a one-to-one correspondence between privacy preserving answers and the extensions of the default logic theory (restricted to the query) obtained by translating the privacy preservation problem into default logic via **trans**. Leveraging this translation, we are able to derive a suite of results on the complexity of maintaining privacy. Finally, we present an algorithm to check for privacy.

2   The Privacy Preservation Problem (P3)

In this section, we provide a simple formulation of the privacy preservation problem (**P3** for short).

We start by assuming the existence of some finite set $\mathcal{U}$ of users. Each member of $\mathcal{U}$ is a string denoting a userid.

We assume the existence of some finite set of constant symbols, function symbols and predicate symbols as well as an enumerable set of variables $x_1, x_2, \ldots$. As usual, a term is inductively defined as follows: (i) Each constant is a term, (ii) Each variable is a term, and (iii) if f is an n-ary predicate symbol and $t_1, \ldots, t_n$ are terms, then $f(t_1, \ldots, t_n)$ is a term. A *ground term* is any term that contains no variable symbols. Similarly, if p is an n-ary predicate symbol and $t_1, \ldots, t_n$ are terms, then $p(t_1, \ldots, t_n)$ is an atom. A *ground atom* is any atom that contains no variable symbols. A well formed formula (wff) is inductively defined as follows. (i) Every atom is a wff, (ii) If F, G are wffs then so are $(F \wedge G), (F \vee G)$ and $\neg F$. As usual, we use $F \rightarrow G$ as an abbreviation for $\neg F \vee G$. WFF denotes the set of all well formed formulas in our language.

Definition 1 (logic database). *A* logic database LDB *is a finite set of ground atoms.*

Note that any standard relational database can be viewed as a logic database—if tuple **t** is a tuple in a relation r, then $r(\mathbf{t})$ is a ground atom.

Example 1. We may have a small medical database containing information about the symptoms and diseases that a person p may have. Such a database may contain two predicates symptom and disease. The database may contain the following facts:

$$
\begin{array}{ll}
\text{symptom}(john, s_1) & \text{disease}(jane, aids) \\
\text{symptom}(john, s_2) & \text{disease}(john, cancer) \\
\text{symptom}(john, s_3) & \text{disease}(ed, polio) \\
\text{symptom}(jane, s_1) & \\
\text{symptom}(jane, s_4) & \\
\end{array}
$$

This little database, which we will call MedDB will be used as a motivating example in this paper.

The database may contain information about various individuals, businesses and organisations. These entities may wish to designate some (or all) of this information as private. For example, John and Jane may want their diseases kept private.

In addition, at any given instance t in time, each user u has some set of *background knowledge*. This background knowledge may be elicited in many ways - one such source is the set of all information disclosed to the user by the system. For example, a hospital accountant may not be allowed to see patient diagnoses, though she may see billing information about them.

Definition 2 (user model). *We assume the existence of a family of functions* $\mathsf{BK}^t : \mathcal{U} \to 2^{\mathsf{WFF}}$ *for each t in time, and a function* $\mathsf{Priv} : \mathcal{U} \to 2^{\mathsf{WFF}}$.

As usual, 2^X is used here to denote the power set of some set X.

Intuitively, $\mathsf{BK}^t(u)$ denotes the background knowledge of user u (which we assume to be consistent) at time t, while $\mathsf{Priv}(u)$ is the set of all formulas that the user wants to keep secret. Note that $\mathsf{BK}^t(u)$ varies as t varies. For example, as the database discloses answers to the user u, his background knowledge may increase. *Throughout most of this paper, we will assume that t is arbitrary but fixed and we address the problem of preserving privacy at time t.* As a consequence, we will usually write $\mathsf{BK}(u)$ and drop the superscript t.

Example 2. Returning to the case of MedDB, John may want to keep the atom disease($john, cancer$) private, while Jane may want to keep disease($jane, aids$) private. In this case, $\mathsf{Priv}(john) = \{\text{disease}(john, cancer)\}$, while $\mathsf{Priv}(jane) = \{\text{disease}(jane, aids)\}$.

Likewise, consider the user acct (denoting the accountant). This person may have the following background knowledge.

$$
\text{symptom}(X, s_1) \land \text{symptom}(X, s_4) \to \text{disease}(X, aids)
$$
$$
\text{symptom}(X, s_2) \land \text{symptom}(X, s_3) \to \text{disease}(X, cancer)
$$

Definition 3 (query). *If $A_1, \ldots, A_n$ are all atoms, then $(\exists)(A_1 \land \cdots \land A_n)$ is a query.*

For example, disease($john, D$) is a query asking what disease D John has.

Definition 4 (answer). *The* answer, ANS(Q), *to query Q w.r.t. a logic database* LDB *is the set* $\{Q\theta \mid Q\theta$ *is ground and* LDB $\models Q\theta\}$ *where, as usual, the symbol* "$\models$" *denotes logical consequence.*

Example 3. Returning to our MedDB example, posing the query disease($john, X$), we would get as an answer the set $\{$disease($john, aids$)$\}$. Likewise, the answer to the query symptom($john, X$) is the set $\{$symptom($john, s_1$), symptom($john, s_2$), symptom($john, s_3$)$\}$.

In our example, we considered the case when John and Jane want their diseases kept private. However, the accountant can violate John's privacy by asking the query symptom($john, X$). The answer she would get back is $\{$symptom($john, s_1$), symptom($john, s_2$), symptom($john, s_3$)$\}$. However, recall that the accountant has some background information - this background information includes the rule symptom(X, s_2) $\wedge$ symptom(X, s_3) $\rightarrow$ disease($X, cancer$). Using this rule and the answer to her query above, the accountant can easily infer that John has cancer. The notion of a privacy preserving answer given below is intended to avoid such situations.

Definition 5 (privacy preserving answer). *Suppose* LDB *is a logic database,* $\mathcal{U}$ *is a set of users, $u_0 \in \mathcal{U}$, and suppose the functions* BK *and* Priv *are specified. Suppose Q is a query. A set $X \subseteq$ WFF is a privacy preserving answer w.r.t.* (LDB, $\mathcal{U}$, BK, Priv, u_0, Q) *iff:*

1. $X \subseteq$ ANS(Q) *and*
2. *For all $u \in \mathcal{U} - \{u_0\}$ and for all $p \in$ Priv(u), if* BK(u_0) $\not\models p$ *then* $X \cup$ BK(u_0) $\not\models p$ *and*
3. *There is no X' such that $X \subset X'$ satisfies the previous two conditions.*

Intuitively, a privacy preserving answer to a query posed by user u_0 is a subset of the actual answer to the query that does not allow him to use his background knowledge to infer any new private information about any other user. Note that when user u_0 poses a query, we are only interested in preserving private information about other users u - clearly, the user u_0 can know private information about herself, as she, presumably, is the one who decides what information about her is to be kept private.

Example 4. Let us return to the MedDB example, and consider the case of the obnoxious accountant. If the system knows that she has the background knowledge listed earlier, when she asks the query symptom($john, X$), then it could return either of the following privacy preserving answers.

$$Ans1 = \{\text{symptom}(john, s_1), \text{symptom}(john, s_2)\}$$
$$Ans2 = \{\text{symptom}(john, s_1), \text{symptom}(john, s_3)\}$$

Either of these two answers returns as much of the real answer as possible without making it possible for the user to infer that John has cancer.

Let us suppose that the above query was asked at time t. In this case, the accountant's background knowledge at time $t + 1$ should be updated so that it includes all his previous background knowledge, plus the additional knowledge that John has symptoms s_1 and s_3. Thus, $\mathsf{BK}^{t+1}(\mathsf{acct}) = \mathsf{BK}^t(\mathsf{acct}) \cup \{\mathsf{symptom}(john, s_1), \mathsf{symptom}(john, s_2)\}$ (assuming the answer returned by the system in response to John's query at time t is $Ans1$ above). *For the sake of simplicity, throughout the rest of this paper, we assume that t is arbitrary but fixed, and that we are only interested in preserving privacy at time t.*

Example 5. Suppose now that the system somehow knows that the accountant already had $\mathsf{disease}(john, cancer)$ in his background knowledge at time t (e.g. the system might know this because a doctor included the accountant on a list of people notified about John's health). In this case, revealing the entire answer $\{\mathsf{symptom}(john, s_1), \mathsf{symptom}(john, s_2), \mathsf{symptom}(john, s_3)\}$ to the query $\mathsf{symptom}(john, X)$ to the accountant would not violate John's privacy as the answer does not allow the accountant to infer any private facts that she did not already know. As a consequence, were the accountant's background knowledge to include the rules mentioned earlier and the additional fact $\mathsf{disease}(john, cancer)$, then there is only one privacy preserving answer, viz. $\{\mathsf{symptom}(john, s_1), \mathsf{symptom}(john, s_2), \mathsf{symptom}(john, s_3)\}$.

We emphasize that the above definition allows the background knowledge to contain some private information. A simpler definition would be to drop the "*if* $\mathsf{BK}(u_0) \not\models p$ *then*" part in (2) above. But then there would be no privacy preserving answers at all if $\mathsf{BK}(u_0)$ contained some private information.

We are now ready to state the Privacy Preservation Problem (**P3**).

*Problem 1 (**P3**($\mathsf{LDB}, \mathcal{U}, \mathsf{BK}, \mathsf{Priv}, u_0, Q$)).* Suppose LDB is a logic database, $\mathcal{U}$ is a finite set of users, BK is a background knowledge function, Priv is a privacy function, u_0 is a user in $\mathcal{U}$ who is posing query Q to the logic database LDB. The *privacy preservation problem* is to find a privacy-preserving answer w.r.t. ($\mathsf{LDB}, \mathcal{U}, \mathsf{BK}, \mathsf{Priv}, u_0, Q$).

The following proposition says that there is always a privacy preserving answer.

Proposition 1. *Every privacy preservation problem* **P3**($\mathsf{LDB}, \mathcal{U}, \mathsf{BK}, \mathsf{Priv}, u_0, Q$) *has at least one privacy preservation answer.*

Proof. If no $X \subseteq \mathsf{ANS}(Q)$ exists such that $X \neq \emptyset$ and $\forall u \in \mathcal{U} - \{u_0\}$ and $\forall p \in \mathsf{Priv}(u)$ $\mathsf{BK}(u_0) \not\models p$ implies $X \cup \mathsf{BK}(u_0) \not\models p$, then $\emptyset$ is a privacy preserving answer.

Obviously, $\emptyset \subseteq \mathsf{ANS}(Q)$ holds trivially, and $\mathsf{BK}(u_0) \not\models p$ implies $\mathsf{BK}(u_0) \not\models p$ is a tautology for arbitrary p. Moreover, no superset of $\emptyset$ is a privacy preserving answer by assumption. $\qquad\square$

A database system that seeks to preserve privacy can use the following algorithm to answer queries posed by user u_0.

algorithm PrivAns(P3(LDB,$\mathcal{U}$, BK, Priv, u_0, Q))

1. Find a privacy preserving answer ANS(Q) to query Q
   w.r.t. (LDB,$\mathcal{U}$, BK, Priv, u_0, Q).
2. Update BK(u_0) = BK(u_0) $\cup$ ANS(Q).
3. Return ANS(Q) to user u_0 and halt.

The key step in this algorithm is step (1). The rest of this paper develops methods to implement step (1).

3   Translating P3 to Default Logic

In this section, we provide a translation **trans** which takes as input, a privacy preservation problem **P3**(LDB,$\mathcal{U}$, BK, Priv, u_0, Q), and returns as output, a default logic theory $\Delta = (D, W)$ such that there is a one-to-one correspondence between the solutions to the privacy preservation problem and the extensions of the default theory (restricted to the query) returned by the translation [1]. The consequence of this translation is that standard (and well studied) methods to evaluate default logic theories may be used to preserve privacy effectively, efficiently, and elegantly.

Definition 6 (translation trans). *Let* **P3**(LDB,$\mathcal{U}$, BK, Priv, u_0, Q) *be a privacy preservation problem. The* translation, ***trans***(LDB,$\mathcal{U}$, BK, Priv, u_0, Q) *of a privacy preservation problem into default logic is the theory* $\Delta = (D, W)$ *where:*

$$W = \mathsf{BK}(u_0).$$
$$D = \{\frac{:\ f}{f} \mid f \in \mathsf{LDB}\} \bigcup$$
$$\{\frac{p\ :}{\neg p} \mid (\exists u \in \mathcal{U} - \{u_0\})\ p \in \mathsf{Priv}(u)\ \text{and}\ \ \mathsf{BK}(u_0) \not\models p\}.$$

We now present an example to show what the result of transforming the privacy preservation problem into default logic looks like.

Example 6. Let us return to the case of the accountant. In this case, W consists of the two rules

$$\mathsf{symptom}(X, s_1) \wedge \mathsf{symptom}(X, s_4) \rightarrow \mathsf{disease}(X, aids)$$
$$\mathsf{symptom}(X, s_2) \wedge \mathsf{symptom}(X, s_3) \rightarrow \mathsf{disease}(X, cancer).$$

In addition, D consists of the following defaults:

$$\frac{: \text{symptom}(john,s_1)}{\text{symptom}(john,s_1)} \qquad \frac{: \text{symptom}(john,s_2)}{\text{symptom}(john,s_2)} \qquad \frac{: \text{symptom}(john,s_3)}{\text{symptom}(john,s_3)}$$

$$\frac{: \text{symptom}(jane,s_1)}{\text{symptom}(jane,s_1)} \qquad \frac{: \text{symptom}(jane,s_4)}{\text{symptom}(jane,s_4)}$$

$$\frac{: \text{disease}(ed,polio)}{\text{disease}(ed,polio)} \qquad \frac{: \text{disease}(jane,aids)}{\text{disease}(jane,aids)} \qquad \frac{: \text{disease}(john,cancer)}{\text{disease}(john,cancer)}$$

$$\frac{\text{disease}(jane,aids) \,:}{\neg\text{disease}(jane,aids)} \qquad \frac{\text{disease}(john,cancer) \,:}{\neg\text{disease}(john,cancer)}$$

Note that we are assuming here that Ed has not marked his disease as being a private fact.

Note that this translation uses linear space. The time complexity of the translation depends on the complexity of checking entailment. For example, assuming a finite number of constants in our language (reasonable) and assuming that all rules in BK are definite clauses, then the translation is implementable in polynomial time. But if BK can consist of arbitrary first order formulas, then the translation can take exponential time.

Before presenting our central theorem, linking privacy preserving answers and extensions of default theories, we remind the reader of some basic terminology associated with default theories. Given a default $d = \frac{\alpha:\beta}{\gamma}$, we use the notation $pre(d)$ to denote α, $j(d)$ to denote β and $c(d)$ to denote γ. In addition, given any default theory $\Delta = (D, W)$, we may associate with Δ, a mapping Γ_Δ which maps sets of wffs to sets of wffs. $\Gamma_\Delta(Y) = \text{CN}(W \cup \{pre(d) \to c(d) \mid j(d) \text{ is consistent with } Y\}$. As usual, the function $\text{CN}(X)$ denotes the set of all first order logical consequences of X. A set Y of wffs is an *extension* of Δ iff $Y = \Gamma_\Delta(Y)$.

We are now ready to present a key result linking the privacy preservation problem and default logic extensions. Suppose we consider any privacy preservation problem. The privacy preserving answers to that privacy preservation problem are in a one-one correspondence with the consistent extensions of the translation (restricted to the query) of the privacy preservation problem into default logic (using the translation **trans** shown in Definition 6).

Theorem 1. *Suppose that A is an atom, that* **P3**$(\text{LDB}, \mathcal{U}, \text{BK}, \text{Priv}, u_0, A)$ *is a privacy preservation problem and* **trans**$(\text{LDB}, \mathcal{U}, \text{BK}, \text{Priv}, u_0, A) = \Delta = (D, W)$. *Then: X is a solution to the above privacy preservation problem iff there is a consistent extension E of $\Delta = (D, W)$ such that $X = \{A\theta \mid A\theta \in E \cap \text{LDB}\}$.*

In order to prove Theorem 1, we first formulate a useful abstract lemma.

Lemma 1. *Let W, LDB and P be consistent sets of formulae s.t. $W \cup LDB$ is consistent as well. Let $D_P = \{\frac{p\,:}{\neg p} \,:\, p \in P\}$ and $D_{LDB} = \{\frac{:\,f}{f} \,:\, f \in LDB\}$.*

Then the consistent extensions of the theory $(D_P \cup D_{LDB}, W)$ *are the sets* $Cn(W \cup \{f : f \in F\})$ *where* F *is a subset of* LDB *that is maximal wrt. set inclusion (i.e. there is no larger set* F' *such that* $W \cup \{f : f \in F'\} \not\models p$ *for all* $p \in P$*).*

Proof. Clearly the sets $Cn(W \cup \{f : f \in F\})$ where F is a maximal subset of LDB are extensions of the default theory: the defaults in D_P do not apply and we are left with a supernormal default theory (the result follows from well-known characterizations in default logic, see eg. [2,3]).

Conversely, let E be a consistent extension. Then no default in D_P applies. Because extensions are grounded and we are dealing with a supernormal theory, E must have the form $Cn(W \cup \{f : f \in F\})$ for a subset F of LDB. Because E is maximal (no other extension can contain E), the set $Cn(W \cup \{f : f \in F\})$ is maximal in the sense defined in the lemma. □

Now we are able to prove Theorem 1:

Proof. The proof of Theorem 1 is an application of Lemma 1. Suppose X is a solution to **P3**(LDB, $\mathcal{U}$, BK, Priv, u_0, A) and let **trans**(LDB, $\mathcal{U}$, BK, Priv, u_0, A) = $\Delta = (D, W)$. Then we let $F := X$, $W := \mathsf{BK}(u_0)$ and $P := \{p : (\exists u \in \mathcal{U} - \{u_0\})$ $p \in \mathsf{Priv}(u)$ and $\mathsf{BK}(u_0) \not\models p\}$ and apply our lemma. The set $Cn(W \cup \{f : f \in F\})$ is an extension (it is maximal because of (3) and (2) in the definition of a privacy preserving answer).

Conversely let a consistent extension E of **trans**(LDB, $\mathcal{U}$, BK, Priv, u_0, A) be given and consider $X := \{A\theta \mid A\theta \in E \cap \mathsf{LDB}\}$. Our lemma implies that X is a subset of LDB that is maximal. Therefore X is also a privacy preserving answer (if there were a larger X' satisfying (2) in the definition of pp answer, then E would not be maximal and thus not be an extension). □

The preceding theorem applies to *atomic* queries. A straightforward extension of the above proof gives us the following corollary, which applies to arbitrary queries.

Corollary 1. *Suppose that* **P3**(LDB, $\mathcal{U}$, BK, Priv, u_0, Q) *is a privacy preservation problem and that* **trans**(LDB, $\mathcal{U}$, BK, Priv, u_0, Q) = $\Delta = (D, W)$. *Then:* X *is a solution to the above privacy preservation problem iff there is a consistent extension* E *of* $\Delta = (D, W)$ *such that* $X = \{Q\theta \mid Q\theta \in E \cap \mathsf{LDB}\}$.

In order to illustrate this theorem, we revisit the example privacy preservation problem and its default logic translation that we presented earlier.

Example 7. Let us return to the MedDB example. Consider the privacy preservation problem of Example 4 and the default logic translation shown in Figure 6. As seen in Example 4, there are two privacy preserving answers to this problem. They are:

$$Ans1 = \{\mathsf{symptom}(john, s_1), \mathsf{symptom}(john, s_2)\}$$
$$Ans2 = \{\mathsf{symptom}(john, s_1), \mathsf{symptom}(john, s_3)\}$$

The default logic translation of this privacy preservation problem shown in Example 6 has exactly four consistent extensions $E_1, \ldots, E_4$.

$$E_1 = \mathsf{CN}(W \cup \{\mathsf{symptom}(john, s_1), \mathsf{symptom}(john, s_2),$$
$$\mathsf{symptom}(jane, s_1), \mathsf{disease}(ed, polio)\})$$
$$E_2 = \mathsf{CN}(W \cup \{\mathsf{symptom}(john, s_1), \mathsf{symptom}(john, s_3),$$
$$\mathsf{symptom}(jane, s_1), \mathsf{disease}(ed, polio)\})$$
$$E_3 = \mathsf{CN}(W \cup \{\mathsf{symptom}(john, s_1), \mathsf{symptom}(john, s_2),$$
$$\mathsf{symptom}(jane, s_4), \mathsf{disease}(ed, polio)\})$$
$$E_4 = \mathsf{CN}(W \cup \{\mathsf{symptom}(john, s_1), \mathsf{symptom}(john, s_3),$$
$$\mathsf{symptom}(jane, s_4), \mathsf{disease}(ed, polio)\})$$

However, if we restrict our interest to answers to the query $\mathsf{symptom}(john, X)$ in the above extensions, then extensions E_1, E_4 only contain $\{\mathsf{symptom}(john, s_1),$ $\mathsf{symptom}(john, s_2)\}$ while E_2, E_3 yield $\{\mathsf{symptom}(john, s_1), \mathsf{symptom}(john, s_3)\}$. These restrictions of the extensions are in a one-one correspondence with the privacy preserving answers to the query posed by the accountant.

4   Complexity of Privacy Preservation

In this section, we analyze the complexity of the privacy preservation problem.

Computing a privacy-preserving answer typically involves "guessing" a subset of answers, and subsequently checking it with respect to privacy preservation and maximality. Intuitively, this computational task has a correspondence to common non-monotonic reasoning tasks, because the maximality condition for privacy-preserving answers has its counterpart as minimality conditions in non-monotonic semantics, while guessing a model candidate and checking it on a set of formulae is even more closely related.

It therefore does not come as a surprise that a non-monotonic logic allows for an apt representation of the privacy preservation problem. Concerning the complexity analysis, we can indeed leverage the translation **trans** to use well-known results concerning the complexity of default logic in order to prove membership of various subclasses of **P3**.

As already shown in [4], default reasoning involving function symbols is undecidable. Note that Definitions 5 and 6 involve checking $\mathsf{BK}(u_0) \not\models p$, which is clearly undecidable for arbitrary first-order formulae. We will therefore focus on decidable fragments. In particular, we will assume in our analysis below that problems are restricted to those for which deciding $\mathsf{BK} \not\models p$, $p \in \mathsf{Priv}$ is feasible in polynomial time. We will focus on theories in a Datalog setting, the data complexity of which corresponds to propositional default theories.

Then, membership can be seen by virtue of **trans** and the structure of formulae in BK and Priv. In particular, brave reasoning for non-disjunctive default theories is NP-complete (see e.g. [5, 6] for such classes), while brave reasoning for arbitrary default theories is Σ_2^P-complete, see [7] and [8].

We thus consider **P3**s with the following restrictions:

1. We vary $BK(u)$ to be an arbitrary theory, a non-disjunctive theory, and a set of facts.
2. We vary $Priv(u)$ to be a set of arbitrary formulas, a non-disjunctive theory, and a set of facts.

Table 1 summarizes our results on the complexity of privacy preservation in the Datalog case.

Table 1. Data Complexity of Privacy Preservation Problems

Priv/BK	Facts	Non-disjunctive	Arbitrary
Facts	P	P	Σ_2^P
Non-disjunctive	NP	NP	Σ_2^P
Arbitrary	Σ_2^P	Σ_2^P	Σ_2^P

Theorem 2. *The data complexity for* **P3** *problems without function symbols under various syntactic restrictions are as reported in Table 1. Completeness holds for* NP *and* Σ_2^P *results.*

Next, we will prove some of the hardness results.

Corollary 2. **P3** *with* BK *containing non-disjunctive rules and* Priv *made of facts is hard for* NP.

Proof. We show NP-hardness by a reduction from 3SAT to a **P3** in which BK contains only rules with negation on LDB predicates and in which Priv contains only one fact: Given a CNF $\phi = \bigwedge_{i=1}^n L_{i,1} \vee L_{i,2} \vee L_{i,3}$, we create a **P3** with LDB $= \{c_i \mid c_i$ is an atom in $\phi\} \cup \{q\}$, two users u_0, u_1, $BK(u_0) = \{L'_{i,1} \wedge L'_{i,2} \wedge L'_{i,3} \rightarrow unsat\}$, where $(\neg x)' = x$ and $x' = \neg x$. Finally, $Priv(u_1) = \{unsat\}$, and $Q = q$. It is not hard to see that q is an answer iff ϕ is satisfiable: If q is an answer, then a truth assignment can be obtained from the subset $X \subseteq$ LDB in which exactly the c_i in X are interpreted as true. Since *unsat* does not hold for this X, no conjunct in ϕ evaluates to false under this assignment, which therefore satisfies ϕ. Conversely, if ϕ is satisfiable, each cardinality maximal satisfying truth assignment induces an $X \subseteq$ LDB, such that $X \cup BK(u_0) \not\models unsat$. □

Corollary 3. **P3** *with empty* BK *and arbitrary* Priv *is hard for* Σ_2^P.

Proof. We show Σ_2^P-hardness by a reduction from a $QBF_{2,\exists}$ to a **P3** in which BK is empty and Priv contains arbitrary formulae. Consider an arbitrary $QBF_{2,\exists}$ formula $\psi = \exists x_1 \cdots \exists x_n \forall y_1 \cdots \forall y_m \phi$, where ϕ is a propositional formula. We create a **P3** with LDB $= \{x_1, \ldots, x_n\} \cup \{q\}$, two users u_0, u_1, $Priv(u_1) = \{\neg E\}$, and $Q = q$. An answer X induces a valuation ν of the existentially quantified variables. Then, no extension ν' of ν to the universally quantified variables can exist such that E is false, hence ψ is valid. Conversely, if ψ is valid, each cardinality maximal satisfying truth assignment for $x_1, \ldots, x_n$ induces an answer. □

This proof can easily be adapted such that $\mathsf{BK}(u_0)$ contains the arbitrary formula $(\neg E) \rightarrow unsat$ and $\mathsf{Priv}(u_1)$ contains only $unsat$.

All complexity results above refer to propositional theories or data complexity, in our setting this means that only LDB is considered as input, while especially BK and Priv are considered to be fixed. For considering program complexity, we can adapt the data complexity results by using techniques from [9]. Due to space constraints, we do not present proofs.

Theorem 3. *The program complexity for* **P3** *problems without function symbols under various syntactic restrictions are as reported in the Table 2.*

Table 2. Program Complexity of Privacy Preservation Problems

Priv/BK	Facts	Non-disj.	Arbitrary
Facts	EXPTIME	EXPTIME	NEXPTIME^{NP}
Non-disj.	NEXPTIME	NEXPTIME	NEXPTIME^{NP}
Arbitrary	NEXPTIME^{NP}	NEXPTIME^{NP}	NEXPTIME^{NP}

To summarize, the results in this section confirm that default logic is indeed a suitable choice to represent **P3**s.

5   Privacy Preservation Algorithm

In this section, we describe an algorithm to preserve privacy that leverages our translation of the privacy preservation problem to default logic. First and foremost, we recall the important observation of [10] that Reiter's Γ_Δ operator is anti-monotonic - hence, the operator Γ_Δ^2 that applies Γ_Δ is monotonic. As a consequence, Γ_Δ^2 has both a least fixpoint and a greatest fixpoint, denoted $\mathsf{lfp}(\Gamma_\Delta^2)$ and $\mathsf{gfp}(\Gamma_\Delta^2)$ respectively.

Theorem 4 ([10]). *Recall the following properties:*

1. *If $Y_1 \subseteq Y_2$ then $\Gamma_\Delta(Y_2) \subseteq \Gamma_\Delta(Y_1)$.*
2. *Γ_Δ^2 has a least and a greatest fixpoint, denoted respectively as $\mathsf{lfp}(\Gamma_\Delta^2)$ and $\mathsf{gfp}(\Gamma_\Delta^2)$.*
3. *$\Gamma_\Delta(\mathsf{lfp}(\Gamma_\Delta^2)) = \mathsf{gfp}(\Gamma_\Delta^2)$.*

An immediate consequence of the above theorem is that one can compute extensions of default theories by first computing $\mathsf{lfp}(\Gamma_\Delta^2)$ and $\mathsf{gfp}(\Gamma_\Delta^2)$. Anything in $\mathsf{lfp}(\Gamma_\Delta^2)$ is true in all extensions, while anything not in $\mathsf{gfp}(\Gamma_\Delta^2)$ is false in all extensions. We can therefore start by computing both $\mathsf{lfp}(\Gamma_\Delta^2)$ and $\mathsf{gfp}(\Gamma_\Delta^2)$. If $\mathsf{lfp}(\Gamma_\Delta^2)$ is not an extension, we nondeterministically add things in $\mathsf{gfp}(\Gamma_\Delta^2)$ to the default theory and iteratively compute the least fixpoint of Γ_Δ^2 w.r.t. the modified theory. This algorithm for arbitrary default theories gives rise to the specialization for computing privacy preserving answers depicted in Figure 1.

P3Alg(LDB, $\mathcal{U}$, BK, Priv, u_0, Q)

$\Delta = \mathbf{trans}(\mathrm{LDB}, \mathcal{U}, \mathrm{BK}, \mathrm{Priv}, u_0, Q) = (D, W);$

$Todo = \mathrm{LDB} \cap (\mathsf{gfp}(\Gamma_\Delta^2) \setminus \mathsf{lfp}(\Gamma_\Delta^2));$

if $\mathsf{lfp}(\Gamma_\Delta^2) = \Gamma_\Delta(\mathsf{lfp}(\Gamma_\Delta^2))$ **then**

    $done = true;$

while $Todo \neq \emptyset \wedge \neg done$ **do**

    Nondeterministically select an $a \in Todo;$

    Let $\Delta = (D, W \cup \{a\});$

    if $\mathsf{lfp}(\Gamma_\Delta^2) = \Gamma_\Delta(\mathsf{lfp}(\Gamma_\Delta^2))$ **then**

        $done = true;$

    else

        $Todo = Todo \setminus \{a\};$

% **end-while**

return $\mathrm{LDB} \cap \mathsf{lfp}(\Gamma_\Delta^2);$

Fig. 1. Algorithm computing privacy preserving answers

The algorithm proceeds as follows: First the problem is translated to a default theory using **trans**. Subsequently, the least and greatest fixpoint of Γ_Δ^2 are computed. Anything which is in the greatest, but not in the least fixpoint can or cannot be true in some extension, so we store it in $Todo$ to nondeterministically assume its truth.

The crucial point here is that we restrict these nondeterministic choices to LDB, which can dramatically decrease the search space. Then we enter the nondeterministic phase of the algorithm, in which a truth assignment for $Todo$ is generated until a fixpoint (i.e., an extension) is reached, if at all. As a final step, a projection of the extension onto LDB is generated.

The following proposition states that the above algorithm is always guaranteed to return the correct answer.

Proposition 2. *Let* **P3**(LDB, $\mathcal{U}$, BK, Priv, u_0, Q) *be a privacy preservation problem. Then the algorithm* **P3Alg**(LDB, $\mathcal{U}$, BK, Priv, u_0, Q) *returns* X *iff* X *is a privacy preserving answer to* **P3**(LDB, $\mathcal{U}$, BK, Priv, u_0, Q).

We have thus given an effective and also efficient (w.r.t. to general algorithms computing answers to default theories) algorithm for computing privacy preserving answers.

6   Related Work and Conclusions

Security and privacy of information are closely related. There has been extensive work on privacy and security for many years now [11, 12, 13, 14]. A body of work in the field [11, 12] set up the security problem as that of inferring a maximal subset of the answer to a query so that no secrets are violated. Algorithms were also given to determine how to update the database so that security and privacy are preserved. Another body of work [14] determines how to generalize answers (rather than choose a subset). Our work is related to the former category.

Many other works focus on enforcing authorization on various levels of detail, for example in [15], a query rewriting method has been worked out, which avoids the disclosure of data to a user who is not entitled to see it. A similar approach has been described in [16], where classified data will basically be substituted by null-values. Both approaches are quite different from ours with respect to the problem addressed and the methodology employed: These works do not provide methods for modelling users' knowledge; rather, it is needed to determine in advance and to specify extensionally what data is to be hidden from the user. Moreover, both works do not employ logical frameworks for solving this problem.

In contrast to the above body of work, we are not aware of any works that ties well known nonmonotonic logic formalisms such as default logic to the privacy preservation problem. This paper is a first step in this regard. As shown by the P3Alg algorithm and the complexity results derived in this paper, the relationships between privacy preservation and default logics can lead to results in one domain being applicable and beneficial to another. Our future work will focus on leveraging the relationship between default logic and privacy even further so that the rich experience gained in implementing default logics can be applied fruitfully to the privacy domain.

In particular, we would like to investigate whether we can utilize Answer Set Programming (ASP) [17] engines like DLV [18], Smodels [19], cmodels [20], or ASSAT [21] to this end. The formalism of these systems (logic programs under the answer set semantics) is comparatively close to default logic, and also the complexity bounds match.

References

1. Cadoli, M., Eiter, T., Gottlob, G.: Default Logic as a Query Language. IEEE Transactions on Knowledge and Data Engineering **9** (1997) 448–463
2. Dix, J.: Default Theories of Poole-Type and a Method for Constructing Cumulative Versions of Default Logic. In Neumann, B., ed.: Proc. of 10th European Conf. on Artificial Intelligence ECAI 92, John Wiley & Sons (1992) 289–293
3. Marek, W., Truszczyński, M.: Nonmonotonic Logics; Context-Dependent Reasoning. 1st edn. Springer, Berlin (1993)
4. Reiter, R.: A Logic for Default Reasoning. Artificial Intelligence **13** (1980) 81–132
5. Kautz, H., Selman, B.: Hard Problems for Simple Default Logics. Artificial Intelligence **49** (1991) 243–279
6. Stillman, J.: It's Not My Default: The Complexity of Membership Problems in Restricted Propositional Default Logic. In: Proceedings AAAI-90. (1990) 571–579
7. Gottlob, G.: Complexity Results for Nonmonotonic Logics. Journal of Logic and Computation **2** (1992) 397–425
8. Stillman, J.: The Complexity of Propositional Default Logic. In: Proceedings AAAI-92. (1992) 794–799

9. Gottlob, G., Leone, N., Veith, H.: Succinctness as a Source of Expression Complexity. Annals of Pure and Applied Logic **97** (1999) 231–260
10. Baral, C., Subrahmanian, V.: Dualities Between Alternative Semantics for Logic Programming and Non-Monotonic Reasoning. Journal of Automated Reasoning **10** (1993) 399–420
11. M. Winslett, K.S., Qian, X.: Formal Query Languages for Secure Relational Databases. ACM Transactions on Database Systems **19** (1994) 626–662
12. P. Bonatti, S.K., Subrahmanian, V.: Foundations of Secure Deductive Databases. IEEE Transactions on Knowledge and Data Engineering **7** (1995) 406–422
13. Cuppens, F., Demolombe, R.: A Modal Logical Framework for Security Policies. In: Proc. ISMIS. (1997) 579–589
14. Samarati, P., Sweeney, L.: Generalizing Data to Provide Anonymity when Disclosing Information. In: Proceedings ACM Symp. on Principles of Database Systems. (1998)
15. Rizvi, S., Mendelzon, A.O., Sudarshan, S., Roy, P.: Extending query rewriting techniques for fine-grained access control. In Weikum, G., König, A.C., Deßloch, S., eds.: Proceedings of the ACM SIGMOD International Conference on Management of Data (SIGMOD 2004), ACM (2004) 551–562
16. LeFevre, K., Agrawal, R., Ercegovac, V., Ramakrishnan, R., Xu, Y., DeWitt, D.J.: Limiting disclosure in hippocratic databases. In Nascimento, M.A., Özsu, M.T., Kossmann, D., Miller, R.J., Blakeley, J.A., Schiefer, K.B., eds.: Proceedings of the Thirtieth International Conference on Very Large Data Bases (VLDB 2004), Morgan Kaufmann (2004) 108–119
17. Gelfond, M., Lifschitz, V.: Classical Negation in Logic Programs and Disjunctive Databases. **9** (1991) 365–385
18. Leone, N., Pfeifer, G., Faber, W., Eiter, T., Gottlob, G., Perri, S., Scarcello, F.: The DLV System for Knowledge Representation and Reasoning. (2005) To appear. Available via http://www.arxiv.org/ps/cs.AI/0211004.
19. Simons, P., Niemelä, I., Soininen, T.: Extending and Implementing the Stable Model Semantics. Artificial Intelligence **138** (2002) 181–234
20. Lierler, Y., Maratea, M.: Cmodels-2: SAT-based Answer Set Solver Enhanced to Non-tight Programs. In Lifschitz, V., Niemelä, I., eds.: Proceedings of the 7th International Conference on Logic Programming and Non-Monotonic Reasoning (LPNMR-7). LNCS, Springer (2004) 346–350
21. Lin, F., Zhao, Y.: ASSAT: Computing Answer Sets of a Logic Program by SAT Solvers. In: Proceedings of the Eighteenth National Conference on Artificial Intelligence (AAAI-2002), Edmonton, Alberta, Canada, AAAI Press / MIT Press (2002)

Comparative Similarity, Tree Automata, and Diophantine Equations

Mikhail Sheremet[1], Dmitry Tishkovsky[2], Frank Wolter[2],
and Michael Zakharyaschev[1]

[1] Department of Computer Science,
King's College London,
Strand, London WC2R 2LS, U.K.
{mikhail, mz}@dcs.kcl.ac.uk
[2] Department of Computer Science,
University of Liverpool,
Liverpool L69 7ZF, U.K.
{dmitry, frank}@csc.liv.ac.uk

Abstract. The notion of comparative similarity 'X is more similar or closer to Y than to Z' has been investigated in both foundational and applied areas of knowledge representation and reasoning, e.g., in concept formation, similarity-based reasoning and areas of bioinformatics such as protein sequence alignment. In this paper we analyse the computational behaviour of the 'propositional' logic with the binary operator 'closer to a set τ_1 than to a set τ_2' and nominals interpreted over various classes of distance (or similarity) spaces. In particular, using a reduction to the emptiness problem for certain tree automata, we show that the satisfiability problem for this logic is ExpTime-complete for the classes of all finite symmetric and all finite (possibly non-symmetric) distance spaces. For finite subspaces of the real line (and higher dimensional Euclidean spaces) we prove the undecidability of satisfiability by a reduction of the solvability problem for Diophantine equations. As our 'closer' operator has the same expressive power as the standard operator $>$ of conditional logic, these results may have interesting implications for conditional logic as well.

1   Introduction

There are two main approaches to defining and classifying concepts in computer science and artificial intelligence. One of them is *logic based*. It uses formalisms like description logics to define concepts by establishing relationships between them, for example,

$$\mathsf{Mother} \equiv \mathsf{Woman} \sqcap \exists \mathsf{hasChild.Person}$$

The main tool for analysing and using such definitions (e.g., to compute the concept hierarchy based on the subsumption relation) is *reasoning*.

G. Sutcliffe and A. Voronkov (Eds.): LPAR 2005, LNAI 3835, pp. 651–665, 2005.
© Springer-Verlag Berlin Heidelberg 2005

Another approach is based on *similarity*.[1] Using various techniques (such as alignment algorithms) we compute suitable similarity measures on (part of) the application domain and then define concepts in terms of similarity, for example,

$$\text{Reddish} \quad \equiv \quad \{\text{Red}\} \Leftarrow \{\text{Green}, \ldots, \text{Black}\}$$

which reads 'a colour is reddish iff it is more similar (with respect to the RGB, HSL or some other explicit or implicit colour model) to the prototypical colour *Red* than to the prototypical colours *Green*, ..., *Black*.' The established tools for dealing with concepts of this sort are *numerical computations* (say, with the help of Voronoi tessellations, nearest neighbour or clustering algorithms).

As more and more application areas—like bioinformatics and linguistics—use both of these ways of defining concepts, we are facing the problem of integrating them. In particular, we need formalisms that are capable of *reasoning* about concepts defined in terms of (explicit or implicit) similarity in the same way as this is done in description logic (DL).

In [6, 17, 8, 18] we presented and investigated rudimentary DL-like formalisms for reasoning about concepts and similarity with concept constructors of the form $\exists^{<^a}\tau$, that is, 'in the a-neighbourhood of τ,' where $a \in \mathbb{Q}^{\geq 0}$. The apparent limitation of these languages is that they can only operate with *concrete* degrees of similarity $a \in \mathbb{Q}^{\geq 0}$, and so require substantial expert knowledge in order to define concepts.

In this paper we propose a purely *qualitative* logic $\mathcal{CSL}$ for knowledge representation and reasoning about *comparative similarity*. Its main ingredients are the binary *closer* operator $\Leftarrow$ as in the example above and individual constants (nominals) for representing prototypical objects (we refer the reader to [7, 16] for a discussion of relations like 'X more similar to Y than to Z'). The logic is interpreted in various natural classes of distance (or similarity) spaces such as finite metric spaces, finite metric spaces without symmetry (see, e.g., [14] for an argumentation that similarity measures are not necessarily symmetric) as well as the finite subspaces of the Euclidean space $\mathbb{R}^n$, $n \geq 1$ (natural similarity measures for weight, length, etc.).

The computational behaviour of $\mathcal{CSL}$ over the class of finite metric spaces (with or without symmetry) turns out be similar to the behaviour of standard description logics: the satisfiability problem is ExpTime-complete which can be established by a reduction to the emptiness problem for certain tree automata. However, it was a great surprise for us to discover that over finite subspaces of the real line $\mathbb{R}$ (as well as any higher dimensional Euclidean space or any $\mathbb{Z}^n$) the logic turns out to be undecidable. This result is proved by a reduction of the (undecidable) solvability problem for Diophantine equations.

Because of the space limit some proofs in this paper are only sketched, some are omitted. For a detailed exposition the reader is referred to the full version [11].

---

[1] "There is nothing more basic to thought and language than our sense of similarity; our sorting of things into kinds." Quine (1969).

2   The Logic of Comparative Similarity

The *logic $\mathcal{CSL}$ of comparative similarity* we consider in this paper is based on the following language:

$$\tau \ ::= \ p_i \ \mid \ \{\ell_i\} \ \mid \ \neg\tau \ \mid \ \tau_1 \sqcap \tau_2 \ \mid \ \tau_1 \Leftarrow \tau_2$$

where the p_i are *atomic terms*, the ℓ_i are *object names*, and $\Leftarrow$ is the *closer operator*. We call $\{\ell_i\}$ a *nominal* and τ a *$\mathcal{CSL}$-term* or simply a *term*.

The intended models for $\mathcal{CSL}$ are based on *distance* (or rather *similarity*) *spaces* $\mathfrak{D} = (\Delta, d)$, where Δ is a nonempty set and d is a map from $\Delta \times \Delta$ to the set $\mathbb{R}^{\geq 0}$ of nonnegative real numbers such that, for all $x, y \in \Delta$, we have $d(x, y) = 0$ iff $x = y$. If the *distance function* d satisfies two additional properties

$$d(x, y) \ = \ d(y, x) \tag{sym}$$
$$d(x, z) \ \leq \ d(x, y) + d(y, z) \tag{tr}$$

then $\mathfrak{D}$ is a standard *metric space*. The *distance $d(X, Y)$* between two nonempty sets X and Y of Δ is defined by taking

$$d(X, Y) \ = \ \inf\{d(x, y) \mid x \in X, \ y \in Y\}.$$

If one of X, Y is empty then $d(X, Y) = \infty$. Finally, if we actually have

$$d(X, Y) \ = \ \min\{d(x, y) \mid x \in X, \ y \in Y\} \tag{min}$$

for any nonempty X and Y, then the distance space $\mathfrak{D}$ is called a *min-space*. Every finite distance space is clearly a min-space.

$\mathcal{CSL}$-*models* are structures of the form

$$\mathfrak{I} \ = \ \left(\Delta^{\mathfrak{I}}, d^{\mathfrak{I}}, \ell_1^{\mathfrak{I}}, \ell_2^{\mathfrak{I}}, \ldots, p_1^{\mathfrak{I}}, p_2^{\mathfrak{I}}, \ldots\right), \tag{1}$$

where $\left(\Delta^{\mathfrak{I}}, d^{\mathfrak{I}}\right)$ is a distance space, the $p_i^{\mathfrak{I}}$ are subsets of $\Delta^{\mathfrak{I}}$, and $\ell_i^{\mathfrak{I}} \in \Delta^{\mathfrak{I}}$ for every i. We call such models *min-models*, *symmetric* or satisfying the *triangle inequality* if the underlying distance space satisfies (min), (sym) or (tr), respectively. If both (sym) and (tr) are satisfied then $\mathfrak{I}$ is called a *metric $\mathcal{CSL}$-model*.

The interpretation of the Boolean operators $\neg$ and $\sqcap$ in $\mathfrak{I}$ is as usual (we will use $\sqcup$, $\rightarrow$, $\bot$ (for $\emptyset$), and $\top$ (for the whole space) as standard abbreviations), $\{\ell\}^{\mathfrak{I}} = \{\ell^{\mathfrak{I}}\}$, and

$$(\tau_1 \Leftarrow \tau_2)^{\mathfrak{I}} \ = \ \{x \in \Delta^{\mathfrak{I}} \mid d^{\mathfrak{I}}(x, \tau_1^{\mathfrak{I}}) < d^{\mathfrak{I}}(x, \tau_2^{\mathfrak{I}})\}. \tag{2}$$

A term τ is *satisfied* in $\mathfrak{I}$ if $\tau^{\mathfrak{I}} \neq \emptyset$. More precisely, we say that $x \in \Delta^{\mathfrak{I}}$ *satisfies* τ whenever $x \in \tau^{\mathfrak{I}}$. τ is *satisfiable* in a class $\mathcal{C}$ of models if it is satisfied in some model from $\mathcal{C}$. Finally, τ is *valid* in $\mathfrak{I}$ if $\tau^{\mathfrak{I}} = \Delta^{\mathfrak{I}}$.

The seemingly simple logic $\mathcal{CSL}$ turns out to be quite expressive. First, the operator $\exists\tau = (\tau \Leftarrow \bot)$ is interpreted by the *existential modality* (in the sense that $\exists\tau$ is the whole space iff τ is not empty); its dual, the *universal modality*, will be denoted by $\forall$. Thus the term $\forall(\tau_1 \rightarrow \tau_2)$ expresses in $\mathcal{CSL}$ the *subsumption relation* $\tau_1 \sqsubseteq \tau_2$ which is usually used in description logic knowledge bases. Note also that the following definable operator $\leftrightarrows$ means 'at the same distance:'

$$\tau_1 \leftrightarrows \tau_2 \;\; = \;\; \neg(\tau_1 \Leftarrow \tau_2) \sqcap \neg(\tau_2 \Leftarrow \tau_1). \tag{3}$$

Second, in metric models the operator $\square$ defined by taking $\square\tau = (\top \Leftarrow \neg\tau)$ is actually interpreted by the *interior operator* of the induced topology. Thus, $\mathcal{CSL}$ contains the full logic $\mathbf{S4}_u$ of topological spaces, and so can be used for spatial representation and reasoning (see, e.g., [1]). The topological aspects of $\mathcal{CSL}$ will be considered elsewhere.

Finally, it is to be noted that the operator $\Leftarrow$ is closely related to the 'implication' $>$ of conditional logics. According to Lewis' [7] semantics for conditionals, propositions are interpreted in a set W of possible worlds that come together with orderings $\preceq_w \subseteq W \times W$, for $w \in W$, which can be understood as follows: $w' \preceq_w w''$ if w' is more similar or closer to w than w''. A formula $\varphi > \psi$ is true at w iff, for every $\preceq_w$-minimal v with $v \models \varphi$, we have $v \models \psi$. Various authors (see, for example, [3, 10]) have considered the case where the relations $\preceq_w$ are induced by min-spaces (Δ, d) (in conditional logic, the requirement (min) is often called the *limit assumption*) by setting

$$w' \preceq_w w'' \quad \text{iff} \quad d(w, w') \leq d(w, w'').$$

Under this interpretation the operators $\Leftarrow$ and $>$ have exactly the same expressive power: for every min-model $\mathfrak{I} = (\Delta^{\mathfrak{I}}, d^{\mathfrak{I}}, p_1^{\mathfrak{I}}, p_2^{\mathfrak{I}}, \ldots)$ we have

$$(p_1 > p_2)^{\mathfrak{I}} \;\; = \;\; \big((p_1 \Leftarrow (p_1 \sqcap \neg p_2)) \sqcup \forall\neg p_1\big)^{\mathfrak{I}}$$

and, conversely,

$$(p_1 \Leftarrow p_2)^{\mathfrak{I}} \;\; = \;\; \big(((p_1 \sqcup p_2) > p_1) \sqcap (p_1 > \neg p_2) \sqcap \neg(p_1 > \bot)\big)^{\mathfrak{I}}.$$

Relations $\preceq_w$ induced by *symmetric* distance spaces have not been considered in the conditional logic literature. According to the classification of [5], our (nominal-free) logic of arbitrary min-spaces corresponds to the conditional logic of frames satisfying the normality, reflexivity, strict centering, uniformity and connectedness conditions.

3   Main Results

In this paper, our main concern is the computational behaviour of $\mathcal{CSL}$ over natural classes of *min-models*, in particular, *finite* models.

Theorem 1. *Let $\mathcal{C}$ be the class of all min-models satisfying any combination of the properties (sym) and (tr), in particular, neither of them. Then the satisfiability problem for $\mathcal{CSL}$-terms in $\mathcal{C}$ is ExpTime-complete. Moreover, a term is satisfiable in $\mathcal{C}$ iff it is satisfiable in a finite model from $\mathcal{C}$.*

Remark 1. For the nominal-free fragment of $\mathcal{CSL}$ over arbitrary min-models, Theorem 1 was essentially proved in [5] in the framework of conditional logic. We provide a new proof here because it serves as a preparation for the more sophisticated proof for the class of *symmetric* min-models.

Remark 2. It is to be noted that in fact the language of $\mathcal{CSL}$ cannot distinguish between models with and without (tr). To see this, let us suppose that τ is satisfied in a model $\mathfrak{I}$ of the form (1) which does not satisfy (tr). Take any strictly monotonic function $f : \mathbb{R}^{\geq 0} \rightarrow (9, 10)$, where $(9, 10)$ is the open interval between 9 and 10. Define a new model $\mathfrak{I}'$ which differs from $\mathfrak{I}$ only in the distance function: $d^{\mathfrak{I}'}(x, y) = f(d^{\mathfrak{I}}(x, y))$ for all $x \neq y$ and $d^{\mathfrak{I}'}(x, x) = 0$ for all x. Clearly, $\mathfrak{I}'$ satisfies the triangle inequality. It is easily checked that τ is satisfied in $\mathfrak{I}'$.

Remark 3. On the other hand, $\mathcal{CSL}$ can distinguish between models with and without (sym). Consider, for example, the term

$$p \sqcap \forall\big((p \rightarrow (q \Leftarrow r)) \sqcap (q \rightarrow (r \Leftarrow p)) \sqcap (r \rightarrow (p \Leftarrow q))\big).$$

One can readily check that it is satisfiable in a three-point model without (sym), say, in the one depicted below where the distance from x to y is the length of the shortest directed path from x to y.

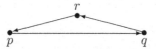

However, this term is not satisfiable in any symmetric min-model. On the other hand, it can be satisfied in the following subspace of $\mathbb{R}$ which is not a min-space:

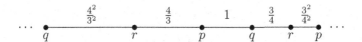

Our second main result is quite surprising: $\mathcal{CSL}$ turns out to be undecidable when interpreted in finite subspaces of $\mathbb{R}$. More precisely, we are going to prove the following:

Theorem 2. *For each $n \geq 1$, the satisfiability problem for $\mathcal{CSL}$-terms is undecidable in the class of finite models and the class of min-models based on subspaces of $\mathbb{R}^n$, or only $\mathbb{Z}^n$.*

Theorem 1 will be proved in the next section: for the lower bound we use a reduction of the global consequence relation for the modal logic $\mathbf{K}$, while the upper bound is established by reduction to the emptiness problem for tree automata. Theorem 2 is proved in Section 5 by reduction of the solvability problem for Diophantine equations (and, for $n \geq 2$, the $\mathbb{Z} \times \mathbb{Z}$ tiling problem).

4   Proof of Theorem 1

The ExpTime lower bound is proved by a reduction of the global consequence relation for the modal logic **K** which is known to be ExpTime-hard [12]. A detailed proof can be found in [11]. We now show how to establish the ExpTime upper bound and the finite model property with respect to the given class $\mathcal{C}$ of models.

Given a term τ, denote by $cl\tau$ the closure under single negation of the set consisting of all subterms of τ, the term $\bot$, and the term $\exists \rho = \rho \sqsubseteq \bot$ for every subterm ρ of τ. A *type* t for τ is a subset of $cl\tau$ such that $\bot \notin t$ and the following Boolean closure conditions are satisfied:

- $\tau_1 \sqcap \tau_2 \in t$ iff $\tau_1, \tau_2 \in t$, for every $\tau_1 \sqcap \tau_2 \in cl\tau$,
- $\neg\rho \in t$ iff $\rho \notin t$, for every $\neg\rho \in cl\tau$.

Clearly, $|cl\tau|$ is a linear function of the *length* $|\tau|$ (say, the number of subterms) of τ.

A 'typical' type is given by an element $w \in \Delta^{\mathfrak{J}}$ from a model $\mathfrak{J}$ of the form (1), namely,

$$t^{\mathfrak{J}}(w) = \{\rho \in cl\tau \mid w \in \rho^{\mathfrak{J}}\}.$$

A τ-*bouquet* is a pair $\mathfrak{B} = (T_{\mathfrak{B}}, \leq_{\mathfrak{B}})$, where $T_{\mathfrak{B}}$ is a set of types for τ such that $2 \leq |T_{\mathfrak{B}}| \leq |cl\tau|$, and $\leq_{\mathfrak{B}}$ is a transitive, reflexive, and connected relation on $T_{\mathfrak{B}}$ with a unique minimal element $t_{\mathfrak{B}} \in T_{\mathfrak{B}}$ for which the following conditions hold:

- $\tau_1 \sqsubseteq \tau_2 \in t_{\mathfrak{B}}$ iff there exists some $t \in T_{\mathfrak{B}}$ such that $\tau_1 \in t$ and $\tau_2 \notin t'$ for any $t' \leq_{\mathfrak{B}} t$,
- $\exists\rho \in t$ for some $t \in T_{\mathfrak{B}}$ iff $\exists\rho \in t$ for all $t \in T_{\mathfrak{B}}$.

We use the following notation:

$$t \sim_{\mathfrak{B}} t' \quad \text{iff} \quad t \leq_{\mathfrak{B}} t' \quad \text{and} \quad t' \leq_{\mathfrak{B}} t$$
$$t <_{\mathfrak{B}} t' \quad \text{iff} \quad t \leq_{\mathfrak{B}} t' \quad \text{and} \quad t \not\sim_{\mathfrak{B}} t'.$$

The intended meaning of a τ-bouquet $\mathfrak{B}$ is to encode the local requirements in order to realise the type $t_{\mathfrak{B}}$. A 'typical' τ-bouquet can be obtained by taking a point w from $\mathfrak{J}$ above and then selecting, for every term $\tau_1 \sqsubseteq \tau_2$ from $t^{\mathfrak{J}}(w)$, a point w' such that $d^{\mathfrak{J}}(w, w')$ is minimal with $w' \in \tau_1^{\mathfrak{J}}$. Denote by V the set of all selected points. Clearly, $|V| < |cl\tau|$ and we can assume that $t^{\mathfrak{J}}(w_1) \neq t^{\mathfrak{J}}(w_2)$ for any two distinct w_1, w_2 from V. If $|V| \geq 1$, then we define the τ-*bouquet* $(T_V^{\mathfrak{J}}(w), \leq_w)$ *induced by* w *and* V *in* $\mathfrak{J}$ by taking

$$T_V^{\mathfrak{J}}(w) = \{t^{\mathfrak{J}}(w)\} \cup \{t^{\mathfrak{J}}(w') \mid w' \in V\},$$
$$t^{\mathfrak{J}}(w') \leq_w t^{\mathfrak{J}}(w'') \quad \text{iff} \quad d^{\mathfrak{J}}(w, w') \leq d^{\mathfrak{J}}(w, w'').$$

Notice that if we require a certain type t satisfied in $\mathfrak{J}$ to be a member of the bouquet then we can add to V a point w' such that $d(w, w')$ is minimal with

$t = t^{\mathfrak{I}}(w')$ and form the bouquet induced by w and $V \cup \{w'\}$. In particular, if $\mathfrak{I}$ satisfies at least two distinct types, then we can always find a set V such that w and V induce a bouquet. In what follows we will only be working with models satisfying at least two distinct types. This is the interesting case because the problem of checking satisfiability in a model with only one type is clearly decidable in NP.

4.1 Non-symmetric Case

First we establish the finite model property and the ExpTime upper bound for satisfiability in min-models that are not necessarily symmetric. Let N be the set of nominals occurring in τ. A set B τ-bouquets is said to be *nominal ready* if there is a set $\{t_\ell \mid \ell \in N\}$ of types for τ such that whenever $\{\ell\} \in t \in T_{\mathfrak{B}}$, for some $\mathfrak{B} \in B$, then $t = t_\ell$.

Let $k = |cl\tau|$. We remind the reader that the *full k-ary tree over* the set $\{1, \ldots, k\}^*$ (of finite sequences of elements of $\{1, \ldots, k\}$) contains the empty sequence ϵ as its root, and the immediate successors (children) of each node α are precisely the nodes αi, where $1 \leq i \leq k$. Given some set L (of labels), a function $K : \{1, \ldots, k\}^* \to L$ will be called an L-*labelled tree over* $\{1, \ldots, k\}^*$.

A *Hintikka tree satisfying* τ is a B-labelled tree K over $\{1, \ldots, k\}^*$, for some nominal ready set B of τ-bouquets, such that the following conditions are satisfied (where, as before, $t_{K(\alpha)}$ denotes the unique $\leq_{K(\alpha)}$-minimal element of the set of types $T_{K(\alpha)}$ in the bouquet $K(\alpha)$):

- $\tau \in t_{K(\epsilon)}$,
- for every nominal $\ell \in N$, there exists a type in $K(\epsilon)$ containing $\{\ell\}$,
- for every $\alpha \in \{1, \ldots, k\}^*$, $K(\alpha)$ is a bouquet such that

$$T_{K(\alpha)} \setminus \{t_{K(\alpha)}\} = \{t_{K(\alpha i)} \mid 1 \leq i \leq k\}$$

and $t_{K(\alpha)} \in T_{K(\alpha i)}$, for $1 \leq i \leq k$.

Lemma 1. *For every term τ, the following conditions are equivalent:*

(a) *τ is satisfiable in some min-model (with at least two distinct types);*
(b) *there exists a Hintikka tree satisfying τ over $\{1, \ldots, k\}^*$, where $k = |cl\tau|$;*
(c) *τ is satisfiable in a finite model (with at least two distinct types).*

Proof. (a) $\Rightarrow$ (b) Suppose that $\tau^{\mathfrak{I}} \neq \emptyset$ in some model $\mathfrak{I} \in \mathcal{C}$ of the form (1) with at least two distinct types. We define a Hintikka tree K satisfying τ by induction as follows. First take some $w \in \tau^{\mathfrak{I}}$ and set

$$K(\epsilon) = (T_{V_\epsilon}^{\mathfrak{I}}(w), \leq_w),$$

where $(T_{V_\epsilon}^{\mathfrak{I}}(w), \leq_w)$ is a bouquet induced by w and a suitable set $V_\epsilon \subseteq W$ containing $\{\ell\}^{\mathfrak{I}}$ for all ℓ that occur in τ. Here and in what follows we assume that we construct the underlying sets of the bouquet as described above in the introduction of bouquets.

Suppose now that we have already defined $K(\alpha)$, for some $\alpha \in \{1, \ldots, k\}^*$:

$$K(\alpha) = (T^{\mathfrak{I}}_{V_\alpha}(w_\alpha), \leq_{w_\alpha}),$$

where $(T^{\mathfrak{I}}_{V_\alpha}(w_\alpha), \leq_{w_\alpha})$ is induced by w_α and a suitable set V_α. Take some surjective map $s : \{1, \ldots, k\} \to V_\alpha$. For each j, $1 \leq j \leq k$, let

$$K(\alpha j) = (T^{\mathfrak{I}}_{V_{\alpha j}}(s(j)), \leq_{s(j)})$$

where $(T^{\mathfrak{I}}_{V_{\alpha j}}(s(j)), \leq_{s(j)})$ is the bouquet induced by $s(j)$ and a suitable set $V_{\alpha j}$ which contains a w' such that $t^{\mathfrak{I}}(w') = t^{\mathfrak{I}}(w_\alpha)$.

It is easy to see that the resulting K is a Hintikka tree satisfying τ.

(b) $\Rightarrow$ (c) Suppose that $K : \{1, \ldots, k\}^* \to B$ with

$$K(\alpha) = (T_\alpha, \leq_\alpha)$$

is a Hintikka tree satisfying τ over a nominal ready set B of τ-bouquets. First we define a distance space (Δ_0, d_0) with the domain $\Delta_0 = \{1, \ldots, k\}^*$ in the following way. Take a finite subset I of the interval $(0, 1)$ and, for each $\alpha \in \Delta_0$, a map

$$f_\alpha : (T_{K(\alpha)} \setminus \{t_{K(\alpha)}\}) \to I$$

for which $t <_{K(\alpha)} t'$ iff $f_\alpha(t) < f_\alpha(t')$. Now set

- $d_0(\alpha, \alpha i) = f_\alpha(t_{K(\alpha i)})$ for all $\alpha \in \Delta_0$ and $1 \leq i \leq k$,
- $d_0(\alpha, \alpha) = 0$ and,
- $d_0(\alpha, \beta) = 1$ for $\beta \notin \{\alpha, \alpha 1, \ldots, \alpha k\}$.

It is not difficult to see that (Δ_0, d_0) is a (non-symmetric) min-space.

For every type t such that $t = t_{K(\alpha)}$ for some $\alpha \in \Delta_0$, we fix exactly one α with this property. Let Δ be the set of the selected α. Construct a finite distance model from $\mathcal{C}$

$$\mathfrak{I} = (\Delta, d, \ell_1^{\mathfrak{I}}, \ldots, p_1^{\mathfrak{I}}, \ldots)$$

by taking $p_i^{\mathfrak{I}} = \{\alpha \in \Delta \mid p_i \in t_{K(\alpha)}\}$, $\ell_i^{\mathfrak{I}} = \alpha$ for the unique $\alpha \in \Delta$ with $\{\ell_i\} \in t_{K(\alpha)}$, and, for $\alpha, \beta \in \Delta$,

$$d(\alpha, \beta) = d_0(\alpha, \{\beta' \in \Delta_0 \mid t_{K(\beta')} = t_{K(\beta)}\}).$$

Now, given a subterm ρ of τ, one can prove by induction on the construction of ρ that $\alpha \in \rho^{\mathfrak{I}}$ iff $\rho \in t_{K(\alpha)}$. Therefore, τ is satisfied in $\mathfrak{I}$.

The implication (c) $\Rightarrow$ (a) is clear.

We are now in a position to prove the ExpTime upper bound by a reduction to the emptiness problem for finite looping tree automata; see [15, 13]. Recall that a *finite looping tree automaton* $\mathcal{A}$ *for infinite k-ary trees* is a quadruple (Σ, Q, Γ, Q_0), where

- Σ is a (nonempty) finite alphabet,
- Q is a (nonempty) finite set of states of the automaton,

- $\Gamma \subseteq \Sigma \times Q \times Q^k$ is a transition relation,
- $Q_0 \subseteq Q$ is a (nonempty) set of start states of the automaton.

Let T be a Σ-labelled tree over $\{1, \ldots, k\}^*$. A *run* of $\mathcal{A}$ on T is a function $R : \{1, \ldots, k\}^* \to Q$ such that

- $R(\epsilon) \in Q_0$, and
- $(T(\alpha), R(\alpha), (R(\alpha 1), \ldots, R(\alpha k))) \in \Gamma$ for all nodes α of T.

$\mathcal{A}$ accepts T if there exists a run R of $\mathcal{A}$ on T. The following *emptiness problem* for looping automata is decidable in polynomial time [13]: given a looping automaton for k-ary trees, decide whether the set of trees it accepts is empty.

To reduce the satisfiability problem for $\mathcal{CSL}$-terms in $\mathcal{C}$, we associate with every term τ and every nominal ready set B of τ-bouquets a finite looping automaton $\mathcal{A}_\tau^B = (\Sigma, Q, \Gamma, Q_0)$ which is defined as follows:

- Σ is the set of types occurring in bouquets from B,
- $Q = B$,
- $Q_0 = \{\mathfrak{B} \in B \mid \tau \in t_\mathfrak{B}, \mathfrak{B} \text{ contains a type containing } \ell, \text{ for every } \ell \text{ in } \tau\}$,
- $(t, \mathfrak{B}_0, (\mathfrak{B}_1, \ldots, \mathfrak{B}_k)) \in \Gamma$ iff $t_{\mathfrak{B}_0} = t$, $T_{\mathfrak{B}_0} \setminus \{t_{\mathfrak{B}_0}\}$ coincides with the set $\{t_{\mathfrak{B}_i} \mid 1 \leq i \leq k\}$, and $t_{\mathfrak{B}_0} \in T_{\mathfrak{B}_i}$, for $1 \leq i \leq k$.

It follows immediately from Lemma 1 and the given definitions that the runs of $\mathcal{A}_\tau^B$ on Σ-labelled trees are exactly the B-labelled Hintikka-trees satisfying τ.

Lemma 2. *A term τ is satisfiable in a min-model (with at least two types) iff there exists a nominal ready set B such that $\mathcal{A}_\tau^B$ accepts at least one tree.*

As there are only exponentially many different nominal ready sets B and as $\mathcal{A}_\tau^B$ is only exponential in $|cl\tau|$, the satisfiability problem in min- (and finite) models is decidable in ExpTime.

4.2   Symmetric Case

The construction is more involved if we deal with the class of symmetric $\mathcal{CSL}$-models. Suppose that B is a nominal ready set of τ-bouquets, $|cl\tau| = k$, and $K : \{1, \ldots, k\}^* \to B$ is a B-labelled Hintikka tree with $K(\alpha) = (T_\alpha, \leq_\alpha)$ and $t_\alpha = t_{K(\alpha)}$, for $\alpha \in \{1, \ldots, k\}^*$.

We 'paint' each node of K in one of three 'colours:' inc (for increasing), const (for constant), and dec (for decreasing). The colour of a node α will be denoted by $c(\alpha)$. It is defined by induction as follows. The root ϵ and its immediate successors are painted with the same colour, say, $c(\epsilon) = c(1) = \cdots = c(k) = \mathsf{inc}$. Suppose now that we have already defined $c(\alpha i)$. Then, for $1 \leq j \leq k$, we set

- $c(\alpha ij) = \mathsf{const}$ iff $t_{\alpha ij} \sim_{\alpha i} t_\alpha$,
- $c(\alpha ij) = \mathsf{dec}$ iff $t_\alpha >_{\alpha i} t_{\alpha ij}$,
- $c(\alpha ij) = \mathsf{inc}$ iff $t_\alpha <_{\alpha i} t_{\alpha ij}$.

Intuitively, the colours determine whether in the symmetric space (Δ_0, d_0) to be constructed from $\{1, \ldots, k\}^*$ we have $d_0(\alpha, \alpha i) = d_0(\alpha i, \alpha i j)$ (the constant case), $d_0(\alpha, \alpha i) < d_0(\alpha i, \alpha i j)$ (the increasing case), or $d_0(\alpha, \alpha i) > d_0(\alpha i, \alpha i j)$ (the decreasing case).

We call K a *min-tree* if its every branch with infinitely many dec nodes also contains infinitely many inc nodes.

We require two simple observations; see [11] for proofs. First, the Hintikka tree K constructed in the proof of Lemma 1 starting from a *symmetric* min-model $\mathfrak{I}$ is a min-tree. And second, if there is a sequence $\alpha, \alpha i_1, \ldots, \alpha i_1 \cdots i_{n+1}$ (for $1 \leq i_j \leq k$) of nodes of K such that

$$(K(\alpha), K(\alpha i_1)) = (K(\alpha i_1 \cdots i_n), K(\alpha i_1 \cdots i_{n+1}))$$

then by 'cutting off' the nodes $\alpha, \ldots, \alpha i_1 \cdots i_{n-1}$ we obtain again a B-labelled Hintikka tree such that the colours of the (renamed) nodes do not change.

We are now in a position to prove a symmetric analogue of Lemma 1.

Lemma 3. *For every term τ, the following conditions are equivalent:*

(a) *τ is satisfiable in some symmetric min-model (with at least two distinct types);*
(b) *there exists a Hintikka min-tree satisfying τ over $\{1, \ldots, k\}^*$, where $k = |cl\,\tau|$;*
(c) *τ is satisfiable in a finite symmetric model (with at least two different types).*

Proof. (a) $\Rightarrow$ (b) is established in precisely the same way as in the proof of Lemma 1 using the first observation above that if we start with a symmetric model then the resulting Hintikka tree is a min-tree. (c) $\Rightarrow$ (a) is again trivial.

(b) $\Rightarrow$ (c) Suppose that $K : \{1, \ldots, k\}^* \rightarrow B$ is a Hintikka min-tree satisfying τ with

$$K(\alpha) = (T_\alpha, \leq_\alpha) \quad \text{and} \quad t_\alpha = t_{K(\alpha)}.$$

By the second observation above, without loss of generality we may assume that if no node in a path of the form $\alpha, \alpha i_1, \ldots, \alpha i_1 \cdots i_n$ is inc then no two dec nodes $\beta i j$ and $\beta' i j$ in it can have predecessors $(\beta, \beta i)$ and $(\beta', \beta' j)$ such that $(K(\beta), K(\beta i)) = (K(\beta'), K(\beta' j))$. It follows that there is a number n_τ (exponential in $|cl\,\tau|$) which bounds the numbers of dec nodes in each such path.

Now we define a symmetric distance space (Δ_0, d_0) with $\Delta_0 = \{1, \ldots, k\}^*$ (symmetry means that $d_0(\alpha, \alpha i) = d_0(\alpha i, \alpha)$ for $\alpha \in \Delta_0$ and $1 \leq i \leq k$). First we take a set $D \subset (9, 10)$ of cardinality $n_\tau \times |cl\,\tau|$. For all $1 \leq i \leq k$ we define $d_0(\epsilon, i)$ to be the maximal numbers in D such that we can satisfy the constraint: $d_0(\epsilon, i) < d_0(\epsilon, j)$ iff $t_{K(i)} <_\epsilon t_{K(j)}$, for $1 \leq i, j \leq k$. Suppose now that $d_0(\alpha, \alpha i) \in D$ is defined. Then we define $d_0(\alpha i, \alpha i j)$ to be the maximal number in D such that we can satisfy the constraints

- $d_0(\alpha i, \alpha i j) = d_0(\alpha, \alpha i)$ for $t_{K(\alpha i j)} = t_{K(\alpha)}$ and
- $d_0(\alpha i, \alpha i j) < d_0(\alpha i, \alpha i j')$ iff $t_{K(\alpha i j)} <_{\alpha i} t_{K(\alpha i j')}$, for $1 \leq j, j' \leq k$.

Notice that this is possible by the definition of n_τ. Finally, set $d_0(\alpha, \alpha) = 0$ and $d_0(\alpha, \beta) = 10$ for all remaining $\alpha \neq \beta$.

Now construct a finite symmetric model $\mathfrak{I} = (\Delta, d, p_1^{\mathfrak{I}}, \ldots, \ell_1^{\mathfrak{I}}, \ldots)$ as follows. Let $\sim$ be the equivalence relation on Δ_0 defined by taking $\alpha \sim \beta$ iff $t_{K(\alpha)} = t_{K(\beta)}$. Then we set

$$[\alpha] = \{\beta \in \Delta_0 \mid \alpha \sim \beta\}, \quad \Delta = \{[\alpha] \mid \alpha \in \{1, \ldots, k\}^*\}, \quad d([\alpha], [\beta]) = d_0([\alpha], [\beta])$$

and $[\alpha] \in p_i^{\mathfrak{I}}$ iff $p_i \in t_{K(\alpha)}$, and $\ell_i^{\mathfrak{I}} = [\alpha]$ for the uniquely determined $[\alpha]$ such that $\{\ell_i\} \in t_{K(\alpha)}$. We leave it to the reader to check that this model is as required.

A *single complemented pair automaton* $\mathcal{A}$ on infinite k-ary trees is a tuple $(\Sigma, Q, \Gamma, Q_0, F)$, where

- (Σ, Q, Γ, Q_0) is a looping tree automaton as defined in Section 4.1,
- F is a pair of disjoint sets of states from Q; it will be convenient for us to assume that $F = (\mathsf{dec}, \mathsf{inc})$ and $\mathsf{dec}, \mathsf{inc} \subseteq Q$.

$\mathcal{A}$ accepts a Σ-labelled tree T over $\{1, \ldots, k\}^*$ iff there exists a run R of $\mathcal{A}$ on T such that, for every path $i_0 i_1 \ldots$ in T, if $R(i_0 i_1 \ldots i_j) \in \mathsf{dec}$ for infinitely many j, then $R(i_0 i_1 \ldots i_j) \in \mathsf{inc}$ for infinitely many j as well.

As was shown in [4], the emptiness problem for single complemented pair automata is decidable in polynomial time. We show now how to reduce the satisfiability problem for $\mathcal{CSL}$-terms in symmetric models to the emptiness problem for these automata.

A *coloured τ-bouquet* is a pair $(\mathfrak{B}, c)$ where $\mathfrak{B} = (T_\mathfrak{B}, \leq_\mathfrak{B})$ is a τ-bouquet and c is a function from $T_\mathfrak{B}$ to $\{\mathsf{dec}, \mathsf{inc}, \mathsf{const}\}$.

With every term τ and every nominal ready set B of coloured τ-bouquets we associate a single complemented pair automaton $\mathcal{A}_\tau^B = (\Sigma, Q, \Delta, Q_0, F)$ by taking

- Σ to be the set of types occurring in coloured bouquets of B,
- $Q = B$,
- $Q_0 = \{(\mathfrak{B}, c) \in B \mid \tau \in t_\mathfrak{B}, \mathfrak{B} \text{ contains a type with } \ell \text{ for every } \ell \text{ in } \tau\}$,
- $\mathsf{dec} = \{(\mathfrak{B}, c) \in B \mid c(t_\mathfrak{B}) = \mathsf{dec}\}$,
- $\mathsf{inc} = \{(\mathfrak{B}, c) \in B \mid c(t_\mathfrak{B}) = \mathsf{inc}\}$,
- $(t, (\mathfrak{B}_0, c_0), (\mathfrak{B}_1, c_1), \ldots, (\mathfrak{B}_k, c_k)) \in \Gamma$ iff $t_{\mathfrak{B}_0} = t$,

$$T_{\mathfrak{B}_0} \setminus \{t_{\mathfrak{B}_0}\} = \{t_{\mathfrak{B}_i} \mid 1 \leq i \leq k\},$$

$t_{\mathfrak{B}_0} \in T_{\mathfrak{B}_i} \setminus \{t_{\mathfrak{B}_i}\}, c_i(t_{\mathfrak{B}_i}) = c_0(t_{\mathfrak{B}_i})$ for $1 \leq i \leq k$, and for all $t' \in T_{\mathfrak{B}_i} \setminus \{t_{\mathfrak{B}_i}\}$,

- $c_i(t') = \mathsf{inc}$ iff $t <_{\mathfrak{B}_i} t'$,
- $c_i(t') = \mathsf{const}$ iff $t' \sim_{\mathfrak{B}_i} t$,
- $c_i(t') = \mathsf{dec}$ iff $t' <_{\mathfrak{B}_i} t$.

It follows immediately from Lemma 3 and the given definitions that the runs of $\mathcal{A}_\tau^B$ on Σ-labelled trees are exactly the B-labelled Hintikka-trees satisfying τ.

Lemma 4. *A term τ is satisfiable in a symmetric min-model (with at least two distinct types) iff there exists a nominal ready set B of coloured τ-bouquets such that $\mathcal{A}_\tau^B$ accepts at least one tree.*

As there are only exponentially many different nominal ready sets B of coloured τ-bouquets and as $\mathcal{A}_\tau^B$ is only exponential in $|cl\tau|$, the satisfiability problem in symmetric min-models is decidable in ExpTime.

This completes the proof of Theorem 1.

5   Proof of Theorem 2

Here we only discuss the idea of the proof; see [11] for details. The proof is by reduction of the decision problem for Diophantine equations (Hilbert's 10th problem) which was shown to be undecidable by Matiyasevich–Robinson–Davis–Putnam (see [9, 2] and references therein). More precisely, we will use the following (still undecidable) variant of this problem:

given arbitrary polynomials g and h with coefficients from $\mathbb{N} \setminus \{0, 1\}$, decide whether the equation $g = h$ has a solution in the set $\mathbb{N} \setminus \{0, 1\}$.

Observe first that we can always deal with models based on *one-dimensional* spaces. Indeed, let $\mathfrak{J}$ be based on $\mathbb{R}^n$. Then, for nominals ℓ_0 and ℓ_1, the term $(\{\ell_0\} \leftrightarrows \{\ell_1\}) \sqcap \forall \neg(\{\ell_0\} \sqcap \{\ell_1\})$, if satisfiable, defines an affine subspace of dimension $n - 1$. By iterating this construction we can reduce dimension to 1.

Let $\mathcal{R}$ be the class of min-models based on subspaces of $\mathbb{R}$. We begin by considering the satisfiability problem for $\mathcal{CSL}$-terms in $\mathcal{R}$; then we discuss how to deal with finite models only. It is easy to see that any polynomial equation can be rewritten equivalently as a set of elementary equations of the form

$$x = y + z, \quad x = y \cdot z, \quad x = y, \quad x = n, \tag{4}$$

where x, y, z are variables and $n \in \mathbb{N} \setminus \{0, 1\}$. Now we are facing the following three tasks:

(a) to ensure that a given model is based on a space similar to $\mathbb{Z}$;
(b) to define in such a model sets of the form $\{lk + j \mid k \in \mathbb{Z}\}$ that will be used to encode the number l;
(c) to encode addition and multiplication on such sets.

For (a) we set $\mathsf{Base}(\mathbf{p})$ to be the term

$$\exists p_0 \sqcap \exists p_1 \sqcap \exists p_2 \ \sqcap \ \forall(p_0 \sqcup p_1 \sqcup p_2) \ \sqcap \ \forall \prod_{i<3}(p_i \ \rightarrow \ \neg p_{i \oplus 1} \sqcap (p_{i \ominus 1} \leftrightarrows p_{i \oplus 1})),$$

where $\mathbf{p}$ is stands for p_0, p_1, p_2, and $\oplus, \ominus$ denote addition and subtraction modulo 3. Then a model $\mathfrak{J} \in \mathcal{R}$ satisfies $\mathsf{Base}(\mathbf{p})$ iff $\mathfrak{J}$ coincides (modulo an affine transformation) with a model $\mathfrak{Z}$ such that $\Delta^{\mathfrak{Z}} = \mathbb{Z}$ and $p_i^{\mathfrak{Z}} = \{3k + i \mid k \in \mathbb{Z}\}$, $i < 3$. Now we can simulate the functions '$+1$' and '-1' with the following analogues of the 'next-time' operator and its inverse (τ is an arbitrary term):

$$\bigcirc \tau = \prod_{i<3}(p_i \rightarrow (p_{i \oplus 1} \leftrightarrows (p_{i \oplus 1} \sqcap \tau))), \quad \bigcirc^{-1} \tau = \prod_{i<3}(p_i \rightarrow (p_{i \ominus 1} \leftrightarrows (p_{i \ominus 1} \sqcap \tau))).$$

Next, to fix an origin and an orientation for our model we take a fresh atom p and consider the term $\exists(p_2 \sqcap \neg p \sqcap \bigcirc p) \sqcap \forall(p \to \bigcirc p)$. It is satisfied in a model $\mathfrak{Z}$ of the above form iff $p^{\mathfrak{Z}} = \{k, k+1, \dots\}$ for some $k \in \mathbb{Z}$, $k \equiv 0 \pmod 3$. Thus we can assume that $p^{\mathfrak{Z}} = \mathbb{N}$. Then $\mathsf{Zero} = p \sqcap \bigcirc^{-1} \neg p$ defines $\{0\}$.

For (b) we take the term

$$\mathsf{Seq}(\mathbf{q}) \;=\; \forall\bigsqcap_{i<3}\left(q_i \;\to\; \neg q_{i\oplus 1} \sqcap (q_{i\oplus 1} \leftrightarrows q_{i\ominus 1})\right) \;\sqcap\; \exists(q_0 \sqcap p \sqcap (q_2 \leftharpoondown (q_2 \sqcap p)))$$

which is satisfied in $\mathfrak{Z}$ iff $q_i^{\mathfrak{Z}} = \{lk + j \mid k \equiv i \pmod 3\}$, $i < 3$, for some $j < l$ in $\mathbb{N}$. We say in this case that $\mathbf{q}$ (and $\{lk+j \mid k \in \mathbb{Z}\}$) *encodes* l with *indent* j. For each term τ, we let $\hat{\tau} = \tau \sqcap p$. If $\mathbf{q}$ encodes l with indent j then j, $j + l$, $j + 2l$ are the nearest points to 0 satisfying $\hat{q}_0$, $\hat{q}_1$ and $\hat{q}_2$, respectively. Clearly, two sets encode the same number iff they either coincide or strictly alternate. This can be expressed by the term

$$\mathsf{Alt}(\mathbf{q}, \mathbf{q}') \;=\; \forall\bigsqcap_{i<3}\left((q_i \to (q_i' \leftharpoondown q_{i\oplus 1})) \;\sqcap\; (q_i' \to (q_i \leftharpoondown q_{i\oplus 1}'))\right)$$

in conjunction with $\mathsf{Seq}(\mathbf{q})$ and $\mathsf{Seq}(\mathbf{q}')$. Note also that to encode a number n we can use the term $\mathsf{Seq}(\mathbf{q}) \sqcap \forall(\mathsf{Zero} \to (\hat{q}_1 \leftrightarrows \bigcirc^{-n}\mathsf{Zero}))$.

For (c), let $\mathbf{q}$, $\mathbf{r}$, $\mathbf{s}$ encode, respectively, the numbers u, v, w with indent 0. Let $v < w$ (which can be expressed by $\forall(\mathsf{Zero} \to (\hat{r}_1 \leftharpoondown \hat{s}_1))$). Then the term

$$\mathsf{Seq}(\mathbf{s}') \;\sqcap\; \mathsf{Alt}(\mathbf{s}, \mathbf{s}') \;\sqcap\; \forall(\mathsf{Zero} \to (\hat{s}_0' \leftrightarrows \hat{r}_1) \sqcap (\hat{s}_1' \leftrightarrows \hat{q}_1))$$

(with some fresh $\mathbf{s}'$) says that $\mathbf{s}'$ encodes w with indent v and that $v + w = u$. The case $w < v$ is symmetrical, while the case $v = w$, i.e., $u = v + v$, can be expressed by $\forall(\mathsf{Zero} \to (\hat{s}_1 \leftrightarrows \hat{r}_1) \sqcap (\hat{s}_2 \leftrightarrows \hat{q}_1))$. To encode multiplication, we use

Fact 1. *Let v, w be integer numbers with $0 < v < w - 1$. Then*

1) *$u = vw$ is the least solution to $u \equiv 0 \pmod w$, $u \equiv v \pmod{(w-1)}$.*
2) *$u = (w-1)w$ is the least positive solution to $u \equiv 0 \pmod w$, $u \equiv 0 \pmod{(w-1)}$.*
3) *$u = w^2$ is the least solution to $u \equiv 0 \pmod w$, $u \equiv 1 \pmod{(w-1)}$, $x > w$.*

Suppose that $v < w - 1$. Take fresh $\mathbf{s}'$, $\mathbf{s}''$ and consider the term

$$\mathsf{Seq}(\mathbf{s}') \;\sqcap\; \mathsf{Seq}(\mathbf{s}'') \;\sqcap\; \mathsf{Alt}(\mathbf{s}', \mathbf{s}'') \;\sqcap\; \forall\big(\mathsf{Zero} \to s_0' \sqcap (\hat{s}_1' \leftrightarrows \bigcirc \hat{s}_1) \sqcap (\hat{s}_0'' \leftrightarrows \hat{r}_1)\big) \quad (5)$$

saying that $\mathbf{s}'$ and $\mathbf{s}''$ encode the same number, this number is $w - 1$, $\mathbf{s}'$ encodes it with indent 0, while $\mathbf{s}''$ with indent v. Let $s_* = s_0 \sqcup s_1 \sqcup s_2$, $s_*'' = s_0'' \sqcup s_1'' \sqcup s_2''$. Then, in view of Fact 1 (1), term (5) means that $v \cdot w$ is the nearest point to 0 satisfying $\hat{s}_* \sqcap \hat{s}_*''$. Therefore, $\forall(\mathsf{Zero} \to (\hat{q}_1 \leftrightarrows (\hat{s}_* \sqcap \hat{s}_*'')))$ in conjunction with (5) ensures that $u = v \cdot w$.

For the cases $v = w - 1$, $v = w$ we use similar constructions by applying Fact 1 (2,3). Thus we can encode any elementary equation from (4), and so the whole system of such equations representing the given polynomial equation.

In the finite case, we modify the terms $\mathsf{Base}(\mathbf{p})$, $\mathsf{Seq}(\mathbf{q})$, $\mathsf{Alt}(\mathbf{q}, \mathbf{q}')$ to take care of the endpoints. And to ensure that two encoding sets represent the same number, we require additionally that they are sufficiently long.

In fact, the undecidability for min-subspaces of $\mathbb{R}^n$, $n \geq 2$, can be proved by reduction of the $\mathbb{Z} \times \mathbb{Z}$ tiling problem. To simulate the $\mathbb{Z} \times \mathbb{Z}$ grid we use

$$\tau \;\; = \;\; \exists p_0 \sqcap \exists p_1 \sqcap \forall \bigsqcap \{p_i \rightarrow \neg p_{i \oplus 1} \sqcap (p_{i \oplus 1} \leftrightarrows p_j) \mid i, j < 7, j \neq i, i \oplus 1\},$$

where $\oplus$ is addition modulo 7. Let $\mathfrak{T}$ be a min-model satisfying τ and based on a subspace of $\mathbb{R}^2$, and let $P_i = p_i^{\mathfrak{T}}$ $(i < 7)$. Then one can show that $P_0 \cup \cdots \cup P_6$ forms a grid as in (6a).

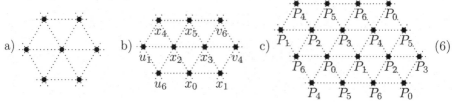

$$(6)$$

To encode tilings, we need to fix some concrete partition of this grid into the sets $P_0, \ldots, P_6$. First we note that, in fact, it suffices to fix such a partition for a few points only. Indeed, suppose that $x_0 \in P_0$, $\ldots$, $x_5 \in P_5$ are located as in (6b). Then we have $u_1 \in P_1$, $v_4 \in P_4$, $u_6, v_6 \in P_6$. This means that neither of the two six-point figures $u_6, x_0, x_1, x_2, x_3, v_4$ and $u_1, x_2, x_3, x_4, x_5, v_6$ contain a pair of points from the same P_i. It follows that the entire grid is as in (6c).

To ensure that such $x_0, \ldots, x_5$ exist, we set, for distinct $i, j, k < 7$,

$$\mu_{ijk} \;\; = \;\; (p_i \leftrightarrows p_j) \sqcap (p_i \leftrightarrows p_k) \sqcap \bigsqcap \{p_i \leftleftarrows p_l \mid l < 7, \ l \neq i, j, k\}.$$

Then $x \in \mathfrak{T}$ satisfies μ_{ijk} iff x is the centre of some small triangle $x_i x_j x_k$ with $x_i \in P_i$, $x_j \in P_j$, $x_k \in P_k$. Consider now the term $\sigma = \mu_{103} \sqcap (\mu_{032} \leftrightarrows p_3)$. Then σ is satisfied in $\mathfrak{T}$ iff there exist small triangles $x_1 x_0 x_3$, $x_0' x_3' x_2$ $(x_i, x_i' \in P_i)$ in our grid such that their centres x and x' belong to $\mathfrak{T}$, and the distances from x to x_3 and x' coincide. This can only be possible if $x_0 = x_0'$, $x_3 = x_3'$. Using this idea one can easily construct a term τ_1 that enforces a configuration of points $x_0 \in P_0$, $\ldots$, $x_5 \in P_5$ as in (6b). Then every model satisfying $\tau \sqcap \tau_1$ will contain a grid of the form (6c), and we can encode the $\mathbb{Z} \times \mathbb{Z}$ tiling problem.

6   Outlook

In this paper, we have investigated the computational complexity of the basic logic $\mathcal{CSL}$ for comparative similarity. The final verdict is that this logic behaves similarly to standard description logics (is ExpTime-complete) over general classes of (finite or min-) distance spaces, but becomes undecidable when interpreted over (finite or min-) subspaces of Euclidean spaces.

Starting from the positive results, one can now investigate combinations of $\mathcal{CSL}$ with 'quantitative' similarity logics from [17, 8] as well as with description logics. On the other hand, it would be interesting to find out how one can avoid the 'negative' results for subspaces of $\mathbb{R}^n$. One promising route is to impose restrictions on the interpretations of set variables. For example, in many applications it seems natural to assume that variables are interpreted as intervals in (subspaces of) $\mathbb{R}$. In this case decidability would follow immediately. Another related question is whether the computational behaviour of the logics depends on the 'crisp' truth-conditions. Exploring more relaxed 'non-punctual' truth-conditions could be important as well in order to take into account unprecise measurements, vagueness, and paradoxes of similarity such as the Sorites paradox.

Acknowledgements. The work on this paper was partially supported by the U.K. EPSRC research grants GR/S61966/01 and GR/S61973/01.

References

1. A. Cohn and S. Hazarika. Qualitative spatial representation and reasoning: an overview. *Fundamenta Informaticae*, 43:2–32, 2001.
2. M. Davis. Unsolvable problems. In J. Barwise, editor, *Handbook of Mathematical Logic*, pages 567–594. North-Holland, Amsterdam, 1977.
3. J. P. Delgrande. Preliminary considerations on the modelling of belief change operators by metric spaces. In *NMR*, pages 118–125, 2004.
4. E. Emerson and C. Jutla. The complexity of tree automata and logics of programs. *SIAM Journal of Computing*, 29:132–158, 1999.
5. N. Friedman and J. Halpern. On the complexity of conditional logics. In *Proceedings of KR'94*, pages 202–213, 1994.
6. O. Kutz, H. Sturm, N.-Y. Suzuki, F. Wolter, and M. Zakharyaschev. Logics of metric spaces. *ACM Transactions on Computational Logic*, 4:260–294, 2003.
7. D. Lewis. *Counterfactuals*. Blackwell, Oxford, 1973.
8. C. Lutz, F. Wolter, and M. Zakharyaschev. A tableau algorithm for reasoning about concepts and similarity. In M. C. Mayer and F. Pirri, editors, *Automated Reasoning with Analytic Tableaux and Related Methods*, volume 2796 of *LNCS*, pages 134–149. Springer, 2003.
9. Yu. V. Matiyasevich. Enumerable sets are Diophantine. *Soviet Mathematics Doklady*, 11:354–358, 1970.
10. K. Schlechta. *Coherent Systems*. Elsevier, 2004.
11. M. Sheremet, D. Tishkovsky, F. Wolter, and M. Zakharyaschev. Comparative similarity, tree automata, and diophantine equations. Available at http://www.csc.liv.ac.uk/~frank/publ/publ.html, 2005.
12. E. Spaan. *Complexity of Modal Logics*. PhD thesis, University of Amsterdam, 1993.
13. W. Thomas. Automata on infinite objects. In *Handbook of Theoretical Computer Science*, volume B, pages 133–191. Elsevier, 1990.
14. A. Tversky. Features of similarity. *Psychological Review*, 84:327–352, 1977.
15. M. Vardi and P. Wolper. Automata-theoretic techniques for modal logics of programs. *Journal of Computer and System Sciences*, 32:183–221, 1986.
16. T. Williamson. First-order logics for comparative similarity. *Notre Dame Journal of Formal Logic*, 29:457–481, 1988.
17. F. Wolter and M. Zakharyaschev. Reasoning about distances. In *Proceedings of the 18th International Joint Conference on Artificial Intelligence (IJCAI 2003)*, pages 1275–1280. Morgan Kaufmann, 2003.
18. F. Wolter and M. Zakharyaschev. A logic for metric and topology. *Journal of Symbolic Logic*, 70:795–828, 2005.

Analytic Tableaux for KLM Preferential and Cumulative Logics*

Laura Giordano[1], Valentina Gliozzi[2], Nicola Olivetti[3], and Gian Luca Pozzato[4]

[1] Dipartimento di Informatica,
Università del Piemonte Orientale A. Avogadro - Alessandria, Italy
laura@mfn.unipmn.it
[2] Dipartimento di Informatica, Università degli Studi di Torino, Italy
gliozzi@di.unito.it
[3] LSIS - UMR CNRS 6168, Université Paul Cézanne (Aix-Marseille 3),
Marseille, France
nicola.olivetti@univ.u-3mrs.fr
[4] Dipartimento di Informatica, Università degli Studi di Torino, Italy
pozzato@di.unito.it

Abstract. We present tableau calculi for some logics of default reasoning, as defined by Kraus, Lehmann and Magidor. We give a tableau proof procedure for preferential and cumulative logics. Our calculi are obtained by introducing suitable modalities to interpret conditional assertions. Moreover, they give a decision procedure for the respective logics and can be used to establish their complexity.

1 Introduction

In the early 90' [11] Kraus, Lehmann and Magidor (from now on KLM) proposed a formalization of non-monotonic reasoning that was early recognized as a landmark. Their work stemmed from two sources: the theory of nonmonotonic consequence relations initiated by Gabbay [6] and the preferential semantics proposed by Shoham [13] as a generalization of Circumscription. Their works lead to a classification of nonmonotonic consequence relations, determining a hierarchy of stronger and stronger systems.

According to the KLM framework, defeasible knowledge is represented by a (finite) set of nonmonotonic conditionals or assertions of the form $A \mathrel{|\!\sim} B$ whose reading is *normally (or typically) the A's are B's*. The operator "$\mathrel{|\!\sim}$" is nonmonotonic, in the sense that $A \mathrel{|\!\sim} B$ does not imply $A \wedge C \mathrel{|\!\sim} B$. For instance, a knowledge base K may contain the following set of conditionals: *adult $\mathrel{|\!\sim}$ work, adult $\mathrel{|\!\sim}$ taxpayer, student $\mathrel{|\!\sim}$ adult, student $\mathrel{|\!\sim}$ ¬work, student $\mathrel{|\!\sim}$ ¬taxpayer, retired $\mathrel{|\!\sim}$ adult, retired $\mathrel{|\!\sim}$ ¬work*, whose meaning is that adults typically work, adults typically pay taxes, students are typically adults, but they typically do not work, nor do they pay taxes, and so on. Observe that if $\mathrel{|\!\sim}$

---

* This research has been partially supported by the project MIUR PRIN 2003 "Logic-based development and verication of multi-agent systems".

were interpreted as classical (or intuitionistic) implication, we simply would get *student* $\vdash \perp$, *retired* $\vdash \perp$, i.e. typically there are not students, nor retired people, thereby obtaining a trivial knowledge base. One can derive new conditional assertions from the knowledge base by means of a set of inference rules.

In KLM framework, the set of adopted inference rules defines some fundamental types of inference systems, namely, from the weakest to the strongest: Cumulative (**C**) , Loop-Cumulative (**CL**), Preferential (**P**) and Rational logic (**R**). All these systems allow one to infer new assertions from K without incurring in the trivialising conclusions of classical logic: regarding our example, in none of them, one can infer *student* $\vdash$ *work* or *retired* $\vdash$ *work*. In cumulative logics (both **C** and **CL**) one can infer *adult* $\wedge$ *student* $\vdash \neg work$ (giving preference to more specific information), in Preferential logic **P** one can also infer that *adult* $\vdash \neg retired$ (i.e. typical adults are not retired). In the rational case **R**, if one further knows that *adult* $\not\vdash \neg married$ (i.e. it is not the case the adults are typically unmarried), one can also infer that *adult* $\wedge$ *married* $\vdash$ *work*.

From a semantic point of view, to the each logic (**C**, **CL**, **P**, **R**) corresponds one kind of models, namely, possible-world structures equipped with a preference relation among worlds or states. More precisely, for **P** we have models with a preference relation (an irreflexive and transitive relation) on worlds. For the stronger **R** the preference relation is further assumed to be *modular*. For the weaker logic **CL**, the preference relation is defined on *states*, where a state can be identified, intuitively, with a set of worlds. In the weakest case of **C**, the preference relation is on states, as for **CL**, but it is no longer assumed to be transitive. In all cases, the meaning of a conditional assertion $A \vdash B$ is that B holds in the *most preferred* worlds/states where A holds.

In KLM framework the operator "$\vdash$" is considered as a meta-language operator, rather than as a connective in the object language. However, it has been readily observed that KLM systems **P** and **R** coincide to a large extent with the flat (i.e. unnested) fragments of well-known conditional logics, once we interpret the operator "$\vdash$" as a binary connective [3], [2], [10].

A recent result by Halpern and Friedman [4] has shown that preferential and rational logic are quite natural and general systems: surprisingly enough, the axiom system of preferential (likewise of rational logic) is complete with respect to a wide spectrum of semantics, from ranked models, to parametrized probabilistic structures, ϵ-semantics and possibilistic structures. The reason is that all these structures are examples of *plausibility structures* and the truth in them is captured by the axioms of preferential (or rational) logic. These results, and their extensions to the first order setting [5] are the source of a renewed interest in KLM framework.

Even if KLM was born as an inferential approach to nonmonotonic reasoning, curiously enough, there has not been much investigation on deductive mechanisms for these logics. In short, the state of the art is as follows:

- Lehmann and Magidor [12] have proved that validity in **P** is **coNP**-complete. Their decision procedure for **P** is more a theoretical tool than a practical algorithm, as it requires to guess sets of indexes and propositional evaluations.

They have also provided another procedure for **P** that exploits its reduction to **R**. However, the reduction of **P** to **R** breaks down if boolean combinations of conditionals are allowed, indeed it is exactly when such combinations are allowed that the difference between **P** and **R** arises.

- A tableau proof procedure for **C** has been given in [1]. Their tableau procedure is fairly complicated; it uses labels and it contains a cut-rule. Moreover, it is not clear how it can be adapted to **CL** and **P**.
- In [7] it is defined a labelled tableau calculus for the conditional logic **CE** whose flat fragment (i.e. without nested conditionals) corresponds to **P**. That calculus needs a fairly complicated loop-checking mechanism to ensure termination. It is not clear if it matches complexity bounds and if it can be adapted in a simple way to **CL**.
- Finally, decidability of **P** and **R** has also been obtained by interpreting them into standard modal logics, as it is done by Boutilier [2]. However, his mapping is not very direct and natural, as we discuss below.
- To the best of our knowledge, for **CL** no decision procedure and complexity bound was known before the present work.

In this work we begin our investigation of tableau procedures for KLM logics, by considering the cases of **P** and **CL**. The investigation of tableau calculi for the weakest **C** and the strongest **R** is left for future work. Our approach is based on a novel interpretation of **P** into modal logics. As a difference with previous approaches (e.g. Lamarre [3] and Boutillier [2]), that take S4 as the modal counterpart of **P**, we consider here modal logic G. Our tableau method provides a sort of run-time translation of **P** into modal logic G.

The idea is simply to interpret the preference relation as an accessibility relation: a conditional $A \mathrel{\vert\!\sim} B$ holds in a model if B is true in all A-worlds w that are minimal. An A-world is minimal if all smaller worlds are not A-worlds. The relation with modal logic G is motivated by the fact that we assume, following KLM, the so-called *smoothness condition*, which is related to the well-known *limit assumption*. This condition ensures indeed that A-minimal worlds exist, by preventing an infinitely descending chain of worlds. This condition is therefore ensured by the finite-chain condition on the accessibility relation (as in modal logic G). Therefore, our interpretation of conditionals is different from the one proposed by Boutilier, who rejects the smoothness condition and then gives a less natural (and more complicated) interpretation of **P** into modal logic S4.

However, we do not give a formal translation of **P** into G, we appeal to the correspondence as far as it is needed to derive the tableau rules for **P**. For deductive purposes, we believe that our approach is more direct, intuitive, and efficient than translating **P** into G and then using a calculus for G.

We are able to extend our approach to the case of **CL** by using a second modality which takes care of states. More precisely, we show that we can map **CL**-models into **P**-models with an additional modality. The very fact that one can interpret **CL** into **P** by means of an additional modality does not seem to be previously known and might be of independent interest. In both cases, **P** and **CL**, we can define a decision procedure and obtain also a complexity bound for these logics, namely that they are both **coNP**-complete. In case of **CL** this bound is new, to the best of our knowledge.

2   KLM Logics

We briefly recall the axiomatizations and semantics of the two KLM systems we consider: **P** and **CL**. For a complete picture of KLM systems, see [11].

2.1   Preferential Logic P

The language of KLM logics consists just of conditional assertions $A \mathrel{|\!\sim} B$. We consider a richer language allowing boolean combinations of assertions and propositional formulas. Our language $\mathcal{L}$ is defined from a set of propositional variables ATM, the boolean connectives and the conditional operator $\mathrel{|\!\sim}$. We use $A, B, C, ...$ to denote propositional formulas, whereas $F, G, ...$ are used to denote all formulas (even conditionals); $\Gamma, \Delta, ...$ represent sets of formulas, whereas $X, Y, ...$ denote sets of sets of formulas. The formulas of $\mathcal{L}$ are defined as follows: if A is a propositional formula, $A \in \mathcal{L}$; if A and B are propositional formulas, $A \mathrel{|\!\sim} B \in \mathcal{L}$; if F is a boolean combination of formulas of $\mathcal{L}$, $F \in \mathcal{L}$.

The axiomatization of **P** consists of all axioms and rules of propositional calculus together with the following axioms and rules (notice that $\vdash$ denotes provability in the propositional calculus):

- REF. $A \mathrel{|\!\sim} A$ (reflexivity)
- LLE. If $\vdash A \leftrightarrow B$, then $(A \mathrel{|\!\sim} C) \to (B \mathrel{|\!\sim} C)$ (left logical equivalence)
- RW. If $\vdash A \to B$, then $(C \mathrel{|\!\sim} A) \to (C \mathrel{|\!\sim} B)$ (right weakening)
- CM. $((A \mathrel{|\!\sim} B) \wedge (A \mathrel{|\!\sim} C)) \to (A \wedge B \mathrel{|\!\sim} C)$ (cautious monotonicity)
- AND. $((A \mathrel{|\!\sim} B) \wedge (A \mathrel{|\!\sim} C)) \to (A \mathrel{|\!\sim} B \wedge C)$
- OR. $((A \mathrel{|\!\sim} C) \wedge (B \mathrel{|\!\sim} C)) \to (A \vee B \mathrel{|\!\sim} C)$

The semantics of **P** is defined by considering possible world structures with a preference relation (a strict partial order) $w < w'$ whose meaning is that w is preferred to w'. We have that $A \mathrel{|\!\sim} B$ holds in a model $\mathcal{M}$ if B holds in all *minimal worlds* (with respect to the relation $<$) where A holds. This definition makes sense provided minimal worlds for A exist whenever there are A-worlds. This is ensured by the *smoothness condition* in the next definition.

Definition 1 (Semantics of P, Definition 16 in [11]). *A preferential model is a triple $\mathcal{M} = \langle \mathcal{W}, <, V \rangle$ where: $\mathcal{W}$ is a non-empty set of items called worlds; $<$ is an irreflexive and transitive relation on $\mathcal{W}$; V is a function $V : \mathcal{W} \longmapsto pow(ATM)$, which assigns to every world w the set of atoms holding in that world. We define the truth conditions for a formula F as follows:*

- *If F is a boolean combination of formulas, $\mathcal{M}, w \models F$ is defined as for propositional logic;*
- *Let A be a propositional formula; we define $Min_<(A) = \{ w \in W \mid \mathcal{M}, w \models A$ and $\forall w'.w' < w$ implies $\mathcal{M}, w' \not\models A \}$;*
- *$\mathcal{M}, w \models A \mathrel{|\!\sim} B$ if for all $w' \in Min_<(A)$ we have $\mathcal{M}, w' \models B$.*

The relation $<$ satisfies the following condition, called smoothness: *if $\mathcal{M}, w \models A$ then $w \in Min_<(A)$ or $\exists w' \in Min_<(A)$ such that $w' < w$.*

We say that a formula F is valid *in a model $\mathcal{M}$, denoted with $\mathcal{M} \models F$, if $\mathcal{M}, w \models F$ for every $w \in \mathcal{W}$. A formula is* valid *if it is valid in every model $\mathcal{M}$.*

Notice that the truth conditions for conditional formulas are given with respect to single possible worlds for uniformity sake. Since the truth value of a conditional only depends on global properties of $\mathcal{M}$, we have that: $\mathcal{M}, w \models A \mathrel{\vdash\mkern-9mu\sim} B$ iff $\mathcal{M} \models A \mathrel{\vdash\mkern-9mu\sim} B$.

Now we introduce the language $\mathcal{L}_P$ of the calculus introduced in the next section. $\mathcal{L}_P$ extends $\mathcal{L}$ by formulas of the form $\Box A$, where A is propositional, whose intuitive meaning is as follows: $\Box A$ holds in a world w if A holds in all the worlds w' such that $w' < w$:

Definition 2 (Truth condition of modality $\Box$). *We define the truth condition of a boxed formula as follows:*

$$\mathcal{M}, w \models \Box A \text{ if for every } w' \in W \text{ if } w' < w \text{ then } \mathcal{M}, w' \models A$$

It is easy to see that $\Box$ has the properties of the modal system G: the accessibility relation (defined as xRy if $y < x$) is transitive and does not have infinite ascending chains. From definition of $Min_<(A)$ in Definition 1 above, and Definition 2, it follows that for any formula A, $w \in Min_<(A)$ iff $\mathcal{M}, w \models A \wedge \Box \neg A$.

2.2   Loop Cumulative Logic CL

The next KLM logic we consider is **CL**, weaker than **P**. The axiomatization of **CL** can be obtained from the axiomatization of **P** by removing the axiom OR and by adding the following infinite set of axioms LOOP:

$$(LOOP) \ (A_0 \mathrel{\vdash\mkern-9mu\sim} A_1) \wedge (A_1 \mathrel{\vdash\mkern-9mu\sim} A_2)...(A_{n-1} \mathrel{\vdash\mkern-9mu\sim} A_n) \wedge (A_n \mathrel{\vdash\mkern-9mu\sim} A_0) \rightarrow (A_0 \mathrel{\vdash\mkern-9mu\sim} A_n)$$

Notice that these axioms are derivable in **P**.

Definition 3 (Loop-cumulative models, Definition 13 in [11]). *A loop-cumulative model is a tuple $\mathcal{M} = \langle S, l, <, V \rangle$. S is a set, whose elements are called* states. *Given a set $\mathcal{U}$ of possible worlds, $l : S \longmapsto 2^{\mathcal{U}}$ is a function that labels every state with a nonempty set of worlds. $<$ is an irreflexive and transitive relation on S. V is a valuation function $V : \mathcal{U} \longmapsto pow(ATM)$, which assigns to every world w the atoms holding in that world. For $s \in S$ and A propositional, we let $s \models A$ if $\forall w \in l(s)$, $w \models A$. Let $Min_<(A)$ be the set of minimal states s such that $s \models A$. We define $\mathcal{M}, s \models A \mathrel{\vdash\mkern-9mu\sim} B$ if $\forall s' \in Min_<(A)$, $s' \models B$. We assume that $<$ satisfies the smoothness condition.*

Here again, we define satisfiability of conditionals with respect to states rather than to models for uniformity reasons. Indeed, a conditional is satisfied by a state of a model only if it is satisfied by all the states of that model, hence by the whole model. We show that we can map loop-cumulative models into preferential models extended with an additional accessibility relation R. We call these preferential models *CL-preferential structures*. The idea is to represent states as sets of possible worlds related by R in such a way that a formula is satisfied in a state s just in case it is satisfied in all possible worlds w' accessible from its corresponding w. The syntactic counterpart of the extra accessibility relation R is a modality L. Given a loop-cumulative model $\mathcal{M}$ and the corresponding CL-structure $\mathcal{M}'$, $\mathcal{M}, s \models A$ iff for its corresponding w, $\mathcal{M}', w \models LA$.

As we will see, this mapping enables us to use a variant of the tableau calculus for **P** to deal with system **CL**. As for **P**, the tableau calculus for **CL** will use boxed formulas. Thus, the formulas that appear in the tableau for **CL** belong to the language $\mathcal{L}_L$ obtained from $\mathcal{L}$ as follows: (i) if A is propositional, then $A \in \mathcal{L}_L$; $LA \in \mathcal{L}_L$; $\Box\neg LA \in \mathcal{L}_L$; ($ii$) if A, B are propositional, then $A \mathrel{\vdash\mkern-9mu\sim} B \in \mathcal{L}_L$; ($iii$) if F is a boolean combination of formulas of $\mathcal{L}_L$, then $F \in \mathcal{L}_L$. Observe that the only allowed combination of $\Box$ and L is in formulas of the form $\Box\neg LA$ where A is propositional.

We can map loop-cumulative models into preferential structures with an additional accessibility relation as defined below:

Definition 4 (CL-preferential structures). *A model has the form* $\mathcal{M} = \langle W, R, <, V \rangle$ *where:* W, $<$, *and* V *are defined as in Definition 1, and* R *is a serial accessibility relation. We add to the truth conditions for preferential models in Definition 1 the following clause:*

$$\mathcal{M}, w \models LA \text{ if for all } w' \text{ } wRw' \text{ implies } \mathcal{M}, w' \models A$$

Moreover, we need to change the truth condition for conditional formulas as follows: $\mathcal{M}, w \models A \mathrel{\vdash\mkern-9mu\sim} B$ *if for all* $w' \in Min_<(LA)$ *we have* $\mathcal{M}, w' \models LB$.

We can prove the following proposition:

Proposition 1. *A set of conditional formulas* $\{(\neg)A_1 \mathrel{\vdash\mkern-9mu\sim} B_1, \ldots, (\neg)A_n \mathrel{\vdash\mkern-9mu\sim} B_n\}$ *is satisfiable in a loop-cumulative model* $\langle S, l, <, V \rangle$ *iff it is satisfiable in a CL-preferential model* $\langle W, R, <, V \rangle$.

3   The Tableau Calculus for Preferential Logic P

In this section we present a tableau calculus for **P** called $\mathcal{T}$**P**, then we analyze it in order to obtain a decision procedure for this logic. We also give an explicit complexity bound for **P**.

Definition 5 (The calculus $\mathcal{T}$P). *The rules of the calculus manipulate sets of formulas* Γ. *We write the shorthand* Γ, F *to denote* $\Gamma \cup \{F\}$. *Moreover, given* Γ *we define the following notation:*

- $\Gamma^\Box = \{\Box A \mid \Box A \in \Gamma\}$ $-\Gamma^{\Box\downarrow} = \{A \mid \Box A \in \Gamma\}$ $-\Gamma^{\vdash\mkern-9mu\sim^+} = \{A \mathrel{\vdash\mkern-9mu\sim} B \mid A \mathrel{\vdash\mkern-9mu\sim} B \in \Gamma\}$
- $\Gamma^{\vdash\mkern-9mu\sim^-} = \{\neg(A \mathrel{\vdash\mkern-9mu\sim} B) \mid \neg(A \mathrel{\vdash\mkern-9mu\sim} B) \in \Gamma\}$ $-\Gamma^{\vdash\mkern-9mu\sim^\pm} = \Gamma^{\vdash\mkern-9mu\sim^+} \cup \Gamma^{\vdash\mkern-9mu\sim^-}$

The tableau rules are given in Figure 1. Due to space limitations, we only give propositional rules for $\neg$ *and* $\wedge$. *We say that a tableau is closed if all its leaves contain both* F *and* $\neg F$, *for a formula* $F \in \mathcal{L}_P$.

$$(\mathbf{AX})\ \Gamma, F, \neg F \qquad\qquad\qquad (\neg)\ \dfrac{\Gamma, \neg\neg F}{\Gamma, F}$$

$$(\vdash^+)\ \dfrac{\Gamma, A \vdash B}{\Gamma, \neg A, A \vdash B \qquad \Gamma, \neg\Box\neg A, A \vdash B \qquad \Gamma, B, A \vdash B}$$

$$(\vdash^-)\ \dfrac{\Gamma, \neg(A \vdash B)}{A, \Box\neg A, \neg B, \Gamma^{\vdash\pm}} \qquad\qquad (\Box^-)\ \dfrac{\Gamma, \neg\Box\neg A}{\Gamma^{\Box}, \Gamma^{\Box\downarrow}, \Gamma^{\vdash\pm}, A, \Box\neg A}$$

$$(\wedge^+)\ \dfrac{\Gamma, F \wedge G}{\Gamma, F, G} \qquad\qquad (\wedge^-)\ \dfrac{\Gamma, \neg(F \wedge G)}{\Gamma, \neg F \qquad \Gamma, \neg G}$$

Fig. 1. Tableau system $\mathcal{TP}$

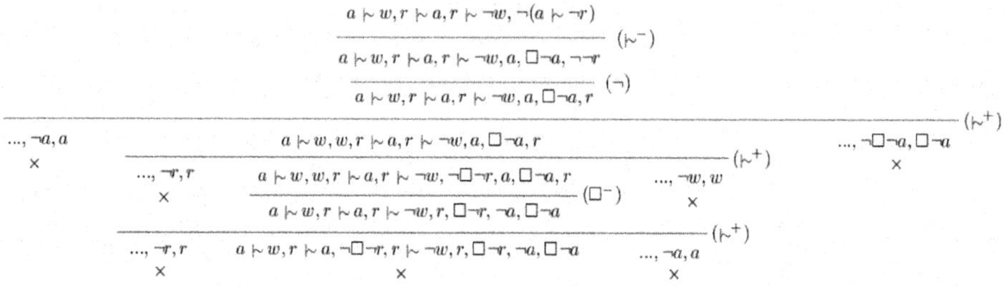

Fig. 2. A derivation of $((adult \vdash work) \wedge (retired \vdash adult) \wedge (retired \vdash \neg work)) \rightarrow (adult \vdash \neg retired)$. For readability, we use a to denote *adult*, r for *retired*, and so on.

Our tableau calculus $\mathcal{TP}$ is based on a runtime translation of conditional assertions into modal logic G. As we have seen this allows a characterization of the minimal worlds satisfying a formula A (i.e., the worlds in $Min_<(A)$) as the worlds w satisfying the formula $A \wedge \Box\neg A$. It is tempting to provide a full translation of the conditionals in the logic G, and then to use the standard tableau calculus for G. To this purpose, we can exploit the transitivity properties of G frames to capture the fact that conditionals are global to all worlds by the formula $\Box(A \wedge \Box\neg A \rightarrow B)$. Hence, the overall translation of a conditional formula $A \vdash B$ could be the following one: $(A \wedge \Box\neg A \rightarrow B) \wedge \Box(A \wedge \Box\neg A \rightarrow B)$. However, there are significant differences between the calculus resulting from the translation and our calculus.

Using the standard tableau rules for G on the translation, we get the rule $(\vdash^+)$ as a derived rule. Instead, the rule for dealing with negated conditionals (which are translated in G into a disjunction of two formulas, namely $(A \wedge \Box\neg A \wedge \neg B) \vee \Diamond(A \wedge \Box\neg A \wedge \neg B)$), is rather different.

Let us first observe that the rule $(\sim^-)$ we have introduced precisely captures the intuition that: (1) conditionals are global (all conditionals are kept in the conclusion of the rule) and (2) when moving to a new minimal world, all the boxed formulas (positive and negated) are removed. Conversely, when the tableau rules for G are applied to the translation of the negated conditionals, we get two branches (due to the disjunction). None of the branches can be eliminated. In both branches all the boxed formulas are kept, while negated conditionals are erased. This is quite different from our rule $(\sim^-)$, and it is not that obvious that the calculus obtained by the translation of **P** conditionals in G is equivalent to $\mathcal{T}\mathbf{P}$.

Also observe that, from the semantic point of view, the model extracted from an open tableau has the structure of a forest, while the model constructed by applying the tableau for G to the translation of conditionals has the structure of a tree. This difference is due to the fact that the above translation of **P** in G uses the same modality $\square$ both for capturing the minimality condition and for modelling the fact that conditionals are global. For this reason, a translation to G as the one proposed above for **P**, would not be applicable to the cumulative logic **C**, as the relation $<$ is not transitive in **C**. Moreover, the treatment of both the logics **C** and **CL** would anyhow require the addition to the language of a new modality to deal with states. The advantage of the runtime translation we have adopted is that of providing a uniform approach to deal with the different logics.

The system $\mathcal{T}\mathbf{P}$ is sound and complete with respect to the semantics.

Theorem 1 (Soundness of $\mathcal{T}\mathbf{P}$). *The system $\mathcal{T}\mathbf{P}$ is sound with respect to the semantics, i.e. if there is a closed tableau for a set Γ, then Γ is unsatisfiable.*

To prove the completeness of $\mathcal{T}\mathbf{P}$ we have to show that if F is unsatisfiable, then there is a closed tableau starting with F. We prove the contrapositive, that is: if there is no closed tableau for F, then there is a model satisfying F. This proof is inspired by [8]. First of all, we distinguish *static* and *dynamic* rules. The rules $(\sim^-)$ and $(\square^-)$ are called *dynamic*, since their conclusion represents another world with respect to the premise; the other rules are called *static*, since the world represented by premise and conclusion(s) is the same. Moreover, we have to introduce the *saturation* of a set of formulas Γ. Given a set of formulas Γ, we say that it is saturated if all the static rules have been applied.

Definition 6 (Saturated sets). *A set of formulas Γ is saturated with respect to the static rules if the following conditions hold:*

- *if $F \wedge G \in \Gamma$ then $F, G \in \Gamma$;*
- *if $\neg(F \wedge G) \in \Gamma$ then $\neg F \in \Gamma$ or $\neg G \in \Gamma$;*
- *if $\neg\neg F \in \Gamma$ then $F \in \Gamma$;*
- *if $A \sim B \in \Gamma$ then $\neg A \in \Gamma$ or $\neg\square\neg A \in \Gamma$ or $B \in \Gamma$.*

Lemma 1. *Given a consistent finite set of formulas Γ, there is a consistent, finite, and saturated set $\Gamma' \supseteq \Gamma$.*

By Lemma 1, we can think of having a function which, given a consistent set Γ, returns one fixed consistent saturated set, denoted by $\mathtt{SAT}(\Gamma)$. Moreover, we denote by $\mathtt{APPLY}(\Gamma, F)$ the result of applying to Γ the rule for the principal connective in F. In case the rule for F has more conclusions (the case of a branching), we suppose that the function $\mathtt{APPLY}$ chooses one consistent conclusion in an arbitrary but fixed manner.

Theorem 2 (Completeness of $\mathcal{T}\mathbf{P}$). $\mathcal{T}\mathbf{P}$ *is complete with respect to the semantics.*

Proof. As mentioned above, we assume that no tableau for Γ_0 is closed, then we construct a model for Γ_0. We build X, the set of worlds of the model, as follows:

1. initialize $X = \{\mathtt{SAT}(\Gamma_0)\}$;
while X contains unresolved nodes do
    2. choose an unresolved Γ from X;
    3. **for** each formula $\neg(A \mathrel{\vdash\!\!\!\sim} B) \in \Gamma$
        3a. let $\Gamma_{\neg(A \mathrel{\vdash\!\!\!\sim} B)} = \mathtt{SAT}(\mathtt{APPLY}(\Gamma, \neg(A \mathrel{\vdash\!\!\!\sim} B)))$;
        3b. if $\Gamma_{\neg(A \mathrel{\vdash\!\!\!\sim} B)} \notin X$ **then** $X = X \cup \{\Gamma_{\neg(A \mathrel{\vdash\!\!\!\sim} B)}\}$;
    4. **for** each formula $\neg\Box\neg A \in \Gamma$, let $\Gamma_{\neg\Box\neg A} = \mathtt{SAT}(\mathtt{APPLY}(\Gamma, \neg\Box\neg A))$;
        4a. add the relation $\Gamma_{\neg\Box\neg A} < \Gamma$;
        4b. if $\Gamma_{\neg\Box\neg A} \notin X$ **then** $X = X \cup \{\Gamma_{\neg\Box\neg A}\}$.
    5. mark Γ as resolved;
endWhile;

This procedure terminates, since the number of possible sets of formulas that can be obtained by applying $\mathcal{T}\mathbf{P}$'s rules to an initial finite set Γ is finite. We construct the model $\mathcal{M} = \langle X, <_X, V \rangle$ for Γ as follows:

- $<_X$ is the transitive closure of the relation $<$;
- $V(\Gamma) = \{P \mid P \in \Gamma \cap ATM\}$

In order to show that $\mathcal{M}$ is a preferential model for Γ, we prove the following:

Fact 1. *The relation $<_X$ is acyclic.*

Fact 2. *For all formulas F and for all sets $\Gamma \in X$ we have that:*

(i) if $F \in \Gamma$ then $\mathcal{M}, \Gamma \models F$; (ii) if $\neg F \in \Gamma$ then $\mathcal{M}, \Gamma \not\models F$.

By the above Facts the proof of the completeness of $\mathcal{T}\mathbf{P}$ is over, since $\mathcal{M}$ is a model for the initial set Γ_0. $\qquad\Box$

A relevant property of the calculus that will be useful to estimate the complexity of logic $\mathbf{P}$ is the so-called *disjunction property* of conditional formulas:

Proposition 2 (Disjunction property). *If there is a closed tableau for $\Gamma, \neg(A \mathrel{\vdash\!\!\!\sim} B), \neg(C \mathrel{\vdash\!\!\!\sim} D)$, then there is a closed tableau either for $\Gamma, \neg(A \mathrel{\vdash\!\!\!\sim} B)$ or for $\Gamma, \neg(C \mathrel{\vdash\!\!\!\sim} D)$.*

The reason why this property holds is that the $(\mathrel{\vdash\!\!\!\sim}^-)$ rule discards all the other formulas that could have been introduced by its previous application.

3.1   Decision Procedure for P

In general, non-termination in tableau calculi can be caused by two different reasons: 1. some rules copy their principal formula in the conclusion, thus can be reapplied over the same formula without any control; 2. dynamic rules can generate infinitely-many worlds, creating infinite branches.

Concerning the second source of non-termination (point 2.) we show that the generation of infinite branches due to the interplay between rules $(\mathrel{|\!\sim}^+)$ and $(\Box^-)$ cannot occur. Indeed, as we will see, the application of $(\Box^-)$ to a formula $\neg\Box\neg A$ (introduced by $(\mathrel{|\!\sim}^+)$) adds the formula $\Box\neg A$ to the conclusion, so that $(\mathrel{|\!\sim}^+)$ can no longer consistently introduce $\neg\Box\neg A$. This is due to the properties of $\Box$ in G, which do not hold in other systems as K4. Furthermore, the $(\mathrel{|\!\sim}^-)$ rule can be applied only once to a given negated conditional on a branch, thus infinitely-many worlds cannot be generated on a branch.

Concerning point 1. the above calculus $\mathcal{T}\mathbf{P}$ does not ensure a terminating proof search due to $(\mathrel{|\!\sim}^+)$, which can be applied without any control. We ensure the termination by putting some constraints on $\mathcal{T}\mathbf{P}$. The intuition is as follows: one does not need to apply $(\mathrel{|\!\sim}^+)$ on the same conditional formula $A \mathrel{|\!\sim} B$ *more than once in the same world*, therefore we keep track of positive conditionals already used by moving them in an additional set Σ in the conclusions of $(\mathrel{|\!\sim}^+)$, and restrict the application of this rule to unused conditionals only. The dynamic rules re-introduce formulas from Σ in order to allow further applications of $(\mathrel{|\!\sim}^+)$ in the other worlds. This machinery is standard.

$$
(\mathrel{|\!\sim}^+) \ \frac{\Gamma, A \mathrel{|\!\sim} B; \Sigma}{\Gamma, \neg A; \Sigma, A \mathrel{|\!\sim} B \quad \Gamma, \neg\Box\neg A; \Sigma, A \mathrel{|\!\sim} B \quad \Gamma, B; \Sigma, A \mathrel{|\!\sim} B}
$$

$$
(\mathrel{|\!\sim}^-) \ \frac{\Gamma, \neg(A \mathrel{|\!\sim} B); \Sigma}{\Sigma, A, \Box\neg A, \neg B, \Gamma^{|\!\sim\pm}; \emptyset} \qquad\qquad (\Box^-) \ \frac{\Gamma, \neg\Box\neg A; \Sigma}{\Sigma, \Gamma^\Box, \Gamma^{\Box\downarrow}, \Gamma^{|\!\sim\pm}, A, \Box\neg A; \emptyset}
$$

Fig. 3. The calculus $\mathcal{T}\mathbf{P^T}$. Propositional rules are as in Figure 1 addicting Σ.

Theorem 4 below shows that no additional machinery is needed to ensure termination. Notice that this would not work in other systems (for instance, in K4 one needs a more sophisticated loop-checking as described in [9]).

The terminating calculus $\mathcal{T}\mathbf{P^T}$ is presented in Figure 3. The calculus $\mathcal{T}\mathbf{P^T}$ is sound and complete with respect to the semantics: the soundness is immediate, and the completeness easily follows from the fact that two successive applications of $(\mathrel{|\!\sim}^+)$ to the same conditional in the same world are useless.

Theorem 3 (Soundness and completeness of $\mathcal{T}\mathbf{P^T}$). *The calculus $\mathcal{T}\mathbf{P^T}$ is sound and complete w.r.t. the semantics.*

In order to prove that $\mathcal{T}\mathbf{P^T}$ ensures a terminating proof search, we define a complexity measure on a set of formulas Γ and the corresponding set of positive conditionals already used Σ, denoted by $m(\Gamma; \Sigma)$, which consists of four measures c_1, c_2, c_3 and c_4 in a lexicographic order. We write $A \mathrel{|\!\sim} B \in_+ \Gamma$ (resp. $A \mathrel{|\!\sim} B \in_- \Gamma$) if $A \mathrel{|\!\sim} B$ occurs positively (resp. negatively) in Γ, where positive and negative occurrences are defined in the standard way. We also denote by $cp(F)$ the complexity of a formula F.

Definition 7 (Lexicographic order). *We define* $m(\Gamma; \Sigma) = \langle c_1, c_2, c_3, c_4 \rangle$ *where:* $c_1 = \mid \{A \mathrel{|\!\sim} B \in_- \Gamma\} \mid$, $c_2 = \mid \{A \mathrel{|\!\sim} B \in_+ \Gamma \cup \Sigma \mid \Box\neg A \notin \Gamma\} \mid$, $c_3 = \mid \{A \mathrel{|\!\sim} B \in_+ \Gamma\} \mid$, *and* $c_4 = \sum_{F \in \Gamma} cp(F)$. *We consider the lexicographic order given by* $m(\Gamma; \Sigma)$.

Intuitively, c_2 represents the number of positive conditionals *which can still create a new world*. The application of $(\Box^-)$ reduces c_2: indeed, if $(\mathrel{|\!\sim}^+)$ is applied to $A \mathrel{|\!\sim} B$, this application introduces a branch containing $\neg\Box\neg A$; when a new world is generated by an application of $(\Box^-)$ on $\neg\Box\neg A$, it contains A and $\Box\neg A$. If $(\mathrel{|\!\sim}^+)$ is applied to $A \mathrel{|\!\sim} B$ once again, then the conclusion where $\neg\Box\neg A$ is introduced is closed, by the presence of $\Box\neg A$ in that branch. c_3 is the number of conditionals not yet considered in that branch.

Theorem 4 (Termination of $\mathcal{T}\mathbf{P^T}$). $\mathcal{T}\mathbf{P^T}$ *ensures a terminating proof search.*

Proof sketch. Let $\Gamma'; \Sigma'$ be obtained by an application of a rule of $\mathcal{T}\mathbf{P^T}$ to a premise $\Gamma; \Sigma$. It can be easily proved that $m(\Gamma'; \Sigma') < m(\Gamma; \Sigma)$.   □

We conclude this section with a complexity analysis of $\mathcal{T}\mathbf{P^T}$, in order to prove that validity in $\mathbf{P}$ is **coNP**-complete. First of all, notice that we could take advantage of the disjunction property (Proposition 2). By this property we can reformulate the $(\mathrel{|\!\sim}^-)$ rule as follows:

$$\frac{\Gamma, \neg(A \mathrel{|\!\sim} B); \Sigma}{\Sigma, A, \Box\neg A, \neg B, \Gamma^{\mathrel{|\!\sim}^+}; \emptyset} \; (\mathrel{|\!\sim}^-)$$

This rule reduces the length of a branch at the price of making the proof search more non-deterministic.

We give a non-deterministic algorithm for testing satisfiability in $\mathbf{P}$ that: (i) takes a set of formulas Γ as input; (ii) returns SAT iff Γ is satisfiable.

By the disjunction property, we can consider a negated conditional at a time. Indeed, for $\Gamma, \neg(A \mathrel{|\!\sim} B), \neg(C \mathrel{|\!\sim} D)$ to be satisfiable, it is sufficient that both $\Gamma, \neg(A \mathrel{|\!\sim} B)$ and $\Gamma, \neg(C \mathrel{|\!\sim} D)$, separately considered, are satisfiable. For each negated conditional, the algorithm GENERAL-CHECK applies the rule $(\mathrel{|\!\sim}^-)$ to it, and calls the algorithm CHECK on the resulting set of formulas. CHECK is a non-deterministic algorithm that tests satisfiability in $\mathbf{P}$ of a set of formulas not containing negated conditionals. One can see that, when a negated conditional at a time is considered, a set of formulas is satisfiable in a preferential model if and only if it is satisfiable in a linearly ordered model (this can be proven directly, by transforming our canonical model in Theorem 2 into a linearly ordered model, and has also been proved in [12]). The algorithm CHECK verifies if there is a *linearly ordered* model satisfying the initial set of formulas. To this purpose, it makes use of a stronger version of the rule ($\Box^-$) in which, roughly speaking, each branch coming from the conclusion represents a possible linear model of the premise. The strengthened version of ($\Box^-$) is the following (we use $\Gamma_{-i}^{\Box^-}$ to denote $\{\neg\Box\neg A_j \vee A_j \mid \neg\Box\neg A_j \in \Gamma \wedge j \neq i\}$):

$$\frac{\Gamma, \neg\Box\neg A_1, \neg\Box\neg A_2, ..., \neg\Box\neg A_n}{\Gamma^{\vdash\pm}, \Gamma^{\Box}, \Gamma^{\Box^!}, A_1, \Box\neg A_1, \Gamma_{-1}^{\Box^-} \mid ... \mid \Gamma^{\vdash\pm}, \Gamma^{\Box}, \Gamma^{\Box^!}, A_n, \Box\neg A_n, \Gamma_{-n}^{\Box^-}} (\Box^-)$$

An important feature of this reformulation with respect to the original ($\Box^-$) rule is that no backtracking on the choice of the formula $\neg\Box\neg A_i$ is needed as all alternatives are kept in the conclusion.

We call $LTP^\mathbf{T}$ the calculus obtained by replacing in $TP^\mathbf{T}$ the initial rules ($\vdash^-$) and ($\Box^-$) with the ones reformulated above. We can prove that $LTP^\mathbf{T}$ is sound and complete w.r.t. the preferential models by proving the following proposition:

Proposition 3. *There is a closed tableau for Γ in $TP^\mathbf{T}$ iff there is a closed tableau for Γ in $LTP^\mathbf{T}$.*

Let EXPAND(Γ) be a procedure that returns one saturated expansion of Γ w.r.t. all static rules. In case of a branching rule, EXPAND nondeterministically selects (guesses) and applies one conclusion of the rule. The algorithm is defined below; in brackets we give the complexity of each operation, considering that $n = |\Gamma|$.

CHECK(Γ)
1. $\Gamma \longleftarrow$ EXPAND(Γ); $(O(n))$
2. if Γ contains an axiom **then return** UNSAT; $(O(n^2))$
3. if $\{\neg\Box\neg A \mid \neg\Box\neg A \in \Gamma\} = \emptyset$ **then return** SAT;
4. **else if** $(\{\neg\Box\neg A \mid \neg\Box\neg A \in \Gamma\} \neq \emptyset)$ **then**
    4a. let $\{\neg\Box\neg A_1, ..., \neg\Box\neg A_k\}$ be all the negated boxed conditionals in Γ;
    4b. choose $i = 1, ..., k$;
    4c. CHECK(APPLY($\Gamma, \neg\Box\neg A_i$));

The above procedure allows to decide the satisfiability of a set of formulas (not containing negated conditionals). To see that the decision problem is in **NP**, observe that: (1) the complexity of each call to the procedure EXPAND is polynomial. Indeed, as the number of different subformulas is at most $O(n)$, EXPAND makes at most $O(n)$ applications of the static rules. (2) The test that a set Γ (of size $O(n)$) of formulas contains an axiom has at most complexity $O(n^2)$. (3) The number of recursive calls to the procedure CHECK is at most $O(n)$, since in a branch the rule ($\Box^-$) can be applied only once to each formula $\neg\Box\neg A_i$, and the number of different negated box formulas is at most $O(n)$.

Let us now define a procedure to decide whether an arbitrary set of formulas Γ (possibly containing negated conditionals) is satisfiable:

```
GENERAL-CHECK(Γ)
1. Γ ⟵ EXPAND(Γ); (O(n))
2. let ¬(A₁ |∼ B₁),..., ¬(Aₖ |∼ Bₖ) be all negated conditionals in Γ;
   2.1. for all i = 1,..., k result[i] ⟵ CHECK(APPLY(Γ, ¬(Aᵢ |∼ Bᵢ))) ;
3. if for all i = 1,..., n result[i]==SAT then return SAT;
   else return UNSAT;
```

By the subformula property, the number of negated conditionals which can occur in Γ is at most $O(n)$. Hence, the procedure GENERAL-CHECK calls to the algorithm CHECK at most $O(n)$ times.

Theorem 5 (Complexity of P). *The problem of deciding validity for preferential logic* **P** *is* **coNP**-*complete.*

Proof. The procedure GENERAL-CHECK allows the satisfiability of a set of formulas of logic **P** to be decided in nondeterministic polynomial time. The validity problem for **P** is therefore in **coNP**. As **coNP**-hardness is immediate (this logic includes classical propositional logic), we conclude that the validity problem for logic **P** is **coNP**-complete.   □

This result matches with the known complexity results for logic **P** [12]. Due to the **coNP** lower bound, the above method provides a computationally optimal reasoning procedure for logic **P**.

4   The Tableau Calculus for Loop Cumulative Logic CL

In this section we develop a tableau calculus $\mathcal{T}\mathbf{CL}$ for **CL**, and we show that it can be turned into a terminating calculus. This provides a decision procedure for **CL** and a **coNP**-membership upper bound for validity in **CL**.

The calculus $\mathcal{T}\mathbf{CL}$ can be obtained from the calculus $\mathcal{T}\mathbf{P}$ for preferential logics, by adding a suitable rule for dealing with the modality L. We define $\Gamma^{L^\downarrow} = \{A \mid LA \in \Gamma\}$. Our tableau system $\mathcal{T}\mathbf{CL}$ for **CL** is shown in Figure 4 and is obtained by introducing the new modality L in the rules of $\mathcal{T}\mathbf{P}$ and by adding the new rule (L^-). Observe that rules $(|\sim^+)$ and $(|\sim^-)$ have been changed as they introduce the modality L in front of the propositional formulas A and B in their conclusions. The new rule (L^-) is a dynamic rule.

The proof of the completeness of the calculus can be done as for the preferential case, provided we suitably modify the procedure for constructing a model for a finite consistent set of formulas Γ of $\mathcal{L}_L$. First of all, we modify the definition of saturated sets as follows:

- if $A \vdash\!\!\!\sim B \in \Gamma$ then $\neg LA \in \Gamma$ or $\neg\Box\neg LA \in \Gamma$ or $LB \in \Gamma$

For this notion of saturated set of formulas we can still prove Lemma 1 for language $\mathcal{L}_L$.

Theorem 6 (Completeness of $\mathcal{T}\mathbf{CL}$). $\mathcal{T}\mathbf{CL}$ *is complete with respect to the semantics.*

$$(\mathop{\sim}\limits^{+}) \; \frac{\Gamma, A \mathrel{\mid\!\sim} B}{\Gamma, \neg LA, A \mathrel{\mid\!\sim} B \quad \Gamma, \neg\Box\neg LA, A \mathrel{\mid\!\sim} B \quad \Gamma, LB, A \mathrel{\mid\!\sim} B} \qquad (\mathop{\sim}\limits^{-}) \; \frac{\Gamma, \neg(A \mathrel{\mid\!\sim} B)}{LA, \Box\neg LA, \neg LB, \Gamma^{\mathrel{\mid\!\sim}\pm}}$$

$$(L^-) \; \frac{\Gamma, \neg LA}{\Gamma^{L^{\downarrow}}, \neg A} \; \text{ where either } \{\neg LA\} \neq \emptyset \text{ or } \Gamma^{L^{\downarrow}} \neq \emptyset \qquad (\Box^-) \; \frac{\Gamma, \neg\Box\neg LA}{\Gamma^{\Box}, \Gamma^{\Box^{\downarrow}}, \Gamma^{\mathrel{\mid\!\sim}\pm}, LA, \Box\neg LA}$$

Fig. 4. Tableau system $\mathcal{T}\mathbf{CL}$. If $\neg LA$ is not in the premise of (L^-) (i.e. $\{\neg LA\} = \emptyset$) the rule allows to step from Γ to $\Gamma^{L^{\downarrow}}$. The boolean rules are omitted.

Proof. We define a procedure for constructing a model satisfying a set of formulas $\Gamma_0 \in \mathcal{L}_L$ by modifying the procedure for the preferential logic $\mathbf{P}$. We add to the procedure two new steps 4' and 4", between step 4 and step 5 as follows:

    4'. **if** $\{\neg LA \mid \neg LA \in \Gamma\} \neq \emptyset$ **then**
        for each $\neg LA \in \Gamma$, let $\Gamma_{\neg LA} = \texttt{SAT}(\texttt{APPLY}(\Gamma, \neg LA))$;
        4' a. add the relation $\Gamma \ R \ \Gamma_{\neg LA}$;
        4' b. **if** $\Gamma_{\neg LA} \notin X$ **then** $X = X \cup \{\Gamma_{\neg LA}\}$;
    4". **else if** $\Gamma^{L^{\downarrow}} \neq \emptyset$ **then**, let $\Gamma' = \texttt{SAT}(\texttt{APPLY}(\Gamma, L^-))$;
        4" a. add the relation $\Gamma \ R \ \Gamma'$;
        4" b. **if** $\Gamma' \notin X$ **then** $X = X \cup \{\Gamma'\}$;

This procedure terminates. We construct the model $\mathcal{M} = \langle X, R_X, <_X, V \rangle$ by defining $<_X$ and V as in the case of $\mathbf{P}$ and by letting R_X the relation obtained from R above augmented with all the pairs (Γ, Γ) such that $\Gamma \in X$ and Γ has no R-successor. It is easy to show that the following properties hold for $\mathcal{M}$:

- for all $\Gamma, \Gamma' \in X$, if $(\Gamma, \Gamma') \in R_X$ and $LA \in \Gamma$ then $A \in \Gamma'$;
- for all formulas F and for all sets $\Gamma \in X$ we have that: (i) if $F \in \Gamma$ then $\mathcal{M}, \Gamma \models F$; (ii) if $\neg F \in \Gamma$ then $\mathcal{M}, \Gamma \not\models F$. $\qquad\square$

4.1 Decision Procedure for CL

Let us now analyze the calculus $\mathcal{T}\mathbf{CL}$ in order to obtain a decision procedure for $\mathbf{CL}$ logic. First of all, we reformulate the calculus as we made for $\mathbf{P}$, obtaining a system called $\mathcal{T}\mathbf{CL}^{\mathbf{T}}$: we reformulate the $(\mathrel{\mid\!\sim}^+)$ rule so that it applies only once to each conditional in each world, by adding of an extra set Σ. We reformulate the other rules accordingly. Notice that the rule (L^-) does not need to be further reformulated since it can only be applied a finite number of times. Exactly as we made for $\mathbf{P}$, we consider a lexicographic order given by $m(\Gamma; \Sigma) = < c_1, c_2, c_3, c_4 >$, and easily prove that each application of the rules of $\mathcal{T}\mathbf{CL}^{\mathbf{T}}$ reduces this measure. Thus, $\mathcal{T}\mathbf{CL}^{\mathbf{T}}$ ensures termination. Furthermore, the decision algorithm for $\mathbf{P}$ described in section 3 can be adapted to $\mathbf{CL}$. The procedure $\texttt{CHECK}$ has to be modified by introducing the following steps 4' and 4" between steps 2 and 3:

4'. **else if** $\{\neg LA \mid \neg LA \in \Gamma\} \neq \emptyset$ **then**
  4'a. **for all** $\neg LA_i \in \Gamma$ **do** CHECK(APPLY($\Gamma, \neg LA_i$));
4". **else if** $\{LA \mid LA \in \Gamma\} \neq \emptyset$ **then**
  4"a. CHECK(APPLY (Γ, L^-));

Observe that the two recursive calls of CHECK in 4'a and 4"a do not generate further recursive calls. By this reason, one obtains the following result:

Theorem 7 (Complexity of CL). *The problem of deciding validity for* **CL** *is* **coNP**-*complete.*

5   Conclusions

In this paper, we have presented tableau calculi for some of the KLM logical systems for default reasoning. We have given a tableau calculus for preferential logic **P** and for loop-cumulative logic **CL**. The calculi presented give a decision procedure for the respective logics, whose complexity is **coNP** for both **P** and **CL**. We will make a detailed comparison with existing works ([1], [7], [12]) in a full paper.

We plan to extend our calculi to the other KLM systems, namely to the weaker **C** and to the stronger **R**. For **C** we conjecture that a complete calculus is given by a variant of $\mathcal{T}\mathbf{CL}$ in which the ($\Box^-$) rule is weakened so that it does not enforce the transitivity of the preferential relation $<$. Another development of our work will be the extension to the first order case. The starting point will be the analysis of first order preferential and rational logics by Friedman, Halpern and Koller in [5].

Acknowledgements. We are grateful to the anonymous referees for their very helpful comments.

References

1. A. Artosi, G. Governatori, and A. Rotolo. Labelled tableaux for non-monotonic reasoning: Cumulative consequence relations. *Journal of Logic and Computation*, 12(6):1027–1060, 2002.
2. C. Boutilier. Conditional logics of normality: a modal approach. *Artificial Intelligence, 68(1)*, pages 87–154, 1994.
3. G. Crocco and P. Lamarre. On the connection between non-monotonic inference systems and conditional logics. *In Proc. of KR '92*, pages 565–571, 1992.
4. N. Friedman and J. Y. Halpern. Plausibility measures and default reasoning. *Journal of the ACM*, 48(4):648–685, 2001.
5. N. Friedman, J. Y. Halpern, and D. Koller. First-order conditional logic for default reasoning revisited. *ACM TOCL, ACM Press*, 1(2):175–207, 2000.
6. D. Gabbay. Theoretical foundations for non-monotonic reasoning in expert systems. *Logics and models of concurrent systems, Springer*, pages 439–457, 1985.
7. L. Giordano, V. Gliozzi, N. Olivetti, and C. Schwind. Tableau calculi for preference-based conditional logics. *In Proc. of TABLEAUX 2003, vulme 2796 of LNAI, Springer*, pages 81–101, 2003.

8. R. Goré. Tableau methods for modal and temporal logics. *In Handbook of Tableau Methods, Kluwer Academic Publishers*, pages 297–396, 1999.
9. A. Heuerding, M. Seyfried, and H. Zimmermann. Efficient loop-check for backward proof search in some non-classical propositional logics. *In Proc. of TABLEAUX 1996, volume 1071 of LNAI, Springer*, pages 210–225, 1996.
10. H. Katsuno and K. Sato. A unified view of consequence relation, belief revision and conditional logic. *In Proc. IJCAI'91*, pages 406–412, 1991.
11. S. Kraus, D. Lehmann, and M. Magidor. Nonmonotonic reasoning, preferential models and cumulative logics. *Artificial Intelligence, 44(1-2)*, pages 167–207, 1990.
12. D. Lehmann and M. Magidor. What does a conditional knowledge base entail? *Artificial Intelligence, Elsevier Science Publishers Ltd.*, 55(1):1–60, 1992.
13. Y. Shoham. A semantical approach to nonmonotonic logics. *In Proceedings of Logics in Computer Science*, pages 275–279, 1987.

Bounding Resource Consumption
with Gödel-Dummett Logics

Dominique Larchey-Wendling

LORIA – CNRS,
Campus scientifique, BP 239,
54 506 Vandœuvre-lès-Nancy, France

Abstract. Gödel-Dummett logic LC and its finite approximations LC_n are the intermediate logics complete w.r.t. linearly ordered Kripke models. In this paper, we use LC_n logics as a tool to bound resource consumption in some process calculi. We introduce a non-deterministic process calculus where the consumption of a particular resource denoted • is explicit and provide an operational semantics which measures the consumption of this resource. We present a linear transformation of a process P into a formula f of LC. We show that the consumption of the resource by P can be bounded by the positive integer n if and only if the formula f admits a counter-model in LC_n. Combining this result with our previous results on proof and counter-model construction for LC_n, we conclude that bounding resource consumption is (linearly) equivalent to searching counter-models in LC_n.

1   Introduction

Gödel-Dummett logic LC and its finitary versions $(LC_n)_{n>0}$ are the intermediate logics (between classical logic CL and intuitionistic logic IL) characterized by linear Kripke models. LC was introduced by Gödel in [1] and later axiomatized by Dummett in [2]. It is now one of the most studied intermediate logics and has been recognized recently as one of the fundamental *t-norm based fuzzy logics* [3]. Proof-search in LC has benefited from the development of proof-search in intuitionistic logic IL with two important seeds: the *contraction-free calculus* of Dyckhoff [4,5,6] and the *hyper-sequent* calculus of Avron [7,8]. Two recent contributions propose an alternative approach based on a set of *local* and *strongly invertible* proof rules (for either sequent [9] or hyper-sequent [7,10] calculus) and a semantic criterion to decide *irreducible (hyper)-sequents* and eventually build a counter-model.

In our previous work, we proposed a new approach to the decision problem in LC [11]. We transform a formula (or a sequent) of LC into a *conditional bi-colored graph* of the same size. Then, we search counter-models of the initial formula by looking for chains of a certain kind in the graph. We call those chains *alternating chains*. This method constitutes a decision procedure for LC and LC_n, thus we have a linear transformation of the decision problem for LC (and also LC_n) into the search for alternating chains problem in conditional graphs. Moreover,

G. Sutcliffe and A. Voronkov (Eds.): LPAR 2005, LNAI 3835, pp. 682–696, 2005.

we propose a procedure based on matrix computation to solve the search of alternating chains [12].

In this paper, we study the reverse transformation. First, we characterize the search for alternating chains in conditional graphs as a resource use bounding problem in some particular process calculus: the processes have *non-deterministic* branching, *conditional* branching, *consume* some particular resource, and can be *recursive*. The conditions are expressed by boolean formulae. We show how to normalize process systems being thus able to view theses processes as conditional graphs. We relate resource consumption by processes to the search for alternating chains in conditional graphs.

Then we show how to encode a conditional graph into a formula of LC (of size linear w.r.t. the size of the graph). We prove the equivalence of the existence of a counter-model for this formula and the existence of an alternating chain into the conditional graph. Therefore we obtain a linear transformation of the search for alternating chains problem in conditional graphs into a decision problem for the family of logics LC_n.

Moreover, this result establishes a characterization of the family of Gödel-Dummett logics LC_n as resource use bounding logics for some particular process calculus. This is the main goal of this paper: to shed some new light of LC and to relate it with processes and resource consumption. In particular, the process calculus we introduce here should not be viewed as a real tool to model complex systems. However, it could be extended or integrated to other process calculi like CCS [13] so as to exploit the LC logic for specifying resource related properties.

2   Logical Syntax for **CL** and **LC**

In this section we present the syntax we use for logical formulae. We either use formulae of classical propositional logic CL or formulae of propositional Gödel-Dummett logic LC. Fortunately they share the same syntax, even though their semantics differ.

The set of propositional *formulae*, denoted Form, is defined inductively, starting from a set of propositional *variables*, denoted by LVar, with an additional bottom constant $\perp$ denoting *absurdity* and using the connectives $\wedge$, $\vee$ and $\supset$:

$$\text{Form :} \quad f ::= \perp \mid x \mid f \wedge f \mid f \vee f \mid f \supset f \quad \text{where } x \in \text{LVar}$$

We use the abbreviations $\neg f \equiv f \supset \perp$ and $\top \equiv \neg\perp$. In conditional graphs (see sections 4 and 6), we even use the notation $\overline{x} \equiv \neg x$ but only for propositional variables. The semantics of classical formulae is as usual: given a *valuation* (or interpretation) of propositional variables $\sigma : \text{LVar} \to \{0, 1\}$, the semantic value of f denoted by $[\![f]\!]_\sigma \in \{0, 1\}$ is defined inductively on the structure of f, the connectives $\perp$, $\supset$, $\wedge$ and $\vee$ being respectively interpreted by their corresponding boolean operator. The semantics of the formulae of LC will be defined later in section 5.1.

3   Resource Consuming Processes

In this section, we present a calculus for processes which consume resources. This calculus features non-determinism, choices, recursion and of course resource consumption. We only model one kind of resources in our calculus, denoted by a big dot •. The processes only consume resources, they do not produce them, neither do they transform them into another kind of resources. So the behavior of processes is characterized by how they consume resources.

Let us consider a set of *process variables* denoted PVar. We define the set of *processes* Proc as follows:

$$\text{Proc}: \quad P ::= X \mid <f> P \mid \bullet P \mid [P + \cdots + P] \quad \text{where } f \in \text{Form}, X \in \text{PVar}$$

The process $\bullet P$ should be viewed as the process which consumes one resource • and then, behaves as P. The process $[P + Q]$ should be understood as the non-deterministic sum of P and Q, i.e. the process that behaves either as P or Q. In particular, the process $[\,]$ does nothing, i.e. does not consume any resource. Given a boolean condition f, the process $<f> P$ is the process which behaves like P if the condition f is fulfilled, and does nothing otherwise.

Non-determinism and conditions are sufficient to represent the if-then-else construct: if f then P else $Q \equiv [<f> P + <\neg f> Q]$. We insist on the fact that the boolean value of the condition f does not evolve during the execution of processes: it is fixed once and for all before the execution starts. And as we are going to describe the operational semantics of processes, it should be noted that conditions (like f) are *external*: even though they influence the behavior of processes, they cannot change because of that behavior.

3.1   Process Systems and Recursion

To represent recursion, i.e. the possibility for processes to become themselves again after having consumed some resources, we use (sets of) recursive equations:

Definition 1 (Process system). *A process system is a pair $(\mathcal{E}, \mathcal{V})$ where $\mathcal{E} = \{X_1 = P_1, \ldots, X_n = P_n\}$ is a finite set of process equations. $X_1, \ldots, X_n$ are supposed are to be n distinct process variables and $\mathcal{V} \subseteq \{X_1, \ldots, X_n\}$ is a subset of relevant variables. $P_1, \ldots, P_n$ are processes. The variables occurring in $\mathcal{E}$ but not in $\mathcal{V}$ are called private variables. A sub-process of $\mathcal{E}$ is either one of $X_1, \ldots, X_n$ or a sub-term of one of $P_1, \ldots, P_n$.*

As an example, consider the system

$$\mathcal{V} = \{X\}$$

$$\mathcal{E} = \begin{cases} X = \bullet <a> Y \\ Y = [<b> X + <\neg a> \bullet Z + Z] \\ Z = [\,] \end{cases}$$

$[<b> X + <\neg a> \bullet Z + Z]$		
X	$<b> X$	$[\,]$
Y	$<a> Y$	$\bullet <a> Y$
Z	$\bullet Z$	$<\neg a> \bullet Z$

The sub-processes are listed on the right-hand side. Intuitively, X is the process which consumes one resource and if a is true becomes Y. Y becomes either X

if b is true, or if a is false consumes one resource and then becomes Z, or Y becomes Z. Z is the process that does nothing.

This calculus should not be viewed as useful for representing real or complex systems. It has too few features for that. But it could be viewed as an *abstraction* calculus: either one could abstract a complex system into our simple formalism to prove resource consumption related properties for this particular system, or one could extend our calculus with further constructs to model more sophisticated systems directly.

3.2   Operational Semantics for Resource Consumption

Given a set of process equations $\mathcal{E}$ and a valuation $\sigma : \mathsf{LVar} \to \{0, 1\}$ of boolean variables, we define the ternary relation $-\!\{\cdot, \sigma, \mathcal{E}\}\!\!\to\bullet \subseteq \mathsf{Proc} \times \mathbb{N} \times \mathsf{Proc}$ by the set of deduction rules presented in figure 1. As the reader might notice, σ and $\mathcal{E}$ are not modified by the application of those rules but they occur in the side conditions of rules [Eq] and [Con], restricting the applicability of those rules. When $\mathcal{E}$ or σ are understood in the context, we might simplify the notation $P -\!\{n, \sigma, \mathcal{E}\}\!\!\to Q$ into $P -\!\{n, \sigma\}\!\!\to Q$ or even $P -\!\{n\}\!\!\to Q$. Intuitively, $P -\!\{n\}\!\!\to Q$ should be read as: the process P has an execution path to Q which consumes exactly n times the resource $\bullet$.

$$\frac{}{P -\!\{0, \sigma, \mathcal{E}\}\!\!\to\bullet P} \; \text{[Id]}$$

$$\frac{P_i -\!\{n, \sigma, \mathcal{E}\}\!\!\to\bullet Q}{[\cdots + P_i + \cdots] -\!\{n, \sigma, \mathcal{E}\}\!\!\to\bullet Q} \; \text{[Sum]}$$

$$\frac{P -\!\{n, \sigma, \mathcal{E}\}\!\!\to\bullet Q}{\bullet P -\!\{n+1, \sigma, \mathcal{E}\}\!\!\to\bullet Q} \; \text{[Res]}$$

$$\frac{P -\!\{n, \sigma, \mathcal{E}\}\!\!\to\bullet Q \qquad X = P \in \mathcal{E}}{X -\!\{n, \sigma, \mathcal{E}\}\!\!\to\bullet Q} \; \text{[Eq]}$$

$$\frac{P -\!\{n, \sigma, \mathcal{E}\}\!\!\to\bullet Q \qquad \llbracket f \rrbracket_\sigma = 1}{<\!f\!> P -\!\{n, \sigma, \mathcal{E}\}\!\!\to\bullet Q} \; \text{[Con]}$$

Fig. 1. Deduction system for resource consumption

Lemma 1. *The [Cut] rule is admissible:*

$$\frac{P -\!\{m\}\!\!\to\bullet Q \qquad Q -\!\{n\}\!\!\to\bullet R}{P -\!\{m+n\}\!\!\to\bullet R} \; [Cut]$$

Proof. We prove the result by induction on the length of the deduction of $P -\!\{m\}\!\!\to\bullet Q$. If $P -\!\{m\}\!\!\to\bullet Q$ is obtained by the axiom [Id], then $Q \equiv P$ and $m = 0$, thus $P -\!\{0 + n\}\!\!\to\bullet R$ is identical to $Q -\!\{n\}\!\!\to\bullet R$. If $P -\!\{m\}\!\!\to\bullet Q$ is obtained by the [Res] rule then $P \equiv \bullet P'$ and we have a shorter (sub-)deduction of $P' -\!\{m - 1\}\!\!\to\bullet Q$. By induction, $P' -\!\{m - 1 + n\}\!\!\to\bullet R$ is deducible and then, applying rule [Res], we obtain $\bullet P' -\!\{m - 1 + n + 1\}\!\!\to\bullet R$, thus $P -\!\{m + n\}\!\!\to\bullet R$. If the last rule is [Eq], then $P \equiv X$ with $X = P' \in \mathcal{E}$ and we have a sub-deduction of $P' -\!\{m\}\!\!\to\bullet Q$. Thus, by induction, we obtain a deduction of $P' -\!\{m + n\}\!\!\to\bullet R$.

Applying rule [Eq], we obtain a deduction of $P \dashv\!\!\lvert m + n\rbrace\!\!\!-\!\!\bullet R$. The cases of rules [Sum] and [Con] are similar.

$\square$

Definition 2 (Boundable resource use). *A process system* $(\mathcal{E}, \mathcal{V})$ *has a resource use boundable by* n *if there exists a valuation* $\sigma : \mathsf{LVar} \to \{0, 1\}$ *such that for any* $X, Y \in \mathcal{V}$ *and* $k \in \mathbb{N}$, *if* $X \dashv\!\!\lvert k, \sigma, \mathcal{E}\rbrace\!\!\!-\!\!\bullet Y$ *holds then* $k \leqslant n$.

This definition means that the resource use *can be bounded* in some context, modeled by the valuation σ. The resource use is not necessarily bounded in every context.

3.3   Normalization

We define the equivalence of process systems and a normalization procedure so that the systems appear in a shape suitable for further transformations. The process systems $(\mathcal{E}, \mathcal{V})$ and $(\mathcal{F}, \mathcal{V})$ are *equivalent* if for any valuation σ, the relations $\dashv\!\!\lvert \cdot, \sigma, \mathcal{E}\rbrace\!\!\!-\!\!\bullet$ and $\dashv\!\!\lvert \cdot, \sigma, \mathcal{F}\rbrace\!\!\!-\!\!\bullet$ have identical restrictions to $\mathcal{V} \times \mathbb{N} \times \mathcal{V}$.

Definition 3 (Normality). *A process equation is* normal *if it contains no nested construct, i.e. it has one of the following forms:* $X = \bullet Y$, $X = {<}f{>}Y$ *or* $X = [Y_1 + \cdots + Y_n]$ *where* Y *and the* Y_i's *are process variables. A process system is* normal *if all its equations are normal.*

Lemma 2 (Normalization). *Let* $(\mathcal{E}, \mathcal{V})$ *be a process system of size* k. *There exists a normal process system* $(\mathcal{E}', \mathcal{V})$ *of size* $\mathcal{O}(k)$ *which is equivalent to* $(\mathcal{E}, \mathcal{V})$.

Proof. Let $(\mathcal{E}, \mathcal{V})$ be a process system of size k. We build the set of equations of the system $\mathcal{E}'$. Let us introduce a new process variable X_P for each strict (i.e. not a process variable) sub-process P of $\mathcal{E}$. For process variables $P \equiv Y$ occurring in $\mathcal{E}$, we choose $X_Y \equiv Y$, so there is no new process variable for atomic sub-processes. Let P be a sub-process of $\mathcal{E}$. If $P \equiv \bullet Q$, we add the equation $X_P = \bullet X_Q$ to $\mathcal{E}'$. If $P \equiv {<}f{>}Q$, we add $X_P = {<}f{>}X_Q$ and if $P \equiv [Q_1 + \cdots + Q_k]$, we add $X_P = [X_{Q_1} + \cdots + X_{Q_k}]$. Finally, if $Y = P$ is an equation of $\mathcal{E}$, we add the equation $Y = [X_P]$ to $\mathcal{E}'$.

Obviously $(\mathcal{E}', \mathcal{V})$ is a normal system and its size (number of symbols) is linear in the size of $(\mathcal{E}, \mathcal{V})$. It is a bit tedious but obvious to show that for any sub-process $P, Q \in \mathcal{E}$, $\sigma : \mathsf{LVar} \to \{0, 1\}$ and $n \in \mathbb{N}$, $P \dashv\!\!\lvert n, \sigma, \mathcal{E}\rbrace\!\!\!-\!\!\bullet Q$ holds if and only if $X_P \dashv\!\!\lvert n, \sigma, \mathcal{E}'\rbrace\!\!\!-\!\!\bullet X_Q$ holds. The proof can be done by induction on the length of deductions. Then, since for any variable Y of $\mathcal{V}$ we have the property $X_Y \equiv Y$, the relation $\dashv\!\!\lvert \cdot, \sigma, \mathcal{E}\rbrace\!\!\!-\!\!\bullet$ and $\dashv\!\!\lvert \cdot, \sigma, \mathcal{E}'\rbrace\!\!\!-\!\!\bullet$ have identical restrictions to $\mathcal{V} \times \mathbb{N} \times \mathcal{V}$.

$\square$

The result of the normalization procedure described previously applied to the example presented in section 3.1 is the following:

$$X = [K_6] \quad Z = [K_5] \quad K_2 = {<}b{>}X \quad K_4 = \bullet Z \quad K_1 = [K_2 + K_7 + Z]$$
$$Y = [K_1] \quad K_6 = \bullet K_3 \quad K_3 = {<}a{>}Y \quad K_5 = [\,] \quad K_7 = {<}\neg a{>}K_4$$

4 Conditional Bi-colored Graphs

In this section, we introduce the notion of *conditional graphs*. Then we show how to transform a normal process system into a conditional graph and the relation between the existence of some chains in those graphs and the operational semantics of the process system.

4.1 Graphs and Instance Graphs

A *bi-colored graph* is a (finite) directed graph with two kinds of arrows: *green* arrows denoted by $\rightarrow$ and *red* arrows denoted by $\Rightarrow$.

Definition 4 (alternating chain). *A n-alternating chain is a chain of the form $(\rightarrow^* \Rightarrow)^n$.*

So a chain contains a n-alternating chain if and only if it contains at least n red arrows $\Rightarrow$.

Definition 5 (Conditional graph). *A* conditional bi-colored graph *is a bicolored graph where green arrows $\rightarrow$ may be indexed with the (propositional) boolean expressions of* Form.

Considering boolean expressions as representatives for boolean functions and given a valuation $\sigma : \mathsf{LVar} \rightarrow \{0, 1\}$, a boolean expression e is instantiated to the boolean value $[\![e]\!]_\sigma \in \{0, 1\}$. We obtain an instance graph: an arrow indexed with a boolean expression e belongs to this instance if and only if $[\![e]\!]_\sigma = 1$. The case of an unconditional (i.e. not indexed) arrow can be treated by considering that it has an implicit boolean conditional which is the tautology $\top$ (and then always evaluates to 1) and non-existing arrows have the implicit boolean condition $\bot$ that always evaluates to 0.

Definition 6 (Instance graph). *Let $\mathcal{G}$ be a conditional bi-colored graph and σ be a valuation of boolean variables in $\{0, 1\}$. We define the* instance graph $\mathcal{G}_\sigma$ *as the bi-colored graph that one obtains when one evaluates boolean expressions indexing arrows and keeping exactly those whose valuation equals 1.*

4.2 From Normal Process Systems to Conditional Graphs

We describe how to build a conditional bi-colored graph from a normal set of process equations. Let $\mathcal{E}$ be a finite set of normal process equations. The equations are of one of the following forms: $X = \bullet Y$, $X = <f>Y$ or $X = [Y_1 + \cdots + Y_k]$ where Y and the Y_i's are process variables.

We build the graph $\mathcal{G}_\mathcal{E}$ (simply denoted $\mathcal{G}$ here). It has the process variables occurring in $\mathcal{E}$ as vertices. We associate to each (normal) equation of $\mathcal{E}$ a set of arrows:

- for the equation $X = \bullet Y$, we associate the arrow $X \Rightarrow Y$;
- for $X = <f>Y$, we associate the arrow $X \rightarrow_f Y$;
- for $X = [Y_1 + \cdots + Y_k]$, we associate the arrows $X \rightarrow Y_1, \ldots, X \rightarrow Y_k$.

Obviously, the graph $\mathcal{G} \equiv \mathcal{G}_\mathcal{E}$ is a conditional bi-colored graph and its size is linear in the size of $\mathcal{E}$. As an example, we display the graph associated with the example of normal process system obtained in section 3.3:

$$X \leftarrow b \text{-} K_2 \longleftarrow K_1 \longrightarrow K_7 \text{-} \overline{a} \rightarrow K_4$$

$$K_6 \Longrightarrow K_3 \text{-} a \rightarrow Y \qquad K_5 \longleftarrow Z$$

4.3   Chains and Resource Consumption

In this section, we relate the consumption of the resource $\bullet$ by the processes of $\mathcal{E}$ to the alternating chains of $\mathcal{G}_\mathcal{E}$.

Theorem 1. *Let $\mathcal{E}$ be a normal set of process equations and $\mathcal{G} = \mathcal{G}_\mathcal{E}$ be its associated conditional graph. Let $\sigma :$ LVar $\rightarrow \{0, 1\}$ be a valuation. Then for any process variables $X, Y \in \mathcal{E}$ and any $n \in \mathbb{N}$, $X \dashv n, \sigma \vdash \bullet Y$ holds if and only if there exists a chain $X (\rightarrow^* \Rightarrow)^n \rightarrow^* Y$ in the instance graph $\mathcal{G}_\sigma$.*

Proof. Let us fix $\mathcal{E}$ and $\sigma :$ LVar $\rightarrow \{0, 1\}$. We consider the conditional graph $\mathcal{G}_\mathcal{E}$ and its instance $\mathcal{G}_\sigma$. Let $X \Rightarrow Y$ be an arrow of $\mathcal{G}_\sigma$. By construction of $\mathcal{G}_\mathcal{E}$, there is an equation $X = \bullet Y$ in $\mathcal{E}$. Thus, $X \dashv 1 \vdash \bullet Y$ holds. Now let us consider an arrow $X \rightarrow Y$ of $\mathcal{G}_\sigma$: either there exists an equation $X = <f> Y$ in $\mathcal{E}$ s.t. $[\![f]\!]_\sigma = 1$ or there exists an equation $X = [\cdots + Y + \cdots]$ in $\mathcal{E}$. In either case, $X \dashv 0 \vdash \bullet Y$ holds. Then by using the derived [Cut] rule of lemma 1, from a chain $X (\rightarrow^* \Rightarrow)^n \rightarrow^* Y$ containing exactly n red arrows $\Rightarrow$, we can deduce that $X \dashv n \vdash \bullet Y$ holds.

Conversely, let us show how to transform a deduction of $X \dashv n \vdash \bullet Y$ into a chain of the form $X (\rightarrow^* \Rightarrow)^n \rightarrow^* Y$ in $\mathcal{G}_\sigma$, by induction on the length of the deduction. Suppose it ends with the [Id] rule. Then $Y \equiv X$ and $n = 0$. Thus $X \rightarrow^0 Y$ is a zero length chain. Considering other rules, we remark that a deduction of $X \dashv n \vdash \bullet Y$ cannot end with rules [Sum], [Res] or [Con] since X is a process variable. We consider the last remaining case where the deduction ends with rule [Eq]. Then there exists an equation $X = P$ in $\mathcal{E}$. As $\mathcal{E}$ is normal, P is in one of the following forms: $\bullet Z$, $<f> Z$ or $[Z_1 + \cdots + Z_k]$, where Z and the Z_i are process variables:

- if $P \equiv \bullet Z$ then there is a (sub-)deduction of $\bullet Z \dashv n \vdash \bullet Y$ and therefore a (sub-)deduction of $Z \dashv n - 1 \vdash \bullet Y$. By induction on deductions, we obtain of chain $Z (\rightarrow^* \Rightarrow)^{n-1} \rightarrow^* Y$ in $\mathcal{G}_\sigma$. Moreover, as $X = \bullet Z \in \mathcal{E}$, we have an arrow $X \Rightarrow Z$ in $\mathcal{G}_\sigma$. Thus there exists a chain $X (\rightarrow^* \Rightarrow)^n \rightarrow^* Y$ in $\mathcal{G}_\sigma$;
- if $P \equiv <f> Z$, then we have a sub-deduction of $<f> Z \dashv n \vdash \bullet Y$. It is necessary that the last rule of this sub-deduction is [Cond] and then $[\![f]\!]_\sigma = 1$. We have a sub-deduction of $Z \dashv n \vdash \bullet Y$. By induction, there is a chain $Z (\rightarrow^* \Rightarrow)^n \rightarrow^* Y$ in $\mathcal{G}_\sigma$. Since $X = <f> Z \in \mathcal{E}$ and $[\![f]\!]_\sigma = 1$, there is an arrow $X \rightarrow Z$ in $\mathcal{G}_\sigma$. Thus there exists a chain $X (\rightarrow^* \Rightarrow)^n \rightarrow^* Y$ in $\mathcal{G}_\sigma$;

– if $P \equiv [Z_1 + \cdots + Z_k]$, then we have a sub-deduction of $[Z_1 + \cdots + Z_k] -\!\!\!\lfloor n \rfloor\!\!-\bullet Y$. It is necessary that the last rule of this sub-deduction is [Sum] and thus, there exists $i \in [1, k]$ and a sub-deduction of $Z_i -\!\!\!\lfloor n \rfloor\!\!-\bullet Y$. By induction, we obtain a chain $Z_i (\rightarrow^\star \Rightarrow)^n \rightarrow^\star Y$. Since $X = [Z_1 + \cdots + Z_k] \in \mathcal{E}$, there is an arrow $X \rightarrow Z_i$ in $\mathcal{G}_\sigma$, and there exists a chain $X (\rightarrow^\star \Rightarrow)^n \rightarrow^\star Y$ in $\mathcal{G}_\sigma$.   □

Corollary 1. *Let $\mathcal{E}$ be a normal set of process equations, $\mathcal{V}$ the set of variables of $\mathcal{E}$, $\mathcal{G}$ its associated conditional graph and $n \in \mathbb{N}$. The process system $(\mathcal{E}, \mathcal{V})$ has a resource use boundable by n if and only if there is an instance graph $\mathcal{G}_\sigma$ with no $(n + 1)$-alternating chain.*

Proof. If $(\mathcal{E}, \mathcal{V})$ has a resource use boundable by n, there exists a valuation $\sigma : \mathsf{LVar} \rightarrow \{0, 1\}$ s.t. for any $X, Y \in \mathcal{V}$ and $k \in \mathbb{N}$, if $X -\!\!\!\lfloor k, \sigma \rfloor\!\!-\bullet Y$ holds then $k \leqslant n$. Suppose there exists a $(n + 1)$-alternating chain $X_0 (\rightarrow^\star \Rightarrow)^{n+1} Y_0$ in the instance graph $\mathcal{G}_\sigma$. Then, by theorem 1, $X_0 -\!\!\!\lfloor n + 1, \sigma \rfloor\!\!-\bullet Y_0$. But $X_0, Y_0 \in \mathcal{V}$ so we get $n + 1 \leqslant n$, that leads to a contradiction. Conversely, let $X_0, Y_0 \in \mathcal{V}$ and $k \in \mathbb{N}$ satisfying $X_0 -\!\!\!\lfloor k, \sigma \rfloor\!\!-\bullet Y_0$. Then, by theorem 1, there is a chain $X_0 (\rightarrow^\star \Rightarrow)^k \rightarrow^\star Y_0$ in the instance graph $\mathcal{G}_\sigma$. If $k > n$ then this chain contains a sub-chain of the form $X_0 (\rightarrow^\star \Rightarrow)^{n+1} Y_1$, contradiction. Consequently $k \leqslant n$.   □

4.4   From Conditional Graphs to Normal Process Systems

We have proved that a normal process system can be transformed into a conditional graph of the same size. Now we present the converse transformation. We show how to recover a process system from a conditional graph.

There is only a slight problem to be addressed: the construction described in section 4.2 does not generate a configuration like for example $X \rightarrow Y$ and $X \Rightarrow Z$ where these two arrows have the same source X. This can only be generated when these two arrows are green $\rightarrow$ using the $[\cdots + \cdots]$ construct. To overcome this difficulty, we propose the following trick: every red arrows $\Rightarrow$ (resp. conditional arrow $\rightarrow_f$) is split into two arrows $\rightarrow\Rightarrow$ (resp. $\rightarrow\rightarrow_f$) introducing a new intermediary node for each red $\Rightarrow$ and conditional $\rightarrow_f$ arrow. These two splits preserve n-alternating chains.

Using such a transformation on a conditional graph $\mathcal{G}$, we obtain a new conditional graph $\mathcal{G}'$ with the following property: every node which is the source of multiple arrows is the source of only unconditional green arrows $\rightarrow$ since the source of a red $\Rightarrow$ (resp. conditional $\rightarrow_f$) arrow is the intermediary node which is specifically introduced for this particular arrow.

The graph $\mathcal{G}'$ can be transformed into a normal set of process equations. Let $\mathcal{V}$ be a set of process variables, one X_v for each vertex v of $\mathcal{G}'$. We build $\mathcal{E}$ as follows. We consider each vertex as a source for some arrows and associate an equation to each vertex:

– if v is the source of a red arrow $v \Rightarrow w$ then v is the source of no other arrow[1] and we add $X_v = \bullet X_w$ to $\mathcal{E}$;

---

[1] v is new and has been introduced in $\mathcal{G}'$ specifically for this purpose.

- if v is the source of a conditional green arrow $v \rightarrow_f w$ then v is the source of no other arrow and we add $X_v = <f> X_w$ to $\mathcal{E}$;
- otherwise v is the source of k (unconditional) green arrows $v \rightarrow w_1, \dots, v \rightarrow w_k$ (k could be 0) and we add $X_v = [X_{w_1} + \cdots + X_{w_k}]$ to $\mathcal{E}$.

$\mathcal{E}$ being built this way, it is obvious that it is a normal set of process equations and that $\mathcal{G}'$ appears as the conditional graph associated with $\mathcal{E}$ by the construction described in section 4.2, i.e. $\mathcal{G}' = \mathcal{G}_{\mathcal{E}}$.

Theorem 2. *Let $\mathcal{G}$ be a conditional graph of size k. There exists a process system $(\mathcal{E}, \mathcal{V})$ of size $\mathcal{O}(k)$ with the following property: for any $n \in \mathbb{N}$, $(\mathcal{E}, \mathcal{V})$ has a resource use boundable by n if and only if there is an instance graph $\mathcal{G}_\sigma$ with no $(n+1)$-alternating chain.*

Proof. Obviously, the size of the graph $\mathcal{G}'$ described earlier in this section is less than $2k$. The size of $\mathcal{E}$ is the same as the size of $\mathcal{G}'$, so is less than $2k$. Let $\mathcal{V}$ be the set of process variables occurring in $\mathcal{E}$. The size of $(\mathcal{E}, \mathcal{V})$ is less than $3k$. Then it is clear that for any $\sigma : \mathsf{LVar} \rightarrow \{0, 1\}$, there is a one-to-one correspondence between a $(n+1)$-alternating chain of $\mathcal{G}_\sigma$ and a $(n+1)$-alternating chain of $\mathcal{G}'_\sigma$, since the splits $\Rightarrow \rightsquigarrow \rightarrow \Rightarrow$ and $\rightarrow_f \rightsquigarrow \rightarrow \rightarrow_f$ preserve alternating chains in every instance. As the identity $\mathcal{G}' = \mathcal{G}_{\mathcal{E}}$ holds, we finish by an application of corollary 1 to $\mathcal{E}$. □

5   From Conditional Graphs to LC

In this section, we introduce the algebraic semantics of the family of propositional Gödel-Dummett logics LC_n. The value n belongs to the set $\overline{\mathbb{N}}^* = \{1, 2, \dots\} \cup \{\infty\}$ of strictly positive natural numbers with its natural order $\leqslant$, augmented with a greatest element ∞. In the case $n = \infty$, the logic LC_∞ is also denoted by LC: this is the usual Gödel-Dummett logic.

After having defined the semantics of LC_n, we show how to transform a conditional graph into a formula[2] of LC_n and we relate the existence of a counter-model for this formula to the alternating chains of the initial graph, and thus to resource consumption.

5.1   The Semantics of LC_n

IL denotes the set of formulae that are provable in any intuitionistic propositional calculus (see [4]) and CL denotes the classically valid formulae. As usual an *intermediate propositional logic* [6] is a set of formulae $\mathcal{L}$ satisfying $\mathsf{IL} \subseteq \mathcal{L} \subseteq \mathsf{CL}$ and closed under the rule of modus ponens (if $A \in \mathcal{L}$ and $A \supset B \in \mathcal{L}$ then $B \in \mathcal{L}$) and under arbitrary substitution (if $A \in \mathcal{L}$ and ρ is any substitution then $A_\rho \in \mathcal{L}$.)

---

[2] In fact, into a sequent which can straightforwardly be transformed into an equivalent formula, see proposition 1.

For any $n \in \overline{\mathbb{N}}^*$, the Gödel-Dummett logic LC_n is an intermediate logic. On the semantic side, it is characterized by the linear Kripke models of size n, see [2]. The following strictly increasing sequence holds:

$$\mathsf{IL} \subset \mathsf{LC} = \mathsf{LC}_\infty \subset \cdots \subset \mathsf{LC}_n \subset \cdots \subset \mathsf{LC}_1 = \mathsf{CL}$$

In the particular case of LC, the logic has a simple Hilbert axiomatic system: $(X \supset Y) \vee (Y \supset X)$ added to the axioms of IL.

In this paper, we will use the algebraic semantic characterization of LC_n [7] rather than the Kripke semantics. Let us fix a particular $n \in \overline{\mathbb{N}}^*$. The algebraic model is the set $\overline{[0,n)} = [0, \ldots, n[\cup \{\infty\}$ composed of $n+1$ elements.[3] A valuation (or interpretation) on propositional variables $\sigma : \mathsf{LVar} \to \overline{[0,n)}$ is inductively extended to formulae:

$$\begin{aligned}
&[\![\bot]\!]_\sigma = 0 && [\![a \vee b]\!]_\sigma = \max(a,b) \\
&[\![x]\!]_\sigma = \sigma_x && [\![a \wedge b]\!]_\sigma = \min(a,b)
\end{aligned} \qquad [\![a \supset b]\!]_\sigma = a \rightarrow b$$

where the operator $\rightarrow$ is defined by $a \rightarrow b =$ if $a \leqslant b$ then ∞ else b. A formula f is *valid* for the valuation σ if the equality $[\![f]\!]_\sigma = \infty$ holds. This interpretation is complete for LC_n. A *counter-model* of a formula f is a valuation σ such that $[\![f]\!] < \infty$.

A *sequent* is a pair $\Gamma \vdash \Delta$ where Γ and Δ are multisets of formulae. Γ, Δ denotes the sum of the two multisets and if Γ is the empty multiset, we write $\vdash \Delta$. Given a sequent $\Gamma \vdash \Delta$ and an interpretation $[\![\cdot]\!]$ of variables, we interpret $\Gamma \equiv a_1, \ldots, a_n$ by $\lfloor\Gamma\rfloor = \min\{[\![a_1]\!], \ldots, [\![a_n]\!]\}$ and $\Delta \equiv b_1, \ldots, b_p$ by $\lceil\Delta\rceil = \max\{[\![b_1]\!], \ldots, [\![b_p]\!]\}$. This sequent is *valid* with respect to the interpretation $[\![\cdot]\!]$ if $\lfloor\Gamma\rfloor \leqslant \lceil\Delta\rceil$ holds. On the other hand, a *counter-model* to this sequent is an interpretation $[\![\cdot]\!]$ such that $\lceil\Delta\rceil < \lfloor\Gamma\rfloor$, i.e. for any pair (i,j), the inequality $[\![b_j]\!] < [\![a_i]\!]$ holds.

Proposition 1. *The sequent $a_1, \ldots, a_n \vdash b_1, \ldots, b_p$ has the same counter-models as the formula $(a_1 \wedge \cdots \wedge a_n) \supset (b_1 \vee \cdots \vee b_p)$.*

The proof of this proposition is trivial. Let f be a propositional formula. It can either be viewed as a boolean formula, or a formula of LC_n. We relate the two semantic interpretations using the double negation. We define the mappings $\phi : \{0,1\} \to \overline{[0,n)}$ and $\psi : \overline{[0,n)} \to \{0,1\}$ by $\phi_0 = 0$, $\phi_1 = \infty$, $\psi_0 = 0$ and $\psi_x = \infty$ for $x > 0$.

Proposition 2. *Let f be a propositional formula and $\sigma : \mathsf{LVar} \to \overline{[0,n)}$ be an interpretation of variables. The identity $[\![\neg\neg f]\!](\sigma) = \phi([\![f]\!](\psi \circ \sigma))$ holds.*

Proof. Let us denote $\neg\neg f$ by f^*. We remark that ϕ commutes with the interpretation of the connectives $\wedge$, $\vee$ and $\supset$; for instance $\max(\phi_x, \phi_y) = \phi(x \vee y)$. Then, the following logical identities hold in LC_n:

---

[3] With the convention $\overline{[0,\infty)} = \mathbb{N} \cup \{\infty\}$. With our particular representation, the algebraic models $\overline{[0,n)}$ form a strictly increasing sequence of subsets of $\overline{\mathbb{N}}$.

$$\llbracket \bot^* \rrbracket_\sigma = \llbracket \bot \rrbracket_\sigma \qquad\qquad \llbracket (a \vee b)^* \rrbracket_\sigma = \max(\llbracket a^* \rrbracket_\sigma, \llbracket b^* \rrbracket_\sigma)$$
$$\llbracket (a \supset b)^* \rrbracket_\sigma = \llbracket a^* \rrbracket_\sigma \rightarrow \llbracket b^* \rrbracket_\sigma \qquad \llbracket (a \wedge b)^* \rrbracket_\sigma = \min(\llbracket a^* \rrbracket_\sigma, \llbracket b^* \rrbracket_\sigma)$$

We prove $\llbracket f^* \rrbracket(\sigma) = \phi(\llbracket f \rrbracket(\psi \circ \sigma))$ by induction on f:

- if $f \equiv \bot$, we obtain $\llbracket \bot^* \rrbracket_\sigma = \llbracket \bot \rrbracket_\sigma = 0$ and $\phi(\llbracket \bot \rrbracket(\psi \circ \sigma)) = 0$;
- if $f \equiv x$, then $\llbracket x^* \rrbracket_\sigma = 0$ if $\sigma_x = 0$ and $\llbracket x^* \rrbracket_\sigma = \infty$ if $\sigma_x > 0$. So $\llbracket x^* \rrbracket_\sigma = \phi(\psi(\sigma_x))$. On the other hand, $\phi(\llbracket x \rrbracket(\psi \circ \sigma)) = \phi(\psi \circ \sigma(x)) = \phi(\psi(\sigma_x))$;
- if $f \equiv a \vee b$, then $\llbracket (a \vee b)^* \rrbracket_\sigma = \llbracket a^* \vee b^* \rrbracket_\sigma = \max(\phi(\llbracket a \rrbracket(\psi \circ \sigma)), \phi(\llbracket b \rrbracket(\psi \circ \sigma))) = \phi(\max(\llbracket a \rrbracket(\psi \circ \sigma), \llbracket b \rrbracket(\psi \circ \sigma))) = \phi(\llbracket a \vee b \rrbracket(\psi \circ \sigma))$;
- the cases $f \equiv a \wedge b$ and $f \equiv a \supset b$ are similar. $\qquad\square$

5.2   Transforming Conditional Graphs into Formulae

Let us consider a conditional graph $\mathcal{G}$. There may be some conditional formulae on green arrows like $\rightarrow_f$. We consider all these formulae and the propositional variables they contain. For each vertex v of $\mathcal{G}$ we introduce a new propositional variable x_v, so that the propositional variables occurring in conditional formulae and the newly introduced x_v do not overlap. We build a sequent $\mathcal{S_G} = \Gamma \vdash \Delta$ by adding one formula to either Γ or Δ for each arrow of $\mathcal{G}$:

- if $v \rightarrow w$ is green arrow of $\mathcal{G}$, we add $x_v \supset x_w$ to Γ;
- if $v \rightarrow_f w$ is conditional green arrow of $\mathcal{G}$, we add $(\neg\neg f) \supset (x_v \supset x_w)$ to Γ;
- if $v \Rightarrow w$ is a red arrow of $\mathcal{G}$, we add $x_w \supset x_v$ to Δ.

Theorem 3. *Let $\mathcal{G}$ be a conditional graph, $\mathcal{S_G}$ its associated sequent and $n \in \mathbb{N}$. There exists a valuation $\sigma : \mathsf{LVar} \rightarrow \{0, 1\}$ such that the instance graph $\mathcal{G}_\sigma$ does not contain a $(n + 1)$-alternating chain if and only if the sequent $\mathcal{S_G}$ has a counter-model in LC_n.*

Proof. First, let us suppose that there exists a valuation $\sigma : \mathsf{LVar} \rightarrow \{0, 1\}$ s.t. the instance graph $\mathcal{G}_\sigma$ does not contain a chain of type $(\rightarrow^*\Rightarrow)^{n+1}$. By theorem 4 of [11], there exists a height h s.t. for every vertices v, w of $\mathcal{G}$ (or $\mathcal{G}_\sigma$, they have the same vertices), $h_v \in [0, n]$, if $v \rightarrow w \in \mathcal{G}_\sigma$ then $h_v \leqslant h_w$ and if $v \Rightarrow w \in \mathcal{G}_\sigma$ then $h_v < h_w$. We define $h'_v = n \rightarrow v$, i.e. $h'_v = h_v$ if $h_v < n$ and $h'_v = \infty$ if $h_v = n$. We define a valuation $\sigma' : \mathsf{LVar} \rightarrow \overline{[0, n)}$. If $x \equiv x_v$ is a variable corresponding to one of the vertices of $\mathcal{G}$ then $\sigma'_{x_v} = h'_v$. Otherwise we define $\sigma'_x = \phi(\sigma_x)$. We recall that the x_v do not overlap with the variables occurring in the conditional formulae of $\mathcal{G}$. We prove that σ' is a counter-model of $\mathcal{S_G} \equiv \Gamma \vdash \Delta$:

- consider the formula $x_v \supset x_w$ occurring in Γ. Then $\llbracket x_v \supset x_w \rrbracket_{\sigma'} = \llbracket x_v \rrbracket_{\sigma'} \rightarrow \llbracket x_w \rrbracket_{\sigma'} = \sigma'(x_v) \rightarrow \sigma'(x_w) = h'_v \rightarrow h'_w = \infty$ because $h'_v \leqslant h'_w$ since $v \rightarrow w$ occurs in $\mathcal{G}_\sigma$. Thus $\llbracket x_v \supset x_w \rrbracket_{\sigma'} = \infty$;
- consider the formula $(\neg\neg f) \supset (x_v \supset x_w)$ occurring in Γ. Then $\llbracket (\neg\neg f) \supset (x_v \supset x_w) \rrbracket_{\sigma'} = \llbracket \neg\neg f \rrbracket_{\sigma'} \rightarrow \llbracket x_v \supset x_w \rrbracket_{\sigma'}$. $\llbracket \neg\neg f \rrbracket_{\sigma'} = \phi(\llbracket f \rrbracket(\psi \circ \sigma')) = \phi(\llbracket f \rrbracket(\psi \circ \phi \circ \sigma)) = \phi(\llbracket f \rrbracket_\sigma)$. If $\llbracket f \rrbracket_\sigma = 0$ and in this case $\llbracket \neg\neg f \rrbracket_{\sigma'} \rightarrow \llbracket x_v \supset x_w \rrbracket_{\sigma'} = 0 \rightarrow \llbracket x_v \supset x_w \rrbracket_{\sigma'} = \infty$. On the other hand, if $\llbracket f \rrbracket_\sigma = 1$, then $v \rightarrow w$ occurs in $\mathcal{G}_\sigma$, and thus $h'_v \leqslant h'_w$. So $\llbracket \neg\neg f \rrbracket_{\sigma'} \rightarrow \llbracket x_v \supset x_w \rrbracket_{\sigma'} = \infty \rightarrow \llbracket x_v \supset x_w \rrbracket_{\sigma'} = \llbracket x_v \supset x_w \rrbracket_{\sigma'} = h'_v \rightarrow h'_w = \infty$. In either case, $\llbracket (\neg\neg f) \supset (x_v \supset x_w) \rrbracket_{\sigma'} = \infty$;

– consider the formula $x_w \supset x_v$ occurring in Δ. Then $v \Rightarrow w$ occurs in $\mathcal{G}_\sigma$. $[\![x_w \supset x_v]\!]_{\sigma'} = h'_w \to h'_v = h'_v$ since $h'_v < h'_w$. Moreover, as $h'_v < h'_w$, we deduce $h'_v < \infty$ and then $[\![x_w \supset x_v]\!]_{\sigma'} < \infty$.

Then $\lceil \Delta \rceil_{\sigma'} < \infty$ and that $\lfloor \Gamma \rfloor_{\sigma'} = \infty$. So σ' is a counter-model of $\mathcal{S}_\mathcal{G}$.

Conversely, consider $\sigma : \mathsf{LVar} \to \overline{[0, n)}$ a counter-model of $\mathcal{S}_\mathcal{G}$. We define $\sigma' = \psi \circ \sigma$. Let us consider a conditional arrow $v \to_f w$ of $\mathcal{G}$. We compute $[\![\neg\neg f]\!]_\sigma = \phi([\![f]\!]_{\sigma'})$. $[\![f]\!]_{\sigma'} = 1$ if and only if there is an arrow $v \to w$ in $\mathcal{G}_{\sigma'}$. If $[\![f]\!]_{\sigma'} = 1$ then $\phi([\![f]\!]_{\sigma'}) = \infty$ and $[\![(\neg\neg f) \supset (x_v \supset x_w)]\!]_\sigma = \infty \to [\![x_v \supset x_w]\!]_\sigma = [\![x_v \supset x_w]\!]_\sigma$. On the other hand, if $[\![f]\!]_{\sigma'} = 0$, then $[\![(\neg\neg f) \supset (x_v \supset x_w)]\!]_\sigma = 0 \to [\![x_v \supset x_w]\!]_\sigma = \infty$. Let use denote Γ' the multiset where we have replaced the formula $(\neg\neg f) \supset (x_v \supset x_w)$ by $x_v \supset x_w$ when $[\![f]\!]_{\sigma'} = 1$ and by nothing (i.e. we simply erase it) when $[\![f]\!]_{\sigma'} = 0$. It is clear that $\lfloor \Gamma' \rfloor_\sigma = \lfloor \Gamma \rfloor_\sigma$. So σ is also a counter-model in LC_n of the implicational sequent $\Gamma' \vdash \Delta$ corresponding to the instance graph $\mathcal{G}_{\sigma'}$. According to theorem 6 of [11], since the implicational sequent $\Gamma' \vdash \Delta$ has a counter-model in LC_n, its instance graph $\mathcal{G}_{\sigma'}$ does not contain a chain of type $(\to^\star \Rightarrow)^{n+1}$. □

It is obvious that the size of $\mathcal{S}_\mathcal{G}$ is linear in the size of $\mathcal{G}$ (of course, the size of $\mathcal{G}$ should account for the size of conditional formulae). So there exists a linear transformation of the problem of resource consumption bounding into the decision problem in LC_n.

Corollary 2. *Let $\mathcal{E}$ be a normal set of process equations of size k and $\mathcal{V}$ the set of variables of $\mathcal{E}$. There exists a formula $f_\mathcal{E}$ of LC of size $\mathcal{O}(k)$ such that for any $n \in \mathbb{N}$, $(\mathcal{E}, \mathcal{V})$ has a resource use boundable by n if and only if $f_\mathcal{E}$ has a counter-model in LC_n.*

Proof. Let $\mathcal{G}$ be the conditional graph associated to $\mathcal{E}$ (see corollary 1), $\mathcal{S}$ be the sequent associated to $\mathcal{G}$ (see theorem 3). Then $f_\mathcal{E}$ is a formula logically equivalent to $\mathcal{S}$, see proposition 1. □

6   Counter-Models of LC_n and Resource Consumption

In this section, we briefly recall some of our previous results which provide the proof of the converse of corollary 2. Given a formula f of LC, we explain how to build a conditional graph $\mathcal{G}_f$ of size linear w.r.t. the size of f which represents the proof-search process on f and on which it is possible to either prove f or extract counter-models of f. For an explanation of the construction in full details, the reader is invited to consult [12].

Let f be a formula of LC. We build a conditional graph $\mathcal{G}_f$ based on the decomposition tree of f, i.e. the set of sub-formula occurrences of f. An occurrence of a sub-formula r can be identified with the root node of the sub-tree corresponding to r. Each node is *polarized* starting with polarity $-$ for the root f^- and propagated the following way: the connectives $\vee$ and $\wedge$ preserve the polarity while the connective $\supset$ preserves the polarity on the right hand side and inverses it on the left-hand side.

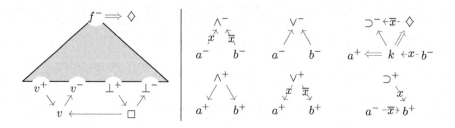

Fig. 2. Counter-model search system for LC

We add a supplementary node for each propositional variable v occurring in f. This is one node per variable, not per occurrence: two occurrences of the same variable only produce one supplementary node. These added nodes are not polarized. Two more nodes are added: $\Diamond$ and $\Box$. Intuitively, $\Diamond$ represents the semantic value ∞ whereas $\Box$ represents the semantic value 0.

Before we describe how we build the arrows of $\mathcal{G}_f$, we precise that we will sometimes introduce new conditional variables denoted x and use either x or its negation $\overline{x} \equiv \neg x$ as a condition indexing some green arrows like $\to_x$ or $\to_{\overline{x}}$. Now we describe how we build the arrows of $\mathcal{G}_f$:

- for the root f^-, we add a red arrows $f \Rightarrow \Diamond$;
- for every added node v corresponding to a propositional variable occurring in f, we add a green arrow $\Box \to v$;
- for a positive occurrence v^+ of a variable in f, we add a green arrow $v^+ \to v$;
- for a negative occurrence v^- of a variable in f, we add a green arrow $v \to v^-$;
- for a positive occurrence of $\bot^+$ in f, we add a green arrow $\bot^+ \to \Box$;
- for a negative occurrence of $\bot^-$ in f, we add a green arrow $\Box \to \bot^-$.

All these rules correspond to the left part of figure 2. Now we describe what we do with internal nodes, which corresponds to the right part of figure 2:

- for each negative occurrence of a sub-formula $r^- \equiv a^- \wedge b^-$, we introduce a new conditional variable x and we add the two conditional green arrows $a^- \to_x r^-$ and $b^- \to_{\overline{x}} r^-$;
- for each positive occurrence of a sub-formula $r^+ \equiv a^+ \wedge b^+$, we add the two green arrows $r^+ \to a^+$ and $r^+ \to b^+$;
- for $r^- \equiv a^- \vee b^-$, we add the two green arrows $a^- \to r^-$ and $b^- \to r^-$;
- for $r^+ \equiv a^+ \vee b^+$, we introduce a new variable x and add the two arrows $r^+ \to_x a^+$ and $r^+ \to_{\overline{x}} b^+$;
- for $r^- \equiv a^+ \supset b^-$, we introduce a new variable x and a new node k and the five arrows $b^- \to_x k$, $k \Rightarrow a^+$, $k \to r^-$, $k \Rightarrow \Diamond$ and $\Diamond \to_{\overline{x}} r^-$;
- for $r^+ \equiv a^- \supset b^+$, we introduce a variable new x and add the two arrows $r^+ \to_x b^+$ and $a^- \to_{\overline{x}} b^+$.

The construction of $\mathcal{G}_f$ is finished after each internal node has been processed. The order in which they are processed is indifferent. We recall the main result[4] of [11], which relates conditional graphs and LC_n:

Theorem 4. *Let f be a formula of LC, $\mathcal{G} \equiv \mathcal{G}_f$ be the conditional graph associated to f by the construction described in this section and $n \in \mathbb{N}$. Then f has a counter-model in LC_n if and only if there exists a valuation σ such that the instance graph $\mathcal{G}_\sigma$ has no $(n+1)$-alternating chain.*

Corollary 3. *Let f be a formula of LC of size k. There exists a process system $(\mathcal{E}, \mathcal{V})$ of size $\mathcal{O}(k)$ such that for any $n \in \mathbb{N}$, $(\mathcal{E}, \mathcal{V})$ has resource use boundable by n if and only if f has a counter-model in LC_n.*

Proof. Let f be a formula of LC. We apply theorem 4 and obtain a conditional graph $\mathcal{G}_f$. The size of $\mathcal{G}_f$ is linear w.r.t. the size of f. Then we apply theorem 2 and obtain a process system $(\mathcal{E}, \mathcal{V})$. The size of $(\mathcal{E}, \mathcal{V})$ is linear w.r.t. the size of $\mathcal{G}_f$, thus also w.r.t. the size of f. $(\mathcal{E}, \mathcal{V})$ has resource use boundable by n if and only if $\mathcal{G}_f$ has no $(n+1)$-alternating chains if and only if f has a counter-model in LC_n. □

7   Conclusion

We have defined a process calculus and an operational semantics that measures resource consumption. We establish a correspondence between normal process systems and conditional bi-colored graphs: a process system has resource use boundable by an integer n if and only if the corresponding graph has no $(n+1)$-alternating chain. Then we show how the absence of $(n+1)$-alternating chain in a graph can be expressed by the refutability of a formula of LC_n. Combining the two results, we get a linear transformation of a resource bounding problem in a process calculus into a decision problem in LC_n.

We recall our previous result on counter-model search in LC [11] and relate it to the process formalism we introduced. Thus, we have a linear transformation of a decision problem in LC_n into a resource bounding problem in a process calculus. This establishes the linear equivalence of the two problems. So LC could be viewed as a logic for specifying some resource related properties. This sheds some new lights on LC.

In further studies, we want to use the process calculus defined in this paper as an abstraction of more complex calculi: by keeping only the basic constructs present in our calculus and abstracting the other constructs. Counter-model search in LC could be used as a tool to bound resource consumption in some specified complex systems.

---

[4] To be precise, the construction of $\mathcal{G}_f$ we present here, and the associated theorem 4 are a slight but obvious modification of the cited result, to integrate the case of the $\perp$ logical constant and to avoid generating conditional red arrows like $\Rightarrow_x$ or $\Rightarrow_{\overline{x}}$.

References

1. Gödel, K.: Zum intuitionistischen Aussagenkalkül. In: Anzeiger Akademie des Wissenschaften Wien. Volume 69. (1932) 65–66
2. Dummett, M.: A Propositional Calculus with a Denumerable matrix. Journal of Symbolic Logic **24** (1959) 96–107
3. Hajek, P.: Metamathematics of Fuzzy Logic. Kluwer Academic Publishers (1998)
4. Dyckhoff, R.: Contraction-free Sequent Calculi for Intuitionistic Logic. Journal of Symbolic Logic **57** (1992) 795–807
5. Dyckhoff, R.: A Deterministic Terminating Sequent Calculus for Gödel-Dummett logic. Logical Journal of the IGPL **7** (1999) 319–326
6. Avellone, A., Ferrari, M., Miglioli, P.: Duplication-Free Tableau Calculi and Related Cut-Free Sequent Calculi for the Interpolable Propositional Intermediate Logics. Logic Journal of the IGPL **7** (1999) 447–480
7. Avron, A.: A Tableau System for Gödel-Dummett Logic Based on a Hypersequent Calculus. In: TABLEAUX 2000. Volume 1847 of LNAI. (2000) 98–111
8. Metcalfe, G., Olivetti, N., Gabbay, D.: Goal-Directed Calculi for Gödel-Dummett Logics. In: CSL. Volume 2803 of LNCS. (2003) 413–426
9. Larchey-Wendling, D.: Combining Proof-Search and Counter-Model Construction for Deciding Gödel-Dummett Logic. In: CADE-18. Volume 2392 of LNAI. (2002) 94–110
10. Baaz, M., Ciabattoni, A., Fermüller, C.: Hypersequent Calculi for Gödel Logics – A Survey. Journal of Logic and Computation **13** (2003) 835–861
11. Larchey-Wendling, D.: Counter-model search in Gödel-Dummett logics. In: IJCAR 2004. Volume 3097 of LNAI. (2004) 274–288
12. Larchey-Wendling, D.: Gödel-Dummett counter-models through matrix computation. Electronic Notes in Theoretical Computer Science **125** (2005) 137–148
13. Milner, R.: Communication and Concurrency. International series in computer science. Prentice Hall (1989)

On Interpolation in Existence Logics

Matthias Baaz and Rosalie Iemhoff[*]

Technical University Vienna, Wiedner Hauptstrasse 8-10, A-1040 Vienna, Austria
{baaz, iemhoff}@logic.at
http://www.logic.at/people/baaz, http://www.logic.at/people/iemhoff

Abstract. In [2] Gentzen calculi for intuitionistic logic extended with an existence predicate were introduced. Such logics were first introduced by Dana Scott, who provided a proof system for it in Hilbert style. The logic seems particularly useful in settings where non constant domain Kripke models play a role. In this paper it is proved that these systems have interpolation and the Beth definability property.

Keywords: Intuitionistic logic, existence predicate, Gentzen calculus, interpolation, Beth definability, cut-elimination, Skolemization, truth-value logics, Gödel logics, Scott logics, Kripke models.

1 Introduction

In this paper we prove that existence logics have interpolation and satisfy the Beth definability property (Corollary 2 and Theorem 5). Existence logics are extensions of intuitionistic predicate logic IQC with an existence predicate E, where the intuitive meaning of Et is that t *exists*[1].

Recall that we say that a single conclusion Gentzen calculus L has *interpolation* if whenever $L \vdash \Gamma_1, \Gamma_2 \Rightarrow C$, there exists an I in the common language of Γ_1 and $\Gamma_2 \cup \{C\}$ such that

$$\Gamma_1 \vdash_L I \text{ and } I, \Gamma_2 \vdash_L C.$$

In the context of existence logics, the *common language* of two multisets Γ_1 and Γ_2, denoted by $\mathcal{L}(\Gamma_1, \Gamma_2)$, consists of all variables, $\top$, $\bot$ and E, and all predicates and non-variable terms that occur both in Γ_1 and Γ_2.

We say that a Gentzen calculus L satisfies the *Beth definability property* if whenever $A(R)$ is a formula with R an n-ary relation symbol in a language $\mathcal{L}$, and R', R'' are two relation symbols not in $\mathcal{L}$ such that

$$L \vdash A(R') \wedge A(R'') \Rightarrow \forall \bar{x}(R'\bar{x} \leftrightarrow R''\bar{x}),$$

---

[*] Supported by the Austrian Science Fund FWF under project P17503.

[1] For a more computational view replace "t exists" by "the evaluation of t terminates". Universal (existential) statements express consequently weak (strong) correctness properties.

G. Sutcliffe and A. Voronkov (Eds.): LPAR 2005, LNAI 3835, pp. 697–711, 2005.

then there is a formula S in $\mathcal{L}$ such that

$$\mathsf{L} \vdash \Rightarrow \forall \bar{x}(S\bar{x} \leftrightarrow R'\bar{x}).$$

Existence logic IQCE was first introduced by D. Scott in [12], where he presented a Hilbert style proof system for the logic. The motivation behind these logics is that in the context of intuitionistic logic it is natural to be able to denote whether a term exists or not. In this system both variables and terms range over arbitrary objects while the quantifiers are assumed to range over existing objects only. Existence logic in which terms range over all objects while quantifiers as well as variables only range over existing objects is denoted by IQCE^+ and has e.g. been used by M. Beeson in [4]. M. Unterhalt thoroughly studied the Kripke semantics of these logics and proved respectively completeness and strong completeness for the systems IQCE and IQCE^+ in [18]. In [2] Gentzen calculi for existence logics were introduced and proved to have cut-elimination. Completeness results for these systems are presented in [1]. Applications that use existence logic are discussed below.

The Gentzen calculi that we introduce in this paper are called LJE and $\mathsf{LJE}(\Sigma_{\mathcal{L}})$, which is LJE extended by axioms $\Sigma_{\mathcal{L}}$, to be defined below. LJE corresponds to Scott's IQCE, and for a specific $\Sigma_{\mathcal{L}}$ the calculus $\mathsf{LJE}(\Sigma_{\mathcal{L}})$ corresponds to IQCE^+ as explained in Section 4.2.

1.1   Applications

Existence logic has many applications, and sometimes leads to surprising solutions of problems that do not seem solvable in pure intuitionistic logic. We do not describe these applications in full detail here, but we try to explain the general idea and give pointers to the literature.

Truth-Value Logics and Linear Frames. One application of the existence predicate is in the context of truth-value logics. These are logics based on truth-value sets V, i.e. closed subsets of the unit interval $[0, 1]$, also called *Gödel sets*. One can, for a given Gödel set V, interpret formulas by mapping them to elements of V. The logical symbols receive a meaning via restrictions on these interpretations, e.g. by stipulating that the interpretation of $\wedge$ is the infimum of the interpretations of the respective conjuncts, or that the interpretation of $\exists x Ax$ is the supremum of the values of Aa for all elements a in the domain. Given these interpretations, one can associate a logic with such a Gödel set V: the logic of all sentences that are mapped to 1 under any interpretation on V.

Gödel logics G_V are an example of truth value logics. Without going into the precise definition of these logics here, we only want to mention that these logics naturally correspond to the logics of linear frames. As has been shown by A. Beckmann and N. Preining this correspondence takes the following form.

Theorem 1. *(A. Beckmann and N. Preining [3]) For every countable linear frame F there exists a Gödel set V such that*

$$G_V \models A \iff A \text{ holds in all Kripke models on } F \text{ with constant domains,} \quad (1)$$

and vice versa: for every Gödel set V there exists a countable linear frame F such that (1).

In [9] so-called *Scott logics* S_V are introduced which correspond to linear frames, but now for possibly non constant domains. That is, we have

Theorem 2. *[9] For every countable linear frame F there exists a Gödel set V such that*

$$S_V \models A \iff A \text{ holds in all Kripke models based on } F, \quad (2)$$

and vice versa: for every countable Gödel set V there exists a countable linear frame F such that (2).

In the same paper it is shown that there is a natural and faithful translation from Scott logics into Gödel logics. This translation $(\cdot)^e$, that makes use of the existence predicate, allows to transfer properties about Gödel logics to Scott logics. $(\cdot)^e$ is defined as follows.

$(P(\bar{t}))^e = P(\bar{t})$ for atomic P and terms $\bar{t}$,
$(\cdot)^e$ commutes with the connectives,
$(\exists x A(x))^e = \exists x (Ex \wedge (A(x))^e)$,
$(\forall x A(x))^e = \forall x (Ex \to (A(x))^e)$.

Given this translation we then have the following theorem.

Lemma 1. *[9] For any Gödel set V, $(\cdot)^e$ is a faithful translation of S_V into G_V, i.e. for all $\mathcal{L}$-sentences A*

$$S_V \models A \iff G_V^e \models A^e.$$

Skolemization. Another application of the existence predicate is in the setting of Skolemization. As is well-known, the classical Skolemization method of replacing strong quantifiers in a formula by fresh function symbols and thus obtaining a equiconsistent formula, is not complete with respect to IQC. That is, there are formulas that are underivable, but for which their Skolemized version is derivable in IQC. For example,

$$IQC \nvdash \forall x(Ax \vee B) \to (\forall x Ax \vee B) \qquad IQC \vdash \forall x(Ax \vee B) \to (Ac \vee B).$$

In [1] an alternative Skolemization method called *eSkolemization* is introduced and is shown to be sound and complete with respect to IQC for a class of formulas larger than the class of formulas for which standard Skolemization is sound and complete. This eSkolemization method makes use of the existence predicate. It replaces negative occurrences of existential quantifiers $\exists x Bx$ by $(Ef(\bar{y}) \wedge Bf(\bar{y}))$, and positive occurrences of universal quantifiers $\forall x Bx$ by $(Ef(\bar{y}) \to Bf(\bar{y}))$. For example, the eSkolemization of the displayed formula above is

$$IQCE \nvdash \forall x(Ax \vee B) \to ((Ec \to Ac) \vee B).$$

We will not proceed with the topic of eSkolemization here but refer the interested reader to [1] instead.

Note the similarity between the different applications of the existence predicate: the translation $(\cdot)^e$ does a similar thing to quantifiers as eSkolemization does. Essentially, it all has to do with the fact that an existence predicate allows us in a Kripke model to name objects that do not exist in the root but come into existence only at a later stage in the model. Both [1] and [9] describe this intuition in more detail.

2   Preliminaries

We consider languages $\mathcal{L} \subseteq \mathcal{L}'$ for intuitionistic predicate logic plus the existence predicate E, without equality. For convenience we assume that $\mathcal{L}$ contains at least one constant and no variables, and that $\mathcal{L}'$ contains infinitely many variables. The languages may or may not contain functional symbols: the results in this paper hold for all cases. The reason for this has to do with the semantics for the Gentzen calculi; a topic we will not proceed with here, but which is discussed in [1].

The languages contain $\perp$, and $\neg A$ is defined as $A \to \perp$. $A, B, C, D, E, ..$ range over formulas in $\mathcal{L}'$, $s, t, ..$ over terms in $\mathcal{L}'$. Γ, Δ, Π range over multisets of formulas in $\mathcal{L}'$. Sequents are expressions of the form $\Gamma \Rightarrow C$, where Γ is a finite multiset. A sequent is in $\mathcal{L}$ if all its formulas are in $\mathcal{L}$. And similarly for $\mathcal{L}'$. A formula is *closed* when it does not contain free variables. A sequent $\Gamma \Rightarrow C$ is closed if C and all formulas in Γ are closed. For terms t and s $A[t/s]$ denotes the result of substituting t for all occurrences (for all free occurrences if s is a variable) of s in A. If for a formula $A(x)$ we write $A(t)$, this indicates the result of replacing some, possibly not all, occurrences of x in A with t. This is a subtlety overlooked in most textbooks, but not in [14], when defining e.g. the right introduction of $\exists$ as

$$\frac{\Gamma \Rightarrow A(t)}{\Gamma \Rightarrow \exists x A[x/t]}$$

In such a system, $R(t, t) \Rightarrow \exists x R(x, t)$ is not derivable. Because of this most proofs of interpolation, although correct, seem to overlook that subtle point.

In one of the final proof systems, $(\Rightarrow Et)$ will hold for the terms in $\mathcal{L}$, but not necessarily for the terms in $\mathcal{L}' \backslash \mathcal{L}$. $\mathcal{T}_\mathcal{L}$ denotes the set of terms in $\mathcal{L}$, $\mathcal{F}_\mathcal{L}$ denotes the set of formulas in $\mathcal{L}$, $\mathcal{S}_\mathcal{L}$ denotes the set of sequents in $\mathcal{L}$, and similarly for $\mathcal{L}'$.

In order not to drown in brackets we often write Ax for $A(x)$.

3   The Proof System

In this section we define the system LJE, a conservative extension of LJ for $\mathcal{L}'$ that covers the intuition that Et means t *exists*. Such a system was first introduced by Dana Scott in [12], but then in a Hilbert style axiomatization, and called IQCE. The Gentzen calculus for this system was first introduced in [2].

Given an existence predicate, terms, including variables, typically range over existing as well as non-existing elements, while the quantifiers range over existing objects only. Proofs are assumed to be trees.

The system LJE

$Ax \quad \Gamma, P \Rightarrow P \quad P$ atomic $\qquad\qquad L\bot \quad \Gamma, \bot \Rightarrow C$

$$L\wedge \quad \frac{\Gamma, A, B \Rightarrow C}{\Gamma, A \wedge B \Rightarrow C} \qquad\qquad R\wedge \quad \frac{\Gamma \Rightarrow A \qquad \Gamma \Rightarrow B}{\Gamma \Rightarrow A \wedge B}$$

$$L\vee \quad \frac{\Gamma, A \Rightarrow C \qquad \Gamma, B \Rightarrow C}{\Gamma, A \vee B \Rightarrow C} \qquad\qquad R\vee \quad \frac{\Gamma \Rightarrow A_i}{\Gamma \Rightarrow A_0 \vee A_1} \, i = 0, 1$$

$$L\rightarrow \quad \frac{\Gamma, A \rightarrow B \Rightarrow A \qquad \Gamma, B \Rightarrow C}{\Gamma, A \rightarrow B \Rightarrow C} \qquad\qquad R\rightarrow \quad \frac{\Gamma, A \Rightarrow B}{\Gamma \Rightarrow A \rightarrow B}$$

$$L\forall \quad \frac{\Gamma, \forall x Ax, At \Rightarrow C \qquad \Gamma, \forall x Ax \Rightarrow Et}{\Gamma, \forall x Ax \Rightarrow C} \qquad\qquad R\forall \quad \frac{\Gamma, Ey \Rightarrow Ay}{\Gamma \Rightarrow \forall x A[x/y]} \, *$$

$$L\exists \quad \frac{\Gamma, Ey, Ay \Rightarrow C}{\Gamma, \exists x A[x/y] \Rightarrow C} \, * \qquad\qquad R\exists \quad \frac{\Gamma \Rightarrow At \qquad \Gamma \Rightarrow Et}{\Gamma \Rightarrow \exists x Ax}$$

$$Cut \quad \frac{\Gamma \Rightarrow A \qquad \Gamma, A \Rightarrow C}{\Gamma \Rightarrow C}$$

Where $(*)$ denotes the condition that y does not occur free in Γ and C.

The principal formula of a rule is defined as usual. In the Cut rule the formula A is called the cut formula, and it is the principal formula of the Cut rule. The formulas Et and Ey are not principal in respectively $L\forall$, $R\exists$ and $R\forall$, $L\exists$.

We write $\mathsf{LJE} \vdash S$ if the sequent S is derivable in LJE. For a set of sequents X and a sequent S, we say that S *is derivable from* X *in* LJE, and write $X \vdash_{\mathsf{LJE}} S$, if S is derivable in the system LJE to which the sequents in X are added as initial sequents. We also denote this system by $\mathsf{LJE}(X)$.

In the system LJE no existence of any term that is not a variable is assumed. This implies e.g. that we cannot derive $\forall x Px \Rightarrow Pt$, but only $\forall x Px, Et \Rightarrow Pt$. Note however that the former is derivable in LJE from $(\Rightarrow Et)$. This is the reason why we consider derivations from extra axioms, especially axioms of the form $(\Rightarrow Et)$. Therefore, we define the following sets of sequents

$$\Sigma_{\mathcal{L}} \equiv_{def} \{\Gamma \Rightarrow Et \mid t \in \mathcal{T}_{\mathcal{L}}, \Gamma \text{ a multiset}\}.$$

Note that because of the assumptions on $\mathcal{L}$, $\Sigma_{\mathcal{L}}$ contains at least one sequent and for all sequents $\Gamma \Rightarrow Et$ in $\Sigma_{\mathcal{L}}$, t is a closed term. Given two languages $\mathcal{L} \subseteq \mathcal{L}'$, we write

$$\mathsf{LJE}(\Sigma_{\mathcal{L}}) \equiv_{def} \{S \in \mathcal{S}_{\mathcal{L}'} \mid \Sigma_{\mathcal{L}} \vdash_{\mathsf{LJE}} \Rightarrow S\}.$$

The $\mathcal{L}'$ is not denoted in $\mathsf{LJE}(\Sigma_{\mathcal{L}})$, but most of the time it is clear what is the "larger" language $\mathcal{L}'$ of which $\mathcal{L}$ is a subset.

Example 1.

$$\nvdash_{\mathsf{LJE}} \Rightarrow \exists x Ex \qquad \vdash_{\mathsf{LJE}} \Rightarrow \forall x Ex.$$

$$\vdash_{\mathsf{LJE}(\Sigma_{\mathcal{L}})} \Rightarrow \exists x Ex \land \forall x Ex.$$

Lemma 2. *For all sequents S in $\mathcal{L}$ that do not contain E:*

$$\mathsf{LJ} \vdash S \text{ implies } \mathsf{LJE}(\Sigma_{\mathcal{L}}) \vdash S.$$

Proof. Since S is a sequent in $\mathcal{L}$, we may assume w.l.o.g. that when S is provable in LJ it has a cut free proof in which all terms that are not eigenvariables are terms in $\mathcal{L}$. Denote this set of terms by X. Clearly, $X^s = \{\Gamma \Rightarrow Et \mid t \in X\}$ is a subset of $\Sigma_{\mathcal{L}}$. At every application of $R\exists$ or $L\forall$, add the appropriate $\Gamma \Rightarrow Et$ as the right hypothesis. At every application of $R\forall$ or $L\exists$ add the appropriate Ey to the antecedent. This gives a proof of $\Gamma \Rightarrow A$ in $\mathsf{LJE}(\Sigma_{\mathcal{L}})$.

Later on, in Proposition 1, we will see that the converse of the above lemma holds too.

4   Cut Elimination

In this section we recall some results from [2] that show that LJE and $\mathsf{LJE}(\Sigma_{\mathcal{L}})$ have a restricted form of cut elimination and have weakening and contraction. Some of these results we will need later on, the others are recalled to show that the systems we consider are well-behaved. The proofs of these results are more or less straightforward, where the ECut theorem, which shows that the systems allow some partial cut-elimination, is the most involved, as usual.

Lemma 3. *(Substitution Lemma)*
For $\mathsf{L} \in \{\mathsf{LJE}(\Sigma_{\mathcal{L}}), \mathsf{LJE}\}$:
If P is a proof in L of a sequent S in $\mathcal{L}'$ and y is a free variable in P, and t is a term in $\mathcal{L}'$ that does not contain eigenvariables or bound variables of P, then $P[t/y]$ is a proof of $S[t/y]$ in L.
In case $\mathsf{L} = \mathsf{LJE}$ the same holds for any term s instead of y.

Lemma 4. *([2]) (Weakening Lemma)*
For $\mathsf{L} \in \{\mathsf{LJE}(\Sigma_{\mathcal{L}}), \mathsf{LJE}\}$: $\mathsf{L} \vdash \Gamma \Rightarrow C$ implies $\mathsf{L} \vdash \Gamma, A \Rightarrow C$.

Lemma 5. *([2]) (Contraction Lemma)*
For $\mathsf{L} \in \{\mathsf{LJE}(\Sigma_{\mathcal{L}}), \mathsf{LJE}\}$: $\mathsf{L} \vdash \Gamma, A, A \Rightarrow C$ implies $\mathsf{L} \vdash \Gamma, A \Rightarrow C$.

Theorem 3. *([2]) (ECut theorem)*
For $\mathsf{L} \in \{\mathsf{LJE}(\Sigma_{\mathcal{L}}), \mathsf{LJE}\}$: Every sequent in $\mathcal{L}'$ provable in L has a proof in L in which the only cuts are instances of the ECut rule:

$$ECut: \quad \frac{\Gamma \Rightarrow Et \in \Sigma_{\mathcal{L}} \qquad \Gamma, Et \Rightarrow C}{\Gamma \Rightarrow C}$$

In particular, LJE *has cut-elimination.*

Corollary 1. *([2])* LJE($\Sigma_{\mathcal{L}}$) *is consistent.*

The cut elimination theorem allows us to prove the following correspondence between LJ and LJE($\Sigma_{\mathcal{L}}$).

Proposition 1. *([2]) For all closed sequents S in $\mathcal{L}$ not containing E:*

$$\text{LJ} \vdash S \ \textit{if and only if} \ \text{LJE}(\Sigma_{\mathcal{L}}) \vdash S.$$

4.1   Uniqueness

Observe that given another predicate E' that satisfies the same rules of LJE as E', it follows that

$$\text{LJE}(\Sigma_{\mathcal{L}}) \vdash Et \Rightarrow E't \ \land \ \text{LJE}(\Sigma_{\mathcal{L}}) \vdash E't \Rightarrow Et.$$

Namely, LJE($\Sigma_{\mathcal{L}}$) $\vdash$ ($\Rightarrow$ ($\forall x Ex \land \forall x E'x$)), and LJE($\Sigma_{\mathcal{L}}$) $\vdash$ ($\forall x Ex, E't \Rightarrow Et$) and LJE($\Sigma_{\mathcal{L}}$) $\vdash$ ($\forall x E'x, Et \Rightarrow E't$). Finally, two cuts do the trick. This shows that the existence predicate E is unique up to provable equivalence.

4.2   IQCE and IQCE$^+$

As remarked above, given an existence predicate, terms typically range over existing as well as non-existing elements, while quantifiers range over existing objects only. As to the choice of the domain for the variables, there have been different approaches. Scott in [12] introduces a system IQCE for the predicate language with the distinguished predicate E, in which variables range over all objects, like in LJE and LJE($\Sigma_{\mathcal{L}}$). On the other hand, Beeson in [4] discusses a system in which variables range over existing objects only.

The formulation of the system IQCE in [12], where logic with an existence predicate was first introduced was in Hilbert style, where the axioms and rules for the quantifiers are the following:

$$\forall x Ax \land Et \to At \qquad\qquad \frac{\overset{\vdots}{B \land Ey \to Ay}}{B \to \forall x Ax} \ *$$

$$\frac{\overset{\vdots}{Ay \land Ey \to B}}{\exists x Ax \to B} \ * \qquad\qquad At \land Et \to \exists x Ax$$

Here $*$ are the usual side conditions on the eigenvariable y.

The following formulation of IQCE in natural deduction style was given in [16]. We call the system NDE (Natural Deduction Existence). It consists of the axioms and quantifier rules of the standard natural deduction formulation of IQC (as e.g. given in [16]), where the quantifier rules are replaced by the following rules:

$$
\forall I \ \frac{\begin{array}{c}[Ey]\\ \vdots\\ Ay\end{array}}{\forall x Ax}\ * \qquad \forall E \ \frac{\begin{array}{cc}\vdots & \vdots\\ \forall x Ax & Et\end{array}}{At}
$$

$$
\exists I \ \frac{\begin{array}{cc}\vdots & \vdots\\ At & Et\end{array}}{\exists x Ax} \qquad \exists E \ \frac{\begin{array}{cc} & [Ay][Ey]\\ \vdots & \vdots\\ \exists x Ax & C\end{array}}{C}\ *
$$

Again, the $*$ are the usual side conditions on the eigenvariable y. It is easy to see that the following holds.

Fact. $\forall A \in \mathcal{F}_{\mathcal{L}'}$: $\vdash_{\mathsf{IQCE}} A$ if and only if $\vdash_{\mathsf{NDE}} A$ if and only if $\vdash_{\mathsf{LJE}} \Rightarrow A$.

Existence logic in which terms range over all objects while quantifiers and variables only range over existing objects is denoted by IQCE^+ and has e.g. been used by M. Beeson in [4]. The logic is the result of leaving out Ey in the two rules for the quantifiers in IQCE given above and adding Ex as axioms for all variables x. A formulation in natural deduction style is obtained from NDE by replacing the $\forall I$ and $\exists E$ by their standard formulations for IQC and adding Ex as axioms for all variables x. We call the system NDE^+. In this case we have the following correspondence.

Fact. $\forall A \in \mathcal{F}_{\mathcal{L}'}$:
$\vdash_{\mathsf{IQCE}^+} A$ iff $\vdash_{\mathsf{NDE}^+} A$ iff $\{\Gamma \Rightarrow Ex \mid x$ a variable, Γ a multiset$\} \vdash_{\mathsf{LJE}(\Sigma_{\mathcal{L}})} \Rightarrow A$.

M. Unterhalt in [18] thoroughly studied the Kripke semantics of these logics and proved respectively completeness and strong completeness for the systems IQCE and IQCE^+. Similar results for the Gentzen calculi presented here can be found in [1].

5   Interpolation

In this section we prove that the calculus LJE and $\mathsf{LJE}(\Sigma_{\mathcal{L}})$ have interpolation. To this end we use a calculus LJE' that is equivalent to LJE but in which the structural rules are not hidden.

The system LJE$'$

$$Ax \quad P \Rightarrow P \qquad P \text{ atomic} \qquad\qquad L\bot \quad \bot \Rightarrow C$$

$$\text{LW} \; \frac{\Gamma \Rightarrow C}{\Gamma, A \Rightarrow C} \qquad\qquad\qquad \text{LC} \; \frac{\Gamma, A, A \Rightarrow C}{\Gamma, A \Rightarrow C}$$

$$\text{L}\wedge \; \frac{\Gamma, A, B \Rightarrow C}{\Gamma, A \wedge B \Rightarrow C} \qquad\qquad \text{R}\wedge \; \frac{\Gamma \Rightarrow A \qquad \Gamma \Rightarrow B}{\Gamma \Rightarrow A \wedge B}$$

$$\text{L}\vee \; \frac{\Gamma, A \Rightarrow C \qquad \Gamma, B \Rightarrow C}{\Gamma, A \vee B \Rightarrow C} \qquad\qquad \text{R}\vee \; \frac{\Gamma \Rightarrow A_i}{\Gamma \Rightarrow A_0 \vee A_1} \; i = 0, 1$$

$$\text{L}\rightarrow \; \frac{\Gamma \Rightarrow A \qquad \Gamma, B \Rightarrow C}{\Gamma, A \rightarrow B \Rightarrow C} \qquad\qquad \text{R}\rightarrow \; \frac{\Gamma, A \Rightarrow B}{\Gamma \Rightarrow A \rightarrow B}$$

$$\text{L}\forall \; \frac{\Gamma, At \Rightarrow C \qquad \Gamma \Rightarrow Et}{\Gamma, \forall x Ax \Rightarrow C} \qquad\qquad \text{R}\forall \; \frac{\Gamma, Ey \Rightarrow Ay}{\Gamma \Rightarrow \forall x A[x/y]} \; *$$

$$\text{L}\exists \; \frac{\Gamma, Ay, Ey \Rightarrow C}{\Gamma, \exists x A[x/y] \Rightarrow C} \; * \qquad\qquad \text{R}\exists \; \frac{\Gamma \Rightarrow At \qquad \Gamma \Rightarrow Et}{\Gamma \Rightarrow \exists x Ax}$$

$$\text{ECut:} \quad \frac{\Gamma \Rightarrow Et \in \Sigma_{\mathcal{L}} \qquad \Gamma, Et \Rightarrow C}{\Gamma \Rightarrow C}$$

The calculus LJE$'(\Sigma_{\mathcal{L}})$ is the system LJE$'$ extended by the axioms $\Sigma_{\mathcal{L}}$ (Section 3).

Lemma 6. *For all formulas A in $\mathcal{L}'$:*

$$\text{LJE} \vdash A \; \Leftrightarrow \; \text{LJE}' \vdash A \qquad \text{LJE}(\Sigma_{\mathcal{L}}) \vdash A \; \Leftrightarrow \; \text{LJE}'(\Sigma_{\mathcal{L}}) \vdash A.$$

Proof. Use Theorem 3 and Lemmas 4 and 5.

Recall that we write $\mathcal{L}(\Gamma_1, \Gamma_2)$ for the common language of Γ_1 and Γ_2, i.e. the language consisting of the predicates and non-variable terms that occur both in Γ_1 and Γ_2, plus $\top$, $\bot$ and E and the variables.

Theorem 4. LJE$'$ *and* LJE$'(\Sigma_{\mathcal{L}})$ *have interpolation.*

Proof. We first prove the theorem for LJE$'$ and then for LJE$'(\Sigma_{\mathcal{L}})$ by showing how this case can be reduced to the LJE$'$ case. We write $\vdash$ for $\vdash_{\text{LJE}'}$ in this proof. Assume $\vdash \Gamma_1, \Gamma_2 \Rightarrow C$. We look for a formula I in the common language $\mathcal{L}(\Gamma_1, \Gamma_2 \cup \{C\})$ of Γ_1 and $\Gamma_2 \cup \{C\}$ such that

$$\vdash \Gamma_1 \Rightarrow I \quad \vdash I, \Gamma_2 \Rightarrow C. \tag{3}$$

We prove the theorem with induction to the depth d of P. Recall that the depth of a sequent in a proof is inductively defined as the sum of the depths of its upper sequents plus 1. Thus axioms have depth 1. The depth of a proof is the depth of its endsequent.

$d = 1$: P is an instance of an axiom. When the axiom is Ax we have $\Gamma_1\Gamma_2, Q \Rightarrow Q$, where Q is an atomic formula. There are two cases: we look for interpolants I and J such that

$$\vdash \Gamma_1, Q \Rightarrow I \quad \vdash I, \Gamma_2 \Rightarrow Q \quad \text{and} \quad \vdash \Gamma_1 \Rightarrow J \quad \vdash J, Q, \Gamma_2 \Rightarrow Q.$$

This case is trivial: take $I = Q$ and $J = \top$. The case that P is an instance of $L\bot$ is equally simple: again there are two possibilities, like above, and the interpolants are $\top$ and $\bot$.

$d > 1$. We distinguish by cases according to the last rule applied in P. If it is a LC, the last lines of P look as follows.

$$\frac{\Gamma_1\Gamma_2, A, A \Rightarrow C}{\Gamma_1\Gamma_2, A \Rightarrow C}$$

Again there are several cases: we look for interpolants

$$\vdash \Gamma_1, A \Rightarrow I \quad \vdash I, \Gamma_2 \Rightarrow C \quad \text{and} \quad \vdash \Gamma_1 \Rightarrow J \quad \vdash J, A, \Gamma_2 \Rightarrow C.$$

By the induction hypothesis there are interpolants I' and J' such that the sequents $\Gamma_1, A, A \Rightarrow I'$ and $I', \Gamma_2 \Rightarrow C$, and $\Gamma_1 \Rightarrow J'$ and $J', A, A, \Gamma_2 \Rightarrow C$ are derivable. Moreover, I' is in $\mathcal{L}(\Gamma_1 \cup \{A\}, \Gamma_2 \cup \{C\})$, and J' is in $\mathcal{L}(\Gamma_1, \Gamma_2 \cup \{A, C\})$. Hence taking $I = I'$ and $J = J'$ and applying contraction gives the desired result. The case LW is equally trivial.

The connective cases are equal to their treatment in proofs of interpolation for LJ. For completeness sake we sketch the proof for the case that the last rule is $L\rightarrow$. Then the last lines of the proof look as follows.

$$\frac{\Gamma_1\Gamma_2 \Rightarrow A \qquad \Gamma_1\Gamma_2, B \Rightarrow C}{\Gamma_1\Gamma_2, A \rightarrow B \Rightarrow C}$$

We have to find I in $\mathcal{L}(\Gamma_1 \cup \{A \rightarrow B\}, \Gamma_2 \cup \{C\})$ and J in $\mathcal{L}(\Gamma_1, \Gamma_2 \cup \{A \rightarrow B, C\})$ such that

$$\vdash \Gamma_1, A \rightarrow B \Rightarrow I \quad \vdash I, \Gamma_2 \Rightarrow C \quad \text{and} \quad \vdash \Gamma_1 \Rightarrow J \quad \vdash J, A \rightarrow B, \Gamma_2 \Rightarrow C.$$

We teat the case I and leave J to the reader. For I, note that by the induction hypothesis there are $I' \in \mathcal{L}(\Gamma_2, \Gamma_1 \cup \{A\})$ and $I'' \in \mathcal{L}(\Gamma_1 \cup \{B\}, \Gamma_2 \cup \{C\})$ such that $\vdash \Gamma_2 \Rightarrow I', \vdash I', \Gamma_1 \Rightarrow A, \vdash \Gamma_1, B \Rightarrow I''$ and $\vdash I'', \Gamma_2 \Rightarrow C$. Hence we can take $I = I' \rightarrow I''$.

The case of the existential quantifier is more or less similar to the corresponding case for LJ. Suppose the last rule is $L\exists$. Then the last two lines of the proof are

$$\frac{\Gamma_1\Gamma_2, Ey, Ay \Rightarrow C}{\Gamma_1\Gamma_2, \exists x A[x/y] \Rightarrow C}$$

We write $\exists x A x$ for $\exists x A[x/y]$. Note that y is not free in $\Gamma_1 \Gamma_2$ and C. We have to find $I \in \mathcal{L}(\Gamma_1 \cup \{\exists x A x\}, \Gamma_2 \cup \{C\})$ and $J \in \mathcal{L}(\Gamma_1, \Gamma_2 \cup \{\exists x A x, C\})$ such that

$$\vdash \Gamma_1, \exists x A x \Rightarrow I \quad \vdash I, \Gamma_2 \Rightarrow C \quad \text{and} \quad \vdash \Gamma_1 \Rightarrow J \quad \vdash J, \exists x A x, \Gamma_2 \Rightarrow C.$$

For I, use that the induction hypothesis gives a I' such that

$$\vdash \Gamma_1, Ey, Ay \Rightarrow I' \quad \vdash I', \Gamma_2 \Rightarrow C.$$

Observe that we have

$$\vdash \Gamma_1, Ey, Ay \Rightarrow \exists z I'[z/y] \quad \vdash \exists z I'[z/y], \Gamma_2 \Rightarrow C,$$

because we also have $\vdash I'(y), \Gamma_2, Ey \Rightarrow C$ by the weakening lemma. An application of L$\exists$ to $\Gamma_1, Ey, Ay \Rightarrow \exists z I'[z/y]$ shows that we can take $I = \exists z I'[z/y]$ as interpolant. Of course, if y is not free in I' we can take $I = I'$ as well.

For J, use that the induction hypothesis gives a J' such that

$$\vdash \Gamma_1 \Rightarrow J' \quad \vdash J', \Gamma_2, Ey, Ay \Rightarrow C.$$

Observe that whe have

$$\vdash \Gamma_1 \Rightarrow \forall z J'[z/y] \quad \vdash \forall z J'[z/y], \Gamma_2, Ey, Ay \Rightarrow C,$$

because we also have

$$\vdash \Gamma_1, Ey \Rightarrow J' \quad \forall z J'[z/y], J', \Gamma_2, Ey, Ay \Rightarrow C \quad \forall z J'[z/y], \Gamma_2, Ey, Ay \Rightarrow Ey$$

by the weakening lemma. An application of L$\exists$ to $\forall z J'[z/y], \Gamma_2, Ey, Ay \Rightarrow C$ shows that we can take $J = \forall z J'[z/y]$ as interpolant. Of course, if y is not free in J' we can take $J = J'$ as well.

Suppose the last rule is R$\exists$:

$$\frac{\Gamma_1 \Gamma_2 \Rightarrow At \qquad \Gamma_1 \Gamma_2 \Rightarrow Et}{\Gamma_1 \Gamma_2 \Rightarrow \exists x A x}$$

We have to find $I \in \mathcal{L}(\Gamma_1, \Gamma_2 \cup \{ExAx\})$ such that $\vdash \Gamma_1 \Rightarrow I$ and $\vdash I \Rightarrow ExAx$.

By the induction hypothesis there are I_1 and I_2 such that

$$\vdash \Gamma_1 \Rightarrow I_1 \quad \vdash I_1, \Gamma_2 \Rightarrow At \quad \vdash \Gamma_1 \Rightarrow I_2 \quad \vdash I_2, \Gamma_2 \Rightarrow Et.$$

Thus we can take $I = I_1 \wedge I_2$ as interpolant.

Finally, we treat the universal quantifier, the most complicated case. Suppose the last rule is R$\forall$:

$$\frac{\Gamma_1 \Gamma_2, Ey \Rightarrow A(y)}{\Gamma_1 \Gamma_2 \Rightarrow \forall x A[x/y]}$$

By the induction hypothesis there is a interpolant $I \in \mathcal{L}(\Gamma_1, \Gamma_2 \cup \{Ey, A(y)\})$ for the upper sequent: $\vdash \Gamma_1 \Rightarrow I$ and $\vdash I, Ey, \Gamma_2 \Rightarrow A(y)$. In case y is not free in I the sequent $I, \Gamma_2 \Rightarrow \forall x A[x/y]$ is derivable too. Hence we can take I as an interpolant of the lower sequent and are done. Therefore, suppose y occurs free in I. By the side conditions y is not free in $\Gamma_1 \Gamma_2$. Hence we have the following derivation:

$$\vdots$$
$$\frac{\Gamma_1, Ey \Rightarrow I}{\Gamma_1 \Rightarrow \forall z I[z/y]}$$

Thus the following derivation shows that $\forall z I[z/y]$ is an interpolant for the lower sequent:

$$\vdots$$
$$\frac{\dfrac{I, Ey, \Gamma_2 \Rightarrow A(y) \qquad Ey, \Gamma_2 \Rightarrow Ey}{\forall z I[z/y], Ey, \Gamma_2 \Rightarrow A(y)}}{\forall z I[z/y], \Gamma_2 \Rightarrow \forall x A[x/y]}$$

Finally, we treat L$\forall$, when the last lines of the proof are:

$$\frac{\Gamma_1 \Gamma_2, A(t) \Rightarrow C \qquad \Gamma_1 \Gamma_2 \Rightarrow Et}{\Gamma_1 \Gamma_2, \forall x A(x) \Rightarrow C}$$

We have to find $I \in \mathcal{L}(\Gamma_1 \cup \{\forall x A(x)\}, \Gamma_2 \cup \{C\})$ and $J \in \mathcal{L}(\Gamma_1, \Gamma_2 \cup \{\forall x A(x), C\})$ such that

$$\vdash \Gamma_1, \forall x A(x) \Rightarrow I \quad \vdash I, \Gamma_2 \Rightarrow C \quad \text{and} \quad \vdash \Gamma_1 \Rightarrow J \quad \vdash J, \forall x A(x), \Gamma_2 \Rightarrow C.$$

First we treat the case J. Note that by the induction hypothesis there are three formulas $I' \in \mathcal{L}(\Gamma_1, \Gamma_2 \cup \{A(t), C\})$, $J' \in \mathcal{L}(\Gamma_1, \Gamma_2 \cup \{Et\})$ and $H' \in \mathcal{L}(\Gamma_2, \Gamma_1 \cup \{Et\})$ such that

$$\vdash \Gamma_1 \Rightarrow I' \quad \vdash I', A(t), \Gamma_2 \Rightarrow C \quad \text{and} \quad \vdash \Gamma_1 \Rightarrow J' \quad \vdash J', \Gamma_2 \Rightarrow Et \quad (4)$$

$$\vdash \Gamma_2 \Rightarrow H' \quad \vdash H', \Gamma_1 \Rightarrow Et.$$

Note that I', J' and H' may contain t. If t does not occur in I' and J' or it occurs in $\mathcal{L}(\Gamma_1, \Gamma_2 \cup \{\forall x A(x), C\})$, then $I', J' \in \mathcal{L}(\Gamma_1, \Gamma_2 \cup \{\forall x A(x), C\})$. Moreover, (4) implies

$$\vdash \Gamma_1 \Rightarrow I' \wedge J' \quad \vdash I' \wedge J', \forall x A(x), \Gamma_2 \Rightarrow C.$$

Thus in this case we can take $J = I' \wedge J'$.

On the other hand, if t does occur in I' or J' and not in $\mathcal{L}(\Gamma_1, \Gamma_2 \cup \{\forall x A(x), C\}$ we proceed as follows. Either t does not occur in Γ_1 or t does not occur in $\Gamma_2 \cup \{\forall x A(x), C\}$. In the first case, it follows that t does not occur in I' and not in J', contradicting our assumptions. Thus t occurs in Γ_1 but not in $\Gamma_2 \cup \{\forall x A(x), C\}$. Hence t does not occur in H'. Note that we have a derivation

$$\frac{\vdots \qquad\qquad \vdots}{\dfrac{H', \Gamma_1 \Rightarrow I' \wedge J' \qquad H', \Gamma_1 \Rightarrow Et}{\dfrac{H', \Gamma_1 \Rightarrow \exists x(I' \wedge J')[x/t]}{\Gamma_1 \Rightarrow \big(H' \to \exists x(I' \wedge J')[x/t]\big)}}}$$

Now note something important: because t does not occur in $\forall x A(x)$, this implies that $\forall x A(x) = \forall x A[x/t]$ (for the difference between $A(x)$ and $A[x/t]$ see the preliminaries, Section 2). Thus also $\forall x(A[y/t])[x/y] = \forall x A(x)$. And because t does not occur in Γ_2 or C, by the substitution lemma, Lemma 3, we also have a derivation for a variable y not occurring in P of

$$\begin{array}{c} \vdots \qquad\qquad\qquad\qquad\qquad\qquad \vdots \\ \dfrac{(I' \wedge J')[y/t], Ey, A[y/t], \Gamma_2 \Rightarrow C \qquad Ey, (I' \wedge J')[y/t], \Gamma_2 \Rightarrow Ey}{\dfrac{Ey, (I' \wedge J')[y/t], \forall x A(x), \Gamma_2 \Rightarrow C}{\dfrac{\exists x(I' \wedge J')[x/t], \forall x A(x), \Gamma_2 \Rightarrow C}{(H' \to \exists x(I' \wedge J')[x/t]), \forall x A(x), \Gamma_2 \Rightarrow C}}} \end{array}$$

with $\dfrac{\vdots}{\Gamma_2 \Rightarrow H'}$ on the left branch.

Hence we can take $J = \big(H' \to \exists x(I' \wedge J')[x/t]\big)$ and we are done.

The last case we have to treat is the one where we look for the interpolant $I \in \mathcal{L}(\Gamma_1 \cup \{\forall x A(x)\}, \Gamma_2 \cup \{C\})$ such that

$$\vdash \Gamma_1, \forall x A(x) \Rightarrow I \quad \vdash I, \Gamma_2 \Rightarrow C. \tag{5}$$

Note that by the induction hypothesis there are $I' \in \mathcal{L}(\Gamma_1 \cup \{A(t)\}, \Gamma_2 \cup \{C\})$, $J' \in \mathcal{L}(\Gamma_2, \Gamma_1 \cup \{Et\})$ and $H' \in \mathcal{L}(\Gamma_2, \Gamma_1 \cup \{Et\})$ such that

$$\vdash \Gamma_1, A(t) \Rightarrow I' \quad \vdash I', \Gamma_2 \Rightarrow C \qquad \text{and} \qquad \vdash \Gamma_2 \Rightarrow J' \quad \vdash J', \Gamma_1 \Rightarrow Et$$

$$\vdash \Gamma_1 \Rightarrow H' \quad \vdash H', \Gamma_2 \Rightarrow Et.$$

Observe that whence we have $\vdash (J' \to I'), \Gamma_2 \Rightarrow C$. Furthermore, we have a derivation

$$\frac{\vdots \qquad\qquad \vdots}{\dfrac{J', A(t), \Gamma_1 \Rightarrow I' \qquad J', \Gamma_1 \Rightarrow Et}{\dfrac{J', \forall x A(x), \Gamma_1 \Rightarrow I'}{\forall x A(x), \Gamma_1 \Rightarrow J' \to I'}}}$$

Thus, in case t belongs to the common language $\mathcal{L}(\Gamma_1 \cup \{\forall x A(x)\}, \Gamma_2 \cup \{C\})$ we can take $I = (J' \to I')$ and we are done. Therefore, assume t does not belong to the common language. In case it does not belong to $\Gamma_2 \cup \{C\}$, it follows that both I' and J' cannot contain t and we can again take $I = (J' \to I')$. Therefore, assume t does not belong to $\Gamma_1 \cup \{\forall x A(x)\}$. Hence H' does not contain t. But then we can infer, by Lemma 3, for a fresh variable y, from $\vdash \forall x A(x), \Gamma_1 \Rightarrow J' \to I'$ above, that we have the following derivation

$$\vdots$$

$$\frac{\forall x A(x), Ey, \Gamma_1 \Rightarrow (J' \to I')[y/t] \qquad \vdots}{\forall x A(x), \Gamma_1 \Rightarrow \forall z(J' \to I')[z/t] \qquad \Gamma_1 \Rightarrow H'}$$
$$\overline{\forall x A(x), \Gamma_1 \Rightarrow \forall z(J' \to I')[z/t] \wedge H'}$$

On the other hand we also have

$$\vdots \qquad\qquad \vdots$$

$$\frac{H', J' \to I', \Gamma_2 \Rightarrow C \qquad H', J' \to I', \Gamma_2 \Rightarrow Et}{H', \forall z(J' \to I')[z/t], \Gamma_2 \Rightarrow C}$$
$$\overline{H' \wedge \forall z(J' \to I')[z/t], \Gamma_2 \Rightarrow C}$$

Hence we take $I = H' \wedge \forall z(J' \to I')[z/t]$ as the interpolant.

It is interesting to note that (5) also holds for $I = (Et \to I') \wedge H'$. But in this case I does not in general belong to the common language.

Finally, we show that $\mathsf{LJE}'(\Sigma_{\mathcal{L}})$ has interpolation too, by reducing this case to the case LJE' in the following way. Given a proof P of $\Gamma_1\Gamma_2 \Rightarrow C$ in $\mathsf{LJE}'(\Sigma_{\mathcal{L}})$ we consider all axioms of the form $\Pi \Rightarrow Et \in \Sigma_{\mathcal{L}}$ that occur in P. Suppose there are n of them: $\Pi_1 \Rightarrow Et_1, \ldots, \Pi_n \Rightarrow Et_n$. Note that all t_i have to be closed. Clearly, there is a proof of $Et_1, \ldots, Et_n, \Gamma_1\Gamma_2 \Rightarrow C$ in LJE' by replacing the axioms $\Pi_i \Rightarrow Et_i$ by the logical axioms $\Pi_i, Et_i \Rightarrow Et_i$. Now we consider the following partition $\Gamma_1'\Gamma_2' \Rightarrow C$ of $Et_1, \ldots, Et_n, \Gamma_1\Gamma_2 \Rightarrow C$:

$$\Gamma_1' = \Gamma_1 \cup \{Et_j \mid j \le n, \ t_j \text{ occurs in } \Gamma_1 \text{ or not in } \Gamma_1 \cup \Gamma_2\}.$$

$$\Gamma_2' = \Gamma_2 \cup \{Et_j \mid j \le n, \ t_j \text{ occurs in } \Gamma_2\}.$$

By the interpolation theorem for LJE' there exists an interpolant I such that $\vdash_{\mathsf{LJE}'} \Gamma_1' \Rightarrow I$ and $\vdash_{\mathsf{LJE}'} I, \Gamma_2' \Rightarrow C$ where I is in the common language of Γ_1' and $\Gamma_2' \cup \{C\}$. It is not difficult to see that whence I is in the common language of Γ_1 and $\Gamma_2 \cup \{C\}$ too. By cutting on the Et_i's we obtain

$$\vdash_{\mathsf{LJE}'(\Sigma_{\mathcal{L}})} \Gamma_1 \Rightarrow I \qquad \vdash_{\mathsf{LJE}'(\Sigma_{\mathcal{L}})} I, \Gamma_2 \Rightarrow C.$$

This proves that $\mathsf{LJE}'(\Sigma_{\mathcal{L}})$ has interpolation too.

Corollary 2. LJE *and* $\mathsf{LJE}(\Sigma_{\mathcal{L}})$ *have interpolation.*

5.1   Interpolation of Fragments

We say that a Gentzen calculus L interpolates for the fragment $\mathcal{F}$ where $\mathcal{F}$ is a set of formulas, if whenever $\mathsf{L} \vdash \Gamma_1, \Gamma_2 \Rightarrow C$, there exists an $I \in \mathcal{F}$ in the common language of Γ_1 and $\Gamma_2 \cup \{C\}$ such that

$$\vdash_{\mathsf{L}} \Gamma_1 \Rightarrow I \qquad \vdash_{\mathsf{L}} I, \Gamma_2 \Rightarrow C.$$

As is well-known, the fragment consisting of formulas containing no other logical symbols as $\wedge, \vee, \forall, \exists$, interpolates for LJ. We conjecture that LJE and $\mathsf{LJE}(\Sigma_{\mathcal{L}})$

do not interpolate for this fragment because of the L∀ case in the proof of the interpolation theorem above.

5.2 Beth's Theorem

Following standard proofs for the Beth definability property of LJ, it is easy to prove the following theorem.

Theorem 5. LJE *and* LJE($\Sigma_{\mathcal{L}}$) *satisfy the Beth definability property.*

References

1. Baaz, M. and Iemhoff, R., Skolemization in intuitionistic logic, *Manuscript*, 2005.
2. Baaz, M. and Iemhoff, R., Gentzen calculi for the existence predicate, *Studia Logica*, to appear.
3. Beckmann, A. and Preining, N., Linear Kripke Frames and Gödel Logics, *Submitted*, 2005.
4. Beeson, M., Foundations of Constructive Mathematics, Springer, Berlin, 1985.
5. Corsi, G.,
   A cut-free calculus for Dummett's LC quantified, *Zeitschrift für Mathematische Logik und Grundlagen der Mathematik* 35, pp. 289-301, 1989.
6. Corsi, G., A logic characterized by the class of connected models with nested domains, *Studia Logica* 48(1), pp. 15-22, 1989.
7. Corsi, G., Completeness theorem for Dummett's LC quantified and some of its extensions, *Studia Logica* 51(2), pp. 317-335, 1992.
8. Heyting, A., Die formalen Regeln der intuitionistische Mathematik II, *Sitzungsberichte der Preussischen Akademie von Wissenschaften. Physikalisch-mathematische Klasse*, pp. 57-71, 1930.
9. Iemhoff, R., A note on linear Kripke models, *Journal of Logic and Computation*, to appear.
10. Mints, G.E., Axiomatization of a Skolem function in intuitionistic logic, *Formalizing the dynamics of information*, Faller, M. (ed.) et al., CSLI Lect. Notes 91, pp. 105-114, 2000.
11. Preining, N., *Complete Recursive Axiomatizability of Gödel Logics*, PhD-thesis, Technical University Vienna, 2003.
12. Scott, D.S., Identity and existence in intuitionistic logic, *Applications of sheaves, Proc. Res. Symp. Durham 1977*, Fourman (ed.) et al., Lect. Notes Math. 753, pp. 660-696, 1979.
13. Takano, M., Another proof of the strong completeness of the intuitionistic fuzzy logic, *Tsukuba J. Math.* 11(1), pp. 101-105, 1987.
14. Takeuti, G. , *Proof Theory*, North-Holland Publishing Company, 1979.
15. Takeuti, G. AND Titani, M., Intuitionistic fuzzy logic and intuitionistic fuzzy set theory, *Journal of Symbolic Logic* 49, pp. 851-866, 1984.
16. Troelstra, A.S., and van Dalen, D., *Constructivism in Mathematics*, vol. I North-Holland, 1988.
17. Troelstra, A.S., and Schwichtenberg, H.,, *Basic Proof Theory*, Cambridge Tracts in Theoretical Computer Science 43, Cambridge University Press, 1996.
18. Unterhalt, M., *Kripke-Semantik mit partieller Existenz*, PhD-thesis, University of Münster, 1986.

Incremental Integrity Checking: Limitations and Possibilities

Henning Christiansen and Davide Martinenghi

Roskilde University, Computer Science Dept.,
P.O. Box 260, DK-4000 Roskilde, Denmark
{henning, dm}@ruc.dk

Abstract. Integrity checking is an essential means for the preservation of the intended semantics of a deductive database. Incrementality is the only feasible approach to checking and can be obtained with respect to given update patterns by exploiting query optimization techniques. By reducing the problem to query containment, we show that no procedure exists that always returns the best incremental test (aka *simplification* of integrity constraints), and this according to any reasonable criterion measuring the checking effort. In spite of this theoretical limitation, we develop an effective procedure allowing general parametric updates that, for given database classes, returns ideal simplifications and also applies to recursive databases. Finally, we point out the improvements with respect to previous methods based on an experimental evaluation.

1 Introduction

Semantic information in databases is conventionally represented under the form of integrity constraints (ICs), i.e., properties that must always be satisfied for the data to be considered *consistent*. Besides simple forms of predefined constraints, of which primary and foreign keys are the most common examples, real-world applications may involve nontrivial integrity requirements that capture complex data dependencies and "business logic". The need for advanced integrity verification tools is testified by the introduction of several standard constructs for integrity support in the SQL language, such as *check* constraints and *assertions*. However, in spite of a long recognition of the importance of such practices, which are part of the SQL standard since 1992, today's DBMSs still lack the ability of efficiently handling non-predefined constraints.

Maintaining compliance of data wrt ICs is an essential requirement: if data lack integrity, answers to queries cannot be trusted; furthermore, satisfaction of ICs can be exploited to improve query evaluation performance by means of so-called semantic query optimization. Databases, however, usually contain very large collections of data that quickly evolve over time. In this regard, DBMSs need to be extended with the ability to automatically verify, in an *incremental* way, that database updates do not introduce any violation of integrity.

Today's practices based on triggers (at the database level) or hand-coding of tests (at the application level) are clearly unsatisfactory, since, by their procedural and *ad hoc* nature, they are prone to errors and difficult to maintain. The need

G. Sutcliffe and A. Voronkov (Eds.): LPAR 2005, LNAI 3835, pp. 712–727, 2005.

for automated integrity maintenance methods has attracted much research in the database as well as the logic programming and artificial intelligence communities. Main approaches to efficient integrity checking that have been proposed since the early eighties include extensions of the SLD(NF) proof procedure [18, 6], partial evaluation [10], update propagation [11], incremental view maintenance [7] and several others. The way we pursue here is the so-called *simplification* of ICs — a principle that has been recognized for more than two decades, dating back to at least [16], and then elaborated by several other authors, e.g., [11, 17, 4, 6, 20, 5]. Our work is an attempt to reconcile and generalize such ideas in a systematic way that may promote applications of deductive databases for use with current database management technology.

Simplification means to generate a set of ICs whose satisfaction in the *current* state implies the satisfaction of the original constraints in the updated state. The input of the procedure is a set of ICs to be maintained on the database as well as an update pattern describing a typology of updates that the database can receive; the produced output is the set of simplified ICs that should be checked upon reception of an update matching the given pattern. We find it important that a proposed simplification algorithm can work on parametric update patterns, not only specific updates. This means that such patterns can be simplified at design time, when only the schema exists and not yet any database state. At runtime the simplified ICs can be instantiated wrt the specific updates and tested in the actual state. The main interest of the simplification process is that the output set of ICs is as *easy* to evaluate as possible. In this sense, simplification proper is only feasible by assuming satisfaction of ICs in the state prior to the update.

We identify as "ideal" a simplification procedure that outputs a set of ICs that is minimal wrt an ordering that represents an approximation of the cost of evaluating the constraints. Although there is no ultimate criterion that, independently of the actual database state, perfectly measures the evaluation effort, natural requirements can be imposed that should be met by any sensible ordering — in particular, that "nothing to check" is the best possible simplification one can hope for. With this assumption, it can be proved that ideal simplification is equivalent to decidability of query containment, which is known not to hold in general (query containment is not decidable, e.g., already for pure DATALOG without negation). In fact, ideal simplification is possible in a class of databases if and only if query containment is decidable in that class.

In spite of this limitation, it can be argued on an experimental basis that simplification procedures that are "almost ideal" can still be of practical use and certainly improve upon non-optimized integrity checking.

2   The Simplification Problem

We adopt the notation and terminology of deductive databases, and focus on DATALOG with stratified negation [1] (aka DATALOG$^\neg$). Our results are, thus, also applicable in the relational setting. Predicates are divided into three pairwise disjoint sets: *intensional, extensional,* and *built-in* predicates. We use vector notation to indicate sequences of terms, e.g., $\vec{t}$. Substitutions are written as $\{\vec{X}/\vec{t}\}$ in order to indicate which variables are mapped to which terms. A *clause* is a formula $A \leftarrow L_1 \wedge \cdots \wedge L_n$ where A is an atom and $L_1, \ldots, L_n$ are literals and with the usual understanding of variables being implicitly universally quantified; A is called the *head* and $L_1 \wedge \cdots \wedge L_n$ the *body* of the clause. If the head is missing (understood as *false*) the clause is called a *denial*. A *rule* is a clause whose head is intensional, and a *fact* is a clause whose head is extensional and ground and whose body is empty (understood as *true*). Clauses are assumed to be *range restricted*, i.e., all clause variables must occur in a positive database literal in the body.

As mentioned, ICs need to be specialized for update patterns rather than for specific updates. For this purpose, we use *parameters* (written in boldface: **a**, **b**, ...) that can appear anywhere in a formula where a constant is expected. Parameters behave like variables that are universally quantified at a metalevel; they are not expected to be part of any actual database nor of any query or update actually given to a database, but we may have parametric expressions of these categories. Unique name axioms are assumed for (non-parametric) constants, i.e., distinct constants denote distinct values. A *parameter substitution* is a mapping from parameters to constants; whenever E is an expression containing parameters, and π is a parameter substitution for those, $E\pi$ is called a *parametric instance* of E.

Definition 1. *A schema S is a pair $\langle IDB, IC \rangle$, where IDB (the intensional database) is a finite set of rules and IC a finite set of denials called a* constraint *theory. A database D on S is a pair $\langle IDB, EDB \rangle$, where EDB (the extensional database) is a finite set of facts; D is based on IDB. Any set $\mathcal{L} \subseteq \mathcal{S}$, where $\mathcal{S}$ is the set of all schemata, is called a* database language.

We express our definitions and operators on schemata, so that ICs are always in the context of an *IDB*; however, when the *IDB* is understood, the schema may be identified with *IC* and the database with *EDB*. When considering different schemata, we assume that they are *compatible*, i.e., they do not redefine each other's predicates. We focus on *stratified* databases [2], that do not allow mixing negation and recursion. We refer to the semantics of the *standard model*, and write $D \models \phi$, where D is a database and ϕ is a closed formula, to indicate that ϕ holds in D's standard model. The notation $A \models B$ is extended to parametric expressions with the meaning that it holds for all its parametric instances; similarly for $\equiv$ and "iff". We say that a database $D = \langle IDB, EDB \rangle$ is *consistent* with *IC* whenever $D \models IC$ (and thus with schema $S = \langle IDB, IC \rangle$, written $D \models S$).

Definition 2. *Given an IDB and an intensional predicate p defined in it by the rules $\{p(\vec{t}_1) \leftarrow F_1, \ldots, p(\vec{t}_n) \leftarrow F_n\}$, where the $\vec{t}_i$'s are sequences of terms and the F_i's are conjunctions of literals, the* defining formula *of p is $(F_1 \wedge \vec{X} = \vec{t}_1)\rho_1 \vee \ldots \vee (F_n \wedge \vec{X} = \vec{t}_n)\rho_n$, where $\vec{X}$ is a sequence of new distinct variables and each ρ_i is a renaming giving fresh new names to the variables of F_i not in $\vec{X}$. The variables in $\vec{X}$ are the* distinguished variables *of the defining formula; all other variables in it are the* non-distinguished variables.

For convenience, we include *queries* in intensional predicates; when no ambiguity arises, a given query may be indicated by means of its defining formula (instead of the predicate name). The *extension* of a database predicate p in a given database D is defined as the set of tuples $\{\vec{a} \mid D \models p(\vec{a})\}$; if p is a query, we refer also to the extension as the *answer* to p in D and denote it $\mathcal{A}_D^p$.

Definition 3. *A predicate update for an extensional predicate p is an expression of the form $p(\vec{X}) \Leftarrow p'(\vec{X})$ where $\Leftarrow p'(\vec{X})$ is a query; p is said to be* affected *by the update. An* update *is a set of predicate updates for distinct predicates. For a given database D and an update U, the* updated *database D^U is as D, but for every extensional predicate p affected by a predicate update $p(\vec{X}) \Leftarrow p'(\vec{X})$ in U, the subset $\{p(\vec{t}) \mid D \models p(\vec{t})\}$ of EDB is replaced by the set $\{p(\vec{t}) \mid D \models p'(\vec{t})\}$.*

This definition subsumes others that separately specify the added and deleted parts of a predicate. As mentioned, updates can be parametric as input to the transformations to follow.

Example 1. Update $U_1 = \{p(X) \Leftarrow p(X) \vee X = a\}$ describes the addition of fact $p(a)$, whereas $U_2 = \{r(X,Y) \Leftarrow (r(X,Y) \wedge X \neq \mathbf{a}) \vee (r(\mathbf{a},Y) \wedge X = \mathbf{b})\}$ is parametric and means "change any $r(\mathbf{a}, X)$ into $r(\mathbf{b}, X)$". Update $U_3 = \{p(X) \Leftarrow q(X), \quad q(X) \Leftarrow p(X)\}$ exchanges the contents of p and q.

To simplify notation, we write in the following $p(\vec{\mathbf{a}})$ as a shorthand for $p(\vec{X}) \Leftarrow p(\vec{X}) \vee \vec{X} = \vec{\mathbf{a}}$ and $\neg p(\vec{\mathbf{a}})$ for $p(\vec{X}) \Leftarrow p(\vec{X}) \wedge \vec{X} \neq \vec{\mathbf{a}}$.

The constraint verification problem asks, given a database D, a constraint theory Γ, such that $D \models \Gamma$, and an update U, whether $D^U \models \Gamma$ holds. Since checking $D^U \models \Gamma$ may be too expensive, a suitable reformulation of the problem is called for. With our approach we look for a constraint theory Γ^U such that $D^U \models \Gamma$ iff $D \models \Gamma^U$ and Γ^U is easier to evaluate than Γ. In other words, condition Γ^U, called a *simplification* of the original constraints Γ, should specialize the original Γ, as specific information coming from U is available, and avoid redundant checks by exploiting the fact that $D \models \Gamma$ holds. We observe that reasoning about the future database state D^U with a condition (Γ^U) that is tested in the present state D, complies with the deferred semantics of IC checking[1] and allows avoiding the execution of illegal updates completely. Formally, this is captured by the notions of conditional weakest precondition (CWP) and weakest precondition (WP).

Definition 4. *Consider compatible schemata $S = \langle IDB, \Gamma \rangle$, $S' = \langle IDB', \Gamma' \rangle$ and update U. S' is a WP (resp., CWP) of S wrt U whenever $D \models \Gamma'$ iff $D^U \models \Gamma$ for any database D based on $IDB \cup IDB'$ (resp., and consistent with Γ).*

A CWP is a necessary and sufficient condition for consistency of a database in the updated state to be checked in the state prior to the update (i.e., a *pre-test*). Among the CWPs, WPs do not exploit the initial consistency of the database.

---

[1] An update can be imagined as a sequence of operations modifying the state. With the *deferred* semantics, satisfaction of ICs is required after the whole update has executed, but not in the intermediate states.

Thus, to qualify as a simplification, a CWP must be at least as good as any WP. For this purpose, we assume, for any schema S and update U, the existence of a reference schema $\bar{S}^U$ representing a WP of S wrt U; we show the construction of such a WP in section 4. We further assume an ordering to sort the different CWPs so that a smallest element in this ordering represents an optimum.

Definition 5. *An* ordering *between schemata is a reflexive and transitive binary relation* $\preceq$ *such that, for any two schemata S and S':*

1. $\langle \emptyset, \emptyset \rangle \preceq S$ *and it is decidable whether* $S \preceq S'$.
2. *If* $S \neq S'$, *either* $S \prec S'$ *or* $S' \prec S$ ($S \prec S'$ *means* $S \preceq S'$ *but not* $S' \preceq S$).
3. *For a given S,* $\{S'' \mid S'' \preceq S\}$ *is finite and its schemata can be enumerated.*

It is essential, for definition 5, to consider as identical expressions that differ only by renaming and orders of operands of commutative and associative connectives.

Definition 6. *Given a schema S and an update U, schema S' is a simplification of S wrt U if $S' \preceq \bar{S}^U$ and S' is a CWP for S wrt U. A procedure with input S, U and output S', written* $\mathsf{Simp}^U(S) = S'$, *is a simplification procedure. The procedure is* ideal *if, for any S and U, there is no other simplification S'' of S wrt U s. t. $S'' \prec S'$.*

According to this definition, any CWP that is at least as small as $\bar{S}^U$ in the $\preceq$ ordering is considered a simplification; the minimal ones, among those, are the ideal simplifications. This distinction makes sense because, as we shall see, it is not always possible to obtain an ideal simplification in all cases, but even a non-ideal simplification can be a significant improvement wrt a non-optimized CWP. This is particularly important when the ordering somehow reflects the effort of checking the satisfaction of the constraint theory in any database state: ideal simplifications do then express the best possible way of checking ICs.

The basic idea is to start with the reference schema and optimize it as much as possible wrt the hypotheses S. For compatible schemata S, S_1, S_2, we write $S_1 \overset{S}{\equiv} S_2$ to indicate that $D \models S_1$ iff $D \models S_2$ in any D consistent with S.

Definition 7. *Schema S_2 is an* optimization *of schema S_1 wrt schema S if $S_1 \overset{S}{\equiv} S_2$ and $S_2 \preceq S_1$. A procedure with input S_1, S and output S_2, written* $\mathsf{Optimize}^S(S_1) = S_2$, *which is idempotent in the sense that $\mathsf{Optimize}^S(S_2) = S_2$, is an* optimization procedure. *The procedure is* ideal *if, for any S and S_1, there is no other optimization S_3 of S_1 wrt S s. t. $S_3 \prec S_2$.*

Obviously, $\mathsf{Optimize}^S(\bar{S}^U)$ is a simplification procedure for S, U, which is ideal if $\mathsf{Optimize}$ is ideal, since for all CWPs S_1, S_2 of some S, we have $S_1 \overset{S}{\equiv} S_2$.

3   Achieving Ideal Simplification

Given two queries $\Leftarrow p(\vec{X})$ and $\Leftarrow q(\vec{X})$, the *query containment* problem (QC) asks whether $\mathcal{A}_D^p$ is contained in $\mathcal{A}_D^q$ for all database D. QC is already undecid-

able for DATALOG without negation [21], and, thus, also for DATALOG¬. There is
a direct correspondence between the problem of ideal simplification and QC.

Theorem 1. *For any database language $\mathcal{L}$, QC is decidable in $\mathcal{L}$ if and only if
$\mathcal{L}$ admits an ideal simplification procedure*[2].

The only-if part of the proof enumerates all theories that are smaller than the
reference WP and tests, by QC, whether they are CWPs until one is found.
This may be impractical (although we assumed that there were finitely many
such theories) so a different strategy is described at the end of this section.
Analogously, an ideal optimization procedure can be constructed from a QC
decision procedure (if it exists) using enumeration.

Theorem 2. *There exists an ideal optimization procedure for a language $\mathcal{L}$ if
and only if QC is decidable in $\mathcal{L}$.*

In order to characterize a transformed IC as an optimal simplification, it must
represent a minimum in some ordering that reflects the effort of actually evaluating it. This can only be an estimate, as the actual execution times depend
on the database state, which is not available at the time of the simplification
process. Furthermore, it is highly dependent on the applied database technology
that may perform optimizations that cannot be included in a general definition.

Several different criteria can be defined. A natural choice is a syntactic order
based on the number of literals: the optimal theories are those in which this
number is minimal (and when the number is the same, another standard ordering, such as the alphabetical ordering, is used). This ordering, indicated as $\prec_\ell$,
may appear a bit coarse, as the number of literals in, say, $\leftarrow 1 = 2$, $\leftarrow p(a)$, and
$\leftarrow p(X)$ is the same. However, it applies within the class of CWPs of the input.

Semantic orderings are also possible (e.g., the weaker the theory, the better),
but testing precedence is generally undecidable and it can be argued that this
does not correctly reflect the evaluation effort either. The notion of *checking
space* is sometimes used [17], i.e., the portion of the Herbrand base that affects
the evaluation of a given constraint theory: the smaller the checking space, the
better the CWP. However, there may be infinitely many theories (e.g., those
that differ by tautologies) having the same checking space. For these reasons,
and since no ordering can perfectly capture the notion of efficiency, we adhere to
the simpler $\prec_\ell$ ordering. We stress that *any* criterion can only approximate optimality. For example, a syntactically minimal query does not necessarily evaluate
faster than an equivalent non-minimal query in all database states; the amount
of computation required to answer a query can be reduced, e.g., by adding a join
with a very small relation. Several refinements can be considered, such as preferring more specific constraints. However, for all such improvements there will be
cases in which efficiency is not measured precisely. For example, $\leftarrow p(X) \land q(Y)$
is likely to be evaluated faster than the more specific $\leftarrow p(X) \land q(X)$, as the
former can be checked by verifying that either p or q are empty, whereas the
latter introduces a join that potentially requires that all tuples in p be looked

---

[2] Theorems 1 and 2 and propositions 1, 2, and 3 are proved in [13].

up in q. Even if we limit such criterion to the preference of ground literals to non-ground ones, we still do not capture the notion of efficiency correctly. For example, $\leftarrow p(X)$ will typically run faster than $\leftarrow p(a)$, as for the former it is sufficient to verify that p is empty, whereas for the latter a lookup in p is needed.

As mentioned, finding an ideal simplification, although feasible in some cases, may be costly. We may thus less ambitiously content ourselves with a *local minimum*, i.e., a constraint theory such that no set of subclauses of its clauses is a simplification. A general procedure to find a local minimum of a given CWP Γ wrt hypotheses Δ consists in repeating the following steps as long as possible.

1. If there exists $\phi \in \Gamma$ such that $\Delta \cup (\Gamma \setminus \phi) \models \phi$ then ϕ is removed from Γ.
2. If there exists $\leftarrow L_1 \wedge \ldots \wedge L_n = \phi \in \Gamma$ such that $\Delta \cup \Gamma \models \leftarrow L_1 \wedge \ldots \wedge L_{i-1} \wedge L_{i+1} \wedge \ldots \wedge L_n = \psi$ for some i s. t. $1 \le i \le n$ then ϕ is replaced by ψ.

After each step we still have a CWP and a local minimum is eventually found.

Example 2. Consider the following constraint theories.

$$\Delta = \{ \leftarrow \neg p(X) \wedge q(X) \wedge r(X), \quad \leftarrow p(X) \wedge \neg q(X), \qquad \leftarrow p(X) \wedge \neg r(X) \},$$
$$\Gamma = \{ \leftarrow s(X) \wedge q(X) \wedge r(X) \}, \quad \Sigma = \{ \leftarrow s(X) \wedge p(X) \}.$$

We have $\Sigma \stackrel{\Delta}{\equiv} \Gamma$, as Δ is an encoding of the equivalence between $p(X)$ and $q(X) \wedge r(X)$. Both Γ and Σ are local minima of $\Gamma \cup \Sigma$ wrt Δ; Σ is the global minimum.

In practice there is often one local minimum. However, when particular dependencies are encoded in the ICs, such as equivalences between (sets of) predicates, like in example 2, then they may differ. The procedure depicted in this section is, however, based on entailment, which is in general undecidable; furthermore, sound and complete proof procedures, based, e.g., on resolution, are not guaranteed to terminate.

Next, we describe a simplification framework implementing a practically relevant approximation of this strategy in which entailment is replaced by specialized sound and terminating proof procedures.

4 A Concrete Simplification Procedure

We now show how to construct the reference WP, given a schema and an update, which was only supposed to exist in the previous section.

Definition 8. *Let $S = \langle IDB, \Gamma \rangle$ be a schema and U an update such that, for each predicate update $p(\vec{X}) \Leftarrow p^U(\vec{X})$ in U, p^U is defined in IDB.*

  – *Let us indicate with Γ^U a copy of Γ in which any atom $p(\vec{t})$ whose predicate is affected by a predicate update $p(\vec{X}) \Leftarrow p^U(\vec{X})$ in U is simultaneously replaced by the expression $p^U(\vec{t})$ and every intensional predicate q is replaced by a new intensional predicate q^U defined in IDB^U below.*

- *Similarly, let us indicate with IDB^U a copy of IDB in which the same replacements are simultaneously made, and let IDB^* be the biggest subset of $IDB \cup IDB^U$ including only definitions of predicates on which Γ^U depends.*

We define $\mathsf{After}^U(S) = \langle IDB^*, \Gamma^U \rangle$.

The IDB^U used in the construction of definition 8 indicates auxiliary views that are needed in order to properly characterize the resulting constraint theory. Often no such views are strictly necessary, whereas, in some other cases (e.g., in the presence of recursion), they cannot be avoided; in the former case, we will omit the specification of the intensional database and refer to the unfolding[3] of the constraint theory wrt IDB^*.

Proposition 1. *For any schema S and update U,* $\mathsf{After}^U(S)$ *is a WP of S wrt U.*

In the construction of After we did not use the hypothesis that the initial constraint theory was satisfied in the state before the update. Since the result of After also refers to the same state, we use an optimization procedure receiving as input After's output theory and, as hypotheses, After's input theory. In other words, After's result is non-optimized and we can pose $\bar{S}^U = \mathsf{After}^U(S)$. We implement $\mathsf{Optimize}$ in terms of sound and terminating rewrite rules that remove from the input theory all denials and literals that can be proved redundant.

Given a denial ϕ, we indicate as ϕ^- its *reduction* [4], i.e., a copy of it in which all tautological (non)equalities are removed and all failing (non)equalities replace ϕ by *true*; variable-term equalities are also removed and cause the variable to be replaced by the equalled term. For example, $(\leftarrow X = a \wedge p(X))^- = \leftarrow p(a)$. Conversely, *expansion* [4] of a denial ϕ, indicated ϕ^+, replaces every constant in a database predicate (or variable already occurring elsewhere in database predicates) by a new variable, and equals it to the replacing item. For example let $(\leftarrow p(X, a, X))^+ = \leftarrow p(X, Y, Z) \wedge Y = a \wedge Z = X$. Obviously, for any denial ϕ we have $\phi^- \equiv \phi \equiv \phi^+$. We write $\Gamma \vdash_R \phi$ if there is a resolution derivation of a denial ψ from the constraint theory Γ^+ such that in each resolution step the resolvent has at most n literals and ψ^- subsumes ϕ, where n is the number of literals of the largest denial in Γ^+. The boundedness on the size of resolvents guarantees termination, as Γ is function-free.

Definition 9. *Given the schemata S_Δ, S_Γ based on IDB, let Δ, Γ be the respective unfolding of their constraint theories wrt IDB;* $\mathsf{Optimize}^{S_\Delta}(S_\Gamma)$ *is the schema $\langle IDB, \Sigma \rangle$, where Σ is the result of applying on Γ the following rules as long as possible; ϕ, ψ are denials, Γ' is a constraint theory.*

$$
\begin{aligned}
\{\phi\} \cup \Gamma' &\Rightarrow \Gamma' \text{ if } \phi^- = true \\
\{\phi\} \cup \Gamma' &\Rightarrow \Gamma' \text{ if } (\Gamma' \cup \Delta) \vdash_R \phi \\
\{\phi\} \cup \Gamma' &\Rightarrow \{\phi^-\} \cup \Gamma' \text{ if } \phi \neq \phi^- \neq true \\
\{\phi\} \cup \Gamma' &\Rightarrow \{\psi^-\} \cup \Gamma' \text{ if } (\{\phi\} \cup \Gamma' \cup \Delta) \vdash_R \psi \text{ and } \psi^- \text{ strictly subsumes } \phi
\end{aligned}
$$

---

[3] The replacement of each nonrecursive intensional predicate with its defining formula, until only extensional or recursive predicates remain; see [13] for details.

The first two rules attempt the removal of a whole denial, while the last two try to remove literals from a denial, according to the strategy shown in the previous section. The described Optimize implements a terminating optimization procedure that can be used, with After, to compose a simplification procedure $\mathsf{Simp}^U(S) = \mathsf{Optimize}^S(\mathsf{After}^U(S))$ for any schema S and an update U.

Example 3. We have $\mathsf{Simp}^{\{p(\mathbf{a})\}}(\{\leftarrow p(X) \wedge q(X)\}) = \{\leftarrow q(\mathbf{a})\}$.

Each step in Optimize reduces the number of literals or instantiates them. The high complexity of Simp does not affect the quality of the approach, as simplification takes place at design time. This is possible thanks to the following property.

Proposition 2. *Let S, S' be schemata, U an update and π a param. substitution for U's parameters. If S' is a CWP of S wrt U then $S'\pi$ is a CWP of S wrt $U\pi$.*

We argue that a syntactic ordering such as the one induced by the strategy for finding local minima captures efficiency for *most* cases, as will be demonstrated in our experiments. Besides, simplification also conforms to the strategy of specializing ICs as much as possible, in that variable/constant equalities are removed by substituting the variable by the constant. So, for example, a denial such as $\phi = \leftarrow X = a \wedge p(X, Y) \wedge q(Y)$ is not transformed into $\leftarrow p(X, Y) \wedge q(Y)$,[4] which has fewer literals but is arguably less efficient to evaluate than ϕ, but to $\leftarrow p(a, Y) \wedge q(Y)$, which contains fewer literals *and* is more specialized than ϕ.

4.1 Refinements for Recursion

For some of the most commonly used recursive patterns (such as left- and right-linear recursion [15]), simplification can be refined by possibly eliminating the introduction of new recursive views; work in this direction was done in [14]. A predicate r is right-linear if it is defined by the *exit* rule $r(\vec{X}, \vec{Y}) \leftarrow q(\vec{X}, \vec{Y})$ and by the *recursive* rule $r(\vec{X}, \vec{Y}) \leftarrow p(\vec{X}, \vec{Z}) \wedge r(\vec{Z}, \vec{Y})$. There may in principle be several exit and recursive rules for the same predicate r, but they can always be reduced to one by introducing suitable new views.

The definition of r can always be decomposed in two parts: a nonrecursive definition $\{r(\vec{X}, \vec{Y}) \leftarrow q(\vec{X}, \vec{Y}), \ r(\vec{X}, \vec{Y}) \leftarrow r_p(\vec{X}, \vec{Z}) \wedge q(\vec{Z}, \vec{Y})\}$ and a transitive closure definition $\{r_p(\vec{X}, \vec{Y}) \leftarrow p(\vec{X}, \vec{Y}), \ r_p(\vec{X}, \vec{Y}) \leftarrow p(\vec{X}, \vec{Z}) \wedge r_p(\vec{Z}, \vec{Y})\}$. The construction is symmetric when r is left-linear.

All occurrences of r in a constraint theory can now be unfolded wrt these definitions, which introduce q and r_p, the latter being the transitive closure of p (which can be thought of as a path in a directed graph of p-edges). Upon the addition U of tuple $p(\vec{a}, \vec{b})$, all added r_p paths are those that pass by the new p-arc and that were not there before the update. If $\delta_U^+ r_p(\vec{X}, \vec{Y})$ indicates that there is a new path from $\vec{X}$ to $\vec{Y}$ after update U, this can be expressed as:

---

[4] Unless a constraint such as $\leftarrow X \neq a \wedge p(X, Y)$ is known to hold, which could then be used by a query optimizer to evaluate $\leftarrow p(X, Y) \wedge q(Y)$ as fast as $\leftarrow p(a, Y) \wedge q(Y)$.

$$\delta_U^+ r_p(\vec{X}, \vec{Y}) \leftarrow (r_p(\vec{X}, \vec{a}) \vee \vec{X} = \vec{a}) \wedge (r_p(\vec{b}, \vec{Y}) \vee \vec{Y} = \vec{b}) \wedge \neg r_p(\vec{X}, \vec{Y}).$$

We can define $\delta_U^- r_p$ in a similar way and unfold, in After, predicate r_p^U wrt the definition $r_p^U(\vec{X}) \leftarrow (r_p(\vec{X}) \wedge \neg \delta_U^- r_p(\vec{X})) \vee \delta_U^+ r_p(\vec{X})$.

Similarly, Simp can be extended to use as extra hypotheses all transitive closure rules in S rewritten as denials, e.g., $\leftarrow \neg r_p(\vec{X}, \vec{Y}) \wedge p(\vec{X}, \vec{Y})$ and $\leftarrow \neg r_p(\vec{X}, \vec{Y}) \wedge p(\vec{X}, \vec{Z}) \wedge r_p(\vec{Z}, \vec{Y})$, for a predicate r_p.

Generally, $\delta_U^- r_p$ requires the evaluation of $\neg r_p^U$, but often $\delta_U^- r_p$ is simplified away. If both the new and the old state are available, as in some trigger implementations, r_p^U can be evaluated as "r_p in the new state". However, these are precisely the cases where the simplification was, to some extent, unsuccessful, as accessing or simulating the new state with a view clearly requires extra work.

Example 4. Consider a schema S representing paths and edges of a directed graph $\{p(X, Y) \leftarrow e(X, Y), p(X, Y) \leftarrow e(X, Z) \wedge p(Z, Y)\}$ for which we impose acyclicity $\{\leftarrow p(X, X)\}$. Let $U = \{e(\mathbf{a}, \mathbf{b})\}$ be an update pattern that adds an arc. We have $\mathsf{Simp}^U(S) = \{\leftarrow p(\mathbf{b}, \mathbf{a}), \leftarrow \mathbf{a} = \mathbf{b}\}$. Note that $\mathsf{Simp}^U(S)$ is a much simpler test than S's IC, as it basically requires to check whether there exists a path between two given nodes, whereas the latter implies testing the existence of a cyclic path for all the nodes in the graph.

4.2   Ideality of Simp

Definition 9 gives an approximation of the procedure described in section 3. The quality of the result depends on how well the described proof procedure implements entailment. It is known that for certain classes of languages, such as the monadic class, Herbrand's class and the one-variable class, sound and complete procedures based on resolution refinements are guaranteed to terminate. In these cases an ideal simplification can be found. The principles of subsumption and reduction are, in practice, sufficient for most cases of denial elimination, and resolution proper is only needed when the ICs encode circularity.

There are other cases in which entailment can be replaced by a terminating proof procedure. We recall that a clause is Horn if, when expressed as a disjunction of literals, it contains at most one positive literal. Then, for a set Γ of Horn denials containing no non-nullary function symbol, no parameters and no equalities, there is a terminating procedure that produces Γ's local minimum.

Proposition 3. *The* Optimize *procedure always returns a local minimum when the inputs are view-less, Horn, parameter-free theories with no equalities.*

This result is in accordance with the decidability of QC for nonrecursive DATALOG [1]; it extends to Horn theories with equalities and parameters provided that proper equality axioms are added to the input set.[5] However, QC is already

---

[5] Actually, reduction takes care of reflexivity and expansion provides substitutivity, whereas symmetry was assumed to be an implicit syntactic property of equality; however, the transitivity axiom ($\leftarrow X \neq Y \wedge X = Z \wedge Z = Y$) needs to be added.

undecidable for nonrecursive DATALOG$^\neg$ [1], so we cannot hope for an ideal procedure in these cases. As for complexity, QC is known to be decidable in exponential time for nonrecursive DATALOG and subsumption is NP-complete in general [8]. The search for a local minimum in these cases is thus also exponential, since it may require solving $n + m$ QC problems, where n is the number of literals and m is the number of denials in the constraint theory. This would suggest that the problem is intractable; however, the complexity is here measured wrt the size of the query and not of the data in the database. Furthermore, simplification is a static process, therefore it is worthwhile to invest resources for compiling the constraints at design time so as to improve run time efficiency.

5   Experiments

In order to demonstrate the effectiveness of the simplification procedure, we have tested it on more complex examples. We show here our experimental results for the nonrecursive case[6]; we refer to [14] for an analysis of the recursive case. The random data sets used for the tests were generated beforehand, so that the different procedures under analysis could run on exactly the same data and thus be compared fairly. All tests were repeated 20 times, so as to have an average measure of the execution time. The symbolic simplifications shown here were obtained with an implementation of the simplification procedure [12].

We first consider the tests presented in [19] where the method of the so-called *inconsistency indicators* (II) was shown to run more efficiently than previous methods, namely [18, 11] and naive constraint checking (i.e., with no simplification). We show that, on their examples, we obtain better performance (indeed, ideal simplifications). Let S_1 be the following schema[7]:

$$
\begin{aligned}
\langle\{ \quad & mother(X,Y) \leftarrow husband(Z,X) \land father(Z,Y), \\
& parent(X,Y) \leftarrow father(X,Y) \lor mother(X,Y), \\
& wife(X,Y) \leftarrow husband(Y,X), \\
& married(X,Y) \leftarrow husband(X,Y) \lor wife(X,Y), \\
& employed(X) \leftarrow occup(X,serv), \\
& student(X) \leftarrow occup(X,stud), \\
& dependent(X,Y) \leftarrow parent(Y,X) \land employed(Y) \land student(X), \\
& dependent(X,Y) \leftarrow married(Y,X) \land employed(Y) \land \neg employed(X), \\
& self(X) \leftarrow married(Y,X) \land \neg employed(Y), \\
& guardian(X,Y) \leftarrow dependent(Y,X) \qquad\qquad\qquad \}, \\
\{ \quad & \leftarrow guardian(X,Y) \land \neg sponsor(X,Y), \\
& \leftarrow married(X_1,Y_1) \land student(X_1), \\
& \leftarrow occup(X_2,Y_2) \land occup(X_2,Z) \land Z \neq Y_2 \qquad\quad \}\rangle
\end{aligned}
$$

---

[6] All tests were run on a machine with a 2.4 GHz processor, 1 GB of RAM and 80 GB of hard disk. For compatibility with the compared method, the tests are run under a Prolog system (SICStus Prolog 3.11).

[7] We use disjunctions for compactness.

The distribution of facts in the initial database considered in [19] is as follows: 177 $father$ facts, 229 $husband$ facts, 620 $occup$ facts and 59 $sponsor$ facts. We considered additions of tuples to the $father$ and $husband$ relations. To test whether an update $U_1 = \{father(\mathbf{a}, \mathbf{b})\}$ leads to inconsistency, the II method proposes the following tests (rewritten with our notation):

$$\{\leftarrow \neg sponsor(\mathbf{a}, \mathbf{b}) \wedge guardian(\mathbf{a}, \mathbf{b}), \quad \leftarrow guardian(X, \mathbf{b}) \wedge \neg sponsor(X, \mathbf{b}) \}.$$

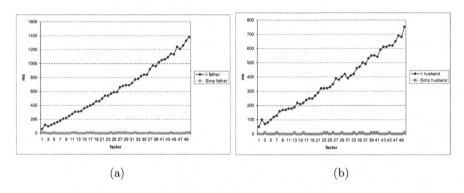

(a)   (b)

Fig. 1. Comparing Simp to the Inconsistency Indicators method

These can be checked by asserting the update as a Prolog fact `father(a,b)` and calling the Prolog query `inconsistent(father(a,b))` on the Prolog program:

```
inconsistent(father(X,Y)) :- \+ sponsor(X,Y), guardian(X,Y).
inconsistent(father(Z,Y)) :- guardian(X,Y), \+ sponsor(X,Y).
```

Their checking strategy is therefore: assert the update, then retract if inconsistency was detected. The simplification given by $\mathsf{Simp}^{U_1}(S_1)$ is more specialized and refers only to the extensional predicates:

$$\{ \leftarrow occup(\mathbf{a}, serv) \wedge occup(\mathbf{b}, stud) \wedge \neg sponsor(\mathbf{a}, \mathbf{b}),$$
$$\leftarrow husband(\mathbf{a}, X) \wedge occup(X, serv) \wedge occup(\mathbf{b}, stud) \wedge \neg sponsor(X, \mathbf{b})\}.$$

Our strategy is: first test, then assert the update if inconsistency was not detected. To see whether the approaches "scale", we ran our tests on databases that are bigger than the initial one by a given factor. Figures 1(a) and 1(b) report this factor on the X-axis and the measured average execution times (in milliseconds) for the additions of 177 $father$ facts and 229 $husband$ facts, respectively, with both approaches. In both tests, the performance worsens very quickly with the II method, whereas it basically remains constant with our approach.

The last example of [19] refers to the following schema S_2:

$\langle\{ \quad parent(X,Y) \leftarrow father(X,Y) \vee mother(X,Y),$
$\quad mother(X,Y) \leftarrow father(Z,Y) \wedge husband(Z,X),$
$\quad age(X,Y) \leftarrow civilst(X,Y,P,Q),$
$\quad dependent(X,Y) \leftarrow parent(Y,X) \wedge occup(Y,serv) \wedge occup(X,stud),$
$\quad occup(X,Y) \leftarrow civilst(X,P,Q,Y) \qquad \},$

$\{ \leftarrow civilst(X,Y_1,Z_1,t_1) \wedge civilst(X,Y_2,Z_2,t_2) \wedge \neg(Y_1 = Y_2 \wedge Z_1 \neq Z_2 \wedge t_1 \neq t_2),$
$\quad \leftarrow father(X_1,Y) \wedge father(X_2,Y) \wedge X_1 \neq X_2,$
$\quad \leftarrow husband(X_1,Y) \wedge husband(X_2,Y) \wedge X_1 \neq X_2,$
$\quad \leftarrow husband(X,Y_1) \wedge husband(X,Y_2) \wedge Y_1 \neq Y_2,$
$\quad \leftarrow civilst(X,Y,Z,Tax) \wedge (\neg(X > 0 \wedge X < 100000 \wedge Y > 0 \wedge Y < 125)$
$\qquad \vee(Z \neq m \wedge Z \neq f) \vee (Tax \neq stud \wedge Tax \neq ret \wedge Tax \neq biz \wedge Tax \neq serv)),$
$\quad \leftarrow (civilst(X,Y,Z,stud) \wedge \neg(Y < 25)) \vee (civilst(X,Y,Z,ret) \wedge \neg(Y > 60)),$
$\quad \leftarrow father(X,Y) \wedge (civilst(X,P,S,Q) \vee civilst(Y,P,S,Q)) \wedge S \neq m,$
$\quad \leftarrow husband(X,Y) \wedge (civilst(X,P,S,Q) \wedge S \neq m) \vee (civilst(Y,P,S,Q) \wedge S \neq f),$
$\quad \leftarrow husband(X,Y) \wedge age(X,P) \wedge age(Y,Q) \wedge (P < 20 \vee Q < 20),$
$\quad \leftarrow civilst(X,Y,Z,Tax) \wedge Y < 20 \wedge Tax \neq stud,$
$\quad \leftarrow dependent(X,Y) \wedge \neg tax(Y,X) \qquad \}\rangle.$

The update in question is a transaction of the form:

$$U_2 = \{ \; civilst(\mathbf{a},\mathbf{p}_a,m,\mathbf{o}_a), civilst(\mathbf{b},\mathbf{p}_b,f,\mathbf{o}_b), civilst(\mathbf{c},\mathbf{p}_c,\mathbf{s}_c,stud),$$
$$husband(\mathbf{a},\mathbf{b}), father(\mathbf{a},\mathbf{c}), tax(\mathbf{a},\mathbf{c}) \qquad \}$$

We observe that in the example it is explicitly assumed that the added family facts were not already in the database; let us indicate this extra hypothesis as Δ. The simplification given by the II method consists of one set of simplified constraints for every single update in U_2. Instead, the simplification wrt the whole transaction given by $\mathsf{Optimize}^\Delta(\mathsf{Simp}^{U_2}(S_2))$ returns $\langle\emptyset,\emptyset\rangle$. The results of [19] have execution times that vary roughly linearly wrt the size of the database. Our simplified theory ($\emptyset$) is clearly a great improvement over these results, since it executes in virtually no time and guarantees, without further checking, that this transaction pattern cannot affect integrity. This example was also used in [10], where the authors, unfortunately, only compared their method to [11], but not to [19]. However, our transactional simplification is clearly unbeatable.

The same author reconsidered in [20] some of the redundancies of [19]. For the extended example discussed in [20], the schema S_3 is as follows.

$\langle \{ mother(X,Y) \leftarrow husband(Z,X) \wedge father(Z,Y),$
$\quad parent(X,Y) \leftarrow father(X,Y) \vee mother(X,Y),$
$\quad agediff(X,Y,n) \leftarrow age(X,n_1) \wedge age(Y,n_2) \wedge minus(n,n_1,n_2)\},$
$\quad \{ \leftarrow parent(X,Y) \wedge agediff(X,Y,n) \wedge n < 15 \; \} \qquad \rangle$

We tested this on the addition of $father$ facts on a distribution similar to that considered for S_1. In this case our simplifications basically correspond to the unfolding of their so-called revised inconsistency indicators (RII), so there is almost no observable difference in the execution times of the two methods. We stress, however, that the method of [20] has a much more restricted expressive power, in that the updates are limited to singleton insertions and no negations are allowed in the database. Furthermore, in this case the update was simple, so the computational effort required for assertion and retraction of facts was little; however, our approach based on early recognition of inconsistency proves yet more efficient for cases in which updates lead to illegal states (dramatically, if the transactions are complex). To see this effect we updated a small database (2 $father$ facts and 2 age facts) with schema S_3 with an illegal $father$ insertion and measured, with the RII method, an answer time approximately four times bigger than with the method based on Simp. This behavior is amplified as the database grows (and it is thus more expensive to add facts for the DBMS): attempting 10000 times the insertion of an illegal $father$ fact on a database with approximately 5000 $father$ facts took about $1s$ with the RII method, but only $70ms$ with Simp. This reflects the fact that with our strategy, upon an illegal update, we just perform a test, whereas the RII method requires to execute the update, perform a consistency test and then roll back the update.

The figures do not report the time employed to obtain a simplification, as this is a design time task. Yet, in our tests (with up to 20 rules, 20 ICs, 10 literals per IC and 5 literals per update) no simplification took more than 500 ms.

5.1   More on Related Work

As mentioned, the ability to check consistency of a possibly updated database *before* execution of the transaction under consideration allows avoiding inconsistent states completely, and thus rollbacks, which may require costly bookkeeping in order to restore the old state. Several approaches to simplification do not comply with this requirement [16, 11, 18, 4, 6, 19, 10]; [19] showed that his II method was more efficient than [11, 18] and we gave evidence of great improvements obtained with Simp wrt II. Methods that as ours, are based on pre-tests are, e.g., [17, 9]. However, the former does not allow more than one update action in a transaction to operate on the same relation; furthermore, no mechanism corresponding to parameters is present, thus requiring to execute the procedure for each specific update. The latter provides low-cost pre-tests which are sufficient conditions that guarantee the integrity of the database; however, if the pre-tests fail (as, e.g., in simple recursive cases), nothing can be concluded about consistency and an exact test, such as ours, needs to be made. Simplification of integrity constraints with respect to given parametric update patterns resembles the notion of program *specialization*, which is the process of creating a specialized version of a given program with respect to known input data. In [10], a partial evaluation of a meta-interpreter is used to produce logic programs that correspond to simplified constraints. However, loop checks needed to ensure termination in the presence of recursion do not partially evaluate satisfactorily, resulting in an explosion of (possibly unreachable) alternatives. Integrity checking is often regarded as an instance of materialized view maintenance: integrity constraints are defined as views that must always remain empty for the database to be consistent; the book [7] provides insightful discussion on the subject. In [5], it is shown how to implement integrity constraint checking by translating first-order logic specifications into SQL triggers. It is interesting to note that the result of our transformations can be combined with similar translation techniques and thus integrated in an active database system. In this way the advantages of declarativity are combined with the efficiency of execution. The idea of embedding integrity control via semi-automatic generation of triggers (without semantic optimization) is originally due to [3].

6   Conclusion and Future Work

We applied program transformation operators to the generation of simplified ICs. A procedure was constructed that makes use of these transformations and produces the simplification searched for according to a criterion of minimality. An important contribution of this paper is the definition of the notion of ideality of a simplification procedure, its connection with the QC problem, and the analysis of different minimality criteria that can be used to characterize an ideal procedure. In particular, we showed that, in any sensible ordering in which *true* represents a minimal element, ideality of simplification corresponds to decidability of QC.

We described an implementation in terms of rewrite rules based on resolution, subsumption and replacement of specific patterns. The ability of producing a necessary and sufficient condition for checking integrity before a database update, together with the generality of the update language, constitutes the main advantage of our method with respect to earlier approaches. This was also demonstrated through a series of experiments. This work could be extended to identify more cases for which useful differential expressions exist and to integrate in the framework rewrite techniques reducing recursive problems to easier ones.

References

1. S.Abiteboul, R.Hull, and V.Vianu. *Foundations of Databases*Addison-Wesley,1995.
2. K. R. Apt, H. A. Blair, and A. Walker. Towards a theory of declarative knowledge. In *Foundations of Deductive Databases and Logic Programming.*, pages 89–148. Morgan Kaufmann, 1988.
3. S. Ceri and J. Widom. Deriving production rules for constraint maintainance. In *Proceedings of VLDB 90*, pages 566–577. Morgan Kaufmann, 1990.
4. U. S. Chakravarthy, J. Grant, and J. Minker. Logic-based approach to semantic query optimization. *ACM Trans. on Database Syst. (TODS)*, 15(2):162–207, 1990.
5. H. Decker. Translating advanced integrity checking technology to sql. In *Database integrity: challenges and solutions*, pages 203–249. Idea Group Publishing, 2002.
6. H. Decker and M. Celma. A slick procedure for integrity checking in deductive databases. In *ICLP 94*, pages 456–469. MIT Press, Cambridge, MA, 1994.
7. A. Gupta and I. S. Mumick, editors. *Materialized views: techniques, implementations, and applications*. MIT Press, 1999.
8. D. Kapur and P. Narendran. Np-completeness of the set unification and matching problems. In *CADE*, pages 489–495, 1986.
9. S. Y. Lee and T. W. Ling. Further improvements on integrity constraint checking for stratifiable deductive databases. In *VLDB'96*, pages 495–505. Kaufmann, 1996.

10. M. Leuschel and D. de Schreye. Creating specialised integrity checks through partial evaluation of meta-interpreters. *JLP*, 36(2):149–193, 1998.
11. J. W. Lloyd, L. Sonenberg, and R. W. Topor. Integrity constraint checking in stratified databases. *JLP*, 4(4):331–343, 1987.
12. D. Martinenghi. http://www.dat.ruc.dk/~dm/spic/index.html, 2005.
13. D. Martinenghi. *Advanced Techniques for Efficient Data Integrity Checking*. PhD thesis, Roskilde University, Denmark, in *Datalogiske Skrifter*, 105, http://www.ruc.dk/dat/forskning/skrifter/DS105.pdf , 2005.
14. D. Martinenghi and H. Christiansen. Efficient integrity checking for databases with recursive views. In *ADBIS 05*, volume 3631 of *LNCS*, pages 109–124. Springer, 2005.
15. J. F. Naughton, R. Ramakrishnan, Y. Sagiv, and J. D. Ullman. Efficient evaluation of right-, left-, and mult-linear rules. In *SIGMOD 89*, pages 235–242. ACM, 1989.
16. J.-M. Nicolas. Logic for improving integrity checking in relational data bases. *Acta Informatica*, 18:227–253, 1982.
17. X. Qian. An effective method for integrity constraint simplification. In *ICDE 88*, pages 338–345. IEEE Computer Society, 1988.
18. F. Sadri and R. Kowalski. A theorem-proving approach to database integrity. In *Foundations of Deductive Databases and Logic Programming*, pages 313–362. Kaufmann, Los Altos, CA, 1988.
19. R. Seljée. A new method for integrity constraint checking in deductive databases. *Data Knowl. Eng.*, 15(1):63–102, 1995.
20. R. Seljée and H. C. M. de Swart. Three types of redundancy in integrity checking: An optimal solution. *Data Knowl. Eng.*, 30(2):135–151, 1999.
21. O. Shmueli. Decidability and expressiveness aspects of logic queries. In *Proceedings of the sixth ACM PODS symposium*, pages 237–249. ACM Press, 1987.

Concepts of Automata Construction from LTL

Carsten Fritz[*]

Institut für Informatik und Praktische Mathematik, CAU Kiel, Germany
fritz@ti.informatik.uni-kiel.de

Abstract. We present an algorithm for the conversion of very weak alternating Büchi automata into nondeterministic Büchi automata (NBA), and we introduce a local optimization criterion for deleting superfluous transitions in these NBA. We show how to use this algorithm in the translation of LTL formulas into NBA, matching the worst-case upper bounds of other LTL-to-NBA translations. We compare the NBA resulting from our translation to the results of two popular algorithms for the translation of LTL to generalized Büchi automata: the translation of Gerth et al. of 1995 (resulting in the GPVW-automaton), and the translation of Daniele et al. of 1999 (resulting in the DGV-automaton), which improves on the GPVW algorithm. We show that the redundancy check by syntactical implication used in the construction of the DGV-automaton is covered by our local optimization, that is, all transitions removed by the redundancy check will also be removed according to our local optimization criterion. Moreover, for a fixed input formula in next normal form, our locally optimized NBA from LTL and the locally optimized GPVW- and DGV-automaton are all essentially the same. Both these results give a "structural" explanation for the syntactic approaches by Gerth et al. and Daniele et al. We show that a bottom-up variant of our algorithm allows to pass simplifications of NBA for subformulas on to the NBA for the entire LTL formula.

1 Introduction

Propositional linear time temporal logic (LTL for short) [17] is a popular language for the specification of system properties. In the standard way of model checking an LTL specification against a system [20, 21], it is necessary to translate the negation of the specification into an equivalent nondeterministic Büchi automaton, which incurs an exponential blow-up in the worst case. Minimizing such a Büchi automaton is computationally difficult: Even testing universality for nondeterministic finite automata on finite strings is PSPACE-hard [10]. This implies that approximating a minimum-size ω-automaton up to a constant factor (or even up to a logarithmic factor [14]) is impossible in polynomial time unless P = PSPACE.

Practical algorithms therefore use various heuristics for the state-space reduction of the resulting automata. Many implementations, e. g., Etessami's TMP [4] and Wring [1] of Somenzi and Bloem, use a tableau-based algorithm of Daniele, Giunchiglia and Vardi [2], which is based on an algorithm of Gerth, Peled, Vardi and Wolper [12], as the starting point for the construction of nondeterministic Büchi automata from LTL.

---

[*] Supported by Deutsche Forschungsgemeinschaft under project no. 223228.

The result of this algorithm is a *generalized* Büchi automaton with propositional labels on the states rather than on the transitions and with multiple initial states. This requires a further processing of the result, to change the acceptance condition and to allow a fruitful application of heuristics like simulation quotienting.

We analyze the automaton resulting from the algorithms of Gerth et al. (henceforth called the *GPVW-automaton*) and of Daniele et al. (the *DGV-automaton*) and show that there is a strong connection between these automata and approaches based on alternating automata [11, 7]. To this end, we first present an algorithm for the conversion of a *very weak* alternating Büchi automaton [18, 15] with n states into an equivalent nondeterministic automaton with at most $(n+1)2^n$ states (Section 3). This algorithm is a specialized and optimized variant of the de-universalization algorithm of Miyano and Hayashi [16] for alternating Büchi automata. As a distinctive feature of our algorithm, an integer counter to check the Büchi condition is an integral part of the states of our automata and the automata construction. We also introduce a simple rule for the deletion of superfluous transitions in the constructed nondeterministic automata, called *local optimization*.

We then turn our de-universalization algorithm into an algorithm to translate an LTL formula of length n into an equivalent nondeterministic Büchi automaton with at most $(n+1)2^n$ states (Section 4).

To analyze the GPVW-automaton and the DGV-automaton (which results from an improved version of the GPVW-algorithm), we then give a new presentation of the automata resulting from the GPVW- and DGV-algorithms in Section 5; in contrast, the focus of [12, 2] is on the pseudo-code presentation of the algorithms and their correctness. We adapt the GPVW-automaton and the DGV-automaton to the format of our Büchi automaton of Sections 3 and 4 (cf. [13] for similar adaptations), and we then show that the redundancy check by syntactical implication, which is an important step in the construction of the DGV-automaton, is covered by our local optimization. That is, if a transition is not constructed because of a successful redundancy check, then it will be removed according to our local optimization criterion. Moreover, the locally optimized versions of the adapted GPVW- and DGV-automaton and of the automaton resulting from our de-universalization are *exactly the same* for all input formulas in next normal form.

We then discuss the possibility to use our algorithm for the inductive construction of nondeterministic automata from LTL (Section 6). That is, we show that a nondeterministic Büchi automaton for an input formula, e. g., $\psi \cup \rho$, can be constructed by merging the automata for the subformulas ψ and ρ into an automaton for $\psi \cup \rho$. This merging process allows us to turn simplifications of the automata for ψ and ρ into simplifications of the new ($\psi \cup \rho$)-automaton. This is interesting if a thorough simplification for the larger formula would be too time-consuming. Our concept of inductive construction can be seen as a specifically tailored variant of temporal logic with automata connectives, cf. [22, 21].

A technical report containing all the proofs is available as [8].

We hope that these results are helpful in the future design of translation algorithms and automata simplification heuristics. The shown tight connection between the tableau-based approach and the automata construction via alternating automata should help to concentrate on the core aspects of these algorithms and ease their analysis.

2   Basic Definitions

By convention, we identify an integer n with the set $\{0,\ldots,n-1\}$. We define $\max \emptyset = 0$, i. e., the maximum of the empty set is 0. For an infinite sequence $(q_i)_{i<\omega}$, $\text{Inf}((q_i)_{i<\omega})$ is the set of elements appearing infinitely often in the sequence, i. e., $\text{Inf}((q_i)_{i<\omega}) = \{q \mid \forall i < \omega \exists j > i\colon q = q_j\}$.

A *nondeterministic Büchi automaton* (NBA) over an alphabet Σ is a tuple $\mathbf{Q} = (Q,\Sigma,q_I,\Delta,F)$ where Q is a finite set of states, $q_I \in Q$ is an initial state, $\Delta \subseteq Q \times \Sigma \times Q$ a transition relation, and $F \subseteq Q$ a set of accepting states.

Such an automaton $\mathbf{Q}$ accepts a word $w\colon \omega \to \Sigma$ if and only if there is a sequence of states $(q_i)_{i<\omega} \in Q^\omega$ such that $q_0 = q_I$, $(q_i,w(i),q_{i+1}) \in \Delta$ for every $i < \omega$, and $\text{Inf}((q_i)_{i<\omega}) \cap F \neq \emptyset$. The *language of* $\mathbf{Q}$ is $L(\mathbf{Q}) = \{w \in \Sigma^\omega \mid \mathbf{Q} \text{ accepts } w\}$.

An *alternating Büchi automaton* (ABA) over an alphabet Σ is defined like an NBA over Σ, but additionally there is a partition of Q into the sets E and U of *existential* and *universal* states, respectively. A run of an ABA is not just a sequence of states but a computation tree in which all possible successors of a universal state have to be incorporated. Such a computation tree is accepting if all its infinite branches fulfill the Büchi acceptance condition. See, e. g., [9] for more details, and see [19] for alternating automata with transitions defined via positive Boolean formulas.

We will also use automata over finite, nonempty sets of propositions. If $\mathbf{Q}$ is an automaton over a set of propositions[1] Σ, then the language of $\mathbf{Q}$ is a set of infinite sequences of subsets of Σ, i. e., a word of the language is an element of $(2^\Sigma)^\omega$. And, following [5], the transitions of automata over a set of propositions are labeled by so-called *terms* over the set of propositions. A term is the (possibly empty) conjunction of literals, i. e., positive and negative propositions. That is, the set of terms over Σ is

$$\text{term}_\Sigma = \{ \bigwedge_{p \in M} p \wedge \bigwedge_{q \in N} \neg q \mid M,N \subseteq \Sigma \} . \tag{1}$$

For a term $t \in \text{term}_\Sigma$, $\text{lit}(t)$ is the set of literals appearing in t, and for a set of literals L, $\text{term}(L)$ is the term $\bigwedge_{l \in L} l$. That is, $t \equiv \text{term}(\text{lit}(t))$. We say that a set $M \subseteq \Sigma$ satisfies a term $t \in \text{term}_\Sigma$ (written as $M \models t$) if $(\text{term}(M) \wedge \bigwedge_{a \in \Sigma \setminus M} \neg a) \to t$ is a tautology.

Note that $\text{tt} \in \text{term}_\Sigma$ (empty conjunction), and $M \models \text{tt}$ for every $M \subseteq \Sigma$. On the other hand, if t is contradictory, i. e., $t \equiv \text{ff}$, then $M \not\models t$ for all $M \subseteq \Sigma$.

An NBA $\mathbf{Q} = (Q,\Sigma,q_I,\Delta,F)$ over a set of propositions Σ is defined like an NBA over an alphabet, with the difference that the transition relation Δ is a subset of $Q \times \text{term}_\Sigma \times Q$. Such an automaton $\mathbf{Q}$ over a set of propositions Σ accepts a word $w\colon \omega \to 2^\Sigma$ if and only if there is a sequence of states $(q_i)_{i<\omega}$ of $\mathbf{Q}$ such that $q_0 = q_I$ and for every $i < \omega$, there is a $t_i \in \text{term}_\Sigma$ such that $(q_i,t_i,q_{i+1}) \in \Delta$ and $w(i) \models t_i$, and $\text{Inf}((q_i)_{i<\omega}) \cap F \neq \emptyset$.

---

[1] We will use the letter Σ both for alphabets and sets of propositions. There is no danger of confusion, because automata over alphabets are only used in Section 3, and automata over sets of propositions are not used in that section.

LTL formulas over a set of propositions Σ are defined inductively by (1) tt and a are LTL formulas for every $a \in \Sigma$, and (2) if ψ and ρ are LTL formulas, then so are $\neg\psi$, $\psi \vee \rho$, $X\psi$ and $\psi \cup \rho$. LTL formulas are interpreted over infinite sequences of subsets of Σ. For every such word $w: \omega \to 2^\Sigma$, we define the relation $\models$ by

$$w \models \text{tt} , \tag{2}$$

$$w \models a \quad \text{iff } a \in w(0) , \tag{3}$$

$$w \models \neg\psi \text{ iff } w \not\models \psi , \tag{4}$$

$$w \models \psi \vee \rho \text{ iff } w \models \psi \text{ or } w \models \rho , \tag{5}$$

$$w \models X\psi \text{ iff } w[1..] \models \psi , \tag{6}$$

$$w \models \psi \cup \rho \text{ iff } \exists i(w[i..] \models \rho \wedge \forall j < i(w[j..] \models \psi)) , \tag{7}$$

where $w[i..]$ is defined by $w[i..](n) = w(i+n)$ for every $n < \omega$. The language of an LTL formula φ is $L(\varphi) = \{w \in (2^\Sigma)^\omega \mid w \models \varphi\}$.

As usual, we will use derived logical operators like ff, $\wedge$, $\to$, and the temporal operators R, F, G defined by $\psi \text{ R } \rho = \neg(\neg\psi \cup \neg\rho)$, $F\psi = \text{tt} \cup \psi$ and $G\psi = \text{ff R } \psi$. See also [3] for the semantics of LTL.

The set of subformulas of an LTL formula φ is denoted $sub(\varphi)$. Literals are regarded as atomic subformulas, i.e., $sub((\neg a) \cup (\neg b)) = \{(\neg a) \cup (\neg b), \neg a, \neg b\}$. The length of an LTL formula φ, denoted $|\varphi|$, is its number of symbols, not counting negations and brackets.

An LTL formula φ is in *negation normal form* if every subformula $\neg\psi$ of φ is of the form $\neg a$ for some $a \in \Sigma$. The formula φ is in *next normal form* if every subformula $X\psi$ is of the form $XX\psi'$, Xa or $X\neg a$ for some $a \in \Sigma$. Using the operators ff, $\wedge$ and R and the equivalence $\neg X\psi \equiv X\neg\psi$, we can compute an equivalent negation normal form for every LTL formula in linear time. Throughout this paper, we will assume LTL formulas to be in negation normal form. The next normal form can be computed in linear time by exploiting the equivalences $X(\psi \cup \rho) \equiv (X\psi) \cup (X\rho)$ and $X(\psi \vee \rho) \equiv (X\psi) \vee (X\rho)$.

3 De-universalization of Very Weak Alternating Büchi Automata

Let $\mathbf{Q} = (Q, \Sigma, q_I, \Delta, E, U, F)$ be an alternating Büchi automaton over the alphabet Σ such that there is an injective mapping $v: Q \to \omega$ such that $(q, a, q') \in \Delta$ implies $v(q) \leq v(q')$ for all $q, q' \in Q, a \in \Sigma$. We say that $\mathbf{Q}$ is *very weak*, cf. [18, 15, 11].

Let $P = \{q \in Q \mid q \notin F \text{ and } \exists a \in \Sigma : (q, a, q) \in \Delta\}$, $k = |P|$ and z a bijection $P \to \{1, \ldots, k\}$. That is, P contains those states in Q in which a run of $\mathbf{Q}$ can "get stuck" without accepting.

For $\mathbf{Q}$, we construct an equivalent nondeterministic Büchi automaton as follows. Let

$$\mathbf{Q}_{nd} = (2^Q \times (k+1), \Sigma, (\{q_I\}, z(q_I)), \Delta_{nd}, 2^Q \times \{0\}) , \tag{8}$$

where $z(q_I) = 0$ if $q_I \notin P$. To define Δ_{nd}, we first define the notion of a *successor set* of a set $M \in 2^Q$ for $a \in \Sigma$. A set $M' \in 2^Q$ is a successor set of M for a if there is a mapping $s_a: Q \to Q$ such that, for every $q \in M \cap E, s_a(q) \in \Delta(q, a)$ and

$$M' = \bigcup_{q \in M \cap U} \Delta(q, a) \cup \{s_a(q) \mid q \in M \cap E\} . \tag{9}$$

That is, a successor set M' of M for a contains all a-successors of the universal states in M and an a-successor for every existential state in M.

For $M, M' \in 2^Q$ and $a \in \Sigma$, we will write sucset(M, a, M') if M' is a successor set of M for a, i.e., sucset is a relation over $2^Q \times \Sigma \times 2^Q$.

We will usually write sucset(M, a) instead of $\{M' \in 2^Q \mid \text{sucset}(M, a, M')\}$ and sucset(M) instead of $\{(a, M') \in \Sigma \times 2^Q \mid \text{sucset}(M, a, M')\}$.

We further define the function next: $2^Q \times (k+1) \to k+1$ by

$$\text{next: } (M, i) \mapsto \max\{z(p) \mid p \in M \cap P, \, z(p) < i\} \; . \tag{10}$$

The function next describes the behavior of the counter component. We use a decreasing counter to keep track of the Büchi acceptance condition. In the following, we are only interested in states $(M, i) \in 2^Q \times (k+1)$ with $i = 0$ or $z^{-1}(i) \in M$. We say that these states are *consistent*.

The relation Δ_{nd} is the smallest set that contains the following transitions, for consistent states $(M, i) \in 2^Q \times (k+1)$.

1. If M' is a successor set of M for a, then $((M, 0), a, (M', \max\{z(p) \mid p \in M' \cap P\})) \in \Delta_{nd}$.
2. If M' is a successor set of $M \setminus \{z^{-1}(i)\}$ for a, N' is a successor set of $\{z^{-1}(i)\}$ for a and $z^{-1}(i) \notin N'$, then $((M, i), a, (M' \cup N', \text{next}(M' \cup N', i))) \in \Delta_{nd}$.
3. If M' is a successor set of $M \setminus \{z^{-1}(i)\}$ for a, N' is a successor set of $\{z^{-1}(i)\}$ for a and $z^{-1}(i) \in N'$, then $((M, i), a, (M' \cup N', i)) \in \Delta_{nd}$.

That is, every reachable state is consistent.

Intuitively, if a run π of $\mathbf{Q}_{nd}$ is in a state (M, i), then the respective run tree of $\mathbf{Q}$ which is compatible with the nondeterministic choices in π, is in all of the states in M simultaneously. The value i of the counter component indicates that, in order to get an accepting run, we currently have the obligation to show that the computation branch which is currently in $z^{-1}(i)$ will not stay there forever (because in that case, the run tree is not accepting). As soon as this computation branch leaves the state $z^{-1}(i)$, the counter is decreased to the next smaller P-state in the current NBA state (our obligation jumps to another computation branch), or to 0, if there is no such state. The counter value 0 indicates that an NBA state is accepting (we have met all obligations), so the counter is reset to point to the z-largest P-state in the next step of the NBA run.

Theorem 1. *Let $\mathbf{Q}$ be a very weak alternating Büchi automaton with n states, k of which belong to its set P. Then $L(\mathbf{Q}) = L(\mathbf{Q}_{nd})$, and $\mathbf{Q}_{nd}$ has at most $(k+1)2^n$ states.*

Note that for a very weak ABA $\mathbf{Q}$ with n states, the usual de-universalization according to [16] results in a nondeterministic automaton with $\Omega(4^n)$ states in the worst case.

We now give a simple rule for the deletion of superfluous transitions in nondeterministic Büchi automata constructed from very weak alternating Büchi automata as described above. In Section 5, we will see that this local optimization of Büchi automata plays a crucial role in the comparison to the GPVW- and DGV-automaton.

Definition 1 (local optimization). *Let $\mathbf{Q}$ be a very weak alternating Büchi automaton. For two transitions $((M, i), a, (N, j))$ and $((M, i), a, (N', j'))$ of $\mathbf{Q}_{nd}$, we say that $((M, i), a, (N', j'))$ is a better transition than $((M, i), a, (N, j))$, if $N' \subseteq N$ and $j' \leq j$.*

The locally optimized automaton $\mathbf{Q}^{lo}_{nd}$ is defined like $\mathbf{Q}_{nd}$, only the set of transitions is different. The set of transitions of $\mathbf{Q}^{lo}_{nd}$ is

$$\Delta^{lo}_{nd} = \Delta_{nd} \setminus \{((M,i),a,(N,j)) \mid \exists((M,i),a,(N',j')) \in \Delta_{nd} :$$
$$((M,i),a,(N',j')) \text{ is better than } ((M,i),a,(N,j))\} \ . \tag{11}$$

That is, $\mathbf{Q}^{lo}_{nd}$ only contains "optimal" transitions. It can be shown that local optimization is correct in the following sense.

Theorem 2. *Let* $\mathbf{Q}$ *be a very weak alternating Büchi automaton. Then* $L(\mathbf{Q}) = L(\mathbf{Q}_{nd}) = L(\mathbf{Q}^{lo}_{nd})$.

4   Application to the Construction of Büchi Automata from LTL

The above construction can be used in a straightforward manner to construct nondeterministic Büchi automata from LTL formulas via very weak alternating Büchi automata, demonstrating that this two-phase construction can yield automata of the same worst-case size as tableau-based constructions.

This approach leads to a top-down construction: For an LTL formula φ of length n with k (syntactically distinct) subformulas of the form $\psi \cup \rho$ or $F\psi$, first a very weak alternating Büchi automaton $\mathbf{Q}(\varphi)$ is constructed, cf. [19, 7]. This automaton has at most $n + 1$ states, k of which belong to its set $P \subseteq Q$ as defined above. The above de-universalization construction can then be applied to $\mathbf{Q}(\varphi)$; the result is a nondeterministic Büchi automaton $\mathbf{Q}(\varphi)_{nd}$ with at most $2^n \cdot (k+1)$ states.

In fact, it is not necessary to use alternating automata explicitly. For an LTL formula φ in negation normal form over a set of propositions Σ, we can directly define a nondeterministic Büchi automaton. The following construction for this top-down automaton will be used in Section 5.

Let P_φ be the set of U- and F-formulas in sub(φ), and let $k_\varphi = |P_\varphi|$. Let z be a bijection $P_\varphi \to \{1, \dots, k_\varphi\}$. We then define a nondeterministic Büchi automaton $\mathbf{Q}^{td}(\varphi)$ with $L(\mathbf{Q}^{td}(\varphi)) = L(\varphi)$ by

$$\mathbf{Q}^{td}(\varphi) = (\mathbf{Q}_\varphi, \Sigma, q_I^\varphi, \Delta^{td}, F_\varphi) \tag{12}$$

where $\mathbf{Q}_\varphi = 2^{\text{sub}(\varphi)} \times (k_\varphi + 1)$, $\Delta^{td} \subseteq \mathbf{Q}_\varphi \times \text{term}_\Sigma \times \mathbf{Q}_\varphi$, and $F_\varphi = 2^{\text{sub}(\varphi)} \times \{0\}$.

In the state set, formulas of the form $\varphi_0 \wedge \varphi_1$ are identified with the union of the conjunctive subformulas, i.e., a state (M,i) with $\varphi_0 \wedge \varphi_1 \in M$ is identified with $(M \cup \{\varphi_0, \varphi_1\} \setminus \{\varphi_0 \wedge \varphi_1\}, i)$. Especially, the formula tt is identified with the empty conjunction, i.e., $(\{\text{tt}\}, 0)$ is identified with $(\emptyset, 0)$. In this sense, the initial state of $\mathbf{Q}^{td}(\varphi)$ is $q_I^\varphi = (\{\varphi\}, \max\{z(\psi) \mid \psi \in \{\varphi\} \cap P_\varphi\})$.

We now define the notion of a successor set for a term $t \in \text{term}_\Sigma$, i.e., sucset now is a relation over $2^{\text{sub}(\varphi)} \times \text{term}_\Sigma \times 2^{\text{sub}(\varphi)}$. The transitions in Δ^{td} are then defined as in Section 3, enumeration items 1 to 3, where the function next is defined as in Equation (10) with $P = P_\varphi$.

The relation sucset is the smallest relation that satisfies the following.

- sucset($\emptyset$, tt, $\emptyset$)
- For singleton sets, we distinguish the following cases.
  - The set $\{$ff$\}$ does not have successor sets. If $\varphi = a$ or $\varphi = \neg a$ for some $a \in \Sigma$, then sucset($\{\varphi\}, \varphi, \emptyset$). (The set $\{$tt$\}$ is identified with $\emptyset$.)
  - For all $t \in \text{term}_\Sigma$, sucset($\{\psi \vee \rho\}, t$) = sucset($\{\psi\}, t$) $\cup$ sucset($\{\rho\}, t$). (The set $\{\psi \wedge \rho\}$ is identified with $\{\psi, \rho\}$.)
  - sucset($\{X\psi\}$, tt, ψ)
  - sucset($\{\psi \cup \rho\}$) = $\{(t, N \cup \{\psi \cup \rho\}) \mid$ sucset($\{\psi\}, t, N$)$\} \cup$ sucset($\{\rho\}$)
    (This also covers the case F$\rho \equiv$ tt $\cup \rho$.)
  - sucset($\{\psi \mathrel{R} \rho\}$) = $\{(t', N' \cup \{\psi \mathrel{R} \rho\}) \mid$ sucset($t', N', \{\rho\}$)$\}$
    $\cup \{(t \wedge t', N \cup N') \mid$ sucset($t, N, \{\psi\}$), sucset($t', N', \{\rho\}$)$\}$
    (This also covers the case G$\rho \equiv$ ff $\mathrel{R} \rho$.)
- If $M \in 2^{\text{sub}(\varphi)}$ such that $|M| > 1$, suppose that $M = \{\varphi_0, \ldots, \varphi_{r-1}\}$.
  Then sucset(M) = $\{(\bigwedge_{i<r} t_i, \bigcup_{i<r} N_i) \mid \forall i < r\colon$ sucset($t_i, N_i, \{\varphi_i\}$)$\}$.

Theorem 3. *Let φ be an LTL formula in negation normal form. Then $L(\varphi) = L(\mathbf{Q}^{td}(\varphi))$.*

We can adapt the local optimization of Definition 1 to this setting by adding a condition regarding the term labels of the transitions. That is, for transitions $((M, i), t, (N, j))$ and $((M, i), t', (N', j'))$ of $\mathbf{Q}^{td}(\varphi)$, we say that $((M, i), t', (N', j'))$ is a better transition than $((M, i), t, (N, j))$ if $N' \subseteq N$, $j' \leq j$ and also $t \to t'$. The locally optimized automaton $\mathbf{Q}^{lo}(\varphi)$ then is defined in analogy to Definition 1.

5   A Comparison of LTL-to-NBA Constructions

In this section, we show that the GPVW-automaton and the DGV-automaton are in most aspects equivalent to our construction. We first give a conversion of the GPVW-automaton and the DGV-automaton to our format in a straightforward manner. We then show that the redundancy check by syntactical implication of [2] is, in effect, almost equivalent to our local optimization. We also show that our locally optimized automaton and the locally optimized GPVW-automaton are the same for input formulas in next normal form.

5.1   The GPVW-Automaton

The GPVW-automaton differs from our top-down automaton in some basic aspects. Let φ be an LTL formula in negation normal form, and let $\mathcal{A}(\varphi) = (Q_\varphi, \Sigma, I, \to, \mathcal{F}, L)$ be the GPVW-automaton for an LTL formula φ. Then $\mathcal{A}(\varphi)$ is a generalized Büchi automaton, i. e., the acceptance condition $\mathcal{F}$ is given as $\mathcal{F} = \{F_0, \ldots, F_{n-1}\} \subseteq 2^{Q_\varphi}$ such that a run $\pi = (q_i)_{i<\omega} \in Q_\varphi^\omega$ of $\mathcal{A}(\varphi)$ is accepting if and only if $\text{Inf}(\pi) \cap F_i \neq \emptyset$ for all $i < n$. Moreover, $I \subseteq Q_\varphi$ is a set of initial states rather than a single initial state, and the terms which are used as labels of the transitions in our construction are labels of the states in the GPVW-automaton while there are no labels on the transitions. That is, L

is a labeling function $Q_\varphi \to \mathrm{term}_\Sigma$, and a sequence $(q_i)_{i<\omega} \in Q_\varphi^\omega$ is a run of the GPVW-automaton on a word $w \in (2^\Sigma)^\omega$ if and only if $q_0 \in I$, $(q_i, q_{i+1}) \in \to$ and $w(i) \models L(q_i)$, for all $i < \omega$.

In the algorithmic definition of the GPVW-automaton in [12], a state of the automaton is described as an object with the fields *Name*, *Incoming*, *New*, *Old*, *Next* and *Father*. Of these, only *Old* and *Next* are necessary to describe a node while the other fields contain auxiliary data. Both *Old* and *Next* are sets of subformulas of the input formula. Consequently, we will describe a state of the GPVW-automaton as an element of $2^{\mathrm{sub}(\varphi)} \times 2^{\mathrm{sub}(\varphi)}$, with the first component representing the *Old*-field and the second component representing the *Next*-field. There is an accepting run for a word $w \in (2^\Sigma)^\omega$ starting from such a state if w satisfies all formulas in the *Old*-field and $w[1..]$ satisfies all formulas in the *Next*-field.

To define the transition relation of the GPVW-automaton, we first define the relation $\leadsto \subseteq 2^{\mathrm{sub}(\varphi)} \times (2^{\mathrm{sub}(\varphi)} \times 2^{\mathrm{sub}(\varphi)})$. We have $N \leadsto (M', N')$ if there is a $t \in \mathrm{term}_\Sigma$ such that $\mathrm{sucset}(N, t, N')$ and $M' = \mathrm{lit}(t) \cup N$. As in Section 4, we identify a subset $\{\psi \wedge \rho\}$ with $\{\psi, \rho\}$.

The GPVW-automaton $\mathcal{A}(\varphi)$ is now defined by

$$\to \; = \; \{((M,N),(M',N')) \in (2^{\mathrm{sub}(\varphi)})^4 \mid N \leadsto (M',N')\} \;, \tag{13}$$

$$Q_\varphi \; = \; \{(M,N) \in 2^{\mathrm{sub}(\varphi)} \times 2^{\mathrm{sub}(\varphi)} \mid (\emptyset, \{\varphi\}) \to^+ (M,N)\} \;, \tag{14}$$

$$I \; = \; \{(M,N) \in Q_\varphi \mid \{\varphi\} \leadsto (M,N)\} \;, \tag{15}$$

$$L: (M,N) \mapsto \bigwedge_{\alpha \in M \text{ a literal}} \alpha \;. \tag{16}$$

To define the set $\mathcal{F}$ of accepting sets, let z be a bijection of the set P_φ of F- and U-formulas in $\mathrm{sub}(\varphi)$ to $\{1, \ldots, k_\varphi\}$. We have $\mathcal{F} = \{F_1, \ldots, F_{k_\varphi}\}$, where

$$F_i = \{(M,N) \in Q_\varphi \mid (z(\psi \cup \rho) = i \wedge \psi \cup \rho \in M) \to \rho \in M\} \;, \tag{17}$$

for $1 \le i \le k_\varphi$; here, a formula Fρ is regarded as tt U ρ.

5.2 The Adjusted GPVW-Automaton

We now adjust the GPVW-automaton to our format. The states of this adjusted GPVW-automaton $\mathcal{A}^{ad}(\varphi)$ are elements of $2^{\mathrm{sub}(\varphi)} \times (k_\varphi + 1)$, as for our top-down automaton. Also as for the top-down automaton, (1) the new single initial state of $\mathcal{A}^{ad}(\varphi)$ is $q_I^{ad} = (\{\varphi\}, \max\{z(\psi) \mid \psi \in \{\varphi\} \cap P_\varphi\})$.

The following definition condenses several steps: (2) The labels of states in Q_φ become labels of the *incoming* transitions. Consequently, the *Next*-field of the states now does not give the formulas which are true *in the next step*, but those which are true *now*. The *Old*-field's remaining function then is in describing the acceptance condition. Since we also (3) switch from a generalized to a normal Büchi condition by introducing a counter, (4) the new states have an integer component instead of an *Old*-field, such that they are in fact elements of $2^{\mathrm{sub}(\varphi)} \times (k_\varphi + 1)$. In a sense, the states in Q_φ are thus split and merged in a new fashion.

We now define the set of reachable states Q_φ^{ad} of $\mathcal{A}^{ad}(\varphi)$ and its set of transitions Δ^{ad} inductively as follows.

- $q_I^{ad} \in Q_\varphi^{ad}$, and if $q_I^{ad} = (N_I, i)$ and $(M, N) \in I$ is an initial state of $\mathcal{A}(\varphi)$, then there is a transition $(q_I^{ad}, \mathcal{L}(M, N), (N, j)) \in \Delta^{ad}$ such that $j = \max\{l \leq k_\varphi \mid (M, N) \notin F_l$ and $i \neq 0 \rightarrow l \leq i\}$, and $(N, j) \in Q_\varphi^{ad}$.
- If $(N, i) \in Q_\varphi^{ad}$, then there is a transition $((N, i), t, (N', j)) \in \Delta^{ad}$ and $(N', j) \in Q_\varphi^{ad}$ if the following holds: There are sets $M, M' \in 2^{\mathrm{sub}(\varphi)}$ such that $(M, N) \rightarrow (M', N')$, $t \equiv \mathcal{L}(M', N')$, and $j = \max\{l \leq k_\varphi \mid (M', N') \notin F_l$ and $i \neq 0 \rightarrow l \leq i\}$.

The set of accepting states is $F^{ad} = Q_\varphi^{ad} \cap (2^{\mathrm{sub}(\varphi)} \times \{0\})$.

Note that a "jumping" decreasing counter as used here and in our definition of optimized de-universalization is similar to the jumping (yet increasing) counter discussed in [13]. Giannakopoulou and Lardi also discuss the translation of term labels to the incoming transitions.

5.3   The DGV-Automaton

An important difference between the DGV-automaton (i.e., the result of the algorithm LTL2AUT in [2]) and the GPVW-automaton is the use of the concept of *syntactical implication* in defining the acceptance sets and for redundancy and contradiction checks. We introduce the notion of syntactical implication following [13].

Definition 2 (syntactical implication, cf. [2,13]). *For sets A, B of LTL formulas over Σ, $\mathrm{SI}(A, B)$ is the set of LTL formulas over Σ defined inductively as follows.*

1. *$\mathrm{tt} \in \mathrm{SI}(A, B)$,*
2. *$\varphi \in \mathrm{SI}(A, B)$, if $\varphi \in A$,*
3. *$\varphi \in \mathrm{SI}(A, B)$, if one of the following holds:*
   - *$\varphi = \mathsf{X}\psi$ and $\psi \in B$, [2] or*
   - *$\varphi = \psi \vee \rho$ and ($\psi \in \mathrm{SI}(A, B)$ or $\rho \in \mathrm{SI}(A, B)$), or*
   - *$\varphi = \psi \wedge \rho$ and $\{\psi, \rho\} \subseteq \mathrm{SI}(A, B)$, or*
   - *$\varphi = \psi \mathsf{U} \rho$ and ($\psi \in \mathrm{SI}(A, B)$ and $\varphi \in B$, or $\rho \in \mathrm{SI}(A, B)$), or*
   - *$\varphi = \psi \mathsf{R} \rho$ and ($\rho \in \mathrm{SI}(A, B)$ and $\varphi \in B$, or $\{\psi, \rho\} \subseteq \mathrm{SI}(A, B)$).*

If $\varphi \in \mathrm{SI}(A, B)$, we say that φ is syntactically implied *by A and B, or that φ is* syntactically redundant *w. r. t. A and B.*

Obviously, if $A' \subseteq A$ and $B' \subseteq B$, then $\mathrm{SI}(A', B') \subseteq \mathrm{SI}(A, B)$. As an intuition, if for $w \in (2^\Sigma)^\omega$, we have $w \models \varphi$ for all $\varphi \in A$ and $w[1..] \models \varphi'$ for all $\varphi' \in B$, then $w \models \varphi''$ for all $\varphi'' \in \mathrm{SI}(A, B)$.

Ignoring redundancy and contradiction checks (which are discussed in the next subsection), the difference to the GPVW-automaton can be described as follows.

- For the DGV-automaton, we have $N \rightsquigarrow (M', N')$ if there is a $t \in \mathrm{term}_\Sigma$ such that $\mathrm{sucset}(N, t, N')$ and $M' = \mathrm{lit}(t)$.
- The acceptance sets in the generalized Büchi condition are $F_i = \{(M, N) \in Q_\varphi \mid (z(\psi \mathsf{U} \rho) = i \wedge \psi \mathsf{U} \rho \in \mathrm{SI}(M, N)) \rightarrow \rho \in \mathrm{SI}(M, N)\}$, for $1 \leq i \leq k_\varphi$.

All other definitions and the adjustments are as for the GPVW-automaton. We write $\mathcal{B}^{ad}(\varphi)$ for the adjusted DGV-automaton for an input formula φ.

Note that the states of $\mathcal{A}^{ad}(\varphi)$ and $\mathcal{B}^{ad}(\varphi)$ are consistent. For $\mathcal{B}^{ad}(\varphi)$, this is because $\psi \mathsf{U} \rho \in \mathrm{SI}(M, N)$ and $\rho \notin \mathrm{SI}(M, N)$ implies $\psi \mathsf{U} \rho \in N$.

---

[2] We add this rule for technical reasons. It is not included in the definition of [13].

5.4   Local Optimization and Syntactical Implication

At this stage, $\mathcal{A}^{ad}(\varphi)$, $\mathcal{B}^{ad}(\varphi)$ and $\mathbf{Q}^{td}(\varphi)$ are *not* the same automaton. For example, if the input formula is $\varphi = (a \cup b) \wedge Gb$, then $\mathcal{A}^{ad}(\varphi)$ has a transition $((\{a \cup b, Gb\}, 1), a \wedge b, (\{a \cup b, Gb\}, 0))$ while $\mathbf{Q}^{td}(\varphi)$ has a transition $((\{a \cup b, Gb\}, 1), a \wedge b, (\{a \cup b, Gb\}, 1))$ instead. In this example, one can observe that, in both automata, the $(a \wedge b)$-labeled transitions are not locally optimal—there is a better transition $((\{a \cup b, Gb\}, 1), b, (\{Gb\}, 0))$ in both automata. We also have $a \cup b \in \mathrm{SI}(\{b\}, \{Gb\})$, i.e., a redundancy check as in [2] can[3]detect that $a \cup b$ is syntactically redundant in $\{a \cup b, Gb\}$, with the effect that the transition $((\{a \cup b, Gb\}, 1), a \wedge b, (\{a \cup b, Gb\}, 0))$ is not added to the DGV-automaton.

This example suggests that there is a connection between syntactical implication and local optimization. This connection is described by the following lemma. Intuitively, part 1 of Lemma 1 says the following: If a successful redundancy check w.r.t. syntactical implication detects that φ is redundant in N with the result that a transition from M to N is not constructed, then, for every possible i such that (M, i) is a state in our automaton, a transition to (N, j) with any possible j is not locally optimal and will be deleted. In this sense, redundancy checks by syntactical implication are covered by local optimization.

Lemma 1. *Let* $((M,i),t,(N,j))$ *be a transition of the nondeterministic Büchi automata* $\mathbf{Q}^{td}(\varphi_0)$, $\mathcal{A}^{ad}(\varphi_0)$ *or* $\mathcal{B}^{ad}(\varphi_0)$, *respectively, for an LTL formula* φ_0. *Let* $\varphi \in M$ *such that for* $(t', N') \in \mathrm{sucset}(M \setminus \{\varphi\})$ *and* $(t'', N'') \in \mathrm{sucset}(\{\varphi\})$, *we have* $t \equiv t' \wedge t''$ *and* $N = N' \cup N''$.

1. *If* $\varphi \in \mathrm{SI}(\mathrm{lit}(t'), N')$ *such that also* $\varphi \notin N'$ *if* φ *is an* U-formula[4], *then there is a transition* $((M,i),t',(N',j'))$ *in* $\mathbf{Q}^{td}(\varphi_0)$, $\mathcal{A}^{ad}(\varphi_0)$ *or* $\mathcal{B}^{ad}(\varphi_0)$, *respectively, which is as least as good as* $((M,i),t,(N,j))$.
2. *If there is a* j' *such that* $((M,i),t',(N',j'))$ *is a transition of* $\mathbf{Q}^{td}(\varphi_0)$, $\mathcal{A}^{ad}(\varphi_0)$ *or* $\mathcal{B}^{ad}(\varphi_0)$, *respectively, which is at least as good as* $((M,i),t,(N,j))$, *then* $\varphi \in \mathrm{SI}(\mathrm{lit}(t'), N')$.

In the following, let $\mathcal{A}^{lo}(\varphi)$ and $\mathcal{B}^{lo}(\varphi)$ be the locally optimized versions of $\mathcal{A}^{ad}(\varphi)$ and $\mathcal{B}^{ad}(\varphi)$, respectively. By Lemma 1, all possible effects of the redundancy checks in the construction of the DGV-automaton are covered by the local optimization. We do not elaborate on the contradiction checks by syntactical implication of [2]; obviously, a set of formulas is contradictory if and only if no accepting run starts from the respective automaton state.

In the example, we have $\mathcal{A}^{lo}(\varphi) = \mathbf{Q}^{lo}(\varphi)$ (and also $\mathcal{B}^{lo}(\varphi) = \mathbf{Q}^{lo}(\varphi)$), because the $(a \wedge b)$-labelled transitions and, consequently, the state $(\{a \cup b, Gb\}, 0)$ of $\mathcal{A}^{ad}(\varphi)$ are deleted. We claim that our observation for the example is not a coincidence: The adjusted and locally optimized GPVW-automaton and DGV-automaton and the locally

---

[3] In fact, the redundancy checks in [2] are performed during the construction of the transitions starting from a state in such a way that their effect depends on the order in which the formulas are processed. That is, it may happen that a formula is processed although it is redundant.

[4] This special rule for U-formulas is in analogy to the special treatment of U-formulas in the redundancy checks of [2, 13].

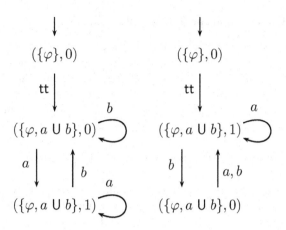

Fig. 1. $\mathcal{A}^{lo}(\varphi)$ (left) and $\mathbf{Q}^{lo}(\varphi)$ (right) for $\varphi = \mathsf{GX}(a \cup b)$

optimized top-down automaton are the same for all LTL formulas in next normal form, provided that the same bijection z is used for the set of U- and F-subformulas. We write, e. g., $\mathbf{Q}_z^{td}(\varphi)$ for the top-down automaton of φ based on a fixed bijection z.

Theorem 4. *Let φ be an LTL formula in next normal form over a set of propositions Σ. Let P_φ be the set of U- and F-subformulas of φ, and let z be a bijection $P_\varphi \to \{1,\dots,|P_\varphi|\}$.*
Then $\mathcal{A}_z^{lo}(\varphi) = \mathcal{B}_z^{lo}(\varphi) = \mathbf{Q}_z^{lo}(\varphi)$.

The transition structure of the three locally optimized automata can be different if the input formula is not in next normal form. For example, with the input formula $\varphi = \mathsf{GX}(a \cup b)$, $\mathcal{A}_z^{lo}(\varphi)$ and $\mathbf{Q}_z^{lo}(\varphi)$ are different (see Figure 1), and for $\varphi = a \wedge \mathsf{X}(a \cup b)$, $\mathcal{A}_z^{lo}(\varphi)$ and $\mathcal{B}^{lo}(\varphi)$ are different. In fact, it is sufficient to require that no U- or F-subformula is within the scope of an X-operator in the input formula.

To proof Theorem 4, it is crucial to observe that for a transition $((M,i),t,(N,j))$ in one of the locally optimized automata resulting from an input formula in next normal form, the value j is determined by i and N only.

Lemma 2. *Let φ be an LTL formula in next normal form. Let $((M,i),t,(N,j))$ be a transition of $\mathbf{Q}_z^{lo}(\varphi)$, $\mathcal{A}_z^{lo}(\varphi)$ or $\mathcal{B}_z^{lo}(\varphi)$, respectively.*
If there is a formula $\varphi' \in N \cap P_\varphi$ such that $z(\varphi') \leq i$, then $z(\varphi') \leq j \leq i$, else $j = 0$. More precisely, $j = \max\{z(\varphi') \leq i \mid \varphi' \in N \cap P_\varphi\}$.

6   Inductive Bottom-Up NBA Construction from LTL

It is also possible to construct an NBA from an LTL formula in a bottom-up fashion, by defining nondeterministic automata inductively over the structure of the formula. For a given LTL formula, the inductive construction described below and the top-down approach of Section 4 yield the same nondeterministic automaton (up to the order induced on the states in P_φ by the bijection z). The main advantage of the bottom-up construction is the possibility to make use of simplifications of automata for subformulas. That is, we can first construct automata for the subformulas and simplify these automata. Then we can merge these automata into an automaton for the whole formula in such a way that this larger automaton inherits the simplifications of the subautomata. For example, the size of $\mathbf{Q}^{td}(\psi \cup \rho)$ may be quadratic in the size of both $\mathbf{Q}^{td}(\psi)$ and $\mathbf{Q}^{td}(\rho)$. It may be too time-consuming to substantially simplify $\mathbf{Q}^{td}(\psi \cup \rho)$, but it may be possible to simplify $\mathbf{Q}^{td}(\psi)$ and $\mathbf{Q}^{td}(\rho)$.

We will first give an inductive construction and then give a sketch of how to apply this construction for simplified subautomata.

We inductively define, for every LTL formula φ in negation normal form over a set of propositions Σ, an equivalent nondeterministic Büchi automaton

$$\mathbf{Q}^{bu}(\varphi) = (\mathbf{Q}_\varphi, \Sigma, q_I^\varphi, \Delta^{bu}, F_\varphi) \tag{18}$$

where the components $\mathbf{Q}_\varphi$, q_I^φ and F_φ are defined as in Section 4. Again, P_φ is the set of U- and F-subformulas in φ and $k_\varphi = |P_\varphi|$.

The transition structure of the defined automaton will be similar to the structure of the top-down automaton defined in Section 4, that is, there is a bijection $z \colon P_\varphi \to \{1, \dots, k_\varphi\}$ such that every transition of the automaton $\mathbf{Q}^{bu}(\varphi)$ defined here is also a transition of the automaton $\mathbf{Q}_z^{td}(\varphi)$ constructed via the top-down approach and vice versa. This underlying bijection $z = z_\varphi$ will be defined inductively together with $\mathbf{Q}^{bu}(\varphi)$.

The construction is as follows. If φ is an atomic formula tt, ff, a or $\neg a$ with $a \in \Sigma$, we take $\mathbf{Q}^{bu}(\varphi) = \mathbf{Q}^{td}(\varphi)$. The mapping z_φ is empty.

We now assume that the automata $\mathbf{Q}^{bu}(\psi)$ and $\mathbf{Q}^{bu}(\rho)$ and the bijections z_ψ and z_ρ are already defined. Due to space constraints, we only give the construction of $\mathbf{Q}^{bu}(\varphi)$ and z_φ for the case $\varphi = \psi \cup \rho$ in this extended abstract. This also covers the case $\varphi = \mathsf{F}\rho \equiv \mathsf{tt} \cup \rho$.

The initial state of $\mathbf{Q}^{bu}(\varphi)$ is $q_I^\varphi = (\{\varphi\}, k_\varphi)$, with $k_\varphi = k_\psi + k_\rho + 1$.

The bijection $z_\varphi \colon P_\varphi \to \{1, \dots, k_\varphi\}$ is defined by

- $z_\varphi(\varphi) = k_\varphi$,
- $z_\varphi(p) = z_\psi(p)$ for $p \in P_\psi$,
- $z_\varphi(p) = z_\rho(p) + k_\psi$ for $p \in P_\rho$.

To define the set of transitions Δ^{bu} of $\mathbf{Q}^{bu}(\varphi)$, let $(M_\varphi, i) \in 2^{\mathrm{sub}(\varphi)} \times (k_\varphi + 1)$ be a state of $\mathbf{Q}^{bu}(\varphi)$.

- If (M_φ, i) is the initial state of $\mathbf{Q}^{bu}(\varphi)$, i.e., $(M_\varphi, i) = (\{\varphi\}, k_\varphi)$, then
  - $((\{\varphi\}, k_\varphi), t, (\{\varphi\} \cup N_\psi, k_\varphi)) \in \Delta^{bu}$ for every transition $(q_I^\psi, t, (N_\psi, j)) \in \Delta_\psi$,
  - $((\{\varphi\}, k_\varphi), t, (N_\rho, 0)) \in \Delta^{bu}$ for every transition $(q_I^\rho, t, (N_\rho, 0)) \in \Delta_\rho$, and
  - $((\{\varphi\}, k_\varphi), t, (N_\rho, j + k_\psi)) \in \Delta^{bu}$ for every transition $(q_I^\rho, t, (N_\rho, j)) \in \Delta_\rho$ such that $j > 0$.
- Now let (M, i) be some state of $\mathbf{Q}^{bu}(\varphi)$ other than the initial state. Let $M_\psi = M \cap 2^{\mathrm{sub}(\psi)}$, $M_\rho = M \cap 2^{\mathrm{sub}(\rho)}$ and $M_\varphi = M \setminus (M_\psi \cup M_\rho)$, i.e., either $M_\varphi = \emptyset$ or $M_\varphi = \{\varphi\}$. (For simplicity in notation, we assume that $((\emptyset, 0), \mathsf{tt}, (\emptyset, 0)) \in \Delta^{bu} \cap \Delta_\psi \cap \Delta_\rho$.) Then there is a transition $((M, i), t_\varphi \wedge t_\psi \wedge t_\rho, (N_\varphi \cup N_\psi \cup N_\rho, j))$ if the terms t_φ, t_ψ and t_ρ, the sets N_φ, N_ψ and N_ρ and the integer j satisfy the following.

- $((M_\varphi, \max\{z(\psi) \mid \psi \in M_\varphi \cap P_\varphi\}), t_\varphi, (N_\varphi, j_\varphi)) \in \Delta^{bu}$
- If $i = k_\psi + k_\rho + 1$ then $((M_\psi, 0), t_\psi, (N_\psi, j_\psi)) \in \Delta_\psi$
  and $((M_\rho, 0), t_\rho, (N_\rho, j_\rho)) \in \Delta_\rho$.
- If $0 \leq i \leq k_\psi$ then $((M_\psi, i), t_\psi, (N_\psi, j_\psi)) \in \Delta_\psi$
  and $((M_\rho, 0), t_\rho, (N_\rho, j_\rho)) \in \Delta_\rho$.
- If $k_\psi < i \leq k_\psi + k_\rho$ then $((M_\psi, 0), t_\psi, (N_\psi, j_\psi)) \in \Delta_\psi$
  and $((M_\rho, i - k_\psi), t_\rho, (N_\rho, j_\rho)) \in \Delta_\rho$.
- $j'_\rho = j_\rho + k_\psi$ if $j_\rho \neq 0$, else $j'_\rho = 0$.
- $j = \max\{0 < l \leq i \mid l \in \{j_\varphi, j_\psi, j'_\rho\}\}$

Theorem 5. *Let φ be an LTL formula in negation normal form. Then $L(\varphi) = L(\mathbf{Q}^{bu}(\varphi))$.*

The basic idea for the propagation of simplifications now is to replace $\mathbf{Q}^{bu}(\psi)$ and $\mathbf{Q}^{bu}(\rho)$ in the above construction by simplified automata $\mathbf{S}(\psi)$ and $\mathbf{S}(\rho)$. Obviously, it is necessary that these simplified automata still have the same inner structure as the bottom-up automaton, i.e., their state set must be a subset of, e.g., $2^{\mathrm{sub}(\psi)} \times (k_\psi + 1)$, the behavior of the counter component and the set of accepting states must be similar etc.

This can be achieved if $\mathbf{S}(\psi)$ is a quotient automaton of $\mathbf{Q}^{bu}(\psi)$ w.r.t. to an appropriate simulation relation $\equiv$, i.e., $\equiv$ may be direct or delayed simulation equivalence [6]. In this case, the states of $\mathbf{S}(\psi)$ are equivalence classes of the states of $\mathbf{Q}^{bu}(\psi)$, i.e., subsets of $2^{\mathrm{sub}(\psi)} \times (k_\psi + 1)$. It is then possible to use a quotient automaton $\mathbf{S}(\psi)$ in the above construction by using some standard representatives of its states (classes) instead of its states during the construction. The technical details have to be omitted in this extended abstract; see [8] for an exhaustive treatment.

7 Conclusion

Starting from an optimized de-universalization algorithm for very weak alternating Büchi automata, we have developed an algorithm for the translation of an LTL formula to an equivalent nondeterministic Büchi automaton which matches the bounds of other LTL-to-NBA translations. The resulting automata feature a clear separation between the locally valid subformulas and the check of the Büchi acceptance condition via an integrated counter component. They allow a natural deletion of superfluous transitions by local optimization.

We have analyzed the automata resulting from the standard tableau-based algorithm of Gerth, Peled, Vardi and Wolper and from the improved algorithm of Daniele, Giunchiglia and Vardi. We have shown that the redundancy check of Daniele et al. is covered by our local optimization, and that, for all LTL formulas in next normal form, the results of these algorithms are essentially equivalent to the results of our algorithm.

We have outlined how to use a variant of our algorithm for an inductive construction in such a way that simplifications of subautomata are inherited by the superautomaton.

Acknowledgments

Thanks to Moshe Vardi for his comments on a draft of this work.

References

1. R. Bloem. Wring: an LTL to Buechi translator. URL: http://vlsi.colorado.edu/~rbloem/wring.html.
2. M. Daniele, F. Giunchiglia, and M. Y. Vardi. Improved automata generation for linear time temporal logic. In N. Halbwachs and D. Peled, editors, *Computer Aided Verification, 11th Internat. Conf., CAV '99, Trento, Italy*, volume 1633 of *Lecture Notes in Computer Science*, pages 249–260. Springer, Berlin, 1999.
3. A. E. Emerson. Temporal and modal logic. In J. van Leeuwen, editor, *Handbook of Theoretical Computer Science*, volume B: Formal Methods and Semantics, pages 995–1072. Elsevier Publishing, Amsterdam, 1990.
4. K. Etessami. Temporal massage parlor. URL: http://www1.bell-labs.com/project/TMP/.
5. K. Etessami and G. Holzmann. Optimizing Büchi automata. In C. Palamidessi, editor, *11th Int. Conf. on Concurrency Theory (CONCUR 2000), University Park, PA, USA*, volume 1877 of *Lecture Notes in Computer Science*, pages 153–167. Springer, Berlin, 2000.
6. K. Etessami, R. Schuller, and Th. Wilke. Fair simulation relations, parity games, and state space reduction for Büchi automata. In F. Orejas, P. Spirakis, and J. van Leeuwen, editors, *Automata, Languages and Programming, 28th Internat. Coll., ICALP 2001, Crete, Greece*, volume 2076 of *Lecture Notes in Computer Science*, pages 694–707. Springer, Berlin, 2001.
7. C. Fritz. Constructing Büchi automata from linear temporal logic using simulation relations for alternating Büchi automata. In O. H. Ibarra and Z. Dang, editors, *Implementation and Application of Automata, 8th Internat. Conf., CIAA 2003, Santa Barbara, CA, USA*, volume 2759 of *Lecture Notes in Computer Science*, pages 35–48. Springer, Berlin, 2003.
8. C. Fritz. Concepts of automata construction from LTL. Technical report, Institut für Informatik, Christian-Albrechts-Universität zu Kiel, 2005. URL: http://www.ti.informatik.uni-kiel.de/~fritz/AutFromLTL-TR.pdf.
9. C. Fritz and Th. Wilke. State space reductions for alternating Büchi automata: Quotienting by simulation equivalences. In M. Agrawal and A. Seth, editors, *22nd Conf. on Foundations of Software Technology and Theoretical Computer Science, Kanpur, India*, volume 2556 of *Lecture Notes in Computer Science*, pages 157–168. Springer, Berlin, 2002.
10. M. R. Garey and D. S. Johnson. *Computers and Intractability: A Guide to the Theory of NP-Completeness*. W.H. Freeman and Co., San Francisco, 1979.
11. P. Gastin and D. Oddoux. Fast LTL to Büchi automata translation. In G. Berry, H. Comon, and A. Finkel, editors, *Computer Aided Verification, 13th Internat. Conf., CAV 2001, Paris, France*, volume 2102 of *Lecture Notes in Computer Science*, pages 53–65. Springer, Berlin, 2001.
12. R. Gerth, D. Peled, M. Y. Vardi, and P. Wolper. Simple on-the-fly automatic verification of linear temporal logic. In *Proc. 15th Workshop on Protocol Specification, Testing, and Verification, Warsaw, Poland*, pages 3–18. Chapman & Hall, London, 1995.
13. D. Giannakopoulou and F. Lerda. From states to transitions: Improving translation of LTL formulae to Büchi automata. In D. Peled and M. Y. Vardi, editors, *Proc. of 22nd IFIP Int. Conf. on Formal Techniques for Networked and Distributed Systems (FORTE 2002), Houston, TX, USA*, volume 2529 of *Lecture Notes in Computer Science*, pages 308–326. Springer, 2002.
14. G. Gramlich and G. Schnitger. Minimizing NFA's and regular expressions. In V. Diekert and B. Durand, editors, *22nd Symp. on Theoretical Aspects of Computer Science, STACS 2005, Stuttgart, Germany*, volume 3404 of *Lecture Notes in Computer Science*, pages 399–411. Springer, Berlin, 2005.

15. O. Kupferman and M. Y. Vardi. Weak alternating automata are not that weak. In *5th Israeli Symposium on the Theory of Computing Systems (ISTCS '97)*, pages 147–158, Ramat-Gan, Israel, 1997. IEEE.

16. S. Miyano and T. Hayashi. Alternating finite automata on ω-words. *Theoretical Computer Science*, 32:321–330, 1984.

17. A. Pnueli. The temporal logic of programs. In *18th Ann. Symp. on Foundations of Computer Science*, pages 46–57, Providence, RI, 1977. IEEE Computer Society.

18. S. Rohde. *Alternating Automata and the Temporal Logic of Ordinals*. PhD thesis, Department of Mathematics, University of Illinois at Urbana-Champaign, 1997.

19. M. Y. Vardi. An automata-theoretic approach to linear temporal logic. In F. Moller and G. Birtwistle, editors, *Logics for Concurrency: Structure versus Automata*, volume 1043 of *Lecture Notes in Computer Science*, pages 238–266. Springer, Berlin, 1996.

20. M. Y. Vardi and P. Wolper. An automata-theoretic approach to automatic program verification. In D. Kozen, editor, *1st Annual IEEE Symposium on Logic in Computer Science (LiCS'86)*, pages 332–344, Cambridge, Mass., USA, 16–18 June 1986. IEEE Computer Society.

21. M. Y. Vardi and P. Wolper. Reasoning about infinite computations. *Information and Computation*, 115(1):1–37, 15 Nov. 1994.

22. P. Wolper. Temporal logic can be more expressive. *Information and Control*, 56(1–2):72–99, 1983.

Author Index

Lecture Notes in Artificial Intelligence (LNAI)